Microsoft©
Office 2007
Introductory Concepts and Techniques

Windows XP Edition

Gary B. Shelly

Thomas J. Cashman

Misty E. Vermaat

Contributing Authors

Steven G. Forsythe

Mary Z. Last

Philip J. Pratt

Jeffrey J. Quasney

Susan L. Sebok

Jeffrey J.Webb

SHELLY CASHMAN SERIES®

THOMSON COURSE TECHNOLOGY   25 THOMSON PLACE   BOSTON MA 02210

Australia • Canada • Denmark • Japan • Mexico • New Zealand • Philippines • Puerto Rico • Singapore • South Africa
Spain • United Kingdom • United States

Microsoft Office 2007
Introductory Concepts and Techniques, Windows XP Edition

Gary B. Shelly

Thomas J. Cashman

Misty E. Vermaat

Executive Editor
Alexandra Arnold

Senior Product Managers
Reed Curry, Mali Jones

Product Manager
Heather Hawkins

Associate Product Manager
Klenda Martinez

Editorial Assistant
Jon Farnham

Senior Marketing Manager
Joy Stark-Vancs

Marketing Coordinator:
Julie Schuster

Print Buyer
Julio Esperas

Director of Production
Patty Stephan

Lead Production Editor
Marissa Falco

Production Editors
Cathie DiMassa,
Matthew Hutchinson,
Jill Klaffky, Phillipa Lehar

Developmental Editors
Jill Batistick, Amanda Brodkin,
Laurie Brown, Lyn Markowicz

Proofreaders
John Bosco,
Kim Kosmatka

Indexer
Rich Carlson

QA Manuscript Reviewers
John Freitas, Serge Palladino,
Chris Scriver, Danielle Shaw,
Marianne Snow, Teresa Storch

Art Director
Bruce Bond

Cover and Text Design
Joel Sadagursky

Cover Photo
Jon Chomitz

Compositor
GEX Publishing Services

Printer
Banta Menasha

Microsoft® Office 2007
Introductory Concepts and Techniques
Windows XP Edition

Contents

Preface	x
To the Student	xxii

Essential Introduction to Computers

Objectives	**COM 1**
What Is a Computer?	**COM 2**
What Does a Computer Do?	**COM 3**
Why Is a Computer so Powerful?	**COM 4**
How Does a Computer Know What to Do?	**COM 4**
What Are the Components of a Computer?	**COM 4**
Input Devices	**COM 5**
The Keyboard	COM 5
The Mouse	COM 7
System Unit	**COM 8**
Processor	COM 8
Memory	COM 8
Output Devices	**COM 9**
Printers	COM 9
Display Devices	COM 10
Storage Devices	**COM 11**
Magnetic Disks	COM 11
Optical Disks	COM 14
Tape	COM 16
Miniature Mobile Storage Media	COM 16
Communications Devices	**COM 18**
Computer Software	**COM 18**
System Software	COM 18
Application Software	COM 19
Networks and the Internet	**COM 20**
The Internet	COM 21
The World Wide Web	COM 21
Electronic Commerce	COM 23
How to Purchase a Personal Computer	**COM 24**
How to Purchase a Desktop Computer	**COM 25**
How to Purchase a Notebook Computer	**COM 32**
How to Purchase a Tablet PC	**COM 35**
How to Purchase a Personal Mobile Device	**COM 37**
Learn It Online	**COM 39**
Case Studies	**COM 39**
Index	**COM 40**
Photo Credits	**COM 40**

Microsoft Windows XP and Office 2007

CHAPTER ONE
Introduction to Microsoft Windows XP

Objectives	**WIN 1**
What Is an Operating System?	**WIN 2**
Versions of the Microsoft Windows XP	
Operating System	**WIN 2**
Overview	WIN 3
Microsoft Windows XP Professional	**WIN 4**
Windows XP Service Pack 2	WIN 4
What Is a User Interface?	WIN 4
Starting Microsoft Windows XP	WIN 5
The Windows XP User Interface	WIN 6
Logging On to the Computer	WIN 7
The Windows XP Desktop	**WIN 8**
The My Computer Window	WIN 13
Summary of Mouse and Windows Operations	WIN 22
The Keyboard and Keyboard Shortcuts	**WIN 22**
Starting an Application Program	**WIN 23**
What Is Internet Explorer?	WIN 23
Uniform Resource Locator	WIN 24
Browsing the World Wide Web	**WIN 25**
Windows Explorer	**WIN 29**
Using a Hierarchical Format to Organize Files	
and Folders	WIN 31
Removable Media and Network Drives	WIN 32
Downloading a Hierarchy of Folders into the	
Freshman Folder	WIN 35
Creating a Document and Folder Using WordPad	**WIN 38**
File Management in Windows Explorer	**WIN 45**
Finding Files or Folders	**WIN 51**
Using Help and Support	**WIN 56**
Logging Off and Turning Off the Computer	**WIN 62**
Chapter Summary	**WIN 65**
Learn It Online	**WIN 66**
In the Lab	**WIN 66**

Microsoft **Word 2007**

CHAPTER ONE
Creating and Editing a Word Document

Objectives	**WD 1**
What Is Microsoft Office Word 2007?	**WD 2**
Project — Document with a Picture	**WD 2**
Overview	WD 4
Starting Word	**WD 4**
The Word Window	**WD 6**
Document Window	WD 6
Ribbon	WD 7
Mini Toolbar and Shortcut Menus	WD 9
Quick Access Toolbar	WD 10
Office Button	WD 11
Key Tips	WD 12
Entering Text	**WD 12**
Wordwrap	WD 14
Spelling and Grammar Check	WD 16
Saving the Project	**WD 18**
Formatting Paragraphs and Characters in a Document	**WD 22**
Fonts, Font Sizes, Styles, and Themes	WD 23
Formatting Single Versus Multiple Paragraphs and Characters	WD 26
Document Formats	WD 36
Inserting and Formatting a Picture in a Word Document	**WD 40**
Scrolling	WD 43
Enhancing the Page	**WD 48**
Changing Document Properties and Saving Again	**WD 50**
Printing a Document	**WD 53**
Quitting Word	**WD 55**
Starting Word and Opening a Document	**WD 55**
Correcting Errors	**WD 57**
Types of Changes Made to Documents	WD 57
Deleting Text from an Existing Document	WD 59
Closing the Entire Document	WD 59
Word Help	**WD 60**
Chapter Summary	**WD 62**
Learn It Online	**WD 63**
Apply Your Knowledge	**WD 63**
Extend Your Knowledge	**WD 65**
Make It Right	**WD 66**
In the Lab	**WD 67**
Cases and Places	**WD 71**

CHAPTER TWO
Creating a Research Paper

Objectives	**WD 73**
Introduction	**WD 74**
Project — Research Paper	**WD 74**
Overview	WD 74
MLA Documentation Style	WD 76

Changing Document Settings	**WD 77**
Adjusting Line and Paragraph Spacing	WD 78
Headers and Footers	WD 79
Typing the Research Paper Text	**WD 83**
Shortcut Keys	WD 86
The AutoCorrect Dialog Box	WD 94
Citations	WD 94
Footnotes	WD 99
Footnote Text Style	WD 102
Working with Footnotes and Endnotes	WD 106
Automatic Page Breaks	WD 107
Creating an Alphabetical Works Cited Page	**WD 111**
Proofing and Revising the Research Paper	**WD 118**
Moving Text	WD 119
Selecting Text	WD 120
Find and Replace Dialog Box	WD 124
The Main and Custom Dictionaries	WD 127
Research Task Pane Options	WD 129
Chapter Summary	**WD 132**
Learn It Online	**WD 133**
Apply Your Knowledge	**WD 133**
Extend Your Knowledge	**WD 135**
Make It Right	**WD 136**
In the Lab	**WD 138**
Cases and Places	**WD 143**

CHAPTER THREE
Creating a Cover Letter and a Resume

Objectives	**WD 145**
Introduction	**WD 146**
Project — Cover Letter and Resume	**WD 146**
Overview	WD 146
Creating a Letterhead	**WD 149**
Mini Toolbar	WD 151
Using Tab Stops to Align Text	WD 158
Tab Stops	WD 159
AutoFormat As You Type	WD 162
Creating a Cover Letter	**WD 165**
Building Blocks vs. AutoCorrect	WD 172
Tables	WD 173
Selecting Table Contents	WD 178
Adding and Deleting Table Rows	WD 180
Using a Template to Create a Resume	**WD 183**
Resume Template	WD 185
Copying and Pasting	WD 188
Paste Options Button	WD 192
Addressing and Printing Envelopes and Mailing Labels	**WD 203**
Envelopes and Labels	WD 204
Chapter Summary	**WD 204**
Learn It Online	**WD 205**
Apply Your Knowledge	**WD 205**
Extend Your Knowledge	**WD 206**
Make It Right	**WD 208**
In the Lab	**WD 209**
Cases and Places	**WD 213**

WEB FEATURE
Creating a Web Page Using Word
Objectives	WD 215
Web Feature Introduction	WD 216
Project — Web Page	WD 216
Overview	WD 216
Saving a Word Document as a Web Page	WD 218
Saving to a Web Server	WD 219
Formatting a Web Page	WD 220
Testing the Web Page	WD 222
Feature Summary	WD 223
In the Lab	WD 224

Microsoft Excel 2007

CHAPTER ONE
Creating a Worksheet and an Embedded Chart
Objectives	EX 1
What Is Microsoft Office Excel 2007?	EX 2
Project — Worksheet with an Embedded Chart	EX 2
Overview	EX 4
Starting Excel	EX 6
The Excel Workbook	EX 7
The Worksheet	EX 7
Worksheet Window	EX 9
Status Bar	EX 9
Ribbon	EX 9
Formula Bar	EX 12
Mini Toolbar and Shortcut Menus	EX 12
Quick Access Toolbar	EX 13
Office Button	EX 14
Key Tips	EX 15
Selecting a Cell	EX 15
Entering Text	EX 15
Entering Text in a Cell	EX 18
Correcting a Mistake while Typing	EX 19
AutoCorrect	EX 19
Entering Numbers	EX 22
Calculating a Sum	EX 24
Using the Fill Handle to Copy a Cell to Adjacent Cells	EX 26
Saving the Project	EX 29
Formatting the Worksheet	EX 33
Font Type, Style, Size, and Color	EX 34
Using the Name Box to Select a Cell	EX 47
Other Ways to Select Cells	EX 48
Adding a 3-D Clustered Column Chart to the Worksheet	EX 49
Changing Document Properties and Saving Again	EX 54
Printing a Worksheet	EX 57
Quitting Excel	EX 59
Starting Excel and Opening a Workbook	EX 60
AutoCalculate	EX 62

Correcting Errors	EX 63
Correcting Errors while You Are Typing Data into a Cell	EX 63
Correcting Errors after Entering Data into a Cell	EX 63
Undoing the Last Cell Entry	EX 65
Clearing a Cell or Range of Cells	EX 66
Clearing the Entire Worksheet	EX 66
Excel Help	EX 67
Chapter Summary	EX 69
Learn It Online	EX 70
Apply Your Knowledge	EX 70
Extend Your Knowledge	EX 72
Make It Right	EX 73
In the Lab	EX 74
Cases and Places	EX 79

CHAPTER TWO
Formulas, Functions, Formatting, and Web Queries
Objectives	EX 81
Introduction	EX 82
Project — Worksheet with Formulas, Functions, and Web Queries	EX 82
Overview	EX 84
Entering the Titles and Numbers into the Worksheet	EX 87
Entering Formulas	EX 90
Arithmetic Operations	EX 92
Order of Operations	EX 92
Smart Tags and Option Buttons	EX 96
Using the AVERAGE, MAX, and MIN Functions	EX 98
Verifying Formulas Using Range Finder	EX 106
Formatting the Worksheet	EX 107
Formatting Numbers Using the Ribbon	EX 114
Conditional Formatting	EX 118
Conditional Formatting Operators	EX 121
Changing the Widths of Columns and Heights of Rows	EX 122
Checking Spelling	EX 127
Additional Spell Checker Considerations	EX 129
Preparing to Print the Worksheet	EX 129
Previewing and Printing the Worksheet	EX 132
Displaying and Printing the Formulas Version of the Worksheet	EX 135
Importing External Data from a Web Source Using a Web Query	EX 137
Changing the Worksheet Names	EX 140
E-Mailing a Workbook from within Excel	EX 142
Chapter Summary	EX 143
Learn It Online	EX 144
Apply Your Knowledge	EX 145
Extend Your Knowledge	EX 147
Make It Right	EX 148
In the Lab	EX 149
Cases and Places	EX 156

CHAPTER THREE
What-If Analysis, Charting, and Working with Large Worksheets

Objectives	EX 161
Introduction	EX 162
Project — Financial Projection Worksheet with What-If Analysis and Chart	EX 162
Overview	EX 165
Rotating Text and Using the Fill Handle to Create a Series	EX 168
Using the Auto Fill Options Menu	EX 171
Copying a Range of Cells to a Nonadjacent Destination Area	EX 174
Using the Paste Options Menu	EX 176
Using Drag and Drop to Move or Copy Cells	EX 177
Using Cut and Paste to Move Cells	EX 177
Inserting and Deleting Cells in a Worksheet	EX 177
Inserting Columns	EX 179
Inserting Single Cells or a Range of Cells	EX 179
Deleting Columns and Rows	EX 180
Deleting Individual Cells or a Range of Cells	EX 180
Entering Numbers with Format Symbols	EX 180
Freezing Worksheet Titles	EX 181
Displaying a System Date	EX 183
Absolute versus Relative Addressing	EX 186
Making Decisions — The IF Function	EX 189
Nested Forms of the IF Function	EX 195
Formatting the Worksheet	EX 195
Copying a Cell's Format Using the Format Painter Button	EX 201
Adding a 3-D Pie Chart to the Workbook	EX 204
Renaming and Reordering the Sheets and Coloring Their Tabs	EX 216
Checking Spelling, Saving, Previewing, and Printing the Workbook	EX 218
Changing the View of the Worksheet	EX 220
What-If Analysis	EX 223
Goal Seeking	EX 227
Chapter Summary	EX 228
Learn It Online	EX 229
Apply Your Knowledge	EX 229
Extend Your Knowledge	EX 230
Make It Right	EX 232
In the Lab	EX 233
Cases and Places	EX 245

WEB FEATURE
Creating Web Pages Using Excel

Objectives	EX 249
Web Feature Introduction	EX 250
Project — Workbook with Chart Saved as a Web Page	EX 251
Overview	EX 252
Using Web Page Preview and Saving an Excel Workbook as a Web Page	EX 252
Saving Workbooks as Web Pages	EX 258
File Management Tools in Excel	EX 259
Web Feature Summary	EX 261
In the Lab	EX 262

Microsoft Access 2007

CHAPTER ONE
Creating and Using a Database

Objectives	AC 1
What Is Microsoft Office Access 2007?	AC 2
Project — Database Creation	AC 3
Overview	AC 4
Designing a Database	AC 6
Database Requirements	AC 6
Naming Tables and Fields	AC 8
Identifying the Tables	AC 8
Determining the Primary Keys	AC 8
Determining Additional Fields	AC 8
Determining and Implementing Relationships Between the Tables	AC 9
Determining Data Types for the Fields	AC 9
Identifying and Removing Redundancy	AC 10
Starting Access	AC 12
Creating a Database	AC 13
The Access Window	AC 17
Navigation Pane and Access Work Area	AC 18
Ribbon	AC 19
Mini Toolbar and Shortcut Menus	AC 21
Quick Access Toolbar	AC 22
Office Button	AC 22
Key Tips	AC 23
Creating a Table	AC 23
Making Changes to the Structure	AC 26
Making Changes to the Data	AC 34
AutoCorrect	AC 34
Quitting Access	AC 35
Starting Access and Opening a Database	AC 36
Previewing and Printing the Contents of a Table	AC 40
Creating a Report	AC 50
Using a Form to View Data	AC 57
Changing Document Properties	AC 60
Access Help	AC 61
Chapter Summary	AC 63
Learn It Online	AC 64
Apply Your Knowledge	AC 64
Extend Your Knowledge	AC 65
Make It Right	AC 66
In the Lab	AC 67
Cases and Places	AC 71

CHAPTER TWO
Querying a Database

Objectives	AC 73
Introduction	AC 74
Project — Querying A Database	AC 74
Overview	AC 76
Starting Access	AC 77

Learn It Online INT 40
In the Lab INT 41
Cases and Places INT 46

Appendices

APPENDIX A
Project Planning Guidelines
Using Project Planning Guidelines APP 1
Determine the Project's Purpose APP 1
Analyze your Audience APP 1
Gather Possible Content APP 2
Determine What Content to Present to your
Audience APP 2
Summary APP 2

APPENDIX B
Microsoft Office 2007
What Is Microsoft Office 2007? APP 3
The User Interface APP 4
The Ribbon APP 4
Quick Access Toolbar APP 5
Mini Toolbar APP 5
The Gallery and Live Preview APP 5
Menus and Toolbars APP 6
Office 2007 and the Internet, World Wide Web,
and Intranets APP 6
Online Collaboration Using Office APP 6
Using Microsoft Office 2007 APP 7
Microsoft Office Word 2007 APP 7
Microsoft Office Excel 2007 APP 9
Microsoft Office Access 2007 APP 12
Microsoft Office PowerPoint 2007 APP 13
Microsoft Office Publisher 2007 APP 16
Microsoft Office Outlook 2007 APP 17
Microsoft Office 2007 Help APP 20
Collaboration and SharePoint APP 21

APPEN
Micro
Using M
The Wo
Sea
Tool
Searchir
Obtainir
Use Hel

APPEN
Publis
Web S
Usir

Usir

APPEN
Custo
Changir
Scre

Customi
Cus

Changir

APPEN
Micro
What is
Pr
Wha

Wha

Index

Quick Re

Creating Queries AC 78
Using Queries AC 80
Entering Criteria AC 85
Creating a Parameter Query AC 89
Using Compound Criteria AC 95
Sorting AC 97
Joining Tables AC 103
Calculations AC 113
Calculating Statistics AC 117
Crosstab Queries AC 122
Chapter Summary AC 127
Learn It Online AC 128
Apply Your Knowledge AC 128
Extend Your Knowledge AC 129
Make It Right AC 130
In the Lab AC 131
Cases and Places AC 135

CHAPTER THREE
Maintaining a Database
Objectives AC 137
Introduction AC 138
Project — Maintaining a Database AC 138
Overview AC 139
Starting Access AC 140
Updating Records AC 141
Adding Records AC 141
Filtering Records AC 148
Filters and Queries AC 156
Changing the Database Structure AC 156
Mass Changes AC 162
Validation Rules AC 165
Updating a Table that Contains Validation Rules AC 169
Changing the Appearance of a Datasheet AC 178
Using the Datasheet Formatting Dialog Box AC 181
Multivalued Field in Queries AC 181
Referential Integrity AC 185
Effect of Referential Integrity AC 189
Ordering Records AC 192
Special Database Operations AC 192
Backup and Recovery AC 193
Compacting and Repairing a Database AC 193
Additional Operations AC 194
Chapter Summary AC 195
Learn It Online AC 196
Apply Your Knowledge AC 196
Extend Your Knowledge AC 197
Make It Right AC 198
In the Lab AC 199
Cases and Places AC 203

INTEGRATION FEATURE
Sharing Data Among Applications
Objectives AC 205
Integration Feature Introduction AC 206
Project — Sharing Data Among Applications AC 206
Overview AC 209

Starting Access AC 210
Importing or Linking Data From Other
Applications to Access AC 211
Using the Access Table AC 215
Linking versus Importing AC 216
The Linked Table Manager AC 216
Importing from or Linking to Data in Another
Access Database AC 217
Text Files AC 218
Using Saved Import Steps AC 219
Exporting Data From Access to Other
Applications AC 220
Using Saved Export Steps AC 225
XML AC 226
Feature Summary AC 230
In The Lab AC 230

Microsoft PowerPoint 2007

CHAPTER ONE
Creating and Editing a Presentation
Objectives PPT 1
What Is Microsoft Office PowerPoint 2007? PPT 2
Project — Presentation with Bulleted Lists PPT 3
Overview PPT 4
Starting PowerPoint PPT 5
The PowerPoint Window PPT 6
PowerPoint Window PPT 6
PowerPoint Views PPT 8
Ribbon PPT 8
Mini Toolbar and Shortcut Menus PPT 11
Quick Access Toolbar PPT 13
Office Button PPT 14
Key Tips PPT 15
Choosing a Document Theme PPT 16
Creating a Title Slide PPT 18
Correcting a Mistake When Typing PPT 19
Paragraphs PPT 19
Formatting Characters in a Presentation PPT 21
Fonts and Font Styles PPT 21
Saving the Project PPT 26
Adding a New Slide to a Presentation PPT 29
Creating a Text Slide with a Single-Level
Bulleted List PPT 31
Creating a Text Slide with a Multi-Level
Bulleted List PPT 33
Ending a Slide Show with a Closing Slide PPT 40
Changing Document Properties and Saving Again PPT 43
Moving to Another Slide in Normal View PPT 46
Viewing the Presentation in Slide Show View PPT 48
Quitting PowerPoint PPT 52
Starting PowerPoint and Opening a Presentation PPT 53
Checking a Presentation for Spelling Errors PPT 55
Correcting Errors PPT 58
Types of Corrections Made to Presentations PPT 58
Deleting Text PPT 58
Replacing Text in an Existing Slide PPT 59

Displaying a Presentation in Grayscale	PPT 59
Printing a Presentation	PPT 61
Making a Transparency	PPT 62
PowerPoint Help	PPT 63
Chapter Summary	PPT 65
Learn It Online	PPT 66
Apply Your Knowledge	PPT 66
Extend Your Knowledge	PPT 67
Make It Right	PPT 68
In the Lab	PPT 69
Cases and Places	PPT 78

CHAPTER TWO

Creating a Presentation with Illustrations and Shapes

Objectives	PPT 81
Introduction	PPT 82
Project — Presentation with Illustrations and a Shape	PPT 82
Overview	PPT 82
Starting PowerPoint	PPT 84
Creating Slides from a Blank Presentation	PPT 85
Changing Views to Review a Presentation	PPT 90
Changing Layouts	PPT 92
Inserting Clip Art and Photographs into Slides	PPT 95
Photographs and the Clip Organizer	PPT 97
Resizing Clip Art and Photographs	PPT 101
Formatting Title and Content Text	PPT 106
Format Painter	PPT 111
Adding and Formatting a Shape	PPT 115
Adding a Transition	PPT 122
Printing a Presentation as an Outline and Handouts	PPT 125
Saving and Quitting PowerPoint	PPT 130
Chapter Summary	PPT 131
Learn It Online	PPT 132
Apply Your Knowledge	PPT 132
Extend Your Knowledge	PPT 134
Make It Right	PPT 135
In the Lab	PPT 136
Cases and Places	PPT 142

INTEGRATION FEATURE

Creating Web Pages Using PowerPoint

Objectives	PPT 145
Web Feature Introduction	PPT 145
Project — Web Page	PPT 146
Overview	PPT 146
Using Web Page Preview and Saving a PowerPoint Presentation as a Web Page	PPT 146
Web Page Format Options	PPT 152
Saving Presentations as Web Pages	PPT 154
File Management Tools in PowerPoint	PPT 155
Web Feature Summary	PPT 157
In the Lab	PPT 158

About Our New Cover Look

Learning styles of students have changed, but the Shelly Cashman Series' dedication to their success has remained steadfast for over 30 years. We are committed to continually updating our approach and content to reflect the way today's students learn and experience new technology.

This focus on the user is reflected in our bold new cover design, which features photographs of real students using the Shelly Cashman Series in their courses. Each book features a different user, reflecting the many ages, experiences, and backgrounds of all of the students learning with our books. When you use the Shelly Cashman Series, you can be assured that you are learning computer skills using the most effective courseware available.

We would like to thank the administration and faculty at the participating schools for their help in making our vision a reality. Most of all, we'd like to thank the wonderful students from all over the world who learn from our texts and now appear on our covers.

Microsoft Office 2007

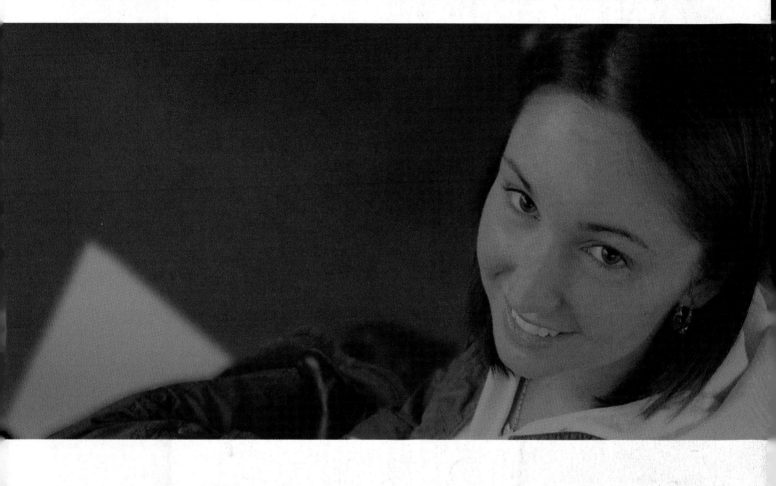

ESSENTIAL
Introduction to Computers

and How to Purchase a Personal Computer

OBJECTIVES

After completing this material, you will be able to:

1. Define the term computer and discuss the four basic computer operations: input, processing, output, and storage

2. Define data and information

3. Explain the principal components of the computer and their use

4. Describe the use of magnetic disks, USB flash drives, and other storage media

5. Discuss computer software and explain the difference between system software and application software

6. Identify several types of personal computer application software

7. Discuss computer communications channels and equipment and the Internet and World Wide Web

8. Define e-commerce

9. Explain how to purchase a personal computer

Computers are everywhere: at work, at school, and at home. In the workplace, employees use computers to create correspondence such as e-mail, memos, and letters; calculate payroll; track inventory; and generate invoices. At school, teachers use computers to assist with classroom instruction. Students complete assignments and do research on computers. At home, people spend hours of leisure time on the computer. They play games, communicate with friends and relatives using e-mail, purchase goods online, chat in chat rooms, listen to music, watch videos and movies, read books and magazines, research genealogy, compose music and videos, retouch photographs, and plan vacations. At work, at school, and at home, computers are helping people do their work faster, more accurately, and in some cases, in ways that previously would not have been possible.

WEB LINK

Computers

For more information, visit scsite.com/ic7/ weblink and then click Computers.

WHAT IS A COMPUTER?

A **computer** is an electronic device, operating under the control of instructions stored in its own memory, that can accept data (input), process the data according to specified rules (process), produce results (output), and store the results (storage) for future use. Generally, the term is used to describe a collection of hardware components that function together as a system. An example of common hardware components that make up a personal computer is shown in Figure 1.

FIGURE 1   Common computer hardware components.

printer
(output device)

portable media player
(output device)

monitor
(output device)   screen

PC video camera
(input device)

CD/DVD drive
(storage device)

hard disk drive
(storage device)

system unit
(processor, memory, and storage devices)

keyboard
(input device)

mouse
(input device)

scanner
(input device)

digital camera
(input device)

microphone
(input device)

external hard disk
(storage device)

modem
(communications device)

card reader/writer
(storage device)

USB flash drive
(storage device)

WHAT DOES A COMPUTER DO?

Computers perform four basic operations — input, process, output, and storage. These operations comprise the **information processing cycle**. Collectively, these operations change data into information and store it for future use.

All computer processing requires data. **Data** is a collection of unprocessed items, which can include text, numbers, images, audio, and video. Computers manipulate data to create information. **Information** conveys meaning and is useful to one or more people. During the output operation, the information that has been created is put into some form, such as a printed report, or it can be written on computer storage for future use. As shown in Figure 2, a computer processes several data items to produce a grade report.

People who use the computer directly or use the information it provides are called **computer users**, **end users**, or sometimes, just **users**.

FIGURE 2   A computer processes data into information. In this example, the student identification number, semester, course codes, and course grades all represent data. The computer processes the data to produce the grade report (information).

A **smart card**, which is similar in size to a credit card or ATM card, stores data on a thin microprocessor embedded in the card. When you insert the smart card in a specialized card reader, the information on the card is read and, if necessary, updated (Figure 26). Uses of smart cards include storing medical records, tracking customer purchases, storing a prepaid amount of money, and authenticating users, such as for Internet purchases.

COMMUNICATIONS DEVICES

A **communications device** is a hardware component that enables a computer to send (transmit) and receive data, instructions, and information to and from one or more computers. A widely used communications device is the telephone or cable modem (Figure 1 on page COM 2).

Communications occur over **transmission media** such as telephone lines, cables, cellular radio networks, and satellites. Some transmission media, such as satellites and cellular radio networks, are **wireless**, which means they have no physical lines or wires. People around the world use computers and communications devices to communicate with each other using one or more transmission media.

COMPUTER SOFTWARE

Computer software is the key to productive use of computers. With the correct software, a computer can become a valuable tool. Software can be categorized into two types: system software and application software.

System Software

WEB LINK

**Operating
Systems**

For more information, visit scsite.com/ic7/ weblink and then click Operating Systems.

System software consists of programs to control the operations of computer equipment. An important part of system software is a set of programs called the operating system. Instructions in the **operating system** tell the computer how to perform the functions of loading, storing, and executing an application program and how to transfer data. For a computer to operate, an operating system must be stored in the computer's memory. When a computer is turned on, the operating system is loaded into the computer's memory from auxiliary storage. This process is called **booting**.

Today, most computers use an operating system that has a **graphical user interface (GUI)** that provides visual cues such as icon symbols to help the user. Each **icon** represents an application such as word processing, or a file or document where data is stored. Microsoft Windows Vista (Figure 27) and Windows XP, Apple Mac OS X, and Linux are four popular personal computer operating systems.

FIGURE 26   A smart card and smart card reader.

FIGURE 27   A graphical user interface, such as Microsoft Windows Vista, makes the computer easier to use.

Application Software

Application software consists of programs designed to make users more productive and/or assist them with personal tasks. Some widely used application software includes Web browsers, personal information managers, project management, accounting, computer-aided design, desktop publishing, paint/image editing, audio and video editing, multimedia authoring, Web page authoring, personal finance, legal, tax preparation, home design/landscaping, educational, reference, and entertainment (games, simulations, etc.). Often, application software is available for purchase from a Web site or store that sells computer products (Figure 28).

Personal computer users regularly use application software. Some of the more commonly used applications are word processing, electronic spreadsheet, database, and presentation graphics.

WORD PROCESSING **Word processing software** (Figure 29) is used to create, edit, format, and print documents. A key advantage of word processing software is that users easily can make changes in documents, such as correcting spelling; changing margins; and adding, deleting, or relocating entire paragraphs. These changes would be difficult and time consuming to make using manual methods such as a typewriter. With a word processor, documents can be printed quickly and accurately and easily stored on a disk for future use. Word processing software is oriented toward working with text, but word processing packages also support features that enable users to manipulate numeric data and utilize graphics.

SPREADSHEET **Electronic spreadsheet software** (Figure 30) allows the user to add, subtract, and perform user-defined calculations on rows and columns of numbers. These numbers can be changed, and the spreadsheet quickly recalculates the new results. Electronic spreadsheet software eliminates the tedious recalculations required with manual methods. Spreadsheet information frequently is converted into a graphic form, such as charts. Graphics capabilities now are included in most spreadsheet packages.

WEB LINK

Word Processing Software

For more information, visit scsite.com/ic7/ weblink and then click Word Processing Software.

WEB LINK

Spreadsheet Software

For more information, visit scsite.com/ic7/ weblink and then click Spreadsheet Software.

FIGURE 28 Stores that sell computer products have shelves stocked with software for sale.

FIGURE 29 Word processing software is used to create letters, memos, newsletters, and other documents.

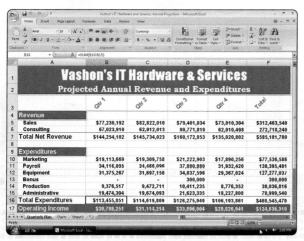

FIGURE 30 Electronic spreadsheet software frequently is used by people who work with numbers. The user enters the data and the formulas to be used on the data, and the computer calculates the results.

How to Purchase a Personal Computer

(a) desktop computer

(b) mobile computer (notebook computer or Tablet PC)

At some point, perhaps while you are taking this course, you may decide to buy a personal computer. The decision is an important one and will require an investment of both time and money. Like many buyers, you may have little computer experience and find yourself unsure of how to proceed. You can get started by talking to your friends, coworkers, and instructors about their computers. What type of computers did they buy? Why? For what purposes do they use their computers? You also should answer the following three questions to help narrow your choices to a specific computer type, before reading this guide. At the end of this guide, you'll also find tips on purchasing PDAs, smart phones, portable media players, and other personal mobile devices such as handheld navigation devices and game consoles.

❶ Do you want a desktop computer or mobile computer?

A desktop computer (Figure 37a) is designed as a stationary device that sits on or below a desk or table in a location such as a home, office, or dormitory room. A desktop computer must be plugged in an electrical outlet to operate. A mobile computer, such as a notebook computer or Tablet PC (Figure 37b), is smaller than a desktop computer, more portable, and has a battery that allows you to operate it for a period without an electrical outlet.

Desktop computers are a good option if you work mostly in one place and have plenty of space in your work area. Desktop computers generally give you more performance for your money.

Increasingly, more corporations are buying mobile computers to take advantage of their portability to work while traveling and at home. The past disadvantages of mobile computers, such as lower processor speeds, poor-quality monitors, weight, short battery life, and significantly higher prices, have all but disappeared. Today, hard drive speed, capacity, processor speed, and graphics capability in notebook computers are equal to, if not better than, desktop computers.

If you are thinking of using a mobile computer to take notes in class or in business meetings, then consider a Tablet PC with handwriting and drawing capabilities. Typically, note-taking involves writing text notes and drawing charts,

FIGURE 37

schematics, and other illustrations. By allowing you to write and draw directly on the screen with a digital pen, a Tablet PC eliminates the distracting sound of the notebook keyboard tapping and allows you to capture drawings. Some notebook computers can convert to Tablet PCs.

Mobile computers used to have several drawbacks, including the lack of high-end capabilities. Today's high-end notebook computers include most of the capabilities of a good desktop computer. Manufacturers have made great strides in improving durability and battery life. Most notebook computers are 1.5 to 2 inches thick and weigh less than 10 pounds, making them very portable and easy to carry.

2 **For what purposes will you use the computer?**
Having a general idea of the purposes for which you want to use your computer will help you decide on the type of computer to buy. At this point in your research, it is not necessary to know the exact application software titles or version numbers you might want to use. Knowing that you plan to use the computer primarily to create word processing, spreadsheet, database, and presentation documents, however, will point you in the direction of a desktop or notebook computer. If you want the portability of a smart phone or PDA, but you need more computing power, then a Tablet PC may be the best alternative. You also must consider that some application software runs only on a Mac, while others run only on a PC with the Windows operating system. Still other software may run only on a PC running the UNIX or Linux operating system.

3 **Should the computer be compatible with the computers at school or work?**
If you plan to bring work home, telecommute, or take distance education courses, then you should purchase a computer that is compatible with those at school or work.

Compatibility is primarily a software issue. If your computer runs the same operating system version, such as Microsoft Windows Vista, and the same application software, such as Microsoft Office, then your computer will be able to read documents created at school or work and vice versa. Incompatible hardware can become an issue if you plan to connect directly to a school or office network using a cable or wireless technology. You usually can obtain the minimum system requirements from the Information Technology department at your school or workplace.

After evaluating the answers to these three questions, you should have a general idea of how you plan to use your computer and the type of computer you want to buy. Once you have decided on the type of computer you want, you can follow the guidelines presented in this guide to help you purchase a specific computer, along with software, peripherals, and other accessories.

Many of the desktop computer guidelines presented also apply to the purchase of a notebook computer and a Tablet PC. Later in this guide, sections on purchasing a notebook computer or Tablet PC address additional considerations specific to those computer types.

This guide concentrates on recommendations for purchasing a desktop computer or mobile computer.

HOW TO PURCHASE A DESKTOP COMPUTER

Once you have decided that a desktop computer is most suited to your computing needs, the next step is to determine specific software, hardware, peripheral devices, and services to purchase, as well as where to buy the computer.

1 **Determine the specific software you want to use on your computer.**
Before deciding to purchase software, be sure it contains the features necessary for the tasks you want to perform. Rely on the computer users in whom you have confidence to help you decide on the software to use. The minimum requirements of the software you select may determine the operating system (Microsoft Windows Vista, Linux, UNIX, Mac OS X) you need. If you have decided to use a particular operating system that does not support software you want to use, you may be able to purchase similar software from other manufacturers.

Many Web sites and trade magazines, such as those listed in Figure 38 on the next page, provide reviews of software products. These Web sites frequently have articles that rate computers and software on cost, performance, and support.

Your hardware requirements depend on the minimum requirements of the software you will run on your computer.

Some software requires more memory and disk space than others, as well as additional input, output, and storage devices. For example, suppose you want to run software that can copy one CD's or DVD's contents directly to another CD or DVD, without first copying the data to your hard disk. To support that, you should consider a desktop computer or a high-end notebook computer, because the computer will need two CD or DVD drives: one that reads from a CD or DVD, and one that reads from and writes on a CD or DVD. If you plan to run software that allows your computer to work as an entertainment system, then you will need a CD or DVD drive, quality speakers, and an upgraded sound card.

Type of Computer	Web Site	Web Address
PC	CNET Shopper	shopper.cnet.com
	PC World Magazine	pcworld.com
	BYTE Magazine	byte.com
	PC Magazine	pcmag.com
	Yahoo! Computers	computers.yahoo.com
	MSN Shopping	shopping.msn.com
	Dave's Guide to Buying a Home Computer	css.msu.edu/PC-Guide
Mac	Macworld Magazine	macworld.com
	Apple	apple.com
	Switch to Mac Campaign	apple.com/switch

For an updated list of hardware and software reviews and their Web site addresses, visit scsite.com/ic7/buyers.

FIGURE 38   Hardware and software reviews.

 Know the System Requirements of the Operating System.

After deciding what software you want to run on your new computer, you need to determine the operating system you want to use. If, however, you purchase a new computer, chances are it will have the latest version of your preferred operating system (Windows Vista, Linux, UNIX, Mac OS X). Figure 39 lists the minimum computer requirements of Windows Vista versions.

Windows Vista Versions	Minimum Computer Requirements
Windows Vista Home Basic	• 800 MHz processor • 512 MB of RAM • DirectX 9 capable graphics processor
Windows Vista Home Premium **Windows Vista Ultimate** **Windows Vista Business** **Windows Vista Enterprise**	• 1 GHz processor • 1 GB of RAM • DirectX 9 capable graphics Windows Vista Enterprise • 40 GB of hard disk capacity (15 GB free space) • DVD-ROM drive • Audio output capability • Internet access capability

FIGURE 39   Hardware requirements for Windows Vista.

 Look for bundled software.

When you purchase a computer, it may come bundled with software. Some sellers even let you choose which software you want. Remember, however, that bundled software has value only if you would have purchased the software even if it had not come with the computer. At the very least, you probably will want word processing software and a browser to access the Internet. If you need additional applications, such as a spreadsheet, a database, or presentation graphics, consider purchasing Microsoft Works, Microsoft Office, OpenOffice.org, or Sun StarOffice, which include several programs at a reduced price.

 Avoid buying the least powerful computer available.

Once you know the application software you want to use, you then can consider the following important criteria about the computer's components: (1) processor speed, (2) size and types of memory (RAM) and storage, (3) types of input/output devices, (4) types of ports and adapter cards, and (5) types of communications devices. You also need to consider if the computer is upgradeable and to what extent you are able to upgrade. For example, all manufacturers limit the amount of memory you can add. The information in Figures 40 and 41 can help you determine what system components are best for you. Figure 40 (on COM 27 to COM 28) outlines considerations for specific hardware components. Figure 41 (on page COM 29) provides a Base Components worksheet that lists PC recommendations for each category of user discussed in this book: Home User, Small Office/Home Office User, Mobile User, Power User, and Large Business User. In the worksheet, the Home User category is divided into two groups: Application Home User and Game Home User. The Mobile User recommendations list criteria for a notebook computer, but do not include the PDA or Tablet PC options.

Computer technology changes rapidly, meaning a computer that seems powerful enough today may not serve your computing needs in a few years. In fact, studies show that many users regret not buying a more powerful computer. To avoid this, plan to buy a computer that will last you for two to three years. You can help delay obsolescence by purchasing the fastest processor, the most memory, and the largest hard disk you can afford. If you must buy a less powerful computer, be sure you can upgrade it with additional memory, components, and peripheral devices as your computer requirements grow.

 Consider upgrades to the mouse, keyboard, monitor, printer, microphone, and speakers.

You use these peripheral devices to interact with your computer, so you should make sure they are up to your standards. Review the peripheral devices listed in Figure 40 on pages COM 27 to COM 28 and then visit both local computer dealers and large retail stores to test the computers on display. Ask the salesperson what input and output devices would be best for you and whether you should upgrade beyond what comes standard. Consider purchasing a wireless keyboard and wireless mouse to eliminate bothersome wires on your desktop. A few extra dollars spent on these components when you initially purchase a computer can extend its usefulness by years.

CD/DVD Drives: Most computers come with a CD-RW drive. A CD-RW drive allows you to create your own custom data CDs for data backup or data transfer purposes. It also will allow you to store and share video files, digital photos, and other large files with other people who have access to a CD-ROM drive. An even better alternative is to upgrade to a DVD±RW combination drive. It allows you to read DVDs and CDs and to write data on (burn) a DVD or CD. A DVD has a capacity of at least 4.7 GB versus the 650 MB capacity of a CD. An HD DVD has a minimum capacity of 45 GB.

Card Reader/Writer: A card reader/writer is useful for transferring data directly to and from a removable flash memory card, such as the ones used in your camera or audio player. Make sure the card reader/writer can read from and write on the flash memory cards that you use.

Digital Camera: Consider an inexpensive point-and-shoot digital camera. They are small enough to carry around, usually operate automatically in terms of lighting and focus, and contain storage cards for storing photographs. A 5-megapixel camera with a 512 MB storage card is fine for creating images for use on the Web or to send via e-mail.

Digital Video Capture Device: A digital video capture device allows you to connect your computer to a camcorder or VCR and record, edit, manage, and then write video back on a VCR tape, a CD, or a DVD. To create quality video (true 30 frames per second, full-sized TV), the digital video capture device should have a USB 2.0 or FireWire port. You also will need sufficient storage: an hour of data on a VCR tape takes up about 5 GB of disk storage.

External Hard Disk: An external hard disk can serve many purposes: it can serve as extra storage for your computer, provide a way to store and transport large files or large quantities of files, and provide security by allowing you to keep all of your data on the external disk without leaving any data on the computer. External hard disks can be purchased with the same amount of capacity as any internal disk. If you are going to use it as a backup to your internal hard disk, you should purchase an external hard drive with at least as much capacity as your internal hard disk.

Hard Disk: It is recommended that you buy a computer with 60 to 80 GB if your primary interests are browsing the Web and using e-mail and Office suite-type applications; 80 to 100 GB if you also want to edit digital photographs; 100 to 200 GB if you plan to edit digital video or manipulate large audio files even occasionally; and 200 to 500 GB if you will edit digital video, movies, or photography often; store audio files and music; or consider yourself to be a power user. It also is recommended that you use Serial ATA (SATA) as opposed to Parallel ATA (PATA). SATA has many advantages over PATA, including support for Plug and Play devices.

Joystick/Wheel: If you use your computer to play games, then you will want to purchase a joystick or a wheel. These devices, especially the more expensive ones, provide for realistic game play with force feedback, programmable buttons, and specialized levers and wheels.

Keyboard: The keyboard is one of the more important devices used to communicate with the computer. For this reason, make sure the keyboard you purchase has 101 to 105 keys, is comfortable and easy to use, and has a USB connection. A wireless keyboard should be considered, especially if you have a small desk area.

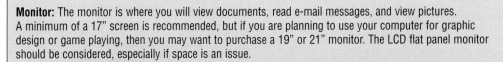

Microphone: If you plan to record audio or use speech recognition to enter text and commands, then purchase a close-talk headset with gain adjustment support.

Modem: Most computers come with a modem so that you can use your telephone line to access the Internet. Some modems also have fax capabilities. Your modem should be rated at 56 Kbps.

Monitor: The monitor is where you will view documents, read e-mail messages, and view pictures. A minimum of a 17" screen is recommended, but if you are planning to use your computer for graphic design or game playing, then you may want to purchase a 19" or 21" monitor. The LCD flat panel monitor should be considered, especially if space is an issue.

Mouse: As you work with your computer, you use the mouse constantly. For this reason, spend a few extra dollars, if necessary, and purchase a mouse with an optical sensor and USB connection. The optical sensor replaces the need for a mouse ball, which means you do not need a mouse pad. For a PC, make sure your mouse has a wheel, which acts as a third button in addition to the top two buttons on the left and right. An ergonomic design is also important because your hand is on the mouse most of the time when you are using your computer. A wireless mouse should be considered to eliminate the cord and allow you to work at short distances from your computer.

FIGURE 40   Hardware guidelines.

(continued next page)

(continued from previous page)

Ports: Depending on how you are using your computer, you may need anywhere from 4 to 10 USB 2.0 ports. USB 2.0 ports have become the connection of choice in the computer industry. They offer an easy way to connect peripheral devices such as printers, digital cameras, portable media players, etc. Many computers intended for home or professional audio/video use have built-in FireWire ports. Most personal computers come with a minimum of six USB 2.0 ports and two FireWire ports.

Port Hub Expander: If you plan to connect several peripheral devices to your computer at the same time, then you need to be concerned with the number of ports available on your computer. If your computer does not have enough ports, then you should purchase a port hub expander. A port hub expander plugs into a single FireWire port or USB port and gives several additional ports.

Printer: Your two basic printer choices are ink-jet and laser. Color ink-jet printers cost on average between $50 and $300. Laser printers cost from $200 to $2,000. In general, the cheaper the printer, the lower the resolution and speed, and the more often you are required to change the ink cartridge or toner. Laser printers print faster and with a higher quality than an ink-jet, and their toner on average costs less. If you want color, then go with a high-end ink-jet printer to ensure quality of print. Duty cycle (the number of pages you expect to print each month) also should be a determining factor. If your duty cycle is on the low end — hundreds of pages per month — then stay with a high-end ink-jet printer, rather than purchasing a laser printer. If you plan to print photographs taken with a digital camera, then you should purchase a photo printer. A photo printer is a dye-sublimation printer or an ink-jet printer with higher resolution and features that allow you to print quality photographs.

Processor: For a PC, an Intel Core 2 Duo processor at 2.66 GHz is more than enough processor power for application home and small office/home office users. Game home, large business, and power users should upgrade to faster processors.

RAM: RAM plays a vital role in the speed of your computer. Make sure the computer you purchase has at least 512 MB of RAM. If you have extra money to invest in your computer, then consider increasing the RAM to 1 GB or more. The extra money for RAM will be well spent.

Scanner: The most popular scanner purchased with a computer today is the flatbed scanner. When evaluating a flatbed scanner, check the color depth and resolution. Do not buy anything less than a color depth of 48 bits and a resolution of 1200 x 2400 dpi. The higher the color depth, the more accurate the color. A higher resolution picks up the more subtle gradations of color.

Sound Card: Many computers come with a standard sound card that supports Dolby 5.1 surround and is capable of recording and playing digital audio. Make sure it is suitable in the event you decide to use your computer as an entertainment or gaming system.

Speakers: Once you have a good sound card, quality speakers and a separate subwoofer that amplifies the bass frequencies of the speakers can turn your computer into a premium stereo system.

PC Video Camera: A PC video camera is a small camera used to capture and display live video (in some cases with sound), primarily on a Web page. You also can capture, edit, and share video and still photos. The camera sits on your monitor or desk. Recommended minimum specifications include 640 x 480 resolution, a video with a rate of 30 frames per second, and a USB 2.0 or FireWire port.

USB Flash Drive: If you work on different computers and need access to the same data and information, then this portable miniature mobile storage device is ideal. USB flash drive capacity varies from 16 MB to 4 GB.

Video Card: Most standard video cards satisfy the monitor display needs of application home and small office users. If you are a game home user or a graphic designer, you will want to upgrade to a higher quality video card. The higher refresh rates will further enhance the display of games, graphics, and movies.

Wireless LAN Access Point: A Wireless LAN Access Point allows you to network several computers, so they can share files and access the Internet through a single cable modem or DSL connection. Each device that you connect requires a wireless card. A Wireless LAN Access Point can offer a range of operations up to several hundred feet, so be sure the device has a high-powered antenna.

BASE COMPONENTS

	Application Home User	Game Home User	Small Office/Home Office User	Mobile User	Large Business User	Power User
HARDWARE						
Processor	Intel Core 2 Duo at 2.66 GHz	Intel Core 2 Duo at 2.93 GHz	Intel Core 2 Duo at 2.93 GHz	Intel Core 2 Duo at 2.33 GHz	Intel Core 2 Duo at 2.66 GHz	Intel Core 2 Extreme
RAM	512 MB	4 GB	1 GB	1 GB	1 GB	2 GB
Cache	512 KB L2	512 KB L2	512 KB L2	512 KB L2	512 KB L2	2 MB L3
Hard Disk	250 GB	300 GB	500 GB	100 GB	500 GB	1.5 TB
LCD Flat Panel	17" or 19"	21"	19" or 21"	17" Wide Display	19" of 21"	23"
Video Card	256 MB	512 MB	256 MB	256 MB	256 MB	256 MB
CD/DVD Bay 1	CD-RW	Blue-ray or HD DVD reader/writer	CD-RW	CD-RW/DVD	CD-RW	Blue-ray or HD DVD reader/writer
CD/DVD Bay 2	DVD±RW	DVD±RW	DVD±RW	DVD±RW	DVD±RW	DVD±RW
Printer	Color Ink-Jet	Color Ink-Jet	18 ppm Laser	Portable Ink-Jet	50 ppm Laser	10 ppm Color Laser
PC Video Camera	Yes	Yes	Yes	Yes	Yes	Yes
Fax/Modem	Yes	Yes	Yes	Yes	Yes	Yes
Microphone	Close-Talk Headset With Gain Adjustment	Close-Talk Headset With Gain Adjustment	Close-Talk Headset With Gain Adjustment	Close-Talk Headset With Gain Adjustment	Close-Talk Headset With Gain Adjustment	Close-Talk Headset With Gain Adjustment
Speakers	5.1 Dolby Surround	5.1 Dolby Surround	5.1 Dolby Surround	Stereo	5.1 Dolby Surround	5.1 Dolby Surround
Pointing Device	IntelliMouse or Optical Mouse	Laser Mouse and Joystick	IntelliMouse or Optical Mouse	Touchpad or Pointing Stick and Laser Mouse	IntelliMouse or Optical Mouse	IntelliMouse or Laser Mouse and Joystick
Keyboard Yes		Yes	Yes	Built-In	Yes	Yes
Backup Disk/Tape Drive	External or Removable Hard Disk	External or Removable Hard Disk	External or Removable Hard Disk	External or Removable Hard Disk	Tape Drive	External or Removable Hard Disk
USB Flash Drive	256 MB	512 MB	512 MB	512 MB	4 GB	2 GB
Sound Card	Sound Blaster Compatible	Sound Blaster Audigy 2	Sound Blaster Compatible	Built-In	Sound Blaster Compatible	Sound Blaster Audigy 2
Network Card	Yes	Yes	Yes	Yes	Yes	Yes
TV-Out Connector	Yes	Yes	Yes	Yes	Yes	Yes
USB 2.0 Port	6	8	6	4	9	10
FireWire Port	2	2	2	1	2	2
SOFTWARE						
Operating System	Windows Vista Home Basic	Windows Vista Home Premium	Windows Vista Business	Windows Vista Business	Windows Vista Enterprise	Windows Vista Ultimate
Application Suite	Office Standard 2007	Office Standard 2007	Office Small Business 2007	Office Small Business 2007	Office Professional 2007	Office Professional 2007
Antivirus	Yes, 12-Mo. Subscription	Yes, 12-Mo. Subscription	Yes, 12-Mo. Subscription	Yes, 12-Mo. Subscription	Yes, 12-Mo. Subscription	Yes, 12-Mo. Subscription
Internet Access	Cable, DSL, or Dial-up	Cable or DSL	Cable or DSL	Wireless or Dial-up	LAN/WAN (T1/T3)	Cable or DSL
OTHER						
Surge Protector	Yes	Yes	Yes	Portable	Yes	Yes
Warranty	3-Year Limited, 1-Year Next Business Day On-Site Service	3-Year Limited, 1-Year Next Business Day On-Site Service	3-year On-Site Service	3-Year Limited, 1-Year Next Business Day On-Site Service	3-year On-Site Service	3-year On-Site Service
Other		Wheel	Postage Printer	Docking Station Carrying Case Fingerprint Scanner Portable Data Projector		Graphics Tablet Plotter or Large-Format Printer

Optional Components for all Categories	
802.11g Wireless Card	Graphics Tablet
Bluetooth Enabled	Portable Media Player
Biometric Input Device	IrDA Port
Card Reader/Writer	Multifunction Peripheral
Digital Camera	Photo Printer
Digital Video Capture Device	Port Hub Expander
Digital Video Camera	Portable Data Projector
Dual-Monitor Support with Second Monitor	Scanner
Ergonomic Keyboard	TV/FM Tuner
External Hard Disk	Uninterruptible Power Supply

FIGURE 41   Base desktop and mobile computer components and optional components. A copy of the Base Components worksheet is part of the Data Files for Students. To obtain a copy of the Data Files for Students, see the inside back cover of this book for instructions.

6 **Determine whether you want to use telephone lines or broadband (cable or DSL) to access the Internet.**

If your computer has a modem, then you can access the Internet using a standard telephone line. Ordinarily, you call a local or toll-free 800 number to connect to an ISP (see Guideline 7 on the next page). Using a dial-up Internet connection is relatively inexpensive but slow.

DSL and cable connections provide much faster Internet connections, which are ideal if you want faster file download speeds for software, digital photos, and music. As you would expect, they also are more expensive. DSL, which is available through local telephone companies, also may require that you subscribe to an ISP. Cable is available through your local cable television provider and some online service providers (OSPs). If you get cable, then you would not use a separate Internet service provider or online service provider.

7 **If you are using a dial-up or wireless connection to connect to the Internet, then select an ISP or OSP.**

You can access the Internet via telephone lines in one of two ways: an ISP or an OSP. Both provide Internet access for a monthly fee that ranges from $6 to $25. Local ISPs offer Internet access to users in a limited geographic region, through local telephone numbers. National ISPs provide access for users nationwide (including mobile users), through local and toll-free telephone numbers and cable. Because of their size, national ISPs generally offer more services and have a larger technical support staff than local ISPs. OSPs furnish Internet access as well as members-only features for users nationwide. Figure 42 lists several national ISPs and OSPs. Before you choose an ISP or OSP, compare such features as the number of access hours, monthly fees, available services (e-mail, Web page hosting, chat), and reliability.

Company	Service	Web Address
America Online	OSP	aol.com
AT&T Worldnet	ISP	www.att.net
Comcast	OSP	comcast.net
CompuServe	OSP	compuserve.com
EarthLink	ISP	earthlink.net
Juno	OSP	juno.com
NetZero	OSP	netzero.com
MSN	OSP	msn.com
Prodigy	ISP/OSP	myhome.prodigy.net

For an updated list of national ISPs and OSPs and their Web site addresses, visit scsite.com/ic7/buyers.

FIGURE 42   National ISPs and OSPs.

8 **Use a worksheet to compare computers, services, and other considerations.**

You can use a separate sheet of paper to take notes on each vendor's computer and then summarize the information on a worksheet, such as the one shown in Figure 43. You can use Figure 43 to compare prices for either a PC or a Mac. Most companies advertise a price for a base computer that includes components housed in the system unit (processor, RAM, sound card, video card), disk drives (hard disk, CD-ROM, CD-RW, DVD-ROM, and DVD6RW), a keyboard, mouse, monitor, printer, speakers, and modem. Be aware, however, that some advertisements list prices for computers with only some of these components. Monitors and printers, for example, often are not included in a base computer's price. Depending on how you plan to use the computer, you may want to invest in additional or more powerful components. When you are comparing the prices of computers, make sure you are comparing identical or similar configurations.

FIGURE 43   A worksheet is an effective tool for summarizing and comparing components and prices of different computer vendors. A copy of the Computer Cost Comparison Worksheet is part of the Data Files for Students. To obtain a copy of the Data Files for Students, see the inside back cover of this book for instructions.

9 **If you are buying a new computer, you have several purchasing options: buying from your school bookstore, a local computer dealer, a local large retail store, or ordering by mail via telephone or the Web.**

Each purchasing option has certain advantages. Many college bookstores, for example, sign exclusive pricing agreements with computer manufacturers and, thus, can offer student discounts. Local dealers and local large retail stores, however, more easily can provide hands-on support. Mail-order companies that sell computers by telephone or online via the Web (Figure 44) often provide the lowest prices, but extend less personal service. Some major mail-order companies, however, have started to provide next-business-day, on-site services. A credit card usually is required to buy from a mail-order company. Figure 45 lists some of the more popular mail-order companies and their Web site addresses.

10 **If you are buying a used computer, stay with name brands such as Dell, Gateway, Hewlett-Packard, and Apple.**

Although brand-name equipment can cost more, most brand-name computers have longer, more comprehensive warranties, are better supported, and have more authorized centers for repair services. As with new computers, you can purchase a used computer from local computer dealers, local large retail stores, or mail order via the telephone or the Web. Classified ads and used computer sellers offer additional outlets for purchasing used computers. Figure 46 lists several major used computer brokers and their Web site addresses.

11 **If you have a computer and are upgrading to a new one, then consider selling or trading in the old one.**

If you are a replacement buyer, your older computer still may have value. If you cannot sell the computer through the classified ads, via a Web site, or to a friend, then ask if the computer dealer will buy your old computer. An increasing number of companies are taking trade-ins, but do not expect too much money for your old computer. Other companies offer free disposal of your old PC.

12 **Be aware of hidden costs.**

Before purchasing, be sure to consider any additional costs associated with buying a computer, such as an additional telephone line, a cable or DSL modem, an uninterruptible power supply (UPS), computer furniture, a USB flash drive, paper, and computer training classes you may want to take. Depending on where you buy your computer, the seller may be willing to include some or all of these in the computer purchase price.

Type of Computer	Company	Web Address
PC	CNET Shopper	shopper.cnet.com
	Hewlett-Packard	hp.com
	CompUSA	compusa.com
	TigerDirect	tigerdirect.com
	Dell	dell.com
	Gateway	gateway.com
Macintosh	Apple Computer	store.apple.com
	ClubMac	clubmac.com
	MacConnection	macconnection.com
	PC & MacExchange	macx.com

For an updated list of mail-order computer companies and their Web site addresses, visit scsite.com/ic7/buyers.

FIGURE 45 Computer mail-order companies.

FIGURE 44 Mail-order companies, such as Dell, sell computers online.

Company	Web Address
Amazon.com	amazon.com
TECHAGAIN	techagain.com
American Computer Express	americancomputerex.com
U.S. Computer Exchange	uscc.org
eBay	ebay.com

For an updated list of used computer mail-order companies and their Web site addresses, visit scsite.com/ic7/buyers.

FIGURE 46 Used computer mail-order companies.

13 Consider more than just price.

The lowest-cost computer may not be the best long-term buy. Consider such intangibles as the vendor's time in business, the vendor's regard for quality, and the vendor's reputation for support. If you need to upgrade your computer often, you may want to consider a leasing arrangement, in which you pay monthly lease fees, but can upgrade or add on to your computer as your equipment needs change. No matter what type of buyer you are, insist on a 30-day, no-questions-asked return policy on your computer.

14 Avoid restocking fees.

Some companies charge a restocking fee of 10 to 20 percent as part of their money-back return policy. In some cases, no restocking fee for hardware is applied, but it is applied for software. Ask about the existence and terms of any restocking policies before you buy.

15 Use a credit card to purchase your new computer.

Many credit cards offer purchase protection and extended warranty benefits that cover you in case of loss of or damage to purchased goods. Paying by credit card also gives you time to install and use the computer before you have to pay for it. Finally, if you are dissatisfied with the computer and are unable to reach an agreement with the seller, paying by credit card gives you certain rights regarding withholding payment until the dispute is resolved. Check your credit card terms for specific details.

15 Consider purchasing an extended warranty or service plan.

If you use your computer for business or require fast resolution to major computer problems, consider purchasing an extended warranty or a service plan through a local dealer or third-party company. Most extended warranties cover the repair and replacement of computer components beyond the standard warranty. Most service plans ensure that your technical support calls receive priority response from technicians. You also can purchase an on-site service plan that states that a technician will come to your home, work, or school within 24 hours. If your computer includes a warranty and service agreement for a year or less, think about extending the service for two or three years when you buy the computer.

CENTURY COMPUTERS
Performance Guarantee
(See reverse for terms & conditions of this contract)

Invoice #: 1984409   Effective Date: 10/12/07
Invoice Date: 10/12/07   Expiration Date: 10/12/10

Customer Name: Leon, Richard   **System & Serial Numbers**
Date: 10/12/07   IMB computer
Address: 1123 Roxbury   S/N: US759290C
       Sycamore, IL 60178
Day phone: (815) 555-0303
Evening Phone: (728) 555-0203

John Smith   10/12/07
Print Name of Century's Authorized Signature   Date

HOW TO PURCHASE A NOTEBOOK COMPUTER

If you need computing capability when you travel or to use in lectures or meetings, you may find a notebook computer to be an appropriate choice. The guidelines mentioned in the previous section also apply to the purchase of a notebook computer. The following are additional considerations unique to notebook computers.

1 Purchase a notebook computer with a sufficiently large active-matrix screen.

Active-matrix screens display high-quality color that is viewable from all angles. Less expensive, passive-matrix screens sometimes are difficult to see in low-light conditions and cannot be viewed from an angle. Notebook computers typically come with a 12.1-inch, 13.3-inch, 14.1-inch, 15.4-inch, or 17-inch display. For most users, a 14.1-inch display is satisfactory. If you intend to use your notebook computer as a desktop computer replacement, however, you may opt for a 15.7-inch or 17-inch display. Dell offers a notebook computer with a 20.1-inch display that looks like a briefcase when closed. Notebook computers with these larger displays weigh seven to ten pounds, however, so if you travel a lot and portability is essential, you might want a lighter computer with a smaller display. The lightest notebook computers, which weigh less than 3 pounds, are equipped with a 12.1-inch display. Regardless of size, the resolution of the display should be at least 1024×768 pixels. To compare the monitor size on various notebook computers, visit the company Web sites in Figure 47.

Type of Notebook	Company	Web Address
PC	Acer	global.acer.com
	Dell	dell.com
	Fujitsu	fujitsu.com
	Gateway	gateway.com
	Hewlett-Packard	hp.com
	Lenovo	lenovo.com/us/en/
	NEC	nec.com
	Sony	sony.com
	Toshiba	toshiba.com
Mac	Apple	apple.com

For an updated list of companies and their Web site addresses, visit scsite.com/ic7/buyers.

FIGURE 47 Companies that sell notebook computers.

2 **Experiment with different keyboards and pointing devices.**

Notebook computer keyboards are far less standardized than those for desktop computers. Some notebook computers, for example, have wide wrist rests, while others have none, and keyboard layouts on notebook computers often vary. Notebook computers also use a range of pointing devices, including pointing sticks, touchpads, and trackballs. Before you purchase a notebook computer, try various types of keyboard and pointing devices to determine which is easiest for you to use. Regardless of the pointing device you select, you also may want to purchase a regular mouse to use when you are working at a desk or other large surface.

3 **Make sure the notebook computer you purchase has a CD and/or DVD drive.**

Most notebook computers come with a CD and/or a DVD drive. Although DVD drives are slightly more expensive, they allow you to play CDs and DVD movies using your notebook computer and a headset.

4 **If necessary, upgrade the processor, memory, and disk storage at the time of purchase.**

As with a desktop computer, upgrading your notebook computer's memory and disk storage usually is less expensive at the time of initial purchase. Some disk storage is custom designed for notebook computer manufacturers, meaning an upgrade might not be available in the future. If you are purchasing a lightweight notebook computer, then it should include at least an Intel Core Duo processor, 512 MB RAM, and 80 GB of storage.

5 **The availability of built-in ports and a port extender on a notebook computer is important.**

A notebook computer does not have a lot of room to add adapter cards. If you know the purpose for which you plan to use your notebook computer, then you can determine the ports you will need. Most notebooks come with common ports, such as a mouse port, IrDA port, serial port, parallel port, video port, a FireWire port, and multiple USB ports. If you plan to connect your notebook computer to a TV, however, then you will need a PCtoTV port. If you want to connect to networks at school or in various offices via a network cable, make sure the notebook computer you purchase has a network port. If your notebook computer does not come with a network port, then you will have to purchase an external network card that slides into an expansion slot in your notebook computer, as well as a network cable. While newer portable media players connect to a USB port, older ones require a FireWire port.

6 **If you plan to use your notebook computer for note-taking at school or in meetings, consider a notebook computer that converts to a Tablet PC.**

Some computer manufacturers have developed convertible notebook computers that allow the screen to rotate 180 degrees on a central hinge and then fold down to cover the keyboard and become a Tablet PC (Figure 48). You then can use a stylus to enter text or drawings into the computer by writing on the screen. Some notebook computers have wide screens for better viewing and editing, and some even have a screen on top of the unit in addition to the regular screen.

FIGURE 48 The HP Compaq tc4200 Tablet PC converts to a notebook computer.

7 **Purchase a notebook computer with a built-in wireless network connection.**

A wireless network connection (Bluetooth, Wi-Fi a/b/g, WiMAX, etc.) can be useful when you travel or as part of a home network. Increasingly more airports, hotels, and cafes have wireless networks that allow you to connect to the Internet. Many users today are setting up wireless home networks. With a wireless home network, the desktop computer functions as the server, and your notebook computer can access the desktop computer from any location in the house to share files and hardware, such as a printer, and browse the Web. Most home wireless networks allow connections from distances of 150 to 800 feet.

8 **If you are going to use your notebook computer for long periods without access to an electrical outlet, purchase a second battery.**

The trend among notebook computer users today is power and size over battery life, and notebook computer manufacturers have picked up on this. Many notebook computer users today are willing to give up longer battery life for a larger screen, faster processor, and more storage. In addition, some manufacturers typically sell the notebook with the lowest capacity battery. For this reason, you need to be careful in choosing a notebook computer if you plan to use it without access to electrical outlets for long periods, such as an airplane flight. You also might want to purchase a second battery as a backup. If you anticipate running your notebook computer on batteries frequently, choose a computer that uses lithium-ion batteries, which last longer than nickel cadmium or nickel hydride batteries.

9 **Purchase a well-padded and well-designed carrying case.**

An amply padded carrying case will protect your notebook computer from the bumps it will receive while traveling. A well-designed carrying case will have room for accessories such as spare CDs and DVDs, a user manual, pens, and paperwork (Figure 49).

FIGURE 49 A well-designed notebook computer carrying case.

10 **If you travel overseas, obtain a set of electrical and telephone adapters.**

Different countries use different outlets for electrical and telephone connections. Several manufacturers sell sets of adapters that will work in most countries.

11 **If you plan to connect your notebook computer to a video projector, make sure the notebook computer is compatible with the video projector.**

You should check, for example, to be sure that your notebook computer will allow you to display an image on the computer screen and projection device at the same time (Figure 50). Also, ensure that your notebook computer has the ports required to connect to the video projector. You also may consider purchasing a notebook computer with a built-in video camera for videoconferencing purposes.

12 **For improved security, consider a fingerprint scanner.**

More than half a million notebook computers are stolen or lost each year. If you have critical information stored on your notebook computer, then consider purchasing one with a fingerprint scanner (Figure 51) to protect the data if your computer is stolen or lost. Fingerprint security offers a level of protection that extends well beyond the standard password protection. If your notebook computer is stolen, the odds of recovering it improve dramatically with anti-theft tracking software. Manufacturers claim recovery rates of 90 percent or more for notebook computers using their product.

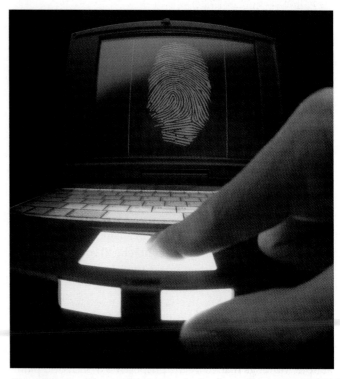

FIGURE 51 Fingerprint scanner technology offers greater security than passwords.

FIGURE 50 A notebook computer connected to a video projector projects the image displayed on the screen.

HOW TO PURCHASE A TABLET PC

The Tablet PC (Figure 52) combines the mobility features of a traditional notebook computer with the simplicity of pencil and paper, because you can create and save Office-type documents by writing and drawing directly on the screen with a digital pen. Tablet PCs use the Windows Tablet Technology in Windows Vista operating system. A notebook computer and a Tablet PC have many similarities. For this reason, if you are considering purchasing a Tablet PC, review the guidelines for purchasing a notebook computer, as well as the guidelines below.

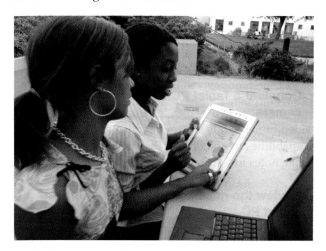

FIGURE 52 The lightweight Tablet PC, with its handwriting capabilities, is the latest addition to the family of mobile computers.

 Make sure the Tablet PC fits your mobile computing needs.

The Tablet PC is not for every mobile user. If you find yourself in need of a computer in class or you are spending more time in meetings than in your office, then the Tablet PC may be the answer. Before you invest money in a Tablet PC, however, determine the programs you plan to use on it. You should not buy a Tablet PC simply because it is an interesting type of computer. For additional information on the Tablet PC, visit the Web sites listed in Figure 53. You may have to

Company	Web Address
Fujitsu	fujitsu.com
Hewlett-Packard	hp.com
Microsoft	microsoft.com/windowsxp/tabletpc
ViewSonic	viewsonic.com

For an updated list of companies and their Web site addresses, visit scsite.com/ic7/buyers.

FIGURE 53 Companies involved with Tablet PCs and their Web sites.

use the search capabilities on the home page of the companies listed to locate information about the Tablet PC.

 Decide whether you want a convertible or pure Tablet PC.

Convertible Tablet PCs have an attached keyboard and look like a notebook computer. You rotate the screen and lay it flat against the computer for note-taking. The pure Tablet PCs are slim and lightweight, weighing less than four pounds. They have the capability of easily docking at a desktop to gain access to a large monitor, keyboard, and mouse. If you spend a lot of time attending lectures or meetings, then the pure Tablet PC is ideal. Acceptable specifications for a Tablet PC are shown in Figure 54.

TABLET PC SPECIFICATIONS

Dimensions	12" × 9" × 1.2"
Weight	Less than 5 Pounds
Processor	Pentium M Processor at 2 GHz
RAM	1 GB
Hard Disk	60 GB
Display	12.1" TFT
Digitizer	Electromagnetic Digitizer
Battery	6-Cell High Capacity Lithium-Ion
USB	3
FireWire	1
Docking Station	Grab and Go with CD-ROM, Keyboard, and Mouse
Bluetooth Port	Yes
Wireless	802.11a/b/g Card
Network Card	10/100 Ethernet
Modem	56 Kbps
Speakers	Internal
Microphone	Internal
Operating System	Windows Vista
Application Software	Office Small Business Edition
Antivirus Software	Yes – 12 Month Subscription
Warranty	1-Year Limited Warranty Parts and Labor

FIGURE 54 Tablet PC specifications.

 Be sure the weight and dimensions are conducive to portability.

The weight and dimensions of the Tablet PC are important because you carry it around like a notepad. The Tablet PC you buy should weigh four pounds or less. Its dimensions should be approximately 12 inches by 9 inches by 1.2 inches.

up arrow button, the area collapses. When you click the double down arrow button, the area expands and the entire contents of the area are visible.

Pointing to a task in the System Tasks area or a folder name in the Other Places area underlines the task or folder name and displays the task or folder name in light blue. Underlined text, such as the task and folder names, is referred to as a **hyperlink**, or simply a **link**. Pointing to a link changes the mouse pointer to a hand icon, and clicking a link displays information associated with the link.

The right pane of the My Computer window contains three groups of icons. The Files Stored on This Computer group contains the Shared Documents and Brad Wilson's Documents folder icons. The Hard Disk Drives group contains the Local Disk C drive icon. The Devices with Removable Storage group contains the DVD-RW Drive D drive icon and label.

To Minimize and Redisplay a Window

The Minimize and the Maximize buttons on the title bar of a window, allow you to control the way a window is displayed on the desktop. The following steps minimize and then redisplay the My Computer window.

1

- Click the Minimize button on the title bar of the My Computer window to minimize the My Computer window (Figure 1–15).

Q&A

What happens to the My Computer window when I click the Minimize button?

The My Computer window is still available, but it is no longer the active window.

Figure 1–15

2

- Click the My Computer button in the taskbar button area to display the My Computer window (Figure 1–16).

Q&A

Why does the My Computer button on the taskbar change?

After you click it, the My Computer button on the taskbar is recessed and the color is medium blue to indicate that the My Computer window is the active window. Notice too that when you move the mouse pointer off the taskbar button the button changes to dark blue, just like the title bar of the My Computer window.

Other Ways

1. Click icon on left side of title bar, click Minimize
2. Right-click title bar, click Minimize
3. Press WINDOWS+M

Figure 1–16

To Maximize and Restore a Window

Sometimes when information is displayed in a window, the information is not completely visible. One method of displaying more content in a window is to enlarge the window using the **Maximize button**, so the window fills the entire screen. The following steps maximize and restore the My Computer window.

1

• Click the Maximize button on the title bar of the My Computer window to maximize the My Computer window (Figure 1–17).

Q&A What happens to the Maximize button on the title bar when I click it?

The Restore Down button replaces the Maximize button on the title bar. You can click the Restore Down button to return the window to its size before maximizing.

Q&A When a window is maximized, can I also minimize it?

Yes. Click the Minimize button to minimize the window.

2

• Click the Restore Down button on the title bar of the My Computer window to return the My Computer window to its previous size (Figure 1–18).

Q&A What happens to the Restore Down button when I click it?

The Maximize button replaces the Restore Down button on the title bar.

Figure 1–17

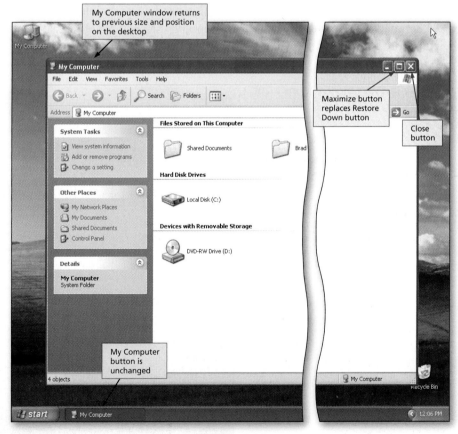

Figure 1–18

To Close a Window

You can click the **Close button** on the title bar of a window to close the window and remove the taskbar button from the taskbar. The following step closes the My Computer window.

● Click the Close button on the title bar of the My Computer window to close the My Computer window (Figure 1–19).

Q&A

What happens to the My Computer window when I click the Close button?

The My Computer window closes and the My Computer button no longer is displayed in the taskbar button area.

Figure 1–19

Other Ways

1. Click icon on left side of title bar, click Close
2. Right-click title bar, click Close on shortcut menu
3. Press ALT+F4

To Open a Window Using the Start Menu

Previously, you opened the My Computer window by double-clicking the My Computer icon on the desktop. Another method of opening a window and viewing the contents of the window is to click a command on the Start menu. The following steps open the My Documents window using the My Documents command on the Start menu.

● Display the Start menu (Figure 1–20).

Figure 1–20

2

- Click My Documents on the Start menu to display the My Documents window (Figure 1–21).

Q&A What happens if I click a folder icon in the right pane?

The icon is highlighted and the left pane might change.

Q&A What happens if I double-click a folder icon in the right pane?

The contents of the folder are displayed in the right pane, and the information in the left pane is changed.

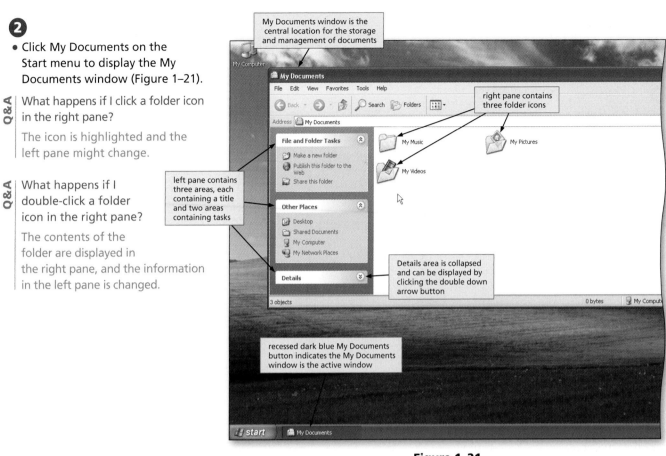

Figure 1–21

Other Ways

1. Click Start button, right-click My Documents icon, click Open on shortcut menu

To Move a Window by Dragging

Drag means you point to an item, hold down the left mouse button, move the item to the desired location, and then release the left mouse button. You can move any open window to another location on the desktop by pointing to the title bar of the window and then dragging the window. The following steps drag the My Documents window to the center of the desktop.

- Point to the My Documents window title bar.

- Hold down the left mouse button, move the mouse so the window moves to the center of the desktop, and release the left mouse button (Figure 1–22).

Figure 1–22

Other Ways

1. Click icon on left side of title bar, click Move, drag window

To Expand an Area

The Details area in the My Documents window is collapsed and a double down arrow button appears to the right of the Details title. The following step expands the Details area in the left pane of the My Documents window.

1

- Click the double down arrow button in the Details area to expand the Details area in the left pane of the My Documents window (Figure 1–23).

Q&A What happens when I click the double up arrow?

Only the area title and a double down arrow are displayed.

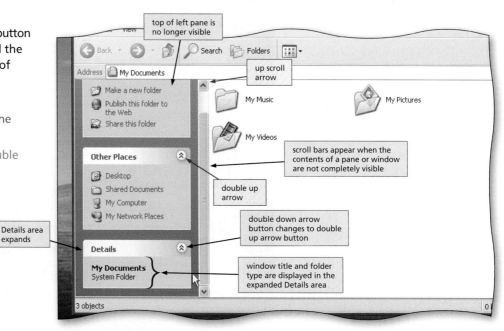

Figure 1–23

To Scroll Using Scroll Arrows

Another method of viewing information that is not visible in a window is to scroll in the window. Scrolling can be accomplished in three ways: (1) click the scroll arrows; (2) click the scroll bar; and (3) drag the scroll box. The following steps scroll the left pane using the scroll arrows.

1

- Click the up scroll arrow two times on the vertical scroll bar to scroll the left pane down (Figure 1–24).

Q&A Why doesn't my window include a scroll bar?

If your window was resized the last time it was opened, it may not include a scroll bar.

Q&A Is scrolling a window the best way to view objects in a window?

Sometimes it is your only option but maximizing the window is more efficient.

Figure 1–24

2

• Click the up scroll arrow two more times to move the scroll box to the top of the scroll bar (Figure 1–25).

Figure 1–25

To Size a Window by Dragging

You can change the size of the window by dragging the border of a window, as the following steps demonstrate.

1

• Point to the bottom border of the My Documents window until the mouse pointer changes to a two-headed arrow.

• Drag the bottom border downward until the Details area on your desktop resembles the Details area shown in Figure 1–26.

Q&A

Can I drag other borders to enlarge the window?

You can drag the left, right, top, and bottom borders and any window corner.

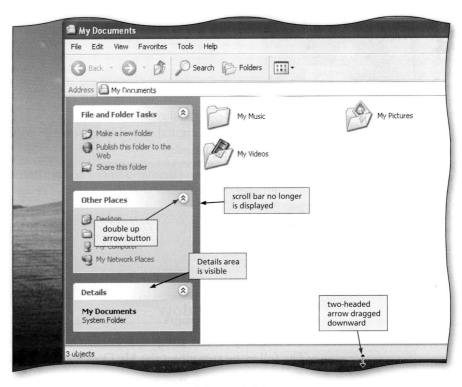

Figure 1–26

O&A

❶

- Click the Address bar to select the URL in the Address bar (Figure 1–34).

Q&A What happens when I click the Address bar?

Internet Explorer selects the URL in the Address bar and the mouse pointer changes to an I-beam.

Figure 1–34

❷

- Type www.scsite.com in the Address bar to display the new URL in the Address bar (Figure 1–35).

Q&A Must I type www.?

No. If you only type scsite.com, Internet Explorer automatically will add www.

Figure 1–35

❸

- Click the Go to button to display the SC Site - Shelly Cashman Series Student Resources Web site (Figure 1–36).

Q&A The Go to button changes after I click it. Why?

When you type the URL, the button changes to the Go to button. After the page is displayed, the button changes to the Refresh button. When you click the Refresh button, the Web page is downloaded again from the Web server, resulting in the most up-to-date version of the page being displayed.

Other Ways
1. On File menu click Open, type URL in Open box, click OK button
2. Press CTRL+O, type URL in Open box, click OK button
3. Press ALT+F, press O, type URL in Open box, press ENTER key

Figure 1–36

To Open a Link in a New Tab

You can view multiple Web pages in a single window using tabbed pages. A tabbed page consists of a tab in the Internet Explorer window and the associated Web page. When you start Internet Explorer only one tab is displayed, but you can open as many tabbed pages as you want. The following steps use the Instant Search box and the Course Technology – Shelly Cashman Series link to open a Web page on a new tabbed page.

1

- Click the Instant Search box and type `Shelly Cashman Series` in the Instant Search box (Figure 1–37).

Q&A

What is an Instant Search box?

It is a text box in which you can type a term which then can be searched for by a search engine. Internet Explorer provides an Instant Search box in the upper-right corner of the window.

Figure 1–37

2

- Click the Search button to the right of the Instant Search box to display the results of the Web search (Figure 1–38).

Figure 1–38

3

- If necessary, scroll to view the Course Technology –Shelly Cashman Series link.

- Right-click the Course Technology – Shelly Cashman Series link to display a shortcut menu (Figure 1–39).

Q&A

What happens when I just click a link?

The Web page will open on the same tabbed page as the search results and will replace the search results.

Figure 1–39

- Click the Open in New Tab command on the shortcut menu to close the shortcut menu and display the Course Technology – Shelly Cashman Series tab (Figure 1–40).

Figure 1–40

To Switch Between Tabs

You can display the contents of any tabbed page by clicking the tab, as shown in the following step.

- Click the Course Technology – Shelly Cashman Series tab to activate the tab and display The Shelly Cashman Series® in the display area (Figure 1–41).

Q&A

What if I don't want to use tabbed browsing?

You can disable the tabbed browsing feature. To do so, click the Tools button on the Command Bar, click Internet Options, click the General tab, in Tabs section click Settings, clear Enable Tab Browsing check box, and then click OK twice.

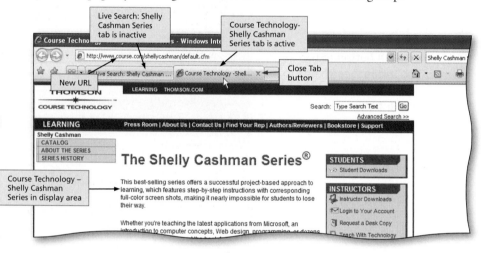

Figure 1–41

To Close a Tab

You can keep as many tabbed pages open as necessary. If you no longer have a need for the tabbed page to be open, you can close the tab using the following steps.

- Click the Close Tab button in the Course Technology –Shelly Cashman Series tab to close the Course Technology –Shelly Cashman Series Web page (Figure 1–42).

- Click the Close button on the title bar to close the Live Search: Shelly Cashman Series - Windows Internet Explorer window.

Figure 1–42

Windows Explorer

Windows Explorer is an application program included with Windows XP. It allows you to view the contents of the computer, the hierarchy of drives and folders on the computer, and the files and folders in each folder. In this section, you will use Windows Explorer to expand and collapse drives and folders, display drive and folder contents, create a new folder, copy a file between folders, and rename and then delete a file. These are common operations that you should understand how to perform.

To Start Windows Explorer and Maximize Its Window

First, you must start the Windows Explorer application. The following steps start Windows Explorer using the Folders button in the My Computer window.

1
- Display the Start menu (Figure 1–43).

Figure 1–43

2
- Click My Computer on the Start menu to display the My Computer window (Figure 1–44).

Figure 1–44

3

- If necessary, double-click the My Computer title bar to maximize the My Computer window.

- If the status bar is not located at the bottom of the My Computer window, click View on the menu bar, and then click Status Bar to display the status bar (Figure 1–45).

Figure 1–45

4

- Click the Folders button on the Standard Buttons toolbar to display the Folders pane (Figure 1–46).

Q&A What is the Folders pane?

The Folders pane displays the hierarchy of folders and drives on your computer.

Q&A Is it possible to display my folders and drives in the right pane differently than what is shown in Figure 1–46?

You can display files and folders in the right pane in several different views. Currently, the drives and folders in the right pane are displayed in Tiles view using Large Icons format.

🔍 **Experiment**

- Click a plus sign in the Folders pane and observe the changes in the window. Then click the minus sign to return the window to its previous status. Do the same thing for another plus sign.

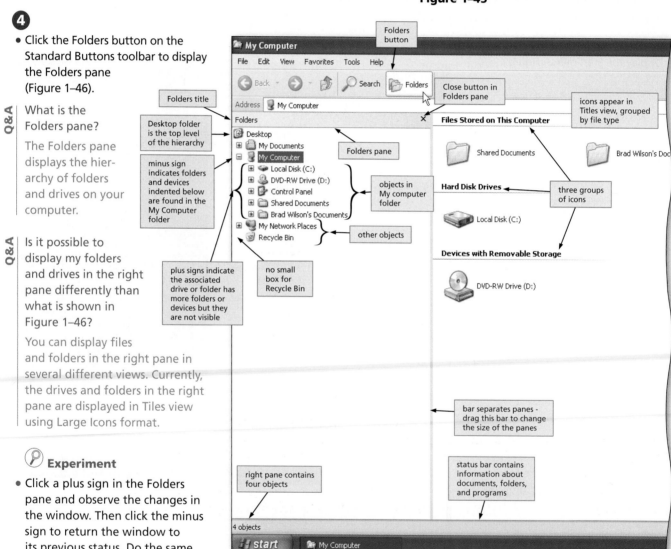

FIGURE 1–46

Other Ways
1. Click Start button, right click My Computer, click Explore on shortcut menu   3. Click Start button, point to All Programs, point to Accessories, click Windows Explorer, click My Computer
2. Right-click Start button or any desktop icon, click Explore on shortcut menu   4. Press WINDOWS+E

Using a Hierarchical Format to Organize Files and Folders

An important task is to be able to create and organize the files and folders on the computer. A file may contain a spreadsheet assignment given by the computer teacher, a research paper assigned by the English teacher, an electronic quiz given by the Business teacher, or a study sheet designed by the Math teacher. These files should be organized and stored in folders to reduce the possibility of misplacing a file and to quickly find a file.

Assume you are a freshman taking four classes (Business, Computer, English, and Math). You want to design a series of folders for the four classes you are taking in the first semester of your freshman year. To accomplish this, you arrange the folders in a **hierarchical format**. The hierarchical structure of folders for the Freshman year is shown in Figure 1–47.

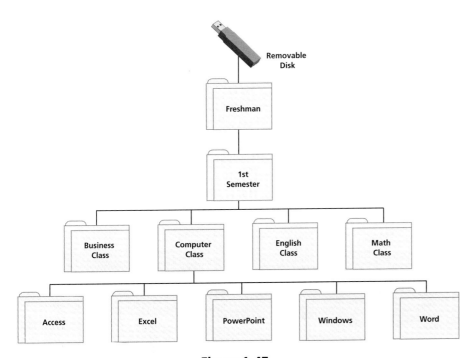

Figure 1–47

The hierarchy contains five levels. The first level contains the UDISK 2.0 (E:) drive, the second level contains the Freshman folder, the third level contains the 1st Semester folder, the fourth level contains four folders (Business Class, Computer Class, English Class, and Math Class), and the fifth level contains five folders (Access, Excel, PowerPoint, Windows, and Word).

The vertical and horizontal lines in the hierarchy chart form a pathway that allows you to navigate to a drive or folder. Each pathway is a means of navigation to a specific location on a computer or network. A path consists of a drive letter and colon (C:), a backslash (\ ), and one or more folder names. Each drive or folder in the hierarchy chart has a corresponding path. When you click a drive or folder icon in the Folders pane, the corresponding path appears in the Address box on the Address bar. Table 1–2 on the following page contains examples of path names and their corresponding drives and folders.

Path	Drive and folder
Table 1–2 Path Names and Corresponding Drives and Folders	
E:\	Drive E (UDISK 2.0 (E:)
E:\ Freshman	Freshman folder on drive E
E:\ Freshman\ 1st Semester	1st Semester folder in Freshman folder on drive E
E:\ Freshman\ 1st Semester\ Computer Class\ Word	Word folder in Computer Class folder in 1st Semester folder in Freshman folder on drive E

When this hierarchy is created, the UDISK 2.0 (E:) drive is said "to contain" the Freshman folder, the Freshman folder is said "to contain" the 1st Semester folder, and so on. In addition, this hierarchy can easily be expanded to include folders from the Sophomore, Junior, and Senior years and any additional semesters.

Removable Media and Network Drives

A removable media (USB flash drive) is ideal for storing files and folders on a computer. A **USB flash drive**, sometimes called a **keychain drive**, is a flash memory storage device that plugs into a USB port on a computer. A **USB port**, short for universal serial bus port, can be found on either the front or back of most computers. USB flash drives, like the one shown in Figure 1–48, are convenient for mobile users because they are small and lightweight enough to be transported on a keychain or in a pocket.

USB ports

USB flash drive

Figure 1–48

A **network** is a collection of computers and devices connected together for the purpose of sharing information between computer users. In some cases, students might be required to store their files on a network drive found on the school's computer network. A **network drive** is a storage device that is connected to the server on the computer network. A **server** controls access to the hardware, software, and other resources on the network and provides a centralized storage area for programs, data, and information. If student files reside on the network drive on the school's network, files may be accessed from a school computer, or from a personal computer with permission from the school. Ask your teacher if the school requires you to use a network drive.

To Plug a USB Flash Drive into a USB Port

Although other removable media may be used for storage, the USB flash drive is one of the more popular drives. To store files and folders on the USB flash drive, you must plug the USB flash drive into a USB port on the computer. Plugging a USB flash drive into a USB port causes the UDISK 2.0 (E:) window to display on the desktop. The removable media drive name on your computer may be different. The following steps plug a USB flash drive into a USB port.

1

- Plug the USB flash drive into a USB port on the computer to display the UDISK 2.0 (E:) window (Figure 1–49).

Q&A What does UDISK mean?

UDISK is the name of the particular type of USB drive used. The name of your USB drive might be different.

Q&A What is drive E?

It is the drive identification; it is similar to C for the hard disk drive on your computer, and your drive identifier may be different.

Figure 1–49

2

- In the UDISK 2.0 (E:) window, click the Folders button on the Standard Buttons toolbar to display the Folders pane (Figure 1–50).

Figure 1–50

5 Scroll down to display the Data Files for Students (Windows) area and then click the Windows XP Chapter 1 Data Files link.

6 When the File Download – Security Warning dialog box is displayed, click the Run button.

7 When the Internet Explorer – Security Warning dialog box is displayed, click the Run button.

8 When the WinZip Self-Extractor dialog box is displayed, type the removable media drive letter of your removable media drive followed by a colon, backslash, and folder name (Freshman) (for example, E:\ Freshman).

9 Click the Unzip button.

10 When Windows displays the WinZip Self-Extractor dialog box, click the OK button.

11 Click the Close button in the WinZip Self-Extractor dialog box.

12 Click the Close button in the SC Site – Shelly Cashman Series Student Resources Web site window.

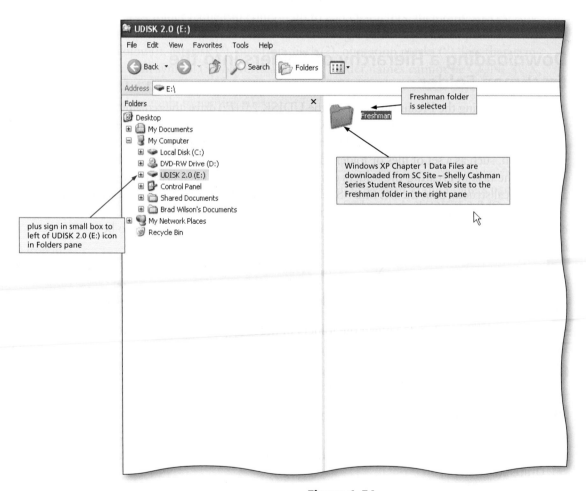

Figure 1–54

Even though you cannot see the folders and files in the Freshman folder, the folders and files are contained in the Freshman folder. Some folders contain files to be used later in this chapter.

To Expand a Drive

Windows Explorer displays the hierarchy of items in the Folders pane and the contents of drives and folders in the right pane. You might want to expand a drive to view its contents in the Folders pane. The following step expands a drive.

1

• Click the plus sign in the small box to the left of the UDISK 2.0 (E:) icon in the Folders pane to display the Freshman folder (Figure 1–55).

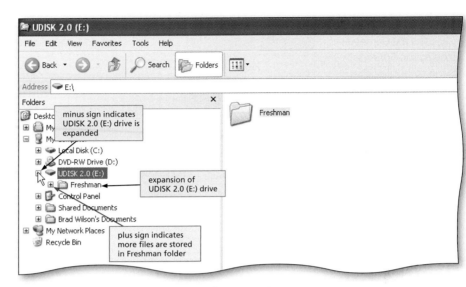

Figure 1–55

Other Ways		
1. Click drive icon in Folders pane	2. Select drive to expand using ARROW keys, press PLUS on numeric keyboard	3. Select drive to expand, press RIGHT ARROW

To Expand a Folder

When a plus sign in a small box is displayed to the left of a folder icon in the Folders pane, you can expand the folder to show all the folders it contains. The following step expands the Freshman folder to view the contents of the Freshman folder.

1

• Click the plus sign in the small box to the left of the Freshman icon to expand the Freshman folder (Figure 1–56).

 Why is the 1st Semester folder indented below the Freshman folder in the Folders pane?

The folder is indented below the Freshman icon to show that the folder is contained within the Freshman folder. A folder with a plus sign contains more folders.

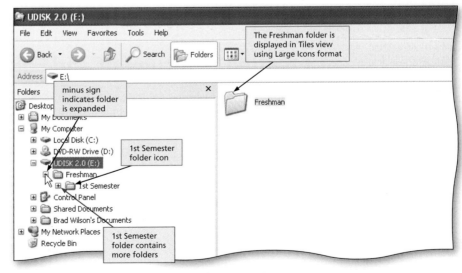

Figure 1–56

To Display the Contents of a Folder

Clicking an icon in the Folders pane displays the contents of the drive or folder in the right pane, expands the hierarchy in the Folders pane, and displays the path in the Address Path text box. The following step displays the contents of the 1st Semester folder.

1

- Click the 1st Semester icon in the Folders pane to display the contents of the 1st Semester folder (Figure 1–57).

Figure 1–57

Other Ways

1. Right-click 1st Semester icon, click Explore on shortcut menu

BTW

About WordPad
WordPad was first included with the Microsoft Windows 95 operating system. More advanced than NotePad, but not as complex as Microsoft Word, WordPad can format and print text, but does not have a spell checker or thesaurus.

Creating a Document and Folder Using WordPad

Previously, the Freshman folder was created in the UDISK 2.0 (E:) drive using Windows Explorer. You also can create a folder anytime you save a file in a Windows application. For example, you can use WordPad to create a document and then save the new document in a folder. **WordPad** is a word processing program included with Windows XP that allows you to create a limited variety of personal and business documents. The following section illustrates how to start WordPad, type text into a WordPad document, save the document in a new folder, and verify the document was saved in the folder.

To Start WordPad

Assume you want to create a document that lists your homework for Friday, April 11 using the WordPad application. The first process is to start the WordPad application. The following steps start WordPad based on a typical installation. You may need to ask your instructor how to start WordPad on your system.

1

- Display the Start menu.

- To display the All Programs submenu, point to All Programs on the Start menu.

- Point to Accessories on the All Programs submenu to display WordPad on the Accessories submenu (Figure 1–58).

 What are Accessories?

Accessories are application programs that accomplish a variety of tasks commonly required on a computer. For example, the Accessories programs include Accessibility programs to help people view a monitor screen and enter data into a computer; Communication programs that aid in installing and maintaining computer communications; and System Tools programs that provide information about the computer; and maintenance tools for maintaining the computer.

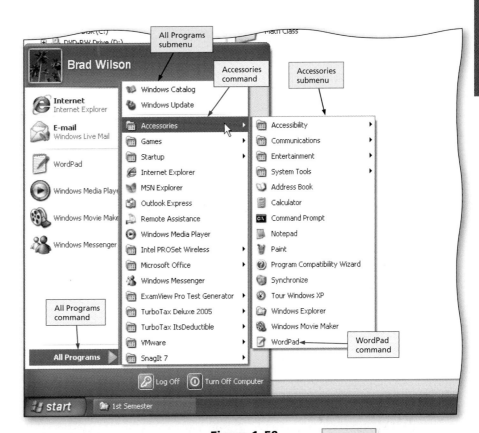

Figure 1–58

2

- Click WordPad to start the WordPad application and display a new blank document in the WordPad window (Figure 1–59).

- If the WordPad window is not maximized, click the Maximize button next to the Close button on its title bar to maximize the window.

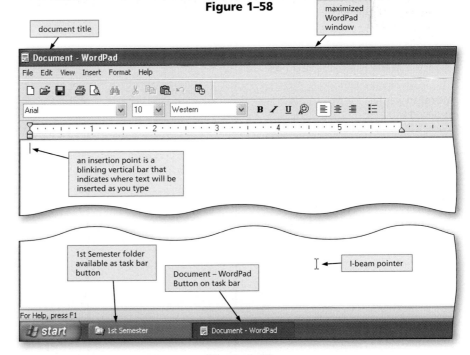

Figure 1–59

To Type Text

After starting WordPad, you can enter the text in the Friday, April 11 WordPad document. To enter text in the document, you type on the keyboard. The following steps show the process of entering the text of the Friday, April 11 WordPad document.

- Type Friday, April 11 and then press the ENTER key twice.

- Type Finish - The Bike Delivers Data Base and then press the ENTER key.

- Type Read - Next Project and then press the ENTER key (Figure 1–60).

Q&A

What if I make an error while typing?

You can press the **BACKSPACE** key until you have deleted the text in error and then retype the text correctly.

Figure 1–60

To Save a WordPad Document in a New Folder

After typing the text of a WordPad document, you can create a folder in which to save the document, and then save the document in the created folder. The following steps save the Friday, April 11 document in a created folder named Homework. The Homework folder is created within the Computer Class folder (see the hierarchy in Figure 1–47 on page WIN 31).

- Click the Save button on the Toolbar to display the Save As dialog box (Figure 1–61).

Q&A

Why is the Document file name selected in the File name text box?

The Document file name is selected in the File name text box as the default file name. You can change the default file name by immediately typing the new name.

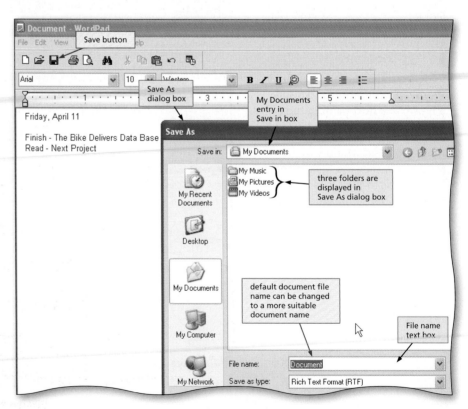

Figure 1–61

2

- Type Friday, April 11 in the File name text box. Do not press the ENTER key after typing the file name (Figure 1–62).

Q&A

What happens if I press the ENTER key after typing the file name?

If you press the ENTER key, the Save As dialog box closes and the file will be saved in the My Documents folder. If you want to save the file in a folder other than the My Documents folder, you must select the desired folder.

Figure 1–62

3

- Click the Save in box arrow to display a list of available drives and folders in which you can save the document (Figure 1–63).

Q&A

Is it okay if my list of drives and folders is different than the one in Figure 1–63?

Yes. The folders and drives can be unique for each computer.

Figure 1–63

● Click UDISK 2.0 (E:) in the Save in
list to display the contents of the
UDISK 2.0 (E:) drive in the Save As
dialog box (Figure 1–64).

Figure 1–64

● Double-click the Freshman folder in
the Save As dialog box to display the
Freshman folder name in the Save in
text box and display the contents of
the Freshman folder in the Save As
dialog box (Figure 1–65).

Figure 1–65

- Double-click the 1st Semester folder icon in the Save As dialog box to display the 1st Semester folder name in the Save in text box and display the contents of the 1st Semester folder in the Save As dialog box (Figure 1–66).

Figure 1–66

- Double-click the Computer Class folder icon in the Save As dialog box to display the Computer Class folder name in the Save in text box and display the contents of the Computer Class folder in the Save As dialog box (Figure 1–67).

Figure 1–67

- Click the Create New Folder button on the Save As dialog box toolbar to create a new folder within the Computer Class folder.

- Type `Homework` as the name of the folder and then press the ENTER key (Figure 1–68).

Figure 1–68

- Click the Open button in the Save As dialog box to open the Homework folder.

- Click the Save button in the Save As dialog box to save the Friday, April 11 file to its new location in the Homework folder.

- Click the Close button in the Friday, April 11 - WordPad window to close the window (Figure 1–69).

Figure 1–69

Other Ways

1. On File menu click Save As, type file name, click Save in box arrow, select drive, click Create New Folder button on toolbar, type folder name, click Open button in Save As dialog box, click Save button in Save As dialog box, click Close button

2. Press CTRL+S, type file name, click Save in box arrow, select drive, click Create New Folder button on toolbar, type folder name, click Open button in Save As dialog box, click Save button in Save As dialog box, click Close button

To Verify the Contents of a Folder

After saving the Friday, April 11 document in the Homework folder, you can verify that the document was correctly saved in the Homework folder. The following step verifies the Homework folder contains the Friday, April 11 document.

1

- Click the plus sign in the small box next to the Computer Class icon in the Folders pane to display the folders within the Computer Class folder.

- Click the Homework icon in the Folders pane to select the Homework folder and display the contents of the Homework folder in the right pane (Figure 1–70).

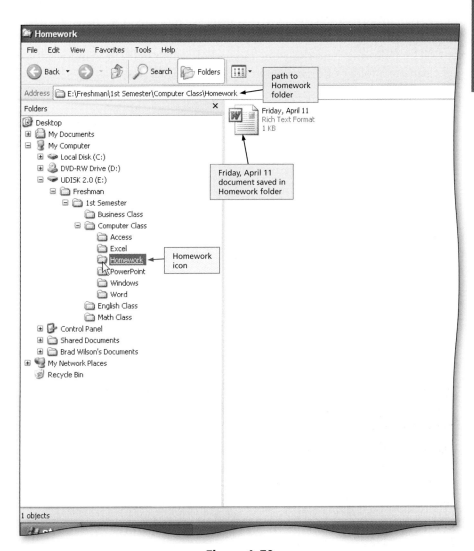

Figure 1–70

File Management in Windows Explorer

Being able to manage the files on the computer is one of the more important computer skills a computer user can possess. File management includes copying, moving, renaming, and deleting files and folders on the computer.

To Copy a File in Windows Explorer by Right-Dragging

When copying files, the drive and folder containing the files to be copied are called the **source drive** and **source folder**, respectively. The drive and folder to which the files are copied are called the **destination drive** and **destination folder**, respectively. In the following steps, the Access folder is the source folder, the Homework folder is the destination folder, and the UDISK 2.0 (E:) drive is both the source drive and the destination drive. The Access folder contains two of the eleven Access database files (SciFi Scene and The Bike Delivers) required to perform the lab assignments in the Access section of this book.

The following steps show one method of copying files in Windows Explorer - right-drag a file icon from the right pane to a folder or drive icon in the Folders pane.

- Click the Access icon in the Folders pane to select the Access folder and display its contents in the right pane (Figure 1–71).

Figure 1–71

- Right-drag the The Bike Delivers icon from the right pane onto the top of the Homework folder icon in the Folders bar to open the shortcut menu (Figure 1–72).

- Click Copy Here on the shortcut menu to copy The Bike Delivers file to the Homework folder.

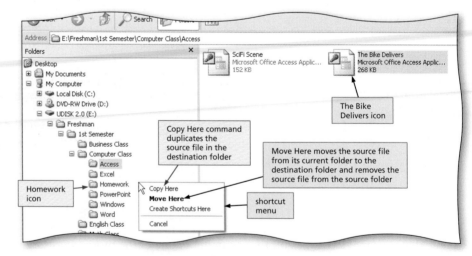

Figure 1–72

Other Ways
1. Right-click file to copy, click Copy on the shortcut menu, right-click Homework icon, click Paste on the shortcut menu   2. Click file to copy, on Edit menu click Copy, click Homework icon, on Edit menu click Paste   3. Select file to copy, press CTRL+C, select Homework icon, press CTRL+V

To Display the Contents of a Folder

After copying a file, you might want to examine the folder or drive where the file was copied to ensure it was copied properly. The following step displays the contents of the Homework folder.

1

• Click the Homework icon in the Folders pane to display the contents of the Homework folder (Figure 1–73).

Q&A

Can I copy or move more than one file at a time?

Yes. To copy or move multiple files, select each file to be copied or moved by clicking the file icon while holding down the CTRL key. Then, right-drag the selected files to the destination folder using the same technique as right-dragging a single file.

Figure 1–73

To Rename a File

In some circumstances, you may want to **rename** a file or a folder. This could occur when you want to distinguish a file in one folder or drive from a copy, or if you decide you need a better name to identify a file. The Word folder in Figure 1–74 contains the three Word documents (Barn and Silo, Fall Harvest, and Lake at Sunset) required to perform the lab assignments in the Word section of this book. In this case, you decide to change the Fall Harvest name to Great Fall Harvest. The following steps change the name of the Fall Harvest file in the Word folder to Great Fall Harvest.

1

• Click the Word folder in the left pane to display the Barn and Silo, Fall Harvest, and Lake at Sunset files in the right pane.

• Right-click the Fall Harvest icon in the right pane to select the Fall Harvest icon and display a shortcut menu (Figure 1–74).

Figure 1–74

2

- Click Rename on the shortcut menu to select the file name for renaming.

- Type `Great Fall Harvest` and then press the ENTER key (Figure 1–75).

Are there any risks to renaming files that are located on the hard disk?

If you inadvertently rename a file that is associated with certain programs, the programs may not be able to find the file and, therefore, may not execute properly. Always use caution when renaming files.

Figure 1–75

Other Ways
1. Right-click icon, press M, type name, press ENTER 2. Select icon, press F2, type name, press ENTER	3. Select icon, on File menu click Rename, type name, press ENTER	4. Select icon, press ALT+F, press M, type name, press ENTER

To Delete a File by Right-Clicking

A final operation you may want to perform in Windows Explorer is to delete a file. Exercise extreme caution when deleting a file or files. When you delete a file from a hard drive, the deleted file is stored in the Recycle Bin where you can recover it until you empty the Recycle Bin. If you delete a file from removable media, the file is gone permanently once you delete it. The following steps delete the Lake at Sunset file.

1

- Right-click the Lake at Sunset icon in the right pane to select the icon and display a shortcut menu (Figure 1–76).

Why are some of the items on my shortcut menu different than the ones shown in Figure 1–76?

Depending on the software installed on your computer, the shortcut commands can differ. The Delete command always is available.

Figure 1–76

2

• Click Delete on the shortcut menu to begin the delete process by displaying the Confirm File Delete dialog box (Figure 1–77).

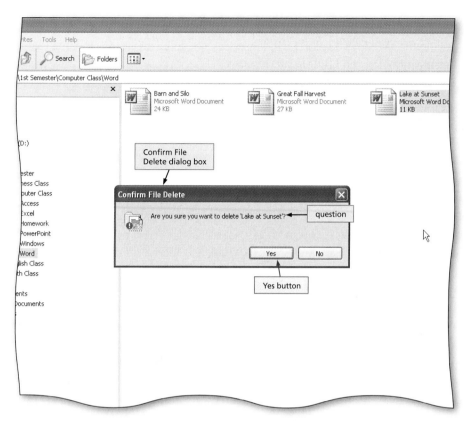

Figure 1–77

3

• Click the Yes button in the Confirm File Delete dialog box to remove the Lake at Sunset file (Figure 1–78).

Can I use this same technique to delete a folder?

Yes. Right-click the folder and then click Delete on the shortcut menu. When you delete a folder, all the files and folders contained in the folder you are deleting, together with all the files and folders on the lower hierarchical levels, are deleted as well.

Figure 1–78

Other Ways

1. Drag icon to Recycle Bin

2. Click icon, on File menu click Delete, click Yes button

3. Select icon, press ALT+F, press D, press Y

Again, you should use extreme caution when deleting files and folders to ensure you do not delete something you may not be able to recover.

To Close Expanded Folders

Sometimes, after you have completed work with expanded folders, you will want to close the expansions while still leaving the Windows Explorer window open. The following steps close the Computer Class folder, 1st Semester folder, Freshman folder, and UDISK 2.0 (E:) drive.

- Click the minus sign to the left of the Computer Class icon in the left pane to collapse the Computer Class folder (Figure 1–79).

Figure 1–79

2

- Click the minus sign to the left of the 1st Semester icon to collapse the icon.

- Click the minus sign to the left of the Freshman icon to collapse the icon.

- Click the minus sign to the left of the UDISK 2.0 (E:) to collapse the icon.

Other Ways

1. Click expanded folder icon, press MINUS SIGN on numeric keypad
2. Click expanded folder icon, press LEFT ARROW

To Quit Windows Explorer

When you have finished working with Windows Explorer, you can quit Windows Explorer by closing the Folders pane or by closing the Windows Explorer (UDISK 2.0 (E:)) window. The following step quits Windows Explorer by closing the UDISK 2.0 (E:) window.

1 Click the Close button on the UDISK 2.0 (E:) window title bar to close the UDISK 2.0 (E:) window.

Finding Files or Folders

You know the location of files you use often and can locate the folder that contains them. In some cases, however, you may know you have a certain file on the computer but you have no idea in what folder it is located.

Search Companion allows you to search for files and folders by name, type, or size. You can search for a file based on when you last worked on the file or search for files containing specific text. You also can choose to search with the help of an animated character.

To Search for a File by Name

If you know the name or partial name of a file, you can use Search Companion to locate the file. The following steps search for a file on the UDISK 2.0 (E:) drive.

1
• Display the Start menu (Figure 1–80).

Figure 1–80

2

- Click Search on the Start menu to display the Search Results window.

- If necessary, maximize the Search Results window (Figure 1–81).

What are all the items in the Search Companion balloon?

They are links you can click to select different search criteria or to find other information. As you use Search, the items in the balloon will change based on the tasks you perform.

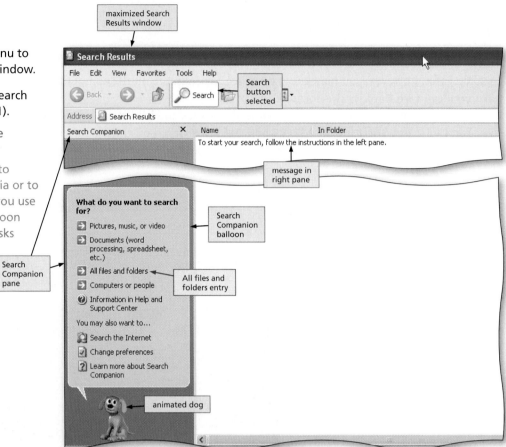

Figure 1–81

3

- Click the 'All files and folders' entry in the Search Companion balloon to display an insertion point in the 'All or part of the file name' text box.

- Type Great Fall Harvest in the 'All or part of the the file name' text box (Figure 1–82).

Do I have to know the exact name of a file to search for it?

No. If you know only a portion of a file's name, you can use an asterisk in the name to represent the remaining characters. For example, if you know the file starts with the letters, win, you can type win* in the text box. All files that begin with the letters win, regardless of what letters follow, will be displayed.

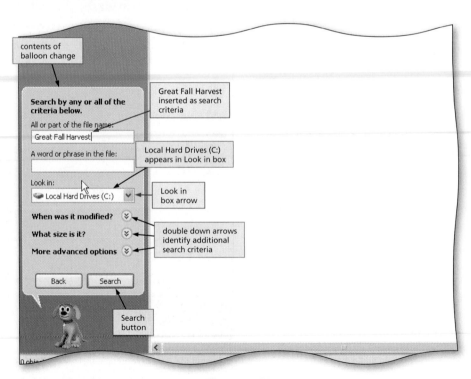

Figure 1–82

4

• Click the Look in box arrow in the Search Companion pane to display the list of locations in which to search (Figure 1–83).

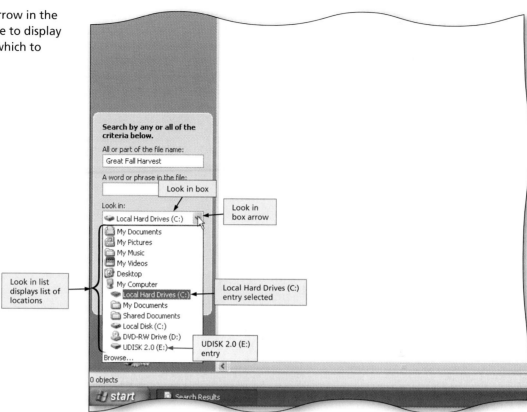

Figure 1–83

5

• Click UDISK 2.0 (E:) in the Look in list to close the Look in list and select the UDISK 2.0 (E:) drive name in the Look in box (Figure 1–84).

Figure 1–84

• Click the Search button to search drive E: for the Great Fall Harvest file (Figure 1–85).

What does the progress bar demonstrate?

While the search continues, Windows momentarily displays a message as well as the locations being searched.

• Click the Close button on the Search Results window title bar to close the Search Results window.

Other Ways

1. Open Windows Explorer, click Search button on Standard Buttons toolbar, click All files and folders, select search criteria, click Search button

2. Press F3 or WINDOWS+F, select search criteria, press ENTER

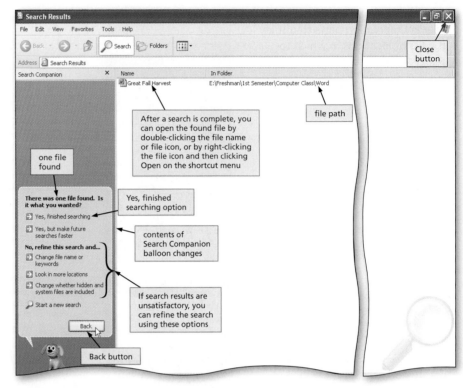

Figure 1–85

Any operation you can accomplish from My Computer or from Windows Explorer can be performed on the files displayed in the right pane of the Search Results window. If the file you are searching for is an executable program file, you can start the program by double-clicking the file icon in the right pane of the Search Results window.

Finding Files
Some would argue that Search is the handiest Windows XP tool. If an application is not represented on the Start menu, many people use Search to display the icon in the Search Results window, and then double-click the icon to start the program.

To Search for a File Using a Word or Phrase in the File

If you want to search for a file knowing only a word or phrase in the file, you can search by typing the word or phrase in the 'A word or phrase in the file' text box in the Search Companion balloon. Assume you want to find all files containing the word, apply, on the UDISK 2.0 (E:) drive. The following steps search for all files containing the word, apply.

• Display the Start menu.

• Click the Search button on the Start menu to display the Search Results window.

• If necessary, maximize the Search Results window.

• Click 'All files and folders' in the Search companion balloon to begin a search (Figure 1–86).

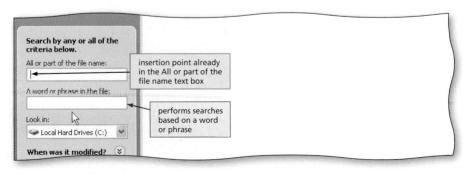

Figure 1–86

2

- Click the 'A word or phrase in the file' text box to prepare to type text.

- Type apply in the 'A word or phrase in the file' text box.

- Click the Look in box arrow to display the Look in list.

- Click UDISK 2.0 (E:) in the Look in list to designate UDISK 2.0 (E:) drive as the drive to search (Figure 1–87).

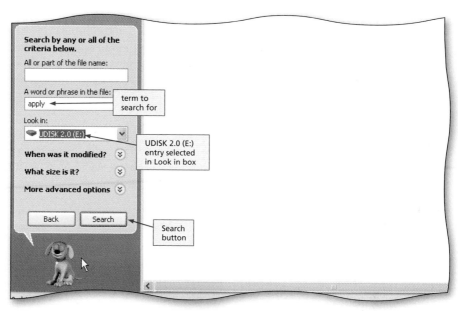

Figure 1–87

3

- Click the Search button in the Search Companion balloon to perform a search (Figure 1–88).

Q&A What if my results are different from those shown in Figure 1–88?

If your results are different, you may have mistyped the search term. To determine if this is the case, click the Back button, review your search criteria, and if necessary, perform the search again.

- Click the Close button on the Search Results window title bar to close the Search Results window.

- Remove the USB flash drive from the USB port.

Q&A Why does the computer make a sound when I unplug the USB flash drive?

Windows XP produces many different sounds for various events. When a device is unplugged, your computer produces a sound to alert that this has happened.

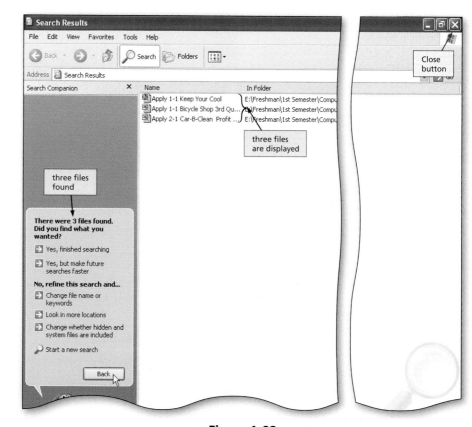

Figure 1–88

Other Ways

1. Open Windows Explorer, click Search button on Standard Buttons toolbar, click All files and folders, select search criteria, click Search button

2. Press F3 or WINDOWS+F, select search criteria, press ENTER

3. Press WINDOWS+F, press L, select search criteria, press ENTER

Using Help and Support

One of the more powerful Windows XP features is Help and Support. **Help and Support** is available when using Windows XP, or when using any application program running under Windows XP. It contains answers to many questions you may ask with respect to the Windows XP operating system.

To Start Help and Support

Before you can access the Help and Support Center services, you must start Help and Support. One method of starting Help and Support uses the Start menu. The following steps start Help and Support.

- Display the Start menu (Figure 1–89).

- Click Help and Support to display the Help and Support Center window.

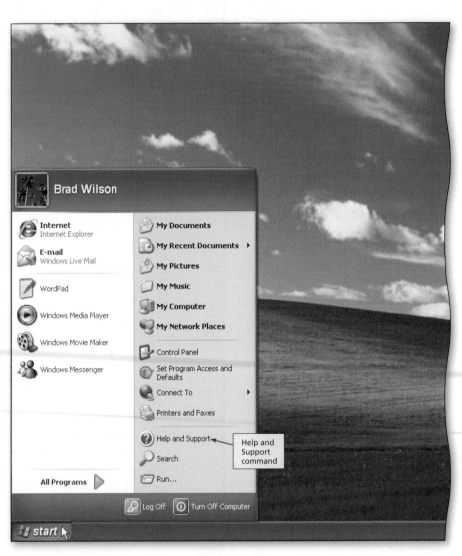

Figure 1–89

2

• If necessary, click the Maximize button on the Help and Support Center title bar to maximize the Help and Support Center window (Figure 1–90).

Q&A

What does the Help and Support Center contain?

The Help and Support Center contains the Help viewer which includes the Navigation toolbar, Search text box, Set search options link, and a table of contents.

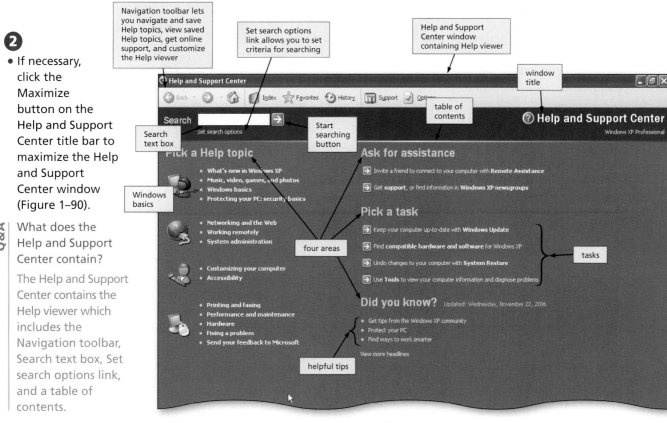

Figure 1–90

Other Ways

1. Press F1
2. Press CTRL+ESC, press H
3. Press WINDOWS+F1

Table 1–3 shows the categories in the Help and Support Center table of contents.

Table 1–3 Help and Support Center Table of Contents

Path	Drive and folder
Pick a Help topic area	Area contains fourteen Help topics arranged in four category groups. Clicking a category displays a list of subcategories and Help topics related to the category.
Ask for assistance area	Area contains Remote Assistance task allowing an individual to connect and control a computer while helping to solve a problem. The Windows XP newsgroups task obtains Help from experts or discusses questions with other Windows XP users.
Pick a task area	The Windows Update task allows you to access a catalog of items that keep your computer up-to-date. The Compatible Hardware and Software task allows you to search for hardware and software compatible with Windows XP. The System Restore task stores the current state of the computer and then restores it without losing information. The Tools task has eight helpful tools to keep the computer running.
Did you know? area	Area is updated daily with helpful tips for using Windows XP.

To Browse for Help Topics in the Table of Contents

After starting Help and Support, the next action is to find the Help topic in which you are interested. The following steps use the table of contents to find a Help topic that describes how to find what you need in the Help and Support Center.

• Click Windows basics in the Pick a Help topic area to display the Navigation Pane and topic pane in the Help and Support Center window (Figure 1–91).

Figure 1–91

• Click the Tips for using Help category to display the Tips for using Help page (Figure 1–92).

Figure 1–92

3

- Click 'Find what you need in Help and Support Center' to display the 'To find what you need in Help and Support Center' topic.

- Read the information in the 'To find what you need in Help and Support Center' topic in the topic pane (Figure 1–93).

Other Ways

1. Press TAB until category or topic is highlighted, press ENTER, repeat for each category or topic

Figure 1–93

To Search for Help Topics Using the Index

A second method of finding answers to your questions about Windows XP is to use the Help and Support Center Index. The **Help and Support Center Index** contains a list of alphabetized entries, each of which references one or more Help topics. The following steps obtain help and information about home networking.

1

- Click the Index button on the Navigation toolbar to display the Index pane.

- Type home networking in the 'Type in the keyword to find' text box in the Navigation Pane (Figure 1–94).

Q&A

What happens if the term I search for is not included in the index?

Try typing the term into the Search box in the Help and Support Center or search the World Wide Web for the term.

Figure 1–94

● Click overview in the list to select
the overview entry in the Index
entries list (Figure 1–95).

Figure 1–95

● Click the Display button to display
the home networking overview
topic in the topic pane (Figure 1–96).

Q&A

Must I always click the Display button
to see the help in the topic pane?

No. You can double-click any topic in
the Index list and the corresponding
help material will be displayed in
the topic pane.

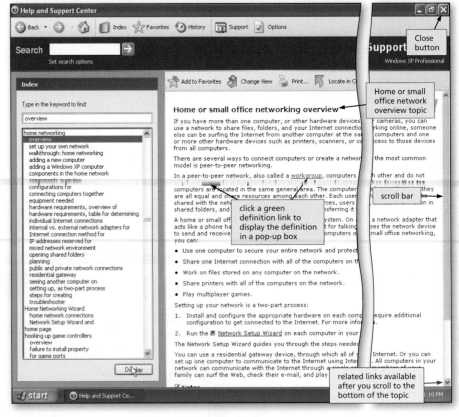

Figure 1–96

Other Ways

1. Press ALT+N, type
   keyword, press DOWN
   ARROW until topic is
   highlighted, press
   ALT+D (or ENTER)

To Display the Related Topics Link

Although not visible in Figure 1–96, the Related Topics link appears at the bottom of the Home or small office networking overview page, underlined, and in blue font. Clicking the Related Topics link displays a list of topics related to the home networking topic. The following step displays the Related Topics link and a pop-up window.

1

• Scroll to the bottom of the Home or small office networking overview topic to display the Related Topics link.

• Click the Related Topics link to display a pop-up window containing a list of related topics (Figure 1–97).

Figure 1–97

To Close the Help and Support Center

The following step shows how to close the Help and Support Center.

1 Click the Close button on the title bar of the Help and Support Center window to close the Help and Support Center window.

Logging Off and Turning Off the Computer

After completing your work with Windows XP, you should close your user account by logging off the computer. Logging off the computer closes any open applications, allows you to save any unsaved documents, ends the Windows XP session, and makes the computer available for other users.

To Log Off from the Computer

The following steps log off the computer.

1
- Display the Start menu (Figure 1–98).

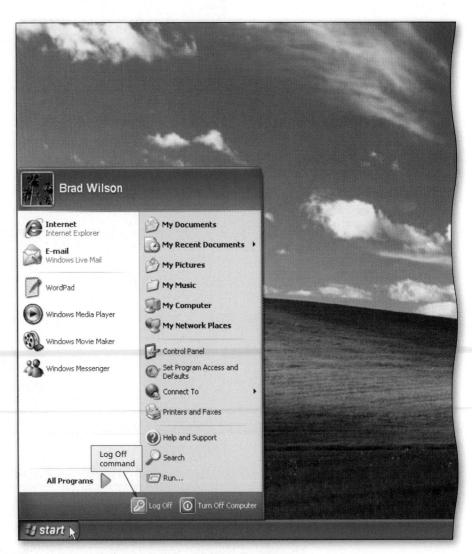

Figure 1–98

2

- Click Log Off on the Start menu to display the Log Off Windows dialog box (Figure 1–99).

 Q&A

Why should I log off the computer?

It is important to log off the computer so you do not lose your work. Some users of Windows XP have turned off their computers without following the log off procedure only to find data they thought they had stored on disk lost.

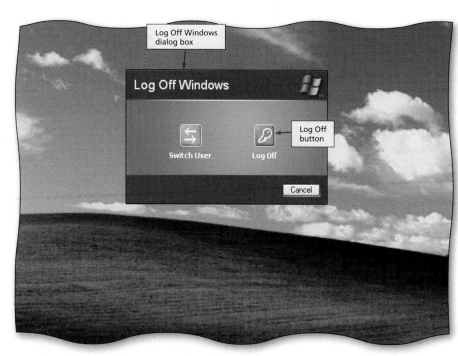

Figure 1–99

3

- Click the Log Off button in the Log Off Windows dialog box to log off from the computer and display the Welcome screen (Figure 1–100).

Q&A

If I accidentally click Log Off on the Start menu and do not want to log off, what should I do?

Click the Cancel button in the Log Off Windows dialog box to display the Start menu.

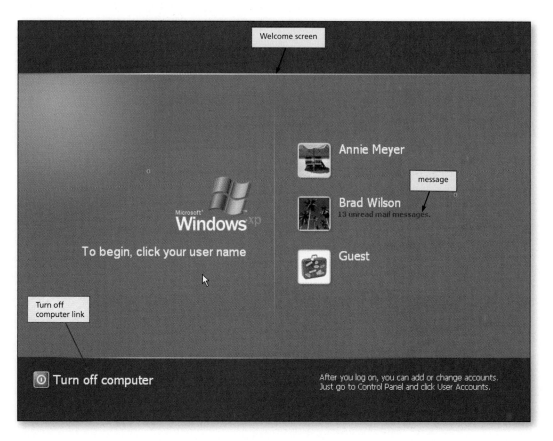

Figure 1–100

Other Ways
1. Press CTRL+ESC, press L, press L

To Turn Off the Computer

After logging off, you also may want to turn off the computer using the Turn off computer link on the Welcome screen. Turning off the computer shuts down Windows XP so you can turn off the power to the computer. Almost all computers turn the power off automatically. The following steps turn off the computer. If you are not sure about turning off the computer, simply read the steps.

1

- Click the Turn off computer link on the Welcome screen (Figure 1–101).

Q&A
What does the Stand By button do?

The Stand By button places the computer in a low-power state so that you can quickly resume your Windows session.

Q&A
Why should I turn off the computer?

Turning off the computer shuts down Windows XP so that you can safely turn off the computer.

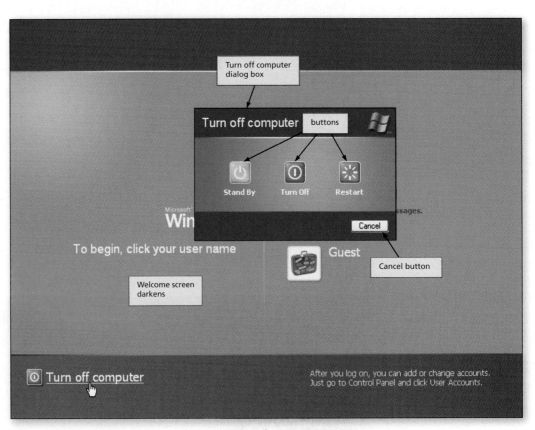

Figure 1–101

2

- Click the Turn Off button in the Turn off computer dialog box.

Q&A
If I accidentally click Turn Off computer on the Welcome screen and I do not want to shut down Windows XP, what should I do?

Click the Cancel button in the Turn off computer dialog box to return to normal Windows XP operation.

Other Ways

1. Press CTRL+ESC, press U, use ARROW KEYS to select Turn Off, press ENTER
2. Press ALT+F4, use ARROW keys to select Turn Off, press ENTER

Chapter Summary

In this chapter you have learned about the Microsoft Windows XP graphical interface, hierarchical format, removable media, and flash drives. You used Windows Explorer, Internet Explorer, and WordPad. You also obtained help about using Microsoft Windows XP. The following list includes all the new skills you have learned in this chapter.

1. Log On to the Computer   (WIN 7)
2. Display the Start Menu   (WIN 8)
3. Add an Icon to the Desktop   (WIN 11)
4. Open a Window by Double-Clicking a Desktop Icon   (WIN 12)
5. Minimize and Redisplay a Window   WIN 14)
6. Maximize and Restore a Window   (WIN 15)
7. Close a Window   (WIN 16, WIN 20)
8. Open a Window Using the Start Menu   (WIN 16)
9. Move a Window by Dragging   (WIN 17)
10. Expand an Area   (WIN 18)
11. Scroll Using Scroll Arrows   (WIN 18)
12. Size a Window by Dragging   (WIN 19)
13. Collapse an Area   (WIN 20)
14. Resize a Window   (WIN 20)
15. Delete a Desktop Icon by Right-Dragging   (WIN 21)
16. Start an Application Using the Start Menu   (WIN 23)
17. Browse the Web by Entering a URL   (WIN 25)
18. Open a Link in a New Tab   (WIN 27)
19. Switch Between Tabs   (WIN 28)
20. Close a Tab   (WIN 28)
21. Start Windows Explorer and Maximize Its Window   (WIN 29)
22. Plug a USB Flash Drive into a USB Port   (WIN 33)
23. Create a Folder on a Removable Drive   (WIN 34)
24. Download a Hierarchy of Folders into the Freshman Folder   (WIN 35)
25. Expand a Drive   (WIN 37)
26. Expand a Folder   (WIN 37)
27. Display the Contents of a Folder   (WIN 38)
28. Start WordPad   (WIN 39)
29. Type Text   (WIN 40)
30. Save a WordPad Document in a New Folder   (WIN 40)
31. Verify the Contents of a Folder   (WIN 45)
32. Copy a File in Windows Explorer by Right-Dragging   (WIN 46)
33. Display the Contents of a Folder   (WIN 47)
34. Rename a File   (WIN 47)
35. Delete a File by Right-Clicking   (WIN 48)
36. Close Expanded Folders   (WIN 50)
37. Quit Windows Explorer   (WIN 50)
38. Search for a File by Name   (WIN 51)
39. Search for a File Using a Word or Phrase in the File   (WIN 54)
40. Start Help and Support   (WIN 56)
41. Browse for Help Topics in the Table of Contents   (WIN 58)
42. Search for Help Topics Using the Index   (WIN 59)
43. Display the Related Topics Link   (WIN 61)
44. Close the Help and Support Center   (WIN 61)
45. Log Off from the Computer   (WIN 62)
46. Turn Off the Computer   (WIN 64)

If you have a SAM user profile, you may have access to hands-on instruction, practice, and assessment. Log in to your SAM account (http://sam2007.course.com) to launch any assigned training activities or exams that relate to the skills covered in this chapter.

Learn It Online

Test your knowledge of chapter content and key terms.

Instructions: To complete the Learn It Online exercises, start your browser, click the Address Path text box, and then enter the Web address scsite.com/winxp2007/learn. When the Windows Learn It Online page is displayed, click the link for the exercise you want to complete and then read the instructions.

Chapter Reinforcement TF, MC, and SA
A series of true/false, multiple choice, and short answer questions that test your knowledge of the chapter content.

Flash Cards
An interactive learning environment where you identify chapter key terms associated with displayed definitions.

Practice Test
A series of multiple choice questions that test your knowledge of chapter content and key terms.

Who Wants To Be a Computer Genius?
An interactive game that challenges your knowledge of chapter content in the style of a television quiz show.

Wheel of Terms
An interactive game that challenges your knowledge of chapter key terms in the style of the television show *Wheel of Fortune*.

Crossword Puzzle Challenge
A crossword puzzle that challenges your knowledge of key terms presented in the chapter.

In the Lab

Using the guidelines, concepts, and skills presented in this chapter complete the following Labs.

Lab 1: Taking the Windows XP Tour
Instructions: Use a computer to perform the following tasks:

Part 1: Starting the Windows XP Tour
1. If necessary, start Microsoft Windows XP and log on to the computer.
2. Click the Start button and then click Help and Support on the Start menu.
3. Click the Maximize button on the Help and Support Center title bar.
4. Click What's new in Windows XP in the Navigation Pane.
5. Click 'Taking a tour or tutorial' in the Navigation Pane. The Taking a tour or tutorial page appears in the topic pane.
6. Click Take the Windows XP tour in the topic pane. The Windows XP Tour dialog box appears.
7. If your computer does not have speakers or earphones, proceed to step 8 below. If your computer has speakers or earphones, follow the steps in Part 2.
8. If your computer does not have speakers or earphones, follow the steps in Part 3.

Part 2: Taking the Windows XP Tour with Sound and Animation
1. Verify the 'Play the animated tour that features text, animation, music, and voice narration' button is selected in the Windows XP Tour dialog box and then click the Next button.
2. Listen to the voice narration of the introduction to the Windows XP tour.

3. Click the gray Windows XP Basics button and answer the following questions.

   a. What is the narrow band at the bottom of the desktop called? _____

   _____

   b. What identifies a shortcut icon? _____

   c. What icons appear on the desktop the first time you start Windows? _____

   _____

   d. What is contained in the notification area? _____

   _____

   e. How does Windows keep the taskbar tidy? _____

   f. What does a right-facing arrow on a Start menu command signify? _____

   _____

   g. In which folders are text, image, and music files placed? _____

   _____

   h. What does the Restore Down button do? _____

   i. What appears when a program needs some information from you before it can complete a command? _____

   j. What do you use to set up user accounts? _____

   _____

   k. Where do you go when you want to interrupt your Windows session and let someone else use the computer? _____

   _____

4. Click the Skip Intro button in the lower corner of the desktop to skip the introduction to the Windows XP tour.

5. Click the yellow Best for Business button and listen to the narration.

6. Click the red Safe and Easy Personal Computing button and listen to the narration.

7. Click the green Unlock the World of Digital Media button and listen to the narration.

8. Click the blue The Connected Home and Office button and listen to the narration.

9. Click the red Exit Tour button on the desktop to exit the Windows XP tour.

10. Click the Close button in the Help and Support Center window.

Part 3: Taking the Windows XP Tour without Sound or Animation

   1. Click the 'Play the non-animated tour that features text and images only' button in the Windows XP Tour dialog box and then click the Next button.

2. Click the Start Here button to read about the basics of the Windows XP operating system.

3. Scroll the Windows XP Basics window and read the paragraph below the Windows Desktop heading. Click the Next button to display the next topic.

4. Scroll the Windows XP Basics window and read the paragraph below the Icons heading. Answer the following questions.

   a. What icon is displayed on the desktop the first time you start Windows? _____

   _____

   b. Does deleting a shortcut icon affect the actual program or file? _____

   _____

Continued >

In the Lab *continued*

5. Click the Next button to display the next topic. Scroll the Windows XP Basics window and read the paragraphs below the Taskbar heading. Answer the following question.

    a. Where is the notification area located? _____

    _____

6. Click the Next button to display the next topic. Scroll the Windows XP Basics window and read the paragraph below the Start Menu heading. Answer the following question.

    a. What does a right-facing arrow mean? _____

    _____

7. Click the Next button to display the next topic. Scroll the Windows XP Basics window and read the paragraph below the Files and Folder heading. Answer the following question.

    a. In which folders are text, image, and music files placed?

    _____

8. Click the Next button to display the next topic. Scroll the Windows XP Basics window and read the paragraphs below the Windows heading. Answer the following question.

    a. What appears if a program needs some information from you before it can complete a command?

    _____

9. Click the Next button to display the next topic. Scroll the Windows XP Basics window and read the paragraphs below the Control Panel heading. Answer the following questions.

    a. What Windows feature do you use to customize computer settings? _____

    _____

    b. Where is this feature located? _____

    _____

10. Click the Next button to display the next topic. Scroll the Windows XP Basics window and read the paragraphs below the Ending Your Session heading. Answer the following question.

    a. What do you do when you want to interrupt your Windows session and let someone else use the computer? _____

    _____

11. Click the Next button repeatedly to display the topics in the remaining four sections of the Windows XP tour.

12. Click the Close button in the window to end the tour.

13. Click the Close button in the Help and Support Center window.

In the Lab

Lab 2: Windows Explorer

Instructions: Use a computer to perform the following tasks.

1. Start Microsoft Windows XP.

2. Right-click the Start button on the taskbar, click Explore on the shortcut menu, and then maximize the Start Menu window.

3. If necessary, scroll to the left in the Folders pane so the Start Menu and Programs icons are visible.

4. Click the Programs icon in the Start Menu folder.

5. Double-click the Internet Explorer shortcut icon in the Contents pane to start the Internet Explorer application. What is the URL of the Web page that appears in the Address bar in the Windows Internet Explorer window? _____

6. Click the URL in the Address Path text box in the Internet Explorer window to select it. Type scsite.com and then press the ENTER key.

7. If necessary, scroll the Web page to display the Browse by Subject navigation pane containing the subject categories. Clicking a subject category displays the book titles in that category.

8. Click Operating Systems in the Browse by Subject navigation pane.

9. Click the Microsoft Windows XP link.

10. Right-click the first Microsoft Windows XP textbook cover image on the Web page, click Save Picture As on the shortcut menu, type Windows XP Cover in the File name box, and then click the Save button in the Save Picture dialog box to save the image in the My Pictures folder.

11. Click the Close button in the Windows Internet Explorer window.

12. If necessary, scroll to the top of the Folders pane to make the drive icon visible.

13. Click the minus sign in the box to the left of the drive icon.

14. Click the My Documents folder name in the Folders pane.

15. Click the My Pictures folder name in the Folders pane.

16. Right-click the Windows XP Cover icon and then click Properties on the shortcut menu.
    a. What type of file is the Windows XP Cover file? _____
    b. When was the file last modified? _____
    c. With what application does this file open? _____

17. Click the Cancel button in the Windows XP Cover Properties dialog box.

18. Insert a USB flash drive into your computer.

19. Right-drag the Windows XP Cover icon to the USB flash drive icon in the Folders pane. Click Move Here on the shortcut menu. Click the USB flash drive icon in the Folders pane.
    a. Is the Windows XP Cover file stored on drive? _____

20. Click the Close button in the USB flash drive window.

In the Lab

Lab 3: Using the Help and Support Center
Instructions: Use Windows Help and Support to perform the following tasks.

Part 1: Using the Question Mark Button
1. If necessary, start Microsoft Windows XP and then log on to the computer.

2. Right-click an open area of the desktop to display a shortcut menu.

3. Click Properties on the shortcut menu to display the Display Properties dialog box.

4. Click the Desktop tab in the Display Properties dialog box.

5. Click the Help button on the title bar. The mouse pointer changes to a block arrow with a question mark.

Continued >

In the Lab *continued*

6. Click the list box in the Desktop sheet. A pop-up window is displayed explaining the list box. Read the information in the pop-up window and then summarize the function of the list box.

_____

7. Click an open area of the Desktop sheet to remove the pop-up window.

8. Click the Help button on the title bar and then click the Customize Desktop button. A pop-up window is displayed explaining what happens when you click this button. Read the information in the pop-up window and then summarize the function of the button.

_____

9. Click an open area in the Desktop sheet to remove the pop-up window.

10. Click the Help button on the title bar and then click the monitor icon in the Desktop sheet. A pop-up window is displayed explaining the function of the monitor. Read the information in the pop-up window and then summarize the function of the monitor.

_____

11. Click an open area in the Desktop sheet to remove the pop-up window.

12. Click the Help button on the title bar and then click the Cancel button. A pop-up window is displayed explaining what happens when you click the button. Read the information in the pop-up window and then summarize the function of the Cancel button.

_____

13. Click an open area in the Desktop sheet to remove the pop-up window.

14. Click the Cancel button in the Display Properties dialog box.

Part 2: Finding What's New in Windows XP

1. Click the Start button and then click Help and Support on the Start menu.

2. If necessary, click the Maximize button on the Help and Support Center title bar.

3. Click What's new in Windows XP in the Navigation Pane.

4. Click What's new in the Navigation Pane. Twelve topics are displayed in the topic pane.

5. Click 'What's new on your desktop' in the topic pane.

6. Click Start menu (or the plus sign in the small box preceding Start menu) to expand the entry. Read the information about the Start menu.

7. Click the Using the Start menu link.

8. Click the Print button on the Help and Support toolbar to print the topic. Click the Print button in the Print dialog box.

9. If necessary, scroll the topic pane to display the Related Topics link. Click the Related Topics link to display a pop-up window containing three related topics. List the three topics.

_____

10. Click 'Display a program at the top of the Start menu' in the pop-up window.

11. Click the Print button on the Help and Support toolbar to print the topic. Click the Print button in the Print dialog box.

Part 3: Viewing Windows XP Articles

1. Click Windows XP articles: Walk through ways to use your PC in the What's new in Windows XP area in the Navigation Pane. A list of overviews, articles, and tutorials are displayed in the topic pane.

2. Click Walkthrough: Making music in the topic pane. Read the Making music article in the topic pane. List four ways in which you can use Windows XP musically.

_____

_____

3. Click Play music in the Making Music area. Scroll to display the Display details about a CD area. List the three steps to display details about a CD.

_____

_____

4. Scroll to the top of the window to display the Making Music area.

5. Click Create CDs in the Making Music area. Scroll to display the steps to burn your own CD. List the six steps to burn a CD.

_____

_____

_____

_____

_____

_____

6. Read other articles of interest to you in the Making Music area.

7. Click the Close button in the Help and Support Center window.

In the Lab

Lab 4: Downloading the Word Chapters 1-3 Data Files

Instructions: Use the SC Site – Shelly Cashman Series Student Resources Web site to download the Word Chapters 1-3 Data Files into the Word folder.

Part 1: Plug the USB Flash Drive into the USB Port

1. If necessary, launch Microsoft Windows XP and log on to the computer.

2. Plug the USB flash drive into the USB port on the computer. The UDISK 2.0 (E:) window should display on the desktop and should contain the Freshman folder.

3. If the Freshman folder is not displayed in the UDISK 2.0 (E:) window, follow the steps in Chapter One to create the hierarchy of folders shown in Figure 1–47 on page WIN 31.

Part 2: Download the Word Chapters 1-3 Data Files into the Word Folder

1. Start Internet Explorer by clicking the Start button on the taskbar and then clicking Internet on the Start menu.

2. Click the Address bar, type `scsite.com` in the Address box, and then click the Go button.

3. When the SC Site – Shelly Cashman Series Student Resources Web site is displayed, use the Browse by Subject navigation bar, click Office Suites, and then click Microsoft Office 2007.

4. In the center of the screen, locate your textbook, and then click the title (for example, Microsoft Office 2007: Introductory Concepts and Techniques, Windows XP Edition.)

5. When the page for your textbook displays, click the Word Chapters 1-3 Data Files link (You may need to scroll down the page).

Continued >

In the Lab *continued*

6. When the File Download – Security Warning dialog box is displayed, click the Run button.

7. When the Internet Explorer – Security Warning dialog box is displayed, click the Run button.

8. When the WinZip Self-Extractor dialog box displays, click the Browse button.

9. Click the plus sign to the left of UDISK 2.0 (E:), click the plus sign to the left of the Freshman folder, click the plus sign to the left of the 1st Semester folder, click the plus sign to the left of the Computer Class folder, and then click the Word folder.

10. Click the OK button in the Browse for Folder dialog box.

11. Click the Unzip button in the WinZip Self-Extractor dialog box.

12. When a smaller WinZip Self-Extractor dialog box appears, click the OK button.

13. Click the Close button in the WinZip Self-Extractor dialog box.

14. Click the Close button in the SC Site – Shelly Cashman Series Student Resources Web site window.

15. Verify the Word Chapters 1-3 Data Files folder is contained in the Word folder.

16. Close the Word window. Unplug the USB flash drive from the USB port.

1 Creating and Editing a Word Document

Objectives

You will have mastered the material in this chapter when you can:

- Start and quit Word
- Describe the Word window
- Enter text in a document
- Check spelling as you type
- Save a document
- Format text, paragraphs, and document elements
- Undo and redo commands or actions

- Insert a picture and format it
- Print a document
- Change document properties
- Open a document
- Correct errors in a document
- Use Word's Help

1 | Creating and Editing a Word Document

What Is Microsoft Office Word 2007?

Microsoft Office Word 2007 is a full-featured word processing program that allows you to create professional-looking documents and revise them easily. A document is a printed or electronic medium people use to communicate with others. With Word, you can develop many types of documents, including flyers, letters, memos, resumes, reports, fax cover sheets, mailing labels, and newsletters. Word also provides tools that enable you to create Web pages. From within Word, you can place these Web pages directly on a Web server.

Word has many features designed to simplify the production of documents and make documents look visually appealing. Using Word, you easily can change the shape, size, and color of text. You can include borders, shading, tables, images, pictures, charts, and Web addresses in documents.

While you are typing, Word performs many tasks automatically. For example, Word detects and corrects spelling and grammar errors in several languages. Word's thesaurus allows you to add variety and precision to your writing. Word also can format text, such as headings, lists, fractions, borders, and Web addresses, as you type.

This latest version of Word has many new features to make you more productive. For example, Word has many predefined text and graphical elements designed to assist you with preparing documents. Word also includes new charting and diagramming tools; uses themes so that you can coordinate colors, fonts, and graphics; and has a feature that enables you to convert a document to a PDF format.

To illustrate the features of Word, this book presents a series of projects that use Word to create documents similar to those you will encounter in academic and business environments.

Project Planning Guidelines	The process of developing a document that communicates specific information requires careful analysis and planning. As a starting point, establish why the document is needed. Once the purpose is determined, analyze the intended readers of the document and their unique needs. Then, gather information about the topic and decide what to include in the document. Finally, determine the document design and style that will be most successful at delivering the message. Details of these guidelines are provided in Appendix A. In addition, each project in this book provides practical applications of these planning considerations.

Project — Document with a Picture

To advertise a sale, promote a business, publicize an event, or convey a message to the community, you may want to create a flyer and post it in a public location. Libraries, schools, churches, grocery stores, and other places often provide bulletin boards or windows for flyers. These flyers announce personal items for sale or rent (car, boat, apartment); garage or block sales; services being offered (animal care, housecleaning, lessons); membership, sponsorship, or donation requests (club, church, charity); and other messages. Flyers are an inexpensive means of reaching the community, yet many go unnoticed because they are designed poorly.

The project in this chapter follows general guidelines and uses Word to create the flyer shown in Figure 1–1. This colorful, eye-catching flyer advertises horseback riding lessons at Tri-Valley Stables. The picture of the horse and rider entices passersby to stop and look at the flyer. The headline on the flyer is large and colorful to draw attention into the text. The body copy below the headline briefly describes key points of the riding lessons, and the bulleted list below the picture concisely highlights important additional information. The signature line of the flyer calls attention to the stable name and telephone number. Finally, the graphical page border nicely frames and complements the contents of the flyer.

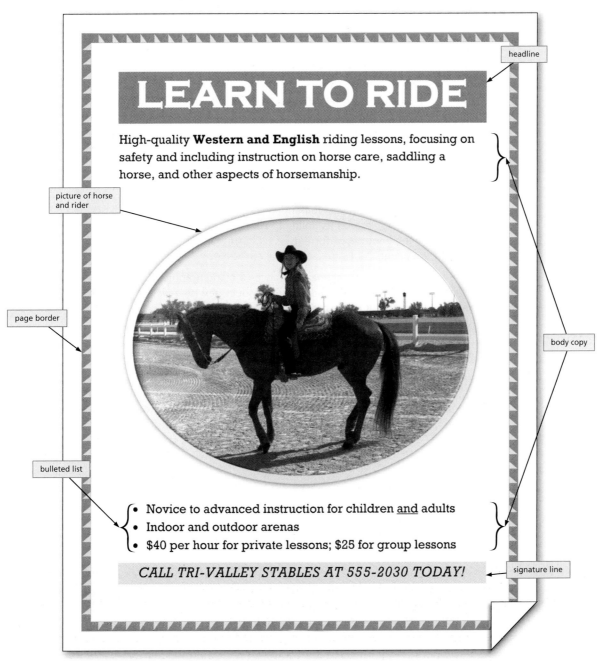

Figure 1–1

Overview

As you read this chapter, you will learn how to create the flyer shown in Figure 1–1 on the previous page by performing these general tasks:

- Enter text in the document.
- Save the document.
- Format the text in the document.
- Insert a picture in the document.
- Format the picture.
- Add a border to the page.
- Print the document.

Plan Ahead

General Project Guidelines

When creating a Word document, the actions you perform and decisions you make will affect the appearance and characteristics of the finished document. As you create a flyer, such as the project shown in Figure 1–1, you should follow these general guidelines:

1. **Choose the words for the text.** Follow the *less is more* principle. The less text, the more likely the flyer will be read. Use as few words as possible to make a point.

2. **Determine where to save the flyer.** You can store a document permanently, or **save** it, on a variety of storage media including a hard disk, USB flash drive, or CD. You also can indicate a specific location on the storage media for saving the document.

3. **Identify how to format various elements of the text.** The overall appearance of a document significantly affects its ability to communicate clearly. Examples of how you can modify the appearance, or **format**, of text include changing its shape, size, color, and position on the page.

4. **Find the appropriate graphical image.** An eye-catching graphical image should convey the flyer's overall message. It could show a product, service, result, or benefit, or visually convey a message that is not expressed easily with words.

5. **Establish where to position and how to format the graphical image.** The position and format of the graphical image should grab the attention of passersby and draw them into reading the flyer.

6. **Determine whether the flyer needs a page border, and if so, its style and format.** A graphical, color-coordinated page border can further draw attention to a flyer and nicely frame its contents. Be careful, however, that a page border does not make the flyer look too cluttered.

When necessary, more specific details concerning the above guidelines are presented at appropriate points in the chapter. The chapter also will identify the actions performed and decisions made regarding these guidelines during the creation of the flyer shown in Figure 1–1.

Starting Word

The Word Window
The screen in Figure 1-3 shows how the Word window looks the first time you start Word after installation on most computers. Your screen may look different depending on your screen resolution and Word settings.

If you are using a computer to step through the project in this chapter and you want your screen to match the figures in this book, you should change your screen's resolution to 1024 × 768. For information about how to change a computer's resolution, read Appendix E.

To Start Word

The following steps, which assume Windows is running, start Word based on a typical installation. You may need to ask your instructor how to start Word for your computer.

- Click the Start button on the Windows taskbar to display the Start menu.

- Point to All Programs on the Start menu to display the All Programs submenu.

- Point to Microsoft Office on the All Programs submenu to display the Microsoft Office submenu (Figure 1–2).

Figure 1–2

- Click Microsoft Office Word 2007 to start Word and display a new blank document in the Word window (Figure 1–3).

- If the Word window is not maximized, click the Maximize button next to the Close button on its title bar to maximize the window.

Q&A What is a maximized window?

A maximized window fills the entire screen. When you maximize a window, the Maximize button changes to a Restore Down button.

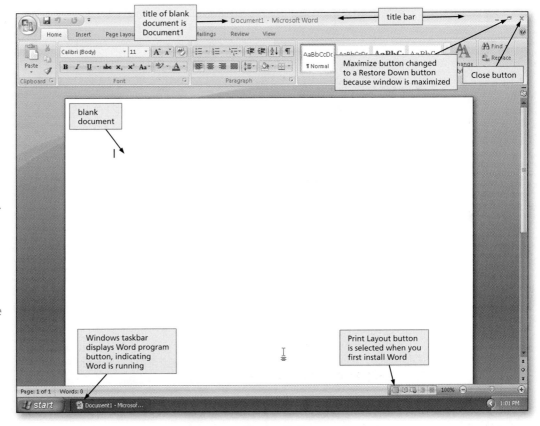

Figure 1–3

- If the Print Layout button is not selected, click it so that your screen layout matches Figure 1–3.

Other Ways
1. Double-click Word icon on desktop, if one is present
2. Click Microsoft Office Word 2007 on Start menu

The Word Window

The Word window consists of a variety of components to make your work more efficient and documents more professional. These include the document window, Ribbon, Mini toolbar and shortcut menus, Quick Access Toolbar, and Office Button. Some of these components are common to other Microsoft Office 2007 programs; others are unique to Word.

Document Window

You view a portion of a document on the screen through a **document window** (Figure 1–4). The default (preset) view is **Print Layout view**, which shows the document on a mock sheet of paper in the document window.

The Word document window in Figure 1–4 contains an insertion point, mouse pointer, scroll bar, and status bar. Other elements that may appear in the document window are discussed later in this and subsequent chapters.

Insertion Point The **insertion point** is a blinking vertical bar that indicates where text, graphics, and other items will be inserted. As you type, the insertion point moves to the right, and when you reach the end of a line, it moves downward to the beginning of the next line.

Figure 1–4

Mouse Pointer The **mouse pointer** becomes different shapes depending on the task you are performing in Word and the pointer's location on the screen. The mouse pointer in Figure 1–4 is the shape of an I-beam.

Scroll Bar You use a **scroll bar** to display different portions of a document in the document window. At the right edge of the document window is a vertical scroll bar. If a document is too wide to fit in the document window, a horizontal scroll bar also appears at the bottom of the document window. On a scroll bar, the position of the **scroll box** reflects the location of the portion of the document that is displayed in the document window. A **scroll arrow** is located at each end of a scroll bar. To scroll through, or display different portions of the document in the document window, you can click a scroll arrow or drag the scroll box.

Status Bar The **status bar**, located at the bottom of the document window above the Windows taskbar, presents information about the document, the progress of current tasks, and the status of certain commands and keys; it also provides controls for viewing the document. As you type text or perform certain commands, various indicators may appear on the status bar.

The left edge of the status bar in Figure 1–4 shows the current page followed by the total number of pages in the document, the number of words in the document, and a button to check spelling and grammar. Toward the right edge are buttons and controls you can use to change the view of a document and adjust the size of the displayed document.

Ribbon

The **Ribbon**, located near the top of the Word window, is the control center in Word (Figure 1–5a). The Ribbon provides easy, central access to the tasks you perform while creating a document. The Ribbon consists of tabs, groups, and commands. Each **tab** surrounds a collection of groups, and each group contains related commands.

When you start Word, the Ribbon displays seven top-level tabs: Home, Insert, Page Layout, References, Mailings, Review, and View. The **Home tab**, called the primary tab, contains the more frequently used commands. To display a different tab on the Ribbon, click the top-level tab. That is, to display the Insert tab, click Insert on the Ribbon. To return to the Home tab, click Home on the Ribbon. The tab currently displayed is called the **active tab**.

To display more of the document in the document window, some users prefer to minimize the Ribbon, which hides the groups on the Ribbon and displays only the top-level tabs (Figure 1–5b). To use commands on a minimized Ribbon, click the top-level tab.

BTW

Minimizing the Ribbon
If you want to minimize the Ribbon, right-click the Ribbon and then click Minimize the Ribbon on the shortcut menu, double-click the active tab, or press CTRL+F1. To restore a minimized Ribbon, right-click the Ribbon and then click Minimize the Ribbon on the shortcut menu, double-click any top-level tab, or press CTRL+F1. To use commands on a minimized Ribbon, click the top-level tab.

Figure 1–5

Each time you start Word, the Ribbon appears the same way it did the last time you used Word. The chapters in this book, however, begin with the Ribbon appearing as it did at the initial installation of the software. If you are stepping through this chapter on a computer and you want your Ribbon to match the figures in this book, read Appendix E.

In addition to the top-level tabs, Word displays other tabs, called **contextual tabs**, when you perform certain tasks or work with objects such as pictures or tables. If you insert a picture in the document, for example, the Picture Tools tab and its related subordinate Format tab appear (Figure 1–6). When you are finished working with the picture, the Picture Tools and Format tabs disappear from the Ribbon. Word determines when contextual tabs should appear and disappear based on tasks you perform. Some contextual tabs, such as the Table Tools tab, have more than one related subordinate tab.

Figure 1–6

Commands on the Ribbon include buttons, boxes (text boxes, check boxes, etc.), and galleries (Figure 1–6). A **gallery** is a set of choices, often graphical, arranged in a grid or in a list. You can scroll through choices on an in-Ribbon gallery by clicking the gallery's scroll arrows. Or, you can click a gallery's More button to view more gallery options on the screen at a time. Some buttons and boxes have arrows that, when clicked, also display a gallery; others always cause a gallery to be displayed when clicked. Most galleries support **live preview**, which is a feature that allows you to point to a gallery choice and see its effect in the document — without actually selecting the choice (Figure 1–7).

Figure 1–7

Some commands on the Ribbon display an image to help you remember their function. When you point to a command on the Ribbon, all or part of the command glows in shades of yellow and orange, and an Enhanced ScreenTip appears on the screen. An **Enhanced ScreenTip** is an on-screen note that provides the name of the command, available keyboard shortcut(s), a description of the command, and sometimes instructions for how to obtain help about the command (Figure 1–8). Enhanced ScreenTips are more detailed than a typical ScreenTip, which usually only displays the name of the command.

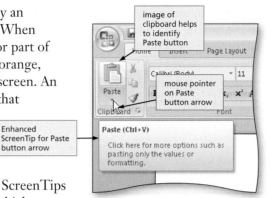

Figure 1–8

The lower-right corner of some groups on the Ribbon has a small arrow, called a **Dialog Box Launcher**, that when clicked, displays a dialog box or a task pane with additional options for the group (Figure 1–9). When presented with a dialog box, you make selections and must close the dialog box before returning to the document. A **task pane**, by contrast, is a window that can remain open and visible while you work in the document.

Figure 1–9

Mini Toolbar and Shortcut Menus

The **Mini toolbar**, which appears automatically based on tasks you perform, contains commands related to changing the appearance of text in a document. All commands on the Mini toolbar also exist on the Ribbon. The purpose of the Mini toolbar is to minimize mouse movement. For example, if you want to use a command that currently is not displayed on the active tab, you can use the command on the Mini toolbar — instead of switching to a different tab to use the command.

When the Mini toolbar appears, it initially is transparent (Figure 1–10a). If you do not use the transparent Mini toolbar, it disappears from the screen. To use the Mini toolbar, move the mouse pointer into the toolbar, which causes the Mini toolbar to change from a transparent to bright appearance (Figure 1–10b).

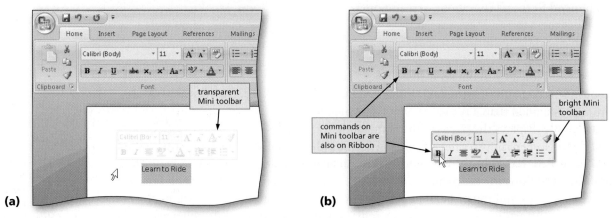

Figure 1–10

A **shortcut menu**, which appears when you right-click an object, is a list of frequently used commands that relate to the right-clicked object. When you right-click a scroll bar, for example, a shortcut menu appears with commands related to the scroll bar. If you right-click an item in the document window, Word displays both the Mini toolbar and a shortcut menu (Figure 1–11).

Figure 1–11

Quick Access Toolbar

The **Quick Access Toolbar**, located by default above the Ribbon, provides easy access to frequently used commands (Figure 1–12a). The commands on the Quick Access Toolbar always are available, regardless of the task you are performing. Initially, the Quick Access Toolbar contains the Save, Undo, and Redo commands. If you click the Customize Quick Access Toolbar button, Word provides a list of commands you quickly can add to and remove from the Quick Access Toolbar (Figure 1–12b).

Figure 1–12

You also can add other commands to or delete commands from the Quick Access Toolbar so that it contains the commands you use most often. As you add commands to the Quick Access Toolbar, its commands may interfere with the document title on the title bar. For this reason, Word provides an option of displaying the Quick Access Toolbar below the Ribbon (Figure 1–13).

Quick Access Toolbar positioned below Ribbon

Figure 1–13

Each time you start Word, the Quick Access Toolbar appears the same way it did the last time you used Word. The chapters in this book, however, begin with the Quick Access Toolbar appearing as it did at the initial installation of the software. If you are stepping through this chapter on a computer and you want your Quick Access Toolbar to match the figures in this book, you should reset your Quick Access Toolbar. For more information about how to reset the Quick Access Toolbar, read Appendix E.

Office Button

While the Ribbon is a control center for creating documents, the **Office Button** is a central location for managing and sharing documents. When you click the Office Button, located in the upper-left corner of the window, Word displays the Office Button menu (Figure 1–14a). A **menu** contains a list of commands.

When you click the New, Open, Save As, and Print commands on the Office Button menu, Word displays a dialog box with additional options. The Save As, Print, Prepare, Send, and Publish commands have an arrow to their right. If you point to this arrow, Word displays a **submenu**, which is a list of additional commands associated with the selected command (Figure 1–14b). For the Prepare, Send, and Publish commands that do not display a dialog box when clicked, you can point either to the command or the arrow to display the submenu.

(a)

(b)

Figure 1–14

Key Tips

If you prefer using the keyboard instead of the mouse, you can press the ALT key on the keyboard to display a **Key Tip badge**, or keyboard code icon, for certain commands (Figure 1–15). To select a command using the keyboard, press its displayed code letter, or **Key Tip**. When you press a Key Tip, additional Key Tips related to the selected command may appear. For example, to select the New command on the Office Button menu, press the ALT key, then press the F key, and then press the N key.

To remove the Key Tip badges from the screen, press the ALT key or the ESC key until all Key Tip badges disappear, or click the mouse anywhere in the Word window.

Figure 1–15

Entering Text

The first step in creating a document is to enter its text by typing on the keyboard. By default, Word positions text you type at the left margin. In a later section of this chapter, you will learn how to format, or change the appearance of, the entered text.

<table>
<tr><td>Plan
Ahead</td><td>

Choose the words for the text.
The text in a flyer is organized into three areas: headline, body copy, and signature line.

- The headline is the first line of text on the flyer. It conveys the product or service being offered, such as a car for sale or personal lessons, or the benefit that will be gained, such as a convenience, better performance, greater security, higher earnings, or more comfort.

- The body text consists of all text between the headline and the signature line. This text highlights the key points of the message in as few words as possible. It should be easy to read and follow. While emphasizing the positive, the body text must be realistic, truthful, and believable.

- The signature line, which is the last line of text on the flyer, contains contact information or identifies a call to action.

</td></tr>
</table>

BTW

Zooming
If text is too small for you to read on the screen, you can zoom the document by dragging the Zoom slider on the status bar or clicking the Zoom Out or Zoom In buttons on the status bar. Changing the zoom has no effect on the printed document.

To Type Text

To begin creating the flyer in this chapter, you type the headline in the document window. The following steps type this first line of text in the document.

• Type `Learn to Ride` as the headline (Figure 1–16).

Q&A What if I make an error while typing?

You can press the **BACKSPACE** key until you have deleted the text in error and then retype the text correctly.

Q&A Why did the Spelling and Grammar Check icon appear on the status bar?

When you begin typing text, the **Spelling and Grammar Check icon** appears on the status bar with an animated pencil writing on paper that indicates Word is checking for spelling and grammar errors. When you stop typing, the pencil changes to a blue check mark (no errors) or a red X (potential errors found). Word flags potential errors in the document with a red or green wavy underline. Later, this chapter shows how to fix flagged errors.

Figure 1–16

• Press the ENTER key to move the insertion point to the beginning of the next line (Figure 1–17).

Q&A Why did blank space appear between the headline and the insertion point?

Each time you press the ENTER key, Word creates a new paragraph and inserts blank space between the two paragraphs. Later in this chapter, you will learn how to adjust the spacing between paragraphs.

Figure 1–17

To Display Formatting Marks

To indicate where in a document you press the ENTER key or SPACEBAR, you may find it helpful to display formatting marks. A **formatting mark**, sometimes called a **nonprinting character**, is a character that Word displays on the screen but is not visible on a printed document. For example, the paragraph mark (¶) is a formatting mark that indicates where you pressed the ENTER key. A raised dot (·) shows where you pressed the SPACEBAR. Other formatting marks are discussed as they appear on the screen.

Depending on settings made during previous Word sessions, your Word screen already may display formatting marks (Figure 1–18). The following step displays formatting marks, if they do not show already on the screen.

- If necessary, click Home on the Ribbon to display the Home tab.

- If it is not selected already, click the Show/Hide ¶ button on the Home tab to display formatting marks on the screen (Figure 1–18).

Q&A

What if I do not want formatting marks to show on the screen?

If you feel the formatting marks clutter the screen, you can hide them by clicking the Show/Hide ¶ button again. It is recommended that you display formatting marks so that you visually can identify when you press the ENTER key, SPACEBAR, and other keys associated with nonprinting characters; therefore, the document windows presented in this book show the formatting marks.

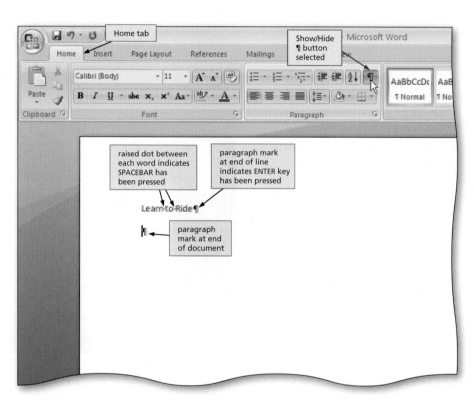

Figure 1–18

Other Ways

1. Press CTRL+SHIFT+*

Wordwrap

Wordwrap allows you to type words in a paragraph continually without pressing the ENTER key at the end of each line. When the insertion point reaches the right margin, Word automatically positions the insertion point at the beginning of the next line. As you type, if a word extends beyond the right margin, Word also automatically positions that word on the next line along with the insertion point.

Word creates a new paragraph each time you press the ENTER key. Thus, as you type text in the document window, do not press the ENTER key when the insertion point reaches the right margin. Instead, press the ENTER key only in these circumstances:

1. To insert blank lines in a document

2. To begin a new paragraph

3. To terminate a short line of text and advance to the next line

4. To respond to questions or prompts in Word dialog boxes, task panes, and other on-screen objects

To Wordwrap Text as You Type

The next step in creating the flyer is to type the body copy. The following step wordwraps the text in the body copy.

- **Type** High-quality Western and English riding lessons, focusing on safety and including instruction on horse care, saddling a horse, and other aspects of horsemanship.

Why does my document wrap on different words?

Differences in wordwrap relate to the printer used by your computer. That is, the printer controls where wordwrap occurs for each line in your document. Thus, it is possible that the same document could wordwrap differently if printed on different printers.

- Press the ENTER key to position the insertion point on the next line in the document (Figure 1–19).

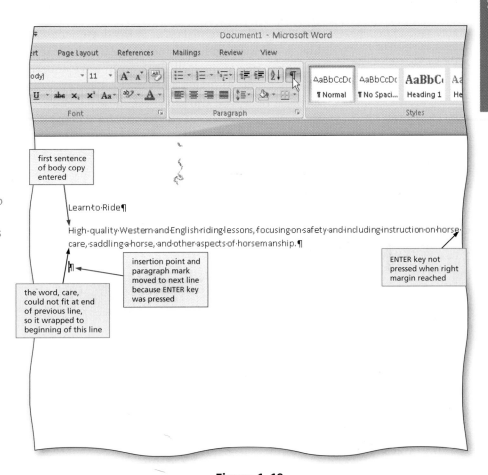

Figure 1–19

To Insert a Blank Line

In the flyer, the picture of the horse and rider should be positioned below the paragraph just entered. The picture will be inserted after all text is entered and formatted. Thus, you will leave a blank line in the document for the picture. To enter a blank line in a document, press the ENTER key without typing any text on the line. The following step inserts one blank line below the first paragraph of body copy.

- Press the ENTER key to insert a blank line in the document (Figure 1–20).

Figure 1–20

BTW

Automatic Spelling Correction
As you type, Word automatically corrects some misspelled words. For example, if you type recieve, Word automatically fixes the misspelling and displays the word, receive, when you press the SPACEBAR or type a punctuation mark. To see a complete list of automatically corrected words, click Office Button, click the Word Options button, click Proofing in the left pane of the Word Options dialog box, click the AutoCorrect Options button, and then scroll through the list of words near the bottom of the dialog box.

Spelling and Grammar Check

As you type text in a document, Word checks your typing for possible spelling and grammar errors. If all of the words you have typed are in Word's dictionary and your grammar is correct, as mentioned earlier, the Spelling and Grammar Check icon on the status bar displays a blue check mark. Otherwise, the icon shows a red X. In this case, Word flags the potential error in the document window with a red or green wavy underline. A red wavy underline means the flagged text is not in Word's dictionary (because it is a proper name or misspelled). A green wavy underline indicates the text may be incorrect grammatically. Although you can check the entire document for spelling and grammar errors at once, you also can check these flagged errors as they appear on the screen.

To display a list of corrections for flagged text, right-click the flagged text. When you right-click a flagged word, for example, a list of suggested spelling corrections appears on the screen. A flagged word, however, is not necessarily misspelled. For example, many names, abbreviations, and specialized terms are not in Word's main dictionary. In these cases, you tell Word to ignore the flagged word. As you type, Word also detects duplicate words while checking for spelling errors. For example, if your document contains the phrase, to the the store, Word places a red wavy underline below the second occurrence of the word, the.

To Check Spelling and Grammar as You Type

In the following steps, the word, instruction, has been misspelled intentionally as intrution to illustrate Word's check spelling as you type feature. If you are doing this project on a computer, your flyer may contain other misspelled words, depending on the accuracy of your typing.

1
- **Type** Novice to advanced intrution **and then press the** SPACEBAR (Figure 1–21).

Q&A

What if Word does not flag my spelling and grammar errors with wavy underlines?

To verify that the check spelling and grammar as you type features are enabled, click the Office Button and then click the Word Options button. When the Word Options dialog box is displayed, click Proofing, and then ensure the 'Check spelling as you type' and 'Mark grammar errors as you type' check boxes have check marks. Also ensure the 'Hide spelling errors in this document only' and 'Hide grammar errors in this document only' check boxes do not have check marks. Click the OK button.

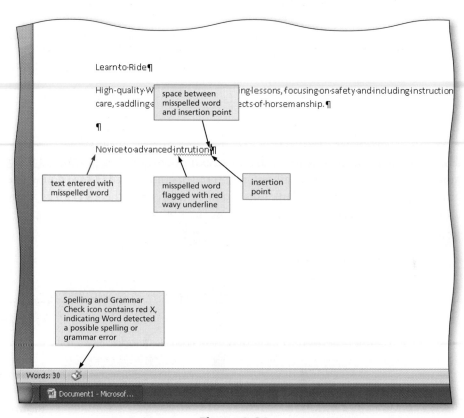

Figure 1–21

2

- Right-click the flagged word (intrution, in this case) to display a shortcut menu that includes a list of suggested spelling corrections for the flagged word (Figure 1–22).

What if, when I right-click the misspelled word, my desired correction is not in the list on the shortcut menu?

You can click outside the shortcut menu to close the menu and then retype the correct word, or you can click Spelling on the shortcut menu to display the Spelling dialog box. Chapter 2 discusses the Spelling dialog box.

What if a flagged word actually is, for example, a proper name and spelled correctly?

Right-click it and then click Ignore All on the shortcut menu to instruct Word not to flag future occurrences of the same word.

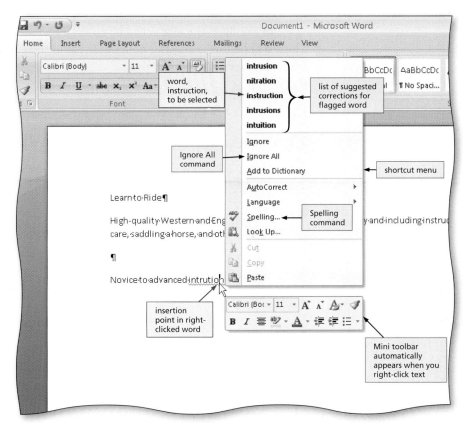

Figure 1–22

3

- Click instruction on the shortcut menu to replace the misspelled word in the document (intrution) with the word, instruction (Figure 1–23).

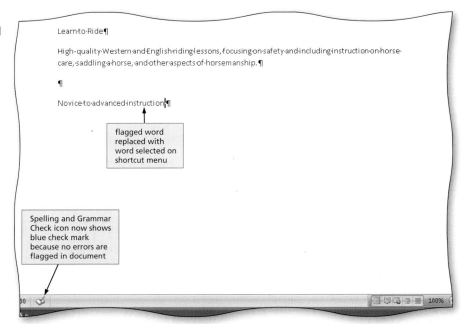

Figure 1–23

Other Ways

1. Click Spelling and Grammar Check icon on status bar, click correct word on shortcut menu

To Enter More Text

In the flyer, the text yet to be entered includes the remainder of the body copy, which will be formatted as a bulleted list, and the signature line. The following steps enter the remainder of text in the flyer.

1 Press the END key to move the insertion point to the end of the current line.

2 Type `for children and adults` and then press the ENTER key.

3 Type `Indoor and outdoor arenas` and then press the ENTER key.

4 Type `$40 per hour for private lessons; $25 for group lessons` and then press the ENTER key.

5 To complete the text in the flyer, type `Call Tri-Valley Stables at 555-2030 today!` (Figure 1–24).

Character Widths
Many word processing documents use variable character fonts, where some characters are wider than others; for example, the letter w takes up more space than the letter i.

Figure 1–24

Saving the Project

While you are creating a document, the computer stores it in memory. When you save a document, the computer places it on a storage medium such as a USB flash drive, CD, or hard disk. A saved document is referred to as a **file**. A **file name** is the name assigned to a file when it is saved.

It is important to save a document frequently for the following reasons:

• The document in memory will be lost if the computer is turned off or you lose electrical power while Word is open.

• If you run out of time before completing your project, you may finish your document at a future time without starting over.

Determine where to save the document.

When saving a document, you must decide which storage medium to use.

- If you always work on the same computer and have no need to transport your projects to a different location, then your computer's hard disk will suffice as a storage location. It is a good idea, however, to save a backup copy of your projects on a separate medium in case the file becomes corrupted or the computer's hard disk fails.

- If you plan to work on your projects in various locations or on multiple computers, then you should save your projects on a portable medium, such as a USB flash drive or CD. The projects in this book use a USB flash drive, which saves files quickly and reliably and can be reused. CDs are easily portable and serve as good backups for the final versions of projects because they generally can save files only one time.

To Save a Document

You have performed many tasks while creating this project and do not want to risk losing the work completed thus far. Accordingly, you should save the document. The following steps save a document on a USB flash drive using the file name, Horseback Riding Lessons Flyer.

1

- With a USB flash drive connected to one of the computer's USB ports, click the Save button on the Quick Access Toolbar to display the Save As dialog box (Figure 1–25).

Q&A

Do I have to save to a USB flash drive?

No. You can save to any device or folder. A **folder** is a specific location on a storage medium. You can save to the default folder or a different folder. You also can create your own folders, which is explained later in this book.

Figure 1–25

2

- Type Horseback Riding Lessons Flyer in the File name text box to change the file name. Do not press the ENTER key after typing the file name (Figure 1–26).

Q&A

What characters can I use in a file name?

A file name can have a maximum of 255 characters, including spaces. The only invalid characters are the backslash (\), slash (/), colon (:), asterisk (*), question mark (?), quotation mark ("), less than symbol (<), greater than symbol (>), and vertical bar (|).

Figure 1–26

3

- Click the Save in box arrow to display a list of available drives and folders (Figure 1–27).

Q&A

Why is my list of files, folders, and drives arranged and named differently from those shown in the figure?

Your computer's configuration determines how the list of files and folders is displayed and how drives are named. You can change the save location by clicking shortcuts on the **My Places bar**.

Q&A

How do I save the file if I am not using a USB flash drive?

Use the same process, but be certain to select your device in the Save in list.

Figure 1–27

4

● Click UDISK 2.0 (E:) in the Save in list to select the USB flash drive, Drive E in this case, as the new save location (Figure 1–28).

Q&A

What if my USB flash drive has a different name or letter?

It is very likely that your USB flash drive will have a different name and drive letter and be connected to a different port. Verify the device in your Save in list is correct.

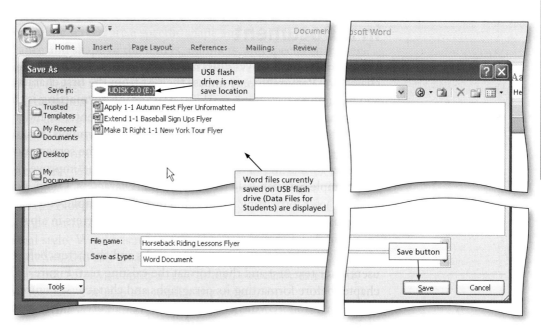

Figure 1–28

5

● Click the Save button in the Save As dialog box to save the document on the USB flash drive with the file name, Horseback Riding Lessons Flyer (Figure 1–29).

Q&A

How do I know that the project is saved?

While Word is saving your file, it briefly displays a message on the status bar indicating the amount of the file saved. In addition, your USB drive may have a light that flashes during the save process.

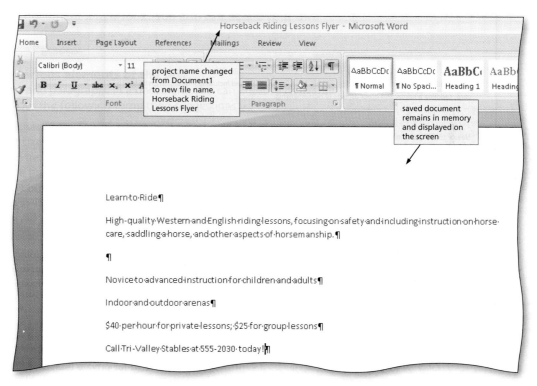

Figure 1–29

Other Ways

1. Click Office Button, click Save, type file name, select drive or folder, click Save button

2. Press CTRL+S or press SHIFT+F12, type file name, select drive or folder, click Save button

To Apply Styles

In the flyer, you want the headline and the signature line to be emphasized more than the other text. Word provides heading styles designed to emphasize this type of text. The first step in formatting the flyer is to apply the Heading 1 style to the headline and the Heading 2 style to the signature line. The default Heading 1 style is a 14-point Cambria bold font. The default Heading 2 style is a 13-point Cambria bold font. The default theme color scheme uses shades of blue for headings.

To apply a style to a paragraph, you first position the insertion point in the paragraph and then apply the style. The following steps apply heading styles to paragraphs.

- Press CTRL+HOME (that is, press and hold down the CTRL key, press the HOME key, and then release both keys) to position the insertion point at the top of the document (Figure 1–31).

Figure 1–31

- Point to Heading 1 in the Styles gallery to display a live preview in the document of the Heading 1 style (Figure 1–32).

Q&A

What happens if I move the mouse pointer?

If you move the mouse pointer away from the gallery, the text containing the insertion point returns to the Normal style.

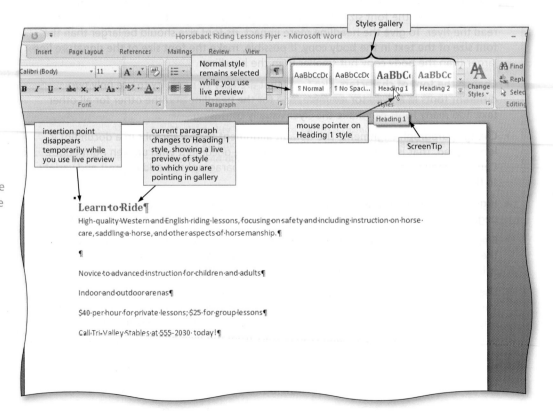

Figure 1–32

3

- Click Heading 1 in the Styles gallery to apply the Heading 1 style to the headline (Figure 1–33).

Q&A

Why did a square appear on the screen near the left edge of the headline?

The square is a nonprinting character, like the paragraph mark, that indicates text to its right has been formatted using a style.

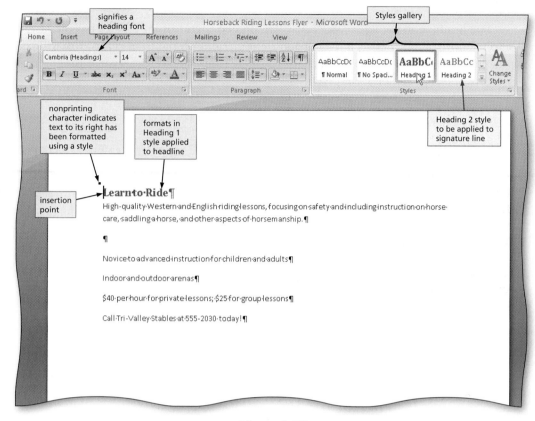

Figure 1–33

4

- Press CTRL+END (that is, press and hold down the CTRL key, press the END key, and then release both keys) to position the insertion point at the end of the document.

- Click Heading 2 in the Styles gallery to apply the Heading 2 style to the signature line (Figure 1–34).

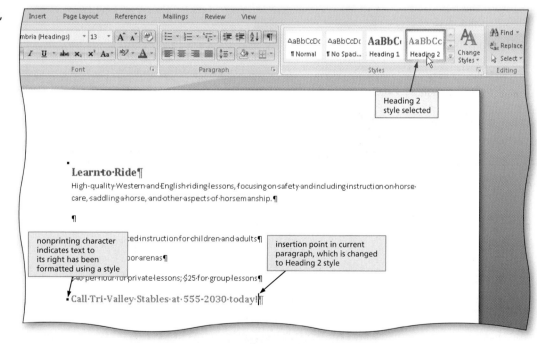

Figure 1–34

Other Ways	
1. Click Styles Dialog Box Launcher, click desired style in Styles task pane	2. Press CTRL+SHIFT+S, click Style Name box arrow in Apply Styles task pane, click desired style in list

To Center a Paragraph

The headline in the flyer currently is left-aligned (Figure 1–35). You want the headline to be **centered**, that is, positioned horizontally between the left and right margins on the page. Thus, you will center the paragraph containing the headline. Recall that Word considers a single short line of text, such as the three-word headline, a paragraph. The following steps center a paragraph.

- Click somewhere in the paragraph to be centered (in this case, the headline) to position the insertion point in the paragraph to be formatted (Figure 1–35).

Figure 1–35

- Click the Center button on the Home tab to center the headline (Figure 1–36).

Q&A

What if I want to return the paragraph to left-aligned?

Click the Align Text Left button on the Home tab.

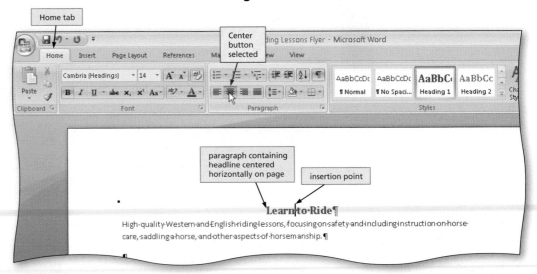

Figure 1–36

Other Ways

1. Right-click paragraph, click Center button on Mini toolbar
2. Right-click paragraph, click Paragraph on shortcut menu, click Indents and Spacing tab, click Alignment box arrow, click Centered, click OK button
3. Click Paragraph Dialog Box Launcher, click Indents and Spacing tab, click Alignment box arrow, click Centered, click OK button
4. Press CTRL+E

Formatting Single Versus Multiple Paragraphs and Characters

As shown in the previous pages, to format a single paragraph, simply move the insertion point in the paragraph and then format the paragraph. Likewise, to format a single word, position the insertion point in the word and then format the word.

To format *multiple* paragraphs or words, however, you first must select the paragraphs or words you want to format and then format the selection. If your screen normally displays dark letters on a light background, which is the default setting in Word, then selected text displays light letters on a dark background.

To Select a Line

The font size of characters in the Heading 1 style, 14 point, is too small for passersby to read in the headline of the flyer. To increase the font size of the characters in the headline, you must first select the line of text containing the headline. The following steps select a line.

- Move the mouse pointer to the left of the line to be selected (in this case, the headline) until the mouse pointer changes to a right-pointing block arrow (Figure 1–37).

Figure 1–37

- While the mouse pointer is a right-pointing block arrow, click the mouse to select the entire line to the right of the mouse pointer (Figure 1–38).

Figure 1–38

Other Ways	
1. Drag mouse through line	2. With insertion point at beginning of desired line, press SHIFT+DOWN ARROW

To Change the Font Size of Selected Text

The next step is to increase the font size of the characters in the selected headline. You would like the headline to be as large as possible and still fit on a single line, which in this case is 48 point. The following steps increase the font size of the headline from 14 to 48 point.

- With the text selected, click the Font Size box arrow on the Home tab to display the Font Size gallery (Figure 1–39).

Why are the font sizes in my Font Size gallery different from those in Figure 1–39?

Font sizes may vary depending on the current font and your printer driver.

Q&A
What happened to the Mini toolbar?

The Mini toolbar disappears if you do not use it. These steps used the Font Size box arrow on the Home tab instead of the Font Size box arrow on the Mini toolbar. If a command exists both on the currently displayed tab and the Mini toolbar, this book uses the command on the tab. When the command is not on the currently displayed tab, the Mini toolbar is used.

Figure 1–39

- Point to 48 in the Font Size gallery to display a live preview of the headline at 48 point (Figure 1–40).

Experiment

- Point to various font sizes in the Font Size gallery and watch the font size of the headline change in the document window.

- Click 48 in the Font Size gallery to increase the font size of the selected text to 48.

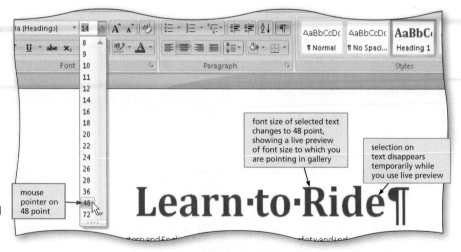

Figure 1–40

Other Ways

1. Click Font Size box arrow on Mini toolbar, click desired font size in Font Size gallery

2. Right-click selected text, click Font on shortcut menu, click Font tab, select desired font size in Size list, click OK button

3. Click Font Dialog Box Launcher, click Font tab, select desired font size in Size list, click OK button

4. Press CTRL+SHIFT+P, click Font tab, select desired font size in Size list, click OK button

To Change the Font of Selected Text

As mentioned earlier, the default Heading 1 style uses the font called Cambria. Word, however, provides many other fonts to add variety to your documents. To draw more attention to the headline, you change its font so it differs from the font of other text in the flyer. The following steps change the font from Cambria to Copperplate Gothic Bold.

1

• With the text selected, click the Font box arrow on the Home tab to display the Font gallery (Figure 1–41).

Q&A

Will the fonts in my Font gallery be the same as those in Figure 1–41?

Your list of available fonts may differ, depending on the type of printer you are using.

Figure 1–41

2

• Scroll through the Font gallery, if necessary, and then point to Copperplate Gothic Bold (or a similar font) to display a live preview of the headline in Copperplate Gothic Bold font (Figure 1–42).

Experiment

• Point to various fonts in the Font gallery and watch the font of the headline change in the document window.

3

• Click Copperplate Gothic Bold (or a similar font) to change the font of the selected text to Copperplate Gothic Bold.

Figure 1–42

Other Ways
1. Click Font box arrow on Mini toolbar, click desired font in Font gallery 2. Right-click selected text, click Font on shortcut menu, click	Font tab, select desired font in Font list, click OK button 3. Click Font Dialog Box Launcher, click Font tab, select desired font in Font list, click OK button	4. Press CTRL+SHIFT+F, click Font tab, select desired font in the Font list, click OK button

To Select Multiple Paragraphs

The next formatting step in creating the flyer is to increase the font size of the characters between the headline and the signature line so that they are easier to read from a distance. To change the font size of the characters in multiple lines, you first must select all the lines to be formatted. The following steps select multiple lines.

- Move the mouse pointer to the left of the first paragraph to be selected until the mouse pointer changes to a right-pointing block arrow (Figure 1–43).

Figure 1–43

- Drag downward to select all lines that will be formatted (Figure 1–44).

Q&A

How do I *drag* the mouse?

Dragging is the process of holding down the mouse button while moving the mouse and then releasing the mouse button.

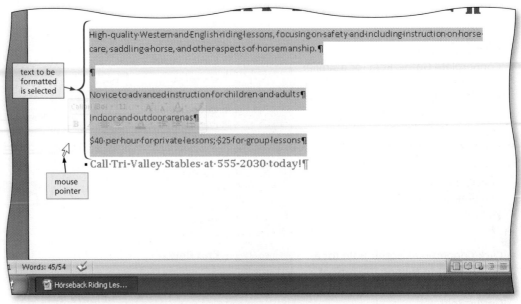

Figure 1–44

Other Ways

1. With insertion point at beginning of desired line, press SHIFT+DOWN ARROW repeatedly until all lines are selected

To Change the Font Size of Selected Text

The characters between the headline and the signature line in the flyer currently are 11 point. To make them easier to read from a distance, this flyer uses 16 point for these characters. The following steps change the font size of the selected text.

1 With the text selected, click the Font Size box arrow on the Home tab to display the Font Size gallery.

2 Click 16 in the Font Size gallery to increase the font size of the selected text to 16.

To Format a Line

In the flyer, the signature line is to be centered to match the paragraph alignment of the headline. Also, its text should have a font size larger than the rest of the body copy. The following steps center the line and increase its font size to 18.

1 Click somewhere in the paragraph to be centered (in this case, the signature line) to position the insertion point in the paragraph to be formatted.

2 Click the Center button on the Home tab to center the signature line.

3 Move the mouse pointer to the left of the line to be selected (in this case, the signature line) until the mouse pointer changes to a right-pointing block arrow and then click to select the line.

4 With the signature line selected, click the Font Size box arrow on the Home tab and then click 18 in the Font Size gallery to increase the font size of the selected text to 18 (Figure 1–45).

Figure 1–45

● Drag the mouse pointer through the last character of the text to be selected, in this case, the h in English (Figure 1–49).

 Why did the mouse pointer shape change again?

When the mouse pointer is positioned in selected text, its shape is a left-pointing block arrow.

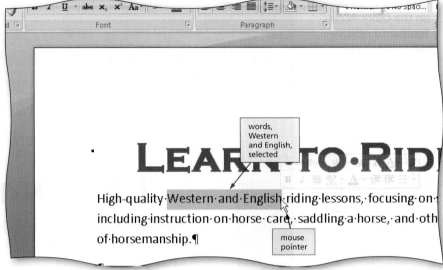

Figure 1–49

Other Ways

1. With insertion point at beginning of first word in group, press CTRL+SHIFT+RIGHT ARROW repeatedly until all words are selected

To Bold Text

Bold characters display somewhat thicker and darker than those that are not bold. The following step formats the selected words, Western and English, as bold.

● With the text selected, click the Bold button on the Home tab to format the selected text in bold (Figure 1–50).

 How would I remove a bold format?

You would click the Bold button a second time, or you immediately could click the Undo button on the Quick Access Toolbar.

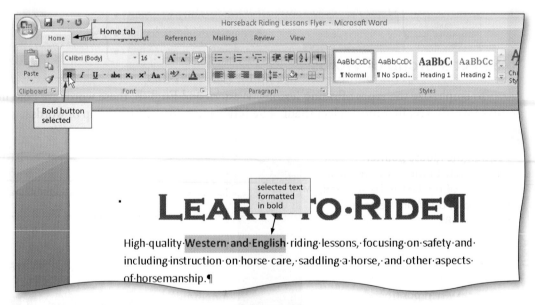

Figure 1–50

Other Ways

1. Click Bold button on Mini toolbar

2. Right-click selected text, click Font on shortcut menu, click Font tab, click Bold in Font style list, click OK button

3. Click Font Dialog Box Launcher, click Font tab, click Bold in Font style list, click OK button

4. Press CTRL+B

To Underline a Word

As with bold text, underlines are used to emphasize or draw attention to specific text. **Underlined** text prints with an underscore (_) below each character. In the flyer, the word, and, in the first bulleted paragraph is emphasized with an underline.

As with a single paragraph, if you want to format a single word, you do not need to select the word. Simply position the insertion point somewhere in the word and apply the desired format. The following step formats a word with an underline.

- Click somewhere in the word to be underlined (and, in this case).

- Click the Underline button on the Home tab to underline the word containing the insertion point (Figure 1–51).

Q&A How would I remove an underline?

You would click the Underline button a second time, or you immediately could click the Undo button on the Quick Access Toolbar.

Q&A Are other types of underlines available?

In addition to the basic solid underline shown in Figure 1–51, Word has many decorative underlines, such as double underlines, dotted underlines, and wavy underlines. You can access the decorative underlines and also change the color of an underline through the Underline gallery.

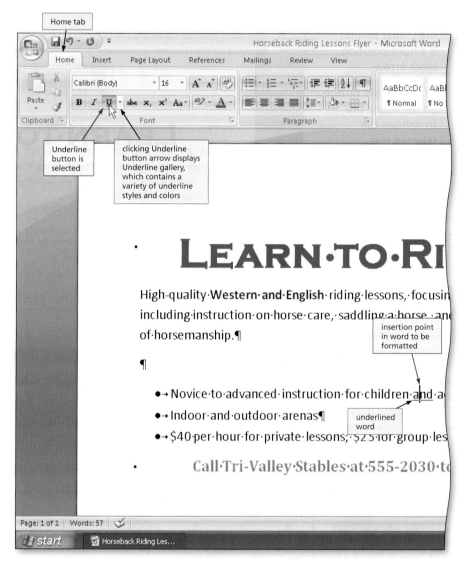

Figure 1–51

Other Ways

1. Right-click text, click Font on shortcut menu, click Font tab, click Underline style box arrow, click desired underline style, click OK button

2. Click Font Dialog Box Launcher, click Font tab, click Underline style box arrow, click desired underline style, click OK button

3. Press CTRL+U

- Point to Style Set on the Change Styles menu to display the Style Set gallery.

- Point to Modern in the Style Set gallery to display a live preview of the formats associated with the Modern style set (Figure 1–54).

 Experiment

- Point to various style sets in the Style Set gallery and watch the formats of the styled text change in the document window.

- Click Modern in the Style Set gallery to change the document style set to Modern.

Q&A What if I want to return to the original style set?

You would click the Change Styles button, click Style Set on the Change Styles menu, and then click Default in the Style Set gallery, or you could click the Undo button on the Quick Access Toolbar.

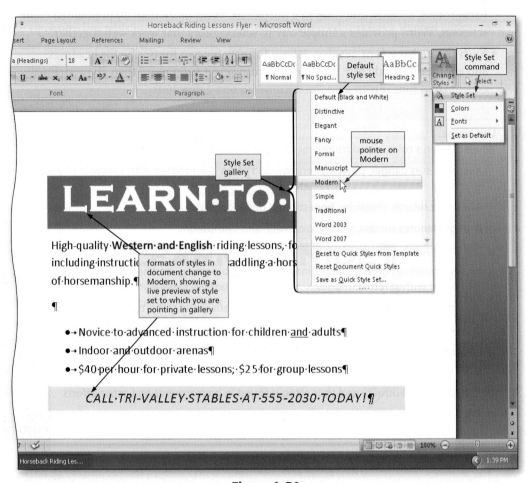

Figure 1–54

BTW

Style Formats

To see the formats assigned to a particular style in a document, click the Styles Dialog Box Launcher on the Home tab and then click the Style Inspector button in the Styles task pane. Position the insertion point in the style and then point to the Paragraph formatting or Text level formatting areas in the Style Inspector task pane to display an Enhanced ScreenTip describing formats assigned to the location of the insertion point. You also can click the Reveal Formatting button in the Style Inspector to display the Reveal Formatting task pane.

To Change Theme Colors

To suggest enthusiasm, success, and honesty, the background colors around the headline and signature line paragraphs in the flyer use shades of orange and brown. In Word, the color scheme called Aspect uses these colors. Thus, you will change the color scheme to Aspect. The following steps change theme colors.

 1

- Click the Change Styles button on the Home tab to display the Change Styles menu.

- Point to Colors on the Change Styles menu to display the Colors gallery.

- Point to Aspect in the Colors gallery to display a live preview of the Aspect color scheme (Figure 1–55).

 Experiment

- Point to various color schemes in the Colors gallery and watch the paragraph background colors change in the document window.

2

- Click Aspect in the Colors gallery to change the document theme colors to Aspect.

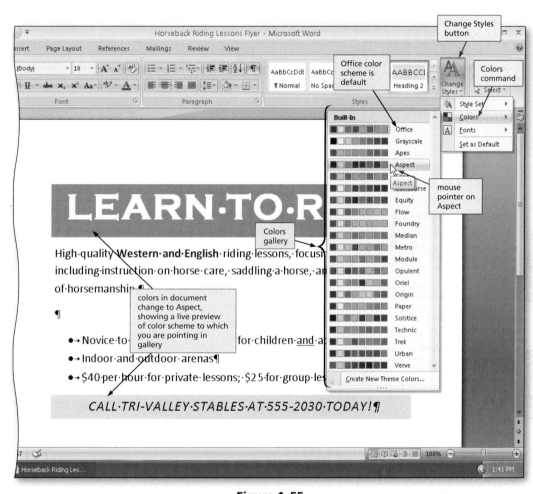

Figure 1–55

Q&A

What if I want to return to the original color scheme?

You would click the Change Styles button, click Colors on the Change Styles menu, and then click Office in the Colors gallery.

Other Ways

1. Click Theme Colors button arrow on Page Layout tab, select desired color scheme

To Change Theme Fonts

Earlier in this chapter, you changed the font of the headline to Copperplate Gothic Bold. In this flyer, all text below the headline should be the Rockwell font, instead of the Calibri font, because it better matches the western tone of the flyer. Thus, the next step is to change the current font set, which is called Office, to a font set called Foundry, which uses the Rockwell font for headings and body text.

If you previously changed a font using buttons on the Ribbon or Mini toolbar, Word will not alter those when you change the font set because changes to the font set are not applied to fonts changed individually. This means the font headline in the flyer will stay as Copperplate Gothic Bold when you change the font set. The following steps change the font set to Foundry.

- Click the Change Styles button on the Home tab.

- Point to Fonts on the Change Styles menu to display the Fonts gallery.

- Scroll through the Fonts gallery until Foundry is displayed and then point to Foundry to display a live preview of the Foundry font set (Figure 1–56).

 Experiment

- Point to various font sets in the Fonts gallery and watch the fonts below the headline change in the document window.

Figure 1–56

2

- Click Foundry in the Fonts gallery to change the document theme fonts to Foundry.

Q&A

What if I want to return to the original font set?

You would click the Change Styles button, click Fonts on the Change Styles menu, and then click Office in the Fonts gallery.

Other Ways

1. Click Theme Fonts button arrow on Page Layout tab, select desired font set

Inserting and Formatting a Picture in a Word Document

With the text formatted in the flyer, the next step is to insert a picture in the flyer and format the picture. Flyers usually contain graphical images, such as a picture, to attract the attention of passersby.

Plan
Ahead

Find the appropriate graphical image.

To use graphical images, also called graphics, in a Word document, the image must be stored digitally in a file. Files containing graphical images are available from a variety of sources:

- Word includes a collection of predefined graphical images that you can insert in a document.

- Microsoft has free digital images on the Web for use in a document. Other Web sites also have images available, some of which are free, while others require a fee.

- You can take a picture with a digital camera and **download** it, which is the process of copying the digital picture from the camera to your computer.

- With a scanner, you can convert a printed picture, drawing, or diagram to a digital file.

  If you receive a picture from a source other than yourself, do not use the file until you are certain it does not contain a virus. A **virus** is a computer program that can damage files and programs on your computer. Use an antivirus program to verify that any files you use are virus free.

Plan
Ahead

Establish where to position and how to format the graphical image.

The content, size, shape, position, and format of a graphic should capture the interest of passersby, enticing them to stop and read the flyer. Often, the graphic is the center of attraction and visually the largest element on a flyer. If you use colors in the graphical image, be sure they are part of the document's color scheme.

To Insert a Picture

The next step in creating the flyer is to insert the picture of the horse and rider so that it is centered on the blank line above the bulleted list. The picture, which was taken with a digital camera, is available on the Data Files for Students. See the inside back cover of this book for instructions on downloading the Data Files for Students, or contact your instructor for information on accessing the required files. The following steps insert a centered picture, which, in this example, is located on the same USB flash drive that contains the saved flyer.

- To position the insertion point where you want the picture to be located, press CTRL+HOME and then press the DOWN ARROW key four times.

- Click the Center button on the Home tab to center the paragraph that will contain the picture.

- Click Insert on the Ribbon to display the Insert tab (Figure 1–57).

Figure 1–57

2

- Click the Insert Picture from File button on the Insert tab to display the Insert Picture dialog box.

- With your USB flash drive connected to one of the computer's USB ports, if necessary, click the Look in box arrow and then click UDISK 2.0 (E:) to select the USB flash drive, Drive E in this case, in the Look in list as the device that contains the picture.

- Click Horse and Rider to select the file name (Figure 1–58).

Q&A

What if the picture is not on a USB flash drive?

Use the same process, but be certain to select the device containing the picture in the Look in list.

Figure 1–58

3

- Click the Insert button in the dialog box to insert the picture at the location of the insertion point in the document (Figure 1–59).

Q&A

What are the symbols around the picture?

A selected graphic appears surrounded by a **selection rectangle**, which has small squares and circles, called **sizing handles**, at each corner and middle location.

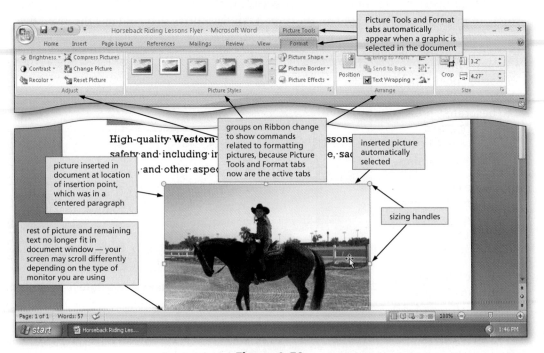

Figure 1–59

Scrolling

As mentioned at the beginning of this chapter, you view only a portion of a document on the screen through the document window. At some point when you type text or insert graphics, Word will **scroll** the top or bottom portion of the document off the screen. Although you cannot see the text and graphics once they scroll off the screen, they remain in the document.

As shown in Figure 1–59, when you insert the picture in the flyer, the text and graphics are too long to fit in the document window. Thus, to see the bottom of the flyer, you will need to scroll downward.

You may use either the mouse or the keyboard to scroll to a different location in a document. With the mouse, you can use the scroll arrows or the scroll box on the scroll bar to display a different portion of the document in the document window, and then click the mouse to move the insertion point to that location. Table 1–1 explains various techniques for using the scroll bar to scroll vertically with the mouse.

BTW

Minimize Wrist Injury
Computer users frequently switch between the keyboard and the mouse during a word processing session; such switching strains the wrist. To help prevent wrist injury, minimize switching. For instance, if your fingers already are on the keyboard, use keyboard keys to scroll. If your hand already is on the mouse, use the mouse to scroll.

Table 1–1 Using the Scroll Bar to Scroll with the Mouse	
SCROLL DIRECTION	**MOUSE ACTION**
Up	Drag the scroll box upward.
Down	Drag the scroll box downward.
Up one screen	Click anywhere above the scroll box on the vertical scroll bar.
Down one screen	Click anywhere below the scroll box on the vertical scroll bar.
Up one line	Click the scroll arrow at the top of the vertical scroll bar.
Down one line	Click the scroll arrow at the bottom of the vertical scroll bar.

When you use the keyboard to scroll, the insertion point automatically moves when you press the appropriate keys. Table 1–2 outlines various techniques to scroll through a document using the keyboard, some of which you have seen used in this chapter.

Table 1–2 Scrolling with the Keyboard	
SCROLL DIRECTION	**KEY(S) TO PRESS**
Left one character	LEFT ARROW
Right one character	RIGHT ARROW
Left one word	CTRL+LEFT ARROW
Right one word	CTRL+RIGHT ARROW
Up one line	UP ARROW
Down one line	DOWN ARROW
To end of line	END
To beginning of line	HOME
Up one paragraph	CTRL+UP ARROW
Down one paragraph	CTRL+DOWN ARROW
Up one screen	PAGE UP
Down one screen	PAGE DOWN
To top of document window	ALT+CTRL+PAGE UP
To bottom of document window	ALT+CTRL+PAGE DOWN
To beginning of document	CTRL+HOME
To end of document	CTRL+END

To Apply a Picture Style

Earlier in this chapter, you applied the heading styles to the headline and signature line in the flyer. Word also provides styles for pictures, allowing you easily to change the basic rectangle format to a more visually appealing style. Word provides a gallery of more than 25 picture styles, which include a variety of shapes, angles, borders, and reflections. The flyer in this chapter uses an oval picture style that has a border around its edges. The following steps apply a picture style to the picture in the flyer.

1

- Click the down scroll arrow on the vertical scroll bar as many times as necessary until the entire picture is displayed in the document window (Figure 1–60).

Q&A

What if the Picture Tools and Format tabs no longer are displayed on my Ribbon?

Double-click the picture to display the Picture Tools and Format tabs.

Figure 1–60

2

- Click the More button in the Picture Styles gallery, which shows more gallery options.

- Point to Metal Oval in the Picture Styles gallery to display a live preview of that style applied to the picture in the document (Figure 1–61).

 Experiment

- Point to various picture styles in the Picture Styles gallery and watch the format of the picture change in the document window.

3

- Click Metal Oval in the Picture Styles gallery to apply the selected style to the picture.

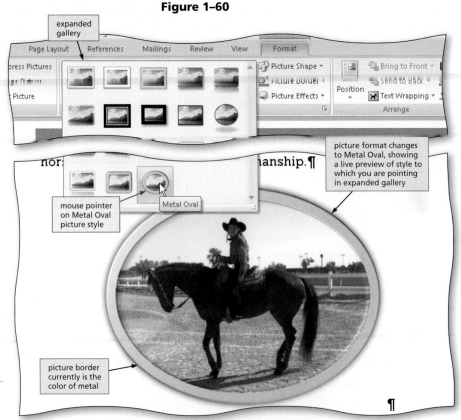

Figure 1–61

To Change a Picture Border Color

The flyer in this chapter has a tan border around the picture. Earlier in this chapter, you changed the color scheme to Aspect. To coordinate the border color with the other colors in the document, you will use a shade of tan in Aspect color scheme for the picture border. Any color galleries you display show colors defined in this current color scheme. The following steps change the picture border color.

1

- Click the Picture Border button on the Format tab to display the Picture Border gallery.

Q&A What if the Picture Tools and Format tabs no longer are displayed on my Ribbon?

Double-click the picture to display the Picture Tools and Format tabs.

- Point to Tan, Background 2 (third theme color from left in the first row) in the Picture Border gallery to display a live preview of that border color on the picture (Figure 1–62).

Experiment

- Point to various colors in the Picture Border gallery and watch the border color on the picture change in the document window.

2

- Click Tan, Background 2 in the Picture Styles gallery to change the picture border color.

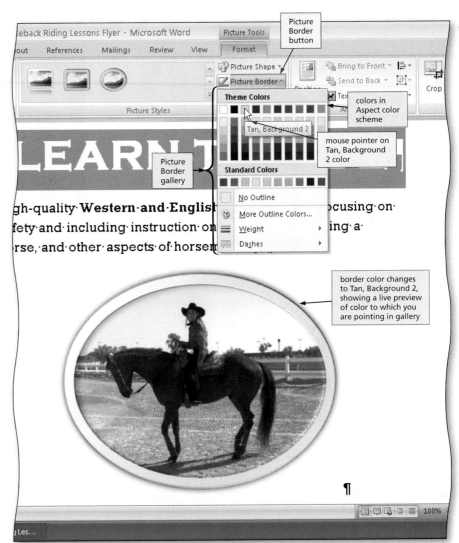

Figure 1–62

To Zoom the Document

The next step in formatting the picture is to resize it. Specifically, you will increase the size of the picture. You do not want it so large, however, that it causes the flyer text to flow to a second page. You can change the zoom so that you can see the entire document on the screen at once. Seeing the entire document at once helps you determine the appropriate size of the picture. The steps on the next page zoom the document.

Experiment

- Repeatedly click the Zoom Out and Zoom In buttons on the status bar and watch the size of the document change in the document window.

2

- Click the Zoom Out or Zoom In button as many times as necessary until the Zoom level button displays 50% on its face (Figure 1–63).

Q&A

If I change the zoom percentage, will the document print differently?

Changing the zoom has no effect on the printed document.

Figure 1–63

Other Ways		
1. Drag Zoom slider on status bar	2. Click Zoom level button on status bar, select desired zoom percent or type, click OK button	3. Click Zoom level button on View tab, select desired zoom percent or type, click OK button

To Resize a Graphic

The next step is to resize the picture. **Resizing** includes both enlarging and reducing the size of a graphic. The picture in the flyer should be as large as possible, without causing any flyer text to flow to a second page.

With the entire document displaying in the document window, you will be able to see how the resized graphic will look on the entire page. The following steps resize a selected graphic.

- With the graphic still selected, point to the upper-right corner sizing handle on the picture so that the mouse pointer shape changes to a two-headed arrow (Figure 1–64).

Q&A

What if my graphic (picture) is not selected?

To select a graphic, click it.

Figure 1–64

2

- Drag the sizing handle diagonally outward until the crosshair mouse pointer is positioned approximately as shown in Figure 1–65.

3

- Release the mouse button to resize the graphic.

Q&A What if the graphic is the wrong size?

Repeat Steps 1 and 2.

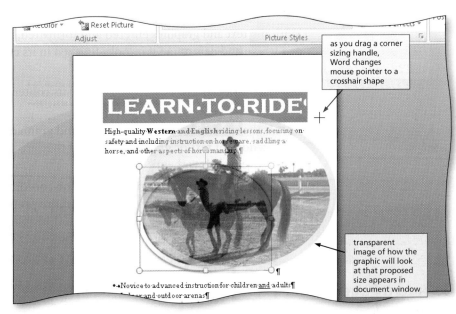

as you drag a corner sizing handle, Word changes mouse pointer to a crosshair shape

transparent image of how the graphic will look at that proposed size appears in document window

Figure 1–65

4

- Click outside the graphic to deselect it (Figure 1–66).

Q&A What happened to the Picture Tools and Format tabs?

When you click outside of a graphic or press a key to scroll through a document, Word deselects the graphic and removes the Picture Tools and Format tabs from the screen.

Q&A What if I want to return a graphic to its original size and start again?

With the graphic selected, click the Size Dialog Box Launcher on the Format tab to display the Size dialog box, click the Size tab, click the Reset button, and then click the Close button.

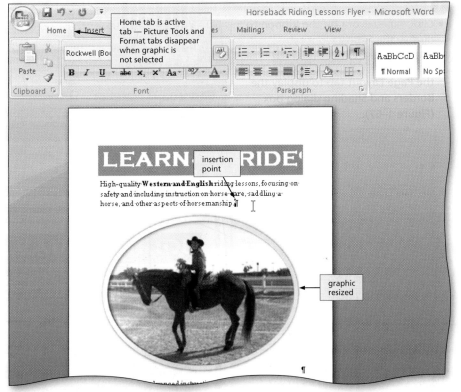

Home tab is active tab — Picture Tools and Format tabs disappear when graphic is not selected

insertion point

graphic resized

Figure 1–66

Other Ways

1. Enter graphic height and width in Shape Height and Shape Width text boxes in Size group on Format tab in Picture Tools tab

2. Click Size Dialog Box Launcher on Format tab in Picture Tools tab, click Size tab, enter desired height and width values in text boxes, click Close button

To Open a Document from Word

Earlier in this chapter you saved your project on a USB flash drive using the file name, Horseback Riding Lessons Flyer. The following steps open the Horseback Riding Lessons Flyer file from the USB flash drive.

1

• With your USB flash drive connected to one of the computer's USB ports, click the Office Button to display the Office Button menu (Figure 1–79).

Q&A What files are shown in the Recent Documents list?

Word displays, by default, the nine most recently opened document file names in this list. If the name of the file you want to open appears in the Recent Documents list, you could click it to open the file.

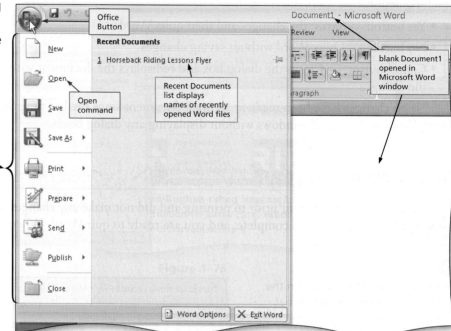

Figure 1–79

2

• Click Open on the Office Button menu to display the Open dialog box.

• If necessary, click the Look in box arrow and then click UDISK 2.0 (E:) to select the USB flash drive, Drive E in this case, in the Look in list as the new open location.

• Click Horseback Riding Lessons Flyer to select the file name (Figure 1–80).

Q&A How do I open the file if I am not using a USB flash drive?

Use the same process, but be certain to select your device in the Look in list.

Figure 1–80

3

- Click the Open button to open the selected file and display the Horseback Riding Lessons Flyer document in the Word window (Figure 1–81).

Q&A

Why is the Word icon and document name on the Windows taskbar?

When you open a Word file, a Word program button is displayed on the taskbar. The button in Figure 1–81 contains an ellipsis because some of its contents do not fit in the allotted button space. If you point to a program button, its entire contents appear in a ScreenTip, which in this case would be the file name followed by the program name.

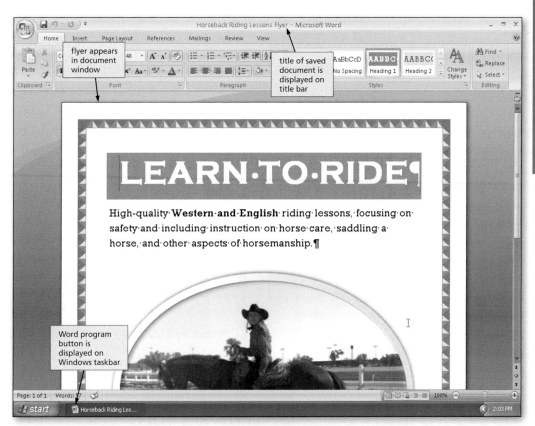

Figure 1–81

Other Ways

1. Click Office Button, double-click file name in Recent Documents list

2. Press CTRL+O, select file name, press ENTER

Correcting Errors

After creating a document, you often will find you must make changes to it. For example, the document may contain an error, or new circumstances may require you to add text to the document.

Types of Changes Made to Documents

The types of changes made to documents normally fall into one of the three following categories: additions, deletions, or modifications.

Additions Additional words, sentences, or paragraphs may be required in a document. Additions occur when you omit text from a document and want to insert it later. For example, additional types of riding lessons may be offered.

BTW

Print Preview
You can preview a document before printing it by clicking the Office Button, pointing to Print, and then clicking Print Preview. When finished previewing the document, click the Close Print Preview button.

Deletions Sometimes, text in a document is incorrect or is no longer needed. For example, group lessons might not be offered. In this case, you would delete the words, $25 for group lessons, from the flyer.

Modifications If an error is made in a document or changes take place that affect the document, you might have to revise a word(s) in the text. For example, the fee per hour may change from $40 to $50 for private lessons.

To Insert Text in an Existing Document

Word inserts text to the left of the insertion point. The text to the right of the insertion point moves to the right and downward to fit the new text. The following steps insert the word, various, to the left of the word, aspects, in the flyer.

1
- Scroll through the document and then click to the left of the location of text to be inserted (in this case, the a in aspects) to position the insertion point where text should be inserted (Figure 1–82).

Figure 1–82

2
- Type various and then press the SPACEBAR to insert the word, various, to the left of the insertion point (Figure 1–83).

 Why did the text move to the right as I typed?

In Word, the default typing mode is **insert mode**, which means as you type a character, Word moves all the characters to the right of the typed character one position to the right. You can change to overtype mode by pressing the INSERT key on the keyboard. In **overtype mode**, Word replaces characters to the right of the insertion point. Pressing the INSERT key again returns Word to insert mode.

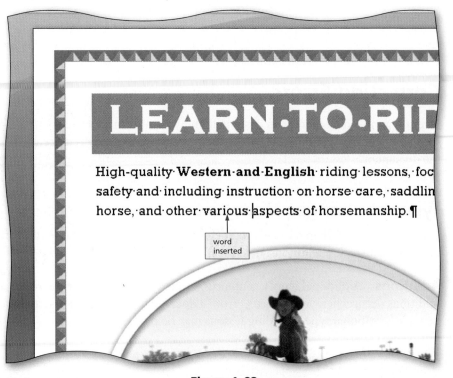

Figure 1–83

Deleting Text from an Existing Document

It is not unusual to type incorrect characters or words in a document. As discussed earlier in this chapter, you can click the Undo button on the Quick Access Toolbar to immediately undo a command or action — this includes typing. Word also provides other methods of correcting typing errors.

To delete an incorrect character in a document, simply click next to the incorrect character and then press the BACKSPACE key to erase to the left of the insertion point, or press the DELETE key to erase to the right of the insertion point.

To Select a Word and Delete It

To delete a word or phrase, you first must select the word or phrase. The following steps select the word, various, that was just added in the previous steps and then delete the selection.

- Position the mouse pointer somewhere in the word to be selected (in this case, various), as shown in Figure 1–84.

Figure 1–84

2

- Double-click the word to select it (Figure 1–85).

3

- With the text selected, press the DELETE key to delete the selected text (shown in Figure 1–82).

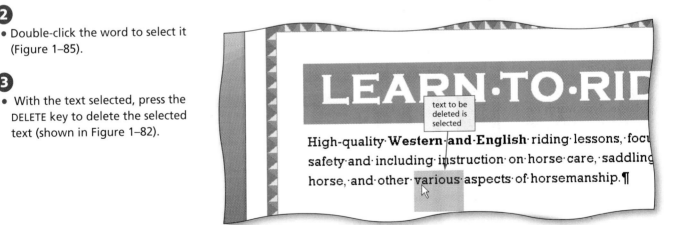

Figure 1–85

Closing the Entire Document

Sometimes, everything goes wrong. If this happens, you may want to close the document entirely and start over with a new document. You also may want to close a document when you are finished with it so you can begin your next document. If you wanted to close a document, you would use the steps on the next page.

the steps on the next page.

*Left margin column (partially visible):*

2

- Press th...
  key to...
  search...

- Click th...
  button...
  Help w...
  to max...
  window...

Where...
window...
Horseb...
Lesson...
docum...

Word is...
backgr...
Word H...
window...
overlai...
on top...
the Wo...
window...
When t...
window...
the doc...
reappe...

3

- Click th...
  informa...
  (Figure...

What is...
at the t...
window...

Use the...
corner...
navigate...
display,...
of conte...
of the w...

4

- Click the...
  Help wi...
  Word He...
  the Wor...

Quick Reference
For a table that lists how to complete the tasks covered in this book using the mouse, Ribbon, shortcut menu, and keyboard, see the Quick Reference Summary at the back of this book, or visit the Word 2007 Quick Reference Web page (scsite.com/wd2007/qr).

To Quit Word

The following steps quit Word.

1 Click the Close button on the right side of the title bar to quit Word.

2 If necessary, click the No button in the Microsoft Office Word dialog box so that any changes you have made are not saved.

Chapter Summary

In this chapter you have learned how to enter text in a document, format text, insert a picture, format a picture, add a page border, and print a document. The items listed below include all the new Word skills you have learned in this chapter.

1. Start Word (WD 5)
2. Type Text (WD 13)
3. Display Formatting Marks (WD 14)
4. Wordwrap Text as You Type (WD 15)
5. Insert a Blank Line (WD 15)
6. Check Spelling and Grammar as You Type (WD 16)
7. Save a New Document (WD 19)
8. Apply Styles (WD 24)
9. Center a Paragraph (WD 26)
10. Select a Line (WD 27)
11. Change the Font Size of Selected Text (WD 28)
12. Change the Font of Selected Text (WD 29)
13. Select Multiple Paragraphs (WD 30)
14. Bullet a List of Paragraphs (WD 32)
15. Undo and Redo an Action (WD 32)
16. Select a Group of Words (WD 33)
17. Bold Text (WD 34)
18. Underline a Word (WD 35)
19. Italicize Text (WD 36)
20. Change the Style Set (WD 37)
21. Change Theme Colors (WD 39)
22. Change Theme Fonts (WD 39)
23. Insert a Picture (WD 41)
24. Apply a Picture Style (WD 44)
25. Change a Picture Border Color (WD 45)
26. Zoom the Document (WD 45)
27. Resize a Graphic (WD 46)
28. Add a Page Border (WD 48)
29. Change Spacing Above and Below Paragraphs (WD 50)
30. Change Document Properties (WD 51)
31. Save an Existing Document with the Same File Name (WD 53)
32. Print a Document (WD 54)
33. Quit Word (WD 55)
34. Open a Document from Word (WD 56)
35. Insert Text in an Existing Document (WD 58)
36. Select a Word and Delete It (WD 59)
37. Close the Entire Document and Start Over (WD 60)
38. Search for Word Help (WD 60)

If you have a SAM user profile, you may have access to hands-on instruction, practice, and assessment. Log in to your SAM account (http://sam2007.course.com) to launch any assigned training activities or exams that relate to the skills covered in this chapter.

Certification
The Microsoft Certified Application Specialist (MCAS) program provides an opportunity for you to obtain a valuable industry credential – proof that you have the Word 2007 skills required by employers. For more information, see Appendix F or visit the Word 2007 Certification Web page (scsite.com/wd2007/cert).

Learn It Online

Test your knowledge of chapter content and key terms.

Instructions: To complete the Learn It Online exercises, start your browser, click the Address bar, and then enter the Web address scsite.com/wd2007/learn. When the Word 2007 Learn It Online page is displayed, click the link for the exercise you want to complete and then read the instructions.

Chapter Reinforcement TF, MC, and SA
A series of true/false, multiple choice, and short answer questions that test your knowledge of the chapter content.

Flash Cards
An interactive learning environment where you identify chapter key terms associated with displayed definitions.

Practice Test
A series of multiple choice questions that test your knowledge of chapter content and key terms.

Who Wants To Be a Computer Genius?
An interactive game that challenges your knowledge of chapter content in the style of a television quiz show.

Wheel of Terms
An interactive game that challenges your knowledge of chapter key terms in the style of the television show *Wheel of Fortune*.

Crossword Puzzle Challenge
A crossword puzzle that challenges your knowledge of key terms presented in the chapter.

Apply Your Knowledge

Reinforce the skills and apply the concepts you learned in this chapter.

Modifying Text and Formatting a Document
Instructions: Start Word. Open the document, Apply 1-1 Autumn Fest Flyer Unformatted, from the Data Files for Students. See the inside back cover of this book for instructions on downloading the Data Files for Students, or contact your instructor for information about accessing the required files.

The document you open is an unformatted flyer. You are to modify text, format paragraphs and characters, and insert a picture in the flyer.

Perform the following tasks:
1. Delete the word, entire, in the sentence of body copy below the headline.
2. Insert the word, Creek, between the text, Honey Farm, in the sentence of body copy below the headline. The sentence should end: …Honey Creek Farm.
3. At the end of the signature line, change the period to an exclamation point. The sentence should end: …This Year's Fest!
4. Apply the Heading 1 style to the headline. Apply the Heading 2 style to the signature line.
5. Center the headline and the signature line.
6. Change the font and font size of the headline to 48-point Cooper Black, or a similar font.
7. Change the font size of body copy between the headline and the signature line to 22 point.
8. Change the font size of the signature line to 28 point.
9. Bullet the three lines (paragraphs) of text above the signature line.
10. Bold the text, October 4 and 5.

Continued >

Apply Your Knowledge *continued*

11. Underline the word, and, in the first bulleted paragraph.

12. Italicize the text in the signature line.

13. Change the theme colors to the Civic color scheme.

14. Change the theme fonts to the Opulent font set.

15. Change the zoom to 50 percent so the entire page is visible in the document window.

16. Change the spacing before the headline paragraph to 0 point. Change the spacing after the headline paragraph to 12 point.

17. Insert the picture of the combine centered on the blank line above the bulleted list. The picture is called Fall Harvest and is available on the Data Files for Students. Apply the Snip Diagonal Corner, White picture style to the inserted picture. Change the color of the picture border to Orange, Accent 6.

18. The entire flyer now should fit on a single page. If it flows to two pages, resize the picture or decrease spacing before and after paragraphs until the entire flyer text fits on a single page.

19. Change the document properties, as specified by your instructor.

20. Click the Office Button and then click Save As. Save the document using the file name, Apply 1-1 Autumn Fest Flyer Formatted.

21. Submit the revised document, shown in Figure 1–89, in the format specified by your instructor.

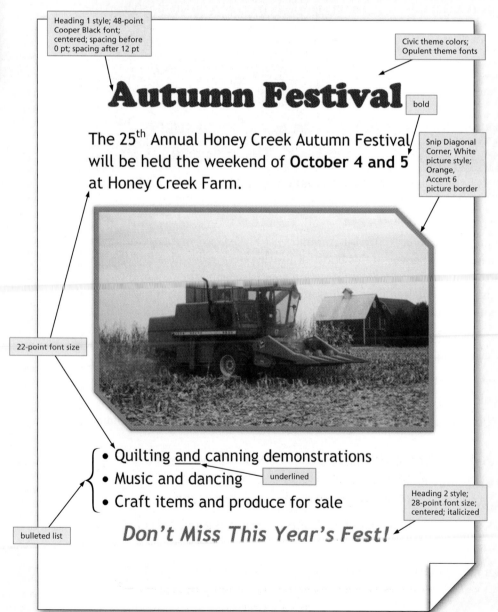

Figure 1–89

Extend Your Knowledge

Extend the skills you learned in this chapter and experiment with new skills. You may need to use Help to complete the assignment.

Modifying Text and Graphics Formats

Instructions: Start Word. Open the document, Extend 1-1 Baseball Sign Ups Flyer, from the Data Files for Students. See the inside back cover of this book for instructions on downloading the Data Files for Students, or contact your instructor for information on accessing the required files.

You will enhance the look of the flyer shown in Figure 1–90.

Perform the following tasks:

1. Use Help to learn about the following formats: grow font, shrink font, change text color, decorative underline, and change bullet.

2. Select the headline and use the Grow Font button to increase its font size just enough so that the headline still fits on a single line. If it wraps to two lines, use the Shrink Font button.

3. Change the font color of all body copy between the headline and the signature line to a color other than Automatic, or Black.

4. Change the picture style of the picture so that it is not the Drop Shadow Rectangle picture style. Add a Glow picture effect to the picture of the baseball player.

5. Change the solid underline below the words, Indoor facility, to a decorative underline.

6. Change the color and width of the border.

7. Change the style of the bullets to a character other than the dot.

8. Change the document properties, as specified by your instructor. Save the revised document with a new file name and then submit it in the format specified by your instructor.

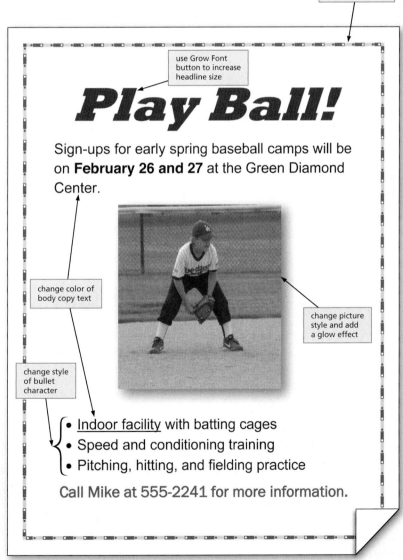

change color and width of border

use Grow Font button to increase headline size

change color of body copy text

change picture style and add a glow effect

change style of bullet character

Play Ball!

Sign-ups for early spring baseball camps will be on **February 26 and 27** at the Green Diamond Center.

- Indoor facility with batting cages
- Speed and conditioning training
- Pitching, hitting, and fielding practice

Call Mike at 555-2241 for more information.

Figure 1–90

Make It Right

Analyze a document and correct all errors and/or improve the design.

Correcting Spelling and Grammar Errors

Instructions: Start Word. Open the document, Make It Right 1-1 New York Tour Flyer, from the Data Files for Students. See the inside back cover of this book for instructions on downloading the Data Files for Students, or contact your instructor for information on accessing the required files.

The document is a flyer that contains spelling and grammar errors, as shown in Figure 1–91. You are to correct each spelling (red wavy underline) and grammar error (green wavy underline) by right-clicking the flagged text and then clicking the appropriate correction on the shortcut menu. If your screen does not display the wavy underlines, click the Office Button and then click the Word Options button. When the Word Options dialog box is displayed, click Proofing, be sure the 'Hide spelling errors in this document only' and 'Hide grammar errors in this document only' check boxes do not have check marks, and then click the OK button. If your screen still does not display the wavy underlines, click the Recheck Document button in the Word Options dialog box.

Change the document properties, as specified by your instructor. Save the revised document with a new file name and then submit it in the format specified by your instructor.

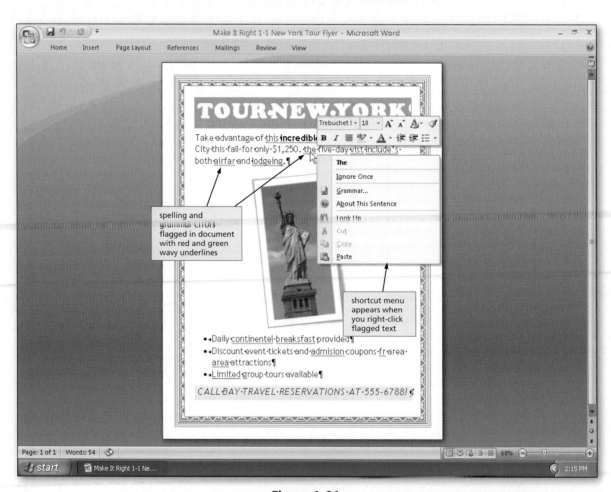

Figure 1–91

In the Lab

Design and/or create a document using the guidelines, concepts, and skills presented in this chapter. Labs are listed in order of increasing difficulty.

Lab 1: Creating a Flyer with a Picture

Problem: You work part-time at Scenic Air. Your boss has asked you to prepare a flyer that advertises aerial tours over the city of Campton. First, you prepare the unformatted flyer shown in Figure 1–92a, and then you format it so that it looks like Figure 1–92b on the next page. *Hint:* Remember, if you make a mistake while formatting the flyer, you can click the Undo button on the Quick Access Toolbar to undo your last action.

Instructions: Perform the following tasks:

1. Display formatting marks on the screen.

2. Type the flyer text, unformatted, as shown in Figure 1–92a. If Word flags any misspelled words as you type, check the spelling of these words and correct them.

3. Save the document on a USB flash drive using the file name, Lab 1-1 Airplane Rides Flyer.

4. Apply the Heading 1 style to the headline. Apply the Heading 2 style to the signature line.

5. Center the headline and the signature line.

6. Change the font and font size of the headline to 48-point Arial Rounded MT Bold, or a similar font.

7. Change the font size of body copy between the headline and the signature line to 22 point.

8. Change the font size of the signature line to 28 point.

9. Bullet the three lines (paragraphs) of text above the signature line.

10. Bold the text, change your view.

11. Italicize the word, aerial.

Figure 1–92a

Continued >

4. Apply the Heading 1 style to the headline. Apply the Heading 2 style to the signature line.

5. Center the headline and the signature line.

6. Change the font and font size of the headline to 48-point Arial Rounded MT Bold, or a similar font.

7. Change the font size of body copy between the headline and the signature line to 22 point.

8. Change the font size of the signature line to 28 point.

9. Bullet the three lines (paragraphs) of text above the signature line.

10. Italicize the word, growing.

11. Bold the text, recently expanded.

12. Underline the word, and, in the third bulleted paragraph.

13. Change the style set to the Traditional.

14. Change the theme colors to the Solstice color scheme.

15. Change the theme fonts to the Flow font set.

16. Change the zoom to 50 percent so the entire page is visible in the document window.

17. Change the spacing before the headline to 0 point. Change the spacing after the first paragraph of body copy to 24 point. Change the spacing before the first bulleted paragraph to 12 point.

18. Insert the picture on the blank line above the bulleted list. The picture is called Bradford Pear in Bloom and is available on the Data Files for Students. Apply the Soft Edge Oval picture style to the inserted picture.

19. The entire flyer should fit on a single page. If it flows to two pages, resize the picture or decrease pacing before and after paragraphs until the entire flyer text fits on a single page.

20. Add the graphic border, shown in Figure 1–93 on the previous page (about one-third down in the Art gallery). Change the color of the border to Tan, Background 2.

21. Change the document properties, as specified by your instructor.

22. Save the flyer again with the same file name.

23. Submit the document, shown in Figure 1–93, in the format specified by your instructor.

In the Lab

Lab 3: Creating a Flyer with a Picture and Resized Border Art

Problem: Your neighbor has asked you to prepare a flyer that promotes her cabin rental business. You prepare the flyer shown in Figure 1–94.

Instructions: Enter the text in the flyer, checking spelling as you type, and then format it as shown in Figure 1–94. The picture to be inserted is called Paddle Boat on Lake and is available on the Data Files for Students. After adding the page border, reduce the point size of its width so that the border is not so predominant on the page. Change the document properties, as specified by your instructor. Save the document on a USB flash drive using the file name, Lab 1-3 Cabin Rentals Flyer. Submit the document, shown in Figure 1–94, in the format specified by your instructor.

Art cabin border; color Accent 6; width 25 pt

Aspect theme colors; Opulent theme fonts

Heading 1 style; 48-point Ravie font; centered; spacing before 0 pt

Rent a Cabin

Enjoy the splendors of nature and relax in a beautiful setting at our **new** lakeside resort. Cabins offer kitchen facilities, water, and electricity.

spacing after 18 point

bold

20-point font size

Bevel Rectangle picture style

spacing after 18 point

- Two- and three-bedroom cabins available
- All cabins are lakeside and include a dock, pier, and paddleboat
- Prices start at $100 per night

bulleted list

underlined

Heading 2 style; 26-point font size; centered; italicized; spacing before 18 pt

Call Sunset Cabins at 555-8404 today!

Figure 1–94

Cases and Places

Apply your creative thinking and problem solving skills to design and implement a solution.

• EASIER •• MORE DIFFICULT

• 1: Design and Create a Grand Reopening Flyer

Your friend owns the Craft Barn, a large, year-round craft fair. She recently has renovated and remodeled the facility and is planning a grand reopening. She has asked you to create a flyer advertising this fact. The flyer should contain the following headline: Craft Barn. The first paragraph of text below the headline should read: Pick up a jar of homemade jam or a handcrafted gift at the completely remodeled and renovated Craft Barn, located at 8701 County Road 300 West. Insert the photograph named, Barn and Silo, which is available on the Data Files for Students. The bullet items

Continued >

Cases and Places *continued*

under the photograph should read as follows: first bullet – Expanded and paved parking; second bullet – More than 150 booths; and third bullet – Open Monday through Saturday, 10:00 a.m. to 7:00 p.m. The last line should read: Call 555-5709 for more information! Use the concepts and techniques presented in this chapter to create and format this flyer. Be sure to check spelling and grammar.

• 2: Design and Create a Property Advertisement Flyer

As a part-time employee of Markum Realty, you have been assigned the task of preparing a flyer advertising lakefront property. The headline should read: Lakefront Lot. The first paragraph of text should read as follows: Build the house of your dreams or a weekend getaway on this beautiful lakeside property located on the north side of Lake Pleasant. Insert the photograph named, Lake at Sunset, which is available on the Data Files for Students. Below the photograph, insert the following bullet items: first bullet — City sewer and water available; second bullet – Lot size 110 × 300; third bullet – List price $65,000. The last line should read: Call Markum Realty at 555-0995 for a tour! Use the concepts and techniques presented in this chapter to create and format this flyer. Be sure to check spelling and grammar.

•• 3: Design and Create a Flyer for the Sale of a Business

After 25 years, your Uncle Mitch has decided to sell his ice cream shop and wants you to help him create a sales flyer. The shop is in a choice location at the corner of 135th and Main Street and has an established customer base. The building has an adjacent, paved parking lot, as well as an outdoor seating area. He wants to sell the store and all its contents, including the equipment, tables, booths, and chairs. The 1200-square-foot shop recently was appraised at $200,000, and your uncle is willing to sell for cash or on contract. Use the concepts and techniques presented in this chapter to create and format a sales flyer. Include a headline, descriptive body copy, a signature line, an appropriate photograph or clip art image, a bulleted list, a decorative underline, and if appropriate, a page border. Be sure to check spelling and grammar in the flyer.

•• 4: Design and Create a Flyer that Advertises You

Make It Personal

Everyone has at least one skill, talent, or special capability, which if shared with others, can lead to opportunity for growth, experience, and personal reward. Perhaps you play a musical instrument. If so, you could offer lessons. Maybe you are a skilled carpenter or other tradesman who could advertise your services. If you speak a second language, you could offer tutoring. Budding athletes might harbor a desire to pass on their knowledge by coaching a youth sports team. You may have a special knack for singing, sewing, knitting, photography, typing, housecleaning, or pet care. Carefully consider your own personal capabilities, skills, and talents and then use the concepts and techniques presented in this chapter to create a flyer advertising a service you can provide. Include a headline, descriptive body copy, a signature line, an appropriate photograph or clip art image, a bulleted list, a decorative underline, and if appropriate, a page border. Be sure to check spelling and grammar in the flyer.

•• 5: Redesign and Enhance a Poorly Designed Flyer

Working Together

Public locations, such as stores, schools, and libraries, have bulletin boards or windows for people to post flyers. Often, these bulletin boards or windows have so many flyers that some go unnoticed. Locate a posted flyer on a bulletin board or window that you think might be overlooked. Copy the text from the flyer and distribute it to each team member. Each member then independently should use this text, together with the techniques presented in this chapter, to create a flyer that would be more likely to catch the attention of passersby. Be sure to check spelling and grammar. As a group, critique each flyer and have team members redesign their flyer based on the group's recommendations. Hand in each team member's original and final flyers.

2 Creating a Research Paper

Objectives

You will have mastered the material in this chapter when you can:

- Describe the MLA documentation style for research papers
- Change line and paragraph spacing in a document
- Use a header to number pages of a document
- Apply formatting using shortcut keys
- Modify paragraph indentation
- Create and modify styles

- Insert and edit citations and their sources
- Add a footnote to a document
- Insert a manual page break
- Create a bibliographical list of sources
- Move text
- Find and replace text
- Use the Research task pane to look up information

2 | Creating a Research Paper

Introduction

In both academic and business environments, you will be asked to write reports. Business reports range from proposals to cost justifications to five-year plans to research findings. Academic reports focus mostly on research findings. A **research paper** is a document you can use to communicate the results of research findings. To write a research paper, you learn about a particular topic from a variety of sources (research), organize your ideas from the research results, and then present relevant facts and/or opinions that support the topic. Your final research paper combines properly credited outside information along with personal insights. Thus, no two research papers — even if about the same topic — will or should be the same.

Project — Research Paper

When preparing a research paper, you should follow a standard documentation style that defines the rules for creating the paper and crediting sources. A variety of documentation styles exists, depending on the nature of the research paper. Each style requires the same basic information; the differences in styles relate to requirements for presenting the information. For example, one documentation style uses the term bibliography for the list of sources, whereas another uses references, and yet a third prefers the title works cited. Two popular documentation styles for research papers are the **Modern Language Association of America (MLA)** and **American Psychological Association (APA)** styles. This chapter uses the MLA documentation style because it is used in a wide range of disciplines.

The project in this chapter follows research paper guidelines and uses Word to create the short research paper shown in Figure 2–1. This paper, which discusses three types of wireless communications, follows the MLA documentation style. Each page contains a page number. The first two pages present the heading (name, course, and date information), paper title, an introduction with a thesis statement, details that support the thesis, and a conclusion. This section of the paper also includes references to research sources. The third page contains a detailed, alphabetical list of the sources used in the research paper.

Overview

As you read through this chapter, you will learn how to create the research paper shown in Figure 2–1 by performing these general tasks:

- Change the document settings.
- Type the research paper.
- Save the research paper.
- Create an alphabetical list of sources.
- Proof and revise the research paper.
- Print the research paper.

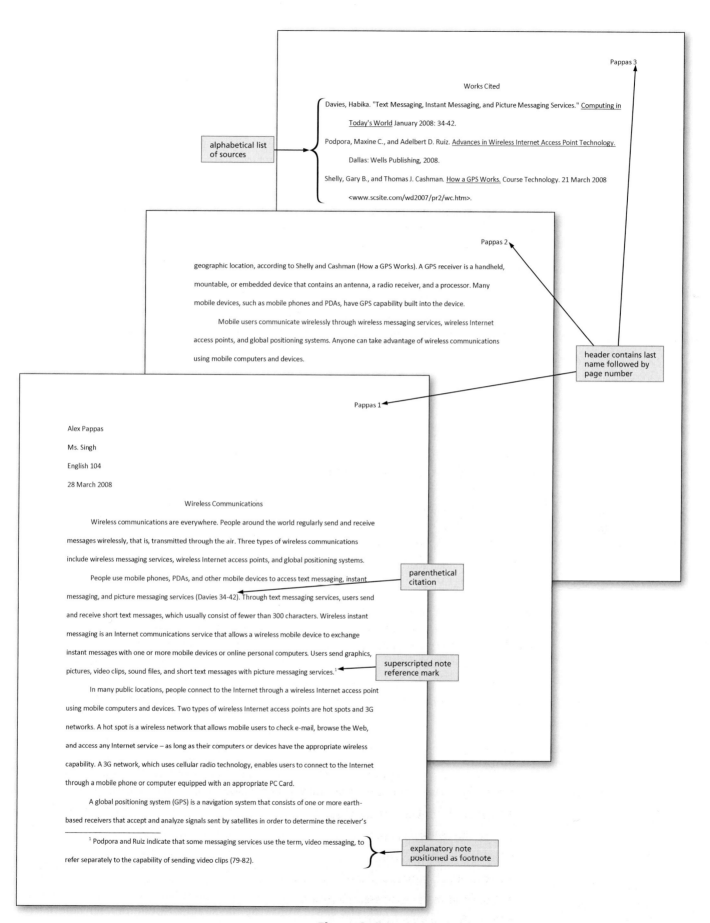

Figure 2–1

**Plan
Ahead**

General Project Guidelines

When creating a Word document, the actions you perform and decisions you make will affect the appearance and characteristics of the finished document. As you create a research paper, such as the project shown in Figure 2–1 on the previous page, you should follow these general guidelines:

1. **Select a topic.** Spend time brainstorming ideas for a topic. Choose one you find interesting. For shorter papers, narrow down the scope of the topic; for longer papers, broaden the scope. Identify a tentative thesis statement, which is a sentence describing the paper's subject matter.

2. **Research the topic and take notes.** Gather credible, relevant information about the topic that supports the thesis statement. Sources of research include books, magazines, newspapers, and the Internet. As you record facts and ideas, list details about the source: title, author, place of publication, publisher, date of publication, etc. When taking notes, be careful not to **plagiarize**. That is, do not use someone else's work and claim it to be your own. If you copy information directly, place it in quotation marks and identify its source.

3. **Organize your ideas.** Classify your notes into related concepts. Make an outline from the categories of notes. In the outline, identify all main ideas and supporting details.

4. **Write the first draft, referencing sources.** From the outline, compose the paper. Every research paper should include an introduction containing the thesis statement, supporting details, and a conclusion. Follow the guidelines identified in the required documentation style. Reference all sources of information.

5. **Create the list of sources.** Using the formats specified in the required documentation style, completely list all sources referenced in the body of the research paper in alphabetical order.

6. **Proofread and revise the paper.** If possible, proofread the paper with a fresh set of eyes, that is, at least one to two days after completing the first draft. Proofreading involves reading the paper with the intent of identifying errors (spelling, grammar, etc.) and looking for ways to improve the paper (wording, transitions, flow, etc.). Try reading the paper out loud, which helps to identify unclear or awkward wording. Ask someone else to proofread the paper and give you suggestions for improvements.

When necessary, more specific details concerning the above guidelines are presented at appropriate points in the chapter. The chapter also will identify the actions performed and decisions made regarding these guidelines during the creation of the research paper shown in Figure 2–1.

BTW

APA Documentation Style
In the APA style, a separate title page is required instead of placing name and course information on the paper's first page. Double-space all pages of the paper with 1.5" top, bottom, left, and right margins. Indent the first word of each paragraph .5" from the left margin. In the upper-right margin of each page, including the title page, place a running head that consists of the page number double-spaced below a brief summary of the paper title.

MLA Documentation Style

The research paper in this project follows the guidelines presented by the MLA. To follow the MLA style, double-space text on all pages of the paper using one-inch top, bottom, left, and right margins. Indent the first word of each paragraph one-half inch from the left margin. At the right margin of each page, place a page number one-half inch from the top margin. On each page, precede the page number by your last name.

The MLA style does not require a title page. Instead, place your name and course information in a block at the left margin beginning one inch from the top of the page. Center the title one double-space below your name and course information.

In the text of the paper, place author references in parentheses with the page number(s) of the referenced information. The MLA style uses in-text **parenthetical citations** instead of noting each source at the bottom of the page or at the end of the paper. In the MLA style, notes are used only for optional explanatory notes.

If used, explanatory notes elaborate on points discussed in the paper. Use a superscript (raised number) to signal that an explanatory note exists, and also to sequence the notes. Position explanatory notes either at the bottom of the page as footnotes or at the end of the paper as endnotes. Indent the first line of each explanatory note one-half inch from the left margin. Place one space following the superscripted number before beginning the note text. Double-space the note text. At the end of the note text, you may list bibliographic information for further reference.

The MLA style uses the term **works cited** to refer to the bibliographic list of sources at the end of the paper. The works cited page alphabetically lists sources that are referenced directly in the paper. Place the list of sources on a separate numbered page. Center the title, Works Cited, one inch from the top margin. Double-space all lines. Begin the first line of each source at the left margin, indenting subsequent lines of the same source one-half inch from the left margin. List each source by the author's last name, or, if the author's name is not available, by the title of the source. Underline or italicize the title of each source.

Changing Document Settings

The MLA documentation style defines some global formats that apply to the entire research paper. Some of these formats are the default in Word. For example, the default left, right, top, and bottom margin settings in Word are one inch, which meets the MLA style. You will modify, however, the paragraph and line spacing and header formats as required by the MLA style.

After starting Word, the following pages adjust line and paragraph spacing and define a header for the current document.

To Start Word

If you are using a computer to step through the project in this chapter and you want your screens to match the figures in this book, you should change your computer's resolution to 1024×768. For information about how to change a computer's resolution, read Appendix E.

The following steps, which assume Windows is running, start Word based on a typical installation. You may need to ask your instructor how to start Word for your computer.

1 Click the Start button on the Windows taskbar to display the Start menu, and then point to All Programs on the Start menu to display the All Programs submenu.

2 Point to Microsoft Office on the All Programs submenu to display the Microsoft Office submenu, and then click Microsoft Office Word 2007 to start Word and display a new blank document in the Word window.

3 If the Word window is not maximized, click the Maximize button next to the Close button on its title bar to maximize the window.

4 If the Print Layout button is not selected, click it so your screen layout matches Figure 2–2 on the next page.

5 If your zoom percent is not 100, click the Zoom Out or Zoom In button as many times as necessary until the Zoom level button displays 100% on its face.

To Display Formatting Marks

As discussed in Chapter 1, it is helpful to display formatting marks that indicate where in the document you pressed the ENTER key, SPACEBAR, and other keys. The following step displays formatting marks.

1 If necessary, click Home on the Ribbon to display the Home tab. If the Show/Hide ¶ button on the Home tab is not selected already, click it to display formatting marks on the screen.

BTW

Line Spacing
If the top of a set of characters or a graphical image is chopped off, then line spacing may be set to Exactly. To remedy the problem, change line spacing to 1.0, 1.15, 1.5, 2.0, 2.5, 3.0 or At least (in the Paragraph dialog box), all of which accommodate the largest font or image.

Adjusting Line and Paragraph Spacing

Line spacing is the amount of vertical space between lines of text in a paragraph. **Paragraph spacing** is the amount of space above and below a paragraph. By default, the Normal style places 10 points of blank space after each paragraph and inserts a vertical space equal to 1.15 lines between each line of text. It also automatically adjusts line height to accommodate various font sizes and graphics.

The MLA documentation style requires that you **double-space** the entire research paper. That is, the amount of vertical space between each line of text and above and below paragraphs should be equal to one blank line. The next sets of steps adjust line spacing and paragraph spacing according to the MLA documentation style.

To Double-Space Text

To double-space the lines in the research paper, change the line spacing to 2.0. The following steps change line spacing to double.

1

- Click the Line spacing button on the Home tab to display the Line spacing gallery (Figure 2–2).

Q&A

What do the numbers in the Line spacing gallery represent?

The default line spacing is 1.15 lines. The options 1.0, 2.0, and 3.0 set line spacing to single, double, and triple, respectively. Similarly, the 1.5 and 2.5 options set line spacing to 1.5 and 2.5 lines. All these options adjust line spacing automatically to accommodate the largest font or graphic on a line.

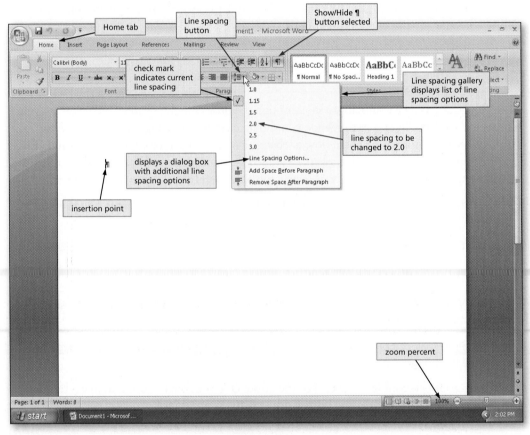

Figure 2–2

2

- Click 2.0 in the Line spacing gallery to change the line spacing to double at the location of the insertion point.

Q&A

Can I change the line spacing of existing text?

Yes. Select the text first and then change the line spacing as described in these steps.

Other Ways
1. Right-click paragraph, click Paragraph on shortcut menu, click Indents and Spacing tab, click Line	spacing box arrow, click Double, click OK button	and Spacing tab, click Line spacing box arrow, click Double, click OK button
	2. Click Paragraph Dialog Box Launcher, click Indents	3. Press CTRL+2

To Remove Space after a Paragraph

The research paper should not have additional blank space after each paragraph. The following steps remove space after a paragraph.

- Click the Line spacing button on the Home tab to display the Line spacing gallery (Figure 2–3).

- Click Remove Space After Paragraph in the Line spacing gallery so that no blank space appears after a paragraph.

Q&A

Can I remove space after existing paragraphs?

Yes. Select the paragraphs first and then remove the space as described in these steps.

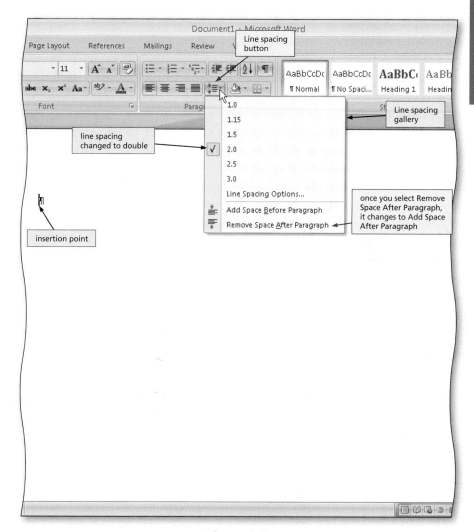

Figure 2–3

Other Ways

1. Click Spacing After box arrow on Page Layout tab until 0 pt is displayed

2. Right-click paragraph, click Paragraph on shortcut menu, click Indents and Spacing tab, click Spacing After box arrow until 0 pt is displayed, click OK button

3. Click Paragraph Dialog Box Launcher, click Indents and Spacing tab, click Spacing After box arrow until 0 pt is displayed, click OK button

Headers and Footers

A **header** is text and graphics that print at the top of each page in a document. Similarly, a **footer** is text and graphics that print at the bottom of every page. In Word, headers print in the top margin one-half inch from the top of every page, and footers print in the bottom margin one-half inch from the bottom of each page, which meets the MLA style. In addition to text and graphics, headers and footers can include document information such as the page number, current date, current time, and author's name.

In this research paper, you are to precede the page number with your last name placed one-half inch from the upper-right edge of each page. The procedures on the following pages enter your name and the page number in the header, as specified by the MLA style.

To Switch to the Header

To enter text in the header, you instruct Word to edit the header. The following steps switch from editing the document text to editing the header.

1

- Click Insert on the Ribbon to display the Insert tab.

- Click the Header button on the Insert tab to display the Header gallery (Figure 2–4).

Q&A Can I use a built-in header for this research paper?

None of the built-in headers adhere to the MLA style. Thus, you enter your own header contents, instead of using a built-in header, for this research paper.

Figure 2–4

2

 Experiment

- Click the down scroll arrow in the Header gallery to see the available built-in headers.

3

- Click the Edit Header command to switch from the document text to the header, which allows you to edit the contents of the header (Figure 2–5).

Figure 2–5

 Q&A How do I remove the Header & Footer Tools and Design tabs from the Ribbon?

When you are finished editing the header, you will close it, which removes the Header & Footer Tools tabs.

Other Ways

1. Double-click dimmed header

To Right-Align a Paragraph

The paragraph in the header currently is left-aligned (Figure 2–5). Your last name and the page number should print **right-aligned**, that is, at the right margin. The following steps right-align a paragraph.

1

- Click Home on the Ribbon to display the Home tab.

- Click the Align Text Right button on the Home tab to right-align the paragraph in the header (Figure 2–6).

Q&A

What if I wanted to return the paragraph to left-aligned?

Click the Align Text Right button again, or click the Align Text Left button.

Other Ways

1. Right-click paragraph, click Paragraph on shortcut menu, click Indents and Spacing tab, click Alignment box arrow, click Right, click OK button

2. Click Paragraph Dialog Box Launcher, click Indents and Spacing tab, click Alignment box arrow, click Right, click OK button

3. Press CTRL+R

Figure 2–6

To Enter Text

The following steps enter your last name right-aligned in the header area.

1 Click Design on the Ribbon to display the Design tab.

2 Type Pappas and then press the SPACEBAR to enter your last name in the header.

BTW

Footers
If you wanted to create a footer, you would click the Footer button on the Insert tab and then select the desired built-in footer or click Edit Footer to create a customized footer.

To Insert a Page Number

The next task is to insert the current page number in the header. The following steps insert a page number at the location of the insertion point.

- Click the Insert Page Number button on the Design tab to display the Insert Page Number menu.

- Point to Current Position on the Insert Page Number menu to display the Current Position gallery (Figure 2–7).

Figure 2–7

 Experiment

- Click the down scroll arrow in the Current Position gallery to see the available page number formats.

- If necessary, scroll to the top of the Current Position gallery. Click Plain Number in the Current Position gallery to insert an unformatted page number at the location of the insertion point (Figure 2–8).

Figure 2–8

Other Ways

1. Click Insert Page Number button on Insert tab

2. Click Quick Parts button on Insert tab or on Design

   tab on Header & Footer Tools tab, click Field on Quick Parts menu, select Page in Field names list, click OK button

To Close the Header

You are finished entering text in the header. Thus, the next task is to switch back to the document text. The following step closes the header.

- Click the Close Header and Footer button on the Design tab (shown in Figure 2–8) to close the header and switch back to the document text (Figure 2–9).

Q&A

How do I make changes to existing header text?

Switch to the header using the steps described on page WD 80, edit the header as you would edit text in the document window, and then switch back to the document text.

Figure 2–9

Other Ways

1. Double-click dimmed document text

Typing the Research Paper Text

The text of the research paper in this chapter encompasses the first two pages of the paper. You will type the text of the research paper and then modify it later in the chapter, so that it matches Figure 2–1 on page WD 75.

Plan Ahead

Write the first draft, referencing sources.
As you write the first draft of your research paper, be sure it includes the proper components, uses credible sources, and does not contain any plagiarism.

- **Include an introduction, body, and conclusion.** The first paragraph of the paper introduces the topic and captures the reader's attention. The body, which follows the introduction, consists of several paragraphs that support the topic. The conclusion summarizes the main points in the body and restates the topic.

- **Evaluate sources for authority, currency, and accuracy.** Be especially wary of information obtained from the Web. Any person, company, or organization can publish a Web page on the Internet. Ask yourself these questions about the source:

  - Authority: Does a reputable institution or group support the source? Is the information presented without bias? Are the author's credentials listed and verifiable?

  - Currency: Is the information up to date? Are dates of sources listed? What is the last date revised or updated?

  - Accuracy: Is the information free of errors? Is it verifiable? Are the sources clearly identified?

- **Acknowledge all sources of information; do not plagiarize.** Not only is plagiarism unethical, but it is considered an academic crime that can have severe punishments such as failing a course or being expelled from school.

  When you summarize, paraphrase (rewrite information in your own words), present facts, give statistics, quote exact words, or show a map, chart, or other graphical image, you

(continued)

**Plan
Ahead**

(continued)

must acknowledge the source. Information that commonly is known or accessible to the audience constitutes common knowledge and does not need to be acknowledged. If, however, you question whether certain information is common knowledge, you should document it — just to be safe.

As discussed earlier in this chapter, the MLA style does not require a separate title page for research papers. Instead, place your name and course information in a block at the top of the page, below the header, at the left margin.

To Enter Name and Course Information

1 Type `Alex Pappas` as the student name and then press the ENTER key.

2 Type `Ms. Singh` as the instructor name and then press the ENTER key.

3 Type `English 104` as the course name and then press the ENTER key.

4 Type `28 March 2008` as the paper due date and then press the ENTER key (Figure 2–10).

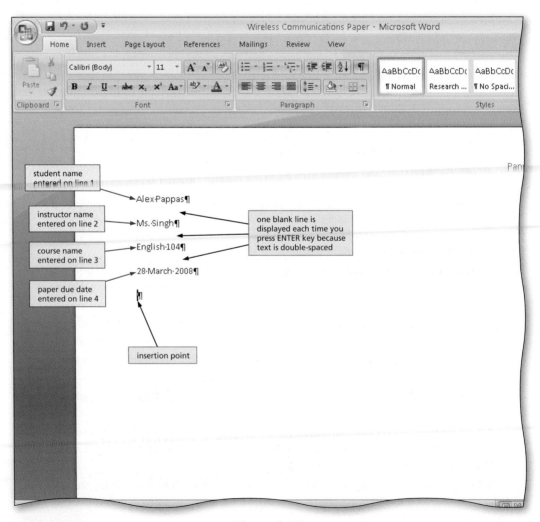

Figure 2–10

To Click and Type

The next step is to enter the title of the research paper centered between the page margins. In Chapter 1, you used the Center button on the Home tab to center text and graphics. As an alternative, you can use **Click and Type** to format and enter text, graphics, and other items. To use Click and Type, you double-click a blank area of the document window. Word automatically formats the item you enter according to the location where you just double-clicked. The next steps use Click and Type to center and then type the title of the research paper.

🔍 **Experiment**

- Move the mouse pointer around the document below the entered name and course information and observe the various icons that appear with the I-beam.

❷

- Position the mouse pointer in the center of the document at the approximate location for the research paper title until a center icon appears below the I-beam (Figure 2–11).

Q&A

What are the other icons that appear in the Click and Type pointer?

A left-align icon appears to the right of the I-beam when the Click and Type pointer is in certain locations on the left side of the document window. A right-align icon appears to the left of the icon when the Click and Type pointer is in certain locations on the right side of the document window.

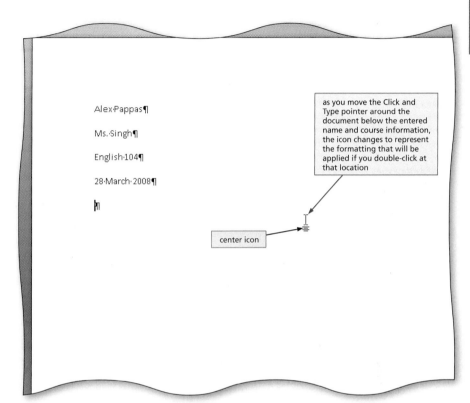

Figure 2–11

❸

- Double-click to center the paragraph mark and insertion point between the left and right margins.

- Type `Wireless Communications` as the paper title and then press the ENTER key (Figure 2–12).

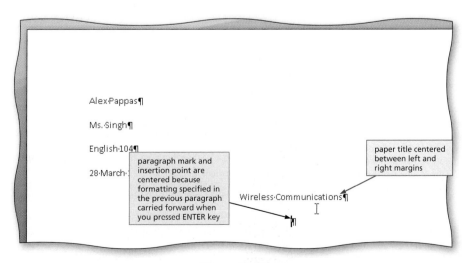

Figure 2–12

Shortcut Keys

Word has many shortcut keys for your convenience while typing. Table 2–1 lists the common shortcut keys for formatting characters. Table 2–2 lists common shortcut keys for formatting paragraphs.

Table 2–1 Shortcut Keys for Formatting Characters

Character Formatting Task	Shortcut Keys	Character Formatting Task	Shortcut Keys
All capital letters	CTRL+SHIFT+A	Italic	CTRL+I
Bold	CTRL+B	Remove character formatting (plain text)	CTRL+SPACEBAR
Case of letters	SHIFT+F3	Small uppercase letters	CTRL+SHIFT+K
Decrease font size	CTRL+SHIFT+<	Subscript	CTRL+EQUAL SIGN
Decrease font size 1 point	CTRL+[	Superscript	CTRL+SHIFT+PLUS SIGN
Double-underline	CTRL+SHIFT+D	Underline	CTRL+U
Increase font size	CTRL+SHIFT+>	Underline words, not spaces	CTRL+SHIFT+W
Increase font size 1 point	CTRL+]		

Table 2–2 Shortcut Keys for Formatting Paragraphs

Paragraph Formatting	Shortcut Keys	Paragraph Formatting	Shortcut Keys
1.5 line spacing	CTRL+5	Justify paragraph	CTRL+J
Add/remove one line above paragraph	CTRL+0 (ZERO)	Left-align paragraph	CTRL+L
Center paragraph	CTRL+E	Remove hanging indent	CTRL+SHIFT+T
Decrease paragraph indent	CTRL+SHIFT+M	Remove paragraph formatting	CTRL+Q
Double-space lines	CTRL+2	Right-align paragraph	CTRL+R
Hanging indent	CTRL+T	Single-space lines	CTRL+1
Increase paragraph indent	CTRL+M		

BTW

Shortcut Keys
To print a complete list of shortcut keys in Word, click the Microsoft Office Word Help button near the upper-right corner of the Word window, type shortcut keys in the 'Type words to search for' text box at the top of the Word Help window, press the ENTER key, click the Keyboard shortcuts for Microsoft Office Word link, click the Show All link in the upper-right corner of the Help window, click the Print button in the Help window, and then click the Print button in the Print dialog box.

To Format Text Using Shortcut Keys

The paragraphs below the paper title should be left-aligned, instead of centered. Thus, the next step is to left-align the paragraph below the paper title. When your fingers are already on the keyboard, you may prefer using **shortcut keys**, or keyboard key combinations, to format text as you type it. The following step left-aligns a paragraph using the shortcut keys CTRL+L. (Recall from Chapter 1 that a notation such as CTRL+L means to press the letter l on the keyboard while holding down the CTRL key.)

1 Press CTRL+L to left-align the current paragraph, that is, the paragraph containing the insertion point.

Q&A Why would I use a keyboard shortcut, instead of the Ribbon, to format text?

Switching between the mouse and the keyboard takes time. If your hands are already on the keyboard, use a keyboard shortcut. If your hand is on the mouse, use the Ribbon.

To Save a Document

You have performed many tasks while creating the research paper and do not want to risk losing the work completed thus far. Accordingly, you should save the document. For a detailed example of the procedure summarized below, refer to pages WD 19 through WD 21 in Chapter 1.

1 With a USB flash drive connected to one of the computer's USB ports, click the Save button on the Quick Access Toolbar to display the Save As dialog box.

2 Type `Wireless Communications Paper` in the File name text box to change the file name.

3 Click the Save in box arrow and then click UDISK 2.0 (E:) in the Save in list to select the USB flash drive as the new save location. (Your USB flash drive may have a different name and letter.)

4 Click the Save button in the Save As dialog box to save the document on the USB flash drive with the file name, Wireless Communications Paper.

To Display the Rulers

According to the MLA style, the first line of each paragraph in the research paper is to be indented one-half inch from the left margin. Although you can use a dialog box to indent paragraphs, Word provides a quicker way through the **horizontal ruler**. This ruler displays at the top edge of the document window just below the Ribbon. Word also provides a **vertical ruler** that displays along the left edge of the Word window. The following step displays the rulers.

1

 Experiment

- Repeatedly click the View Ruler button on the vertical scroll bar to see the how this button is used to both show and hide the rulers.

2

- If the rulers are not displayed, click the View Ruler button on the vertical scroll bar because you want to use the ruler to indent paragraphs (Figure 2–13).

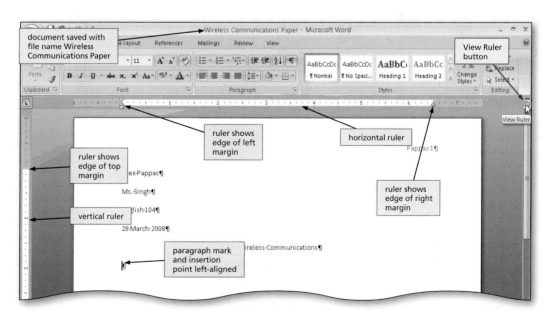

Figure 2–13

Q&A

Can I use the rulers for other tasks?

In addition to indenting paragraphs, you can use the rulers to set tab stops, change page margins, and adjust column widths.

Other Ways
1. Click View Ruler check box on View tab

To First-Line Indent Paragraphs

The first line of each paragraph in the research paper is to be indented one-half inch from the left margin. You can use the horizontal ruler, usually simply called the **ruler**, to indent just the first line of a paragraph, called **first-line indent**.

The left margin on the ruler contains two triangles above a square. The **First Line Indent marker** is the top triangle at the 0" mark on the ruler (Figure 2–14). The bottom triangle is discussed later in this chapter. The small square at the 0" mark is the Left Indent marker. The **Left Indent marker** allows you to change the entire left margin, whereas the First Line Indent marker indents only the first line of the paragraph. The following steps first-line indent paragraphs in the research paper.

- With the insertion point on the paragraph mark below the research paper title, point to the First Line Indent marker on the ruler (Figure 2–14).

Figure 2–14

❷

- Drag the First Line Indent marker to the .5" mark on the ruler to display a vertical dotted line in the document window, which indicates the proposed location of the first line of the paragraph (Figure 2–15).

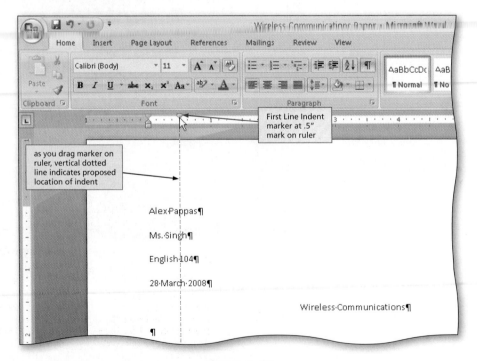

Figure 2–15

3

- Release the mouse button to place the First Line Indent marker at the .5" mark on the ruler, or one-half inch from the left margin (Figure 2–16).

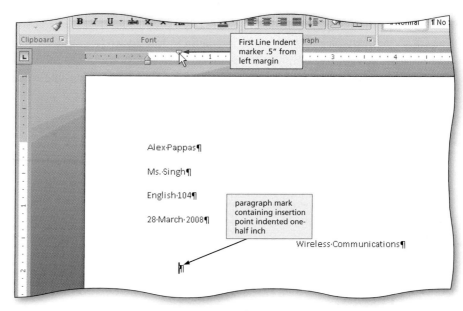

Figure 2–16

4

- Type `Wireless communications are everywhere. People around the world regularly send and receive messages wirelessly, that is, transmitted through the air.` and notice that Word automatically indented the first line of the paragraph by one-half inch (Figure 2–17).

Will I have to set first-line indent for each paragraph in the paper?

No. Each time you press the ENTER key, paragraph formatting in the previous paragraph carries forward to the next paragraph. Thus, once you set the first-line indent, its format carries forward automatically to each subsequent paragraph you type.

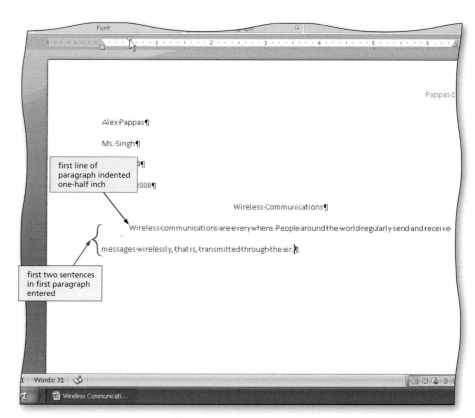

Figure 2–17

Other Ways

1. Right-click paragraph, click Paragraph on shortcut menu, click Indents and Spacing tab, click Special box arrow, click First line, click OK button

2. Click Paragraph Dialog Box Launcher, click Indents and Spacing tab, click Special box arrow, click First line, click OK button

3. Press TAB key at beginning of paragraph

To Create a Quick Style

Recall from Chapter 1 that a Quick Style is a predefined style that appears in the Styles gallery on the Ribbon. You use styles in the Styles gallery to apply defined formats to text. Later in this chapter, you will apply the formats of the research paper paragraph to the paragraphs in the footnote. To accomplish this task, you can create a Quick Style based on the formats in the current paragraph. That is, text is double-spaced with the first line of the paragraph indented and no space after the paragraph. The following steps first select the paragraph and then create a Quick Style based on the formats in the selected paragraph.

- Position the mouse pointer in the paragraph below the title and then triple-click; that is, press the mouse button three times in rapid succession, to select the paragraph.

- Right-click the selected paragraph to display a shortcut menu.

- Point to Styles on the shortcut menu to display the Styles submenu (Figure 2–18).

Figure 2–18

- Click Save Selection as a New Quick Style on the Styles submenu to display the Create New Style from Formatting dialog box.

- Type Research Paper Paragraphs in the Name text box (Figure 2–19).

Figure 2–19

3

- Click the OK button to create the new Quick Style and add it to the Styles gallery (Figure 2–20).

Q&A

How can I see the formats assigned to a Quick Style?

Click the Styles Dialog Box Launcher. When the Styles task pane appears, position the mouse pointer on any style to display its formats. When finished, click the Close button in the task pane.

Research Paper Paragraphs Quick Style added to Styles gallery

Styles Dialog Box Launcher

Figure 2–20

Other Ways
1. Click More button in Styles gallery on Home tab, click Save Selection as a New   Quick Style, enter name of new Quick Style, click OK button

To AutoCorrect as You Type

As you type, you may make typing, spelling, capitalization, or grammar errors. For this reason, Word provides an **AutoCorrect** feature that automatically corrects these kinds of errors as you type them in the document. For example, if you type the text ahve, Word automatically changes it to the correct spelling, have, when you press the SPACEBAR or a punctuation mark key such as a period or comma.

Word has predefined many commonly misspelled words, which it automatically corrects for you. In the following steps, the word wireless is misspelled intentionally as wreless to illustrate the AutoCorrect as you type feature.

1

- Press CTRL+END to move the insertion point to the end of the document.

- Press the SPACEBAR.

- Type the beginning of the next sentence, misspelling the word, wireless, as follows: `Three types of wireless communications include wireless messaging services, wreless` (Figure 2–21).

Pappas 1¶

Alex·Pappas¶

Ms.·Singh¶

English·104¶

28·March·2008¶

beginning of sentence entered

less·Communications¶

Wireless·communications·are·everywhere.·People·around·the·world·regularly·send·and·receive·

messages·wirelessly,·that·is,·transmitted·through·the·air.·Three·types·of·wireless·communications·

include·wireless·messaging·services,·wreless¶

misspelled word

insertion point immediately follows last character in misspelled word

Communicati...

Figure 2–21

- Press the SPACEBAR and watch how Word automatically corrects the misspelled word.

- Type the rest of the sentence (Figure 2–22): `Internet access points, and global positioning systems.`

as soon as you press the SPACEBAR, Word detects the misspelling and corrects the misspelled word

rest of sentence entered

Figure 2–22

To Use the AutoCorrect Options Button

When you position the mouse pointer on text that Word automatically corrected, a small blue box appears below the text. If you point to the small blue box, Word displays the AutoCorrect Options button. When you click the **AutoCorrect Options button**, Word displays a menu that allows you to undo a correction or change how Word handles future automatic corrections of this type. The following steps illustrate the AutoCorrect Options button and menu.

- Position the mouse pointer in the text automatically corrected by Word (in this case, the word wireless) to display a small blue box below the automatically corrected word (Figure 2–23).

clicking the small blue box will display the AutoCorrect Options button

mouse pointer is in automatically corrected text

Figure 2–23

- Point to the small blue box to display the AutoCorrect Options button.

- Click the AutoCorrect Options button to display the AutoCorrect Options menu (Figure 2–24).

- Press the ESCAPE key to remove the AutoCorrect Options menu from the screen.

AutoCorrect Options button

AutoCorrect Options menu

Change back to "wreless"

Stop Automatically Correcting "wreless"

Control AutoCorrect Options...

clicking this command will display the AutoCorrect dialog box

Figure 2–24

Q&A

Do I need to remove the AutoCorrect Options button from the screen?

No. When you move the mouse pointer, the AutoCorrect Options button will disappear from the screen. If, for some reason, you wanted to remove the AutoCorrect Options button from the screen, you could press the ESCAPE key a second time.

To Create an AutoCorrect Entry

In addition to the predefined list of AutoCorrect spelling, capitalization, and grammar errors, you can create your own AutoCorrect entries to add to the list. For example, if you tend to type the word mobile as moble, you should create an AutoCorrect entry for it. The following steps create an AutoCorrect entry.

- Click the Office Button to display the Office Button menu (Figure 2–25).

Figure 2–25

- Click the Word Options button on the Office Button menu to display the Word Options dialog box.

- Click Proofing in the left pane to display proofing options in the right pane.

- Click the AutoCorrect Options button in the right pane to display the AutoCorrect dialog box.

- When Word displays the AutoCorrect dialog box, type moble in the Replace text box.

- Press the TAB key and then type mobile in the With text box (Figure 2–26).

Figure 2–26

- Click the Add button in the AutoCorrect dialog box. (If your dialog box displays a Replace button instead, click it and then click the Yes button in the Microsoft Office Word dialog box.)

- Click the OK button to add the entry alphabetically to the list of words to correct automatically as you type.

- Click the OK button in the Word Options dialog box.

To Insert a Footnote Reference Mark

The following step inserts a footnote reference mark in the document at the location of the insertion point and also at the location where the footnote text will be typed.

1

- With the insertion point positioned as shown in Figure 2–35 on the previous page, click the Insert Footnote button on the References tab to display a note reference mark (a superscripted 1) in two places: (1) in the document window at the location of the insertion point and (2) at the bottom of the page where the footnote will be positioned, just below a separator line (Figure 2–36).

Q&A

What if I wanted explanatory notes to be positioned as endnotes instead of as footnotes?

You would click the Insert Endnote button on the References tab, which places the separator line and the endnote text at the end of the document, instead of the bottom of the page containing the reference.

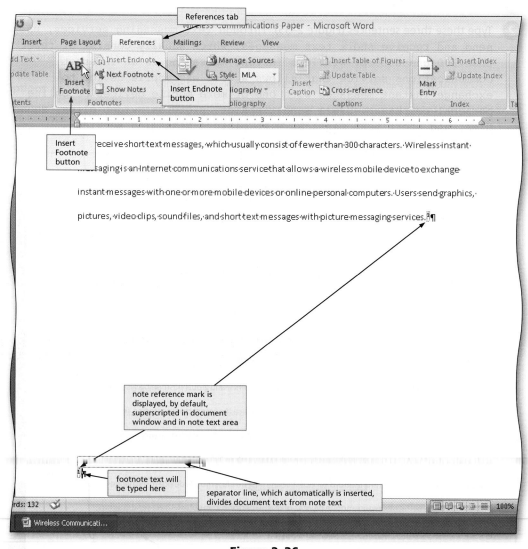

Figure 2–36

Other Ways

1. Press CTRL+ALT+F

To Enter Footnote Text

The next step is to type the footnote text to the right of the note reference mark below the separator line.

1 Type the footnote text up to the citation: `Podpora and Ruiz indicate that some messaging services use the term, video messaging, to refer separately to the capability of sending video clips` **and then press the** SPACEBAR.

To Insert a Citation Placeholder

Earlier in this chapter, you inserted a citation and its source at once. Sometimes, you may not have the source information readily available and would prefer entering it at a later time.

In the footnote, you will insert a placeholder for the citation and enter the source information later. The following steps insert a citation placeholder.

- With the insertion point positioned as shown in Figure 2–37, click the Insert Citation button on the References tab to display the Insert Citation menu (Figure 2–37).

Figure 2–37

- Click Add New Placeholder on the Insert Citation menu to display the Placeholder Name dialog box.

- Type Podpora as the tag name for the source (Figure 2–38).

Q&A

What is a tag name?

A tag name is an identifier that links a citation to a source. Word automatically creates a tag name when you enter a source. When you create a citation placeholder, enter a meaningful tag name, which will appear in the citation placeholder until you edit the source.

- Click the OK button to close the dialog box and insert the tag name in the citation placeholder.

- Press the PERIOD key to end the sentence.

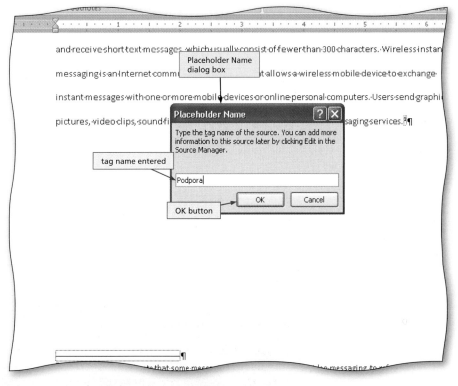

Figure 2–38

Footnote Text Style

When you insert a footnote, Word formats it using the Footnote Text style, which does not adhere to the MLA documentation style. For example, notice in Figure 2–38 on the previous page that the footnote text is single-spaced, left-aligned, and a smaller font size than the text in the research paper. According to the MLA style, notes should be formatted like all other paragraphs in the paper.

You could change the paragraph formatting of the footnote text to first-line indent and double-spacing and then change the font size from 10 to 11 point. If you use this technique, however, you will need to change the format of the footnote text for each footnote you enter into the document.

A more efficient technique is to modify the format of the Footnote Text style so that every footnote you enter into the document will use the formats defined in this style.

To Modify a Style Using a Shortcut Menu

The Footnote Text style should be based on the Research Paper Paragraphs style defined earlier in this chapter. Because the Footnote Text style specifically set paragraphs to single-spaced and the font size to 10 point, you will need to modify those formats to double-spaced paragraphs and 11-point font. The following steps modify the Footnote Text style.

- Right-click the note text in the footnote to display a shortcut menu related to footnotes (Figure 2–39).

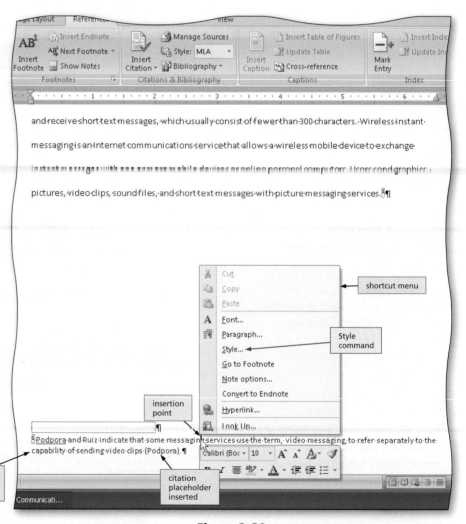

Figure 2–39

2

- Click Style on the shortcut menu to display the Style dialog box. If necessary, click Footnote Text in the Styles list.

- Click the Modify button in the Style dialog box to display the Modify Style dialog box.

- Click the 'Style based on' box arrow and then click Research Paper Paragraphs so that the Footnote Text style is based on the Research Paper Paragraphs style.

- Click the 'Style for following paragraph' box arrow and then scroll to and click Research Paper Paragraphs so that the additional footnote paragraphs are based on the Research Paper Paragraphs style.

Figure 2–40

- Click the Font Size box arrow and then click 11 in the Font Size list to change the font size to 11.

- Click the Double Space button to set the line spacing to double (Figure 2–40).

3

- Click the OK button in the Modify Style dialog box to close the dialog box.

- Click the Apply button in the Style dialog box to apply the style changes to the footnote text (Figure 2–41).

Figure 2–41

Q&A

Will all footnotes use this modified style?

Yes. Any future footnotes entered into the document will use an 11-point font with the paragraphs first-line indented and double-spaced.

Other Ways

1. Click Styles Dialog Box Launcher, click Footnote Text in list, click Footnote Text box arrow, click Modify, change settings, click OK button

2. Click Styles Dialog Box Launcher, click Manage Styles button, scroll to Footnote Text and then select it, click Modify button, change settings, click OK button in each dialog box

Working with Footnotes and Endnotes

You edit footnote text just as you edit any other text in the document. To delete or move a note reference mark, however, you must be in the document text (not in the footnote text).

To delete a note, select the note reference mark in the document text (not in the footnote text) by dragging through the note reference mark and then click the Cut button on the Home tab. Another way to delete a note is to click immediately to the right of the note reference mark in the document text and then press the BACKSPACE key twice, or to click immediately to the left of the note reference mark in the document text and then press the DELETE key twice.

To move a note to a different location in a document, select the note reference mark in the document text (not in the footnote text), click the Cut button on the Home tab, click the location where you want to move the note, and then click the Paste button on the Home tab. When you move or delete notes, Word automatically renumbers any remaining notes in the correct sequence.

If you position the mouse pointer on the note reference mark, the note text displays above the note reference mark as a ScreenTip. To remove the ScreenTip, move the mouse pointer.

If, for some reason, you wanted to change the format of note reference marks in footnotes or endnotes (i.e., from 1, 2, 3, to A, B, C), you would click the Footnotes Dialog Box Launcher to display the Footnote and Endnote dialog box, click the Number format box arrow, click the desired number format in the list, and then click the OK button.

If, for some reason, you wanted to convert footnotes to endnotes, you would click the Footnotes Dialog Box Launcher to display the Footnote and Endnote dialog box, click the Convert button, make sure the Convert all footnotes to endnotes option button is selected, click the OK button, and then click the Close button in the Footnote and Endnote dialog box.

To Enter More Text

The next step is to continue typing text in the body of the research paper.

1 Position the insertion point after the note reference mark in the document, and then press the ENTER key.

2 Type the third paragraph of the research paper (Figure 2–45): In many public locations, people connect to the Internet through a wireless Internet access point using mobile computers and devices. Two types of wireless Internet access points are hot spots and 3-G networks. A 3-G network, which uses cellular radio technology, enables users to connect to the Internet through a mobile phone or computer equipped with an appropriate PC Card. A hot spot is a wireless network that allows mobile users to check e-mail, browse the Web, and access any Internet service - as long as their computers or devices have the proper wireless capability.

BTW

Spacing after Punctuation
Because word processing documents use variable character fonts, it often is difficult to determine in a printed document how many times someone has pressed the SPACEBAR between sentences. The rule is to press the SPACEBAR only once after periods, colons, and other punctuation marks.

To Count Words

Often when you write papers, you are required to compose the papers with a minimum number of words. The minimum requirement for the research paper in this chapter is 325 words. You can look on the status bar and see the total number of words thus far in a document. For example, Figure 2–45 shows the research paper has 250 words, but you are not sure if that count includes the words in your footnote. The following steps display the Word Count dialog box, so that you can verify whether the footnote text is included in the count.

1

- Click the Word Count indicator on the status bar to display the Word Count dialog box.

- If necessary, place a check mark in the 'Include textboxes, footnotes and endnotes' check box.

Q&A
Why do the statistics in my Word Count dialog box differ from Figure 2–45?

Depending on the accuracy of your typing, your statistics may differ.

2

- Click the Close button to close the dialog box.

Q&A
Can I display statistics for just a section of the document?

Yes. Select the section and then click the Word Count indicator on the status bar to display statistics about the selected text.

Figure 2–45

Other Ways

1. Click Word Count button on Review tab
2. Press CTRL+SHIFT+G

Automatic Page Breaks

As you type documents that exceed one page, Word automatically inserts page breaks, called **automatic page breaks** or **soft page breaks**, when it determines the text has filled one page according to paper size, margin settings, line spacing, and other settings. If you add text, delete text, or modify text on a page, Word recomputes the location of automatic page breaks and adjusts them accordingly.

Word performs page recomputation between the keystrokes, that is, in between the pauses in your typing. Thus, Word refers to the automatic page break task as **background repagination**. The steps on the next page illustrate Word's automatic page break feature.

To Change Document Properties

Before saving the research paper again, you want to add your name, course information, and some keywords as document properties. The following steps use the Document Information Panel to change document properties.

1 Click the Office Button to display the Office Button menu, point to Prepare on the Office Button menu, and then click Properties on the Prepare submenu to display the Document Information Panel.

2 Click the Author text box, if necessary, and then type your name as the Author property. If a name already is displayed in the Author text box, delete it before typing your name.

3 Click the Subject text box, if necessary delete any existing text, and then type your course and section as the Subject property.

4 Click the Keywords text box, if necessary delete any existing text, and then type `instant messaging, Internet access points, global positioning systems` as the Keywords property.

5 Click the Close the Document Information Panel button so that the Document Information Panel no longer is displayed.

BTW

Conserving Ink and Toner
You can instruct Word to print draft quality documents to conserve ink or toner by clicking the Office Button, clicking the Word Options button, clicking Advanced in the left pane of the Word Options dialog box, scrolling to the Print area, placing a check mark in the 'Use draft quality' check box, and then clicking the OK button. Click the Office Button, point to Print, and then click Quick Print.

To Save an Existing Document with the Same File Name

The document now is complete. You should save the research paper again. The following step saves the document again.

1 Click the Save button on the Quick Access Toolbar to overwrite the previous Wireless Communications Paper file on the USB flash drive.

To Print Document Properties and then the Document

With the document properties entered and the completed document saved, you may want to print the document properties along with the document. The following steps print the document properties, followed by the contents of the saved Wireless Communications Paper project.

1
• Click the Office Button to display the Office Button menu and then point to Print on the Office Button menu to display the Print submenu (Figure 2–77).

Figure 2–77

2

- Click Print on the Print submenu to display the Print dialog box.

- Click the Print what box arrow and then click Document properties to instruct Word to print the document properties instead of the document (Figure 2–78).

Figure 2–78

3

- Click the OK button to print the document properties (Figure 2–79).

4

- Click the Office Button again to display the Office Button menu, point to Print on the Office Button menu, and then click Quick Print on the Print submenu to print the research paper (shown in Figure 2–1 on page WD 75).

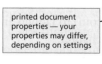

printed document properties — your properties may differ, depending on settings

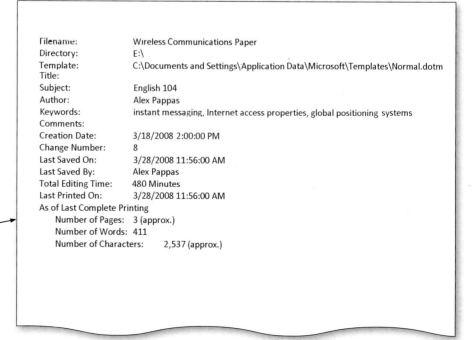

Filename:	Wireless Communications Paper
Directory:	E:\
Template:	C:\Documents and Settings\Application Data\Microsoft\Templates\Normal.dotm
Title:	
Subject:	English 104
Author:	Alex Pappas
Keywords:	instant messaging, Internet access properties, global positioning systems
Comments:	
Creation Date:	3/18/2008 2:00:00 PM
Change Number:	8
Last Saved On:	3/28/2008 11:56:00 AM
Last Saved By:	Alex Pappas
Total Editing Time:	480 Minutes
Last Printed On:	3/28/2008 11:56:00 AM

As of Last Complete Printing
    Number of Pages: 3 (approx.)
    Number of Words: 411
    Number of Characters: 2,537 (approx.)

Figure 2–79

Apply Your Knowledge *continued*

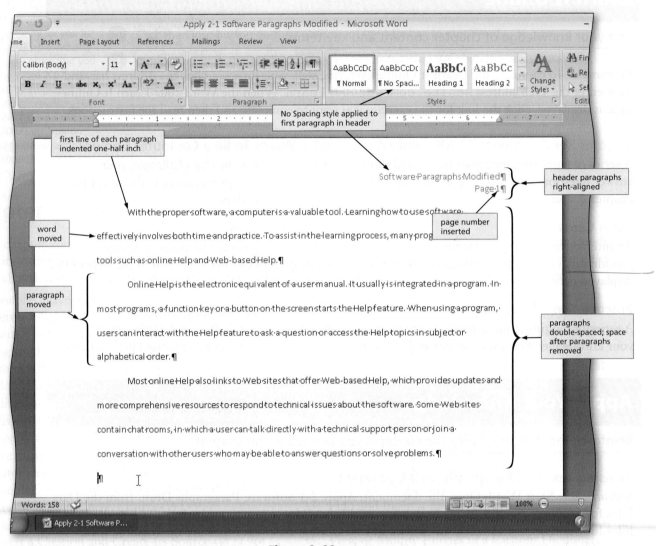

Figure 2–80

6. With the paragraphs still selected, use Line spacing box arrow to remove extra space below (after) the paragraphs. Click anywhere to remove the selection.

7. Use the Find and Replace dialog box to replace all occurrences of the word, Internet, with the word, Web. How many replacements were made?

8. Use Word's thesaurus to change the word, incorporated, to the word, integrated, in the first sentence of the second paragraph.

9. Switch to the header so you can edit it. In the first line of the header, change the word, Draft, to the word, Modified, so it reads: Software Paragraphs Modified. Change the first line of the header from the Normal style to the No Spacing style.

10. In the second line of the header, insert and center the page number (with no formatting) one space after the word, Page.

11. Change the alignment of both lines of text in the header from left-aligned to right-aligned. Switch back to the document text.

12. Change the document properties, as specified by your instructor.

13. Click the Office Button and then click Save As. Save the document using the file name, Apply 2-1 Software Paragraphs Modified.

14. Print the document properties and then print the revised document, shown in Figure 2–80.

15. Use the Research task pane to look up the definition of the word, online, in the first sentence of the second paragraph. Handwrite the COMPUTING definition of the word, online, on your printout.

16. Display the Research Options dialog box and on your printout, handwrite the currently active Reference Books, Research Sites, and Business and Financial Sites. If your instructor approves, activate one of the services.

Extend Your Knowledge

Extend the skills you learned in this chapter and experiment with new skills. You may need to use Help to complete the assignment.

Working with References and Proofing Tools

Instructions: Start Word. Open the document, Extend 2-1 Computing Options Paper Draft, from the Data Files for Students. See the inside back cover of this book for instructions on downloading the Data Files for Students, or contact your instructor for information on accessing the required files.

You will add another footnote to the paper, use the thesaurus, convert the document from MLA to APA style, convert the footnotes to endnotes, modify the Endnote Text style, change the format of the note reference marks, and translate the document to another language.

Perform the following tasks:

1. Insert a second footnote at an appropriate place in the research paper. Use the following footnote text: The Americans with Disabilities Act (ADA) requires any company with 15 or more employees to make reasonable attempts to accommodate the needs of physically challenged workers.

2. Use the Find dialog box to find the word, imagine, in the document and use Word to help you determine an appropriate synonym.

3. Save the document with a new file name and then print it. Select the entire document and then change the style of the citations and bibliography from MLA to APA. Save the APA version of the document with a new file name and then print it. Compare the two versions. Circle the differences between the two documents.

4. Convert the footnotes to endnotes.

5. Modify the Endnote Text style to 11-point Calibri font, double-spaced text with a first-line indent.

6. Change the format of the note reference marks to capital letters (A, B, etc.).

7. Save the revised document with endnotes with a new file name and then print it. On the printout with the endnotes, write the number of words, characters without spaces, characters with spaces, paragraphs, and lines in the document. Be sure to include endnote text in the statistics.

8. Translate the research paper into a language of your choice (Figure 2–81 on the next page) using the Translate button on the Review tab. Print the translated document.

Continued >

STUDENT ASSIGNMENTS

Extend Your Knowledge *continued*

Figure 2–81

Make It Right

Analyze a document and correct all errors and/or improve the design.

Inserting Missing Elements in an MLA Style Research Paper

Instructions: Start Word. Open the document, Make It Right 2-1 Certification Paper Draft, from the Data Files for Students. See the inside back cover of this book for instructions on downloading the Data Files for Students, or contact your instructor for information on accessing the required files.

The document is a research paper that is missing several elements. You are to insert these missing elements, all formatted according to the MLA documentation style: header with a page number, heading (name, course, and date information), paper title, footnote, and source information for the first citation and the citation in the footnote.

Perform the following tasks:

1. Insert a header with a page number, heading (use your own information: name, course information, and date), and an appropriate paper title, all formatted according to the MLA style.

2. Use the Select Browse Object button to go to page 2. How many bibliographical entries currently are on the Works Cited page? You will create additional source entries in Steps 3 and 4.

3. The Otoole placeholder (tag name) is missing its source information (Figure 2–82). Use the following source information to edit the source: magazine article titled "Career Builders and Boosts," written by Sarah W. O'Toole, magazine name is *IT World and Certifications*, publication date is March 2008, article is on pages 88-93. Edit the citation so it displays the author name and the page numbers.

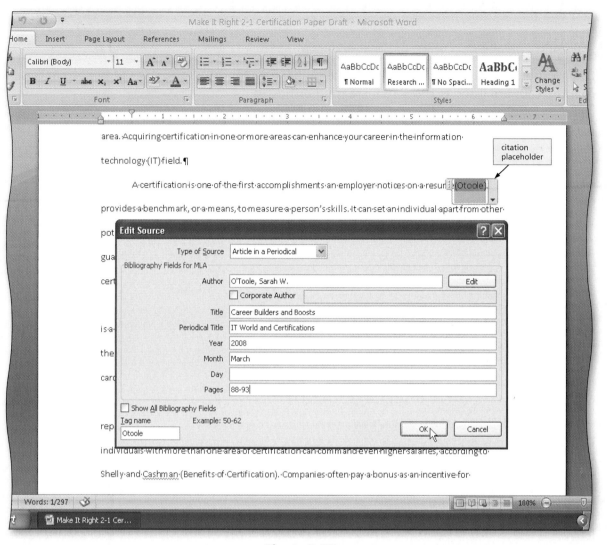

Figure 2–82

4. Insert the following footnote with the note reference at an appropriate place in the paper, formatted according to the MLA style: Debbins points out that, as an additional bonus, some certification training can be used for college credit. The citation for this footnote should be at the end of the footnote. The source information is as follows: book named *Preparing for the Future: IT Strategies*, authored by Floyd I. Debbins, published in 2008 at IT World Press in Boston, pages 99-104. Edit the citation so it only displays page numbers.

5. Use the Select Browse Object button to go to page 3. Be sure the bibliographical list on the Works Cited page contains all three entries. If necessary, use the F9 key to update the bibliographical list. Format the bibliographical paragraphs with a one-half inch hanging indent.

6. Use the Select Browse Object button to go to the footnote. Be sure the footnote is formatted properly.

7. Change the document properties, as specified by your instructor. Save the revised document with a new file name and then submit it in the format specified by your instructor.

In the Lab

Design and/or create a document using the guidelines, concepts, and skills presented in this chapter. Labs are listed in order of increasing difficulty.

Lab 1: Preparing a Short Research Paper

Problem: You are a college student currently enrolled in an introductory business class. Your assignment is to prepare a short research paper (300-350 words) about a computer-related job. The requirements are that the paper be presented according to the MLA documentation style and have three references. One of the three references must be from the Web. You prepare the paper shown in Figure 2–83, which discusses the computer forensics specialist.

Hankins 1

Mary Hankins

Mr. Habib

Business 102

14 March 2008

Computer Forensics Specialist

Computer forensics, also called digital forensics, network forensics, or cyberforensics, is a rapidly growing field that involves gathering and analyzing evidence from computers and networks. Because computers and the Internet are the fastest growing technology used for criminal activity, the need for computer forensics specialists will increase in years to come.

A computer forensics specialist examines computer media, programs, data, and log files on computers, servers, and networks. According to Shelly and Cashman (Computer Careers), many areas employ computer forensics specialists, including law enforcement, criminal prosecutors, military intelligence, insurance agencies, and information security departments in the private sector. A computer forensics specialist must have knowledge of the law, technical experience with many types of hardware and software products, superior communication skills, a willingness to learn and update skills, and a knack for problem solving.

When a problem occurs, it is the responsibility of the computer forensics specialist to carefully take several steps to identify and retrieve possible evidence that may exist on a suspect's computer. These steps include protecting the suspect's computer, discovering all files, recovering deleted files, revealing hidden files, accessing protected or encrypted files, analyzing all the data, and providing expert consultation and/or testimony as required (Reinman 52-58).

A computer forensics specialist must have knowledge of all aspects of the computer, from the operating system to computer architecture and hardware design. In the past, many computer forensics specialists were self-taught computer users. Today, extensive training, usually from several different

(a)

Figure 2–83

(b)

Hankins 2

sources, is required. A degree in Computer Science should be supplemented with graduate courses and university-level professional development certificates. Entry level salaries range from $45,000 to $75,000. With experience and certifications, salaries can exceed $125,000 (Turell 44-55).

    With the growing use of computers in all areas of life, the number of computer crimes surely will continue to rise. As a result, the need for skilled specialists to battle these crimes will increase for many years to come.

(c)

Hankins 3

Works Cited

Reinman, David P. "Fighting Cybercriminals." Cybertech Monthly February 2008: 52-58.

Shelly, Gary B., and Thomas J. Cashman. "Computer Careers." Course Technology. 7 March 2008 <www.scsite.com/wd2007/pr2/wc.htm>.

Turell, Marcia O., and Alex N. Gutierrez. Cybercrimes and Criminals. El Paso: Legal Works Publishing Company, 2008.

Figure 2–83 (continued)

Instructions: Perform the following tasks:

1. If necessary, display formatting marks on the screen.

2. Adjust line spacing to double.

3. Remove space below (after) paragraphs.

4. Create a header to number pages.

5. Type the name and course information at the left margin. Center and type the title.

6. Set first-line indent for paragraphs in the body of the research paper.

7. Create a Quick Style for the research paper paragraphs.

8. Type the research paper as shown in Figures 2–83a and 2–83b. Change the bibliography style to MLA. As you insert citations, enter their source information (shown in Figure 2–83c). Edit the citations so they display according to Figures 2–83a and 2–83b.

9. At the end of the research paper text, press the ENTER key and then insert a manual page break so the Works Cited page begins on a new page. Enter and format the works cited title (Figure 2–83c). Use Word to insert the bibliographical list. Format the paragraphs in the list with a hanging indent.

10. Check the spelling and grammar of the paper at once.

11. Save the document on a USB flash drive using Lab 2-1 Computer Forensics Paper as the file name.

12. Print the research paper. Handwrite the number of words, paragraphs, and characters in the research paper above the title of your printed research paper.

In the Lab

Lab 2: Preparing a Research Report with a Footnote

Problem: You are a college student enrolled in an introductory English class. Your assignment is to prepare a short research paper in any area of interest to you. The requirements are that the paper be presented according to the MLA documentation style, contain at least one explanatory note positioned as a footnote, and have three references. One of the three references must be from the Internet. You prepare a paper about antivirus programs (Figure 2–84).

Yadav 1

Pahdi Yadav

Professor Milton

English 101

5 May 2008

Antivirus Programs

Today, people rely on computers to create, store, and manage critical information, many times via a home computer network. Information transmitted over networks has a higher degree of security risk than information kept in a user's home or company premises. Thus, it is crucial that they take measures to protect their computers and data from loss, damage, and misuse resulting from computer security risks. Antivirus programs are an effective way to protect a computer against viruses.

An antivirus program protects a computer against viruses by identifying and removing any computer viruses found in memory, on storage media, or on incoming files.[1] When you purchase a new computer, it often includes antivirus software. Antivirus programs work by scanning for programs that attempt to modify the boot program, the operating system, and other programs that normally are read from but not modified. In addition, many antivirus programs automatically scan files downloaded from the Web, e-mail attachments, opened files, and all types of removable media inserted in the computer (Karanos 201-205).

One technique that antivirus programs use to identify a virus is to look for virus signatures, or virus definitions, which are known specific patterns of virus code. According to Shelly and Cashman (Antivirus Programs), many vendors of antivirus programs allow registered users to update virus signature files automatically from the Web at no cost for a specified time. Updating the antivirus

---

[1] Bulowski points out that most antivirus programs also protect against worms and Trojan horses (55-61).

(a)

Figure 2–84

Yadav 2

program's signature files regularly is important, because it will download any new virus definitions that
have been added since the last update.

Methods that guarantee a computer or network is safe from computer viruses simply do not
exist. Installing, updating, and using an antivirus program, though, is an effective technique to safeguard
your computer from loss.

(b)

Figure 2–84 (continued)

Instructions: Perform the following tasks:

1. Adjust line spacing to double and remove space below (after) paragraphs. Create a header to number pages. Type the name and course information at the left margin. Center and type the title. Set first-line indent for paragraphs in the body of the research paper. Create a Quick Style for the research paper paragraphs.

2. Type the research paper as shown in Figures 2–84a and 2–84b. Add the footnote as shown in Figure 2–84a. Change the Footnote Text style to the format specified in the MLA style. As you insert citations, use the following source information:

   a. Type of Source: Periodical
      Author: Bulowski, Dana
      Title: Protection and Precaution: Keeping Your Computer Healthy
      Periodical Title: Computing Today
      Year: 2008
      Month: February
      Pages 55-61
   b. Type of Source: Book
      Author: Karanos, Hector
      Title: Internet Security
      Year: 2008
      City: Indianapolis
      Publisher: Citywide Cyber Press
   c. Type of Source: Document From Web site
      Author: Shelly, Gary B., and Thomas J. Cashman
      Name of Web page: Antivirus Programs
      Production Company: Course Technology
      Year Accessed: 2008
      Month Accessed: February
      Day Accessed: 7
      URL: www.scsite.com/wd2007/pr2/wc.htm

3. At the end of the research paper text, press the ENTER key once and insert a manual page break so the Works Cited page begins on a new page. Enter and format the works cited title. Use Word to insert the bibliographical list. Format the paragraphs in the list with a hanging indent.

4. Check the spelling and grammar of the paper.

5. Save the document on a USB flash drive using Lab 2-2 Antivirus Programs Paper as the file name.

6. Print the research paper. Handwrite the number of words, including the footnotes, in the research paper above the title of your printed research paper.

In the Lab

Lab 3: Composing a Research Paper from Notes

Problem: You have drafted the notes shown in Figure 2–85. Your assignment is to prepare a short research paper from these notes.

Home networks:
- Home users connect multiple computers and devices together in a home network.
- Home networking saves money and provides conveniences.
- Approximately 39 million homes have more than one computer.
- Many vendors offer home networking packages that include all the necessary hardware and software to network a home using wired or wireless techniques.

Three types of wired home networks: Ethernet, powerline cable, and phoneline (source: "Wired vs. Wireless Networks," an article on pages 24-29 in March 2008 issue of Modern Networking by Mark A. Travis).
- Traditional Ethernet networks require that each computer have built-in network capabilities or contain a network card, which connects to a central network hub or similar device with a physical cable. This may involve running cable through walls, ceilings, and floors in the house.
- The hardware and software of an Ethernet network can be difficult to configure for the average home user (source: a book called <u>Home Networking</u> by Frank A. Deakins, published at Current Press in New York in 2008).
- A phoneline network is an easy-to-install and inexpensive network that uses existing telephone lines in the home.
- A home powerline cable network is a network that uses the same lines that bring electricity into the house. This network requires no additional wiring.

Two types of wireless home networks: HomeRF and Wi-Fi (source: a Web site titled "Wired and Wireless Networks" by Gary B. Shelly and Thomas J. Cashman of Course Technology, viewed on April 23, 2008. Web address is www.scsite.com/wd2007/pr2/wc.htm).
- Wireless networks have the disadvantage of interference, because walls, ceilings, and other electrical devices such as cordless telephones and microwave ovens can disrupt wireless communications.
- A HomeRF (radio frequency) network uses radio waves, instead of cables, to transmit data.
- A Wi-Fi network sends signals over a wider distance than the Home RF network, which can be up to 1,500 feet in some configurations.

Figure 2–85

Instructions: Perform the following tasks:

1. Review the notes in Figure 2–85 and then rearrange and reword them. Embellish the paper as you deem necessary. Present the paper according to the MLA documentation style. Create an AutoCorrect entry that automatically corrects the spelling of the misspelled word, wird, to the correct spelling, wired. Add a footnote that refers the reader to the Web for more information. Enter citations and their sources as shown. Create the works cited page from the listed sources.

2. Check the spelling and grammar of the paper. Save the document on a USB flash drive using Lab 2-3 Home Networks Paper as the file name.

3. Use the Research task pane to look up a definition of a word in the paper. Copy and insert the definition into the document as a footnote. Be sure to quote the definition and cite the source.

4. Print the research paper. Handwrite the number of words, including the footnotes, in the research paper above the title of the printed research paper.

Cases and Places

Apply your creative thinking and problem solving skills to design and implement a solution.

• EASIER •• MORE DIFFICULT

• 1: Create a Research Paper about Word Using the MLA Documentation Style

Chapter 1 of this book discussed the components of the Word window (pages WD 6 through 11). Using the material presented on those pages, write a short research paper (350–400 words) that describes the purpose and functionality of one or more of these components: document window, Ribbon, Mini toolbar and shortcut menus, Quick Access Toolbar, and Office Button. Use your textbook and Word Help as sources. Include at least two citations and one explanatory note positioned as a footnote. Add an AutoCorrect entry to correct a word you commonly mistype. Use the concepts and techniques presented in this chapter to format the paper according to the MLA documentation style. Check spelling and grammar of the finished paper.

•• 2: Create the Research Paper Presented in this Chapter Using the APA Documentation Style

As discussed in this chapter, two popular documentation styles for research papers are the Modern Language Association of America (MLA) and American Psychological Association (APA) styles. In this chapter, you created a research paper that followed guidelines of the MLA documentation style. Using the school library, this textbook, other textbooks, the Internet, magazines, or other sources, research the guidelines of the APA documentation style. Then, prepare the Wireless Communications Paper from this chapter following the guidelines of the APA documentation style. Use Figure 2–1 on page WD 75 as a starting point for the text and source information. Check spelling and grammar of the finished paper.

•• 3: Create a Research Paper that Compares Documentation Styles

This chapter discussed the requirements of the MLA documentation style. The American Psychological Association (APA) and the Chicago Manual of Style (CMS) are two other documentation styles supported by Word. Using the school library, this textbook, other textbooks, the Internet, magazines, or other sources, research the guidelines of the APA and CMS documentation styles to learn more about the differences among the MLA, APA, and CMS documentation styles. Using what you learn, write a short research paper (450-500 words) that compares the requirements and formats of the three documentation styles. Include at least two references and one explanatory note positioned as a footnote. Use the documentation style specified by your instructor to format the paper. Check spelling and grammar of the finished paper.

•• 4: Create a Research Paper about the Month You Were Born

Make It Personal

Did you ever wonder what world events took place during the month you were born (besides your birth)? For example, what happened with respect to politics, world affairs, and the economy? What made headline news? Were there any scientific breakthroughs? What was on television and at the box office? Were any famous people born? Did anyone famous die? What songs topped the charts? What was happening in the world of sports? Research the newsworthy events that took place during the month and year you were born (i.e., July 1981) by looking through newspapers, magazines, searching the Web, and/or interviewing family and friends. Write a short research paper (450-500 words) that summarizes your findings. Include at least two references and one explanatory note. Use the documentation style specified by your instructor to format the paper. Check spelling and grammar of the finished paper.

Continued >

Cases and Places *continued*

•• 5: Create a Research Paper about Spring Break Vacation Destinations

Working Together

With spring break just two months away, you and your fellow classmates are thinking about various spring break vacation destinations. Many options are available. Should you vacation close to home or travel across the country? Stay at a hotel, rent a condominium, or camp outdoors? Travel by car, train, or airplane? Book through a travel agent or the Web? Each team member is to research the attractions, accommodations, required transportation, and total cost of one spring break destination by looking through newspapers, magazines, searching the Web, and/or visiting a travel agency. Each team member is to write a minimum of 200 words summarizing his or her findings. Each team member also is to write at least one explanatory note and supply his or her source information for the citation and bibliography. Then, the team should meet as a group to compose a research paper that includes all team members' write-ups. Start by copying and pasting the text into a single document and then write an introduction and conclusion as a group. Use the documentation style specified by your instructor to format the paper. Check spelling and grammar of the finished paper. Set the default dictionary. If Word flags any of your last names as an error, add the name(s) to the custom dictionary. Hand in printouts of each team member's original write-up, as well as the final research paper.

3 Creating a Cover Letter and a Resume

Objectives

You will have mastered the material in this chapter when you can:

- Format characters and paragraphs
- Insert and format clip art
- Set and use tab stops
- Identify the components of a business letter
- Insert the current date
- Create and insert a building block
- Insert a Word table, enter data in the table, and format the table
- Use a template to create a document

- Fill in a document template
- Copy and paste using the Office Clipboard
- Indent paragraphs
- Insert a Quick Part
- Sort a List
- Use print preview to view and print a document
- Address and print an envelope

3 | Creating a Cover Letter and a Resume

Introduction

In a business environment, people use documents to communicate with others. Business documents can include letters, memos, newsletters, proposals, and resumes. An effective business document clearly and concisely conveys its message and has a professional, organized appearance.

Some people prefer to use their own creative skills to design and compose business documents. Using Word, for example, you can develop the content and decide on the location of each item in a document. On occasion, however, you may have difficulty composing a particular type of document. To assist with the task of creating certain types of documents, such as resumes and fax cover letters, Word provides templates. A **template** is similar to a form with prewritten text; that is, Word prepares the requested document with text and/or formatting common to all documents of this nature. After Word creates a document from a template, you fill in the blanks or replace prewritten words in the document.

Project — Cover Letter and Resume

At some time in your professional life, you will prepare a cover letter along with a resume to send to prospective employers. In addition to some personal information, a **resume** usually contains the applicant's educational background and job experience. Employers review many resumes for each vacant position. Thus, you should design your resume carefully so that it presents you as the best candidate for the job. You also should attach a personalized cover letter to each resume you send. A **cover letter** enables you to elaborate on positive points in your resume; it also provides you with an opportunity to show a potential employer your writing skills.

The project in this chapter follows generally accepted guidelines for writing letters and resumes and uses Word to create the cover letter shown in Figure 3–1 and the resume shown in Figure 3–2 on page WD 148. The personalized cover letter to the prospective employer (Juniper Culinary Academy) includes a custom-made letterhead, as well as all essential business letter components. The resume for Lana Halima Canaan, a recent graduate of the culinary arts program, uses a Word template to present relevant information to a potential employer.

Overview

As you read through this chapter, you will learn how to create the cover letter and resume shown in Figures 3–1 and 3–2 by performing these general tasks:

- Design and compose a letterhead.
- Compose a cover letter.
- Print the cover letter.
- Use a template to create a resume.
- Print the resume.
- Address and print an envelope.

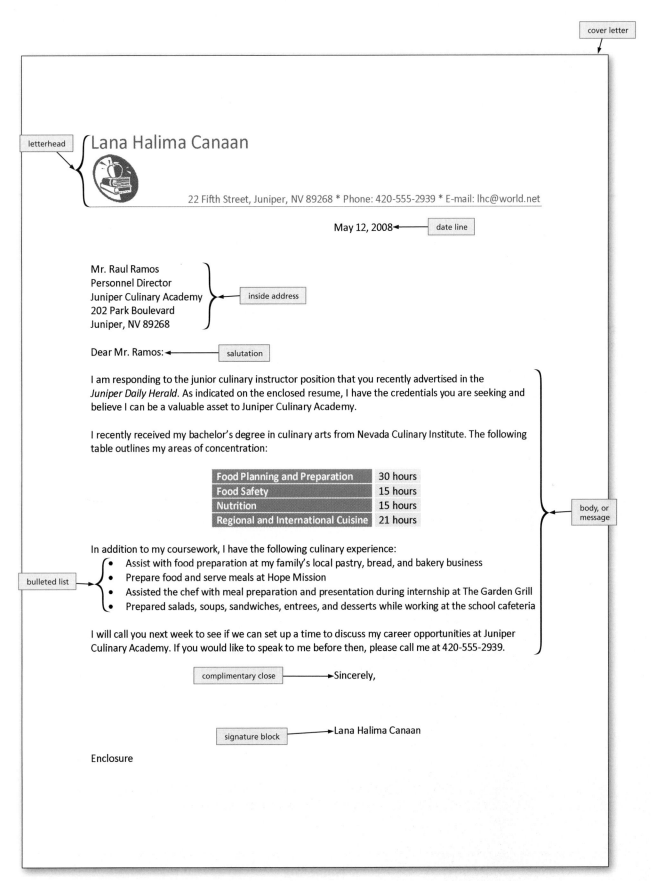

cover letter

letterhead

Lana Halima Canaan

22 Fifth Street, Juniper, NV 89268 * Phone: 420-555-2939 * E-mail: lhc@world.net

May 12, 2008 ← date line

Mr. Raul Ramos
Personnel Director
Juniper Culinary Academy ← inside address
202 Park Boulevard
Juniper, NV 89268

Dear Mr. Ramos: ← salutation

I am responding to the junior culinary instructor position that you recently advertised in the *Juniper Daily Herald*. As indicated on the enclosed resume, I have the credentials you are seeking and believe I can be a valuable asset to Juniper Culinary Academy.

I recently received my bachelor's degree in culinary arts from Nevada Culinary Institute. The following table outlines my areas of concentration:

Food Planning and Preparation	30 hours
Food Safety	15 hours
Nutrition	15 hours
Regional and International Cuisine	21 hours

body, or message

In addition to my coursework, I have the following culinary experience:
- Assist with food preparation at my family's local pastry, bread, and bakery business
- Prepare food and serve meals at Hope Mission
- Assisted the chef with meal preparation and presentation during internship at The Garden Grill
- Prepared salads, soups, sandwiches, entrees, and desserts while working at the school cafeteria

bulleted list

I will call you next week to see if we can set up a time to discuss my career opportunities at Juniper Culinary Academy. If you would like to speak to me before then, please call me at 420-555-2939.

complimentary close → Sincerely,

signature block → Lana Halima Canaan

Enclosure

Figure 3–1

resume

Lana Halima Canaan

22 Fifth Street, Juniper, NV 89268
Phone: 420-555-2939
E-mail: lhc@world.net

Objectives

To obtain a full-time culinary instructor position with a culinary academy, school, or institute in the Juniper area.

Education

B.S. Culinary Arts (Nevada Culinary Institute, May 2008)

- Dean's List, six semesters
- Moeller Nutrition Award, January 2008
- Marge Rae Outstanding Student Scholarship, 2006 – 2008
- Baker Food Preparation Contest, 1ˢᵗ Place, November 2008
- Areas of concentration:
  Food Planning and Preparation
  Food Safety
  Nutrition
  Regional and International Cuisine

Experience

Chef Intern (September 2006 – May 2008)
    The Garden Grill (Juniper, NV)
    Assisted chef with meal selection, preparation, and presentation. Assumed chef responsibilities during last semester of school.

Assistant Cook (September 2004 – August 2006)
    Nevada Culinary Institute Cafeteria (Juniper, NV)
    Planned meals for staff and students. Prepared salads, soups, sandwiches, entrees, and desserts.

Skills

- Culinary Arts Association
- National Honor Society
- Nevada Restaurant Federation
- Nutrition Services of America
- Student Government Association, President

Community Service

Prepare food and serve meals at Hope Mission every week.

Figure 3–2

General Project Guidelines

When creating a Word document, the actions you perform and decisions you make will affect the appearance and characteristics of the finished document. As you create a cover letter and resume, such as the project shown in Figure 3–1 on page WD 147 and Figure 3–2, you should follow these general guidelines:

1. **Design a creative letterhead.** Use text, graphics, formats, and colors that reflect your personality or employment goals. Include your name, postal mailing address, and telephone number. If you have an e-mail address and Web address, include those as well.

2. **Compose an effective cover letter.** A finished business letter (i.e., cover letter) should look like a symmetrically framed picture with evenly spaced margins, all balanced below an attractive letterhead. A well-written, properly formatted cover letter presents solid evidence of your writing skills and provides insight into your personality. The content of a letter should contain proper grammar, correct spelling, logically constructed sentences, flowing paragraphs, and sound ideas. Be sure to proofread it carefully.

3. **Craft a successful resume.** Your resume should present, at a minimum, your contact information, objective, educational background, and work experience to a potential employer. It should honestly present all your positive points. As with the cover letter, the resume should be error free. Ask someone else to proofread your resume and give you suggestions for improvements.

When necessary, more specific details concerning the above guidelines are presented at appropriate points in the chapter. The chapter also will identify the actions performed and decisions made regarding these guidelines during the creation of the cover letter shown in Figure 3–1 and the resume shown in Figure 3–2.

Creating a Letterhead

In many businesses, letterhead is preprinted on stationery that everyone in the company uses for correspondence. For personal letters, the cost of preprinted letterhead can be high. An alternative is to create your own letterhead and save it in a file. At a later time, when you want to create a letter using the letterhead, simply open the letterhead file and then save the file with a new name to preserve the original letterhead file. The letterhead in this project (Figure 3–1), follows this process; that is, you design and create a letterhead and then save it in a file.

Design a creative letterhead.

A letterhead often is the first section a reader notices on a letter. Thus, it is important your letterhead appropriately reflect the essence of the individual or business (i.e., formal, youthful, technical, etc.). The letterhead should leave ample room for the contents of the letter. When designing a letterhead, consider its contents, placement, and appearance.

- **Contents of letterhead.** A letterhead should contain these elements:

  - Complete legal name of the individual, group, or company

  - Complete mailing address: street address including building, room, suite number, or post office box, along with city, state, and postal code

  - Telephone number(s) and fax number, if one exists

  Many letterheads also include a Web address, e-mail address, and a logo or other image. If you use an image, select one that expresses your personality or goals.

(continued)

**Plan
Ahead**

(continued)

- **Placement of elements in the letterhead.** Some letterheads center their elements across the top of the page. Others align some or all of the elements with the left or right margins. Sometimes, the elements are split between the top and bottom of the page. For example, a name and logo may be at the top of the page with the address at the bottom of the page.

- **Appearance of letterhead elements.** Use fonts that are easy to read. Give your name impact by making its font size larger than the rest of the text in the letterhead. For additional emphasis, consider formatting the name in bold or italic. Choose colors that complement each other and convey your goals or personality.

   When finished designing the letterhead, determine if a divider line would help to visually separate the letterhead from the text of the letter.

The following pages start Word, enter and format the text and graphics in the letterhead, shown in Figure 3–1 on page WD 147, and then save the personal letterhead file.

To Start Word and Display Formatting Marks

If you are using a computer to step through the project in this chapter and you want your screens to match the figures in this book, you should change your computer's resolution to 1024×768. For information about how to change a computer's resolution, read Appendix D.

The following steps start Word and display formatting marks.

1 Start Word. If necessary, maximize the Word window.

2 If the Print Layout button is not selected, click it so that your screen layout matches Figure 3–3.

3 If your zoom level is not 100%, change it to 100%.

4 If the Show/Hide ¶ button on the Home tab is not selected already, click it to display formatting marks on the screen.

To Apply a Quick Style

When you press the ENTER key in the letterhead, you want the insertion point to advance to the next line, with no blank space between the lines. Recall that, by default, the Normal style in Word places 10 points of blank space after each paragraph and inserts a blank space equal to 1.15 lines between each line of text. The No Spacing style, however, does not put any extra blank space between lines when you press the ENTER key. The following step applies the No Spacing style to the current paragraph.

1 Click No Spacing in the Styles gallery to apply the No Spacing style to the current paragraph.

To Change Theme Colors

Recall that Word provides document themes that contain a variety of color schemes to assist you in selecting complementary colors in a document. In your own letterhead, you would select a color scheme that reflects your personality or goals. This letterhead uses the Urban color scheme. The following steps change theme colors.

1 Click the Change Styles button on the Home tab to display the Change Styles menu, and then point to Colors on the Change Styles menu to display the Colors gallery.

2 Click Urban in the Colors gallery to change the document theme colors to Urban.

Normal Style
If your screen settings differ from Figure 3–3, it is possible the default settings in your Normal style have been changed. Normal style settings are saved in the normal.dotm file. To restore the original Normal style settings, quit Word and use Windows Explorer to locate the normal.dotm file (be sure that hidden files and folders are displayed and include system and hidden files in your search). Rename the normal.dotm file to oldnormal.dotm file. After renaming the normal.dotm file, it will no longer exist as normal.dotm. The next time you start Word, it will recreate a normal .dotm file using the original default settings.

To Type Text

To begin creating the personal letterhead file in this chapter, type your name in the document window. The following step types this first line of text in the document.

1 Type Lana Halima Canaan and then press the ENTER key.

Q&A

Why not type the name in all capital letters?

Studies show that all capital letters can be more difficult to read.

Mini Toolbar

Recall from Chapter 1 that the Mini toolbar, which automatically appears based on certain tasks you perform, contains commands related to changing the appearance of text in a document. All commands on the Mini toolbar also exist on the Ribbon.

When the Mini toolbar appears, it initially is transparent. If you do not use the transparent Mini toolbar, it disappears from the screen. To use the Mini toolbar, move the mouse pointer into the toolbar, which causes the Mini toolbar to change from a transparent to a bright appearance. The following steps illustrate the use of the Mini toolbar.

To Use the Grow Font Button to Increase Font Size

You want the font size of the name to be larger than the rest of the text in the letterhead. In previous chapters, you used the Font Size box arrow on the Home tab to change the font size of text. Word also provides a Grow Font button, which increases the font size of selected text each time you click the button. The following steps use the Grow Font button on the Mini toolbar to increase the font size of the name.

1

- Move the mouse pointer to the left of the line to be selected (in this case, the line containing your name) until the mouse pointer changes to a right-pointing block arrow, and then click the mouse to select the line (Figure 3–3).

Figure 3–3

2

- Move the mouse pointer into the transparent Mini toolbar, so that it changes to a bright toolbar.

- Repeatedly click the Grow Font button on the Mini toolbar until the Font Size box displays 20, for 20 point (Figure 3–4).

Q&A What if I click the Grow Font button too many times and make the font size too big?

Click the Shrink Font button until the desired font size is displayed.

Figure 3–4

3

Experiment

- Repeatedly click the Grow Font and Shrink Font buttons on the Mini toolbar and watch the font size of the selected name change in the document window. When you have finished experimenting, set the font size to 20 point.

Other Ways

1. Click Grow Font button on Home tab
2. Press CTRL+>

To Color Text

The text in the letterhead is to be a shade of teal. The following steps change the color of the entered text.

1

- With the text still selected and the Mini toolbar still displaying, click the Font Color button arrow on the Mini toolbar to display the Font Color gallery (Figure 3–5).

Q&A What if my Mini toolbar no longer is displayed?

Use the Font Color button arrow on the Home tab.

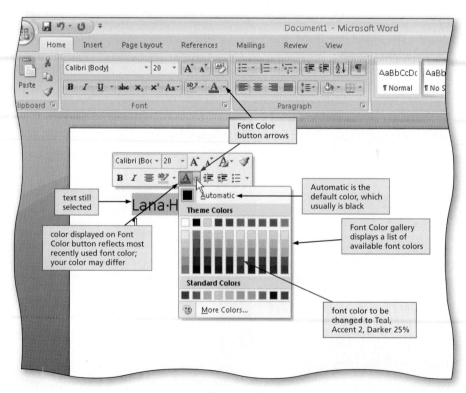

Figure 3–5

②

- Click Teal, Accent 2, Darker 25%, which is the sixth color in the fifth row in the Theme Colors area, to change the color of the selected text to a shade of teal.

- Click the paragraph mark below the name to deselect the text and position the insertion point on line 2 of the document (Figure 3–6).

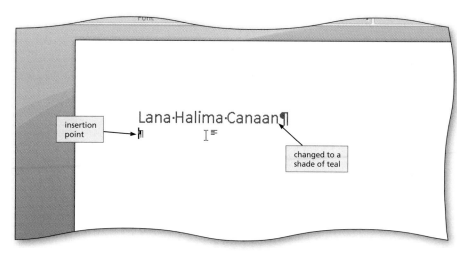

Figure 3–6

Q&A How would I change the text color back to black?

If, for some reason, you wanted to change the text color back to black at this point, you would select the text, click the Font Color button arrow again, and then click Automatic on the Font Color gallery.

Other Ways		
1. Click the Font Color button arrow on Home tab, click desired color	2. Click Font Dialog Box Launcher, click Font tab, click Font color box arrow,	click desired color, click OK button

To Insert Clip Art

Files containing graphical images, or **graphics**, are available from a variety of sources. In Chapter 1, you inserted a digital picture taken with a digital camera into a document. In this project, you insert **clip art**, which is a predefined graphic. In the Microsoft Office programs, clip art is located in the **Clip Organizer**, which contains a collection of clip art, photographs, sounds, and videos.

The letterhead in this project contains clip art of an apple on a stack of books (Figure 3–1 on page WD 147), which represents Lana's desire to be a instructor. Thus, the next steps insert clip art on line 2 of the letterhead below the job seeker's name.

①

- With the insertion point on line 2 below the name, click Insert on the Ribbon to display the Insert tab.

- Click the Clip Art button on the Insert tab to display the Clip Art task pane.

Q&A What is a task pane?

A **task pane** is a separate window that enables you to carry out some Word tasks more efficiently.

- If the Search for text box displays text, drag through the text to select it.

- Type teacher in the Search for text box (Figure 3–7).

Figure 3–7

2

- Click the Go button to display a list of clips that match the description, teacher (Figure 3–8).

Q&A

Why is my list of clips different from Figure 3–8?

If you are connected to the Internet, the Clip Art task pane displays clips from the Web as well as those installed on your hard disk.

Go button

Clip Art

Search for:
teacher | Go

Search in:
All collections

Results should be:
All media file types

list of clips that matches description

globe icon indicates clip art from the Web

a·Canaan¶

Organize clips...
Clip art on Office Online
Tips for finding clips

Figure 3–8

3

- Click the clip art of the apple on the stack of books to insert it in the document at the location of the insertion point (Figure 3–9).

4

- Click the Close button on the Clip Art task pane title bar to close the task pane.

Picture Tools tab automatically appears because a graphic is selected in the document window

Close button

Document1 - M

Insert   Page Layout   References

Format

Compress Pictures
Change Picture
Reset Picture
Adjust

Picture Shape
Picture Border
Picture Effects

Send to Back
Text Wrapping
Arrange

1.85"
Crop
Size

Clip Art

Search for:
teacher | Go

Search in:
All collections

Results should be:
All media file types

clip art selected

box arrow is displayed when you click or point to clip art; clicking box arrow displays a menu

inserted clip art is selected automatically

Lana·Halima·Canaan¶

Figure 3–9

To Resize a Graphic Using the Size Dialog Box

In this project, the graphic is 35 percent of its original size. Instead of dragging the sizing handle to change the graphic's size, as you learned how to do in Chapter 1, you can use the Size dialog box to set exact size percentages. The following steps resize a graphic using the Size dialog box.

1

- With the graphic still selected, click the Size Dialog Box Launcher on the Format tab to display the Size dialog box (Figure 3–10).

Q&A What if Format tab is not the active tab on my Ribbon?

Double-click the graphic or click Format on the Ribbon to display the Format tab.

Figure 3–10

2

- In the Scale area, triple-click the Height box to select it.

- Type 35 and then press the TAB key to display 35% in the Height and Width boxes and resize the selected graphic to 35 percent of its original size (Figure 3–11).

Q&A How do I know to use 35 percent for the resized graphic?

The larger graphic consumed too much room on the page. Try various percentages to determine the size that works best in the letterhead design.

3

- Click the Close button in the Size dialog box to close the dialog box.

Figure 3–11

Other Ways
1. Right-click graphic, click Size on shortcut menu, click Size tab, enter Height and Width values, click Close button

To Recolor a Graphic

The clip art currently is bright red and black, which does not blend well with the current color scheme. In Word, you can change the color of a graphic. The following steps change the color of the graphic to a shade in the current color scheme.

1

- With the graphic still selected, click the Recolor button on the Format tab to display the Recolor gallery (Figure 3–12).

Figure 3–12

2

- Click Accent color 2 Light in the Recolor gallery (third color in Light Variations area) to change the color of the selected graphic in the document window (Figure 3–13).

Q&A

How would I change a graphic back to its original colors?

With the graphic selected, you would click the Reset Picture button on the Format tab or click No Recolor in the Recolor gallery.

Figure 3–13

Other Ways

1. Right-click graphic, click Format Picture on shortcut menu, click Picture in left pane, click Recolor button, select color, click Close button

To Set a Transparent Color in a Graphic

Although the graphic now is the right color scheme, it is difficult to distinguish the objects in the graphic because they use shades of the same color. In Word, you can make one color in a graphic transparent, that is, remove the color. In this project, you make the lighter shades of teal in the graphic transparent, which results in a graphic that is teal and white — making the image easier to identify. The following steps set a transparent color in a graphic.

- With the graphic still selected, click the Recolor button on the Format tab to display the Recolor gallery (Figure 3–14).

Figure 3–14

- Click Set Transparent Color in the Recolor gallery to display a pen mouse pointer in the document window.

- Position the pen mouse pointer in the graphic where you want to make the color transparent (Figure 3–15).

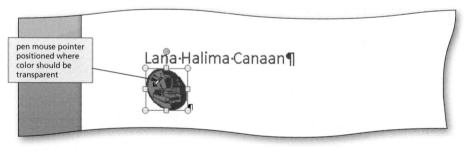

Figure 3–15

③

- Click the location in the graphic where you want the color to be transparent (Figure 3–16).

- Press the END key to deselect the graphic and move the insertion point to the end of the line, which is between the graphic and the paragraph mark.

Figure 3–16

Using Tab Stops to Align Text

In the letterhead, the graphic of the apple and the stack of books is left-aligned (Figure 3–16 on the previous page). The address, phone, and e-mail information in the letterhead is to be positioned at the right margin on the same line. In Word, a paragraph cannot be both left-aligned and right-aligned. If you click the Align Text Right button on the Ribbon, for example, the graphic will be right-aligned. To place text at the right margin of a left-aligned paragraph, you set a tab stop at the right margin. A **tab stop** is a location on the horizontal ruler that tells Word where to position the insertion point when you press the TAB key on the keyboard.

To Display the Ruler

You want to see the location of tab stops on the horizontal ruler. The following step displays the ruler in the document window.

 If the rulers are not displayed already, click the View Ruler button on the vertical scroll bar.

To Set Custom Tab Stops Using the Tabs Dialog Box

Word, by default, places a tab stop at every .5" mark on the ruler (shown in Figure 3–17). These default tab stops are indicated at the bottom of the horizontal ruler by small vertical tick marks. You also can set your own custom tab stops.

The next step in creating the letterhead for this project is to set a custom tab stop at the right margin, that is, at the 6.5" mark on the ruler, because you want the address, phone, and e-mail information at the right margin. One method of setting custom tab stops is to click the ruler at the desired location of the tab stop. You cannot click, however, at the right margin location. Thus, the following steps use the Tabs dialog box to set a custom tab stop.

1
• With the insertion point positioned between the paragraph mark and the graphic, click the Paragraph Dialog Box Launcher to display the Paragraph dialog box (Figure 3–17).

Figure 3–17

2

- Click the Tabs button in the Paragraph dialog box to display the Tabs dialog box.

- Type 6.5 in the Tab stop position text box.

- Click Right in the Alignment area to specify alignment for text at the tab stop (Figure 3–18).

Figure 3–18

3

- Click the Set button in the Tabs dialog box to set a right-aligned custom tab stop.

- Click the OK button to place a right tab marker at the 6.5" mark on the ruler (Figure 3–19).

What happened to all the default tab stops on the ruler?

When you set a custom tab stop, Word clears all default tab stops to the left of the newly set custom tab stop on the ruler.

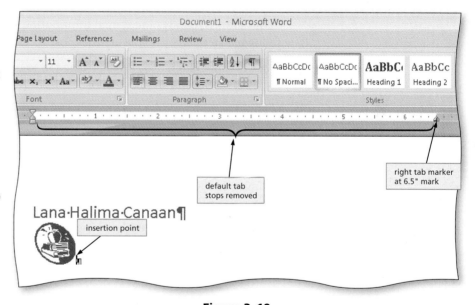

Figure 3–19

Other Ways

1. Right-click paragraph, click Paragraph on shortcut menu, click Tabs button

Tab Stops

Tab settings are a paragraph format. Thus, each time you press the ENTER key, any custom tab stops are carried forward to the next paragraph.

To move the insertion point from one tab stop to another, press the TAB key on the keyboard. When you press the TAB key, a **tab character** formatting mark appears in the empty space between the tab stops.

When you set a custom tab stop, you specify how the text will align at a tab stop. The tab marker on the ruler reflects the alignment of the characters at the location of the tab stop. Table 3–1 shows types of tab stop alignments in Word and their corresponding tab markers. To change an existing tab stop's alignment, double-click the tab marker on the ruler to display the Tabs dialog box (or display the Tabs dialog box as described in the steps on the previous page), click the tab stop position you wish to change, click the new alignment, and then click the OK button. You can remove an existing tab stop by clicking the tab stop position in the Tabs dialog box and then clicking the Clear button in the dialog box. To remove all tab stops, click the Clear All button in the Tabs dialog box.

Table 3–1 Types of Tab Stop Alignments

Tab Stop	Tab Marker	Result of Pressing Tab Key	Example
Left Tab	L	Left-aligns text at the location of the tab stop	toolbar ruler
Center Tab	⊥	Centers text at location of the tab stop	toolbar ruler
Right Tab	⅃	Right-aligns text at location of the tab stop	toolbar ruler
Decimal Tab	⊥	Aligns text on decimal point at location of the tab stop	45.72 223.75
Bar Tab	I	Aligns text at a bar character at the location of the tab stop	toolbar ruler

To Specify Font Color before Typing

The address, phone, and e-mail information should be the same color as the name. The following steps enter text using the most recently defined color.

1 Click the Font Color button on the Home tab so that the text you type will be the color displayed on the face of the button.

Q&A What if the color I want is not displayed on the face of the Font Color button?

Click the Font Color button arrow and then click the desired color in the Font Color gallery.

2 With the insertion point positioned between the graphic and the paragraph mark (as shown in Figure 3–19 on the previous page), press the TAB key to move the insertion point to the 6.5" mark on the ruler.

3 Type 22 Fifth Street, Juniper, NV 89268 * Phone: 420-555-2939 * E-mail: lhc@world.net in the letterhead (Figure 3–20).

Figure 3–20

To Bottom Border a Paragraph

The letterhead in this project has a horizontal line that extends from the left margin to the right margin immediately below the address, phone, and e-mail information. In Word, you can draw a solid line, called a **border**, at any edge of a paragraph. That is, borders may be added above or below a paragraph, to the left or right of a paragraph, or in any combination of these sides. The following steps add a bottom border to the paragraph containing address, phone, and e-mail information.

1

- With the insertion point in the paragraph to border, click the Border button arrow on the Home tab to display the Border gallery (Figure 3–21).

Figure 3–21

2

- Click Bottom Border in the Border gallery to place a border below the paragraph containing the insertion point (Figure 3–22).

Q&A
If the face of the Border button displays the border icon I want to use, can I click the Border button instead of using the Border button arrow?

Yes.

Figure 3–22

Q&A
How would I remove an existing border from a paragraph?

If, for some reason, you wanted to remove a border from a paragraph, you would position the insertion point in the paragraph, click the Border button arrow on the Home tab, and then click No Border (Figure 3–21) in the Border gallery.

Other Ways
1. Click Page Borders on Page Layout tab, click Borders tab in Borders and Shading   dialog box, select desired border, click OK

To Clear Formatting

The next step is to position the insertion point below the letterhead, so that you can type the content of the letter. When you press the ENTER key at the end of a paragraph containing a border, Word moves the border forward to the next paragraph. It also retains all current settings. That is, the paragraph text will be teal and will have a bottom border. Instead, you want the paragraph and characters on the new line to use the Normal style: black font with no border. In Word, the term, **clear formatting**, refers to returning the formatting to the Normal style. The following steps clear formatting at the location of the insertion point.

- With the insertion point between the e-mail address and paragraph mark (as shown in Figure 3–22 on the previous page), press the ENTER key (Figure 3–23).

Figure 3–23

- Click the Clear Formatting button on the Home tab to apply the Normal style to the location of the insertion point (Figure 3–24).

Figure 3–24

Other Ways

1. Click More button in Styles gallery on Home tab, click Clear Formatting
2. Click Styles Dialog Box Launcher, click Clear All in Styles task pane
3. Press CTRL+SPACEBAR, press CTRL+Q

AutoFormat As You Type

As you type text in a document, Word automatically formats it for you. For example, when you press the ENTER key or SPACEBAR after typing an e-mail address or Web address, Word automatically formats the address as a hyperlink, that is, colored blue and underlined. In Figure 3–23, Word formatted the e-mail address as a hyperlink because you pressed the ENTER key at the end of the line. Table 3–2 outlines commonly used AutoFormat As You Type options and their results.

Table 3–2 Commonly Used AutoFormat As You Type Options

Typed Text	AutoFormat Feature	Example
Quotation marks or apostrophes	Changes straight quotation marks or apostrophes to curly ones	"the" becomes "the"
Text, a space, one hyphen, one or no spaces, text, space	Changes the hyphen to an en dash	ages 20 - 45 becomes ages 20 – 45
Text, two hyphens, text, space	Changes the two hyphens to an em dash	Two types--yellow and red becomes Two types—yellow and red
Web or e-mail address followed by SPACEBAR or ENTER key	Formats Web or e-mail address as a hyperlink	www.scsite.com becomes www.scsite.com
Three hyphens, underscores, equal signs, asterisks, tildes, or number signs and then ENTER key	Places a border above a paragraph	--- This line becomes This line

Number followed by a period, hyphen, right parenthesis, or greater than sign and then a space or tab followed by text	Creates a numbered list when you press the SPACEBAR or TAB key	1. Word
		2. Excel
		becomes
		   1. Word
		   2. Excel

Asterisk, hyphen, or greater than sign and then a space or tab followed by text	Creates a bulleted list when you press the SPACEBAR or TAB key	* Home tab
		* Insert tab
		becomes
		   • Home tab
		   • Insert tab

Fraction and then a space or hyphen	Condenses the fraction entry so that it consumes one space instead of three	1/2 becomes ½
Ordinal and then a space or hyphen	Makes part of the ordinal a superscript	3rd becomes 3rd

To Convert a Hyperlink to Regular Text

The e-mail address in the letterhead should be formatted as regular text; that is, it should not be blue or underlined. Thus, the next step is to remove the hyperlink format from the e-mail address in the letterhead.

1
- Right-click the hyperlink (in this case, the e-mail address) to display the Mini toolbar and a shortcut menu (Figure 3–25).

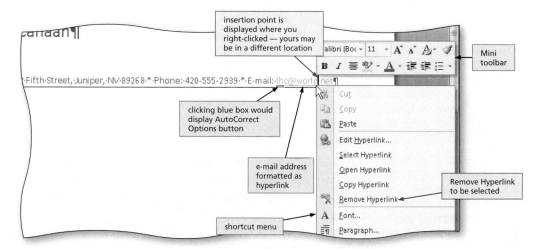

insertion point is displayed where you right-clicked — yours may be in a different location

Mini toolbar

clicking blue box would display AutoCorrect Options button

e-mail address formatted as hyperlink

Remove Hyperlink to be selected

shortcut menu

Cut
Copy
Paste
Edit Hyperlink...
Select Hyperlink
Open Hyperlink
Copy Hyperlink
Remove Hyperlink
Font...
Paragraph...

Figure 3–25

2

- Click Remove Hyperlink on the shortcut menu to remove the hyperlink format from the e-mail address.

- Position the insertion point on the paragraph mark below the border (Figure 3-26).

Q&A

Could I have used the AutoCorrect Options button instead of the Remove Hyperlink command?

Yes. Alternatively, you could have pointed to the small blue box at the beginning of the hyperlink, clicked the AutoCorrect Options button, and then clicked Undo Hyperlink on the AutoCorrect Options menu.

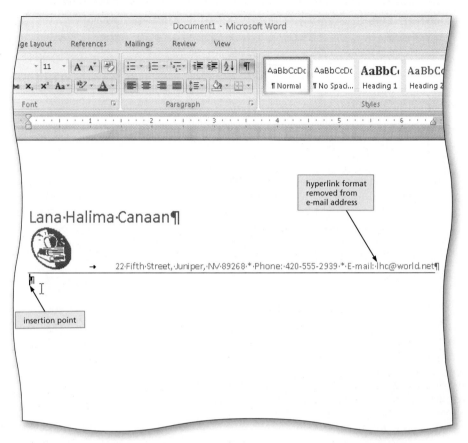

Figure 3–26

Other Ways

1. With insertion point in hyperlink, click Hyperlink button on Insert tab, click Remove Link button

To Save the Letterhead

The letterhead now is complete. Thus, you should save it in a file. For a detailed example of the procedure summarized below, refer to pages WD 19 through WD 21 in Chapter 1.

1 With a USB flash drive connected to one of the computer's USB ports, click the Save button on the Quick Access Toolbar to display the Save As dialog box.

2 Type `Canaan Letterhead` in the File name text box to change the file name.

3 Click the Save in box arrow and select the USB flash drive as the new save location.

4 Click the Save button in the Save As dialog box to save the document on the USB flash drive with the file name, Canaan Letterhead.

Q&A

How can I keep reusing this same letterhead file for every letter I create?

If the letterhead file is not yet opened, you can instruct Word to create a new document window that contains the contents of an existing document. If the letterhead file is already opened, you can save the file with a new file name.

BTW

Saving a Template
As an alternative to saving the letterhead as a Word document, you could save it as a template by clicking the Office Button, pointing to Save As, clicking Word Template, clicking Trusted Templates in the My Places bar, entering the template name, and then clicking the Save button. To use the template, click the Office Button, click New, click My templates in the left pane, and then double-click the template icon or name.

To Create a New File from an Existing File

If you wish to open a new document window that contains the contents of an existing file, you would follow these steps.

1. Click the Office Button and then click New to display the New Document dialog box.
2. Click 'New from existing' in the Templates area to display the New from Existing Document dialog box.
3. If necessary, click the Look in box arrow and then locate and select the file from which you wish to create a new file.
4. Click the Create New button.

Creating a Cover Letter

You have created a letterhead for the cover letter. The next step is to compose the cover letter. The following pages use Word to compose a cover letter that contains a table and a bulleted list.

Compose an effective cover letter.
You always should send a personalized cover letter with a resume. The cover letter should highlight aspects of your background relevant to the position. To help you recall past achievements and activities, keep a personal file containing documents that outline your accomplishments.

A cover letter is a type of business letter. When composing a business letter, you need to be sure to include all essential elements and to decide which letter style to use.

- **Include all essential letter elements.** All business letters, including cover letters, contain the same basic elements. Essential business letter elements include the date line, inside address, message, and signature block (shown in Figure 3–1 on page WD 147).

- **Determine which letter style to use.** You can follow many different styles when creating business letters. A letter style specifies guidelines for the alignment and spacing of elements in the business letter.

Plan
Ahead

To Save the Document with a New File Name

The current open file has the name Canaan Letterhead, which is the name of the personal letterhead. You want the letterhead to remain intact. Thus, the following steps save the document with a new file name.

1 With a USB flash drive connected to one of the computer's USB ports, click the Office Button to display the Office Button menu and then click Save As on the Office Button menu to display the Save As dialog box.

2 Type Canaan Cover Letter in the File name text box to change the file name.

3 If necessary, click the Save in box arrow and then select the USB flash drive as the new save location.

4 Click the Save button in the Save As dialog box to save the document on the USB flash drive with the file name, Canaan Cover Letter.

To Apply a Quick Style

When you press the ENTER key in the letter, you want the insertion point to advance to the next line, with no blank space between the lines. Recall that, by default, the Normal style in Word places 10 points of blank space after each paragraph and inserts a blank space equal to 1.15 lines between each line of text. The No Spacing style, however, does not put any blank space between lines when you press the ENTER key. Thus, the following step applies the No Spacing style to the current paragraph.

 Click No Spacing in the Styles gallery to apply the No Spacing style to the current paragraph.

Plan Ahead

> **Include all essential letter elements.**
> Be sure to include all essential business letter elements, properly spaced, in your cover letter.
>
> - The **date line**, which consists of the month, day, and year, is positioned two to six lines below the letterhead.
>
> - The **inside address**, placed three to eight lines below the date line, usually contains the addressee's courtesy title plus full name, job title, business affiliation, and full geographical address.
>
> - The **salutation**, if present, begins two lines below the last line of the inside address. If you do not know the recipient's name, avoid using the salutation "To whom it may concern" — it is impersonal. Instead, use the recipient's title in the salutation, e.g., Dear Personnel Director.
>
> - The body of the letter, the **message**, begins two lines below the salutation. Within the message, paragraphs are single-spaced with one blank line between paragraphs.
>
> - Two lines below the last line of the message, the **complimentary close** is displayed. Capitalize only the first word in a complimentary close.
>
> - Type the **signature block** at least four blank lines below the complimentary close, allowing room for the author to sign his or her name.

Plan Ahead

> **Determine which letter style to use.**
> Three common business letter styles are the block, the modified block, and the modified semi-block. Each style specifies different alignments and indentations.
>
> - In the block letter style, all components of the letter begin flush with the left margin.
>
> - In the modified block letter style, the date, complimentary close, and signature block are positioned approximately one-half inch to the right of center, or at the right margin. All other components of the letter begin flush with the left margin.
>
> - In the modified semi-block letter style, the date, complimentary close, and signature block are centered, positioned approximately one-half inch to the right of center, or at the right margin. The first line of each paragraph in the body of the letter is indented one-half to one inch from the left margin. All other components of the letter begin flush with the left margin.
>
> The cover letter in this project follows the modified block style.

To Set Custom Tab Stops Using the Ruler

The first required element of the cover letter is the date line, which in this letter is to be positioned two lines below the letterhead. The date line contains the month, day, and year, and begins 3.5 inches from the left margin, or approximately one-half inch to the right of center. Thus, you should set a custom tab stop at the 3.5" mark on the ruler. Earlier you used the Tabs dialog box to set a tab stop because you could not use the ruler to set a tab stop at the right margin. The following steps set a left-aligned tab stop using the ruler.

1

- With the insertion point on the paragraph mark below the border, press the ENTER key so that a blank line appears between the letterhead and the date line.

- If necessary, click the tab selector at the left edge of the horizontal ruler until it displays the Left Tab icon.

- Position the mouse pointer on the 3.5" mark on the ruler (Figure 3–27).

Q&A What is the purpose of the tab selector?

Before using the ruler to set a tab stop, you must ensure the correct tab stop icon appears in the tab selector. Each time you click the tab selector, its icon changes. For a list of the types of tab stops, see Table 3–1 on page WD 160.

Figure 3–27

2

- Click the 3.5" mark on the ruler to place a left tab marker at that location on the ruler (Figure 3–28).

Q&A What if I click the wrong location on the ruler?

You can move a custom tab stop by dragging the tab marker to the desired location on the ruler. Or, you can remove a custom tab stop by pointing to the tab marker on the ruler and then dragging the tab marker down and out of the ruler.

Figure 3–28

To Insert the Current Date in a Document

The next step is to enter the current date at the 3.5" tab stop in the document, as specified in the guidelines for a modified block style letter. Word provides a method of inserting a computer's system date in a document. The following steps insert the current date in the cover letter.

- Press the TAB key.

- Click Insert on the Ribbon to display the Insert tab.

- Click the Insert Date and Time button on the Insert tab to display the Date and Time dialog box.

- Click the desired format (in this case, May 12, 2008) in the dialog box.

- If the Update automatically check box is selected, click the check box to remove the check mark (Figure 3–29).

Why should the Update automatically check box not be selected?

In this project, the date at the top of the letter should always show today's date. If, however, you wanted the date always to change to reflect the current computer date, for example showing the date you open or print the letter, then you would put a check mark in this check box.

Figure 3–29

2

● Click the OK button to insert the current date at the location of the insertion point (Figure 3–30).

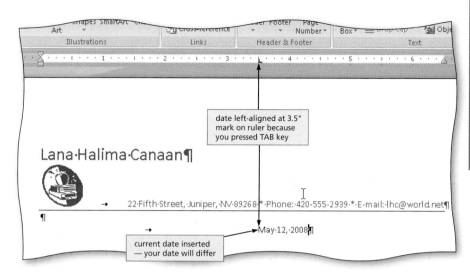

date left-aligned at 3.5" mark on ruler because you pressed TAB key

Lana·Halima·Canaan¶

→ 22·Fifth·Street,·Juniper,·NV·89268·*·Phone:·420-555-2939·*·E-mail:·lhc@world.net¶
¶
→ ►May·12,·2008¶

current date inserted — your date will differ

Figure 3–30

To Enter the Inside Address and Salutation

The next step in composing the cover letter is to type the inside address and salutation.

1 With the insertion point at the end of the date, press the ENTER key three times.

2 Type Mr. Raul Ramos and then press the ENTER key.

3 Type Personnel Director and then press the ENTER key.

4 Type Juniper Culinary Academy and then press the ENTER key.

5 Type 202 Park Boulevard and then press the ENTER key.

6 Type Juniper, NV 89268 and then press the ENTER key twice.

7 Type Dear Mr. Ramos and then press the COLON key (:) to complete the entries of the inside address and salutation (Figure 3–31).

Lana·Halima·Canaan¶

→ 22·Fifth·Street,·Juniper,·NV·89268·*·Phone:·420-555-2939·*·E-mail:·lhc@world.net¶
¶
→ May·12,·2008¶
¶
¶
Mr.·Raul·Ramos¶
Personnel·Director¶
Juniper·Culinary·Academy¶
202·Park·Boulevard¶
Juniper,·NV·89268¶
¶
Dear·Mr.·Ramos:¶

inside address entered

salutation entered

Figure 3–31

To Create a Building Block

If you use the same text or graphic frequently, you can store the text or graphic in a **building block** and then use the stored building block entry in the open document, as well as in future documents. That is, you can create the entry once as a building block, and for all future occurrences of the text or graphic, you can insert the building block as you need it. In this way, you avoid entering the text or graphics inconsistently or incorrectly in different locations throughout the same document.

The next steps create a building block for the prospective employer's name, Juniper Culinary Academy. Later in the chapter, you will insert the building block in the document instead of typing the employer's name.

- Select the text to be a building block, in this case, Juniper Culinary Academy. Do not select the paragraph mark at the end of the text.

Why is the paragraph mark not part of the building block?

Only select the paragraph mark if you want to store paragraph formatting, such as indentation and line spacing, as part of the building block.

- Click the Quick Parts button on the Insert tab to display the Quick Parts menu (Figure 3–32).

Figure 3–32

- Click Save Selection to Quick Part Gallery on the Quick Parts menu to display the Create New Building Block dialog box.

- Type jca in the Name text box to replace the proposed building block name (Juniper Culinary) with a shorter building block name (Figure 3–33).

Figure 3–33

- Click the OK button to store the building block entry and close the dialog box.

- If Word displays another dialog box, click the Yes button.

Other Ways

1. Select text, press ALT+F3

To Insert a Nonbreaking Space

Some compound words, such as proper nouns, dates, units of time and measure, abbreviations, and geographic destinations, should not be divided at the end of a line. These words either should fit as a unit at the end of a line or be wrapped together to the next line.

Word provides two special characters to assist with this task: nonbreaking space and nonbreaking hyphen. A **nonbreaking space** is a special space character that prevents two words from splitting if the first word falls at the end of a line. Similarly, a **nonbreaking hyphen** is a special type of hyphen that prevents two words separated by a hyphen from splitting at the end of a line.

The following steps insert a nonbreaking space between the words in the newspaper name.

- Click to the right of the colon in the salutation and then press the ENTER key twice to position the insertion point one blank line below the salutation.

- Type I am responding to the junior culinary instructor position that you recently advertised in the and then press the SPACEBAR.

- Press CTRL+I to turn on italics. Type Juniper as the first word in the newspaper name and then press CTRL+SHIFT+SPACEBAR to insert a nonbreaking space after the word, Juniper (Figure 3–34).

Figure 3–34

2

- Type Daily and then press CTRL+SHIFT+SPACEBAR to insert another nonbreaking space after the word, Daily.

- Type Herald and then press CTRL+I to turn off italics. Press the PERIOD key (Figure 3–35).

Figure 3–35

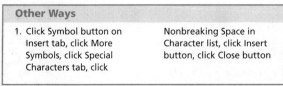

Other Ways
1. Click Symbol button on Insert tab, click More Symbols, click Special Characters tab, click   Nonbreaking Space in Character list, click Insert button, click Close button

To Insert a Building Block

At the end of the next sentence in the body of the cover letter, you want the prospective employer name, Juniper Culinary Academy, to be displayed. Recall that earlier in this chapter, you created a building block name of jca for Juniper Culinary Academy. Thus, you will type the building block name and then instruct Word to replace the building block name with the stored building block entry of Juniper Culinary Academy. The following steps insert a building block.

- Press the SPACEBAR. Type As indicated on the enclosed resume, I have the credentials you are seeking and believe I can be a valuable asset to jca as shown in Figure 3–36.

Figure 3–36

- Press the F3 key to instruct word to replace the building block name (jca) with the stored building block entry (Juniper Culinary Academy).

- Press the PERIOD key (Figure 3–37).

Figure 3–37

Other Ways

1. Click Quick Parts button on Insert tab, click desired building block

Building Blocks vs. AutoCorrect

In Project 2, you learned how to use the AutoCorrect feature, which enables you to insert and create AutoCorrect entries, similarly to how you created and inserted building blocks in this chapter. The difference between an AutoCorrect entry and a building block entry is that the AutoCorrect feature makes corrections for you automatically as soon as you press the SPACEBAR or type a punctuation mark, whereas you must instruct Word to insert a building block. That is, you enter the building block name and then press the F3 key, or click the Quick Parts button and select the building block from the list.

To Enter a Paragraph

The next step in creating the cover letter is to enter a paragraph of text.

1. Press the ENTER key twice to place a blank line between paragraphs, according to the guidelines of the modified block letter style.

2 Type I recently received my bachelor's degree in culinary arts from Nevada Culinary Institute. The following table outlines my areas of concentration:

3 Press the ENTER key twice.

Tables

The next step in composing the cover letter is to place a table listing the number of credit hours for areas of concentration (shown in Figure 3–1 on page WD 147). A Word **table** is a collection of rows and columns. The intersection of a row and a column is called a **cell**, and cells are filled with text.

The first step in creating a table is to insert an empty table into the document. When inserting a table, you must specify the total number of rows and columns required, which is called the **dimension** of the table. The table in this project has two columns. You often do not know the total number of rows in a table. Thus, many Word users create one row initially and then add more rows as needed. In Word, the first number in a dimension is the number of columns, and the second is the number of rows. For example, in Word, a 2 × 1 (pronounced "two by one") table consists of two columns and one row.

To Insert an Empty Table

The next step is to insert an empty table in the cover letter. The following steps insert a table with two columns and one row at the location of the insertion point.

1

• Click the Table button on the Insert tab to display the Table gallery.

🔍 **Experiment**

• Point to various cells on the grid to see a preview of the table in the document window.

2

• Position the mouse pointer on the cell in the first row and second column of the grid to preview the desired table dimension (Figure 3–38).

Figure 3–38

3

- Click the cell in the first row and second column of the grid to insert an empty table with one row and two columns in the document (Figure 3–39).

Q&A

What are the small circles in the table cells?

Each table cell has an **end-of-cell mark**, which is a formatting mark that assists you with selecting and formatting cells. Similarly, each row has an **end-of-row mark**, which you can use to add columns to the right of a table. Recall that formatting marks do not print on a hard copy. The end-of-cell marks currently are left-aligned, that is, positioned at the left edge of each cell.

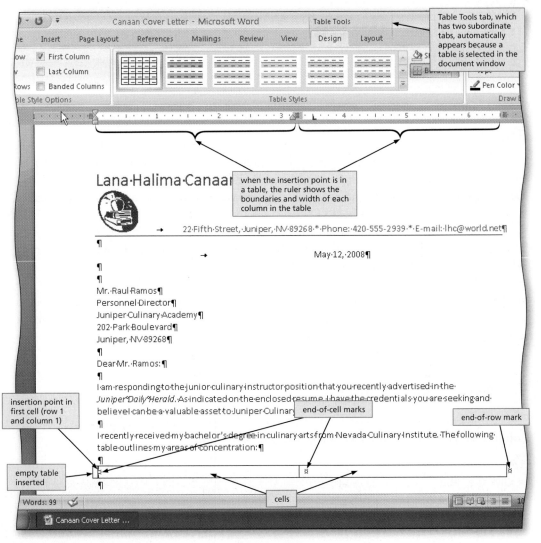

Figure 3–39

Other Ways

1. Click Table on Insert tab, click Insert Table on Table gallery, enter number of columns and rows, click OK

To Enter Data in a Table

The next step is to enter data in the cells of the empty table. The data you enter in a cell wordwraps just as text wordwraps between the margins of a document. To place data in a cell, you click the cell and then type.

To advance rightward from one cell to the next, press the TAB key. When you are at the rightmost cell in a row, press the TAB key to move to the first cell in the next row; do not press the ENTER key. The ENTER key is used to begin a new paragraph within a cell. One way to add new rows to a table is to press the TAB key when the insertion point is positioned in the bottom-right corner cell of the table. The next steps enter data in the table, adding rows as necessary.

1

- If necessary, scroll the table up in the document window.

- With the insertion point in the left cell of the table, type Food Planning and Preparation and then press the TAB key to advance the insertion point to the next cell.

- Type 30 hours and then press the TAB key to add a second row to the table and position the insertion point in the first column of that row (Figure 3–40).

Q&A

How do I edit cell contents if I make a mistake?

Click in the cell and then correct the entry.

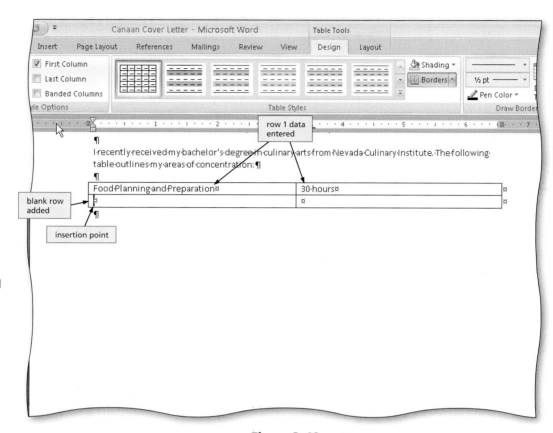

Figure 3–40

2

- Type Food Safety and then press the TAB key. Type 15 hours and then press the TAB key.

- Type Nutrition and then press the TAB key. Type 15 hours and then press the TAB key.

- Type Regional and International Cuisine and then press the TAB key. Type 21 hours to complete the entries in the table (Figure 3–41).

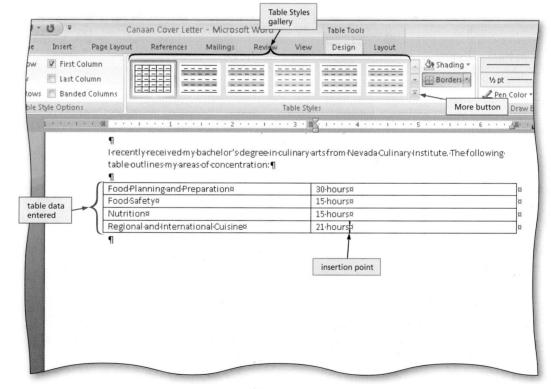

Figure 3–41

To Apply a Table Style

The next step is to apply a table style to the table. Word provides a Table Styles gallery, allowing you to change the basic table format to a more visually appealing style. Word provides a gallery of more than 90 table styles, which include a variety of colors and shading. In this project, you do not want the heading rows or alternating rows to use a different format; that is, you want the formatting applied to the rows in the table to be the same. The following steps apply a table style to the table in the cover letter.

1

- With the insertion point in the table, remove the check marks from the Header Row and Banded Rows check boxes in the Design tab so that all rows in the table will be formatted the same.

Q&A

What if the Design tab in the Table Tools tab no longer is the active tab?

Click in the table and then click Design on the Ribbon.

2

- Click the More button in the Table Styles gallery (shown in Figure 3–41 on the previous page) to expand the Table Styles gallery.

- Scroll and then point to Medium Grid 3 - Accent 2 In the Table Styles gallery to display a live preview of that style applied to the table in the document (Figure 3–42).

Experiment

- Point to various table styles in the Table Styles gallery and watch the format of the table change in the document window.

Figure 3–42

- Click Medium Grid
  3 - Accent 2 in the
  Table Styles gallery
  to apply the selected
  style to the table
  (Figure 3–43).

Figure 3–43

To Resize Table Columns to Fit Table Contents

The table in this project currently extends from the left margin to the right margin of the document. You want each column only to be as wide as the longest entry in the table. That is, the first column must be wide enough to accommodate the words, Regional and International Cuisine, and the second column should be only as wide as the hours entered. The following steps instruct Word to fit the width of the columns to the contents of the table automatically.

- With the insertion
  point in the table,
  click Layout on the
  Ribbon to display
  the Layout tab.

- Click the AutoFit
  button on the
  Layout tab
  (Figure 3–44).

Figure 3–44

2

- Click AutoFit Contents on the AutoFit menu, so that Word automatically adjusts the widths of the columns based on the text in the table (Figure 3–45).

Q&A

Can I resize columns manually?

Yes, you can drag a **column boundary**, the border to the right of a column, until the column is the desired width. Similarly, you can resize a row by dragging the **row boundary**, the border at the bottom of a row, until the row is the desired height. You also can resize the entire table by dragging the **table resize handle**, which is a small square that appears when you point to a corner of the table (shown in Figure 3–46).

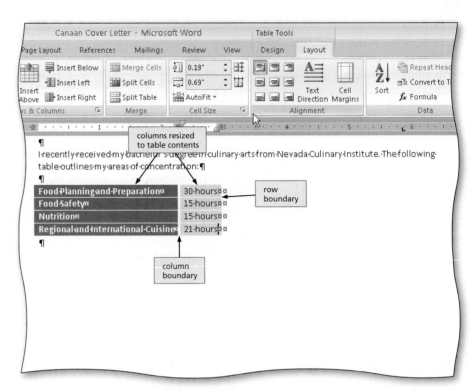

Figure 3–45

Other Ways

1. Right-click table, point to AutoFit on shortcut menu, click AutoFit to Contents
2. Double-click column boundary

Selecting Table Contents

When working with tables, you may need to select the contents of cells, rows, columns, or the entire table. Table 3–3 identifies ways to select various items in a table.

Table 3–3 Selecting Items in a Table	
Item to Select	**Action**
Cell	Click left edge of cell
Column	Click border at top of column
Multiple cells, rows, or columns adjacent to one another	Drag through cells, rows, or columns
Multiple cells, rows, or columns not adjacent to one another	Select first cell, row, or column and then hold down CTRL key while selecting next cell, row, or column
Next cell	Press TAB key
Previous cell	Press SHIFT+TAB
Row	Click to left of row
Table	Click table move handle

BTW

Tab Character
In a table, the TAB key advances the insertion point from one cell to the next in a table. To insert a tab character in a cell, you must press CTRL+TAB.

To Select a Table

When you first create a table, it is left-aligned, that is, flush with the left margin. In this cover letter, the table should be centered. To center a table, you first select the entire table.

1

- Position the mouse pointer in the table so that the table move handle appears.

- Click the table move handle to select the entire table (Figure 3–46).

Figure 3–46

Other Ways

1. Click Select button on Layout tab, click Select Table on Select menu

To Center a Selected Table

The following steps center the selected table between the margins.

1 Move the mouse pointer into the Mini toolbar, so that the toolbar changes to a bright toolbar.

2 Click the Center button on the Mini toolbar to center the selected table between the left and right margins (Figure 3–47).

Q&A When should I use the Mini toolbar versus the Ribbon?

If the command you want to use is not on the currently displayed tab on the Ribbon and it is available on the Mini toolbar, use the Mini toolbar instead of switching to a different tab. This technique minimizes mouse movement.

Q&A How would I center the contents of the table cells instead of the entire table?

If you wanted to center the contents of the cells, you would select the cells by dragging through them and then click the Center button.

BTW

Tables
For simple tables, such as the one just created, Word users often select the table dimension in the grid to create the table. For more complex tables, such as one with a varying number of columns per row, Word has a Draw Table feature that allows users to draw a table in the document using a pencil pointer. To use this feature, click Table on the Insert tab and then click Draw Table.

Figure 3–47

Adding and Deleting Table Rows

As discussed in the previous steps, you can add a row to the end of a table by positioning the insertion point in the bottom-right corner cell and then pressing the TAB key. You also can add rows to a table by clicking the Insert Above button or Insert Below button on the Layout tab to insert a row above or below the location of the insertion point in the table. Similarly, you can right-click the table, point to Insert on the shortcut menu, and then click Insert Rows Above or Insert Rows Below.

To add columns to a table, click the Insert Left button or Insert Right button on the Layout tab to insert a column to the left or right of the location of the insertion point in the table. Similarly, you can right-click the table, point to Insert on the shortcut menu, and then click Insert Columns to the Left or Insert Columns to the Right.

If you want to delete row(s) or delete column(s) from a table, position the insertion point in the row(s) or column(s) to delete, click the Delete button on the Layout tab, and then click Delete Rows or Delete Columns. Or, select the row or column to delete, right-click the selection, and then click Delete Rows or Delete Columns on the shortcut menu.

To delete the contents of a cell, select the cell contents by pointing to the left edge of a cell and clicking when the mouse pointer changes direction, and then press the DELETE key. You also can drag and drop or cut and paste the contents of cells.

BTW

Table Rows and Columns
To change the width of a column to an exact measurement, hold down the ALT key while dragging markers on the ruler. Or, enter values in the Table Row Height and Table Column Width boxes in the Layout tab.

To Add More Text

The next step is to add more text below the table.

1 Position the insertion point on the paragraph mark below the table and then press the ENTER key.

2 Type `In addition to my coursework, I have the following culinary experience:` and then press the ENTER key.

To Bullet a List as You Type

In Chapter 1, you learned how to apply bullets to existing paragraphs. If you know before you type that a list should be bulleted, you can use Word's AutoFormat As You Type feature to bullet the paragraphs as you type them (Table 3–2 on page WD 163). The following steps add bullets to a list as you type.

1

- Press the ASTERISK key (*) as the first character on the line (Figure 3–48).

Figure 3–48

2

- Press the SPACEBAR to convert the asterisk to a bullet character.

 Q&A
What if I did not want the asterisk converted to a bullet character?

You would undo the AutoFormat by clicking the Undo button, or by clicking the AutoCorrect Options button and then clicking Undo Automatic Bullets on the AutoCorrect Options menu, or by clicking the Bullets button on the Home tab.

- Type Assist with food preparation at my family's local pastry, bread, and bakery business as the first bulleted item.

- Press the ENTER key to place another bullet character at the beginning of the next line (Figure 3–49).

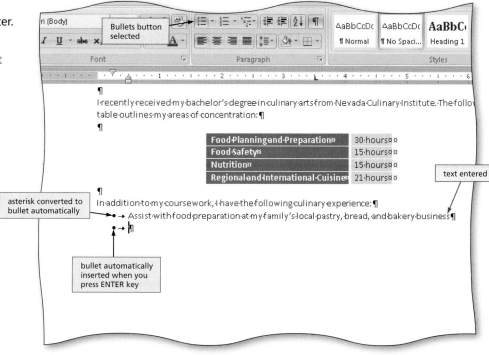

Figure 3–49

3

- Type Prepare food and serve meals at Hope Mission and then press the ENTER key.

- Type Assisted the chef with meal preparation and presentation during internship at The Garden Grill and then press the ENTER key.

- Type Prepared salads, soups, sandwiches, en-trees, and desserts while working at the school cafeteria and then press the ENTER key.

- Press the ENTER key to turn off automatic bullets as you type (Figure 3–50).

Q&A
Why did automatic bullets stop?

When you press the ENTER key without entering any text after the automatic bullet character, Word turns off the automatic bullets feature.

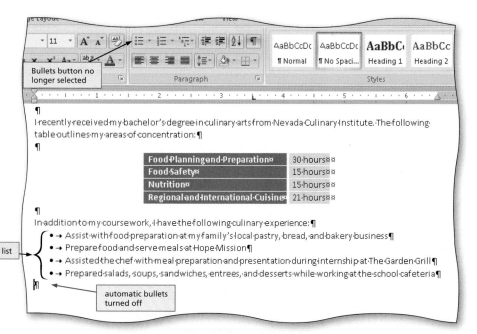

Figure 3–50

Other Ways
1. Click Bullets button on Home tab
2. Right-click paragraph to be bulleted, click bullets button on Mini toolbar
3. Right-click paragraph to be bulleted, point to Bullets on shortcut menu, click desired bullet style

To Enter the Remainder of the Cover Letter

The next step is to enter the remainder of the cover letter.

1 Press the ENTER key and then type the paragraph shown in Figure 3–51, making certain you use the building block name, jca, to insert the employer name.

2 Press the ENTER key twice. Press the TAB key. Type Sincerely and then press the COMMA key.

3 Press the ENTER key four times. Press the TAB key. Type Lana Halima Canaan and then press the ENTER key twice. Type Enclosure as the final text in the cover letter (Figure 3–51).

Figure 3–51

To Change Document Properties

Before saving the research paper again, you want to add your name, course and section, and some keywords as document properties. The following steps use the Document Information Panel to change document properties.

1 Display the Office Button menu, point to Prepare on the Office Button menu, and then click Properties on the Prepare submenu to display the Document Information Panel.

2 Click the Author text box, if necessary, and then type your name as the Author property. If a name already is displayed in the Author text box, delete it before typing your name. Click the Subject text box, if necessary delete any existing text, and then type your course and section as the Subject property. Click the Keywords text box, if necessary delete any existing text, and then type cover letter as the Keywords property.

3 Close the Document Information Panel.

To Save an Existing Document and Print It

The document now is complete. You should save the cover letter again. The following steps save the document again and then print it. Do not close the Canaan Cover Letter file. You will use it again later in this chapter to copy the address, phone, and e-mail information to the resume.

1 Click the Save button on the Quick Access Toolbar to overwrite the previous Canaan Cover Letter file on the USB flash drive.

2 Display the Office Button menu, point to Print, and then click Quick Print to print the cover letter (shown in Figure 3–1 on page WD 147).

Using a Template to Create a Resume

The next step in this project is to create the resume (Figure 3–2 on page WD 148). Although you could compose a resume in a blank document window, this chapter shows instead how to use a template, where Word formats the resume with appropriate headings and spacing. You customize the resume created by the template by filling in blanks and by selecting and replacing text.

Plan
Ahead

Craft a successful resume.

Two types of resumes are the chronological resume and the functional resume. A chronological resume sequences information by time, with the most recent listed first. This type of resume highlights a job seeker's job continuity and growth. A functional resume groups information by skills and accomplishments. This resume emphasizes a job seeker's experience and qualifications in specialized areas. Some resumes use a combination of the two formats. For an entry-level job search, experts recommend a chronological resume or a combination of the two types of resumes.

When creating your resume, be sure to include necessary information and present it appropriately. Keep descriptions short and concise, using action words and bulleted lists.

- **Include necessary information.** Your resume should include contact information, a clearly written objective, educational background, and experience. Use your complete legal name and mailing address, along with phone number and e-mail address, if one exists. Other sections you might consider including are organizations, recognitions and awards, and skills. Do not include your social security number, marital status, age, height, weight, gender, physical appearance, health, citizenship, previous pay rates, reasons for leaving a prior job, current date, high-school information (if you are a college graduate), and references. Employers assume you will give references, if asked, and this information simply clutters a resume.

- **Present your resume appropriately.** For printed resumes, use a high-quality ink-jet or laser printer to print your resume (and cover letter) on standard letter-size white or ivory paper. Consider using paper that contains cotton fibers for a professional look. Select envelopes that are the same quality and grade as the paper. If you e-mail the resume, consider that the potential employer may not have the same software you used to create the resume and thus may not be able to open it up. As an alternative, you could save the file in a format, such as a PDF, that can be viewed with a reader program. Many job seekers also post their resume on the Web.

BTW

Saving in the PDF Format
To save a Word document in the PDF format, you need to install the Save as PDF add-in from Microsoft. Use Help to search for the term, PDF, to assist with this process. Once installed, the PDF or XPS command will appear when you point to Save As on the Office Button menu. Both the PDF and XPS formats are intended to enable users to share documents easily with other users.

To Use a Template

Word installs a variety of templates for letters, fax cover sheets, reports, and resumes on your hard disk. The templates are grouped into five styles: Equity, Median, Oriel, Origin, and Urban. The templates in each style use similar formatting, themes, etc., enabling users to create a set of documents that complement one another. In this chapter, you will create a resume from the template in the Origin style. The following steps create a new document based on a template.

1
- Display the Office Button menu (Figure 3–52).

Figure 3–52

2

- Click New on the Office Button menu to display the New Document dialog box.

- Click Installed Templates in the Templates area to display the list of templates on the hard disk.

Experiment

- Click various installed templates in the Templates list and watch the preview of the template display at the right edge of the dialog box.

Figure 3–53

3

- Scroll through the Installed Templates list and then click Origin Resume to select it (Figure 3–53).

Q&A How do I access a template on the Web?

If you are connected to the Internet when you click the desired template in the Microsoft Office Online area of the New Document dialog box, Word automatically displays templates from the Microsoft Office Online Web page that you can download.

4

- Click the Create button to create a new document based on the selected template (Figure 3–54).

Figure 3–54

To Print the Resume

To see the entire resume created by the resume template, print the document shown in the Word window.

1 Ready the printer. Display the Office Button menu, point to Print, and then click Quick Print to print the resume created from the template (Figure 3–55).

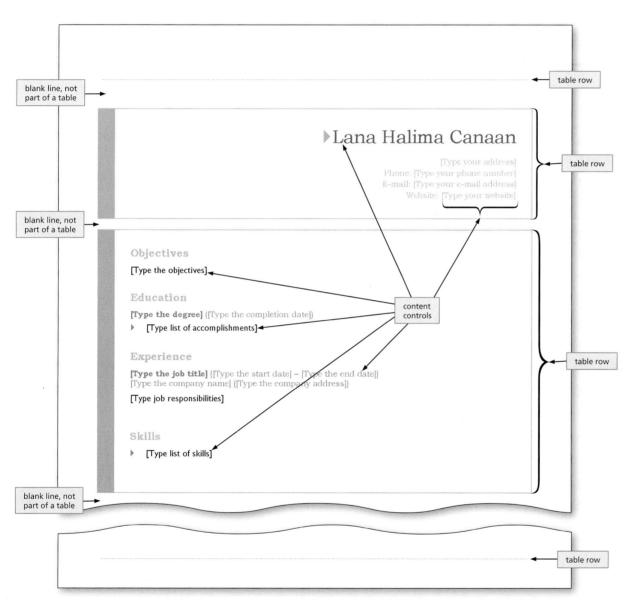

Figure 3–55

Resume Template

The resume created from the template, shown in Figure 3–55, consists of four individual tables, each with one row and one column. The first and last tables contain a decorative blue line; the second table contains the labels and content controls for the job seeker's contact information; and the third table contains labels and content controls for the Objectives, Education, Experience, and Skills sections of the resume. A **content control** contains instructions for filling areas of the template. To select a content control, you click it. As soon as you begin typing in the selected content control, your typing replaces the instruction in the control. Thus, you do not need to delete the selection before you begin typing.

The next step is to personalize the resume. The following pages personalize the resume created by the resume template.

To Delete Rows

The first and last rows of the resume created from the template contain a decorative line. The resume in this project deletes those rows to provide more space for the contents of the resume. The following steps delete the first and last rows on the resume.

- With the insertion point at the top of the document, click Layout on the Ribbon to display the Layout tab.

- Click the Delete button on the Layout tab to display the Delete menu (Figure 3–56).

Figure 3–56

- Click Delete Rows on the Delete menu to delete the row containing the insertion point (Figure 3–57).

What happened to the Table Tools tab on the Ribbon?

It is a contextual tab that appears only when the insertion point is in a table. With the row deleted, the insertion point is above the table row containing contact information.

Figure 3–57

- Press CTRL+END and then press the DOWN ARROW key to position the insertion point at the bottom of the document in the last row.

- Click Layout on the Ribbon to display the Layout tab.

- Click the Delete button on the Layout tab to display the Delete menu (Figure 3–58).

- Click Delete Rows on the Delete menu to delete the row containing the insertion point.

Figure 3–58

> **Other Ways**
>
> 1. Right-click selected rows, click Delete Rows on shortcut menu

To Modify Text in a Content Control

The next step is to select text that the template inserted into the resume and replace it with personal information. The name area on your resume may contain a name, which Word copied from the Word Options dialog box, or it may contain the instruction, Type your name. This content control should contain your name. In this project, the name is bold to give it more emphasis on the resume. It also uses the same color as the name on the cover letter.

The following steps modify the text in the content control that contains the job seeker's name.

- Press CTRL+HOME to position the insertion point at the top of the document.

- Click the name content control to select it (if it already contains a name, instead of the instruction, Type name here, drag through the name to select it). Then, type Lana Halima Canaan as the name.

- Triple-click the name content control to select its contents, so that you can format the name (Figure 3–59).

Figure 3–59

2

- Move the mouse pointer into the transparent Mini toolbar, so that it changes to a bright toolbar.

- Click the Bold button on the Mini toolbar to bold the selected name.

- Click the Font Color button on the Mini toolbar to change the font color of the selected name to the most recently used font color, which was the color of the name in the cover letter (Figure 3–60).

Q&A Instead of using buttons on the Mini toolbar, can I use the Bold and Font Color buttons on the Home tab?

Yes.

Figure 3–60

BTW

Windows Taskbar
If your Windows taskbar does not display a separate program button for each open Word document (as shown in Figure 3-61), click the Office Button, click the Word Options button, click Advanced in the left pane, scroll to the Display area in the right pane, place a check mark in the Show all windows in the Taskbar check box, and then click the OK button.

To Save the Resume

You have completed several tasks on the resume. Thus, you should save it in a file.

1 Display the Office Button menu and then click Save As to display the Save As dialog box.

2 Save the file on your USB flash drive using `Canaan Resume` as the file name.

Copying and Pasting

The next step in personalizing the resume is to enter the address, phone, and e-mail information in the content controls. One way to enter this information in the resume is to type it. Recall, however, that you already typed this information in the cover letter. Thus, a timesaving alternative would be to use the Office Clipboard to copy it from the cover letter to the resume. The **Office Clipboard** is a temporary storage area that holds up to 24 items (text or graphics) copied from any Office program.

Through the Office Clipboard, you can copy multiple items from any Office document and then paste them into the same or another Office document by following these general guidelines:

BTW

Clipboard
The Windows Clipboard, which can hold only one item at a time, is not the same as the Office Clipboard. When you collect multiple items on the Office Clipboard, however, the last copied item is copied to the Windows Clipboard as well. When you clear the Office Clipboard, the Windows Clipboard also is cleared.

1. Items are copied *from* a **source document**. If the source document is not the active document, display it in the document window.

2. Display the Office Clipboard task pane and then copy items from the source document to the Office Clipboard.

3. Items are copied *to* a **destination document**. If the destination document is not the active document, display the destination document in the document window.

4. Paste items from the Office Clipboard to the destination document.

The following pages use these guidelines to copy the address, phone, and e-mail information from the letterhead to the resume.

To Switch from One Open Document to Another

The step below switches from the open resume document to the open cover letter document, which is the source document in this case.

- Click the Canaan Cover Letter - Microsoft Word program button on the Windows taskbar to switch from the resume document to the cover letter document (Figure 3–61).

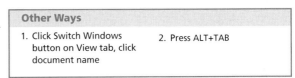

Figure 3–61

Other Ways

1. Click Switch Windows button on View tab, click document name

2. Press ALT+TAB

To Copy Items to the Office Clipboard

You can copy multiple items to the Office Clipboard through the Clipboard task pane and then paste them later. The following steps copy three items from the source document, the Canaan Cover Letter document, to the Office Clipboard.

- If necessary, scroll to the top of the cover letter, so that the items to be copied are visible in the document window.

- Click the Clipboard Dialog Box Launcher on the Home tab to display the Clipboard task pane.

- If the Office Clipboard in the Clipboard task pane is not empty, click the Clear All button in the Clipboard task pane (Figure 3–62).

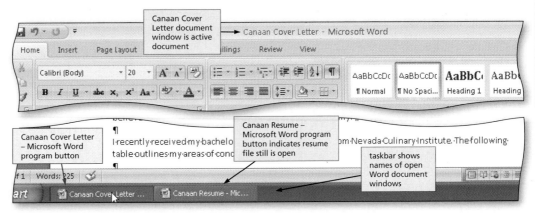

Figure 3–62

2

- In the cover letter, select the address, 22 Fifth Street, Juniper, NV 89268, which is the first item to be copied. Do not include the spaces to the right and left of the address.

- Click the Copy button on the Home tab to copy the selection to the Office Clipboard (Figure 3–63).

Q&A Does the copied item always display in its entirety in the Office Clipboard?

No. If the entry is too long, only the first portion is displayed.

Q&A What appears in the Office Clipboard if I copy a graphic instead of text?

A thumbnail of the copied graphic is displayed.

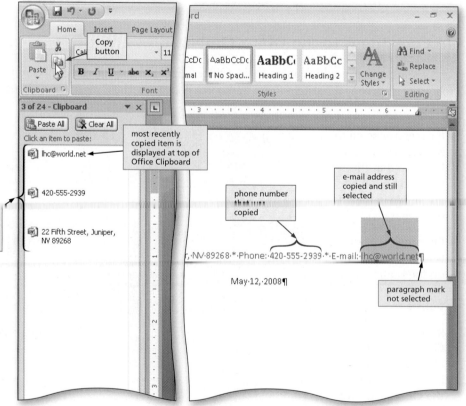

Figure 3–63

Figure 3–64

3

- Select the phone number (just the number, not the word Phone: and no spaces before or after the number) and then click the Copy button on the Home tab to copy the selection to the Office Clipboard.

- Select the e-mail address (just the e-mail address, not the word E-mail: and no spaces before or after the address) and then click the Copy button on the Home tab to copy the selection to the Office Clipboard (Figure 3–64).

Q&A What if I copy more than the maximum 24 items allowed in the Office Clipboard?

When you copy a 25th item, Word deletes the first item to make room for the new item.

Q&A Can I delete an item from the Office Clipboard?

Yes. Point to the item in the gallery, click the box arrow to the right of the item, and then click Delete.

Other Ways

1. With Clipboard task pane displayed, right-click selected item, click Copy on shortcut menu

2. With Clipboard task pane displayed and item to copy selected, press CTRL+C

To Paste from the Office Clipboard

The next step is to paste the copied items (the address, phone, and e-mail information) into the destination document, in this case, the resume document. Recall that the address, phone, and e-mail address are part of content controls in the resume.

The following steps paste the address, phone, and e-mail information from the Office Clipboard into the resume.

1

- Click the Canaan Resume - Microsoft Word program button on the Windows taskbar to display the resume document.

Q&A Does the destination document have to be a different document?

No. The source and destination documents can be the same document.

- If the Clipboard task pane is not displayed on the screen, click the Clipboard Dialog Box Launcher on the Home tab to display the Clipboard task pane.

- Click the content control in the resume with the instruction, Type your address, to select it (Figure 3–65).

Q&A What is the function of the Paste All button?

It pastes all items in a row, without any characters between them, at the location of the insertion point or selection.

Figure 3–65

BTW

Clipboard Task Pane
The Clipboard task pane may appear on the screen if you click the Copy button or the Cut button twice in succession, or if you copy and paste an item and then copy another item. You can display the Clipboard task pane by clicking the Office Clipboard icon, if it appears in the notification area on the Windows taskbar. If the Office Clipboard icon does not appear, click the Options button at the bottom of the Clipboard task pane and then click Show Office Clipboard Icon on Taskbar.

- Click the address entry in the Office Clipboard to paste it in the document at the location of the selected content control (Figure 3–66).

Q&A

Are the contents of the Office Clipboard erased when you paste?

No.

Figure 3–66

- Click the content control in the resume with the instruction, Type your phone number, to select it.

- Click the phone entry in the Office Clipboard to paste it in the document at the location of the selected content control.

- Click the content control in the resume with the instruction, Type your e-mail address, to select it.

- Click the e-mail entry in the Office Clipboard to paste it in the document at the location of the selected content control (Figure 3–67).

Figure 3–67

④

- Click the Close button on the Clipboard task pane title bar.

Other Ways

1. With Clipboard task pane displayed, right-click selected item, click Paste on shortcut menu
2. With Clipboard task pane displayed, press CTRL+V

Paste Options Button

When you paste items into a document, Word automatically displays the Paste Options button on the screen. The Paste Options button allows you to change the format of pasted items. For example, you can instruct Word to format the pasted text the same as the text from where it was copied or format it the same as the text to where it was pasted. You also can have Word remove all extra non-text characters that were pasted. For example, if you included a paragraph mark when copying at the end of a line in the address of the resume, the Paste Options button allows you to remove the paragraph mark from the pasted text.

To Change Font Color

The phone and e-mail labels should be the same color as the other contact information. Currently, they are a shade different from each other. The following steps change text color to the most recently used color.

 Drag through the text, Phone:, to select it. Move the mouse pointer into the transparent Mini toolbar, so that it changes to a bright toolbar. Click the Font Color button on the Mini toolbar to change the color of the Phone: label to the color displayed on the button.

 Drag through the text, E-mail:, to select it. Move the mouse pointer into the transparent Mini toolbar, so that it changes to a bright toolbar. Click the Font Color button on the Mini toolbar to change the color of the E-mail: label.

To Delete Text and Lines

You do not have a Web address. Thus, the Website content control, its corresponding label, and the line should be deleted. The following steps delete text.

1
- Drag through the text to be deleted, as shown in Figure 3–68.

2
- Press the DELETE key to delete the label and content control.

- Press the UP ARROW key to position the insertion point at the end of the e-mail address.

Figure 3–68

- Press the DELETE key to delete the extra paragraph mark and line below the e-mail address.

Other Ways		
1. With text selected, click Cut button on Home tab	2. Right-click selected text, click Cut on shortcut menu	3. With text selected, press CTRL+X

To Zoom the Document

The text in the resume is a little small for you to read. The following step changes the zoom to 110 percent.

1 Use the Zoom slider to change the zoom to 110% (Figure 3–69).

Figure 3–69

To Enter More Text in Content Controls

The next step is to select content controls in the resume and replace their instructions with personal information. The following steps enter text in the Objectives and some of the Education sections of the resume.

1 Scroll to position the Objectives section near the top of the document window. In the Objectives section of the resume, click the content control with the instruction, Type the objectives. Type `To obtain a full-time culinary instructor position with a culinary academy, school, or institute in the Juniper area.`

2 In the Education section of the resume, click the content control with the instruction, Type the degree. Type `B.S. Culinary Arts` and then click the content control with the instruction, Type the completion date.

3 Type `Nevada Culinary Institute, May 2008` and then click the content control with the instruction, Type list of accomplishments. Type `Dean's List, six semesters` and then press the ENTER key. Type `Moeller Nutrition Award, January 2008` and then press the ENTER key. Type `Marge Rae Outstanding Student Scholarship, 2006 – 2008` and then press the ENTER key. Type `Baker Food Preparation, 1st Place, November 2008` (Figure 3–70).

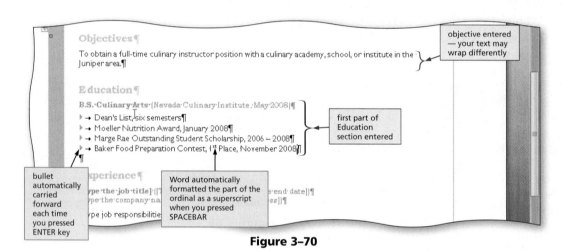

Figure 3–70

To Enter a Line Break

The next step in personalizing the resume is to enter the areas of concentration in the education section. You want only the first line that says, Areas of concentration:, to begin with a bullet. If you press the ENTER key on subsequent lines, Word automatically will carry forward the paragraph formatting, which includes the bullet. Thus, you will not press the ENTER key between each line. Instead, you will create a **line break**, which advances the insertion point to the beginning of the next physical line, ignoring any paragraph formatting. The following steps enter the areas of concentration using a line break, instead of a paragraph break, between each line.

- Press the ENTER key.

- Type `Areas of concentration:` and then press SHIFT+ENTER to insert a line break character and move the insertion point to the beginning of the next physical line (Figure 3–71).

Figure 3–71

2

- Type `Food Planning and Preparation` and then press SHIFT+ENTER.

- Type `Food Safety` and then press SHIFT+ENTER.

- Type `Nutrition` and then press SHIFT+ENTER.

- Type `Regional and International Cuisine` as the last entry. Do not press SHIFT+ENTER at the end of this line (Figure 3–72).

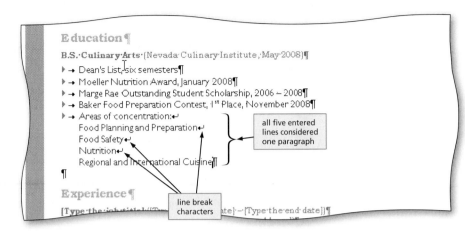

Figure 3–72

BTW

Line Break Character
Line break characters do not print. A line break character is a formatting mark that indicates a line break at the end of the line.

To Change Spacing Below Paragraphs

The blank paragraph below the Education section has spacing after (below) of 6 point. You do not want space below this paragraph because you want enough room for all the resume text. The following steps change the spacing after to 0 point.

1 Position the insertion point in the paragraph to be adjusted, in this case, the paragraph mark below the Education section on the resume.

2 Display the Page Layout tab.

3 Click the Spacing After box down arrow on the Page Layout tab as many times as necessary until 0 pt is displayed in the Spacing After box (Figure 3–73).

Figure 3–73

To Enter More Text in Content Controls

The next step is to select content controls in the Experience section of the resume and replace their instructions with personalized information.

1 In the Experience section of the resume, click the content control with the instruction, Type the job title.

2 Type `Chef Intern` and then bold the text, Chef Intern.

3 Click the content control with the instruction, Type the start date.

4 Type `September 2006` and then click the content control with the instruction, Type the end date.

5 Type `May 2008` and then click the content control with the instruction, Type the company name.

6 Type `The Garden Grill` and then click the content control with the instruction, Type the company address.

7 Type `Juniper, NV` as the company address.

To Indent a Paragraph

In the resume, the lines below the job title that contain the company name and job responsibilities are to be indented, so that the job titles are easier to see. The following step indents the left edge of a paragraph.

1

- Display the Home tab.

- With the insertion point in the paragraph to indent, click the Increase Indent button on the Home tab to indent the paragraph one-half inch (Figure 3–74).

 Experiment

- Repeatedly click the Increase Indent and Decrease Indent buttons on the Home tab and watch the left indent of the current paragraph change. When you have finished experimenting, use the Increase Indent and Decrease Indent buttons to set the left margin to the one-inch mark on the ruler.

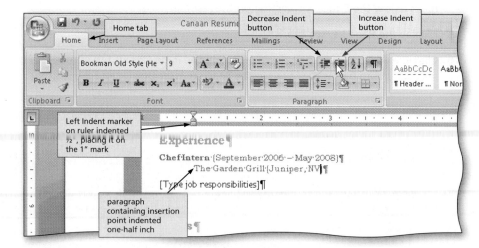

Figure 3–74

Q&A

Why did the paragraph indent one-half inch?

Each time you click the Increase Indent button, the current paragraph indents one-half inch. Similarly, when you click the Decrease Indent button, the paragraph decreases the indent by one-half inch.

Other Ways

1. Drag Left Indent marker on ruler

2. Enter value in Indent Left box on Page Layout tab

3. Click Paragraph Dialog Box Launcher on Home tab, click

   Indents and Spacing sheet, set indentation in Left box, click OK

4. Right-click text, click Paragraph on shortcut menu, click Indents

   and Spacing sheet, set indentation in Left box, click OK

5. Press CTRL+M

To Change Spacing Below Paragraphs

The next step is to remove the blank space below the company name paragraph, so that the company name and job description paragraphs are closer together. The following steps change the spacing after to 0 point.

1 Display the Page Layout tab.

2 With the insertion point in the paragraph to be adjusted, as shown in Figure 3–74, click the Spacing After box down arrow on the Page Layout tab as many times as necessary until 0 pt is displayed in the Spacing After box.

To Enter and Format More Text in Content Controls

The next step is to select the job responsibilities content control in the Experience section of the resume and replace its instructions with personal information.

1 In the Experience section of the resume, click the content control with the instruction, Type job responsibilities.

2 Type `Assisted chef with meal selection, preparation, and presentation. Assumed chef responsibilities during last semester of school.`

3 With the insertion point in the paragraph to be adjusted, in this case, the job responsibilities paragraph, click the Spacing After box down arrow on the Page Layout tab as many times as necessary until 6 pt is displayed in the Spacing After box.

4 Display the Home tab.

5 Click the Increase Indent button on the Home tab to indent the paragraph one-half inch (Figure 3–75).

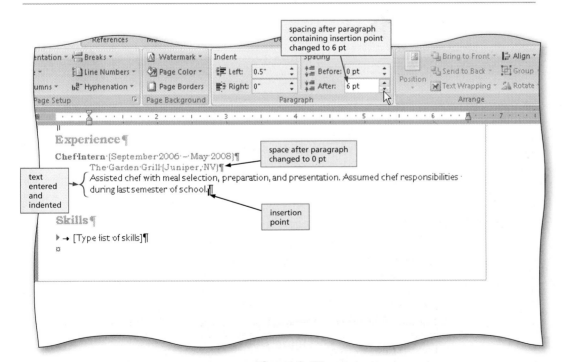

Figure 3–75

To Insert a Building Block Using the Quick Parts Gallery

In this resume, the Experience section contains two jobs. The template, however, inserted content controls for only one job. Word has defined the sections and subsections of the resume in the building blocks, which you can insert in the document. In this case, you want to insert the Experience Subsection building block. The following steps insert a building block.

- Scroll to display the Experience section at the top of the document window.

- Position the insertion point on the paragraph mark below the first job entry.

- Display the Insert tab.

- Click the Quick Parts button on the Insert tab and then scroll through the Quick Parts gallery until Experience Subsection is displayed (Figure 3–76).

Figure 3–76

- Click the Experience Subsection to insert the building block in the document at the location of the insertion point.

- Press the DELETE key to remove the extra paragraph mark inserted with the building block (Figure 3–77).

Figure 3–77

To Enter and Format the Experience Subsection and the Skills Section

The next step is to select content controls in the Experience Subsection building block just inserted and the Skills section in the resume and replace the instructions with personal information.

1 Enter `Assistant Cook` as the job title and then bold the job title. Enter `September 2004` as the start date. Enter `August 2006` as the end date. Enter `Nevada Culinary Institute Cafeteria` as the company name. Enter `Juniper, NV` as the company address.

2 Display the Home tab. With the insertion point in the paragraph to indent (company address line), click the Increase Indent button on the Home tab to indent the paragraph one-half inch.

3 Display the Page Layout tab. With the insertion point in the paragraph to be adjusted (company address line), change the Spacing After to 0 point.

4 Enter this text for the job responsibilities: `Planned meals for staff and students. Prepared salads, soups, sandwiches, entrees, and desserts.`

5 With the insertion point in the paragraph to be adjusted, in this case, the job responsibilities paragraph, change Spacing After to 0 point.

6 Display the Home tab. Click the Increase Indent button on the Home tab to indent the paragraph one-half inch.

7 In the Skills section, click the content control with the instruction, Type list of skills, to select it. Type `National Honor Society` and then press the ENTER key. Type `Culinary Arts Association` and then press the ENTER key. Type `Nutrition Services of America` and then press the ENTER key. Type `Student Government Association, President` and then press the ENTER key. Enter `Nevada Restaurant Federation` as the last skill (Figure 3–78).

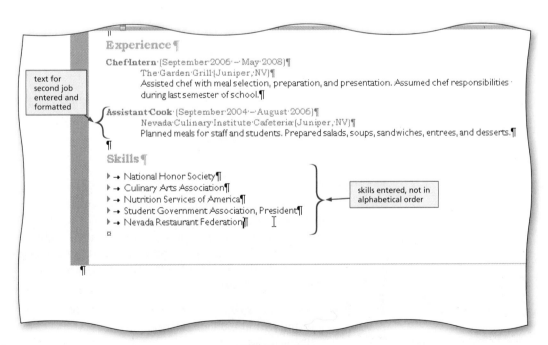

Figure 3–78

To Sort Paragraphs

The next step is to alphabetize the paragraphs in the Skills section of the resume. In Word, you can arrange paragraphs in alphabetic, numeric, or date order based on the first character in each paragraph. Ordering characters in this manner is called **sorting**. The following steps sort paragraphs.

 1

- Drag through the paragraphs to be sorted, in this case, the list of skills.

- Display the Home tab.

- Click the Sort button on the Home tab to display the Sort Text dialog box (Figure 3–79).

Q&A

What does ascending mean?

Ascending means to sort in alphabetic, numeric or earliest-to-latest date order.

Figure 3–79

2

- Click the OK button to close the dialog box and instruct Word to alphabetize the selected paragraphs.

To Insert Another Building Block

The last section of the resume is the Community Service section. No building block exists for this section; however, the format of the Reference Section building block is the same format you would like for the Community Service section. Thus, you will insert the Reference Section building block and modify its text. The following steps insert a building block.

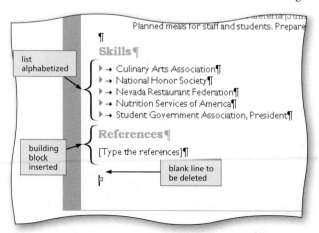

Figure 3–80

1 Position the insertion point on the line below the Skills section on the resume. Display the Insert tab. Click the Quick Parts button on the Insert tab and then scroll through the Quick Parts gallery until Reference Section is displayed. Click Reference Section to insert the building block in the document at the location of the insertion point (Figure 3–80).

2 Press the BACKSPACE key to remove the extra blank line inserted with the building block.

To Enter and Format the Community Service Section

The next step is to select content controls in the section just inserted in the resume and replace its instructions with community service information.

1 Change the title, References, to Community Service.

2 Display the Page Layout tab. With the insertion point in the paragraph to be adjusted (Community Service heading), change the Spacing Before to 12 point.

3 In the last content control, type `Prepare food and serve meals at Hope Mission every week.`

4 With the insertion point in the paragraph to be adjusted, in this case, the community services paragraph, change Spacing After to 0 point (Figure 3–81).

5 If the document flows to a second page, reduce the space after internal paragraphs so that it fits on a single page.

Figure 3–81

To Change Theme Colors

The cover letter created earlier in this chapter used the Urban color scheme. Because you will be mailing the resume along with the cover letter, you decide also to use the Urban color scheme for the resume. The following step changes theme colors.

1 Display the Home tab. Click the Change Styles button on the Home tab, point to Colors on the Change Styles menu, and then click Urban in the Colors gallery to change the document theme colors to Urban.

To Print Preview a Document

To see exactly how a document will look when you print it, you could display it in print preview. **Print preview** displays the entire document in reduced size on the Word screen. In print preview, you can edit and format text, adjust margins, view multiple pages, reduce the document to fit on a single page, and print the document. The following steps view and print the resume in print preview.

1

• Click the Office Button and then point to Print on the Office Button menu (Figure 3–82).

Figure 3–82

2

- Click Print Preview on the Print submenu to display the document in print preview (Figure 3–83).

- Click the Print button on the Print Preview tab and then click the OK button in the Print dialog box to print the resume, as shown in Figure 3–2 on page WD 148.

- Click the Close Print Preview button on the Print Preview tab to redisplay the resume in the document window.

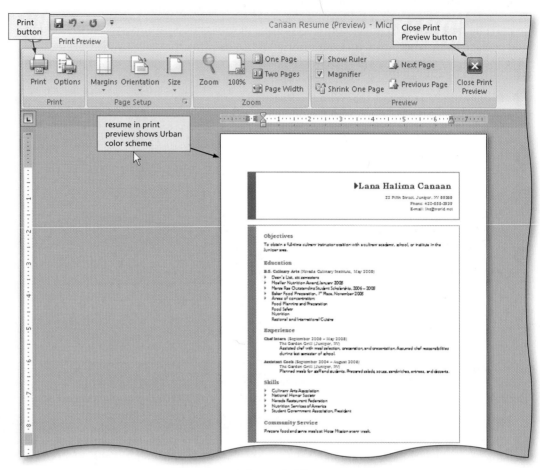

Figure 3–83

Print Preview
If you want to display two pages in print preview, click the Two Pages button on the Print Preview tab. With the Magnifier check box on the Print Preview tab selected, you can click in the document to zoom in or out. Magnifying a page does not affect the printed document. To edit a document, remove the check mark from the Magnifier check box and then edit the text. If a document spills onto a second page by a line or two, click the Shrink One Page button and Word will try to fit all content on a single page.

To Change Document Properties and Save Again

Before saving the resume a final time, you want to add your name, course and section, and some keywords as document properties. The following steps use the Document Information Panel to change document properties and then save the document again.

1 Display the Office Button menu, point to Prepare on the Office Button menu, and then click Properties on the Prepare submenu to display the Document Information Panel.

2 Enter your name in the Author text box. Enter your course and section in the Subject text box. Enter the text, resume, in the Keywords text box.

3 Close the Document Information Panel.

4 Click the Save button on the Quick Access Toolbar to overwrite the previous Canaan Resume file on the USB flash drive.

Addressing and Printing Envelopes and Mailing Labels

BTW

Quick Reference
For a table that lists how to complete the tasks covered in this book using the mouse, Ribbon, shortcut menu, and keyboard, see the Quick Reference Summary at the back of this book, or visit the Word 2007 Quick Reference Web page (scsite.com/wd2007/qr).

With Word, you can print address information on an envelope or on a mailing label. Computer-printed addresses look more professional than handwritten ones. Thus, the following steps address and print an envelope.

To Address and Print an Envelope

1

- Switch to the cover letter by clicking its program button on the Windows taskbar.

- Close the Clipboard task pane.

- Scroll through the cover letter to display the inside address in the document window.

- Drag through the inside address to select it (Figure 3–84).

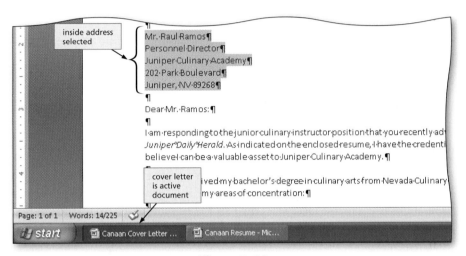

Figure 3–84

2

- Click Mailings on the Ribbon to display the Mailings tab.

- Click the Envelopes button on the Mailings tab to display the Envelopes and Labels dialog box.

- If necessary, click the Envelopes tab in the dialog box.

- Click the Return address text box.

- Type `Lana Halima Canaan` and then press the ENTER key.

- Type `22 Fifth Street` and then press the ENTER key.

- Type `Juniper, NV 89268` (Figure 3–85).

- Insert an envelope into your printer, as shown in the Feed area of the dialog box (your Feed area may be different depending on your printer).

- Click the Print button in the Envelopes and Labels dialog box to print the envelope.

- If a dialog box is displayed, click the No button.

Figure 3–85

BTW

Certification
The Microsoft Certified Application Specialist (MCAS) program provides an opportunity for you to obtain a valuable industry credential – proof that you have the Word 2007 skills required by employers. For more information, see Appendix F or visit the Word 2007 Certification Web page (scsite.com/wd2007/cert).

Envelopes and Labels

Instead of printing the envelope immediately, you can add it to the document by clicking the Add to Document button in the Envelopes and Labels dialog box. To specify a different envelope or label type (identified by a number on the box of envelopes or labels), click the Options button in the Envelopes and Labels dialog box.

Instead of printing an envelope, you can print a mailing label. To do this, click the Labels tab in the Envelopes and Labels dialog box (Figure 3–85 on the previous page). Type the delivery address in the Address box. To print the same address on all labels on the page, click Full page of the same label. Click the Print button in the dialog box.

To Quit Word

This project is complete. The following step quits Word.

 1 Click the Close button on the right side of the title bar to quit Word.

Chapter Summary

In this chapter, you have learned how to use Word to insert and format clip art, set and use tab stops, create and insert building blocks, insert the current date, insert and format tables, use print preview, copy and paste, and use templates. The items listed below include all the new Word skills you have learned in this chapter.

1. Use the Grow Font Button to Increase Font Size (WD 151)
2. Color Text (WD 152)
3. Insert Clip Art (WD 153)
4. Resize a Graphic Using the Size Dialog Box (WD 155)
5. Recolor a Graphic (WD 156)
6. Set a Transparent Color in a Graphic (WD 157)
7. Set Custom Tab Stops Using the Tabs Dialog Box (WD 158)
8. Bottom Border a Paragraph (WD 161)
9. Clear Formatting (WD 162)
10. Convert a Hyperlink to Regular Text (WD 163)
11. Create a New File from an Existing File (WD 165)
12. Set Custom Tab Stops Using the Ruler (WD 167)
13. Insert the Current Date in a Document (WD 168)
14. Create a Building Block (WD 170)
15. Insert a Nonbreaking Space (WD 171)
16. Insert a Building Block (WD 172)
17. Insert an Empty Table (WD 173)
18. Enter Data in a Table (WD 175)
19. Apply a Table Style (WD 176)
20. Resize Table Columns to Fit Table Contents (WD 177)
21. Bullet a List as You Type (WD 180)
22. Use a Template (WD 183)
23. Delete Rows (WD 186)
24. Modify Text in a Content Control (WD 187)
25. Switch from One Open Document to Another (WD 189)
26. Copy Items to the Office Clipboard (WD 189)
27. Paste from the Office Clipboard (WD 191)
28. Delete Text and Lines (WD 193)
29. Enter a Line Break (WD 194)
30. Indent a Paragraph (WD 196)
31. Insert a Building Block Using the Quick Parts Gallery (WD 198)
32. Sort Paragraphs (WD 200)
33. Print Preview a Document (WD 201)
34. Address and Print an Envelope (WD 203)

 If you have a SAM user profile, you may have access to hands-on instruction, practice, and assessment. Log in to your SAM account (http://sam2007.course.com) to launch any assigned training activities or exams that relate to the skills covered in this chapter.

Learn It Online

Test your knowledge of chapter content and key terms.

Instructions: To complete the Learn It Online exercises, start your browser, click the Address bar, and then enter the Web address `scsite.com/wd2007/learn`. When the Word 2007 Learn It Online page is displayed, click the link for the exercise you want to complete and then read the instructions.

Chapter Reinforcement TF, MC, and SA
A series of true/false, multiple choice, and short answer questions that test your knowledge of the chapter content.

Flash Cards
An interactive learning environment where you identify chapter key terms associated with displayed definitions.

Practice Test
A series of multiple choice questions that test your knowledge of chapter content and key terms.

Who Wants To Be a Computer Genius?
An interactive game that challenges your knowledge of chapter content in the style of a television quiz show.

Wheel of Terms
An interactive game that challenges your knowledge of chapter key terms in the style of the television show *Wheel of Fortune*.

Crossword Puzzle Challenge
A crossword puzzle that challenges your knowledge of key terms presented in the chapter.

Apply Your Knowledge

Reinforce the skills and apply the concepts you learned in this chapter.

Working with Tabs and a Table
Instructions: Start Word. Open the document, Apply 3-1 Expenses Table Draft, from the Data Files for Students. See the inside back cover of this book for instructions on downloading the Data Files for Students, or contact your instructor for information about accessing the required files.

The document is a Word table that you are to edit and format. The revised table is shown in Figure 3–86.

Monthly Club Expenses

	January	February	March	April
Decorations	170.88	129.72	74.43	167.85
Postage	65.90	62.90	40.19	69.91
Computer Supplies	17.29	18.50	72.50	19.12
Paper Supplies	46.57	41.67	38.82	48.70
Food/Beverages	122.04	99.88	55.43	100.00
Hall Rental	120.00	120.00	120.00	120.00
Total	542.68	472.67	401.37	525.58

Figure 3–86

Continued >

Perform the following tasks:

1. In the line containing the table title, Monthly Club Table, remove the tab stop at the 1" mark on the ruler.

2. Set a centered tab at the 3.25" mark on the ruler.

3. Bold the characters in the title. Increase their font size to 14. Change their color to Red, Accent 2, Darker 25%.

4. Add a new row to the bottom of the table. In the first cell of the new row, type Total as the entry. Enter these values in the next four cells: January – 542.68; February – 472.67; April – 525.58.

5. Delete the row containing the Duplicating Fees expenses.

6. Insert a column between the February and April columns. Fill in the column as follows: Column Title – March; Decorations – 74.43; Postage – 40.19; Computer Supplies – 72.50; Paper Supplies – 38.82; Food/Beverages – 55.43; Hall Rental – 120.00; Total – 401.37.

7. In the Design tab, remove the check mark from the Banded Rows check box. Place a check mark in the Total Row check box. The three check boxes that should have check marks are Header Row, Total Row, and First Column. Apply the Medium Grid 3 - Accent 1 style to the table.

8. Make all columns as wide as their contents (AutoFit Contents).

9. Center the table between the left and right margins of the page.

10. Change the document properties, as specified by your instructor.

11. Click the Office Button and then click Save As. Save the document using the file name, Apply 3-1 Expenses Table Modified.

12. Print the document properties.

13. Print the revised table, shown in Figure 3–86.

Extend Your Knowledge

Extend the skills you learned in this chapter and experiment with new skills. You may need to use Help to complete the assignment.

Working with Pictures, Symbols, Borders, and Tables

Instructions: Start Word. Open the document, Extend 3-1 Club Letter Draft, from the Data Files for Students. See the inside back cover of this book for instructions on downloading the Data Files for Students, or contact your instructor for information on accessing the required files.

You will flip the clip art, insert symbols, add a decorative border, add totals to the table, modify the table style, and print mailing labels.

Perform the following tasks:

1. Use Help to learn about rotating objects, inserting symbols, working with borders, entering formulas, and printing mailing labels.

2. Flip the image in the letterhead horizontally so that the fruit faces toward the middle of the letter instead of toward the margin.

3. In the letterhead, replace the asterisk characters that separate the address, phone, and e-mail information with a symbol in one of the Wingdings fonts (Figure 3–87).

4. Remove the bottom border in the letterhead. Add a new bottom border that has a color and style different from the default Word border.

5. Add a row to the bottom of the table with a label indicating it contains totals. For each of the columns, use the Formula button on the Layout tab to sum the contents of the column. Write down the formula that Word uses to sum the contents of a column. Add a column to the right of the table with a label indicating it contains totals. For each of the rows, use a formula to sum the row. Write down the formula that Word uses to sum the contents of a row.

6. Change the table style. One at a time, select and deselect each check box in the Table Style Options group. Write down the function of each check box: Header Row, Total Row, Banded Rows, First Column, Last Column, and Banded Columns. Select the check boxes you prefer for the table.

7. Change the document properties, as specified by your instructor. Save the revised document using a new file name and then submit it in the format specified by your instructor.

8. Print a single mailing label for the letter.

9. Print a full page of mailing labels, each containing the address shown in Figure 3-87.

Figure 3–87

Make It Right

Analyze a document and correct all errors and/or improve the design.

Formatting a Business Letter

Instructions: Start Word. Open the document, Make It Right 3-1 Cover Letter Draft, from the Data Files for Students. See the inside back cover of this book for instructions on downloading the Data Files for Students, or contact your instructor for information on accessing the required files.

The document is a cover letter that is missing elements and formatted incorrectly (Figure 3–88). You are to insert and format clip art in the letterhead, change the color of the text and graphic, change the letter style from block to modified block, and format the table.

Figure 3–88

Perform the following tasks:

1. Locate and insert an appropriate clip art image. If you have access to the Internet, use one from the Web. Resize the graphic, if necessary.

2. Change the color of the text in the letterhead. Recolor the graphic to match the color of the text. Format one color in the graphic as transparent.

3. The letter currently is the block letter style. It should be the modified block letter style. Format the appropriate paragraphs by setting custom tab stops and then positioning those paragraphs at the tab stops. Be sure to position the insertion point in the paragraph before setting the tab stop.

4. Center the table. Apply a table style of your choice. Resize the table columns to fit the contents of the cells.

5. Change the document properties, as specified by your instructor. Save the revised document using a new file name and then submit it in the format specified by your instructor.

In the Lab

Design and/or create a document using the guidelines, concepts, and skills presented in this chapter. Labs are listed in order of increasing difficulty.

Lab 1: Creating a Cover Letter with a Table

Problem: You are a student at Norson Central College. Graduation is approaching quickly and you would like a part-time job while furthering your studies. Thus, you prepare the cover letter shown in Figure 3–89.

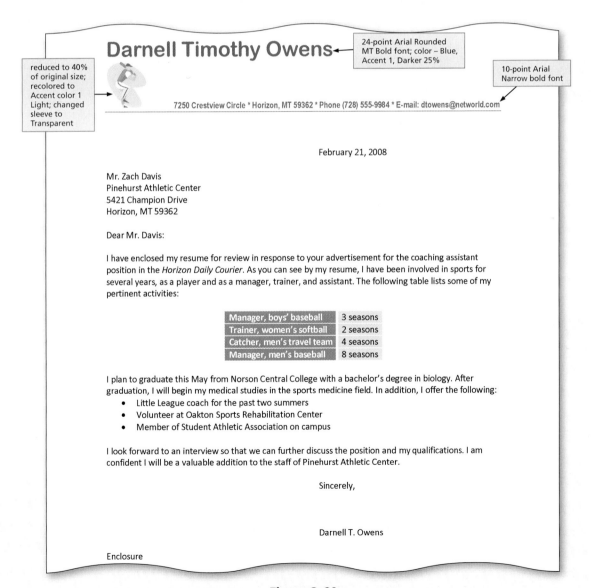

Figure 3–89

Continued >

In the Lab *continued*

Perform the following tasks:

1. Create the letterhead shown at the top of Figure 3–89 on the previous page. Remove the hyperlink format from the e-mail address. Save the letterhead with the file name, Lab 3-1 Owens Letterhead.

2. Create the letter shown in Figure 3–89. Set a tab stop at the 3.5" mark on the ruler for the date line, complimentary close, and signature block. Insert the current date. After entering the inside address, create a building block for Pinehurst Athletic Center and insert the building block whenever you have to enter the company name. Insert nonbreaking space characters in the newspaper name. Insert and center the table. Format the table using the Medium Grid 3 - Accent 1 table style. Select only the First Column check box in the Table Style Options group. Adjust the column widths so that they are as wide as the contents of the cells. Bullet the list as you type it.

3. Check the spelling of the letter. Change the document properties, as specified by your instructor. Save the letter with Lab 3-1 Owens Cover Letter as the file name.

4. View and print the cover letter from within print preview.

5. Address and print an envelope and a mailing label using the inside and return addresses in the cover letter.

In the Lab

Lab 2: Creating a Resume from a Template

Problem: You are a nursing student at Ferrell College. As graduation is approaching quickly, you prepare the resume shown in Figure 3–90 using one of Word's resume templates.

Perform the following tasks:

1. Use the Equity Resume template to create a resume.

2. Personalize the resume as shown in Figure 3–90. Use your own name and address information when you personalize the resume. If necessary, drag the blue-dotted column border to the right of the name to the right, to make room for a name with a larger font size. Insert the Experience Subsection building block, so that you can enter the second job. Indent the text in the Experience section as shown. Enter line break characters between the job responsibility lines. Adjust line spacing in the Experience section, so that it matches Figure 3–90. Change the title, Skills, to the word, Activities.

3. Change the theme fonts to Aspect.

4. Check the spelling of the resume. Change the document properties, as specified by your instructor. Save the resume with Lab 3-2 Marsh Resume as the file name.

5. View and print the resume from within print preview.

Constance Leah Marsh

Phone: 504-555-8272

322 East Center Street
Apollo, WY 83163
E-mail: clmarsh@world.net

Objectives

To secure a nursing position at a primary care facility.

Education

May 2008 | Ferrell College, Apollo, Wyoming
- B.S., Nursing
- Certified Nursing Assistant

Experience

January 2007 – May 2008 | Health Care Assistant
Prime Assisted Living | Apollo, Wyoming
Organized daily activities and events for patients
Acted as receptionist at front desk as needed
Assisted patients with personal care, grooming, and medical needs

September 2005 – December 2006 |Nursing Assistant
Clearview Hospital | Apollo, Wyoming
Assisted nursing staff with patient care
Directed calls and patient visitors
Updated files and charts

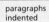

paragraphs
indented

Activities
- Volunteer at a local hospital reading to patients
- Teach Pilates class for seniors at Halwell Physical Therapy Center
- Member of local women's outreach group promoting literacy
- Volunteer at Women's Health Center twice a month

Figure 3–90

In the Lab

Lab 3: Creating a Letter

Problem: You are a president of the Parents Educational Organization for the local high school. The organization currently is taking nominations for outstanding teacher award and you write thank-you letters to nominators, also asking them for donations.

Instructions: Prepare the letter shown in Figure 3–91. Follow the guidelines in the modified semi-block letter style. Use proper spacing between elements of the letter. Check the spelling of the letter. Change the document properties, as specified by your instructor. Save the letter with Lab 3-3 Ling Letter as the file name.

Kim S. Ling
Parents Educational Organization
99 Ohio Avenue, Harrust, NH 03891
(317) 555-1865 * E-mail: ksling@net.com

February 14, 2008

Ms. Laura Ennis
74 MacEnroe Court
Fairview, IN 46142

Dear Ms. Ennis:

Thank you for your recent nomination of Mr. Serensi from Bakersville North High School for our outstanding teacher award. He will be pleased that you believe he was a great influence in your decision to become a teacher.

In addition to the honor of being selected outstanding teacher, we present our candidates with a monetary gift. They use the funds for future classroom needs, including:

- Reading materials to be kept in the classroom
- Emergency funds to assist students in need of supplies
- Supplies for additional projects to be determined by teacher
- Guest author and speaker visits

If you are interested in donating to this worthy cause, please contact me via e-mail or telephone. All donors' names are engraved on a plaque on display in the school auditorium. Listed in the table below are the donation levels.

Donation Level	Donation Amount
Gold	$500
Silver	$250
Bronze	$100

Again, we thank you for your interest in our project.

Yours truly,

Kim Ling
President

Figure 3–91

Cases and Places

Apply your creative thinking and problem solving skills to design and implement a solution.

● Easier   ●● More Difficult

● 1: Create a Fax Cover Sheet from a Template

Your boss has asked you to send a fax that includes a fax cover sheet. In the New Document dialog box, click Installed Templates in the Templates pane and then click Equity Fax in the Installed Templates list. Click in each area to enter the following information in the fax cover sheet: the fax is from your boss, Max Henreich; the fax should go to Shirelle Bradley; her fax number is (317) 555-0922; the fax contains three pages; and the phone is (317) 555-1350. Use today's date for the date. The Re: area should contain the following text: Site visit materials. Leave the CC: field blank. The For Review check box should be checked, and your boss wants the following comment on the cover sheet: Here are the notes for tomorrow's site visit.

● 2: Create this Chapter's Resume Using a Different Template

Information can look and be perceived completely differently simply by virtue of the way it is presented. Take the resume created in this chapter and create it using a different template. For example, try the Equity, Median, Oreil, or Urban Resume template in the Installed Templates list. Make sure each section of the resume in this chapter is presented in the new document. You may need to rename or delete sections and add building blocks. Open the resume you created in this chapter and use the copy and paste commands to simplify entering the text. Select a theme you like best for the finished resume.

●● 3: Create a Memo Using a Template from the Web

As assistant director of programs at a local park, you are responsible for soliciting ideas from employees regarding future programs and activities. In the New Document dialog box, click Memos in the Microsoft Office Online area to create a memo. Select a template you like. Use the following information to complete the memo: the memo should go to all staff members; the meeting will be held in room A42 on March 14, 2008 at 3:00 p.m.; attendees should be prepared to discuss their ideas for spring and summer activities; and attendance is mandatory. Mention that if anyone is to be on vacation or unavailable, he or she should contact you prior to the meeting to arrange for submission of activities lists.

●● 4: Create Your Resume and Cover Letter for a Potential Job

Make It Personal

Assume you are graduating this semester and need to find a job immediately after graduation. Check a local newspaper or online employment source to find an advertisement for a job relating to your major or a job for which you believe you are qualified. Use the techniques you learned in this chapter to create your resume and a cover letter. Tailor your cover letter and your resume to fit the job description. Make sure you include an objective, education, and work experience section. Also include any other pertinent sections. Use the copy and paste commands to copy your name and address information from one document to the other.

Continued >

Cases and Places *continued*

•• 5: Create a Memo Using a Template from the Web

Working Together

As active members of your school's Travel and Leisure Club, you have been assigned the task of publicizing the club's upcoming activities and soliciting new memberships. Assign each team member one of the following tasks: create a calendar listing various club activities for a three-month period, including any scheduled trips, parties, or meetings; design an award or certificate for excellence or other recognition presented to your club by another campus group; compose a letter of thanks from a past member; and create an invitation to join the Travel and Leisure Club. Visit Microsoft Office Online to obtain templates for awards and certificates, calendars, and invitations. Then, as a group, write a cover letter soliciting memberships and listing the reasons why students should join the club. Include a table or bulleted list similar to those used in this chapter. Make the package attractive and eye-catching.

3

- Click Other For
  on the Save As
  menu to display
  Save As dialog |

- Type `Canaan`
  `Resume Web P`
  in the File name
  box to change t
  file name. If nec
  sary, change the
  Save in location
  UDISK 2.0 (E:). ('
  USB flash drive |
  have a different
  name and letter

- Click the Save as
  box arrow; scroll
  and then click Si
  File Web Page.

- Click the Change
  Title button to
  display the Set P.
  Title dialog box.

- Type `Canaan Re`
  the Page title te>

4

- Click the OK butt
  Page Title dialog

- Click the Save but
  As dialog box to s
  as a Web page an
  document windo\
  Word displays a d
  compatibility with
  click the Continue
  dialog box.)

Saving to a \

If you have ad
page directly to the
As dialog box (Figu
FTP site, then you
the Save in list. To |
Microsoft Office pr

Web Feature
Creating a Web Page Using Word

Objectives

You will have mastered the material in this feature when you can:

- Save a Word document as a Web page
- Insert a hyperlink

- Add a background color with a pattern
- Use Windows Explorer to view a Web page

To Add a Pattern Fill Effect to a Background

When you changed the background color in the previous steps, Word placed a solid background color on the screen. For this resume Web page, the solid background color is a little too intense. To soften the background color, you can add patterns to it. The following steps add a pattern to the blue background.

- Click the Page Color button on the Page Layout tab (shown in Figure 8 on the previous page) to display the Page Color gallery again.

- Click Fill Effects in the Page Color gallery (shown in Figure 8) to display the Fill Effects dialog box.

- Click the Pattern tab to display the Pattern sheet in the dialog box.

- Click the Outlined diamond pattern (rightmost pattern in the fifth row) to select it (Figure 9).

Figure 9

- Click the OK button to add the outlined diamond pattern to the blue background color (Figure 10).

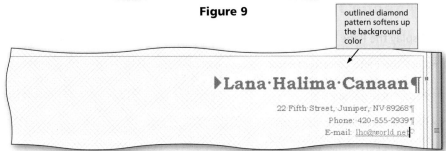

Figure 10

To Save a

The fo
feature on a
you did not o

- Start Word
  open the fi
  Canaan Res
  created in (

- With the re
  open in the
  ment windo
  the Office B
  and then po
  Save As on
  Button men
  display the
  submenu (F

To Save an Existing Document and Quit Word

The Web page document now is complete. The following steps save the document again and quit Word.

1 Click the Save button on the Quick Access Toolbar to overwrite the previous Canaan Resume Web Page file on the USB flash drive.

2 Click the Close button on the right side of the title bar to quit Word.

Testing the Web Page

After creating and saving a Web page, you will want to test it in at least one browser to be sure it looks and works the way you intended.

To Test the Web Page in a Web Browser

The following steps use Windows Explorer to display the resume Web page in the Internet Explorer Web browser.

1

- Click the Start button on the Windows taskbar to display the Start menu.

- Click My Computer on the Start menu to display the My Computer window.

- If necessary, maximize the My Computer window (Figure 11).

Figure 11

2

- Double-click the USB flash drive icon in the My Computer window to display the contents of the USB flash drive in an Explorer window (Figure 12).

3

- Double-click the file name, Canaan Resume Web Page, to start the Internet Explorer Web browser and display the file in the browser window (shown in Figure 1a on page WD 217).

- With the Web page document displaying in the Web browser, click the e-mail address link to ensure it displays the e-mail window, as shown in Figure 1b on page WD 217.

Figure 12

4

- Close all open windows.

BTW

Quick Reference
For a table that lists how to complete the tasks covered in this book using the mouse, Ribbon, shortcut menu, and keyboard, see the Quick Reference Summary at the back of this book, or visit the Word 2007 Quick Reference Web page (scsite.com/wd2007/qr).

Feature Summary

In this feature, you have learned how to save a Word document as a Web page, insert a hyperlink, add background color, and view a Web page. The items listed below include all the new Word skills you have learned in this feature.

1. Save a Word Document as a Web Page (WD 218)
2. Format Text as a Hyperlink (WD 220)
3. Add a Background Color (WD 221)
4. Add a Pattern Fill Effect to a Background (WD 222)
5. Test the Web Page in a Web Browser (WD 223)

If you have a SAM user profile, you may have access to hands-on instruction, practice, and assessment. Log in to your SAM account (http://sam2007.course.com) to launch any assigned training activities or exams that relate to the skills covered in this chapter.

1 | Creating a Worksheet and an Embedded Chart

What Is Microsoft Office Excel 2007?

Microsoft Office Excel 2007 is a powerful spreadsheet program that allows users to organize data, complete calculations, make decisions, graph data, develop professional looking reports (Figure 1–1), publish organized data to the Web, and access real-time data from Web sites. The four major parts of Excel are:

- **Workbooks and Worksheets** Workbooks are a collection of worksheets. Worksheets allow users to enter, calculate, manipulate, and analyze data such as numbers and text. The terms worksheet and spreadsheet are interchangeable.

- **Charts** Excel can draw a variety of charts.

- **Tables** Tables organize and store data within worksheets. For example, once a user enters data into a worksheet, an Excel table can sort the data, search for specific data, and select data that satisfies defined criteria.

- **Web Support** Web support allows users to save Excel worksheets or parts of a worksheet in HTML format, so a user can view and manipulate the worksheet using a browser. Excel Web support also provides access to real-time data, such as stock quotes, using Web queries.

This latest version of Excel makes it much easier than in previous versions to perform common functions by introducing a new style of user interface. It also offers the capability of creating larger worksheets, improved formatting and printing, improved charting and table functionality, industry-standard XML support that simplifies the sharing of data within and outside an organization, improved business intelligence functionality, and the capability of performing complex tasks on a server.

In this chapter, you will create a worksheet that includes a chart. The data in the worksheet and chart includes sales data for several stores that a company owns and operates.

Project Planning Guidelines

The process of developing a worksheet that communicates specific information requires careful analysis and planning. As a starting point, establish why the worksheet is needed. Once the purpose is determined, analyze the intended users of the worksheet and their unique needs. Then, gather information about the topic and decide what to include in the worksheet. Finally, determine the worksheet design and style that will be most successful at delivering the message. Details of these guidelines are provided in Appendix A. In addition, each project developed in this book provides practical applications of these planning considerations.

Project — Worksheet with an Embedded Chart

The project in this chapter follows proper design guidelines and uses Excel to create the worksheet shown in Figure 1–1. The worksheet contains sales data for Walk and Rock Music stores. The Walk and Rock Music product line includes a variety of MP3 music players, called Rock-It MP3, including players that show pictures and video, as well as a complete line of headphones and other accessories. The company sells its products at kiosks in several malls throughout the United States. By concentrating its stores near colleges and universities and keeping the newest items in stock, the Walk and Rock Music stores quickly became trendy. As sales continued to grow in the past year, senior management requested an easy-to-read worksheet that shows product sales for the first quarter by region. In addition, they asked for a chart showing first quarter sales, because the president of the company likes to have a graphical representation of sales that allows him quickly to identify stronger and weaker product types by region.

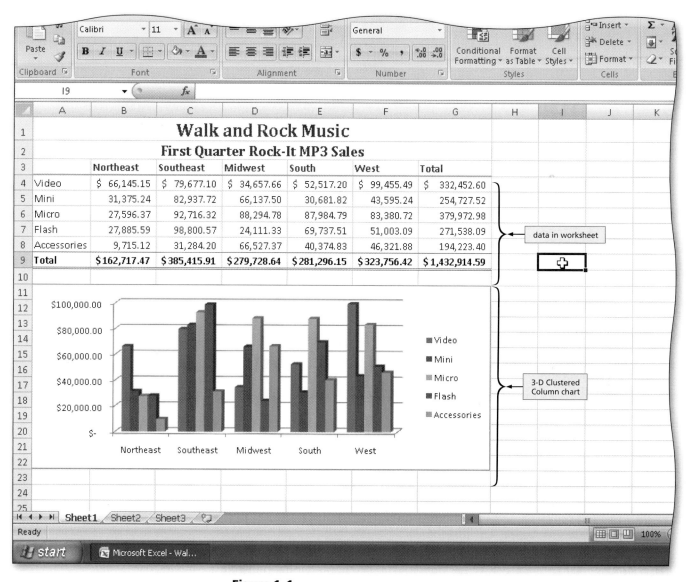

Figure 1–1

The first step in creating an effective worksheet is to make sure you understand what is required. The person or persons requesting the worksheet should supply their requirements in a requirements document. A **requirements document** includes a needs

BTW

Excel 2007 Features
With its what-if
analysis tools, research
capabilities, collaboration
tools, streamlined user
interface, smart tags,
charting features, Web
capabilities, hundreds of
functions, and enhanced
formatting capabilities,
Excel 2007 is one of the
easier and more powerful
spreadsheet packages
available.

statement, source of data, summary of calculations, and any other special requirements for the worksheet, such as charting and Web support. Figure 1–2 shows the requirements document for the new workbook to be created in this chapter.

requirements
document

REQUEST FOR NEW WORKBOOK

Date Submitted:	April 15, 2008
Submitted By:	Trisha Samuels
Worksheet Title:	Walk and Rock Music First Quarter Sales
Needs:	An easy-to-read worksheet that shows Walk and Rock Music's first quarter sales for each of our sales regions in which we operate (Northeast, Southeast, Midwest, South, West). The worksheet also should include total sales for each region, total sales for each product type, and total company sales for the first quarter.
Source of Data:	The data for the worksheet is available for the end of the first quarter from the chief financial officer (CFO) of Walk and Rock Music.
Calculations:	The following calculations must be made for the worksheet: (a) total first quarter sales for each of the five regions; (b) total first quarter sales for each of the five product types; and (c) total first quarter sales for the company.
Chart Requirements:	Below the data in the worksheet, construct a 3-D Clustered Column chart that compares the total sales for each region within each type of product.

Approvals

Approval Status:	X	Approved
		Rejected
Approved By:	Stan Maderbek	
Date:	April 22, 2008	
Assigned To:	J. Quasney, Spreadsheet Specialist	

Figure 1–2

BTW

Worksheet Development Cycle
Spreadsheet specialists
do not sit down and
start entering text,
formulas, and data into
a blank Excel worksheet
as soon as they have a
spreadsheet assignment.
Instead, they follow
an organized plan,
or methodology, that
breaks the development
cycle into a series of
tasks. The recommended
methodology for creating
worksheets includes:
(1) analyze require-
ments (supplied in a
requirements document);
(2) design solution;
(3) validate design;
(4) implement design;
(5) test solution; and
(6) document solution.

Overview

As you read this chapter, you will learn how to create the worksheet shown in Figure 1–1 by performing these general tasks:

- Enter text in the worksheet
- Add totals to the worksheet
- Save the workbook that contains the worksheet
- Format the text in the worksheet
- Insert a chart in the worksheet
- Save the workbook a second time using the same file name
- Print the worksheet

Plan Ahead

General Project Guidelines

While creating an Excel worksheet, you need to make several decisions that will determine the appearance and characteristics of the finished worksheet. As you create the worksheet shown in Figure 1–1, you should follow these general guidelines:

1. **Select titles and subtitles for the worksheet.** Follow the *less is more* guideline. The less text in the titles and subtitles, the more impact the titles and subtitles will have. Use the fewest words possible to specify the information presented in the worksheet to the intended audience.

(continued)

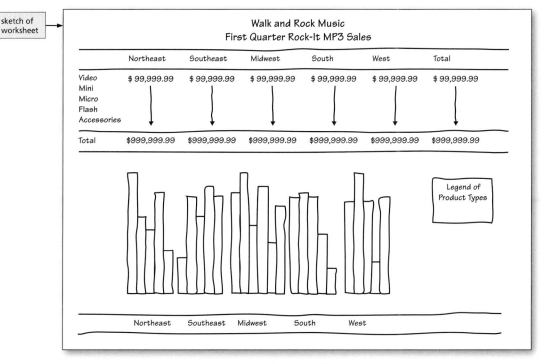

sketch of worksheet

Figure 1–3

Plan
Ahead

(continued)

2. **Determine the contents for rows and columns.** Rows typically contain information that is analogous to items in a list, such as the products sold by a company. Columns typically contain descriptive information about items in rows or contain information that helps to group the data in the worksheet, such as company regions.

3. **Determine the calculations that are needed.** You can decide to total data in a variety of ways, such as across rows or in columns. You also can include a grand total.

4. **Determine where to save the workbook.** You can store a workbook permanently, or **save** it, on a variety of storage media including a hard disk, USB flash drive, or CD. You also can indicate a specific location on the storage media for saving the workbook.

5. **Identify how to format various elements of the worksheet.** The overall appearance of a worksheet significantly affects its ability to communicate clearly. Examples of how you can modify the appearance, or **format**, of text include changing its shape, size, color, and position on the worksheet.

6. **Decide on the type of chart needed.** Excel includes the capability of creating many different types of charts, such as bar charts and pie charts. Each chart type relays a different message about the data in the worksheet. Choose a chart type that relays the message that you want to convey.

7. **Establish where to position and how to format the chart.** The position and format of the chart should command the attention of the intended audience. If possible, position the chart so that it prints with the worksheet data on a single page.

When necessary, more specific details concerning the above guidelines are presented at appropriate points in the chapter. The chapter also will identify the actions performed and decisions made regarding these guidelines during the creation of the worksheet shown in Figure 1–1 on page EX 2.

After carefully reviewing the requirements document (Figure 1–2 on page EX 4) and necessary decisions, the next step is to design a solution or draw a sketch of the worksheet based on the requirements, including titles, column and row headings, location of data values, and the 3-D Clustered Column chart, as shown in Figure 1–3 on page EX 5. The dollar signs, 9s, and commas that you see in the sketch of the worksheet indicate formatted numeric values.

With a good understanding of the requirements document, an understanding of the necessary decisions, and a sketch of the worksheet, the next step is to use Excel to create the worksheet and chart.

Starting Excel

If you are using a computer to step through the project in this chapter and you want your screen to match the figures in this book, you should change your computer's resolution to 1024 × 768. For information about how to change a computer's resolution, read Appendix E.

To Start Excel

The following steps, which assume Windows is running, start Excel based on a typical installation of Microsoft Office on your computer. You may need to ask your instructor how to start Excel for your computer.

1

- Click the Start button on the Windows taskbar to display the Start menu.

- Point to All Programs on the Start menu to display the All Programs submenu.

- Point to Microsoft Office in the All Programs submenu to display the Microsoft Office submenu (Figure 1–4).

Figure 1–4

②

- Click Microsoft Office Excel 2007 to start Excel and display a new blank workbook titled Book1 in the Excel window (Figure 1–5).

- If the Excel window is not maximized, click the Maximize button next to the Close button on its title bar to maximize the window.

- If the worksheet window in Excel is not maximized, click the Maximize button next to the Close button on its title bar to maximize the worksheet window within Excel.

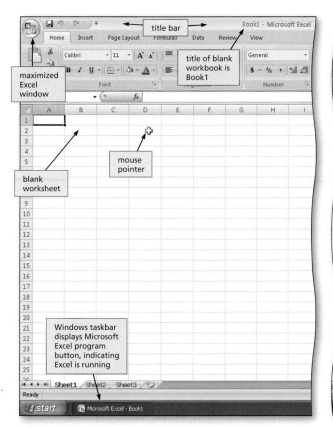

Figure 1–5

The Excel Workbook

The Excel window consists of a variety of components to make your work more efficient and worksheets more professional. These include the document window, Ribbon, Mini toolbar and shortcut menus, Quick Access Toolbar, and Office Button. Some of these components are common to other Microsoft Office 2007 programs; others are unique to Excel.

When Excel starts, it creates a new blank workbook, called Book1. The **workbook** (Figure 1–6) is like a notebook. Inside the workbook are sheets, each of which is called a **worksheet**. Excel opens a new workbook with three worksheets.

If necessary, you can add additional worksheets as long as your computer has enough memory to accommodate them. Each worksheet has a sheet name that appears on a **sheet tab** at the bottom of the workbook. For example, Sheet1 is the name of the active worksheet displayed in the Book1 workbook. If you click the sheet tab labeled Sheet2, Excel displays the Sheet2 worksheet. The project in this chapter uses only the Sheet1 worksheet.

The Worksheet

The worksheet is organized into a rectangular grid containing vertical columns and horizontal rows. A column letter above the grid, also called the **column heading**, identifies each column. A row number on the left side of the grid, also called the **row heading**, identifies each row. With the screen resolution set to 1024 × 768 and the Excel window maximized, Excel displays 15 columns (A through O) and 25 rows (1 through 25) of the worksheet on the screen, as shown in Figure 1–6.

Figure 1–6

Worksheet Development

The key to developing a useful worksheet is careful planning. Careful planning can reduce your effort significantly and result in a worksheet that is accurate, easy to read, flexible, and useful. When analyzing a problem and designing a worksheet solution, you should follow these steps: (1) define the problem, including need, source of data, calculations, charting, and Web or special requirements; (2) design the worksheet; (3) enter the data and formulas; and (4) test the worksheet.

The intersection of each column and row is a cell. A **cell** is the basic unit of a worksheet into which you enter data. Each worksheet in a workbook has 16,384 columns and 1,048,576 rows for a total of 17,179,869,180 cells. Only a small fraction of the active worksheet appears on the screen at one time.

A cell is referred to by its unique address, or **cell reference**, which is the coordinates of the intersection of a column and a row. To identify a cell, specify the column letter first, followed by the row number. For example, cell reference D11 refers to the cell located at the intersection of column D and row 11 (Figure 1–6).

One cell on the worksheet, designated the **active cell**, is the one into which you can enter data. The active cell in Figure 1–6 is A1. The active cell is identified in three ways. First, a heavy border surrounds the cell; second, the active cell reference shows immediately above column A in the Name box; and third, the column heading A and row heading 1 are highlighted so it is easy to see which cell is active (Figure 1–6).

The horizontal and vertical lines on the worksheet itself are called **gridlines**. Gridlines make it easier to see and identify each cell in the worksheet. If desired, you can turn the gridlines off so they do not show on the worksheet, but it is recommended that you leave them on for now.

The mouse pointer in Figure 1–6 has the shape of a block plus sign. The mouse pointer appears as a block plus sign whenever it is located in a cell on the worksheet. Another common shape of the mouse pointer is the block arrow. The mouse pointer turns into the block arrow whenever you move it outside the worksheet or when you drag cell contents between rows or columns. The other mouse pointer shapes are described when they appear on the screen.

Worksheet Window

You view the portion of the worksheet displayed on the screen through a **worksheet window** (Figure 1–6). The default (preset) view is **normal view**. Below and to the right of the worksheet window are **scroll bars**, **scroll arrows**, and **scroll boxes** that you can use to move the worksheet window around to view different parts of the active worksheet. To the right of the sheet tabs at the bottom of the screen is the tab split box. You can drag the **tab split box** to increase or decrease the view of the sheet tabs (Figure 1–6). When you decrease the view of the sheet tabs, you increase the length of the horizontal scroll bar, and vice versa.

Status Bar

The status bar is located immediately above the Windows taskbar at the bottom of the screen (Figure 1–6). The **status bar** presents information about the worksheet, the function of the button the mouse pointer is pointing to, or the mode of Excel. **Mode indicators**, such as Enter and Ready, appear on the status bar and specify the current mode of Excel. When the mode is **Ready**, Excel is ready to accept the next command or data entry. When the mode indicator reads **Enter**, Excel is in the process of accepting data through the keyboard into the active cell.

Keyboard indicators, such as Scroll Lock, show which toggle keys are engaged. Keyboard indicators appear to the right of the mode indicator. Toward the right edge of the status bar are buttons and controls you can use to change the view of a document and adjust the size of the displayed document.

Ribbon

The **Ribbon**, located near the top of the Excel window, is the control center in Excel (Figure 1–7a). The Ribbon provides easy, central access to the tasks you perform while creating a worksheet. The Ribbon consists of tabs, groups, and commands. Each **tab** surrounds a collection of groups, and each **group** contains related commands.

BTW

The Worksheet Size and Window
Excel's 16,384 columns and 1,048,576 rows make for a huge worksheet that – if you could imagine – takes up the entire side of a building to display in its entirety. Your computer screen, by comparison, is a small window that allows you to view only a minute area of the worksheet at one time. While you cannot see the entire worksheet, you can move the window over the worksheet to view any part of it.

BTW

Increasing the Viewing Area
You can increase the size of the Excel window or viewing area to show more of the worksheet. Two ways exist to increase what you can see in the viewing area: (1) on the View tab on the Ribbon, click Full Screen; and (2) change to a higher resolution. See Appendix E for information about how to change to a higher resolution.

(a) The Excel Ribbon

(b) The Excel Ribbon Minimized

Figure 1–7

BTW

Minimizing the Ribbon
If you want to minimize
the Ribbon, right-click
the Ribbon and then click
Minimize the Ribbon
on the shortcut menu,
double-click the active
tab, or press CTRL+F1.
To restore a minimized
Ribbon, right-click the
Ribbon and then click
Minimize the Ribbon
on the shortcut menu,
double-click any top-level
tab, or press CTRL+F1.
To use commands on a
minimized Ribbon, click
the top-level tab.

When you start Excel, the Ribbon displays seven top-level tabs: Home, Insert, Page Layout, Formulas, Data, Review, and View. The **Home tab**, called the primary tab, contains groups with the more frequently used commands. To display a different tab on the Ribbon, click the top-level tab. That is, to display the Insert tab, click Insert on the Ribbon. To return to the Home tab, click Home on the Ribbon. The tab currently displayed is called the **active tab**.

To display more of the document in the document window, some users prefer to minimize the Ribbon, which hides the groups on the Ribbon and displays only the top-level tabs (Figure 1–7b). To use commands on a minimized Ribbon, click the top-level tab.

Each time you start Excel, the Ribbon appears the same way it did the last time you used Excel. The chapters in this book, however, begin with the Ribbon appearing as it did at the initial installation of the software. If you are stepping through this chapter on a computer and you want your Ribbon to match the figures in this book, read Appendix E.

In addition to the top-level tabs, Excel displays other tabs, called **contextual tabs**, when you perform certain tasks or work with objects such as charts or tables. If you insert a chart in the worksheet, for example, the Chart Tools tab and its related subordinate Design tab appear (Figure 1–8). When you are finished working with the chart, the Chart Tools and Design tabs disappear from the Ribbon. Excel determines when contextual tabs should appear and disappear, based on the tasks you perform.

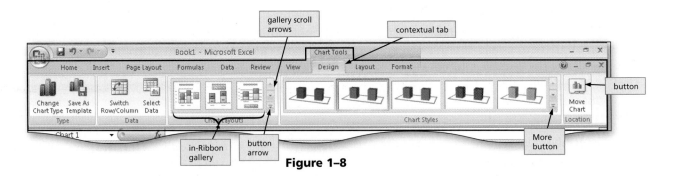

Figure 1–8

Ribbon commands include buttons, boxes (text boxes, check boxes, etc.), and galleries (Figure 1–8). A **gallery** is a set of choices, often graphical, arranged in a grid or in a list. You can scroll through choices on an in-Ribbon gallery by clicking the gallery's scroll arrows. An **in-Ribbon** gallery shows common gallery choices on the Ribbon rather than in a dropdown list. Or, you can click a gallery's More button to view more gallery options on the screen at a time. Some buttons and boxes have arrows that, when clicked, also display a gallery; others always cause a gallery to be displayed when clicked. Most galleries support **live preview**, which is a feature that allows you to point to a gallery choice and see its effect in the worksheet without actually selecting the choice (Figure 1–9).

Some commands on the Ribbon display an image to help you remember their function. When you point to a command on the Ribbon, all or part of the command glows in shades of yellow and orange, and an Enhanced ScreenTip appears on the screen. An **Enhanced ScreenTip** is an on-screen note that provides the name of the command, available keyboard shortcut(s), a description of the command, and sometimes instructions for how to obtain Help about the command (Figure 1–10). Enhanced ScreenTips are more detailed than a typical **ScreenTip**, which usually displays only the name of the command.

The lower-right corner of some groups on the Ribbon has a small arrow, called a **Dialog Box Launcher**, that when clicked displays a dialog box or a task pane (Figure 1–11). A **dialog box** contains additional commands and options for the group. When presented with a dialog box, you make selections and must close the dialog box before returning to the worksheet. A **task pane**, by contrast, is a window that contains additional commands and can stay open and visible while you work on the worksheet.

Figure 1–9

Figure 1–10

Figure 1–11

Formula Bar

The formula bar appears below the Ribbon (Figure 1–12a). As you type, Excel displays the entry in the **formula bar**. You can make the formula bar larger by dragging the sizing handle (Figure 1–7) on the formula bar or clicking the expand button to the right of the formula bar. Excel also displays the active cell reference in the **Name box** on the left side of the formula bar.

Mini Toolbar and Shortcut Menus

The **Mini toolbar**, which appears automatically based on tasks you perform (such as selecting text), contains commands related to changing the appearance of text in a worksheet. All commands on the Mini toolbar also exist on the Ribbon. The purpose of the Mini toolbar is to minimize mouse movement. For example, if you want to format text using a command that currently is not displayed on the active tab, you can use the command on the Mini toolbar — instead of switching to a different tab to use the command.

When the Mini toolbar appears, it initially is transparent (Figure 1–12a). If you do not use the transparent Mini toolbar, it disappears from the screen. To use the Mini toolbar, move the mouse pointer into the toolbar, which causes the Mini toolbar to change from a transparent to bright appearance (Figure 1–12b).

(a) Transparent Mini Toolbar

(b) Bright Mini Toolbar

Figure 1–12

Figure 1–13

A **shortcut menu**, which appears when you right-click an object, is a list of frequently used commands that relate to the right-clicked object. If you right-click an item in the document window such as a cell, Excel displays both the Mini toolbar and a shortcut menu (Figure 1–13).

Quick Access Toolbar

The **Quick Access Toolbar**, located by default above the Ribbon, provides easy access to frequently used commands (Figure 1–14a). The commands on the Quick Access Toolbar always are available, regardless of the task you are performing. Initially, the Quick Access Toolbar contains the Save, Undo, and Redo buttons. If you click the Customize Quick Access Toolbar button, Excel provides a list of commands you quickly can add to and remove from the Quick Access Toolbar (Figure 1–14b).

You also can add other commands to or delete commands from the Quick Access Toolbar so that it contains the commands you use most often. As you add commands to the Quick Access Toolbar, its commands may interfere with the workbook title on the title bar. For this reason, Excel provides an option of displaying the Quick Access Toolbar below the Ribbon (Figure 1–14c).

BTW

Quick Access Toolbar Commands
To add a Ribbon command as a button to the Quick Access Toolbar, right-click the command on the Ribbon and then click Add to Quick Access Toolbar on the shortcut menu. To delete a button from the Quick Access Toolbar, right-click the button on the Quick Access Toolbar and then click Remove from Quick Access Toolbar on the shortcut menu. To display the Quick Access Toolbar below the Ribbon, right-click the Quick Access Toolbar and then click Show Quick Access Toolbar below the Ribbon on the shortcut menu.

(a) Quick Access Toolbar above Ribbon

(c) Quick Access Toolbar below Ribbon

(b) Customize Quick Access Toolbar Menu

Figure 1–14

Each time you start Excel, the Quick Access Toolbar appears the same way it did the last time you used Excel. The chapters in this book, however, begin with the Quick Access Toolbar appearing as it did at the initial installation of the software. If you are stepping through this chapter on a computer and you want your Quick Access Toolbar to match the figures in this book, you should reset your Quick Access Toolbar. For more information about how to reset the Quick Access Toolbar, read Appendix E.

Office Button

While the Ribbon is a control center for creating worksheets, the **Office Button** is a central location for managing and sharing workbooks. When you click the Office Button, located in the upper-left corner of the window, Excel displays the Office Button menu (Figure 1–15). A **menu** contains a list of commands.

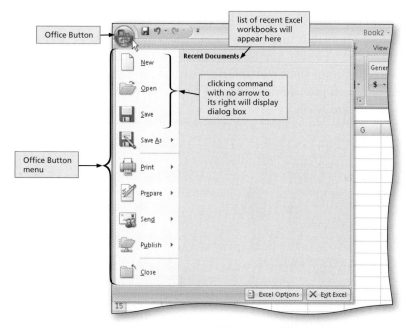

Figure 1–15

When you click the New, Open, Save As, and Print commands on the Office Button menu, Excel displays a dialog box with additional options. The Save As, Print, Prepare, Send, and Publish commands have an arrow to their right. If you point to a button that includes an arrow, Excel displays a **submenu**, which is a list of additional commands associated with the selected command (Figure 1–16). For the Prepare, Send, and Publish commands that do not display a dialog box when clicked, you can point either to the command or the arrow to display the submenu.

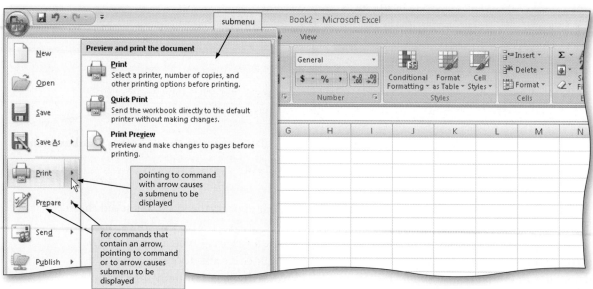

Figure 1–16

Key Tips

If you prefer using the keyboard, instead of the mouse, you can press the ALT key on the keyboard to display a **Key Tip badge**, or keyboard code icon, for certain commands (Figure 1–17). To select a command using the keyboard, press its displayed code letter, or **Key Tip**. When you press a Key Tip, additional Key Tips related to the selected command appear. For example, to select the New command on the Office Button menu, press the ALT key, then press the F key, then press the N key.

Figure 1–17

To remove the Key Tip badges from the screen, press the ALT key or the ESC key on the keyboard until all Key Tip badges disappear or click the mouse anywhere in the Excel window.

Selecting a Cell

To enter data into a cell, you first must select it. The easiest way **to select a cell** (make it active) is to use the mouse to move the block plus sign mouse pointer to the cell and then click.

An alternative method is to use the arrow keys that are located just to the right of the typewriter keys on the keyboard. An arrow key selects the cell adjacent to the active cell in the direction of the arrow on the key.

You know a cell is selected, or active, when a heavy border surrounds the cell and the active cell reference appears in the Name box on the left side of the formula bar. Excel also changes the active cell's column heading and row heading to a gold color.

Entering Text

In Excel, any set of characters containing a letter, hyphen (as in a telephone number), or space is considered text. **Text** is used to place titles, such as worksheet titles, column titles, and row titles, on the worksheet.

<table>
<tr><td>Plan
Ahead</td><td>**Select titles and subtitles for the worksheet.**
As previously stated, worksheet titles and subtitles should be as brief and meaningful as possible. As shown in Figure 1–18, the worksheet title, Walk and Rock Music, identifies the company for whom the worksheet is being created in Chapter 1. The worksheet subtitle, First Quarter Rock-It MP3 Sales, identifies the type of report.</td></tr>
</table>

<table>
<tr><td>Plan
Ahead</td><td>**Determine the contents of rows and columns.**
As previously mentioned, rows typically contain information that is similar to items in a list. For the Walk and Rock Music sales data, the list of product types meets this criterion. It is more likely that in the future, the company will add more product types as opposed to more regions. Each product type, therefore, should be placed in its own row. The row titles in column A (Video, Mini, Micro, Flash, Accessories, and Total) identify the numbers in each row.

Columns typically contain descriptive information about items in rows or contain information that helps to group the data in the worksheet. In the case of the Walk and Rock Music sales data, the regions classify the sales of each product type. The regions, therefore, are placed in columns. The column titles in row 3 (Northeast, Southeast, Midwest, South, West, and Total) identify the numbers in each column.</td></tr>
</table>

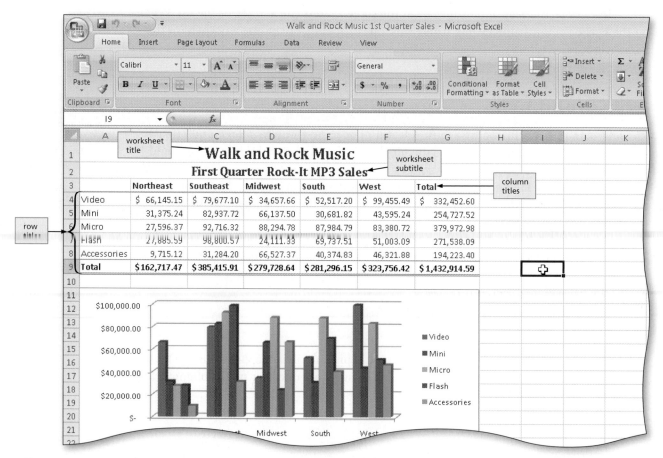

Figure 1–18

To Enter the Worksheet Titles

The following steps show how to enter the worksheet titles in cells A1 and A2. Later in this chapter, the worksheet titles will be formatted so they appear as shown in Figure 1–18.

1
- Click cell A1 to make cell A1 the active cell (Figure 1–19).

Figure 1–19

2
- Type Walk and Rock Music in cell A1, and then point to the Enter box in the formula bar.

Q&A Why did the appearance of the formula bar change?

Excel displays the title in the formula bar and in cell A1. When you begin typing a cell entry, Excel displays two additional boxes in the formula bar: the Cancel box and the Enter box. Clicking the **Enter box** completes an entry. Clicking the **Cancel box** cancels an entry.

Q&A What is the vertical line in cell A1?

In Figure 1–20, the text in cell A1 is followed by the insertion point. The **insertion point** is a blinking vertical line that indicates where the next typed character will appear.

Figure 1–20

- Click the Enter box to complete the entry and enter the worksheet title in cell A1 (Figure 1–21).

Figure 1–21

- Click cell A2 to select it.

- Type First Quarter Rock-It MP3 Sales as the cell entry.

- Click the Enter box to complete the entry and enter the worksheet subtitle in cell A2 (Figure 1–22).

Figure 1–22

Other Ways

1. To complete entry, click any cell other than active cell

2. To complete entry, press ENTER key

3. To complete entry, press HOME, PAGE UP, PAGE DOWN, or END key

Entering Text in a Cell

When you complete a text entry into a cell, a series of events occurs. First, Excel positions the text left-aligned in the cell. **Left-aligned** means the cell entry is positioned at the far left in the cell. Therefore, the W in the worksheet title, Walk and Rock Music, begins in the leftmost position of cell A1.

Second, when the text is longer than the width of a column, Excel displays the overflow characters in adjacent cells to the right as long as these adjacent cells contain no data. In Figure 1–22, the width of cell A1 is approximately nine characters. The text consists of 19 characters. Therefore, Excel displays the overflow characters from cell A1 in cells B1 and C1, because cells B1 and C1 are empty. If cell B1 contained data, Excel would hide the overflow characters, so that only the first nine characters in cell A1 would appear on the worksheet. Excel stores the overflow characters in cell A1 and displays them in the formula bar whenever cell A1 is the active cell.

Third, when you complete an entry by clicking the Enter box, the cell in which the text is entered remains the active cell.

Correcting a Mistake while Typing

If you type the wrong letter and notice the error before clicking the Enter box or pressing the ENTER key, use the BACKSPACE key to delete all the characters back to and including the incorrect letter. To cancel the entire entry before entering it into the cell, click the Cancel box in the formula bar or press the ESC key. If you see an error in a cell after entering the text, select the cell and retype the entry. Later in this chapter, additional error-correction techniques are discussed.

AutoCorrect

The **AutoCorrect feature** of Excel works behind the scenes, correcting common mistakes when you complete a text entry in a cell. AutoCorrect makes three types of corrections for you:

1. Corrects two initial capital letters by changing the second letter to lowercase.

2. Capitalizes the first letter in the names of days.

3. Replaces commonly misspelled words with their correct spelling. For example, it will change the misspelled word *recieve* to *receive* when you complete the entry. AutoCorrect will correct the spelling of hundreds of commonly misspelled words automatically.

BTW

The ENTER Key
When you first install Excel, the ENTER key not only completes the entry, but it also moves the selection to an adjacent cell. You can instruct Excel not to move the selection after pressing the ENTER key by clicking the Excel Options button on the Office Button menu, clicking the Advanced option, removing the checkmark from the 'After pressing Enter, move selection' check box, and then clicking the OK button.

To Enter Column Titles

To enter the column titles in row 3, select the appropriate cell and then enter the text. The following steps enter the column titles in row 3.

- Click cell B3 to make cell B3 the active cell (Figure 1–23).

Figure 1–23

2

- Type Northeast in cell B3 (Figure 1–24).

Figure 1–24

3

- Press the RIGHT ARROW key to enter the column title, Northeast, in cell B3 and make cell C3 the active cell (Figure 1–25).

Q&A

Why is the RIGHT ARROW key used to complete the entry in the cell?

If the next entry is in an adjacent cell, use the arrow keys to complete the entry in a cell. When you press an arrow key to complete an entry, the adjacent cell in the direction of the arrow (up, down, left, or right) becomes the active cell. If the next entry is in a nonadjacent cell, complete an entry by clicking the next cell in which you plan to enter data. You also can click the Enter box or press the ENTER key and then click the appropriate cell for the next entry.

Figure 1–25

4

- Repeat Steps 2 and 3 to enter the remaining column titles in row 3; that is, enter `Southeast` in cell C3, `Midwest` in cell D3, `South` in cell E3, `West` in cell F3, and `Total` in cell G3 (complete the last entry in cell G3 by clicking the Enter box in the formula bar) (Figure 1–26).

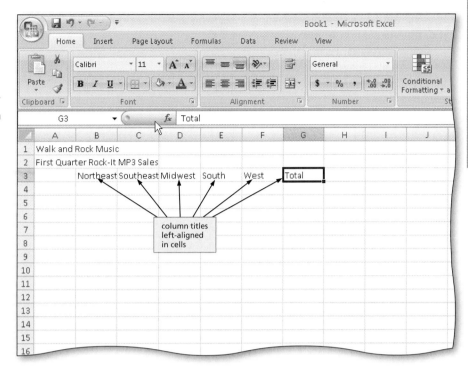

Figure 1–26

To Enter Row Titles

The next step in developing the worksheet for this project is to enter the row titles in column A. This process is similar to entering the column titles. The following steps enter the row titles in the worksheet.

1

- Click cell A4 to select it.

- Type `Video` and then press the DOWN ARROW key to enter the row title and make cell A5 the active cell (Figure 1–27).

Figure 1–27

2

- Repeat Step 1 to enter the remaining row titles in column A; that is, enter Mini in cell A5, Micro in cell A6, Flash in cell A7, Accessories in cell A8, and Total in cell A9 (Figure 1–28).

Q&A

Why is the text left-aligned in the cells?

When you enter text, Excel automatically left-aligns the text in the cell. Excel treats any combination of numbers, spaces, and nonnumeric characters as text. For example, the following entries are text:

401AX21, 921-231, 619 321, 883XTY

You can change the text alignment in a cell by realigning it. Several alignment techniques are discussed later in the chapter.

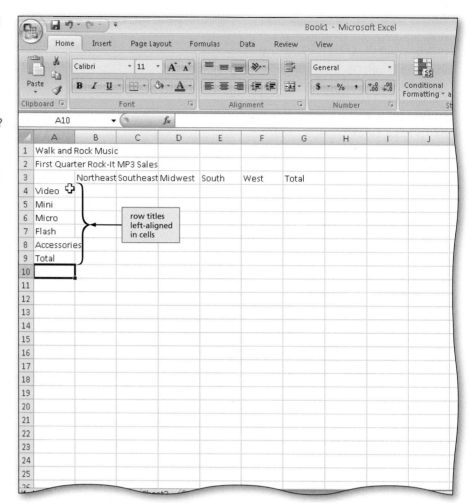

Figure 1–28

Entering Numbers

BTW

Numeric Limitations
In Excel, a number can be between approximately -1×10^{308} and 1×10^{308}, that is, between a negative 1 followed by 308 zeros and a positive 1 followed by 308 zeros. To enter a number such as 6,000,000,000,000,000, you can type 6,000,000,000,000,000, or you can type 6E15, which stands for 6×10^{15}.

In Excel, you can enter numbers into cells to represent amounts. A **number** can contain only the following characters:

0 1 2 3 4 5 6 7 8 9 + - ( ) , / . $ % E e

If a cell entry contains any other keyboard character (including spaces), Excel interprets the entry as text and treats it accordingly. The use of the special characters is explained when they are used in this book.

To Enter Numbers

The Walk and Rock Music First Quarter Rock-It MP3 Sales numbers used in Chapter 1 are summarized in Table 1–1. These numbers, which represent sales revenue for each of the product types and regions, must be entered in rows 4, 5, 6, 7, and 8.

Table 1–1 Walk and Rock Music First Quarter Rock-It MP3 Sales					
	Northeast	**Southeast**	**Midwest**	**South**	**West**
Video	66145.15	79677.10	34657.66	52517.20	99455.49
Mini	31375.24	82937.72	66137.50	30681.82	43595.24
Micro	27596.37	92716.32	88294.78	87984.79	83380.72
Flash	27885.59	98800.57	24111.33	69737.51	51003.09
Accessories	9715.12	31284.20	66527.37	40374.83	46321.88

The following steps enter the numbers in Table 1–1 one row at a time.

- Click cell B4.

- Type 66145.15 and then press the RIGHT ARROW key to enter the data in cell B4 and make cell C4 the active cell (Figure 1–29).

Q&A

Do I need to enter dollar signs, commas, or trailing zeros for the quarterly sales numbers?

You are not required to type dollar signs, commas, or trailing zeros. When you enter a dollar value that has cents, however, you must add the decimal point and the numbers representing the cents. Later in this chapter, the numbers will be formatted to use dollar signs, commas, and trailing zeros to improve the appearance and readability of the numbers.

Figure 1–29

- Enter 79677.1 in cell C4, 34657.66 in cell D4, 52517.2 in cell E4, and 99455.49 in cell F4 (Figure 1–30).

Figure 1–30

3

- Click cell B5.

- Enter the remaining first quarter sales numbers provided in Table 1–1 for each of the four remaining offerings in rows 5, 6, 7, and 8 to display the quarterly sales in the worksheet (Figure 1–31).

row title partially displayed because adjacent cell on right contains data

data entered into worksheet

Figure 1–31

Calculating a Sum

The next step in creating the worksheet is to perform any necessary calculations, such as calculating the column and row totals.

Plan Ahead

Determine calculations that are needed.
As stated in the requirements document in Figure 1–2 on page EX 4, totals are required for each region, each product type, and the company. The first calculation is to determine the quarterly sales for the stores in the Northeast region in column B. To calculate this value in cell B9, Excel must add, or sum, the numbers in cells B4, B5, B6, B7, and B8. Excel's **SUM function**, which adds all of the numbers in a range of cells, provides a convenient means to accomplish this task.

A **range** is a series of two or more adjacent cells in a column or row or a rectangular group of cells. For example, the group of adjacent cells B4, B5, B6, B7, and B8 is called a range. Many Excel operations, such as summing numbers, take place on a range of cells.

After the total quarterly sales for the stores in the Northeast region in column B is determined, the totals for the remaining regions and totals for each product type will be determined.

Entering Numbers as Text
Sometimes, you will want Excel to treat numbers, such as Zip codes and telephone numbers, as text. To enter a number as text, start the entry with an apostrophe (').

Calculating Sums
Excel calculates sums for a variety of data types. For example, Boolean values, such as TRUE and FALSE, can be summed. Excel treats the value of TRUE as 1 and the value of FALSE as 0. Times also can be summed. For example, Excel treats the sum of 1:15 and 2:45 as 4:00.

To Sum a Column of Numbers

The following steps sum the numbers in column B.

1

- Click cell B9 to make it the active cell and then point to the SUM button on the Ribbon (Figure 1–32).

Figure 1–32

2

- Click the Sum button on the Ribbon to display =SUM(B4:B8) in the formula bar and in the active cell B9 (Figure 1–33).

Q&A

How does Excel know which cells to sum?

When you enter the SUM function using the Sum button, Excel automatically selects what it considers to be your choice of the range to sum. When proposing the range to sum, Excel first looks for a range of cells with numbers above the active cell and then to the left. If Excel proposes the wrong range, you can correct it by dragging through the correct range before pressing the ENTER key. You also can enter the correct range by typing the beginning cell reference, a colon (:), and the ending cell reference.

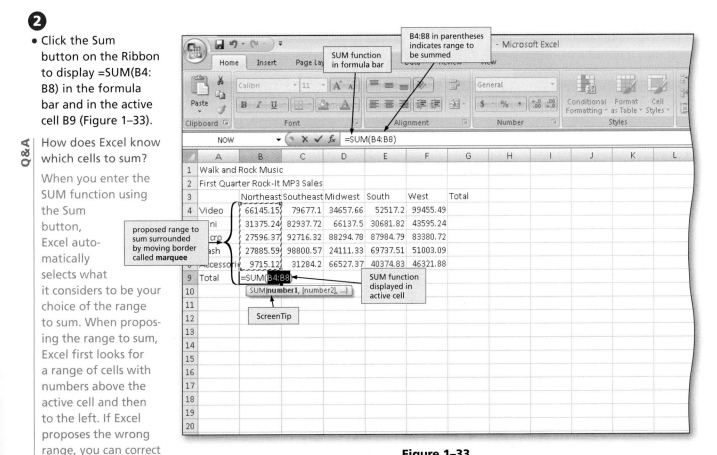

Figure 1–33

3

- Click the Enter box in the formula bar to enter the sum of the first quarter sales for the five product types for the Northeast region in cell B9.

- Select cell B9 to display the SUM function assigned to cell B9 in the formula bar (Figure 1–34).

What is the purpose of the Sum button arrow?

If you click the Sum button arrow on the right side of the Sum button (Figure 1–34), Excel displays a list of often-used functions from which you can choose. The list includes functions that allow you to determine the average, the number of items in the selected range, the minimum value, or the maximum value of a range of numbers.

Figure 1–34

Other Ways

1. Click Function Wizard button in formula bar, select SUM in Select a function list, click OK button, select range, click OK button

2. Click Sum button arrow on Ribbon, click More Functions, select SUM in Select a function list, click OK button, select range, click OK button

3. Type = s in cell, select SUM from list, select range

4. Press ALT + EQUAL SIGN (=) twice

Using the Fill Handle to Copy a Cell to Adjacent Cells

Excel also must calculate the totals for the Southeast in cell C9, the Midwest in cell D9, the South in cell E9, and for the West in cell F9. Table 1–2 illustrates the similarities between the entry in cell B9 and the entries required to sum the totals in cells C9, D9, E9, and F9.

Table 1–2 Sum Function Entries in Row 9

Cell	Sum Function Entries	Remark
B9	=SUM(B4:B8)	Sums cells B4, B5, B6, B7, and B8
C9	=SUM(C4:C8)	Sums cells C4, C5, C6, C7, and C8
D9	=SUM(D4:D8)	Sums cells D4, D5, D6, D7, and D8
E9	=SUM(E4:E8)	Sums cells E4, E5, E6, E7, and E8
F9	=SUM(F4:F8)	Sums cells F4, F5, F6, F7, and F8

To place the SUM functions in cells C9, D9, E9, and F9, you could follow the same steps shown previously in Figures 1–32 through 1–34. A second, more efficient method is to copy the SUM function from cell B9 to the range C9:F9. The cell being copied is called the **source area** or **copy area**. The range of cells receiving the copy is called the **destination area** or **paste area**.

Although the SUM function entries in Table 1–2 are similar, they are not exact copies. The range in each SUM function entry uses cell references that are one column to the right of the previous column. When you copy cell references, Excel automatically adjusts them for each new position, resulting in the SUM function entries illustrated in Table 1–2. Each adjusted cell reference is called a **relative reference**.

To Copy a Cell to Adjacent Cells in a Row

The easiest way to copy the SUM formula from cell B9 to cells C9, D9, E9, and F9 is to use the fill handle. The **fill handle** is the small black square located in the lower-right corner of the heavy border around the active cell. The following steps use the fill handle to copy cell B9 to the adjacent cells C9:F9.

- With cell B9 active, point to the fill handle (Figure 1–35).

Figure 1–35

- Drag the fill handle to select the destination area, range C9:F9, to display a shaded border around the destination area, range C9:F9, and the source area, cell B9 (Figure 1–36). Do not release the mouse button.

Figure 1–36

• Release the mouse button to copy the SUM function in cell B9 to the range C9:F9 (Figure 1–37) and calculate the sums in cells C9, D9, E9, and F9.

Q&A

What is the purpose of the Auto Fill Options button?

When you copy one range to another, Excel displays an Auto Fill Options button (Figure 1–37). The Auto Fill Options button allows you to choose whether you want to copy the values from the source area to the destination area with formatting, without formatting, or copy only the format. To view the available fill options, click the Auto Fill Options button. The Auto Fill Options button disappears when you begin another activity.

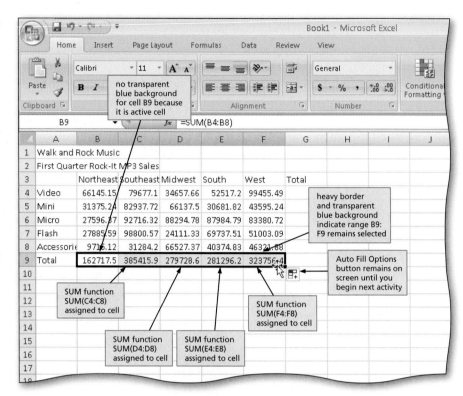

Figure 1–37

Other Ways

1. Select source area, click Copy button on Ribbon, select destination area, click Paste button on Ribbon

2. Right-click source area, click Copy on shortcut menu, right-click destination area, click Paste on shortcut menu

3. Select source area and then point to border of range; while holding down CTRL key, drag source area to destination area

---

To Determine Multiple Totals at the Same Time

The next step in building the worksheet is to determine the quarterly sales for each product type and total quarterly sales for the company in column G. To calculate these totals, you can use the SUM function much as it was used to total the quarterly sales by region in row 9. In this example, however, Excel will determine totals for all of the rows at the same time. The following steps illustrate this process.

1

• Click cell G4 to make it the active cell (Figure 1–38).

Figure 1–38

2

- With the mouse pointer in cell G4 and in the shape of a block plus sign, drag the mouse pointer down to cell G9 to highlight the range G4:G9 with a transparent view (Figure 1–39).

Figure 1–39

3

- Click the Sum button on the Ribbon to calculate and display the sums of the corresponding rows of sales in cells G4, G5, G6, G7, G8, and G9 (Figure 1–40).

4

- Select cell A10 to deselect the range G4:G9.

Q&A

Why does Excel create totals for each row?

If each cell in a selected range is next to a row of numbers, Excel assigns the SUM function to each cell when you click the Sum button.

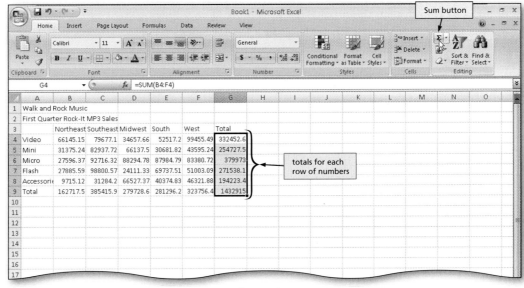

Figure 1–40

Saving the Project

While you are building a worksheet in a workbook, the computer stores it in memory. When you save a workbook, the computer places it on a storage medium such as a USB flash drive, CD, or hard disk. A saved workbook is referred to as a **file**. A **file name** is the name assigned to a file when it is saved. It is important to save the workbook frequently for the following reasons:

- The worksheet in memory will be lost if the computer is turned off or you lose electrical power while Excel is open.
- If you run out of time before completing your workbook, you may finish your worksheet at a future time without starting over.

BTW

Saving

Excel allows you to save a workbook in more than 30 different file formats. Choose the file format by clicking the 'Save as type' box arrow at the bottom of the Save As dialog box (Figure 1–41 on the next page). Excel Workbook is the default file format.

<table>
<tr>
<td>Plan
Ahead</td>
<td>

Determine where to save the workbook.
When saving a workbook, you must decide which storage medium to use.

• If you always work on the same computer and have no need to transport your projects to a different location, then your computer's hard drive will suffice as a storage location. It is a good idea, however, to save a backup copy of your projects on a separate medium in case the file becomes corrupted or the computer's hard drive fails.

• If you plan to work on your workbooks in various locations or on multiple computers, then you should save your workbooks on a portable medium, such as a USB flash drive or CD. The workbooks used in this book are saved to a USB flash drive, which saves files quickly and reliably and can be reused. CDs are easily portable and serve as good backups for the final versions of workbooks because they generally can save files only one time.

</td>
</tr>
</table>

To Save a Workbook

You have performed many tasks while creating this project and do not want to risk losing the work completed thus far. Accordingly, you should save the workbook. The following steps save a workbook on a USB flash drive using the file name, Walk and Rock Music 1st Quarter Sales.

• With a USB flash drive connected to one of the computer's USB ports, click the Save button on the Quick Access Toolbar to display the Save As dialog box (Figure 1–41).

Q&A

Do I have to save to a USB flash drive?

No. You can save to any device or folder. A folder is a specific location on a storage medium. You can save to the default folder or a different folder. You also can create your own folders, which is explained later in this book.

Figure 1–41

2

• Type Walk and Rock Music 1st Quarter Sales in the File name text box to change the file name. Do not press the ENTER key after typing the file name (Figure 1–42).

Q&A

What characters can I use in a file name?

A file name can have a maximum of 255 characters, including spaces. The only invalid characters are the backslash (\ ), slash (/), colon (:), asterisk (*), question mark (?), quotation mark ("), less than symbol (<), greater than symbol (>), and vertical bar (|).

selected words in default file name automatically are replaced when you type new file name

clicking Cancel button will close Save As dialog box

Figure 1–42

3

• Click the Save in box arrow to display a list of available drives and folders (Figure 1–43).

Q&A

Why is my list of files, folders, and drives arranged and named differently from those shown in the figure?

Your computer's configuration determines how the list of files and folders is displayed and how drives are named. You can change the save location by clicking shortcuts on the **My Places bar**.

Q&A

How do I save the file if I am not using a USB flash drive?

Use the same process, but be certain to select your device in the Save in list.

Save in box arrow

list of available drives and folders is displayed in Save in list

workbook to be saved on USB flash drive

shortcuts on My Places bar allow you to change save location

Figure 1–43

4

• Click UDISK 2.0 (E:) in the Save in list to select the USB flash drive, Drive E in this case, as the new save location (Figure 1–44).

Q&A

What if my USB flash drive has a different name or letter?

It is very likely that your USB flash drive will have a different name and drive letter and be connected to a different port.

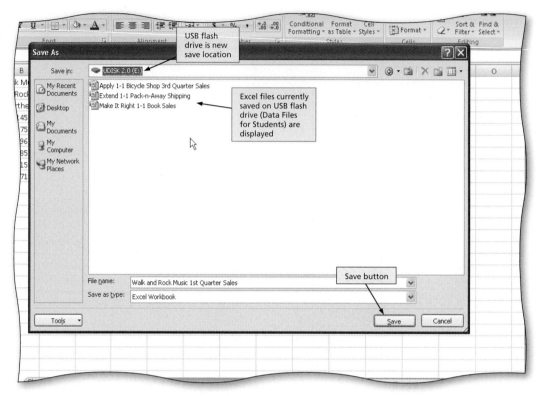

Figure 1–44

5

• Click the Save button in the Save As dialog box to save the workbook on the USB flash drive with the file name, Walk and Rock Music 1st Quarter Sales (Figure 1–45).

Q&A

How do I know that Excel saved the workbook?

While Excel is saving your file, it briefly displays a message on the status bar indicating the amount of the file saved. In addition, your USB drive may have a light that flashes during the save process.

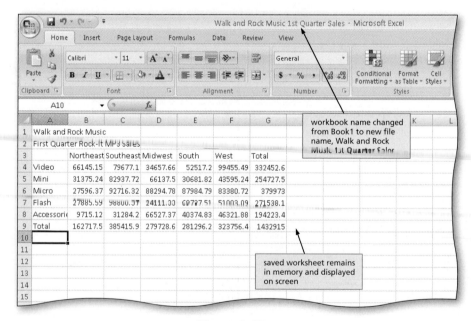

Figure 1–45

Other Ways

1. Click Office Button, click Save, type file name, select drive or folder, click Save button
2. Press CTRL+S or press SHIFT+F12, type file name, select drive or folder, click Save button

Formatting the Worksheet

The text, numeric entries, and functions for the worksheet now are complete. The next step is to format the worksheet. You **format** a worksheet to emphasize certain entries and make the worksheet easier to read and understand.

Figure 1–46a shows the worksheet before formatting. Figure 1–46b shows the worksheet after formatting. As you can see from the two figures, a worksheet that is formatted not only is easier to read but also looks more professional.

(a) Before Formatting

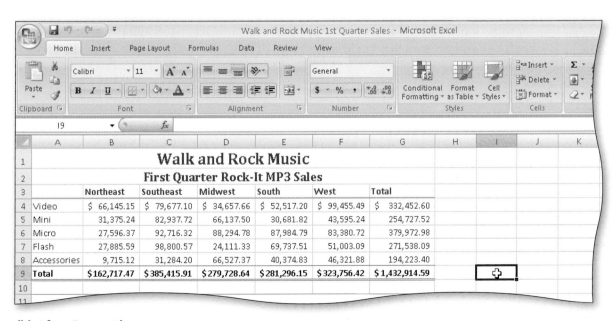

(b) After Formatting

Figure 1–46

<table>
<tr>
<td>Plan
Ahead</td>
<td>

Identify how to format various elements of the worksheet.
To change the unformatted worksheet in Figure 1–46a to the formatted worksheet in Figure 1–46b, the following tasks must be completed:

1. Change the font type, change the font style to bold, increase the font size, and change the font color of the worksheet titles in cells A1 and A2. These changes make the worksheet title prominently display to the user and inform the user of the purpose of the worksheet.

2. Center the worksheet titles in cells A1 and A2 across columns A through G.

3. Format the body of the worksheet. The body of the worksheet, range A3:G9, includes the column titles, row titles, and numbers. Formatting the body of the worksheet changes the numbers to use a dollars-and-cents format, with dollar signs in the first row (row 4) and the total row (row 9); adds underlining that emphasizes portions of the worksheet; and modifies the column widths to make the text and numbers readable.

</td>
</tr>
</table>

The remainder of this section explains the process required to format the worksheet. Although the format procedures are explained in the order described above, you should be aware that you could make these format changes in any order. Modifying the column widths, however, usually is done last.

BTW

Fonts
In general, use no more than two font types in a worksheet.

BTW

Fonts and Themes
Excel uses default recommended fonts based on the workbook's theme. A theme is a collection of fonts and color schemes. The default theme is named Office, and the two recommended fonts for the Office theme are Calibri and Cambria. Excel, however, allows you to apply any font to a cell or range as long as the font is installed on your computer.

Font Type, Style, Size, and Color

The characters that Excel displays on the screen are a specific font type, style, size, and color. The **font type**, or font face, defines the appearance and shape of the letters, numbers, and special characters. Examples of font types include Calibri, Cambria, Times New Roman, Arial, and Courier. **Font style** indicates how the characters are emphasized. Common font styles include regular, bold, underline, or italic. The **font size** specifies the size of the characters on the screen. Font size is gauged by a measurement system called points. A single point is about 1/72 of one inch in height. Thus, a character with a **point size** of 10 is about 10/72 of one inch in height. The **font color** defines the color of the characters. Excel can display characters in a wide variety of colors, including black, red, orange, and blue.

When Excel begins, the preset font type for the entire workbook is Calibri, with a font size, font style, and font color of 11-point regular black. Excel allows you to change the font characteristics in a single cell, a range of cells, the entire worksheet, or the entire workbook.

To Change a Cell Style

Excel includes the capability of changing several characteristics of a cell, such as font type, font size, and font color, all at once by assigning a predefined cell style to a cell. The following steps assign the Title cell style to the worksheet title in cell A1.

1

- Click cell A1 to make cell A1 the active cell.

- Click the Cell Styles button on the Ribbon to display the Cell Styles gallery (Figure 1–47).

Figure 1–47

2

- Point to the Title cell style in the Titles and Headings area of the Cell Styles gallery to see a live preview of the cell style in cell A1 (Figure 1–48).

 Experiment

- Point to several other cell styles in the Cell Styles gallery to see a live preview of other cell styles in cell A1.

Q&A Why does the font type, font size, and font color change in cell A1 when I point to it?

The change in cell A1 is a result of live preview. Live preview is a feature of Excel 2007 that allows you to preview cell styles as you point to them in the Cell Styles gallery.

Figure 1–48

3

- Click the Title cell style to apply the cell style to cell A1 (Figure 1–49).

Why do several items in the Font group on the Ribbon change?

The changes to the Font box, Bold button, and Font Size box indicate the font changes applied to the active cell, cell A1, as a result of applying the Title cell style.

Figure 1–49

To Change the Font Type

Different font types often are used in a worksheet to make it more appealing to the reader. The following steps show how to change the worksheet subtitle's font type from Calibri to Cambria.

1

- Click cell A2 to make cell A2 the active cell.

- Click the Font box arrow on the Ribbon to display the Font gallery (Figure 1–50)

Which fonts are displayed in the Font gallery?

Because many applications supply additional font types beyond what comes with the Windows operating system, the number of font types available on your computer will depend on the applications installed. This book uses only font types that come with the Windows operating system and Microsoft Office.

Figure 1–50

2

- Point to Cambria in the Theme Fonts area of the Font gallery to see a live preview of the Cambria font in cell A2 (Figure 1–51).

 Experiment

- Point to several other fonts in the Font gallery to see a live preview of other fonts in cell A2.

Q&A

What is the Theme Fonts area?

Excel applies the same default theme to any new workbook that you start. A **theme** is a collection of cell styles and other styles that have common characteristics, such as a color scheme and font type. The default theme for an Excel workbook is the Office theme. The Theme Fonts area of the Font gallery includes the fonts included in the default Office theme. Cambria is recommended for headings and Calibri is recommended for cells in the body of the worksheet (Figure 1–51).

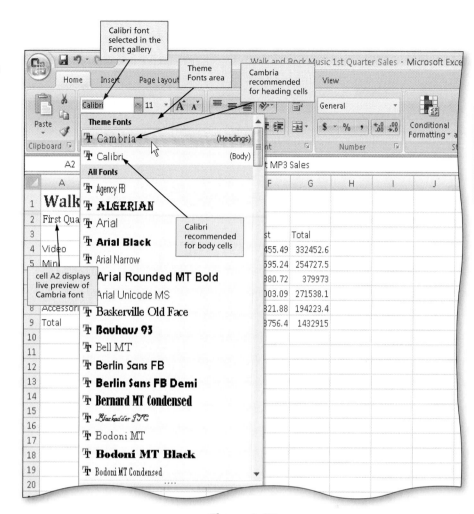

Figure 1–51

3

- Click Cambria in the Theme Fonts area to change the font type of the worksheet subtitle in cell A2 from Calibri to Cambria (Figure 1–52).

Figure 1–52

Other Ways

1. Select font type from Font list on Mini toolbar

2. Right-click cell, click Format Cells on shortcut menu, click Font tab, click desired font type, click OK button

To Bold a Cell

You **bold** an entry in a cell to emphasize it or make it stand out from the rest of the worksheet. The following step shows how to bold the worksheet subtitle in cell A2.

1

- With cell A2 active, click the Bold button on the Ribbon to change the font style of the worksheet subtitle to bold (Figure 1–53).

Q&A What if a cell already includes a bold style?

If you point to the Bold button and the active cell already is bold, then Excel displays the button with a transparent orange background.

Q&A How do I remove the bold style from a cell?

Clicking the Bold button a second time removes the bold font style.

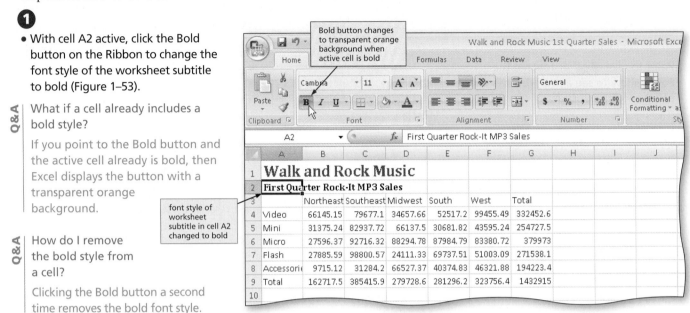

Figure 1–53

Other Ways

1. Click Bold button on Mini toolbar
2. Right-click cell, click Format Cells on shortcut menu, click Font tab, click Bold, click OK button
3. Press CTRL+B

To Increase the Font Size of a Cell Entry

Increasing the font size is the next step in formatting the worksheet subtitle. You increase the font size of a cell so the entry stands out and is easier to read. The following steps increase the font size of the worksheet subtitle in cell A2.

1

- With cell A2 selected, click the Font Size box arrow on the Ribbon to display the Font Size list.

- Point to 14 in the Font Size list to see a live preview of cell A2 with a font size of 14 (Figure 1–54).

Experiment

- Point to several other font sizes in the Font Size list to see a live preview of other font sizes in cell A2.

Figure 1–54

2

- Click 14 in the Font Size list to change the font in cell A2 from 11 point to 14 point (Figure 1–55).

Q&A

Can I assign a font size that is not in the Font Size list?

Yes. An alternative to clicking a font size in the Font Size list is to click the Font Size box, type the font size, and then press the ENTER key. This procedure allows you to assign a font size not available in the Font Size list to a selected cell entry.

Figure 1–55

Other Ways

1. Click Increase Font Size button or Decrease Font Size button on Ribbon
2. Select font size from Font Size list on Mini toolbar
3. Right-click cell, click Format Cells on shortcut menu, click Font tab, select font size in Size box, click OK button

To Change the Font Color of a Cell Entry

The next step is to change the color of the font in cell A2 from black to dark blue. The following steps change the font color of a cell entry.

1

- With cell A2 selected, click the Font Color button arrow on the Ribbon to display the Font Color palette.

- Point to Dark Blue, Text 2 (dark blue color in column 4, row 1) in the Theme Colors area of the Font Color palette to see a live preview of the font color in cell A2 (Figure 1–56).

Experiment

- Point to several other colors in the Font Color palette to see a live preview of other font colors in cell A2.

Q&A

Which colors does Excel make available on the Font Color palette?

You can choose from more than 60 different font colors on the Font Color palette (Figure 1–56). Your Font Color palette may have more or fewer colors, depending on color settings of your operating system. The Theme Colors area includes colors that are included in the current workbook's theme.

Figure 1–56

2

- Click Dark Blue, Text 2 (column 4, row 1) on the Font Color palette to change the font of the worksheet subtitle in cell A2 from black to dark blue (Figure 1–57).

Q&A

Why does the Font Color button change after I select the new font color?

When you choose a color on the Font Color palette, Excel changes the Font Color button on the Formatting toolbar to the chosen color. Thus, to change the font color of the cell entry in another cell to the same color, you need only to select the cell and then click the Font Color button.

Figure 1–57

Other Ways

1. Select font color from Font Color list on Mini toolbar

2. Right-click cell, click Format Cells on shortcut menu, click Font tab, select color on Font Color palette, click OK button

To Center Cell Entries across Columns by Merging Cells

The final step in formatting the worksheet title and subtitle is to center them across columns A through G. Centering a title across the columns used in the body of the worksheet improves the worksheet's appearance. To do this, the seven cells in the range A1:G1 are combined, or merged, into a single cell that is the width of the columns in the body of the worksheet. The seven cells in the range A2:G2 also are merged in a similar manner. **Merging cells** involves creating a single cell by combining two or more selected cells. The following steps center the worksheet title and subtitle across columns by merging cells.

1

- Select cell A1 and then drag to cell G1 to highlight the range A1:G1 (Figure 1–58).

Q&A

What if a cell in the range B1:G1 contained data?

For the Merge and Center button to work properly, all the cells except the leftmost cell in the selected range must be empty.

Figure 1–58

❷

- Click the Merge and Center button on the Ribbon to merge cells A1 through G1 and center the contents of cell A1 across columns A through G (Figure 1–59).

Q&A

What happened to cells B1 through G1?

After the merge, cells B1 through G1 no longer exist. Cell A1 now extends across columns A through G.

Figure 1–59

❸

- Repeat Steps 1 and 2 to merge and center the worksheet subtitle across cells A2 through G2 (Figure 1–60).

Q&A

Are cells B1 through G1 and B2 through G2 lost forever?

No. The opposite of merging cells is **splitting a merged cell**. After you have merged multiple cells to create one merged cell, you can unmerge, or split, the merged cell to display the original cells on the worksheet. You split a merged cell by selecting it and clicking the Merge and Center button. For example, if you click the Merge and Center button a second time in Step 2, it will split the merged cell A1 to cells A1, B1, C1, D1, E1, F1, and G1.

Figure 1–60

Other Ways	
1. Right-click selection, click Merge and Center button on Mini toolbar	2. Right-click selection, click Format Cells on shortcut menu, click Alignment tab, select Center Across Selection in Horizontal list, click OK button

To Format Column Titles and the Total Row

The next step to format the worksheet is to format the column titles in row 3 and the total row, row 9. Column titles and the total row should be formatted so anyone who views the worksheet can quickly distinguish the column titles and total row from the data in the body of the worksheet. The following steps format the column titles and total row using cell styles in the default worksheet theme.

1

- Click cell A3 and then drag the mouse pointer to cell G3 to select the range A3:G3.

- Point to the Cell Styles button on the Ribbon (Figure 1–61).

Q&A Why is cell A3 selected in the range for the column headings?

The style to be applied to the column headings includes an underline that will help to distinguish the column headings from the rest of the worksheet. Including cell A3 in the range ensures that the cell will include the underline, which is visually appealing and further helps to separate the data in the worksheet.

Figure 1–61

2

- Click the Cell Styles button to display the Cell Styles gallery.

- Point to the Heading 3 cell style in the Titles and Headings area of the Cell Styles gallery to see a live preview of the cell style in the range A3:G3 (Figure 1–62).

Experiment

- Point to other cell styles in the Titles and Headings area of the Cell Styles gallery to see a live preview of other cell styles in the range A3:G3.

Figure 1–62

❸

- Click the Heading 3 cell style to apply the cell style to the range A3:G3.

- Click cell A9 and then drag the mouse pointer to cell G9 to select the range A9:G9.

- Point to the Cell Styles button on the Ribbon (Figure 1–63).

Q&A

Why should I choose Heading 3 instead of another heading cell style?

Excel includes many types of headings, such as Heading 1 and Heading 2, because worksheets often include many levels of headings above columns. In the case of the worksheet created for this project, the Heading 3 title includes formatting that makes the column titles' font size smaller than the title and subtitle and makes the column title stand out from the data in the body of the worksheet.

Figure 1–63

❹

- Click the Cell Styles button on the Ribbon to display the Cell Styles gallery and then click the Total cell style in the Titles and Headings area to apply the Total cell style to the cells in the range A9:G9.

- Click cell A11 to select the cell (Figure 1–64).

Figure 1–64

To Format Numbers in the Worksheet

As previously noted, the numbers in the worksheet should be formatted to use a dollar-and-cents format, with dollar signs in the first row (row 4) and the total row (row 9). Excel allows you to format numbers in a variety of ways, and these methods are discussed in other chapters in this book. The following steps use buttons on the Ribbon to format the numbers in the worksheet.

- Select cell B4 and drag the mouse pointer to cell G4 to select the range B4:G4.

- Point to the Accounting Number Format button on the Ribbon to display the Enhanced ScreenTip (Figure 1–65).

Figure 1–65

- Click the Accounting Number Format button on the Ribbon to apply the Accounting Number Format to the cells in the range B4:G4.

- Select the range B5:G8 (Figure 1–66).

Q&A

What effect does the Accounting Number Format have on the selected cells?

The Accounting Number Format causes the cells to display with two decimal places so that decimal places in cells below the selected cells align vertically. Cell widths are automatically adjusted to accommodate the new formatting.

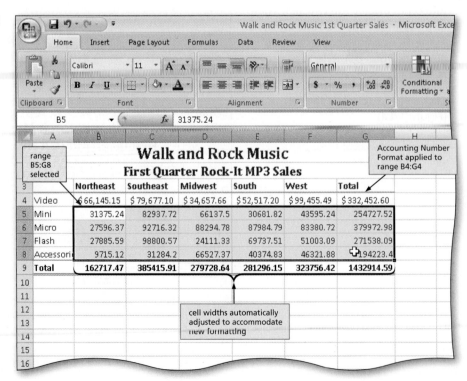

Figure 1–66

3

- Click the Comma Style button on the Ribbon to apply the Comma Style to the range B5:G8.

- Select the range B9:G9 (Figure 1–67).

Q&A

What effect does the Comma Style format have on the selected cells?

The Comma Style format causes the cells to display with two decimal places and commas as thousands separators.

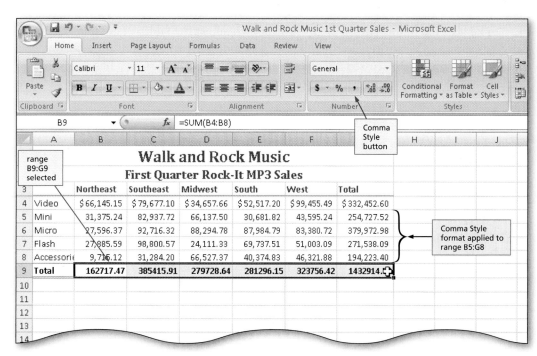

Figure 1–67

4

- Click the Accounting Number Format button on the Ribbon to apply the Accounting Number format to the cells in the range B9:G9.

- Select cell A11 (Figure 1-68).

Figure 1–68

Other Ways
1. Click Accounting Number Format or Comma button on Mini toolbar   2. Right-click selection, click Format Cells on the shortcut menu, select Accounting in Category list or select Number and click Use 1000 Separator, click OK button

To Adjust the Column Width

The last step in formatting the worksheet is to adjust the width of column A so that the word Accessories in cell A8 is shown in its entirety in the cell. Excel includes several methods for adjusting cell widths and row heights, and these methods are discussed later in this book. The following steps adjust the width of column A so that the contents of cell A8 are displayed in the cell.

- Point to the boundary on the right side of the column A heading above row 1 to change the mouse pointer to a split double arrow (Figure 1–69).

Figure 1–69

- Double-click on the boundary to adjust the width of column A to the width of the largest item in the column (Figure 1–70).

Q&A

What if none of the items in column A extended through the entire width of the column?

If all of the items in column A were shorter in length than the width of the column when you double-click the right side of the column A heading, then Excel still would adjust the column width to the largest item in the column. That is, Excel would reduce the width of the column to the largest item.

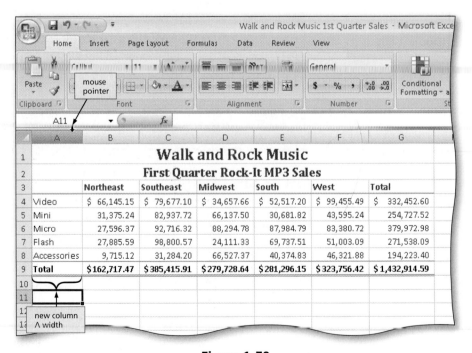

Figure 1–70

Using the Name Box to Select a Cell

The next step is to chart the quarterly sales for the five product types sold by the company. To create the chart, you must select the cell in the upper-left corner of the range to chart (cell A3). Rather than clicking cell A3 to select it, the next section describes how to use the Name box to select the cell.

To Use the Name Box to Select a Cell

As previously noted, the Name box is located on the left side of the formula bar. To select any cell, click the Name box and enter the cell reference of the cell you want to select. The following steps select cell A3.

1

- Click the Name box in the formula bar and then type a3 as the cell to select (Figure 1–71).

Q&A

Why is cell A11 still selected?

Even though cell A11 is the active cell, Excel displays the typed cell reference a3 in the Name box until you press the ENTER key.

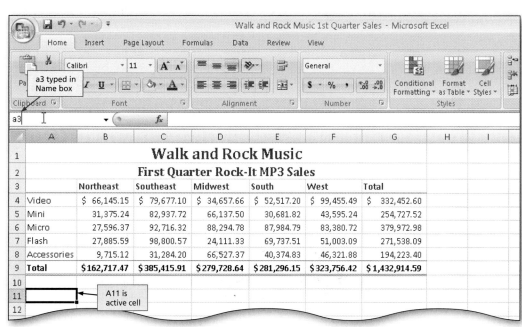

Figure 1–71

2

- Press the ENTER key to change the active cell from A11 to cell A3 (Figure 1–72).

Figure 1–72

Other Ways to Select Cells

As you will see in later chapters, in addition to using the Name box to select any cell in a worksheet, you also can use it to assign names to a cell or range of cells. Excel supports several additional ways to select a cell, as summarized in Table 1–3.

BTW

Find & Select
You can find and select cells based on their content. Click the Find & Select button on the Home tab on the Ribbon. Then, click the Go To Special command. Choose your desired option in the Select area of the Go To Special dialog box and then click the OK button.

Table 1–3 Selecting Cells in Excel

Key, Box, or Command	Function
ALT+PAGE DOWN	Selects the cell one worksheet window to the right and moves the worksheet window accordingly.
ALT+PAGE UP	Selects the cell one worksheet window to the left and moves the worksheet window accordingly.
ARROW	Selects the adjacent cell in the direction of the arrow on the key.
CTRL+ARROW	Selects the border cell of the worksheet in combination with the arrow keys and moves the worksheet window accordingly. For example, to select the rightmost cell in the row that contains the active cell, press CTRL+RIGHT ARROW. You also can press the END key, release it, and then press the appropriate arrow key to accomplish the same task.
CTRL+HOME	Selects cell A1 or the cell one column and one row below and to the right of frozen titles and moves the worksheet window accordingly.
Find command on Edit menu or SHIFT+F5	Finds and selects a cell that contains specific contents that you enter in the Find dialog box. If necessary, Excel moves the worksheet window to display the cell. You also can press CTRL+F to display the Find dialog box.
Go To command on Edit menu or F5	Selects the cell that corresponds to the cell reference you enter in the Go To dialog box and moves the worksheet window accordingly. You also can press CTRL+G to display the Go To dialog box.
HOME	Selects the cell at the beginning of the row that contains the active cell and moves the worksheet window accordingly.
Name box	Selects the cell in the workbook that corresponds to the cell reference you enter in the Name box.
PAGE DOWN	Selects the cell down one worksheet window from the active cell and moves the worksheet window accordingly.
PAGE UP	Selects the cell up one worksheet window from the active cell and moves the worksheet window accordingly.

Plan Ahead

Decide on the type of chart needed.
Excel includes 11 chart types from which you can choose including column, line, pie, bar, area, X Y (scatter), stock, surface, doughnut, bubble, and radar. The type of chart you choose depends on the type of data that you have, how much data you have, and the message you want to convey.

A column chart is a good way to compare values side-by-side. A Clustered Column chart can go even further in comparing values across categories. In the case of the Walk and Rock Music quarterly sales data, comparisons of product types within each region can be made side-by-side with a Clustered Column chart.

Establish where to position and how to format the chart.

- When possible, try to position charts so that both the data and chart appear on the screen on the worksheet together and so that the data and chart can be printed in the most readable manner possible. By placing the chart below the data on the Walk and Rock Music 1st Quarter Sales worksheet, both of these goals are accomplished.

- When choosing/selecting colors for a chart, consider the color scheme of the rest of the worksheet. The chart should not present colors that are in stark contrast to the rest of the worksheet. If the chart will be printed in color, minimize the amount of dark colors on the chart so that the chart both prints quickly and preserves ink.

Adding a 3-D Clustered Column Chart to the Worksheet

As outlined in the requirements document in Figure 1–2 on page EX 4, the worksheet should include a 3-D Clustered Column chart to graphically represent quarterly sales for each product type that the company sells. The 3-D Clustered Column chart shown in Figure 1–73 is called an **embedded chart** because it is drawn on the same worksheet as the data.

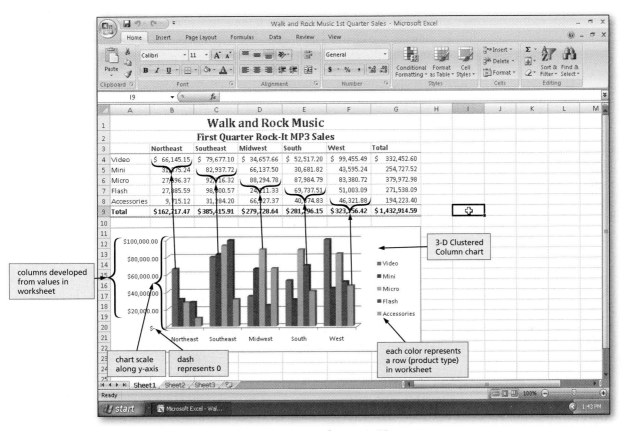

Figure 1–73

The chart uses different colored columns to represent sales for different product types. Each region uses the same color scheme for identifying product types, which allows for easy identification and comparison. For the Northeast sales region, for example, the dark blue column representing Video products shows quarterly sales of $66,145.15; for the Southeast sales region, the maroon column representing Mini products shows quarterly sales of $82,937.72; for the Midwest sales region, the pale green column representing Micro products shows quarterly sales of $88,294.78; for the South sales region, the violet column representing Flash products shows quarterly sales of $69,737.51; and for the West sales region, the light blue column representing Accessories shows quarterly sales of $46,321.88. Because the same color scheme is used in each region to represent the five product types, you easily can compare sales of product types among the sales regions. The totals from the worksheet are not represented, because the totals are not in the range specified for charting.

BTW

Cell Values and Charting
When you change a cell value on which a chart is dependent, Excel redraws the chart instantaneously, unless automatic recalculation is disabled. If automatic recalculation is disabled, then you must press the F9 key to redraw the chart. To enable or disable automatic recalculation, click the Calculations Options button on the Formulas tab on the Ribbon.

Excel derives the chart scale based on the values in the worksheet and then displays the scale along the vertical axis (also called the **y-axis** or **value axis**) of the chart. For example, no value in the range B4:F8 is less than 0 or greater than $100,000.00, so the scale ranges from 0 to $100,000.00. Excel also determines the $10,000.00 increments of the scale automatically. For the numbers along the y-axis, Excel uses a format that includes representing the 0 value with a dash (Figure 1–73 on the previous page).

To Add a 3-D Clustered Column Chart to the Worksheet

The commands to insert a chart are located on the Insert tab. With the range to chart selected, you click the Column button on the Ribbon to initiate drawing the chart. The area on the worksheet where the chart appears is called the chart location. As shown in Figure 1–73, the chart location in this worksheet is the range A11:G22, immediately below the worksheet data.

The following steps draw a 3-D Clustered Column chart that compares the quarterly sales by product type for the five sales regions.

- Click cell A3 and then drag the mouse pointer to the cell F8 to select the range A3:F8 (Figure 1–74).

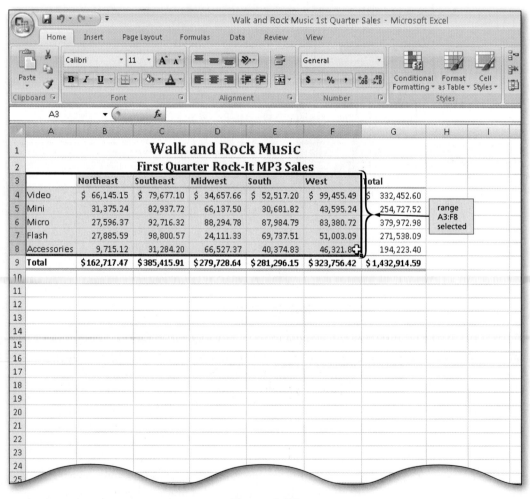

Figure 1–74

2

- Click the Insert tab to make the Insert tab the active tab (Figure 1–75).

Q&A

What tasks can I perform with the Insert tab?

The Insert tab includes commands that allow you to insert various objects, such as shapes, tables, illustrations, and charts, into a work-sheet. These objects will be discussed as they are used throughout this book.

Figure 1–75

3

- Click the Column button on the Ribbon to display the Column gallery.

- Point to the 3-D Clustered Column chart type in the 3-D Column area of the Column gallery (Figure 1–76).

Figure 1–76

④

- Click the 3-D Clustered Column chart type in the 3-D Column area of the Column gallery to add a 3-D Clustered Column chart to the middle of the worksheet in a selection rectangle.

- Click the top-right edge of the selection rectangle but do not release the mouse to grab the chart and change the mouse pointer to a cross hair with four arrowheads (Figure 1–77).

 Q&A Why is a new tab displayed on the Ribbon?

When you select objects such as shapes or charts, Excel displays contextual tabs that include special commands that are used to work with the type of object selected. Because a chart is selected, Excel displays the Chart Tools contextual tab. The three tabs below the Chart Tools contextual tab, Design, Layout, and Format, are tabs that include commands to work with charts.

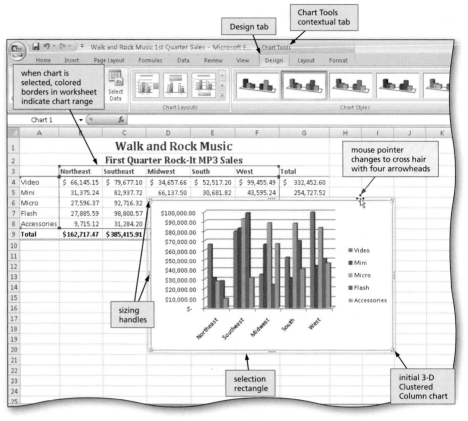

Figure 1–77

⑤

- Continue holding down the left mouse button while dragging the chart down and to the left to position the upper-left corner of the dotted line rectangle over the upper-left corner of cell A11. Release the mouse button to complete the move of the chart.

- Click the middle sizing handle on the right edge of the chart and do not release the mouse button (Figure 1–78).

Q&A How does Excel know how to create the chart?

Excel automatically selects the entries in the topmost row of the chart range (row 3) as the titles for the horizontal axis (also called the **x-axis** or **category axis**) and draws a column for each of the 25 cells in the range containing numbers.

Figure 1–78

6

- While continuing to hold down the mouse button, press the ALT key and drag the right edge of the chart to the right edge of column G and then release the mouse button to resize the chart.

- Point to the middle sizing handle on the bottom edge of the selection rectangle and do not release the mouse button (Figure 1–79).

Why should I hold the ALT key down while I resize a chart?

Holding down the ALT key while you drag a chart **snaps** (aligns) the edge of the chart area to the worksheet gridlines. If you do not hold down the ALT key, then you can place an edge of a chart in the middle of a column or row.

Figure 1–79

7

- While continuing to hold down the mouse button, press the ALT key and drag the bottom edge of the chart up to the bottom edge of row 22 and then release the mouse button to resize the chart.

- Click the More button in the Chart Styles gallery to expand the gallery and point to Style 2 in the gallery (column 2, row 1) (Figure 1–80).

Figure 1–80

8

- Click Style 2 in the Chart Styles gallery to apply the chart style Style 2 to the chart.

🔍 **Experiment**

- Select other chart styles in the Chart Styles gallery to apply other chart styles to the chart, but select Style 2 as your final choice.

- Click cell I9 to deselect the chart and complete the worksheet (Figure 1–81).

Q&A

What is the purpose of the items on the right side of the chart?

The items to the right of the column chart in Figure 1–81 are the **legend**, which identifies the colors assigned to each bar in the chart. Excel automatically selects the entries in the leftmost column of the chart range (column A) as titles within the legend.

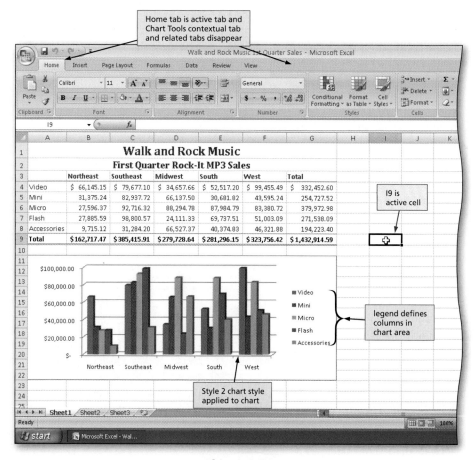

Figure 1–81

Changing Document Properties and Saving Again

BTW

Document Properties
Excel allows you to assign additional document properties by clicking the Document Properties button arrow in the Document Information panel and then clicking Advanced Properties. You can assign custom properties, such as Department, Purpose, and Editor. Or, you can create your own document properties.

Excel helps you organize and identify your files by using **document properties**, which are the details about a file. Document properties, also known as **metadata**, can include such information as the project author, title, or subject. **Keywords** are words or phrases that further describe the document. For example, a class name or worksheet topic can describe the file's purpose or content. Document properties are valuable for a variety of reasons:

- Users can save time locating a particular file because they can view a document's properties without opening the workbook.

- By creating consistent properties for files having similar content, users can better organize their workbooks.

- Some organizations require Excel users to add document properties so that other employees can view details about these files.

Five different types of document properties exist, but the more common ones used in this book are standard and automatically updated properties. **Standard properties** are associated with all Microsoft Office documents and include author, title, and subject. **Automatically updated properties** include file system properties, such as the date you create or change a file, and statistics, such as the file size.

To Change Document Properties

The **Document Information Panel** contains areas where you can view and enter document properties. You can view and change information in this panel at any time while you are creating your workbook. Before saving the workbook again, you want to add your name and class name as document properties. The following steps use the Document Information Panel to change document properties.

1

- Click the Office Button to display the Office Button menu.

- Point to Prepare on the Office Button menu to display the Prepare submenu (Figure 1–82).

Q&A What other types of actions besides changing properties can you take to prepare a document for distribution?

The Prepare submenu provides commands related to sharing a document with others, such as allowing or restricting people to view and modify your document, checking to see if your worksheet will work in earlier versions of Excel, and searching for hidden personal information.

Figure 1–82

2

- Click Properties on the Prepare submenu to display the Document Information Panel (Figure 1–83).

Q&A Why are some of the document properties in my Document Information Panel already filled in?

The person who installed Microsoft Office 2007 on your computer or network may have set or customized the properties.

Figure 1–83

3

- Click the Author text box and then type your name as the Author property. If a name already is displayed in the Author text box, delete it before typing your name.

- Click the Subject text box, if necessary delete any existing text, and then type your course and section as the Subject property.

- Click the Keywords text box, if necessary delete any existing text, and then type `First Quarter Rock-It MP3 Sales` (Figure 1–84).

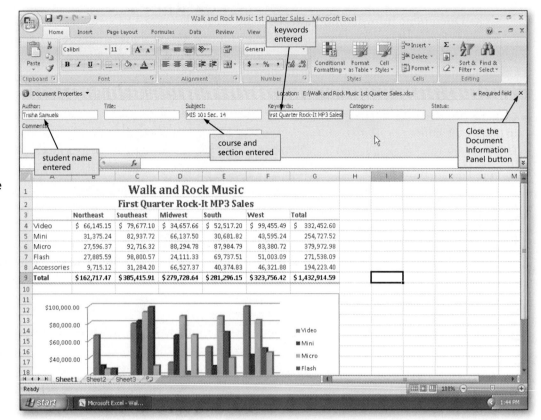

Figure 1–84

Q&A What types of document properties does Excel collect automatically?

Excel records such details as how long you worked at creating your project, how many times you revised the document, and what fonts and themes are used.

4

- Click the Close the Document Information Panel button so that the Document Information Panel no longer is displayed.

To Save an Existing Workbook with the Same File Name

Saving frequently cannot be overemphasized. Several modifications have been made to the workbook since it was saved earlier in the chapter. Earlier in this chapter, the Save button on the Quick Access Toolbar caused the Save As dialog box to appear, and the file name, Walk and Rock Music 1st Quarter Sales, was entered. Clicking the Save button on the Quick Access Toolbar causes Excel to save the changes made to the workbook since the last time it was saved. The following step saves the workbook again.

❶

- With your USB flash drive connected to one of the computer's USB ports, click the Save button on the Quick Access Toolbar to overwrite the previous Walk and Rock Music 1st Quarter Sales file on the USB flash drive (Figure 1–85).

Q&A

Why did the Save As dialog box not appear?

Excel overwrites the document using the settings specified the first time the document was saved. To save the file with a different file name or on different media, display the Save As dialog box by clicking the Office Button and then clicking Save As on the Office But-ton menu. Then, fill in the Save As dialog box as described in Steps 2 through 5 on pages EX 31 and EX 32.

Figure 1–85

Other Ways

1. Press CTRL+S or press SHIFT+F12, press ENTER

Printing a Worksheet

After you create a worksheet, you often want to print it. A printed version of the worksheet is called a **hard copy** or **printout**. Printed copies of your worksheet can be useful for the following reasons:

- Many people prefer proofreading a hard copy of the worksheet rather than viewing the worksheet on the screen to check for errors and readability.
- Someone without computer access can view the worksheet's content.
- Copies can be distributed as handouts to people during a meeting or presentation.
- Hard copies can serve as reference material if your storage medium is lost or becomes corrupted and you need to recreate the worksheet.

It is a good practice to save a workbook before printing it, in the event you experi-ence difficulties with the printer.

BTW

Conserving Ink and Toner

You can print a presentation in black and white to conserve ink or toner by clicking the Office Button, pointing to Print on the Office Button menu, and then clicking Print Preview on the Print submenu. Click the Options button on the Print Preview tab, point to Color/Grayscale on the Options button menu, and then click Pure Black and White on the Color/Grayscale submenu. Click the Office Button, point to Print, and then click Quick Print.

To Print a Worksheet

With the completed worksheet saved, you may want to print it. The following steps print the worksheet in the saved Walk and Rock Music 1st Quarter Sales workbook.

- Click the Office Button to display the Office Button menu.

- Point to Print on the Office Button menu to display the Print submenu (Figure 1–86).

Figure 1–86

- Click Quick Print on the Print submenu to print the document (Figure 1-87).

Q&A

Can I print my document in black and white to conserve ink or toner?

Yes. Click the Office Button and then click the Excel Options button on the Office Button menu. When the Excel Options dialog box is displayed, click Advanced, scroll to the Print area, place a check mark in the Use draft quality check box if it is displayed, and then click the OK button. Click the Office Button, point to Print, and then click Quick Print.

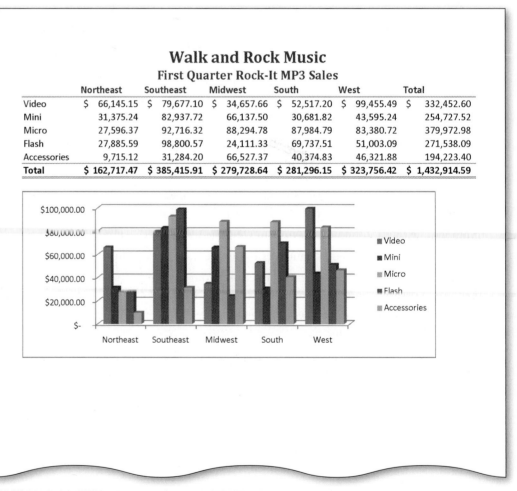

Figure 1–87

Other Ways

1. Press CTRL+P, press ENTER

Quitting Excel

When you close a workbook, if you have made changes to a workbook since the last time the file was saved, Excel displays a dialog box asking if you want to save the changes you made to the file before it closes that window. The dialog box contains three buttons with these resulting actions:

- Yes button — Saves the changes and then quits Excel
- No button — Quits Excel without saving changes
- Cancel button — Closes the dialog box and redisplays the worksheet without saving the changes

If no changes have been made to an open workbook since the last time the file was saved, Excel will close all windows without displaying any dialog boxes.

To Quit Excel

The Walk and Rock 1st Quarter Sales worksheet is complete. The following steps quit Excel if only one workbook is open.

1
- Point to the Close button on the right side of the Excel title bar (Figure 1–88).

2
- Click the Close button to quit Excel.

Q&A

Why are there two Minimize and Restore buttons in the Microsoft Excel window?

You can see that the Excel window includes two Minimize and two Restore icons (Figure 1–88). The Minimize button and Restore button on the title bar are used to minimize and restore the entire Excel window. The Minimize button and Restore button next to the Help icon are used to minimize and restore the worksheet within the Excel window.

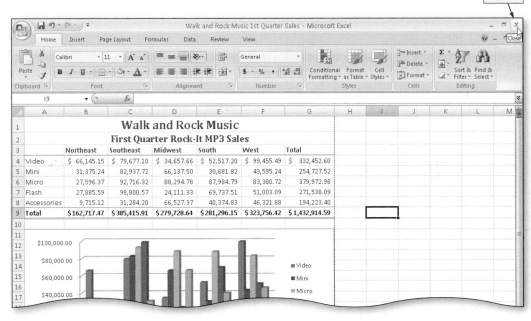

Figure 1–88

Other Ways

1. Double-click Office Button
2. Click Office Button, click Exit Excel on Office Button menu
3. Right-click Microsoft Excel button on Windows taskbar, click Close on shortcut menu
4. Press ALT+F4

BTW

Print Preview
You can preview the printout on your screen using the Print Preview command on the Print submenu (Figure 1–86 on page EX 58), make adjustments to the worksheet, and then print it only when it appears exactly as you want. Each time you preview rather than print, you save both ink and paper.

Starting Excel and Opening a Workbook

Once you have created and saved a workbook, you may need to retrieve it from your storage medium. For example, you might want to revise a worksheet or reprint it. Opening a workbook requires that Excel is running on your computer.

To Start Excel

The following steps, which assume Windows is running, start Excel.

1 Click the Start button on the Windows taskbar to display the Start menu.

2 Point to All Programs on the Start menu to display the All Programs submenu and then point to Microsoft Office in the All Programs submenu to display the Microsoft Office submenu.

3 Click Microsoft Office Excel 2007 on the Microsoft Office submenu to start Excel and display a new blank worksheet in the Excel window.

4 If the Excel window is not maximized, click the Maximize button on its title bar to maximize the window.

To Open a Workbook from Excel

Earlier in this chapter, you saved your workbook on a USB flash drive using the file name, Walk and Rock Music 1st Quarter Sales. The following steps open the Walk and Rock Music 1st Quarter Sales file from the USB flash drive.

1

• With your USB flash drive connected to one of the computer's USB ports, click the Office Button to display the Office Button menu (Figure 1–89).

Q&A What files are shown in the Recent Documents list?

Excel displays the most recently opened document file names in this list. If the name of the file you want to open appears in the Recent Documents list, you could double-click it to open the file.

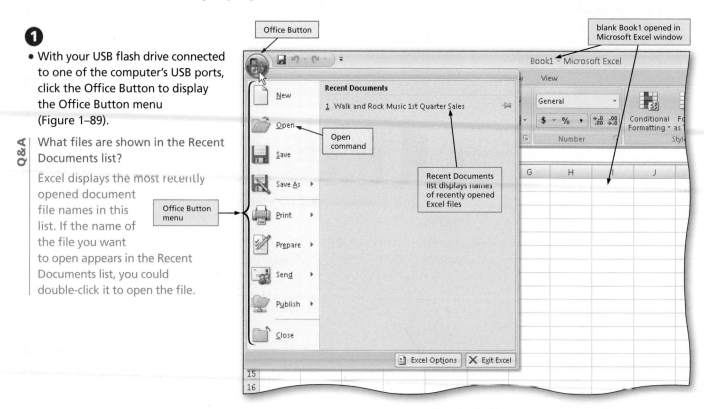

Figure 1–89

2

- Click Open on the Office Button menu to display the Open dialog box.

- If necessary, click the Look in box arrow and then click UDISK 2.0 (E:) to select the USB flash drive, Drive E in this case, in the Look in list as the new open location.

- Click Walk and Rock Music 1st Quarter Sales to select the file name (Figure 1–90).

Q&A How do I open the file if I am not using a USB flash drive?

Use the same process, but be certain to select your device in the Look in list.

Figure 1–90

3

- Click the Open button to open the selected file and display the worksheet in the Excel window (Figure 1–91).

Q&A Why do I see the Microsoft Excel icon and name on the Windows taskbar?

When you open an Excel file, the application name (Microsoft Excel) is displayed on a selected button on the taskbar. If you point to this button, the file name also appears in a ScreenTip.

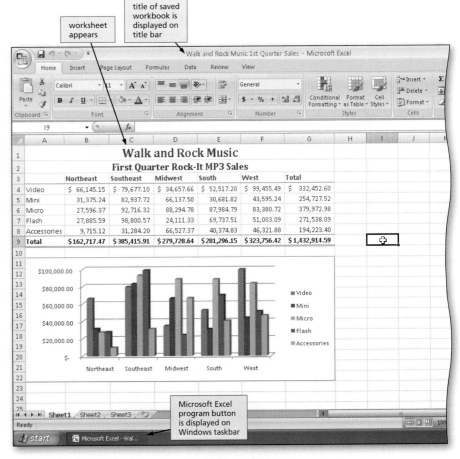

Figure 1–91

Other Ways

1. Click Office Button, double-click file name in Recent Documents list

2. Press CTRL+O, select file name, press ENTER

BTW

AutoCalculate
Use the AutoCalculate area on the status bar to check your work as you enter data in a worksheet. If you enter large amounts of data, you select a range of data and then check the AutoCalculate area to provide insight into statistics about the data you entered. Often, you will have an intuitive feel for whether the numbers are accurate or if you may have made a mistake while entering the data.

AutoCalculate

You easily can obtain a total, an average, or other information about the numbers in a range by using the **AutoCalculate area** on the status bar. First, select the range of cells containing the numbers you want to check. Next, right-click the AutoCalculate area to display the Status Bar Configuration shortcut menu (Figure 1–92). The check mark to the left of the active functions (Average, Count, and Sum) indicates that the sum, count, and average of the selected range are displayed in the AutoCalculate area on the status bar. The functions of the AutoCalculate commands on the Status Bar Configuration shortcut menu are described in Table 1–4.

Table 1–4 AutoCalculate Shortcut Menu Commands	
Command	**Function**
Average	AutoCalculate area displays the average of the numbers in the selected range
Count	AutoCalculate area displays the number of nonblank cells in the selected range
Numerical Count	AutoCalculate area displays the number of cells containing numbers in the selected range
Minimum	AutoCalculate area displays the lowest value in the selected range
Maximum	AutoCalculate area displays the highest value in the selected range
Sum	AutoCalculate area displays the sum of the numbers in the selected range

To Use the AutoCalculate Area to Determine a Maximum

The following steps show how to display the largest quarterly sales for any region for the Micro product type.

1

- Select the range B6:F6 and then right-click the AutoCalculate area on the status bar to display the Status Bar Configuration shortcut menu (Figure 1–92).

Q&A

What is displayed on the Status Bar Configuration shortcut menu?

This shortcut menu includes several commands that allow you to control the items displayed on the Customize Status Bar shortcut menu. The AutoCalculate area of the shortcut menu includes six commands as well as the result of the associated calculation on the right side of the menu.

Figure 1–92

- Click Maximum on the shortcut menu to display the Maximum value in the range B6:F6 in the AutoCalculate area of the status bar.

- Click anywhere on the worksheet to cause the shortcut menu to disappear (Figure 1–93).

- Right-click the AutoCalculate area and then click Maximum on the shortcut menu to cause the Maximum value to no longer appear in the AutoCalculate area.

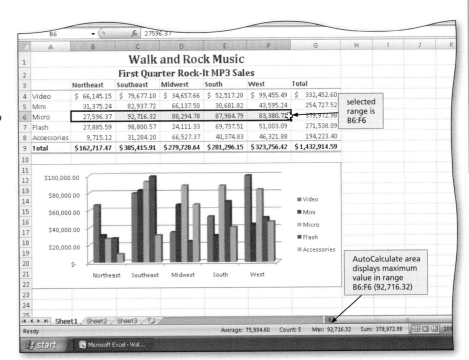

Figure 1–93

Correcting Errors

You can correct errors on a worksheet using one of several methods. The method you choose will depend on the extent of the error and whether you notice it while typing the data or after you have entered the incorrect data into the cell.

Correcting Errors while You Are Typing Data into a Cell

If you notice an error while you are typing data into a cell, press the BACKSPACE key to erase the incorrect characters and then type the correct characters. If the error is a major one, click the Cancel box in the formula bar or press the ESC key to erase the entire entry and then reenter the data from the beginning.

Correcting Errors after Entering Data into a Cell

If you find an error in the worksheet after entering the data, you can correct the error in one of two ways:

1. If the entry is short, select the cell, retype the entry correctly, and then click the Enter box or press the ENTER key. The new entry will replace the old entry.

2. If the entry in the cell is long and the errors are minor, using Edit mode may be a better choice than retyping the cell entry. Use the Edit mode as described below.

   a. Double-click the cell containing the error to switch Excel to Edit mode. In **Edit mode**, Excel displays the active cell entry in the formula bar and a flashing

BTW

In-Cell Editing
An alternative to double-clicking the cell to edit it is to select the cell and then press the F2 key.

insertion point in the active cell (Figure 1–94). With Excel in Edit mode, you can edit the contents directly in the cell — a procedure called **in-cell editing**.

b. Make changes using in-cell editing, as indicated below.

(1) To insert new characters between two characters, place the insertion point between the two characters and begin typing. Excel inserts the new characters at the location of the insertion point.

(2) To delete a character in the cell, move the insertion point to the left of the character you want to delete and then press the DELETE key or place the insertion point to the right of the character you want to delete and then press the BACKSPACE key. You also can use the mouse to drag through the character or adjacent characters you want to delete and then press the DELETE key or click the Cut button on the Standard toolbar.

(3) When you are finished editing an entry, click the Enter box or press the ENTER key.

Figure 1–94

When Excel enters the Edit mode, the keyboard usually is in Insert mode. In **Insert mode**, as you type a character, Excel inserts the character and moves all characters to the right of the typed character one position to the right. You can change to Overtype mode by pressing the INSERT key. In **Overtype mode**, Excel overtypes, or replaces, the character to the right of the insertion point. The INSERT key toggles the keyboard between Insert mode and Overtype mode.

While in Edit mode, you may have reason to move the insertion point to various points in the cell, select portions of the data in the cell, or switch from inserting characters to overtyping characters. Table 1–5 summarizes the more common tasks used during in-cell editing.

BTW

Editing the Contents of a Cell
Rather than using in-cell editing, you can select the cell and then click the formula bar to edit the contents.

Table 1–5 Summary of In-Cell Editing Tasks

	Task	Mouse	Keyboard
1	Move the insertion point to the beginning of data in a cell.	Point to the left of the first character and click.	Press HOME
2	Move the insertion point to the end of data in a cell.	Point to the right of the last character and click.	Press END
3	Move the insertion point anywhere in a cell.	Point to the appropriate position and click the character.	Press RIGHT ARROW or LEFT ARROW
4	Highlight one or more adjacent characters.	Drag the mouse pointer through adjacent characters.	Press SHIFT+RIGHT ARROW or SHIFT+LEFT ARROW
5	Select all data in a cell.	Double-click the cell with the insertion point in the cell.	
6	Delete selected characters.	Click the Cut button on the Standard toolbar.	Press DELETE
7	Delete characters to the left of the insertion point.		Press BACKSPACE
8	Delete characters to the right of the insertion point.		Press DELETE
9	Toggle between Insert and Overtype modes.		Press INSERT

Undoing the Last Cell Entry

Excel provides the Undo command on the Quick Access Toolbar (Figure 1–95), which allows you to erase recent cell entries. Thus, if you enter incorrect data in a cell and notice it immediately, click the Undo button and Excel changes the cell entry to what it was prior to the incorrect data entry.

Figure 1–95

Excel remembers the last 100 actions you have completed. Thus, you can undo up to 100 previous actions by clicking the Undo button arrow to display the Undo list and then clicking the action to be undone (Figure 1–95). You can drag through several actions in the Undo list to undo all of them at once. If no actions are available for Excel to undo, then the Undo button is dimmed and inoperative.

The Redo button, next to the Undo button on the Quick Access Toolbar, allows you to repeat previous actions.

Clearing a Cell or Range of Cells

If you enter data into the wrong cell or range of cells, you can erase, or clear, the data using one of the first four methods listed below. The fifth method clears the formatting from the selected cells.

To Clear Cell Entries Using the Fill Handle

1. Select the cell or range of cells and then point to the fill handle so the mouse pointer changes to a cross hair.
2. Drag the fill handle back into the selected cell or range until a shadow covers the cell or cells you want to erase. Release the mouse button.

To Clear Cell Entries Using the Shortcut Menu

1. Select the cell or range of cells to be cleared.
2. Right-click the selection.
3. Click Clear Contents on the shortcut menu.

To Clear Cell Entries Using the delete Key

1. Select the cell or range of cells to be cleared.
2. Press the DELETE key.

To Clear Cell Entries and Formatting Using the Clear Button

1. Select the cell or range of cells to be cleared.
2. Click the Clear button on the Home tab (Figure 1–95 on the previous page).
3. Click Clear Contents on the menu.

To Clear Formatting Using the Cell Styles Button

1. Select the cell or range of cells from which you want to remove the formatting.
2. Click the Cell Styles button on the Home tab and point to Normal.
3. Click Normal in the Live Preview Gallery.

The Clear button on the Home tab is the only command that clears both the cell entry and the cell formatting. As you are clearing cell entries, always remember that you should *never press the* SPACEBAR *to clear a cell*. Pressing the SPACEBAR enters a blank character. A blank character is text and is different from an empty cell, even though the cell may appear empty.

Clearing the Entire Worksheet

If required worksheet edits are extremely extensive, you may want to clear the entire worksheet and start over. To clear the worksheet or delete an embedded chart, use the following steps.

To Clear the Entire Worksheet

1. Click the Select All button on the worksheet (Figure 1–95).
2. Click the Clear button on the Home tab to delete both the entries and formats.

The Select All button selects the entire worksheet. Instead of clicking the Select All button, you also can press CTRL+A. To clear an unsaved workbook, click the workbook's Close Window button or click the Close command on the Office Button menu. Click the No button if the Microsoft Excel dialog box asks if you want to save changes. To start a new, blank workbook, click the New command on the Office Button menu.

To delete an embedded chart, complete the following steps.

TO DELETE AN EMBEDDED CHART

1. Click the chart to select it.
2. Press the DELETE key.

BTW

Excel Help
The best way to become familiar with Excel Help is to use it. Appendix C includes detailed information about Excel Help and exercises that will help you gain confidence in using it.

Excel Help

At any time while using Excel, you can find answers to questions and display information about various topics through **Excel Help**. This section introduces you to Excel Help.

To Search for Excel Help

Using Excel Help, you can search for information based on phrases such as save a workbook or format a chart, or key terms such as copy, save, or format. Excel Help responds with a list of search results displayed as links to a variety of resources. The following steps, which use Excel Help to search for information about formatting a chart, assume you are connected to the Internet.

- Click the Microsoft Office Excel Help button near the upper-right corner of the Excel window to open the Excel Help window.

- Type format a chart in the Type words to search for text box at the top of the Excel Help window (Figure 1–96).

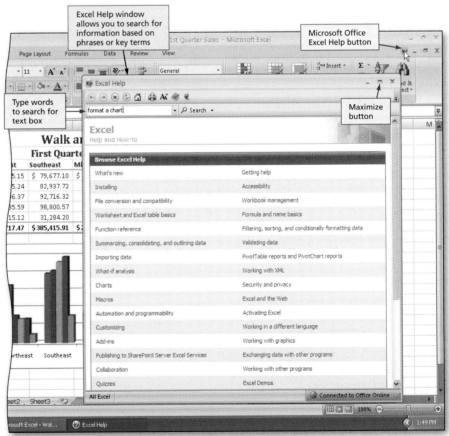

Figure 1–96

2

- Press the ENTER key to display the search results.

- Click the Maximize button on the Excel Help window title bar to maximize the Help window (Figure 1–97).

Q&A

Where is the Excel window with the Walk and Rock Music 1st Quarter Sales worksheet?

Excel is open in the background, but the Excel Help window is overlaid on top of the Microsoft Excel window. When the Excel Help window is closed, the worksheet will reappear.

Figure 1–97

3

- Click the Format chart elements link to display information regarding formatting chart elements (Figure 1–98).

Q&A

What is the purpose of the buttons at the top of the Excel Help window?

Use the buttons in the upper-left corner of the Excel Help window to navigate through the Help system, change the display, show the Excel Help table of contents, and print the contents of the window.

Figure 1–98

4

- Click the Close button on the Excel Help window title bar to close the Excel Help window and make Excel active.

Other Ways

1. Press F1

To Quit Excel

The following steps quit Excel.

1 Click the Close button on the right side of the title bar to quit Excel.

2 If necessary, click the No button in the Microsoft Office Excel dialog box so that any changes you have made are not saved.

BTW

Quitting Excel
Do not forget to remove your USB flash drive from the USB port after quitting Excel, especially if you are working in a laboratory environment. Nothing can be more frustrating than leaving all of your hard work behind on a USB flash drive for the next user.

Chapter Summary

In this chapter you have learned about the Excel window, how to enter text and numbers to create a worksheet, how to select a range, how to use the Sum button, save a workbook, format cells, insert a chart, print a worksheet, quit Excel, and use Excel Help. The items listed below include all the new Excel skills you have learned in this chapter.

1. Start Excel (EX 6)
2. Enter the Worksheet Titles (EX 17)
3. Enter Column Titles (EX 19)
4. Enter Row Titles (EX 21)
5. Enter Numbers (EX 23)
6. Sum a Column of Numbers (EX 25)
7. Copy a Cell to Adjacent Cells in a Row (EX 27)
8. Determine Multiple Totals at the Same Time (EX 28)
9. Save a Workbook (EX 30)
10. Change a Cell Style (EX 35)
11. Change the Font Type (EX 36)
12. Bold a Cell (EX 38)
13. Increase the Font Size of a Cell Entry (EX 38)
14. Change the Font Color of a Cell Entry (EX 39)
15. Center Cell Entries across Columns by Merging Cells (EX 40)
16. Format Column Titles and the Total Row (EX 42)
17. Format Numbers in the Worksheet (EX 44)
18. Adjust the Column Width (EX 46)
19. Use the Name Box to Select a Cell (EX 47)
20. Add a 3-D Clustered Column Chart to the Worksheet (EX 50)
21. Change Document Properties (EX 55)
22. Save an Existing Workbook with the Same File Name (EX 58)
23. Print a Worksheet (EX 58)
24. Quit Excel (EX 59)
25. Open a Workbook from Excel (EX 60)
26. Use the AutoCalculate Area to Determine a Maximum (EX 62)
27. Clear Cell Entries Using the Fill Handle (EX 66)
28. Clear Cell Entries Using the Shortcut Menu (EX 66)
29. Clear Cell Entries Using the DELETE Key (EX 66)
30. Clear Cell Entries and Formatting Using the Clear Button (EX 66)
31. Clear Formatting Using the Cell Styles Button (EX 66)
32. Clear the Entire Worksheet (EX 66)
33. Delete an Embedded Chart (EX 67)
34. Search for Excel Help (EX 67)

If you have a SAM user profile, you may have access to hands-on instruction, practice, and assessment. Log in to your SAM account (http://sam2007.course.com) to launch any assigned training activities or exams that relate to the skills covered in this chapter.

Learn It Online

Test your knowledge of chapter content and key terms.

Instructions: To complete the Learn It Online exercises, start your browser, click the Address bar, and then enter the Web address scsite.com/ex2007/learn. When the Excel 2007 Learn It Online page is displayed, click the link for the exercise you want to complete and then read the instructions.

Chapter Reinforcement TF, MC, and SA

A series of true/false, multiple choice, and short answer questions that test your knowledge of the chapter content.

Flash Cards

An interactive learning environment where you identify chapter key terms associated with displayed definitions.

Practice Test

A series of multiple choice questions that test your knowledge of chapter content and key terms.

Who Wants To Be a Computer Genius?

An interactive game that challenges your knowledge of chapter content in the style of a television quiz show.

Wheel of Terms

An interactive game that challenges your knowledge of chapter key terms in the style of the television show *Wheel of Fortune*.

Crossword Puzzle Challenge

A crossword puzzle that challenges your knowledge of key terms presented in the chapter.

Apply Your Knowledge

Reinforce the skills and apply the concepts you learned in this chapter.

Changing the Values in a Worksheet

Instructions: Start Excel. Open the workbook Apply 1-1 Bicycle Shop 3rd Quarter Sales (Figure 1–99a). See the inside back cover of this book for instructions for downloading the Data Files for Students, or see your instructor for information on accessing the files required in this book.

1. Make the changes to the worksheet described in Table 1–6 so that the worksheet appears as shown in Figure 1–99b. As you edit the values in the cells containing numeric data, watch the totals in row 8, the totals in column G, and the chart change.

2. Change the worksheet title in cell A1 to the Title cell style and then merge and center it across columns A through G. Use commands in the Font group on the Home tab on the Ribbon to change the worksheet subtitle in cell A2 to 16-point Corbel red, bold font and then center it across columns A through G. Use the Accent 1 theme color (column 5, row 1 on the Font palette) for the red font color.

3. Update the document properties with your name, course number, and name for the workbook. Save the workbook using the file name, Apply 1-1 Spoke-Up Bicycle Shop 3rd Quarter Sales. Submit the assignment as requested by your instructor.

Table 1–6 New Worksheet Data	
Cell	**Change Cell Contents To**
A1	Spoke-Up Bicycle Shop
B4	11869.2
E4	9157.83
D6	5217.92
F6	6239.46
B7	3437.64

(a) Before

(b) After
Figure 1–99

Extend Your Knowledge

Extend the skills you learned in this chapter and experiment with new skills. You may need to use Help to complete the assignment.

Formatting Cells and Inserting Multiple Charts

Instructions: Start Excel. Open the workbook Extend 1-1 Pack-n-Away Shipping. See the inside back cover of this book for instructions for downloading the Data Files for Students, or see your instructor for information on accessing the files required in this book. Perform the following tasks to format cells in the worksheet and to add two charts to the worksheet.

1. Use the commands in the Font group on the Home tab on the Ribbon to change the font of the title in cell A1 to 24-point Arial, red, bold and subtitle of the worksheet to 16-point Arial Narrow, blue, bold.

2. Select the range A3:E8, click the Insert tab on the Ribbon and then click the More button in the lower-right corner of the Charts group on the Ribbon to open the Insert Chart dialog box (Figure 1–100).

Figure 1–100

3. Insert a Stacked Line chart by clicking the Stacked Line chart in the gallery and then clicking the OK button. Move the chart either below or to the right of the data in the worksheet. Click the Design tab and apply a chart style to the chart.

4. With the same range selected, follow Step 3 above to insert a 3-D Area chart in the worksheet. You may need to use the scroll box on the right side of the Insert Chart dialog box to view the Area charts in the gallery. Move the chart either below or to the right of the data so that each chart does not overlap the Stacked Line chart. Choose a different chart style for this chart than the one you selected for the Stacked Line chart.

5. Resize each chart so that each snaps to the worksheet gridlines. Make certain that both charts are visible with the worksheet data without the need to scroll the worksheet.

6. Update the document properties with your name, course number, and name for the workbook.

7. Save the workbook using the file name, Extend 1-1 Pack-n-Away Shipping Charts. Submit the assignment as requested by your instructor.

Make It Right

Analyze a workbook and correct all errors and/or improve the design.

Correcting Formatting and Values in a Worksheet

Instructions: Start Excel. Open the workbook Make It Right 1-1 Book Sales. See the inside back cover of this book for instructions for downloading the Data Files for Students, or see your instructor for information on accessing the files required for this book. Correct the following formatting problems and data errors (Figure 1–101) in the worksheet, while keeping in mind the guidelines presented in this chapter.

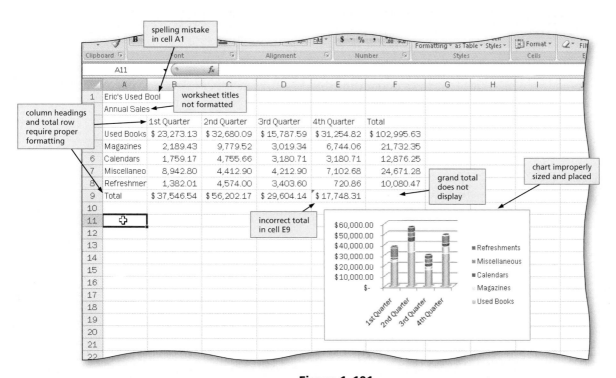

Figure 1–101

1. Merge and center the worksheet title and subtitle appropriately.

2. Format the worksheet title with a cell style appropriate for a worksheet title.

3. Format the subtitle using commands in the Font group on the Ribbon.

4. Correct the spelling mistake in cell A1 by changing Bool to Books.

5. Apply proper formatting to the column headers and total row.

Continued >

STUDENT ASSIGNMENTS

Make It Right *continued*

6. Adjust column sizes so that all data in each column is visible.

7. Use the SUM function to create the grand total for annual sales.

8. The SUM function in cell E9 does not sum all of the numbers in the column. Correct this error by editing the range for the SUM function in the cell.

9. Resize and move the chart so that it is below the worksheet data and does not extend past the right edge of the worksheet data. Be certain to snap the chart to the worksheet gridlines by holding down the ALT key as you resize the chart.

10. Update the document properties with your name, course number, and name for the workbook. Save the workbook using the file name, Make It Right 1-1 Eric's Used Books Annual Sales. Submit the assignment as requested by your instructor.

In the Lab

Design and/or create a workbook using the guidelines, concepts, and skills presented in this chapter. Labs 1, 2, and 3 are listed in order of increasing difficulty.

Lab 1: Annual Cost of Goods Worksheet

Problem: You work part-time as a spreadsheet specialist for Kona's Expresso Coffee, one of the up-and-coming coffee franchises in the United States. Your manager has asked you to develop an annual cost of goods analysis worksheet similar to the one shown in Figure 1–102.

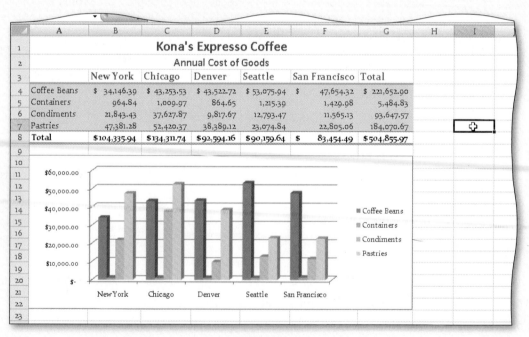

Figure 1–102

Instructions: Perform the following tasks.

1. Start Excel. Enter the worksheet title, Kona's Expresso Coffee, in cell A1 and the worksheet subtitle, Annual Cost of Goods, in cell A2. Beginning in row 3, enter the store locations, costs of goods, and supplies categories shown in Table 1–7.

Table 1–7 Kona's Expresso Coffee Annual Cost of Goods

	New York	Chicago	Denver	Seattle	San Franscisco
Coffee Beans	34146.39	43253.53	43522.72	53075.94	47654.32
Containers	964.84	1009.97	864.65	1215.39	1429.98
Condiments	21843.43	37627.87	9817.67	12793.47	11565.13
Pastries	47381.28	52420.37	38389.12	23074.84	22805.06

2. Use the SUM function to determine the totals for each store location, type of supply, and company grand total.

3. Use Cell Styles in the Styles group on the Home tab on the Ribbon to format the worksheet title with the Title cell style. Center the title across columns A through G. Do not be concerned if the edges of the worksheet title are not displayed.

4. Use buttons in the Font group on the Home tab on the Ribbon to format the worksheet subtitle to 14-point Calibri dark blue, bold font and center it across columns A through G.

5. Use Cell Styles in the Styles group on the Home tab on the Ribbon to format the range A3:G3 with the Heading 2 cell style, the range A4:G7 with the Accent1 - 20% cell style, and the range A8:G8 with the Total cell style. Use the buttons in the Number group on the Home tab on the Ribbon to apply the Accounting Number format to the range B4:G4 and the range B8:G8. Use the buttons in the Number group on the Home tab on the Ribbon to apply the Comma Style to the range B5:G7. Adjust any column widths to the widest text entry in each column.

6. Select the range A3:F7 and then insert a 3-D Clustered Column chart. Apply the Style 8 chart style to the chart. Move and resize the chart so that it appears in the range A10:G22. If the labels along the horizontal axis (x-axis) do not appear as shown in Figure 1-102, then drag the right side of the chart so that it is displayed in the range A10:H22.

7. Update the document properties with your name, course number, and name for the workbook.

8. Save the workbook using the file name Lab 1-1 Konas Expresso Coffee Annual Cost of Goods.

9. Print the worksheet.

10. Make the following two corrections to the sales amounts: $9,648.12 for Seattle Condiments (cell E6), $12,844.79 for Chicago Pastries (cell C7). After you enter the corrections, the company totals in cell G8 should equal $462,135.04.

11. Print the revised worksheet. Close the workbook without saving the changes. Submit the assignment as requested by your instructor.

In the Lab

Lab 2: Annual Sales Analysis Worksheet

Problem: As the chief accountant for Scissors Office Supply, Inc., you have been asked by the sales manager to create a worksheet to analyze the annual sales for the company by location and customer type category (Figure 1–103). The office locations and corresponding sales by customer type for the year are shown in Table 1–8.

Continued >

In the Lab *continued*

Instructions Part 1:   Using the numbers in Table 1–9, create the worksheet shown in columns A through F in Figure 1–104. Format the worksheet title as Calibri 24-point bold red. Merge and center the worksheet title in cell A1 across columns A through F. Format the worksheet subtitles in cells A2 and A11 as Calibri 16-point bold green. Format the ranges A3:F3 and A12:F12 with the Heading 2 cell style, the ranges A4:F9 and A13:F17 with the Accent 1 - 20% style, and the ranges A10:F10 and A18:F18 with the Total cell style.

Update the document properties, including the addition of at least one keyword to the properties, and save the workbook using the file name, Lab 1-3 Part 1 College Cost and Financial Support. Print the worksheet. Submit the assignment as requested by your instructor.

Screenshot showing worksheet with the following data:

Cell reference box: A20

	A	B	C	D	E	F
1	**College Cost and Financial Support**					
2	**Cost**					
3		**Freshman**	**Sophomore**	**Junior**	**Senior**	**Total**
4	Books	$ 450.00	$ 477.00	$ 505.62	$ 535.95	$ 1,968.57
5	Room & Board	7,500.00	7,950.00	8,427.00	8,932.62	32,809.62
6	Tuition	8,200.00	8,692.00	9,213.52	9,766.33	35,871.85
7	Entertainment	1,325.00	1,404.50	1,488.77	1,578.10	5,796.37
8	Miscellaneous	950.00	1,007.00	1,067.42	1,131.47	4,155.89
9	Clothes	725.00	768.50	814.61	863.49	3,171.60
10	**Total**	**$19,150.00**	**$ 20,299.00**	**$21,516.94**	**$22,807.96**	**$83,773.90**
11	**Financial Support**					
12		**Freshman**	**Sophomore**	**Junior**	**Senior**	**Total**
13	Job	$ 3,400.00	$ 3,604.00	$ 3,820.24	$ 4,049.45	$14,873.69
14	Savings	4,350.00	4,611.00	4,887.66	5,180.92	19,029.58
15	Parents	4,700.00	4,982.00	5,280.92	5,597.78	20,560.70
16	Financial Aid	5,500.00	5,830.00	6,179.80	6,550.59	24,060.39
17	Other	1,200.00	1,272.00	1,348.32	1,429.22	5,249.54
18	**Total**	**$19,150.00**	**$ 20,299.00**	**$21,516.94**	**$22,807.96**	**$83,773.90**

Chart: Freshman Expenses (pie) with legend: Books, Room & Board, Tuition, Entertainment, Miscellaneous, Clothes

Chart: Freshman Financial Support (pie) with legend: Job, Savings, Parents, Financial Aid, Other

Figure 1–104

After reviewing the numbers, you realize you need to increase manually each of the Junior-year expenses in column D by $600. Change the Junior-year expenses to reflect this change. Manually change the financial aid for the Junior year by the amount required to cover the increase in costs. The totals in cells F10 and F18 should equal $87,373.90. Print the worksheet. Close the workbook without saving changes.

Instructions Part 2:   Open the workbook Lab 1-3 Part 1 College Cost and Financial Support. Insert an Exploded pie in 3-D chart in the range G3:K10 to show the contribution of each category of cost for the Freshman year. Chart the range A4:B9 and apply the Style 8 chart style to the chart. Add the Pie chart title as shown in cell G2 in Figure 1–104. Insert an Exploded pie in 3-D chart in the range G12:K18 to show the contribution of each category of financial support for the Freshman year. Chart the range A13:B17 and apply the Style 8 chart style to the chart. Add the Pie chart title shown in cell G11 in Figure 1–104. Update the identification area with the exercise part number and save the workbook using the file name, Lab 1-3 Part 2 College Cost and Financial Support. Print the worksheet. Submit the assignment as requested by your instructor.

Instructions Part 3:   Open the workbook Lab 1-3 Part 2 College Cost and Financial Support. A close inspection of Table 1–9 shows that both cost and financial support figures increase 6% each year. Use Excel Help to learn how to enter the data for the last three years using a formula and the Copy and Paste buttons on the Home tab on the Ribbon. For example, the formula to enter in cell C4 is =B4*1.06. Enter formulas to replace all the numbers in the range C4:E9 and C13:E17. If necessary, reformat the tables, as described in Part 1. The worksheet should appear as shown in Figure 1–104, except that some of the totals will be off by 0.01 due to rounding errors. Save the worksheet using the file name, Lab 1-3 Part 3 College Cost and Financial Support. Print the worksheet. Press CTRL+ACCENT MARK (`) to display the formulas. Print the formulas version. Submit the assignment as requested by your instructor. Close the workbook without saving changes.

Cases and Places

Apply your creative thinking and problem solving skills to design and implement a solution.

● EASIER   ●● MORE DIFFICULT

● 1: Design and Create a Workbook to Analyze Yearly Sales

You are working as a summer intern for Hit-the-Road Mobile Services. Your manager has asked you to prepare a worksheet to help her analyze historical yearly sales by type of product (Table 1–10). Use the concepts and techniques presented in this chapter to create the worksheet and an embedded 3-D Clustered Column chart.

Table 1–10 Hit-the-Road Mobile Services Sales				
	2005	**2006**	**2007**	**2008**
Standard Mobile Phones	87598	99087	129791	188785
Camera Phones	71035	75909	96886	100512
Music Phones	65942	24923	34590	15696
Wireless PDAs	67604	58793	44483	35095
Satellite Radios	15161	27293	34763	43367
Headsets	9549	6264	2600	4048
Other Accessories	47963	108059	100025	62367

● 2: Design and Create a Worksheet and Chart to Analyze a Budget

To estimate the funds needed by your school's Environmental Club to make it through the upcoming year, you decide to create a budget for the club itemizing the expected quarterly expenses. The anticipated expenses are listed in Table 1–11. Use the concepts and techniques presented in this chapter to create the worksheet and an embedded 3-D Column chart using an appropriate chart style that compares the quarterly cost of each expense. Use the AutoCalculate area to determine the average amount spent per quarter on each expense. Manually insert the averages with appropriate titles in an empty area on the worksheet.

Table 1–11 Quarterly Environmental Club Budget				
	Jan – Mar	**April – June**	**July – Sept**	**Oct – Dec**
Meeting Room Rent	300	300	150	450
Copies and Supplies	390	725	325	640
Travel	450	755	275	850
Refreshments	105	85	215	155
Speaker Fees	200	200	0	500
Miscellaneous	125	110	75	215

Continued >

Cases and Places *continued*

•• 3: Create a 3-D Pie Chart to Analyze Quarterly Revenue

In-the-Villa DVD Rental is a DVD movie rental store. The owner of the store is trying to decide if it is feasible to hire more employees during certain times of the year. You have been asked to develop a worksheet totaling all the revenue received last year by quarter. The revenue per quarter is: Quarter 1, $52,699.23; Quarter 2, $111,244.32; Quarter 3, $70,905.03; and Quarter 4, $87,560.10. Create a 3-D Pie chart to illustrate quarterly revenue contribution by quarter. Use the AutoCalculate area to find the average, maximum, and minimum quarterly revenue and manually enter them and their corresponding identifiers in an empty area of the worksheet.

•• 4: Design and Create a Workbook to Analyze Your Field of Interest

Make It Personal

Based on your college major, area of interest, or career, use an Internet search engine or other research material to determine the total number of people employed in your chosen field of interest in the country over the past five years. For each year, break the yearly number down into two or more categories. For example, the number for each year can be broken into management and nonmanagement employees. Create an Excel worksheet that includes this data. Place the data in appropriate rows and columns for each year and category. Create totals for each row, totals for each column, and a grand total. Format the worksheet title, column headings, and data using the concepts presented in this chapter. Create a properly formatted 3-D Clustered Cone chart for the data and place it below the data in the worksheet. Make certain that years are on the X axis and number of employees is on the Y axis.

•• 5: Design and Create a Workbook to Analyze Your School

Working Together

Visit the registrar's office at your school and obtain data, such as age, gender, and full-time versus part-time status, for the students majoring in at least six different academic departments this semester. Have each member of your team divide the data into different categories. For example, separate the data by:

1. Age, divided into four different age groups
2. Gender, divided into male and female
3. Status, divided into full-time and part-time

After coordinating the data as a group, have each member independently use the concepts and techniques presented in this chapter to create a worksheet and appropriate chart to show the total students by characteristics by academic department. As a group, critique each worksheet and have each member modify his or her worksheet based on the group recommendations.

2 Formulas, Functions, Formatting, and Web Queries

Objectives

You will have mastered the material in this chapter when you can:

- Enter formulas using the keyboard and Point mode
- Apply the AVERAGE, MAX, and MIN functions
- Verify a formula using Range Finder
- Apply a theme to a workbook
- Add conditional formatting to cells
- Change column width and row height
- Check the spelling of a worksheet

- Set margins, headers and footers in Page Layout View
- Preview and print versions of a worksheet
- Use a Web query to get real-time data from a Web site
- Rename sheets in a workbook
- E-mail the active workbook from within Excel

2 | Formulas, Functions, Formatting, and Web Queries

Introduction

In Chapter 1, you learned how to enter data, sum values, format the worksheet to make it easier to read, and draw a chart. You also learned about using Help and saving, printing, and opening a workbook. This chapter continues to highlight these topics and presents some new ones.

The new topics covered in this chapter include using formulas and functions to create a worksheet. A **function** is a prewritten formula that is built into Excel. Other new topics include smart tags and option buttons, verifying formulas, applying a theme to a worksheet, adding borders, formatting numbers and text, using conditional formatting, changing the widths of columns and heights of rows, spell checking, e-mailing from within an application, renaming worksheets, using alternative types of worksheet displays and printouts, and adding page headers and footers to a worksheet. One alternative worksheet display and printout shows the formulas in the worksheet, instead of the values. When you display the formulas in the worksheet, you see exactly what text, data, formulas, and functions you have entered into it. Finally, this chapter covers Web queries to obtain real-time data from a Web site.

Project — Worksheet with Formulas, Functions, and Web Queries

The project in the chapter follows proper design guidelines and uses Excel to create the two worksheets shown in Figure 2–1. The Silver Dollars Stock Club was started and is owned by a national academic fraternity, which pools contributions from a number of local chapters. Each local chapter contributes $150 per month; the money is then invested in the stock market for the benefit of the organization and as a tool to help members learn about investing. At the end of each month, the club's treasurer summarizes the club's financial status in a portfolio summary. This summary includes information such as the stocks owned by the club, the cost of the stocks to the club, and the gain or loss that the club has seen over time on the stock. As the complexity of the task of creating the summary increases, the treasurer wants to use Excel to create the monthly portfolio summary. The treasurer also sees an opportunity to use Excel's built-in capability to access real-time stock quotes over the Internet.

Recall that the first step in creating an effective worksheet is to make sure you understand what is required. The people who will use the worksheet usually provide requirements. The requirements document for the Silver Dollars Stock Club Portfolio Summary worksheet includes the following: needs, source of data, summary of calculations, Web requirements, and other facts about its development (Figure 2–2 on page EX 84). The real-time stock quotes (shown in Figure 2–1b) will be accessed via a Web query. The stock quotes will be returned to the active workbook on a separate worksheet. Microsoft determines the content and format of the Real-Time Stock Quotes worksheet.

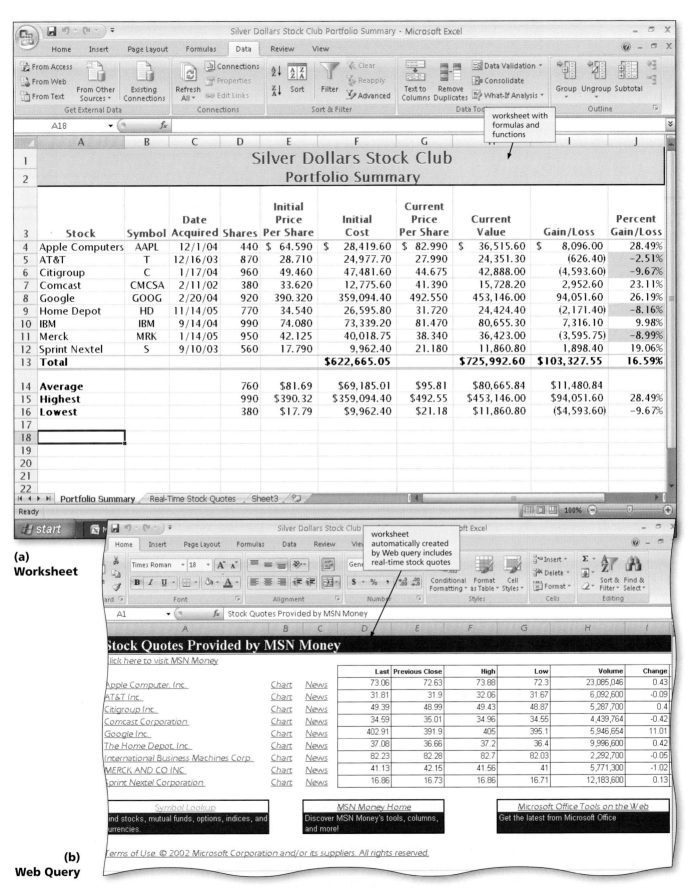

**(a)
Worksheet**

**(b)
Web Query**

Figure 2–1

REQUEST FOR NEW WORKSHEET

Date Submitted:	April 8, 2008
Submitted By:	Juan Castillo
Worksheet Title:	Silver Dollars Stock Club Portfolio Summary
Needs:	An easy-to-read worksheet that summarizes the club's investments (Figure 2-3). For each stock, the worksheet is to include the stock name, stock symbol, date acquired, shares, initial price per share, initial cost, current price per share, current value, gain/loss, and percent gain/loss. Also include totals and the average, highest value, and lowest value for each column of numbers. Use the import data capabilities of Excel to access real-time stock quotes using Web queries.
Source of Data:	The data supplied by Juan includes the stock names, symbols, dates acquired, number of shares, initial price per share, and current price per share. This data is shown in Table 2-1 on page EX 88.
Calculations:	The following calculations must be made for each of the stocks: 1. Initial Cost = Shares × Initial Price Per Share 2. Current Value = Shares × Current Price Per Share 3. Gain/Loss = Current Value − Initial Cost 4. Percent Gain/Loss = Gain/Loss / Initial Cost 5. Compute the totals for initial cost, current value, and gain/loss. 6. Use the AVERAGE function to determine the average for the number of shares, initial price per share, initial cost per share, current price per share, current value, and gain/loss. 7. Use the MAX and MIN functions to determine the highest and lowest values for the number of shares, initial price per share, initial cost per share, current price per share, current value, gain/loss, and percent gain/loss.
Web Requirements:	Use the Web query feature of Excel to get real-time stock quotes for the stocks owned by the Silver Dollars Stock Club.

Approvals

Approval Status:	X	Approved
		Rejected
Approved By:	Members of the Silver Dollars Stock Club	
Date:	April 15, 2008	
Assigned To:	J. Quasney, Spreadsheet Specialist	

Figure 2–2

BTW

Aesthetics versus Function
In designing a worksheet, functional considerations should come first, before visual aesthetics. The function, or purpose, of a worksheet is to provide a user with direct ways to accomplish tasks. Avoid the temptation to use flashy or confusing visual elements within the worksheet, unless they will help the user more easily complete a task.

Overview

As you read this chapter, you will learn how to create the worksheet shown in Figure 2–1 by performing these general tasks:

- Enter formulas and apply functions in the worksheet
- Add conditional formatting to the worksheet
- Apply a theme to the worksheet
- Work with the worksheet in Page Layout View
- Print a part of the worksheet
- Perform a Web query to get real-time data from a Web site and create a new worksheet
- E-mail the worksheet

General Project Decisions

While creating an Excel worksheet, you need to make several decisions that will determine the appearance and characteristics of the finished worksheet. As you create the worksheet required to meet the requirements shown in Figure 2–2, you should follow these general guidelines:

1. **Plan the layout of the worksheet.** As discussed in Chapter 1 and shown in Figure 2–3, rows typically contain items analogous to items in a list. In the case of the stock club's data, the individual stocks serve this purpose and each stock should be placed in a row. As the club adds more stocks, the number of rows in the worksheet will increase. Information about each stock and associated calculations should appear in columns.

2. **Determine the necessary formulas and functions needed.** Values such as initial cost and current value are calculated from known values. The formulas for these calculations should be known in advance of creating the worksheet. Values such as the average, highest, and lowest values can be calculated using Excel functions as opposed to relying on complex formulas.

3. **Identify how to format various elements of the worksheet.** As discussed in Chapter 1 and shown in Figure 2–3, the appearance of the worksheet affects its ability to communicate clearly. Numeric data should be formatted in generally accepted formats, such as using commas as thousands separators and parentheses for negative values.

4. **Establish rules for conditional formatting.** Conditional formatting allows you to format a cell based on the contents of the cell. Decide under which circumstances you would like a cell to stand out from similar cells and determine in what way the cell will stand out. In the case of the Percent Gain/Loss column on the worksheet, placing a different background color in cells that show losses is an appropriate format for the column.

5. **Specify how the printed worksheet should appear.** When it is possible that a person will want to print a worksheet, care should be taken in the development of the worksheet to ensure that the contents can be printed in a readable manner. Excel prints worksheets in landscape or portrait orientation and margins can be adjusted to fit more or less data on each page. Headers and footers add an additional level of customization to the printed page.

(continued)

Plan
Ahead

Figure 2–3

To Change Workbook Properties and Save the Workbook

With the data entered into the worksheet, the following steps save the workbook using the file name, Silver Dollars Stock Club Portfolio Summary. As you are building a workbook, it is a good idea to save it often so that you do not lose your work if the computer is turned off or if you lose electrical power. The first time you save a workbook, you should change the workbook properties.

1 Click the Office Button, click Prepare on the Office Button menu, and then click Properties.

2 Update the document properties with your name and any other information required.

3 Click the Close button on the Properties pane.

4 With a USB flash drive connected to one of the computer's USB ports, click the Save button on the Quick Access toolbar.

5 When Excel displays the Save As dialog box, type `Silver Dollars Stock Club Portfolio Summary` in the File name text box.

6 If necessary, click UDISK 2.0 (E:) in the Save in list (your USB flash drive may have a different name and letter). Click the Save button in the Save As dialog box to save the workbook on the USB flash drive using the file name, Silver Dollars Stock Club Portfolio Summary.

Entering Formulas

One of the reasons Excel is such a valuable tool is that you can assign a **formula** to a cell and Excel will calculate the result. Consider, for example, what would happen if you had to multiply 440 × 64.59 and then manually enter the product, 28,419.60, in cell F4. Every time the values in cells D4 or E4 changed, you would have to recalculate the product and enter the new value in cell F4. By contrast, if you enter a formula in cell F4 to multiply the values in cells D4 and E4, Excel recalculates the product whenever new values are entered into those cells and displays the result in cell F4.

Determine the necessary formulas and functions needed.
The formulas needed in the worksheet are noted in the requirements document as follows:

1. Initial Cost (column F) = Shares × Initial Price Per Share

2. Current Value (column H) = Shares × Current Price Per Share

3. Gain/Loss (column I) = Current Value − Initial Cost

4. Percent Gain/Loss (column J) = Gain/Loss / Initial Cost

The necessary functions to determine the average, highest, and lowest numbers are discussed shortly.

To Enter a Formula Using the Keyboard

The initial cost for each stock, which appears in column F, is equal to the number of shares in column D times the initial price per share in column E. Thus, the initial cost for Apple Computers in cell F4 is obtained by multiplying 440 (cell D4) by 64.59 (cell E4) or =D4*E4. The following steps enter the initial cost formula in cell F4 using the keyboard.

1

- With cell F4 selected, type =d4*e4 in the cell to display the formula in the formula bar and in cell F4 and to display colored borders around the cells referenced in the formula (Figure 2–5).

Q&A

What is happening on the worksheet as I enter the formula?

The **equal sign** (=) preceding d4*e4 is an important part of the formula. It alerts Excel that you are entering a formula or function and not text. Because the most common error when entering a formula is to reference the wrong cell in a formula mistakenly, Excel colors the borders of the cells referenced in the formula. The coloring helps in the reviewing process to ensure the cell references are correct. The **asterisk** (*) following d4 is the arithmetic operator that directs Excel to perform the multiplication operation.

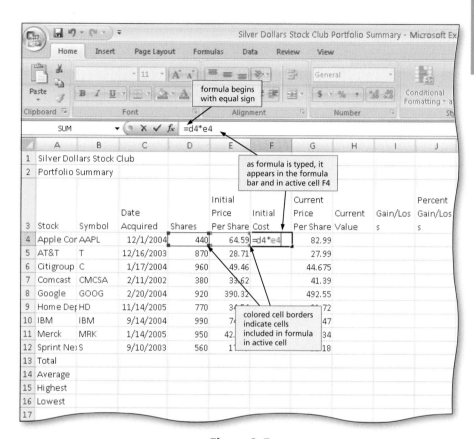

Figure 2–5

2

- Press the RIGHT ARROW key twice to complete the arithmetic operation indicated by the formula, display the result, 28419.6, and to select cell H4 (Figure 2–6).

Figure 2–6

Arithmetic Operations

Table 2–2 describes multiplication and other valid Excel arithmetic operators.

Table 2–2 Summary of Arithmetic Operators

Arithmetic Operator	Meaning	Example of Usage	Meaning
–	Negation	–34	Negative 34
%	Percentage	=72%	Multiplies 72 by 0.01
^	Exponentiation	=4 ^ 6	Raises 4 to the sixth power
*	Multiplication	=22.6 * F4	Multiplies the contents of cell F4 by 22.6
/	Division	=C3 / C6	Divides the contents of cell C3 by the contents of cell C6
+	Addition	=7 + 3	Adds 7 and 3
–	Subtraction	=F12 – 22	Subtracts 22 from the contents of cell F12

BTW

Troubling Formulas
If Excel does not accept a formula, remove the equal sign from the left side and complete the entry as text. Later, after you have entered additional data or determined the error, reinsert the equal sign to change the text back to a formula and edit the formula as needed.

You can enter the cell references in formulas in uppercase or lowercase, and you can add spaces before and after arithmetic operators to make the formulas easier to read. The formula, =d4*e4, is the same as the formulas, =d4 * e4, =D4 * e4, or =D4 * E4.

Order of Operations

When more than one arithmetic operator is involved in a formula, Excel follows the same basic order of operations that you use in algebra. Moving from left to right in a formula, the **order of operations** is as follows: first negation (–), then all percentages (%), then all exponentiations (^), then all multiplications (*) and divisions (/), and finally, all additions (+) and subtractions (–).

You can use parentheses to override the order of operations. For example, if Excel follows the order of operations, 5 * 9 + 8 equals 53. If you use parentheses, however, to change the formula to 5 * (9 + 8), the result is 85, because the parentheses instruct Excel to add 9 and 8 before multiplying by 5. Table 2–3 illustrates several examples of valid Excel formulas and explains the order of operations.

Table 2–3 Examples of Excel Formulas

Formula	Meaning
=K12	Assigns the value in cell K12 to the active cell.
=10 + 4^2	Assigns the sum of 10 + 16 (or 26) to the active cell.
=3 * C20 or =C20 * 3 or =(3 * C20)	Assigns three times the contents of cell C20 to the active cell.
=50% * 12	Assigns the product of 0.50 times 12 (or 6) to the active cell.
– (H3 * Q30)	Assigns the negative value of the product of the values contained in cells H3 and Q30 to the active cell.
–12 * (N8 – Q8)	Assigns the product of 12 times the difference between the values contained in cells N8 and Q8 to the active cell.
=M9 / Z8 – C3 * Q19 + A3 ^ B3	Completes the following operations, from left to right: exponentiation (A3 ^ B3), then division (M9 / Z8), then multiplication (C3 * Q19), then subtraction (M9 / Z8) – (C3 * Q19), and finally addition (M9 / Z8 – C3 * Q19) + (A3 ^ B3). If cells A3 = 2, B3 = 4, C3 = 6, M9 = 3, Q19 = 4, and Z8 = 3, then Excel assigns the active cell the value 18; that is, 3 / 3 – 6 * 4 + 2 ^ 4 = -7.

To Enter Formulas Using Point Mode

The sketch of the worksheet in Figure 2–3 on page EX 85 calls for the current value, gain/loss, and percent gain/loss of each stock to appear in columns H, I, and J respectively. All three of these values are calculated using formulas in row 4:

Current Value (cell H4) = Shares × Current Price Per Share or =D4*G4

Gain/Loss (cell I4) = Current Value − Initial Cost or H4-F4

Percent Gain/Loss (cell J4) = Gain/Loss / Initial Cost or I4/F4

An alternative to entering the formulas in cells H4, I4, and J4 using the keyboard is to enter the formulas using the mouse and Point mode. **Point mode** allows you to select cells for use in a formula by using the mouse. The following steps enter formulas using Point mode.

- With cell H4 selected, type = (equal sign) to begin the formula and then click cell D4 to add a reference to cell D4 to the formula (Figure 2–7).

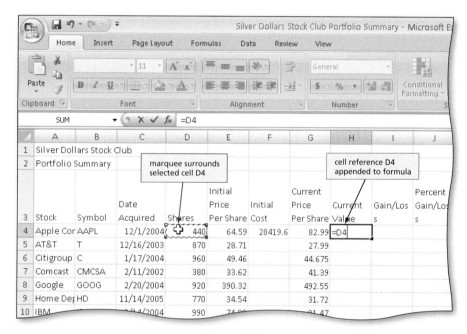

Figure 2–7

②
- Type * (asterisk) and then click cell G4 to add a multiplication operator and reference to cell G4 to the formula (Figure 2–8).

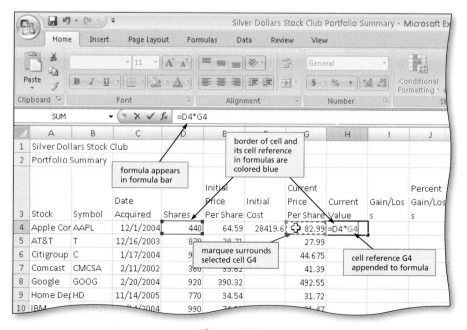

Figure 2–8

❸

- Click the Enter box and then click cell I4 to select cell I4.

- Type = (equal sign) and then click cell H4 to add a reference to cell H4 to the formula.

- Type – (minus sign) and then click cell F4 to add a subtraction operator and reference to cell F4 to the formula (Figure 2–9).

Q&A When should I use Point mode to enter formulas?

Using Point mode to enter formulas often is faster and more accurate than using the keyboard to type the entire formula when the cell you want to select does not require you to scroll. In many instances, as in these steps, you may want to use both the keyboard and mouse when entering a formula in a cell. You can use the keyboard to begin the formula, for example, and then use the mouse to select a range of cells.

Figure 2–9

❹

- Click the Enter box to enter the formula in cell I4.

- Select cell J4. Type = (equal sign) and then click cell I4 to add a reference to cell I4 to the formula.

- Type / (forward slash) and then click cell F4 to add a reference to cell F4 to the formula.

- Click the Enter box to enter the formula in cell J4 (Figure 2–10).

Q&A Why do only six decimal places show in cell J4?

The actual value assigned by Excel to cell J4 from the division operation in Step 4 is 0.284873819. While not all the decimal places appear in Figure 2–10, Excel maintains all of them for computational purposes. Thus, if referencing cell J4 in a formula, the value used for computational purposes is 0.284873819, not 0.284874. Excel displays the value in cell J4 as 0.284874 because the cell formatting is set to display only six digits after the decimal point. If you change the cell formatting of column J to display 15 digits after the decimal point, then Excel displays the true value 0.284873819.

Figure 2–10

To Copy Formulas Using the Fill Handle

The four formulas for Apple Computers in cells F4, H4, I4, and J4 now are complete. You could enter the same four formulas one at a time for the eight remaining stocks. A much easier method of entering the formulas, however, is to select the formulas in row 4 and then use the fill handle to copy them through row 12. Recall from Chapter 1 that the fill handle is a small rectangle in the lower-right corner of the active cell or active range. The following steps copy the formulas using the fill handle.

- Select cell F4 and then point to the fill handle.

- Drag the fill handle down through cell F12 and continue to hold the mouse button to select the destination range (Figure 2–11).

Figure 2–11

- Release the mouse button to copy the formula in cell F4 to the cells in the range F5:F12.

- Select the range H4:J4 and then point to the fill handle (Figure 2–12).

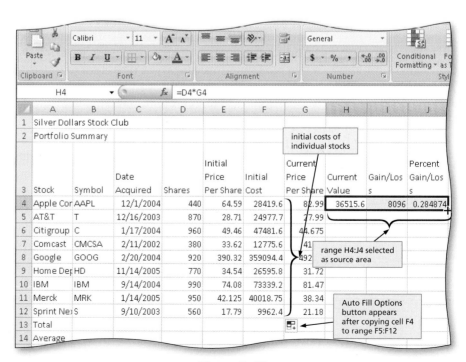

Figure 2–12

3

- Drag the fill handle down through the range H5:J12 to copy the three formulas =D4*G4 in cell H4, =H4-F4 in cell I4, and =I4/F4 in cell J4 to the range H5:J12 (Figure 2–13).

Q&A

How does Excel adjust the cell references in the formulas in the destination area?

Recall that when you copy a formula, Excel adjusts the cell references so the new formulas contain references corresponding to the new location and performs calculations using the appropriate values. Thus, if you copy downward, Excel adjusts the row portion of cell references. If you copy across, then Excel adjusts the column portion of cell references. These cell references are called **relative cell references**.

	A	B	C	D	E	F	G	H	I	J	K	L	M
								H4		=D4*G4			
1	Silver Dollars Stock Club												
2	Portfolio Summary												
3	Stock	Symbol	Date Acquired	Shares	Initial Price Per Share	Initial Cost	Current Price Per Share	Current Value	Gain/Loss	Percent Gain/Loss			
4	Apple Cor	AAPL	12/1/2004				82.99	36515.6	8096	0.284874			
5	AT&T	T	12/16/2003				27.99	24351.3	-626.4	-0.02508			
6	Citigroup	C	1/17/2004				44.65	42888	-4593.6	-0.09674			
7	Comcast	CMCSA	2/11/2002				41.39	15728.2	2952.6	0.231112			
8	Google	GOOG	2/20/2004	920	390.32	359094.4	492.55	453146	94051.6	0.261913			
9	Home Dep	HD	11/14/2005	770	34.54	26595.8	31.72	24424.4	-2171.4	-0.08164			
10	IBM	IBM	9/14/2004	990	74.08	73339.2	81.47	80655.3	7316.1	0.099757			
11	Merck	MRK	1/14/2005	950	42.125	40018.75	38.34	36423	-3595.75	-0.08985			
12	Sprint Ne	S	9/10/2003	560	17.79	9962.4	21.18	11860.8	1898.4	0.190556			
13	Total												
14	Average												
15	Highest												
16	Lowest												

current value, gain/loss, and percent gain/loss formulas in range H4:J4 copies to range H5:J12

Auto Fill Options button appears after copying the range H4:J4 to range H5:J12

Figure 2–13

Other Ways

1. Select source area, click Copy button on Ribbon, select destination area, click Paste button on Ribbon
2. Select source area, right-click copy area, click Copy on shortcut menu, select destination area, right-click paste area, click Paste on shortcut menu

Smart Tags and Option Buttons

Excel can identify certain actions to take on specific data in workbooks using **smart tags**. Data labeled with smart tags includes dates, financial symbols, people's names, and more. To use smart tags, you must turn on smart tags using the AutoCorrect Options in the Excel Options dialog box. To change AutoCorrect options, click the Office Button, click the Excel Options button on the Office Button menu, point to Proofing, and then click AutoCorrect Options. Once smart tags are turned on, Excel places a small purple triangle, called a **smart tag indicator**, in a cell to indicate that a smart tag is available. When you move the insertion point over the smart tag indicator, the Smart Tag Actions button appears. Clicking the Smart Tag Actions button arrow produces a list of actions you can perform on the data in that specific cell.

In addition to smart tags, Excel also displays Options buttons in a workbook while you are working on it to indicate that you can complete an operation using automatic features such as AutoCorrect, Auto Fill, error checking, and others. For example, the Auto Fill Options button shown in Figure 2–13 appears after a fill operation, such as dragging the fill handle. When an error occurs in a formula in a cell, Excel displays the Trace Error button next to the cell and identifies the cell with the error by placing a green triangle in the upper left of the cell.

Table 2–4 summarizes the smart tag and Options buttons available in Excel. When one of these buttons appears on your worksheet, click the button arrow to produce the list of options for modifying the operation or to obtain additional information.

Table 2–4 Smart Tag and Options Buttons in Excel

Button	Name	Menu Function
	Auto Fill Options	Gives options for how to fill cells following a fill operation, such as dragging the fill handle
	AutoCorrect Options	Undoes an automatic correction, stops future automatic corrections of this type, or causes Excel to display the AutoCorrect Options dialog box
	Insert Options	Lists formatting options following an insertion of cells, rows, or columns
	Paste Options	Specifies how moved or pasted items should appear (for example, with original formatting, without formatting, or with different formatting)
	Smart Tag Actions	Lists information options for a cell containing data recognized by Excel, such as a stock symbol
	Trace Error	Lists error checking options following the assignment of an invalid formula to a cell

To Determine Totals Using the Sum Button

The next step is to determine the totals in row 13 for the initial cost in column F, current value in column H, and gain/loss in column I. To determine the total initial cost in column F, the values in the range F4 through F12 must be summed. To do so, enter the function =sum(f4:f12) in cell F13 or select cell F13 and then click the Sum button on the Ribbon and then press the ENTER key. Recall that a function is a prewritten formula that is built into Excel. Similar SUM functions or the Sum button can be used in cells H13 and I13 to determine total current value and total gain/loss, respectively.

1 Select cell F13. Click the Sum button on the Ribbon and then click the Enter button.

2 Select the range H13:I13. Click the Sum button on the Ribbon to display the totals in row 13 as shown in Figure 2–14.

BTW

Selecting a Range
You can select a range using the keyboard. Press the F8 key and then use the arrow keys to select the desired range. After you are finished, make sure to press the F8 key to turn off the selection or you will continue to select ranges.

Figure 2–14

To Determine the Total Percent Gain/Loss

With the totals in row 13 determined, the next step is to copy the percent gain/loss formula in cell J12 to cell J13 as performed in the following steps.

1 Select cell J12 and then point to the fill handle.

2 Drag the fill handle down through cell J13 to copy the formula in cell J12 to cell J13 (Figure 2–15).

Q&A Why was the formula I13/F13 not copied to cell J13 earlier?

The formula, I13/F13, was not copied to cell J13 when cell J4 was copied to the range J5:J12 because both cells involved in the computation (I13 and F13) were blank, or zero, at the time. A **blank cell** in Excel has a numerical value of zero, which would have resulted in an error message in cell J13. Once the totals were determined, both cells I13 and F13 (especially F13, because it is the divisor) had nonzero numerical values.

	Stock	Symbol	Date Acquired	Shares	Initial Price Per Share	Initial Cost	Current Price Per Share	Current Value	Gain/Loss	Percent Gain/Loss	
3	Stock	Symbol	Acquired	Shares	Per Share	Cost	Per Share	Value	s	s	
4	Apple Cor	AAPL	12/1/2004	440	64.59	28419.6	82.99	36515.6	8096	0.284874	
5	AT&T	T	12/16/2003	870	28.71	24977.7	27.99	24351.3	-626.4	-0.02508	
6	Citigroup	C	1/17/2004	960	49.46	47481.6	44.675	42888	-4593.6	-0.09674	
7	Comcast	CMCSA	2/11/2002	380	33.62	12775.6	41.39	15728.2	2952.6	0.231112	formula is =I12/F12
8	Google	GOOG	2/20/2004	920	390.32	359094.4	492.55	453146	94051.6	0.261913	
9	Home Dep	HD	11/14/2005	770	34.54	26595.8	31.72	24424.4	-2171.4	-0.08164	
10	IBM	IBM	9/14/2004	990	74.08	73339.2	81.47	80655.3	7316.1	0.099757	formula is =I13/F13
11	Merck	MRK	1/14/2005	950	42.125	40018.75	38.34	36423	-3595.75	-0.08985	
12	Sprint Nex	S	9/10/2003	560	17.79	9962.4	21.18	11860.8	1898.4	0.190556	
13	Total					622665.1		725992.6	103327.6	0.165944	Auto Fill Options button appears after copying cell J12 to cell J13
14	Average										
15	Highest										
16	Lowest										

Figure 2–15

BTW

Entering Functions
You can drag the Function Arguments dialog box (Figure 2–20 on page EX 101) out of the way in order to select a range. You also can click the Collapse Dialog button to the right of the Number 1 box to hide the Function Arguments dialog box. After selecting the range, click the Collapse Dialog button a second time.

BTW

Statistical Functions
Excel usually considers a blank cell to be equal to 0. The statistical functions, however, ignore blank cells. Excel thus calculates the average of 3 cells with values of 7, blank, and 5 to be 6 or (7 + 5) / 2 and not 4 or (7 + 0 + 5) / 3.

Using the AVERAGE, MAX, and MIN Functions

The next step in creating the Silver Dollars Stock Club Portfolio Summary worksheet is to compute the average, highest value, and lowest value for the number of shares listed in the range D4:D12 using the AVERAGE, MAX, and MIN functions in the range D14:D16. Once the values are determined for column D, the entries can be copied across to the other columns.

Excel includes prewritten formulas called functions to help you compute these statistics. A **function** takes a value or values, performs an operation, and returns a result to the cell. The values that you use with a function are called **arguments**. All functions begin with an equal sign and include the arguments in parentheses after the function name. For example, in the function =AVERAGE(D4:D12), the function name is AVERAGE, and the argument is the range D4:D12.

With Excel, you can enter functions using one of five methods: (1) the keyboard or mouse; (2) the Insert Function box in the formula bar; (3) the Sum menu; (4) the AutoSum command on the Formulas tab on the Ribbon; and (5) the Name box area in the formula bar (Figure 2–16). The method you choose will depend on your typing skills and whether you can recall the function name and required arguments.

In the following pages, each of the first three methods will be used. The keyboard and mouse method will be used to determine the average number of shares (cell D14). The Insert Function button in the formula bar method will be used to determine the highest number of shares (cell D15). The Sum menu method will be used to determine the lowest number of shares (cell D16).

To Determine the Average of a Range of Numbers Using the Keyboard and Mouse

The **AVERAGE function** sums the numbers in the specified range and then divides the sum by the number of nonzero cells in the range. The following steps use the AVERAGE function to determine the average of the numbers in the range D4:D12.

- Select cell D14.

- Type =av in the cell to display the Formula AutoComplete list.

- Point to the AVERAGE function name (Figure 2–16).

Q&A

What is happening as I type?

As you type the equal sign followed by the characters in the name of a function, Excel displays the Formula AutoComplete list. This list contains those functions that alphabetically match the letters you have typed. Because you typed =av, Excel displays all the functions that begin with the letters av.

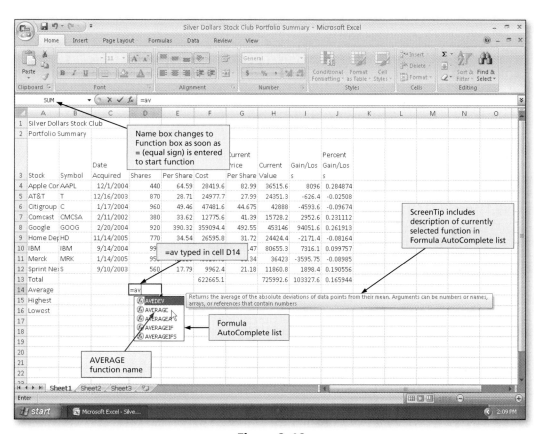

Figure 2–16

2

- Double-click AVERAGE in the Formula AutoComplete list to select the AVERAGE function.

- Select the range D4:D12 to insert the range as the argument to the AVERAGE function (Figure 2–17).

Q&A As I drag, why does the function in cell D14 change?

When you click cell D4, Excel appends cell D4 to the left parenthesis in the formula bar and surrounds cell D4 with a marquee. When you begin dragging, Excel appends to the argument a colon (:) and the cell reference of the cell where the mouse pointer is located.

3

- Click the Enter box to compute the average of the nine numbers in the range D4:D12 and display the result in cell D14 (Figure 2–18).

Q&A Can I use the arrow keys to complete the entry instead?

No. When you use Point mode you cannot use the arrow keys to complete the entry. While in Point mode, the arrow keys change the selected cell reference in the range you are selecting.

Q&A What is the purpose of the parentheses in the function?

The AVERAGE function requires that the argument (in this case, the range D4:D12) be included within parentheses following the function name. Excel automatically appends the right parenthesis to complete the AVERAGE function when you click the Enter box or press the ENTER key.

Figure 2–17

Figure 2–18

Other Ways

1. Click Insert Function box in formula bar, click AVERAGE function

2. Click Sum button arrow on Ribbon, click Average function

3. Click Formulas tab on Ribbon, click AutoSum button, click Average function

To Determine the Highest Number in a Range of Numbers Using the Insert Function Box

The next step is to select cell D15 and determine the highest (maximum) number in the range D4:D12. Excel has a function called the **MAX function** that displays the highest value in a range. Although you could enter the MAX function using the keyboard and Point mode as described in the previous steps, an alternative method to entering the function is to use the Insert Function box in the formula bar, as performed in the following steps.

- Select cell D15.

- Click the Insert Function box in the formula bar to display the Insert Function dialog box.

- When Excel displays the Insert Function dialog box, click MAX in the 'Select a function list' (Figure 2–19).

Figure 2–19

- Click the OK button.

- When Excel displays the Function Arguments dialog box, type d4:d12 in the Number 1 box (Figure 2–20).

Q&A

Why did numbers appear in the Function Arguments dialog box?

As shown in Figure 2–20, Excel displays the value the MAX function will return to cell D15 in the Function Arguments dialog box. It also lists the first few numbers in the selected range, next to the Number 1 box.

Figure 2–20

- Click the OK button to display the highest value in the range D4:D12 in cell D15 (Figure 2–21).

Q&A

Why should I not just enter the highest value that I see in the range D4:D12 in cell D15?

In this example, rather than entering the MAX function, you easily could scan the range D4:D12, determine that the highest number of shares is 990, and manually enter the number 990 as a constant in cell D15. Excel would display the number the same as in Figure 2–21. Because it contains a constant, however, Excel will continue to display 990 in cell D15, even if the values in the range D4:D12 change. If you use the MAX function, Excel will recalculate the highest value in the range D4:D9 each time a new value is entered into the worksheet.

Figure 2–21

Other Ways

1. Click Sum button arrow on Ribbon, click Max function
2. Click Formulas tab on Ribbon, click AutoSum button, click Max function
3. Type =MAX in cell

To Determine the Lowest Number in a Range of Numbers Using the Sum Menu

The next step is to enter the **MIN function** in cell D16 to determine the lowest (**minimum**) number in the range D4:D12. Although you can enter the MIN function using either of the methods used to enter the AVERAGE and MAX functions, the following steps perform an alternative using the Sum button on the Ribbon.

- Select cell D16.
- Click the Sum button arrow on the Ribbon to display the Sum button menu (Figure 2–22).

Q&A

Why should I use the Sum button menu?

Using the Sum button menu allows you to enter one of five often-used functions easily into a cell, without having to memorize its name or the required arguments.

Figure 2–22

2

- Click Min to display the function =MIN(D14:D15) in the formula bar and in cell D16 (Figure 2–23).

Q&A

Why does Excel select the range D14:D15?

The range D14:D15 automatically selected by Excel is not correct. Excel attempts to guess which cells you want to include in the function by looking for adjacent ranges to the selected cell that contain numeric data.

Figure 2–23

3

- Click cell D4 and then drag through cell D12 to display the function in the formula bar and in cell D14 with the new range (Figure 2–24).

Figure 2–24

4

- Click the Enter box to determine the lowest value in D4:D12 and display the result in the formula bar and in cell D14 (Figure 2–25).

Q&A

How can I use other functions?

Excel has more than 400 additional functions that perform just about every type of calculation you can imagine. These functions are categorized in the Insert Function dialog box shown in Figure 2–19 on page EX 101. To view the categories, click the 'Or select a category' box arrow. To obtain a description of a selected function, select its name in the Insert Function dialog box. Excel displays the description of the function below the Select a function list in the dialog box.

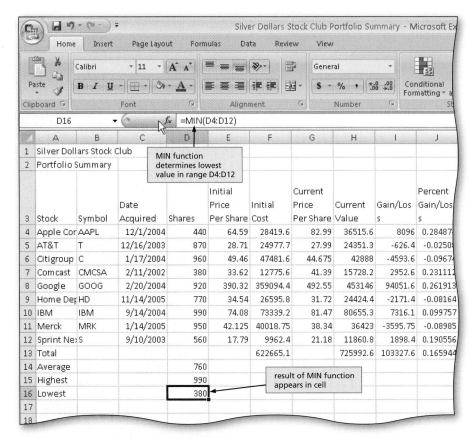

Figure 2–25

| | | | | | Initial | | Current | | | Percent |
Stock	Symbol	Date Acquired	Shares	Price Per Share	Initial Cost	Price Per Share	Current Value	Gain/Loss	Gain/Loss
Apple Cor	AAPL	12/1/2004	440	64.59	28419.6	82.99	36515.6	8096	0.28487
AT&T	T	12/16/2003	870	28.71	24977.7	27.99	24351.3	-626.4	-0.02505
Citigroup	C	1/17/2004	960	49.46	47481.6	44.675	42888	-4593.6	-0.09674
Comcast	CMCSA	2/11/2002	380	33.62	12775.6	41.39	15728.2	2952.6	0.231111
Google	GOOG	2/20/2004	920	390.32	359094.4	492.55	453146	94051.6	0.261913
Home Dep	HD	11/14/2005	770	34.54	26595.8	31.72	24424.4	-2171.4	-0.08164
IBM	IBM	9/14/2004	990	74.08	73339.2	81.47	80655.3	7316.1	0.099757
Merck	MRK	1/14/2005	950	42.125	40018.75	38.34	36423	-3595.75	-0.08985
Sprint Nex	S	9/10/2003	560	17.79	9962.4	21.18	11860.8	1898.4	0.190556
Total					622665.1		725992.6	103327.6	0.165944
Average			760						
Highest			990						
Lowest			380						

Other Ways

1. Click Insert Function box in formula bar, click MIN function
2. Click Formulas tab on Ribbon, click AutoSum button, click Min function
3. Type =MIN in cell

To Copy a Range of Cells across Columns to an Adjacent Range Using the Fill Handle

The next step is to copy the AVERAGE, MAX, and MIN functions in the range D14:D16 to the adjacent range E14:J16. The following steps use the fill handle to copy the functions.

1

- Select the range D14:D16.

- Drag the fill handle in the lower-right corner of the selected range through cell J16 and continue to hold down the mouse button (Figure 2–26).

Figure 2–26

2

- Release the mouse button to copy the three functions to the range E14:J16 (Figure 2–27).

Q&A How can I be sure that the function arguments are proper for the cells in range E14:J16?

Remember that Excel adjusts the cell references in the copied functions so each function refers to the range of numbers above it in the same column. Review the numbers in rows 14 through 16 in Figure 2–27. You should see that the functions in each column return the appropriate values, based on the numbers in rows 4 through 12 of that column.

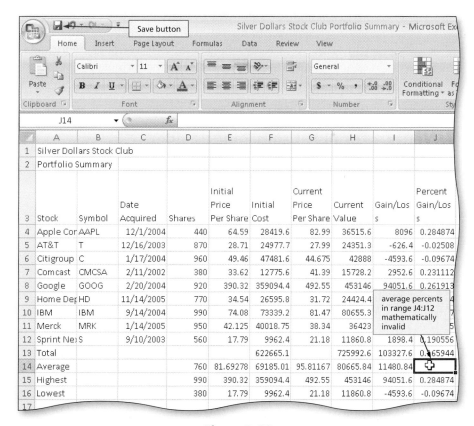

Figure 2–27

3

- Select cell J14 and press the DELETE key to delete the average of the percent gain/loss (Figure 2–28).

Q&A Why is the formula in cell J14 deleted?

The average of the percent gain/loss in cell J14 is deleted because an average of percentages of this type is mathematically invalid.

Other Ways

1. Select source area and point to border of range, while holding down CTRL key, drag source area to destination area

2. Select source area, on Ribbon click Copy button, select destination area, on Ribbon click Paste button

3. Right-click source area, click Copy on shortcut menu, right-click destination area, click Paste on shortcut menu

4. Select source area, press CTRL+C, select destination area, press CTRL+V

Figure 2–28

To Save a Workbook Using the Same File Name

Earlier in this project, an intermediate version of the workbook was saved using the file name, Silver Dollars Stock Club Portfolio Summary. The following step saves the workbook a second time using the same file name.

1 Click the Save button on the Quick Access toolbar to save the workbook on the USB flash drive using the file name, Silver Dollars Stock Club Portfolio Summary.

Q&A Why did Excel not display the Save As dialog box?

When you save a workbook a second time using the same file name, Excel will not display the Save As dialog box as it does the first time you save the workbook. Excel automatically stores the latest version of the workbook using the same file name, Silver Dollars Stock Club Portfolio Summary. You also can click Save on the Office Button menu or press SHIFT+F12 or CTRL+S to save a workbook again.

Verifying Formulas Using Range Finder

One of the more common mistakes made with Excel is to include a wrong cell reference in a formula. An easy way to verify that a formula references the cells you want it to reference is to use Excel's Range Finder. Use the **Range Finder** to check which cells are referenced in the formula assigned to the active cell. Range Finder allows you to make immediate changes to the cells referenced in a formula.

To use Range Finder to verify that a formula contains the intended cell references, double-click the cell with the formula you want to check. Excel responds by highlighting the cells referenced in the formula so you can check that the cell references are correct.

To Verify a Formula Using Range Finder

The following steps use Range Finder to check the formula in cell J4.

1
- Double-click cell J4 to activate Range Finder (Figure 2–29).

2
- Press the ESC key to quit Range Finder and then select cell A18.

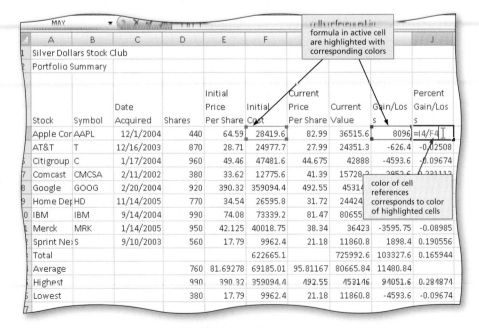

Figure 2–29

Formatting the Worksheet

Although the worksheet contains the appropriate data, formulas, and functions, the text and numbers need to be formatted to improve their appearance and readability.

In Chapter 1, cell styles were used to format much of the worksheet. This section describes how to change the unformatted worksheet in Figure 2–30a to the formatted worksheet in Figure 2–30b using a theme and other commands on the Ribbon. A **theme** is a predefined set of colors, fonts, chart styles, cell styles, and fill effects that can be applied to an entire workbook. Every new workbook that you create is assigned a default theme named Office. The colors and fonts that are used in the worksheet shown in Figure 2–30b are those that are associated with the Concourse theme.

(a) Unformatted Worksheet

(b) Formatted Worksheet

Figure 2–30

Identify how to format various elements of the worksheet.

The following outlines the formatting suggested in the sketch of the worksheet in Figure 2–3 on page EX 85:

1. Workbook theme - Concourse

2. Worksheet title and subtitle

   a. Alignment — center across columns A through J

   b. Cell style —Title

   c. Font size — title 18; subtitle 16

   d. Background color (range A1:J2) — Turquoise Accent 1, Lighter 60%

   e. Border — thick box border around range A1:J2

3. Column titles

   a. Cell style — Heading 3

   b. Alignment — center

4. Data

   a. Alignment — center data in column B

   b. Dates in column C — mm/dd/yy format

   c. Numbers in top row (range E4:I4) — Accounting style

   d. Numbers below top row (range E5:I12) — Comma style and decimal places

5. Total line

   a. Cell style — Total

   b. Numbers — Accounting style

6. Average, Highest, and Lowest rows

   a. Font style of row titles in range A14:A16 — bold

   b. Numbers — Currency style with floating dollar sign in the range E14:I16

7. Percentages in column J

   a. Numbers — Percentage style with two decimal places; if a cell in range J4:J12 is less than zero, then cell appears with background color of light red

8. Column widths

   a. Column A — 14.11 characters

   b. Columns B and C — best fit

   c. Column D — 6.00 characters

   d. Column E, G, and J — 9.00 characters

   e. Columns F, H, and I — 12.67 characters

9. Row heights

   a. Row 3 — 60.00 points

   b. Row 14 — 26.25 points

   c. Remaining rows — default

To Change the Workbook Theme

The Concourse theme includes fonts and colors that provide the worksheet a professional and subtly colored appearance. The following steps change the workbook theme to the Concourse theme.

1

- Click the Page Layout tab on the Ribbon.

- Click the Themes button on the Ribbon to display the Theme gallery (Figure 2–31).

Experiment

- Point to several themes in the Theme gallery to see a live preview of the themes.

Q&A Why should I change the theme of a workbook?

A company or department may standardize on a specific theme so that all of their documents have a similar appearance. Similarly, an individual may want to have a theme that sets their work apart from others. Other Office applications, such as Word and Power-Point, include the same themes included with Excel, meaning that all of your Microsoft Office documents can share a common theme.

Figure 2–31

2

- Click Concourse in the Theme gallery to change the workbook theme to Concourse (Figure 2–32).

Q&A Why did the cells in the worksheet change?

The cells in the worksheet originally were formatted with the default font for the default Office theme. The default font for the Concourse theme is different than that of the default font for the Office theme and therefore changed on the worksheet when you changed the theme. If you had modified the font for any of the cells, those cells would not receive the default font for the Concourse theme.

Figure 2–32

To Format the Worksheet Titles

The following steps merge and center the worksheet titles, apply the Title cells style to the worksheet titles, and decrease the font of the worksheet subtitle.

1 Click the Home tab on the Ribbon.

2 Select the range A1:J1 and then click the Merge and Center button on the Ribbon.

3 Select the range A2:J2 and then click the Merge and Center button on the Ribbon.

4 Select the range A1:A2, click the Cell Styles button on the Ribbon, and then click the Title cell style in the Cell Styles gallery.

5 Select cell A2 and then click the Decrease Font Size button on the Ribbon (Figure 2–33).

Q&A What is the effect of clicking the Decrease Font Size button?

When you click the Decrease Font Size button Excel assigns the next lowest font size in the Font Size gallery to the selected range. The Increase Font Size button works in a similar manner, but causes Excel to assign the next highest font size in the Font Size gallery to the selected range.

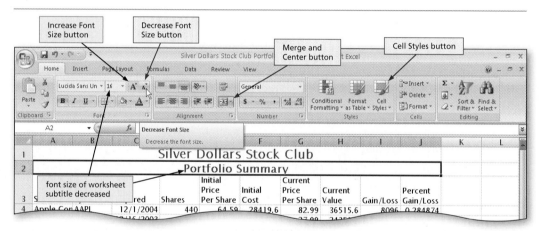

Figure 2–33

To Change the Background Color and Apply a Box Border to the Worksheet Title and Subtitle

The final formats assigned to the worksheet title and subtitle are the turquoise background color and thick box border (Figure 2–30b on page EX 107). The following steps complete the formatting of the worksheet titles.

- Select the range A1:A2 and then click the Fill Color button arrow on the Ribbon to display the Fill Color palette (Figure 2–34).

Figure 2–34

2

- Click Turquoise Accent 1, lighter 60% (column 5, row 3) on the Fill Color palette to change the background color of cells A1 and A2 from white to turquoise (Figure 2–35).

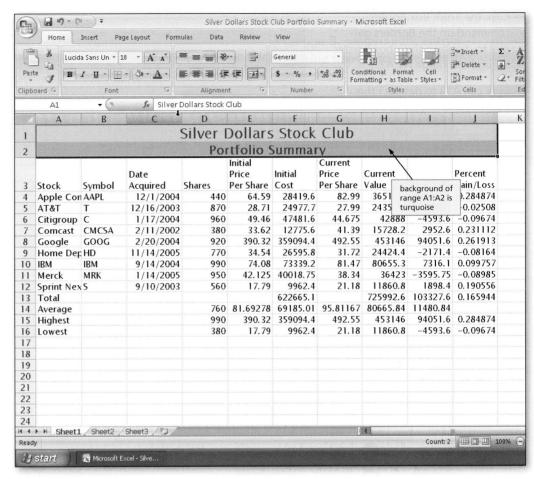

Figure 2–35

3

- Click the Borders button arrow on the Ribbon to display the Borders gallery (Figure 2–36).

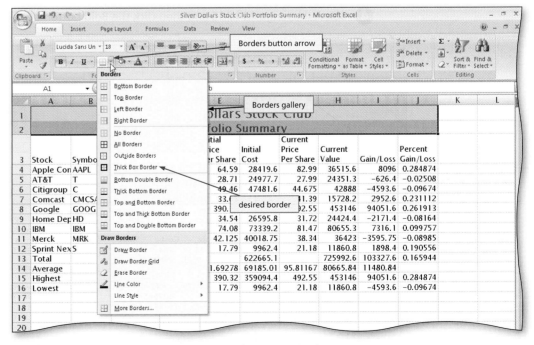

Figure 2–36

3

- Click cell E4.

- While holding down the CTRL key, select cell G4.

- Click the Increase Decimal button on the Ribbon to increase the number of decimal places displayed in cell E4 and G4.

- Select the range E5:E12. While holding down the CTRL key, select the range G5:G12.

- Click the Increase Decimal button on the Ribbon to increase the number of decimal places displayed in selected ranges (Figure 2–43).

Q&A

What is the effect of clicking the Increase Decimal button?

The Increase Decimal button instructs Excel to display additional decimal places in a cell. Each time you click the Increase Decimal button, Excel adds a decimal place to the selected cell.

Figure 2–43

To Apply a Currency Style Format with a Floating Dollar Sign Using the Format Cells Dialog Box

The following steps use the Format Cells dialog box to apply the Currency style format with a floating dollar sign to the numbers in the ranges E14:I16.

1

- Select the range E14:I16 and then point to the Format Cells: Number Dialog Box Launcher on the Ribbon (Figure 2–44).

ired	Shares	Per Share	Initial Cost	Share	Value	Gain/Loss
2/1/04	440	$ 64.590	$ 28,419.60	$ 82.990	$ 36,515.60	$ 8,096.00
/16/03	870	28.710	24,977.70	27.990	24,351.30	(626.40)
/17/0			47,481....		888.00	
	950	42.1...		38.340		....75)
/10/03	560	17.790	9,962.40	21.180	11,860.80	1,898.40
			$ 622,665.05		$ 725,992.60	$ 103,327.55
	760	81.69278	69185.00556	95.81167	80665.84444	11480.83889
	990	390.32	359094.4	492.55	453146	94051.6
	380	17.79	9962.4	21.18	11860.8	−4593.6

Figure 2–44

2

- Click the Format Cells: Number Dialog Box Launcher.

- If necessary, click the Number tab in the Format Cells dialog box.

- Click Currency in the Category list and then click the third style ($1,234.10) in the Negative numbers list (Figure 2–45).

Q&A How do I select the proper format?

You can choose from 12 categories of formats. Once you select a category, you can select the number of decimal places, whether or not a dollar sign should be displayed, and how negative numbers should appear. Selecting the appropriate negative numbers format is important, because doing so adds a space to the right of the number in order to align the numbers in the worksheet on the decimal points. Some of the available negative number formats do not align the numbers in the worksheet on the decimal points.

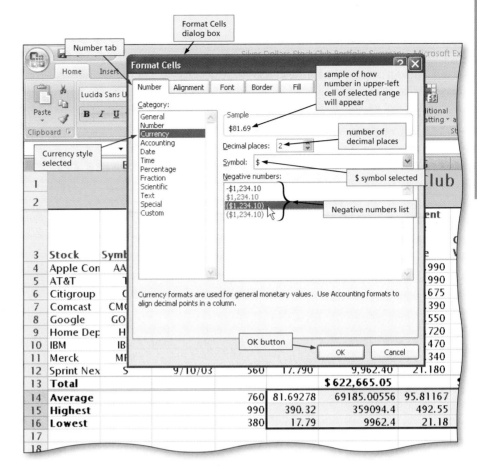

Figure 2–45

3

- Click the OK button to assign the Currency style format with a floating dollar sign to the range E14:I16 (Figure 2–46).

Q&A Should I click the Accounting Number Style button on the Ribbon or use the Format Cells dialog box?

Recall that a floating dollar sign always appears immediately to the left of the first digit, and the fixed dollar sign always appears on the left side of the cell. Cell E4, for example, has a fixed dollar sign, while cell E14 has a floating dollar sign. The Currency style was assigned to cell E14 using the Format Cells dialog box and the result is a floating dollar sign.

Figure 2–46

Other Ways
1. Press CTRL+1, click Number tab, click Currency in Category list, select format, click OK button	2. Press CTRL+SHIFT+ DOLLAR SIGN (\$)

To Apply a Percent Style Format and Use the Increase Decimal Button

The next step is to format the percent gain/loss in column J. Currently, Excel displays the numbers in column J as a decimal fraction (for example, 0.284874 in cell J4). The following steps format the range J4:J16 to the Percent style format with two decimal places.

- Select the range J4:J16.

- Click the Percent Style button on the Ribbon to display the numbers in column J as a rounded whole percent.

Q&A

What is the result of clicking the Percent Style button?

The Percent Style button instructs Excel to display a value as a percentage, determined by multiplying the cell entry by 100, rounding the result to the nearest percent, and adding a percent sign. For example, when cell J4 is formatted using the Percent Style and Increase Decimal buttons, Excel displays the actual value 0.284874 as 28.49%.

- Click the Increase Decimal button on the Ribbon two times to display the numbers in column J with the Percent style format and two decimal places (Figure 2–47).

Figure 2–47

Other Ways

1. Right-click range, click Format Cells on shortcut menu, click Number tab, click Percentage in Category list, select format, click OK button

2. Press CTRL+1, click Number tab, click Percentage in Category list, select format, click OK button

3. Press CTRL+SHIFT+ PERCENT SIGN (%)

Conditional Formatting

The next step is to emphasize the negative percentages in column J by formatting them to appear with a tinted background. The Conditional Formatting button on the Ribbon will be used to complete this task.

Excel lets you apply formatting that appears only when the value in a cell meets conditions that you specify. This type of formatting is called **conditional formatting**. You can apply conditional formatting to a cell, a range of cells, the entire worksheet, or the entire workbook. Usually, you apply conditional formatting to a range of cells that contains values you want to highlight, if conditions warrant. For example, you can instruct Excel to change the color of the background of a cell if the value in the cell meets a condition, such as being less than 0 as shown in Figure 2–48.

A **condition**, which is made up of two values and a relational operator, is true or false for each cell in the range. If the condition is true, then Excel applies the formatting. If the condition is false, then Excel suppresses the formatting. What makes conditional formatting so powerful is that the cell's appearance can change as you enter new values in the worksheet.

To Apply Conditional Formatting

The following steps assign conditional formatting to the range J4:J12, so that any cell value less than zero will cause Excel to display the number in the cell with a light red background.

1

- Select the range J4:J12.

- Click the Conditional Formatting button on the Ribbon to display the Conditional Formatting gallery (Figure 2–48).

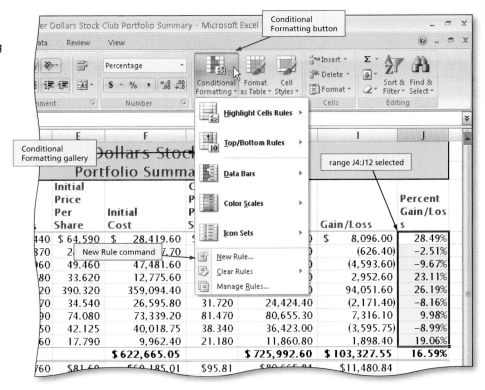

Figure 2–48

2

- Click New Rule in the Conditional Formatting gallery to display the New Formatting Rule dialog box.

- Click 'Format only cells that contain' in the Select a Rule Type area.

- In the Edit the Rule Description area, click the box arrow in the relational operator box (second text box) and then select less than.

- Type 0 (zero) in the rightmost box in the Edit the Rule Description area (Figure 2–49).

Figure 2–49

- Click the Format button.

- When Excel displays the Format Cells dialog box, click the Fill tab and then click the light red color in column 6, row 2 (Figure 2–50).

Figure 2–50

④

- Click the OK button to close the Format Cells dialog box and display the New Formatting Rule dialog box with the desired color displayed in the Preview box (Figure 2–51).

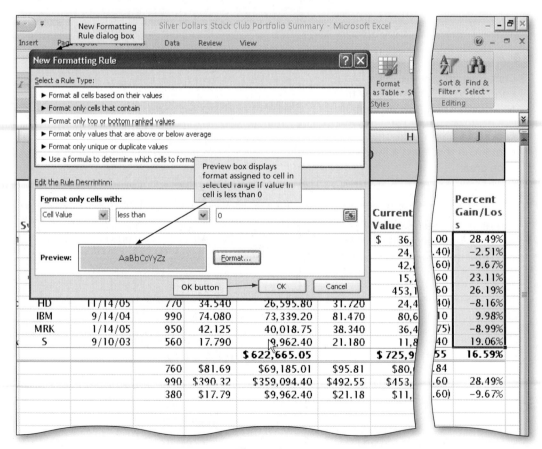

Figure 2–51

5
- Click the OK button to assign the conditional format to the range J4:J12.

- Click cell A18 to deselect the range J4:J12 (Figure 2–52).

Figure 2–52

Conditional Formatting Operators

As shown in Figure 2–49 on page EX 119, the second text box in the New Formatting Rule dialog box allows you to select a relational operator, such as less than, to use in the condition. The eight different relational operators from which you can choose for conditional formatting in the New Formatting Rule dialog box are summarized in Table 2–5.

Table 2–5 Summary of Conditional Formatting Relational Operators

Relational Operator	Description
Between	Cell value is between two numbers
Not between	Cell value is not between two numbers
Equal to	Cell value is equal to a number
Not equal to	Cell value is not equal to a number
Greater than	Cell value is greater than a number
Less than	Cell value is less than a number
Greater than or equal to	Cell value is greater than or equal to a number
Less than or equal to	Cell value is less than or equal to a number

BTW

Hidden Columns
Trying to unhide a range of columns using the mouse can be frustrating. An alternative is to use the keyboard: select the columns to the right and left of the hidden columns and then press CTRL+SHIFT+) (RIGHT PARENTHESIS). To use the keyboard to hide a range of columns, press CTRL+0 (ZERO).

Changing the Widths of Columns and Heights of Rows

When Excel starts and displays a blank worksheet on the screen, all of the columns have a default width of 8.43 characters, or 64 pixels. A character is defined as a letter, number, symbol, or punctuation mark in 11-point Calibri font, the default font used by Excel. An average of 8.43 characters in 11-point Calibri font will fit in a cell.

Another measure of the height and width of cells is pixels, which is short for picture element. A **pixel** is a dot on the screen that contains a color. The size of the dot is based on your screen's resolution. At a common resolution of 1024 × 768, 1024 pixels appear across the screen and 768 pixels appear down the screen for a total of 786,432 pixels. It is these 786,432 pixels that form the font and other items you see on the screen.

The default row height in a blank worksheet is 15 points (or 20 pixels). Recall from Chapter 1 that a point is equal to 1/72 of an inch. Thus, 15 points is equal to about 1/5 of an inch. You can change the width of the columns or height of the rows at any time to make the worksheet easier to read or to ensure that Excel displays an entry properly in a cell.

To Change the Widths of Columns

When changing the column width, you can set the width manually or you can instruct Excel to size the column to best fit. **Best fit** means that the width of the column will be increased or decreased so the widest entry will fit in the column. Sometimes, you may prefer more or less white space in a column than best fit provides. Excel thus allows you to change column widths manually.

When the format you assign to a cell causes the entry to exceed the width of a column, Excel automatically changes the column width to best fit. If you do not assign a format to a cell or cells in a column, the column width will remain 8.43 characters. To set a column width to best fit, double-click the right boundary of the column heading above row 1.

The following steps change the column widths: column A to 14.11 characters; columns B and C to best fit; column D to 6.00 characters; columns E, G, and J to 9.00 characters; and columns F, H, and I to 12.67 characters.

1

• Point to the boundary on the right side of the column A heading above row 1.

• When the mouse pointer changes to a split double arrow, drag until the ScreenTip indicates Width: 14.11 (134 pixels). Do not release the mouse button (Figure 2–53).

Q&A

What happens if I change the column width to zero (0)?

If you decrease the column width to 0, the column is hidden. **Hiding cells** is a technique you can use to hide data that might not be relevant to a particular report or sensitive data that you do not want others to see. To instruct Excel to display a hidden column, position the mouse pointer to the right of the column heading boundary where the hidden column is located and then drag to the right.

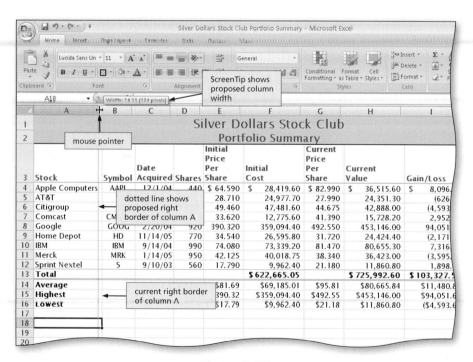

Figure 2–53

2

- Release the mouse button.

- Drag through column headings B and C above row 1.

- Point to the boundary on the right side of column heading C to cause the mouse pointer to become a split double arrow (Figure 2–54).

Q&A

What if I want to make a large change to the column width?

If you want to increase or decrease column width significantly, you can right-click a column heading and then use the Column Width command on the shortcut menu to change the column's width. To use this command, however, you must select one or more entire columns.

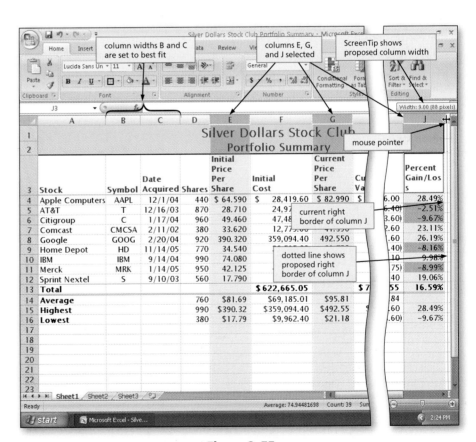

Figure 2–54

3

- Double-click the right boundary of column heading C to change the width of columns B and C to best fit.

- Click the column E heading above row 1.

- While holding down the CTRL key, click the column G heading and then the column J heading above row 1 so that columns E, G, and J are selected.

- Point to the boundary on the right side of the column J heading above row 1.

- Drag until the ScreenTip indicates Width: 9.00 (88 pixels). Do not release the mouse button (Figure 2–55).

Figure 2–55

4

- Release the mouse button.

- Click the column F heading above row 1 to select column F.

- While holding down the CTRL key, click the column H heading and then the column I heading above row 1, to select columns F, H, and I.

- Point to the boundary on the right side of the column I heading above row 1.

- Drag to the left until the ScreenTip indicates Width: 12.67 (121 pixels). Do not release the mouse button (Figure 2–56).

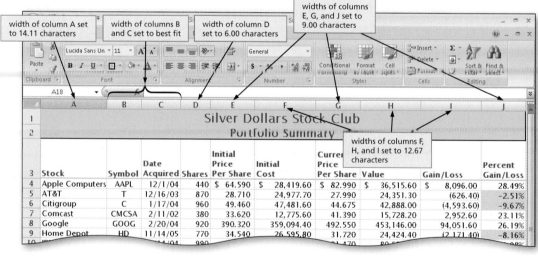

Figure 2–56

5

- Release the mouse button.

- Point to the boundary on the right side of the column D heading above row 1.

- Drag to the left until the ScreenTip indicates Width: 6.00 (61 pixels) and then release the mouse button to display the worksheet with the new column widths.

- Click cell A18 to deselect columns F, H, and I (Figure 2–57).

Figure 2–57

Other Ways

1. Right-click column heading or drag through multiple column headings and right-click, click Column Width on shortcut menu, enter desired

   column width, click OK button

2. Right-click column heading or drag through multiple column headings and right-

   click, click Format button on Ribbon, click Column Width in Format gallery, enter desired column width, click OK button

To Change the Heights of Rows

When you increase the font size of a cell entry, such as the title in cell A1, Excel automatically increases the row height to best fit so it can display the characters properly. Recall that Excel did this earlier when multiple lines were entered in a cell in row 3, and when the cell style of the worksheet title and subtitle was changed.

You also can increase or decrease the height of a row manually to improve the appearance of the worksheet. The following steps show how to improve the appearance of the worksheet by decreasing the height of row 3 to 60.00 points, and increasing the height of row 14 to 26.25 points.

1

- Point to the boundary below row heading 3.

- Drag up until the ScreenTip indicates Height: 60.00 (80 pixels). Do not release the mouse button (Figure 2–58).

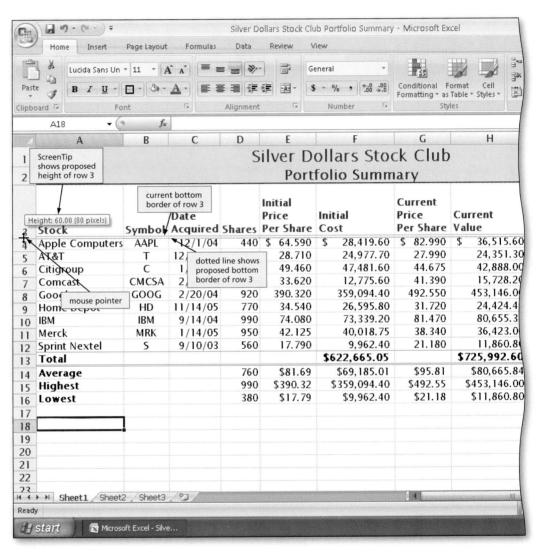

Figure 2–58

2

• Release the mouse button.

• Point to the boundary below row heading 14.

• Drag down until the ScreenTip indicates Height: 26.25 (35 pixels). Do not release the mouse button (Figure 2–59).

A18

	A	B	C	D	E	F	G
1					Silver Dollars Stock Club		
2					Portfolio Summary		
3	Stock	Symbol	Date Acquired	Shares	Initial Price Per Share	Initial Cost	Current Price Per Share
4	Apple Computers	AAPL	12/1/04	440	$ 64.590	$ 28,419.60	$ 82.990
5	AT&T	T	12/16/03	870	28.710	24,977.70	27.990
6	Citigroup	C	1/17/04	960	49.460	47,481.60	44.675
7	Comcast	CMCSA	2/11/02	380	33.620	12,775.60	41.390
8	Google	GOOG	2/20/04	920	390.320	359,094.40	492.550
9	Home Depot	HD	11/14/05	770	34.540	26,595.80	31.720
10	IBM	IBM	9/14/04	990	74.080	73,339.20	81.470
11	Merck			950		40,018.75	38.340
12	Sprint Nextel			560		9,962.40	21.180
13						$622,665.05	
14	Average			760	$81.69	$69,185.01	$95.81
15	Highest			990	$390.32	$359,094.40	$492.55
16	Lowest				$17.79	$9,962.40	$21.18
17							
18							

row 3 height is 60.00 points

ScreenTip shows proposed height of row 14

dotted line shows proposed bottom border of row 14

Height: 26.25 (35 pixels)

mouse pointer

current bottom border of row 14

Figure 2–59

3

• Release the mouse button to change the row height of row 14 to 26.25.

• Select cells A3:J3 and then click the Center button on the Ribbon to center the column headings.

• Select cell A18 (Figure 2–60).

Can I hide a row?

Yes. As with column widths, when you decrease the row height to 0, the row is hidden. To instruct Excel to display a hidden row, position the mouse pointer just below the row heading boundary where the row is hidden and then drag down. To set a row height to best fit, double-click the bottom boundary of the row heading.

Clipboard | Font | Align | Number | Formatting

formatting of worksheet complete

A18

	A	B	C	D	E	F	G
1					Silver Dollars Stock Club		
2					Portfolio Summary		
3	Stock	Symbol	Date Acquired	Shares	Initial Price Per Share	Initial Cost	Current Price Per Share
4	Apple Computers	AAPL	12/1/04	440	$ 64.590	$ 28,419.60	$ 82.990
5	AT&T	T	12/16/03	870	28.710	24,977.70	27.990
6	Citigroup	C	1/17/04	960	49.460	47,481.60	44.675
7	Comcast	CMCSA	2/11/02	380	33.620	12,775.60	41.390
8	Google	GOOG	2/20/04	920	390.320	359,094.40	492.550
9	Home Depot	HD	11/14/05	770	34.540	26,595.80	31.720
10	IBM	IBM	9/14/04	990	74.080	73,339.20	81.470
11	Merck	MRK	1/14/05			40,018.75	38.340
12	Sprint Nextel	S	9/10/03			9,962.40	21.180
13	Total					$622,665.05	
14	Average			760	$81.69	$69,185.01	$95.81
15	Highest			990	$390.32	$359,094.40	$492.55
16	Lowest			380	$17.79	$9,962.40	$21.18
17							
18							

row 14 height is 26.25 points

added white space in row 14 improves appearance of worksheet

Figure 2–60

Other Ways

1. Right-click row heading or drag through multiple row headings and right-click, click Row Height on shortcut menu, enter desired row height, click OK button

Checking Spelling

Excel has a **spell checker** you can use to check the worksheet for spelling errors. The spell checker looks for spelling errors by comparing words on the worksheet against words contained in its standard dictionary. If you often use specialized terms that are not in the standard dictionary, you may want to add them to a custom dictionary using the Spelling dialog box.

When the spell checker finds a word that is not in either dictionary, it displays the word in the Spelling dialog box. You then can correct it if it is misspelled.

BTW

Hidden Rows
You can use the keyboard to unhide a range of rows by selecting the rows immediately above and below the hidden rows and then pressing CTRL+SHIFT+((LEFT PARENTHESIS). To use the keyboard to hide a range of rows, press CTRL+9.

To Check Spelling on the Worksheet

To illustrate how Excel responds to a misspelled word, the word, Stock, in cell A3 is misspelled purposely as the word, Stcok, as shown in Figure 2–61.

1 *Start* ✓

- Click cell A3 and then type Stcok to misspell the word Stock.

- Click cell A1.

- Click the Review tab on the Ribbon.

- Click the Spelling button on the Ribbon to run the spell checker and display the misspelled word, Stcok, in the Spelling dialog box (Figure 2–61).

Q&A

What happens when the spell checker finds a misspelled word?

When the spell checker identifies that a cell contains a word not in its standard or custom dictionary, it selects that cell as the active cell and displays the Spelling dialog box (Figure 2–61) lists the word not found in the dictionary and a list of suggested corrections.

Figure 2–61

2

- With the word Stock highlighted in the Suggestions list, click the Change button to change the misspelled word, Stcok, to the correct word, Stock and then select cell A18 (Figure 2–62).

- If the Microsoft Office Excel dialog box is displayed, click the OK button.

3

- Click the Close button.

- Click the Home tab on the Ribbon.

- Click the Save button on the Quick Access toolbar to save the workbook.

 What other actions can I take in the Spelling dialog box?

If one of the words in the Suggestions list is correct, click it and then click the Change button. If none of the suggestions is correct, type the correct word in the Not in Dictionary text box and then click the Change button. To change the word throughout the worksheet, click the Change All button instead of the Change button. To skip correcting the word, click the Ignore Once button. To have Excel ignore the word for the remainder of the worksheet, click the Ignore All button.

Other Ways

1. Press F7

	A	B	C	D	E	F	G
1					**Silver Dollars Stock Club**		
2					**Portfolio Summary**		
3	**Stock**	**Symbol**	**Date Acquired**	**Shares**	**Initial Price Per Share**	**Initial Cost**	**Current Price Per Share**
4	Apple Computers	AAPL	12/1/04	440	$ 64.590	$ 28,419.60	$ 82.990
5	AT&T	T	12/16/03	870	28.710	24,977.70	27.990
6	Citigroup	C	1/17/04	960	49.460	47,481.60	44.675
7	Comcast	CMCSA	2/11/02	380	33.620	12,775.60	41.390
8	Google	GOOG	2/20/04	920	390.320	359,094.40	492.550
9	Home Depot	HD	11/14/05	770	34.540	26,595.80	31.720
10	IBM	IBM	9/14/04	990	74.080	73,339.20	81.470
11	Merck	MRK	1/14/05	950	42.125	40,018.75	38.340
12	Sprint Nextel	S	9/10/03	560	17.790	9,962.40	21.180
13	**Total**					**$622,665.05**	
14	**Average**			760	$81.69	$69,185.01	$95.81
15	**Highest**			990	$390.32	$359,094.40	$492.55
16	**Lowest**			380	$17.79	$9,962.40	$21.18
17							
18							
19							
20							
21							
22							

Stcok changed to Stock

Figure 2–62

Additional Spell Checker Considerations

Consider these additional guidelines when using the spell checker:

- To check the spelling of the text in a single cell, double-click the cell to make the formula bar active and then click the Spelling button on the Review tab on the Ribbon.

- If you select a single cell so that the formula bar is not active and then start the spell checker, Excel checks the remainder of the worksheet, including notes and embedded charts.

- If you select a cell other than cell A1 before you start the spell checker, Excel will display a dialog box when the spell checker reaches the end of the worksheet, asking if you want to continue checking at the beginning.

- If you select a range of cells before starting the spell checker, Excel checks the spelling of the words only in the selected range.

- To check the spelling of all the sheets in a workbook, click Select All Sheets on the sheet tab shortcut menu and then start the spell checker. To instruct Excel to display the sheet tab shortcut menu, right-click any sheet tab.

- To add words to the dictionary such as your last name, click the Add to Dictionary button in the Spelling dialog box (Figure 2–61 on page EX 127) when Excel identifies the word as not in the dictionary.

- Click the AutoCorrect button (Figure 2–61) to add the misspelled word and the correct version of the word to the AutoCorrect list. For example, suppose you misspell the word, do, as the word, dox. When the spell checker displays the Spelling dialog box with the correct word, do, in the Change to box, click the AutoCorrect button. Then, anytime in the future that you type the word, dox, Excel automatically will change it to the word, do.

Preparing to Print the Worksheet

Excel allows for a great deal of customization in how a worksheet appears when printed. For example, the margins on the page can be adjusted. A header or footer can be added to each printed page as well. Excel also has the capability to work on the worksheet in Page Layout View. **Page Layout View** allows you to create or modify a worksheet while viewing how it will look in printed format. The default view that you have worked in up until this point in the book is called **Normal View**.

Specify how the printed worksheet should appear.

Before printing a worksheet, you should consider how the worksheet will appear when printed. In order to fit as much information on the printed page as possible, the margins of the worksheet should be set to a reasonably small width and height. The current Portfolio Summary worksheet will print on one page. If, however, the club added more data to the worksheet, then it may extend to multiple pages. It is, therefore, a good idea to add a page header to the worksheet that prints in the top margin of each page.

In Chapter 1, the worksheet was printed in **portrait orientation**, which means the printout is printed across the width of the page. **Landscape orientation** means the printout is printed across the length of the page. Landscape orientation is a good choice for the Silver Dollars Stock Club Portfolio Summary because the printed worksheet's width is greater than its length.

To Change the Worksheet's Margins, Header, and Orientation in Page Layout View

The following steps change to Page Layout View, narrow the margins of the worksheet, change the header of the worksheet, and set the orientation of the worksheet to landscape.

1

- Click the Page Layout View button on the status bar to view the worksheet in Page Layout View (Figure 2–63).

Q&A

What are some key features of Page Layout View?

Page Layout View shows the worksheet divided into pages. A blue background separates each page. The white areas surrounding each page indicate the print margins. The top of each page includes a Header area, and the bottom of each page includes a Footer area. Page Layout View also includes a ruler at the top of the page that assists you in placing objects on the page, such as charts and pictures.

Figure 2–63

2

- Click the Page Layout tab on the Ribbon.

- Click the Margins button on the Ribbon to display the Margins gallery (Figure 2–64).

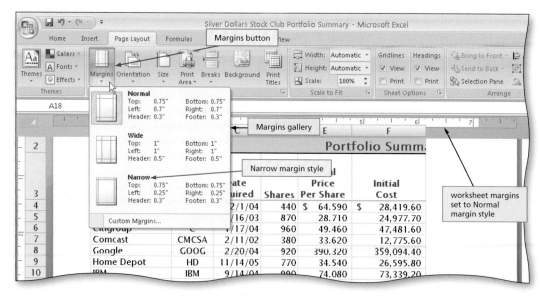

Figure 2–64

❸

- Click Narrow in the Margins gallery to change the worksheet margins to the Narrow margin style.

- Drag the scroll bar on the right side of the worksheet to the top so that row 1 of the worksheet is displayed.

- Click above the worksheet title in cell A1 in the Header area.

- Type `Treasurer: Juan Castillo` and then press the ENTER key. Type `castillo_ juan37@hotmail. com` to complete the worksheet header (Figure 2–65).

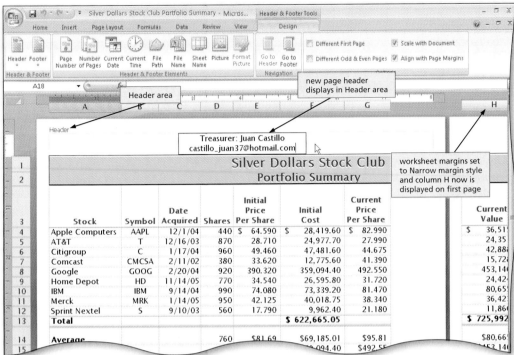

Figure 2–65

❹

- Select cell B16 to deselect the header. Click the Orientation button on the Ribbon to display the Orientation gallery.

- Point to Landscape but do not click the mouse button (Figure 2–66).

Figure 2–66

- Click Landscape in the Orientation gallery to change the worksheet's orientation to landscape (Figure 2–67).

Q&A

Do I need to change the orientation every time I want to print the worksheet?

No. Once you change the orientation and save the workbook, Excel will save the orientation setting for that workbook until you change it. When you open a new workbook, Excel sets the orientation to portrait.

Figure 2–67

Other Ways

1. Click Page Layout tab on Ribbon, click Page Setup Dialog Box Launcher button, click appropriate tab, change desired options, click OK button

---

Previewing and Printing the Worksheet

In Chapter 1, the worksheet was printed without first previewing it on the screen. By **previewing the worksheet**, however, you see exactly how it will look without generating a printout. Previewing a worksheet using the Print Preview command can save time, paper, and the frustration of waiting for a printout only to discover it is not what you want.

To Preview and Print a Worksheet

The following steps preview and then print the worksheet.

- Click the Office Button and then point to Print on the Office Button menu to display the Print submenu (Figure 2–68).

Figure 2–68

2

- Click Print Preview on the Print submenu to display a preview of the worksheet in landscape orientation (Figure 2–69).

What is the purpose of the buttons in the Print Preview area?

The Print button displays the Print dialog box and allows you to print the worksheet. The Page Setup button displays the Page Setup dialog box. The Zoom button allows you to zoom in and out of the page displayed in the Preview window.

You also can click the previewed page in the Preview window when the mouse pointer shape is a magnifying glass to carry out the function of the Zoom button.

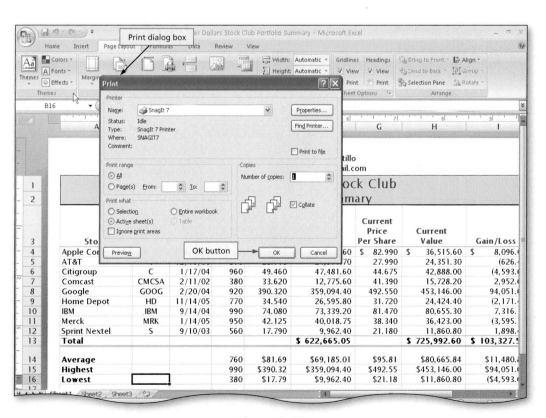

Figure 2–69

3

- Click the Print button to display the Print dialog box (Figure 2–70).

How can I use the Print dialog box?

When you click the Print command on the Print submenu of the Office Button menu or a Print button in a dialog box or Preview window, Excel displays the Print dialog box shown in Figure 2–70. Excel does not display the Print dialog box when you use the Print button on the Quick Access toolbar, as was the case in Chapter 1. The Print dialog box allows you to select a printer, instruct Excel what to print, and indicate how many copies of the printout you want.

Figure 2–70

- Click the OK
  button to print
  the worksheet
  (Figure 2–71).

worksheet printed in
landscape orientation

Treasurer: Juan Castillo
castillo_juan37@hotmail.com

Silver Dollars Stock Club
Portfolio Summary

Stock	Symbol	Date Acquired	Shares	Initial Price Per Share	Initial Cost	Current Price Per Share	Current Value	Gain/Loss
Apple Computers	AAPL	12/1/04	440	$ 64.590	$ 28,419.60	$ 82.990	$ 36,515.60	$ 8,096.00
AT&T	T	12/16/03	870	28.710	24,977.70	27.990	24,351.30	(626.40)
Citigroup	C	1/17/04	960	49.460	47,481.60	44.675	42,888.00	(4,593.60)
Comcast	CMCSA	2/11/02	380	33.620	12,775.60	41.390	15,728.20	2,952.60
Google	GOOG	2/20/04	920	390.320	359,094.40	492.550	453,146.00	94,051.60
Home Depot	HD	11/14/05	770	34.540	26,595.80	31.720	24,424.40	(2,171.40)
IBM	IBM	9/14/04	990	74.080	73,339.20	81.470	80,655.30	7,316.10
Merck	MRK	1/14/05	950	42.125	40,018.75	38.340	36,423.00	(3,595.75)
Sprint Nextel	S	9/10/03	560	17.790	9,962.40	21.180	11,860.80	1,898.40
Total					$ 622,665.05		$ 725,992.60	$ 103,327.55
Average			760	$81.69	$69,185.01	$95.81	$80,665.84	$11,480.84
Highest			990	$390.32	$359,094.40	$492.55	$453,146.00	$94,051.60
Lowest			380	$17.79	$9,962.40	$21.18	$11,860.80	($4,593.60)

Figure 2–71

Other Ways

1. Click Page Layout tab
   on Ribbon, click Page
   Setup Dialog Box
   Launcher button, click
   appropriate tab, change
   desired options, click
   OK button

To Print a Section of the Worksheet

You might not always want to print the entire worksheet. You can print portions of the worksheet by selecting the range of cells to print and then clicking the Selection option button in the Print what area in the Print dialog box. The following steps print the range A3:F16.

- Select the range A3:F16.

- Click the Office Button and then click Print on the Office Button menu to display the Print dialog box.

- Click Selection in the Print what area to instruct Excel to print only the selected range (Figure 2–72).

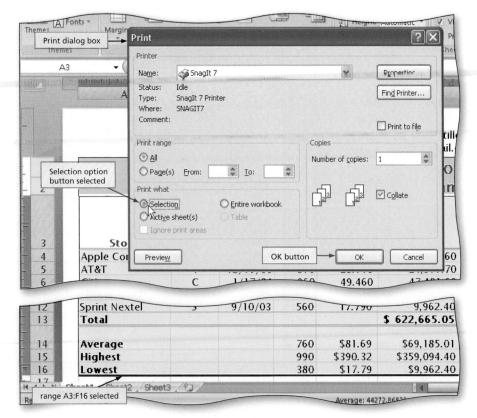

Figure 2–72

2

- Click the OK button to print the selected range of the worksheet on the printer (Figure 2–73).

- Click the Normal View button on the status bar.

- Click cell A18 to deselect the range A3:F13.

Q&A

What are the options in the Print what area?

The Print what area of the Print dialog box includes three option buttons (Figure 2–72). As shown in the previous steps, the Selection option button instructs Excel to print the selected range. The Active sheet(s) option button instructs Excel to print the active worksheet (the worksheet currently on the screen) or the selected worksheets. Finally, the Entire workbook option button instructs Excel to print all of the worksheets in the workbook.

header prints → Treasurer: Juan Castillo
castillo_juan37@hotmail.com ← selected range prints

Stock	Symbol	Date Acquired	Shares	Initial Price Per Share	Initial Cost
Apple Computers	AAPL	12/1/04	440	$ 64.590	$ 28,419.60
AT&T	T	12/16/03	870	28.710	24,977.70
Citigroup	C	1/17/04	960	49.460	47,481.60
Comcast	CMCSA	2/11/02	380	33.620	12,775.60
Google	GOOG	2/20/04	920	390.320	359,094.40
Home Depot	HD	11/14/05	770	34.540	26,595.80
IBM	IBM	9/14/04	990	74.080	73,339.20
Merck	MRK	1/14/05	950	42.125	40,018.75
Sprint Nextel	S	9/10/03	560	17.790	9,962.40
Total					$ 622,665.05
Average			760	$81.69	$69,185.01
Highest			990	$390.32	$359,094.40
Lowest			380	$17.79	$9,962.40

Figure 2–73

Other Ways

1. Select range, click Page Layout tab on Ribbon, click Print Area button, click Quick Print button on Quick Access toolbar, click Print Area button, click Clear Print Area button

Displaying and Printing the Formulas Version of the Worksheet

Thus far, you have been working with the **values version** of the worksheet, which shows the results of the formulas you have entered, rather than the actual formulas. Excel also can display and print the **formulas version** of the worksheet, which shows the actual formulas you have entered, rather than the resulting values. You can toggle between the values version and formulas version by holding down the CTRL key while pressing the ACCENT MARK (`) key, which is located to the left of the number 1 key on the keyboard.

The formulas version is useful for debugging a worksheet. **Debugging** is the process of finding and correcting errors in the worksheet. Viewing and printing the formulas version instead of the values version makes it easier to see any mistakes in the formulas.

When you change from the values version to the formulas version, Excel increases the width of the columns so the formulas and text do not overflow into adjacent cells on the right. The formulas version of the worksheet thus usually is significantly wider than the values version. To fit the wide printout on one page, you can use landscape orientation, which has already been selected for the workbook, and the Fit to option in the Page sheet in the Page Setup dialog box.

BTW

Values versus Formulas
When completing class assignments, do not enter numbers in cells that require formulas. Most instructors require their students to hand in both the values version and formulas version of the worksheet. The formulas version verifies that you entered formulas, rather than numbers, in formula-based cells.

Chapter 2

the Formulas in the Worksheet and Fit the Printout on One Page

wing steps change the view of the worksheet from the values version to the formulas version of the
hen print the formulas version on one page.

- Press CTRL+ACCENT MARK (`).

- When Excel displays the formulas version of the worksheet, click the right horizontal scroll arrow until column J appears to display the worksheet with formulas (Figure 2–74).

	G	H	I	J	K
1	lb				
2					
3	Current Price Per Share	Current Value	Gain/Loss	Percent Gain/Loss	
4	82.99	=D4*G4	=H4–F4	=I4/F4	
5	27.99	=D5*G5	=H5–F5	=I5/F5	
6	44.675	=D6*G6	=H6–F6	=I6/F6	
7	41.39	=D7*G7	=H7–F7	=I7/F7	
8	492.55	=D8*G8	=H8–F8	=I8/F8	
9	31.72	=D9*G9	=H9–F9	=I9/F9	
10	81.47	=D10*G10	=H10–F10	=I10/F10	
11	38.34	=D11*G11	=H11–F11	=I11/F11	
12	21.18	=D12*G12	=H12–F12	=I12/F12	
13		=SUM(H4:H12)	=SUM(I4:I12)	=I13/F13	
14	=AVERAGE(G4:G12)	=AVERAGE(H4:H12)	=AVERAGE(I4:I12)		
15	=MAX(G4:G12)	=MAX(H4:H12)	=MAX(I4:I12)	=MAX(J4:J12)	
16	=MIN(G4:G12)	=MIN(H4:H12)	=MIN(I4:I12)	=MIN(J4:J12)	
17					

numbers displayed using General format

formulas displayed as entered

Figure 2–74

2

- If necessary, click the Page Layout tab on the Ribbon and then click the Page Setup Dialog Box Launcher to display the Page Setup dialog box.

- If necessary, click Landscape to select it and then click Fit to in the Scaling area.

3

- Click the Print button in the Page Setup dialog box to print the formulas in the worksheet on one page in landscape orientation (Figure 2–75).

- When Excel displays the Print dialog box, click the OK button.

Treasurer: Juan Castillo
castillo_juan37@hotmail.com

Silver Dollars Stock Club
Portfolio Summary

Stock	Symbol	Date Acquired	Shares	Initial Price Per Share	Initial Cost	Current Price Per Share	Current Value	Gain/Loss	Percent Gain/Loss
Apple Computers	AAPL	38122	440	64.59	=D4*E4	82.99	=D4*G4	=H4–F4	=I4/F4
AT&T	T	37971	870	28.71	=D5*E5	27.99	=D5*G5	=H5–F5	=I5/F5
Citigroup	C	38092	940	41.48	=D6*E6	44.675	=D6*G6	=H6–F6	=I6/F6
Comcast	CMCSA	37298	380	31.62	=D7*E7	41.39	=D7*G7	=H7–F7	=I7/F7
Google	GOOG	38037	920	390.32	=D8*E8	492.55	=D8*G8	=H8–F8	=I8/F8
Home Depot	HD	38670	770	34.54	=D9*E9	31.72	=D9*G9	=H9–F9	=I9/F9
IBM	IBM	38244	990	74.08	=D10*E10	81.47	=D10*G10	=H10–F10	=I10/F10
Merck	MRK	38366	950	42.125	=D11*E11	38.34	=D11*G11	=H11–F11	=I11/F11
Sprint Nextel	S	37874	560	17.79	=D12*E12	21.18	=D12*G12	=H12–F12	=I12/F12
Total					=SUM(F4:F12)		=SUM(H4:H12)	=SUM(I4:I12)	=I13/F13
Average		=AVERAGE(D4:D12)	=AVERAGE(E4:E12)	=AVERAGE(F4:F12)		=AVERAGE(G4:G12)	=AVERAGE(H4:H12)	=AVERAGE(I4:I12)	
Highest		=MAX(D4:D12)	=MAX(E4:E12)	=MAX(F4:F12)		=MAX(G4:G12)	=MAX(H4:H12)	=MAX(I4:I12)	=MAX(J4:J12)
Lowest		=MIN(D4:D12)	=MIN(E4:E12)	=MIN(F4:F12)		=MIN(G4:G12)	=MIN(H4:H12)	=MIN(I4:I12)	=MIN(J4:J12)

formulas instead of values printed

font size automatically reduced so worksheet fits on one page

Figure 2–75

4

- After viewing and printing the formulas version, press CTRL+ACCENT MARK (`) to instruct Excel to display the values version.

- Click the left horizontal scroll arrow until column A appears.

Other Ways

1. Click Show Formulas button on Formulas tab on Ribbon

To Change the Print Scaling Option Back to 100%

Depending on your printer, you may have to change the Print Scaling option back to 100% after using the Fit to option. The following steps reset the Print Scaling option so future worksheets print at 100%, instead of being resized to print on one page.

1 If necessary, click the Page Layout tab on the Ribbon and then click the Page Setup Dialog Box Launcher to display the Page Setup dialog box.

2 Click Adjust to in the Scaling area.

3 If necessary, type 100 in the Adjust to box.

4 Click the OK button to set the print scaling to normal.

5 Click the Home tab on the Ribbon.

Q&A What is the purpose of the Adjust to box in the Page Setup dialog box?

The Adjust to box allows you to specify the percentage of reduction or enlargement in the printout of a worksheet. The default percentage is 100%. When you click the Fit to option, this percentage automatically changes to the percentage required to fit the printout on one page.

Importing External Data from a Web Source Using a Web Query

One of the major features of Excel is its capability of importing external data from Web sites. To import external data from a Web site, you must have access to the Internet. You then can import data stored on a Web site using a **Web query**. When you run a Web query, Excel imports the external data in the form of a worksheet. As described in Table 2–6, three Web queries are available when you first install Excel. All three Web queries relate to investment and stock market activities.

BTW

Web Queries
Most Excel specialists that build Web queries use the worksheet returned from the Web query as an engine to supply data to another worksheet in the workbook. With 3-D cell references, you can create a worksheet similar to the Silver Dollars Stock Club worksheet to feed the Web query stock symbols and get refreshed stock prices in return.

Table 2–6 Excel Web Queries

Query	External Data Returned
MSN MoneyCentral Investor Currency Rates	Currency rates
MSN MoneyCentral Investor Major Indices	Major indices
MSN MoneyCentral Investor Stock Quotes	Up to 20 stocks of your choice

Plan Ahead

Gather information regarding the needed Web query.
As shown in Table 2–6, the MSN Money Central Investor Stock Quotes feature that is included with Excel allows you to retrieve information on up to 20 stocks of your choice. The Web query requires that you supply the stock symbols. The stock symbols are located in column B of the Portfolio Summary worksheet.

To Import Data from a Web Source Using a Web Query

Although you can have a Web query return data to a blank workbook, the following steps have the data for the nine stock symbols in column B of the Portfolio Summary worksheet returned to a blank worksheet in the Silver Dollars Stock Club Portfolio Summary workbook. The data returned by the stock-related Web queries is real time in the sense that it is no more than 20 minutes old during the business day.

- With the Silver Dollars Stock Club Portfolio Summary workbook open, click the Sheet2 tab at the bottom of the window.

- With cell A1 active, click the Data tab on the Ribbon, and then click the Existing Connections button to display the Existing Connections dialog box (Figure 2–76).

Figure 2–76

2

- Double-click MSN MoneyCentral Investor Stock Quotes to display the Import Data dialog box (Figure 2-77).

Figure 2–77

3

- Click the OK button.

- When Excel displays the Enter Parameter Value dialog box, type the nine stock symbols `aapl t c cmcsa goog hd ibm mrk s` in the text box.

- Click the 'Use this value/reference for future refreshes' check box to select it (Figure 2–78).

Q&A

What is the purpose of clicking the check box?

Once Excel displays the worksheet, you can refresh the data as often as you want. To refresh the data for all the stocks, click the Refresh All button on the Data tab on the Ribbon. Because the 'Use this value/reference for future refreshes' check box was selected, Excel will continue to use the same stock symbols each time it refreshes.

Figure 2–78

4

- Click the OK button to retrieve the stock quotes and display a new worksheet with the desired data (Figure 2–79).

Q&A

What composes the new worksheet?

As shown in Figure 2–79, Excel displays the data returned from the Web query in an organized, formatted worksheet, which has a worksheet title, column titles, and a row of data for each stock symbol entered. Other than the first column, which contains the stock name and stock symbol, you have no control over the remaining columns of data returned. The latest price of each stock appears in column D.

Figure 2–79

Other Ways

1. Press ALT+A, X, select data source

Changing the Worksheet Names

The sheet tabs at the bottom of the window allow you to view any worksheet in the workbook. You click the sheet tab of the worksheet you want to view in the Excel window. By default, Excel presets the names of the worksheets to Sheet1, Sheet2, and so on. The worksheet names become increasingly important as you move towards more sophisticated workbooks, especially workbooks in which you reference cells between worksheets.

Plan Ahead

Choose names for the worksheets.
Use simple, meaningful names for each worksheet. Name the first worksheet that includes the portfolio summary Portfolio Summary. The second worksheet that includes the stock quotes should be named Real-Time Stock Quotes to reflect its contents.

To Change the Worksheet Names

The following steps show how to rename worksheets by double-clicking the sheet tabs.

1

- Double-click the sheet tab labeled Sheet2 in the lower-left corner of the window.

- Type `Real-Time Stock Quotes` as the worksheet name and then press the ENTER key to display the new worksheet name on the sheet tab (Figure 2–80).

Q&A What is the maximum length for a worksheet tab?

Worksheet names can be up to 31 characters (including spaces) in length. Longer worksheet names, however, mean that fewer sheet tabs will show. To view more sheet tabs, you can drag the tab split box (Figure 2–81) to the right. This will reduce the size of the scroll bar at the bottom of the screen. Double-click the tab split box to reset it to its normal position.

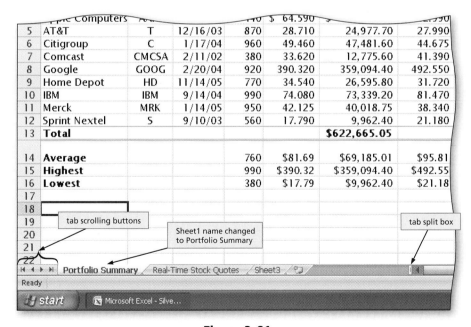

Figure 2–80

2

- Double-click the sheet tab labeled Sheet1 in the lower-left corner of the window.

- Type `Portfolio Summary` as the worksheet name and then press the ENTER key to change the name of the worksheet from Sheet 1 to Portfolio Summary (Figure 2–81).

Q&A How can I quickly move between worksheet tabs?

You can use the tab scrolling buttons to the left of the sheet tabs (Figure 2–81) to move between worksheets. The leftmost and rightmost scroll buttons move to the first or last worksheet in the workbook. The two middle scroll buttons move one worksheet to the left or right.

Figure 2–81

3

- Click the Home tab on the Ribbon.

Obtaining an E-Mail Account
Several Web sites that allow you to sign up for free e-mail are available. Some choices are MSN Hotmail, Yahoo! Mail, and Google Gmail.

E-Mailing a Workbook from within Excel

The most popular service on the Internet is electronic mail, or **e-mail**, which is the electronic transmission of messages and files to and from other computers using the Internet. Using e-mail, you can converse with friends across the room or on another continent. One of the features of e-mail is the capability to attach Office files, such as Word documents or Excel workbooks, to an e-mail message and send it to a coworker. In the past, if you wanted to e-mail a workbook, you saved the workbook, closed the file, started your e-mail program, and then attached the workbook to the e-mail message before sending it. With Excel, you have the capability of e-mailing a worksheet or workbook directly from within Excel. For these steps to work properly, you must have an e-mail address and one of the following as your e-mail program: Microsoft Outlook, Microsoft Outlook Express, Microsoft Exchange Client, or another 32-bit e-mail program compatible with Messaging Application Programming Interface.

To E-Mail a Workbook from within Excel

The following steps show how to e-mail the Silver Dollars Stock Club Portfolio Summary workbook from within Excel to Juan Castillo at the e-mail address castillo_juan37@hotmail.com.

1

• With the Silver Dollars Stock Club Portfolio Summary workbook open, click the Office Button and then click Send to display the Send submenu (Figure 2–82).

Figure 2–82

- Click E-mail on the Send submenu.

- When the e-mail Message window appears, type castillo_ juan37@hotmail. com in the To text box.

- Type the message shown in the message area in Figure 2–83.

Figure 2–83

- Click the Send button to send the e-mail with the attached workbook to castillo_juan37@ hotmail.com.

Q&A

How can the recipient use the attached workbook?

Because the workbook was sent as an attachment, Juan Castillo can double-click the attachment in the e-mail to open it in Excel, or he can save it on disk and then open it later.

To Save the Workbook and Quit Excel

With the workbook complete and e-mailed, the following steps save the workbook and quit Excel.

1 Click the Save button on the Quick Access toolbar.

2 Click the Close button on the upper-right corner of the title bar.

BTW

Quick Reference
For a table that lists how to complete the tasks covered in this book using the mouse, Ribbon, shortcut menu, and keyboard, see the Quick Reference Summary at the back of this book, or visit the Excel 2007 Quick Reference Web page (scsite.com/ex2007/qr).

Chapter Summary

In creating the Silver Dollars Stock Club Portfolio Summary workbook, you learned how to enter formulas, calculate an average, find the highest and lowest numbers in a range, verify formulas using Range Finder, draw borders, align text, format numbers, change column widths and row heights, and add conditional formatting to a range of numbers. In addition, you learned to spell check a worksheet, preview a worksheet, print a section of a worksheet, display and print the formulas version of the worksheet using the Fit to option, complete a Web query, rename sheet tabs, and send an e-mail directly from within Excel with the opened workbook as an attachment. The items listed below include all the new Excel skills you have learned in this chapter.

1. Enter a Formula Using the Keyboard (EX 91)
2. Enter Formulas Using Point Mode (EX 93)
3. Copy Formulas Using the Fill Handle (EX 95)
4. Determine the Average of a Range of Numbers Using the Keyboard and Mouse (EX 99)
5. Determine the Highest Number in a Range of Numbers Using the Insert Function Box (EX 101)
6. Determine the Lowest Number in a Range of Numbers Using the Sum Menu (EX 102)
7. Copy a Range of Cells across Columns to an Adjacent Range Using the Fill Handle (EX 104)
8. Verify a Formula Using Range Finder (EX 106)
9. Change the Workbook Theme (EX 109)
10. Change the Background Color and Apply a Box Border to the Worksheet Title and Subtitle (EX 110)
11. Center Data in Cells and Format Dates (EX 113)
12. Apply an Accounting Number Format and Comma Style Format Using the Ribbon (EX 115)
13. Apply a Currency Style Format with a Floating Dollar Sign Using the Format Cells Dialog Box (EX 116)
14. Apply a Percent Style Format and Use the Increase Decimal Button (EX 118)
15. Apply Conditional Formatting (EX 119)
16. Change the Widths of Columns (EX 122)
17. Change the Heights of Rows (EX 125)
18. Check Spelling on the Worksheet (EX 127)
19. Change the Worksheet's Margins, Header, and Orientation in Page Layout View (EX 130)
20. Preview and Print a Worksheet (EX 132)
21. Print a Section of the Worksheet (EX 134)
22. Display the Formulas in the Worksheet and Fit the Printout on One Page (EX 136)
23. Import Data from a Web Source Using a Web Query (EX 138)
24. Change the Worksheet Names (EX 141)
25. E-Mail a Workbook from within Excel (EX 142)

 If you have a SAM user profile, you may have access to hands-on instruction, practice, and assessment. Log in to your SAM account (http://sam2007.course.com) to launch any assigned training activities or exams that relate to the skills covered in this chapter.

Learn It Online

Learn It Online is a series of online student exercises that test your knowledge of chapter content and key terms.

Instructions: To complete the Learn It Online exercises, start your browser, click the Address bar, and then enter the Web address scsite.com/ex2007/learn. When the Excel 2007 Learn It Online page is displayed, click the link for the exercise you want to complete and then read the instructions.

Chapter Reinforcement TF, MC, and SA
A series of true/false, multiple choice, and short answer questions that test your knowledge of the chapter content.

Flash Cards
An interactive learning environment where you identify chapter key terms associated with displayed definitions.

Practice Test
A series of multiple choice questions that test your knowledge of chapter content and key terms.

Who Wants To Be a Computer Genius?
An interactive game that challenges your knowledge of chapter content in the style of a television quiz show.

Wheel of Terms
An interactive game that challenges your knowledge of chapter key terms in the style of the television show *Wheel of Fortune.*

Crossword Puzzle Challenge
A crossword puzzle that challenges your knowledge of key terms presented in the chapter.

Apply Your knowledge

Reinforce the skills and apply the concepts you learned in this chapter.

Profit Analysis Worksheet

Instructions Part 1: Start Excel. Open the workbook Apply 2-1 Car-B-Clean Profit Analysis. See the inside back cover of this book for instructions for downloading the Data Files for Students or see your instructor for information on accessing the files required in this book. The purpose of this exercise is to open a partially completed workbook, enter formulas and functions, copy the formulas and functions, and then format the worksheet titles and numbers. As shown in Figure 2–84, the completed worksheet analyzes profits by product.

	A	B	C	D	E	F	G	H
1			Car-B-Clean Accessories					
2			Profit Analysis					
3	Item	Unit Cost	Unit Profit	Units Sold	Total Sales	Total Profit	% Total Profit	
4	Brush	$ 5.84	$ 3.15	36,751	$ 330,391.49	$ 115,765.65	35.039%	
5	Bucket	7.14	2.75	57,758	571,226.62	158,834.50	27.806%	
6	Drying Cloth	3.52	1.17	42,555	199,582.95	49,789.35	24.947%	
7	Duster	2.55	1.04	78,816	282,949.44	81,968.64	28.969%	
8	Polish	7.19	7.80	57,758	865,792.42	450,512.40	52.035%	
9	Soap	8.52	4.09	50,646	638,646.06	207,142.14	32.435%	
10	Sponge	2.05	1.84	23,154	90,069.06	42,603.36	47.301%	
11	Wax	10.15	7.44	53,099	934,011.41	395,056.56	42.297%	
12	Vacuum	43.91	33.09	17,780	1,369,060.00	588,340.20	42.974%	
13	Totals			418,317	$5,281,729.45	$2,090,012.80	39.571%	
14	Lowest	$2.05	$1.04	17,780	$90,069.06	$42,603.36	24.947%	
15	Highest	$43.91	$33.09	78,816	$1,369,060.00	$588,340.20	52.035%	
16	Average	$10.10	$6.93	46,480	$586,858.83	$232,223.64		
17								
18								
19								
20								
21								

Figure 2–84

Perform the following tasks.

1. Use the following formulas in cells E4, F4, and G4:

   Total Sales (cell E4) = Units Sold * (Unit Cost + Unit Profit) or =D4 * (B4 + C4)

   Total Profit (cell F4) = Units Sold * Unit Profit or = D4 * C4

   % Total Profit (cell G4) = Total Profit / Total Sales or = F4 / E4

   Use the fill handle to copy the three formulas in the range E4:G4 to the range E5:G12.

2. Determine totals for the units sold, total sales, and total profit in row 13. Copy cell G12 to G13 to assign the formula in cell G12 to G13 in the total line.

Continued >

Apply Your Knowledge *continued*

3. In the range B14:B16, determine the lowest value, highest value, and average value, respectively, for the values in the range B4:B12. Use the fill handle to copy the three functions to the range C14:G16. Delete the average from cell G16, because an average of percentages of this type is mathematically invalid.

4. Format the worksheet as follows:

   a. change the workbook theme to Concourse by using the Themes button on the Page Layout tab on the Ribbon

   b. cell A1 — change to font size 24 with a green (column 6 of standard colors) background and white font color by using the buttons in the Font group on the Home tab on the Ribbon

   c. cell A2 — change to a green (column 6 of standard colors) background and white font color

   d. cells B4:C4, E4:F4, and E13:F13 — Accounting style format with two decimal places and fixed dollar signs (use the Accounting Style button on the Home tab on the Ribbon)

   e. cells B5:C12 and E5:F12 — Comma style format with two decimal places (use the Comma Style button on the Home tab on the Ribbon)

   f. cells D4:D16 — Comma style format with no decimal places

   g. cells G4:G15 — Percent style format with three decimal places

   h. cells B14:C16 and E14:F16 — Currency style format with floating dollar signs (use the Format Cells: Number Dialog Box Launcher on the Home tab on the Ribbon)

5. Switch to Page Layout view and enter your name, course, laboratory assignment number (Apply 2-1), date, and any other information requested by your instructor in the Header area. Preview and print the worksheet in landscape orientation. Change the document properties, as specified by your instructor. Save the workbook using the file name, Apply 2-1 Car-B-Clean Profit Analysis Complete in the format specified by your instructor.

6. Use Range Finder to verify the formula in cell F4.

7. Print the range A3:E16. Press CTRL+ACCENT MARK (`) to change the display from the values version of the worksheet to the formulas version. Print the formulas version in landscape orientation on one page (Figure 2–85) by using the Fit to option in the Page sheet in the Page Setup dialog box. Press CTRL+ACCENT MARK (`) to change the display of the worksheet back to the values version. Do not save the workbook. If requested, submit the three printouts to your instructor.

Instructions Part 2:

1. In column C, use the keyboard to add manually $1.00 to the profit of each product with a unit profit less than $7.00 and $3.00 to the profits of all other products. You should end up with $2,765,603.80 in cell F13.

2. Print the worksheet. Do not save the workbook. If requested, submit the revised workbook in the format specified by your instructor.

Jeff Quasney
Apply Your Knowledge 2–1

Car-B-Clean Accessories
Profit Analysis

Item	Unit Cost	Unit Profit	Units Sold	Total Sales	Total Profit	% Total Profit
Brush	5.84	3.15	36751	=D4*(B4+C4)	=D4*C4	=F4/E4
Bucket	7.14	2.75	57758	=D5*(B5+C5)	=D5*C5	=F5/E5
Drying Cloth	3.52	1.17	42555	=D6*(B6+C6)	=D6*C6	=F6/E6
Duster	2.55	1.04	78816	=D7*(B7+C7)	=D7*C7	=F7/E7
Polish	7.19	7.8	57758	=D8*(B8+C8)	=D8*C8	=F8/E8
Soap	8.52	4.09	50646	=D9*(B9+C9)	=D9*C9	=F9/E9
Sponge	2.05	1.84	23154	=D10*(B10+C10)	=D10*C10	=F10/E10
Wax	10.15	7.44	53099	=D11*(B11+C11)	=D11*C11	=F11/E11
Vacuum	43.91	33.09	17780	=D12*(B12+C12)	=D12*C12	=F12/E12
Totals			=SUM(D4:D12)	=SUM(E4:E12)	=SUM(F4:F12)	=F13/E13
Lowest	=MIN(B4:B12)	=MIN(C4:C12)	=MIN(D4:D12)	=MIN(E4:E12)	=MIN(F4:F12)	=MIN(G4:G12)
Highest	=MAX(B4:B12)	=MAX(C4:C12)	=MAX(D4:D12)	=MAX(E4:E12)	=MAX(F4:F12)	=MAX(G4:G12)
Average	=AVERAGE(B4:B12)	=AVERAGE(C4:C12)	=AVERAGE(D4:D12)	=AVERAGE(E4:E12)	=AVERAGE(F4:F12)	=AVERAGE(F4:F12)

Figure 2–85

Extend Your Knowledge

Extend the skills you learned in this chapter and experiment with new skills. You may need to use Help to complete the assignment.

Applying Conditional Formatting to Cells

Instructions: Start Excel. Open the workbook Extend 2-1 Biology 201 Midterm Scores. See the inside back cover of this book for instructions for downloading the Data Files for Students, or see your instructor for information on accessing the files required in this book. Perform the following tasks to apply new conditional formatting to the worksheet.

1. Select the range C4:C18. Click the Conditional Formatting button on the Home tab on the Ribbon and then select New Rule in the Conditional Formatting gallery. Select 'Format only top or bottom ranked values' in the Select a Rule Type area (Figure 2–86). Enter a value between 20 and 35 of your choosing in the text box in the Edit the Rule Description area and click the '% of selected range' check box to select it. Click the Format button and choose a format to assign to this conditional format. Click the OK button in each dialog box to close the dialog boxes and view the worksheet.

2. With range C4:C18 selected, apply a conditional format to the range that highlights scores that are below average.

3. With range D4:D18 selected, apply a conditional format to the range that highlights any grade that is a D or an F.

4. With range B4:B18 selected, apply a conditional format to the range that uses a red color to highlight any duplicate student names.

5. Change the document properties, as specified by your instructor. Change the worksheet header with your name, course number, and other information requested by your instructor. Save the workbook using the file name, Extend 2-1 Biology 201 Midterm Scores Complete, and submit the revised workbook as specified by your instructor.

Figure 2–86

Make It Right

Analyze a workbook and correct all errors and/or improve the design.

Correcting Functions and Formulas in a Worksheet

Instructions: Start Excel. Open the workbook Make It Right 2-1 El Centro Diner Payroll Report. See the inside back cover of this book for instructions for downloading the Data Files for Students, or see your instructor for information on accessing the files required for this book. Correct the following formatting, function, and formula problems (Figure 2–87) in the worksheet.

	A	B	C	D	E	F	G	H	I
1				**El Centro Diner**					
2				**Payrol Report**					
3	Employee	Dependents	Rate per Hou	Hours Worked	Gross Pay	Federal Tax	State Tax	Net Pay	% Taxes
4	Vincent Flores	1	$9.90	20.00	$198.00	$34.97	$7.92	$162.03	21.660%
5	Wonda Jefferson	2	11.20	40.00	448.00	80.33	17.92	365.67	21.931%
6	Anthony Sanchez	2	15.90	21.25	337.88	58.31	13.52	277.57	21.257%
7	Alexa Martin	3	11.30	23.50	265.55	39.21	10.62	223.34	18.765%
8	Maria Reyes	1	10.30	21.25	218.88	39.14	8.76	178.73	21.883%
9	Lori Romanoff	2	10.75	40.00	430.00	76.73	17.20	351.27	21.845%
10	Carmen Alvarez	1	12.60	21.50	270.90	49.55	10.84	220.35	22.289%
11	Peter Lane	4	14.50	37.50	543.75	90.21	21.75	449.54	20.591%
12	Claudi Moreno	1	16.00	33.00	528.00	100.97	21.12	426.03	23.122%
13	Wayne Vargas	3	8.00	29.25	234.00	32.90	9.36	198.10	18.059%
14	**Totals**				287.25	$3,474.95	$ 602.31	$ 139.00	$2,852.64	21.333%
15	Average	1.8888889	$12.49	28.67	$360.11	$60.23	$13.90	$294.95	21.140%
16	Highest	4	$16.00	40.00	$543.75	$100.97	$21.75	$449.54	23.122%
17	Lowest	1	$8.00	20.00	$198.00	$32.90	$7.92	$162.03	18.059%

Figure 2–87

1. Adjust the width of column B to 11.25 pixels so that the word in the column header does not wrap.
2. Spell check the worksheet and correct any spelling mistakes that are found, but ignore any spelling mistakes found with the worksheet title and the employee names.
3. The averages in several columns do not include the employee in row 13. Adjust the functions in these cells so that all employees are included in the calculation.
4. The net pay calculation should be:

    Net Pay = Gross Pay – (Federal Taxes + State Taxes)

    Adjust the formulas in the range H4:H13 so that the correct formula is used.
5. The value for the highest value in column C was entered as a number rather than as a function. Replace the value with the appropriate function.
6. The currency values in row 4 should be formatted with the Accounting Number Format button on the Home tab on the Ribbon. They are currently formatted with the Currency format.
7. Delete the function in the cell containing the average of % Taxes because it is mathematically invalid.

8. Change the document properties, as specified by your instructor. Change the worksheet header with your name, course number, and other information requested by your instructor. Save the workbook using the file name, Make It Right 2-1 El Centro Diner Payroll Report Corrected. Submit the revised workbook as specified by your instructor.

In the Lab

Create a workbook using the guidelines, concepts, and skills presented in this chapter. Labs are listed in order of increasing difficulty.

Lab 1: Sales Analysis Worksheet

Problem: You have been asked to build a sales analysis worksheet for Facade Importers that determines the sales quota and percentage of quota met for the sales representatives in Table 2–8. The desired worksheet is shown in Figure 2–88.

Table 2–8 Facade Importers Sales Data

Sales Representative	Sales Amount	Sales Return	Sales Quota
Polizzi, Bernard	591518	12638	765130
Li, Grace	895050	12015	776381
Volpe, Pamela	716502	18141	733309
Khan, Anwer	709672	22326	566940
Hudson, Emma	802525	11138	712222
Huerta, Teresa	885156	18721	778060

	A	B	C	D	E	F
	\multicolumn{6}{c}{**Facade Importers**}					
	\multicolumn{6}{c}{**Sales Analysis**}					
	Sales Representative	Sales Amount	Sales Return	Net Sales	Sales Quota	Above Quota
	Polizzi, Bernard	$591,518.00	$12,638.00	$578,880.00	$765,130.00	($186,250.00)
	Li, Grace	895,050.00	12,015.00	883,035.00	776,381.00	106,654.00
	Volpe, Pamela	716,502.00	18,141.00	698,361.00	733,309.00	(34,948.00)
	Khan, Anwer	709,672.00	22,326.00	687,346.00	566,940.00	120,406.00
	Hudson, Emma	802,525.00	11,138.00	791,387.00	712,222.00	79,165.00
	Huerta, Terese	885,156.00	18,721.00	866,435.00	778,060.00	88,375.00
	Total	$4,600,423.00	$94,979.00	$4,505,444.00	$4,332,042.00	$173,402.00
	Average	$766,737.17	$15,829.83	$750,907.33	$722,007.00	$28,900.33
	Highest	$895,050.00	$22,326.00	$883,035.00	$778,060.00	$120,406.00
	Lowest	$591,518.00	$11,138.00	$578,880.00	$566,940.00	($186,250.00)
	% of Quota Sold ====>	104.00%				

Figure 2–88

Continued >

In the Lab *continued*

Instructions Part 1:   Perform the following tasks to build the worksheet shown in Figure 2–88.

1. Apply the Aspect theme to the worksheet by using the Themes button on the Page Layout tab on the Ribbon.

2. Increase the width of column A to 19.00 points and the width of columns B through F to 13.50 points.

3. Enter the worksheet title `Facade Importers` in cell A1 and the worksheet subtitle `Sales Analysis` in cell A2. Enter the column titles in row 3 as shown in Figure 2–88. In row 3, use ALT+ENTER to start a new line in a cell.

4. Enter the sales data described in Table 2–8 in columns A, B, C, and E in rows 4 through 9. Enter the row titles in the range A10:A14 as shown in Figure 2–88 on the previous page.

5. Obtain the net sales in column D by subtracting the sales returns in column C from the sales amount in column B. Enter the formula in cell D4 and copy it to the range D5:D9.

6. Obtain the above quota amounts in column F by subtracting the sales quota in column E from the net sales in column D. Enter the formula in cell F4 and copy it to the range F5:F9.

7. Obtain the totals in row 10 by adding the column values for each salesperson. In the range B11:B13, use the AVERAGE, MAX, and MIN functions to determine the average, highest value, and lowest value in the range B4:B9. Copy the range B11:B13 to the range C11:F13.

8. Determine the percent of quota sold in cell B14 by dividing the total net sales amount in cell D10 by the total sales quota amount in cell E10. Center this value in the cell.

9. If necessary, click the Home tab on the Ribbon. One at a time, merge and center the worksheet title and subtitle across columns A through F. Select cells A1 and A2 and change the background color to red (column 2 in the Standard Colors area on the Fill Color palette). Apply the Title cell style to cells A1 and B1 by clicking the Cell Styles button on the Home tab on the Ribbon and clicking the Title cell style in the Titles and Headings area in the Cell Styles gallery. Change the worksheet title in cell A1 to 28-point white (column 1, row 1 on the Font Color gallery). Change the worksheet subtitle to the same color. Assign a thick box border from the Borders gallery to the range A1:A2.

10. Center the titles in row 3, columns A through F. Apply the Heading 3 cell style to the range A3:F3. Use the Italic button on the Home tab on the Ribbon to italicize the column titles in row 3 and the row titles in the range A10:A14.

11. Apply the Total cell style to the range A10:F10. Assign a thick box to cell B14. Change the background and font colors for cell B14 to the same colors applied to the worksheet title in Step 9.

12. Change the row heights of row 3 to 33.00 points and rows 11 and 14 to 30.00 points.

13. Select cell B14 and then click the Percent Style button on the Home tab on the Ribbon. Click the Increase Decimal button on the Ribbon twice to display the percent in cell B14 to hundredths.

14. Use the CTRL key to select the ranges B4:F4 and B10:F13. That is, select the range B4:F4 and then while holding down the CTRL key, select the range B10:F13. Use the Format Cells: Number Dialog Box Launcher button on the Home tab on the Ribbon to display the Format Cells dialog box to assign the selected ranges a Floating Dollar Sign style format with two decimal places and parentheses to represent negative numbers. Select the range B5:F9 and click the Comma Style button on the Home tab on the Ribbon.

15. Rename the sheet tab as Sales Analysis. Change the document properties, as specified by your instructor. Change the worksheet header with your name, course number, and other information requested by your instructor.

16. Save the workbook using the file name Lab 2-1 Part 1 Facade Importers Sales Analysis. Print the entire worksheet in landscape orientation. Print only the range A3:B10.

17. Display the formulas version by pressing CTRL+ACCENT MARK (`). Print the formulas version using the Fit to option button in the Scaling area on the Page tab in the Page Setup dialog box. After printing the worksheet, reset the Scaling option by selecting the Adjust to option button on the Page tab in the Page Setup dialog box and changing the percent value to 100%. Change the display from the formulas version to the values version by pressing CTRL+ACCENT MARK (`). Do not save the workbook.

18. Submit the assignment as specified by your instructor.

Instructions Part 2:　With the workbook created in Part 1, manually decrement each of the six values in the net sales column by $10,000.00 until the percent of quota sold in cell B14 is below, yet as close as possible to, 100%. All six values in column E must be incremented the same number of times. The percent of quota sold in B14 should equal 99.85%. Update the worksheet header and save the workbook as Lab 2-1 Part 2 Facade Importers Sales Analysis. Print the worksheet. Submit the assignment as specified by your instructor.

Instructions Part 3:　With the percent of quota sold in cell B14 equal to 99.85% from Part 2, manually decrement each of the six values in the sales return column by $1,000.00 until the percent of quota sold in cell B14 is above, yet as close as possible to, 100%. Decrement all six values in column C the same number of times. Your worksheet is correct when the percent of quota sold in cell B14 is equal to 100.12%. Update the worksheet header and save the workbook as Lab 2-1 Part 3 Facade Importers Sales Analysis. Print the worksheet. Submit the assignment as specified by your instructor.

In the Lab

Lab 2: Balance Due Worksheet

Problem:　You are a spreadsheet intern for Jackson's Bright Ideas, a popular Denver-based light fixture store with outlets in major cities across the western United States. You have been asked to use Excel to generate a report (Figure 2–89) that summarizes the monthly balance due. A graphic breakdown of the data also is desired. The customer data in Table 2–9 is available for test purposes.

Table 2–9 Jackson's Bright Ideas Monthly Balance Due Data				
Customer	**Beginning Balance**	**Credits**	**Payments**	**Purchases**
Costa, Dan	160.68	18.70	99.33	68.28
Hernandez, Abraham	138.11	48.47	75.81	46.72
Mc Cartan, John	820.15	32.11	31.23	29.19
Paoli, Pam	167.35	59.32	52.91	33.90
Ramirez, Alberto	568.34	55.17	18.53	36.34
Vaughn, Noah	449.92	25.90	82.05	99.77
Xiong, James	390.73	48.12	19.35	92.13

Continued >

In the Lab *continued*

Instructions Part 1: Create a worksheet similar to the one shown in Figure 2–89. Include the five columns of customer data in Table 2–9 in the report, plus two additional columns to compute a service charge and a new balance for each customer. Assume no negative unpaid monthly balances.

	Customer	Beginning Balance	Credits	Payments	Purchases	Service Charge	New Balance	
	Jackson's Bright Ideas							
	Monthly Balance Due Report							
Costa, Dan	$160.68	$18.70	$99.33	$68.28	$1.17	$112.10
Hernandez, Abraham	138.11	48.47	75.81	46.72	0.38	60.93
Mc Cartan, John	820.15	32.11	31.23	29.19	20.81	806.81
Paoli, Pam	167.35	59.32	52.91	33.90	1.52	90.54
Ramirez, Alberto	568.34	55.17	18.53	36.34	13.60	544.58
Vaughn, Noah	449.92	25.90	82.05	99.77	9.40	451.14
Xiong, James	390.73	48.12	19.35	92.13	8.89	424.28
Totals	**$2,695.28**	**$287.79**	**$379.21**	**$406.33**	**$55.78**	**$2,490.39**
Highest	$820.15	$59.32	$99.33	$99.77	$20.81	$806.81
Lowest	$138.11	$18.70	$18.53	$29.19	$0.38	$60.93
Average	$385.04	$41.11	$54.17	$58.05	$7.97	$355.77

Figure 2–89

Perform the following tasks:

1. Enter and format the worksheet title `Jackson's Bright Ideas` and worksheet subtitle `Monthly Balance Due Report` in cells A1 and A2. Change the theme of the worksheet to the Technic theme. Apply the Title cell style to cells A1 and A2. Change the font size in cell A1 to 28 points. One at a time, merge and center the worksheet title and subtitle across columns A through G. Change the background color of cells A1 and A2 to yellow (column 4 in the Standard Colors area in the Font Color palette). Draw a thick box border around the range A1:A2.

2. Change the width of column A to 20.00 characters. Change the widths of columns B through G to 12.00. Change the heights of row 3 to 36.00 and row 12 to 30.00 points.

3. Enter the column titles in row 3 and row titles in the range A11:A14 as shown in Figure 2–89. Center the column titles in the range A3:G3. Apply the Heading 3 cell style to the range A3:G3. Bold the titles in the range A11:A14. Apply the Total cell style to the range A11:G11. Change the font size of the cells in the range A3:G14 to 12 points.

4. Enter the data in Table 2–9 in the range A4:E10.

5. Use the following formulas to determine the service charge in column F and the new balance in column G for the first customer. Copy the two formulas down through the remaining customers.

   a. Service Charge (cell F4) = 2.75% * (Beginning Balance – Payments – Credits)
      or = 0.0275 * (B4 – C4 – D4)

   b. New Balance (G4) = Beginning Balance + Purchases – Credits – Payments + Service Charge
      or =B4 + E4 – C4 – D4 + F4

6. Determine the totals in row 11.

7. Determine the maximum, minimum, and average values in cells B12:B14 for the range B4:B10 and then copy the range B12:B14 to C12:G14.

8. Use the Format Cells command on the shortcut menu to format the numbers as follows: (a) assign the Currency style with a floating dollar sign to the cells containing numeric data in the ranges B4:G4 and B11:G14; and (b) assign the Comma style (currency with no dollar sign) to the range B5:G10.

9. Use conditional formatting to change the formatting to white bold font on a red background in any cell in the range C4:C10 that contains a value greater than 50.

10. Change the worksheet name from Sheet1 to Balance Due. Change the document properties, as specified by your instructor. Change the worksheet header with your name, course number, and other information requested by your instructor.

11. Spell check the worksheet. Preview and then print the worksheet in landscape orientation. Save the workbook using the file name, Lab 2-2 Part 1 Jackson's Bright Ideas Monthly Balance Due Report.

12. Print the range A3:D14. Print the formulas version on one page. Close the workbook without saving the changes. Submit the assignment as specified by your instructor.

Instructions Part 2: This part requires that a 3-D Bar chart with a cylindrical shape be inserted on a new worksheet in the workbook. If necessary, use Excel Help to obtain information on inserting a chart on a separate sheet in the workbook.

1. With the Lab 2-2 Part 1 Jackson's Bright Ideas Monthly Balance Due Report workbook open, draw the 3-D Bar chart with cylindrical shape showing each customer's total new balance as shown in Figure 2–90.

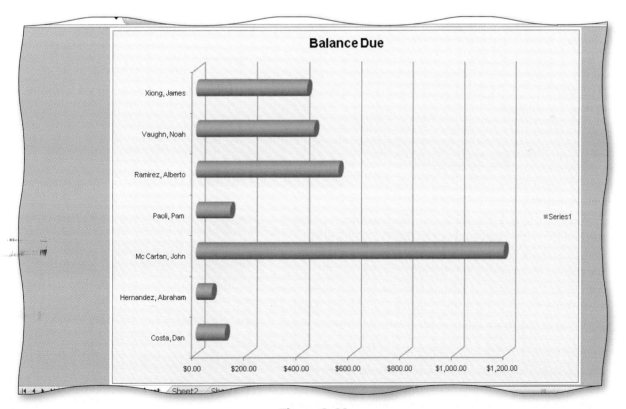

Figure 2–90

2. Use the CTRL key and mouse to select the nonadjacent chart ranges A4:A10 and G4:G10. That is, select the range A4:A10 and then while holding down the CTRL key, select the range G4:G10. The customer names in the range A4:A10 will identify the cylindrical bars, while the data series in the range G4:G10 will determine the length of the bars.

Continued >

In the Lab *continued*

3. Click the Insert tab on the Ribbon. Click the Bar button in the Charts group on the Ribbon and then select Clustered Horizontal Cylinder in the Cylinder area. When the chart is displayed on the worksheet, click the Move Chart button on the Ribbon. When the Move Chart dialog box appears, click New sheet and then type Bar Chart for the sheet name. Click the OK button.

4. When the chart is displayed on the new worksheet, click the wall behind the bars and then click the Format contextual tab. Click the Shape Fill button on the Ribbon and then select Gold, Accent 2, Lighter 80% in the gallery (column 6, row 2). Click the Layout contextual tab. Click the Chart Title button on the Ribbon and then select Above Chart in the Chart Title gallery. If necessary, use the scroll bar on the right side of the worksheet to scroll to the top of the chart. Click the chart title to select it and then type Balance Due as the chart title.

5. Drag the Balance Due tab at the bottom of the worksheet to the left of the Bar Chart tab to reorder the sheets in the workbook. Preview and print the chart.

6. Click the Balance Due sheet tab. Change the following purchases: customer John Mc Cartan to $406.58, and customer Pam Paoli to $74.99. The company also decided to change the service charge from 2.75% to 3.25% for all customers. After copying the adjusted formula in cell F4 to the range F5:F10, click the Auto Fill Options button and then click Fill without Formatting to maintain the original formatting in the range F5:F10. The total new balance in cell G11 should equal $2,919.01.

7. Select both sheets by holding down the SHIFT key and then clicking the Bar Chart tab. Preview and print the selected sheets. Submit the assignment as requested by your instructor. Save the worksheet using the file name, Lab 2-2 Part 2 Jackson's Bright Ideas Monthly Balance Due Report.

8. Submit the assignment as specified by your instructor.

Instructions Part 3: With your instructor's permission, e-mail the workbook created in this exercise with the changes indicated in Part 2 as an attachment to your instructor. Close the workbook without saving the changes.

In the Lab

Lab 3: Equity Web Queries

Problem: A friend of your family, Benson Yackley, has learned that Excel can connect to the Web, download real-time stock data into a worksheet, and then refresh the data as often as needed. Because you have had courses in Excel and the Internet, he has hired you as a consultant to develop a stock analysis workbook. His portfolio is shown in Table 2–10.

Table 2–10 Benson Yackley's Stock Portfolio	
Company	**Stock Symbol**
Exxon Mobil	XOM
Dell	DELL
Hewlett-Packard	HPQ
Intel	INTC
MetLife	MET
PepsiCo	PEP

Instructions Part 1: Start Excel. If necessary, connect to the Internet. Perform a Web query to obtain multiple stock quotes (Figure 2–91), using the stock symbols in the second column of Table 2–10. Place the results of the Web query in a new worksheet. Rename the worksheet Real-Time Stock Quotes. Change the document properties, as specified by your instructor. Add a header with your name, course number, and other information requested by your instructor. Save the workbook using the file name, Lab 2-3 Part 1 Benson Yackley Equities Online. Preview and then print the worksheet in landscape orientation using the Fit to option.

Click the following links and print the Web page that appears in the browser window: Click here to visit MSN Money; Dell Inc.; Chart (to the right of MetLife, Inc.); and News (to the right of PepsiCo, Inc.). Submit the assignment as specified by your instructor.

Figure 2–91

Instructions Part 2: While connected to the Internet and with the Lab 2-3 Benson Yackley Equities Online workbook open, create a worksheet listing the major indices and their current values on Sheet2 of the workbook (Figure 2–92). After clicking the Sheet2 tab, create the worksheet by double-clicking MSN MoneyCentral Investor Major Indices in the Select Data Source dialog box. The dialog box is displayed when you click the Existing Connections button on the Data tab on the Ribbon. Rename the worksheet Major Indices. Preview and then print the Major Indices worksheet in landscape orientation using the Fit to option. Save the workbook using the same file name as in Part 1. Submit the assignment as specified by your instructor.

Figure 2–92

Cases and Places

Apply your creative thinking and problem solving skills to design and implement a solution.

● EASIER ● ● MORE DIFFICULT

● 1: Design and Create a Weight-Loss Plan Worksheet

As a summer intern working for Choose to Lose, a local weight-loss clinic, you have been asked to create a worksheet that estimates the monthly weight lost for an individual based on recommended average daily activities. You have been given the numbers of calories burned per hour and the average number of hours for each activity (Table 2–11). Use the following formulas:

Formula A: Total Calories Burned per Day = Calories burned per Hour $\times$ Average Hours Daily

Formula B: Total Pounds Lost per Month (30 days) = 30 $\times$ Total Calories Burned per Day $\times$ 3500

Formula C: Average function

Formula D: Max function

Formula E: Min function

Use the concepts and techniques presented in this project to create and format the worksheet. Include an embedded 3-D Pie chart that shows the contribution of each activity to the total calories burned per day. Use Microsoft Excel Help to create a professional looking 3-D Pie chart with title and data labels.

Table 2–11 Activities with Corresponding Calories Burned per Hour and Worksheet Layout				
Activity	**Calories Burned per Hour**	**Average Hours Daily**	**Total Calories Burned per Day**	**Total Pounds Lost per Month (30 Days)**
Aerobics class	450	0.50	Formula A	Formula B
Brisk walking	350	0.50		
House work	150	1.00		
Office work/sitting	120	6.00		
Sleeping	70	9.00		
Standing	105	2.00		
Swimming	290	0.50		
Tennis	315	0.25		
Walking	240	1.25		
Totals	—		—	—
Average	Formula C			
Highest	Formula D			
Lowest	Formula E			

• 2: Create a Profit Potential Worksheet

You work part-time for Doze-Now, a retailer of sleep-related products. Your manager wants to know the profit potential of their inventory based on the categories of inventory in Table 2–12. Table 2–12 contains the format of the desired report. The required formulas are shown in Table 2–13. Use the concepts and techniques developed in this project to create and format the worksheet. Submit a printout of the values version and formulas version of the worksheet. The company just received a shipment of 175 additional comforters and 273 items of sleepwear. Update the appropriate cells in the Units on Hand column.

Table 2–12 Doze-Now Profit Potential Data and Worksheet Layout

Item	Units on Hand	Average Unit Cost	Total Cost	Average Unit Price	Total Value	Potential Profit
Comforters	216	46.52	Formula A	Formula B	Formula C	Formula D
Night lights	4,283	6.89				
Pillows	691	47.64				
Sleep sound machines	103	45.06				
Sleepwear	489	16.77				
Total	—		—	—	—	—
Average	Formula E					
Lowest	Formula F					
Highest	Formula G					

Table 2–13 Doze-Now Profit Potential Formulas

Formula A = Units on Hand * Average Unit Cost

Formula B = Average Unit Cost * (1 / (1 − .58))

Formula C = Units on Hand * Average Unit Price

Formula D = Total Value − Total Cost

Formula E = AVERAGE function

Formula F = MIN function

Formula G = MAX function

Continued >

Cases and Places continued

•• 3: Create a Fund-Raising Analysis Worksheet

You are the chairperson of the fund-raising committee for a local charity. You want to compare various fund-raising ideas to determine which will give you the best profit. The data obtained from six businesses about their products and the format of the desired report are shown in Table 2–14. The required formulas are shown in Table 2–15. Use the concepts and techniques presented in this project to create and format the worksheet.

Table 2–14 Fund-Raising Data and Worksheet Layout

Product	Company	Cost per Unit	Margin	Selling Price	Profit per 2000 Sales	Profit per 5000 Sales
Candles	Woodland Farms	$4.75	40%	Formula A	Formula B	Formula C
Candy	Polkandy	3.00	70%			
Coffee	Garcia Coffee	6.50	45%			
Cookie dough	Oh, Dough!	2.90	65%			
Flower bulbs	Early Bloom	2.40	50%			
T-shirts	Zed's Sports	5.75	42%			
Minimum		Formula D				
Maximum		Formula E				

Table 2–15 Band Fund-Raising Formulas

Formula A = Cost per Unit / (1 – Margin)

Formula B = 2000 * (Selling Price – Cost per Unit)

Formula C = 5000 *110% * (Selling Price – Cost per Unit)

Formula D = MIN function

Formula E = MAX function

•• 4: Design and Create a Projected Budget

Make It Personal

For the next six month period, forecast your income for each month, your base expenditures for each month, and your special expenditures for each month. Base expenditures include expenses that occur each month, such as food and loan payments. Special expenditures include expenses that are out of the ordinary, such as the purchase of gifts, automobile insurance, and medical expenses. With this data, develop a worksheet calculating the amount of remaining money at the end of each month. You can determine this amount by subtracting both expenses from the anticipated income.

Include a total, average value, highest value, and lowest value for income, base expenditures, special expenditures, and remaining money. Use the concepts and techniques presented in this project to create and format the worksheet.

Create a 3-D Pie chart on a separate sheet illustrating the portion each month's special expenditures deducts from the total remaining money after all six months have passed. Use Microsoft Excel Help to create a professional looking 3-D Pie chart with title and data labels.

•• 5: Design and Create a Stock Analysis Worksheet

Working Together

Have each member of your team select six stocks — two bank stocks, two communications stocks, and two Internet stocks. Each member should submit the stock names, stock symbols, and an approximate six-month-old price. Create a worksheet that lists the stock names, symbols, price, and number of shares for each stock (use 350 shares as the number of shares for all stocks). Format the worksheet so that it has a professional appearance and is as informative as possible.

Have the group do research on the use of 3-D references, which is a reference to a range that spans two or more worksheets in a workbook (use Microsoft Excel Help). Use what the group learns to create a Web query on the Sheet2 worksheet by referencing the stock symbols on the Sheet1 worksheet. On the Sheet1 worksheet, change the cells that list current price per share numbers on the Sheet1 worksheet so that they use 3-D cell references that refer to the worksheet created by the Web query on the Sheet2 worksheet. Present your workbook and findings to the class.

3 What-If Analysis, Charting, and Working with Large Worksheets

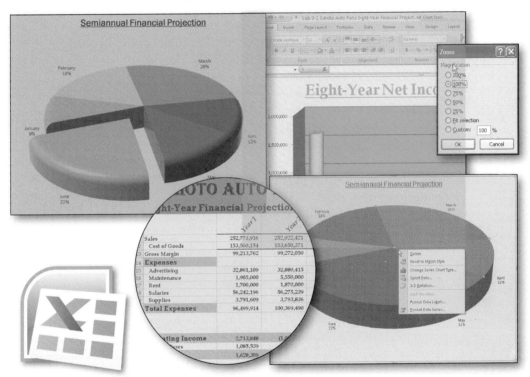

Objectives

You will have mastered the material in this chapter when you can:

- Rotate text in a cell
- Create a series of month names
- Copy, paste, insert, and delete cells
- Format numbers using format symbols
- Freeze and unfreeze titles
- Show and format the system date
- Use absolute cell references in a formula
- Use the IF function to perform a logical test

- Use the Format Painter button to format cells
- Create a 3-D Pie chart on a separate chart sheet
- Color and rearrange worksheet tabs
- Change the worksheet view
- Answer what-if questions
- Goal seek to answer what-if questions

3 | What-If Analysis, Charting, and Working with Large Worksheets

Introduction

Worksheets normally are much larger than those created in the previous chapters, often extending beyond the size of the window. Because you cannot see the entire worksheet on the screen at one time, working with a large worksheet sometimes can be frustrating. This chapter introduces several Excel commands that allow you to control what displays on the screen so you can view critical parts of a large worksheet at one time. One command lets you freeze the row and column titles so Excel always displays them on the screen. Another command splits the worksheet into separate window panes so you can view different parts of a worksheet on the screen at one time. Hiding the Ribbon will allow a larger portion of the worksheet to be visible.

When you set up a worksheet, you should use cell references in formulas whenever possible, rather than constant values. The use of a cell reference allows you to change a value in multiple formulas by changing the value in a single cell. The cell references in a formula are called assumptions. Assumptions are values in cells that you can change to determine new values for formulas. This chapter emphasizes the use of assumptions and shows how to use Excel to answer what-if questions such as, what happens to the semi-annual operating income if you decrease the marketing expenses assumption by 2%? Being able to analyze quickly the effect of changing values in a worksheet is an important skill in making business decisions.

This chapter also introduces you to techniques that will enhance your ability to create worksheets and draw charts. From your work in Chapter 1, you are aware of how easily you can create charts. This chapter covers additional charting techniques that allow you to convey your message in a dramatic pictorial fashion such as an exploded 3-D Pie chart. This chapter also covers other methods for entering values in cells, such as allowing Excel to enter values for you based on a pattern of values that you create, and formatting these values. In addition, you will learn how to use absolute cell references and how to use the IF function to assign a value to a cell based on a logical test.

Project — Financial Projection Worksheet with What-If Analysis and Chart

The project in the chapter follows proper design guidelines and uses Excel to create the worksheet and pie chart shown in Figure 3–1. Campus Clothiers manufactures and sells customized clothing to college students on campuses around the country. Each June and December, the director of finance and accounting submits a plan to the management team to show projected monthly revenues, costs of goods, gross margin, expenses, and operating income for the next six months. The director requires an easy-to-read worksheet that shows financial projections for the next six months. The worksheet should allow for quick analysis if projections for certain numbers change, such as the percentage of expenses allocated to marketing. In addition, a 3-D Pie chart is required that shows the projected operating income contribution for each of the six months.

Home   Insert   Page Layout   Formulas   Data   Review   View   Editing

J28

	A	B	C	D	E	F	G	H
1	**Campus Clothiers**							
2	**Semiannual Projected Gross Margin, Expenses, and Operating Income**							2/1/2007
3		*January*	*February*	*March*	*April*	*May*	*June*	*Total*
4	Sales	$3,383,909.82	$6,880,576.15	$9,742,702.37	$4,818,493.53	$4,566,722.63	$8,527,504.39	$37,919,908.89
5	Cost of Goods Sold	1,319,724.83	2,683,424.70	3,799,653.92	1,879,212.48	1,781,021.83	3,325,726.71	14,788,764.47
6	Gross Margin	$2,064,184.99	$4,197,151.45	$5,943,048.45	$2,939,281.05	$2,785,700.80	$5,201,777.68	$23,131,144.42
7								
8	Expenses							
9	Bonus	$0.00	$100,000.00	$100,000.00	$100,000.00	$0.00	$100,000.00	$400,000.00
10	Commission	109,977.07	223,618.72	316,637.83	156,601.04	148,418.49	277,143.89	1,232,397.04
11	Marketing	304,551.88	619,251.85	876,843.21	433,664.42	411,005.04	767,475.40	3,412,791.80
12	Research and Development	194,574.81	395,633.13	560,205.39	277,063.38	262,586.55	490,331.50	2,180,394.76
13	Support, General, and Administrative	575,264.67	1,169,697.95	1,656,259.40	819,143.90	776,342.85	1,449,675.75	6,446,384.51
14	Total Expenses	$1,184,368.44	$2,508,201.65	$3,509,945.83	$1,786,472.74	$1,598,352.92	$3,084,626.54	$13,671,968.11
15								
16	Operating Income	$879,816.55	$1,688,949.80	$2,433,102.62	$1,152,808.32	$1,187,347.88	$2,117,151.14	$9,459,176.31
17								
18	*What-If Assumptions*							
19	Bonus	$100,000.00						
20	Commission	3.25%						
21	Margin	61.00%						
22	Marketing	9.00%						
23	Research and Development	5.75%						
24	Revenue for Bonus	$4,750,000.00						
25	Support, General, and Administrative	17.00%						
26								

(a) Worksheet

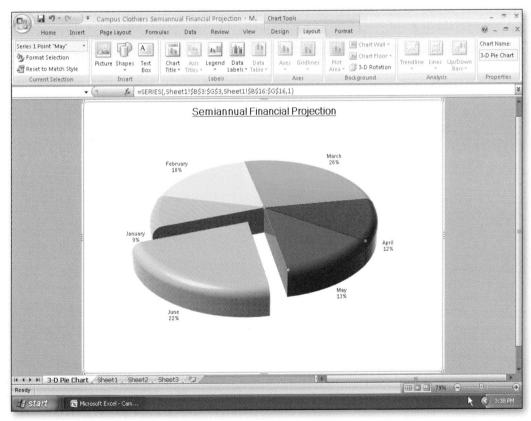

(b) 3-D Pie Chart

Figure 3–1

Correctness

Studies have shown that more than 25 percent of all business worksheets have errors. If you are not careful entering data and formulas, then your worksheet is prone to errors. You can ensure correctness in your formulas by carefully checking them using Range Finder. The Formula Auditing group on the Formulas tab on the Ribbon also can be helpful when verifying formulas.

The requirements document for the Campus Clothiers Semiannual Financial Projection worksheet is shown in Figure 3–2. It includes the needs, source of data, summary of calculations, chart requirements, and other facts about its development.

REQUEST FOR NEW WORKBOOK

Date Submitted:	October 27, 2008
Submitted By:	Norm Armand
Worksheet Title:	Campus Clothiers Semiannual Projected Gross Margin, Expenses, and Operating Income
Needs:	The needs are: (1) a worksheet (Figure 3-3a) that shows Campus Clothiers's projected monthly sales, cost of goods, gross margin, expenses, and operating income for a six-month period; and (2) a 3-D Pie chart (Figure 3-3b) that shows the projected contribution of each month's operating income to the six-month period operating income.
Source of Data:	The data supplied by the Finance department includes projections of the monthly sales and expenses (Table 3-1) that are based on prior years. All the remaining numbers in the worksheet are determined from these 13 numbers using formulas.
Calculations:	The following calculations must be made for each month: 1. Cost of Goods = Sales − Sales * Margin 2. Gross Margin = Sales − Cost of Goods 3. Bonus Expense = $100,000.00 if the Sales exceeds the Revenue for Bonus; otherwise Bonus Expense = 0 4. Commission Expense = Commission Assumption * Sales 5. Marketing Expense = Marketing Assumption * Sales 6. Research and Development = Research and Development Assumption * Sales 7. Support, General, and Administrative Expense = Support, General, and Administrative Assumption * Sales 8. Total Expenses = Sum of Expenses 9. Operating Income = Gross Margin − Total Expenses
Chart Requirements:	A 3-D Pie chart is required on a separate sheet (Figure 3-3b) to show the contribution of each month's operating income to the six month period operating Income. The chart should also emphasize the month with the greatest operating income.

Approvals

Approval Status:	X	Approved
		Rejected
Approved By:		Shauna Hendricks, CFO
Date:		November 1, 2008
Assigned To:		J. Quasney, Spreadsheet Specialist

Figure 3–2

Excel's Usefulness

Just a few short years ago, a what-if question of any complexity only could be answered using a large, expensive computer programmed by highly paid computer professionals. Generating a result could take days. Excel gives the noncomputer professional the ability to get complex business-related questions answered instantaneously and economically.

Overview

As you read this chapter, you will learn how to create the worksheet shown in Figure 3–1 by performing these general tasks:

- Create a series of month names
- Use absolute cell references in a formula
- Use the IF function to perform a logical test
- Use the Format Painter button to format cells
- Create a 3-D Pie chart on a separate chart sheet
- Answer what-if questions
- Manipulate large worksheets

Plan
Ahead

General Project Decisions

While creating an Excel worksheet, you need to make several decisions that will determine the appearance and characteristics of the finished worksheet. As you create the worksheet required to meet the requirements shown in Figure 3–2, you should follow these general guidelines:

1. Plan the layout of the worksheet. The requirements state that six months are necessary in the worksheet. It is therefore sensible to place the months across columns so that the financial headings can be placed in rows. The what-if assumptions should not clutter the worksheet, but they should be placed in an easily located portion of the worksheet.

2. Determine the necessary formulas and functions needed. Except for the monthly sales numbers, the remaining numbers in the main portion of the worksheet are calculated based on the numbers in the what-if portion of the worksheet. The formulas are stated in the requirements document (Figure 3–2). The Bonus expense is included only if a certain condition is met. A function can check for the condition and include the bonus when necessary.

3. Identify how to format various elements of the worksheet. Sales and Expenses are two distinct categories of financial data and should be separated visually. Gross Margin and Total Expenses should stand out because they are subtotals. The Operating Income is the key piece of information being calculated in the worksheet and, therefore, should be formatted in such a manner as to draw the reader's attention. The what-if assumptions should be formatted in a manner which indicates that they are separate from the main area of the worksheet.

4. Specify how the chart should convey necessary information. The requirements document indicates that the chart should be a 3-D Pie chart and emphasize the month with the greatest operating income. A 3-D Pie chart is a good way to compare visually a small set of numbers. The month, which is emphasized, also should appear closer to the reader in order to draw the reader's attention.

5. Perform what-if analysis and goal seeking using the best techniques. What-if analysis allows you quickly to answer questions regarding various predictions. In Campus Clothiers Semiannual Financial Projection worksheet, the only cells that you should change when performing what-if analysis are those in the what-if portion of the worksheet. All other values in the worksheet, except for the projected sales, are calculated. Goal seeking allows you automatically to modify values in the what-if area of the worksheet based on a goal that you have for another cell in the worksheet.

(continued)

Plan Ahead

(continued)

   In addition, using a sketch of the worksheet can help you visualize its design. The sketch of the worksheet (Figure 3-3a) consists of titles, column and row headings, location of data values, calculations, and a rough idea of the desired formatting. The sketch of the 3-D Pie chart (Figure 3–3b) shows the expected contribution of each month's operating income to the semiannual operating income. The projected monthly sales will be entered in row 4 of the worksheet. The assumptions will be entered below the operating income (Figure 3-3a). The projected monthly sales and the assumptions will be used to calculate the remaining numbers in the worksheet.

   When necessary, more specific details concerning the above guidelines are presented at appropriate points in the chapter. The chapter also will identify the actions you perform and decisions made regarding these guidelines during the creation of the worksheet shown in Figure 3–1 on page EX 163.

(a) Worksheet

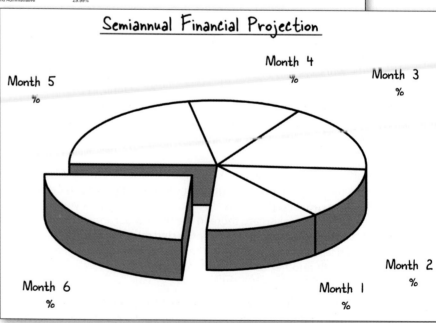

(b) 3-D Pie Chart

Figure 3–3

With a good understanding of the requirements document, an understanding of the necessary decisions, and a sketch of the worksheet, the next step is to use Excel to create the worksheet.

Table 3–1 Campus Clothiers Semiannual Financial Projections Data and What-If Assumptions	
Projected Monthly Total Net Revenues	
January	$3,383,909.82
February	6,880,576.15
March	9,742,702.37
April	4,818,493.53
May	4,566,722.63
June	8,527,504.39
What-If Assumptions	
Bonus	$100,000.00
Commission	3.25%
Margin	61.00%
Marketing	9.00%
Research and Development	5.75%
Revenue for Bonus	$4,750,000.00
Support, General, and Administrative	17.00%

To Start Excel

If you are using a computer to step through the project in this chapter and you want your screen to match the figures in this book, you should change your computer's resolution to 1024 × 768. For information about how to change a computer's resolution, see page APP 36 in Appendix E.

The following steps, which assume Windows is running, start Excel based on a typical installation of Microsoft Office on your computer. You may need to ask your instructor how to start Excel for your computer.

1 Click the Start button on the Windows taskbar to display the Start menu.

2 Point to All Programs on the Start menu and then point to Microsoft Office in the All Programs submenu.

3 Click Microsoft Office Excel 2007 on the Microsoft Office submenu.

4 If the Excel window is not maximized, click the Maximize button next to the Close button on its title bar to maximize the window.

5 If the worksheet window in Excel is not maximized, click the Maximize button next to the Close button on its title bar to maximize the worksheet window within Excel.

BTW

The Startup Submenu
Any application on the Startup submenu starts automatically when you turn your computer on. To add Excel to the Startup submenu, do the following: (1) Click the Start button on the Windows taskbar, point to All Programs on the Start menu, and then point to Microsoft Office on the All Programs submenu; (2) Right-drag Microsoft Office Excel 2007 from the Microsoft Office submenu to the Startup submenu; (3) When the shortcut menu appears, click Copy Here. The next time you turn your computer on, Excel will start automatically.

To Enter the Worksheet Titles, Change Workbook Properties, Apply a Theme, and Save the Workbook

The worksheet contains two titles, one in cell A1 and another in cell A2. In the previous chapters, titles were centered across the worksheet. With large worksheets that extend beyond the size of a window, it is best to enter titles in the upper-left corner as shown in the sketch of the worksheet in Figure 3–3a. The following steps enter the worksheet titles and save the workbook.

1 Click cell A1 and then enter `Campus Clothiers` as the worksheet title.

2 Click cell A2 and then enter `Semiannual Projected Gross Margin, Expenses, and Operating Income` as the worksheet subtitle and then press the ENTER key.

3 Click the Office Button, click Prepare on the Office Button menu, and then click Properties.

4 Update the document properties with your name and any other relevant information.

5 Click the Close button in the Document Properties pane.

6 Apply the Trek theme to the worksheet by clicking the Themes button on the Page Layout tab on the Ribbon and then return to the Home tab on the Ribbon.

7 With a USB flash drive connected to one of the computer's USB ports, click the Save button on the Quick Access Toolbar.

8 When Excel displays the Save As dialog box, type `Campus Clothiers Semiannual Financial Projection` in the File name text box.

9 If necessary, click UDISK 2.0 (E:) in the Save in list (your USB flash drive may have a different name and letter). Click the Save button in the Save As dialog box to save the workbook.

Rotating Text in a Cell
In Excel, you use the Alignment sheet of the Format Cells dialog box, as shown in Figure 3-5, to position data in a cell by centering, left-aligning, or right-aligning; indenting; aligning at the top, bottom, or center; and rotating. If you enter 90 in the Degrees box in the Orientation area, the text will appear vertically and read from bottom to top in the cell.

Rotating Text and Using the Fill Handle to Create a Series

The data on the worksheet, including month names and the What-If Assumptions section, now can be added to the worksheet.

Plan Ahead

> **Plan the layout of the worksheet.**
> The design of the worksheet calls specifically for only six months of data. Because there always will be only six months of data in the worksheet, the months should be placed across the top of the worksheet as column headings rather than as row headings. There are more data items regarding each month than there are months, and it is possible that more expense categories could be added in the future. A proper layout, therefore, includes placing the data items for each month as row headings. The What-If Assumptions section should be placed in an area of the worksheet that is easily accessible, yet does not impair the view of the main section of the worksheet. As shown in Figure 3–3a, the What-If Assumptions should be placed below the calculations in the worksheet.

When you first enter text, its angle is zero degrees (0°), and it reads from left to right in a cell. Text in a cell can be rotated counterclockwise by entering a number between 1° and 90° in the Alignment sheet in the Format Cells dialog box.

To Rotate Text and Use the Fill Handle to Create a Series of Month Names

Chapters 1 and 2 used the fill handle to copy a cell or a range of cells to adjacent cells. The fill handle also can be used to create a series of numbers, dates, or month names automatically. The following steps enter the month name, January, in cell B3; format cell B3 (including rotating the text); and then use the fill handle to enter the remaining month names in the range C3:G3.

- Select cell B3.

- Type January as the cell entry and then click the Enter box.

- Click the Format Cells: Alignment Dialog Box Launcher on the Ribbon to display the Format Cells dialog box (Figure 3-4).

Figure 3–4

- Click the 45° point in the Orientation area to move the Text hand in the Orientation area to the 45° point and to display 45 in the Degrees box (Figure 3–5).

Figure 3–5

- Click the OK button to rotate the text in cell B3 at a 45° angle and automatically increase the height of row 3 to best fit the rotated text (Figure 3–6).

- Point to the fill handle on the lower-right corner of cell B3.

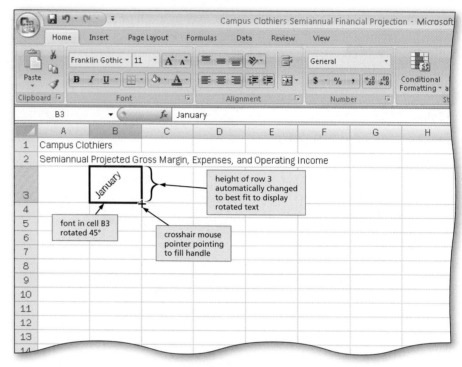

Figure 3–6

❹

- Drag the fill handle to the right to select the range C3:G3. Do not release the mouse button (Figure 3–7).

Figure 3–7

5

- Release the mouse button to create a month name series January through June in the range B3:G3 and copy the format in cell B3 to the range C3:G3.

- Click the Auto Fill Options button below the lower-right corner of the fill area to display the Auto Fill Options menu (Figure 3–8).

Q&A

What if I do not want to copy the format of cell B3 during the auto fill operation?

In addition to creating a series of values, dragging the fill handle instructs Excel to copy the format of cell B3 to the range C3:G3. With some fill operations, you may not want to copy the formats of the source cell or range to the destination cell or range. If this is the case, click the Auto Fill Options button after the range fills (Figure 3–8) and then select the option you desire on the Auto Fill Options menu.

Figure 3–8

6

- Click the Auto Fill Options button to hide the Auto Fill Options menu.

- Click cell H3, type Total, and then press the RIGHT ARROW key.

Q&A

Why is the word Total automatically formatted with the Heading 3 cell style and 45° rotation?

Excel tries to save you time by automatically recognizing the adjacent cell format in cell G3 and applying it to cell H3. The Heading 3 cell style in cell G3 causes this action to occur.

Other Ways

1. Enter start month in cell, apply formatting, right-drag fill handle in direction to fill, click Fill Months on shortcut menu

2. Enter start month in cell, apply formatting, select range, click Fill button on Home tab on Ribbon, click Series, click AutoFill

Using the Auto Fill Options Menu

As shown in Figure 3–8, Fill Series is the default option that Excel uses to fill the area, which means it fills the destination area with a series, using the same formatting as the source area. If you choose another option on the Auto Fill Options menu, then Excel immediately changes the contents of the destination range. Following the use of the fill handle, the Auto Fill Options button remains active until you begin the next Excel operation. Table 3–2 summarizes the options on the Auto Fill Options menu.

BTW

The Mighty Fill Handle
If you drag the fill handle to the left or up, Excel will decrement the series rather than increment the series. To copy a word, such as January or Monday, which Excel might interpret as the start of a series, hold down the CTRL key while you drag the fill handle to a destination area. If you drag the fill handle back into the middle of a cell, Excel erases the contents.

Table 3–2 Options Available on the Auto Fill Options Menu

Auto Fill Option	Description
Copy Cells	Fill destination area with contents using format of source area. Do not create a series.
Fill Series	Fill destination area with series using format of source area. This option is the default.
Fill Formatting Only	Fill destination area using format of source area. No content is copied unless fill is series.
Fill Without Formatting	Fill destination area with contents, without the formatting of source area.
Fill Months	Fill destination area with series of months using format of source area. Same as Fill Series and shows as an option only if source area contains a month.

You can use the fill handle to create a series longer than the one shown in Figure 3–8. If you drag the fill handle past cell G3 in Step 4, Excel continues to increment the months and logically will repeat January, February, and so on, if you extend the range far enough to the right.

You can create several different types of series using the fill handle. Table 3–3 illustrates several examples. Notice in examples 4 through 7, 9, and 11 that, if you use the fill handle to create a series of numbers or nonsequential months, you must enter the first item in the series in one cell and the second item in the series in an adjacent cell. Next, select both cells and drag the fill handle through the destination area.

Table 3–3 Examples of Series Using the Fill Handle

Example	Contents of Cell(s) Copied Using the Fill Handle	Next Three Values of Extended Series
1	2:00	3:00, 4:00, 5:00
2	Qtr3	Qtr4, Qtr1, Qtr2
3	Quarter 1	Quarter 2, Quarter 3, Quarter 4
4	5-Jan, 5-Mar	5 May, 5-Jul, 5 Sep
5	2007, 2008	2009, 2010, 2011
6	1, 2	3, 4, 5
7	430, 410	390, 370, 350
8	Sun	Mon, Tue, Wed
9	Sunday, Tuesday	Thursday, Saturday, Monday
10	4th Section	5th Section, 6th Section, 7th Section
11	−205, −208	−211, −214, −217

To Increase Column Widths and Enter Row Titles

In Chapter 2, the column widths were increased after the values were entered into the worksheet. Sometimes, you may want to increase the column widths before you enter the values and, if necessary, adjust them later. The following steps increase the column widths and then enter the row titles in column A down to What-If Assumptions in cell A18.

- Move the mouse pointer to the boundary between column heading A and column heading B so that the mouse pointer changes to a split double arrow.

- Drag the mouse pointer to the right until the ScreenTip displays, Width: 35.00 (322 pixels). Do not release the mouse button (Figure 3–9).

Figure 3–9

- Release the mouse button to change the width of column A.

- Click column heading B and then drag through column heading G to select columns B through G.

- Move the mouse pointer to the boundary between column headings B and C and then drag the mouse to the right until the ScreenTip displays, Width: 14.00 (133 pixels). Do not release the mouse button (Figure 3–10).

Figure 3–10

3

- Release the mouse button to change the width of columns B through G.

- Use the technique described in Step 1 to increase the width of column H to 15.00.

- Enter the row titles in the range A4:A18 as shown in Figure 3–11, but without the indents.

- Click cell A5 and then click the Increase Indent button on the Ribbon.

- Select the range A9:A13 and then click the Increase Indent button on the Ribbon.

- Click cell A19 to finish entering the row titles (Figure 3–11).

Q&A

What happens when I click the Increase Indent button?

The Increase Indent button indents the contents of a cell to the right by three spaces each time you click it. The Decrease Indent button decreases the indent by three spaces each time you click it.

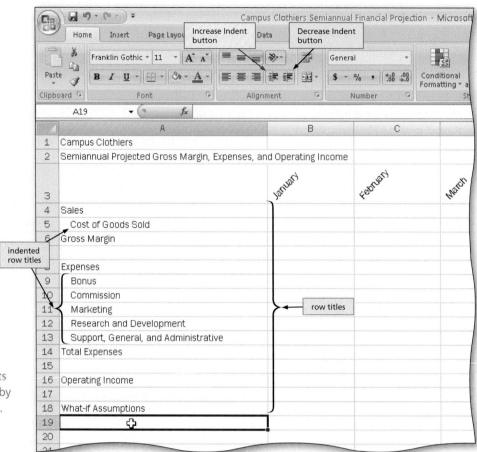

Figure 3–11

Other Ways

1. To indent, right-click range, click Format Cells on shortcut menu, click Alignment tab, click Left (Indent) in Horizontal list, type number of spaces to indent in Indent text box, click OK button

---

BTW

Fitting Entries in a Cell
An alternative to increasing the column widths or row heights is to shrink the characters in the cell to fit the current width of the column. To shrink to fit, click Format Cells: Alignment Dialog Box Button Launcher on the Ribbon, and click Shrink to fit in the Text control area. After shrinking entries to fit in a cell, consider using the Zoom slider on the status bar to make the entries more readable.

Copying a Range of Cells to a Nonadjacent Destination Area

As shown in the sketch of the worksheet (Figure 3–3a on page EX 166), the row titles in the Expenses area are the same as the row titles in the What-If Assumptions table, with the exception of the two additional entries in cells A21 (Margin) and A24 (Revenue for Bonus). Hence, the What-If Assumptions table row titles can be created by copying the range A9:A13 to the range A19:A23 and then inserting two rows for the additional entries in cells A21 and A24. The source area (range A9:A13) is not adjacent to the destination area (range A19:A23). The first two chapters used the fill handle to copy a source area to an adjacent destination area. To copy a source area to a nonadjacent destination area, however, you cannot use the fill handle.

A more versatile method of copying a source area is to use the Copy button and Paste button on the Home tab on the Ribbon. You can use these two buttons to copy a source area to an adjacent or nonadjacent destination area.

The Copy button copies the contents and format of the source area to the **Office Clipboard,** a reserved place in the computer's memory that allows you to collect text and graphic items from an Office document and then paste them into any Office document. The Copy command on the Edit menu or shortcut menu works the same as the Copy button. The Paste button copies the item from the Office Clipboard to the destination area.

To Copy a Range of Cells to a Nonadjacent Destination Area

The following steps use the Copy and Paste buttons to copy the range A9:A13 to the nonadjacent range A19:A23.

1

- Select the range A9:A13 and then click the Copy button on the Home tab on the Ribbon to copy the values and formats of the range A9:A13 to the Office Clipboard.

- Click cell A19, the top cell in the destination area (Figure 3–12).

Q&A

Why do I not need to select the entire destination area?

You are not required to select the entire destination area (range A19:A23) before clicking the Paste button. Excel needs to know only the upper-left cell of the destination area. In the case of a single column range, such as A19:A23, the top cell of the destination area (cell A19) also is the upper-left cell of the destination area.

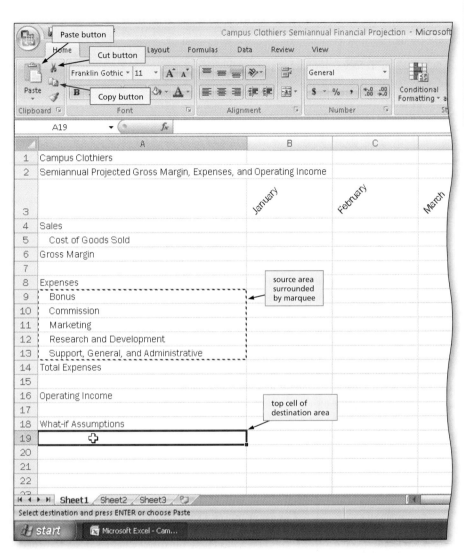

Figure 3–12

2

- Click the Paste button on the Ribbon to copy the values and formats of the last item placed on the Office Clipboard (range A9:A13) to the destination area A19:A23.

- Scroll down so row 5 appears at the top of the window (Figure 3–13).

 Q&A

What if data already existed in the destination area?

When you complete a copy, the values and formats in the destination area are replaced with the values and formats of the source area. Any data contained in the destination area prior to the copy and paste is lost. If you accidentally delete valuable data, immediately click the Undo button on the Quick Access Toolbar.

3

- Press the ESC key to remove the marquee from the source area and disable the Paste button on the Ribbon.

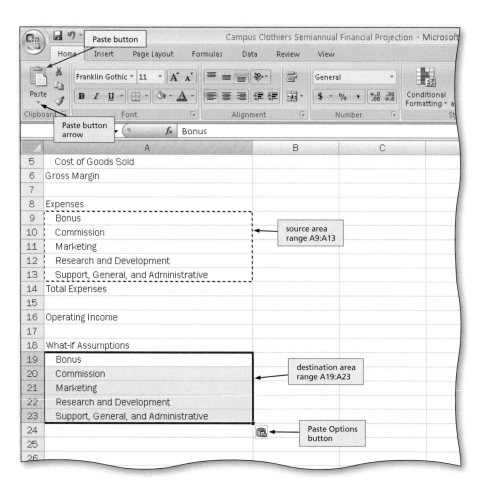

Figure 3–13

Using the Paste Options Menu

After the Paste button is clicked, Excel immediately displays the Paste Options button, as shown in Figure 3–13. If you click the Paste Options button arrow and select an option on the Paste Options menu, Excel modifies the most recent paste operation based on your selection. Table 3–4 summarizes the options available on the Paste Options menu.

Table 3–4 Options Available on the Paste Options Menu	
Paste Option	**Description**
Keep Source Formatting	Copy contents and format of source area. This option is the default.
Match Destination Formatting	Copy contents of source area, but not the format.
Values and Number Formatting	Copy contents and format of source area for numbers or formulas, but use format of destination area for text.
Keep Source Column Widths	Copy contents and format of source area. Change destination column widths to source column widths.
Formatting Only	Copy format of source area, but not the contents.
Link Cells	Copy contents and format and link cells so that a change to the cells in source area updates the corresponding cells in destination area.

The Paste button on the Ribbon (Figure 3–13) includes an arrow, which displays a list of advanced paste options (Paste, Paste Special, and Paste Hyperlink). These options will be discussed when they are used.

An alternative to clicking the Paste button is to press the ENTER key. The ENTER key completes the paste operation, removes the marquee from the source area, and disables the Paste button so that you cannot paste the copied source area to other destination areas. The ENTER key was not used in the previous set of steps so that the capabilities of the Paste Options button could be discussed. The Paste Options button does not appear on the screen when you use the ENTER key to complete the paste operation.

Using Drag and Drop to Move or Copy Cells

You also can use the mouse to move or copy cells. First, you select the source area and point to the border of the cell or range. You know you are pointing to the border of the cell or range when the mouse pointer changes to a block arrow. To move the selected cell or cells, drag the selection to the destination area. To copy a selection, hold down the CTRL key while dragging the selection to the destination area. You know Excel is in copy mode when a small plus sign appears next to the block arrow mouse pointer. Be sure to release the mouse button before you release the CTRL key. Using the mouse to move or copy cells is called **drag and drop**.

Using Cut and Paste to Move Cells

Another way to move cells is to select them, click the Cut button on the Ribbon (Figure 3–12 on page EX 175) to remove them from the worksheet and copy them to the Office Clipboard, select the destination area, and then click the Paste button on the Ribbon or press the ENTER key. You also can use the Cut command on the shortcut menu, instead of the Cut button.

Inserting and Deleting Cells in a Worksheet

At any time while the worksheet is on the screen, you can insert cells to enter new data or delete cells to remove unwanted data. You can insert or delete individual cells; a range of cells, rows, columns; or entire worksheets.

To Insert a Row

The Insert command on the shortcut menu allows you to insert rows between rows that already contain data. According to the sketch of the worksheet in Figure 3–3a on page EX 166, two rows must be inserted in the What-If Assumptions table, one between Commission and Marketing for the Margin assumption and another between Research and Development and Support, General, and Administrative for the Revenue for Bonus assumption. The following steps accomplish the task of inserting the new rows into the worksheet.

* Right-click row heading 21, the row below where you want to insert a row, to display the shortcut menu and the Mini toolbar (Figure 3–14).

Figure 3–14

* Click Insert on the shortcut menu to insert a new row in the worksheet by shifting the selected row 21 and all rows below it down one row.

* Click cell A21 in the new row and then enter Margin as the row title (Figure 3-15).

Q&A

What is the resulting format of the new row?

The cells in the new row inherit the formats of the cells in the row above them. You can change this by clicking the Insert Options button that appears immediately above the inserted row. Following the insertion of a row, the Insert Options button lets you select from the following options: (1) Format Same As Above; (2) Format Same As Below; and (3) Clear Formatting. The Format Same as Above option is the default. The Insert Options button remains active until you begin the next Excel operation.

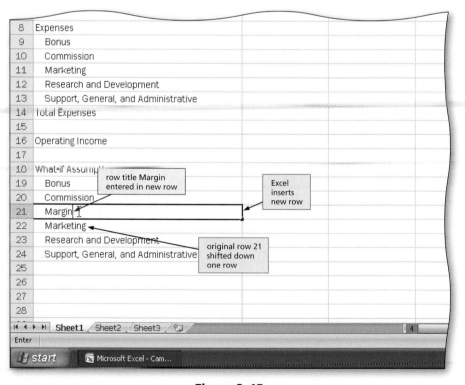

Figure 3–15

3

- Right-click row heading 24 and then click Insert on the shortcut menu to insert a new row in the worksheet.

- Click cell A24 in the new row and then enter `Revenue for Bonus` as the row title (Figure 3–16).

Q&A

What would happen if cells in the shifted rows are included in formulas?

If the rows that are shifted down include cell references in formulas located in the worksheet, Excel automatically adjusts the cell references in the formulas to their new locations. Thus, in Step 2, if a formula in the worksheet references a cell in row 21 before the insert, then the cell reference in the formula is adjusted to row 22 after the insert.

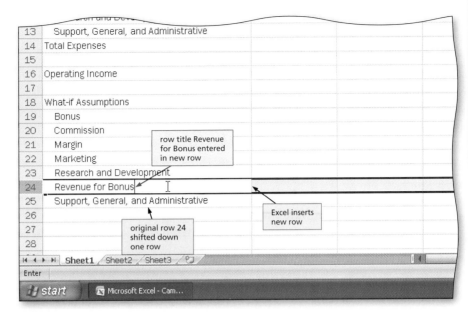

Figure 3–16

Other Ways
1. On Home tab on Ribbon, click Insert, click Insert Sheet Rows
2. Press CTRL+SHIFT+PLUS SIGN, click Entire Row, click OK button

Inserting Columns

You insert columns into a worksheet in the same way you insert rows. To insert columns, select one or more columns immediately to the right of where you want Excel to insert the new column or columns. Select the number of columns you want to insert. Next, click the Insert tab on the Ribbon and then click Insert Sheet Rows in the Insert gallery or click Insert on the shortcut menu. The Insert command on the shortcut menu requires that you select an entire column (or columns) to insert a column (or columns). Following the insertion of a column, Excel displays the Insert Options button, which allows you to modify the insertion in a fashion similar to that discussed earlier when inserting rows.

Inserting Single Cells or a Range of Cells

The Insert command on the shortcut menu or the Cells command on the Insert gallery of the Insert button on the Ribbon allows you to insert a single cell or a range of cells. You should be aware that if you shift a single cell or a range of cells, however, it no longer may be lined up with its associated cells. To ensure that the values in the worksheet do not get out of order, it is recommended that you insert only entire rows or entire columns. When you insert a single cell or a range of cells, Excel displays the Insert Options button so that you can change the format of the inserted cell, using options similar to those for inserting rows and columns.

BTW

Dragging Ranges
You can move and insert a selected cell or range between existing cells by holding down the SHIFT key while you drag the selection to the gridline where you want to insert. You also can copy and insert by holding down the CTRL+SHIFT keys while you drag the selection to the desired gridline.

BTW

The Insert Options Button
When you insert columns or rows, Excel only displays the Insert Options button if formats are assigned to the leftmost column or top row of the selection.

Deleting Columns and Rows

The Delete button on the Ribbon or the Delete command on the shortcut menu removes cells (including the data and format) from the worksheet. Deleting cells is not the same as clearing cells. The Clear command, which was described earlier in Chapter 1 on page EX 66, clears the data from the cells, but the cells remain in the worksheet. The Delete command removes the cells from the worksheet and shifts the remaining rows up (when you delete rows) or shifts the remaining columns to the left (when you delete columns). If formulas located in other cells reference cells in the deleted row or column, Excel does not adjust these cell references. Excel displays the error message **#REF!** in those cells to indicate a cell reference error. For example, if cell A7 contains the formula =A4+A5 and you delete row 5, Excel assigns the formula =A4+#REF! to cell A6 (originally cell A7) and displays the error message #REF! in cell A6. It also displays an Error Options button when you select the cell containing the error message #REF!, which allows you to select options to determine the nature of the problem.

Deleting Individual Cells or a Range of Cells

Although Excel allows you to delete an individual cell or range of cells, you should be aware that if you shift a cell or range of cells on the worksheet, it no longer may be lined up with its associated cells. For this reason, it is recommended that you delete only entire rows or entire columns.

Entering Numbers with Format Symbols

The next step in creating the Semiannual Financial Projection worksheet is to enter the what-if assumptions values in the range B19:B25. The numbers in the table can be entered and then formatted as in Chapters 1 and 2, or each one can be entered with format symbols. When a number is entered with a **format symbol**, Excel immediately displays it with the assigned format. Valid format symbols include the dollar sign ($), comma (,), and percent sign (%).

If you enter a whole number, it appears without any decimal places. If you enter a number with one or more decimal places and a format symbol, Excel displays the number with two decimal places. Table 3–5 illustrates several examples of numbers entered with format symbols. The number in parentheses in column 4 indicates the number of decimal places.

Table 3–5 Numbers Entered with Format Symbols			
Format Symbol	**Typed in Formula Bar**	**Displays in Cell**	**Comparable Format**
,	83,341	83,341	Comma (0)
	1,675.8	1,675.80	Comma (2)
$	$278	$278	Currency (0)
	$3818.54	$3,818.54	Currency (2)
	$45,612.3	$45,612.30	Currency (2)
%	23%	23%	Percent (0)
	97.50%	97.50%	Percent (2)
	39.833%	39.83%	Percent (2)

To Enter Numbers with Format Symbols

The following step enters the numbers in the What-If Assumptions table with format symbols.

- Enter 100,000.00 in cell B19, 3.25% in cell B20, 61.00% in cell B21, 9.00% in cell B22, 5.75% in cell B23, 4,750,000.00 in cell B24, and 17.00% in cell B25 to display the entries using a format based on the format symbols entered with the numbers (Figure 3–17).

Figure 3–17

Other Ways

1. Right-click range, click Format Cells on shortcut menu, click Number tab, click category in Category list, [select desired format], click OK button

2. Press CTRL+1, click Number tab, click category in Category list, [select desired format], click OK button

Freezing Worksheet Titles

Freezing worksheet titles is a useful technique for viewing large worksheets that extend beyond the window. Normally, when you scroll down or to the right, the column titles in row 3 and the row titles in column A that define the numbers no longer appear on the screen. This makes it difficult to remember what the numbers in these rows and columns represent. To alleviate this problem, Excel allows you to **freeze the titles**, so that Excel displays the titles on the screen, no matter how far down or to the right you scroll.

BTW

Freezing Titles
If you want to freeze only column headings, select the appropriate cell in column A before you click the Freeze Panes button on the View tab on the Ribbon. If you only want to freeze row titles, then select the appropriate cell in row 1. To freeze both column headings and row titles, select the cell that is the intersection of the column and row titles before you click the Freeze Panes button on the View tab on the Ribbon.

To Freeze Column and Row Titles

The following steps use the Freeze Panes button on the View tab on the Ribbon to freeze the worksheet title and column titles in rows 1, 2, and 3, and the row titles in column A.

- Press CTRL+HOME to select cell A1 and ensure that Excel displays row 1 and column A on the screen.

- Select cell B4.

- Click the View tab on the Ribbon and then click the Freeze Panes button on the Ribbon to display the Freeze Panes gallery (Figure 3–18).

Figure 3–18

Q&A Why is cell A1 selected first?

Before freezing the titles, it is important that Excel displays cell A1 in the upper-left corner of the screen. For example, if cell B4 was selected without first selecting cell A1 to ensure Excel displays the upper-left corner of the screen, then Excel would freeze the titles and also hide rows 1 and 2. Excel thus would not be able to display rows 1 and 2 until they are unfrozen.

- Click Freeze Panes in the Freeze Panes gallery to freeze column A and rows 1 through 3 (Figure 3–19).

Q&A What happens after I click the Freeze Panes command?

Excel displays a thin black line on the right side of column A, indicating the split between the frozen row titles in column A and the rest of the worksheet. It also displays a thin black line below row 3, indicating the split between the frozen column titles in rows 1 through 3 and the rest of the worksheet (Figure 3–19).

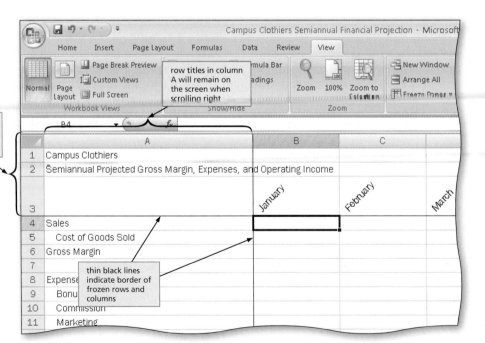

Figure 3–19

To Enter the Projected Monthly Sales

The following steps enter the projected monthly sales, listed earlier in Table 3–1 on page EX 167, in row 4 and compute the projected semiannual sales in cell H4.

1 If necessary, click the Home tab on the Ribbon.

2 Enter 3383909.82 in cell B4, 6880576.15 in cell C4, 9742702.37 in cell D4, 4818493.53 in cell E4, 4566722.63 in cell F4, and 8527504.39 in cell G4.

3 Click cell H4 and then click the Sum button on the Ribbon twice to total the semiannual sales in cell H4 (Figure 3–20).

BTW

Your Age in Days
How many days have you been alive? Enter today's date (e.g., 12/5/2008) in cell A1. Next, enter your birth date (e.g., 6/22/1986) in cell A2. Select cell A3 and enter the formula =A1 - A2. Format cell A3 to the General style using the Number Dialog Box Launcher. Cell A3 will display your age in days.

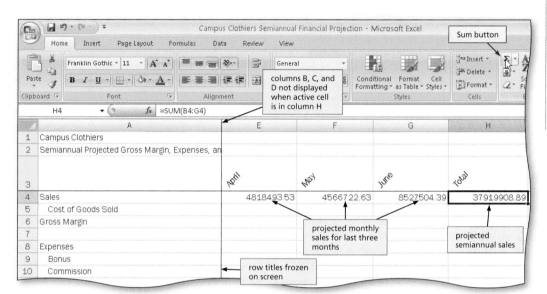

Figure 3–20

Displaying a System Date

The sketch of the worksheet in Figure 3–3a on page EX 166 includes a date stamp on the right side of the heading section. A **date stamp** shows the date a workbook, report, or other document was created or the period it represents. In business, a report often is meaningless without a date stamp. For example, if a printout of the worksheet in this chapter were distributed to the company's analysts, the date stamp would show when the six-month projections were made, as well as what period the report represents.

A simple way to create a date stamp is to use the NOW function to enter the system date tracked by your computer in a cell in the worksheet. The **NOW function** is one of 14 date and time functions available in Excel. When assigned to a cell, the NOW function returns a number that corresponds to the system date and time beginning with December 31, 1899. For example, January 1, 1900 equals 1, January 2, 1900 equals 2, and so on. Noon equals .5. Thus, noon on January 1, 1900 equals 1.5 and 6 P.M. on January 1, 1900 equals 1.75. If the computer's system date is set to the current date, which normally it is, then the date stamp is equivalent to the current date.

Excel automatically formats this number as a date, using the date and time format, mm/dd/yyyy hh:mm, where the first mm is the month, dd is the day of the month, yyyy is the year, hh is the hour of the day, and mm is the minutes past the hour.

BTW

Updating the System Date and Time
If the system date and time appear in an active worksheet, Excel will not update the date and time in the cell until you enter data in another cell or complete some other activity, such as undoing a previous activity or pressing function key F9.

To Enter and Format the System Date

The following steps enter the NOW function and change the format from mm/dd/yyyy hh:mm to mm/dd/yyyy.

- Click cell H2 and then click the Insert Function box in the formula bar.

- When Excel displays the Insert Function dialog box, click the 'Or select a category' box arrow, and then select Date & Time in the list.

- Scroll down in the Select a function list and then click NOW (Figure 3–21).

Figure 3–21

- Click the OK button.

- When Excel displays the Function Arguments dialog box, click the OK button to display the system date and time in cell H2, using the default date and time format mm/dd/yyyy hh:mm.

- Right-click cell H2 to display the shortcut menu (Figure 3–22).

Figure 3–22

3

- Click Format Cells on the shortcut menu.

- When Excel displays the Format Cells dialog box, if necessary, click the Number tab.

- Click Date in the Category list. Scroll down in the Type list and then click 3/14/2001 to display a sample of the data in the active cell (H2) using the selected format in the Sample area (Figure 3–23).

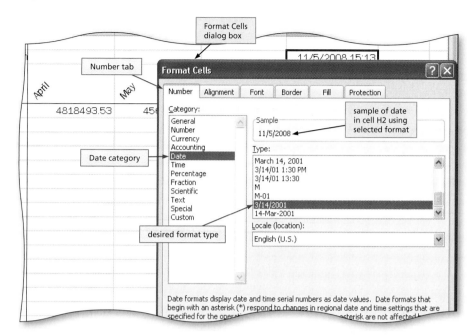

Figure 3–23

4

- Click the OK button in the Format Cells dialog box to display the system date in the form mm/dd/yyyy (Figure 3–24).

Q&A

How does Excel format a date?

In Figure 3–24, the date is displayed right-aligned in the cell because Excel treats a date as a number formatted to display as a date. If you assign the General format (Excel's default format for numbers) to a date in a cell, the date is displayed as a number with two decimal places. For example, if the system time and date is 6:00 PM on December 28, 2007 and the cell containing the NOW function is assigned the General format, then Excel displays the following number in the cell:

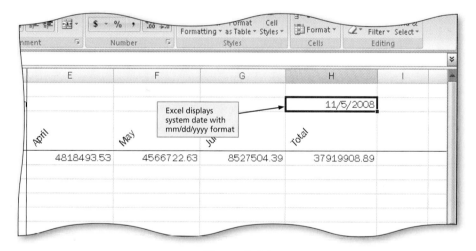

Figure 3–24

$$39444.75$$

| Number of days since December 31, 1899 | time of day is 6:00 PM (portion of day complete) |

The whole number portion of the number (39444) represents the number of days since December 31, 1899. The decimal portion of the number (.75) represents 6:00 PM as the time of day, at which point 3/4 of the day is complete. To assign the General format to a cell, click General in the Category list in the Format Cells dialog box (Figure 3–23).

Other Ways

1. On Formulas tab on Ribbon, click Date & Time, click NOW

2. Press CTRL+SEMICOLON (not a volatile date)

3. Press CTRL+SHIFT+# to format date to day-month-year

Absolute versus Relative Addressing

The next sections describe the formulas and functions needed to complete the calculations in the worksheet.

Plan Ahead

Determine necessary formulas and functions needed.

The next step is to enter the formulas that calculate the following values for January: cost of goods sold (cell B5), gross margin (cell B6), expenses (range B9:B13), total expenses (cell B14), and the operating income (cell B16). The formulas are based on the projected monthly sales in cell B4 and the assumptions in the range B19:B25.

The formulas for each column (month) are the same, except for the reference to the projected monthly sales in row 4, which varies according to the month (B4 for January, C4 for February, and so on). Thus, the formulas for January can be entered in column B and then copied to columns C through G. Table 3–6 shows the formulas for determining the January costs of goods, gross margin, expenses, total expenses, and operating income in column B.

If the formulas are entered as shown in Table 3–6 in column B for January and then copied to columns C through G (February through June) in the worksheet, Excel will adjust the cell references for each column automatically. Thus, after the copy, the February Commission expense in cell C10 would be =C4 * C20. While the cell reference C4 (February Sales) is correct, the cell reference C20 references an empty cell. The formula for cell C7 should read =C4 * B20, rather than =C4 * C20, because B20 references the Commission % value in the What-If Assumptions table. In this instance, a way is needed to keep a cell reference in a formula the same, or constant, when it is copied.

Table 3–6 Formulas for Determining Cost of Goods, Margin, Expenses, Total Expenses, and Operating Income for January

Cell	Row Title	Formula	Comment
B5	Cost of Goods Sold	=B4 * (1 − B21)	Sales times (1 minus Margin %)
B6	Gross Margin	= B4 − B5	Sales minus Cost of Goods
B9	Bonus	=IF(B4 >= B24, B19, 0)	Bonus equals value in B19 or 0
B10	Commission	=B4 * B20	Sales times Commission %
B11	Marketing	=B4 * B22	Sales times Marketing %
B12	Research and Development	=B4 * B23	Sales times Research and Development %
B13	Support, General, and Administrative	=B4 * B25	Sales times Support, General, and Administrative %
B14	Total Expenses	=SUM(B9:B13)	Sum of January Expenses
B16	Operating Income	=B6 − B14	Gross Margin minus Total Expense

BTW

Absolute Referencing
Absolute referencing is one of the more difficult worksheet concepts to understand. One point to keep in mind is that the paste operation is the only operation affected by an absolute cell reference. An absolute cell reference instructs the paste operation to keep the same cell reference as it copies a formula from one cell to another.

To keep a cell reference constant when copying a formula or function, Excel uses a technique called absolute cell referencing. To specify an absolute cell reference in a formula, enter a dollar sign ($) before any column letters or row numbers you want to keep constant in formulas you plan to copy. For example, B20 is an absolute cell reference, while B20 is a relative cell reference. Both reference the same cell. The difference becomes apparent when they are copied to a destination area. A formula using the **absolute cell reference** B20 instructs Excel to keep the cell reference B20 constant (absolute) in the formula as it copies it to the destination area. A formula using the **relative cell reference** B20 instructs Excel to adjust the cell reference as it copies it to the destination area. A cell reference with only one dollar sign before either the column or the row is called a **mixed cell reference**. Table 3–7 gives some additional examples of absolute, relative, and mixed cell references.

Table 3–7 Examples of Absolute, Relative, and Mixed Cell References		
Cell Reference	**Type of Reference**	**Meaning**
B20	Absolute cell reference	Both column and row references remain the same when you copy this cell, because the cell references are absolute.
B$20	Mixed reference	This cell reference is mixed. The column reference changes when you copy this cell to another column because it is relative. The row reference does not change because it is absolute.
$B20	Mixed reference	This cell reference is mixed. The column reference does not change because it is absolute. The row reference changes when you copy this cell reference to another row because it is relative.
B20	Relative cell reference	Both column and row references are relative. When copied to another cell, both the column and row in the cell reference are adjusted to reflect the new location.

To Enter a Formula Containing Absolute Cell References

The following steps enter the cost of goods formula = B4*(1 − B21) in cell B5 using Point mode. To enter an absolute cell reference, you can type the dollar sign ($) as part of the cell reference or enter it by pressing F4 with the insertion point in or to the right of the cell reference to change to absolute.

- Press CTRL+HOME and then click cell B5.

- Type = (equal sign), click cell B4, type *(1–b21 and then press F4 to change b21 from a relative cell reference to an absolute cell reference.

- Type) to complete the formula (Figure 3–25).

Q&A

Is an absolute reference required in this formula?

No, because a mixed cell reference could have been used. The formula in cell B4 will be copied across columns, rather than down rows. So, the formula entered in cell B4 in Step 1 could have been entered as =B4*(1-$B21), rather than =B4*(1-B21). That is, the formula could have included the mixed cell reference $B21, rather than the absolute cell reference B21. When you copy a formula across columns, the row does not change anyway. The key is to ensure that column B remains constant as you copy the formula across rows. To change the absolute cell reference to a mixed cell reference, continue to press the F4 key until you get the desired cell reference.

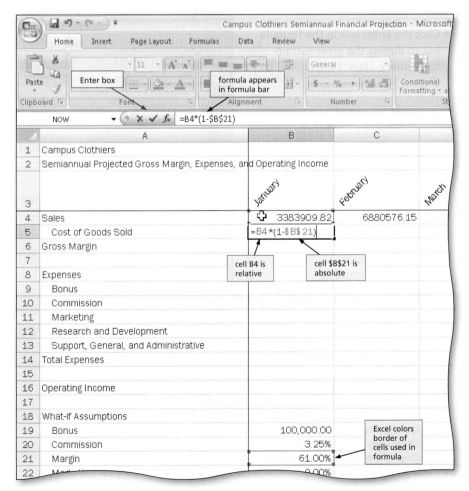

Figure 3–25

To Enter an IF Function

The following steps assign the IF function =IF(B4>=B24,B19,0) to cell B9. This IF function determines whether or not the worksheet assigns a bonus for January.

1

- Click cell B9. Type =if(b4>=b24,b19,0) in the cell (Figure 3–28).

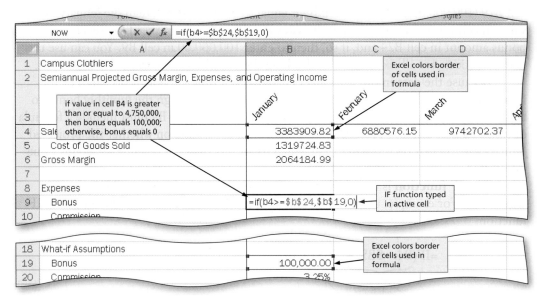

Figure 3–28

2

- Click the Enter box in the formula bar to display 0 in cell B9 (Figure 3–29), because the value in cell B4 (3383909.82) is less than the value in cell B24 (4,750,000) (Figure 3-29).

Q&A

Why does the value 0 display in cell B9?

The value that Excel displays in cell B9 depends on the values assigned to cells B4, B19, and B24. For example, if the value for January sales in cell B4 is reduced below 4,750,000.00, then the IF function in cell B9 will cause Excel to display a 0. If you change the bonus in cell B19 from 100,000.00 to another number and the value in cell B4 is greater than or equal to the value in cell B24, it will change the results in cell B9 as well. Finally, increasing the revenue for bonus in cell B24 so that it is greater than the value in cell B4 will change the result in cell B9.

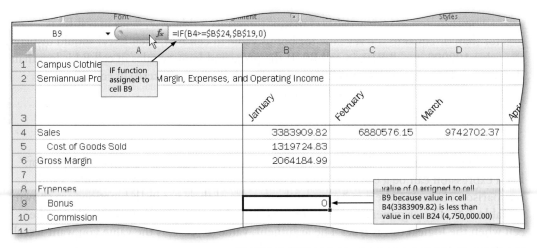

Figure 3–29

Other Ways

1. On Formulas tab on Ribbon, click Logical button, click IF

2. Click Insert Function box in formula bar, click Logical in 'Or select a category list', click IF in drop-down list, click OK button

To Enter the Remaining January Formulas

The January commission expense in cell B10 is equal to the sales in cell B4 times the commission assumption in cell B20 (3.25%). The January marketing expense in cell B11 is equal to the projected January sales in cell B4 times the marketing assumption in cell B22 (9.00%). Similar formulas determine the remaining January expenses in cells B12 and B13.

The total expenses value in cell B14 is equal to the sum of the expenses in the range B9:B13. The operating income in cell B16 is equal to the gross margin in cell B6 minus the total expenses in cell B14. The formulas are short, and therefore, they are typed in the following steps, rather than entered using Point mode.

① Click cell B10. Type =b4*b20 and then press the DOWN ARROW key. Type =b4*b22 and then press the DOWN ARROW key. Type =b4*b23 and then press the DOWN ARROW key. Type =b4*b25 and then press the DOWN ARROW key.

② With cell B14 selected, click the Sum button on the Home tab on the Ribbon twice. Click cell B16. Type =b6–b14 and then press the ENTER key (Figure 3–30a).

③ Press CTRL+ACCENT MARK (`) to instruct Excel to display the formulas version of the worksheet (Figure 3–30b).

④ When you are finished viewing the formulas version, press CTRL+ACCENT MARK (`) to instruct Excel to display the values version of the worksheet.

Q&A Why should I view the formulas version of the worksheet?

Viewing the formulas version (Figure 3–30b) of the worksheet allows you to check the formulas assigned to the range B5:B16. Recall that formulas were entered in lowercase. You can see that Excel converts all the formulas from lowercase to uppercase.

BTW

Replacing a Formula with a Constant
You can replace a formula with its result so it remains constant. Do the following: (1) Click the cell with the formula; (2) press F2 or click in the formula bar; (3) press F9 to display the value in the formula bar; and (4) press the ENTER key.

(a) Values Version

(b) Formulas Version

Figure 3–30

To Copy Formulas with Absolute Cell References Using the Fill Handle

The following steps show how to use the fill handle to copy the January formulas in column B to the other five months in columns C through G.

1

- Select the range B5:B16 and then point to the fill handle in the lower-right corner of cell B16 (Figure 3–31).

Figure 3–31

2

- Drag the fill handle to the right to select the destination area C5:G16 to copy the formulas from the source area (B5:B16) to the destination area (C5:G16) and display the calculated amounts and Auto Fill Options button (Figure 3–32).

Q&A

What happens to the formulas after the copy is made?

Because the formulas in the range B5:B16 use absolute cell references, the formulas still refer to the current values in the Assumptions table when the formulas are copied to the range C5:G16.

Q&A

What happened to columns B, C, and D?

As shown in Figure 3–32, as the fill handle is dragged to the right, columns B, C, and D no longer appear on the screen. Column A, however, remains on the screen, because the row titles were frozen earlier in this chapter.

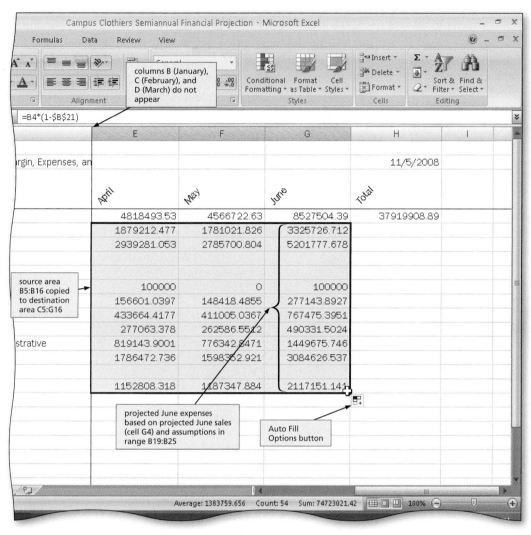

Figure 3–32

Error Messages

When Excel cannot calculate a formula, it displays an error message in a cell. These error messages always begin with a number sign (#). The more commonly occurring error messages are: #DIV/0! (tries to divide by zero); #NAME? (uses a name Excel does not recognize); #N/A (refers to a value not available); #NULL! (specifies an invalid intersection of two areas); #NUM! (uses a number incorrectly); #REF (refers to a cell that is not valid); #VALUE! (uses an incorrect argument or operand); and ##### (cell not wide enough to display entire entry).

To Determine Row Totals in Nonadjacent Cells

The following steps determine the row totals in column H. To determine the row totals using the Sum button, select only the cells in column H containing numbers in adjacent cells to the left. If, for example, you select the range H5:H16, Excel will display 0s as the sum of empty rows in cells H7, H8, and H15.

1 Select the range H5:H6. Hold down the CTRL key and select the range H9:H14 and cell H16 as shown in Figure 3–33.

2 Click the Sum button on the Ribbon to display the row totals in column H (Figure 3–33).

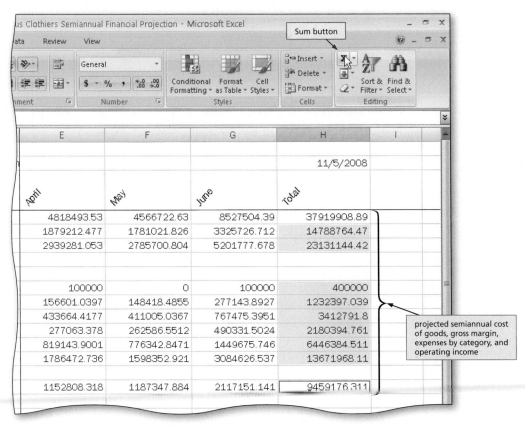

Figure 3–33

Toggle Commands

Many of the commands on the Ribbon, in the galleries, and the shortcut keys function as a toggle. For example, if you click the Freeze Panes command on the Freeze Panes gallery, the command changes to Unfreeze Panes the next time you view the gallery. These types of commands work like an on-off switch, or toggle.

To Unfreeze the Worksheet Titles and Save the Workbook

All the text, data, and formulas have been entered into the worksheet. The following steps unfreeze the titles and save the workbook using its current file name, Campus Clothiers Semiannual Financial Projection.

1 Press CTRL+HOME to select cell B4 and view the upper-left corner of the screen.

2 Click the View tab on the Ribbon and then click the Freeze Panes button on the Ribbon to display the Freeze Panes gallery (Figure 3–34).

3 Click Unfreeze Panes in the Freeze Panes gallery to unfreeze the titles.

4 Click the Home tab on the Ribbon and then click the Save button on the Quick Access Toolbar.

Q&A Why does pressing CTRL+HOME select cell B4?

When the titles are frozen and you press CTRL+HOME, Excel selects the upper-left cell of the unfrozen section of the worksheet. For example, in Step 1 of the previous steps, Excel selected cell B4. When the titles are unfrozen, then pressing CTRL+HOME selects cell A1.

BTW

Work Days

Assume that you have two dates: one in cell F3 and the other in cell F4. The date in cell F3 is your starting date and the date in cell F4 is the ending date. To calculate the work days between the two dates (excludes weekends), use the following formula: =NETWORKDAYS(F3, F4). For this function to work, make sure the Analysis ToolPak add-in is installed. You can install it on the Add-Ins page of the Excel Options dialog box.

Figure 3–34

Nested Forms of the IF Function

A **nested IF function** is one in which the action to be taken for the true or false case includes yet another IF function. The second IF function is considered to be nested, or layered, within the first. Study the nested IF function below, which determines the eligibility of a person to vote. Assume the following in this example: (1) the nested IF function is assigned to cell K12, which instructs Excel to display one of three messages in the cell; (2) cell H12 contains a person's age; and (3) cell I12 contains a Y or N, based on whether the person is registered to vote.

=IF(H12>=18, IF(I12="Y","Registered","Eligible and Not Registered"),"Not Eligible to Register")

The nested IF function instructs Excel to display one, and only one, of the following three messages in cell K12: (1) Registered; or (2) Eligible and Not Registered; or (3) Not Eligible to Register.

You can nest IF functions as deep as you want, but after you get beyond a nest of three IF functions, the logic becomes difficult to follow and alternative solutions, such as the use of multiple cells and simple IF functions, should be considered.

Formatting the Worksheet

The worksheet created thus far shows the financial projections for the six-month period, from January to June. Its appearance is uninteresting, however, even though some minimal formatting (formatting assumptions numbers, changing the column widths, and formatting the date) was performed earlier. This section will complete the formatting of the worksheet to make the numbers easier to read and to emphasize the titles, assumptions, categories, and totals.

Plan Ahead

Identify how to format various elements of the worksheet.
The worksheet will be formatted in the following manner so it appears as shown in Figure 3–35: (1) format the numbers; (2) format the worksheet title, column titles, row titles, and operating income row; and (3) format the assumptions table. Numbers in heading rows and total rows should be formatted with a currency symbol. Other dollar amounts should be formatted with a Comma style. The assumptions table should be diminished in its formatting so it does not distract from the main calculations and data in the worksheet. Assigning the data in the assumptions table a font size of 8-point would set it apart from other data formatted with a font size of 11-point.

Selecting Nonadjacent Ranges
One of the more difficult tasks to learn is selecting nonadjacent ranges. To complete this task, do not hold down the CTRL key when you select the first range because Excel will consider the current active cell to be the first selection. Once the first range is selected, hold down the CTRL key and drag through the nonadjacent ranges. If a desired range is not visible in the window, use the scroll arrows to view the range. It is not necessary to hold down the CTRL key while you scroll.

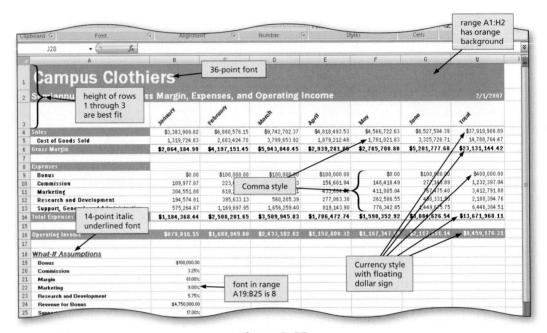

Figure 3–35

To Assign Formats to Nonadjacent Ranges

The numbers in the range B4:H16 are to be formatted as follows:

1. Assign the Currency style with a floating dollar sign to rows 4, 6, 9, 14, and 16.

2. Assign a Comma style to rows 5 and 10 through 13.

To assign a Currency style with a floating dollar sign, use the Format Cells dialog box rather than the Accounting Style button on the Ribbon, which assigns a fixed dollar sign. Also use the Format Cells dialog box to assign the Comma style, because the Comma Style button on the Ribbon assigns a format that displays a dash (-) when a cell has a value of 0. The specifications for this worksheet call for displaying a value of 0 as 0.00 (see cell B9 in Figure 3–35), rather than as a dash. To create a Comma style using the Format Cells dialog box, you can assign a Currency style with no dollar sign. The following steps assign formats to the numbers in rows 4 through 16.

- Select the range B4:H4.

- While holding down the CTRL key, select the nonadjacent ranges B6:H6, B9:H9, B14:H14, and B16:H16, and then release the CTRL key.

- Click the Format Cells: Number Dialog Box Launcher on the Ribbon to display the Format Cells dialog box (Figure 3–36).

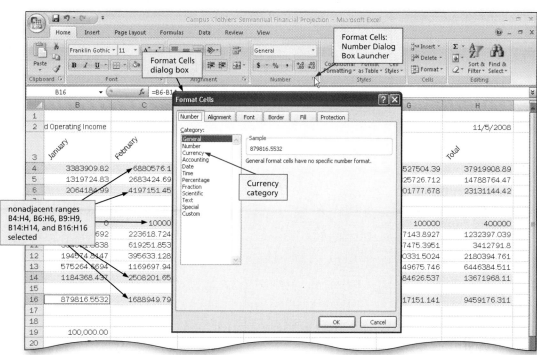

Figure 3–36

2

- Click Currency in the Category list, select 2 in the Decimal places box, click $ in the Symbol list to ensure a dollar sign shows, and click the black font color ($1,234.10) in the Negative numbers list (Figure 3–37).

Q&A

Why was the particular style chosen for the negative numbers?

In accounting, negative numbers often are shown with parentheses surrounding the value rather than with a negative sign preceding the value. Thus, the format (1,234.10) in the

Figure 3–37

Negative numbers list was clicked. The data being used in this chapter contains no negative numbers. However, you must select a format for negative numbers, and you must be consistent if you are choosing different formats in a column, otherwise the decimal points may not line up.

3

- Click the OK button.

- Select the range B5:H5.

- While holding down the CTRL key, select the range B10:H13, and then release the CTRL key.

- Click the Format Cells: Number Dialog Box Launcher on the Ribbon to display the Format Cells dialog box.

- When Excel displays the Format Cells dialog box, click Currency in the Category list, select 2 in the Decimal places box, click None in the Symbol list so a dollar sign does not show, and click the black font color (1,234.10) in the Negative numbers list (Figure 3–38).

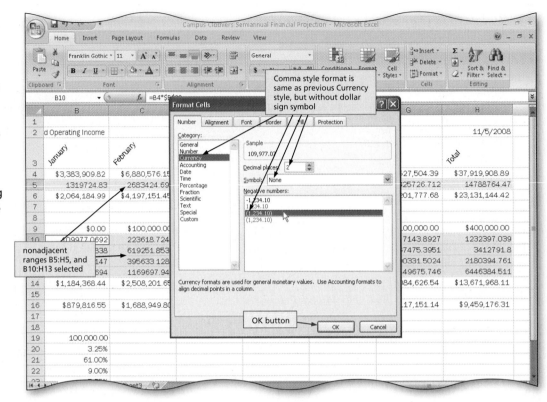

Figure 3–38

4

- Click the OK button.

- Press CTRL+HOME to select cell A1 to display the formatted numbers as shown in Figure 3–39.

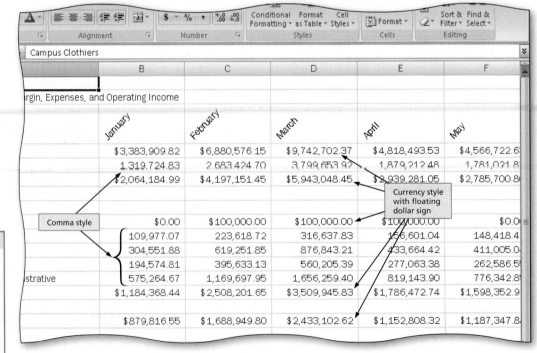

Figure 3–39

Other Ways

1. Right-click range, click Format Cells on shortcut menu, click Number tab, click category in Category list, select format, click OK button

2. Press CTRL+1, click Number tab, click category in Category list, select format, click OK button

To Format the Worksheet Titles

The following steps emphasize the worksheet titles in cells A1 and A2 by changing the font type, size, and color. The steps also format all of the row headers in column A with a Bold font style.

- Click the column A heading to select column A.

- Click the Bold button on the Ribbon to bold all of the data in column A (Figure 3–40).

Figure 3–40

- Click cell A1 to select it. Click the Font Size box arrow on the Ribbon, and then click 36 in the Font Size list.

- Click cell A2, click the Font Size box arrow, and then click 18 in the Font Size list (Figure 3–41).

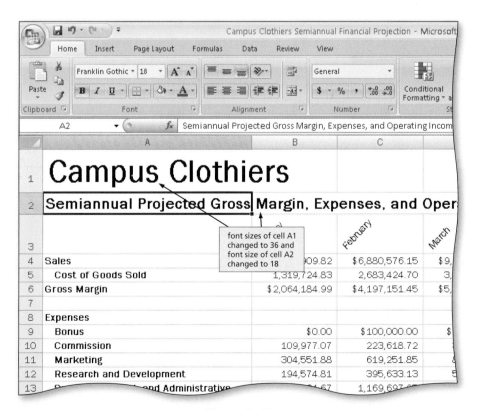

Figure 3–41

3

- Select the range A1:H2 and then click the Fill Color button arrow on the Ribbon.

- Click Orange, Accent 1 (column 5, row 1) on the Fill Color palette.

- Click the Font Color button arrow on the Ribbon and then select White, Background 1 (column 1, row 1) on the Font Color palette (Figure 3–42).

Figure 3–42

Other Ways

1. Right-click range, click Format Cells on shortcut menu, click Fill tab to color background (or click Font tab to color font), click OK button

2. Press CTRL+1, click Fill tab to color background (or click Font tab to color font), click OK button

To Assign Cell Styles to Nonadjacent Rows and Colors to a Cell

The next step to improving the appearance of the worksheet is to format the heading in row 3 and the totals in rows 4, 14, and 16. The following steps format the heading in row 3 with the Heading 3 cell style and the totals in rows 4, 14, and 16 with the Total cell style. Cell A4 also is formatted.

1 Select the range A3:H3 and apply the Heading 3 cell style.

2 Select the range A6:H6 and while holding down the CTRL key, select the ranges A14:H14 and A16:H16.

3 Apply the Total cell style.

4 Click cell A4, click the Fill Color button arrow on the Ribbon, and then click the Orange, Accent 1 color (column 5, row 1) on the Fill Color palette.

5 Click the Font Color button arrow on the Ribbon, and then click the White, Background 1 color (column 1, row 1) on the Font Color palette (Figure 3–43).

The Fill and Font Color Button

You may have noticed that the color bar at the bottom of the Fill Color and Font Color buttons on the Home tab on the Ribbon (Figure 3-42) changes to the most recently selected color. To apply this same color to a cell background or text, select a cell and then click the Fill Color button to use the color as a background or click the Font Color button to use the color as a font color.

Figure 3–43

Copying a Cell's Format Using the Format Painter Button

Using the Format Painter button on the Ribbon, you can format a cell quickly by copying a cell's format to another cell or a range of cells.

To Copy a Cell's Format Using the Format Painter Button

The following steps format cells A6, A14, and the range A16:H16 using the Format Painter button.

 1

- Select cell A4.

- Click the Format Painter button on the Ribbon and then move the mouse pointer onto the worksheet to cause the mouse pointer to change to a block plus sign with a paintbrush (Figure 3–44).

Figure 3–44

• Click cell A6 to assign the format of cell A4 to cell A6 (Figure 3–45).

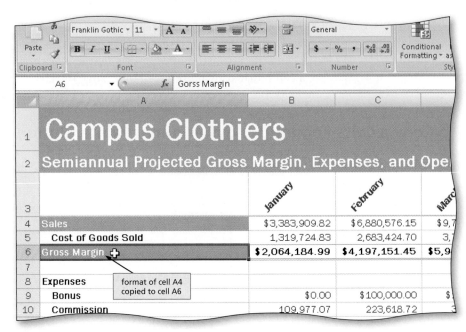

Figure 3–45

• With cell A6 selected, click the Format Painter button on the Ribbon and then click cell A14.

• With cell A14 selected, click the Format Painter button on the Ribbon and then click cell A16.

• Select the range B16:H16, click the Fill Color button on the Ribbon, and then click the Orange, Accent 1 color (column 5, row 1) on the Fill Color palette.

• Click the Font Color button on the Ribbon, and then click the Background 1 color (column 1, row 1) on the Font Color palette (Figure 3–46).

• Apply the Currency style to the range B16:G16.

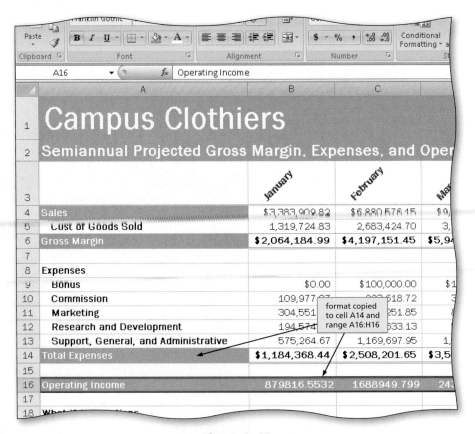

Figure 3–46

To Format the What-If Assumptions Table and Save the Workbook

The last step to improving the appearance of the worksheet is to format the What-If Assumptions table in the range A18:B25. The specifications in Figure 3–35 on page EX 196 require a 14-point italic underlined font for the title in cell A18 and 8-point font in the range A19:B25. The following steps format the What-If Assumptions table.

1 Scroll down to view rows 18 through 25 and then click cell A18.

2 Click the Font Size box arrow on the Ribbon and then click 14 in the Font Size list. Click the Italic button and then click the Underline button on the Ribbon.

3 Select the range A19:B25, click the Font Size button on the Ribbon, and then click 8 in the Font Size list.

4 Click cell D25 to deselect the range A19:B25 and display the What-If Assumptions table as shown in Figure 3–47.

5 Click the Save button on the Quick Access Toolbar.

Q&A What happens when I click the Italic and Underline buttons?

Recall that when you assign the italic font style to a cell, Excel slants the characters slightly to the right as shown in cell A18 in Figure 3–47. The **underline** format underlines only the characters in the cell, rather than the entire cell, as is the case when you assign a cell a bottom border.

BTW

Painting a Format to Nonadjacent Ranges
Double-click the Format Painter button on the Home tab on the Ribbon and then drag through the nonadjacent ranges to paint the formats to the ranges. Click the Format Painter button to deactivate it.

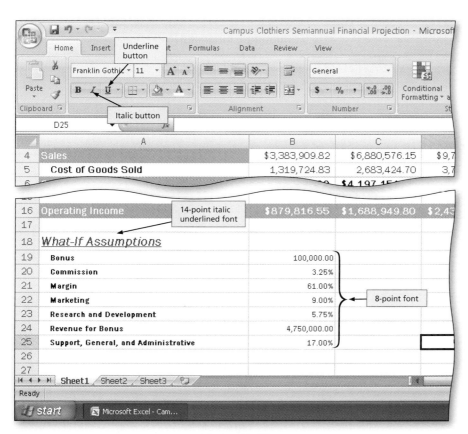

Figure 3–47

Adding a 3-D Pie Chart to the Workbook

The next step in the chapter is to draw the 3-D Pie chart on a separate sheet in the workbook, as shown in Figure 3–48. Use a **Pie chart** to show the relationship or proportion of parts to a whole. Each slice (or wedge) of the pie shows what percent that slice contributes to the total (100%).

> **Specify how the chart should convey necessary information.**
> The 3-D Pie chart in Figure 3–48 shows the contribution of each month's projected operating income to the six-month projected operating income. The 3-D Pie chart makes it easy to evaluate the contribution of one month in comparison to the other months.
>
> Unlike the 3-D Column chart created in Chapter 1, the 3-D Pie chart shown in Figure 3–48 is not embedded in the worksheet. Instead, the Pie chart resides on a separate sheet, called a **chart sheet**, which contains only the chart.
>
> In this worksheet, the ranges to chart are the nonadjacent ranges B3:G3 (month names) and B16:G16 (monthly operating incomes). The month names in the range B3:G3 will identify the slices of the Pie chart; these entries are called **category names**. The range B16:G16 contains the data that determines the size of the slices in the pie; these entries are called the **data series**. Because six months are being charted, the 3-D Pie chart contains six slices.
>
> The sketch of the 3-D Pie chart in Figure 3–3b on page EX 166 also calls for emphasizing the month of June by offsetting its slice from the main portion. A Pie chart with one or more slices offset is called an **exploded Pie chart**.

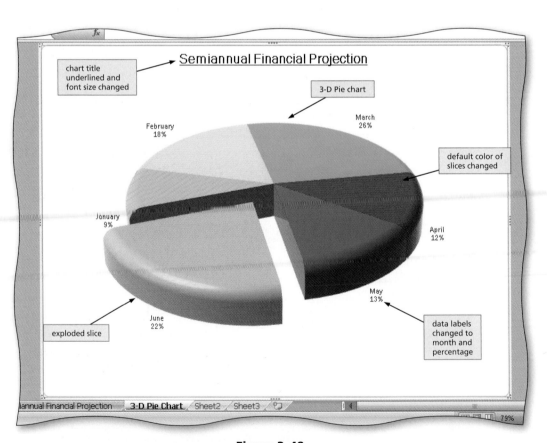

Figure 3–48

As shown in Figure 3–48, the default 3-D Pie chart also has been enhanced by rotating it, changing the colors of the slices, adding a bevel, and modifying the chart title and labels that identify the slices.

To Draw a 3-D Pie Chart on a Separate Chart Sheet

The following steps draw the 3-D Pie chart on a separate chart sheet.

- Select the range B3:G3.

- While holding down the CTRL key, select the range B16:G16.

- Click the Insert tab on the Ribbon.

- Click the Pie button on the Ribbon to display the Pie gallery (Figure 3–49).

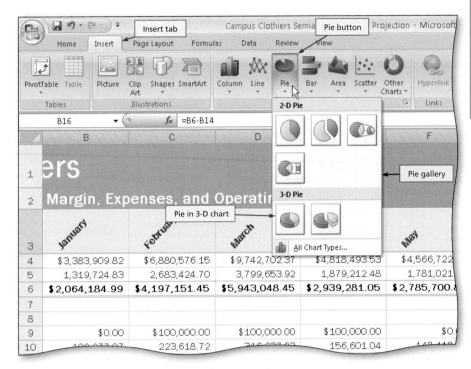

Figure 3–49

2

- Click Pie in 3-D chart in the Pie gallery.

- When Excel draws the chart, click the Move Chart button on the Ribbon to display the Move Chart dialog box (Figure 3–50).

Figure 3–50

- Click the New sheet option button and then type `3-D Pie Chart` in the New sheet name textbox.

- Click the OK button to move the chart to a new chart sheet with the name 3-D Pie Chart (Figure 3–51).

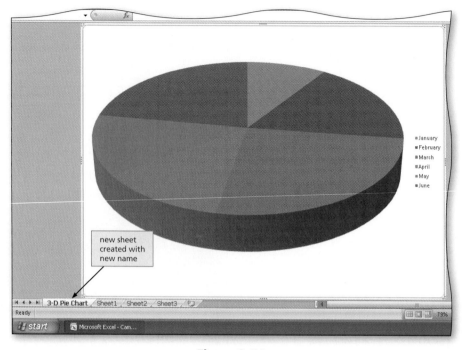

Figure 3–51

Other Ways

1. Select range to chart, press F11

To Insert a Chart Title and Data Labels

The next step is to insert a chart title and labels that identify the slices. Before you can format a chart item, such as the chart title or data labels, you must select it. You can format a selected chart item using the Ribbon or shortcut menu. The following steps insert a chart title, remove the legend, and add data labels.

- Click anywhere in the chart area outside the chart.

- Click the Layout tab on the Ribbon and then click the Chart Title button.

- Click the Centered Overlay Title command in the Chart Title gallery.

- Select the text in the chart title and then type `Semiannual Financial Projection` as the new chart title (Figure 3–52).

Figure 3–52

- Select the text in the new title and then click the Home tab on the Ribbon.

- Click the Underline button to assign an underline font style to the chart title (Figure 3–53).

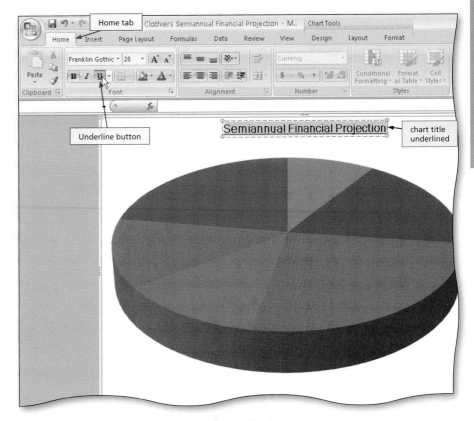

Figure 3–53

3

- Click the Layout tab on the Ribbon and then click the Legend button to display the Legend gallery.

- Point to None in the Legend gallery (Figure 3–54).

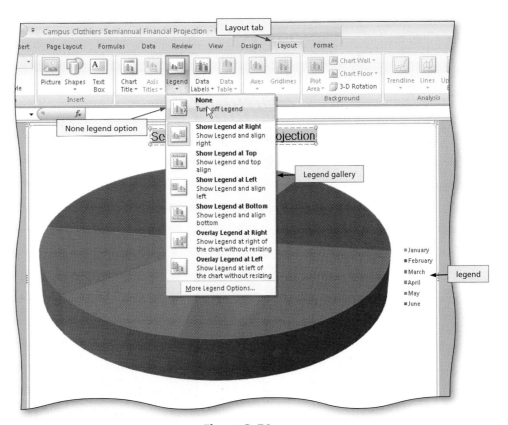

Figure 3–54

4

- Click None to turn off the legend on the chart.

- Click the Data Labels button on the Ribbon and then click Outside End in the Data Labels gallery to display data labels outside the chart at the end of each slice (Figure 3–55).

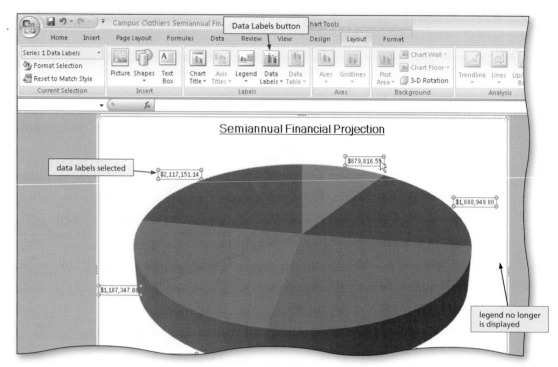

Figure 3–55

5

- If necessary, right-click any data label to select all of the data labels on the chart and to display the shortcut menu.

- Click the Format Data Labels command on the short-cut menu to display the Format Data Labels dialog box.

- If necessary, click the Series Name, Value, and Show Leader Lines check boxes to deselect them and then click the Category Name and Percentage check boxes to select them (Figure 3–56).

Figure 3–56

6

- Click the Close button to close the Format Data Labels dialog box and display the chart as shown in Figure 3–57.

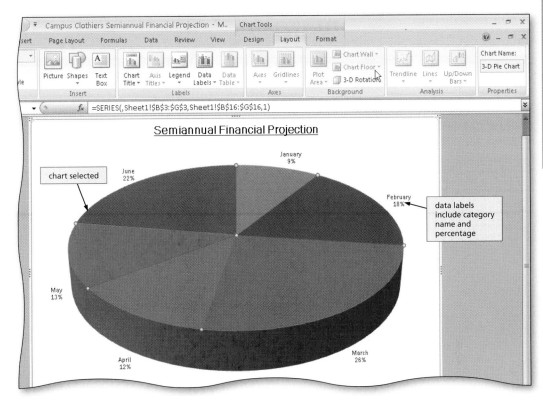

Figure 3–57

To Rotate the 3-D Pie Chart

With a three-dimensional chart, you can change the view to better show the section of the chart you are trying to emphasize. Excel allows you to control the rotation angle, elevation, perspective, height, and angle of the axes by using the Format Chart Area dialog box.

When Excel initially draws a Pie chart, it always positions the chart so that one of the dividing lines between two slices is a straight line pointing to 12 o'clock (or 0°). As shown in Figure 3–57, the line that divides the January and June slices currently is set to 0°. This line defines the rotation angle of the 3-D Pie chart.

To obtain a better view of the offset June slice, the 3-D Pie chart can be rotated 250° to the right. The following steps show how to rotate the 3-D Pie chart.

1

- Click the 3-D Rotation button on the Ribbon to display the Format Chart Area dialog box.

- Click the Increase X Rotation button in the Rotation area of the Format Chart Area dialog box until the X rotation is at 250° (Figure 3–58).

Q&A

What happens as I click the Increase X Rotation button?

Excel rotates the chart 10° in a clockwise direction each time you click the Increase X Rotation button. The Y box in the Rotation area allows you to control the tilt, or elevation, of the chart. You can tilt the chart towards or away from your view in order to enhance the view of the chart.

Figure 3–58

2

- Click the Close button in the Format Chart Area dialog box to display the rotated chart (Figure 3–59).

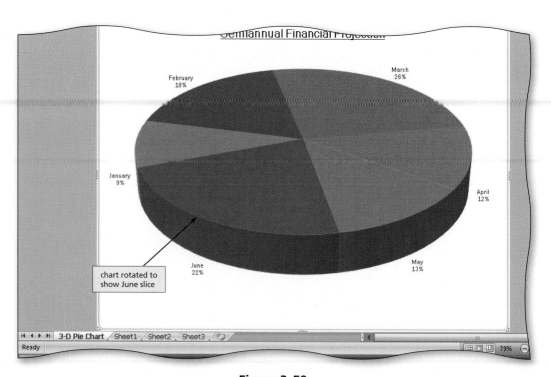

Figure 3–59

To Apply a 3-D Format to the Pie Chart

Excel allows you to apply dramatic 3-D visual effects to charts. The chart shown in Figure 3–59 could be enhanced with a bevel along the top edge. A bevel is a curve that is applied to soften the appearance of a straight edge. Excel also allows you to change the appearance of the material from which the surface of the chart appears to be constructed. The following steps apply a bevel to the chart and change the surface of the chart to a softer-looking material.

1

- Right-click the chart to display the shortcut menu (Figure 3–60).

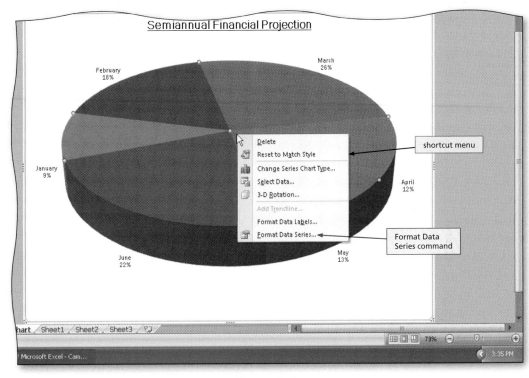

Figure 3–60

2

- Click the Format Data Series command on the shortcut menu to display the Format Data Series dialog box and then click the 3-D Format category on the left side of the dialog box.

- Click the Top button in the Bevel area to display the Bevel gallery (Figure 3–61).

Figure 3–61

3

- Click the Circle bevel button (column 1, row 1) in the Bevel gallery to add a bevel to the chart.

- Type 50 pt in the top Width box in the Bevel area of the dialog box and then type 50 pt in the uppermost Height box in the Bevel area of the dialog box to increase the width and height of the bevel on the chart (Figure 3–62).

Figure 3–62

4

- Click the Material button in the Surface area of the Format Data Series dialog box and then point to the Soft Edge button (column 2, row 2) in the Material gallery (Figure 3–63).

Figure 3–63

5
- Click the Soft Edge button and then click the Close button in the Format Data Series dialog box (Figure 3-64).

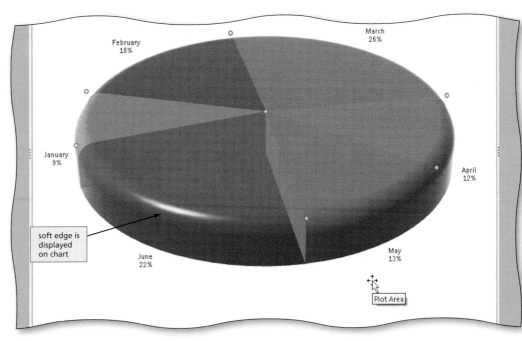

soft edge is displayed on chart

Plot Area

Figure 3–64

To Explode the 3-D Pie Chart and Change the Color of a Slice

The next step is to emphasize the slice representing June by **offsetting**, or exploding, it from the rest of the slices so that it stands out. The following steps explode a slice of the 3-D Pie chart and then change its color.

1
- Click the slice labeled June twice (do not double-click) to select only the June slice.

- Right-click the slice labeled June to display the shortcut menu and then point to Format Data Point (Figure 3–65).

- Click Format Data Point.

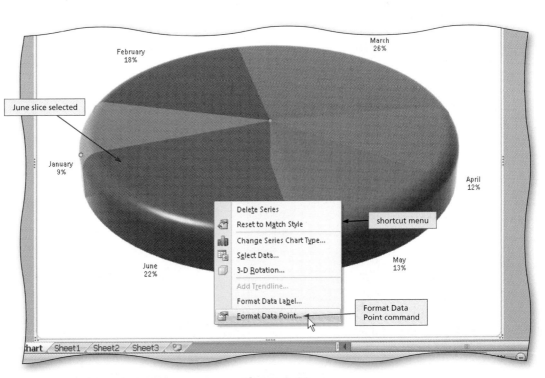

June slice selected

shortcut menu

Format Data Point command

Figure 3–65

2

- When Excel displays the Format Data Point dialog box, drag the Point Explosion slider to the right until the Point Explosion box reads 28% (Figure 3–66).

Q&A

Should I offset more slices?

You can offset as many slices as you want, but remember that the reason for offsetting a slice is to emphasize it. Offsetting multiple slices tends to reduce the impact on the reader and reduces the overall size of the Pie chart.

Figure 3–66

3

- Click the Fill category on the left side of the dialog box.

- Click the Solid fill option button and then click the Color button to display the color palette.

- Point to the Orange color in the Standard Colors area (Figure 3–67).

4

- Click the Orange color on the color palette and then click the Close button on the Format Data Point dialog box to change the color of the slice labeled June to orange.

Figure 3–67

To Change the Colors of the Remaining Slices

BTW

**Exploding a
3-D Pie Chart**
If you click the 3-D Pie
chart so that all of the
slices are selected, you can
drag one of the slices to
explode all of the slices.

The colors of the remaining slices also can be changed to enhance the appeal of the chart. The following steps change the color of the remaining fives chart slices.

1 Click the slice labeled January twice (do not double-click) to select only the January slice.

2 Right-click the slice labeled January to display the shortcut menu and then point to Format Data Point.

3 Click the Fill category on the left side of the dialog box.

4 Click the Solid fill option button and then click the Color button to display the color palette.

5 Click the Green color on the color palette and then click the Close button in the Format Data Point dialog box to change the color of the slice labeled January to green.

6 Repeat steps 1 through 5 for the remaining four slices. Assign the following colors in the Standard Colors area of the color palette to each slice: February – Yellow; March – Light Blue; April – Red; May – Blue. The completed chart appears as shown in Figure 3–68.

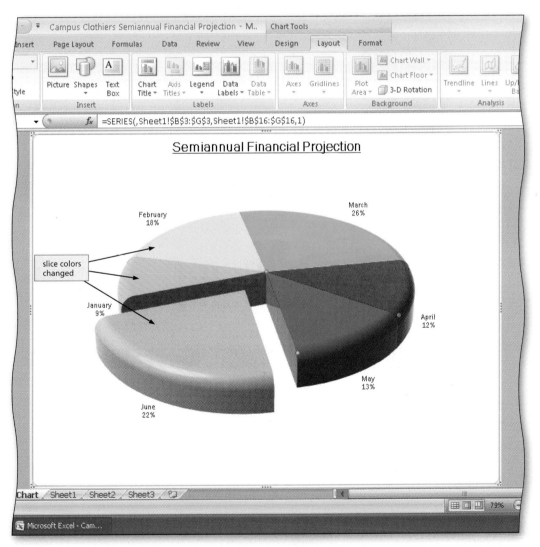

Figure 3–68

Renaming and Reordering the Sheets and Coloring Their Tabs

The final step in creating the workbook is to reorder the sheets and modify the tabs at the bottom of the screen.

To Rename and Reorder the Sheets and Color Their Tabs

The following steps rename the sheets, color the tabs, and reorder the sheets so the worksheet precedes the chart sheet in the workbook.

1

- Right-click the tab labeled 3-D Pie Chart at the bottom of the screen to display the shortcut menu.

- Point to the Tab Color command to display the color palette (Figure 3–69).

Figure 3–69

- Click Brown, Accent 2 (column 6, row 1) in the Theme Colors area to change the color of the tab to brown.

- Double-click the tab labeled Sheet1 at the bottom of the screen.

- Type Semiannual Financial Projection as the new sheet name and then press the ENTER key.

- Right-click the tab and then click Tab Color on the shortcut menu.

- Point to the Orange, Accent 1 (column 5, row 1) color in the Theme Colors area of the palette (Figure 3–70).

3

- Click Orange, Accent 1 (column 5, row 1) in the Theme Colors area to change the color of the tab to orange.

- Drag the Semiannual Financial Projection tab to the left in front of the 3-D Pie Chart tab to rearrange the sequence of the sheets and then click cell E18 (Figure 3–71).

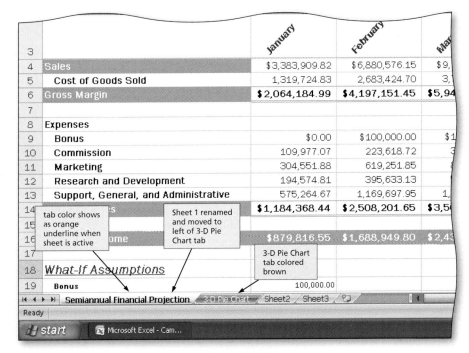

Figure 3–70

Figure 3–71

Other Ways

1. To rename sheet, right-click sheet tab, click Rename on shortcut menu
2. To move sheet, right-click sheet tab, click Move or Copy on shortcut menu

BTW

Checking Spelling
Unless you first select a range of cells or an object before starting the spell checker, Excel checks the selected worksheet, including all cell values, cell comments, embedded charts, text boxes, buttons, and headers and footers.

Checking Spelling, Saving, Previewing, and Printing the Workbook

With the workbook complete, this section checks spelling, saves, previews, and then prints the workbook. Each set of steps concludes with saving the workbook to ensure that the latest changes are saved.

To Check Spelling in Multiple Sheets

By default, the spell checker checks the spelling only in the selected sheets. It will check all the cells in the selected sheets, unless you select a range of two or more cells. Before checking the spelling, the following steps select the 3-D Pie Chart sheet so that the entire workbook is checked for spelling errors.

1 With the Semiannual Financial Projection sheet active, press CTRL+HOME to select cell A1. Hold down the CTRL key and then click the 3-D Pie Chart tab.

2 Click the Review tab on the Ribbon and then click the Spelling button on the Ribbon.

3 Correct any errors and then click the OK button when the spell check is complete.

4 Click the Save button on the Quick Access Toolbar.

BTW

Printing in Black and White
You can speed up the printing process and save ink if you print worksheets with color in black and white. To print a worksheet in black and white on a color printer, do the following: (1) Click the Page Setup Dialog Box Launcher on the Page Layout tab on the Ribbon, click the Sheet tab, and then click 'Black and white' in the Print area. (2) Click the Preview button to see that Excel has removed the colored backgrounds, click the Close button, and then click the OK button. You are now ready to print economically, in black and white.

To Preview and Print the Workbook

After checking the spelling, the next step is to preview and print the sheets. As with spelling, Excel previews and prints only the selected sheets. In addition, because the worksheet is too wide to print in portrait orientation, the orientation must be changed to landscape. The following steps adjust the orientation and scale, preview the workbook, and then print the workbook.

1 Ready the printer. If both sheets are not selected, hold down the CTRL key and then click the tab of the inactive sheet.

2 Click the Page Layout tab on the Ribbon and then click the Page Setup Dialog Box Launcher. Click the Page tab and then click Landscape. Click Fit to in the Scaling area.

3 Click the Print Preview button in the Page Setup dialog box. When the preview of the first of the selected sheets appears, click the Next Page button at the top of the Print Preview window to view the next sheet. Click the Previous Page button to redisplay the first sheet.

4 Click the Print button at the top of the Print Preview window. When Excel displays the Print dialog box, click the OK button to print the worksheet and chart (Figure 3–72).

5 Right-click the Semiannual Financial Projection tab. Click Ungroup Sheets on the shortcut menu to deselect the 3-D Pie Chart tab.

6 Click the Save button on the Quick Access Toolbar.

BTW

Quick Reference
For a table that lists how to complete the tasks covered in this book using the mouse, Ribbon, shortcut menu, and keyboard, see the Quick Reference Summary at the back of this book, or visit the Excel 2007 Quick Reference Web page (scsite.com/ex2007/qr).

(a) Worksheet

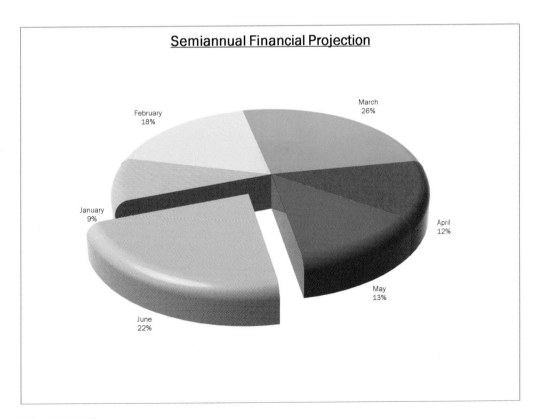

(b) 3-D Pie Chart

Figure 3–72

BTW

Zooming
You can use the Zoom In and Zoom Out buttons on the status bar to zoom from 10% to 400% to reduce or enlarge the display of the worksheet.

Changing the View of the Worksheet

With Excel, you easily can change the view of the worksheet. For example, you can magnify or shrink the worksheet on the screen. You also can view different parts of the worksheet through window panes.

To Shrink and Magnify the View of a Worksheet or Chart

You can magnify (zoom in) or shrink (zoom out) the appearance of a worksheet or chart by using the Zoom button on the View tab on the Ribbon. When you magnify a worksheet, Excel enlarges the view of the characters on the screen, but displays fewer columns and rows. Alternatively, when you shrink a worksheet, Excel is able to display more columns and rows. Magnifying or shrinking a worksheet affects only the view; it does not change the window size or printout of the worksheet or chart. The following steps shrink and magnify the view of the worksheet.

1

• If cell A1 is not active, press CTRL+HOME.

• Click the View tab on the Ribbon and then click the Zoom button on the Ribbon to display a list of Magnifications in the Zoom dialog box (Figure 3–73).

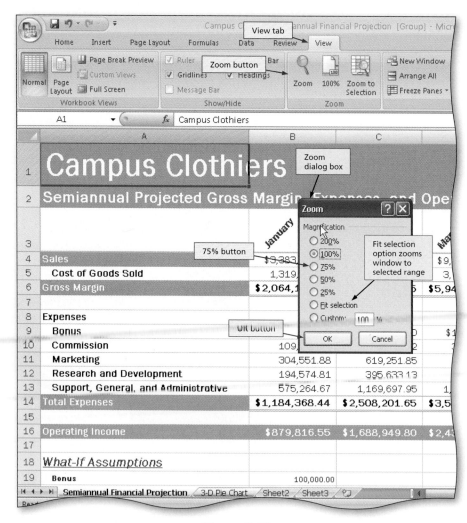

Figure 3–73

2

- Click 75% and then click the OK button to shrink the display of the worksheet to 75% of its normal display (Figure 3–74).

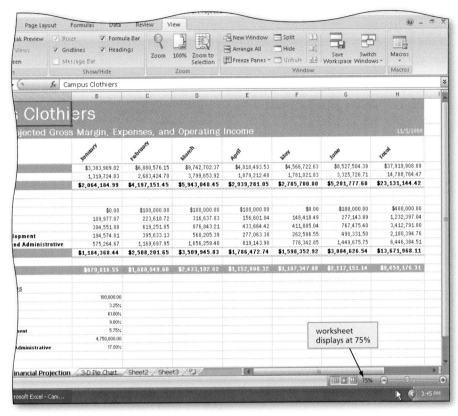

Figure 3–74

3

- Click the Zoom In button on the status bar until the worksheet displays at 100% (Figure 3–75).

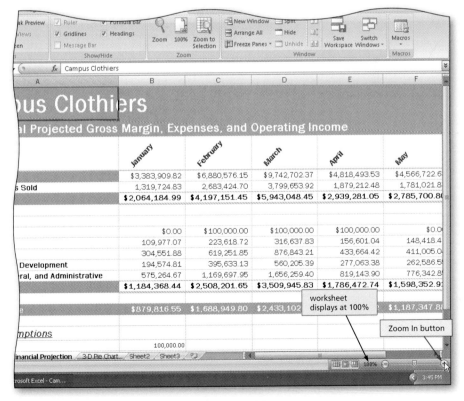

Figure 3–75

To Split a Window into Panes

When working with a large worksheet, you can split the window into two or four panes to view different parts of the worksheet at the same time. Splitting the Excel window into four panes at cell D7 allows you to view all four corners of the worksheet easily. The following steps split the Excel window into four panes.

- Select cell D7, the intersection of the four proposed panes.

- If necessary, click the View tab on the Ribbon and then point to the Split button on the Ribbon (Figure 3–76).

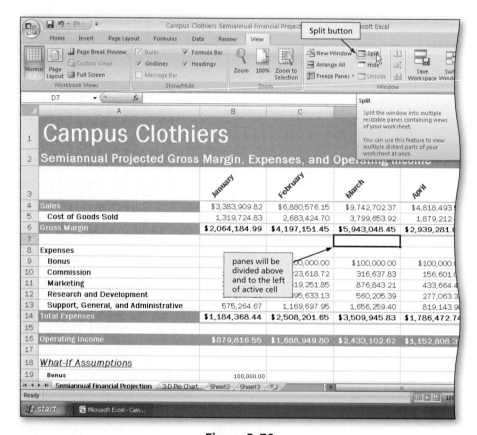

Figure 3–76

2

- Click the Split button to divide the window into four panes.

- Use the scroll arrows to show the four corners of the worksheet at the same time (Figure 3–77).

Q&A

What is shown in the four panes?

The four panes in Figure 3–77 are used to show the following: (1) range A1:C6 in the upper-left pane; (2) range G1:I6 in the upper-right pane; (3) range A14:C26 in the lower-left pane; and (4) range G14:I26 in the lower-right pane. The vertical split bar is the vertical bar going up and down the middle of the window. The horizontal split bar is the horizontal bar going across the middle of the window. If you use the scroll bars below the window and to the right of the window to scroll the window, you will see that the panes split by the horizontal split bar scroll together vertically. The panes split by the vertical split bar scroll together horizontally. To resize the panes, drag either split bar to the desired location in the window.

Figure 3–77

Other Ways

1. Drag horizontal split box and vertical split box to desired locations

To Remove the Panes from the Window

1 Position the mouse pointer at the intersection of the horizontal and vertical split bars.

2 When the mouse pointer changes to a four-headed arrow, double-click to remove the four panes from the window.

What-If Analysis

The automatic recalculation feature of Excel is a powerful tool that can be used to analyze worksheet data. Using Excel to scrutinize the impact of changing values in cells that are referenced by a formula in another cell is called **what-if analysis** or **sensitivity analysis**. When new data is entered, Excel not only recalculates all formulas in a worksheet, but also redraws any associated charts.

BTW

Window Panes

If you want to split the window into two panes, rather than four, drag the vertical split box to the far left of the window or horizontal split box to the top of the window (Figure 3-78 on the next page). You also can drag the center of the four panes in any direction to change the size of the panes.

In the workbook created in this chapter, many of the formulas are dependent on the assumptions in the range B19:B25. Thus, if you change any of the assumption values, Excel immediately recalculates all formulas. Excel redraws the 3-D Pie chart as well, because it is based on these numbers.

To Analyze Data in a Worksheet by Changing Values

A what-if question for the worksheet in Chapter 3 might be *what* would happen to the semiannual operating income in cell H16 *if* the Bonus, Commission, Support, General, and Administrative assumptions in the What-If Assumptions table are changed as follows: Bonus $100,000.00 to $75,000.00; Commission 3.25% to 2.25%; Support, General, and Administrative 17.00% to 14.50%? To answer a question like this, you need to change only the first, second, and seventh values in the What-If Assumptions table as shown in the following steps. The steps also divide the window into two vertical panes. Excel instantaneously recalculates the formulas in the worksheet and redraws the 3-D Pie chart to answer the question.

- Use the vertical scroll bar to move the window so cell A6 is in the upper-left corner of the screen.

- Drag the vertical split box from the lower-right corner of the screen to the left so that the vertical split bar is positioned as shown in Figure 3-78.

- Use the right scroll arrow to view the totals in column H in the right pane.

- Enter 75000 in cell B19, 2.25 in cell B20, and 14.50 in cell B25 (Figure 3–78), which causes the semiannual operating income in cell H16 to increase from $9,459,176.31 to $10,886,373.12.

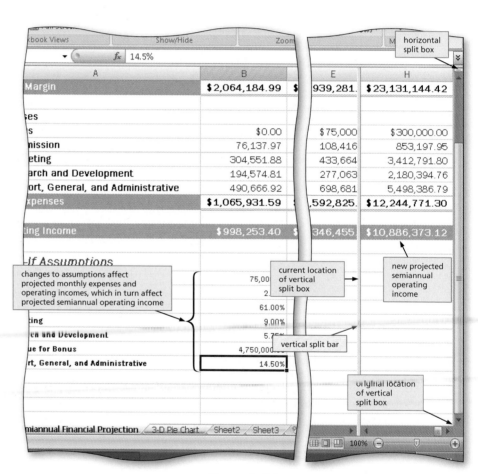

Figure 3–78

To Goal Seek

If you know the result you want a formula to produce, you can use **goal seeking** to determine the value of a cell on which the formula depends. The following steps close and reopen the Campus Clothiers Semiannual Financial Projection workbook. They then show how to use the Goal Seek command on the Data tab on the Ribbon to determine the Support, General, and Administrative percentage in cell B25 that will yield a semi annual operating income of $10,500,000 in cell H16, rather than the original $9,459,176.31.

1

- Close the workbook without saving changes and then reopen it.

- Drag the vertical split box so that the vertical split bar is positioned as shown in Figure 3–79.

- Show column H in the right pane.

- Click cell H16, the cell that contains the semiannual operating income.

- Click the Data tab on the Ribbon and then click the What-If Analysis button on the Ribbon to display the What-If Analysis menu (Figure 3–79).

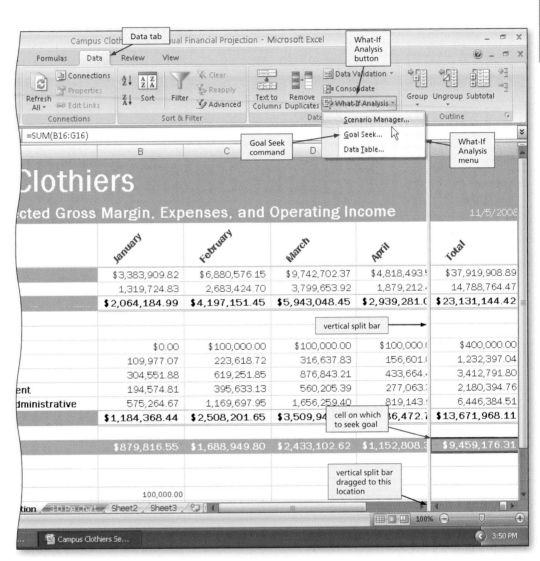

Figure 3–79

2

- Click Goal Seek to display the Goal Seek dialog box with the Set cell box set to the selected cell, H16.

- When Excel displays the Goal Seek dialog box, click the To value text box, type 10500000 and then click the By changing cell box.

- Scroll down so row 4 is at the top of the screen.

- Click cell B25 on the worksheet to assign cell B25 to the By changing cell box (Figure 3–80).

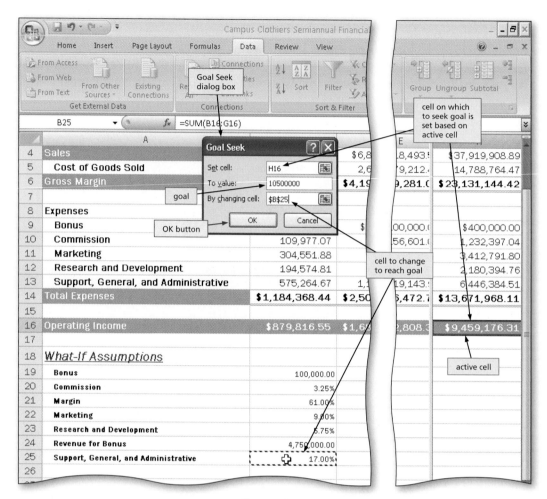

Figure 3–80

3

- Click the OK button to goal seek for the value $10,500,000.00 in cell H16 (Figure 3–81).

Q&A

What happens when I click the OK button?

Excel immediately changes cell H16 from $9,459,176.31 to the desired value of $10,500,000.00. More importantly, Excel changes the Support, General, and Administrative assumption in cell B25 from 17.00% to 14.26% (Figure 3–81). Excel also displays the Goal Seek Status dialog box. If you click the OK button, Excel keeps the new values in the worksheet. If you click the Cancel button, Excel redisplays the original values.

Figure 3–81

4

- Click the Cancel button in the Goal Seek Status dialog box.

Other Ways
1. Press ALT+T, G

Goal Seeking

Goal seeking assumes you can change the value of only one cell referenced directly or indirectly to reach a specific goal for a value in another cell. In this example, to change the semiannual operating income in cell H16 to $10,500,000.00, the Support, General, and Administrative percentage in cell B25 must decrease by 2.74% from 17.00% to 14.26%.

You can see from this goal seeking example that the cell to change (cell B25) does not have to be referenced directly in the formula or function. For example, the semiannual operating income in cell H16 is calculated by the function =SUM(B16:G16). Cell B25 is not referenced in this function. Instead, cell B25 is referenced in the formulas in rows 9 through 13, on which the monthly operating incomes in row 16 are based. Excel thus is capable of goal seeking on the semiannual operating income by varying the value for the Support, General, and Administrative assumption.

BTW

Undoing What You Did
The Undo button is ideal for returning the worksheet to its original state after you have changed the values in a worksheet to answer a what-if question. To view the original worksheet after answering a what-if question, click the Undo button on the Quick Access Toolbar for each value you changed.

To Quit Excel

To quit Excel, complete the following steps.

1 Click the Close button on the title bar.

2 If the Microsoft Excel dialog box is displayed, click the No button.

Chapter Summary

In this chapter you learned how to work with large worksheets that extend beyond the window, how to use the fill handle to create a series, new formatting techniques, about the difference between absolute cell references and relative cell references, how to use the IF function, how to rotate text in a cell, freeze titles, change the magnification of the worksheet, show different parts of the worksheet at the same time through multiple panes, create a 3-D Pie chart, and improve the appearance of a 3-D Pie chart. This chapter also introduced you to using Excel to do what-if analysis by changing values in cells and goal seeking. The items listed below include all the new Excel skills you have learned in this chapter.

1. Rotate Text and Use the Fill Handle to Create a Series of Month Names (EX 169)
2. Increase Column Widths and Enter Row Titles (EX 173)
3. Copy a Range of Cells to a Nonadjacent Destination Area (EX 175)
4. Insert a Row (EX 177)
5. Enter Numbers with Format Symbols (EX 181)
6. Freeze Column and Row Titles (EX 182)
7. Enter and Format the System Date (EX 184)
8. Enter a Formula Containing Absolute Cell References (EX 187)
9. Enter an IF Function (EX 190)
10. Copy Formulas with Absolute Cell References Using the Fill Handle (EX 192)
11. Assign Formats to Nonadjacent Ranges (EX 196)
12. Format the Worksheet Titles (EX 199)
13. Copy a Cell's Format Using the Format Painter Button (EX 201)
14. Draw a 3-D Pie Chart on a Separate Chart Sheet (EX 205)
15. Insert a Chart Title and Data Labels (EX 206)
16. Rotate the 3-D Pie Chart (EX 209)
17. Apply a 3-D Format to the Pie Chart (EX 211)
18. Explode the 3-D Pie Chart and Change the Color of a Slice (EX 213)
19. Rename and Reorder the Sheets and Color Their Tabs (EX 216)
20. Shrink and Magnify the View of a Worksheet or Chart (EX 220)
21. Split a Window into Panes (EX 222)
22. Analyze Data in a Worksheet by Changing Values (EX 224)
23. Goal Seek (EX 225)

 If you have a SAM user profile, you may have access to hands-on instruction, practice, and assessment. Log in to your SAM account (http://sam2007.course.com) to launch any assigned training activities or exams that relate to the skills covered in this chapter.

Learn It Online

Learn It Online is a series of online student exercises that test your knowledge of chapter content and key terms.

Instructions: To complete the Learn It Online exercises, start your browser, click the Address bar, and then enter the Web address `scsite.com/off2007/learn`. When the Office 2007 Learn It Online page is displayed, click the link for the exercise you want to complete and then read the instructions.

Chapter Reinforcement TF, MC, and SA
A series of true/false, multiple choice, and short answer questions that test your knowledge of the chapter content.

Flash Cards
An interactive learning environment where you identify chapter key terms associated with displayed definitions.

Practice Test
A series of multiple choice questions that test your knowledge of chapter content and key terms.

Who Wants To Be a Computer Genius?
An interactive game that challenges your knowledge of chapter content in the style of a television quiz show.

Wheel of Terms
An interactive game that challenges your knowledge of chapter key terms in the style of the television show *Wheel of Fortune*.

Crossword Puzzle Challenge
A crossword puzzle that challenges your knowledge of key terms presented in the chapter.

Apply Your Knowledge

Reinforce the skills and apply the concepts you learned in this chapter.

Understanding Logical Tests and Absolute Cell Referencing
Instructions Part 1: Determine the truth value (true or false) of the following logical tests, given the following cell values: X4 = 25; Y3 = 28; K7 = 110; Z2 = 15; and Q9 = 35. Enter true or false.

a. Y3 < X4   Truth value: _____

b. Q9 = K7   Truth value: _____

c. X4 + 15 * Z2 / 5 <> K7   Truth value: _____

d. K7 / Z2 > X4 − Y3   Truth value: _____

e. Q9 * 2 − 42 < (X4 + Y3 − 8) / 9   Truth value: _____

f. K7 + 300 <= X4 * Z2 + 10   Truth value: _____

g. Q9 + K7 > 2 * (Q9 + 25)   Truth value: _____

h. Y3 = 4 * (Q9 / 5)   Truth value: _____

Instructions Part 2: Write cell K23 as a relative reference, absolute reference, mixed reference with the row varying, and mixed reference with the column varying.

_____ _____ _____ _____

Instructions Part 3: Start Excel. Open the workbook Apply 3-1 Absolute Cell References. See the inside back cover of this book for instructions for downloading the Data Files for Students, or see your instructor for information on accessing the files required in this book. You will recreate the numerical grid pictured in Figure 3–82.

Continued >

In the Lab *continued*

3. Select the legend on the right side of the chart and delete it. Add the chart title by clicking the Layout tab on the Ribbon, then clicking the Chart Title button. Click Above Chart in the Chart Title gallery. Format the chart title as shown in Figure 3–86.

4. To change the color of the cylinders, click one of the cylinders and use the Shape Fill button on the Format tab on the Ribbon. To change the color of the wall, click the wall behind the cylinders and use the Shape Fill button on the Format tab on the Ribbon. Use the same procedure to change the color of the base of the wall.

5. Rename the sheet tabs Eight-Year Financial Projection and 3-D Cylinder Chart. Rearrange the sheets so that the worksheet is leftmost, and color their tabs as shown in Figure 3–86.

6. Click the Eight-Year Financial Projection tab to display the worksheet. Save the workbook using the same file name (Lab 3-1 Salioto Auto Parts Eight-Year Financial Projection) as defined in Part 1. Submit the workbook as requested by your instructor.

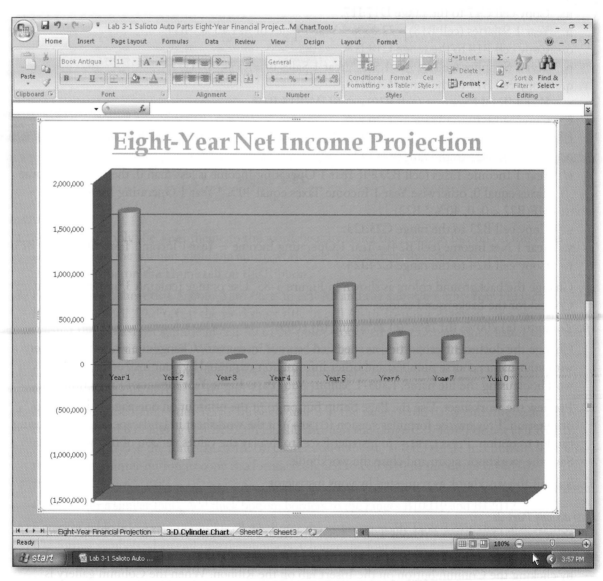

Figure 3–86

Instructions Part 3:

1. Start Excel. Open the workbook Lab 3-1 Salioto Auto Parts Eight-Year Financial Projection. Divide the window into two panes by dragging the horizontal split box between rows 6 and 7. Use the scroll bars to show both the top and bottom of the worksheet. Using the numbers in columns 2 and 3 of Table 3-10, analyze the effect of changing the annual sales growth (cell B4) and annual price decrease (cell B5) on the net incomes in row 24. The resulting answers are in column 4 of Table 3–10. Submit the workbook or results of the what-if analysis for each case as requested by your instructor.

Table 3–10 Salioto Auto Parts Data to Analyze and Results			
Case	**Annual Sales Growth**	**Annual Price Decrease**	**Year 8 Resulting Net Income in Cell I24**
1	7.45%	5.25%	174,568
2	12.75%	−3.00%	6,677,903
3	−7.25%	1.65%	(3,552,156)

2. Close the workbook without saving it, and then reopen it. Use the What-If Analysis button on the Data tab on the Ribbon to goal seek. Determine a margin (cell B6) that would result in a Year 8 net income of $2,000,000 (cell I24). You should end up with a margin of 40.68% in cell B6. Submit the workbook with the new values or the results of the goal seek as requested by your instructor. Do not save the workbook with the latest changes.

In the Lab

Lab 2: Modifying a Weekly Payroll Worksheet

Problem: As a summer intern at Britney's Music Emporium, you have been asked to modify the weekly payroll report shown in Figure 3–87a. The workbook, Lab 3-2 Britney's Music Emporium Weekly Payroll Report, is included with the Data Files for Students. See the inside back cover of this book for instructions for downloading the Data Files for Students, or see your instructor for information on accessing the files required for this book.

The major modifications to the payroll report to be made in this exercise include: (1) reformatting the worksheet; (2) adding computations of time-and-a-half for hours worked greater than 40; (3) adding calculations to charge no federal tax in certain situations; (4) adding Social Security and Medicare deductions; (5) adding and deleting employees; and (6) changing employee information. The final payroll report is shown in Figure 3–87b.

(a) Before

(b) After

Figure 3–87

Instructions Part 1:

1. Start Excel. Open the workbook, Lab 3-2 Britney's Music Emporium Weekly Payroll Report.

2. Select the worksheet by clicking the Select All button. Click the Clear button on the Home tab on the Ribbon and then click Clear Formats on the Clear menu to clear the formatting. Bold the entire worksheet.

3. Delete rows 11 through 13 to remove the statistics below the Totals row. Change all the row heights back to the default height (12.75).

4. Insert four rows above row 1 by selecting rows 1 through 4, right-clicking the selection, and clicking Insert on the shortcut menu.

5. Change the row heights as follows: row 5 = 48.00; rows 6 and 7 = 25.50. One at a time, select cells D7, E7, and G7. For each cell, press the F2 key and then the ENTER key to display the column headings on multiple rows. Center the range B7:J7.

6. Delete column B by right-clicking the column heading and clicking Delete on the shortcut menu.

7. Insert a new column between columns C and D. Change the column widths as follows: A = 25.00; D = 13.00; and E through K = 9.71. Enter the new column D title **YTD Soc. Sec.** in cell D7.

8. Insert two new columns between columns F and G. Enter the new column G title **Soc. Sec.** in cell G7. Enter the new column H title **Medicare** in cell H7.

9. Enhance the worksheet title in cell A5 by using a 36-point light blue Arial Rounded MT Bold (or a similar font) font style as shown in Figure 3–87b.

10. Assign the NOW function to cell B6 and format it to the 3/14/2001 style.

11. Delete employee James, Delmar (row 12). Change Raul Aquire's (row 8) hours worked to 2.5. Change Casimir Kwasny's (row 9) number of dependents to 7 and rate per hour to $8.25. Change Tepin Ruiz's (row 11) hours worked to 49.5 and Fred Holkavich's (row 12) hours worked to 57.

12. Freeze column A and rows 1 through 7 by selecting cell B8, clicking the Freeze Panes button on the View tab on the Ribbon, and then clicking Freeze Panes on the Freeze Panes menu.

13. In column D, enter the YTD Soc. Sec. values listed in Table 3–11.

14. Insert two new rows immediately above the Totals row. Add the new employee data as listed in Table 3–12.

Table 3–11 The Britney Music Emporium's YTD Social Security Values

Employee	YTD Soc. Sec.
Aquire, Raul	767.00
Kwasny, Casimir	1307.75
Mohammed, Aadil	930.25
Ruiz, Tepin	7458.75
Holkavich, Fred	7457.75

Table 3–12 The Britney Music Emporium's New Employee Data

Employee	Dependents	Rate per Hour	YTD Soc. Sec.	Hours Worked
Jordan, Leon	4	13.50	2952.78	37.25
Wright, Louis	5	23.25	7430.00	46.75

15. Center the range B6:B14. Use the Currency category in the Format Cells dialog box to assign a Comma style (no dollar signs) with two decimal places and negative numbers within parentheses to the range C8:K15. Assign a Percent style and two decimal places to the range L8:L15. Draw a thick bottom border in the ranges A7:L7 and A14:L14.

16. As shown in Figure 3–87b, enter and format the Social Security (7.65% with a maximum of $7,458.75) and Medicare tax (1.45%) information in the range A1:B3. Use format symbols where applicable.

17. Change the formulas to determine the gross pay in column F and the federal tax in column I as follows:

   a. In cell F8, enter an IF function that applies the following logic and then copy it to the range F9:F14. If Hours Worked <= 40, then Rate per Hour * Hours Worked, otherwise Rate per Hour * Hours Worked + 0.5 * Rate per Hour * (Hours Worked − 40) or =IF(E8 <= 40, C8 * E8, C8 * E8 + 0.5 * C8 *(E8 − 40))

   b. In cell I8, enter the IF function that applies the following logic and then copy it to the range I9:I14. If (Gross Pay − Dependents * 22.09 > 0, then 20% * (Gross Pay − Dependents * 22.09), otherwise 0 or =IF(F8 − B8 * 22.09 > 0, 20% * (F8 − B8 * 22.09), 0)

Continued >

Table 3–18 Chesterton Trib Bimonthly Projected Earnings and Expenditures

Revenue	February	April	June	August	October	December
Subscriptions	12178.30	8391.50	15714.50	16340.10	12567.25	12800.15
Advertising	4130.20	6425.00	4123.15	5023.30	7015.75	9273.20
Assumptions						
Marketing	15.60%					
Payroll	21.50%					
Commissions on Advertising	3.25%					
Production Costs	12.50%					
Reportorial Expenses	5.00%					

One shareholder lobbied to reduce marketing expenditures by 3% and payroll costs by 5%. Perform a what-if-analysis reflecting the proposed changes in expenditure assumptions. The reduction in expenditures should result in a total operating income of $59,696.91 or an increase of $9,118.59. Submit the workbook and results of the what-if analysis as requested by your instructor.

•• 3: Projected Used-Truck Savings

Cousin Abe and Aunt Esther own a paint company. Their good friend Billie Bob is retiring after 35 years of delivering the morning newspaper. Billie Bob has offered them the opportunity to take his place next year. The job requires, however, that they own a truck. They need to save enough money over the next six months to buy a $10,000 used truck.

They have job orders at their paint company for the next six months: $22,150 in July, $22,480 in August, $32,900 in September, $31,200 in October, $45,301 in November, and $32,190 in December. Each month, they spend 34.55% of the job order income on material, 3.00% on rollers and brushes, 4.75% on their retirement account, and 39.5% on food and clothing. The remaining profits (orders − total expenses) will be put aside for the used truck. Aunt Esther's retired parents have agreed to provide a bonus of $250 whenever the monthly profit exceeds $2,000. Use the concepts and techniques presented in this project to create and format the worksheet.

Cousin Abe has asked you to create a worksheet that shows orders, expenses, profits, bonuses, and savings for the next six months, and totals for each category. Aunt Esther would like to save for another used truck for $17,000. She has asked you to (a) perform a what-if analysis to determine the effect on the savings by reducing the percentage spent on material to 25% (answer total savings = $16,084.49), and (b) with the original assumptions, goal seek to determine what percentage of profits to spend on food and clothing if $15,000 is needed for the used truck (answer = 29.165%). Submit the workbook and results of the what-if analysis as requested by your instructor.

•• 4: College Expense and Resource Projections

Make It Personal

Attending college with limited resources can be a trying experience. One way to alleviate some of the financial stress is to plan ahead. Develop a worksheet following the general layout in Table 3–19 that shows the projected expenses and resources for four years of college. Use the formulas listed in Table 3–20 and the concepts and techniques presented in this project to create the worksheet.

Table 3–19 College Expense and Resource Projections

Expenses	Freshman	Sophomore	Junior	Senior	Total
Room & Board	$6,125.00	Formula A		→	—
Tuition & Books	8,750.00	Formula A		→	—
Clothes	750.00	Formula A		→	—
Entertainment	1,025.00	Formula A		→	—
Miscellaneous	675.00	Formula A		→	—
Total Expenses	—	—	—	—	—

Resources	Freshman	Sophomore	Junior	Senior	Total
Savings	Formula B		→		—
Parents	Formula B		→		—
Job	Formula B		→		—
Loans	Formula B		→		—
Scholarships	Formula B		→		—
Total Resources	—	—	—	—	—

Assumptions	
Savings	10.00%
Parents	20.00%
Job	10.00%
Loans	30.00%
Scholarships	30.00%
Annual Rate Increase	7.50%

After creating the worksheet:
(a) perform what-if analysis by changing the percents of the resource assumptions; (b) perform a what-if analysis to determine the effect on the resources by increasing the Annual Rate Increase to 9%; and (c) with the original assumptions, goal seek to determine what the Annual Rate Increase would be for the total expenses to be $100,000. Submit the workbook and results of the what-if analysis as requested by your instructor.

Table 3–20 College Expense and Resource Projections Formulas

Formula A = Prior Year's Expense * (1 + Annual Rate Increase)

Formula B = Total Expenses for Year * Corresponding Assumption

•• 5: Cost of Storing Radio Isotopes

Working Together

A government agency plans to conduct experiments that will result in some radioactive waste. Although the isotopes will break apart into atoms of other elements over time, agency watchdogs are concerned about containment costs while the material still is radioactive. The agency director has asked your group to prepare a worksheet showing the amount of radioactive material remaining, containment costs, estimated agency appropriations, and the percentage of appropriations that will be spent on containment every year for the next decade. The director has outlined the desired worksheet as shown in Table 3–21 on the next page.

Continued >

Cases and Places *continued*

These formulas have been supplied:

Formula A: Amount Remaining = Original Amount $\times$ 0.5(Number of Years Stored / Half-Life)

Formula B: Containment Costs = Containment Cost Per Kilogram $\times$ Total Amount Remaining

Formula C: Estimated Appropriations = Appropriations $\times$ (1 + Estimated Yearly Increase) (Number of Years Stored / Half-Life)

Formula D: Percentage Spent on Containment = Containment Costs / Estimated Appropriations

The director has asked your group to include a function that prints "Acceptable" below the percentage spent on containment whenever the percentage is less than 1%, otherwise print "Not Acceptable."

Have each member of your team submit a sketch of the proposed worksheet and then implement the best one. Use the concepts and techniques presented in this project to create and format the worksheet. Submit the sketches and workbook as requested by your instructor.

Table 3–21 Cost of Storing Radioactive Isotopes

	Number of Years Stored				
Number of Years Stored	1	2	3	....	10
Amount of Isotope X Remaining (in kg)	Formula A				
Amount of Isotope Y Remaining (in kg)	Formula A				
Total Remaining (in kg)	—	—	—	....	—
Containment Costs	Formula B				
Estimated Appropriations	Formula C				
Percentage Spent on Containment	Formula D				
	Message				

Assumptions	
Original Amount of Isotope X Remaining (in kg)	650
Half-Life of Isotope X (in years)	1
Containment Cost per Kilogram	1000
Estimated Yearly Increase	10.00%
Original Amount of Isotope Y Remaining (in kg)	3000
Half-Life of Isotope Y (in years)	0.45
Appropriations	6000000

Web Feature
Creating Web Pages Using Excel

Objectives

You will have mastered the material in this Web feature when you can:

- Customize the Quick Access Toolbar

- Publish a worksheet and chart as a Web page

- Display Web pages published in Excel in a browser

- Complete file management tasks within Excel

Web Feature Introduction

Excel provides fast, easy methods for saving workbooks as Web pages that can be stored on the World Wide Web, a company's intranet, or a local hard disk. A user then can display the workbook using a browser, rather than Excel.

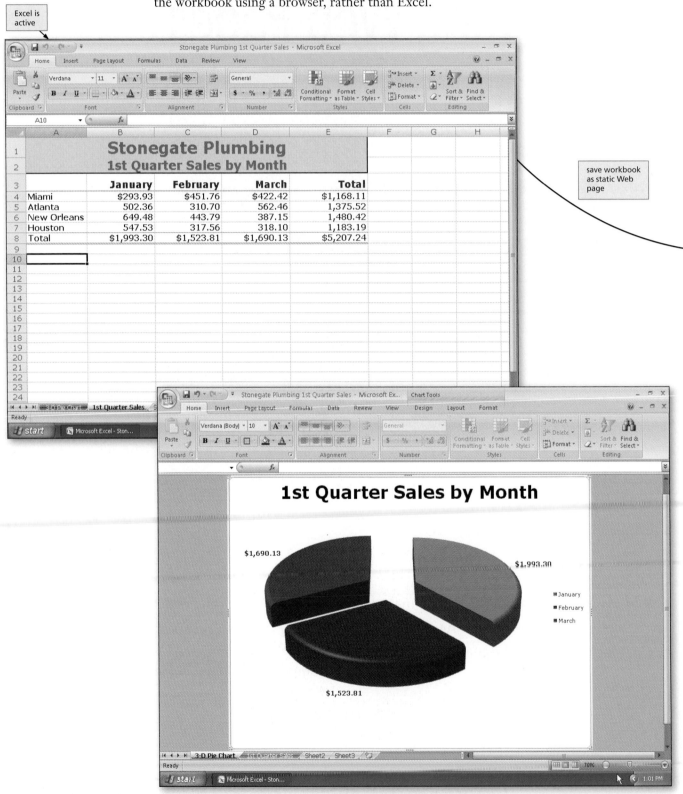

(a) Workbook Viewed in Excel

Figure 1

Project — Workbook with Chart Saved as a Web Page

Figure 1a shows the workbook for Stonegate Plumbing's 1st quarter sales by month. The chief financial officer for the company requests that the information in the worksheet, including the chart, be made available on the company's intranet for others in the company to view. In order to accomplish this task, you must save the workbook as a Web page.

You can save a workbook, or a portion of a workbook, as a Web page. The saved **Web page** is a snapshot of the workbook. It is similar to a printed report in that you can view it, but you cannot modify it. In the browser window, the workbook appears as it would in Microsoft Excel, including sheet tabs that you can click to switch between worksheets. As illustrated in Figure 1, this Web feature shows you how to save a workbook (Figure 1a) as a Web page (Figure 1b) and view it using your browser.

When you use the Save As command on the Office Button menu and choose to save a workbook as a Web page, Excel allows you to **publish workbooks**, which is the process of making a workbook available to others; for example, on the World Wide Web or on a

(b) Static Web Page Viewed in Browser

BTW

Web Folders and FTP Locations
You can save any type of file to a Web folder or on an FTP location, just as you would save to a folder on your hard disk. Web folders and FTP locations are particularly useful because they appear as standard folders in Windows Explorer or in the Save in list. For additional information, see Appendix D.

company's intranet. If you have access to a Web server, you can publish Web pages by saving them on a Web server or on an FTP location. To learn more about publishing Web pages on a Web server or on an FTP location using Microsoft Office applications, refer to Appendix D.

This Web feature illustrates how to create and save the Web pages on a USB flash drive, rather than on a Web server. This feature also demonstrates how to preview a workbook as a Web page and create a new folder using the Save As dialog box.

Overview

As you read through this Web feature, you will learn how to create the worksheet shown in Figure 1 on pages EX 250 and 251 by performing these general tasks:

- Save a Workbook as a Web page
- Preview the Workbook in a Web browser
- Complete file management tasks within Excel

Using Web Page Preview and Saving an Excel Workbook as a Web Page

At any time during the construction of a workbook, you can preview it as a Web page by using the Web Page Preview command. The Web Page Preview command is not available on the Ribbon, but you can add the command to the Quick Access Toolbar. When you invoke the Web Page Preview command, it starts your browser and displays the active sheet in the workbook as a Web page. If the preview is acceptable, then you can save the workbook as a Web page.

To Add a Button to the Quick Access Toolbar

Many commands available in Excel are not included on any of the tabs on the Ribbon. You can, however, add such commands to the Quick Access Toolbar. One such command allows you to preview a document in a Web browser. This command, Web Page Preview, needs to be added to the Quick Access Toolbar so that the Web page can be previewed. The following steps add the Web Page Preview command to the Quick Access Toolbar.

- Connect a USB flash drive with the Data Files for Students on it to one of the computer's USB ports.

- Start Excel and then open the workbook, Stonegate Plumbing 1st Quarter Sales, from the Data Files for students.

- Click the Customize Quick Access Toolbar button to display the Customize Quick Access Toolbar menu (Figure 2).

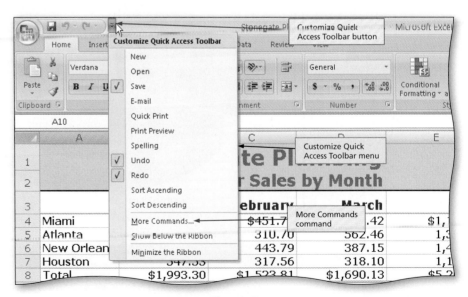

Figure 2

3

• Click the More Commands command on the Customize Quick Access Toolbar menu.

• When the Excel Options dialog box is displayed, click the 'Choose commands from' box arrow to display the 'Choose commands from' list (Figure 3).

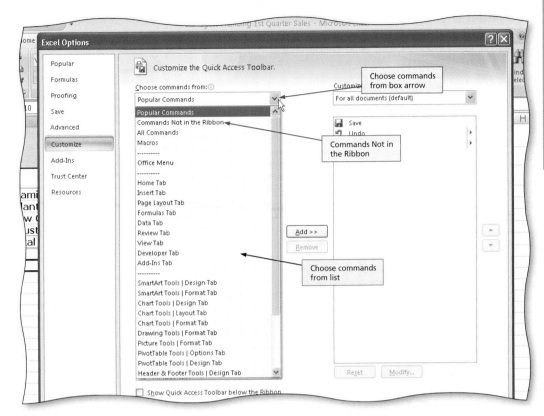

Figure 3

4

• Click Commands Not in the Ribbon in the 'Choose commands from' list to display a list of commands not in the Ribbon (Figure 4).

Figure 4

5

- Scroll to the bottom of the list, click Web Page Preview, and then click the Add button to add the button to the Quick Access Toolbar (Figure 5).

Figure 5

6

- Click the OK button to close the Excel Options dialog box and display the Quick Access Toolbar with the Web Page Preview button added to it (Figure 6).

Q&A

Will the Web Page Preview command be on the Quick Access Toolbar the next time that I start Excel?

Yes. When you change the Quick Access Toolbar, the changes remain even after you restart Excel. If you share a computer with somebody else or if the Quick Access Toolbar becomes cluttered, Excel allows you to remove commands from the Quick Access Toolbar. The Web Page Preview button is removed from the Quick Access Toolbar later in this Web feature.

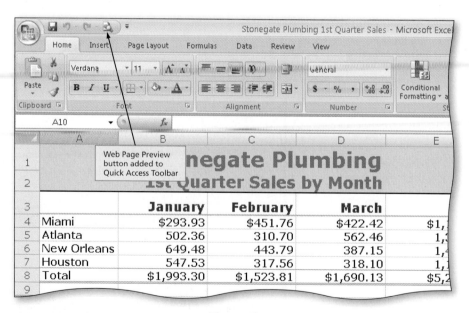

Figure 6

To Preview the Web Page

The following steps preview the Web page version of the workbook in a browser.

1

- Click the Web Page Preview button on the Quick Access Toolbar to display the Web page in your browser.

- If necessary, click the Maximize button on your browser's title bar (Figure 7).

Q&A What happens when I click the Web Page Preview button?

Excel starts your browser. The browser displays a preview of how the 1st Quarter Sales sheet will appear as a Web page (Figure 7). The Web page preview in the browser is nearly identical to the display of the worksheet in Excel. A highlighted browser button appears on the Windows taskbar indicating it is active. The Excel button on the Windows taskbar no longer is highlighted.

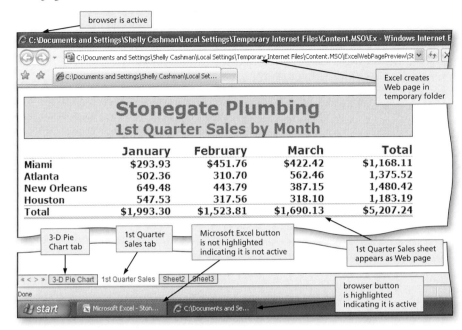

Figure 7

2

- Click the 3-D Pie Chart tab at the bottom of the Web page to display the 3-D Pie chart in the browser (Figure 8).

3

- After viewing the Web page preview of the Stonegate Plumbing 1st Quarter Sales workbook, click the Close button on the right side of the browser title bar to close the browser and make Excel active again.

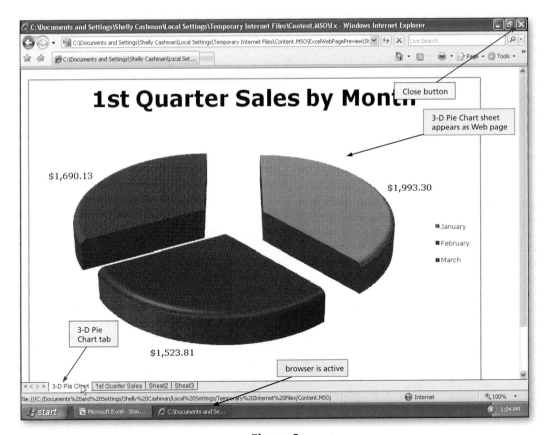

Figure 8

To Save an Excel Workbook as a Web Page in a Newly Created Folder

Once the preview of the workbook as a Web page is acceptable, you can save the workbook as a Web page so that others can view it using a Web browser, such as Internet Explorer or Mozilla Firefox.

Two Web page formats exist in which you can save workbooks. Both formats convert the contents of the workbook into HTML (HyperText Markup Language), which is a language browsers can interpret. One format is called **Single File Web Page format**, which saves all of the components of the Web page in a single file with an .mht extension. This format is useful particularly for e-mailing workbooks in HTML format. The second format, called **Web Page format**, saves the Web page in a file and some of its components in a folder. This format is useful if you need access to the components, such as images, that make up the Web page.

Experienced users organize the files saved on a storage medium, such as a USB flash drive or hard disk, by creating folders. They then save related files in a common folder. Excel allows you to create folders before saving a file using the Save As dialog box. The following steps create a new folder on the USB flash drive and save the workbook as a Web page in the new folder.

- With the Stonegate Plumbing 1st Quarter Sales workbook open, click the Office Button.

- Click Save As on the Office Button menu to display the Save As dialog box (Figure 9).

Figure 9

- Type Stonegate Plumbing 1st Quarter Sales Web Page in the File name box.

- Click the 'Save as type' box arrow and then click Single File Web Page.

- Click the Save in box arrow, select UDISK 2.0 (E:) (your USB flash drive name and letter may be different), and then click the Create New Folder button to display the New Folder dialog box.

- When Excel displays the New Folder dialog box, type Web Feature in the Name text box (Figure 10).

Figure 10

- Click the OK button in the New Folder dialog box.

  What does Excel do when I click the OK button?

  Excel automatically selects the new folder named Web Feature in the Save in box (Figure 11). The Entire Workbook option button in the Save area instructs Excel to save all sheets in the workbook as Web pages.

4

- Click the Save button in the Save As dialog box to save the workbook in a single file in HTML format in the Web Feature folder on the USB flash drive.

- If the Microsoft Office Excel dialog box is displayed, click the Yes button.

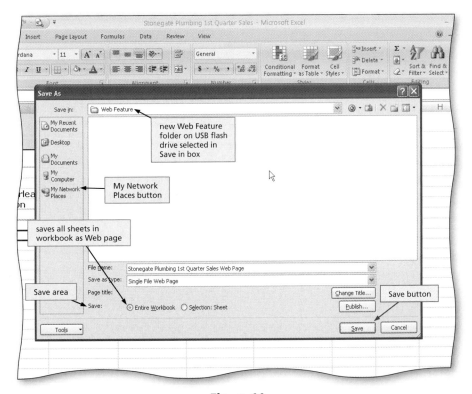

Figure 11

BTW

Creating Links
You can add hyperlinks to an Excel workbook before you save it as a Web page. The hyperlinks in the Excel workbook can link to a Web page, a location in a Web page, or an e-mail address that automatically starts the viewer's e-mail program.

Saving Workbooks as Web Pages

The Save As dialog box changes when you select Single File Web Page, which is in MHTML format, in the 'Save as type' box. When you use the Single File Web Page format, a Save area appears in the dialog box. Within the Save area are two option buttons and a Publish button (Figure 11). You can select only one of the option buttons. The Entire Workbook option button is selected by default. This indicates Excel will save all the active sheets (1st Quarter Sales and 3-D Pie Chart) in the workbook as a Web page. The alternative is the Selection: Sheet option button. If you select this option, Excel will save only the active sheet (the one that currently is displaying in the Excel window) in the workbook. The Publish button in the Save As dialog box in Figure 11 is an alternative to the Save button. It allows you to customize the Web page further.

If you have access to a Web server and it allows you to save files in a Web folder, then you can save the Web page directly on the Web server by clicking the My Network Places button in the Save in bar of the Save As dialog box (Figure 11). If you have access to a Web server that allows you to save on an FTP site, then you can select the FTP site below FTP locations in the Save in box just as you select any folder in which to save a file. To learn more about publishing Web pages in a Web folder or on an FTP location using Office applications, refer to Appendix D.

After Excel saves the workbook in Step 4, it displays the MHTML file in the Excel window. Excel can continue to display the workbook in HTML format, because, within the MHTML file that it created, it also saved the Excel formats that allow it to display the MHTML file in Excel.

BTW

Viewing Source Code
To view the HTML source code for a Web page created in Excel, use your browser to display the Web page, click View on the menu bar, and then click Source.

To Reset the Quick Access Toolbar and Quit Excel

The necessary work with the Excel workbook is complete. The following steps remove the Web Page Preview button from the Quick Access Toolbar and quit Excel.

1 Click the Customize the Quick Access Toolbar button on the Ribbon.

2 Click the More Commands command.

3 When the Excel Options dialog box is displayed, click the Reset button. If the Reset Customizations dialog box is displayed, click the Yes button.

4 Click the OK button in the Excel Options dialog box to close it.

5 Click the Close button on the Microsoft Excel title bar.

Q&A

Do I need to remove the button from the Quick Access Toolbar?

No. For consistency, in this book the Quick Access Toolbar is reset after the added buttons no longer are needed. If you share a computer with others, you should reset the Quick Access Toolbar when you are finished using the computer.

File Management Tools in Excel

In the previous set of steps, Excel automatically inserts the new folder name in the Save in box when you click the OK button in the New Folder dialog box (Figure 11 on page EX 257). It actually was not necessary to create a new folder earlier in this Web feature; the Web page could have been saved on the USB flash drive in the same manner files were saved on the USB flash drive in the previous projects. Creating a new folder, however, allows you to organize your work.

Finally, once you create a folder, you can right-click it while the Save As dialog box is active and perform many file management tasks directly in Excel (Figure 12). For example, once the shortcut menu appears, you can rename the selected folder, delete it, copy it, display its properties, and perform other file management functions.

BTW

Quick Reference
For a table that lists how to complete the tasks covered in this book using the mouse, Ribbon, shortcut menu, and keyboard, see the Quick Reference Summary at the back of this book, or visit the Excel 2007 Quick Reference Web page (scsite.com/ex2007/qr).

BTW

Certification
The Microsoft Certified Application Specialist (MCAS) program provides an opportunity for you to obtain a valuable industry credential – proof that you have the Excel 2007 skills required by employers. For more information, see Appendix F or visit the Excel 2007 Certification Web page (scsite.com/ex2007/cert).

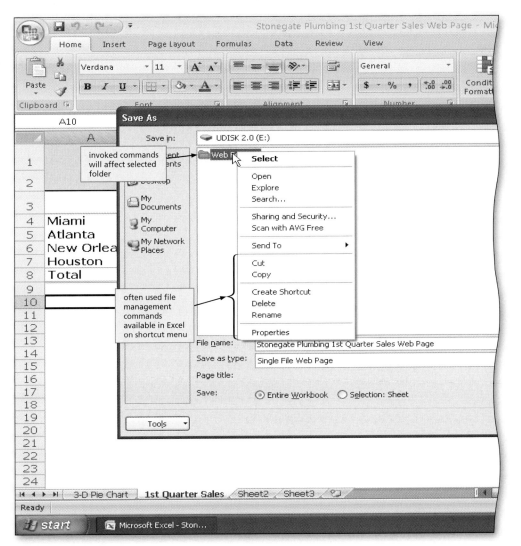

Figure 12

To View and Manipulate the Web Page Using a Browser

With the Web page saved in the Web Feature folder on the USB flash drive, you can now view it using a browser, as shown in the following steps.

- If necessary, connect the USB flash drive with the Data Files for Students to one of the computer's USB ports.

- Click the Start button on the Windows taskbar, point to All Programs on the Start menu, and then click Internet Explorer on the All Programs submenu.

- When the Internet Explorer window opens, type e:\web feature\ stonegate plumbing 1st quarter sales web page.mht in the Address box and then press the ENTER key to display the Web page in your browser (Figure 13). (Your USB flash drive may have a different name and letter.)

- If the Information Bar appears, right-click it and then click Allow Blocked Content on the shortcut menu.

- If the Security Warning dialog box is displayed, click the Yes button.

Figure 13

2

- Click the 3-D Pie Chart sheet tab at the bottom of the window to display the 3-D Pie chart in your browser (Figure 14).

- Use the scroll arrows to display the lower portion of the chart.

Q&A

What are the benefits of using a browser to view a workbook?

You can see from Figures 13 and 14 that a Web page is an ideal way to distribute information to a large group of people. For example, the Web page could be published on a Web server connected to the Internet and made available to anyone with a computer, browser, and the address of the Web page. It also can be e-mailed easily, because the Web page resides in a single file, rather than in a file and folder. Publishing a workbook as a Web page, therefore, is an excellent alternative to distributing printed copies of the workbook.

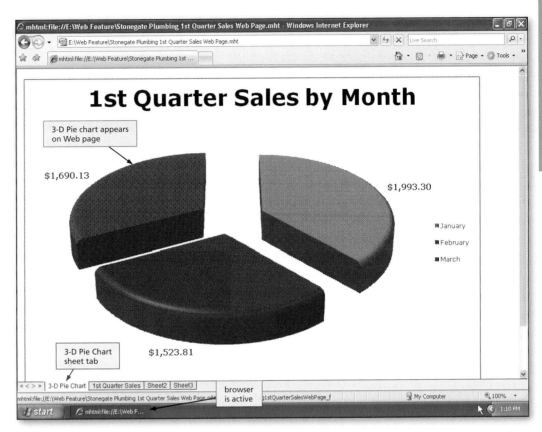

Figure 14

3

- Click the Close button on the right side of the browser title bar to close the browser.

Web Feature Summary

This Web feature introduced you to customizing the Quick Access Toolbar, previewing a workbook as a Web page, creating a new folder on a USB flash drive, and publishing and viewing a Web page. The items listed below include all the new Office 2007 skills you have learned in this Web feature.

1. Add a Button to the Quick Access Toolbar (EX 252)
2. Preview the Web Page (EX 255)
3. Save an Excel Workbook as a Web Page in a Newly Created Folder (EX 256)
4. View and Manipulate the Web Page Using a Browser (EX 260)

If you have a SAM user profile, you may have access to hands-on instruction, practice, and assessment. Log in to your SAM account (http://sam2007.course.com) to launch any assigned training activities or exams that relate to the skills covered in this chapter.

In the Lab

Create a Web page using the guidelines, concepts, and skills presented in this Web feature. Labs are listed in order of increasing difficulty.

1 Creating a Web Page I

Problem: You are a spreadsheet specialist for Aunt Leona's Pizza, a national chain of pizzerias. Your manager has asked you to create a Web page from the company's annual sales workbook.

Instructions Part 1: Start Excel and open the Lab WF-1 Aunt Leonas Pizza Annual Sales workbook from the Data Files for Students. Perform the following tasks:

1. Add the Web Page Preview command to the Quick Access Toolbar.

2. Review the worksheet and chart so you have an idea of what the workbook contains. Preview the workbook as a Web page. Close the browser.

3. Save the workbook as a single file Web page in a new folder titled Web Feature Exercises using the file name, Lab WF-1 Aunt Leonas Pizza Annual Sales Web Page. Make sure you select Entire Workbook in the Save area before you click the Save button. Reset the Quick Access Toolbar and then quit Excel.

4. Start your browser. With the Web page located on the USB flash drive, type `e:\web feature exercises\lab wf-1 aunt leonas pizza annual sales web page.mht` in the Address box (your USB flash drive may have a different name and letter). When the browser displays the Web page, click the tabs at the bottom of the window to view the sheets. Close the browser. Submit the assignment as requested by your instructor.

In the Lab

2 Creating a Web Page II

Problem: You work part-time as a spreadsheet analyst for What-a-Racket Tennis Club. You have been asked to create a Web page from the workbook that the company uses to project membership dues and payroll expenses.

Instructions Part 1: Start Excel and open the Lab WF-2 What-a-Racket Tennis Club Projections workbook from the Data Files for Students. Perform the following tasks:

1. Add the Web Page Preview command to the Quick Access Toolbar.

2. Review the 3-D Bar Chart sheet and the Projected Expenses sheet in Excel. Preview the workbook as a Web page. Close the browser.

3. Save the workbook as a Web page (select Web Page in the Save as type box) in the Web Feature Exercises folder using the file name, Lab WF-2 What-a-Racket Tennis Club Projections Web Page. Make sure you select Entire Workbook in the Save area before you click the Save button. Reset the Quick Access Toolbar and then quit Excel. Saving the workbook as a Web page, rather than a single file Web page, will result in an additional folder being added to the Web Feature Exercises folder.

4. Start your browser. Type `e:\web feature exercises\lab wf-2 what-a-racket tennis club projections web page.htm` in the Address box (your USB flash drive may have a different name and letter). When the browser displays the Web page, click the tabs at the bottom of the window to view the sheets. Close the browser. Submit the assignment as requested by your instructor.

In the Lab

3 File Management within Excel

Problem: Your manager at What-a-Racket Tennis Club has asked you to teach her to complete basic file management tasks from within Excel.

Instructions: Start Excel and click the Open command on the Office Button menu. When Excel displays the Open dialog box, create a new folder called In the Lab 3. Click the Up One Level button to reselect the drive in the Look in box. Use the shortcut menu to complete the following tasks: (1) rename the In the Lab 3 folder to In the Lab 3A; (2) show the properties of the In the Lab 3A folder; and (3) delete the In the Lab 3A folder.

1 Creating and Using a Database

Objectives

You will have mastered the material in this chapter when you can:

- Describe databases and database management systems
- Design a database to satisfy a collection of requirements
- Start Access
- Describe the features of the Access window
- Create a database
- Create a table and add records

- Close a table
- Close a database and quit Access
- Open a database
- Print the contents of a table
- Create and print custom reports
- Create and use a split form
- Use the Access Help system

The rows in the tables are called **records**. A record contains information about a given person, product, or event. A row in the Client table, for example, contains information about a specific client.

The columns in the tables are called fields. A **field** contains a specific piece of information within a record. In the Client table, for example, the fourth field, City, contains the city where the client is located.

The first field in the Client table is the Client Number. JSP Recruiters assigns a number to each client. As is common to the way in which many organizations format client numbers, JSP Recruiters calls it a *number*, although it actually contains letters. The JSP client numbers consist of two uppercase letters followed by a two-digit number.

These numbers are unique; that is, no two clients are assigned the same number. Such a field can be used as a **unique identifier**. This simply means that a given client number will appear only in a single record in the table. Only one record exists, for example, in which the client number is BH72. A unique identifier also is called a **primary key**. Thus, the Client Number field is the primary key for the Client table.

The next seven fields in the Client table are Client Name, Street, City, State, Postal Code, Amount Paid, and Current Due. Note that the default width of the columns cuts off the names of some of the columns. The Amount Paid column contains the amount that the client has paid JSP Recruiters year to date (YTD) prior to the current period. The Current Due column contains the amount due to JSP for the current period. For example, client BL12 is Benton Labs. The address is 12 Mountain in Denton, Colorado. The postal code is 80412. The client has paid $16,500 for recruiting services so far this year. The amount due for the current period is $38,225.

JSP assigns each client a single recruiter. The last column in the Client table, Recruiter Number, gives the number of the client's recruiter.

The first field in the Recruiter table, Recruiter Number, is the number JSP Recruiters assigns to the recruiter. These numbers are unique, so Recruiter Number is the primary key of the Recruiter table.

The other fields in the Recruiter table are Last Name, First Name, Street, City, State, Postal Code, Rate, and Commission. The Rate field contains the percentage of the client fee that the recruiter earns, and the Commission field contains the total amount that JSP has paid the recruiter so far this year. For example, Recruiter 27 is Jaime Fernandez. His address is 265 Maxwell in Charleston, Colorado. The Postal Code is 80380. His commission rate is .09 (9%), and his commission is $9,450.

The recruiter number appears in both the Client table and the Recruiter table. It relates clients and recruiters. For example, in the Client table, you see that the recruiter number for client BL12 is 24. To find the name of this recruiter, look for the row in the Recruiter table that contains 24 in the Recruiter Number column. After you have found it, you know the client is assigned to Camden Reeves. To find all the clients assigned to Camden Reeves, you must look through the Client table for all the clients that contain 24 in the Recruiter Number column. His clients are BH72 (Berls Hospital), BL12 (Benton Labs), FH22 (Family Health), MH56 (Maun Hospital), and WL56 (West Labs).

The last recruiter in the Recruiter table, Jan Lee, has not been assigned any clients yet; therefore, her recruiter number, 34, does not appear on any row in the Client table.

Overview

As you read this chapter, you will learn how to create the database shown in Figure 1–1 on the previous page by performing these general tasks:

- Design the database.
- Create a new blank database.

- Create a table and add the records.
- Preview and print the contents of a table.
- Create a second table and add the records.
- Create four reports.
- Create a form.

Plan
Ahead

Database design guidelines.

Database design refers to the arrangement of data into tables and fields. In the example in this chapter the design is specified, but in many cases, you will have to determine the design based on what you want the system to accomplish.

When designing a database, the actions you take and the decisions you make will determine the tables and fields that will be included in the database. As you create a database, such as the project shown in Figure 1–1 on page AC 3, you should follow these general guidelines:

1. **Identify the tables.** Examine the requirements for the database in order to identify the main objects that are involved. There will be a table for each object you identified.

   In one database, for example, the main objects might be departments and employees. Thus, there would be two tables: one for departments and the other for employees. In another database, the main objects might be clients and recruiters. In this case, there would also be two tables: one for clients and the other for recruiters. In still another database, the main objects might be books, publishers, and authors. Here there would be three tables: one for books, a second for publishers, and a third for authors.

2. **Determine the primary keys.** Recall that the primary key is the unique identifier for records in the table. For each table, determine the unique identifier, if there is one. For a Department table, for example, the unique identifier might be the Department Code. For a Book table, the unique identifier might be the ISBN number.

3. **Determine the additional fields.** The primary key will be a field or combination of fields in a table. There typically will be many additional fields, each of which contains a type of data. Examine the project requirements to determine these additional fields. For example, in an Employee table, the additional fields might include such fields as Employee Name, Street Address, City, State, Postal Code, Date Hired, Salary, and so on.

4. **Determine relationships among the tables.** Examine the list of tables you have created to see which tables are related. When you determine two tables are related, include matching fields in the two tables. For example, in a database containing employees and departments, there is a relationship between the two tables because one department can have many employees assigned to it. Department Code could be the matching field in the two tables.

5. **Determine data types for the fields.** For each field, determine the type of data the field can contain. One field, for example, might contain only numbers. Another field might contain currency amounts, while a third field might contain only dates. Some fields contain text data, meaning any combination of letters, numbers and special characters (!, ;, ', &, and so on). For example, in an Employee table, the Date Hired field would contain dates, the Salary field would contain currency amounts, and the Hours Worked field would contain numbers. The other fields in the Employee table would contain text data, such as Employee Name and Department Code.

6. **Identify and remove any unwanted redundancy. Redundancy** is the storing of a piece of data in more than one place. Redundancy usually, but not always, causes problems, such as wasted space, difficulties with update, and possible data inconsistency. Examine each table you have created to see if it contains redundancy and, if so, determine whether the redundancy causes these problems. If it does, remove the redundancy by splitting the table into two tables. For example, you may have a single table of employees. In addition to typical employee data (name, address, earnings, and so on), the table might contain Department Number and Department Name. If so, the Department Name could repeat multiple times.

(continued)

**Plan
Ahead**

(continued)

Every employee whose department number is 12, for example, would have the same department name. It would be better to split the table into two tables, one for Employees and one for Department. In the Department table, the Department Name is stored only once.

7. **Determine a location for the database. The database you have designed will be stored in a single file. You need to determine a location in which to store the file.**

When necessary, more specific details concerning the above guidelines are presented at appropriate points in the chapter. The chapter also will identify the actions performed and decisions made regarding these guidelines during the creation of the database shown in Figure 1–1 on page AC 3.

BTW

Database Design
For more information on database design methods and for techniques for identifying and eliminating redundancy, visit the Access 2007 Database Design Web page (scsite.com/ac2007/dbdesign).

Designing a Database

This section illustrates the database design process by showing how you would design the database for JSP Recruiters from a set of requirements. In this section, you will use a commonly accepted shorthand to represent the tables and fields that make up the database as well as the primary keys for the tables. For each table, you give the name of the table followed by a set of parentheses. Within the parentheses is a list of the fields in the table separated by columns. You underline the primary key. For example,

Product (<u>Product Code</u>, Description, On Hand, Price)

represents a table called Product. The Product table contains four fields: Product Code, Description, On Hand, and Price. The Product Code field is the primary key.

Database Requirements

JSP Recruiters needs to maintain information on both clients and recruiters. It currently keeps this data in the two Word tables and two Excel workbooks shown in Figure 1–2. They use Word tables for address information and Excel workbooks for financial information.

Client Number	Client Name	Street	City	State	Postal Code
AC34	Alys Clinic	134 Central	Berridge	CO	80330
BH72	Berls Hospital	415 Main	Berls	CO	80349
BL12	Benton Labs	12 Mountain	Denton	CO	80412
EA45	ENT Assoc.	867 Ridge	Fort Stewart	CO	80336
FD89	Ferb Dentistry	34 Crestview	Berridge	CO	80330
FH22	Family Health	123 Second	Tarleton	CO	80409
MH56	Maun Hospital	76 Dixon	Mason	CO	80356
PR11	Peel Radiology	151 Valleyview	Fort Stewart	CO	80336
TC37	Tarleton Clinic	451 Hull	Tarleton	CO	80409
WL56	West Labs	785 Main	Berls	CO	80349

**(a)
Client Address
Information
(Word Table)**

Figure 1–2

(b) Client Financial Information (Excel Workbook)

	A	B	C	D
1	Client Number	Client Name	Amount Paid	Current Due
2	AC34	Alys Clinic	$0.00	$17,500.00
3	BH72	Berls Hospital	$29,200.00	$0.00
4	BL12	Benton Labs	$16,500.00	$38,225.00
5	EA45	ENT Assoc.	$12,750.00	$15,000.00
6	FD89	Ferb Dentistry	$21,000.00	$12,500.00
7	FH22	Family Health	$0.00	$0.00
8	MH56	Maun Hospital	$0.00	$43,025.00
9	PR11	Peel Radiology	$31,750.00	$0.00
10	TC37	Tarleton Clinic	$18,750.00	$31,500.00
11	WL56	West Labs	$14,000.00	$0.00

(c) Recruiter Address Information (Word Table)

Recruiter Number	Last Name	First Name	Street	City	State	Postal Code
21	Kerry	Alyssa	261 Pointer	Tourin	CO	80416
24	Reeves	Camden	3135 Brill	Denton	CO	80412
27	Fernandez	Jaime	265 Maxwell	Charleston	CO	80380
34	Lee	Jan	1827 Oak	Denton	CO	80413

(d) Recruiter Financial Information (Excel Workbook)

	A	B	C	D	E
1	Recruiter Number	Last Name	First Name	Rate	Commission
2	21	Kerry	Alyssa	0.10	$17,600.00
3	24	Reeves	Camden	0.10	$19,900.00
4	27	Fernandez	Jaime	0.09	$9,450.00
5	34	Lee	Jan	0.08	$0.00

Figure 1–2 (continued)

For clients, JSP needs to maintain address data. It currently keeps this address data in a Word table (Figure 1–2a). It also maintains financial data for each client. This includes the amount paid and the current due from the client. It keeps these amounts along with the client name and number in the Excel workbook shown in Figure 1–2b.

JSP keeps recruiter address data in a Word table as shown in Figure 1–2c. Just as with clients, it keeps financial data for recruiters, including their rate and commission, in a separate Excel workbook, as shown in Figure 1–2d.

Finally, it keeps track of which clients are assigned to which recruiters. Currently, for example, clients AC34 (Alys Clinic), FD89 (Ferb Dentistry), and PR11 (Peel Radiology) are assigned to recruiter 21 (Alyssa Kerry). Clients BH72 (Berls Hospital), BL12 (Benton Labs), FH22 (Family Health), MH56 (Maun Hospital), and WL56 (West Labs) are assigned to recruiter 24 (Camden Reeves). Clients EA45 (ENT Assoc.) and TC37 (Tarleton Clinic) are assigned to recruiter 27 (Jaime Fernandez). JSP has an additional recruiter, Jan Lee, whose number has been assigned as 34, but who has not yet been assigned any clients.

Naming Tables and Fields

In designing your database, you must name the tables and fields. Thus, before beginning the design process, you must understand the rules for table and field names, which are:

1. Names can be up to 64 characters in length.
2. Names can contain letters, digits, and spaces, as well as most of the punctuation symbols.
3. Names cannot contain periods (.), exclamation points (!), accent graves (`), or square brackets ([ ]).
4. The same name cannot be used for two different fields in the same table.

The approach to naming tables and fields used in this text is to begin the names with an uppercase letter and to use lowercase for the other letters. In multiple-word names, each word begins with an uppercase letter, and there is a space between words (for example, Client Number). You should know that there are other approaches. Some people omit the space (ClientNumber). Still others use an underscore in place of the space (Client_Number). Finally, some use an underscore in place of a space, but use the same case for all letters (CLIENT_NUMBER or client_number).

BTW

Naming Fields
Access 2007 has a number of reserved words, words that have a special meaning to Access. You cannot use these reserved words as field names. For example, Name is a reserved word and could not be used in the Client table to describe a client's name. For a complete list of reserved words in Access 2007, consult Access Help.

Identifying the Tables

Now that you know the rules for naming tables and fields, you are ready to begin the design process. The first step is to identify the main objects involved in the requirements. For the JSP Recruiters database, the main objects are clients and recruiters. This leads to two tables, which you must name. Reasonable names for these two tables are:

Client

Recruiter

Determining the Primary Keys

The next step is to identify the fields that will be the primary keys. Client numbers uniquely identify clients, and recruiter numbers uniquely identify recruiters. Thus, the primary key for the Client table is the client number, and the primary key for the Recruiter table is the recruiter number. Reasonable names for these fields would be Client Number and Recruiter Number, respectively. Adding these primary keys to the tables gives:

Client (<u>Client Number</u>)

Recruiter (<u>Recruiter Number</u>)

BTW

Database Design Language (DBDL)
DBDL is a commonly accepted shorthand representation for showing the structure of a relational database. You write the name of the table and then within parentheses you list all the columns in the table. If the columns continue beyond one line, indent the subsequent lines.

Determining Additional Fields

After identifying the primary keys, you need to determine and name the additional fields. In addition to the client number, the Client Address Information shown in Figure 1–2a contains the client name, street, city, state, and postal code. These would be fields in the Client table. The Client Financial Information shown in Figure 1–2b on the previous page also contains the client number and client name, which are already included in the Client table. The financial information also contains the amount paid and the current due. Adding the amount paid and current due fields to those already identified in the Client table and assigning reasonable names gives:

Client (<u>Client Number</u>, Client Name, Street, City, State, Postal Code,
    Amount Paid, Current Due)

Similarly, examining the Recruiter Address Information in Figure 1–2c on page AC 7 adds the last name, first name, street, city, state, and postal code fields to the Recruiter table. In addition to the recruiter number, last name, and first name, the Recruiter Financial Information in Figure 1–2d would add the rate and commission. Adding these fields to the Recruiter table and assigning reasonable names gives:

Recruiter (<u>Recruiter Number</u>, Last Name, First Name, Street, City,

State, Postal Code, Rate, Commission)

Determining and Implementing Relationships Between the Tables

Plan
Ahead

> **Determine relationships among the tables.**
> The most common type of relationship you will encounter between tables is the **one-to-many relationship**. This means that each row in the first table may be associated with *many* rows in the second table, but each row in the second table is associated with only *one* row in the first. The first table is called the "one" table and the second is called the "many" table. For example, there may be a relationship between departments and employees, in which each department can have many employees, but each employee is assigned to only one department. In this relationship, there would be two tables, Department and Employee. The Department table would be the "one" table in the relationship. The Employee table would be the "many" table.
>   To determine relationships among tables, you can follow these general guidelines:
>
> 1. Identify the "one" table.
>
> 2. Identify the "many" table.
>
> 3. Include the primary key from the "one" table as a field in the "many" table.

According to the requirements, each client has one recruiter, but each recruiter can have many clients. Thus, the Recruiter table is the "one" table, and the Client table is the "many" table. To implement this one-to-many relationship between recruiters and clients, add the Recruiter Number field (the primary key of the Recruiter table) to the Client table. This produces:

Client (<u>Client Number</u>, Client Name, Street, City, State, Postal Code, Amount Paid,
    Current Due, Recruiter Number)

Recruiter (<u>Recruiter Number</u>, Last Name, First Name, Street, City, State, Postal
    Code, Rate, Commission)

Determining Data Types for the Fields

BTW

Currency Symbols
To show the symbol for the Euro (€) instead of the dollar sign, change the Format property for the field whose data type is currency. To change the default symbols for currency, change the settings in the operating system using the Control Panel.

Each field has a **data type**. This indicates the type of data that can be stored in the field. Three of the most commonly used data types are:

1. **Text** — The field can contain any characters. A maximum number of 255 characters is allowed in a field whose data type is Text.

2. **Number** — The field can contain only numbers. The numbers either can be positive or negative. Fields are assigned this type so they can be used in arithmetic operations. Fields that contain numbers but will not be used for arithmetic operations usually are assigned a data type of Text.

3. **Currency** — The field can contain only monetary data. The values will appear with currency symbols, such as dollar signs, commas, and decimal points, and with

two digits following the decimal point. Like numeric fields, you can use currency fields in arithmetic operations. Access assigns a size to currency fields automatically. Table 1–1 shows the other data types that are available.

Table 1–1 Additional Data Types	
Data Type	**Description**
Memo	Field can store a variable amount of text or combinations of text and numbers where the total number of characters may exceed 255.
Date/Time	Field can store dates and times.
AutoNumber	Field can store a unique sequential number that Access assigns to a record. Access will increment the number by 1 as each new record is added.
Yes/No	Field can store only one of two values. The choices are Yes/No, True/False, or On/Off.
OLE Object	Field can store an OLE object, which is an object linked to or embedded in the table.
Hyperlink	Field can store text that can be used as a hyperlink address.
Attachment	Field can contain an attached file. Images, spreadsheets, documents, charts, and so on can be attached to this field in a record in the database. You can view and edit the attached file.

In the Client table, because the Client Number, Client Name, Street, City, and State can all contain letters, their data types should be Text. The data type for Postal Code is Text instead of Number, because postal codes are not used in arithmetic operations. You do not add postal codes or find an average postal code, for example. The Amount Paid and Current Due fields both contain monetary data, so their data types should be Currency.

Similarly, in the Recruiter table, the data type for the Recruiter Number, Last Name, First Name, Street, City, State, and Postal Code fields all should be Text. The Commission field contains monetary amounts, so its data type should be Currency. The Rate field contains a number that is not a currency amount, so its data type should be Number.

Identifying and Removing Redundancy

Redundancy means storing the same fact in more than one place. It usually results from placing too many fields in a table — fields that really belong in separate tables — and often causes serious problems. If you had not realized there were two objects, clients and recruiters, for example, you might have placed all the data in a single Client table. Figure 1–3 shows a portion of this table with some sample data. Notice that the data for a given Recruiter (number, name, address, and so on) occurs on more than one record. The data for Camden Reeves is repeated in the figure.

Client Table

clients of recruiter 24

name of recruiter 24 appears more than once

Client Number	Client Name	Street	...	Recruiter Number	Last Name	First Name	...
AC34	Alys Clinic	134 Central	...	21	Kerry	Alyssa	...
BH72	Berls Hospital	415 Main	...	24	Reeves	Camden	...
BL12	Benton Labs	12 Mountain	...	24	Reeves	Camden	...
...	...	...	...	...	...	...	...

Figure 1–3

Storing this data on multiple records is an example of redundancy, which causes several problems, including:

1. Wasted storage space. The name of Recruiter 24 (Camden Reeves), for example, should be stored only once. Storing this fact several times is wasteful.

2. More difficult database updates. If, for example, Camden Reeves's name is spelled wrong and needs to be changed in the database, his name would need to be changed in several different places.

3. A possibility of inconsistent data. There is nothing to prohibit the recruiter's last name from being Reeves on client BH72's record and Reed on client BL12's record. The data would be inconsistent. In both cases, the recruiter number is 24, but the last names are different.

The solution to the problem is to place the redundant data in a separate table, one in which the data no longer will be redundant. If, for example, you place the data for recruiters in a separate table (Figure 1–4), the data for each recruiter will appear only once.

Client Table

Client Number	Client Name	Street	...	Recruiter Number
AC34	Alys Clinic	134 Central	...	21
BH72	Berls Hospital	415 Main	...	24 ← clients of recruiter 24
BL12	Benton Labs	12 Mountain	...	24 ←
...	...	...	...	...

Recruiter Table

Recruiter Number	Last Name	First Name	...
21	Kerry	Alyssa	...
24	Reeves ← name of recruiter 24 appears only once	Camden	...
...	...	...	...

Figure 1–4

Notice that you need to have the recruiter number in both tables. Without it, there would be no way to tell which recruiter is associated with which client. The remaining recruiter data, however, was removed from the Client table and placed in the Recruiter table. This new arrangement corrects the problems of redundancy in the following ways:

1. Because the data for each recruiter is stored only once, space is not wasted.

2. Changing the name of a recruiter is easy. You have only to change one row in the Recruiter table.

3. Because the data for a recruiter is stored only once, inconsistent data cannot occur. Designing to omit redundancy will help you to produce good and valid database designs.

You should always examine your design to see if it contains redundancy. If it does, you should decide whether you need to remove the redundancy by creating a separate table.

BTW

Postal Codes
Some organizations with many customers spread throughout the country will, in fact, have a separate table of postal codes, cities, and states. If you call such an organization to place an order, they typically will ask you for your postal code (or ZIP code), rather than asking for your city, state, and postal code. They then will indicate the city and state that correspond to that postal code and ask you if that is correct.

If you examine your design, you'll see that there is one area of redundancy (see the data in Figure 1–1 on page AC 3). Cities and states are both repeated. Every client whose postal code is 80330, for example, has Berridge as the city and CO as the state. To remove this redundancy, you would create a table whose primary key is Postal Code and that contains City and State as additional fields. City and State would be removed from the Client table. Having City, State, and Postal Code in a table is very common, however, and usually you would not take such action. There is no other redundancy in your tables.

Starting Access

If you are using a computer to step through the project in this chapter, and you want your screen to match the figures in this book, you should change your screen's resolution to 1024 × 768. For information about how to change a computer's resolution, read Appendix E.

To Start Access

The following steps, which assume Windows is running, start Access based on a typical installation. You may need to ask your instructor how to start Access for your computer.

1
- Click the Start button on the Windows taskbar to display the Start menu.

- Point to All Programs on the Start menu to display the All Programs submenu.

- Point to Microsoft Office on the All Programs submenu to display the Microsoft Office submenu (Figure 1–5).

Figure 1–5

2

- Click Microsoft Office Access 2007 to start Access and display the Getting Started with Microsoft Office Access screen (Figure 1–6).

- If the Access window is not maximized, click the Maximize button next to the Close button on its title bar to maximize the window.

Q&A

What is a maximized window?

A maximized window fills the entire screen. When you maximize a window, the Maximize button changes to a Restore Down button.

Figure 1–6

Creating a Database

In Access, all the tables, reports, forms, and queries that you create are stored in a single file called a database. Thus, before creating any of these objects, you first must create the database that will hold them. You can use either the Blank Database option or a template to create a new database. If you already know the tables and fields you want in your database, you would use the Blank Database option. If not, you can use a template. Templates can guide you by suggesting some commonly used databases. If you choose to create a database using a template, you would use the following steps.

TO CREATE A DATABASE USING A TEMPLATE

1. If the template you wish to use is not already visible on the Getting Started with Microsoft Office Access page, double-click the links in the Template Categories pane to display the desired template.

2. Click the template you wish to use.

3. Enter a file name (or accept the suggested file name) and select a location for the database.

4. Click the Create button to create the database or the Download button to download the database and create the database, if necessary.

When you create a database, the computer places it on a storage medium, such as a USB flash drive, CD, or hard disk. A saved database is referred to as a **file**. A **file name** is the name assigned to a file when it is saved.

Other Ways

1. Double-click Access icon on desktop, if one is present

2. Click Microsoft Office Access 2007 on Start menu

BTW

Naming Files
File names can be a maximum of 255 characters including the file extension. The file extension for Access 2007 is .accdb. You can use either uppercase or lowercase letters in file names.

Determine where to create the database.
When creating a database, you must decide which storage medium to use.

   If you always work on the same computer and have no need to transport your database to a different location, then your computer's hard drive will suffice as a storage location. It is a good idea, however, to save a backup copy of your database on a separate medium in case the file becomes corrupted, or the computer's hard drive fails.

   If you plan to work on your database in various locations or on multiple computers, then you can consider saving your projects on a portable medium, such as a USB flash drive or CD. The projects in this book are stored on a USB flash drive, which saves files quickly and reliably and can be reused. CDs are easily portable and serve as good backups for the final versions of projects because they generally can save files only one time.

To Create a Database

   Because you already know the tables and fields you want in the JSP Recruiters database, you would use the Blank Database option rather than using a template. The following steps create a database, using the file name JSP Recruiters, on a USB flash drive.

- With a USB flash drive connected to one of the computer's USB ports, click Blank Database to create a new blank database (Figure 1–7).

Figure 1–7

2

- Repeatedly press the DELETE key to delete the default name of Database1.

- Type JSP Recruiters in the File Name text box to replace the default file name of Database1 (your screen may show Database1.accdb). Do not press the ENTER key after typing the file name (Figure 1–8).

Q&A

What characters can I use in a file name?

A file name can have a maximum of 255 characters, including spaces. The only invalid characters are the backslash (\), slash (/), colon (:), asterisk (*), question mark (?), quotation mark ("), less than symbol (<), greater than symbol (>), and vertical bar (|).

Figure 1–8

3

- Click the 'Browse for a location to put your database' button to display the File New Database dialog box (Figure 1–9).

Q&A

Do I have to save to a USB flash drive?

No. You can save to any device or folder. A **folder** is a specific location on a storage medium. You can save to the default folder or a different folder. You also can create your own folders, which is explained later in this book.

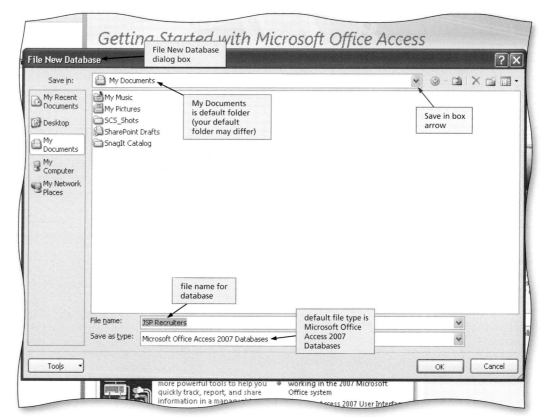

Figure 1–9

4

- Click the Save in box arrow to display a list of available drives and folders (Figure 1–10).

Q&A Why is my list of files, folders, and drives arranged and named differently from those shown in the figure?

Your computer's configuration determines how the list of files and folders is displayed and how drives are named. You can change the save location by clicking shortcuts on the My Places bar.

Q&A How do I save the file if I am not using a USB flash drive?

Use the same process, but be certain to select your device in the Save in list.

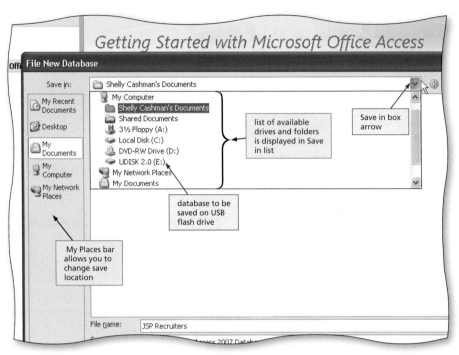

Figure 1–10

5

- Click UDISK 2.0 (E:) in the Save in list to select the USB flash drive, Drive E in this case, as the new save location (Figure 1–11).

Q&A What if my USB flash drive has a different name or letter?

It is very likely that your USB flash drive will have a different name and drive letter and be connected to a different port. Verify that the device in your Save in list is correct.

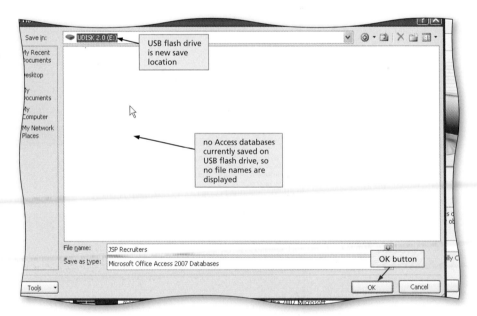

Figure 1–11

6

- Click the OK button to select the USB flash drive as the location for the database and to return to the Getting Started with Microsoft Office Access screen (Figure 1–12).

Figure 1–12

7

- Click the Create button to create the database on the USB flash drive with the file name, JSP Recruiters (Figure 1–13).

How do I know that the JSP Recruiters database is created?

The name of the database appears in the title bar.

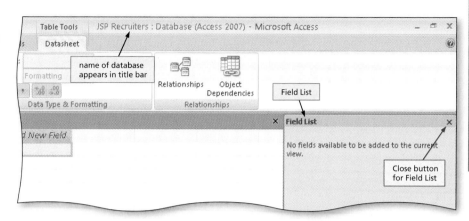

Figure 1–13

8

- If a Field List appears, click its Close button to remove the Field List from the screen (Figure 1–14).

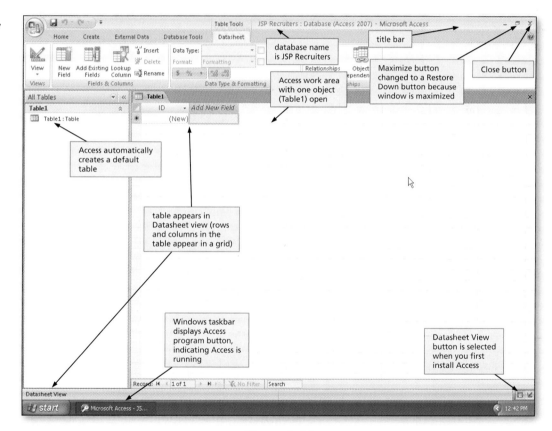

Figure 1–14

Other Ways

1. Click Office Button, click Save, type file name, select drive or folder, click Save button

2. Press CTRL+S or press SHIFT+F12 or press ALT and then 1, type file name, select drive or folder, click Save button

The Access Window

The Access window consists of a variety of components to make your work more efficient and documents more professional. These include the Navigation pane, Access work area, Ribbon, Mini toolbar and shortcut menus, Quick Access Toolbar, and Office Button. Some of these components are common to other Microsoft Office 2007 programs; others are unique to Access.

Navigation Pane and Access Work Area

You work on objects such as tables, forms, and reports in the **Access work area**. In the work area in Figure 1–14 on the previous page, a single table, Table1, is open in the work area. Figure 1–15 shows a work area with multiple objects open. **Object tabs** for the open objects appear at the top of the work area. You can select one of the open objects by clicking its tab. In the figure the Client Form is the selected object. To the left of the work area is the Navigation pane. The Navigation pane contains a list of all the objects in the database. You use this pane to open an object. You also can customize the way objects are displayed in the Navigation pane.

Figure 1–15

The Access work area in Figure 1–15 contains an insertion point, mouse pointer, scroll bar, and status bar. Other elements that may appear in the work area are discussed later in this and subsequent chapters.

Insertion Point   The **insertion point** is a blinking vertical bar that indicates where text, graphics, and other items will be inserted. As you type, the insertion point moves to the right.

Mouse Pointer   The **mouse pointer** becomes different shapes depending on the task you are performing in Access and the pointer's location on the screen. The mouse pointer in Figure 1–15 is the shape of an I-beam.

Scroll Bar   You use a **scroll bar** to display different portions of a database object in the Access window. At the right edge of the window is a **vertical scroll bar**. If an object is too wide to fit in the Access window, a **horizontal scroll bar** also appears at the bottom of the window. On a scroll bar, the position of the **scroll box** reflects the location of the portion of the database object that is displayed in the Access window. A **scroll arrow** is located at each end of a scroll bar. To scroll through, or display different portions of the object in the Access window, you can click a scroll arrow or drag the scroll box.

Status Bar   The **status bar**, located at the bottom of the Access window above the Windows taskbar, presents information about the database object, the progress of current tasks, and the status of certain commands and keys; it also provides controls for viewing the object. As you type text or perform certain commands, various indicators may appear on the status bar.

The left edge of the status bar in Figure 1–15 shows that the form object is open in Form view. Toward the right edge are View buttons, which you can use to change the view that is currently displayed.

Ribbon

The **Ribbon**, located near the top of the Access window, is the control center in Access (Figure 1–16a). The Ribbon provides easy, central access to the tasks you perform while creating a database object. The Ribbon consists of tabs, groups, and commands. Each **tab** surrounds a collection of groups, and each group contains related commands.

When you start Access, the Ribbon displays four top-level tabs: Home, Create, External Data, and Database Tools. The **Home tab**, called the primary tab, contains the more frequently used commands. To display a different tab on the Ribbon, click the top-level tab. That is, to display the Create tab, click Create on the Ribbon. To return to the Home tab, click Home on the Ribbon. The tab currently displayed is called the **active tab**.

To allow more space in the Access work area, some users prefer to minimize the Ribbon, which hides the groups on the Ribbon and displays only the top-level tabs (Figure 1–16b). To use commands on a minimized Ribbon, click the top-level tab.

Each time you start Access, the Ribbon appears the same way it did the last time you used Access. The chapters in this book, however, begin with the Ribbon appearing as it did at the initial installation of the software. If you are stepping through this chapter on a computer and you want your Ribbon to match the figures in this book, read Appendix E.

BTW

Minimizing the Ribbon
If you want to minimize the Ribbon, right-click the Ribbon and then click Minimize the Ribbon on the shortcut menu, double-click the active tab, or press CTRL+F1. To restore a minimized Ribbon, right-click the Ribbon and then click Minimize the Ribbon on the shortcut menu, double-click any top-level tab, or press CTRL+F1. To use commands on a minimized Ribbon, click the top-level tab.

(a) Ribbon at Initial Installation (Default Ribbon)

(b) Minimized Ribbon

Figure 1–16

In addition to the top-level tabs, Access displays other tabs, called **contextual tabs**, when you perform certain tasks or work with objects such as datasheets. If you are working with a table in Datasheet view, for example, the Table Tools tab and its related subordinate Datasheet tab appear (Figure 1–17). When you are finished working with the table, the Table Tools and Datasheet tabs disappear from the Ribbon. Access determines when contextual tabs should appear and disappear based on tasks you perform. Some contextual tabs have more than one related subordinate tab.

Figure 1–17

Figure 1–18

Commands on the Ribbon include buttons, boxes (text boxes, check boxes, etc.), and galleries (Figure 1–18). A **gallery** is a set of choices, often graphical, arranged in a grid or in a list. You can scroll through choices on an in-Ribbon gallery by clicking the gallery's scroll arrows. Or, you can click a gallery's More button to view more gallery options on the screen at a time. Some buttons and boxes have arrows that, when clicked, also display a gallery; others always cause a gallery to be displayed when clicked. Many galleries support **live preview**, which is a feature that allows you to point to a gallery choice and see its effect in the database object — without actually selecting the choice.

Some commands on the Ribbon display an image to help you remember their function. When you point to a command on the Ribbon, all or part of the command glows in shades of yellow and orange, and an Enhanced ScreenTip appears on the screen. An **Enhanced ScreenTip** is an on-screen note that provides the name of the command, available keyboard shortcut(s), a description of the command, and sometimes instructions for how to obtain help about the command (Figure 1–19). Enhanced ScreenTips are more detailed than a typical ScreenTip, which usually only displays the name of the command.

The lower-right corner of some groups on the Ribbon has a small arrow, called a **Dialog Box Launcher**, which, when clicked, displays a dialog box or a task pane with additional options for the group (Figure 1–20). When presented with a dialog box, you make selections and must close the dialog box before returning to the database object. A **task pane**, by contrast, is a window that can remain open and visible while you work in the database object.

Figure 1–19

Figure 1–20

Mini Toolbar and Shortcut Menus

The **Mini toolbar**, which appears automatically based on tasks you perform, contains commands related to changing the appearance of text in a database object. All commands on the Mini toolbar also exist on the Ribbon. The purpose of the Mini toolbar is to minimize mouse movement. For example, if you want to use a command that currently is not displayed on the active tab, you can use the command on the Mini toolbar — instead of switching to a different tab to use the command.

When the Mini toolbar appears, it initially is transparent (Figure 1–21a). If you do not use the transparent Mini toolbar, it disappears from the screen. To use the Mini toolbar, move the mouse pointer into the toolbar, which causes the Mini toolbar to change from a transparent to bright appearance (Figure 1–21b).

A **shortcut menu**, which appears when you right-click an object, is a list of frequently used commands that relate to the right-clicked object. When you right-click a table, for example, a shortcut menu appears with commands related to the table (Figure 1–21c).

(a) Transparent Mini Toolbar

(b) Bright Mini Toolbar

(c) Shortcut Menu

Figure 1–21

Quick Access Toolbar

The **Quick Access Toolbar**, located by default above the Ribbon, provides easy access to frequently used commands (Figure 1–22a). The commands on the Quick Access Toolbar always are available, regardless of the task you are performing. Initially, the Quick Access Toolbar contains the Save, Undo, and Redo commands. If you click the Customize Quick Access Toolbar button, Access provides a list of commands you quickly can add to and remove from the Quick Access Toolbar (Figure 1–22b).

You also can add other commands to or delete commands from the Quick Access Toolbar so that it contains the commands you use most often. As you add commands to the Quick Access Toolbar, its commands may interfere with the title of the database object on the title bar. For this reason, Access provides an option of displaying the Quick Access Toolbar below the Ribbon (Figure 1–22c).

Figure 1-22

Each time you start Access, the Quick Access Toolbar appears the same way it did the last time you used Access. The chapters in this book, however, begin with the Quick Access Toolbar appearing as it did at the initial installation of the software. If you are stepping through this chapter on a computer, and you want your Quick Access Toolbar to match the figures in this book, you should reset your Quick Access Toolbar. For more information about how to reset the Quick Access Toolbar, read Appendix E.

Office Button

While the Ribbon is a control center for creating database objects, the **Office Button** is a central location for managing and sharing database objects. When you click the Office Button, located in the upper-left corner of the window, Access displays the Office Button menu (Figure 1–23). A **menu** contains a list of commands.

When you click the New, Open, and Print commands on the Office Button menu, Access displays a dialog box with additional options. The Save As, Print, Manage, and Publish commands have an arrow to their right. If you point to this arrow, Access displays a **submenu**, which is a list of additional commands associated with the selected command (Figure 1–24). For the Save As, Print, Manage, and Publish commands that do not display a dialog box when clicked, you can point either to the command or the arrow to display the submenu.

Figure 1–23

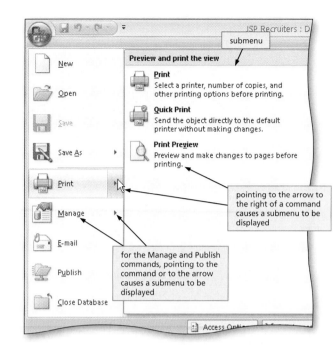

Figure 1–24

Key Tips

If you prefer using the keyboard instead of the mouse, you can press the ALT key on the keyboard to display a **Key Tip badge**, or keyboard code icon, for certain commands (Figure 1–25). To select a command using the keyboard, press its displayed code letter, or **Key Tip**. When you press a Key Tip, additional Key Tips related to the selected command may appear. For example, to select the New command on the Office Button menu, press the ALT key, then press the F key, then press the N key.

To remove the Key Tip badges from the screen, press the ALT key or the ESC key until all Key Tip badges disappear, or click the mouse anywhere in the Access window.

Figure 1–25

Creating a Table

When you first create your database, Access automatically creates a table for you. You can immediately begin defining the fields. If, for whatever reason, you do not have this table or inadvertently delete it, you can create the table by clicking Create on the Ribbon and then clicking the Table button on the Create tab. In either case, you are ready to define the fields.

To Define the Fields in a Table

With the table already created, the next step is to define the fields in the table and to assign them data types. The fields in the Client table are Client Number, Client Name, Street, City, State, Postal Code, Amount Paid, Current Due, and Recruiter Number. The data type for the Amount Paid and Current Due fields is Currency. The data type for all other fields is Text. The following steps define the fields in the table.

- Right-click Add New Field to display a shortcut menu (Figure 1–26).

Q&A Why don't I delete the ID field first, before adding other fields?

You cannot delete the primary key in Datasheet view; you only can delete it in Design view. After adding the other fields, you will move to Design view, delete the ID field, and then make the Client Number the primary key.

Q&A Why does my shortcut menu look different?

You right-clicked within the column instead of right-clicking the column heading.

Figure 1–26

- Click Rename Column on the shortcut menu to display an insertion point.

- Type `Client Number` to assign a name to the new field.

- Press the DOWN ARROW key to complete the addition of the field (Figure 1–27).

Q&A Why doesn't the whole name appear?

The default column size is not large enough for Client Number to appear in its entirety. Later in this book, you will learn how to resize columns so that the entire name can appear.

Figure 1–27

- Right-click Add New Field to display a shortcut menu, click Rename Column on the shortcut menu to display an insertion point, type `Client Name` to assign a name to the new field, and then press the DOWN ARROW key to complete the addition of the field.

Did I have to press the DOWN ARROW key? Couldn't I have just moved to the next field or pressed the ENTER key?

You could have pressed the TAB key or the ENTER key to move to the column heading for the next field. Pressing the DOWN ARROW key, however, completes the entry of the Client Number field and allows you to ensure that the column is assigned the correct data type.

- Using the same technique add the fields in the Client table up through and including the Amount Paid field.

- Click the Data Type box arrow to display the Data Type box menu (Figure 1–28).

Figure 1–28

- Click Currency to select Currency as the data type for the Amount Paid field (Figure 1–29).

Why does Currency appear twice?

The second Currency is the format, which indicates how the data will be displayed. For the Currency data type, Access automatically sets the format to Currency, which is usually what you would want. You could change it to something else, if desired, by clicking the arrow and selecting the desired format.

Figure 1–29

- Click the right scroll arrow to shift the fields to the left and display the Add New Field column (Figure 1–30).

Figure 1–30

- Make the remaining entries from the Client table structure shown in Figure 1–31 to complete the structure. Be sure to select Currency as the data type for the Current Due field.

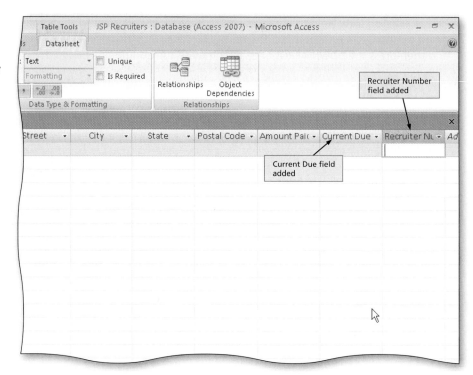

Figure 1–31

Creating a Table: Table Templates
Access includes table templates that assist you in creating some commonly used tables and fields. To use a template, click Create on the ribbon and then click the Table Templates button on the Create tab. Click the desired template, make any adjustments you wish to the table that Access creates, and then save the table.

Making Changes to the Structure

When creating a table, check the entries carefully to ensure they are correct. If you discover a mistake while still typing the entry, you can correct the error by repeatedly pressing the BACKSPACE key until the incorrect characters are removed. Then, type the correct characters. If you do not discover a mistake until later, you can use the following techniques to make the necessary changes to the structure:

- To undo your most recent change, click the Undo button on the Quick Access Toolbar. If there is nothing that Access can undo, this button will be dim, and clicking it will have no effect.
- To delete a field, right-click the column heading for the field (the position containing the field name), and then click Delete Column on the shortcut menu.
- To change the name of a field, right-click the column heading for the field, click Rename Column on the shortcut menu, and then type the desired field name.
- To insert a field as the last field, right-click the Add New Field column heading, click Rename Column on the shortcut menu, type the desired field name, click the down arrow, and then ensure the correct data type is already selected.
- To insert a field between existing fields, right-click the column heading for the field that will follow the new field, and then click Insert Column on the shortcut menu. You then proceed just as you do when you insert a field as the last field.

As an alternative to these steps, you may want to start over. To do so, click the Close button for the window containing the table, and then click the No button in the Microsoft Office Access dialog box. Click Create on the Ribbon and then click the Table button to create a table. You then can repeat the process you used earlier to define the fields in the table.

To Save a Table

The Client table structure now is complete. The final step is to save and close the table within the database. At this time, you should give the table a name.

The following steps save the table, giving it the name, Client.

• Click the Save button on the Quick Access Toolbar to save the structure of the table (Figure 1–32).

Q&A

I have an extra row between the row containing the field names and the row that begins with the asterisk. What happened? Is this a problem? If so, how do I fix it?

You inadvertently added a record to the table by pressing some key after you pressed the DOWN ARROW key. Even pressing the SPACEBAR would add a record. You now have a record you do not want and it will cause problems when you attempt to assign a different primary key. To fix it, you need to delete the record, which you will do in Step 3.

Figure 1–32

❷

• Type Client to change the name to be assigned to the table (Figure 1–33).

Figure 1–33

❸

• Click the OK button to save the structure with the name, Client (Figure 1–34).

• If you have an additional record between the field names and the asterisk, click the record selector (the box at the beginning of the record), press the DELETE key, and then click the Yes button when Access asks you if you want to delete the record.

Figure 1–34

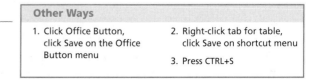

Other Ways
1. Click Office Button, click Save on the Office Button menu	2. Right-click tab for table, click Save on shortcut menu
	3. Press CTRL+S

To Change the Primary Key

To change the primary key, you must first delete the ID field that Access created automatically. You then can designate the Client Number field as the primary key. To delete the ID field, the table must appear in Design view rather than Datasheet view. You also can designate the Client Number field as the primary key within Design view. As you define or modify the fields, the **row selector**, the small box or bar that, when you click it, selects the entire row, indicates the field you currently are describing. The following steps move to Design view and then change the primary key.

- Click the Design View button on the status bar to move to Design view.

- Confirm that your data types match those shown in the figure. Make any necessary corrections to the data types (Figure 1–35).

Q&A

Did I have to save the table before moving to Design view?

Yes. If you had not saved it yourself, Access would have asked you to save it.

Figure 1–35

- Click the row selector for the ID field to select the field.

- Press the DELETE key to delete the field (Figure 1–36).

Q&A

What if I click the row selector for the wrong field before pressing the DELETE key?

Click the No button in the Microsoft Office Access dialog box. If you inadvertently clicked the Yes button, you have deleted the wrong field. You can fix this by clicking the Close button for the Client table, and then clicking the No button when asked if you want to save your changes.

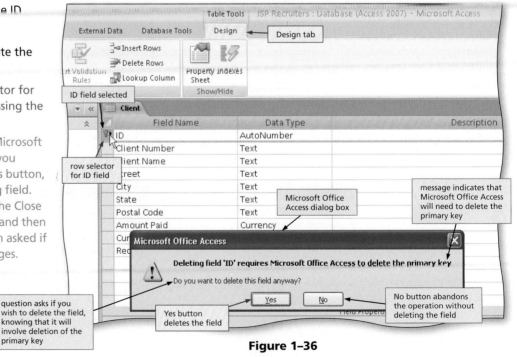

Figure 1–36

3

- Click the Yes button to complete the deletion of the field.

- With the Client Number field selected, click the Primary Key button to designate the Client Number field as the primary key.

- Click the Save button to save the changes (Figure 1–37).

 When I attempted to save the table I got an error message that indicates index or primary key cannot contain a null value. What did I do wrong and how do I fix it?

You inadvertently added a record to the table by pressing some key after you pressed the DOWN ARROW key. To fix it, click the OK button (you will need to do it twice) and then click the Primary Key button to remove the primary key. Click the Save button to save the table and then click the View button near the upper-left corner of the screen to return to datasheet view. Click the little box immediately to the left of the record you added and press the DELETE key. Click the Yes button when Access asks if it is OK to delete the record. Click the View button again and continue with these steps.

Figure 1–37

4

- Close the Client table by clicking the Close 'Client' button (Figure 1–38).

Figure 1–38

To Add Records to a Table

Creating a table by building the structure and saving the table is the first step in a two-step process. The second step is to add records to the table. To add records to a table, the table must be open. When making changes to tables, you work in Datasheet view. In **Datasheet view**, the table is represented as a collection of rows and columns called a **datasheet**.

You often add records in phases. You may, for example, not have enough time to add all the records in one session. The following steps open the Client table in Datasheet view and then add the first two records in the Client table (Figure 1–39).

Client Numb ▾	Client Name ▾	Street ▾	City ▾	State ▾	Postal Code ▾	Amount Paic ▾	Current Due ▾	Recruiter Nu ▾
AC34	Alys Clinic	134 Central	Berridge	CO	80330	$0.00	$17,500.00	21
BH72	Berls Hospital	415 Main	Berls	CO	80349	$29,200.00	$0.00	24

Figure 1–39

1

- Right-click the Client table in the Navigation pane to display the shortcut menu (Figure 1–40).

Figure 1–40

- Click Open on the shortcut menu to open the Client table in Datasheet view.

Q&A

What if I want to return to Design view?

There are two ways to get to Design view. You could click Design View on the shortcut menu. Alternatively, you could click Open on the shortcut menu to open the table in Datasheet view and then click the Design View button on the Access status bar.

- Click the Shutter Bar Open/Close Button to hide the Navigation pane (Figure 1–41).

Figure 1–41

- Click in the Client Number field and type AC34 to enter the first client number. Be sure you type the letters in uppercase so they are entered in the database correctly (Figure 1–42).

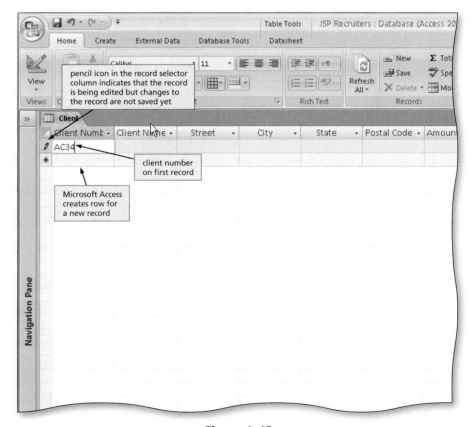

Figure 1–42

4

- Press the TAB key to complete the entry for the Client Number field.

- Enter the client name, street, city, state, and postal code by typing the following entries, pressing the TAB key after each one: Alys Clinic as the client name, 134 Central as the street, Berridge as the city, CO as the state, and 80330 as the postal code.

- Type 0 to enter the amount paid (Figure 1–43).

 Q&A

Do I need to type a dollar sign?

You do not need to type dollar signs or commas. In addition, because the digits to the right of the decimal point are both zeros, you do not need to type either the decimal point or the zeros.

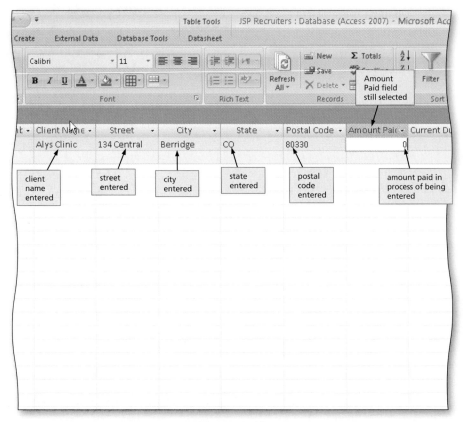

Figure 1–43

5

- Press the TAB key to complete the entry for the Amount Paid field.

- Type 17500 to enter the current due amount and then press the TAB key to move to the next field.

- Type 21 as the Recruiter number to complete data entry for the record (Figure 1–44).

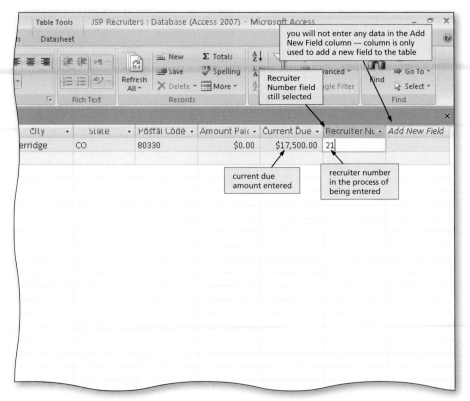

Figure 1–44

6

- Press the TAB key to complete the entry of the first record (Figure 1–45).

How and when do I save the record?

As soon as you have entered or modified a record and moved to another record, the original record is saved. This is different from other applications. The rows entered in an Excel worksheet, for example, are not saved until the entire worksheet is saved.

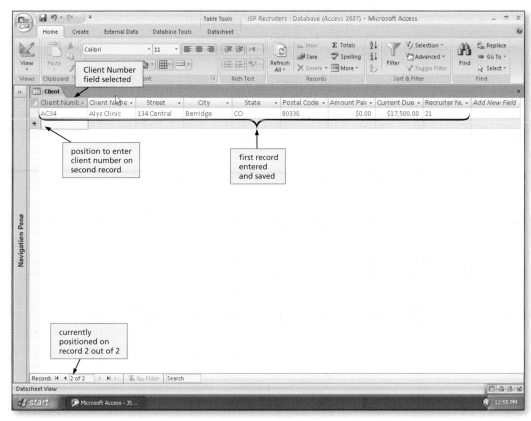

Figure 1–45

7

- Use the techniques shown in Steps 3 through 6 to enter the data for the second record in the Client table (Figure 1–46).

Figure 1–46

Undo and Redo
You also can undo multiple actions. To see a list of recent actions that you can undo, click the down arrow next to the Undo button on the Quick Access Toolbar. To redo the most recent action, click the Redo button on the Quick Access Toolbar. You also can redo multiple actions by clicking the down arrow next to the button.

Making Changes to the Data

Check your entries carefully to ensure they are correct. If you make a mistake and discover it before you press the TAB key, correct it by pressing the BACKSPACE key until the incorrect characters are removed and then typing the correct characters. If you do not discover a mistake until later, you can use the following techniques to make the necessary corrections to the data:

- To undo your most recent change, click the Undo button on the Quick Access Toolbar. If there is nothing that Access can undo, this button will be dim, and clicking it will have no effect.

- To add a record, click the New (blank) record button, shown in Figure 1–46 on the previous page, and then add the record. Do not worry about it being in the correct position in the table. Access will reposition the record based on the primary key, in this case, the Client Number.

- To delete a record, click the Record selector, shown in Figure 1–46, for the record to be deleted. Then press the DELETE key to delete the record, and click the Yes button when Access asks you to verify that you do indeed wish to delete the record.

- To change the contents of one or more fields in a record, the record must be on the screen. If it is not, use any appropriate technique, such as the UP ARROW and DOWN ARROW keys or the vertical scroll bar, to move to it. If the field you want to correct is not visible on the screen, use the horizontal scroll bar along the bottom of the screen to shift all the fields until the one you want appears. If the value in the field is currently highlighted, you can simply type the new value. If you would rather edit the existing value, you must have an insertion point in the field. You can place the insertion point by clicking in the field or by pressing F2. Once you have produced an insertion point, you can use the arrow keys, the DELETE key, and the BACKSPACE key in making the correction. You also can use the INSERT key to switch between Insert and Overtype mode. When you have made the change, press the TAB key to move to the next field.

If you cannot determine how to correct the data, you may find that you are "stuck" on the record. Access neither allows you to move to any other record until you have made the correction, nor allows you to close the table. If you encounter this situation, simply press the ESC key. Pressing the ESC key will remove from the screen the record you are trying to add. You then can move to any other record, close the table, or take any other action you desire.

AutoCorrect Options
Using the Office AutoCorrect feature, you can create entries that will replace abbreviations with spelled-out names and phrases automatically. For example, you can create the abbreviated entry *dbms* for *database management system*. Whenever you type dbms followed by a space or punctuation mark, Access automatically replaces dbms with database management system. To specify AutoCorrect rules and exceptions to the rules, click Access Options on the Office Button menu and then click Proofing in the Access Options dialog box.

AutoCorrect

Not visible in the Access window, the **AutoCorrect** feature of Access works behind the scenes, correcting common mistakes when you complete a text entry in a cell. AutoCorrect makes three types of corrections for you:

1. Corrects two initial capital letters by changing the second letter to lowercase.

2. Capitalizes the first letter in the names of days.

3. Replaces commonly misspelled words with their correct spelling. For example, it changes the misspelled word *recieve* to *receive* when you complete the entry. AutoCorrect will correct the spelling automatically of more than 400 commonly misspelled words.

To Close a Table

    It is a good idea to close a table as soon as you have finished working with it. It keeps the screen from getting cluttered and prevents you from making accidental changes to the data in the table. The following steps close the Client table.

- Click the Close 'Client' button, shown in Figure 1–46 on page AC 33, to close the table (Figure 1–47).

Figure 1–47

Other Ways

1. Right-click tab for table, click Close on shortcut menu

Quitting Access

If you save the object on which you are currently working and then quit Access, all Access windows close. If you have made changes to an object since the last time the object was saved, Access displays a dialog box asking if you want to save the changes you made before it closes that window. The dialog box contains three buttons with these resulting actions:

- Yes button — Saves the changes and then quits Access
- No button — Quits Access without saving changes
- Cancel button — Closes the dialog box and redisplays the database without saving the changes

    If no changes have been made to any object since the last time the object was saved, Access will close all windows without displaying any dialog boxes.

To Quit Access

You saved your changes to the table and did not make any additional changes. You are ready to quit Access. The following step quits Access.

1 Click the Close button on the right side of the Access title bar, shown in Figure 1–47 on the previous page, to quit Access.

Starting Access and Opening a Database

Once you have created and later closed a database, you will need to open it in the future in order to use it. Opening a database requires that Access is running on your computer.

To Start Access

The following steps, which assume Windows is running, start Access.

1 Click the Start button on the Windows taskbar to display the Start menu.

2 Point to All Programs on the Start menu to display the All Programs submenu and then point to Microsoft Office on the All Programs submenu to display the Microsoft Office submenu.

3 Click Microsoft Office Access 2007 on the Microsoft Office submenu to start Access and display the Getting Started with Microsoft Office Access window (Figure 1–48).

4 If the Access window is not maximized, click the Maximize button on its title bar to maximize the window.

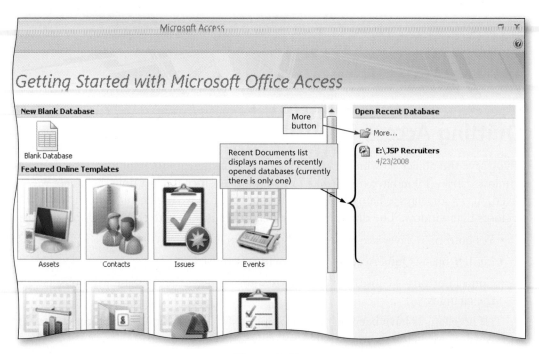

Figure 1–48

To Open a Database from Access

Earlier in this chapter you created your database on a USB flash drive using the file name, JSP Recruiters. There are two ways to open the file containing your database. If the file you created appears in the Recent Documents list, you could click it to open the file. If not, you can use the More button to open the file. The following steps use the More button to open the JSP Recruiters database from the USB flash drive.

1

• With your USB flash drive connected to one of the computer's USB ports, click the More button, shown in Figure 1–48, to display the Open dialog box.

• If necessary, click the Look in box arrow and then click UDISK 2.0 (E:) to select the USB flash drive, Drive E in this case, in the Look in list as the new open location.

• Click JSP Recruiters to select the file name (Figure 1–49).

 How do I open the file if I am not using a USB flash drive?

Use the same process, but be certain to select your device in the Look in list. You might need to open multiple folders.

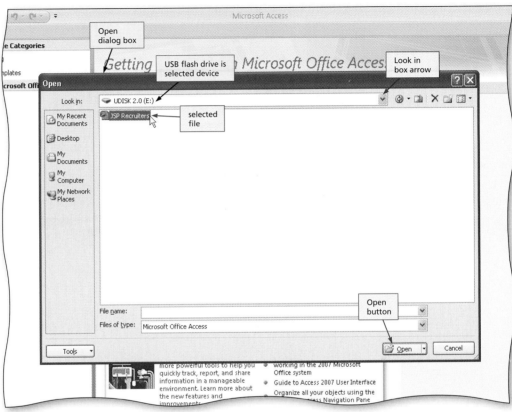

Figure 1–49

2

• Click the Open button to open the database (Figure 1–50).

 Why do I see the Access icon and name on the Windows taskbar?

When you open an Access database, an Access program button is displayed on the taskbar. If the contents of a button cannot fit in the allotted button space, an ellipsis appears. If you point to a program button, its entire contents appear in a ScreenTip, which in this case would be the program name followed by the file name.

Figure 1–50

• If a Security Warning appears, as shown in Figure 1–50 on the previous page, click the Options button to display the Microsoft Office Security Options dialog box (Figure 1–51).

• Click the 'Enable this content' option button.

• Click the OK button to enable the content.

Q&A When would I want to disable the content?

You would want to disable the content if you suspected that your database might contain harmful content or damaging macros. Because you are the one who created the database and no one else has used it, you should have no such suspicions.

Figure 1–51

Other Ways

1. Click Office Button, double-click file name in Recent Documents list

2. Press CTRL+O, select file name, press ENTER

To Add Additional Records to a Table

You can add records to a table that already contains data using a process almost identical to that used to add records to an empty table. The only difference is that you place the insertion point after the last data record before you enter the additional data. To do so, use the **Navigation buttons**, which are buttons used to move within a table, found near the lower-left corner of the screen when a table is open. The purpose of each of the Navigation buttons is described in Table 1–2.

Table 1–2 Navigation Buttons in Datasheet View	
Button	**Purpose**
First record	Moves to the first record in the table
Previous record	Moves to the previous record
Next record	Moves to the next record
Last record	Moves to the last record in the table
New (blank) record	Moves to the end of the table to a position for entering a new record

The following steps add the remaining records (Figure 1–52) to the Client table.

Client Numb ▾	Client Name ▾	Street ▾	City ▾	State ▾	Postal Code ▾	Amount Paic ▾	Current Due ▾	Recruiter Nu ▾
BL12	Benton Labs	12 Mountain	Denton	CO	80412	$16,500.00	$38,225.00	24
EA45	ENT Assoc.	867 Ridge	Fort Stewart	CO	80336	$12,750.00	$15,000.00	27
FD89	Ferb Dentistry	34 Crestview	Berridge	CO	80330	$21,000.00	$12,500.00	21
FH22	Family Health	123 Second	Tarleton	CO	80409	$0.00	$0.00	24
MH56	Maun Hospital	76 Dixon	Mason	CO	80356	$0.00	$43,025.00	24
PR11	Peel Radiology	151 Valleyview	Fort Stewart	CO	80336	$31,750.00	$0.00	21
TC37	Tarleton Clinic	451 Hull	Tarleton	CO	80409	$18,750.00	$31,500.00	27
WL56	West Labs	785 Main	Berls	CO	80349	$14,000.00	$0.00	24

Figure 1–52

- If the Navigation pane is hidden, click the Shutter Bar Open/Close Button, shown in Figure 1–51, to show the Navigation pane (Figure 1–53).

Figure 1–53

- Right-click the Client table in the Navigation pane to display a shortcut menu.

- Click Open on the shortcut menu to open the Client table in Datasheet view.

- Hide the Navigation pane by clicking the Shutter Bar Open/Close button (Figure 1–54).

Figure 1–54

3

- Click the New (blank) record button to move to a position to enter a new record (Figure 1–55).

Why click the New (blank) record button? Could you just click the Client Number on the first open record and then add the record?

You could click the Client Number on the first open record, provided that record appears on the screen. With only two records in the table, this is not a problem. Once a table contains more records than will fit on the screen, it is easier to click the New (blank) record button.

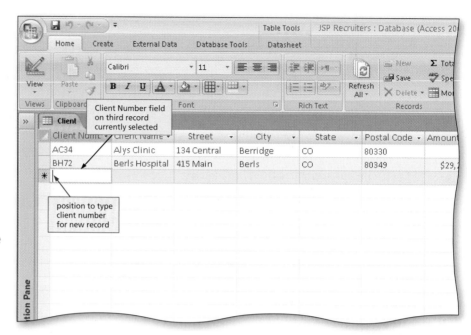

Figure 1–55

4

- Add the records shown in Figure 1–52, using the same techniques you used to add the first two records (Figure 1–56).

5

- Click the Close 'Client' button to close the table.

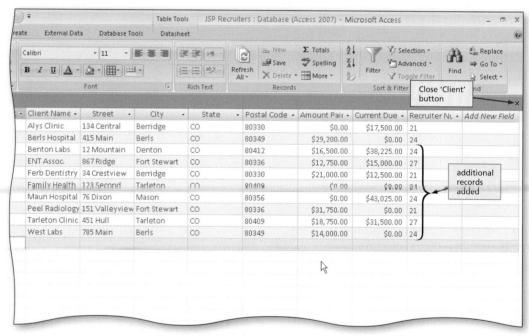

Figure 1–56

Other Ways

1. Click New button on Ribbon
2. Press CTRL+PLUS SIGN (+)

Previewing and Printing the Contents of a Table

When working with a database, you often will need to print a copy of the table contents. Figure 1–57 shows a printed copy of the contents of the Client table. (Yours may look slightly different, depending on your printer.) Because the Client table is wider substantially than the screen, it also will be wider than the normal printed page in portrait orientation. **Portrait orientation** means the printout is across the width of the page.

Client Number	Client Name	Street	City	State	Postal Code	Amount Paid	Current Due	Recruiter Numb
AC34	Alys Clinic	134 Central	Berridge	CO	80330	$0.00	$17,500.00	21
BH72	Berls Hospital	415 Main	Berls	CO	80349	$29,200.00	$0.00	24
BL12	Benton Labs	12 Mountain	Denton	CO	80412	$16,500.00	$38,225.00	24
EA45	ENT Assoc.	867 Ridge	Fort Stewart	CO	80336	$12,750.00	$15,000.00	27
FD89	Ferb Dentistry	34 Crestview	Berridge	CO	80330	$21,000.00	$12,500.00	21
FH22	Family Health	123 Second	Tarleton	CO	80409	$0.00	$0.00	24
MH56	Maun Hospital	76 Dixon	Mason	CO	80356	$0.00	$43,025.00	24
PR11	Peel Radiology	151 Valleyview	Fort Stewart	CO	80336	$31,750.00	$0.00	21
TC37	Tarleton Clinic	451 Hull	Tarleton	CO	80409	$18,750.00	$31,500.00	27
WL56	West Labs	785 Main	Berls	CO	80349	$14,000.00	$0.00	24

Client   4/23/2008

Figure 1–57

Landscape orientation means the printout is across the length (height) of the page. Thus, to print the wide database table, use landscape orientation. If you are printing the contents of a table that fit on the screen, you will not need landscape orientation. A convenient way to change to landscape orientation is to preview what the printed copy will look like by using Print Preview. This allows you to determine whether landscape orientation is necessary and, if it is, to change the orientation easily to landscape. In addition, you also can use Print Preview to determine whether any adjustments are necessary to the page margins.

To Preview and Print the Contents of a Table

The following steps use Print Preview to preview and then print the Client table.

1
- If the Navigation pane is hidden, show the Navigation pane by clicking the Shutter Bar Open/Close Button.

- Be sure the Client table is selected (Figure 1–58).

Q&A
Why do I have to be sure the Client table is selected? It is the only object in the database.

There is no issue when the database contains only one object. Ensuring that the correct object is selected is a good habit to form, however, to make sure that the object you print is the one you want.

Figure 1–58

- Click the Office Button to display the Office Button menu.

- Point to the Print command arrow to display the Print submenu (Figure 1–59).

Figure 1–59

❸

- Click Print Preview on the Print submenu to display a preview of the report (Figure 1–60).

Q & A

I can't read the report. Can I magnify a portion of the report?

Yes. Point the mouse pointer, whose shape will change to a magnifying glass, at the portion of the report that you wish to magnify, and then click. You can return the view of the report to the one shown in the figure by clicking a second time.

Figure 1–60

4

- Click the mouse pointer in the position shown in Figure 1–60 to magnify the upper-right section of the report (Figure 1–61).

Q&A

My report was already magnified in a different area. How can I see the area shown in the figure?

There are two ways. You can use the scroll bars to move to the desired portion of the report. You also can click the mouse pointer anywhere in the report to produce a screen like the one in Figure 1–60, and then click in the location shown in the figure.

Figure 1–61

5

- Click the Landscape button to change to landscape orientation (Figure 1–62).

6

- Click the Print button on the Print Preview tab to print the report.

- When the printer stops, retrieve the hard copy of the Client table.

- Click the Close 'Client' button to close the Print Preview window.

Q&A

How can I print multiple copies of my document other than clicking the Print button multiple times?

Click the Office Button, point to the arrow next to Print on the Office Button menu, click Print on the Print submenu, increase the number in the Number of Copies: box, and then click the OK button.

Q&A

How can I print a range of pages rather than printing the whole report?

Click the Office Button, point to the arrow next to Print on the Office Button menu, click Print on the Print submenu, click the Pages option button in the Print Range box, enter the desired page range, and then click the OK button.

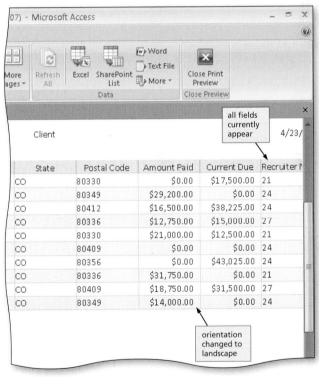

Figure 1–62

Other Ways

1. Press CTRL+P, press ENTER

To Create an Additional Table

The JSP Recruiters database contains two tables, the Client table and the Recruiter table. You need to create the Recruiter table and add records to it. Because you already used the default table that Access created when you created the database, you will need to first create the table. You can then add fields as you did with the Client table. The fields to be added are Recruiter Number, Last Name, First Name, Street, City, State, Postal Code, Rate, and Commission. The data type for the Rate field is Number, and the data type for the Commission field is Currency. The data type for all other fields is Text. The following steps create the Recruiter table.

- Click Create on the Ribbon to display the Create tab (Figure 1–63).

Figure 1–63

2

- Click the Table button on the Create tab to create a new table (Figure 1–64).

Q&A

Could I save the table now so I can assign it the name I want, rather than Table1?

You certainly can. Be aware, however, that you will still need to save it again once you have added all your fields.

Figure 1–64

- Right-click Add New Field to display a shortcut menu.

- Click Rename Column on the shortcut menu to display an insertion point.

- Type `Recruiter Number` to assign a name to the new field.

- Press the DOWN ARROW key to complete the addition of the field.

- Using the same technique, add the Last Name, First Name, Street, City, State, Postal Code, and Rate fields.

- Click the Data Type box arrow to display the Data Type box menu (Figure 1–65).

Figure 1–65

- Click Number on the Data Type box menu to select the Number data type and assign the Number data type to the Rate field.

- Add the Commission field and assign it the Currency data type.

- Click the Save button to display the Save As dialog box (Figure 1–66).

Figure 1–66

- Type `Recruiter` to assign a name to the table.

- Click the OK button (Figure 1–67).

Figure 1–67

To Modify the Primary Key and Field Properties

Fields whose data type is Number often require you to change the field size. Table 1–3 shows the possible field sizes for Number fields.

Table 1–3 Field Sizes for Number Fields	
Field Size	**Description**
Byte	Integer value in the range of 0 to 255.
Integer	Integer value in the range of -32,768 to 32,767.
Long Integer	Integer value in the range of -2,147,483,648 to 2,147,483,647.
Single	Numeric values with decimal places to seven significant digits — requires four bytes of storage.
Double	Numeric values with decimal places to more accuracy than Single — requires eight bytes of storage.
Replication ID	Special identifier required for replication.
Decimal	Numeric values with decimal places to more accuracy than Single — requires 12 bytes of storage.

Because the values in the Rate field have decimal places, only Single, Double, or Decimal would be possible choices. The difference between these choices concerns the amount of accuracy. Double is more accurate than Single, for example, but requires more storage space. Because the rates are only two decimal places, Single is a perfectly acceptable choice.

In addition to changing the field size, you should also change the format to Fixed (a fixed number of decimal places) and the number of decimal places to 2.

The following steps move to Design view, delete the ID field, and make the Recruiter Number field the primary key. They then change the field size of the Rate field to Single, the format to Fixed, and the number of decimal places to 2.

1

- Click the Design View button on the status bar to move to Design view (Figure 1–68).

Figure 1–68

2

- Click the row selector for the ID field to select the field.

- Press the DELETE key to delete the field.

- Click the Yes button to complete the deletion of the field.

- With the Recruiter Number field selected, click the Primary Key button to designate the Recruiter Number field as the primary key.

- Click the row selector for the Rate field to select the field (Figure 1–69).

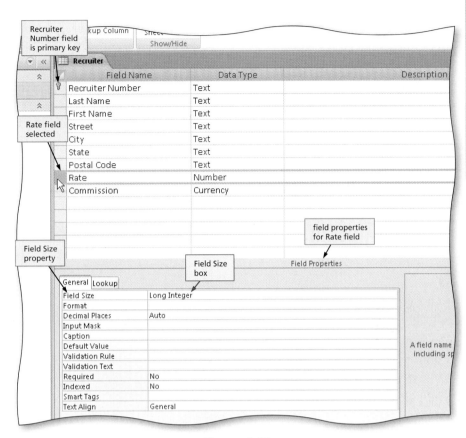

Figure 1–69

3

- Click the Field Size box to display the Field Size box arrow.

- Click the Field Size box arrow to display the Field Size box menu (Figure 1–70).

Q&A

What would happen if I left the field size set to Integer?

If the field size is Integer, no decimal places can be stored. Thus a value of .10 would be stored as 0. If you enter your rates and the values all appear as 0, chances are you did not change the field size.

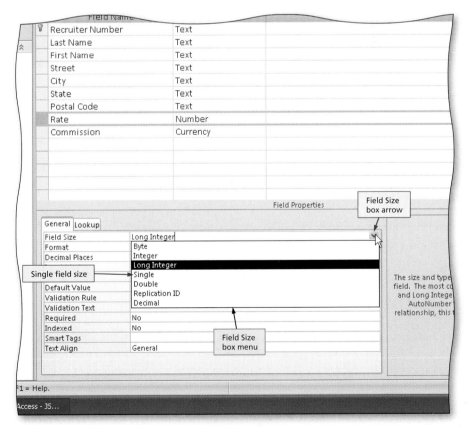

Figure 1–70

4

- Click Single to select single precision as the field size.

- Click the Format box to display the Format box arrow (Figure 1–71).

- Click the Format box arrow to open the Format box menu.

Figure 1–71

5

- Click Fixed to select fixed as the format.

- Click the Decimal Places box to display the Decimal Places box arrow.

- Click the Decimal Places box arrow to enter the number of decimal places.

- Click 2 to select 2 as the number of decimal places.

- Click the Save button to save your changes (Figure 1–72).

Q&A What is the purpose of the error checking button?

You changed the number of decimal places. The error checking button gives you a quick way of making the same change everywhere Rate appears. So far, you have not added any data, nor have you created any forms or reports that use the Rate field, so no such changes are necessary.

Figure 1–72

6

- Close the Recruiter table by clicking the Close 'Recruiter' button (Figure 1–73).

Figure 1–73

To Add Records to an Additional Table

The following steps add the records shown in Figure 1–74 to the Recruiter table.

Recruiter Nu ▾	Last Name ▾	First Name ▾	Street ▾	City ▾	State ▾	Postal Code ▾	Rate ▾	Commission ▾
21	Kerry	Alyssa	261 Pointer	Tourin	CO	80416	0.10	$17,600.00
24	Reeves	Camden	3135 Brill	Denton	CO	80412	0.10	$19,900.00
27	Fernandez	Jaime	265 Maxwell	Charleston	CO	80380	0.09	$9,450.00
34	Lee	Jan	1827 Oak	Denton	CO	80413	0.08	$0.00

Figure 1–74

1

- Open the Recruiter table in Datasheet view by right-clicking the Recruiter table in the Navigation pane and then clicking Open on the shortcut menu.

- Enter the Recruiter data from Figure 1–74 (Figure 1–75).

 Experiment

- Click in the Rate field on any of the records. Be sure the Datasheet tab is selected. Click the Format box arrow and then click each of the formats in the Format box menu to see the effect on the values in the Rate field. When finished, click Fixed in the Format box menu.

Figure 1–75

2

- Click the Close 'Recruiter' button to close the table and remove the datasheet from the screen.

Creating a Report

JSP Recruiters needs the following reports. You will create the four reports shown in Figure 1–76 in this section.

Figure 1–76

To Create a Report

You will first create the report shown in Figure 1–76a. The records in the report are sorted (ordered) by Client Number. To ensure that the records appear in this order, you will specify that the records are to be sorted on the Client Number field. The following steps create the report in Figure 1–76a.

1

- Be sure the Client table is selected in the Navigation pane.

- Click Create on the Ribbon to display the Create tab.

- Click the Report Wizard button to display the Report Wizard dialog box (Figure 1–77).

What would have happened if the Recruiter table were selected instead of the Client table?

The list of available fields would have contained fields from the Recruiter table rather than the Client table.

If the list contained Recruiter table fields, how could I make it contain Client table fields?

Click the arrow in the Tables/ Queries box and then click the Client table in the list that appears.

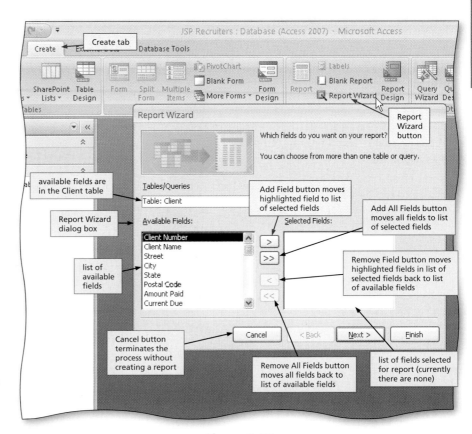

Figure 1–77

2

- Click the Add Field button to add the Client Number field.

- Click the Add Field button to add the Client Name field.

- Click the Amount Paid field, and then click the Add Field button to add the Amount Paid field.

- Click the Add Field button to add the Current Due field.

- Click the Add Field button to add the Recruiter Number field (Figure 1–78).

Figure 1–78

3

- Click the Next button to display the next Report Wizard screen (Figure 1–79).

What is grouping?

Grouping means creating separate collections of records sharing some common characteristic. For example, you might want to group clients in the same Postal code or that have the same recruiter.

What if I realize that I have selected the wrong fields?

You can click the Back button to return to the previous screen and then correct the list of fields. You also could click the Cancel button and start over.

Figure 1–79

4

- Because you will not specify any grouping, click the Next button in the Report Wizard dialog box to display the next Report Wizard screen.

- Click the box arrow in the text box labeled 1 to display a list of available fields for sorting (Figure 1–80).

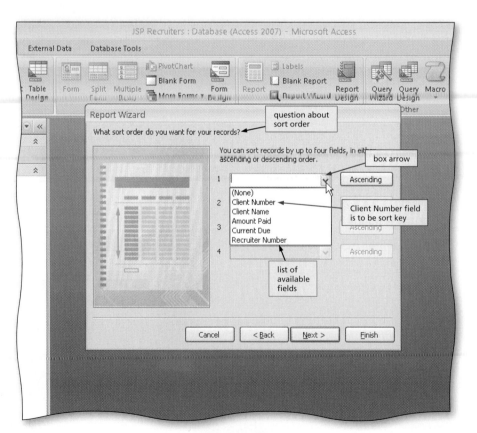

Figure 1–80

5

- Click the Client Number field to select the field as the sort key (Figure 1–81).

 Q&A

What if I want Descending order?

Click the Ascending button next to the sort key to change Ascending order to Descending. If you decide you want Ascending after all, click the button a second time.

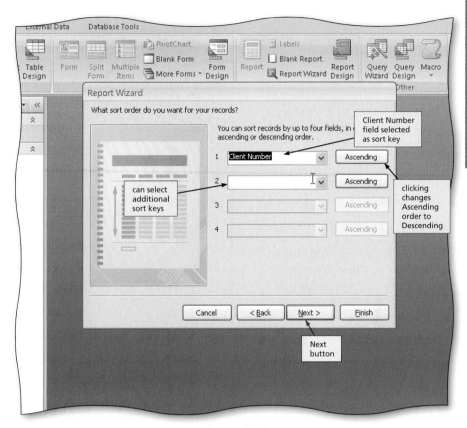

Figure 1–81

6

- Click the Next button to display the next Report Wizard screen (Figure 1–82).

Experiment

- Click different layouts and orientations and observe the effect on the sample report. When you have finished experimenting, click the Tabular option button for the layout and the Portrait option button for the orientation.

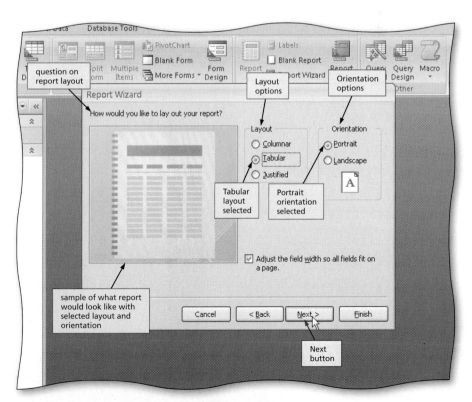

Figure 1–82

7

- Make sure that Tabular is selected as the Layout. (If it is not, click the Tabular option button to select Tabular layout.)

- Make sure Portrait is selected as the Orientation. (If it is not, click the Portrait option button to select Portrait orientation.)

- Click the Next button to display the next Report Wizard screen (Figure 1–83).

🔎 **Experiment**

- Click different styles and observe the effect on the sample report. When you have finished experimenting, click the Module style.

Figure 1–83

8

- Be sure the Module style is selected. (If it is not, click Module to select the Module style.)

- Click the Next button to display the next Report Wizard screen (Figure 1–84).

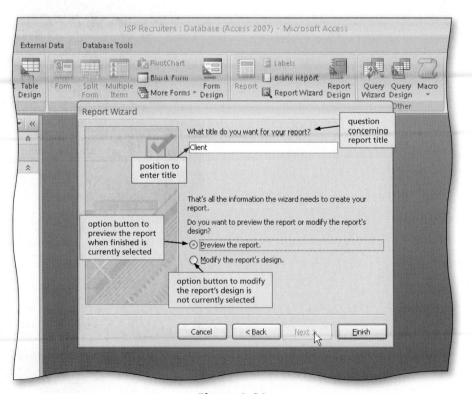

Figure 1–84

9

- Erase the current title, and then type Client Financial Report as the new title (Figure 1–85).

 How do I erase the title?

You can highlight the existing title and then press the DELETE key. You can click at the end of the title and repeatedly press the BACKSPACE key. You can click at the beginning of the title and repeatedly press the DELETE key.

 Could I just click after the word, Client, press the Spacebar, and then type Financial Report?

Yes. In general, you can edit the current title to produce the new title using the method with which you are most comfortable.

Figure 1–85

- Click the Finish button to produce the report (Figure 1–86).

10

- Click the Close 'Client Financial Report' button to remove the report from the screen.

 Why didn't I have to save the report?

The Report Wizard saves the report automatically.

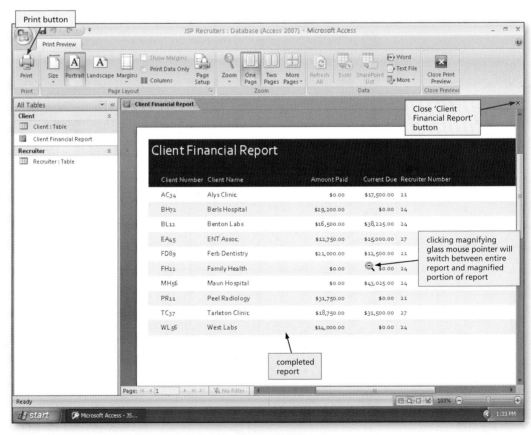

Figure 1–86

BTW

Quick Reference
For a table that lists how to complete the tasks covered in this book using the mouse, Ribbon, shortcut menu, and keyboard, see the Quick Reference Summary at the back of this book, or visit the Access 2007 Quick Reference Web page (scsite.com/ac2007/qr).

To Print a Report

Once you have created a report, you can print it at any time. The printed layout will reflect the layout you created. The data in the report will always reflect current data. The following step prints the Client Financial Report.

- With the Client Financial Report selected in the Navigation pane, click the Office Button.

- Point to the arrow next to Print on the Office Button menu and then click Quick Print on the Print submenu to print the report.

To Create Additional Reports

The following steps produce the reports shown in Figure 1–76b, Figure 1–76c, and Figure 1–76d on page AC 50.

1 If necessary, click Create on the Ribbon to display the Create tab, and then click the Report Wizard button to display the Report Wizard dialog box.

2 Add the Client Number, Client Name, Street, City, State, and Postal Code fields by clicking each field and then clicking the Add Field button.

3 Click the Next button to move to the screen asking about grouping, and then click the Next button a second time to move to the screen asking about sort order.

4 Click the box arrow in the text box labeled 1, click the Client Number field to select the field as the sort key, and then click the Next button.

5 Make sure that Tabular is selected as the Layout and that Portrait is selected as the Orientation, and then click the Next button.

6 Make sure the Module style is selected, and then click the Next button.

7 Enter `Client Address Report` as the title and click the Finish button to produce the report.

8 Click the Close 'Client Address Report' button to close the Print Preview window.

9 Click the Recruiter table in the Navigation pane, and then use the techniques shown in Steps 1 through 8 to produce the Recruiter Financial Report. The report is to contain the Recruiter Number, Last Name, First Name, Rate, and Commission fields. It is to be sorted by Recruiter Number. It is to have tabular layout, portrait orientation, and the Module Style. The title is to be Recruiter Financial Report.

10 With the Recruiter table selected in the Navigation pane, use the techniques shown in Steps 1 through 8 to produce the Recruiter Address Report. The report is to contain the Recruiter Number, Last Name, First Name, Street, City, State, and Postal Code fields. It is to be sorted by Recruiter Number. It is to have tabular layout, landscape orientation, and the Module Style. The title is to be Recruiter Address Report.

11 Click the Close 'Recruiter Address Report' button to close the Print Preview window.

Using a Form to View Data

In Datasheet view, you can view many records at once. If there are many fields, however, only some of the fields in each record might be visible at a time. In **Form view**, where data is displayed in a form on the screen, you usually can see all the fields, but only for one record. To get the advantages from both, many database management systems allow you to easily switch between Datasheet view and Form view while maintaining position within the database. In Access 2007, you can view both a datasheet and a form simultaneously using a split form.

To Create a Split Form

A **split form** combines both a datasheet and a form, thus giving the advantages of both views. The following steps create a split form.

1

- Select the Client table in the Navigation pane.

- If necessary, click Create on the Ribbon to display the Create tab (Figure 1–87).

Figure 1–87

2

- Click the Split Form button to create a split form. If a Field List appears, click its Close button to remove the Field List from the screen (Figure 1–88).

Q&A Is the form automatically saved the way the report was created when I used the Report Wizard?

No. You must take specific action if you wish to save the form.

Figure 1–88

- Click the Save button to display the Save As dialog box (Figure 1–89).

Figure 1–89

- Type `Client Form` as the form name, and then click the OK button to save the form.

- If the form appears in Layout view, click the Form View button on the Access status bar to display the form in Form view (Figure 1–90).

Q&A

How can I recognize Layout view?

There are three ways. The left end of the Status bar will contain the words Layout View. There will be shading around the outside of the selected field in the form. The Layout View button will be selected in the right end of the Status bar.

Figure 1–90

To Use a Split Form

After you have saved a form, you can use it at any time by right-clicking the form in the Navigation pane and then clicking Open in the shortcut menu. If you plan to use the form to enter data, you must ensure you are viewing the form in Form view.

1

- Click the Next Record button four times to move to record 5 (Figure 1–91).

Q&A I inadvertently closed the form at the end of the previous steps. What should I do?

Right-click the form in the Navigation pane and then click Open on the shortcut menu.

Q&A Do I have to take any special action for the form to be positioned on the same record as the datasheet?

No. The advantage to the split form is that changing the position on either the datasheet or the form automatically changes the position on the other.

Figure 1–91

2

- Click the Postal Code field on the second record in the datasheet to select the second record in both the datasheet and the form (Figure 1–92).

Experiment

- Click several fields in various records in the datasheet and observe the effect on the form.

3

- Click the Close 'Client Form' button to remove the form from the screen.

Figure 1–92

Changing Document Properties

Access helps you organize and identify your databases by using **database properties,** which are the details about a file. Database properties, also known as **metadata**, can include such information as the project author, title, or subject. **Keywords** are words or phrases that further describe the database. For example, a class name or database topic can describe the file's purpose or content.

Five different types of document properties exist, but the more common ones used in this book are standard and automatically updated properties. **Standard properties** are associated with all Microsoft Office documents and include author, title, and subject. **Automatically updated properties** include file system properties, such as the date you create or change a file, and statistics, such as the file size.

To Change Database Properties

The Database Properties dialog box contains areas where you can view and enter document properties. You can view and change information in this dialog box at any time while you are working on your database. It is a good idea to add your name and class name as database properties. The following steps use the Properties dialog box to change database properties.

1
- Click the Office Button to display the Office Button menu.

- Point to Manage on the Office Button menu to display the Manage submenu (Figure 1–93).

Q&A What other types of actions besides changing properties can you take to prepare a database for distribution?

The Manage submenu provides commands to compact and repair a database as well as to back up a database.

Figure 1–93

2
- Click Database Properties on the Manage submenu to display the JSP Recruiters.accdb Properties dialog box (Figure 1–94).

Q&A Why are some of the document properties in my Properties dialog box already filled in?

The person who installed Microsoft Office 2007 on your computer or network may have set or customized the properties.

Figure 1–94

- If necessary, click the Summary tab.

- Click the Author text box and then type your name as the Author property. If a name already is displayed in the Author text box, delete it before typing your name.

- Click the Subject text box, if necessary delete any existing text, and then type your course and section as the Subject property.

- Click the Keywords text box, if necessary delete any existing text, and then type `Healthcare, Recruiter` as the Keywords property (Figure 1–95).

Q&A

What types of properties does Access collect automatically?

Access records such details as when the database was created, when it was last modified, total editing time, and the various objects contained in the database.

Figure 1–95

- Click the OK button to save your changes and remove the JSP Recruiters.accdb Properties dialog box from the screen.

Access Help

At any time while using Access, you can find answers to questions and display information about various topics through **Access Help**. Used properly, this form of assistance can increase your productivity and reduce your frustrations by minimizing the time you spend learning how to use Access.

This section introduces you to Access Help. Additional information about using Access Help is available in Appendix C.

To Search for Access Help

Using Access Help, you can search for information based on phrases, such as create a form or change a data type, or key terms, such as copy, save, or format. Access Help responds with a list of search results displayed as links to a variety of resources. The following steps, which use Access Help to search for information about creating a form, assume you are connected to the Internet.

1

- Click the Microsoft Office Access Help button near the upper-right corner of the Access window to open the Access Help window.

- Type create a form in the 'Type words to search for' text box at the top of the Access Help window (Figure 1–96).

Figure 1–96

2

- Press the ENTER key to display the search results.

- Click the Maximize button on the Access Help window title bar to maximize the Help window unless it is already maximized (Figure 1–97).

Q&A

Where is the Access window with the JSP Recruiters database?

Access is open in the background, but the Access Help window sits on top of the Microsoft Access window. When the Access Help window is closed, the database will reappear.

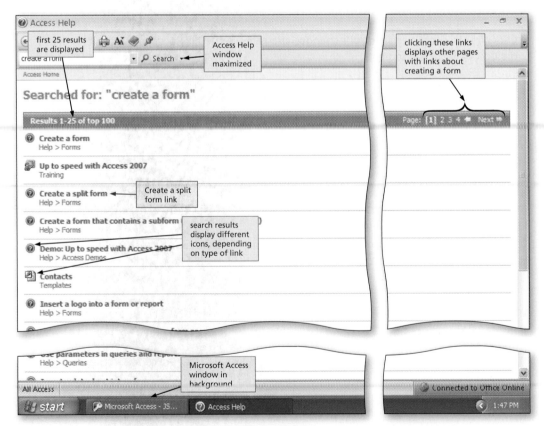

Figure 1–97

3

- Click the Create a split form link to display information regarding creating a split form (Figure 1–98).

Q&A

What is the purpose of the buttons at the top of the Access Help window?

Use the buttons in the upper-left corner of the Access Help window to navigate through the Help system, change the display, show the Access Help table of contents, and print the contents of the window.

4

- Click the Close button on the Access Help window title bar to close the Access Help window and make the database active.

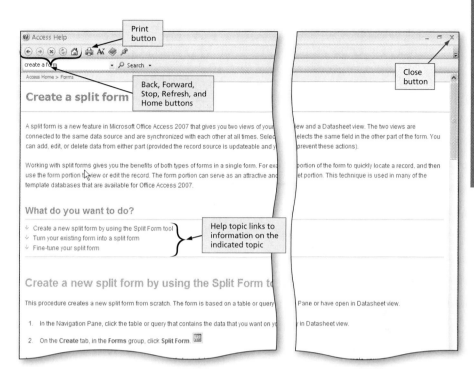

Figure 1–98

Other Ways
1. Press F1

To Quit Access

You saved all your changes and are ready to quit Access. The following step quits Access.

1 Click the Close button on the right side of the Access title bar to quit Access.

Chapter Summary

In this chapter you have learned to design a database, create an Access database, create tables and add records to them, print the contents of tables, create reports, and create forms. The items listed below include all the new Access skills you have learned in this chapter.

1. Start Access (AC 12)
2. Create a Database Using a Template (AC 13)
3. Create a Database (AC 14)
4. Define the Fields in a Table (AC 24)
5. Create a Table Using a Template (AC 26)
6. Save a Table (AC 27)
7. Change the Primary Key (AC 28)
8. Add Records to a Table (AC 30)
9. Close a Table (AC 35)
10. Quit Access (AC 36)
11. Start Access (AC 36)
12. Open a Database from Access (AC 37)
13. Add Additional Records to a Table (AC 38)
14. Preview and Print the Contents of a Table (AC 41)
15. Create an Additional Table (AC 44)
16. Modify the Primary Key and Field Properties (AC 46)
17. Add Records to an Additional Table (AC 49)
18. Create a Report (AC 51)
19. Print a Report (AC 56)

20. Create Additional Reports (AC 56)
21. Create a Split Form (AC 57)
22. Use a Split Form (AC 58)

23. Change Database Properties (AC 60)
24. Search for Access Help (AC 62)
25. Quit Access (AC 63)

If you have a SAM user profile, you may have access to hands-on instruction, practice, and assessment. Log in to your SAM account (http://sam2007.course.com) to launch any assigned training activities or exams that relate to the skills covered in this chapter.

Learn It Online

Test your knowledge of chapter content and key terms.

Instructions: To complete the Learn It Online exercises, start your browser, click the Address bar, and then enter the Web address `scsite.com/ac2007/learn`. When the Access 2007 Learn It Online page is displayed, click the link for the exercise you want to complete and then read the instructions.

Chapter Reinforcement TF, MC, and SA
A series of true/false, multiple choice, and short answer questions that test your knowledge of the chapter content.

Flash Cards
An interactive learning environment where you identify chapter key terms associated with displayed definitions.

Practice Test
A series of multiple choice questions that test your knowledge of chapter content and key terms.

Who Wants To Be a Computer Genius?
An interactive game that challenges your knowledge of chapter content in the style of a television quiz show.

Wheel of Terms
An interactive game that challenges your knowledge of chapter key terms in the style of the television show *Wheel of Fortune*.

Crossword Puzzle Challenge
A crossword puzzle that challenges your knowledge of key terms presented in the chapter.

Apply Your Knowledge

Reinforce the skills and apply the concepts you learned in this chapter.

Changing Data, Creating a Form, and Creating a Report
Instructions: Start Access. Open the The Bike Delivers database. See the inside back cover of this book for instructions for downloading the Data Files for Students, or see your instructor for information on accessing the files required in this book.

The Bike Delivers uses motorbikes to provide courier services for local businesses. The Bike Delivers has a database that keeps track of its couriers and customers. The database has two tables. The Customer table (Figure 1–99a) contains data on the customers who use the services of The Bike Delivers. The Courier table (Figure 1–99b) contains data on the individuals employed by The Bike Delivers.

(a) Customer Table

(b) Courier Table

Figure 1–99

Perform the following tasks:

1. Open the Customer table and change the Courier Number for customer KL55 to 113.

2. Close the Customer table.

3. Create a split form for the Courier table. Use the name Courier for the form.

4. Open the form you created and change the street address for Michelle Hyde to 65 Park.

5. Close the Courier form.

6. Create the report shown in Figure 1–100 for the Customer table. The report uses the Module style.

7. Change the database properties, as specified by your instructor. Submit the revised database in the format specified by your instructor.

Figure 1–100

Extend Your Knowledge

Extend the skills you learned in this chapter and experiment with new skills. You may need to use Help to complete the assignment.

Changing Formats and Creating Grouped and Sorted Reports

Instructions: Start Access. Open the Camden Scott College database. See the inside back cover of this book for instructions for downloading the Data Files for Students, or see your instructor for information on accessing the files required in this book.

Continued >

Extend Your Knowledge *continued*

Camden Scott College is a small liberal arts college. The Human Resources Director has created an Access database in which to store information about candidates applying for faculty positions. You will make some changes to the Candidate table so that it looks like that shown in Figure 1–101 and create a report that both groups records and sorts them in ascending order.

Figure 1–101

Perform the following tasks:

1. Open the Candidate table in Datasheet view and change the column heading for the ID field to Candidate ID.

2. Save the change and open the table in Design view.

3. Select a format for the App Date field that will produce the look shown in Figure 1–101.

4. Change the data type for the Documentation field so that it will match that shown in Figure 1–101.

5. Save the changes.

6. Open the table in Datasheet view. The Human Resources department has received an application from Edward Klinger. Edward applied for the same position as Sarah Klinger on the same date as Sarah. Edward's phone number is 610-555-1111. He did submit all his documentation with his application. Add this record.

7. Add the Quick Print button to the Quick Access Toolbar.

8. Create a report for the Candidate table that lists the Department Code, App Date, Last Name, and First Name. Group the report by Department Code. Sort the report by App Date, Last Name, and then First Name. Choose your own report style and use Candidate by Department as the title of the report.

9. Remove the Quick Print button from the Quick Access Toolbar.

10. Change the database properties, as specified by your instructor. Submit the revised database in the format specified by your instructor.

Make It Right

Analyze a database and correct all errors and/or improve the design.

Correcting Errors in the Table Structure

Instructions: Start Access. Open the SciFi Scene database. See the inside back cover of this book for instructions for downloading the Data Files for Students, or see your instructor for information on accessing the files required in this book.

SciFi Scene is a database containing information on science fiction books. The Book table shown in Figure 1–102 contains a number of errors in the table structure. You are to correct these errors before any additional records can be added to the table. Book Code, not ID, is the primary key for the Book table. The column heading Titel is misspelled. The On Hand field represents the number of books on hand. The field will be used in arithmetic operations. Only whole numbers should be stored in the field. The Price field represents the price of the book. The current data type does not reflect this information.

Change the database properties, as specified by your instructor. Submit the revised database in the format specified by your instructor.

Figure 1–102

In the Lab

Design, create, modify, and/or use a database using the guidelines, concepts, and skills presented in this chapter. Labs are listed in order of increasing difficulty.

Lab 1: Creating the JMS TechWizards Database

Problem: JMS TechWizards is a local company that provides technical services to several small businesses in the area. The company currently keeps its records in two Excel workbooks. One Excel workbook (Figure 1–103a) contains information on the clients that JMS TechWizards serves. The other Excel workbook (Figure 1–103b) contains information on the technicians that JMS employs. JMS would like to store this data in a database and has asked for your help.

(a) Client Data (Excel Workbook)

(b) Technician Data (Excel Workbook)

Figure 1–103

Continued >

In the Lab *continued*

Instructions: Perform the following tasks:

1. Create a new database in which to store all the objects related to the technical services data. Call the database JMS TechWizards.

2. Create a table in which to store the data related to clients. Use the name Client for the table. The fields for the Client table are: Client Number, Client Name, Street, City, State, Postal Code, Telephone Number, Billed, Paid, and Technician Number. Client Number is the primary key. The Billed and Paid fields are currency data type.

3. Create a table in which to store the data related to technicians. Use the name Technician for the table. The fields for the Technician table are: Technician Number, Last Name, First Name, Street, City, State, Postal Code, Hourly Rate, and YTD Earnings. The primary key for the Technician table is Technician Number. Hourly rate and YTD Earnings are currency data type.

4. Add the data from the Client workbook in Figure 1–103a to the Client table.

5. Add the data from the Technician workbook in Figure 1–103b to the Technician table.

6. Create and save the reports shown in Figure 1–104a for the Client table and Figure 1–104b for the Technician table.

7. Change the database properties, as specified by your instructor. Submit the revised database in the format specified by your instructor.

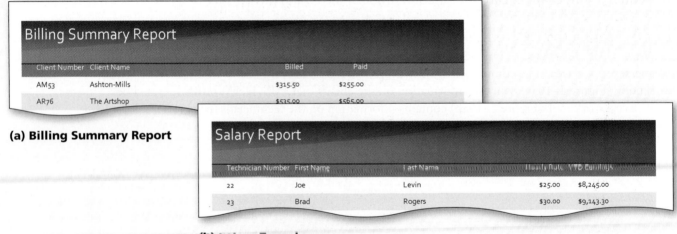

(a) Billing Summary Report

Client Number	Client Name	Billed	Paid
AM53	Ashton-Mills	$315.50	$255.00
AR76	The Artshop	$535.00	$565.00

Billing Summary Report

Salary Report

Technician Number	First Name	Last Name	Hourly Rate	YTD Earnings
22	Joe	Levin	$25.00	$8,245.00
23	Brad	Rogers	$30.00	$9,143.30

(b) Salary Report

Figure 1–104

In the Lab

Lab 2: Creating the Hockey Fan Zone Database

Problem: Your town has a minor league hockey team. The team store sells a variety of items with the team logo. The store purchases the items from suppliers that deal in specialty items for sports teams. Currently, the information about the items and suppliers is stored in the Excel workbook shown in Figure 1–105. You work part-time at the store, and your boss has asked you to create a database that will store the item and supplier information. You have already determined that you need two tables: an Item table and a Supplier table in which to store the information.

Instructions: Perform the following tasks:

1. Design a new database in which to store all the objects related to the items for sale. Call the database Hockey Fan Zone.

2. Use the information shown in Figure 1–105 to determine the primary keys and determine additional fields. Then, determine the relationships among tables and the data types.

3. Create the Item table using the information shown in Figure 1–105.

4. Create the Supplier table using the information shown in Figure 1–105.

5. Add the appropriate data to the Item table.

6. Add the appropriate data to the Supplier table.

7. Create a split form for the Item table. Use the name Item for the form.

8. Create the report shown in Figure 1–106 for the Item table.

9. Change the database properties, as specified by your instructor. Submit the database in the format specified by your instructor.

	A	B	C	D	E	F	G	H
1	Item Number	Description	On Hand	Cost	Selling Price	Supplier Code	Supplier Name	Telephone Number
2	3663	Ball Cap	30	$11.15	$18.95	LG	Logo Goods	517-555-3853
3	3683	Bumper Sticker	50	$0.95	$1.50	MN	Mary's Novelties	317-555-4747
4	4563	Earrings	10	$4.50	$7.00	LG	Logo Goods	517-555-3853
5	4593	Foam Finger	25	$2.95	$5.00	LG	Logo Goods	517-555-3853
6	5923	Jersey	12	$21.45	$24.75	AC	Ace Clothes	616-555-9228
7	6189	Koozies	35	$2.00	$4.00	MN	Mary's Novelties	317-555-4747
8	6343	Note Cube	7	$5.75	$8.00	MN	Mary's Novelties	317-555-4747
9	7810	Tee Shirt	32	$9.50	$14.95	AC	Ace Clothes	616-555-9228
10	7930	Visor	9	$11.95	$17.00	LG	Logo Goods	517-555-3853
11								

Figure 1–105

Inventory Status Report

Item Number	Description	On Hand	Cost
3663	Ball Cap	30	$11.15
3683	Bumper Sticker	50	$0.95

Figure 1–106

In the Lab

Lab 3: Creating the Ada Beauty Supply Database

Problem: A distribution company supplies local beauty salons with items needed in the beauty industry. The distributor employs sales representatives who receive a base salary as well as a commission on sales. Currently, the distributor keeps data on customers and sales reps in two Word documents and two Excel workbooks.

Instructions: Using the data shown in Figure 1–107, design the Ada Beauty Supply database. Use the database design guidelines in this chapter to help you in the design process.

Continued >

In the Lab continued

Customer Number	Customer Name	Street	Telephone
AM23	Amy's Salon	223 Johnson	555-2150
BB34	Bob the Barber	1939 Jackson	555-1939
BL15	Blondie's	3294 Devon	555-7510
CM09	Cut Mane	3140 Halsted	555-0604
CS12	Curl n Style	1632 Clark	555-0804
EG07	Elegante	1805 Boardway	555-1404
JS34	Just Cuts	2200 Lawrence	555-0313
LB20	Le Beauty	13 Devon	555-5161
NC25	Nancy's Place	1027 Wells	555-4210
RD03	Rose's Day Spa	787 Monroe	555-7657
TT21	Tan and Tone	1939 Congress	555-6554

(a) Customer Address Information (Word table)

E15

	A	B	C	D	E
1	Customer Number	Customer Name	Balance	Amount Paid	Sales Rep Num
2	AM23	Amy's Salon	$195.00	$1,695.00	44
3	BB34	Bob the Barber	$150.00	$0.00	51
4	BL15	Blondie's	$555.00	$1,350.00	49
5	CM09	Cut Mane	$295.00	$1,080.00	51
6	CS12	Curl n Style	$145.00	$710.00	49
7	EG07	Elegante	$0.00	$1,700.00	44
8	JS34	Just Cuts	$360.00	$700.00	49
9	LB20	Le Beauty	$200.00	$1,250.00	51
10	NC25	Nancy's Place	$240.00	$550.00	44
11	RD03	Rose's Day Spa	$0.00	$975.00	51
12	TT21	Tan and Tone	$160.00	$725.00	44
13					
14					
15					
16					

(c) Customer Financial Information (Excel Workbook)

Sales Rep Number	Last Name	First Name	Street	City	State	Postal Code
44	Jones	Pat	43 Third	Lawncrest	WA	98084
49	Gupta	Pinn	678 Hillcrest	Manton	WA	98085
51	Ortiz	Gabe	982 Victoria	Lawncrest	WA	98084
55	Sinson	Terry	45 Elm	Manton	WA	98084

(b) Sales Rep Address Information (Word table)

	A	B	C	D	E	F
1	Sales Rep Number	Last Name	First Name	Salary	Comm Rate	Commission
2	44	Jones	Pat	$ 23,000.00	0.05	$613.50
3	49	Gupta	Pinn	$ 24,000.00	0.06	$616.60
4	51	Ortiz	Gabe	$ 22,500.00	0.05	$492.75
5	55	Sinson	Terry	$ 20,000.00	0.05	$0.00
6						

(d) Sales Rep Financial Information (Excel Workbook)

Figure 1–107

When you have completed the database design, create the database, create the tables, and add the data to the appropriate tables. Be sure to determine the correct data types.

Finally, prepare the Customer Status Report shown in Figure 1–108a and the Sales Rep Salary Report shown in Figure 1–108b. Change the database properties, as specified by your instructor. Submit the database in the format specified by your instructor.

Customer Status Report

Customer Name	Telephone	Balance	Amount Paid	Sales Rep Number
Amy's Salon	555-2150	$195.00	$1,695.00	44
Blondie's	555-7510	$555.00	$1,350.00	49

(a) Customer Status Report

Sales Rep Salary Report

Last Name	First Name	Salary	mm Rate	Commission
Gupta	Pinn	$24,000.00	0.06	$616.60
Jones	Pat	$23,000.00	0.05	$613.50

(b) Sales Rep Salary Report

Figure 1–108

Cases and Places

Apply your creative thinking and problem solving skills to design and implement a solution.

● EASIER   ●● MORE DIFFICULT

● 1: Design and Create an E-Commerce Database

Students often have very little money to furnish dorm rooms and apartments. You and two of your friends have decided to use the skills you learned in your e-Commerce class to create a Web site specifically for college students to buy and sell used household furnishings.

Design and create a database to store the data that you need to manage this new business. Then create the necessary tables and enter the data from the Case 1-1 Second-Hand Goods document. See the inside back cover of this book for instructions for downloading the Data Files for Students, or see your instructor for information on accessing the files required in this book. Submit your assignment in the format specified by your instructor.

● 2: Design and Create a Rental Database

You are a part-time employee of BeachCondo Rentals. BeachCondo Rentals provides a rental service for condo owners who want to rent their units. The company rents units by the week. Currently, the company keeps information about its rentals in an Excel workbook.

Design and create a database to store the rental data. Then create the necessary tables and enter the data from the Case 1-2 BeachCondo Rentals workbook. See the inside back cover of this book for instructions for downloading the Data Files for Students, or see your instructor for information on accessing the files required in this book. Create an Available Rentals Report that lists the unit number, weekly rate, and owner number. Submit your assignment in the format specified by your instructor.

●● 3: Design and Create a Restaurant Database

Your school is sponsoring a conference that will draw participants from a wide geographical area. The conference director has asked for your help in preparing a database of restaurants that might be of interest to the participants. At a minimum, she needs to know the following: the type of restaurant (vegetarian, fast-food, fine dining, and so on), street address, telephone number, and opening and closing times and days. Because most of the participants will stay on campus, she also would like to know the approximate distance from campus. Additionally, she would like to know about any unique or special features the restaurants may have.

Design and create a database to meet the conference director's needs. Create the necessary tables, determine the necessary fields, enter some sample data, and prepare a sample report to show the director. Submit your assignment in the format specified by your instructor.

●● 4: Design and Create a Database to Help You Find a Job

Make It Personal

Conducting a job search requires careful preparation. In addition to preparing a resume and cover letter, you will need to research the companies for which you are interested in working and contact these companies to let them know of your interest and qualifications.

Microsoft Access includes a Contacts table template that can create a table that will help you keep track of your job contacts. Create a database to keep track of the companies that are of interest to you. Submit your assignment in the format specified by your instructor.

Continued >

•• 5: Design a Database that Tracks Student Data

Working Together

Keeping track of students is an enormous task for school administrators. Microsoft Access can help school administrators manage student data. The Database Wizard includes a Students template that can create a database that will maintain many different types of data on students, such as allergies, medications, and emergency contact information.

Have each member of your team explore the features of the Database Wizard and determine individually which tables and fields should be included in a Students database. As a group, review your choices and decide on one common design. Prepare a short paper for your instructor that explains why your team chose the particular database design.

After agreeing on the database design, assign one member to create the database using the Database Wizard. Every other team member should contribute data and add the data to the database. Submit your assignment in the format specified by your instructor.

2 Querying a Database

Objectives:

You will have mastered the material in this chapter when you can:

- Create queries using the Simple Query Wizard
- Print query results
- Create queries using Design view
- Include fields in the design grid
- Use text and numeric data in criteria
- Create and use parameter queries
- Save a query and use the saved query

- Use compound criteria in queries
- Sort data in queries
- Join tables in queries
- Create a report from a query
- Perform calculations in queries
- Calculate statistics in queries
- Create crosstab queries
- Customize the Navigation pane

2 | Querying a Database

Introduction

A database management system such as Access offers many useful features, among them the capability of answering questions, the answers to which are found in the database. When you pose a question to Access, or any other database management system, the question is called a query. A **query** is simply a question presented in a way that Access can process.

Thus, to find the answer to a question, you first create a corresponding query using the techniques illustrated in this chapter. After you have created the query, you instruct Access to display the query results; that is, to perform the steps necessary to obtain the answer. Access then displays the answer in Datasheet view.

Project — Querying A Database

Organizations and individuals achieve several benefits from storing data in a database and using Access to manage the database. One of the most important benefits is the capability of easily finding the answers to questions such as those shown in Figure 2–1 and the following, which concern the data in the JSP Recruiters database:

1. What are the number, name, the amount paid, and the current due of client FD89?
2. Which clients' names begin with Be?
3. Which clients are located in Berridge?
4. Which clients have a current due of $0.00?
5. Which clients have an amount paid that is more than $20,000.00?
6. Which clients of recruiter 21 have an amount paid that is more than $20,000.00?
7. In what cities are all the clients located?
8. What is the total amount (amount paid + current due) for each client?
9. What is the client number and name of each client, and what is the number and name of the recruiter to whom each client is assigned?

In addition to these questions, JSP Recruiters needs to find information about clients located in a specific city, but they want to enter a different city each time they ask the question. A parameter query would enable this. The agency also has a special way it wants to summarize data. A crosstab query will present the data in the desired form.

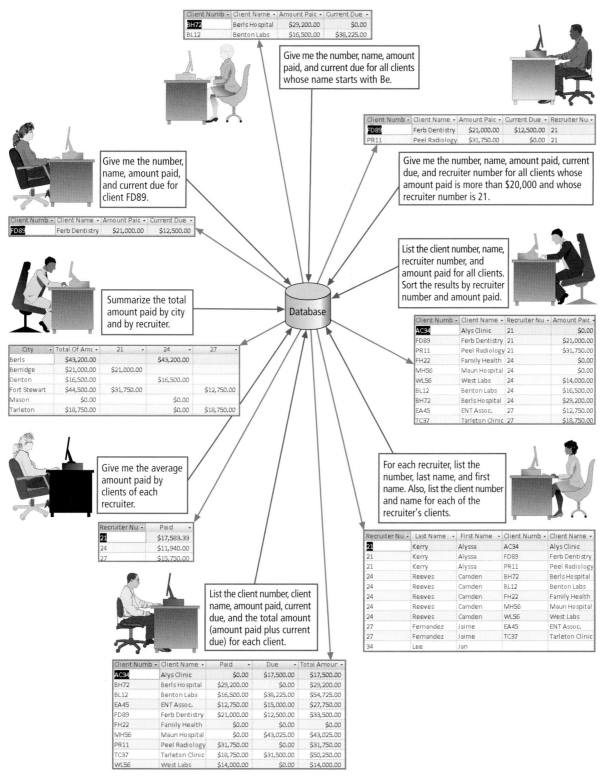

Client Numb ▾	Client Name ▾	Amount Paic ▾	Current Due ▾
BH72	Berls Hospital	$29,200.00	$0.00
BL12	Benton Labs	$16,500.00	$38,225.00

Give me the number, name, amount paid, and current due for all clients whose name starts with Be.

Client Numb ▾	Client Name ▾	Amount Paic ▾	Current Due ▾	Recruiter Nu ▾
FD89	Ferb Dentistry	$21,000.00	$12,500.00	21
PR11	Peel Radiology	$31,750.00	$0.00	21

Give me the number, name, amount paid, current due, and recruiter number for all clients whose amount paid is more than $20,000 and whose recruiter number is 21.

Give me the number, name, amount paid, and current due for client FD89.

Client Numb ▾	Client Name ▾	Amount Paic ▾	Current Due ▾
FD89	Ferb Dentistry	$21,000.00	$12,500.00

List the client number, name, recruiter number, and amount paid for all clients. Sort the results by recruiter number and amount paid.

Summarize the total amount paid by city and by recruiter.

City ▾	Total Of Amc ▾	21 ▾	24 ▾	27 ▾
Berls	$43,200.00		$43,200.00	
Berridge	$21,000.00	$21,000.00		
Denton	$16,500.00		$16,500.00	
Fort Stewart	$44,500.00	$31,750.00		$12,750.00
Mason	$0.00		$0.00	
Tarleton	$18,750.00		$0.00	$18,750.00

Client Numb ▾	Client Name ▾	Recruiter Nu ▾	Amount Paic ▾
AC34	Alys Clinic	21	$0.00
FD89	Ferb Dentistry	21	$21,000.00
PR11	Peel Radiology	21	$31,750.00
FH22	Family Health	24	$0.00
MH56	Maun Hospital	24	$0.00
WL56	West Labs	24	$14,000.00
BL12	Benton Labs	24	$16,500.00
BH72	Berls Hospital	24	$29,200.00
EA45	ENT Assoc.	27	$12,750.00
TC37	Tarleton Clinic	27	$18,750.00

Give me the average amount paid by clients of each recruiter.

For each recruiter, list the number, last name, and first name. Also, list the client number and name for each of the recruiter's clients.

Recruiter Nu ▾	Paid ▾
21	$17,583.33
24	$11,940.00
27	$15,750.00

Recruiter Nu ▾	Last Name ▾	First Name ▾	Client Numb ▾	Client Name ▾
21	Kerry	Alyssa	AC34	Alys Clinic
21	Kerry	Alyssa	FD89	Ferb Dentistry
21	Kerry	Alyssa	PR11	Peel Radiology
24	Reeves	Camden	BH72	Berls Hospital
24	Reeves	Camden	BL12	Benton Labs
24	Reeves	Camden	FH22	Family Health
24	Reeves	Camden	MH56	Maun Hospital
24	Reeves	Camden	WL56	West Labs
27	Fernandez	Jaime	EA45	ENT Assoc.
27	Fernandez	Jaime	TC37	Tarleton Clinic
34	Lee	Jan		

List the client number, client name, amount paid, current due, and the total amount (amount paid plus current due) for each client.

Client Numb ▾	Client Name ▾	Paid ▾	Due ▾	Total Amour ▾
AC34	Alys Clinic	$0.00	$17,500.00	$17,500.00
BH72	Berls Hospital	$29,200.00	$0.00	$29,200.00
BL12	Benton Labs	$16,500.00	$38,225.00	$54,725.00
EA45	ENT Assoc.	$12,750.00	$15,000.00	$27,750.00
FD89	Ferb Dentistry	$21,000.00	$12,500.00	$33,500.00
FH22	Family Health	$0.00	$0.00	$0.00
MH56	Maun Hospital	$0.00	$43,025.00	$43,025.00
PR11	Peel Radiology	$31,750.00	$0.00	$31,750.00
TC37	Tarleton Clinic	$18,750.00	$31,500.00	$50,250.00
WL56	West Labs	$14,000.00	$0.00	$14,000.00

Figure 2–1

Overview

As you read this chapter, you will learn how to query a database by performing these general tasks:

- Create queries using the Simple Query Wizard and Design view
- Use criteria in queries
- Create and use parameter queries
- Sort data in queries
- Join tables in queries
- Perform calculations in queries
- Create crosstab queries

Plan
Ahead

Query Design Guidelines

When posing a question to Access, you must design an appropriate query. In the process of designing a query, the decisions you make will determine the fields, tables, criteria, order, and special calculations included in the query. To design a query, you should follow these general guidelines:

1. **Identify the fields.** Examine the question or request to determine which fields from the tables in the database are involved. Examine the contents of these fields to make sure you understand how the data is stored.

2. **Identify restrictions.** Unless the question or request calls for all records, determine the restrictions, that is, the conditions records must satisfy in order to be included in the results.

3. **Determine whether special order is required.** Examine the question or request to determine whether the results must appear in some specific order.

4. **Determine whether more than one table is required.** If all the fields identified in Step 1 are in the same table, no special action is required. If this is not the case, identify all tables represented by those fields.

5. **Determine whether calculations are required.** Examine the question or request to determine whether, in addition to the fields determined in Step 1, calculations must be included. Results of mathematical operations typically are not stored in the database because they can be calculated easily when necessary. Such calculations include individual record calculations (for example, adding the values in two fields) or group calculations (for example, finding the total of the values in a particular field on all the records).

6. **If data is to be summarized, determine whether a crosstab query would be appropriate.** If data is to be grouped by two different types of information, you can use a crosstab query. You will need to identify the two types of information. One of the types will form the row headings and the other will form the column headings in the query results.

   When necessary, more specific details concerning the above decisions and/or actions are presented at appropriate points in the chapter.

Starting Access

If you are using a computer to step through the project in this chapter and you want your screen to match the figures in this book, you should change your screen's resolution to 1024 × 768. For information about how to change a computer's resolution, read Appendix E.

To Start Access

The following steps, which assume Windows is running, start Access.

1 Click the Start button on the Windows taskbar to display the Start menu.

2 Point to All Programs on the Start menu to display the All Programs submenu and then point to Microsoft Office on the All Programs submenu to display the Microsoft Office submenu.

3 Click Microsoft Office Access 2007 on the Microsoft Office submenu to start Access and display the Getting Started with Microsoft Office Access window.

4 If the Access window is not maximized, click the Maximize button on its title bar to maximize the window.

To Open a Database

In Chapter 1, you created your database on a USB flash drive using the file name, JSP Recruiters. There are two ways to open the file containing your database. If the file you created appears in the Recent Documents list, you can click it to open the file. If not, you can use the More button to open the file. The following steps use the More button to open the JSP Recruiters database from the USB flash drive.

1 With your USB flash drive connected to one of the computer's USB ports, click the More button to display the Open dialog box.

2 If necessary, click the Look in box arrow and then click UDISK 2.0 (E:) to select the USB flash drive in the Look in list as the new open location. (Your drive letter might be different.)

3 Click JSP Recruiters to select the file name.

4 Click the Open button to open the database.

5 If a Security Warning appears, click the Options button to display the Microsoft Office Security Options dialog box.

6 With the option button to enable this content selected, click the OK button to enable the content.

Creating Queries

Queries are simply questions, the answers to which are in the database. Access contains a powerful query feature. Through the use of this feature, you can find the answers to a wide variety of complex questions.

To Use the Simple Query Wizard to Create a Query

Once you have examined the question you wish to ask to determine the fields involved in the question, you can begin creating the query. If there are no restrictions involved in the query, nor any special order or calculations, you can use the Simple Query wizard. The following steps use the Simple Query wizard to create a query to display the number, name, and recruiter number of all clients.

1

- If the Navigation pane is hidden, click the Shutter Bar Open/Close Button to show the Navigation pane.

- Be sure the Client table is selected.

- Click Create on the Ribbon to display the Create tab.

- Click the Query Wizard button on the Create tab to display the New Query dialog box (Figure 2–2).

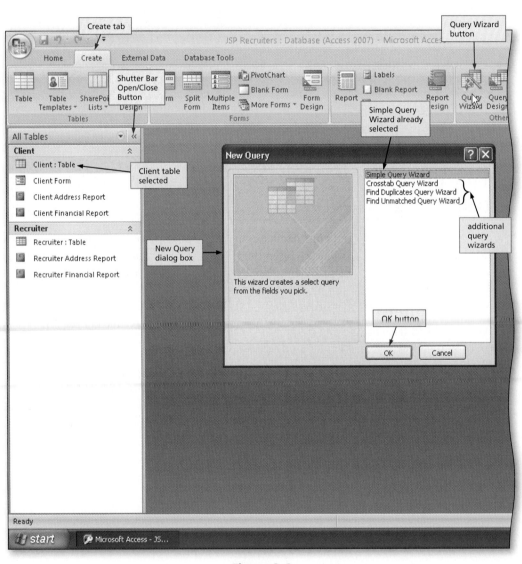

Figure 2–2

2

- Be sure Simple Query Wizard is selected, and then click the OK button to display the Simple Query Wizard dialog box (Figure 2–3).

Q&A

This looks like the screen I saw in the Report Wizard. Do I select fields in the same way?

Yes. In fact, you will see a similar screen in other wizards and you always select the fields just as you did in the Report Wizard.

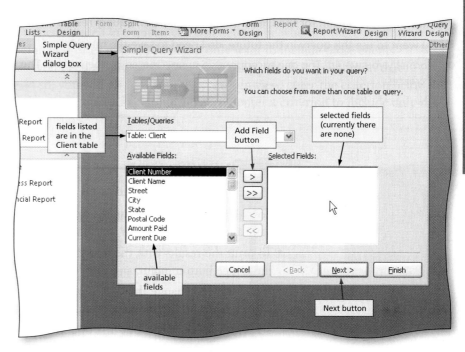

Figure 2–3

3

- Click the Add Field button to add the Client Number field.

- Click the Add Field button a second time to add the Client Name field.

- Click the Recruiter Number field, and then click the Add Field button to add the Recruiter Number field.

- Click the Next button.

- Be sure the title of the query is Client Query.

- Click the Finish button to create the query (Figure 2–4).

Figure 2–4

2

- With the Client table selected, click the Add button in the Show Table dialog box to add the Client table to the query.

- Click the Close button in the Show Table dialog box to remove the dialog box from the screen.

Q&A

What if I inadvertently add the wrong table?

Right-click the table that you added in error and click Remove Table on the shortcut menu. You also can just close the query, indicate that you don't want to save it, and then start over.

- Drag the lower edge of the field box down far enough so all fields in the Client table appear (Figure 2–11).

Figure 2–11

Q&A

How do I drag the lower edge?

Point to the lower edge, press and hold the left mouse button, move the mouse pointer to the new position for the lower edge, and then release the left mouse button. While the mouse pointer points to the lower edge of the field list, its shape changes to a two-headed arrow.

Q&A

Is it essential that I resize the field box?

No. You can always scroll through the list of fields using the scroll bar. If you can resize the field box so all fields appear, it is usually more convenient.

To Add Fields to the Design Grid

Once you have a new query displayed in Design view, you are ready to create the query by making entries in the design grid in the lower pane of the window. You add the fields you want included in the Field row in the grid. Only the fields that appear in the design grid will be included in the results of the query. The following step includes the client number, client name, amount paid, and current due for all clients by adding only those fields in the design grid.

1

- Double-click the Client Number field in the field list to add the Client Number field to the query.

Q&A What if I add the wrong field?

Click just above the field name in the design grid to select the column and then press the DELETE key to remove the field.

- Double-click the Client Name field in the field list to add the Client Name field to the query.

- Add the Amount Paid field to the query by double-clicking the Amount Paid field in the field list.

- Add the Current Due field to the query (Figure 2–12).

Q&A What if I want to include all fields? Do I have to add each field individually?

No. Instead of adding individual fields, you can double-click the asterisk (*) to add the asterisk to the design grid.

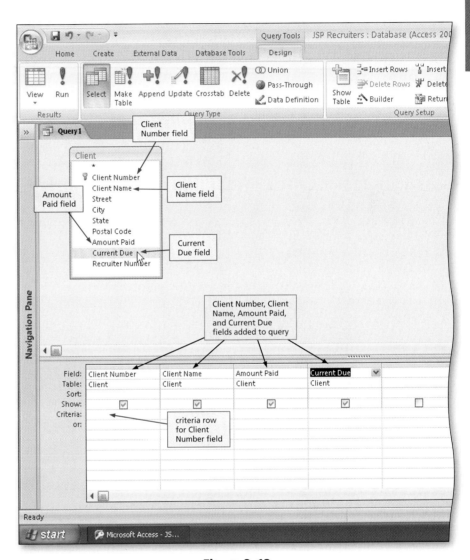

Figure 2–12

Entering Criteria

When you use queries, usually you are looking for those records that satisfy some criterion. In the simple query you created earlier, for example, you entered a criterion to restrict the records that were included to those on which the recruiter number was 24. In another query, you might want the name, amount paid, and current due amounts of the client whose number is FD89, for example, or of those clients whose names start with the letters, Be. You enter criteria in the Criteria row in the design grid below the field name to which the criterion applies. For example, to indicate that the client number must be FD89, you first must add the Client Number field to the design grid. You then would type FD89 in the Criteria row below the Client Number field.

To Use Text Data in a Criterion

To use **text data** (data in a field whose data type is Text) in criteria, simply type the text in the Criteria row below the corresponding field name. The following steps query the Client table and display the client number, client name, amount paid, and current due amount of client FD89.

- Click the Criteria row for the Client Number field to produce an insertion point.

- Type FD89 as the criterion (Figure 2–13).

Figure 2–13

- Click the View button to display the query results (Figure 2–14).

Q&A

I noticed that there is a View button on both the Home tab and the Design tab. Do they both have the same effect?

Yes. Use whichever one you find most convenient.

Figure 2–14

To Use a Wildcard

Microsoft Access supports wildcards. **Wildcards** are symbols that represent any character or combination of characters. One common wildcard, the **asterisk** (*), represents any collection of characters. Thus Be* represents the letters, Be, followed by any collection of characters. Another wildcard symbol is the **question mark** (?), which represents any individual character. Thus T?m represents the letter, T, followed by any single character followed by the letter, m, such as Tim or Tom.

The following steps use a wildcard to find the number, name, and address of those clients whose names begin with Be. Because you do not know how many characters will follow the Be, the asterisk is appropriate.

1

- Click the View button to return to Design view.

- If necessary, click the Criteria row below the Client Number field to produce an insertion point.

- Use the DELETE or BACKSPACE key as necessary to delete the current entry.

- Click the Criteria row below the Client Name field to produce an insertion point.

- Type Be* as the criterion (Figure 2–15).

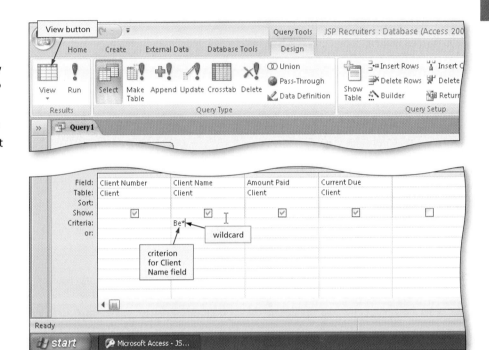

Figure 2–15

2

- View the query results by clicking the View button (Figure 2–16).

 Experiment

- Vary the case of the letters in the criteria and view the results to determine whether case makes a difference when entering a wildcard.

Figure 2–16

To Use Criteria for a Field Not Included in the Results

In some cases, you may have criteria for a particular field that should not appear in the results of the query. For example, you may want to see the client number, client name, address, and amount paid for all clients located in Berridge. The criteria involve the City field, which is not one of the fields to be included in the results.

To enter a criterion for the City field, it must be included in the design grid. Normally, this also would mean it would appear in the results. To prevent this from happening, remove the check mark from its Show check box in the Show row of the grid. The following steps display the client number, client name, amount paid, and current due for clients located in Berridge.

- Click the View button to return to Design view.

- Erase the criterion in the Client Name field.

- Include the City field in the query.

- Type Berridge as the criterion for the City field (Figure 2–17).

Figure 2–17

- Click the Show check box for the City field to remove the check mark (Figure 2–18).

Q&A

Could I have removed the check mark before entering the criterion?

Yes. The order in which you performed the two operations does not matter.

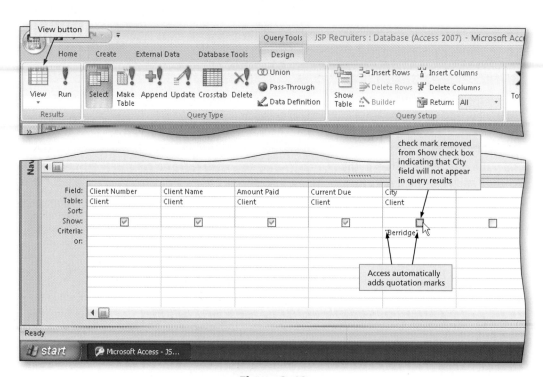

Figure 2–18

❸

● View the query results (Figure 2–19).

🔎 **Experiment**

● Click the View button to return to Design view, enter a different city name, and view the results. Repeat this process with a variety of city names, including at least one city name that is not in the database.

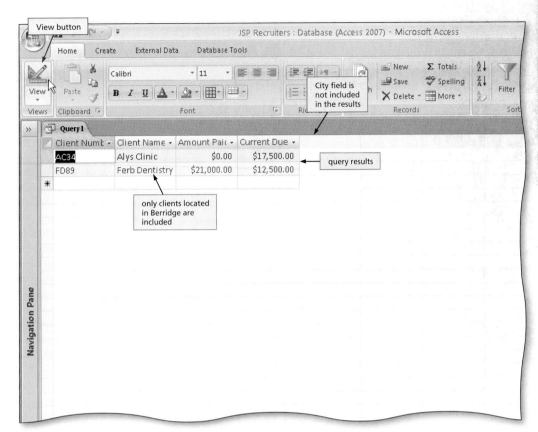

Figure 2–19

Creating a Parameter Query

If you wanted to find clients located in Fort Stewart rather than Berridge, you would either have to create a new query or modify the existing query by replacing Berridge with Fort Stewart as the criterion. Rather than giving a specific criterion when you first create the query, on occasion, you may want to be able to enter part of the criterion when you view the query results and then have the appropriate results appear. For example, to include all the clients located in Berridge, you could enter Berridge as a criterion in the City field. From that point on, every time you ran the query, only the clients in Berridge would appear.

A better way is to allow the user to enter the city at the time the user wants to view the results. Thus a user could view the query results, enter Berridge as the city and then see all the clients in Berridge. Later, the user could use the same query, but enter Fort Stewart as the city, and then see all the clients in Fort Stewart.

To enable this flexibility, you create a **parameter query**, which is a query that prompts for input whenever it is used. You enter a parameter, rather than a specific value, as the criterion. You create a parameter by enclosing a value in a criterion in square brackets. It is important that the value in the brackets does not match the name of any field. If you enter a field name in square brackets, Access assumes you want that particular field and does not prompt the user for input. For example, you could place [Enter City] as the criterion in the City field.

BTW

Removing a Table from a Query
If you add the wrong table to a query or have an extra table in the query, you can remove it by right-clicking the field list for the table and then clicking Remove Table on the shortcut menu.

To Create a Parameter Query

The following steps create a parameter query that prompts the user to enter a city, and then displays the client number, client name, amount paid, and current due for all clients located in that city.

- Return to Design view.

- Erase the current criterion in the City column, and then type [Enter City] as the new criterion (Figure 2–20).

Q&A

What is the purpose of the square brackets?

The square brackets indicate that the text entered is not text that the value in the column must match. Without the brackets, for example, Access would search for records on which the city is Enter City.

Q&A

What if I typed a field name in the square brackets?

Access would simply use the value in that field. In order to create a parameter query, it is essential that the text typed in the square brackets not be a field name.

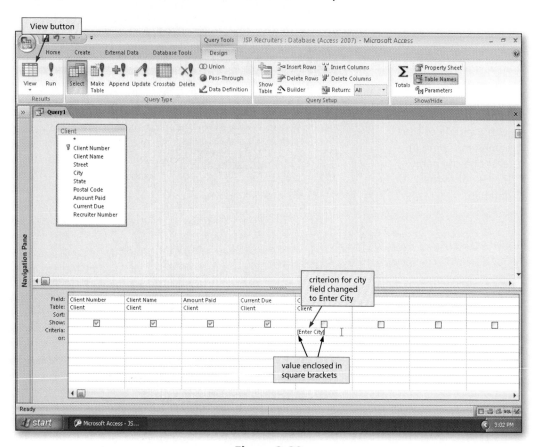

Figure 2–20

- Click the View button to display the Enter Parameter Value dialog box (Figure 2–21).

Figure 2–21

3

- Type `Fort Stewart` as the parameter value in the Enter City text box and then click the OK button (Figure 2–22).

🔎 **Experiment**

- Try other characters between the square brackets. In each case, view the results. When finished, change the characters between the square brackets back to Enter City.

query results

only clients located in Fort Stewart are included

Figure 2–22

Each time you use this query, you will be asked to enter a city. Only clients in the city you enter will be included in the results.

To Save a Query

In many cases, you will want to repeatedly use the queries you construct. By saving the query, you eliminate the need to repeat all your entries. The following steps save the query you just have created and assign it the name Client-City Query.

1

- Click the Save button on the Quick Access Toolbar to open the Save As dialog box.

Q&A Can I also save from Design view?

Yes. You can save the query when you view it in Design view just as you can save the query when you view the query results in Datasheet view.

- Type `Client-City Query` in the Query Name text box (Figure 2–23).

Save button

Save As dialog box

name of query

OK button

Figure 2–23

- Click the OK button to save the query (Figure 2–24).

- Click the Close 'Client-City Query' button to close the query and remove it from the screen.

Other Ways
1. Right-click tab for query, click Save on shortcut menu
2. Press CTRL+S

Figure 2–24

To Use a Saved Query

Once you have saved a query, you can use and manipulate it at any time in the future by opening it. When you right-click the query in the Navigation pane, Access displays a shortcut menu containing commands that allow you to open and change the design of the query. You also can print the results by clicking the Office Button, pointing to Print on the Office button menu, and then clicking Quick Print on the Print submenu.

The query always uses the data that is currently in the table. Thus, if changes have been made to the data since the last time you ran the query, the results of the query may be different. The following steps use the query named Client-City Query.

- Show the Navigation pane.

- Right-click the Client-City Query to produce a shortcut menu.

- Click Open on the shortcut menu to open the query and display the Enter Parameter Value dialog box (Figure 2–25)

Q&A

What would have happened if there were no parameters?

You would immediately see the results without needing to furnish any additional information.

Figure 2–25

- Type `Fort Stewart` in the Enter City text box, and then click the OK button to display the results using Fort Stewart as the city as shown in Figure 2–24.

- Click the Close 'Client-City Query' button, shown in Figure 2–24, to close the query.

To Use a Number in a Criterion

To enter a number in a criterion, type the number without any dollar signs or commas. The following steps display all clients whose current due amount is $0.00.

1

- Hide the Navigation pane.

- Click Create on the Ribbon to display the Create tab.

- Click the Query Design button to create a new query.

- With the Client table selected, click the Add button in the Show Table dialog box to add the Client table to the query.

- Click the Close button in the Show Table dialog box to remove the dialog box from the screen.

- Drag the lower edge of the field box down far enough so all fields in the Client table are displayed.

- Include the Client Number, Client Name, Amount Paid, and Current Due fields in the query.

- Type 0 as the criterion for the Current Due field (Figure 2–26).

 Q&A Do I need to enter a dollar sign and decimal point?

No. Access will interpret 0 as $0.00, because the data type for the Current Due field is currency.

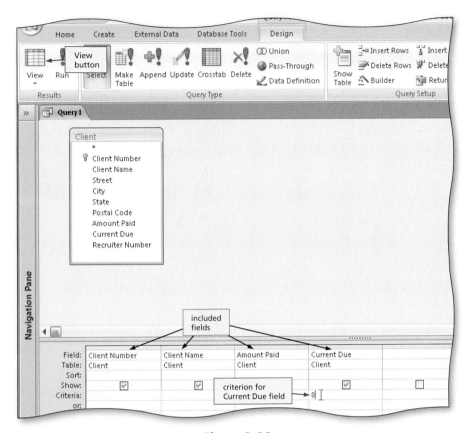

Figure 2–26

2

- View the query results (Figure 2–27).

Q&A Why did Access display the results as $0.00 when I only entered 0?

Access uses the format for the field to determine how to display the result. In this case the format indicated that Access should include the dollar sign and decimal point.

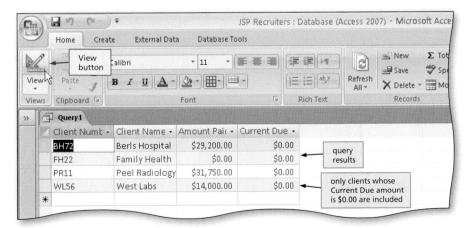

Figure 2–27

To Use a Comparison Operator in a Criterion

Unless you specify otherwise, Access assumes that the criteria you enter involve equality (exact matches). In the last query, for example, you were requesting those clients whose current due amount is equal to 0 (zero). If you want something other than an exact match, you must enter the appropriate **comparison operator**. The comparison operators are > (greater than), < (less than), >= (greater than or equal to), <= (less than or equal to), and NOT (not equal to).

The following steps use the > operator to find all clients whose amount paid is more than $20,000.00.

- Return to Design view.

- Erase the 0 in the Current Due column.

- Type >20000 as the criterion for the Amount Paid field (Figure 2–28).

Figure 2–28

- View the query results (Figure 2–29).

Experiment

- Return to Design view. Try a different criterion involving a comparison operator in the Amount Paid field and view the results. When finished, return to Design view, enter the original criterion (>20000) in the Amount Paid field, and view the results.

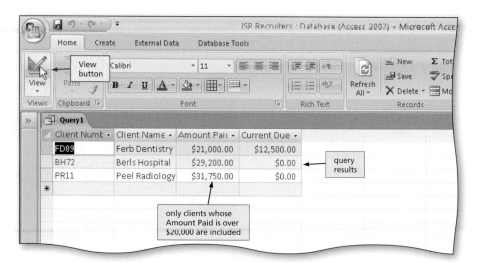

Figure 2–29

Using Compound Criteria

Often you will have more than one criterion that the data for which you are searching must satisfy. This type of criterion is called a **compound criterion**. Two types of compound criteria exist.

In an **AND criterion**, each individual criterion must be true in order for the compound criterion to be true. For example, an AND criterion would allow you to find those clients that have an amount paid greater than $20,000.00 and whose recruiter is recruiter 21.

Conversely, an **OR criterion** is true provided either individual criterion is true. An OR criterion would allow you to find those clients that have an amount paid greater than $20,000.00 or whose recruiter is recruiter 21. In this case, any client whose amount paid is greater than $20,000.00 would be included in the answer, regardless of whether the client's recruiter is recruiter 21. Likewise, any client whose recruiter is recruiter 21 would be included, regardless of whether the client had an amount paid greater than $20,000.00.

BTW

The BETWEEN Operator
The BETWEEN operator allows you to search for a range of values in one field. For example, to find all clients whose amount paid is between $10,000 and $20,000, you would enter Between 10000 and 20000 in the Criteria row for the Amount Paid field.

To Use a Compound Criterion Involving AND

To combine criteria with AND, place the criteria on the same line. The following steps use an AND criterion to find those clients whose amount paid is greater than $20,000.00 and whose recruiter is recruiter 21.

1

- Return to Design view.

- Include the Recruiter Number field in the query.

- Type 21 as the criterion for the Recruiter Number field (Figure 2–30).

Figure 2–30

- View the query results (Figure 2–31).

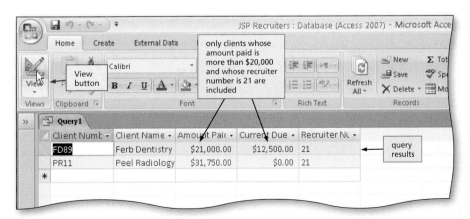

Figure 2–31

To Use a Compound Criterion Involving OR

To combine criteria with OR, the criteria must go on separate lines in the Criteria area of the grid. The following steps use an OR criterion to find those clients whose amount paid is greater than $20,000.00 or whose recruiter is recruiter 21 (or both).

- Return to Design view.

- If necessary, click the Criteria entry for the Recruiter Number field and then use the BACKSPACE key or the DELETE key to erase the entry ("21").

- Click the or: row (the row below the Criteria row) for the Recruiter Number field and then type 21 as the entry (Figure 2–32).

Figure 2–32

- View the query results (Figure 2–33).

Figure 2–33

Sorting

In some queries, the order in which the records appear really does not matter. All you need to be concerned about are the records that appear in the results. It does not matter which one is first or which one is last.

In other queries, however, the order can be very important. You may want to see the cities in which clients are located and would like them arranged alphabetically. Perhaps you want to see the clients listed by recruiter number. Further, within all the clients of any given recruiter, you might want them to be listed by amount paid from largest amount to smallest.

To order the records in the answer to a query in a particular way, you **sort** the records. The field or fields on which the records are sorted is called the **sort key**. If you are sorting on more than one field (such as sorting by amount paid within recruiter number), the more important field (Recruiter Number) is called the **major key** (also called the **primary sort key**) and the less important field (Amount Paid) is called the **minor key** (also called the **secondary sort key**).

To sort in Microsoft Access, specify the sort order in the Sort row of the design grid below the field that is the sort key. If you specify more than one sort key, the sort key on the left will be the major sort key and the one on the right will be the minor key.

The following are guidelines related to sorting in queries.

Plan Ahead

Determine whether special order is required.

1. **Determine whether sorting is required.** Examine the query or request to see if it contains words such as "order" or "sort" that would imply that the order of the query results is important. If so, you need to sort the query.

2. **Determine the sort key(s).** If sorting is required, identify the field or fields on which the results are to be sorted. Look for words such as "ordered by" or "sort the results by," both of which would indicate that the specified field is a sort key.

3. **If using two sort keys, determine major and minor key.** If you are using two sort keys, determine which one is more important. That will be the major key. Look for words such as "sort by amount paid within recruiter number," which imply that the overall order is by recruiter number. Thus, the Recruiter Number field would be the major sort key and the Amount Paid field would be the minor sort key.

4. **Determine sort order.** Words such as "increasing," "ascending," or "low-to-high" imply Ascending order. Words such as "decreasing," "descending," or "high-to-low" imply Descending order. Sorting in alphabetical order implies Ascending order. If there are no words to imply a particular order, you would typically use Ascending.

5. **Determine restrictions.** Examine the query or request to see if there are any special restrictions. One common restriction is to exclude duplicates. Another common restriction is to list only a certain number of records, for example to list only the first five records.

To Clear the Design Grid

If the fields you want to include in the next query are different from those in the previous query, it is usually simpler to start with a clear grid, that is, one with no fields already in the design grid. You always can clear the entries in the design grid by closing the query and then starting over. A simpler approach to clearing the entries is to select all the entries and then press the DELETE key. The following steps return to Design view and clear the design grid.

- Return to Design view.

- Click just above the Client Number column heading in the grid to select the column.

I clicked above the column heading, but the column is not selected. What should I do?

You didn't point to the correct location. Be sure the mouse pointer turns to a down-pointing arrow and then click again.

- Hold the SHIFT key down and click just above the Recruiter Number column heading to select all the columns (Figure 2–34).

Figure 2–34

- Press the DELETE key to clear the design grid.

To Sort Data in a Query

If you have determined in the design process that a query is to be sorted, you must identify the sort key, that is, the field on which the results are to be sorted. In creating the query, you will need to specify the sort key to Access. The following steps sort the cities in the Client table by indicating that the City field is to be sorted. The steps specify Ascending sort order.

- Include the City field in the design grid.

- Click the Sort row below the City field, and then click the Sort row arrow to display a menu of possible sort orders (Figure 2–35).

Figure 2–35

2

- Click Ascending to select Ascending sort order (Figure 2–36).

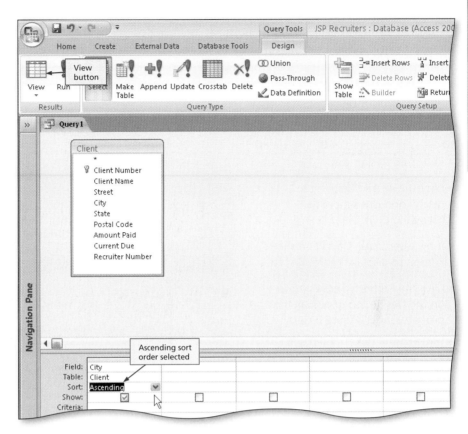

Figure 2–36

3

- View the query results (Figure 2–37).

Experiment

- Return to Design view and change the sort order to Descending. View the results. Return to Design view and change the sort order back to Ascending. View the results.

Q&A

Why do some cities appear more than once?

More than one client is located in those cities.

Figure 2–37

To Omit Duplicates

When you sort data, duplicates normally are included. In Figure 2–37 on the previous page, for example, Berridge appeared twice, as did Fort Stewart and Tarleton. These duplicates do not add any value, so you can eliminate them from the results. To eliminate duplicates, display the query's property sheet. A **property sheet** is a window containing the various properties of the object. To omit duplicates, you will use the property sheet to change the Unique Values property from No to Yes.

The following steps produce a sorted list of the cities in the Client table in which each city is listed only once.

- Return to Design view.

- Click the second field in the design grid (the empty field following City).

- If necessary, click Design on the Ribbon to display the Design tab.

- Click the Property Sheet button on the Design tab to display the property sheet (Figure 2–38).

Q&A

My property sheet looks different. What should I do?

If your sheet looks different, you clicked the wrong place and will have to close the property sheet and repeat this step.

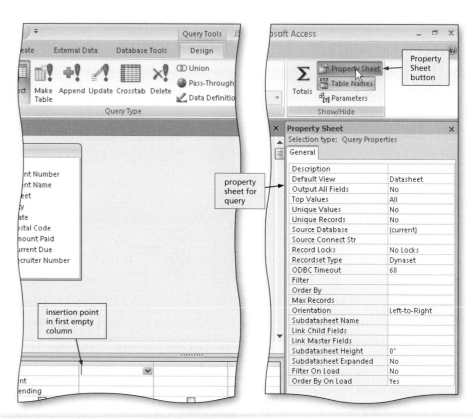

Figure 2–38

2

- Click the Unique Values property box, and then click the arrow that appears to produce a menu of available choices for Unique Values (Figure 2–39).

Figure 2–39

3

- Click Yes and then close the Query Properties sheet by clicking its Close button.

- View the query results (Figure 2–40).

query results

each city listed only once

Figure 2–40

To Sort on Multiple Keys

The following steps sort on multiple keys. Specifically, the data is to be sorted by amount paid (low to high) within recruiter number, which means that the Recruiter Number field is the major key and the Amount Paid field is the minor key.

1

- Return to Design view.

- Clear the design grid.

- Include the Client Number, Client Name, Recruiter Number, and Amount Paid fields in the query in this order.

- Select Ascending as the sort order for both the Recruiter Number field and the Amount Paid field (Figure 2–41).

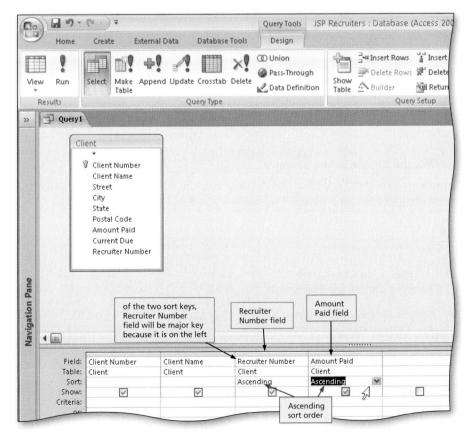

of the two sort keys, Recruiter Number field will be major key because it is on the left

Recruiter Number field

Amount Paid field

Ascending sort order

Figure 2–41

2

- View the query results (Figure 2–42).

 Experiment

- Return to Design view and try other sort combinations for the Recruiter Number and Amount Paid fields, such as Ascending for Recruiter Number and Descending for Amount Paid. In each case, view the results to see the effect of the changes. When finished, select Ascending as the sort order for both fields.

Q&A

What if the Amount Paid field is to the left of the Recruiter Number?

It is important to remember that the major sort key must appear to the left of the minor sort key in the design grid. If you attempted to sort by amount paid within recruiter number, but placed the Amount Paid field to the left of the Recruiter Number field, your results would be incorrect.

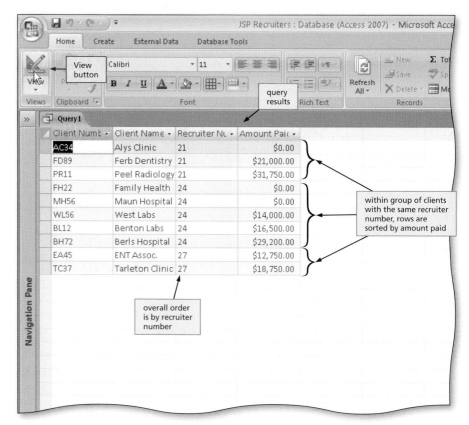

Figure 2–42

To Create a Top-Values Query

Rather than show all the results of a query, you may want to show only a specified number of records or a percentage of records. Creating a **top-values query** allows you to quantify the results. When you sort records, you can limit results to those records having the highest (descending sort) or lowest (ascending sort) values. To do so, first create a query that sorts the data in the desired order. Next, use the Return box on the Design tab to change the number of records to be included from All to the desired number or percentage. The following steps show the first five records that were included in the results of the previous query.

1

- Return to Design view.

- If necessary, click Design on the Ribbon to display the Design tab.

- Click the Return box arrow on the Design tab to display the Return box menu (Figure 2–43).

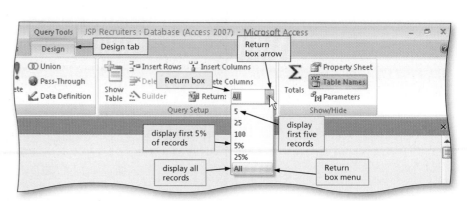

Figure 2–43

②

- Click 5 in the Return box menu to specify that the query results should contain the first five rows.

Q&A Could I have typed the 5? What about other numbers that do not appear in the list?

Yes, you could have typed the 5. For numbers not appearing in the list, you must type the number.

- View the query results (Figure 2–44).

③

- Close the query by clicking the Close 'Query1' button.

- When asked if you want to save your changes, click the No button.

Q&A Do I need to close the query before creating my next query?

Not necessarily. When you use a top-values query, however, it is important to change the value in the Return box back to All. If you do not change the Return value back to All, the previous value will remain in effect. Consequently, you may very well not get all the records you should in the next query. A good practice whenever you use a top-values query is to close the query as soon as you are done. That way, you will begin your next query from scratch, which guarantees that the value is set back to All.

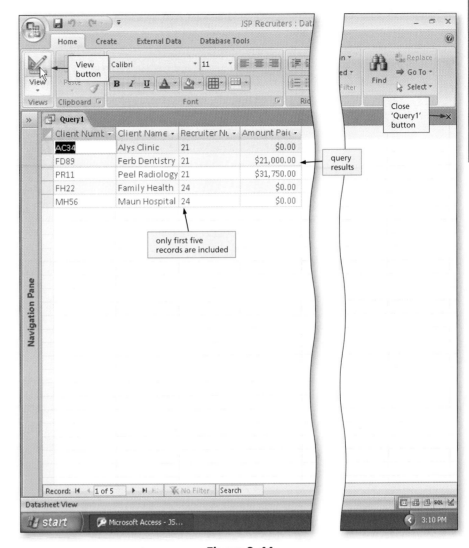

Figure 2–44

Joining Tables

In designing a query, you need to determine whether more than one table is required. If the question being asked involves data from both the Client and Recruiter tables, for example, both tables are required for the query. Such a query may require listing the number and name of each client along with the number and name of the client's recruiter. The client's name is in the Client table, whereas the recruiter's name is in the Recruiter table. Thus, this query cannot be completed using a single table; both the Client and Recruiter tables are required. You need to **join** the tables; that is, to find records in the two tables that have identical values in matching fields (Figure 2–45). In this example, you need to find records in the Client table and the Recruiter table that have the same value in the Recruiter Number fields.

> Give me the number and name of each client along with the number and name of each client's recruiter.

Client table

Client Number	Name	...	Recruiter Number
AC34	Alys Clinic	...	21
BH72	Berls Hospital	...	24
BL12	Benton Labs	...	24
EA45	ENT Assoc.	...	27
FD89	Ferb Dentistry	...	21
FH22	Family Health	...	24
MH56	Maun Hospital	...	24
PR11	Peel Radiology	...	21
TC37	Tarleton Clinic	...	27
WL56	West Labs	...	24

Recruiter table

Recruiter Number	Last Name	First Name	...
21	Kerry	Alyssa	...
24	Reeves	Camden	...
27	Fernandez	Jaime	...
34	Lee	Jan	...

Join Types
The type of join that finds records from both tables that have identical values in matching fields is called an inner join. An inner join is the default join in Access. Outer joins are used to show all the records in one table as well as the common records; that is, the records that share the same value in the join field. In a left outer join, all rows from the table on the left are included. In a right outer join, all rows from the table on the right are included.

Join of Client and Recruiter tables

Client Number	Name	...	Recruiter Number	Last Name	First Name	...
AC34	Alys Clinic	...	21	Kerry	Alyssa	...
BH72	Berls Hospital	...	24	Reeves	Camden	...
BL12	Benton Labs	...	24	Reeves	Camden	...
EA45	ENT Assoc.	...	27	Fernandez	Jaime	...
FD89	Ferb Dentistry	...	21	Kerry	Alyssa	...
FH22	Family Health	...	24	Reeves	Camden	...
MH56	Maun Hospital	...	24	Reeves	Camden	...
PR11	Peel Radiology	...	21	Kerry	Alyssa	...
TC37	Tarleton Clinic	...	27	Fernandez	Jaime	...
WL56	West Labs	...	24	Reeves	Camden	...

Figure 2–45

The following are guidelines related to joining tables.

Plan Ahead

Determine whether more than one table is required.

1. **Determine whether more than one table is required.** Examine the query or request to see if all the fields involved in the request are in one table. If the fields are in two (or more) tables, you need to join the tables.

2. **Determine the matching fields.** If joining is required, identify the matching fields in the two tables that have identical values. Look for the same column name in the two tables or for column names that are similar.

(continued)

(continued)

Plan
Ahead

3. **Determine whether sorting is required**. Queries that join tables often are used as the basis for a report. If this is the case, it may be necessary to sort the results. For example, the Recruiter-Client Report is based on a query that joins the Recruiter and Client tables. The query is sorted by recruiter number and client number.

4. **Determine restrictions**. Examine the query or request to see if there are any special restrictions. For example, the query may only want clients whose current due amount is $0.00.

5. **Determine join properties**. Examine the query or request to see if you only want records from both tables that have identical values in matching fields. If you want to see records in one of the tables that do not have identical values, then you need to change the join properties. When two tables have fields with the same name, you also need to determine which table contains the field to be used in the query. For example, if you want to see all recruiters, even if they have no clients, then you should include the recruiter number from the Recruiter table in the design grid. If you want only records with identical values in matching fields, then it does not matter which matching field you select.

To Join Tables

If you have determined in the design process that you need to join tables, you will first bring field lists for both tables to the upper pane of the Query window. Access will draw a line, called a **join line**, between matching fields in the two tables indicating that the tables are related. You then can select fields from either table. Access joins the tables automatically.

The first step is to create a new query and add the Recruiter table to the query. Then, add the Client table to the query. A join line will appear connecting the Recruiter Number fields in the two field lists. This join line indicates how the tables are related; that is, linked through these matching fields. (If you fail to give the matching fields the same name, Access will not insert the line. You can insert it manually, however, by clicking one of the two matching fields and dragging the mouse pointer to the other matching field.)

The following steps create a new query, add the Client table, and then select the appropriate fields.

1

• Click Create on the Ribbon to display the Create tab.

• Click the Query Design button to create a new query.

• Click the Recruiter table in the Show Table dialog box to select the table.

• Click the Add button to add a field list for the Recruiter table to the query (Figure 2–46).

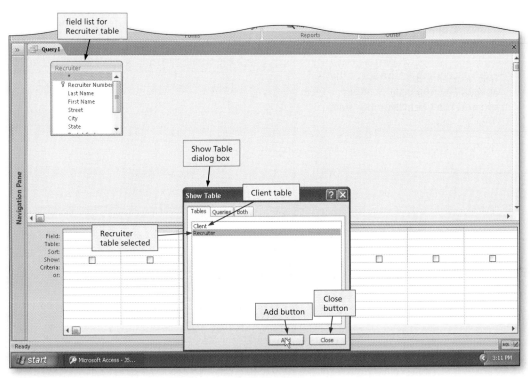

Figure 2–46

2

- Click the Client table in the Show Table dialog box.

- Click the Add button to add a field list for the Client table.

- Close the Show Table dialog box by clicking the Close button.

- Expand the size of the field lists so all the fields in the Recruiter and Client tables appear (Figure 2–47).

Q&A

I didn't get a join line. What should I do?

Ensure that the names of the matching fields are exactly the same, the data types are the same, and the matching field is the primary key in one of the two tables. If all of these are true and you still don't have a join line, you can produce one by pointing to one of the matching fields and dragging to the other matching field.

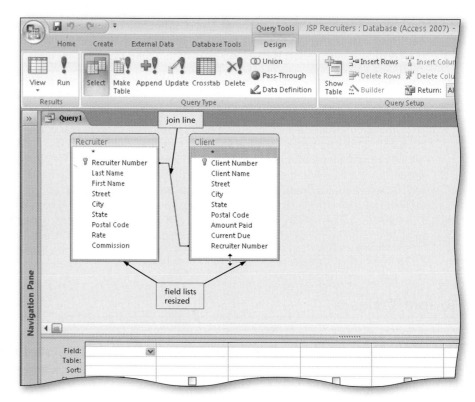

Figure 2–47

3

- In the design grid, include the Recruiter Number, Last Name, and First Name fields from the Recruiter table as well as the Client Number and Client Name fields from the Client table.

- Select Ascending as the sort order for both the Recruiter Number field and the Client Number field (Figure 2–48).

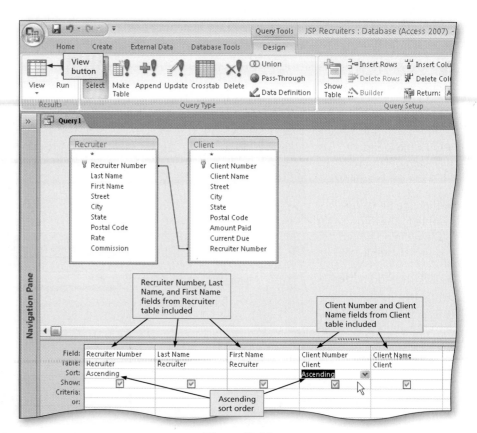

Figure 2–48

4
- View the query results (Figure 2–49).

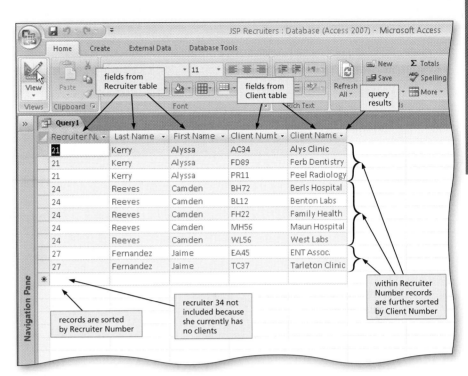

Figure 2–49

To Save the Query

The following steps save the query.

1
- Click the Save button on the Quick Access Toolbar to display the Save As dialog box.

- Type `Recruiter-Client Query` as the query name (Figure 2–50).

2
- Click the OK button to save the query.

Figure 2–50

To Change Join Properties

Normally records that do not match do not appear in the results of a join query. A recruiter such as Jan Lee, for whom no clients currently exist, for example, would not appear. To cause such a record to be displayed, you need to change the **join properties**, which are the properties that indicate which records appear in a join, of the query, as in the following steps.

- Return to Design view.

- Right-click the join line to produce a shortcut menu (Figure 2–51).

Q&A I don't see Join Properties on my shortcut menu. What should I do?

If Join Properties does not appear on your shortcut menu, you did not point to the appropriate portion of the join line. You will need to point to the correct portion and right-click again.

Figure 2–51

- Click Join Properties on the shortcut menu to display the Join Properties dialog box (Figure 2–52).

Q&A How do the options in the Join Properties dialog box match the various types of joins described earlier?

Option button 1 gives an inner join, option button 2 gives a left join, and option button 3 gives a right join.

Figure 2–52

- Click option button 2 to include all records from the Recruiter table regardless of whether they match any clients.

- Click the OK button.

- View the query results by clicking the View button (Figure 2–53).

- Click the Save button on the Quick Access Toolbar.

Experiment

- Return to Design view, change the Join properties, and select option button 3. View the results to see the effect of this option. When done, return to Design view, change the Join properties, and once again select option button 2.

Figure 2–53

- Close the Recruiter-Client Query by clicking the Close 'Recruiter-Client Query' button.

To Create a Report Involving a Join

The following steps create the report shown in Figure 2–54. The records in the report are sorted (ordered) by Client Number within Recruiter Number. To ensure that the records appear in this order, the steps specify that the Recruiter Number and Client Number fields are sort keys.

Recruiter-Client Report

Recruiter Number	Last Name	First Name	Client Number	Client Name
21	Kerry	Alyssa	AC34	Alys Clinic
21	Kerry	Alyssa	FD89	Ferb Dentistry
21	Kerry	Alyssa	PR11	Peel Radiology
24	Reeves	Camden	BH72	Berls Hospital
24	Reeves	Camden	BL12	Benton Labs
24	Reeves	Camden	FH22	Family Health
24	Reeves	Camden	MH56	Maun Hospital
24	Reeves	Camden	WL56	West Labs
27	Fernandez	Jaime	EA45	ENT Assoc.
27	Fernandez	Jaime	TC37	Tarleton Clinic
34	Lee	Jan		

Figure 2–54

1

- Show the Navigation pane and be sure the Recruiter-Client Query is selected in the Navigation pane.

Q&A

I have two copies of Recruiter-Client Query. Does it matter which one I use?

No. There are two copies because the recruiter-Client Query involves two tables. It does not matter which one you select.

- Click Create on the Ribbon to display the Create tab.

- Click the Report Wizard button to display the Report Wizard dialog box (Figure 2–55).

Figure 2–55

2

- Click the Add All Fields button to add all the fields in the Recruiter-Client Query.

- Click the Next button to display the next Report Wizard screen (Figure 2–56).

Figure 2–56

3

• Because you will not specify any grouping, click the Next button in the Report Wizard dialog box to display the next Report Wizard screen.

• Because you already specified the sort order in the query, click the Next button again to display the next Report Wizard screen.

• Make sure that Tabular is selected as the Layout and Portrait is selected as the Orientation.

• Click the Next button to display the next Report Wizard screen.

• Be sure the Module style is selected.

• Click the Next button to display the next Report Wizard screen.

Figure 2–57

• Erase the current title, and then type `Recruiter-Client Report` as the new title.

• Click the Finish button to produce the report (Figure 2–57).

4

• Click the Close button for the Recruiter-Client Report to remove the report from the screen.

To Print a Report

Once you have created a report, you can print it at any time. The layout will reflect the layout you created. The data in the report will always reflect current data. The following step prints the Recruiter-Client Report.

1 With the Recruiter-Client Report selected in the Navigation pane, click the Office Button, point to Print on the Office button menu, and then click Quick Print on the Print submenu to print the report.

To Restrict the Records in a Join

Sometimes you will want to join tables, but you will not want to include all possible records. For example, you would like to create a report showing only those clients whose Amount Paid is greater than $20,000, but you do not want the Amount Paid field to appear in the results. In such cases, you will relate the tables and include fields just as you did before. You also will include criteria. To include only those clients whose amount paid is more than $20,000.00, you will include >20000 as a criterion for the Amount Paid field.

The following steps modify the Recruiter-Client query to restrict the records that will be included in the join.

● Open the Recruiter-Client Query in Design view and hide the Navigation pane.

● Add the Amount Paid field to the query.

● Type >20000 as the criterion for the Amount Paid field and then click the Show check box for the Amount Paid field to remove the check mark (Figure 2–58).

Figure 2–58

● View the query results (Figure 2–59).

● Close the query by clicking the Close 'Recruiter-Client Query' button.

● When asked if you want to save your changes, click the No button.

Figure 2–59

Calculations

If you have determined that a special calculation is required for a query, you then need to determine whether the calculation is an individual record calculation (for example, adding the values in two fields) or a group calculation (for example, finding the total of the values in a particular field on all the records).

JSP Recruiters may want to know the total amount (amount paid plus current due) from each client. This would seem to pose a problem because the Client table does not include a field for total amount. You can calculate it, however, because the total amount is equal to the amount paid plus the current due. A field that can be computed from other fields is called a **calculated field**. A calculated field is an individual record calculation.

JSP also may want to calculate the average amount paid for the clients of each recruiter. That is, they want the average for the clients of recruiter 21, the average for the clients of recruiter 24, and so on. This type of calculation is called a group calculation, because it involves groups of records. In this example, the clients of recruiter 21 would form one group, the clients of recruiter 24 would be a second, and the clients of recruiter 27 form a third group.

The following are guidelines related to calculations in queries.

BTW

Expression Builder
Access includes a tool to help you create complex expressions. If you click Build on the shortcut menu (see Figure 2-60 on the next page), Access displays the Expression Builder dialog box. The dialog box includes an expression box, operator buttons, and expression elements. You use the expression box to build the expression. You can type parts of the expression directly and paste operator buttons and expression elements into the box. You also can use functions in expressions.

Plan Ahead

Determine whether calculations are required.

1. **Determine whether calculations are required.** Examine the query or request to see if there are special calculations to be included. Look for words such as "total," "sum," "compute," or "calculate."

2. **Determine a name for the calculated field.** If calculations are required, decide on the name for the field. Assign a name that helps identify the contents of the field. For example, if you are adding the cost of a number of items, the name "Total Cost" would be appropriate. The name, also called an **alias**, becomes the column name when the query is run.

3. **Determine the format for the calculated field.** Determine how the calculated field should appear. If the calculation involves monetary amounts, you would use the currency format. If the calculated value contains decimals, determine how many decimal places to display.

To Use a Calculated Field in a Query

If you have determined that you need a calculated field in a query, you enter a name (alias) for the calculated field, a colon, and then the expression in one of the columns in the Field row. Any fields included in the expression must be enclosed in square brackets [ ]. For the total amount, for example, you will type Total Amount:[Amount Paid]+[Current Due] as the expression.

You can type the expression directly into the Field row. You will not be able to see the entire entry, however, because the Field row is not large enough. The preferred way is to select the column in the Field row and then use the Zoom command on its shortcut menu. When Access displays the Zoom dialog box, you can enter the expression.

You are not restricted to addition in calculations. You can use subtraction (-), multiplication (*), or division (/). You also can include parentheses in your calculations to indicate which calculations should be done first.

The steps on the next page use a calculated field to display the number, name, amount paid, current due, and the total amount for all clients.

1

- Create a query with a field list for the Client table.

- Add the Client Number, Client Name, Amount Paid, and Current Due fields to the query.

- Right-click the Field row in the first open column in the design grid to display a shortcut menu (Figure 2–60).

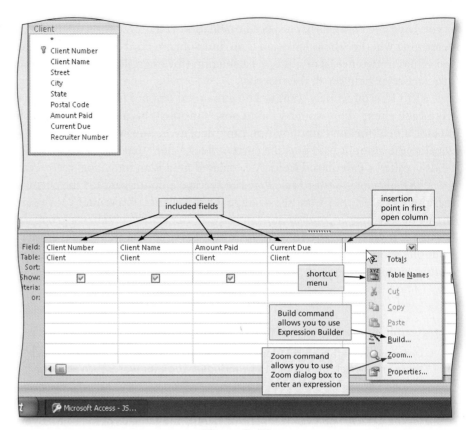

Figure 2–60

2

- Click Zoom on the shortcut menu to display the Zoom dialog box.

- Type Total Amount:[Amount Paid]+[Current Due] in the Zoom dialog box (Figure 2–61).

Do I always need to put square brackets around field names?

If the field name does not contain spaces, square brackets are technically not necessary, although it is still acceptable to use the brackets. It is a good practice, however, to get in the habit of using the brackets.

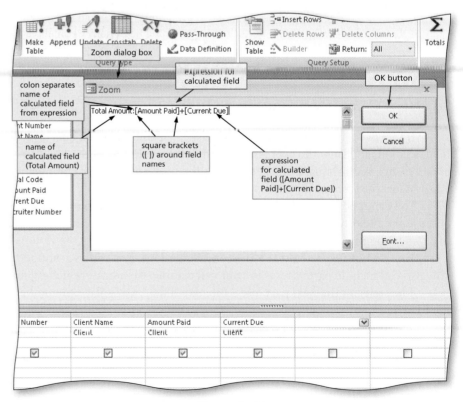

Figure 2–61

3

- Click the OK button to enter the expression (Figure 2–62).

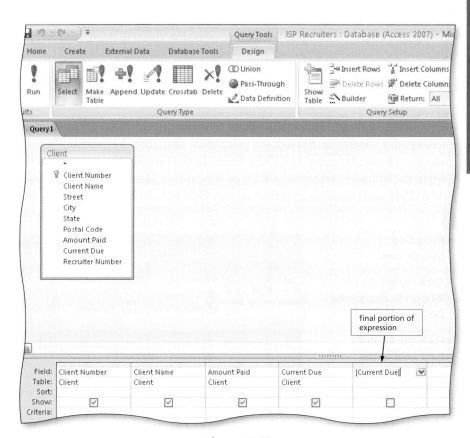

Figure 2–62

4

- View the query results (Figure 2–63).

Experiment

- Return to Design view and try other expressions. In at least one case, omit the Total Amount and the colon. In at least one case, intentionally misspell a field name. In each case, view the results to see the effect of your changes. When finished, re-enter the original expression.

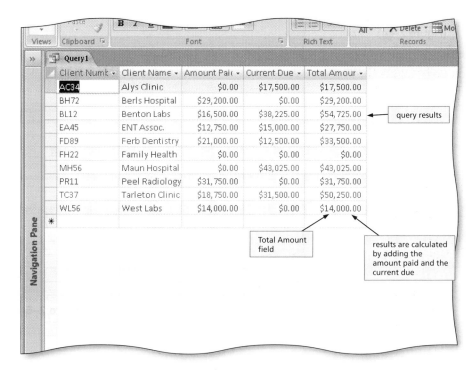

Figure 2–63

Learn It Online

Test your knowledge of chapter content and key terms.

Instructions: To complete the Learn It Online exercises, start your browser, click the Address bar, and then enter the Web address scsite.com/ac2007/learn. When the Access 2007 Learn It Online page is displayed, click the link for the exercise you want to complete and then read the instructions.

Chapter Reinforcement TF, MC, and SA
A series of true/false, multiple choice, and short answer questions that test your knowledge of the chapter content.

Flash Cards
An interactive learning environment where you identify chapter key terms associated with displayed definitions.

Practice Test
A series of multiple choice questions that test your knowledge of chapter content and key terms.

Who Wants To Be a Computer Genius?
An interactive game that challenges your knowledge of chapter content in the style of a television quiz show.

Wheel of Terms
An interactive game that challenges your knowledge of chapter key terms in the style of the television show *Wheel of Fortune*.

Crossword Puzzle Challenge
A crossword puzzle that challenges your knowledge of key terms presented in the chapter.

Apply Your Knowledge

Reinforce the skills and apply the concepts you learned in this chapter.

Using the Query Wizard, Creating a Parameter Query, Joining Tables, and Creating a Report
Instructions: Start Access. Open the The Bike Delivers database that you modified in Apply Your Knowledge in Chapter 1 on page AC 64. (If you did not complete this exercise, see your instructor for a copy of the modified database.)

Perform the following tasks:

1. Use the Simple Query Wizard to create a query for the Customer table. Include the Customer Name, Balance, and Courier Number in the query. Assign the name, Customer Query, to the query.

2. Create a query for the Customer table and add the Customer Number, Customer Name, Courier Number, and Balance fields to the design grid. Sort the records in descending order by Balance. Add a criterion for the Courier Number field that allows the user to enter a different courier each time the query is run. Save the query as Courier Parameter Query.

3. Create a query that joins the Courier and the Customer tables. Add the Courier Number, First Name, and Last Name fields from the Courier table and the Customer Number and Customer Name fields from the Customer table. Sort the records in ascending order by Courier Number and Customer Number. All couriers should appear in the result even if they currently have no customers. Save the query as Courier-Customer Query.

4. Create the report shown in Figure 2–84. The report uses the Courier-Customer Query.

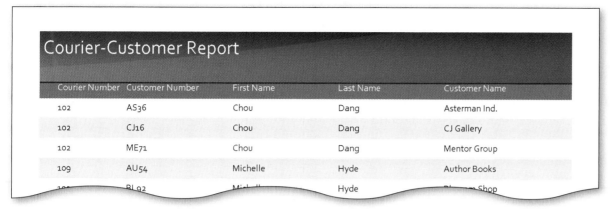

Figure 2–84

5. Submit the revised database in the format specified by your instructor.

Extend Your Knowledge

Extend the skills you learned in this chapter and experiment with new skills. You may need to use Help to complete the assignment.

Creating Crosstab Queries, Creating Queries Using Criteria

Instructions: Start Access. Open the Groom n Fluff database. See the inside back cover of this book for instructions for downloading the Data Files for Students, or see your instructor for information on accessing the files required in this book.

Groom n Fluff is a small pet grooming business. The owner has created an Access database in which to store information about the customers she serves and the pet groomers she employs. You will create the crosstab query shown in Figure 2–85. You also will query the database using specified criteria.

Figure 2–85

Continued >

STUDENT ASSIGNMENTS

Perform the following tasks:

1. Create the crosstab query shown in Figure 2–85 on the previous page. The crosstab groups average of customers' balances by city and groomer number.

2. Create a query to find all customers who do not live in Grant City. Include the Customer Number, Last Name, and Balance fields in the design grid. Save the query as Not Criteria Query.

3. Create a query to find all customers who do not have a telephone number. Include the Customer Number, Last Name, First Name, Street, and City fields in the query results. Save the query as Missing Values Query.

4. Create a query to find all customers whose balance is between $20.00 and $60.00. Include the Customer Number, Last Name, and Balance fields in the design grid. Save the query as Number Range Query.

5. Create a query to find all customers where the groomer number is 203 or 205 and the balance is greater than $40.00. Include the Customer Number, Last Name, First Name, Balance, and Groomer Number fields in the design grid. Save the query as Compound Criteria Query.

6. Change the database properties, as specified by your instructor. Submit the revised database in the format specified by your instructor.

Make It Right

Analyze a database and correct all errors and/or improve the design.

Correcting Errors in the Query Design

Instructions: Start Access. Open the Keep It Green database. See the inside back cover of this book for instructions for downloading the Data Files for Students, or see your instructor for information on accessing the files required in this book.

Keep It Green is a database maintained by a small landscaping business. The queries shown in Figure 2–86 contain a number of errors that need to be corrected before the queries run properly. The sort query shown in Figure 2–86a displays the query results in the proper order (First Name, Last Name, Street, City) but it is sorted incorrectly. The query results should be sorted by last name within city in ascending order. Also the caption for the Street field should be Address. Save the query with your changes.

When you try to run the join query for the Keep It Green database, the message shown in Figure 2–86b appears. The query joins the Worker table and the Customer table. It also calculates the total amount for each customer. The query should be sorted in alphabetical order by worker last name and customer last name. Correct the error that is causing the message shown in Figure 2–86b and sort the records properly. Save the query with your changes.

Change the database properties, as specified by your instructor. Submit the revised database in the format specified by your instructor.

(a) Incorrect Sort Query

(b) Incorrect Join Query

Figure 2–86

In the Lab

Design, create, modify, and/or use a database following the guidelines, concepts, and skills presented in this chapter. Labs are listed in order of increasing difficulty.

Lab 1: Querying the JMS TechWizards Database

Problem: The management of JMS TechWizards has determined a number of questions it wants the database management system to answer. You must obtain answers to the questions posed by management.

Instructions: Use the database created in the In the Lab 1 of Chapter 1 on page AC 67 for this assignment or see your instructor for information on accessing the files required for this book. Perform the following tasks:

1. Open the JMS TechWizards database and create a new query for the Client table that includes the Client Number, Client Name, and Technician Number fields in the design grid for all clients where the technician number is 23. Save the query as Lab 2-1 Step 1 Query.

2. Create a query that includes the Client Number, Client Name, and Paid fields for all clients located in Liberty Corner with a paid amount greater than $500.00. Save the query as Lab2-1 Step 2 Query.

3. Create a query that includes the Client Number, Client Name, Street, and City fields for all clients whose names begin with Gr. Save the query as Lab 2-1 Step 3 Query.

4. Create a query that lists all cities in descending order. Each city should appear only once. Save the query as Lab 2-1 Step 4 Query.

5. Create a query that allows the user to enter the city to search when the query is run. The query results should display the Client Number, Client Name, and Billed. Test the query by searching for those records where the client is located in Anderson. Save the query as Client-City Query.

Continued >

6. Include the Client Number, Client Name, and Billed fields in the design grid. Sort the records in descending order by the Billed field. Display only the top 25 percent of the records in the query result. Save the query as Lab 2-1 Step 6 Query.

7. Join the Technician and the Client table. Include the Technician Number, First Name, and Last Name fields from the Technician table. Include the Client Number, Client Name, and Billed from the Client table. Sort the records in ascending order by technician's last name and client name. All technicians should appear in the result even if they currently have no clients. Save the query as Technician-Client query.

8. Open the Technician-Client query in Design view and remove the Client table. Add the Hourly Rate field to the design grid following the Last Name field. Calculate the number of hours each technician has worked (YTD Earnings/Hourly Rate). Assign the alias Hours Worked to the calculated field. Change the caption for the Hourly Rate field to Rate. Display hours worked as an integer (0 decimal places). Use the Save As command to save the query as Lab 2-1 Step 8 Query.

9. Create a query to display the average billed amount for all clients. Save the query as Lab 2-1 Step 9 Query.

10. Create a query to count the number of clients for technician 23. Save the query as Lab 2-1 Step 10 Query.

11. Create a query to display the average billed amount for each technician. Save the query as Lab 2-1 Step 11 Query.

12. Create the crosstab shown in Figure 2–87. The crosstab groups total of clients' paid amounts by city and technician number. Save the crosstab as City-Technician Crosstab.

13. Submit the revised database in the format specified by your instructor.

City	Total Of Paic	22	23	29
Anderson	$1,005.00	$255.00	$0.00	$750.00
Kingston	$548.50	$548.50	$0.00	
Liberty Corner	$565.00		$565.00	

Figure 2–87

In the Lab

Lab 2: Querying the Hockey Fan Zone Database

Problem: The management of the Hockey Fan Zone store has determined a number of questions it wants the database management system to answer. You must obtain answers to the questions posed by management.

Instructions: Use the database created in the In the Lab 2 of Chapter 1 on page AC 68 for this assignment, or see your instructor for information on accessing the files required for this book. Perform the following tasks:

1. Open the Hockey Fan Zone database and use the query wizard to create a query that includes the Item Number, Description, On Hand, and Cost fields for all records in the Item table. Name the query Lab 2-2 Step 1 Query.

2. Create a query that includes the Item Number, Description, Cost, and Supplier Code fields for all products where the Supplier Code is LG. Save the query as Lab 2-2 Step 2 Query.

3. Create a query that includes the Item Number and Description fields for all products where the description starts with the letter B. Save the query as Lab 2-2 Step 3 Query.

4. Create a query that includes the Item Number and Description field for all products with a cost less than $5.00. Save the query as Lab 2-2 Step 4 Query.

5. Create a query that includes the Item Number and Description field for all products with a selling price greater than $15.00. Save the query as Lab 2-2 Step 5 Query.

6. Create a query that includes all fields for all products with a selling price greater than $10.00 and where the number on hand is fewer than 10. Save the query as Lab 2-2 Step 6 Query.

7. Create a query that includes all fields for all products that have a selling price greater than $15.00 or a supplier code of AC. Save the query as Lab 2-2 Step 7 Query.

8. Join the Supplier table and the Item table. Include the Supplier Code and Supplier Name fields from the Supplier table and the Item Number, Description, On Hand, and Cost fields from the Item table. Sort the records in ascending order by Supplier Code and Item Number. Save the query as Supplier-Item Query. Note that the Report Wizard limits the size of the On Hand column header because it is a number field.

9. Create the report shown in Figure 2–88. The report uses the Supplier-Item query and the Module style.

Supplier-Item Report

Supplier Code	Item Number	Supplier Name	Description	Hand	Cost
AC	5923	Ace Clothes	Jersey	12	$21.45
AC	7810	Ace Clothes	Tee Shirt	32	$9.50
LG	3663	Logo Goods	Ball Cap	30	$11.15
LG	4563	Logo Goods	Earrings	10	$4.50
LG	4593	Logo Goods	Foam Finger	25	$2.95
LG	7930	Logo Goods	Visor	9	$11.95
MN	3683	Mary's Novelties	Bumper Sticker	50	$0.95
MN	6189	Mary's Novelties	Koozies	35	$2.00
MN	6343	Mary's Novelties	Note Cube	7	$5.75

Figure 2–88

10. Create a query that includes the Item Number, Description, On Hand, and Cost fields. Calculate the inventory value (on hand * cost) for all records in the table. Change the caption for the On Hand column to In Stock. Format inventory value as currency with two decimal places. Sort the records in descending order by inventory value. Save the query as Lab 2-2 Step 10 Query.

11. Create a query that calculates and displays the average cost of all items. Save the query as Lab 2-2 Step 11 Query.

12. Create a query that calculates and displays the average cost of items grouped by supplier code. Save the query as Lab 2-2 Step 12 Query.

13. Submit the revised database in the format specified by your instructor.

Continued >

In the Lab *continued*

In the Lab

Lab 3: Querying the Ada Beauty Supply Database

Problem: The management of Ada Beauty Supply has determined a number of questions it wants the database management system to answer. You must obtain answers to the questions posed by management.

Instructions: Use the database created in the In the Lab 3 of Chapter 1 on page AC 69 for this assignment, or see your instructor for information on accessing the files required for this book. For Part 1 and Part 3, save each query using a format similar to the following: Lab 2-3 Part 1a Query, Lab 2-3 Part 3a Query, and so on. Submit the revised database in the format specified by your instructor.

Instructions Part 1: Create a new query for the Customer table and include the Customer Number, Customer Name, Balance, and Amount Paid fields in the design grid. Answer the following questions: (a) Which customers' names begin with C? (b) Which customers are located on Devon? (c) Which customers have a balance of $0.00? (d) Which customers have a balance greater than $200.00 and have an amount paid less than $800.00? (e) Which two customers have the highest balances? (f) For each customer, what is the total of the balance and amount paid amounts?

Instructions Part 2: Join the Sales Rep and the Customer table. Include the Sales Rep Number, First Name, and Last Name from the Sales Rep table and the Customer Number, Customer Name, and Amount Paid from the Customer table in the design grid. Sort the records in ascending order by Sales Rep Number and Customer Number. All sales reps should appear in the result even if they currently have no customers. Save the query as Sales Rep-Customer Query.

Instructions Part 3: Calculate the following statistics: (a) What is the average balance for customers assigned to sales rep 44? (b) What is the total balance for all customers? (c) What is the total amount paid for each sales rep?

Cases and Places

Apply your creative thinking and problem solving skills to design and implement a solution.

• EASIER   •• MORE DIFFICULT

• 1: Querying the Second Hand Goods Database

Use the Second Hand Goods database you created in Cases and Places 1 in Chapter 1 on page AC 71 for this assignment, or see your instructor for information on accessing the files required for this book. Create queries for the following:

a. Find the number and description of all items that contain the word Table.

b. Find the item number, description, and condition of the item that has the earliest posting date.

c. Find the total price of each item available for sale. Show the item description and total price.

d. Find the seller of each item. Show the seller's first name and last name as well as the item description, price, quantity, and date posted. Sort the results by item description within seller last name.

e. Create a parameter query that will allow the user to enter an item description when the query is run. The user should see all fields in the query result.

f. Find all items posted between April 1, 2008 and April 4, 2008. The user should see all fields in the query result.

Submit the revised database in the format specified by your instructor.

• 2: Querying the BeachCondo Rentals Database

Use the BeachCondo Rentals database you created in Cases and Places 2 in Chapter 1 on page AC 71 for this assignment, or see your instructor for information on accessing the files required for this book. Create queries for the following:

a. Find all units that rent for less than $1,000 per week and have at least two bedrooms. The user should see all fields in the query result.

b. Find all units that are on the fourth floor. (Hint: The first digit of the Unit Number field indicates the floor.) Include the Unit Number and the Weekly Rate fields in the query result.

c. Find all units that have more than one bedroom and more than one bathroom and provide linens. Include the Unit Number, Bedrooms, and Weekly Rate fields in the query result.

d. Owner BE20 offers a 15 percent discount on the weekly rate if renters rent for more than one week. What is the discounted weekly rental rate for his units? Your result should include the unit number, bedrooms, bathrooms, sleeps, and discounted weekly rate in your result. Be sure the discounted rate appears as currency.

e. List the owner's first and last name as well as telephone number. Also include the unit number and the weekly rate. All owners should appear in the result even if they currently have no rental units.

f. Find the highest and lowest weekly rate.

Submit the revised database in the format specified by your instructor.

•• 3: Querying the Restaurant Database

Use the restaurant database you created in Cases and Places 3 in Chapter 1 on page AC 71 for this assignment, or see your instructor for information on accessing the files required for this book. Using the Plan Ahead guidelines presented in this chapter, determine at least five questions the conference director might want to ask the database. Using a word processing program, such as Microsoft Word, write the questions in your own words. Then, design the queries for Access. Run and save each query. Submit the Word document and the revised database in the format specified by your instructor.

Continued >

To Use a Form to Add Records

Once a form is open in Form view you can add records using the same techniques you used to add records in Datasheet view. The following steps use the form just created to add records.

- Click the New (blank) record button on the Navigation bar to enter a new record, and then type the data for the new record as shown in Figure 3–5. Press the TAB key after typing the data in each field, except after typing the data for the final field (Recruiter Number).

2

- Press the TAB key to complete the entry of the record.

- Click the Close 'Client' button to close the Client form.

- Click the No button when asked if you want to save your changes.

Q&A

Why not save the form?

If you wish to use this form frequently in the future, you would probably save it. It is very easy to re-create the form whenever you need it, however.

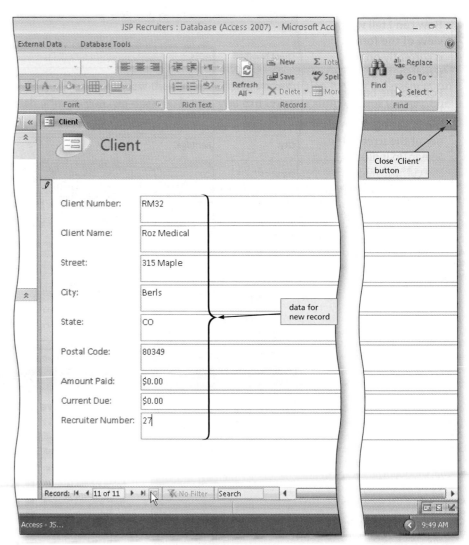

Figure 3–5

Other Ways

1. Click New button on Ribbon
2. Press CTRL+PLUS SIGN (+)

To Search for a Record

In the database environment, **searching** means looking for records that satisfy some criteria. Looking for the client whose number is MH56 is an example of searching. The queries in Chapter 2 also were examples of searching. Access had to locate those records that satisfied the criteria.

A need for searching also exists when using Form view or Datasheet view. To update client MH56, for example, first you need to find the client.

The following steps show how to search for the client whose number is MH56.

1

• Right-click Client Form in the Navigation pane and click Open on the shortcut menu to open the form in Form view.

• Hide the Navigation pane (Figure 3–6).

Which command on the shortcut menu gives me Form view? I see both Layout view and Design view, but no option for Form view.

The Open command opens the form in Form view.

Figure 3–6

2

- Click the Find button on the Home tab to display the Find and Replace dialog box.

- Type MH56 in the Find What text box.

- Click the Find Next button in the Find and Replace dialog box to find client MH56 (Figure 3–7).

Can I also find records in Datasheet view or in Form view?

Yes. You use the same process to find records whether you are viewing the data with split form, in Datasheet view, or in Form view.

🔍 **Experiment**

- Find records using other client numbers. Try to find a record using a client number that does not exist. Click in a different field and try to find records based on the value in that field. Try to use wildcards just as you did in queries. When done, once again locate client MH56.

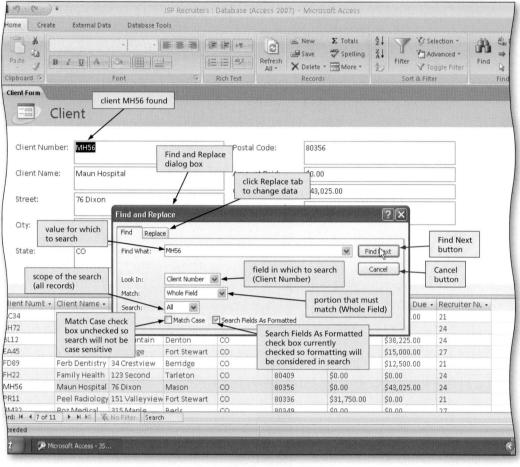

Figure 3–7

3

- Click the Cancel button in the Find and Replace dialog box to remove the dialog box from the screen.

Why does the button in the dialog box read Find Next rather than simply Find?

In some cases, after locating a record that satisfies a criterion, you might need to find the next record that satisfies the same criterion. For example, if you just found the first client whose recruiter number is 24, you then may want to find the second such client, then the third, and so on. To do so, click the Find Next button. You will not need to retype the value each time.

Can I replace one value with another using this dialog box?

Yes. Either click the Replace button on the Ribbon or the Replace tab in the Find and Replace dialog box. You then can enter both the value to find and the replacement value.

Other Ways
1. Press CTRL+F

To Update the Contents of a Record

After locating the record to be changed, select the field to be changed by clicking the field. You also can press the TAB key repeatedly. Then make the appropriate changes. (Clicking the field automatically produces an insertion point. If you use the TAB key, you will need to press F2 to produce an insertion point.)

The following step uses Form view to change the name of client MH56 from Maun Hospital to Munn Hospital by deleting the letters au and then inserting the letters un after the letter M.

1

- Click in the Client Name field in the datasheet for client MH56 after the letter M to select the field.

- Press the DELETE key twice to delete the letters au.

- Type the letters un after the letter M.

- Press the TAB key to complete the change and move to the next field (Figure 3–8).

Q&A Could I have changed the contents of the field in the form?

Yes. You first will need to ensure the record to be changed appears in the form. You can then change the value just as in the datasheet.

Q&A Do I need to save my change?

No. Once you move to another record or close this table, the change to the name will become permanent.

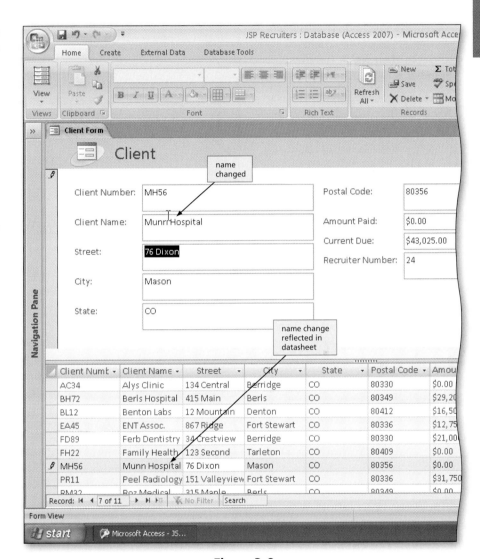

Figure 3–8

To Delete a Record

When records no longer are needed, **delete the records** (remove them) from the table. If client EA45 no longer is served by JSP Recruiters and its final payment is made, the record can be deleted. The following steps delete client EA45.

- With the Client Form open, click the record selector in the datasheet (the small box that appears to the left of the first field) of the record on which the client number is EA45 (Figure 3–9).

Q&A

That technique works in the datasheet portion. How do I select the record in the form portion?

With the desired record appearing in the form, click the record selector (the triangle in front of the record) to select the entire record.

Figure 3–9

- Press the DELETE key to delete the record (Figure 3–10).

- Click the Yes button to complete the deletion.

- Close the Client Form by clicking the Close 'Client Form' button.

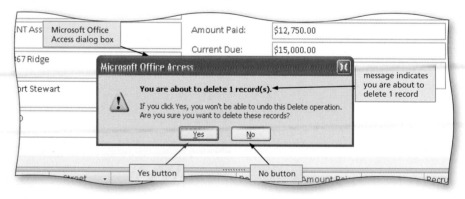

Figure 3–10

Other Ways

1. Click Delete button on Ribbon

Filtering Records

You can use the Find button in either Datasheet view or Form view to locate a record quickly that satisfies some criterion (for example, the client number is MH56). All records appear, however, not just the record or records that satisfy the criterion. To have only the record or records that satisfy the criterion appear, use a **filter**. Four types of filters are available: Filter By Selection, Common Filters, Filter By Form, and Advanced Filter/Sort. You can use a filter in either Datasheet view or Form view.

Plan
Ahead

Determine whether you should filter records.

If you determine that it is desirable to have only those records that satisfy some criterion appear, you have two choices. You can create a query or create a filter. The following guidelines apply to this decision.

1. If you think that you frequently will want to display records that satisfy precisely this same criterion, you should consider creating a query whose results only contain the records that satisfy the criterion. To display those records in the future, simply open the query.

2. If you are viewing data in a datasheet or form and decide you want to restrict the records to be included, it is easier to create a filter than create a query. You can create and use the filter while you are viewing the data.

3. If you have created a filter that you would like to be able to use again in the future, you can save the filter as a query.

   If you have decided that it is appropriate to use a filter, you need to decide which type of filter to use.

1. If your criterion for filtering is that the value in a particular field matches or does not match a certain specific value, you can use Filter By Selection.

2. If your criterion only involves a single field but is more complex, for example, that the value in the field begins with a certain collection of letters, you can use a Common Filter.

3. If your criterion involves more than one field, use Filter By Form.

4. If your criterion involves more than a single And or Or, or if it involves sorting, you will probably find it simpler to use Advanced Filter/Sort.

To Use Filter By Selection

The simplest type of filter is called **Filter By Selection**. To use Filter By Selection, you give Access an example of the data you want by selecting the data within the table. You then choose the option you want on the Selection menu. If you have determined that you only want to display those clients located in Berridge, Filter By Selection is appropriate. The following steps use Filter By Selection in Datasheet view to display only the records for clients in Berridge.

- Open the Client form and hide the Navigation pane.

- Click the City field on the first record in the datasheet portion of the form to select Berridge as the city (Figure 3–11).

Q&A

Could I have selected the City field on the fourth record, which is also Berridge?

Yes. It does not matter which record you select as long as the city is Berridge.

Figure 3–11

2

- Click the Selection button on the Home tab to display the Selection menu (Figure 3–12).

Figure 3–12

3

- Click Equals "Berridge" to select only those clients whose city is Berridge (Figure 3–13).

Q&A

Can I also filter in Datasheet view or in Form view?

Yes. Filtering works the same whether you are viewing the data with split form, in Datasheet view, or in Form view.

Experiment

- Try each of the other values in the Selection menu to see their effect. When done, once again select those clients whose city is Berridge.

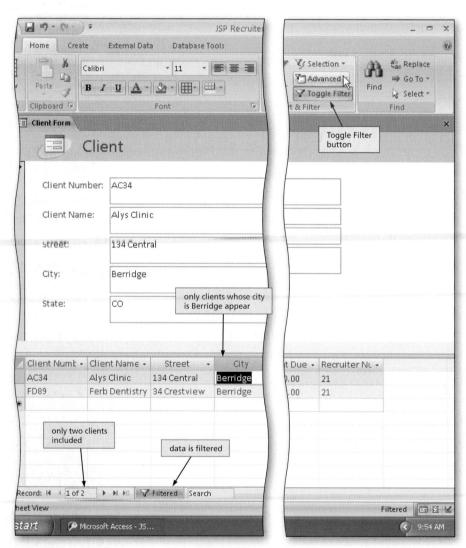

Figure 3–13

To Toggle a Filter

The following step toggles the filter to redisplay all records.

1

- Click the Toggle Filter button on the Home tab to toggle the filter and redisplay all records (Figure 3–14).

Does that action clear the filter?

No. The filter is still in place. If you click the Toggle Filter button a second time, you again will see only the filtered records.

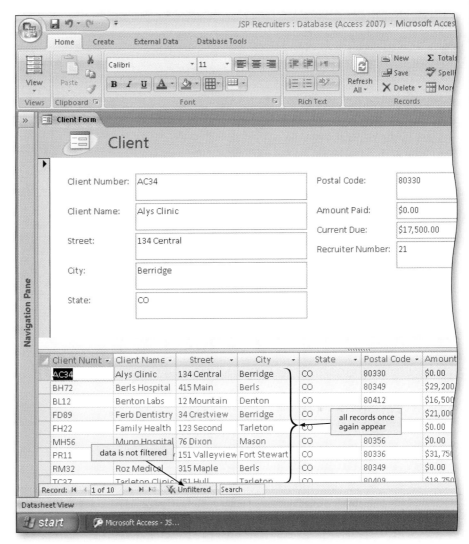

Figure 3–14

To Clear a Filter

Once you have finished using a filter, you can clear the filter. After doing so, you no longer will be able to use the filter by pressing the Toggle Filter button. To clear a filter, you use the following steps.

1. Click the Advanced button on the Home tab.
2. Click Clear All Filters on the Advanced menu.

BTW

Using Wildcards in Filters
Both the question mark (?) and the asterisk (*) wildcards can be used in filters created using Advanced Filter/Sort.

To Use a Common Filter

You can filter individual fields by clicking the arrow to the right of the field name and using a Common Filter. If you have determined you want to include those clients whose city begins with Ber, Filter By Selection would not be appropriate. You would need to use a Common Filter. The following steps use a common filter to include only those clients whose city begins with Ber.

- Be sure the Home tab is selected.

- Click the City arrow to display the common filter menu.

- Point to the Text Filters command to display the custom text filters (Figure 3–15).

Q&A

I selected the City field and then clicked the Filter button on the Home tab. My screen looks the same. Is this right?

Yes. That is another legitimate way to display the common filter menu.

Figure 3–15

- Click Begins With to display the Custom Filter dialog box.

- Type Ber as the City begins with value (Figure 3–16).

Q&A

If I wanted certain cities included, could I use the check boxes?

Yes. Be sure the cities you want are the only ones checked. One way to do this is to click the Select All check box to remove all the check marks and then click the check boxes for the cities you want to include. Another way is to clear the check boxes for the cities you don't want. Use whichever technique you find more convenient.

🔍 **Experiment**

- Try other options in the Common Filter menu to see their effect. When done, once again select those clients whose city begins with Ber.

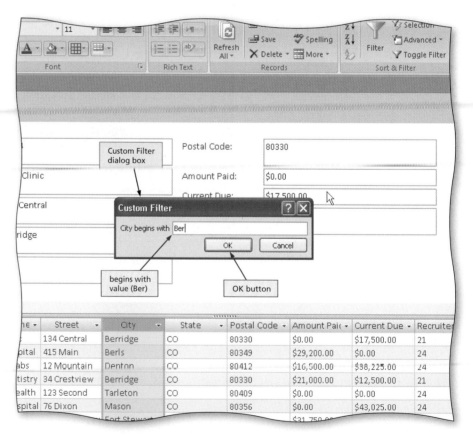

Figure 3–16

3

- Click the OK button to filter the records (Figure 3–17). (Your order may be different.)

Q&A

Can I use the same technique in Form view?

In Form view, you would need to click the field and then click the Filter button to display the Common Filter menu. The rest of the process would be the same.

4

- Click the Toggle Filter button on the Home tab to toggle the filter and redisplay all records.

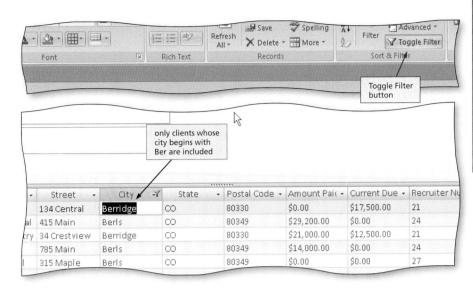

Figure 3–17

To Use Filter By Form

Filter By Selection is a quick and easy way to filter by the value in a single field. For more complex criteria, however, it is not appropriate. For example, if you determined you only wanted those clients whose postal code is 80330 and whose amount paid is 0, you could not use either the Filter by Selection or the Common Filter processes. Rather, you would use **Filter By Form**. The following steps use Filter By Form to restrict the records that appear.

1

- Click the Advanced button on the Home tab to display the Advanced menu (Figure 3–18).

Figure 3–18

2

- Click Clear All Filters on the Advanced menu to clear the existing filter.

- Click the Advanced button on the Home tab to display the Advanced menu a second time.

- Click Filter By Form on the Advanced menu.

- Click the Postal Code field, click the arrow that appears, and then click 80330.

- Click the Amount Paid field, click the arrow that appears, and then click 0 (Figure 3–19).

Q&A

Is there any difference in the process if I am viewing a table in Datasheet view rather than in Form view or in a split form?

In Datasheet view, you will make your entries in a datasheet rather than a form. Otherwise, the process is the same.

- Click the Toggle Filter button on the Home tab to apply the filter (Figure 3–20).

Experiment

- Select Filter By Form again and enter different criteria. In each case, toggle the filter to see the effect of your selection. When done, once again select those clients whose postal code is 80330 and whose amount paid is 0.

Figure 3–19

Figure 3–20

To Use Advanced Filter/Sort

In some cases, your criteria may be too complex even for Filter By Form. You might decide you want to include any client for which the postal code is 80330 and the amount paid is $0. You also may want to include any client whose amount paid is greater than $20,000, no matter where the client is located. Further, you might want to have the results sorted by name. To filter records using complex criteria, you need to use Advanced Filter/Sort as in the following steps.

- Click the Advanced button on the Home tab to display the Advanced menu, and then click Clear All Filters on the Advanced menu to clear the existing filter.

- Click the Advanced button on the Home tab to display the Advanced menu a second time.

- Click Advanced Filter/Sort on the Advanced menu.

- Expand the size of the field list so all the fields in the Client Table appear.

- Include the Client Number field and select Ascending as the sort order.

- Include the Postal Code field and enter 80330 as the criterion.

- Include the Amount Paid field and enter 0 as the criterion in the Criteria row and >20000 as the criterion in the Or row (Figure 3–21).

Figure 3–21

2

- Click the Toggle Filter button on the Home tab to toggle the filter and view the results. Click the Client Form tab to view the Client table (Figure 3–22).

Experiment

- Select Advanced Filter/Sort again and enter different sorting options and criteria. In each case, toggle the filter to see the effect of your selection. When done, change back to the sorting options and criteria you entered in Step 1.

3

- Click Clear All Filters on the Advanced menu.

- Close the Client Form.

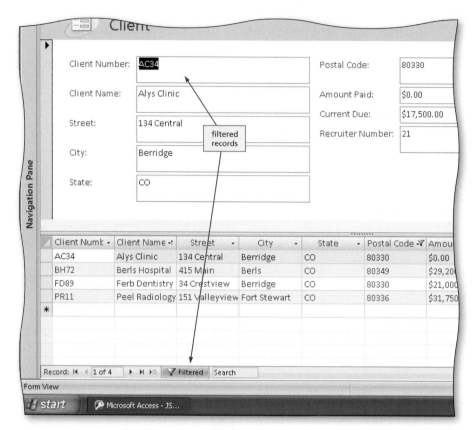

Figure 3–22

Filters and Queries

Filters and queries are related in three ways.

1. You can apply a filter to the results of a query just as you can apply a filter to a table.

2. When you have created a filter using either Filter By Form or Advanced Filter/ Sort, you can save the filter settings as a query by using the Save As Query command on the Advanced menu.

3. You can restore filter settings that you previously saved in a query by using the Load From Query command on the Advanced menu.

Changing the Database Structure

When you initially create a database, you define its **structure**; that is, you assign names and types to all the fields. In many cases, the structure you first define will not continue to be appropriate as you use the database.

Perhaps a field currently in the table no longer is necessary. If no one ever uses a particular field, it is not needed in the table. Because it is occupying space and serving no useful purpose, you should remove it from the table. You also would need to delete the field from any forms, reports, or queries that include it.

More commonly, an organization will find that it needs to maintain additional information that was not anticipated at the time the database was first designed. The organization's own requirements may have changed. In addition, outside regulations that the organization must satisfy may change as well. In either case, the organization must add additional fields to an existing table.

To make any of these changes, you first must open the table in Design view.

TO DELETE A FIELD

If a field in one of your tables no longer is needed; for example, it serves no useful purpose or it may have been included by mistake, you should delete the field. To delete a field you would use the following steps.

1. Open the table in Design view.
2. Click the row selector for the field to be deleted.
3. Press the DELETE key.
4. When Access displays the dialog box requesting confirmation that you want to delete the field, click the Yes button.

To Add a New Field

You can add fields to a table in a database. JSP Recruiters has decided that it needs to categorize its clients. To do so requires an additional field, Client Type. The possible values for Client Type are MED (which indicates the client is a medical institution), DNT (which indicates the client is a dental organization), or LAB (which indicates the client is a lab). The following steps add the Client Type to the Client table immediately after the Postal Code field.

- Show the Navigation pane, and then right-click the Client table to display a shortcut menu.

- Click Design View on the shortcut menu to open the Client table in Design view.

- Click the row selector for the Amount Paid field, and then press the INSERT key to insert a blank row above the Amount Paid row (Figure 3–23).

- Click the Field Name column for the new field. If necessary, erase any text that appears.

- Type Client Type as the field name and then press the TAB key.

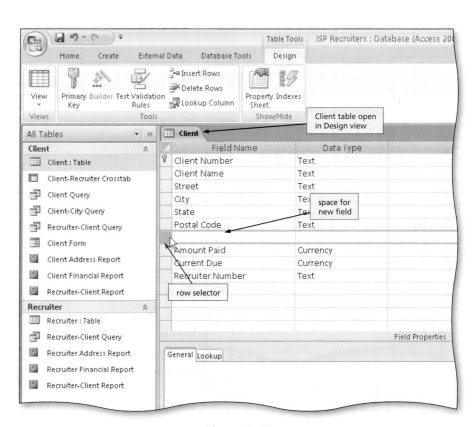

Figure 3–23

Other Ways
1. Click Insert Rows button on Ribbon

To Specify a Format

To affect the way data appears in a field, you can use a **format**. To use a format with a Text field, you enter a special symbol, called a **format symbol**, in the field's Format property box. The Format property uses different settings for different data types. The following step specifies a format for the Client Number field in the Client table and illustrates the way you enter a format. The format symbol used in the example is >, which causes Access to display lowercase letters automatically as uppercase letters. The format symbol < causes Access to display uppercase letters automatically as lowercase letters.

- Select the Client Number field.

- Click the Format property box and then type > (Figure 3–37).

Q&A What is the effect of this change?

From this point on, any lowercase letters will appear automatically as uppercase when users add records or change the value in the Client Number field.

Q&A Client numbers are supposed to be four characters long. Is there a way to ensure users don't type more than four characters?

Yes. The Field Size property dictates how many characters the users can type, so if you wanted to ensure that a maximum of four characters be allowed, you could change the field size from 255 to 4.

Figure 3–37

To Save the Validation Rules, Default Values, and Formats

The following steps save the validation rules, default values, and formats.

1

- Click the Save button on the Quick Access Toolbar to save the changes (Figure 3–38).

2

- Click the No button to save the changes without testing current data.

- Close the Client table.

Q&A

Should I always click the No button when saving validation rules?

If this were a database used to run a business or to solve some other critical need, you would click Yes. You would want to be sure that the data already in the database does not violate the rules.

Figure 3–38

Updating a Table that Contains Validation Rules

When updating a table that contains validation rules, Access provides assistance in making sure the data entered is valid. It helps in making sure that data is formatted correctly. Access also will not accept invalid data. Entering a number that is out of the required range, for example, or entering a value that is not one of the possible choices, will produce an error message in the form of a dialog box. The database will not be updated until the error is corrected.

If the client number entered contains lowercase letters, such am49 (Figure 3–39), Access will display the data automatically as AM49 (Figure 3–40).

Figure 3–39

Figure 3–40

If the client type is not valid, such as xxx, Access will display the text message you specified (Figure 3–41) and not allow the data to enter the database.

Figure 3–41

If the amount paid value is not valid, such as 125000, which is too large, Access also displays the appropriate message (Figure 3–42) and refuses to accept the data.

Figure 3–42

If a required field contains no data, Access indicates this by displaying an error message as soon as you attempt to leave the record (Figure 3–43). The field must contain a valid entry before Access will move to a different record.

Figure 3–43

When entering data into a field with a validation rule, you may find that Access displays the error message and you are unable to make the necessary correction. It may be that you cannot remember the validation rule you created or it was created incorrectly. In such a case, you neither can leave the field nor close the table because you have entered data into a field that violates the validation rule.

If this happens, first try again to type an acceptable entry. If this does not work, repeatedly press the BACKSPACE key to erase the contents of the field and then try to leave the field. If you are unsuccessful using this procedure, press the ESC key until the record is removed from the screen. The record will not be added to the database.

Should the need arise to take this drastic action, you probably have a faulty validation rule. Use the techniques of the previous sections to correct the existing validation rules for the field.

To Use a Lookup Field

Earlier, you changed all the entries in the Client Type field to MED. Thus, you have created a rule that will ensure that only legitimate values (MED, DNT, or LAB) can be entered in the field. You also made Client Type a Lookup field using a mass change. You can make changes to a Lookup field by clicking the field to be changed, clicking the arrow that appears in the field, and then selecting the desired value from the list.

The following steps change the Client Type value on the third record to DNT and on the ninth record to LAB.

- Open the Client table in Datasheet view and ensure the Navigation pane is hidden.

- Click in the Client Type field on the third record to display the arrow (Figure 3–44).

Figure 3–44

2

- Click the down arrow to display the drop-down list of available choices for the Client Type field (Figure 3–45).

Q&A Could I type the value instead of selecting it from the list?

Yes. Once you have either deleted the previous value or selected the entire previous value, you can begin typing. You do not have to type the full entry. When you begin with the letter, D, for example, Access will automatically add the NT.

Figure 3–45

Experiment

- Select the Client Type field on the first record. Try to change the client type by typing various values. Try to type an invalid Client Type (like SPT). When finished, change the value on the record to MED.

3

- Click DNT to change the value.

- In a similar fashion, change MED on the ninth record to LAB (Figure 3–46).

Figure 3–46

To Use a Multivalued Lookup Field

Using a multivalued Lookup field is similar to using a regular Lookup field. The difference is that when you drop down the list, the entries all will be preceded by check boxes. You then can check all the entries that you want. The appropriate entries are shown in Figure 3–47. As indicated in the figure, the specialties needed for client AC34 are CNA, PA, Phy, and RN.

Client Number	Client Name	Specialties Needed
AC34	Alys Clinic	CNA, PA, Phy, RN
BH72	Berls Hospital	CLS, OT, PA, Phy, PT, RN
FD89	Ferb Dentistry	DH, Dnt
FH22	Family Health	NP, Phy, RN
MH56	Munn Hospital	CRNA, OT, Phy, PT, RN
PR11	Peel Radiology	RT
RM32	Roz Medical	CNA, NP, PA, Phy, RN
TC37	Tarleton Clinic	NP, PA, Phy, RN
WL56	West Labs	CLS

Figure 3–47

The following steps make the appropriate entries for the Specialties Needed field.

1

- Click the Specialties Needed field on the first record to display the arrow.

- Click the arrow to display the list of available specialties (Figure 3–48).

Q&A

All the specialties currently appear in the box. What if there were too many specialties to fit?

Access would automatically include a scroll bar that you could use to scroll through all the choices.

Figure 3–48

2

- Click the CNA, PA, Phy, and RN check boxes to select the specialties for the first client (Figure 3–49).

Figure 3–49

3

- Click the OK button to complete the selection.

- Using the same technique, enter the specialties given in Figure 3–47 on the previous page for the remaining clients (Figure 3–50).

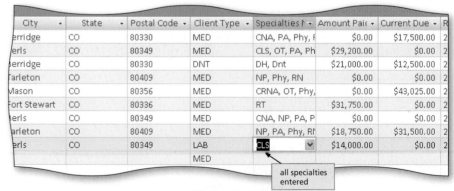

Figure 3–50

To Resize a Column in a Datasheet

The Access default column sizes do not always allow all the data in the field to appear. In some cases, the data may appear, but not the entire field name. You can correct this problem by **resizing** the column (changing its size) in the datasheet. In some instances, you may want to reduce the size of a column. The State field, for example, is short enough that it does not require all the space on the screen that is allotted to it. Changing a column width changes the **layout**, or design, of a table.

The following steps resize the columns in the Client table and save the changes to the layout.

1

• Point to the right boundary of the field selector for the Specialties Needed field (Figure 3–51) so that the mouse pointer becomes a doubled-ended arrow.

Figure 3–51

2

• Double-click the right boundary of the field selector for the Specialties Needed field to resize the field so that it best fits the data (Figure 3–52).

Figure 3–52

- Use the same technique to resize all the other fields to best fit the data. To resize the Amount Paid, Current Due, and Recruiter Number fields, you will need to scroll the fields by clicking the right scroll arrow shown in Figure 3–52 on the previous page (Figure 3-53).

- Save the changes to the layout by clicking the Save button on the Quick Access Toolbar.

- Close the Client table.

What if I closed the table without saving the layout changes?

You would be asked if you want to save the changes.

Figure 3–53

Other Ways
1. Right-click field name, click Column Width

To Include Totals in a Datasheet

It is possible to include totals and other statistics at the bottom of a datasheet in a special row called the Total row. The following steps display the total of the commissions and the average of the rates for recruiters in the Total row.

- Open the Recruiter table in Datasheet view and hide the Navigation pane.

- Click the Totals button on the Home tab to include the Total row in the datasheet (Figure 3–54).

Figure 3–54

2

- Click the Total row in the Commission column to display an arrow.

- Click the arrow to display a menu of available computations (Figure 3–55).

Will I always get the same list?

No. You only will get the items that make sense for the type of data in the column. You cannot calculate the sum of text data, for example.

3

- Click Sum to calculate the sum of the commissions.

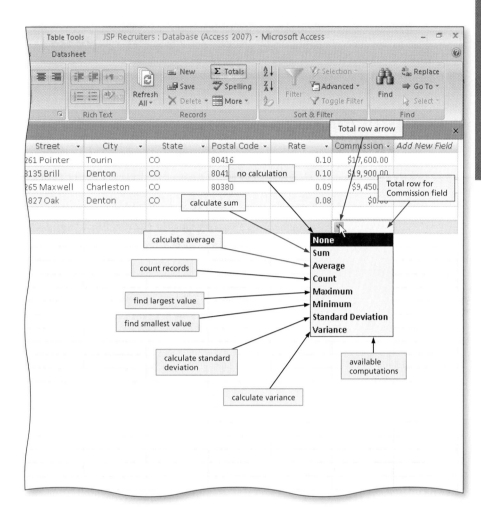

Figure 3–55

4

- Click the Total row in the Rate column to display an arrow.

- Click the arrow to display a menu of available computations.

- Click Average to calculate the average of the rates (Figure 3–56).

Experiment

- Experiment with other statistics. When finished, once again select the sum of the commissions and the average of the rates.

Figure 3–56

To Remove Totals from a Datasheet

If you no longer want the totals to appear as part of the datasheet, you can remove the Total row. The following step removes the Total row.

- Click the Totals button on the Home tab to remove the Total row from the datasheet.

Changing the Appearance of a Datasheet

In addition to resizing columns and displaying totals, you can change the appearance of a datasheet in a variety of other ways. For example, you can change the appearance of gridlines or change the text colors and font. Figure 3–57 shows the various buttons, found on the Home tab, that are available to change the Datasheet appearance.

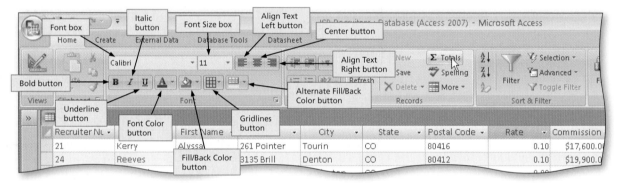

Figure 3–57

The changes to the datasheet will be reflected not only on the screen, but also when you print or preview the datasheet.

Plan Ahead

Determine whether changes to the format of a datasheet are desirable.
You need to decide if changes to the format of a datasheet would improve its appearance and/or its usefulness. The following are the decisions you would make.

1. Would totals or other calculations be useful in the datasheet? If so, include the Total row and select the appropriate computations.

2. Would different gridlines make the datasheet more useful? If so, change to the desired gridlines.

3. Would alternating colors in the rows make them easier to read? If so, change the alternate fill color.

4. Would a different font and/or font color make the text stand out better? If so, change the font color and/or the font.

5. Is the font size appropriate? Can you see enough data at one time on the screen and yet have the data be readable? If not, change the font size to an appropriate value.

6. Is the column spacing appropriate? Are some columns wider than they need to be? Are there some columns where not all the data is visible? If so, change the column size.

As a general guideline, once you have decided on a particular look for a datasheet, all your datasheets should have the same look, unless there is a compelling reason for one of your datasheets to differ.

To Change Gridlines in a Datasheet

One of the changes you can make to a datasheet is which gridlines appear. You may feel that the appearance would be improved by having only horizontal gridlines. The following steps change the datasheet so that only horizontal gridlines are included.

- Open the Recruiter table in Datasheet view, if it is not already open.

- Click the box in the upper-left corner of the Datasheet selector to select the entire datasheet (Figure 3–58).

Figure 3–58

- Click the Gridlines button on the Home tab to display the Gridlines gallery (Figure 3–59).

Does it matter whether I click the button or the arrow?

In this case, it does not matter. Either one will produce the same result.

- Click the Gridlines: Horizontal command in the Gridlines gallery to include only horizontal gridlines.

 Experiment

- Experiment with other gridline options. When finished, once again select horizontal gridlines.

Figure 3–59

To Change the Colors and Font in a Datasheet

You also may decide that you can improve the datasheet by changing the colors and the font. The following steps change the Alternate Fill color, a color that appears on every other row in the datasheet. They also change the font color, the font, and the font size.

- With the datasheet for the Recruiter table selected, click the Alternate Fill/Back Color button arrow to display the color palette (Figure 3–60).

Q&A Does it matter whether I click the button or the arrow?

Yes. Clicking the arrow produces a color palette. Clicking the button applies the currently selected color. When in doubt, you should click the arrow.

Figure 3–60

- Click Aqua Blue (the second from the right color in the standard colors) to select aqua blue as the alternate color.

- Click the Font Color arrow, and then click Red (the second color in the bottom row) in the lower-left corner of standard colors to select Red as the font color.

- Click the Font box arrow, and then select Bodoni MT as the font. (If it is not available, select any font of your choice.)

- Click the Font Size box arrow, and select 10 as the font size (Figure 3–61).

Figure 3–61

Q&A Does the order in which I make these selections make a difference?

No. You could have made these selections in any order.

 Experiment

- Experiment with other colors, fonts, and font sizes. When finished, return to the options selected in this step.

Using the Datasheet Formatting Dialog Box

As an alternative to using the individual buttons, you can click the Datasheet Formatting arrow, shown in Figure 3–61, to display the Datasheet Formatting dialog box (Figure 3–62). You can use the various options within the dialog box to make changes to the datasheet format. Once you are finished, click the OK button to apply your changes.

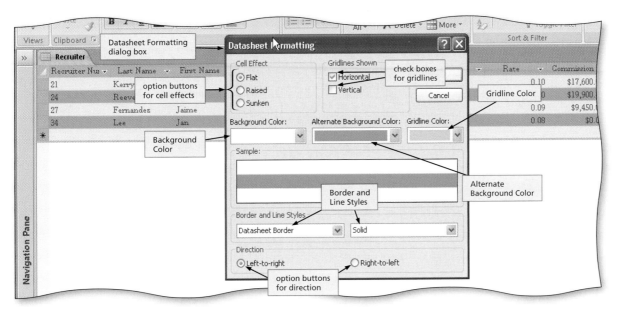

Figure 3–62

To Close the Datasheet Without Saving the Format Changes

The following steps show how to close the datasheet without saving the changes to the format. Because the changes are not saved, the next time you open the Recruiter table it will appear in the original format. If you had saved the changes, the changes would be reflected in its appearance.

1 Click the Close 'Recruiter' button to close the Recruiter table.

2 Click the No button in the Microsoft Office Access dialog box when asked if you want to save your changes.

Multivalued Field in Queries

You can use multivalued fields in queries just as you can use other fields. You have a choice concerning how the multiple values appear. You can choose to have them on a single row or on multiple rows.

To Query a Multivalued Field Showing Multiple Values on a Single Row

To include a multivalued field in the results of a query, place the field in the design grid just like any other field. The results will list all of the values for the multivalued field on a single row, just as in a datasheet. The following steps create a query to display the client number, client name, client type, and specialties needed for all clients.

- Create a query for the Client table and hide the Navigation pane.

- Include the Client Number, Client Name, Client Type, and Specialties Needed fields (Figure 3–63).

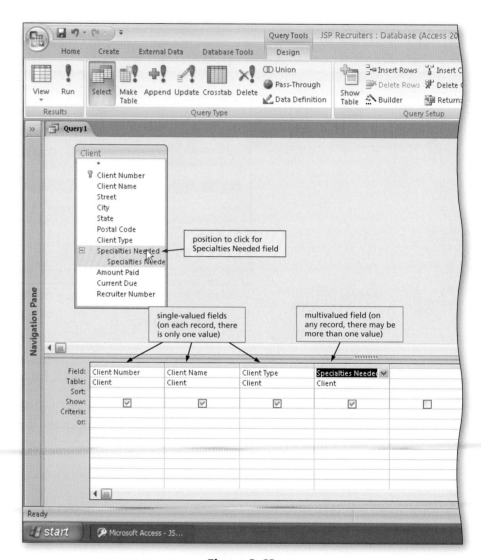

Figure 3–63

2

- View the results (Figure 3–64).

Q&A Can I include criteria for the multi-valued field?

You can include criteria for the multivalued field when all the entries are displayed on a single row.

Experiment

- Return to Design view and enter various criteria in the Specialties Needed field. Run the queries. When finished, return to the options selected in this step.

Figure 3–64

To Query a Multivalued Field Showing Multiple Values on Multiple Rows

You may be interested in those clients requiring a particular specialty, for example, those clients needing an RN. Unfortunately, you cannot simply put the desired specialty in the Criteria row just as you would with other fields. Instead you need to change the query so that each specialty occurs on a different row by using the Value property. Once you have done so, you can enter criteria just as you would in any other query.

The following steps use the Value property to display each specialty on a separate row.

1

- Return to Design view and ensure the Client Number, Client Name, Client Type, and Specialties Needed fields are selected.

- Click the Specialties Needed field to produce an insertion point, and then type a period and the word `Value` after the word, Needed, to use the Value property (Figure 3–65).

Q&A I don't see the word, Specialties. Did I do something wrong?

No. There is not enough room to display the entire name. If you wanted to see it, you could point to the right boundary of the column selector and then either drag or double-click.

Figure 3–65

Q&A Do I need to type the word Value?

No. You also can double-click the second Specialties Needed entry in the field list.

2

- View the results (Figure 3–66).

Q&A Can I now include criteria for the multivalued field?

Yes. This is now just like any other query. There are no multiple values on any row.

3

- Close the query by clicking the Close 'Query1' button.

- When asked if you want to save the query, click the No button.

Figure 3–66

Referential Integrity

The property that ensures that the value in a foreign key must match that of another table's primary key is called **referential integrity**. A **foreign key** is a field in one table whose values are required to match the *primary key* of another table. In the Client table, the Recruiter Number field is a foreign key that must match the primary key of the Recruiter table; that is, the Recruiter number for any client must be a recruiter currently in the Recruiter table. A client whose Recruiter number is 92, for example, should not be stored because no such recruiter exists.

In Access, to specify referential integrity, you must define a relationship between the tables by using the Relationships command. Access then prohibits any updates to the database that would violate the referential integrity.

The type of relationship between two tables specified by the Relationships command is referred to as a **one-to-many relationship**. This means that *one* record in the first table is related to (matches) *many* records in the second table, but each record in the second table is related to only *one* record in the first. In the JSP Recruiters database, for example, a one-to-many relationship exists between the Recruiter table and the Client table. *One* recruiter is associated with *many* clients, but each client is associated with only a single recruiter. In general, the table containing the foreign key will be the *many* part of the relationship.

Plan Ahead

Identify related tables in order to implement relationships between the tables.
When specifying referential integrity, you need to decide how to handle deletions. In the relationship between clients and recruiters, for example, deletion of a recruiter for whom clients exist, such as recruiter number 21, would violate referential integrity. Any clients for recruiter 21 no longer would relate to any recruiter in the database. You can handle this in two ways. For each relationship, you need to decide which of the approaches is appropriate.

1. The normal way to avoid this problem is to prohibit such a deletion.

2. The other option is to **cascade the delete.** This means that Access would allow the deletion but then delete all related records. For example, it would allow the deletion of the recruiter but then automatically delete any clients related to the deleted recruiter.

You also need to decide how to handle the update of the primary key. In the relationship between recruiters and clients, for example, changing the recruiter number for recruiter 21 to 12 in the Recruiter table would cause a problem. Clients are in the Client table on which the recruiter number is 21. These clients no longer would relate to any recruiter. You can handle this in two ways. For each relationship, you need to decide which of the approaches is appropriate.

1. The normal way of avoiding the problem is to prohibit this type of update.

2. The other option is to **cascade the update.** This means to allow the change, but make the corresponding change in the foreign key on all related records. In the relationship between clients and recruiters, for example, Access would allow the update but then automatically make the corresponding change for any client whose recruiter number was 21. It now will be 12.

To Specify Referential Integrity

The following steps use the Relationships command to specify referential integrity by specifying a relationship between the Recruiter and Client tables. The steps also ensure that update will cascade, but that delete will not.

1

• Click Database Tools on the Ribbon to display the Database Tools tab (Figure 3–67).

Figure 3–67

2

• Click the Relationships button on the Database Tools tab to open the Relationships window and display the Show Table dialog box (Figure 3–68).

Figure 3–68

- Click the Recruiter table and then click the Add button to add the Recruiter table.

- Click the Client table and then click the Add button to add the Client table.

- Click the Close button in the Show Table dialog box to close the dialog box.

- Resize the field lists that appear so all fields are visible (Figure 3–69).

Q&A Do I need to resize the field lists?

No. You can use the scroll bars. Before completing the next step, however, you would need to make sure the Recruiter Number fields in both tables appear on the screen.

- Drag the Recruiter Number field in the Recruiter table field list to the Recruiter Number field in the Client table field list to open the Edit Relationships dialog box to create a relationship.

Q&A Do I actually move the field from the Recruiter table to the Client table?

No. The mouse pointer will change shape to indicate you are in the process of dragging, but the field does not move.

- Click the Enforce Referential Integrity check box.

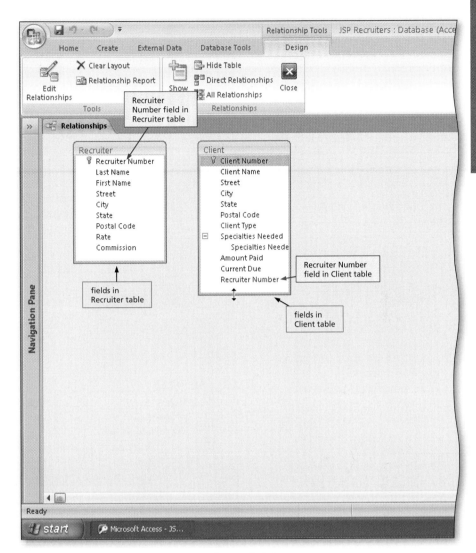

Figure 3–69

- Click the Cascade Update Related Fields check box (Figure 3–70).

Q&A The Cascade check boxes were dim until I clicked the Enforce Referential Integrity check box. Is that correct?

Yes. Until you have chosen to enforce referential integrity, the cascade options have no meaning.

Q&A Can I change the **join type** like I can in queries?

Yes. Click the Join Type button in the Edit Relationships dialog box. Just as with queries, option button 1 creates an INNER join, option button 2 creates a LEFT join, and option button 3 creates a RIGHT join.

Figure 3–70

- Click the Create button to complete the creation of the relationship (Figure 3–71).

Q&A What is the symbol at the lower end of the join line?

It is the mathematical symbol for infinity. It is used here to denote the "many" end of the relationship.

Q&A Can I print a copy of the relationship?

Yes. Click the Relationship Report button on the Design tab to produce a report of the relationship. You can print the report. You also can save it as a report in the database for future use. If you do not want to save it, close the report after you have printed it and do not save the changes.

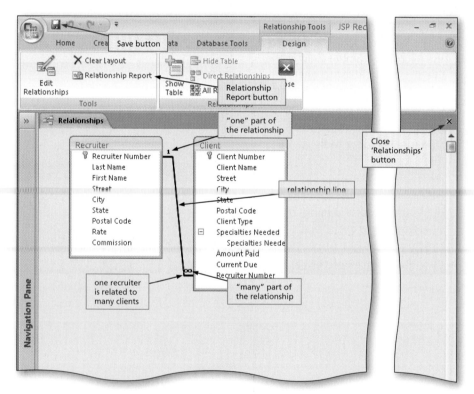

Figure 3–71

6

- Click the Save button on the Quick Access Toolbar to save the relationship you created.

- Close the Relationships window by clicking the Close 'Relationships' button.

Q&A Can I later modify the relationship if I want to change it in some way?

Yes. Click the Relationships button on the Database Tools tab. To add another table, click the Show Table button on the Design tab. To remove a table, click the Hide table button. To edit a relationship, select the relationship and click the Edit Relationships button.

Effect of Referential Integrity

Referential integrity now exists between the Recruiter and Client tables. Access now will reject any number in the Recruiter Number field in the Client table that does not match a Recruiter number in the Recruiter table. Attempting to change the recruiter number for a client to one that does not match any recruiter in the Recruiter table would result in the error message shown in Figure 3–72. Similarly, attempting to add a client whose recruiter number does not match would lead to the same error message.

Figure 3–72

Access also will reject the deletion of a recruiter for whom related clients exist. Attempting to delete recruiter 21 from the Recruiter table, for example, would result in the message shown in Figure 3–73.

Figure 3–73

Access would, however, allow the change of a recruiter number in the Recruiter table. Then it automatically makes the corresponding change to the recruiter number for all the recruiter's clients. For example, if you changed the recruiter number of recruiter 21 to 12, the same 12 would appear in the recruiter number field for clients.

To Use a Subdatasheet

Now that the Recruiter table is related to the Client table, it is possible to view the clients of a given recruiter when you are viewing the datasheet for the Recruiter table. The clients for the recruiter will appear below the recruiter in a **subdatasheet**. The availability of such a subdatasheet is indicated by a plus sign that appears in front of the rows in the Recruiter table. The following steps display the subdatasheet for recruiter 24.

• Open the Recruiter table and hide the Navigation pane (Figure 3–74).

Figure 3–74

2

- Click the plus sign in front of the row for Recruiter 24 to display the subdatasheet (Figure 3–75).

Q&A
How do I hide the subdatasheet when I no longer want it to appear?

When you clicked the plus sign, it changed to a minus sign. Click the minus sign.

 Experiment

- Display subdatasheets for other recruiters. Display more than one subdatasheet at a time. Remove the subdatasheets from the screen.

Figure 3–75

3

- Close the datasheet for the Recruiter table.

TO FIND DUPLICATE RECORDS

One reason to include a primary key for a table is to eliminate duplicate records. A possibility still exists, however, that duplicate records can get into your database. Perhaps the same client was inadvertently added to the database with a new client number. You can detect this type of redundancy by searching to see if any client's names are duplicated. The **Find Duplicates Query Wizard** allows you to find duplicate records. The following steps illustrate how to use the Find Duplicates Query Wizard to find duplicate records.

1. Click Create on the Ribbon, and then click the Query Wizard button on the Create tab.
2. When Access displays the New Query dialog box, click the Find Duplicates Query Wizard and then click the OK button.
3. Identify the table and field or fields that might contain duplicate information.
4. Indicate any other fields you want displayed.
5. Finish the wizard to see any duplicate records.

TO FIND UNMATCHED RECORDS

Occasionally, you may want to find records in one table that have no matching records in another table. For example, you may want to determine which recruiters currently have no clients. The **Find Unmatched Query Wizard** allows you to find unmatched records. The following steps illustrate how to find unmatched records using the Find Unmatched Query Wizard.

1. Click Create on the Ribbon, and then click the Query Wizard button on the Create tab.
2. When Access displays the New Query dialog box, click the Find Unmatched Query Wizard and then click the OK button.
3. Identify the table that may contain unmatched records and then identify the related table.
4. Indicate the fields you want displayed.
5. Finish the wizard to see any duplicate records.

Ordering Records

Normally, Access sequences the records in the Client table by client number whenever listing them because the Client Number field is the primary key. You can change this order, if desired.

To Use the Ascending Button to Order Records

To change the order in which records appear, use the Ascending or Descending buttons. Either button reorders the records based on the field in which the insertion point is located.

The following steps order the records by city using the Ascending button.

- Open the Client table in Datasheet view and hide the Navigation pane.
- Click the City field on the first record to select the field (Figure 3–76).

Q&A

Did I have to click the field on the first record?

No. Any other record would have worked as well.

Figure 3–76

- Click the Ascending button on the Home tab to sort the records by City (Figure 3–77).

Q&A

What if I wanted the cities to appear in reverse alphabetical order?

Click the Descending button.

Figure 3–77

Experiment

Sort the records by city in reverse order. When done, sort the records by city in the original order.

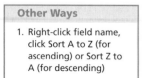

- Close the table. When asked if you want to save your changes, click the No button.

Other Ways

1. Right-click field name, click Sort A to Z (for ascending) or Sort Z to A (for descending)

Special Database Operations

The special operations involved in maintaining a database are backup, recovery, compacting a database, and repairing a database.

Backup and Recovery

It is possible to damage or destroy a database. Users can enter data that is incorrect; programs that are updating the database can end abnormally during an update; a hardware problem can occur; and so on. After any such event has occurred, the database may contain invalid data. It even may be totally destroyed.

Obviously, you cannot allow a situation in which data has been damaged or destroyed to go uncorrected. You must somehow return the database to a correct state. This process is called recovery; that is, you **recover** the database.

The simplest approach to recovery involves periodically making a copy of the database (called a **backup copy** or a **save copy**). This is referred to as **backing up** the database. If a problem occurs, you correct the problem by copying this backup copy over the actual database, often referred to as the **live database**.

To backup the database that is currently open, you use the Back Up Database command on the Manage submenu on the Office Button menu. In the process, Access suggests a name that is a combination of the database name and the current date. For example, if you back up the JSP Recruiters database on April 20, 2008, Access will suggest the name JSP Recruiters_2008-04-20. You can change this name if you desire, although it is a good idea to use this name. By doing so, it will be easy to distinguish between all the backup copies you have made to determine which is the most recent. In addition, if you discover that a critical problem occurred on April 18, 2008, you may want to go back to the most recent backup before April 18. If, for example, the database was not backed up on April 17 but was backed up on April 16, you would use JSP Recruiters_2008-04-16.

The following steps back up a database to a file on a hard disk or high-capacity removable disk. You should check with your instructor before completing these steps.

To Back Up a Database

1. Open the database to be backed up.
2. Click the Office Button, and then point to Manage on the Office Button menu.
3. Click Back Up Database on the Manage submenu.
4. Select the desired location in the Save in box. If you do not want the name Access has suggested, enter the desired name in the File name text box.
5. Click the Save button.

Access creates a backup copy with the desired name in the desired location. Should you ever need to recover the database using this backup copy, you can simply copy it over the live version.

Compacting and Repairing a Database

As you add more data to a database, it naturally grows larger. When you delete an object (records, tables, forms, or queries), the space previously occupied by the object does not become available for additional objects. Instead, the additional objects are given new space, that is, space that was not already allocated. To remove this wasted space from the database, you must **compact** the database. The same option that compacts the database also repairs problems that may have occurred in the database.

To Compact and Repair a Database

1. Open the database to be compacted.
2. Click the Office Button, and then point to Manage on the Office Button menu.
3. Click Compact and Repair Database on the Manage submenu.

The database now is the compacted form of the original.

Additional Operations

Additional special operations include opening another database, closing a database without exiting Access, and saving a database with another name. They also include deleting a table (or other object) as well as renaming an object. Finally, you can change properties of a table or other object, such as the object's description.

When you open another database, Access automatically will close the database that had been open. Before deleting or renaming an object, you should ensure that the object has no dependent objects, that is, other objects that depend on the object you wish to delete.

The following steps describe how you could perform these operations.

To Open Another Database

1. Click the Office Button.
2. Click Open on the Office Button menu.
3. Select the database to be opened.
4. Click the Open button.

To Close a Database without Exiting Access

1. Click the Office Button.
2. Click Close Database on the Office Button menu.

To Save a Database with Another Name

1. Click the Office Button.
2. Point to Save As on the Office Button menu.
3. Select the Desired format.
4. Enter a name and select a location for the new version.
5. Click the Save button.

To Check for Dependent Objects

1. Ensure that the object you wish to check is selected.
2. Click Database Tools on the Ribbon to display the Database Tools tab.
3. Click the Object Dependencies button on the Database Tools tab.
4. Click the 'Objects that depend on me' option button to display any objects that depend on the selected object.

To Delete a Table or Other Object

1. Right-click the object.
2. Click Delete on the shortcut menu.
3. Click the Yes button in the Microsoft Office Access dialog box.

To Rename an Object

1. Right-click the object.
2. Click Rename on the shortcut menu.
3. Type the new name and press the ENTER key.

To Change Object Properties

1. Right-click the object.

2. Click Table Properties (if the object is a table) or Object Properties on the shortcut menu.

3. Change the desired property and click the OK button.

To Quit Access

You saved all your changes and are ready to quit Access. The following step quits Access.

 Click the Close button on the right side of the Access title bar to quit Access.

Chapter Summary

In this chapter you have learned how to use a form to add records to a table; search for records; delete records; filter records; create and use Lookup fields; create and use multivalued fields; make mass changes; create validation rules; change the appearance of a datasheet; specify referential integrity; and use subdatasheets. The following list includes all the new Access skills you have learned in this chapter.

1. Create a Simple Form (AC 142)
2. Use a Form to Add Records (AC 144)
3. Search for a Record (AC 145)
4. Update the Contents of a Record (AC 147)
5. Delete a Record (AC 148)
6. Use Filter By Selection (AC 149)
7. Toggle a Filter (AC 151)
8. Clear a Filter (AC 151)
9. Use a Common Filter (AC 152)
10. Use Filter By Form (AC 153)
11. Use Advanced Filter/Sort (AC 155)
12. Delete a Field (AC 157)
13. Add a New Field (AC 157)
14. Create a Lookup Field (AC 158)
15. Add a Multivalued Field (AC 160)
16. Save the Changes and Close the Table (AC 161)
17. Modify Single or Multivalued Lookup Fields (AC 161)
18. Use an Update Query (AC 162)
19. Use a Delete Query (AC 163)
20. Use an Append Query (AC 165)
21. Use a Make-Table Query (AC 165)
22. Specify a Required Field (AC 166)
23. Specify a Range (AC 166)
24. Specify a Default Value (AC 167)
25. Specify a Collection of Allowable Values (AC 167)
26. Specify a Format (AC 168)
27. Save the Validation Rules, Default Values, and Formats (AC 169)
28. Use a Lookup Field (AC 172)
29. Use a Multivalued Lookup Field (AC 173)
30. Resize a Column in a Datasheet (AC 175)
31. Include Totals in a Datasheet (AC 176)
32. Remove Totals from a Datasheet (AC 178)
33. Change Gridlines in a Datasheet (AC 179)
34. Change the Colors and Font in a Datasheet (AC 180)
35. Close the Datasheet Without Saving the Format Changes (AC 181)
36. Query a Multivalued Field Showing Multiple Values on a Single Row (AC 182)
37. Query a Multivalued Field Showing Multiple Values on Multiple Rows (AC 183)
38. Specify Referential Integrity (AC 186)
39. Use a Subdatasheet (AC 190)
40. Find Duplicate Records (AC 191)
41. Find Unmatched Records (AC 191)
42. Use the Ascending Button to Order Records (AC 192)
43. Backup a Database (AC 193)
44. Compact and Repair a Database (AC 193)
45. Open Another Database (AC 194)
46. Close a Database Without Exiting Access (AC 194)
47. Save a Database with Another Name (AC 194)
48. Check for Dependent Objects (AC 194)
49. Delete a Table or Other Object (AC 194)
50. Rename an Object (AC 194)
51. Change Object Properties (AC 194)

 If you have a SAM user profile, you may have access to hands-on instruction, practice, and assessment. Log in to your SAM account (http://sam2007.course.com) to launch any assigned training activities or exams that relate to the skills covered in this chapter.

Learn It Online

Test your knowledge of chapter content and key terms.

Instructions: To complete the Learn It Online exercises, start your browser, click the Address bar, and then enter the Web address `scsite.com/ac2007/learn`. When the Access 2007 Learn It Online page is displayed, click the link for the exercise you want to complete and then read the instructions.

Chapter Reinforcement TF, MC, and SA
A series of true/false, multiple choice, and short answer questions that test your knowledge of the chapter content.

Flash Cards
An interactive learning environment where you identify chapter key terms associated with displayed definitions.

Practice Test
A series of multiple choice questions that test your knowledge of chapter content and key terms.

Who Wants To Be a Computer Genius?
An interactive game that challenges your knowledge of chapter content in the style of a television quiz show.

Wheel of Terms
An interactive game that challenges your knowledge of chapter key terms in the style of the television show *Wheel of Fortune*.

Crossword Puzzle Challenge
A crossword puzzle that challenges your knowledge of key terms presented in the chapter.

Apply Your Knowledge

Reinforce the skills and apply the concepts you learned in this chapter.

Specifying Validation Rules, Updating Records, Formatting a Datasheet, and Creating Relationships

Instructions: Start Access. Open The Bike Delivers database that you modified in Apply Your Knowledge in Chapter 2 on page AC 128. (If you did not complete this exercise, see your instructor for a copy of the modified database.)

Perform the following tasks:

1. Open the Customer table in Design view as shown in Figure 3–78.

Figure 3–78

2. Format the Customer Number field so any lowercase letters appear in uppercase and make the Customer Name field a required field.

3. Specify that balance amounts must be between $0.0 and $1,000. Include validation text.

4. Save the changes to the Customer table.

5. Create a simple form for the Customer table and find the record for ME71 and change the customer name to Mentor Group Limited. Save the form as Customer Simple Form and close the form.

6. Open the Customer table in Datasheet view and use Filter By Selection to find the record for CI76. Delete the record. Remove the filter.

7. Resize all columns to best fit and remove the gridlines from the datasheet. Save the changes to the layout of the table. Close the Customer table.

8. Establish referential integrity between the Courier table (the one table) and the Customer table (the many table). Cascade the update but do not cascade the delete.

9. Submit the revised database in the format specified by your instructor.

Extend Your Knowledge

Extend the skills you learned in this chapter and experiment with new skills. You may need to use Help to complete the assignment.

Creating Action Queries, Changing Table Properties

Instructions: See the inside back cover of this book for instructions for downloading the Data Files for Students, or see your instructor for information on accessing the files required in this book.

Backyard is a retail business that specializes in products for the outdoors. The owner has created an Access database in which to store information about the products he sells. He recently acquired the inventory of a store that is going out of business. The inventory currently is stored in the Inventory database.

Perform the following tasks:

1. The owner needs to add the items stored in the Product table of the Inventory database to the Item table of the Backyard database. Create and run an append query to create the Item table for the Backyard database shown in Figure 3–79.

Item Code	Description	On Hand	Cost	Selling Price	Add New Field
BA35	Bat House	14	$43.50	$45.50	
BB01	Bird Bath	2	$54.00	$62.00	
BE19	Bee Sculpture	7	$39.80	$42.50	
BL06	Bug Mister	9	$14.35	$15.99	
BO22	Barn Owl Sculp	2	$37.50	$42.99	
BS10	Bunny Sprinkle	4	$41.95	$50.00	
BU24	Butterfly Stake	6	$36.10	$37.75	
FS11	Froggie Sprinkl	5	$41.95	$50.00	
GF12	Globe Feeder	12	$14.80	$16.25	
HF01	Hummingbird F	5	$11.35	$14.25	
LM05	Leaf Mister	3	$29.95	$35.95	
PM05	Purple Martin H	3	$67.10	$69.95	
SF03	Suet Feeder	7	$8.05	$9.95	
WF10	Window feede	10	$14.25	$15.95	

Figure 3–79

Continued >

STUDENT ASSIGNMENTS

Extend Your Knowledge *continued*

2. Open the Item table in the Backyard database and change the description for WF10 to Window Bird Feeder. Resize all columns to best fit the data.

3. Sort the datasheet in ascending order by Description.

4. Add a totals row to the datasheet and display the sum of the on hand items, and the average cost and average selling price.

5. Save the changes to the layout of the table. Close the table and rename it Product.

6. Update the table properties for the Product table to include the description, Updated to include items from Inventory database.

7. Using a query, delete all records in the Product table where the description starts with the letter S. Save the query as Delete Query.

8. Change the database properties, as specified by your instructor. Submit the revised database in the format specified by your instructor.

Make It Right

Analyze a database and correct all errors and/or improve the design.

Correcting Table Design Errors

Instructions: Start Access. Open the Care4Pets database. See the inside back cover of this book for instructions for downloading the Data Files for Students, or see your instructor for information on accessing the files required in this book.

Care4Pets provides a variety of services to pet owners. The owner of Care4Pets has decided that she could better manage her business if she added a multivalued field that lists the various types of pets her customers have. She created the field shown in Figure 3–80 but forgot to add Rabbit as one of the pet types. Modify the multivalued Lookup field to include Rabbit as a pet type.

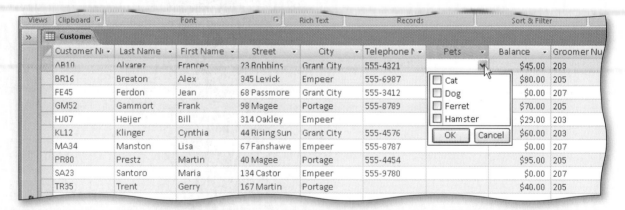

Figure 3–80

Finally, she wanted to add referential integrity between the Groomer table and the Customer table. The relationship shown in Figure 3–81 is not correct and must be fixed. She does not want to cascade the update or the delete.

Figure 3–81

Submit the revised database in the format specified by your instructor.

In the Lab

Design, create, modify, and/or use a database following the guidelines, concepts, and skills presented in this chapter. Labs are listed in order of increasing difficulty.

Lab 1: Maintaining the JMS TechWizards Database

Problem: JMS TechWizards is expanding rapidly and needs to make some database changes to handle the expansion. The company needs to know more about its clients, such as the type of business, and it needs to ensure that data that is entered is valid. It also needs to update the records in the database.

Instructions: Use the database created in the In the Lab 1 of Chapter 1 on page AC 67 for this assignment or see your instructor for information on accessing the files required for this book.

Perform the following tasks:

1. Open the JMS TechWizards database and then open the Client table in Design view.

2. Add a Lookup field, Client Type, to the Client table. The field should appear after the Telephone Number field. The field will contain data on the type of client. The client types are MAN (Manufacturing), RET (Retail), and SER (Service). Save these changes to the structure.

3. Using a query, change all the entries in the Client Type column to RET. Save the query as Client Type Update Query.

4. Open the Client table and make the following changes. You can use either the Find button or Filter By Selection to locate the records to change:

   a. Change the client type for clients AM53 and SA56 to MAN.

   b. Change the client type for clients GR56, JE77, and ME17 to SER.

   c. Change the name of client SA56 to Sawyer Industries.

   d. Change the name of client ST21 to Steed's Department Store.

5. Resize all columns to best fit the data and remove the vertical gridlines. Save the changes to the layout of the table.

Continued >

6. Create the following validation rules for the Client table and save the changes.

   a. Specify the legal values MAN, RET, and SER for the Client Type field. Include validation text.

   b. Assign a default value of RET to the Client Type field.

   c. Ensure that any letters entered in the Client Number field appear as uppercase.

   d. Specify that the billed amount must be less than or equal to $1,500.00. Include validation text.

7. Open the Client table and use Filter By Form to find all records where the client is located in Anderson and has a client type of SER. Delete these records.

8. JMS has signed up a new retail store, Cray Meat Market (Client Number CR21) and needs to add the record to the Client table. The Meat Market is at 72 Main in Anderson, TX 78077. The phone number is 512-555-7766. Lee Torres is the technician assigned to the account. To date, they have not been billed for any services. Create a split form for the Client table and use this split form to add the record.

9. Specify referential integrity between the Technician table (the one table) and the Client table (the many table). Cascade the update but not the delete.

10. Compact the database and then back up the database.

11. Submit the revised database in the format specified by your instructor.

In the Lab

Lab 2: Maintaining the Hockey Fan Zone Database

Problem: The management of the Hockey Fan Zone store needs to change the database structure, add validation rules, and update records.

Instructions: Use the database created in the In the Lab 2 of Chapter 1 on page AC 68 for this assignment, or see your instructor for information on accessing the files required for this book.

Perform the following tasks:

1. Open the Hockey Fan Zone database and then open the Item table in Design view.

2. Add a Lookup field, Item Type to the Item table. The field should appear after the Description field. The field will contain data on the type of item for sale. The item types are CAP (caps and hats), CLO (clothing), and NOV (Novelties).

3. Make the following changes to the Item table:

   a. Change the field size for the On Hand field to Integer. The Format should be fixed and the decimal places should be 0.

   b. Make Description a required field.

   c. Specify the legal values CAP, CLO, and NOV for the Item Type field. Include validation text.

   d. Specify that number on hand must be between 0 and 75. Include validation text.

4. Save the changes to the table design. If a dialog box appears indicating that some data may be lost, click the Yes button.

5. Using a query, assign the value NOV to the Item Type field for all records. Save the query as Update Query.

6. Delete the split form for the Item table that you created in Chapter 1. The form does not include the Item Type field. Recreate the split form for the Item table.

7. Use the split form to change the item type for item numbers 3663 and 7930 to CAP. Change the item type for item numbers 5923 and 7810 to CLO.

8. Add the following items to the Item table.

3673	Blanket	NOV	5	$29.90	$34.00	AC
6078	Key Chain	NOV	20	$3.00	$5.00	MN
7550	Sweatshirt	CLO	8	$19.90	$22.95	LG

9. Create an advanced filter for the Item table. The filter should display the item number, item type, description, and number on hand for all items with less than 10 items on hand. Sort the filter by item type and description. Save the filter settings as a query and name the filter Reorder Filter.

10. Resize all columns in the Item table and the Supplier table to best fit.

11. Using a query, delete all records in the Item table where the description starts with the letter F. Save the query as Delete Query.

12. Specify referential integrity between the Supplier table (the one table) and the Item table (the many table). Cascade the update but not the delete.

13. Compact the database.

14. Submit the revised database in the format specified by your instructor.

In the Lab

Lab 3: Maintaining the Ada Beauty Supply Database

Problem: The management of Ada Beauty Supply has determined that some changes must be made to the database structure. A multivalued field must be added. Validation rules need to be added. Finally, some additions and deletions are required to the database.

Instructions: Use the Ada Beauty Supply database created in the In the Lab 3 of Chapter 1 on page AC 69 for this assignment, or see your instructor for information on accessing the files required for this book. Submit the revised database in the format specified by your instructor.

Instructions Part 1: Several changes must be made to the database structure. For example, management would like a multivalued field that lists the type of services each beauty salon offers. This knowledge can help the sales representatives better meet the needs of their customers. Table 3-2 lists the service abbreviations and descriptions that management would like in a Services Offered multivalued field.

Table 3–2 Service Abbreviations and Descriptions	
Service Abbreviation	**Description**
FAC	Facial
HRS	Hair Styling
MNC	Manicure
PED	Pedicure
MST	Massage Therapy
TAN	Tanning

Management wants to ensure that an entry always appears in the Customer Name field and that any letters entered in the Customer Number field appear in uppercase. It also requires that the amount in the Balance field is never less than 0 or greater than $1,000. Make the changes to the database structure. Place the Services Offered field after the Telephone field.

Continued >

In the Lab *continued*

Instructions Part 2: The data for the Services Offered field shown in Figure 3–82 must be added to the database. The address for Elegante is incorrect. It should be 180 Broadway. Le Beauty has changed its name to Le Beauty Day Spa. Nancy's Place has gone out of business. A new salon, PamperMe Day Spa, just opened. The address for the salon is 2125 Lawrence and the phone number is 555-2401. The spa provides all services except hair styling and tanning.

 Management wants to use PA10 as the customer number and Terry Sinson is the sales rep. The new spa has purchased $750 worth of supplies but has not paid for them. Format the datasheet to best fit the data.

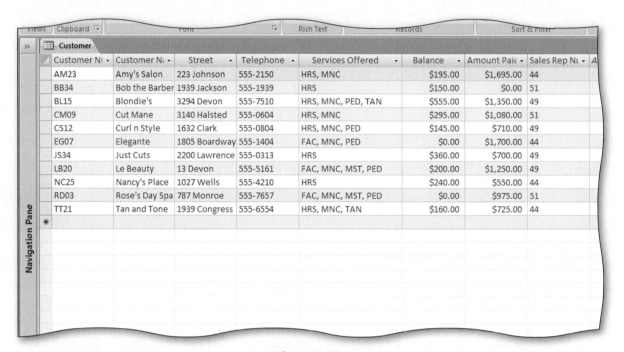

Customer Nu	Customer Na	Street	Telephone	Services Offered	Balance	Amount Paid	Sales Rep Nu	A
AM23	Amy's Salon	223 Johnson	555-2150	HRS, MNC	$195.00	$1,695.00	44	
BB34	Bob the Barber	1939 Jackson	555-1939	HRS	$150.00	$0.00	51	
BL15	Blondie's	3294 Devon	555-7510	HRS, MNC, PED, TAN	$555.00	$1,350.00	49	
CM09	Cut Mane	3140 Halsted	555-0604	HRS, MNC	$295.00	$1,080.00	51	
CS12	Curl n Style	1632 Clark	555-0804	HRS, MNC, PED	$145.00	$710.00	49	
EG07	Elegante	1805 Boardway	555-1404	FAC, MNC, PED	$0.00	$1,700.00	44	
JS34	Just Cuts	2200 Lawrence	555-0313	HRS	$360.00	$700.00	49	
LB20	Le Beauty	13 Devon	555-5161	FAC, MNC, MST, PED	$200.00	$1,250.00	49	
NC25	Nancy's Place	1027 Wells	555-4210	HRS	$240.00	$550.00	44	
RD03	Rose's Day Spa	787 Monroe	555-7657	FAC, MNC, MST, PED	$0.00	$975.00	51	
TT21	Tan and Tone	1939 Congress	555-6554	HRS, MNC, TAN	$160.00	$725.00	44	

Figure 3–82

Instructions Part 3: Because the sales reps work on commission, management wants to make sure that customers are not assigned to a sales rep who is not in the database. It also wants the ability to change a sales rep number in the Sales Rep table and have the change applied to the Customer table. Create the appropriate relationship that would satisfy management's needs.

Cases and Places

Apply your creative thinking and problem solving skills to design and implement a solution.

● EASIER   ●● MORE DIFFICULT

● 1: Maintaining the Second-Hand Goods Database

Use the Second-Hand Goods database you created in Cases and Places 1 in Chapter 1 on page AC 71 for this assignment, or see your instructor for information on accessing the files required for this book. Perform each of the following tasks:

a. The Condition field should be a Lookup field. Only the current values in the database should be legal values.

b. A better description for the bookcases is 3-Shelf Bookcase.

c. The duvet has been sold.

d. The minimum price of any item is $2.00.

e. It would be easier to find items for sale if the default sort order for the item table were by description rather than by item number. Also, some of the descriptions are not displayed completely in Datasheet view.

f. Specify referential integrity. Cascade the update and the delete.

Submit the revised database in the format specified by your instructor.

● 2: Maintaining the BeachCondo Rentals database

Use the BeachCondo Rentals database you created in Cases and Places 2 in Chapter 1 on page AC 71 for this assignment, or see your instructor for information on accessing the files required for this book. Perform each of the following tasks:

a. Add the field, For Sale to the Condo Unit, to indicate whether a condo unit is for sale. The field is a Yes/No field and should appear after the weekly rate.

b. All units owned by Alonso Bonita are for sale.

c. The Bedrooms, Bathrooms, and Sleeps fields always should contain data.

d. Most common condo units have one bedroom, one bathroom, and sleep two people. All condo units should have a minimum of one bedroom, one bathroom, and sleep two people.

e. No unit rents for less than $700 or more than $1,500.

f. Management has just received a new listing from Mark Graty. It is unit 300. The unit sleeps 10, has three bedrooms, has 2.5 bathrooms, and includes linens. The weekly rate is $1,400 and the owner is interested in selling the unit.

Submit the revised database in the format specified by your instructor.

●● 3: Maintaining the Restaurant Database

Use the restaurant database you created in Cases and Places 3 in Chapter 1 on page AC 71 for this assignment, or see your instructor for information on accessing the files required for this book. Using the Plan Ahead guidelines presented in this chapter, determine what changes need to be made to your database. For example, a multivalued field could be useful to record opening days and times of a restaurant. Another multivalued field could record restaurant specialties. Use a word processing program, such as Microsoft Word, to explain the changes you need to make to the database. Then, make the changes to the database. Submit the Word document and the revised database in the format specified by your instructor.

Continued >

Cases and Places *continued*

•• 4: Updating Your Contacts Database

Make It Personal

Use the contacts database you created in Cases and Places 4 in Chapter 1 on page AC 71 for this assignment, or see your instructor for information on accessing the files required for this book. Consider your own personal job situation. Has the focus of your job search changed? Are there specific jobs within the companies of interest that appeal to you? Have you contacted an individual within a company to express your interest? Create a multivalued field to store those specific positions that would interest you. Review the fields in the contacts database. Are there any fields you need to add? Are there any fields you need to delete? Are there any tables that need to be deleted? Are there companies that need to be added to your database? Make any necessary changes to your database structure and update the database. Using a word processing program, such as Microsoft Word, explain what changes you made to your database and why you made the changes. Submit the Word document and the revised database in the format specified by your instructor.

•• 5: Understanding Action Queries, Query Wizards, and Table Design Changes

Working Together

With a make-table query, a user can create a new table from one or more tables in the database. The table can be stored in the same database or a new database. As a team, use the Access Help system to learn more about make-table queries. Then, choose either the Cases and Places 1 database or the Cases and Places 2 database and create a make-table query. For example, for the Hockey Fan Zone, the management could create a table named Supplier Call List that would include the item code, description, and cost of each item as well as the supplier name and telephone number. Write a one-page paper that (1) explains the purpose for which the new table is intended and (2) suggests at least two additional uses for make-table queries. Submit the paper and the database in the format specified by your instructor.

Open the Students database that you created in Chapter 1. As a team, review the data types for each of the fields that are in the database. Do any of these data types need to be changed? For example, is there a field that should store multiple values? Are there any fields that should contain validation rules? Change the data types and add validation rules as necessary. Examine the tables in your database. Delete any tables that you do not need. Write a one-page paper that explains your reasons for changing (or not changing) the structure of the database. Submit the paper and the database in the format specified by your instructor.

Save the Ada Beauty Supply database as Ada Team Beauty Supply. Research the purpose of the Find Unmatched Query Wizard and the Find Duplicates query Wizard. Use the Ada Team database and create queries using each of these wizards. Did the queries perform as expected? Open each query in Design view and modify it, for example, add another field to the query. What happened to the query results? Write a one-page paper that explains the purpose of each query wizard and describes the team's experiences with creating and modifying the queries. Submit the paper and database in the format specified by your instructor.

Integration Feature

Sharing Data Among Applications

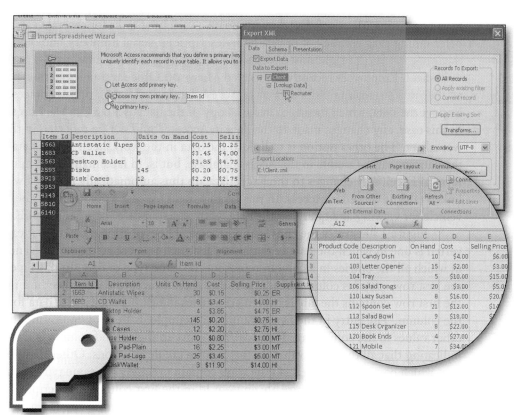

Objectives

You will have mastered the material in this Integration Feature when you can:

- Import from or link to an Excel worksheet

- Import from or link to an Access database

- Import from or link to a text file

- Export data to Excel, Word, and text files

- Publish a report

- Export and import XML data

Starting Access

If you are using a computer to step through the project in this chapter and you want your screen to match the figures in this book, you should change your screen's resolution to 1024 × 768. For information about how to change a computer's resolution, read Appendix E.

To Start Access

The following steps, which assume Windows is running, start Access.

1 Click the Start button on the Windows taskbar to display the Start menu.

2 Point to All Programs on the Start menu to display the All Programs submenu and then point to Microsoft Office on the All Programs submenu to display the Microsoft Office submenu.

3 Click Microsoft Office Access 2007 on the Microsoft Office submenu to start Access and display the Getting Started with Microsoft Office Access window.

4 If the Access window is not maximized, click the Maximize button on its title bar to maximize the window.

To Create a New Database

Before importing data from another application to an Access database, you must ensure that a database exists. If there is no database, then you need to create one. The following steps create a database on a USB flash drive that will store the items for Camashaly.

1 With a USB flash drive connected to one of the computer's USB ports, click Blank Database in the Getting Started with Microsoft Office Access screen to create a new blank database.

2 Type Camashaly in the File Name text box and then click the 'Browse for a location to put your database' button to display the File New Database dialog box.

3 Click the Save in box arrow to display a list of available drives and folders and then click UDISK 2.0 (E:) (your letter may be different) in the Save in list to select the USB flash drive as the new save location.

4 Click the OK button to select the USB flash drive as the location for the database and to return to the Getting Started with Microsoft Office Access screen.

5 Click the Create button to create the database on the USB flash drive with the file name, Camashaly.

Importing or Linking Data From Other Applications to Access

The process of importing or linking an Access database uses a wizard. Specifically, if the data is imported from an Excel worksheet, the process will use the **Import Spreadsheet Wizard**; if the data is linked to an Excel worksheet, the process will use the **Link Spreadsheet Wizard**. The wizard takes you through some basic steps, asking a few simple questions. After you have answered the questions, the wizard will import or link the data.

Identify sources of external data for the database: Excel worksheet.
You need to decide whether it is appropriate for data you currently keep in an Excel worksheet to be kept in a database instead. The following are some common reasons for using a database instead of a worksheet:

1. The worksheet contains a great deal of redundant data. As discussed in Chapter 1 on pages AC 10 and AC 12, databases can be designed to eliminate redundant data.

2. The data to be maintained consists of multiple interrelated items. For example, the JSP Recruiters database maintains data on two items, clients and recruiters, and these items are interrelated. A client has a single recruiter and each recruiter is responsible for several clients. The JSP Recruiters database is a very simple one. Databases easily can contain many separate, but interrelated, items.

3. You want to use the powerful query and report capabilities of Microsoft Access.

Plan Ahead

Determine whether the data you have identified is in an appropriate format: Excel worksheet.
Before importing or linking the Excel worksheet you have identified, you need to make sure it is in an appropriate format. The following are some of the actions you should take to ensure correct format:

1. Make sure the data is in the form of a list, a collection of rows and columns in which all the entries in a column represent the same type of data.

2. Make sure that there are no blank rows within the list. If there are, remove them prior to importing or linking.

3. Make sure there are no blank columns within the list. If there are, remove them prior to importing or linking.

4. Determine whether the first row contains column headings that will make appropriate field names in the resulting table. If not, you might consider adding such a row. In general, the process is simpler if the first row in the worksheet contains appropriate column headings.

Plan Ahead

To Import an Excel Worksheet

After Camashaly managers identified that a worksheet named Computer Items contains data that should be in a table in the database, they would import the data. You import a worksheet by using the Import Spreadsheet Wizard. In the process, you will indicate that the first row in the Computer Items worksheet contains the column headings. These column headings then will become the field names in the Access table. In addition, you will indicate the primary key for the table. As part of the process, you could, if appropriate, choose not to include all the fields from the worksheet in the resulting table.

The following steps import the Computer Items Excel worksheet.

- Click External Data on the Ribbon to display the External Data tab (Figure 3).

Figure 3

2

- Click the Excel button in the Import group on the External Data tab to display the Get External Data – Excel Spreadsheet dialog box.

- Click the Browse button in the Get External Data – Excel Spreadsheet dialog box.

- If necessary, click the Look in box arrow and then click UDISK 2.0 (E:) to select the USB flash drive in the Look in list as the new open location. (Your drive letter might be different.)

- Click the Computer Items workbook, and then click the Open button to select the workbook (Figure 4).

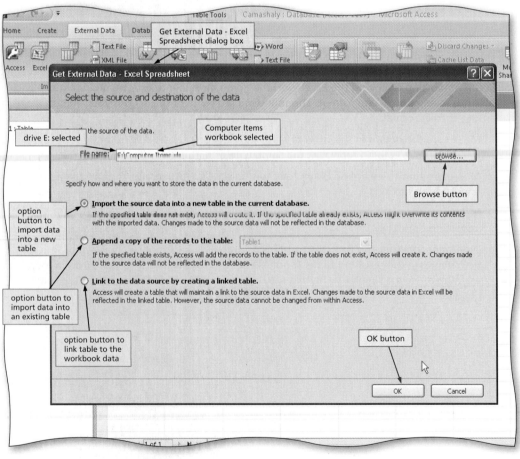

Figure 4

❸

• With the option button to import the data to a new table selected, click the OK button to display the Import Spreadsheet Wizard dialog box (Figure 5).

Q&A

What happens if I select the option button to append records to an existing table?

Instead of the records being placed in a new table, they will be added to the existing table, provided the value in the primary key field does not duplicate that on an existing record.

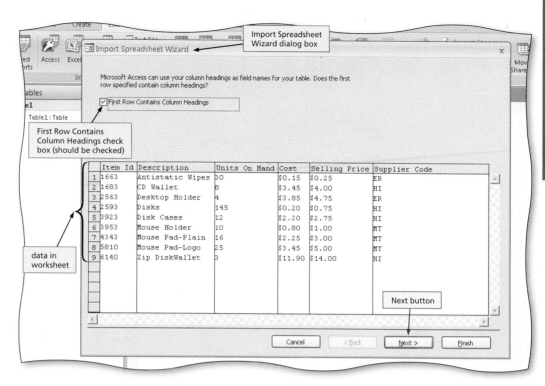

Figure 5

❹

• If necessary, click First Row Contains Column Headings to select it.

• Click the Next button (Figure 6).

Q&A

When would I use the options on this screen?

You would use these options if you wanted to change properties for one or more fields. You can change the name, the data type, and whether the field is indexed. You also can indicate that some fields are not to be imported.

Figure 6

- Because the Field Options need not be specified, click the Next button (Figure 7).

Figure 7

- Click the 'Choose my own primary key.' option button (Figure 8).

Q&A

How do I decide which option button to select?

If one of the fields is an appropriate primary key, choose your own primary key from the list of fields. If you are sure you do not want a primary key, choose No primary key. Otherwise, let Access add the primary key.

Figure 8

- Because the Item Id field, which is the correct field, is already selected as the primary key, click the Next button.

- Be sure Item appears in the Import to Table text box.

- Click the Finish button to import the data (Figure 9).

Figure 9

8

- Click the Save import steps check box to display the Save import steps options.

- If necessary, type `Import-Computer Items` in the Save as text box.

- Type `Import data from Computer Items workbook into Item table` in the Description text box (Figure 10).

Q&A When would I create an Outlook task?

If the import operation is one you will repeat on a regular basis, you can create and schedule the import process just as you can schedule any other Outlook task.

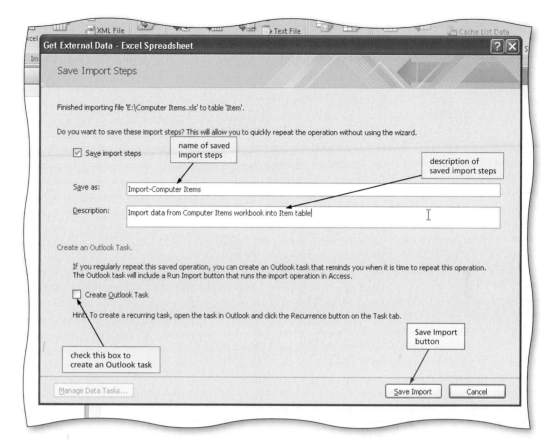

Figure 10

9

- Click the Save Import button to save the import steps (Figure 11).

Figure 11

Other Ways

1. Right-click Table1 : Table in Navigation pane, point to Import, click appropriate file format

Using the Access Table

After the Access version of the table has been created, you can use it as you would any other table. You can open the table in Datasheet view (Figure 1b on page AC 207). You can make changes to the data. You can create queries or reports that use the data in the table.

By clicking Design View on the table's shortcut menu, you can view the table's structure and make any necessary changes to the structure. The changes may include changing field sizes and types (for those that may not be correct), creating indexes, specifying the primary key, or adding additional fields. If you have imported multiple tables that are to be related, you will need to relate the tables. To accomplish any of these tasks, use the same steps you used in Chapter 3.

BTW

Saving Import Steps
When you save the steps that import data from a Microsoft Office Excel 2007 workbook, Access stores the name of the Excel workbook, the name of the destination database, and other details, including whether the data was appended to a table or added to a new table, primary key information, field names, and so on.

Linking versus Importing

When an external table or worksheet is imported, or converted, into an Access database, a copy of the data is placed as a table in the database. The original data still exists, just as it did before, but no further connection exists between it and the data in the database. Changes to the original data do not affect the data in the database. Likewise, changes in the database do not affect the original data.

It also is possible to link data stored in a variety of formats to Access databases by selecting the 'Link to the data source by creating a linked table' option button on the Get External Data - Excel Spreadsheet dialog box rather than the 'Import the source data into a new table in the current database' option button (Figure 4 on page AC 212). With linking, the connection is maintained.

When an Excel worksheet is linked, for example, the worksheet is not stored in the database. Instead Access simply establishes a connection to the worksheet so you can view the data in either Access or Excel. Any change made in the worksheet will be visible immediately in the table. For example, if you change an address in Excel and then view the table in Access, you would see the new address. If you add a new row in Excel and then view the table in Access, the row would appear as a new record. You cannot make changes to the table in Access. If you want to add, change, or delete data, you must make the changes in the worksheet because the data is stored in an Excel workbook.

To identify that a table is linked to other data, Access places an arrow in front of the table (Figure 12). In addition, the Excel icon in front of the name indicates that the data is linked to an Excel worksheet.

Figure 12

The Linked Table Manager

After you link tables between a worksheet and a database or between two databases, you can modify many of the linked table's features. For example, you can rename the linked table, set view properties, and set links between tables in queries. If you move, rename, or modify linked tables, you can use the **Linked Table Manager** to update the links. To do so, click Database Tools on the Ribbon to display the Database Tools tab. Then click the Linked Table Manager button on the Database Tools tab. The Linked Table Manager dialog box that appears includes instructions on how to update the links.

To Close a Database

The following steps show how to close the database.

1 Click the Office Button to display the Office Button menu.

2 Click Close Database on the Office Button menu.

Importing from or Linking to Data in Another Access Database

Just as you can import data from an Excel worksheet, you can import data from another Access database. Similarly, just as you can link to data in an Excel worksheet, you can link to data in another Access database.

Plan
Ahead

Identify sources of external data for the database: Access database.
You need to decide whether it is appropriate for you to import or link data in another Access database. The following are some common reasons for importing from or linking to another database:

1. You want to combine two databases into one. By importing, you can copy all objects (tables, queries, forms, reports, and so on) from one database to the other.

2. You want to create tables that are similar to tables in another database. When importing, you can choose to copy the table structure without the data. The table created in the process will have all the fields and field properties of the original, but will be empty.

3. You want to copy a collection of related objects from another database. In one operation you could, for example, copy a table along with all queries, forms, and reports that are based on that table.

4. You have several databases, but data in some tables is the same, for example, the Client table must be shared between some of the databases. By linking, any updates to the table in the source database are immediately available to anyone using any of the other databases.

TO IMPORT DATA FROM ANOTHER ACCESS DATABASE

The following steps would import data from another Access database into the database that is currently open.

1. Click the Access button in the Import group on the External Data tab.

2. Select the database containing the data to be imported.

3. Be sure the 'Import tables, queries, forms, reports, macros, and modules into the current database' option button is selected and click the OK button.

4. In the Import Objects dialog box, select the tables, queries, forms, reports, macros, and/or modules you wish to import and then click the OK button.

5. Decide if you wish to save the import steps.

TO LINK TO DATA IN ANOTHER ACCESS DATABASE

The following steps would link tables in another Access database into the database that is currently open.

1. Click the Access button in the Import group on the External Data tab.

2. Select the database containing the tables to be linked.

3. Click the 'Link to the data source by creating a linked table' option button to link and then click the OK button.

4. In the Link tables dialog box, select the tables you wish to link and then click the OK button.

Text Files

Text files contain unformatted characters including both readable characters, such as numbers and letters, and some special characters, such as tabs, carriage returns, and line feeds. Typical extensions for text files that can be imported or linked into Access databases are txt, csv, asc, and tab.

To be able to use a text file for importing or linking, it must be organized into records (rows) and fields (columns). Records and fields can be organized in two ways: delimited files and fixed-width files.

In **delimited files**, each record is on a separate line and the fields are separated by a special character, called the **delimiter**. Common delimiters are tabs, semicolon, commas, and spaces. You also can choose any other value that does not appear within the field contents. The csv (comma separated values) file often used in Excel is an example of a delimited file.

In **fixed-width files**, the width of any field is the same on every record. For example, if the width of the first field on the first record is 12 characters, the width of the first field on every other record also must be 12 characters.

Plan Ahead

Identify sources of external data for the database: text file.

You need to decide whether it is appropriate for you to use external data stored in a text file. The following are some common reasons for using a text file for this purpose:

1. Data that you want to import is not available in a format that Access recognizes. You first would export the data from the original application to a text file and then import that text file into Access.

2. You manage data in Access but regularly receive data in text files from other users that needs to be incorporated into your database.

Plan Ahead

Determine whether the data you have identified is in an appropriate format: text file.

Before importing or linking the text file you have identified, you need to make sure it is in an appropriate format. The following are some of the actions you should take to ensure correct format:

1. Make sure the data in the text file consistently follows one of the available formats (delimited or fixed width). If the file is delimited, identify the delimiter and make sure the same one is used throughout. If the file is fixed-width, make sure each field on each record is the same width.

2. Make sure that there are no blank records within the file. If there are, remove them prior to importing or linking.

3. Make sure there are no blank fields within the list. If there are, remove them prior to importing or linking.

4. For each field, make sure the entries in each record represent the same type of data.

5. If it is a delimited file, determine whether the first row contains column headings that will make appropriate field names in the resulting table. If not, you should add such a row. In general, the process is simpler if the first row in a delimited file contains appropriate column headings.

6. Make sure there are no extra paragraph (carriage) returns at the end of the file. If there are, remove them prior to importing or linking.

TO IMPORT DATA FROM OR LINK DATA TO A TEXT FILE

To import data from or link data to a text file, you would use the following steps.

1. Click the Text File button in the Import group on the External Data tab.

2. Select the text file containing the data to be imported.

3. Be sure the 'Import the source into a new table in the current database' option button is selected if you wish to create a new table. Click the 'Append a copy of the records to the table' option button if you wish to add to an existing table, and then select the table. Click the 'Link to the data source by creating a linked table' option button if you wish to link the data. Once you have selected the correct option button, click the OK button.

4. Select the Delimited option button for a delimited file or the Fixed Width option button for a fixed-width file, and then click the Next button.

5a. For a delimited file, select the character that delimits the field values. If you know the file uses a text qualifier, which is a symbol used to enclose character values, select either the double quotation mark (") or the single quotation mark ('). If the first row contains field names, click the First Row contains Field Names check box. Once you have made your selections, click the Next button.

5b. For a fixed-width file, review the structure that Access recommends. If the recommended structure is not appropriate, follow the directions on the screen to add, remove, or adjust the lines. Once you have finished, click the Next button.

6. You can use the next screen if you need to change properties of one or more fields. When finished, click the Next button.

7. If you are importing, select the appropriate primary key, and then click the Next button. If you are linking, you will not have an opportunity to select a primary key.

8. Be sure the table name is correct, and then click the Finish button to import or link the data. Decide if you wish to save the import steps.

Using Saved Import Steps

You can use a set of saved import steps from within Access by clicking the Saved Imports button on the External Data tab. You then will see the Manage Data Tasks dialog box, as shown in Figure 13 on the next page. Select the set of saved import steps you want to repeat. (In this case only the import named Import-Computer Items exists.) Click the Run button to repeat the import steps you saved earlier. If you have created an Outlook task, you can schedule the import operation just as you schedule any other Outlook task.

Figure 13

Exporting Data From Access to Other Applications

Exporting is the process of copying database objects to another database, to a worksheet, or to some other format so another application (for example, Excel) can use the data. Businesses need the flexibility of using the same data in different applications. For example, numerical data in a table exported to Excel could be analyzed using Excel's powerful statistical functions. Data also could be exported as an RTF file for use in marketing brochures.

To Open a Database

Before exporting the JSP Recruiters data, you first must open the database. The following steps open the database.

1 With your USB flash drive connected to one of the computer's USB ports, click the More button to display the Open dialog box.

2 If necessary, click the Look in box arrow and then click UDISK 2.0 (E:) to select the USB flash drive in the Look in list as the new open location. (Your drive letter might be different.)

3 Click JSP Recruiters to select the file name.

Click the Open button to open the database.

 If a Security Warning appears, click the Options button to display the Microsoft Office Security Options dialog box.

 Click the 'Enable this content' option button and then click the OK button to enable the content.

To Export Data to Excel

Once JSP Recruiters has decided to make the Recruiter-Client Query available to Excel users, it needs to export the data. To export data to Excel, select the table or query to be exported, and then click the Excel button in the Export group on the External Data tab. The following steps export the Client-Recruiter Query to Excel and save the export steps.

- Click the Recruiter-Client Query in the Navigation pane to select it.

- Click External Data on the Ribbon to display the External Data tab (Figure 14).

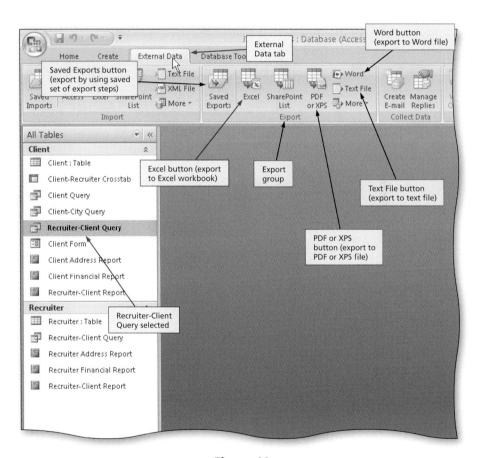

Figure 14

2

- Click the Excel button in the Export group on the External Data tab to display the Export – Excel Spreadsheet dialog box.

- Click the Browse button and select your USB flash drive as the file location.

- Be sure the file name is Recruiter-Client Query and then click the Save button (Figure 15).

Q&A Did I need to browse?

No. You could type the appropriate file location.

Q&A Could I change the name of the file?

You could change it. Simply replace the current file name with the one you want.

Q&A What if the file I want to export already exists?

Access will indicate that the file already exists and ask if you want to replace it. If you click the Yes button, the file you export will replace the old file. If you click the No button, you must either change the name of the export file or cancel the process.

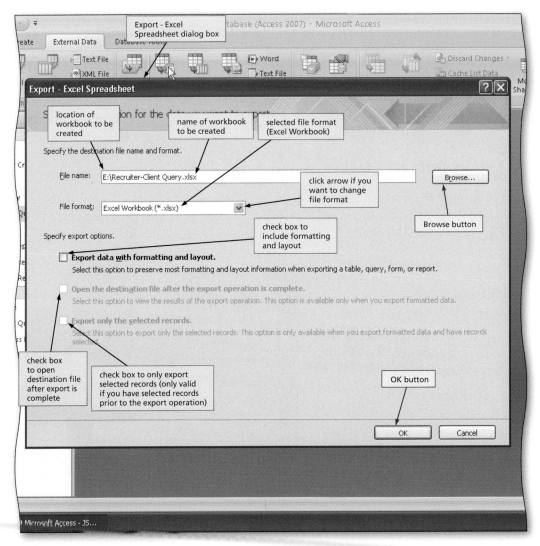

Figure 15

3

- Click the OK button to export the data (Figure 16).

4

- Click the Save export steps check box to display the Save export steps options.

- If necessary, type `Export-Recruiter-Client Query` in the Save as text box.

- Type `Export the Recruiter-Client Query without formatting` in the Description text box.

- Click the Save Export button to save the export steps.

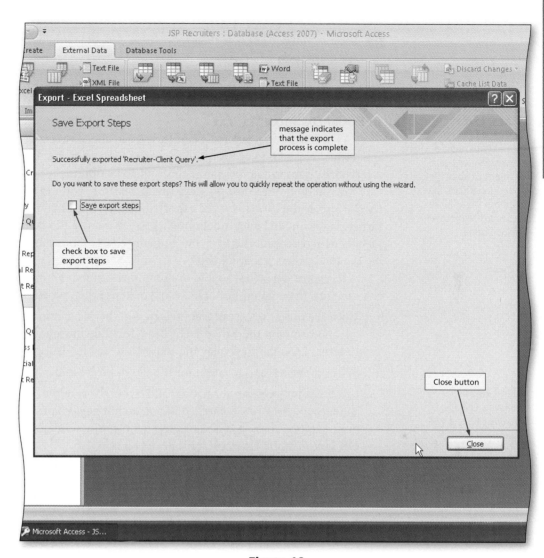

Figure 16

Other Ways

1. Right-click database object in Navigation pane, point to Export, click appropriate file format

To Export Data to Word

Once JSP Recruiters has decided to also make the Recruiter-Client Query available to Word, it needs to export the data. There is a problem, however. It is not possible to export data to the standard Word format. It is possible, however to export the data as an RTF (rich text file), which Word can access. The following steps export the data to an RTF file. They do not save the export steps.

1 With the Recruiter-Client Query selected in the Navigation pane and the External Data tab appearing on the screen, click the Word button in the Export group on the External Data tab to display the Export - RTF file dialog box.

2 Select your USB drive as the file location and make sure that Recruiter-Client Query is the file name.

3 If necessary, click the Save button and then click the OK button to export the data.

4 Because you will not save the export steps, click the Close button to close the Export - RTF File dialog box.

TO EXPORT DATA TO A TEXT FILE

When exporting data to a text file, you can choose to export the data with formatting and layout. This option preserves much of the formatting and layout in tables, queries, forms, and reports. For forms and reports, this is the only option.

If you do not need to preserve the formatting, you can choose either delimited or fixed-width as the format for the exported file. The most common option, especially if formatting is not an issue, is delimited. You can choose the delimiter and also whether to include field names on the first row. In many cases, delimiting with a comma and including the field names is a good choice.

To export data from a table or query to a comma delimited file in which the first row contains the column headings, you would use the following steps.

1. With the object to be exported selected in the Navigation pane and the External Data tab appearing on the Ribbon, click the Text File button in the Export group on the External Data tab to display the Export - Text File dialog box.

2. Select the name and location for the file to be created.

3. If you need to preserve formatting and layout, be sure the 'Export data with formatting and layout' check box is checked. If you do not need to preserve formatting and layout, make sure the check box is not checked. Once you have made your selection, click the OK button in the Export - Text File dialog box.

4. To create a delimited file, be sure the Delimited option button is selected. To create a fixed-width file, be sure the Fixed Width option button is selected. Once you have made your selection, click the Next button.

5a. If you are exporting to a delimited file, choose the delimiter that you want to separate your fields, such as a comma. Decide whether to include field names on the first row and, if so, click the Include Field Names on First Row check box. If you want to select a text qualifier, select it in the Text Qualifier list. When you have made your selections, click the Next button.

5b. If you are exporting to a fixed-width file, review the position of the vertical lines that separate your fields. If any lines are not positioned correctly, follow the directions on the screen to reposition them. When you have finished, click the Next button.

6. Click the Finish button to export the data.

7. Save the export steps if you wish, or simply click the Close button in the Export - Text File dialog box to close the dialog box without saving the export steps.

To Publish a Report

At JSP Recruiters, the staff would like to make the Recruiter Financial Report available through e-mail, which they can do by publishing the report as either a PDF or XPS file. The following steps publish the Recruiter Financial Report as an XPS file.

1

- Click the Recruiter Financial Report in the Navigation pane to select it.

- Click the 'PDF or XPS' button in the Export group on the External Data tab (see Figure 14 on page AC 221) to display the Publish as PDF or XPS dialog box.

- Select your USB drive as the file location. Make sure that Recruiter Financial Report is the file name and that XPS Document is the file type. If necessary, remove the check mark in the 'Open file after publishing' check box.

Figure 17

- Click the 'Standard (publishing online and printing)' option button to create a file that is appropriate for both publishing online and printing (Figure 17).

 Q&A
How do I publish as PDF?

Change XPS Document to PDF in the Save as type box.

2

- Click the Publish button to publish the report as an XPS file.

- Because you will not save the export steps, click the Close button to close the Export - XPS dialog box.

Using Saved Export Steps

You can use a set of saved Export steps from within Access by clicking the Saved Exports button on the External Data tab. You then select the set of saved export steps you want to repeat and click the Run button in the Manage Data Tasks dialog box. If you have created an Outlook task, you can schedule the export operation just as you can schedule any other Outlook task.

BTW

Viewing or Printing the Report
To view or print the report stored in the XPS file, use the XML Paper Specification Viewer. If the XML Paper Specification Viewer is not installed on your system, you can obtain it from Microsoft. If you are unable to view or print XPS files, you alternatively can publish the report as a PDF. To do so, change the Save as type from XPS Document to PDF before clicking the Publish button.

XML

Just as Hypertext Markup Language (HTML) is the standard language for creating and displaying Web pages, **Extensible Markup Language (XML)** is the standard language for describing and delivering data on the Web. Another way of viewing the difference is that HTML handles the *appearance* of data within a Web page, whereas XML handles the *meaning* of data. XML is a data interchange standard that allows you to exchange data between dissimilar systems or applications. With XML, you can describe both the data and the structure **(schema)** of the data. You can export tables, queries, forms, or reports.

When exporting XML data, you can choose to export multiple related tables in a single operation to a single XML file. If you later import this XML data to another database, you will import all the tables in a single operation. Thus, the new database would contain each of the tables. All the fields would have the correct data types and sizes and the primary keys would be correct.

To Export XML Data

In exporting XML data, you indicate whether to just save the data or to save both the data and the schema (that is, the structure). If you have made changes to the appearance of the data, such as changing the font, and want these changes saved as well, you save what is known as the **presentation**. The data is saved in a file with the XML extension, the schema is saved in a file with the XSD extension, and the presentation is saved in a file with the XSL extension. The default choice, which usually is appropriate, is to save both the data and schema, but not the presentation. If multiple tables are related, such as the Client and Recruiter tables in the JSP Recruiters data, you can export both tables to a single file.

The following steps export both the Client and Recruiter tables to a single XML file called Client. The steps save the data and the schema, but do not save the presentation.

1

- Click the Client table in the Navigation pane to select it.

- Click the More button in the Export group on the External Data tab to display the More button menu with additional export options (Figure 18).

Figure 18

2

- Click XML File on the More button menu to display the Export - XML File dialog box.

- Select your USB drive as the file location and make sure that Client is the file name (Figure 19).

Figure 19

❸

- Click the OK button to display the Export XML dialog box (Figure 20).

Figure 20

❹

- Click the More Options button to specify additional options (Figure 21).

Q&A

What is the purpose of the other tabs in this dialog box?

You can use the Schema tab to indicate whether you want primary key, index information, table properties, and field properties included (normally they are) and whether the schema information is to be stored in a separate file (normally it is). If you want to export the presentation, you can use the Presentation tab to indicate this fact and also specify options concerning how the Presentation will be exported.

Figure 21

❺

- Click the expand indicator (the plus sign) to the left of [Lookup Data], and then click the Recruiter check box to select the Recruiter table (Figure 22).

❻

- Click the OK button to export the data.

- Because you will not save the export steps, click the Close button to close the Export - XML File dialog box.

- Click the Close Database command on the Office Button menu.

Figure 22

To Create a New Database

Before importing the data from the JSP Recruiters database, you need to create the new JSP Consulting database that will contain the data. The following steps create the JSP Consulting database on a USB flash drive.

① With a USB flash drive connected to one of the computer's USB ports, click Blank Database in the Getting Started with Microsoft Office Access screen to create a new blank database.

② Type `JSP Consulting` in the File Name text box and then click the 'Browse for a location to put your database' button to display the File New Database dialog box.

③ Click the Save in box arrow to display a list of available drives and folders and then click UDISK 2.0 (E:) (your letter may be different) in the Save in list to select the USB flash drive as the new save location.

④ Click the OK button to select the USB flash drive as the location for the database and to return to the Getting Started with Microsoft Office Access screen.

⑤ Click the Create button to create the database on the USB flash drive with the file name, JSP Consulting.

To Import XML Data

The following steps import both the Client and Recruiter tables stored in the XML file called Client. In addition to having the same data, the fields in both tables will have precisely the same data types and sizes as in the original database. Also, the same fields will have been designated primary keys.

①

- With the JSP Consulting database open, click External Data on the Ribbon to display the External Data tab.

- Click the XML File button in the Import group on the External Data tab to display the Get External Data - XML File dialog box.

- Click the Browse button in the Get External Data - XML File dialog box to display the File Open dialog box.

- If necessary, select UDISK 2.0 (E:) in the Look in list.

- Click the Client file to select it (Figure 23).

Should I click the xsd version?

No. If you do, you will import both tables, but none of the data. That is, the tables will be empty.

Figure 23

• Click the Open button to return to the Get External Data - XML File dialog box (Figure 24).

Figure 24

❸

• Click the OK button to display the Import XML dialog box (Figure 25).

• Be sure the Structure and Data option button is selected and then click the OK button to import the data.

• Because you will not save the import steps, click the Close button to close the Get External Data - XML File dialog box.

Figure 25

To Quit Access

You are ready to quit Access. The following step quits Access.

❶ Click the Close button on the right side of the Access title bar to quit Access.

BTW

Certification
The Microsoft Certified Application Specialist (MCAS) program provides an opportunity for you to obtain a valuable industry credential— proof that you have the Access 2007 skills required by employers. For more information, see Appendix F or visit the Access 2007 Certification Web page (scsite.com/ac2007/cert).

Feature Summary

In this feature you have learned to import from and link to data in Excel worksheets, other Access databases, and text files; export data to Excel worksheets, Word documents, and text files; publish reports; and export and import XML data. The items listed below include all the new Access skills you have learned in this chapter.

1. Import an Excel Worksheet (AC 212)
2. Import Data from Another Access Database (AC 217)
3. Link to Data in Another Access Database (AC 217)
4. Import Data from or Link Data to a Text File (AC 219)
5. Export Data to Excel (AC 221)
6. Export Data to Word (AC 223)
7. Export Data to a Text File (AC 224)
8. Publish a Report (AC 225)
9. Export XML Data (AC 226)
10. Import XML Data (AC 228)

If you have a SAM user profile, you may have access to hands-on instruction, practice, and assessment. Log in to your SAM account (http://sam2007.course.com) to launch any assigned training activities or exams that relate to the skills covered in this chapter.

In The Lab

Design, create, modify, and/or use a database following the guidelines, concepts, and skills presented in this feature. Labs are listed in order of increasing difficulty.

Lab 1: Importing Data to an Access Database

Problem: TAL Woodworks sells custom wood accessories for the home. TAL uses worksheets to keep track of inventory and customers. TAL realizes that customer data would be better handled if maintained in an Access database. The company wants to maintain the products inventory in Excel but also would like to be able to use the query and report features of Access.

Instructions: For this assignment, you will need two files: Customer.csv and Product.xlsx. See the inside back cover of this book for instructions for downloading the Data Files for Students, or see your instructor for information on accessing the files required in this book. Perform the following tasks:

1. Start Access and create a new database in which to store all the objects for TAL Woodworks. Call the database TAL Woodworks.

2. Import the Customer worksheet shown in Figure 26 into Access. The worksheet is saved as a .csv file.

	A	B	C	D	E	F	G	H	I	J	K
1	Customer Number	Name	Address	City	State	Balance					
2	AD23	Adson Gifts	407 Mallory	Tourin	CO	$ 205.00					
3	AR75	Arthur's Interiors	200 Mimberly	Denton	CO	$ 180.00					
4	BE28	Becker Design	224 Harbor Oak	Charleston	CO	$ 170.00					
5	CR66	Casa Grande	506 Mallory	Tourin	CO	$0.00					
6	DL60	Dee's Things	123 Village	Denton	CO	$ 235.00					
7	GR36	Grande Casa	1345 Fern	Charleston	CO	$ 204.00					
8	HA09	Hal's Gifts	568 Denmer	Berridge	CO	$ 245.00					
9	ME17	My House	879 Vinca	Berls	CO	$ 268.00					
10	RO44	Royal Interiors	677 Liatris	Berridge	CO	$0.00					
11	ST22	Steedman's	889 Lantana	Berls	CO	$ 123.00					
12											
13											
14											

Figure 26

3. Use Customer as the name of the table and Customer Number as the primary key.

4. Save the import steps. Be sure to enter a description for the saved steps.

5. Link the Product worksheet shown in Figure 27 to the database.

	A	B	C	D	E	F	G	H	I	J	K	L
1	Product Code	Description	On Hand	Cost	Selling Price							
2	101	Candy Dish	10	$4.00	$6.00							
3	103	Letter Opener	15	$2.00	$3.00							
4	104	Tray	5	$10.00	$15.00							
5	106	Salad Tongs	20	$3.00	$5.00							
6	110	Lazy Susan	8	$16.00	$20.00							
7	112	Spoon Set	21	$12.00	$14.00							
8	113	Salad Bowl	9	$18.00	$25.00							
9	115	Desk Organizer	8	$22.00	$30.00							
10	120	Book Ends	4	$27.00	$34.00							
11	121	Mobile	7	$34.00	$40.00							
12												
13												
14												

Figure 27

6. Rename the linked Product table as Inventory. Then, use the Linked Table Manager to update the link between the Excel worksheet and the Access table.

7. Import the Sales Rep table from the Ada Beauty Supply database that you modified in In the Lab 3 in Chapter 3 on page AC 201. (If you did not complete this exercise, see your instructor for a copy of the modified database.) Sales reps of Ada often sell gift items to salons.

8. Change the database properties, as specified by your instructor. Submit the database in the format specified by your instructor.

1 | Creating and Editing a Presentation

What Is Microsoft Office PowerPoint 2007?

Microsoft Office PowerPoint 2007 is a complete presentation graphics program that allows you to produce professional-looking presentations (Figure 1–1). A PowerPoint **presentation** also is called a **slide show**.

PowerPoint contains several features to simplify creating a slide show. For example, the results-oriented user interface can boost productivity by making tasks and options readily accessible. Professionally designed standard layouts help you save time by formatting and creating content. You then can modify these layouts to create custom slides to fit your specific needs. To make your presentation more impressive, you can add diagrams, tables, pictures, video, sound, and animation effects. Additional PowerPoint features include the following:

- **Word processing** — Create bulleted lists, combine words and images, find and replace text, and use multiple fonts and type sizes.
- **Outlining** — Develop your presentation using an outline format. You also can import outlines from Microsoft Word or other word processing programs.
- **Charting** — Create and insert charts into your presentations and then add effects and chart elements.
- **Drawing** — Form and modify diagrams using shapes such as arcs, arrows, cubes, rectangles, stars, and triangles. Then apply Quick Styles to customize and add effects. Arrange these objects by sizing, scaling, and rotating.
- **Inserting multimedia** — Insert artwork and multimedia effects into your slide show. The Microsoft Clip Organizer contains hundreds of media files, including pictures, photos, sounds, and movies.
- **Saving to the Web** — Save presentations or parts of a presentation in HTML format so they can be viewed and manipulated using a browser. You can publish your slide show to the Internet or to an intranet.
- **E-mailing** — Send your entire slide show as an attachment to an e-mail message.
- **Collaborating** — Share your presentation with friends and coworkers. Ask them to review the slides and then insert comments that offer suggestions to enhance the presentation.
- **Preparing delivery** — Rehearse integrating PowerPoint slides into your speech by setting timings, using presentation tools, showing only selected slides in a presentation, and packaging the presentation for a CD.

This latest version of PowerPoint has many new features to increase your productivity. Graphics and other shape effects allow you to add glow, shadowing, 3-D effects, and other appealing visuals. Typography effects enhance the design's impact. PowerPoint themes apply a consistent look to each graphic, font, and table color in an entire presentation. Digital signatures enable you to verify that no one has altered your presentation since you created it, and the Document Inspector removes private data, such as comments and hidden text.

PowerPoint gives you the flexibility to make presentations using a projection device attached to a personal computer or using overhead transparencies. In addition, you can take advantage of the World Wide Web and run virtual presentations on the Internet. PowerPoint also can create paper printouts of the individual slides, outlines, and speaker notes.

Project Planning Guidlines

The process of developing a presentation that communicates specific information requires careful analysis and planning. As a starting point, establish why the presentation is needed. Next, analyze the intended audience for the presentation and their unique needs. Then, gather information about the topic and decide what to include in the presentation. Finally, determine the presentation design and style that will be most successful at delivering the message. Details of these guidelines are provided in Appendix A. In addition, each project in this book provides practical applications of these planning considerations.

Project — Presentation with Bulleted Lists

In Project 1, you will follow proper design guidelines and learn to use PowerPoint to create, save, and print the slides shown in Figures 1–1a through 1–1e on this page and the next. The objective is to produce a presentation, called A World Beneath the Waves, to help the Student Government Association (SGA) President, Dave Ehlin, promote the annual spring break diving and snorkeling trip to Cabo San Lucas, Mexico. This slide show presents the highlights of this trip and promotes the included amenities, tour prices, and the inviting Pacific waters. Some of the text will have formatting and color enhancements. In addition, you will print handouts of your slides to distribute to students.

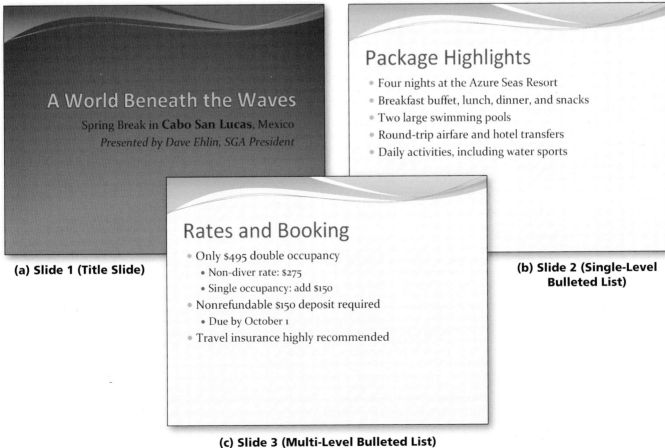

(a) Slide 1 (Title Slide)

(b) Slide 2 (Single-Level Bulleted List)

(c) Slide 3 (Multi-Level Bulleted List)

Figure 1–1

(d) Slide 4 (Multi-Level Bulleted List)   **(e) Slide 5 (Closing Slide)**

Figure 1–1 (continued)

PowerPoint allows you to produce slides to use in an academic, business, or other environment. One of the more common uses of these slides is to enhance an oral presentation. A speaker may desire to convey information, such as urging students to participate in a food drive, explaining first aid, or describing the changes in an employee benefit package. The PowerPoint slides should reinforce the speaker's message and help the audience members retain the information presented. An accompanying handout gives audience members reference notes and review material after the presentation's conclusion.

Overview

As you read this chapter, you will learn how to create the presentation shown in Figure 1–1 by performing these general tasks:

- Select an appropriate document theme.
- Enter titles and text on slides.
- Change the size, color, and style of text.
- View the presentation on your computer.
- Save the presentation so you can modify and view it at a later time.
- Print handouts of your slides.

**Plan
Ahead**

General Project Guidelines

When creating a PowerPoint document, the actions you perform and decisions you make will affect the appearance and characteristics of the finished document. As you create a presentation such as the project shown in Figure 1–1, you should follow these general guidelines:

1. **Find the appropriate theme.** The overall appearance of a presentation significantly affects its capability to communicate information clearly. The slides' graphical appearance should support the presentation's overall message. Colors, fonts, and layouts affect how audience members perceive and react to the slide content.

2. **Choose words for each slide.** Use the less is more principle. The less text, the more likely the slides will enhance your speech. Use the fewest words possible to make a point.

(continued)

(continued)

3. **Format specific elements of the text.** Examples of how you can modify the appearance, or **format**, of text include changing its shape, size, color, and position on the slide.

4. **Determine where to save the presentation.** You can store a document permanently, or **save** it, on a variety of storage media including a hard disk, USB flash drive, or CD. You also can indicate a specific location on the storage media for saving the document.

When necessary, more specific details concerning the above guidelines are presented at appropriate points in the chapter. The chapter also will identify the actions performed and decisions made regarding these guidelines during the creation of the slides shown in Figure 1–1.

Plan Ahead

Starting PowerPoint

If you are using a computer to step through the project in this chapter and you want your screen to match the figures in this book, you should change your screen's resolution to 1024 × 768. For information about how to change a computer's resolution, read Appendix E.

BTW

Decreasing Resolution
You may need to decrease your computer's resolution if you know you are going to run your presentation on another computer that uses a lower resolution, such as 800 × 600 or 640 × 480. This lower resolution, however, may affect the appearance of your slides.

To Start PowerPoint

The following steps, which assume Windows is running, start PowerPoint based on a typical installation. You may need to ask your instructor how to start PowerPoint for your computer.

1

• Click the Start button on the Windows taskbar to display the Start menu.

• Point to All Programs on the Start menu to display the All Programs submenu.

• Point to Microsoft Office on the All Programs submenu to display the Microsoft Office submenu (Figure 1–2).

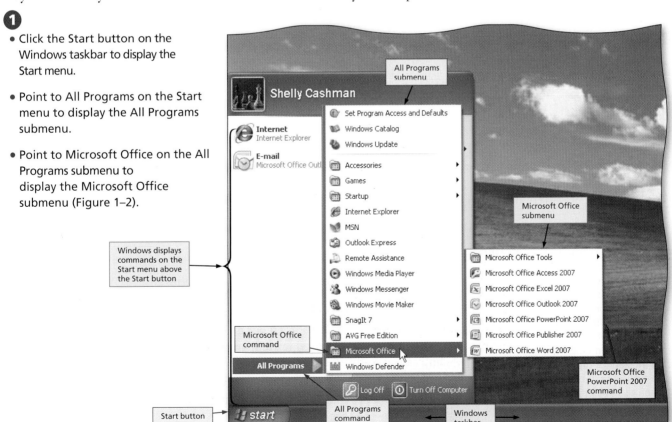

Figure 1–2

2

- Click Microsoft Office PowerPoint 2007 to start PowerPoint and display a new blank document in the PowerPoint window (Figure 1–3).

- If the PowerPoint window is not maximized, click the Maximize button next to the Close button on its title bar to maximize the window.

Q&A

What is a maximized window?

A maximized window fills the entire screen. When you maximize a window, the Maximize button changes to a Restore Down button. When you restore a maximized window, the Restore Down button changes to a Maximize button.

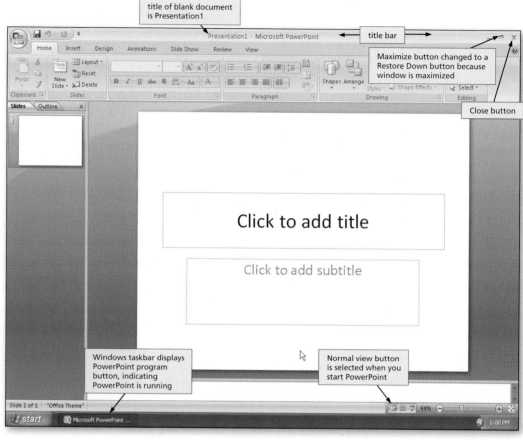

Figure 1–3

Other Ways

1. Double-click PowerPoint icon on desktop, if one is present

2. Click Microsoft Office PowerPoint 2007 on Start menu

BTW

Portrait Page Orientation

If your slide content is dominantly vertical, such as a skyscraper or a person, consider changing the slide layout to a portrait page orientation. To change the orientation, click the Slide Orientation button in the Page Setup group in the Design tab and then click the desired orientation. You can use both slide and portrait orientation in the same slide show.

The PowerPoint Window

The PowerPoint window consists of a variety of components to make your work more efficient and documents more professional. These include the document window, Ribbon, Mini toolbar and shortcut menus, Quick Access Toolbar, and Office Button. Some of these components are common to other Microsoft Office 2007 programs; others are unique to PowerPoint.

PowerPoint Window

The basic unit of a PowerPoint presentation is a **slide**. A slide may contain text and objects, such as graphics, tables, charts, and drawings. **Layouts** are used to position this content on the slide. When you open a new presentation, the default **Title Slide** layout appears (Figure 1–4). The purpose of this layout is to introduce the presentation to the audience. PowerPoint includes eight other built-in standard layouts.

The default (preset) slide layouts are set up in **landscape orientation**, where the slide width is greater than its height. In landscape orientation, the slide size is preset to 10 inches wide and 7.5 inches high when printed on a standard sheet of paper measuring 11 inches wide and 8.5 inches high.

The PowerPoint window in Figure 1–4 contains placeholders, a mouse pointer, and a status bar. Other elements that may appear in the window are discussed later in this and subsequent chapters.

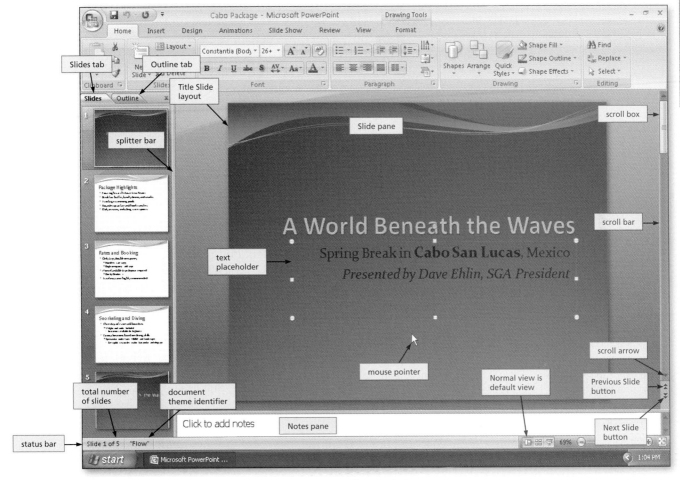

Figure 1–4

PLACEHOLDERS **Placeholders** are boxes with dotted or hatch-marked borders that are displayed when you create a new slide. All layouts except the Blank slide layout contain place-holders. Depending on the particular slide layout selected, title and subtitle placeholders are displayed for the slide title and subtitle; a content text placeholder is displayed for text, art, or a table, chart, picture, graphic, or movie. The title slide in Figure 1–4 has two text placehold-ers where you will type the main heading, or title, of a new slide and the subtitle.

MOUSE POINTER The **mouse pointer** becomes different shapes depending on the task you are performing in PowerPoint and the pointer's location on the screen. The mouse pointer in Figure 1–4 is the shape of a block arrow.

SCROLL BAR You use the **vertical scroll bar** to display different slides in the document window. When you add a second slide to a presentation, this vertical scroll bar appears on the right side of the Slide pane. On the scroll bar, the position of the **scroll box** reflects the location of the slide in the presentation that is displayed in the document window. A **scroll arrow** is located at each end of a scroll bar. To scroll through, or display different portions of the document in the document window, you can click a scroll arrow or drag the scroll box to move forward or backward through the presentation.

The Previous Slide button and the Next Slide button appear at the bottom of the vertical scroll bar. Click one of these buttons to advance through the slides backwards or forwards.

The **horizontal scroll bar** also may appear. It is located on the bottom of the Slide pane and allows you to display a portion of the slide when the entire slide does not fit on the screen.

STATUS BAR The **status bar**, located at the bottom of the document window above the Windows taskbar, presents information about the document, the progress of current tasks, and the status of certain commands and keys; it also provides controls for viewing the document. As you type text or perform certain commands, various indicators may appear on the status bar.

The left edge of the status bar in Figure 1–4 shows the current slide number followed by the total number of slides in the document and a document theme identifier. A **document theme** provides consistency in design and color throughout the entire presentation by setting the color scheme, font and font size, and layout of a presentation. Toward the right edge are buttons and controls you can use to change the view of a slide and adjust the size of the displayed document.

PowerPoint Views

The PowerPoint window display varies depending on the view. A **view** is the mode in which the presentation appears on the screen. PowerPoint has three main views: Normal, Slide Sorter, and Slide Show, and also Notes Page. The default view is **Normal view**, which is composed of three working areas that allow you to work on various aspects of a presentation simultaneously. The left side of the screen has a Tabs pane that consists of a **Slides tab** and an **Outline tab** that alternate between views of the presentation in a thumbnail, or miniature, view of the slides and an outline of the slide text. You can type the text of the presentation on the Outline tab and easily rearrange bulleted lists, paragraphs, and individual slides. As you type, you can view this text in the **Slide pane**, which shows a large view of the current slide on the right side of the window. You also can enter text, graphics, animations, and hyperlinks directly in the Slide pane. The **Notes pane** at the bottom of the window is an area where you can type notes and additional information. This text can consist of notes to yourself or remarks to share with your audience. If you want to work with your notes in full page format, you can display them in **Notes Page view**.

In Normal view, you can adjust the width of the Slide pane by dragging the **splitter bar** and the height of the Notes pane by dragging the pane borders. After you have created at least two slides, **scroll bars**, **scroll arrows**, and **scroll boxes** will appear on the right edge of the window.

Ribbon

The **Ribbon**, located near the top of the PowerPoint window, is the control center in PowerPoint (Figure 1–5a). The Ribbon provides easy, central access to the tasks you perform while creating a slide show. The Ribbon consists of tabs, groups, and commands. Each **tab** surrounds a collection of groups, and each group contains related commands.

Figure 1–5(a)

When you start PowerPoint, the Ribbon displays seven top-level tabs: Home, Insert, Design, Animations, Slide Show, Review, and View. The **Home tab**, called the primary tab, contains the more frequently used commands. To display a different tab on the Ribbon, click the top-level tab. That is, to display the Insert tab, click Insert on the Ribbon. To return to the Home tab, click Home on the Ribbon. The tab currently displayed is called the **active tab**.

To display more of the document in the document window, some users prefer to minimize the Ribbon, which hides the groups on the Ribbon and displays only the top-level tabs (Figure 1–5b). To use commands on a minimized Ribbon, click the top-level tab.

Each time you start PowerPoint, the Ribbon appears the same way it did the last time you used PowerPoint. The chapters in this book, however, begin with the Ribbon appearing as it did at the initial installation of the software. If you are stepping through this chapter on a computer and you want your Ribbon to match the figures in this book, read Appendix E.

Figure 1–5(b)

In addition to the top-level tabs, PowerPoint displays other tabs, called **contextual tabs**, when you perform certain tasks or work with objects such as pictures or tables. If you insert a picture in a slide, for example, the Picture Tools tab and its related subordinate Format tab appear (Figure 1–6). When you are finished working with the picture, the Picture Tools and Format tabs disappear from the Ribbon. PowerPoint determines when contextual tabs should appear and disappear based on tasks you perform. Some contextual tabs, such as the Chart Tools tab, have more than one related subordinate tab.

Figure 1–6

Commands on the Ribbon include buttons, boxes (text boxes, check boxes, etc.), and galleries (Figure 1–6). A **gallery** is a set of choices, often graphical, arranged in a grid or in a list. You can scroll through choices on an in-Ribbon gallery by clicking the gallery's scroll arrows. Or, you can click a gallery's More button to view more gallery options on the screen at a time. Some buttons and boxes have arrows that, when clicked, also display a gallery; others always cause a gallery to be displayed when clicked. Most galleries support **live preview**, which is a feature that allows you to point to a gallery choice and see its effect in the document - without actually selecting the choice (Figure 1–7).

Figure 1–7

Some commands on the Ribbon display an image to help you remember their function. When you point to a command on the Ribbon, all or part of the command glows in shades of yellow and orange, and an Enhanced ScreenTip appears on the screen. An **Enhanced ScreenTip** is an on-screen note that provides the name of the command, available keyboard shortcut(s), a description of the command, and sometimes instructions for how to obtain help about the command (Figure 1–8). Enhanced ScreenTips are more detailed than a typical ScreenTip, which usually only displays the name of the command.

Figure 1–8

The lower-right corner of some groups on the Ribbon has a small arrow, called a **Dialog Box Launcher**, that when clicked displays a dialog box or a task pane with additional options for the group (Figure 1–9). When presented with a dialog box, you make selections and must close the dialog box before returning to the document. A **task pane**, by contrast, is a window that can remain open and visible while you work in the document.

Figure 1–9

Mini Toolbar and Shortcut Menus

The **Mini toolbar**, which appears automatically based on tasks you perform, contains commands related to changing the appearance of text in a slide. All commands on the Mini toolbar also exist on the Ribbon. The purpose of the Mini toolbar is to minimize mouse movement. For example, if you want to use a command that currently is not displayed on the active tab, you can use the command on the Mini toolbar - instead of switching to a different tab to use the command.

When the Mini toolbar appears, it initially is transparent (Figure 1–10a on the next page). If you do not use the transparent Mini toolbar, it disappears from the screen. To use the Mini toolbar, move the mouse pointer into the toolbar, which causes the Mini toolbar to change from a transparent to bright appearance (Figure 1–10b on the next page).

BTW

Turning Off the Mini Toolbar
If you do not want the Mini toolbar to display, click the Office Button, click the PowerPoint Options button on the Office Button menu, and then clear the 'Show Mini Toolbar on selection' check box in the Popular panel.

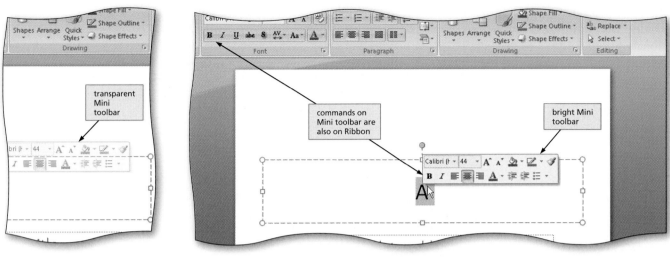

(a) Transparent Mini Toolbar

(b) Bright Mini Toolbar

Figure 1–10

A **shortcut menu**, which appears when you right-click an object, is a list of frequently used commands that relate to the right-clicked object. When you right-click a scroll bar, for example, a shortcut menu appears with commands related to the scroll bar. If you right-click an item in the document window, PowerPoint displays both the Mini toolbar and a shortcut menu (Figure 1–11).

Figure 1–11

Quick Access Toolbar

The **Quick Access Toolbar**, located by default above the Ribbon, provides easy access to frequently used commands (Figure 1–12a). The commands on the Quick Access Toolbar always are available, regardless of the task you are performing. Initially, the Quick Access Toolbar contains the Save, Undo, and Redo commands. If you click the Customize Quick Access Toolbar button, PowerPoint provides a list of commands you quickly can add to and remove from the Quick Access Toolbar (Figure 1–12b).

Figure 1–12(a) Quick Access Toolbar above Ribbon

Figure 1–12(b) Customize Quick Access Toolbar

BTW

Quick Access Toolbar Commands
To add a Ribbon command to the Quick Access Toolbar, right-click the command on the Ribbon and then click Add to Quick Access Toolbar on the shortcut menu. To delete a command from the Quick Access Toolbar, right-click the command on the Quick Access Toolbar and then click Remove from Quick Access Toolbar on the shortcut menu. To display the Quick Access Toolbar below the Ribbon, right-click the Quick Access Toolbar and then click Place Quick Access Toolbar below the Ribbon on the shortcut menu.

You also can add other commands to or delete commands from the Quick Access Toolbar so that it contains the commands you use most often. As you add commands to the Quick Access Toolbar, its commands may interfere with the document title on the title bar. For this reason, PowerPoint provides an option of displaying the Quick Access Toolbar below the Ribbon (Figure 1–12c).

Figure 1–12(c) Quick Access Toolbar below Ribbon

Each time you start PowerPoint, the Quick Access Toolbar appears the same way it did the last time you used PowerPoint. The chapters in this book, however, begin with the Quick Access Toolbar appearing as it did at the initial installation of the software. If you are stepping through this chapter on a computer and you want your Quick Access Toolbar to match the figures in this book, you should reset your Quick Access Toolbar. For more information about how to reset the Quick Access Toolbar, read Appendix E.

Office Button

While the Ribbon is a control center for creating documents, the **Office Button** is a central location for managing and sharing documents. When you click the Office Button, located in the upper-left corner of the window, PowerPoint displays the Office Button menu (Figure 1–13). A **menu** contains a list of commands.

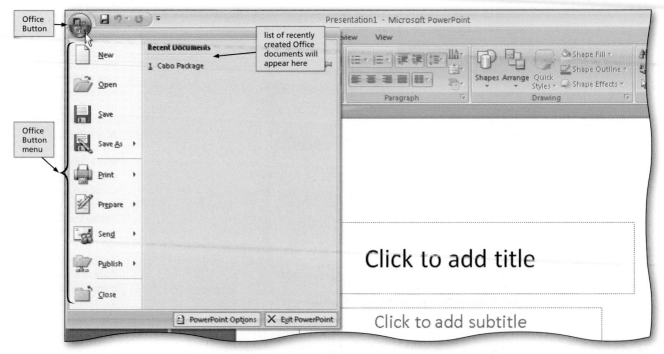

Figure 1–13

When you click the New, Open, Save As, and Print commands on the Office Button menu, PowerPoint displays a dialog box with additional options. The Save As, Print, Prepare, Send, and Publish commands have an arrow to their right. If you point to this arrow, PowerPoint displays a **submenu**, which is a list of additional commands associated with the selected command (Figure 1–14). For the Prepare, Send, and Publish commands that do not display a dialog box when clicked, you can point either to the command or the arrow to display the submenu.

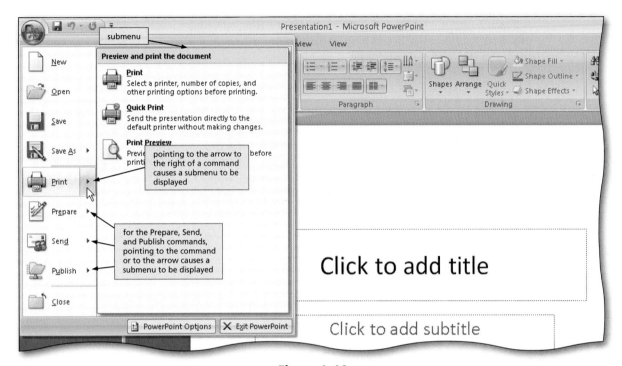

Figure 1–14

Key Tips

If you prefer using the keyboard instead of the mouse, you can press the ALT key on the keyboard to display a **Key Tip badge**, or keyboard code icon, for certain commands (Figure 1–15). To select a command using the keyboard, press its displayed code letter, or **Key Tip**. When you press a Key Tip, additional Key Tips related to the selected command may appear. For example, to select the New command on the Office Button menu, press the ALT key, then press the F key, then press the N key.

Figure 1–15

To remove the Key Tip badges from the screen, press the ALT key or the ESC key until all Key Tip badges disappear, or click the mouse anywhere in the PowerPoint window.

Choosing a Document Theme

You easily can give a presentation a professional and consistent appearance by using a document theme. This collection of formatting choices includes a set of colors (the color theme), a set of heading and content text fonts (the font theme), and a set of lines and fill effects (the effects theme). These themes allow you to choose and change the appearance of all the slides or individual slides in your presentation.

<table>
<tr><td>

**Plan
Ahead**

</td><td>

Find the appropriate theme.
In the initial steps of this project, you will select a document theme by locating a particular built-in theme in the Themes group. You could, however, apply a theme at any time while creating the presentation. Some PowerPoint slide show designers create presentations using the default Office Theme. This blank design allows them to concentrate on the words being used to convey the message and does not distract them with colors and various text attributes. Once the text is entered, the designers then select an appropriate document theme.

</td></tr>
</table>

To Choose a Document Theme

The document theme identifier shows the theme currently used in the slide show. PowerPoint initially uses the **Office Theme** until you select a different theme. The following steps change the theme for this presentation from the Office Theme to the Flow document theme.

- Click Design on the Ribbon to display the Design tab (Figure 1–16).

Figure 1–16

2

- Click the More button in the Themes gallery to expand the gallery, which shows more Built-In theme gallery options (Figure 1–17).

 Experiment

- Point to various document themes in the Themes gallery and watch the colors and fonts change on the title slide.

Q&A Are the themes displayed in a specific order?

Yes. They are arranged in alphabetical order running from left to right. If you point to a theme, a ScreenTip with the design's name appears on the screen.

Q&A What if I change my mind and do not want to select a new theme?

Click anywhere outside the All Themes gallery to close the gallery.

Figure 1–17

3

- Click the Flow theme to apply this theme to Slide 1 (Figure 1–18).

Q&A If I decide at some future time that this design does not fit the theme of my presentation, can I apply a different design?

Yes. You can repeat these steps at any time while creating your presentation.

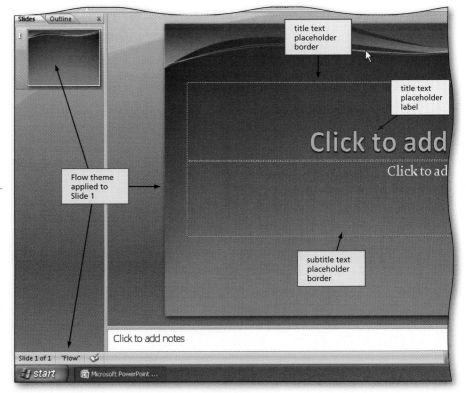

Figure 1–18

Creating a Title Slide

With the exception of a blank slide and a slide with a picture and caption, PowerPoint assumes every new slide has a title. Many of PowerPoint's layouts have both a title text placeholder and at least one content placeholder. To make creating a presentation easier, any text you type after a new slide appears becomes title text in the title text placeholder. The following steps create the title slide for this presentation.

<table>
<tr><td>Plan
Ahead</td><td>

Choose the words for the slide.
No doubt you have heard the phrase, "You get only one chance to make a first impression." The same philosophy holds true for a PowerPoint presentation. The title slide gives your audience an initial sense of what they are about to see and hear. It is, therefore, extremely important to choose the text for this slide carefully. Avoid stating the obvious in the title. Instead, create interest and curiosity using key ideas from the presentation.
Some PowerPoint users create the title slide as their last step in the design process so that it reflects the tone of the presentation. They begin by planning the final slide in the presentation so that they know where and how they want to end the slide show. All the slides in the presentation should work toward meeting this final slide.

</td></tr>
</table>

To Enter the Presentation Title

As you begin typing text in the title text placeholder, the title text also is displayed in the Slide 1 thumbnail in the Slides tab. PowerPoint **line wraps** text that exceeds the width of the placeholder. The presentation title for Project 1 is A World Beneath the Waves. This title creates interest by introducing the concept of exploring the life under water. The following step creates the slide show's title.

• Click the label, Click to add title, located inside the title text placeholder to select the placeholder (Figure 1–19).

Figure 1–19

2

- Type A World Beneath the Waves in the title text placeholder. Do not press the ENTER key (Figure 1–20).

Q&A

What if a button with two lines and two arrows appears on the left side of the title text placeholder?

The **AutoFit** button displays because PowerPoint attempts to reduce the size of the letters when the title text does not fit on a single line. If you are creating a slide and need to squeeze an extra line in the text placeholder, you can click this button to resize the existing text in the placeholder so the spillover text will fit on the slide.

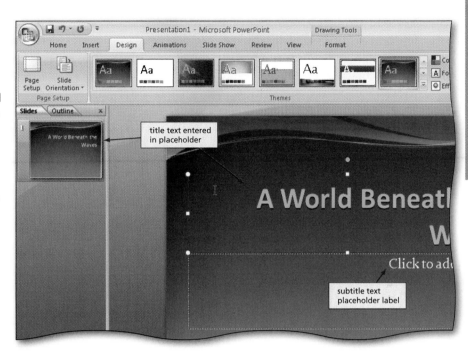

Figure 1–20

Correcting a Mistake When Typing

If you type the wrong letter, press the BACKSPACE key to erase all the characters back to and including the one that is incorrect. If you mistakenly press the ENTER key after typing the title and the insertion point is on the new line, simply press the BACKSPACE key to return the insertion point to the right of the letter s in the word Waves.

When you install PowerPoint, the default setting allows you to reverse up to the last 20 changes by clicking the Undo button on the Quick Access Toolbar. The ScreenTip that appears when you point to the Undo button changes to indicate the type of change just made. For example, if you type text in the title text placeholder and then point to the Undo button, the ScreenTip that appears is Undo Typing. For clarity, when referencing the Undo button in this project, the name displaying in the ScreenTip is referenced. You can reapply a change that you reversed with the Undo button by clicking the Redo button on the Quick Access Toolbar. Clicking the Redo button reverses the last undo action. The ScreenTip name reflects the type of reversal last performed.

Paragraphs

Subtitle text in the subtitle text placeholder supports the title text. It can appear on one or more lines in the placeholder. To create more than one subtitle line, you press the ENTER key after typing some words. PowerPoint creates a new line, which is the second paragraph in the placeholder. A **paragraph** is a segment of text with the same format that begins when you press the ENTER key and ends when you press the ENTER key again. This new paragraph is the same level as the previous paragraph. A **level** is a position within a structure, such as an outline, that indicates the magnitude of importance. PowerPoint allows for five paragraph levels.

To Enter the Presentation Subtitle Paragraph

The first subtitle paragraph links to the title by giving specific details about the vacation location, and the second paragraph gives information about the person who will be speaking to the audience. The following steps enter the presentation subtitle.

- Click the label, Click to add subtitle, located inside the subtitle text placeholder to select the placeholder (Figure 1–21).

Figure 1–21

- Type Spring Break in Cabo San Lucas, Mexico and then press the ENTER key.

- Type Presented by Dave Ehlin, SGA President but do not press the ENTER key (Figure 1–22).

Q&A Why do red wavy lines appear below the words, Cabo and Ehlin?

The lines indicate possible spelling errors.

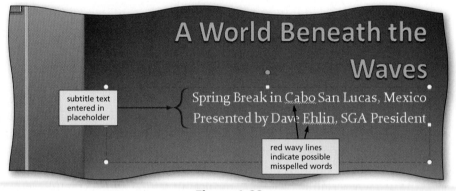

Figure 1–22

Plan Ahead	**Identify how to format specific elements of the text.**

Most of the time, you use the document theme's text attributes, color scheme, and layout. Occasionally, you may want to change the way a presentation looks, however, and still keep a particular document theme. PowerPoint gives you that flexibility.

Graphic designers use several rules when formatting text.

- Avoid all capital letters, if possible. Audiences have difficulty comprehending sentences typed in all capital letters, especially when the lines exceed seven words. All capital letters leaves no room for emphasis or inflection, so readers get confused about what material deserves particular attention. Some document themes, however, have a default title text style of all capital letters.

- Avoid text with a font size less than 24 point. Audience members generally will sit a maximum of 50 feet from a screen, and at this distance 24-point type is the smallest size text they can read comfortably without straining.

- Make careful color choices. Color evokes emotions, and a careless color choice may elicit the incorrect psychological response. PowerPoint provides a color palette with hundreds of colors. The built-in document themes use complementary colors that work well together. If you stray from these themes and add your own color choices, without a good reason to make the changes, your presentation is apt to become ineffective.

Formatting Characters in a Presentation

Recall that each document theme determines the color scheme, font and font size, and layout of a presentation. You can use a specific document theme and then change the characters' formats any time before, during, or after you type the text.

Fonts and Font Styles

Characters that appear on the screen are a specific shape and size. Examples of how you can modify the appearance, or **format**, of these typed characters on the screen and in print include changing the font, style, size, and color. The **font**, or typeface, defines the appearance and shape of the letters, numbers, punctuation marks, and symbols. **Style** indicates how the characters are formatted. PowerPoint's text font styles include regular, italic, bold, and bold italic. **Size** specifies the height of the characters and is gauged by a measurement system that uses points. A **point** is 1/72 of an inch in height. Thus, a character with a point size of 36 is 36/72 (or 1/2) of an inch in height. **Color** defines the hue of the characters.

This presentation uses the Flow document theme, which uses particular font styles and font sizes. The Flow document theme default title text font is named Calibri. It has a bold style with no special effects, and its size is 56 point. The Flow document theme default subtitle text font is Constantia with a font size of 26 point.

BTW

Formatting Words
To format one word, position the insertion point anywhere in the word. Then make the formatting changes you desire. The entire word does not need to be selected for the change to occur.

To Select a Paragraph

You can use many techniques to format characters. When you want to apply the same formats to multiple words or paragraphs, it is efficient to select the desired text and then make the desired changes to all the characters simultaneously. The first formatting change you will make will apply to the second paragraph of the title slide subtitle. The following step selects this paragraph.

1

- Triple-click the paragraph, Presented by Dave Ehlin, SGA President, in the subtitle text placeholder to select the paragraph (Figure 1–23).

Q&A

Can I select the paragraph using a technique other than triple-clicking?

Yes. You can move your mouse pointer to the left of the first paragraph and then drag it to the end of the line.

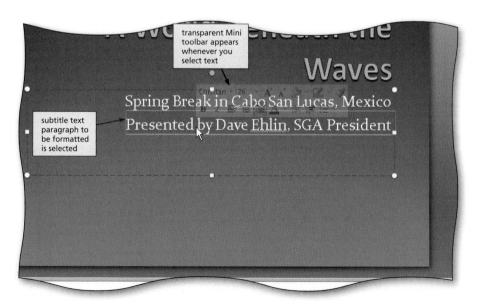

Figure 1–23

To Italicize Text

Different font styles often are used on slides to make them more appealing to the reader and to emphasize particular text. Italic type, used sparingly, draws the readers' eyes to these characters. The following step adds emphasis to the second line of the subtitle text by changing regular text to italic text.

- With the subtitle text still selected, click the Italic button on the Mini toolbar to italicize that text on the slide and on the slide thumbnail (Figure 1–24).

Q&A

If I change my mind and decide not to italicize the text, how can I remove this style?

Select the italicized text and then click the Italic button. As a result, the Italic button will not be selected, and the text will not have the italic font style.

Figure 1–24

Other Ways
1. Right-click selected text, click Font on shortcut menu, click Italic in Font style list   2. Click Home tab, click Italic in Font group   3. Press CTRL+I

To Select Multiple Paragraphs

Each of the subtitle lines is a separate paragraph. As previously discussed, PowerPoint creates a new paragraph each time you press the ENTER key. To change the character formatting in both paragraphs, it is efficient to select the desired text and then make the desired changes to all the characters simultaneously.

The next formatting change you will make will apply to both title slide subtitle paragraphs. The following step selects the first paragraph so that you can format both paragraphs concurrently.

- With the second subtitle text paragraph selected, press the CTRL key and then triple-click the first subtitle text paragraph, Spring Break in Cabo San Lucas, Mexico, to select both paragraphs (Figure 1–25).

Q&A

Can I use a different technique to select both subtitle text paragraphs?

Yes. Click the placeholder border so that it appears as a solid line. When the placeholder is selected in this manner, formatting changes will apply to all text in the placeholder.

Figure 1–25

<table>
<tr><td>

Identify how to format specific elements of the text.
When selecting text colors, try to limit using red. At least 15 percent of men have difficulty distinguishing varying shades of green or red. They also often see the color purple as blue and the color brown as green. This problem is more pronounced when the colors appear in small areas, such as slide paragraphs or line chart bars.

</td><td>

Plan
Ahead

</td></tr>
</table>

To Change the Text Color

PowerPoint allows you to use one or more text colors in a presentation. To add more emphasis to the title slide subtitle text, you decide to change the color. The following steps add emphasis to both subtitle text paragraphs by changing the font color from white to dark blue.

- With both paragraphs selected, click the Font Color arrow on the Mini toolbar to display the palette of Theme Colors and Standard Colors (Figure 1–26).

 If the Mini toolbar disappears from the screen, how can I display it once again?

Right-click the text, and the Mini toolbar should appear.

Figure 1–26

❷

- Click the Dark Blue button in the Standard Colors row on the Mini toolbar (row 1, column 9) to change the font color to dark blue (Figure 1–27).

 Why did I select the color, dark blue?

Dark blue is one of the 10 standard colors associated with every document theme, and it works well with the shades of blue already on the slide. An additional consideration is that dark colors print well.

Figure 1–27

❸

- Click outside the selected area to deselect the two paragraphs.

Other Ways
1. Right-click selected text, click Font on shortcut menu, click Font color button, click Dark Blue in Standard Colors row
2. Click Home tab, click Font Color arrow in Font group, click Dark Blue in Standard Colors row

To Select a Group of Words

PowerPoint designers use many techniques to format characters. To apply the same formats to multiple words or paragraphs, they select the desired text and then make the desired changes to all the characters simultaneously.

To add emphasis to the vacation destination, you want to increase the font size and change the font style to bold for the words, Cabo San Lucas. You could perform these actions separately, but it is more efficient to select this group of words and then change the font attributes. The following steps select a group of words.

- Position the mouse pointer immediately to the left of the first character of the text to be selected (in this case, the C in Cabo) (Figure 1–28).

Figure 1–28

- Drag the mouse pointer through the last character of the text to be selected (in this case, the s in Lucas) (Figure 1–29).

Figure 1–29

To Increase Font Size

To add emphasis, you increase the font size for Cabo San Lucas. The Increase Font Size button on the Mini toolbar increases the font size in preset increments. The following step uses this button to increase the font size.

- Click the Increase Font Size button on the Mini toolbar once to increase the font size of the selected text from 26 to 28 point (Figure 1–30).

Other Ways

1. Click Home tab, click Increase Font Size button in Font group
2. Click Home tab, click Font Size box arrow, click new font size
3. Press CTRL+SHIFT+>

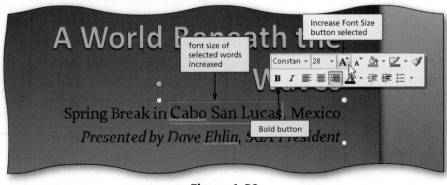

Figure 1–30

To Bold Text

Bold characters display somewhat thicker and darker than those that display in a regular font style. Clicking the Bold button on the Mini toolbar is an efficient method of bolding text. To add more emphasis to the vacation destination, you want to bold the words, Cabo San Lucas. The following step bolds this text.

- Click the Bold button on the Mini toolbar to bold the three selected words (Figure 1–31).

Figure 1–31

Other Ways
1. Click Home tab, click Bold button in Font group
2. Press CTRL+B

Identify how to format specific elements of the text.
Avoid line wraps. Your audience's eyes want to stop at the end of a line. Thus, you must plan your words carefully or adjust the font size so that each point displays on only one line.

Plan
Ahead

To Decrease the Title Slide Title Text Font Size

The last word of the title text, Waves, appears on a line by itself. For aesthetic reasons, it is advantageous to have this word appear with the rest of the title on a single line. One way to fit text on one line is to decrease the font size. The process is similar to increasing the font size. Clicking the Decrease Font Size button on the Mini toolbar decreases the size in preset increments. The following steps decrease the font size from 56 to 48 point.

- Select the title slide title text, A World Beneath the Waves (Figure 1–32).

Figure 1–32

2
- Click the Decrease Font Size button on the Mini toolbar twice to decrease the font size from 56 to 48 point (Figure 1–33).

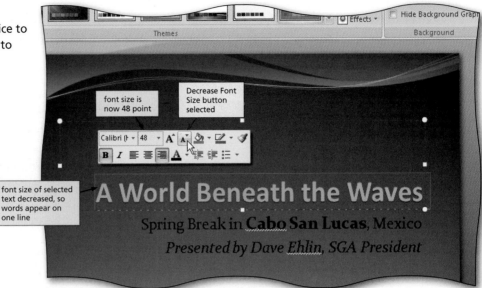

Figure 1–33

Saving the Project

While you are building a presentation, the computer stores it in memory. When you save a presentation, the computer places it on a storage medium such as a USB flash drive, CD, or hard disk. A saved presentation is referred to as a **file**. A **file name** is the name assigned to a file when it is saved.

It is important to save the presentation frequently for the following reasons:

- The presentation in memory will be lost if the computer is turned off or you lose electrical power while PowerPoint is open.
- If you run out of time before completing your project, you may finish your presentation at a future time without starting over.

Plan Ahead

BTW

Saving in a Previous PowerPoint Format
To ensure that your presentation will open in an earlier version of PowerPoint, you must save your file in PowerPoint 97–2003 format. Files saved in this format have the .ppt extension.

Determine where to save the document.
When saving a document, you must decide which storage medium to use.

- If you always work on the same computer and have no need to transport your projects to a different location, then your computer's hard drive will suffice as a storage location. It is a good idea, however, to save a backup copy of your projects on a separate medium in case the file becomes corrupted or the computer's hard drive fails.

- If you plan to work on your projects in various locations or on multiple computers, then you should save your projects on a portable medium, such as a USB flash drive or CD. The projects in this book use a USB flash drive, which saves files quickly and reliably and can be reused. CDs are easily portable and serve as good backups for the final versions of projects because they generally can save files only one time.

To Save a Presentation

You have performed many tasks and do not want to lose the work completed thus far. Thus, you should save the presentation. The following steps save a presentation on a USB flash drive using the file name, Cabo Package.

1

• With a USB flash drive connected to one of the computer's USB ports, click the Save button on the Quick Access Toolbar to display the Save As dialog box. (Figure 1–34).

Q&A Do I have to save to a USB flash drive?

No. You can save to any device or folder. A **folder** is a specific location on a storage medium. You can save to the default folder or a different folder. You also can create your own folders, which is explained later in this book.

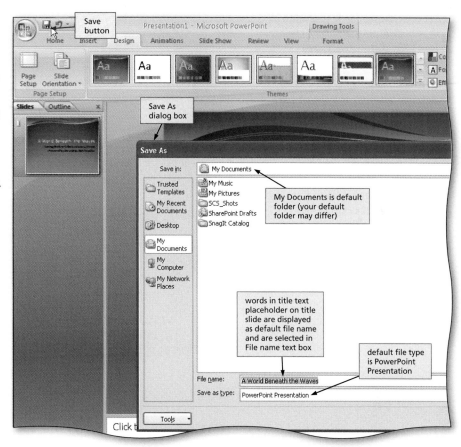

Figure 1–34

2

• Type Cabo Package in the File name box to change the file name. Do not press the ENTER key after typing the file name (Figure 1–35).

Q&A What characters can I use in a file name?

A file name can have a maximum of 255 characters, including spaces. The only invalid characters are the backslash (\), slash (/), colon (:), asterisk (*), question mark (?), quotation mark ("), less than symbol (<), greater than symbol (>), and vertical bar (|).

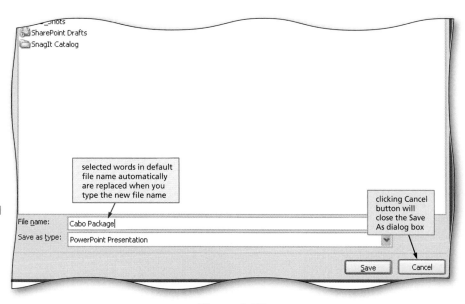

Figure 1–35

3

- Click the Save in box arrow to display a list of available drives and folders (Figure 1–36).

Q&A Why is my list of files, folders, and drives arranged and named differently from those shown in the figure?

Your computer's configuration determines how the list of files and folders is displayed and how drives are named. You can change the save location by clicking shortcuts on the **My Places bar**.

Q&A How do I save the file if I am not using a USB flash drive?

Use the same process, but be certain to select your device in the Save in list.

Figure 1–36

4

- Click UDISK 2.0 (E:) in the Save in list to select the USB flash drive, Drive E in this case, as the new save location (Figure 1–37).

Q&A What if my USB flash drive has a different name or letter?

It is very likely that your USB flash drive will have a different name and drive letter and be connected to a different port. Verify the device in your Save in list is correct.

Figure 1–37

5

- Click the Save button in the Save As dialog box to save the presentation on the USB flash drive with the file name, Cabo Package (Figure 1–38).

Q&A

How do I know that the project is saved?

While PowerPoint is saving your file, it briefly displays a message on the status bar indicating the amount of the file saved. In addition, your USB drive may have a light that flashes during the save process.

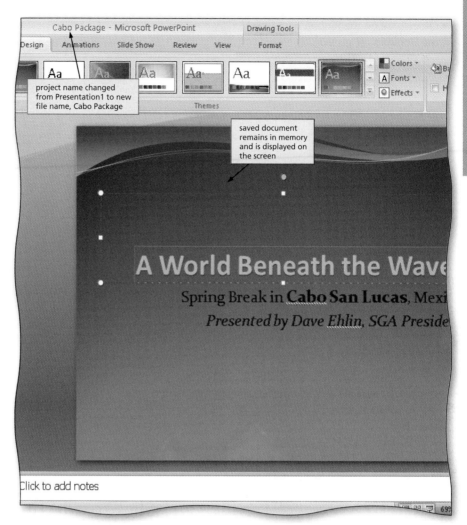

Figure 1–38

Adding a New Slide to a Presentation

With the title slide for the presentation created, the next step is to add the first text slide immediately after the title slide. Usually, when you create a presentation, you add slides with text, graphics, or charts. Some placeholders allow you to double-click the placeholder and then access other objects, such as media clips, charts, diagrams, and organization charts. You can change the layout for a slide at any time during the creation of a presentation.

To Add a New Text Slide with a Bulleted List

When you add a new slide, PowerPoint uses the Title and Content slide layout. This layout provides a title placeholder and a content area for text, art, charts, and other graphics. A vertical scroll bar appears in the Slide pane when you add the second slide so that you can move from slide to slide easily. A thumbnail of this slide also appears in the Slides tab. The following steps add a new slide with the Title and Content slide layout.

Other Ways

1. Click Office Button, click Save, type file name, select drive or folder, click Save button

2. Press CTRL+S or press SHIFT+F12, type file name, select drive or folder, click Save button

● Click Home on the Ribbon to display the Home tab (Figure 1–39).

Figure 1–39

2

● Click the New Slide button in the Slides group to insert a new slide with the Title and Content layout (Figure 1–40).

Q&A
Why does the bullet character display a blue dot?

The Flow document theme determines the bullet characters. Each paragraph level has an associated bullet character.

Q&A
I clicked the New Slide arrow instead of the New Slide button. What should I do?

Click the Title and Content slide thumbnail in the layout gallery.

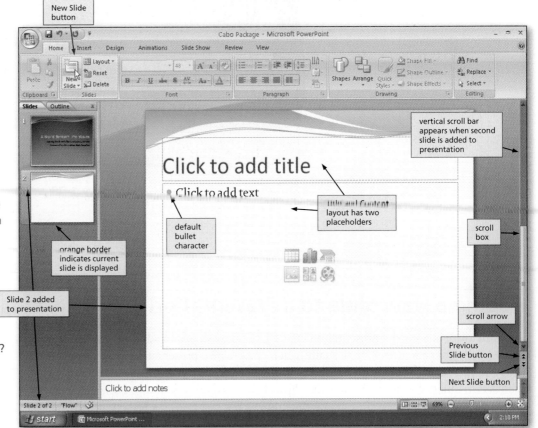

Figure 1–40

Other Ways
1. Press CTRL+M

**Plan
Ahead**

> **Choose the words for the slide.**
> All presentations should follow the 7 × 7 rule which states that each slide should have a maximum of seven lines, and each line should have a maximum of seven words. PowerPoint designers must choose their words carefully and, in turn, help viewers read the slides easily.

Creating a Text Slide with a Single-Level Bulleted List

The information in the Slide 2 text placeholder is presented in a bulleted list. All the bullets appear at the same paragraph level, called the first level.

To Enter a Slide Title

PowerPoint assumes every new slide has a title. The title for Slide 2 is Package Highlights. The following step enters this title.

- Click the label, Click to add title, to select it and then type `Package Highlights` in the placeholder. Do not press the ENTER key (Figure 1–41).

Q&A What are those six icons grouped in the middle of the slide?

You can click one of the icons to insert a specific type of content: table, chart, SmartArt graphic, picture, clip art, or media clip.

Figure 1–41

To Select a Text Placeholder

Before you can type text into the text placeholder, you first must select it. The following step selects the text placeholder on Slide 2.

- Click the label, Click to add text, to select the text placeholder (Figure 1–42).

Q&A Why does my mouse pointer have a different shape?

If you move the mouse pointer away from the bullet, it will change shape.

Figure 1–42

Other Ways
1. Press CTRL+ENTER

To Type a Single-Level Bulleted List

The content placeholder provides an area for the text characters. When you click inside a placeholder, you then can type or paste text. If your text exceeds the size of the placeholder, PowerPoint will attempt to make the text fit by reducing the text size and line spacing. **Line spacing** is the amount of vertical space between the lines of text.

As discussed previously, a bulleted list is a list of paragraphs, each of which is preceded by a bullet. A paragraph is a segment of text ended by pressing the ENTER key. The next step is to type the single-level bulleted list, which consists of five paragraphs (Figure 1–1b on page PPT 3). The following steps create a single-level bulleted list.

- **Type** Four nights at the Azure Seas Resort and then press the ENTER key to begin a new bulleted first-level paragraph (Figure 1–43).

Q&A Can I delete bullets on a slide?

Yes. If you do not want bullets to display on a particular paragraph, click the Bullets button in the Paragraph group on the Home tab or right-click the paragraph and then click the Bullets button on the Mini toolbar.

Figure 1–43

- **Type** Breakfast buffet, lunch, dinner, and snacks and then press the ENTER key.

- **Type** Two large swimming pools and then press the ENTER key.

- **Type** Round-trip airfare and hotel transfers and then press the ENTER key.

- **Type** Daily activities, including water sports but do not press the ENTER key (Figure 1–44).

Q&A I pressed the ENTER key in error, and now a new bullet appears after the last entry on this slide. How can I remove this extra bullet?

Press the BACKSPACE key.

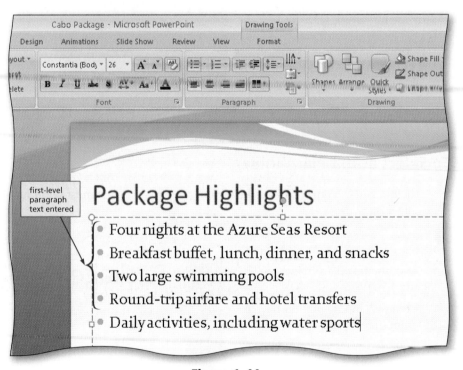

Figure 1–44

Creating a Text Slide with a Multi-Level Bulleted List

Slides 3 and 4 in Figure 1–1 on pages PPT 3 and 4 contain more than one level of bulleted text. A slide that consists of more than one level of bulleted text is called a **multi-level bulleted list slide**. Beginning with the second level, each paragraph indents to the right of the preceding level and is pushed down to a lower level. For example, if you increase the indent of a first-level paragraph, it becomes a second-level paragraph.

Creating a text slide with a multi-level bulleted list requires several steps. Initially, you enter a slide title in the title text placeholder. Next, you select the content text placeholder. Then, you type the text for the multi-level bulleted list, increasing and decreasing the indents as needed. The next several sections add a slide with a multi-level bulleted list.

To Add a New Slide and Enter a Slide Title

When you add a new slide to a presentation, PowerPoint keeps the same layout used on the previous slide. PowerPoint assumes every new slide has a title. The title for Slide 3 is Rates and Booking. The following steps add a new slide (Slide 3) and enter a title.

1
- Click the New Slide button in the Slides group on the Home tab to insert a new slide with the Title and Content layout (Figure 1–45).

Figure 1–45

- Click the title text placeholder and then type Rates and Booking in this placeholder. Do not press the ENTER key (Figure 1–46).

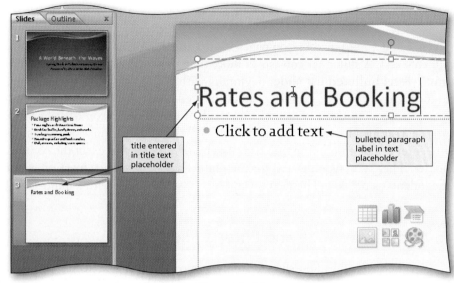

Figure 1–46

To Type a Multi-Level Bulleted List

In a multi-level bulleted list, a lower-level paragraph is a subset of a higher-level paragraph. It usually contains information that supports the topic in the paragraph immediately above it.

The next step is to select the content text placeholder and then type the multi-level bulleted list, which consists of six entries (Figure 1–1c on page PPT 3). Creating a lower-level paragraph is called **demoting** text; creating a higher-level paragraph is called **promoting** text. The following steps create a list consisting of three levels.

- Click the bulleted paragraph text placeholder.

- Type Only $495 double occupancy and then press the ENTER key (Figure 1–47).

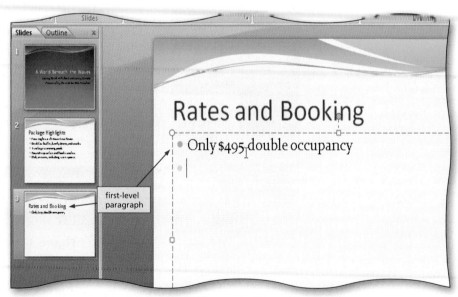

Figure 1–47

2

- Click the Increase List Level button in the Paragraph group to indent the second paragraph below the first and create a second-level paragraph (Figure 1–48).

Q&A

Why does the bullet for this paragraph have a different size and color?

A different bullet is assigned to each paragraph level.

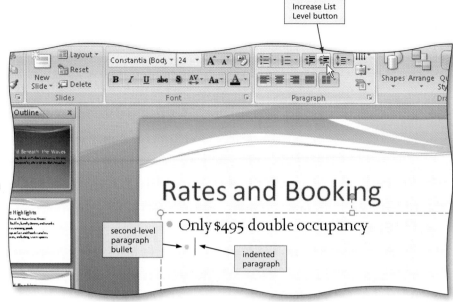

Figure 1–48

3

- Type `Non-diver rate: $275` and then press the ENTER key to add a new paragraph at the same level as the previous paragraph.

- Type `Single occupancy: add $150` and then press the ENTER key (Figure 1–49).

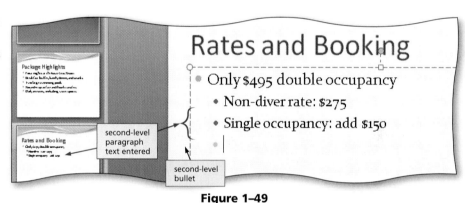

Figure 1–49

4

- Click the Decrease List Level button in the Paragraph group so that the second-level paragraph becomes a first-level paragraph (Figure 1–50).

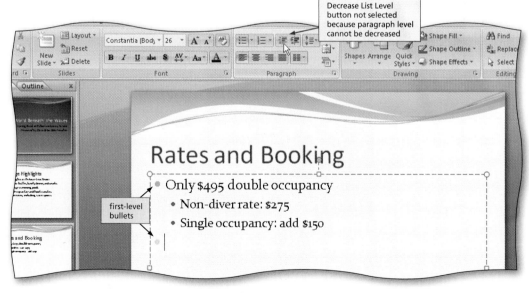

Other Ways

1. Press TAB to promote paragraph; press SHIFT+TAB to demote paragraph

Figure 1–50

To Type the Remaining Text for Slide 3

The following steps complete the text for Slide 3.

1 Type `Nonrefundable $150 deposit required` and then press the ENTER key.

2 Click the Increase List Level button in the Paragraph group to demote the paragraph.

3 Type `Due by October 1` and then press the ENTER key.

4 Click the Decrease List Level button in the Paragraph group to promote the paragraph.

5 Type `Travel insurance highly recommended` but do not press the ENTER key (Figure 1–51).

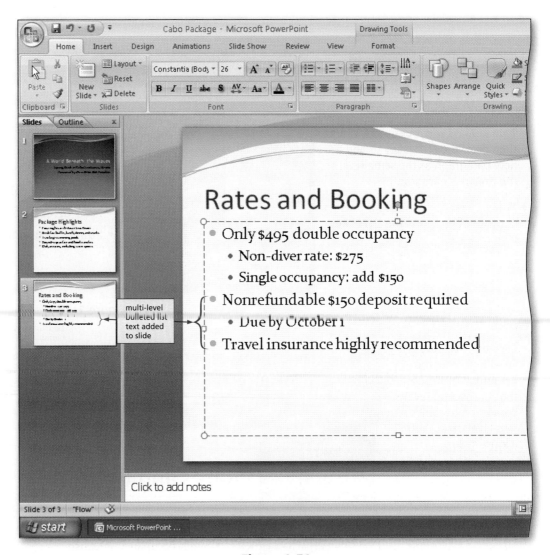

Figure 1–51

To Create Slide 4

Slide 4 is the final multi-level bulleted text slide in this presentation. It has three levels. The following steps create Slide 4.

1 Click the New Slide button in the Slides group.

2 Type `Snorkeling and Diving` in the title text placeholder.

3 Press CTRL+ENTER to move the insertion point to the text placeholder.

4 Type `Three days of two-tank boat dives` and then press the ENTER key.

5 Click the Increase List Level button. Type `Weights and tanks included` and then press the ENTER key (Figure 1–52).

Figure 1–52

To Create a Third-Level Paragraph

Slide 4 contains detailed information about the particular dives. Each additional paragraph becomes more specific and supports the information in the paragraph above it.

The next line in Slide 4 is indented an additional level, to the third level. The following steps demote the text to a third-level paragraph.

• Click the Increase List Level button so that the second-level paragraph becomes a third-level paragraph (Figure 1–53).

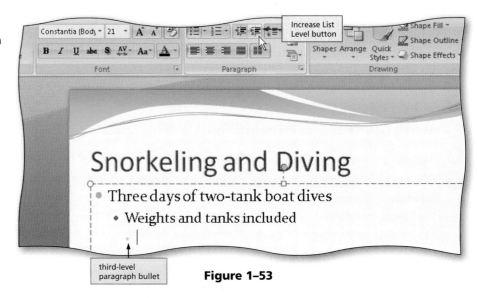

Figure 1–53

2

• Type `Instructors available for beginners` and then press the ENTER key to create a second third-level paragraph (Figure 1–54).

Figure 1–54

3

• Click the Decrease List Level button two times so that the insertion point appears at the first level (Figure 1–55).

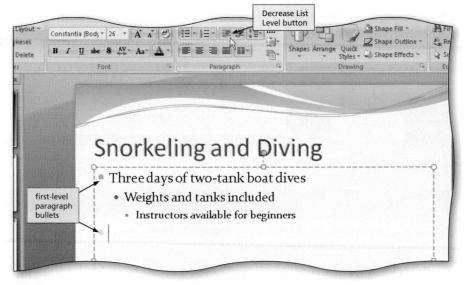

Figure 1–55

To Type the Remaining Text for Slide 4

The next three paragraphs concern what divers and snorkelers will view. The following steps type the remaining text for Slide 4.

1 Type `Various locations based on diving skills` and then press the ENTER key.

2 Press the TAB key to increase the indent to the second level.

3 Type `Spectacular underwater wildlife and landscapes` and then press the ENTER key.

4 Press the TAB key to increase the indent to the third level.

5 Type `See squids, sea turtles, snakes, barracudas, and stingrays` but do not press the ENTER key (Figure 1–56).

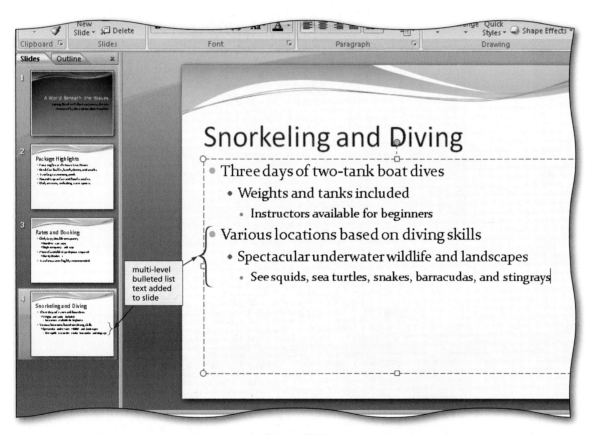

Figure 1–56

Choose the words for the slide.
After the last bulleted list slide in the slide show appears during a slide show, the default PowerPoint setting is to end the presentation with a **black slide**. This black slide appears only when the slide show is running and concludes the slide show, so your audience never sees the PowerPoint window. It is a good idea, however, to end the presentation with a final, closing slide to display at the end of the presentation. This slide ends the presentation gracefully and should be an exact copy, or a very similar copy, of your title slide. The audience will recognize that the presentation is drawing to a close when this slide appears. It can remain on the screen when the audience asks questions, approaches the speaker for further information, or exits the room.

Ending a Slide Show with a Closing Slide

All the text slides are created for the Cabo Package slide show. This presentation thus far consists of a title slide, one text slide with a single-level bulleted list, and two text slides with a multi-level bulleted list. A closing slide that resembles the title slide is the final slide to create.

To Duplicate a Slide

When two slides contain similar information and have the same format, duplicating one slide and then making minor modifications to the new slide saves time and increases consistency.

Slide 5 will have the same layout and design as Slide 1. The most expedient method of creating this slide is to copy Slide 1 and then make minor modifications to the new slide. The following steps duplicate the title slide.

1
- Click the Slide 1 thumbnail in the Slides tab to display Slide 1 (Figure 1–57).

Figure 1–57

2
- Click the New Slide arrow in the Slides group on the Home tab to display the Flow layout gallery (Figure 1–58).

Figure 1–58

3

- Click Duplicate Selected Slides in the Flow layout gallery to create a new Slide 2, which is a duplicate of Slide 1 (Figure 1–59).

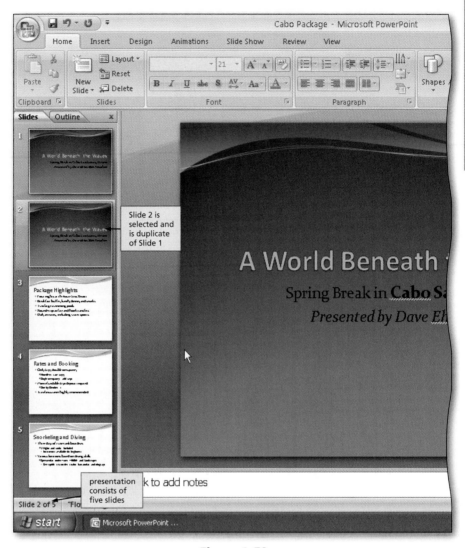

Figure 1–59

To Arrange a Slide

The new Slide 2 was inserted directly below Slide 1 because Slide 1 was the selected slide. This duplicate slide needs to display at the end of the presentation directly after the final title and content slide.

Changing slide order is an easy process and is best performed in the Tabs pane. When you click the slide thumbnail and begin to drag it to a new location, a line indicates the new location of the selected slide. When you release the mouse button, the slide drops into the desired location. Hence, this process of dragging and then dropping the thumbnail in a new location is called **drag and drop**. You can use the drag-and-drop method to move any selected item, including text and graphics. The following step moves the new Slide 2 to the end of the presentation so that it becomes a closing slide.

1

• With Slide 2 selected, drag the Slide 2 slide thumbnail in the Slides pane below the last slide thumbnail (Figure 1–60).

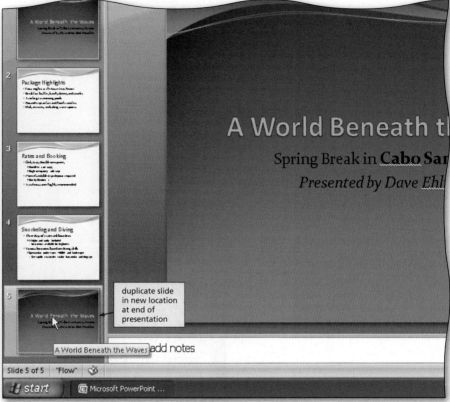

Figure 1–60

To Delete All Text in a Placeholder

To keep the ending slide clean and simple, you want only the slide show title, A World Beneath the Waves, to display on Slide 5. The following steps delete both paragraphs in the subtitle placeholder.

1

• With Slide 5 selected, click the subtitle text placeholder to select it (Figure 1–61).

Figure 1–61

• Click the subtitle text placeholder border to change the border from a dashed line to a solid line (Figure 1–62).

Figure 1–62

• Click the Cut button in the Clipboard group on the Home tab to delete all the text in the subtitle text placeholder (Figure 1–63).

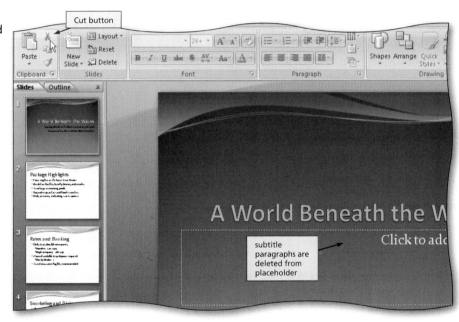

Figure 1–63

Other Ways

1. Right-click selected text, click Cut on shortcut menu
2. Select text, press DELETE key
3. Select text, press CTRL+X

Changing Document Properties and Saving Again

PowerPoint helps you organize and identify your files by using document properties, which are the details about a file. **Document properties**, also known as **metadata**, can include such information as the project author, title, or subject. **Keywords** are words or phrases that further describe the document. For example, a class name or document topic can describe the file's purpose or content.

Document properties are valuable for a variety of reasons:

• Users can save time locating a particular file because they can view a document's properties without opening the document.

• By creating consistent properties for files having similar content, users can better organize their documents.

• Some organizations require PowerPoint users to add document properties so that other employees can view details about these files.

Five different types of document properties exist, but the more common ones used in this book are standard and automatically updated properties. **Standard properties**

BTW

Converters for Earlier PowerPoint Versions
The Microsoft Web site has updates and converters if you are using earlier versions of PowerPoint. The Microsoft Office Compatibility Pack for Word, Excel and PowerPoint 2007 File Format will allow you to open, edit, and save Office 2007 documents that you receive without saving them in the earlier version's file format.

are associated with all Microsoft Office documents and include author, title, and subject. **Automatically updated properties** include file system properties, such as the date you create or change a file, and statistics, such as the file size.

To Change Document Properties

The **Document Information Panel** contains areas where you can view and enter document properties. You can view and change information in this panel at any time while you are creating a document. Before saving the presentation again, you want to add your name and class name as document properties. The following steps use the Document Information Panel to change document properties.

1

- Click the Office Button to display the Office Button menu.
- Point to Prepare on the Office Button menu to display the Prepare submenu (Figure 1–64).

Q&A What other types of actions besides changing properties can you take to set up a document for distribution?

The Prepare submenu provides commands related to sharing a document with others, such as allowing or restricting people to view and modify your document, checking to see if your presentation will run in earlier versions of PowerPoint, and searching for hidden personal information.

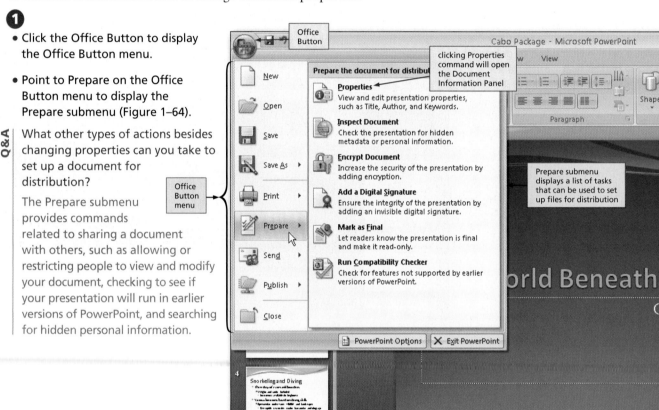

Figure 1–64

2

- Click Properties on the Prepare submenu to display the Document Information Panel (Figure 1–65).

Q&A Why are some of the document properties in my Document Information Panel already filled in?

The person who installed Microsoft Office 2007 on your computer or network may have set or customized the properties.

Figure 1–65

3

- Click the Author text box, if necessary, and then type your name as the Author property. If a name already is displayed in the Author text box, delete it before typing your name.

- Click the Subject text box, if necessary delete any existing text, and then type your course number and section as the Subject property (Figure 1–66).

 What types of document properties does PowerPoint collect automatically?

PowerPoint records such details as how long you worked at creating your project, how many times you revised the document, and what fonts and themes are used.

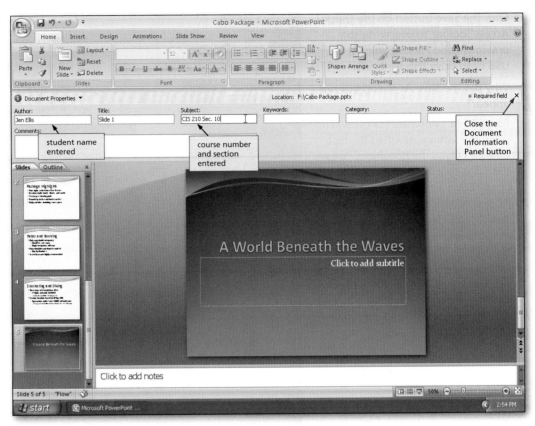

Figure 1–66

4

- Click the Close the Document Information Panel button so that the Document Information Panel no longer is displayed.

To Save an Existing Presentation with the Same File Name

Saving frequently cannot be overemphasized. You have made several modifications to the presentation since you saved it earlier in the chapter. When you first saved the document, you clicked the Save button on the Quick Access Toolbar, the Save As dialog box appeared, and you entered the file name, Cabo Package. If you want to use the same file name to save the changes made to the document, you again click the Save button on the Quick Access Toolbar. The following step saves the presentation again.

3

• Release the mouse button so that Slide 1 appears in the Slide pane and the Slide 1 thumbnail has an orange border in the Slides tab (Figure 1–70).

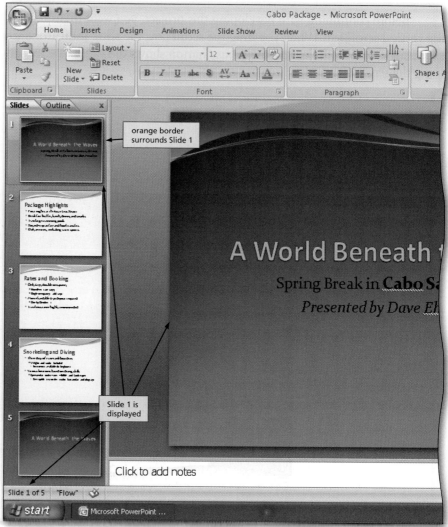

Figure 1–70

Other Ways

1. Click Next Slide button or Previous Slide button to move forward or back one slide

2. Press PAGE DOWN or PAGE UP to move forward or back one slide

Viewing the Presentation in Slide Show View

The Slide Show button, located in the lower-right corner of the PowerPoint window above the status bar, allows you to show a presentation using a computer. The computer acts like a slide projector, displaying each slide on a full screen. The full-screen slide hides the toolbars, menus, and other PowerPoint window elements.

To Start Slide Show View

When making a presentation, you use **Slide Show view**. You can start Slide Show view from Normal view or Slide Sorter view. Slide Show view begins when you click the Slide Show button in the lower-right corner of the PowerPoint window on the status bar. PowerPoint then shows the current slide on the full screen without any of the PowerPoint window objects, such as the menu bar or toolbars. The following steps start Slide Show view.

1

- Point to the Slide Show button in the lower-right corner of the PowerPoint window on the status bar (Figure 1–71).

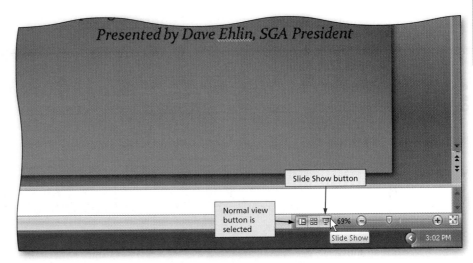

Figure 1–71

2

- Click the Slide Show button to display the title slide (Figure 1–72).

Q&A

Where is the PowerPoint window?

When you run a slide show, the PowerPoint window is hidden. It will reappear once you end your slide show.

Other Ways

1. Click Slide Show tab, click From Beginning button in Start Slide Show group
2. Press F5

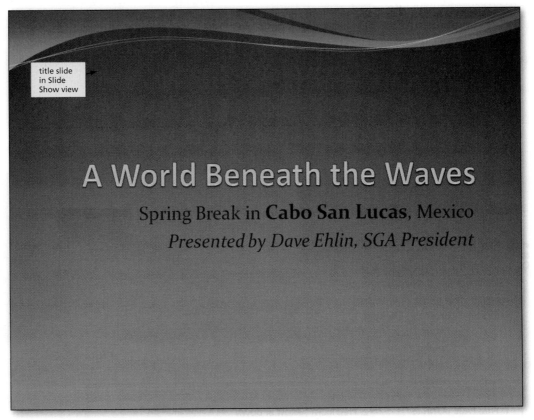

Figure 1–72

To Open a Presentation from PowerPoint

Earlier in this chapter you saved your project on a USB flash drive using the file name, Cabo Package. The following steps open the Cabo Package file from the USB flash drive.

• With your USB flash drive connected to one of the computer's USB ports, click the Office Button to display the Office Button menu (Figure 1–78).

Q&A

What files are shown in the Recent Documents list?

PowerPoint displays the most recently opened document file names in this list. If the name of the file you want to open appears in the Recent Documents list, you could click it to open the file.

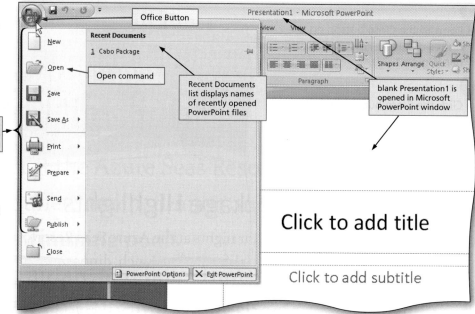

Figure 1–78

• Click Open on the Office Button menu to display the Open dialog box.

• If necessary, click the Look in box arrow and then click UDISK 2.0 (E:) to select the USB flash drive, Drive E in this case, in the Look in list as the new open location.

• Click Cabo Package to select the file name (Figure 1–79).

Q&A

How do I open the file if I am not using a USB flash drive?

Use the same process, but be certain to select your device in the Look in list.

Figure 1–79

❸
- Click the Open button to open the selected file and display Slide 1 in the PowerPoint window (Figure 1–80).

Q&A

Why do I see the PowerPoint icon and name on the Windows taskbar?

When you open a PowerPoint file, a PowerPoint program button is displayed on the taskbar. The button contains an ellipsis because some of its contents do not fit in the allotted button space. If you point to a program button, its entire contents appear in a ScreenTip, which in this case would be the program name followed by the file name.

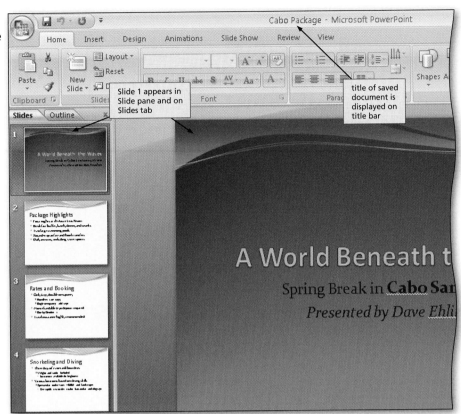

Figure 1–80

Checking a Presentation for Spelling Errors

After you create a presentation, you should check it visually for spelling errors and style consistency. In addition, you use PowerPoint's Spelling tool to identify possible misspellings. Do not rely on the spelling checker to catch all your mistakes. While PowerPoint's spelling checker is a valuable tool, it is not infallible. You should proofread your presentation carefully by pointing to each word and saying it aloud as you point to it. Be mindful of commonly misused words such as its and it's, through and though, and to and too.

PowerPoint checks the entire presentation for spelling mistakes using a standard dictionary contained in the Microsoft Office group. This dictionary is shared with the other Microsoft Office applications such as Word and Excel. A **custom dictionary** is available if you want to add special words such as proper names, cities, and acronyms. When checking a presentation for spelling errors, PowerPoint opens the standard dictionary and the custom dictionary file, if one exists. When a word appears in the Spelling dialog box, you can perform one of several actions.

Table 1–1 Spelling Dialog Box Buttons and Actions

Button Name	When To Use	Action
Ignore	Word is spelled correctly but not found in dictionaries	Continues checking rest of the presentation but will flag that word again if it appears later in document
Ignore All	Word is spelled correctly but not found in dictionaries	Ignores all occurrences of the word and continues checking rest of presentation
Change	Word is misspelled	Click proper spelling of the word in Suggestions list. PowerPoint corrects word, continues checking rest of presentation, but will flag that word again if it appears later in document.
Change All	Word is misspelled	Click proper spelling of word in Suggestions list. PowerPoint changes all occurrences of misspelled word and continues checking rest of presentation.
Add	Add word to custom dictionary	PowerPoint opens custom dictionary, adds word, and continues checking rest of presentation.
Suggest	Correct spelling is uncertain	Lists alternative spellings. Click the correct word from the Suggestions box or type the proper spelling. Corrects the word and continues checking the rest of the presentation.
AutoCorrect	Add spelling error to AutoCorrect list	PowerPoint adds spelling error and its correction to AutoCorrect list. Any future misspelling of word is corrected automatically as you type.
Close	Stop spelling checker	PowerPoint closes spelling checker and returns to PowerPoint window.

To Check Spelling

The standard dictionary contains commonly used English words. It does not, however, contain many proper names, abbreviations, technical terms, poetic contractions, or antiquated terms. PowerPoint treats words not found in the dictionaries as misspellings. The following steps check the spelling on all slides in the Cabo Package presentation.

- Click **Review** on the Ribbon to display the Review tab (Figure 1–81).

Figure 1–81

2

● Click the Spelling button in the Proofing group to start the spelling checker and display the Spelling dialog box (Figure 1–82).

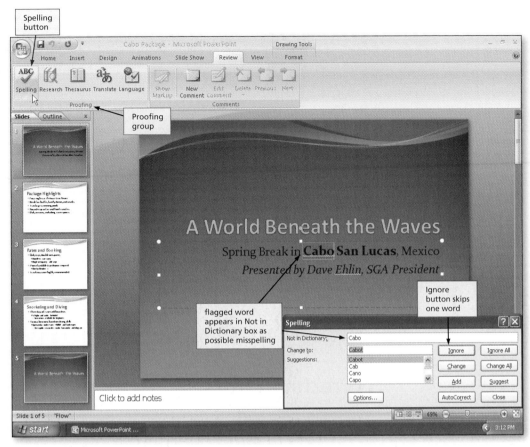

Figure 1–82

3

● Click the Ignore button to skip the word, Cabo (Figure 1–83).

Q&A

Cabo is not flagged as a possible misspelled word. Why not?

Your custom dictionary contains the word, so it is recognized as a correct word.

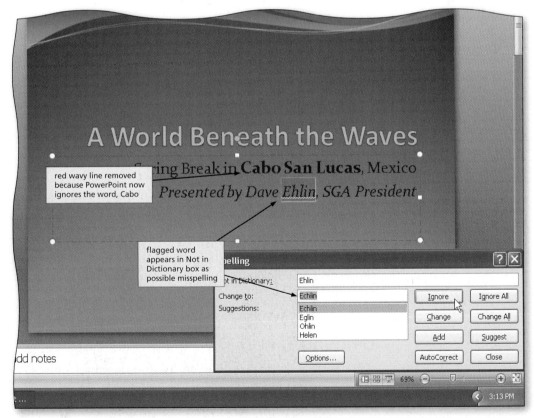

Figure 1–83

4
- Click the Ignore button to skip the word, Ehlin.

- When the Microsoft Office PowerPoint dialog box appears, click the OK button to close the spelling checker and return to the current slide, Slide 1, or to the slide where a possible misspelled word appeared.

- Click the slide to remove the box from the word, Ehlin (Figure 1–84).

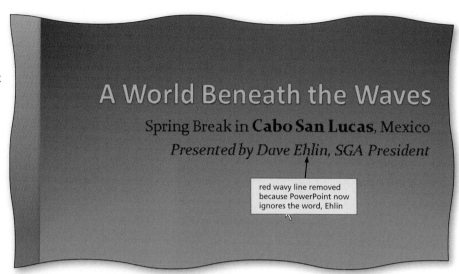

Figure 1–84

Correcting Errors

After creating a presentation and running the spelling checker, you may find that you must make changes. Changes may be required because a slide contains an error, the scope of the presentation shifts, or the style is inconsistent. This section explains the types of errors that commonly occur when creating a presentation.

Types of Corrections Made to Presentations

You generally make three types of corrections to text in a presentation: additions, deletions, and replacements.

- Additions are necessary when you omit text from a slide and need to add it later. You may need to insert text in the form of a sentence, word, or single character. For example, you may want to add the presenter's middle name on the title slide.
- Deletions are required when text on a slide is incorrect or no longer is relevant to the presentation. For example, a slide may look cluttered. Therefore, you may want to remove one of the bulleted paragraphs to add more space.
- Replacements are needed when you want to revise the text in a presentation. For example, you may want to substitute the word, their, for the word, there.

Editing text in PowerPoint basically is the same as editing text in a word processing program. The following sections illustrate the most common changes made to text in a presentation.

BTW

Certification
The Microsoft Certified Application Specialist (MCAS) program provides an opportunity for you to obtain a valuable industry credential – proof that you have the PowerPoint 2007 skills required by employers. For more information see Appendix F or visit the PowerPoint 2007 Certification Web page (scsite.com/ppt2007/cert).

Deleting Text

You can delete text using one of three methods. One is to use the BACKSPACE key to remove text just typed. The second is to position the insertion point to the left of the text you wish to delete and then press the DELETE key. The third method is to drag through the text you wish to delete and then press the DELETE key. Use the third method when deleting large sections of text.

Replacing Text in an Existing Slide

When you need to correct a word or phrase, you can replace the text by selecting the text to be replaced and then typing the new text. As soon as you press any key on the keyboard, the selected text is deleted and the new text is displayed.

PowerPoint inserts text to the left of the insertion point. The text to the right of the insertion point moves to the right (and shifts downward if necessary) to accommodate the added text.

Displaying a Presentation in Grayscale

Printing handouts of a presentation allows you to use them to make overhead transparencies. The Color/Grayscale button on the Color/Grayscale group on the View tab shows the presentation in black and white before you print. Pure Black and White alters the slides' appearance so that black lines display on a white background. Shadows and other graphical effects are hidden. Grayscale shows varying degrees of gray.

To Display a Presentation in Grayscale

The Color/Grayscale button on the Color/Grayscale group on the View tab changes from color bars to shades of black, called grayscale, and white. After you view the text objects in the presentation in grayscale, you can make any changes that will enhance printouts produced from a black and white printer or photocopier. The following steps display the presentation in grayscale.

1
- Click View on the Ribbon to display the View tab (Figure 1–85).

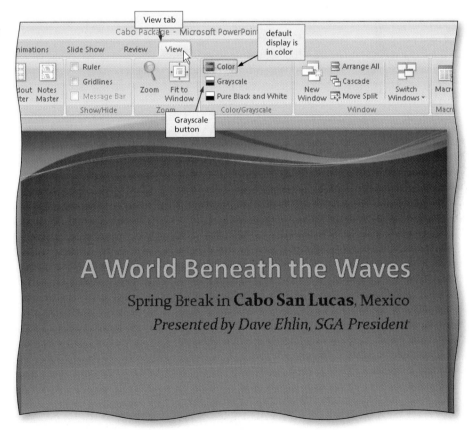

Figure 1–85

2
- Click Grayscale in the Color/Grayscale group to display Slide 1 in grayscale in the Slide pane (Figure 1–86).

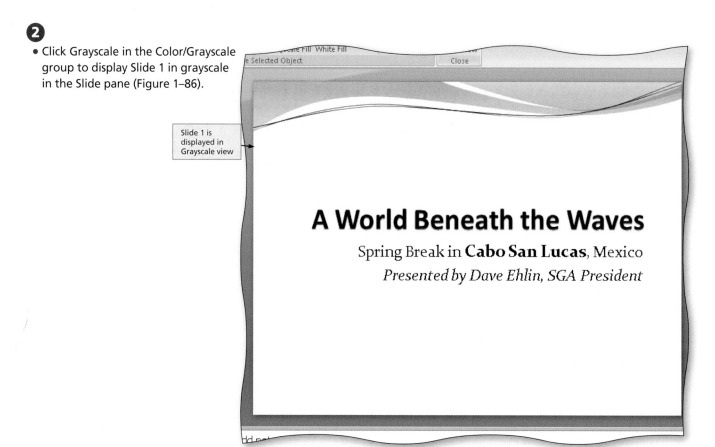

Figure 1–86

3
- Click the Next Slide button four times to view all slides in the presentation in grayscale (Figure 1–87).

Figure 1–87

4
- Click the Back To Color View button in the Close group to return to the previous tab and display Slide 5 with the default Flow color scheme (Figure 1–88).

Figure 1–88

Printing a Presentation

After you create a presentation, you often want to print it. A printed version of the presentation is called a **hard copy** or **printout**.

Printed copies of your presentation can be useful for the following reasons:

- Many people prefer proofreading a hard copy of the presentation rather than viewing the slides on the screen to check for errors and readability.
- Someone without computer access or who could not attend your live presentation can view the slides' content.
- Copies can be distributed as handouts to people viewing your presentation.
- Hard copies can serve as reference material if your storage medium is lost or becomes corrupted and you need to re-create the presentation.

It is a good practice to save a presentation before printing it, in the event you experience difficulties with the printer.

To Print a Presentation

With the completed presentation saved, you may want to print it. The following steps print all five completed presentation slides in the saved Cabo Package project.

1
- Click the Office Button to display the Office Button menu.

- Point to Print on the Office Button menu to display the Print submenu (Figure 1–89).

Q&A

Can I print my presentation in black and white to conserve ink or toner?

Yes. Click the Office Button, point to the arrow next to Print on the Office Button menu, and then click Print Preview on the Print submenu. Click the Options button on the Print Preview tab, point to Color/Grayscale on the Options button menu, and then click Pure Black and White on the Color/Grayscale submenu. Click the Print button on the Print submenu.

Figure 1–89

2

- Click Quick Print on the Print submenu to print the slides.

- When the printer stops, retrieve the hard copy of the five Cabo Package slides (Figures 1–90a through 1–90e).

Q&A

How can I print multiple copies of my document other than clicking the Print button twice?

Click the Office Button, point to Print on the Office Button menu, click Print on the Print submenu, increase the number in the Number of copies box, and then click the OK button.

Q&A

Do I have to wait until my presentation is complete to print it?

No, you can follow these steps to print your slides at any time while you are creating your presentation.

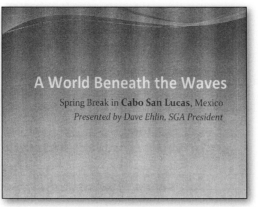

(a) Slide 1

(b) Slide 2

(c) Slide 3

(d) Slide 4

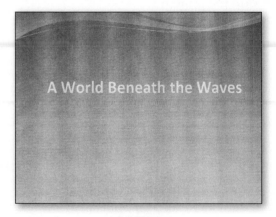

(e) Slide 5

Figure 1–90

Other Ways

1. Press CTRL+P

Making a Transparency

With the handouts printed, you now can make overhead transparencies using one of several devices. One device is a printer attached to your computer, such as an inkjet printer or a laser printer. Transparencies produced on a printer may be in black and white or color, depending on the printer. Another device is a photocopier. Because each of these devices requires a special transparency film, check the user's manual for the film requirement of your specific device, or ask your instructor.

PowerPoint Help

At any time while using PowerPoint, you can find answers to questions and display information about various topics through **PowerPoint Help**. Used properly, this form of assistance can increase your productivity and reduce your frustrations by minimizing the time you spend learning how to use PowerPoint.

This section introduces you to PowerPoint Help. Additional information about using PowerPoint Help is available in Appendix C.

BTW

PowerPoint Help
The best way to become familiar with PowerPoint Help is to use it. Appendix C includes detailed information about PowerPoint Help and exercises that will help you gain confidence in using it.

To Search for PowerPoint Help

Using PowerPoint Help, you can search for information based on phrases such as save a presentation or format a chart, or key terms such as copy, save, or format. PowerPoint Help responds with a list of search results displayed as links to a variety of resources. The following steps, which use PowerPoint Help to search for information about using document themes, assume you are connected to the Internet.

1

- Click the Microsoft Office PowerPoint Help button near the upper right-corner of the PowerPoint window to open the PowerPoint Help window.

- Type document theme in the Type words to search for text box at the top of the PowerPoint Help window (Figure 1–91).

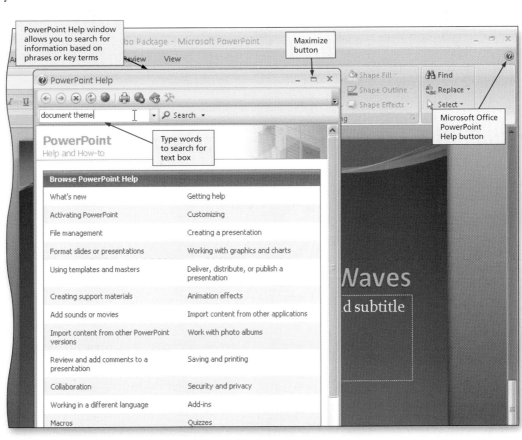

Figure 1–91

2

- Press the ENTER key to display the search results.

- Click the Maximize button on the PowerPoint Help window title bar to maximize the Help window (Figure 1–92).

Where is the PowerPoint window with Slide 1?

PowerPoint is open in the background, but the PowerPoint Help window is overlaid on top of the Microsoft PowerPoint window. When the PowerPoint Help window is closed, the slide will reappear.

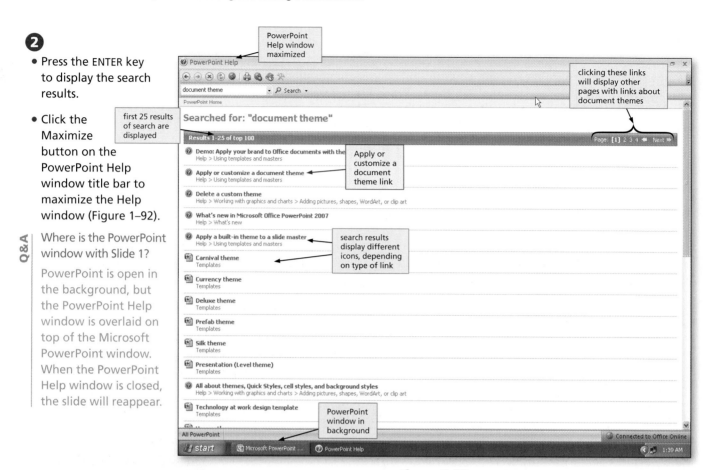

Figure 1–92

3

- Click the 'Apply or customize a document theme' link to display information regarding applying or customizing themes (Figure 1–93).

What is the purpose of the buttons at the top of the PowerPoint Help window?

Use the buttons in the upper-left corner of the PowerPoint Help window to navigate through the Help system, change the display, show the PowerPoint Help table of contents, and print the contents of the window.

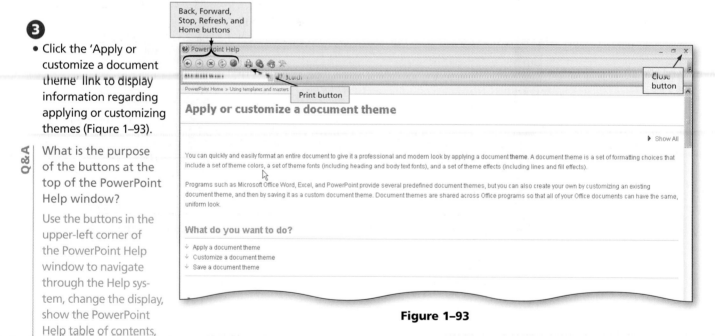

Figure 1–93

4

- Click the Close button on the PowerPoint Help window title bar to close the PowerPoint Help window and display Slide 5.

Other Ways
1. Press F1

To Quit PowerPoint

The following steps quit PowerPoint.

1 Click the Close button on the right side of the title bar to quit PowerPoint.

2 If necessary, click the 'No button in the Microsoft Office PowerPoint' dialog box so that any changes you have made are not saved.

Chapter Summary

In this chapter you have learned how to apply a document theme, create a title slide and text slides with bulleted lists, format text, view the presentation in Slide Show view, and print slides as handouts. The items listed below include all the new PowerPoint skills you have learned in this chapter.

1. Start PowerPoint (PPT 5)
2. Choose a Document Theme (PPT 16)
3. Enter the Presentation Title (PPT 18)
4. Enter the Presentation Subtitle Paragraph (PPT 20)
5. Select a Paragraph (PPT 21)
6. Italicize Text (PPT 22)
7. Select Multiple Paragraphs (PPT 22)
8. Change the Text Color (PPT 23)
9. Select a Group of Words (PPT 24)
10. Increase Font Size (PPT 24)
11. Bold Text (PPT 25)
12. Decrease the Title Slide Title Text Font Size (PPT 25)
13. Save a Presentation (PPT 27)
14. Add a New Text Slide with a Bulleted List (PPT 29)
15. Enter a Slide Title (PPT 31)
16. Select a Text Placeholder (PPT 31)
17. Type a Single-Level Bulleted List (PPT 32)
18. Add a New Slide and Enter a Slide Title (PPT 33)
19. Type a Multi-Level Bulleted List (PPT 34)
20. Create a Third-Level Paragraph (PPT 37)
21. Duplicate a Slide (PPT 40)
22. Arrange a Slide (PPT 41)
23. Delete All Text in a Placeholder (PPT 42)
24. Change Document Properties (PPT 44)
25. Save an Existing Presentation with the Same File Name (PPT 45)
26. Use the Scroll Box on the Slide Pane to Move to Another Slide (PPT 47)
27. Start Slide Show View (PPT 49)
28. Move Manually through Slides in a Slide Show (PPT 50)
29. Display the Pop-Up Menu and Go to a Specific Slide (PPT 51)
30. Use the Pop-Up Menu to End a Slide Show (PPT 52)
31. Quit PowerPoint (PPT 53)
32. Open a Presentation from PowerPoint (PPT 54)
33. Check Spelling (PPT 55)
34. Display a Presentation in Grayscale (PPT 59)
35. Print a Presentation (PPT 61)
36. Search for PowerPoint Help (PPT 63)

 If you have a SAM user profile, you may have access to hands-on instruction, practice, and assessment. Log in to your SAM account (http://sam2007.course.com) to launch any assigned training activities or exams that relate to the skills covered in this chapter.

Learn It Online

Test your knowledge of chapter content and key terms.

Instructions: To complete the Learn It Online exercises, start your browser, click the Address bar, and then enter the Web address scsite.com/ppt2007/learn. When the Office 2007 Learn It Online page is displayed, click the link for the exercise you want to complete and then read the instructions.

Chapter Reinforcement TF, MC, and SA

A series of true/false, multiple choice, and short answer questions that test your knowledge of the chapter content.

Flash Cards

An interactive learning environment where you identify chapter key terms associated with displayed definitions.

Practice Test

A series of multiple choice questions that test your knowledge of chapter content and key terms.

Who Wants To Be a Computer Genius?

An interactive game that challenges your knowledge of chapter content in the style of a television quiz show.

Wheel of Terms

An interactive game that challenges your knowledge of chapter key terms in the style of the television show Wheel of Fortune.

Crossword Puzzle Challenge

A crossword puzzle that challenges your knowledge of key terms presented in the chapter.

Apply Your Knowledge

Reinforce the skills and apply the concepts you learned in this chapter.

Modifying Character Formats and Paragraph Levels

Instructions: Start PowerPoint. Open the presentation, Apply 1-1 Keep Your Cool, from the Data Files for Students. See the inside back cover of this book for instructions on downloading the Data Files for Students, or contact your instructor for more information about accessing the required files.

The two slides in the presentation stress the importance of drinking plenty of water on hot days. The document you open is an unformatted presentation. You are to modify the document theme and text, indent the paragraphs, and format the text so the slides look like Figure 1–94.

Perform the following tasks:

1. Change the document theme to Trek. Note that the Trek theme uses all capital letters for the title text. On the title slide, use your name in place of Student Name and bold and italicize your name. Increase the title text font size to 44 point.

(a) Slide 1 (Title Slide)

Figure 1–94

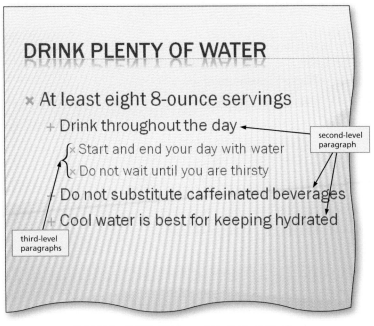

(b) Slide 2 (Multi-Level Bulleted List)
Figure 1–94 (continued)

2. On Slide 2, increase the indent of the second, fifth, and sixth paragraphs (Drink throughout the day; Do not substitute caffeinated beverages; Cool water is best for keeping hydrated) to second-level paragraphs. Then change paragraphs three and four (Start and end your day with water; Do not wait until you are thirsty) to third-level paragraphs.

3. Check the spelling, and then display the revised presentation in grayscale.

4. Change the document properties, as specified by your instructor. Save the presentation using the file name, Apply 1-1 Drink Water. Submit the revised document in the format specified by your instructor.

Extend Your Knowledge

Extend the skills you learned in this chapter and experiment with new skills. You may need to use Help to complete the assignment.

Changing Slide Theme and Text

Instructions: Start PowerPoint. Open the presentation, Extend 1-1 Nutrition, from the Data Files for Students. See the inside back cover of this book for instructions on downloading the Data Files for Students, or contact your instructor for more information about accessing the required files.

You will choose a theme (Figure 1–95), format slides, and create a closing slide.

Perform the following tasks:

1. Apply an appropriate document theme.

2. On Slide 1, use your name in place of Student Name. Format the text using techniques you learned in this chapter, such as changing the font size and color and also bolding and italicizing words.

Figure 1–95

Continued >

3. On Slide 2, adjust the paragraph levels so that the lines of text are arranged under vegetable and fruit categories. Edit the text so that the slide meets the 7 × 7 rule, which states that each line should have a maximum of seven words, and each slide should have a maximum of seven lines.

4. On Slides 3 and 4, create paragraphs and adjust the paragraph levels.

5. Create an appropriate closing slide using the title slide as a guide.

6. Change the document properties, as specified by your instructor. Save the presentation using the file name, Extend 1-1 Fruit and Vegetables.

7. Add the Print button to the Quick Access Toolbar and then click this button to print the slides.

8. Delete the Print button from the Quick Access Toolbar.

9. Submit the revised document in the format specified by your instructor.

Make It Right

Analyze a presentation and correct all errors and/or improve the design.

Correcting Formatting and List Levels

Instructions: Start PowerPoint. Open the presentation, Make It Right 1-1 Indulge, from the Data Files for Students. See the inside back cover of this book for instructions on downloading the Data Files for Students, or contact your instructor for more information about accessing the required files.

Correct the formatting problems and errors in the presentation while keeping in mind the guidelines presented in this chapter.

Perform the following tasks:

1. Change the document theme from Metro, shown in Figure 1–96, to Opulent.

2. On Slide 1, replace the words, Full Semester, with your name. Format your name so that it displays prominently on the slide.

3. Move Slide 2 to the end of the presentation so that it becomes the new Slide 4.

4. Use the spell checker to correct the misspellings. Analyze the slides for other word usage errors that the spell checker did not find.

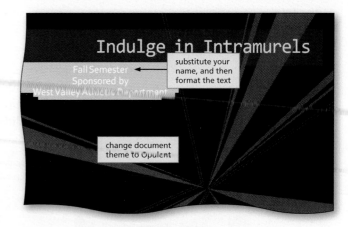

Figure 1–96

5. On Slide 2, increase the Slide 2 title (Athletic Events) font size to 40. Make the indent levels for paragraphs 2, 4, and 6 the same level.

6. On Slide 3, change the title text (Awards Ceremony) font size to 40. Make the indent levels for paragraphs 3 and 5 the same level.

7. Change the document properties, as specified by your instructor. Save the presentation using the file name, Make It Right 1-1 Intramurals.

8. Submit the revised document in the format specified by your instructor.

In the Lab

Design and/or create a presentation using the guidelines, concepts, and skills presented in this chapter. Labs 1, 2, and 3 are listed in order of increasing difficulty.

Lab 1: Creating a Presentation with Bulleted Lists

Problem: Many of the important steps you will take in your life are influenced by your credit report. Buying a car, renting an apartment, and even applying for a job often require a credit check. Your credit score can make or break your ability to obtain the goods you truly want and need. One of your assignments in your economics class is to give a speech about establishing credit. You develop the outline shown in Figure 1–97 and then prepare the PowerPoint presentation shown in Figures 1–98a through 1–98d.

Instructions: Perform the following tasks.

1. Create a new presentation using the Aspect document theme.

2. Using the typed notes illustrated in Figure 1–97, create the title slide shown in Figure 1–98a using your name in place of Marc Kantlon. Italicize your name. Decrease the font size of the title paragraph, Give Yourself Some Credit, to 40. Increase the font size of the first paragraph of the subtitle text, Understanding Your Credit Report, to 28.

3. Using the typed notes in Figure 1–97, create the three text slides with bulleted lists shown in Figures 1–98b through 1–98d.

Give Yourself Some Credit
Understanding Your Credit Report
Marc Kantlon
Economics 101

Credit Report Fundamentals
Generated by three companies
Experian, Equifax, TransUnion
Factors
How much you owe to each company
Payment history for each company
Includes utilities, medical expenses, rent

How FICO Is Calculated
Range - 760 (excellent) to 620 (poor)
35% - Payment history
30% - Amounts owed
15% - Credit history length
10% - New credit
10% - Credit types

Improve Your FICO Score
Pay bills on time
Avoid opening many new accounts
Open only if you intend to use
Keep balances low
Less than 25% of credit limit
Review credit report yearly

Figure 1–97

Continued >

In the Lab *continued*

4. On Slide 3, change the font color of the number, 760, to green and the number, 620, to red.

5. Check the spelling and correct any errors.

6. Drag the scroll box to display Slide 1. Click the Slide Show button to start Slide Show view. Then click to display each slide.

7. Change the document properties, as specified by your instructor. Save the presentation using the file name, Lab 1-1 Credit.

8. Submit the document in the format specified by your instructor.

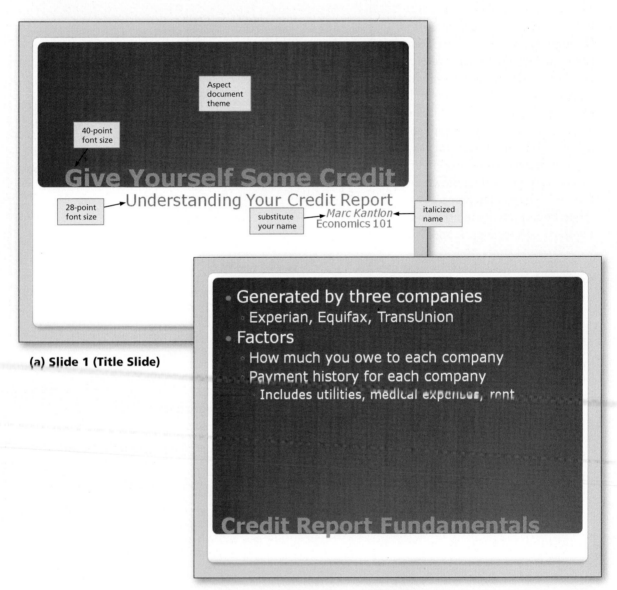

(a) Slide 1 (Title Slide)

(b) Slide 2

Figure 1–98

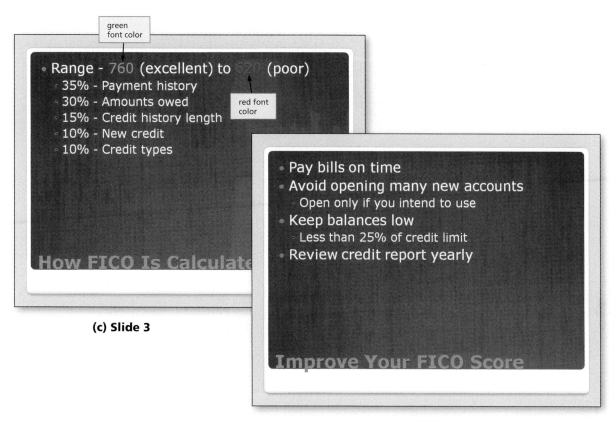

(c) Slide 3

(d) Slide 4

Figure 1–98 (continued)

In the Lab

Lab 2: Creating a Presentation with Bulleted Lists and a Closing Slide

Problem: Hybrid vehicles have received much attention in recent years. Everyone from environmentalists to movie stars are driving them, and potential buyers wait for months until the vehicles arrive in dealers' showrooms. You work part-time at Midwest State Bank, and the loan department manager, Jen Westbrook, has asked you to develop a PowerPoint presentation to accompany her upcoming speech. She hands you the outline shown in Figure 1–99 and asks you to create the presentation shown in Figures 1–100a through 1–100e.

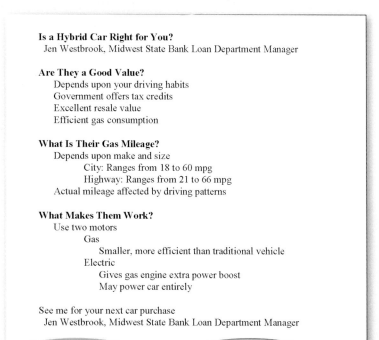

Is a Hybrid Car Right for You?
Jen Westbrook, Midwest State Bank Loan Department Manager

Are They a Good Value?
Depends upon your driving habits
Government offers tax credits
Excellent resale value
Efficient gas consumption

What Is Their Gas Mileage?
Depends upon make and size
City: Ranges from 18 to 60 mpg
Highway: Ranges from 21 to 66 mpg
Actual mileage affected by driving patterns

What Makes Them Work?
Use two motors
Gas
Smaller, more efficient than traditional vehicle
Electric
Gives gas engine extra power boost
May power car entirely

See me for your next car purchase
Jen Westbrook, Midwest State Bank Loan Department Manager

Figure 1–99

Continued >

In the Lab *continued*

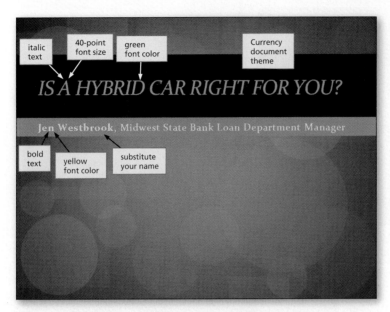

(a) Slide 1 (Title Slide)

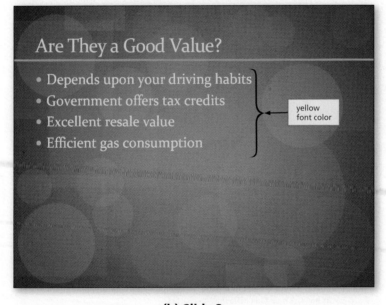

(b) Slide 2

Figure 1–100

Instructions: Perform the following tasks.

1. Create a new presentation using the Currency document theme.

2. Using the typed notes illustrated in Figure 1–99, create the title slide shown in Figure 1–100a using your name in place of Jan Westbrook. Bold your name. Italicize the title, Is a Hybrid Car Right for You?, and decrease the font size to 40. Change the font color of the title text to green and the subtitle text to yellow.

3. Using the typed notes in Figure 1–99, create the three text slides with bulleted lists shown in Figures 1–100b through 1–100d. Change the color of all the bulleted list paragraph text to yellow.

4. Duplicate the title slide and then move the new closing slide to the end of the presentation. Change the Slide 5 title text, decrease the font size to 32, and remove the italics.

5. Check the spelling and correct any errors.

6. Drag the scroll box to display Slide 1. Click the Slide Show button to start Slide Show view. Then click to display each slide.

7. Change the document properties, as specified by your instructor. Save the presentation using the file name, Lab 1-2 Hybrids.

8. Submit the revised document in the format specified by your instructor.

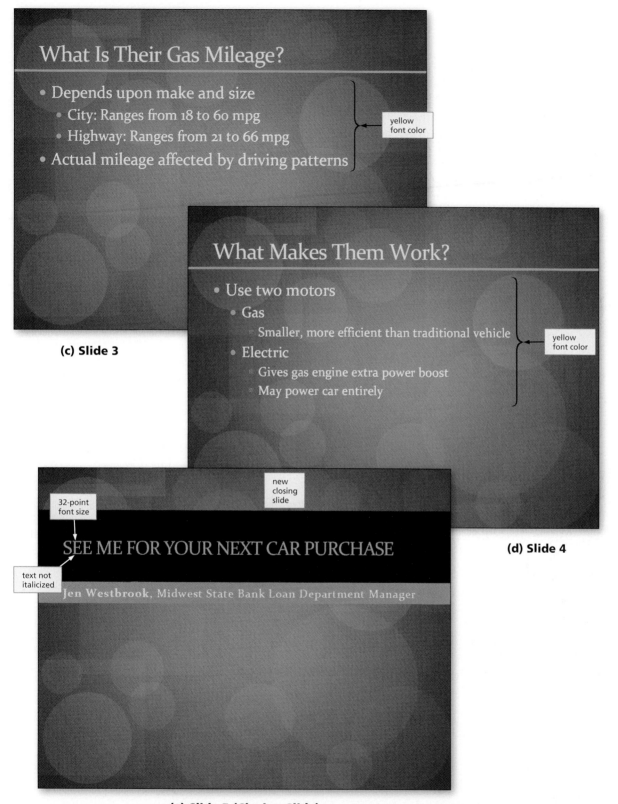

(c) Slide 3

(d) Slide 4

(e) Slide 5 (Closing Slide)

Figure 1–100 (continued)

In the Lab

Lab 3: Creating and Updating Presentations

Problem: Bobbie Willis, the public relations director for the South Haven Park District, plans activities every season for community residents and promotes the offerings using a PowerPoint presentation. The new seminars for senior citizens this spring are quilting and t'ai chi. Adults can register for gourmet cooking lessons and kickball. Teens can enroll in sailing and fencing lessons.

South Haven Park District
New Spring Seminars
Bobbie Willis, Director

Seniors' Seminars
    Quilting
        Quilts made from donated fabrics
        Sewing machines provided
    T'ai Chi
        Gentle warm-ups
        12 slow, continuous movements
        Easy cool-down exercises

Adults' Seminars
    Almost Gourmet
        Learn techniques from a professional chef
            Everyone prepares and enjoys the dinners
                Come hungry!
    Kickball
        Learn techniques and rules

Teens' Seminars
    Sailing
        Sail a 30-foot sailboat at your first class
    Fencing
        Three levels
            Level 1 – Beginning Foil
           Level 2 – Foil, Epee, and Saber
           Level 3 – Open Strip Fencing

Figure 1–101

Instructions Part 1: Using the outline in Figure 1–101, create the presentation shown in Figure 1–102. Use the Oriel document theme. On the title slide shown in Figure 1–102a, type your name in place of Bobbie Willis, increase the font size of the title paragraph, South Haven Park District, to 60 and change the text font style to italic. Increase the font size of the subtitle paragraph, New Spring Seminars, to 32, and change the font size of the subtitle paragraph with your name to 37 or to a size that displays all the text on one line. Create the three text slides with multi-level bulleted lists shown in Figures 1–102b through 1–102d.

Correct any spelling mistakes. Change the document properties, as specified by your instructor. Save the presentation using the file name, Lab 1-3 Part One Spring Seminars. Display the presentation in grayscale.

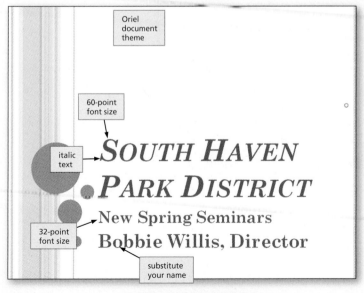

(a) Slide 1 (Title Slide)
Figure 1–102

(b) Slide 2

(c) Slide 3

(d) Slide 4

Figure 1–102 (continued)

Instructions Part 2: The South Haven Park District staff members want to update this presentation to promote the new Fall seminars. Modify the presentation created in Part 1 to create the presentation shown in Figure 1–103. Change the document theme to Civic. On the title slide, remove the italics from the title paragraph, South Haven Park District, decrease the font size to 44, and bold the text. Change the first subtitle paragraph to New Fall Seminars. Then change your title in the second subtitle paragraph to Executive Director and change the font size of the entire paragraph to 28.

On Slide 2, change the first first-level paragraph, Quilting, to Quilting for the Holidays. Change the first second-level paragraph, Quilts made from donated fabrics, to Quilts will be raffled at Annual Bazaar. Change the title of the second seminar to Intermediate T'ai Chi.

On Slide 3, change the first second-level paragraph under Almost Gourmet to Holiday feasts and parties. Then change the second-level paragraph under Kickball to Seminar concludes with single elimination tournament.

On Slide 4, change the first class from Sailing to Climbing and then change the course description second-level paragraph to Covers verbal signals, rope, knots, harnesses, belaying.

Continued >

In the Lab *continued*

Correct any spelling mistakes, and then view the slide show. Change the document properties, as specified by your instructor. Save the presentation using the file name, Lab 1-3 Part Two Fall Seminars. Display the presentation in grayscale. Submit both Part One and Part Two documents in the format specified by your instructor.

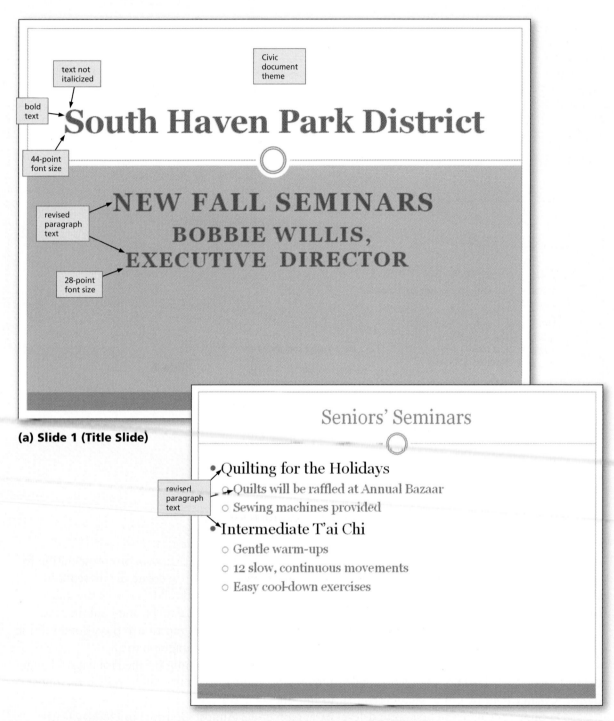

(a) Slide 1 (Title Slide)

(b) Slide 2

Figure 1–103

(c) Slide 3

(d) Slide 4

Figure 1–103 (continued)

Cases and Places

Apply your creative thinking and problem solving skills to design and implement a solution.

• EASIER   •• MORE DIFFICULT

Note: Remember to use the 7 × 7 rule as you design the presentations: a maximum of seven words on a line and a maximum of seven lines on one slide.

• 1: Design and Create an Ocean and Seas Presentation

Salt water covers more than two-thirds of the Earth's surface. This water flows freely between the Earth's five oceans and seas, which all are connected. In preparation for your next snorkeling and diving adventure, you have been reading about the oceans and seas. You decide to prepare a PowerPoint presentation to accompany a speech that is required in your Earth Science class. You create the outline shown in Figure 1–104 about these waters. Use this outline along with the concepts and techniques presented in this chapter to develop and format a slide show with a title slide and three text slides with bulleted lists. Be sure to check spelling.

Water, Water, Everywhere
The Earth's Oceans and Seas
Jamel Thomas
Earth Science 203

Major Bodies of Water
 Four oceans: Pacific, Atlantic, Indian, and Arctic
  Pacific is largest and deepest
   64,186,300 square miles
   12,925 feet average depth
 Fifth ocean delimited in 2000
   Southern Ocean north of Antarctica

Coral Reefs
 Form in shallow, warm seas
 Made of coral polyps' skeletons
  Grow on top of old skeletons
 Spend adult lives fixed to same spot
 Coral diseases increasing dramatically past 10 years
  Responding to onset of bacteria, fungi, viruses

Ocean Zones
  Sunlit (down to 650 feet)
    Sea plants and many animals
  Twilight (down to 3,300 feet)
    Many different fish
  Sunless (down to 13,100 feet)
    Animals feed on dead food from above

Figure 1–104

• 2: Design and Create an Industrial Revolution Presentation

The Industrial Revolution changed the way people worked and lived in many parts of the world. With its roots in Britain in the 18th century, the Industrial Revolution introduced new machines, steam power, and trains. As part of your World History homework assignments, you develop the outline shown in Figure 1–105 about the Industrial Revolution and then create an accompanying PowerPoint presentation. Use the concepts and techniques presented in this chapter to develop and format this slide show with a title slide, three text slides with bulleted lists, and a closing slide. Be sure to check spelling.

The Industrial Revolution
1700 - 1850
Sonia Banks
World History 108

British Inventors
   First machines spun and wove cloth quickly
      Wealthy businessmen built factories
        Spinning Jenny machine spun 16 threads simultaneously
   Angered people who made cloth at home
      Luddites protested by smashing machines
        Led by Ned Ludd

Steam Power
   James Watt invented first steam engine in 1782
      Hundreds of his engines used throughout Britain
   George Stephenson designed steam train, The Rocket
      Peak speed: 30 mph
      Used to transport goods in 1829

Coal Mining
   Coal needed to boil water to create steam
   Mining towns boomed
      Deep mines dug
      Men, women, and children worked long hours
        Many people killed and injured

Figure 1–105

Continued >

Cases and Places *continued*

•• 3: Design and Create a Recycling Presentation

Many communities require recycling of household waste. Residents are required to separate paper, plastics, and glass and put each material in special bins or bags. Electronic equipment also can be recycled. Your community has developed a special program for broken or obsolete computers and peripherals, office equipment and products, small home appliances, and entertainment equipment. These items include personal computers, printers, cellular telephones, toasters, televisions, DVD players, and video game consoles. Community officials will be collecting these items during the next two Fridays at your local police station and a nearby shopping center. They will not accept air conditioners, humidifiers, and hazardous wastes. Using the concepts and techniques presented in this chapter, develop a short PowerPoint presentation to show at various businesses and offices in your community. Emphasize that recycling is important because electronic products have very short useful lives. They produce waste and may contain hazardous materials, but many components can be salvaged. Include one slide with acceptable products and another with unacceptable products.

•• 4 Design and Create Your Favorite or Dream Car Presentation

Make It Personal

Ever since Henry Ford rolled the first Model T off his assembly line in 1908, people have been obsessed with cars. From the sporty Corvette to the environmentally friendly Prius, everyone has a favorite car or dream car. Use the concepts and techniques presented in this chapter to create a slide show promoting a particular vehicle. Include a title slide, at least three text slides with bulleted lists, and a closing slide. Format the text using colors, bolding, and italics where needed for emphasis. Be sure to check spelling.

•• 5: Design and Create a Financial Institutions Presentation

Working Together

Financial institutions such as banks, savings and loans, and credit unions offer a variety of products. Have each member of your team visit, telephone, or view Web sites of three local financial institutions. Gather data about:

1) Savings accounts

2) Checking accounts

3) Mortgages

4) Certificates of deposit

After coordinating the data, create a presentation with at least one slide showcasing each financial institution. As a group, critique each slide. Submit your assignment in the format specified by your instructor.

2 Creating a Presentation with Illustrations and Shapes

Objectives

You will have mastered the material in this chapter when you can:

- Create slides from a blank presentation
- Change views to review a presentation
- Change slide layouts
- Add a background style
- Insert, move, and size clip art
- Insert a photograph from a file
- Delete a placeholder

- Change font color
- Format text using the Format Painter
- Add and size a shape
- Apply Quick Styles to placeholders and shapes
- Select slide transitions
- Preview and print an outline and handout

2 | Creating a Presentation with Illustrations and Shapes

Introduction

In our visual culture, audience members enjoy viewing effective graphics. Whether reading a document or viewing a PowerPoint presentation, people increasingly want to see photographs, artwork, graphics, and a variety of type. Researchers have known for decades that documents with visual elements are more effective than those that consist of only text because the illustrations motivate audiences to study the material. People remember at least one-third more information when the document they are seeing or reading contains visual elements. These graphics help clarify and emphasize details, so they appeal to audience members with differing backgrounds, reading levels, attention spans, and motivations.

BTW

Delivery Skills
While illustrations and shapes help audience members retain important points in a slide show, keep in mind that a speaker's presentation skills are the most effective part of a presentation. The presenter's posture, eye contact, volume, gestures, and rate establish the tone and tempo of the presentation. A good presentation rarely overcomes poor delivery skills.

Project — Presentation with Illustrations and a Shape

The project in this chapter follows graphical guidelines and uses PowerPoint to create the presentation shown in Figure 2–1. This slide show, which discusses identity theft, has a variety of illustrations and visual elements inserted on a gray background. Clip art and photographs add interest. Transitions help one slide flow gracefully into the next during a slide show. Slide titles have a style that blends well with the background and illustrations. The slide handouts include an outline of the slides and print all four slides on one page.

This presentation uses Quick Styles, which are collections of formatting options for objects and documents. The Quick Styles, like the document themes introduced in Chapter 1, are created by Microsoft's visual designers and give your presentation a professional look. When you rest your mouse pointer on a Quick Style thumbnail in the Quick Style gallery, you will see how the various colors, fonts, and effects are combined, and you can select the image that best fits the impression you want to present in your slide show.

Overview

As you read through this chapter, you will learn how to create the presentation shown in Figure 2–1 by performing these general tasks:

- Create a new presentation from a blank presentation.
- Review presentation in a variety of views.
- Insert and format shapes.
- Insert photographs and clips.
- Print an outline and a handout.

(a)

(c)

(b)

(d)

Figure 2–1

Plan Ahead

General Project Guidelines

When creating a PowerPoint presentation, the actions you perform and decisions you make will affect the appearance and characteristics of the finished document. As you create a presentation with illustrations, such as the project shown in Figure 2–1, you should follow these general guidelines:

1. **Focus on slide text content.** Give some careful thought to the words you choose to use. Some graphic designers advise starting with a blank screen so that the document theme does not distract from or influence the words.

2. **Use single quotation marks.** PowerPoint slides generally use a single quotation mark in several instances.

   - The introduction of an unfamiliar term
   - A quotation
   - Nicknames
   - Composition titles

3. **Adhere to copyright regulations.** Copyright laws apply to printed and Web-based materials. You can copy an existing photograph or artwork if it is in the public domain, if your company owns the graphic, or if you have obtained permission to use it. Be certain you have the legal right to use a desired graphic in your presentation.

4. **Use color effectively.** Your audience's eyes are drawn to color on a slide. Used appropriately, color can create interest by emphasizing material and promoting understanding. Be aware of symbolic meanings attached to colors, such as red generally representing danger, electricity, and heat.

5. **Use serif fonts for titles and sans serif fonts for body text.** Typefaces are divided into two categories: serif and sans serif. A serif letter generally has thin and thick areas, with the thin areas at the end of the lines. A sans serif letter generally is the same thickness. The letters in this box are sans serif.

6. **Choose graphics that serve a purpose.** Illustrations and art should help your audience remember and understand information. They should be uncluttered and visually appealing. Determine why you need each graphic and the kind of information it communicates.

7. **Consider graphics for multicultural audiences.** In today's intercultural society, your presentation might be viewed by people whose first language is different from yours. Some graphics have meanings specific to a culture, so be certain to learn about your intended audience and their views.

When necessary, more specific details concerning the above guidelines are presented at appropriate points in the chapter. The chapter also will identify the actions you perform and decisions made regarding these guidelines during the creation of the presentation shown in Figure 2–1.

Starting PowerPoint

Chapter 1 introduced you to starting PowerPoint, selecting a document theme, creating slides with bulleted lists, and printing a presentation. The following steps summarize starting a new presentation. To start PowerPoint, Windows must be running. If you are using a computer to step through the project in this chapter and you want your screen to match the figures in this book, you should change your computer's resolution to 1024 × 768. For more information about how to change a computer's resolution, see Appendix E.

To Start PowerPoint

1 Click the Start button on the Windows taskbar to display the Start menu.

2 Point to All Programs on the Start menu and then point to Microsoft Office on the All Programs submenu.

3 Click Microsoft Office PowerPoint 2007 on the Microsoft Office submenu.

4 If the PowerPoint window is not maximized, click the Maximize button on its title bar.

Plan Ahead

Focus on slide text content.
Once you have researched your presentation topic, many methods exist to begin developing slide content.

• Select a document theme and then enter text, illustration, and tables.

• Open an existing presentation and modify the slides and theme.

• Import an outline created in Microsoft Word.

• Start with a blank presentation that uses the default Office Theme. Consider this practice similar to an artist who begins creating a painting with a blank, white canvas.

Experiment using different methods of developing the initial content for slides. Experienced PowerPoint users sometimes find one technique works better than another to stimulate creativity or help them organize their ideas in a particular circumstance.

Creating Slides from a Blank Presentation

In Chapter 1, you selected a document theme and then typed the content for the title and text slides using single- and multi-level bulleted lists. In this chapter, you will type the slide content for the title and text slides, select a background, and then format the text.

To Create a Title Slide

Recall from Chapter 1 that the title slide introduces the presentation to the audience. In addition to introducing the presentation, this project uses the title slide to capture the audience's attention by using title text and a shape, which is a movable, resizable graphical element. You will add this shape after you have typed the text for all four slides. The following step creates the slide show's title.

1 Type `Protect Your Good Name` in the title text placeholder (Figure 2-2 on the next page).

BTW

Introducing the Presentation
Before your audience enters the room, start the presentation and display Slide 1. This slide should be visually appealing and provide general interest in the presentation. An effective title slide gives a good first impression.

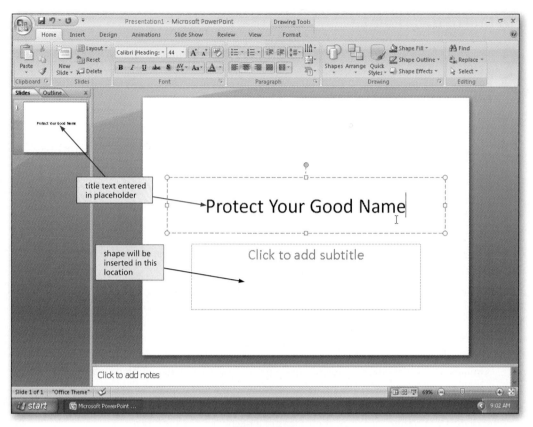

Figure 2–2

Plan
Ahead

> **Use sans serif fonts for content text.**
> When a new slide is displayed during your presentation, your audience members focus on the title and then read the words in the content placeholder. Generally more words appear in the content placeholder, so designers use sans serif typefaces to decrease reading time.

To Create the First Text Slide with a Single-Level Bulleted List

The first text slide you create in Chapter 2 describes tips for helping prevent thieves from accessing personal information. The four suggestions are displayed as second-level paragraphs. The following steps add a new slide (Slide 2) and then create a text slide with a single-level bulleted list.

1 Click the New Slide button in the Slides group.

2 Type Reduce Access to Personal Data in the title text placeholder.

3 Press CTRL+ENTER, type Shred credit card offers in the content text placeholder, and then press the ENTER key.

4 Type Use a locked mailbox and then press the ENTER key.

⑤ Type `Mail envelopes inside the post office` and then press the ENTER key.

⑥ Type `Remove listing from telephone directory` but do not press the ENTER key.

⑦ Italicize the word, inside, in the third bulleted paragraph (Figure 2–3).

To Char

You from Norr

①

• Click the view but lower rig the Powe window the prese Slide Sor (Figure 2

Why is SI selected

It is the in the sli

To Ch

No design de select the tone of y **backgro effects** a style to a

①

• Click D Ribbon the Des

• Click th Styles the Bac group Backgro gallery

• Point to styles th Backgro gallery the bac change

Are the displaye specific

Yes. Th in order the mid you poi

To Cha

You to Norma between attractive from Slid

①

• Click th view bu lower ri PowerP to displ sentatic view (Fi

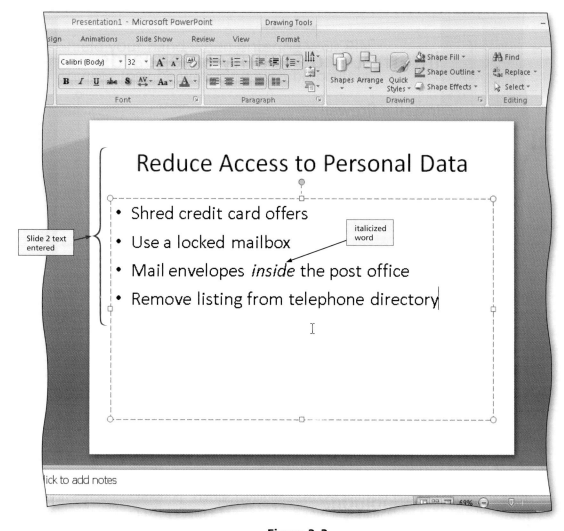

Figure 2–3

To Create the Second Text Slide with a Single-Level Bulleted List

The second text slide contains suggestions to help computer users protect their sensitive electronic files from cyber-intruders. The following steps add a new slide (Slide 3) and then create a text slide with a single-level bulleted list.

① Click the New Slide button in the Slides group.

② Type `Internet and Security Safeguards` in the title text placeholder.

③ Press CTRL+ENTER, type `Install a firewall` in the content text placeholder, and then press the ENTER key.

④ Type `Install and update virus protection software` and then press the ENTER key.

2

• Clic
 Styl
 bac
 slid

Q&A

If I
 this
 styl
 the
 pre
 I ap
 bac

 Yes
 the
 tim
 you

Q&A

Wl
 ap
 sty

 Wl
 is
 rig
 de
 th
 Se

2

• Click the Insert
 Picture from File
 icon in the content
 placeholder to
 display the Insert
 Picture dialog box.

• With your USB flash
 drive connected to
 one of the computer's
 USB ports, if neces-
 sary, click the Look in
 box arrow and then
 click UDISK 2.0 (E:) to
 select the USB flash
 drive, Drive E in this
 case, in the Look in
 list as the device that
 contains the picture.

• Click ATM to select
 the file name
 (Figure 2–18).

Q&A

What if the
 photograph is not
 on a USB flash drive?

Use the same process, but be certain to select the device containing the photograph in the
Look in list.

3

• Click the Insert button in the
 dialog box to insert the picture
 into Slide 4 (Figure 2–19).

Figure 2–18

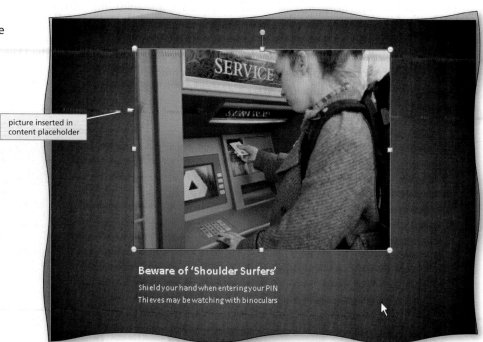

Figure 2–19

BTW

Ex
 Nc
 As
 co
 Po
 wi
 ta
 Ta
 th
 Ta
 th
 ta
 Ta
 ta
 th
 Pr

Resizing Clip Art and Photographs

Sometimes it is necessary to change the size of clip art. **Resizing** includes both enlarging and reducing the size of a clip art graphic. You can resize clip art using a variety of techniques. One method involves changing the size of a clip by specifying exact dimensions in a dialog box. Another method involves dragging one of the graphic's sizing handles to the desired location. A selected graphic appears surrounded by a **selection rectangle**, which has small squares and circles, called **sizing handles** or move handles, at each corner and middle location.

To Resize Clip Art

On Slide 2, much space appears around the clip, so you can increase its size. The photograph on Slide 3 is too large for the slide, so you should reduce its size. To change the size, drag the corner sizing handles to view how the clip will look on the slide. Using these corner handles maintains the graphic's original proportions. Dragging the square sizing handles alters the proportions so that the graphic becomes more or less high or more or less wide. The following steps increase the size of the Slide 2 clip using a corner sizing handle.

1

- Click the Previous Slide button two times to display Slide 2.

- Click the shredder clip to select it and display the selection rectangle.

- Point to the upper-left corner sizing handle on the clip so that the mouse pointer shape changes to a two-headed arrow (Figure 2–20).

Figure 2–20

2

- Drag the sizing handle diagonally toward the center of the slide until the mouse pointer is positioned approximately as shown in Figure 2–21.

Q&A

What if the clip is not the same size shown in Figure 2–21?

Repeat Steps 1 and 2.

Figure 2–21

3

- Release the mouse button to resize the clip. If necessary, select the clip and then use the ARROW keys to position the clip as shown in Figure 2-21.

4

- Click outside the clip to deselect it (Figure 2–22).

Q&A

What happened to the Picture Tools and Format tabs?

When you click outside the clip, PowerPoint deselects the clip and removes the Picture Tools and Format tabs from the screen.

Q&A

What if I want to return the clip to its original size and start again?

With the graphic selected, click the Reset button in the Slides group on the Home tab.

Figure 2–22

To Resize a Photograph

The credit card picture in Slide 3 fills the middle of the slide and covers some text, so you should reduce its size. The following steps resize this photograph using a sizing handle.

1 Click the Next Slide button to display Slide 3.

2 Click the credit card photograph to select it.

3 Drag the upper-left corner sizing handle on the photograph diagonally inward until the photograph is resized approximately as shown in Figure 2–23.

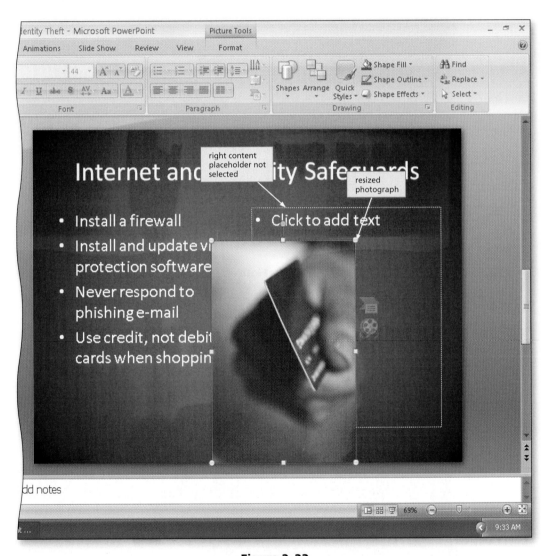

Figure 2–23

To Delete a Placeholder

The credit card photograph was inserted into the slide and not into a content placeholder. The right content placeholder, therefore, is not needed, so you can delete it from the slide. The following steps delete this placeholder.

1
- Click the right content placeholder to select it.

- Click the edge of the placeholder so the border is displayed as a solid line (Figure 2–24).

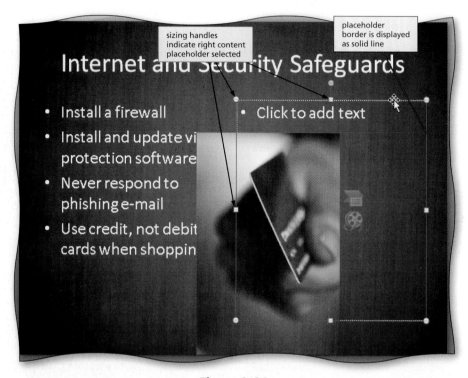

Figure 2–24

2
- Press the DELETE key to delete the placeholder from Slide 2 (Figure 2–25).

Figure 2–25

To Move Clips

After you insert clip art or a picture on a slide, you may want to reposition it. The credit card photograph on Slide 3 and the shredder clip on Slide 2 could be centered in the spaces between the bulleted text and the right edge of the slide. The following steps move these graphics.

- Click the credit card photograph on Slide 3 to select it and then press and hold down the mouse button.

- Drag the photograph diagonally upward toward the word, Safeguards (Figure 2–26).

Figure 2–26

- Click the Previous Slide button to display Slide 2.

- Click the shredder clip to select it, press and hold down the mouse button, and then drag the photograph toward the right side of the slide (Figure 2–27).

Figure 2–27

BTW

Inserting Special Characters
You can insert characters not found on your keyboard, such as the Euro sign (€), the copyright sign (©), and Greek capital letters (e.g., Δ, Ε, Θ). To insert these characters, click the Insert tab on the Ribbon, and then click the Symbol button in the Text group. When the Symbol dialog box is displayed, you can use the same font you currently are using in your presentation, or you can select another font. The Webdings, Webdings 2, and Webdings 3 fonts have a variety of symbols.

To Save an Existing Presentation with the Same File Name

You have made several changes to your presentation since you last saved it. Thus, you should save it again. The following step saves the presentation again.

1 Click the Save button on the Quick Access Toolbar to overwrite the previous Identity Theft file on the USB flash drive.

Formatting Title and Content Text

Choosing well-coordinated colors and styles for text and objects in a presentation is possible by using **Quick Styles**, which are defined combinations of formatting options. The styles in the Quick Styles Gallery have a wide variety of font, background, and border colors. You even can create a custom Quick Style and give it a unique name. Once you select a particular Quick Style and make any other font changes, you then can copy these changes to other text using the **Format Painter**. The Format Painter allows you to copy all formatting changes from one object to another.

To Format Title Text Using Quick Styles

The 42 Quick Styles are displayed in thumbnails in the Quick Style gallery. When you place your mouse pointer over a Quick Style thumbnail, PowerPoint changes the text and shows how the Quick Style affects the formatting. The title text in this presentation will have a light orange background, a dark orange border, and black letters. The following steps apply a Quick Style to the title text.

1

- Click the Slide 2 title text placeholder to select it.

- Click the Quick Styles button in the Drawing group in the Home tab to display the Quick Styles gallery. Point to the Subtle Effect – Accent 6 Quick Style (row 4, column 7) to display a live preview of the style (Figure 2–28).

Experiment

- Point to various styles in the Quick Styles gallery and watch the format of the text, backgrounds, and borders change in the placeholder.

Figure 2–28

2

- Click the Subtle Effect – Accent 6 Quick Style (row 4, column 7) to apply this format to the title text placeholder (Figure 2–29).

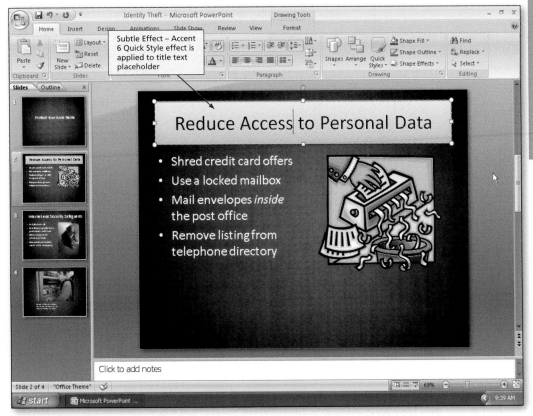

Figure 2–29

To Format Remaining Title Text Using Quick Styles

Once you have applied a Quick Style to one title text placeholder, it is a good idea to use the same style for consistency. The following steps apply the Subtle Effect – Accent 6 Quick Style to the title text placeholder on Slides 3 and 4.

1 Click the Next Slide button to display Slide 3. Click the title text placeholder and then click the Quick Styles button in the Drawing group to display the Quick Styles gallery.

2 Click the Subtle Effect – Accent 6 Quick Style (row 4, column 7) to apply this format to the title text placeholder.

3 Click the Next Slide button to display Slide 4. Click the title text placeholder, click the Quick Styles button, and then click the Subtle Effect – Accent 6 Quick Style (row 4, column 7) to apply this format to the title text placeholder (Figure 2–30).

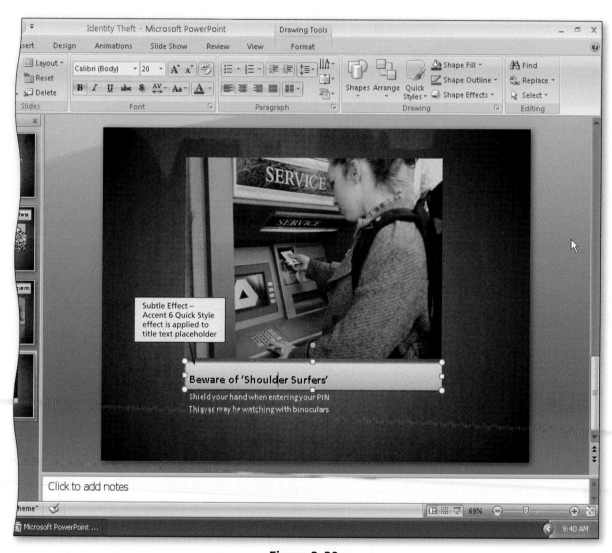

Figure 2–30

Plan Ahead

Use serif fonts for titles.
The design guidelines for title text differ from the guidelines for content body text. You would like your audience members to remember the main points of your presentation, and you can help their retention by having them read the title text more slowly than they read the words in the content text placeholder. The uneven lines in serif typefaces cause eye movement to slow down. Designers, therefore, often use serif fonts for the slide title text.

To Change the Heading Font

The default Office Theme heading and body text font is Calibri with a font size of 28 point. Calibri is a sans serif font, and designers recommend using a serif font to draw more attention to the slide title text. The following steps change the font from Calibri to Cambria.

- Click the Previous Slide button two times to display Slide 2. Triple-click the title text paragraph. With the text selected, click the Font box arrow in the Font group on the Home tab to display the Font gallery (Figure 2–31).

Q&A Will the fonts in my Font gallery be the same as those in Figure 2–31?

Your list of available fonts may differ, depending on the type of printer you are using.

- Scroll through the Font gallery, if necessary, and then point to Cambria (or a similar font) to display a live preview of the title text in Cambria font.

Experiment

- Point to various fonts in the Font gallery and watch the font of the title text change in the document window.

Figure 2–31

3

- Click Cambria (or a similar font) to change the font of the selected text to Cambria (Figure 2–32).

Figure 2–32

Other Ways

1. Click Font box arrow on Mini toolbar, click desired font in Font gallery
2. Right-click selected text, click Font on shortcut menu, click Font tab, select desired font
   in Font list or type a font in Font box, click OK button
3. Click Dialog Box Launcher in Font group, click Font tab, select desired font in Font
   list or type a font in Font box, click OK button
4. Press CTRL+SHIFT+F, click Font tab, select desired font in the Font list, click OK button

To Shadow Text

A **shadow** helps the letters display prominently by adding a shadow behind the text. The following step adds a shadow to the selected title text, Reduce Access to Personal Data.

- With the text selected, click the Text Shadow button in the Font group on the Home tab to add a shadow to the selected text (Figure 2–33).

Q&A

How would I remove a shadow?

You would click the Shadow button a second time, or you immediately could click the Undo button on the Quick Access Toolbar.

Figure 2–33

To Change Font Color

Color is used to emphasize or draw attention to specific text. The following step changes the title text font color from black to dark red.

- With the text selected, click the Font Color box arrow in the Font group on the Home tab to display the Font Color gallery (Figure 2–34).

Q&A

What is the difference between the colors shown in the Theme Colors area and the Standard Colors?

The ten colors in the top row of the Theme Colors area are two text, two background, and six accent colors in the Office Theme; the five colors in each column under the top row display different transparencies. The ten standard colors are available in every document theme.

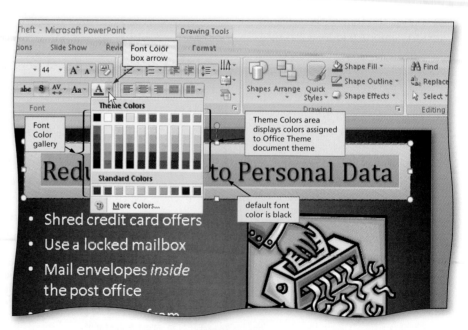

Figure 2–34

②

- Point to the Dark Red color in the Standard Colors row to display a live preview of the title text in a Dark Red color (Figure 2–35).

🔎 **Experiment**

- Point to various colors in the Font Color gallery and watch the title text color change in the slide.

③

- Click Dark Red to change the title text font color.

Q&A How would I change a color?

You would click the Font Color box arrow and then select another color in the Font Color gallery.

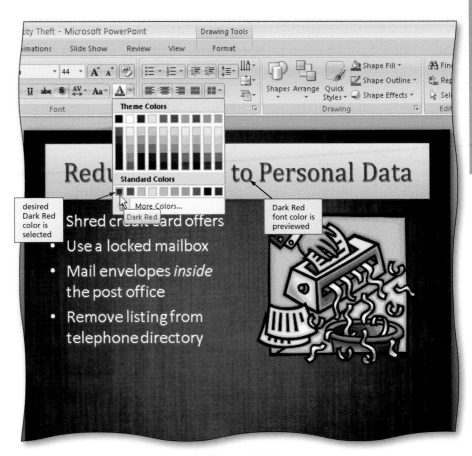

Figure 2–35

Other Ways

1. Click Font color box arrow on Mini toolbar, click desired color in Font Color gallery

2. Right-click selected text, click Font on shortcut menu, click Font tab, select desired color in Font color list, click OK button

3. Click Dialog Box Launcher in Font group, click Font tab, select desired color in Font color list, click OK button

4. Press CTRL+SHIFT+F, click Font tab, select desired color in Font color list, click OK button

Format Painter

To save time and avoid formatting errors, you can use the Format Painter to apply custom formatting to other places in your presentation quickly and easily. You can use this feature in three ways:

- To copy only character attributes, such as font and font effects, select text that has these qualities.
- To copy both paragraph attributes, such as alignment and indentation and character attributes, select the entire paragraph.
- To apply the same formatting to multiple words, phrases, or paragraphs, double-click the Format Painter button and then select each item you want to format. You then can press the ESC key or click the Format Painter button to turn off this feature.

BTW

Deleting WordArt
If you decide you no longer want the WordArt text to display on your slide, select this text, click the Format tab on the Ribbon, click the Quick Styles button, and then click Clear WordArt.

To Format Slide 3 Text Using the Format Painter

To save time and duplicated effort, you quickly can use the Format Painter to copy formatting attributes from the Slide 2 title text and apply them to Slides 3. The following steps use the Format Painter to copy formatting features.

- With the Slide 2 title text still selected, double-click the Format Painter button in the Clipboard group in the Home tab (Figure 2–36).

- Move the mouse pointer off the Ribbon.

Q&A

Why did my mouse pointer change shape?

The mouse pointer changed shape by adding a paint brush to indicate that the Format Painter function is active.

Figure 2–36

- Click the Next Slide button to display Slide 3. Triple-click the title text placeholder to apply the format to all the title text (Figure 2–37).

Figure 2–37

To Format Remaining Title Text

Once you have applied formatting characteristics to one text placeholder, you should maintain consistency and apply the same formats to the other title text characters. The following steps use the Format Painter to change the font and font color and apply a shadow to the Slide 4 and Slide 1 title text.

1 Click the Next Slide button to display Slide 4. Triple-click the title text placeholder to apply the format to all title text characters.

Q&A What happened to all the letters in my title?

The Format Painter applied a style that does not fit in the current placeholder. You will adjust the font size so that all the words are displayed.

2 Click the Previous Slide button three times to display Slide 1. Triple-click the title text placeholder to apply the format to all title text characters.

3 Press the ESC key to turn off the Format Painter feature (Figure 2–38).

Other Ways

1. Click Format Painter button on Mini toolbar

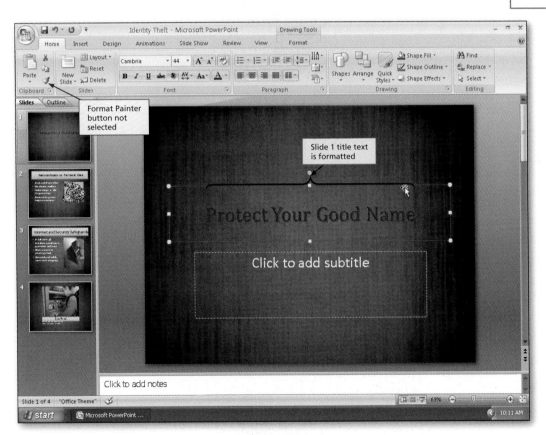

Figure 2–38

To Size Slide 4 Text

The Slide 4 title text placeholder is too small to accommodate the formatting characteristics you applied to the text. The text will fit if you reduce the font size. In addition, the body text should be enlarged for readability. The following steps adjust the size of the Slide 4 title and body text.

1 Click the Next Slide button three times to display Slide 4.

2 Select both body text paragraphs in the content text placeholder and then click the Increase Font Size button on the Mini toolbar four times to increase the font size to 24 point.

3 Triple-click the title text placeholder and then click the Decrease Font Size button on the Mini toolbar three times to reduce the font size to 32 point (Figure 2–39).

4 Click the slide anywhere outside the placeholders to deselect it.

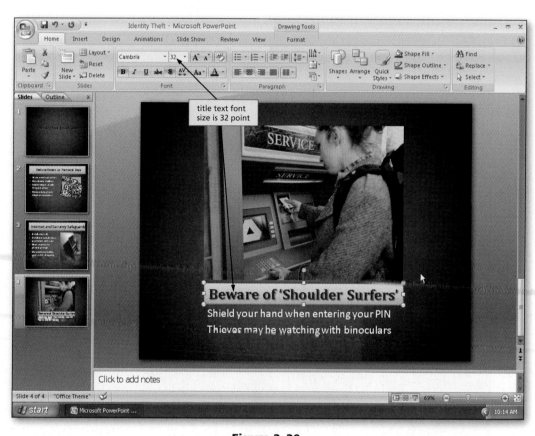

Figure 2–39

Adding and Formatting a Shape

One method of getting the audience's attention at the start of a slide show is to have graphical elements on the title slide. PowerPoint provides a wide variety of shapes that can add visual interest to a slide. Shape elements include lines, basic geometrical shapes, arrows, equation shapes, flowchart symbols, stars, banners, and callouts.

Slide 1 in this presentation is enhanced in a variety of ways. First, the title text font size is increased to aid readability and to catch the audience's attention. Then a shape is inserted below the title text with additional formatted text. Finally, the subtitle text placeholder is deleted because it no longer is needed.

To Increase Title Slide Font Size

The title on a slide should be large enough to stimulate the audience's interest and announce the topic of the presentation. The following steps increase the Slide 1 title text.

1 Click the Previous Slide button three times to display Slide 1.

2 Select the Slide 1 title text, Protect Your Good Name. Click the Increase Font Size button on the Mini toolbar six times until the font size is 80 point (Figure 2–40).

3 Click the slide anywhere outside the title text placeholder to deselect it.

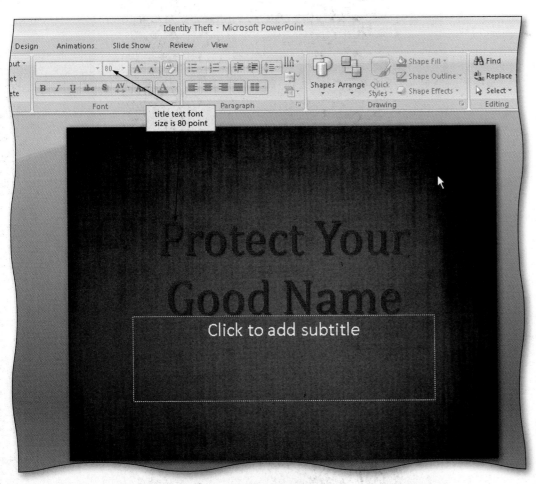

Figure 2–40

To Add a Shape

After adding a shape to a slide, you can change its default characteristics by adding text, bullets, numbers, and Quick Styles. You also can combine multiple shapes to create a more complex graphic. The following steps add a banner shape to Slide 1.

- Click the Shapes button in the Drawing group on the Home tab to display the Shapes gallery. Point to the Wave banner shape in the Stars and Banners area (Figure 2–41).

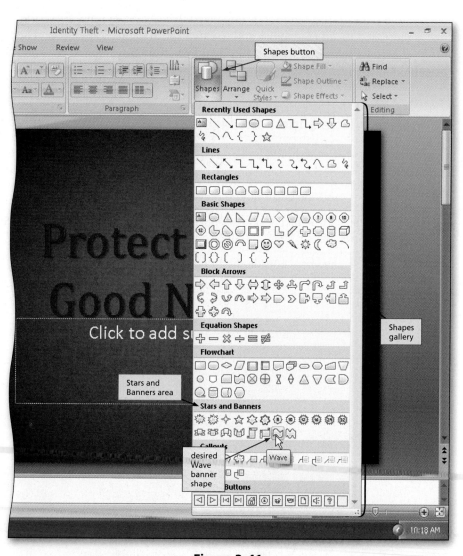

Figure 2–41

2

- Click the Wave shape (Figure 2–42).

Q&A

Why did my pointer change shape?
The pointer changed to a plus shape to indicate the Wave shape has been added to the Clipboard.

Figure 2–42

- Click Slide 1 anywhere below the title text to insert the Wave shape (Figure 2–43).

Figure 2–43

Other Ways

1. Click More button in Insert Shapes group on Format tab in Drawing Tools tab

To Resize a Shape

The next step is to resize the Wave shape. The shape should be enlarged so that it appears prominently on the slide and can hold the subtitle text. The following steps resize the selected Wave shape.

- With the Wave shape still selected, point to the lower-right corner sizing handle on the picture so that the mouse pointer shape changes to a two-headed arrow (Figure 2–44).

Q&A What if my shape is not selected?

To select a shape, click it.

Figure 2–44

- Drag the sizing handle diagonally outward and downward until the Wave shape is the approximate size of the one shown in Figure 2–45.

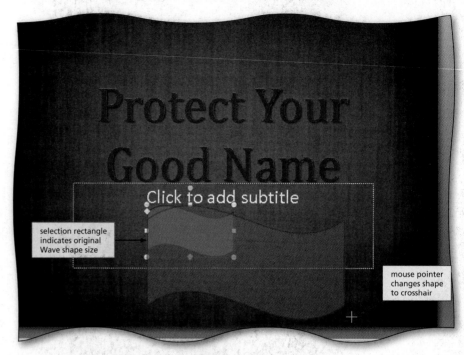

selection rectangle indicates original Wave shape size

mouse pointer changes shape to crosshair

Figure 2–45

- Release the mouse button to resize the shape (Figure 2–46).

Q&A What if the shape is the wrong size?

Repeat Steps 1 and 2.

Q&A What if I want to move the shape to a different location on the slide?

With the shape selected, press the Arrow keys or drag the shape to the desired location.

Other Ways

1. Enter shape height and width in Height and Width text boxes in Size group on Format tab in Drawing Tools contextual tabs

2. Click Dialog Box Launcher in Size group on Format tab in Drawing Tools contextual tabs, click Size tab, enter desired height and width values in text boxes, click Close button

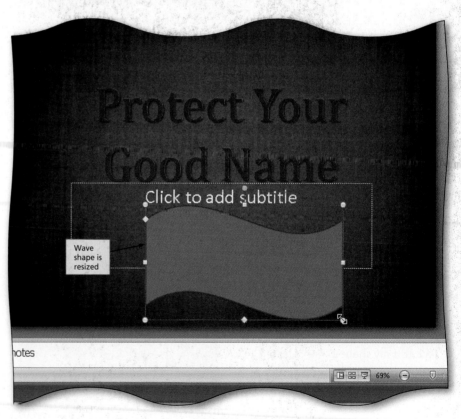

Wave shape is resized

Figure 2–46

To Add Text to a Shape

The banner shape is displayed on Slide 1 in the correct location. The next step is to add text stating that the presentation will cover strategies to help prevent identity theft. The following step describes how to add this information to the shape.

- With the Wave banner shape se-lected, type Reduce Your Risk of Identity Theft in the shape (Figure 2–47).

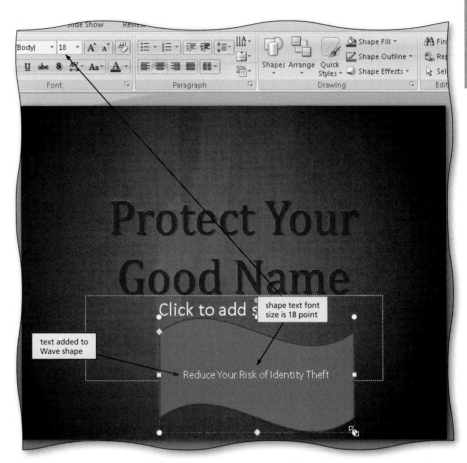

Figure 2–47

To Format Shape Text and Add a Shape Quick Style

Formatting text in a shape follows the same techniques as formatting text in a placeholder. You can change font, font color and size, and alignment, and you also can apply a Shape Quick Style. The following steps describe how to format the shape text by increasing the font size and adding a Shape Quick Style.

- Triple-click the Wave shape text to select it and then click the Increase Font Size button on the Mini toolbar five times until the font size is 36 point (Figure 2–48).

Figure 2–48

2

- Click the Shape Quick Styles button in the Drawing group on the Home tab to display the Quick Styles gallery (Figure 2–49).

- Point to the Subtle Effect – Accent 6 Shape Quick Style (row 4, column 7) to display a live preview of the style.

Experiment

- Point to various styles in the Quick Styles gallery and watch the format of the text, backgrounds, and borders change in the Wave shape.

3

- Click the Subtle Effect – Accent 6 Shape Quick Style (row 4, column 7) to apply this format to the shape.

Figure 2–49

4

- Click outside the shape to deselect it (Figure 2–50).

Figure 2–50

To Delete a Placeholder

The subtitle placeholder no longer is necessary on Slide 1 because the shape fills the area below the title text. The following steps delete the Slide 1 subtitle placeholder.

1

- Click the subtitle text placeholder border two times to change the border to a solid line (Figure 2–51).

Figure 2–51

2

- Press the DELETE key to delete the placeholder. If necessary, select the shape and then use the ARROW keys to center the shape under the title text (Figure 2–52).

Figure 2–52

Plan
Ahead

> **Use simple transitions.**
> Transitions help segue one slide into the next seamlessly. They should not be used decoratively or be something on which an audience member focuses. For consistency, use the same transition throughout the presentation unless you have a special circumstance that warrants a different effect.

BTW

Certification
The Microsoft Certified Application Specialist (MCAS) program provides an opportunity for you to obtain a valuable industry credential – proof that you have the PowerPoint 2007 skills required by employers. For more information see Appendix F or visit the PowerPoint 2007 Certification Web page (scsite.com/ppt2007/cert).

Adding a Transition

PowerPoint provides many animation effects to add interest and make a slide show presentation look professional. **Animation** includes special visual and sound effects applied to text or content. A **slide transition** is a special animation effect used to progress from one slide to the next in a slide show. You can control the speed of the transition effect and add a sound.

PowerPoint provides more than 50 different transitions in the Quick Styles group. They are arranged into five categories that describe the types of effects:

- Fades and Dissolves - Blend one slide seamlessly into the next slide
- Wipes - Gently uncover one slide to reveal the next
- Push and Cover - Appear to move one slide off the screen
- Stripes and Bars – Use blinds and checkerboard patterns
- Random – Use vertical and horizontal bars or an arbitrary pattern that changes each time you run the presentation.

To Add a Transition between Slides

In this presentation, you apply the Uncover Right transition in the Wipes category to all slides and change the transition speed to Medium. The following steps apply this transition to the presentation.

1

- Click the Animations tab on the Ribbon and then point to the More button in the Transition to This Slide group (Figure 2–53).

Q&A

Is a transition applied now?

No. The first slide icon in the Transitions group has an orange border, which indicates no transition has been applied.

Figure 2–53

2

- Click the More button to expand the Transitions gallery.

- Point to the Uncover Right transition (row 2, column 2) in the Wipes category in the Transitions gallery to display a live preview of this transition (Figure 2–54).

 Experiment

- Point to various styles in the Transitions gallery and watch the transitions on the slide.

Figure 2–54

3

- Click Uncover Right in the Wipes category in the Transitions gallery to apply the Uncover Right transition to the title slide.

Q&A Why does a star appear next to Slide 1 in the Slides tab?

The star indicates that a transition animation effect is applied to that slide.

- Click the Transition Speed arrow in the Transition to This Slide group on the Animations tab to display three possible speeds: Slow, Medium, and Fast (Figure 2–55).

Figure 2–55

- Click Medium to change the transition speed for Slide 1 to Medium.

- Click the Apply to All button in the Transition to This Slide group on the Animations tab to apply the Uncover Right transition and Medium speed to all four slides in the presentation (Figure 2–56).

Q&A

What if I want to apply a different transition and speed to each slide in the presentation?

Repeat Steps 2 through 5 for each slide individually.

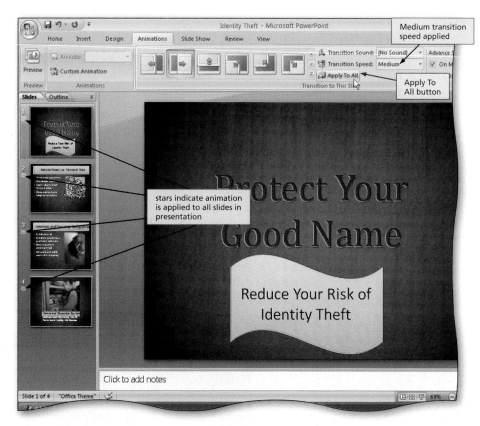

Figure 2–56

To Change Document Properties

Before saving the presentation again, you want to add your name, class name, and some keywords as document properties. The following steps use the Document Information Panel to change document properties.

1 Click the Office Button to display the Office Button menu, point to Prepare on the Office Button menu, and then click Properties on the Prepare submenu to display the Document Information Panel.

2 Click the Author text box, if necessary, and then type your name as the Author property. If a name already is displayed in the Author text box, delete it before typing your name.

3 Click the Subject text box, if necessary delete any existing text, and then type your course and section as the Subject property.

4 Click the Keywords text box, if necessary delete any existing text, and then type identity theft, Internet safeguards, PIN as the Keywords properties.

5 Click the Close the Document Information Panel button so that the Document Information Panel no longer is displayed.

To Save an Existing Presentation with the Same File Name

You have made several changes to the presentation since you last saved it. Thus, you should save it again. The following step saves the document again.

1 Click the Save button on the Quick Access Toolbar to overwrite the previous Identity Theft file on the USB flash drive.

To Run an Animated Slide Show

All changes are complete, and the presentation is saved. You now can view the Identity Theft presentation. The following step starts Slide Show view.

1 Click the Slide Show button to display the title slide (Figure 2–57).

2 Click each slide and view the transition effect and slides.

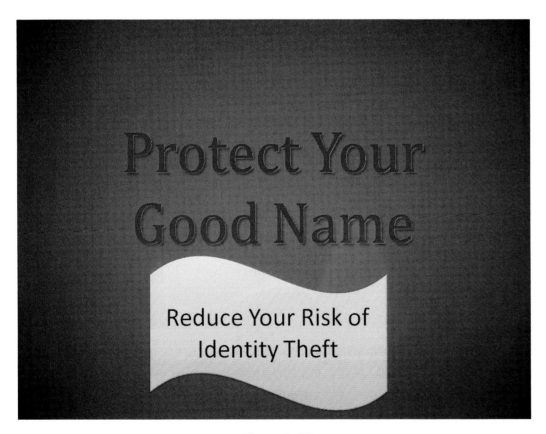

Figure 2–57

Printing a Presentation as an Outline and Handouts

During the development of a lengthy presentation, it often is easier to review an outline in print rather than on the screen. Printing an outline also is useful for audience handouts or when your supervisor or instructor wants to review your subject matter before you

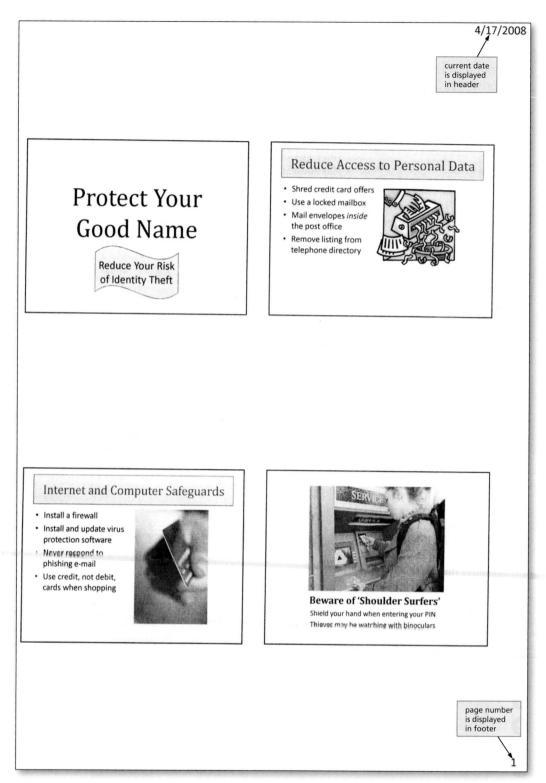

Figure 2–64

Saving and Quitting PowerPoint

If you made any changes to your presentation since your last save, you should save it again before quitting PowerPoint. The following steps save changes to the presentation and quit PowerPoint.

To Quit PowerPoint

This project is complete. The following steps quit PowerPoint.

1 Click the Close button on the right side of the title bar to quit PowerPoint.

2 If necessary, click the Yes button in the Microsoft Office PowerPoint dialog box so that any changes you have made are saved.

Chapter Summary

In this chapter you have learned how to create slides from a blank presentation, change slide layouts, add a background style, insert clip art and pictures, size graphic elements, apply Quick Styles, select slide transitions, and preview and print an outline and handout. The items listed below include all the new PowerPoint skills you have learned in this chapter.

1. Choose a Background Style (PPT 89)
2. Change the View to Slide Sorter View (PPT 91)
3. Change the View to Normal View (PPT 91)
4. Change the Slide Layout to Two Content (PPT 92)
5. Change the Slide Layout to Picture with Caption (PPT 94)
6. Insert a Clip from the Clip Organizer into a Content Placeholder (PPT 96)
7. Insert a Photograph from the Clip Organizer into a Slide (PPT 98)
8. Insert a Photograph from a File into a Slide (PPT 99)
9. Resize Clip Art (PPT 100)
10. Resize a Photograph (PPT 103)
11. Delete a Placeholder (PPT 104)
12. Move Clips (PPT 105)
13. Format Title Text Using Quick Styles (PPT 106)
14. Format Remaining Title Text Using Quick Styles (PPT 107)
15. Change the Heading Font (PPT 109)
16. Shadow Text (PPT 110)
17. Change Font Color (PPT 110)
18. Format Text Using the Format Painter (PPT 112)
19. Format Remaining Title Text (PPT 113)
20. Add a Shape (PPT 116)
21. Resize a Shape (PPT 117)
22. Add Text to a Shape (PPT 119)
23. Format Shape Text and Add a Shape Quick Style (PPT 119)
24. Add a Transition between Slides (PPT 122)
25. Preview and Print an Outline (PPT 122)
26. Preview and Print Handouts (PPT 129)

 If you have a SAM user profile, you may have access to hands-on instruction, practice, and assessment. Log in to your SAM account (http://sam2007.course.com) to launch any assigned training activities or exams that relate to the skills covered in this chapter.

Learn It Online

Test your knowledge of chapter content and key terms.

Instructions: To complete the Learn It Online exercises, start your browser, click the Address bar, and then enter the Web address scsite.com/ppt2007/learn. When the Office 2007 Learn It Online page is displayed, click the link for the exercise you want to complete and then read the instructions.

Chapter Reinforcement TF, MC, and SA
A series of true/false, multiple choice, and short answer questions that test your knowledge of the chapter content.

Flash Cards
An interactive learning environment where you identify chapter key terms associated with displayed definitions.

Practice Test
A series of multiple choice questions that test your knowledge of chapter content and key terms.

Who Wants To Be a Computer Genius?
An interactive game that challenges your knowledge of chapter content in the style of a television quiz show.

Wheel of Terms
An interactive game that challenges your knowledge of chapter key terms in the style of the television show *Wheel of Fortune*.

Crossword Puzzle Challenge
A crossword puzzle that challenges your knowledge of key terms presented in the chapter.

Apply Your Knowledge

Reinforce the skills and apply the concepts you learned in this chapter.

Changing the Background and Adding Photographs and a Quick Style
Instructions: Start PowerPoint. Open the presentation, Apply 2-1 Lifestyle, from the Data Files for Students. See the inside back cover this book for instructions on downloading the Data Files for Students, or contact your instructor for more information about accessing the required files.

The four slides in the presentation present basic guidelines for maintaining a healthy lifestyle and focus on proper weight, exercise, and food choices. The document you open is an unformatted presentation. You are to add and size photographs, change the background style, change slide layouts, apply a transition, and use the Format Painter so the slides look like Figure 2-65.

Perform the following tasks:
1. Change the background style to Style 11 (row 3, column 3). On the title slide, use your name in place of Student Name and bold and italicize your name and change the font color to orange. Increase the title text font size to 72 point, change the font to Baskerville Old Face, and change the font color to Dark Blue.

2. On Slides 2 and 4, change the layout to Two Content and then insert the photographs shown in Figure 2-65b and 2-65d from the Microsoft Clip Organizer.

3. On Slide 3, change the layout to Picture with Caption and then insert the picture shown in Figure 2-65c from the Microsoft Clip Organizer. Delete the text placeholder. Change the title text font size to 44 point, center this text, and then add the italic font style and shadow effect. Use the Format Painter to format the title text on Slides 2 and 4.

4. Apply the Subtle Effect – Accent 1 Quick Style (row 4, column 2) to the Slides 2, 3, and 4 title text placeholders. Apply the Uncover Left wipe transition (row 2, column 1) to all slides.

5. Check the spelling, and then display the revised presentation in Slide Sorter view.

6. Change the document properties, as specified by your instructor. Save the presentation using the file name, Apply 2–1 Healthy Lifestyle. Submit the revised document in the format specified by your instructor.

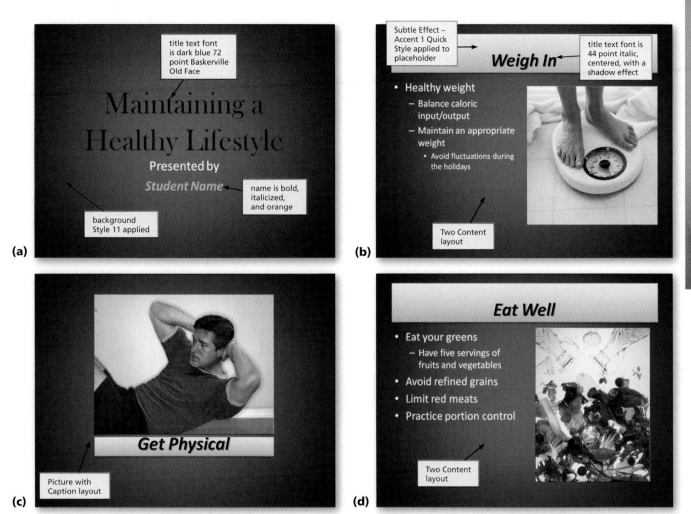

Figure 2–65

Extend Your Knowledge

Extend the skills you learned in this chapter and experiment with new skills. You may need to use Help to complete the assignment.

Changing Slide Layouts and Moving Clips

Instructions: Start PowerPoint. Open the presentation, Extend 2-1 Fats, from the Data Files for Students. See the inside back cover of this book for instructions on downloading the Data Files for Students, or contact your instructor for more information on accessing the required files.

You will choose a background, format slides, and copy clips (Figure 2–66).

Perform the following tasks:

1. Add an appropriate background style.

2. On Slide 1, use your name in place of Student Name. Format the text using techniques you learned and applied in this chapter, such as changing the font size and color and also bolding and italicizing words.

3. Slide 7 contains a variety of clips downloaded from the Microsoft Clip Organizer. Review the slides in the presentation and then move clips from Slide 7 to the appropriate slides. You do not need to use all the clips. Delete Slide 7 when you have finished moving the desired clips to the slides.

4. Change the slide layouts to accommodate the clips. Size the clips when necessary. Edit the text so that each slide meets the 7 × 7 rule, which states that each line should have a maximum of seven words, and each slide should have a maximum of seven lines.

5. Apply an appropriate transition to all slides.

6. Change the document properties, as specified by your instructor. Save the presentation using the file name, Extend 2-1 Enhanced Fats.

7. Submit the revised document in the format specified by your instructor.

variety of clips to consider moving to previous slides in presentation

Figure 2–66

Make It Right

Analyze a presentation and correct all errors and/or improve the design.

Applying Background and Quick Styles

Instructions: Start PowerPoint. Open the presentation, Make It Right 2-1 Safety, from the Data Files for Students. See the back inside cover of this book for instructions on downloading the Data Files for Students, or contact your instructor for more information on accessing the required files.

Correct the formatting problems and errors in the presentation while keeping in mind the guidelines presented in this chapter.

Perform the following tasks:

1. Change the document theme from Verve, shown in Figure 2–67, to Paper. Apply the Style 7 background style (row 2, column 3).

2. On Slide 1, replace the words, Student Name, with your name. Apply a Quick Style to your name and the title text so that they display prominently on the slide.

3. Move Slide 2 to the end of the presentation so that it becomes the new Slide 5.

4. Use the spell checker to correct the misspellings. Analyze the slides for other word usage errors that the spell checker did not find.

5. Adjust the clip art sizes so they do not overlap text and are the appropriate dimensions for the slide content.

6. Select a Quick Style to apply to the Slides 2 through 5 title text. Center the title text and apply a shadow.

7. Apply an appropriate transition to all slides. Change the speed to Slow.

8. Change the document properties, as specified by your instructor. Save the presentation using the file name, Make It Right 2-1 Home Safety.

9. Submit the revised document in the format specified by your instructor.

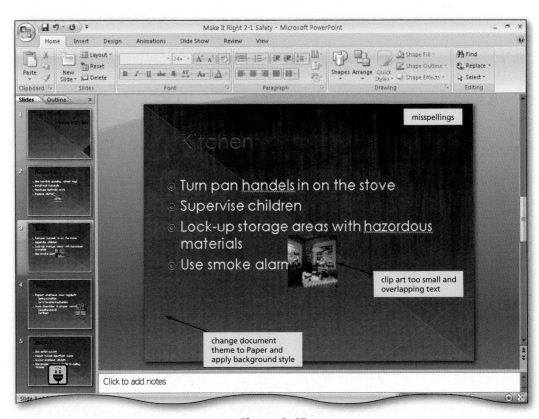

Figure 2–67

In the Lab

Design and/or create a presentation using the guidelines, concepts, and skills presented in this chapter. Labs 1, 2, and 3 are listed in order of increasing difficulty.

Lab 1: Creating a Presentation with a Clip and Shapes

Problem: The ear affects balance while it enables us to hear. This organ can be divided into three parts for analysis: outer, middle, and inner. The outer ear is composed of a flap and the auditory canal. The middle ear has three tiny bones called the auditory ossicles and the eustachian tube, which links the ear to the nose. The inner ear contains the spiral-shaped cochlea and also the semicircular canals and the vestibule, which control balance. You are studying the ear as a unit in your health class, so you decide to develop a PowerPoint slide that names these parts to help you study for a quiz. Create the slide shown in Figure 2–68 from a blank presentation.

Instructions: Perform the following tasks.

1. Apply the Style 6 background style (row 2, column 2) to the slide. Change the layout to Content with Caption. Import the ear diagram clip from the Microsoft Clip Organizer.

2. Type the slide title and caption body text shown in Figure 2–68. Use your name in place of Bill Tracy, and then italicize this text and change the font color to Blue (color 8 in the Standard Colors row). Change the color of the title text to Dark Red (color 1 in the Standard Colors row) and increase the font size to 24.

3. Use the Right Arrow, Left Arrow, Up Arrow, and Down Arrow shapes in the Block Arrow section to point to the parts of the ear shown in Figure 2–68. Add the number to each arrow. Apply the Subtle Effect – Accent 3 Quick Style (row 4, column 4) to each arrow. Change the font size of each arrow text to 24 point and bold these numbers.

4. Check the spelling and correct any errors.

5. Change the document properties, as specified by your instructor. Save the presentation using the file name, Lab 2-1 Ear.

6. Submit the revised document in the format specified by your instructor.

Figure 2–68

In the Lab

Lab 2: Creating a Presentation with Photographs Inserted from a File

Problem: Destructive insects damage specific species of trees throughout the world. You have learned in your Botany 202 class that the Asian Longhorn Beetle, the Emerald Ash Borer, the Gypsy Moth, and the Western Pine Beetle are among trees' biggest pests. One of your assignments in your botany class is to give a speech about common tree pests. You develop the outline shown in Figure 2–69 and then prepare the PowerPoint presentation shown in Figures 2–70a through 2–70f. You have obtained permission from the U.S. Forestry Department to copy photographs from its Web site to your slide show; these photographs are on your Data Files for Students.

Tree Pests
Creatures That Bug Our Trees
Jim DeYoung
Botany 202

Asian Longhorn Beetle
- Native to China
- Transported to United States in infested packing material

Emerald Ash Borer
- Killed 20 million trees in Michigan, Ohio, and Indiana
- Firewood quarantines to prevent new infestations

Gypsy Moth
- Spread to U.S. in 1870
- Oaks and Aspens are most common hosts
- Larva defoliate trees
- Small mammals and birds are predators

Western Pine Beetle
- Infest Ponderosa and Coulter pine trees
  - Mainly Western states
- Tree loss considered normal ecological process

Acknowledgements
- Photos and information courtesy of the USDA Forest Service
  - forestry.about.com

Figure 2–69

Continued >

In the Lab *continued*

Instructions: *Perform the following tasks.*

1. Create a new presentation using the Foundry document theme. Apply the Style 7 background style (row 2, column 3).

2. Using the typed notes illustrated in Figure 2–69, create the title slide shown in Figure 2–70a using your name in place of Jim DeYoung. Bold your name and apply a shadow.

3. Insert the Isosceles Triangle shape (row 1, column 3 in the Basic Shapes category) in the top center of Slide 1. Size the shape so that the top and bottom align with the edges of the brown area of the slide, as shown in Figure 2–70a.

4. Using the typed notes in Figure 2–69, create the five text slides with bulleted lists shown in Figures 2–70b through 2–70f. Use the Two Content slide layout for Slides 2 through 5 and the Title and Content slide layout for Slide 6.

5. Insert the appropriate pictures from your Data Files for Students on Slides 2 through 5.

6. Apply the Wedge transition (row 1, column 5 in the Wipes category) to all slides. Change the speed to Medium. Check the spelling and correct any errors.

7. Review the slides in Slide Sorter view to check for consistency, and then change the view to Normal.

8. Drag the scroll box to display Slide 1. Click the Slide Show button to start Slide Show view. Then click to display each slide.

9. Change the document properties, as specified by your instructor. Save the presentation using the file name, Lab 2-2 Tree Pests.

10. Submit the document in the format specified by your instructor.

(a)

(b)

Figure 2–70

(c)

(d)

(e)

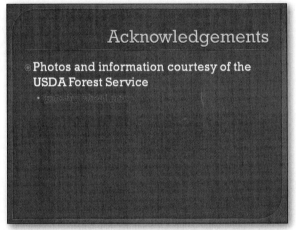

(f)

Figure 2–70

In the Lab

Lab 3: Creating a Presentation with Clips and Shapes

Problem: Snowboarding's popularity has soared in recent years; even Cameron Diaz and Space Shuttle astronauts have a passion for the sport. But with this increase in snowboarders has come a corresponding increase in injuries. The most common injuries are caused by a failure to follow common sense precautions. In order to maximize the time on the slopes, snowboarders need to prepare for the sport by wearing proper equipment, getting into condition, and snowboarding under control. Bryan Howell owns a local ski and snowboard shop in your town and has asked you to prepare a PowerPoint presentation that he can share with equipment buyers and renters. He hands you the outline shown in Figure 2–71 and asks you to create the presentation shown in Figures 2–72a through 2–72d.

Prepare for Snowboarding Season
Vertical Slope Shop
Bryan Howell, Owner

Dress for the Ride
- Loose fitting layers
  - Moisture wicking inner
  - Insulating middle
  - Waterproof outer shell
- Goggles
- Helmet, wrist guards

Get into Condition
- Stretch for 10 minutes
  - Do lateral squats, hops
- Eat complex carbohydrates
- Drink plenty of water
  - Dehydration is common

Snowboard under Control
- Be aware of traffic
  - Where trails merge
- Stick to slopes designed for your ability
- Be aware of changing conditions

Figure 2–71

Instructions: Perform the following tasks.

1. Use the typed notes illustrated in Figure 2–71 to create four slides shown in Figures 2–72a through 2–72d from a blank presentation. Apply the Style 7 background style (row 2, column 3). Use your name in place of Bryan Howell on the title slide shown in Figure 2–72a. Bold your name.

2. Insert the Right Triangle shape (row 1, column 4 in the Basic Shapes category) on Slide 1. With the shape selected, click the Arrange button in the Drawing group on the Home tab, point to Rotate in the Position Objects group, and then click Flip Horizontal to turn the triangle shape. Drag the shape to the lower-right corner of the slide, increase the size to that shown in Figure 2–72a, and apply the Colored Outline - Accent 3 Quick Style (row 1, column 4).

3. Italicize the Slide 1 title text, Prepare for Snowboarding Season, align the text left, and change the font color to Black. Align the subtitle text left and change the font color to Green (color 6 in the Standard Colors row).

4. Add the photographs and clip art shown in Figures 2–72a through 2–72d from the Microsoft Clip Organizer. Adjust the clip sizes when necessary.

5. Change the Slide 2 title text font size to 54 point, change the font to Forte, and then change the color to Green. Use the Format Painter to format the title text on Slides 3 and 4 with the same features as on Slide 2.

6. Apply the Newsflash transition (row 6, column 2 in the Wipes category) to all slides. Change the speed to Medium. Check the spelling and correct any errors.

7. Click the Slide Sorter view button, view the slides for consistency, and then click the Normal view button.

8. Change the document properties, as specified by your instructor. Save the presentation using the file name, Lab 2-3 Snowboarding.

9. Submit the revised document in the format specified by your instructor.

(a)

(b)

(c)

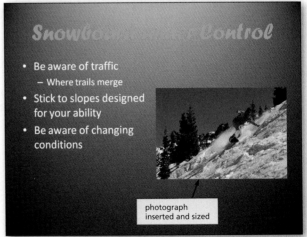

(d)

Figure 2–72

Cases and Places

Apply your creative thinking and problem solving skills to design and implement a solution.

• EASIER   •• MORE DIFFICULT

Note: Remember to use the 7×7 rule as you design the presentations: a maximum of seven words on a line and a maximum of seven lines on one slide.

• 1: Design and Create an Energy Efficiency Presentation

Global demand, industry deregulation, and regional conflicts have increased energy prices. The United States Department of Energy predicts energy use will grow 33 percent by 2030. Despite these staggering numbers, homeowners can undertake relatively simple measures to be energy efficient. Create a presentation using the outline in Figure 2–73. Apply at least three objectives found at the beginning of this chapter to develop the presentation. Add a title slide with a shape and a closing slide that cites your references. Be sure to check spelling.

Home Energy Savings Tips

Save Money While You Help the Environment

Bright Ideas
- Lighting accounts for more than 10 percent of electric bill
- Change to compact florescent lights (CFLs)
  - Use 50-75 percent less energy
  - Last up to ten times longer than conventional bulbs

Keep It Clean
- Wash only *full* loads of clothes and dishes
- Keep dryer vents clean
- Air dry dishes when possible
- Use ENERGY STAR products

Stay Out of Hot Water
- Heating water accounts for 13 percent of energy bill
- Use low-flow fixtures
- Repair leaks
- Lower thermostat
- Insulate heater

References
- www1.eere.energy.gov/consumer/tips/save_energy.html
- www.exeloncorp.com/comedcare/
- www.energystar.gov/

Figure 2–73

• 2: Design and Create a Hypertension Presentation

According to the National Heart, Lung, and Blood Institute, nearly one-third of American adults are inflicted by the "silent killer," high blood pressure. This disease affects people of all ages and ethnicities. Use the concepts and techniques presented in this chapter to create a presentation following the outline in Figure 2–74, which includes the definition of hypertension and hypertension categories, has tips on controlling high blood pressure, and lists Web sites to view for further information. Insert photographs and clips, and apply a subtle slide transition to all slides. Be sure to check spelling.

Blood Pressure 101
Taking Control of the Silent Killer

Blood Pressure Definition
- Force of blood on vein walls
  - Pressure units: milligrams of mercury (mgHg)
- Defined by two numbers
  - Systolic: Pressure during beats
  - Diastolic: Pressure between beats
- Read as the systolic over diastolic level
  - Example: 125 over 74

Adult Blood Pressure Categories
- Normal
  - Systolic < 120
  - Diastolic < 80
- Prehypertension
  - Systolic 120 – 139
  - Diastolic 80 – 89
- Hypertension
  - Systolic > 140
  - Diastolic > 90

Detection
- No symptoms
- Person must be tested
  - Sphygmomanometer and stethoscope used

Hypertension Prevention Tips
- Eat healthy
  - Fruits, vegetables
  - Low fat diet
- Maintain weight
- Exercise regularly

References
- National Heart, Lung, and Blood Institute
  - www.nhlbi.nih.gov
- American Heart Association
  - www.americanheart.org/presenter.jhtml

Figure 2–74

Continued >

STUDENT ASSIGNMENTS

Cases and Places *continued*

•• 3: Design and Create a Portable Media Player Presentation

Video tape recorders were immensely popular more than three decades ago with several competing standards introduced in the market. Each technology touted different features. Today, the situation is similar with portable media players and cellular telephones that can download music from the Internet or rip files from your computer. Your supervisor at NextPhase Electronics recognizes buyers need assistance learning about these devices. She has asked you to prepare a presentation summarizing one of these players for next month's Saturday Seminar Series at the store. Research a specific portable media player and create a slide for each of the following attributes: featured model, user interface, and finding and loading songs. Select art and photographs from the Microsoft Clip Organizer, and add a title slide and summary slide to complete your presentation. Format the title slide with a shape and the text with colors and bolding where needed for emphasis.

•• 4: Design and Create a Campus Orientation Presentation

Make It Personal

Feedback from new students at your school cites difficulties navigating your campus. Incoming students mention the library, registrar, and health services as locations most often sought. To address these concerns, you volunteered as a member of the New Student Orientation Team to create a presentation and distribute a handout showing frequently accessed areas of the school. Use the concepts and techniques presented in this chapter to develop and format a slide show with a title slide and at least three text slides with bulleted lists. Create a slide for each landmark that briefly describes its location, and use clips and text to annotate it. Obtain a map of your campus and import it as a picture into your presentation. Select slide layouts that permit both the map and a bulleted list to appear on each slide. Use the arrow shapes to indicate the location of the landmark on the map. Add a background style and slide transitions. Be sure to check spelling. Print a handout with two slides on each page to distribute to new students on campus.

•• 5: Design and Create a Wellness Program Presentation

Working Together

Health care costs continue to rise at nearly double the inflation rate. Many health insurance companies are becoming proactive in containing those costs by offering reimbursement for wellness programs. Have each member of your team visit, telephone, or view Web sites of three health insurance companies. Gather information about:

1) Health screenings

2) Fitness center amenities

3) Self-Improvement classes

4) Wellness program benefits

After coordinating the data, create a presentation with a least one slide showcasing each topic. As a group, critique each slide. Submit your assignment in the format specified by your instructor.

Web Feature

Creating Web Pages Using PowerPoint

Objectives

You will have mastered the material in this Web feature when you can:

- Preview and save a presentation as a Web page
- Customize the Quick Access Toolbar

- Display Web pages created in PowerPoint in a browser
- Complete file management tasks within PowerPoint

Web Feature Introduction

The graphic design power of PowerPoint allows you to create vibrant presentations that convey information in a clear, interesting manner. Some of these presentations are created for small, specific audiences, such as student club members planning a fundraising activity. In this case, the presentation may be shown in an office. Other presentations are designed for large, general audiences, such as potential students planning a campus visit. These students can view the presentation on their school's **intranet**, which is an internal network that uses Internet technologies. On a grand scale, you can inform the entire world about the contents of your presentation by posting your slide show to the World Wide Web.

Project — Web Page

Figure 1a shows the presentation describing yoga fundamentals in Slide Sorter view. The Fitness Center director at your school requests that the information in the slide be made available on the school's intranet for employees and student workers to view. In order to accomplish this task, you must save the presentation as a Web page.

You can save a presentation, or a portion of a presentation as a Web page. The saved **Web page** is a snapshot of the presentation. It is similar to a running slide show in that you can view it, but you cannot modify it. In the browser window, the presentation appears as it would in Microsoft PowerPoint, including a Next Slide button you can click to advance the slides. As illustrated in Figure 1, this Web feature shows you how to save a presentation (Figure 1a) as a Web page (Figures 1b through 1e) and view it using your browser.

PowerPoint allows you to **publish presentations**, which is the process of making existing presentations available to others on the World Wide Web or on a company's intranet, when you use the Save As command on the Office Button menu and choose to save a presentation as a Web page. If you have access to a Web server, you can publish Web pages by saving them on a Web server or on an FTP location. To learn more about publishing Web pages on a Web server or on an FTP location using Microsoft Office applications, refer to Appendix D.

This Web feature illustrates how to create and save the Web pages on a USB flash drive, rather than on a Web server. This feature also demonstrates how to preview a presentation on a Web page and create a new folder using the Save As dialog box.

Overview

As you read through this feature, you will learn how to create the yoga Web pages shown in Figures 1b, 1c, 1d, and 1e by performing these general tasks:

- Preview and save PowerPoint presentations as Web pages.
- Add a button to the Quick Access Toolbar.
- Use Windows Explorer to view Web pages.

Using Web Page Preview and Saving a PowerPoint Presentation as a Web Page

At any time during the construction of a presentation, PowerPoint makes it easy to preview how it will display on an intranet or on the World Wide Web by using the Web Page Preview command. When you invoke the Web Page Preview command, it starts your browser and displays the active slide in the presentation as a Web page without saving files. By previewing your slide show, you can decide which features look good and which need modification. The left side of the window includes the navigation frame, which is the outline of the presentation. The outline contains a table of contents consisting of each slide's title text. You can click the Expand/Collapse Outline button below the navigation frame to view the complete slide text. The right side of the window shows the complete slide in the slide frame. The speaker notes, if present, are displayed in the notes frame below the slide frame. Once the preview is acceptable, you then can save the presentation as a Web page. The Web Page Preview command is not available on the Ribbon, but you can add the command to the Quick Access Toolbar.

Figure 1

Plan
Ahead

General Project Guidelines

When creating the yoga Web pages, the actions you perform and decisions you make will affect the appearance and characteristics of the finished presentation. As you create Web pages, such as the project shown in Figure 1, you should follow these general guidelines:

1. **Develop an effective presentation.** Your slide show should provide essential information to a specific audience. Text should be essential and meaningful. Graphics, such as illustrations, and color should add visual appeal and promote understanding. Ask someone else to view your presentation and give you suggestions for improvements.

2. **Preview and review the Web pages created from your PowerPoint presentation.** Preview the Web page to assess readability and visual interest. Be certain to test your finished Web page document in at least one browser program to check if it looks and works as you intended.

3. **Publish your Web page.** Once you have created a Web page, you can publish it, which makes it available to others on a network, such as the World Wide Web or a company's intranet. Many Internet service providers offer storage space on their Web servers at no cost to their subscribers. The procedures for using Microsoft Office to publish a Web page are discussed in Appendix D.

This Web Feature focuses on the second guideline, identifying the actions you perform and the decisions you make during the creation of the Web pages shown in Figure 1. Chapters 1 and 2 presented details about how to accomplish the goals of the first guideline listed above, and Appendix D presents details about how to achieve the goals of the last guideline.

To Add a Button to the Quick Access Toolbar

Many commands available in PowerPoint are not included on any of the tabs on the Ribbon. You can, however, add such commands to the Quick Access Toolbar. One such command allows you to preview a document in a Web browser. This command, Web Page Preview, needs to be added to the Quick Access Toolbar so that the Web page can be previewed. The following steps add the Web Page Preview command to the Quick Access Toolbar.

- Connect a USB flash drive to one of the computer's USB ports.

- Start PowerPoint and then open the presentation, Yoga, from the Data Files for Students.

- Click the Customize Quick Access Toolbar button to display the Customize Quick Access Toolbar menu (Figure 2).

Figure 2

3

- Click the More Commands command on the Customize Quick Access Toolbar menu.

- When the PowerPoint Options dialog box is displayed, click the 'Choose commands from' box arrow to display the 'Choose commands from' list (Figure 3).

Figure 3

4

- Click Commands Not in the Ribbon in the 'Choose commands from' list to display a list of commands not in the Ribbon (Figure 4).

Figure 4

• Scroll to the bottom of the list, click Web Page Preview, and then click the Add button to add the button to the Quick Access Toolbar (Figure 5).

Figure 5

• Click the OK button to close the PowerPoint Options dialog box and display the Quick Access Toolbar with the Web Page Preview button added to it (Figure 6).

Q&A

Will the Web Page Preview command be in the Quick Access Toolbar the next time I start PowerPoint?

Yes. When you change the Quick Access Toolbar, the changes remain even after you restart PowerPoint. If you share a computer with somebody else or if the Quick Access Toolbar becomes cluttered, PowerPoint allows you to remove commands from the Quick Access Toolbar. You will remove the Web Page Preview button from the Quick Access Toolbar later in this Web feature.

Figure 6

To Preview the Web Page

The following steps preview the presentation in a browser.

- Click the Web Page Preview button on the Quick Access Toolbar to display the Web page in your browser.

- If necessary, click the Maximize button on your browser's title bar (Figure 7).

Q&A What happens when I click the Web Page Preview button?

PowerPoint starts your browser and it displays a preview of how Slide 1 will appear as a Web page (Figure 7). The Web page preview is nearly identical to the display of the slide in PowerPoint.

Figure 7

2

- Click the Full Screen Slide Show button to have Slide 1 fill the entire screen (Figure 8). If the Information Bar appears asking for an add-on from Microsoft, see your instructor.

Q&A Must I always view the full screen of each slide?

No. Viewing the slides in a full screen helps you review their style and spelling easily and allows you to see how the slides will display when viewed in a browser.

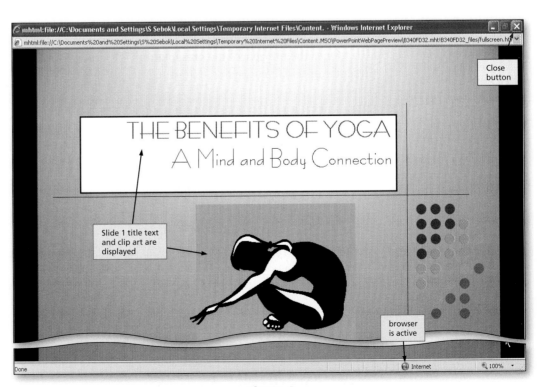

Figure 8

3

- Press the SPACE BAR to display the Slide 2 title text. Continue pressing the SPACE BAR to view each line of Slide 2 body text.

- Continue pressing the SPACE BAR to view each slide in the presentation.

- When the black slide is displayed, press the SPACE BAR again to return to Web Page preview of Slide 1 in the browser window (Figure 9).

- Click the Close button on the right side of the browser title bar to close the browser and make PowerPoint active again.

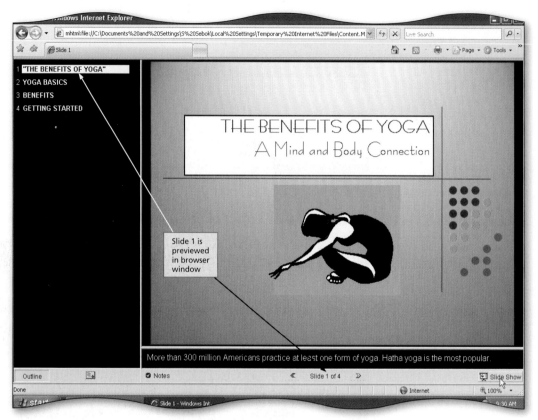

Figure 9

BTW

Viewing Transitions
If slide transitions do not appear when you are previewing your Web Page, you should check your Web Options settings. To do this, click the Office Button, click the PowerPoint Options button, click Advanced, scroll down and then click the Web Options button in the PowerPoint Options dialog box, if necessary click the General tab in the Web Options dialog box, and then click Show slide animation while browsing if it is not selected already.

Web Page Format Options

Once the preview of the presentation as a Web page is acceptable, you can save the presentation as a Web page so that others can view it using a Web browser, such as Internet Explorer or Mozilla Firefox.

You can save the presentation in one of two Web page formats. Both formats convert the contents of the presentation into HTML (HyperText Markup Language), which is a language browsers can interpret. One format is called **Single File Web Page format**, which saves all of the components of the Web page in a single file with an .mht extension. This format is useful particularly for e-mailing presentations in HTML format. The second format, called **Web Page format,** saves the Web page in a file and some of its components in a folder. This format is useful if you need access to the components, such as illustrations, that comprise the Web page.

To Save a PowerPoint Presentation as a Web Page in a Newly Created Folder

Experienced users organize the files saved on a storage medium, such as a USB flash drive or hard disk, by creating folders. They then save related files in a common folder. PowerPoint allows you to create folders before saving a file using the Save As dialog box. The following steps create a new folder on the USB flash drive and then save the Yoga presentation as a Web page in the new folder.

- With the Yoga presentation open, click the Office Button.

- Click Save As on the Office Button menu to display the Save As dialog box (Figure 10).

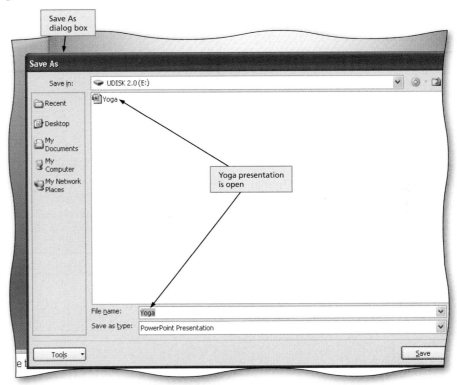

Figure 10

❷

- Type Yoga Web Page in the File name text box.

- Click the 'Save as type' box arrow and then scroll down and click Single File Web Page.

- If the name of your USB flash drive does not appear in the Save in box, click the Save in box arrow and then select UDISK 2.0 (E:) (your USB flash drive name and letter may be different).

- Click the Create New Folder button to display the New Folder dialog box.

- When PowerPoint displays the New Folder dialog box, type Web Feature in the Name text box (Figure 11).

Figure 11

3

- Click the OK button in the New Folder dialog box.

Q&A What does PowerPoint do when I click the OK button?

PowerPoint automatically selects the new folder Web Feature in the Save in box (Figure 12). The Entire Presentation option in the Save area instructs PowerPoint to save all slides in the presentation as Web pages.

4

- Click the Save button in the Save As dialog box to save the presentation in a single file in HTML format in the Web Feature folder on the USB flash drive.

- If the Microsoft Office PowerPoint dialog box is displayed, click the Yes button.

Figure 12

BTW

Certification
The Microsoft Certified Application Specialist (MCAS) program provides an opportunity for you to obtain a valuable industry credential – proof that you have the PowerPoint 2007 skills required by employers. For more information see Appendix G or visit the PowerPoint 2007 Certification Web page (scsite.com/ppt2007/cert).

Saving Presentations as Web Pages

The Save As dialog box changes when you select Single File Web Page in the 'Save as type' box. When you use the Single File Web Page format, a Save area appears in the dialog box. Within the Save area are two option buttons, and a Publish button (Figure 12). You can select only one of the option buttons. The Entire Presentation option button is selected by default. This indicates PowerPoint will save all four slides in the presentation as a Web page.

In the previous set of steps, the Save button was used to save the PowerPoint presentation as a Web page. The Publish button in the Save As dialog box shown in Figure 12 is an alternative to the Save button. It allows you to customize the Web page further.

If you have access to a Web server that allows you to save files in a Web folder, then you can save the Web page directly on the Web server by clicking the My Network Places button in the Save in bar of the Save As dialog box (Figure 12). If you have access to a Web server that allows you to save on an FTP site, then you can select the FTP site below FTP locations in the Save in box just as you select any folder on which to save a file. To learn more about publishing Web pages in a Web folder or on an FTP location using Office applications, refer to Appendix D.

After PowerPoint saves the presentation in Step 4, it displays the MHTML file – not the presentation – in the PowerPoint window. PowerPoint can continue to display the presentation in HTML format, because within the MHTML file that it created, it also saved the PowerPoint formats that allow it to display the MHTML file in PowerPoint. This is referred to as **round tripping** the MHTML file back to the application in which it was created.

To Reset the Quick Access Toolbar and Quit PowerPoint

Your work with the PowerPoint presentation is complete. The following steps remove the Web Page Preview button from the Quick Access Toolbar and quit PowerPoint.

1 Click the Customize the Quick Access Toolbar button on the Ribbon.

2 Click the More Commands command.

3 When the PowerPoint Options dialog box is displayed, click the Reset button. If the Reset Customizations dialog box is displayed, click the Yes button.

4 Click the OK button on the PowerPoint Options dialog box to close it.

5 Click the Close button on the Microsoft PowerPoint title bar.

Q&A Do I need to remove the button from the Quick Access Toolbar?

No. For consistency, the Quick Access Toolbar is reset after the added buttons are no longer needed. If you share a computer with others, you should reset the Quick Access Toolbar.

File Management Tools in PowerPoint

In the previous set of steps, PowerPoint automatically inserted the new folder name in the Save in box when you clicked the OK button in the New Folder dialog box (Figure 12). It was not necessary to create a new folder earlier in this Web feature. You nevertheless could have saved the Web page on the USB flash drive in the same manner in which you saved files on the USB flash drive in the previous projects. Creating a new folder, however, allows you to organize your work.

Finally, once you create a folder, you can right-click it while the Save As dialog box is active and perform many file management tasks directly in PowerPoint (Figure 13). For example, once the shortcut menu appears, you can rename the selected folder, delete it, copy it, display its properties, and perform other file management functions.

BTW

Quick Reference
For a table that lists how to complete the tasks covered in this book using the mouse, Ribbon, shortcut menu, and keyboard, see the Quick Reference Summary at the back of this book, or visit the PowerPoint 2007 Quick Reference Web page (scsite.com/ppt2007/qr).

Figure 13

To View the Web Page Using a Browser

With the Web page saved in the Web Feature folder on the USB flash drive, you now can view it using a browser. If you want to display or hide the navigation frame, click the Show/Hide Outline button below the outline. Later, if you want to redisplay the navigation frame, click the Show/Hide Outline button again. Similarly, the Show/Hide Notes button below the slide frame allows you to display or conceal the speaker notes, if present, on a particular slide. To review a slide you have seen already, click the Previous Slide button. The following steps view the Yoga Web page using your browser.

- If necessary, connect the USB flash drive to one of the computer's USB ports.

- Click the Start button on the Windows taskbar, point to All Programs on the Start menu, and then click Internet Explorer on the All Programs submenu.

- When the Internet Explorer window appears, type
  `E:\Web Feature\`
  `Yoga Web Page.mht`
  in the Address box and then press the ENTER key to display the Web page in your browser (Figure 14). (Your USB flash drive may have a different name and letter).

Figure 14

- If the Information Bar appears, right-click it and then click Allow Blocked Content on the shortcut menu.

- If the Security Warning dialog box is displayed, click the Yes button.

Q&A What are the benefits of using a browser to view a presentation?

You can see from Figures 14 and 15 that a Web page is an ideal way to distribute information to a large group of people. For example, the Web page could be published on a Web server connected to the Internet and made available to anyone with a computer, browser, and the address of the Web page. It also can be e-mailed easily, because the Web page resides in a single file, rather than in a file and folder. Publishing a Web page of a presentation, thus, is an excellent alternative to distributing printed copies of the presentation.

Q&A Can I review a slide I have seen already?

Yes. Click the Previous Slide button.

- Click the Expand/
  Collapse Outline but-
  ton at the bottom
  of the window to
  display the text of
  each slide in outline
  form in the naviga-
  tion frame.

- Click the Next Slide
  button three times
  to view all four slides
  in your browser
  (Figure 15).

Q&A What if I want to
display or hide the
navigation and notes
frames?

To hide the naviga-
tion frame, click the
Show/Hide Outline
button below the
outline. Later, if
you want to redis-
play the navigation
frame, click the
Show/Hide Outline
button again. Similarly,
the Show/Hide Notes button below the slide frame allows you to display or conceal the speaker notes, if present, on a
particular slide.

Figure 15

❸

- Click the Close button on the right side of the browser title bar to close the browser.

Web Feature Summary

This Web feature introduced you to customizing the Quick Access Toolbar, previewing a presentation as a Web
page, creating a new folder on a USB flash drive, and viewing a Web page. The items listed below include all the
new Office 2007 skills you have learned in this Web feature.

1. Add a Button to the Quick Access Toolbar
   (PPT 148)
2. Preview the Web Page (PPT 151)
3. Save a PowerPoint Presentation as a Web Page in a
   Newly Created Folder (PPT 153)

4. Reset the Quick Access Toolbar and Quit Power
   Point (PPT 155)
5. View the Web Page Using a Browser (PPT 156)

If you have a SAM user profile, you may have access to hands-on instruction, practice, and
assessment. Log in to your SAM account (http://sam2007.course.com) to launch any assigned
training activities or exams that relate to the skills covered in this chapter.

In the Lab

Create a Web page using the guidelines, concepts, and skills presented in this Web feature. Labs are listed in order of increasing difficulty.

Lab 1: Creating a Web Page from the A World Beneath the Waves Presentation

Problem: Dave Ehlin, the Student Government Association (SGA) president, wants to expand the visibility of the A World Beneath the Waves presentation you created in Chapter 1. He believes a Web page would be an excellent vehicle to help promote the spring break trip to Cabo San Lucas, Mexico and has asked you to help transfer the presentation to the Internet.

Instructions:

1. Open the Cabo Package presentation shown in Figure 1-1 on page PPT 5 that you created in Chapter 1. (If you did not create this presentation, see your instructor for a copy.)

2. Add the Web Page Preview command to the Quick Access Toolbar.

3. Review the five slides in the Cabo Package presentation, and then preview the presentation as a Web page. Close the browser.

4. Save the presentation as a single file Web page in a new folder titled Web Feature Exercises using the file name, Lab WF-1 Cabo Package Web Page. Reset the Quick Access Toolbar and then quit PowerPoint.

5. Start your browser. With the Web page located on the USB flash drive, type `E:\Web Feature Exercises\Lab WF-1 Cabo Package Web Page.mht` in the Address box (your USB flash drive may have a different name and letter). When the browser displays the Web page, click the Expand/Collapse Outline button at the bottom of the window to display the text of each slide in outline form.

6. Click the Next Slide button at the bottom of the window to view the slides. Close the browser. Submit the assignment as requested by your instructor.

In the Lab

Lab 2: Creating and Printing a Web Page from the Identity Theft Presentation

Problem: The Identity Theft presentation you developed in Chapter 2 could provide useful information for consumers, so you want to save this presentation as a Web page and post it to the Internet.

Instructions:

1. Open the Identity Theft presentation shown in Figure 2-1 on page PPT 83 that you created in Chapter 2. (If you did not create this presentation, see your instructor for a copy.)

2. Add the Web Page Preview command to the Quick Access Toolbar.

3. Review the four slides in the Identity Theft presentation, and then preview the presentation as a Web page. Close the browser.

4. Save the presentation as a Web page (select Web Page in the Save as type box) in the Web Feature Exercises folder using the file name, Lab WF-2 Identity Theft Web Page. Reset the Quick Access Toolbar and then quit PowerPoint. Saving the presentation as a Web page, rather than a single file Web page, will result in an additional folder being added to the Web Feature Exercises folder.

5. Start your browser. Type
   `E:\Web Feature Exercises\Lab WF-2 Identity Theft Web Page.mht` in the Address box (your USB flash drive may have a different name and letter). When the browser displays the Web page, click the Next Slide button at the bottom of the window to view the slides.

6. Print the Web page by clicking the Print button on the Toolbar.

7. Close the browser. Submit the assignment as requested by your instructor.

Continued >

In the Lab

Lab 3: File Management within PowerPoint

Problem: One of your classmates has asked you to teach him how to perform basic file management tasks from within PowerPoint.

Instructions:

1. Start PowerPoint and then click the Open command on the Office Button menu. When PowerPoint displays the Open dialog box, create a new folder called In the Lab 3 on your USB flash drive.

2. Click the Up One Level button to reselect the drive in the Look in box. Use the shortcut menu to complete the following tasks: (1) rename the In the Lab 3 folder to In the Lab 3A; (2) show the properties of the In the Lab 3A folder; and (3) delete the In the Lab 3A folder.

1 Managing E-Mail and Contacts with Outlook

Objectives

You will have mastered the material in this chapter when you can:

- Start and quit Outlook

- Open, read, print, reply to, and delete electronic mail messages

- View a file attachment

- Create and insert an e-mail signature

- Compose, format, and send e-mail messages

- Insert a file attachment in an e-mail message

- Flag, categorize, sort, and filter e-mail messages

- Set e-mail importance, sensitivity, and delivery options

- Create a personal folder

- Create and print a contact list

- Use the Find a Contact feature

- Organize the contact list

- Track activities of a contact

- Use Outlook's Help

1 Managing E-Mail and Contacts with Outlook

What Is Microsoft Office Outlook 2007?

Microsoft Office Outlook 2007, usually referred to as simply Outlook, is a powerful communications and scheduling program that helps you communicate with others (Figure 1-1), keep track of your contacts, and organize your calendar. Personal information management (PIM) programs such as Outlook provide a way for individuals and workgroups to organize, find, view, and share information easily. Outlook allows you to send and receive electronic mail (e-mail) and permits you to engage in real-time messaging with family, friends, or coworkers using instant messaging. Outlook also provides you with the means to organize your contacts. Users can track e-mail messages, meetings, and notes related to a particular contact. Outlook's Calendar, Contacts, Tasks, and Notes components aid in this organization. Contact information readily is available from the Outlook Calendar, Mail, Contacts, and Task components by accessing the Find a Contact feature.

Electronic mail (e-mail) is the transmission of messages and files over a computer network. E-mail has become an important means of exchanging information and files between business associates, classmates and instructors, friends, and family. Businesses find that using e-mail to send documents electronically saves both time and money. Parents with students away at college or relatives who are scattered across the country find that communicating by e-mail is an inexpensive and easy way to stay in touch with their family members. In fact, exchanging e-mail messages is one of the more widely used features of the Internet.

This latest version of Outlook has many new features to help make you more productive. For example, Outlook now offers Instant Search, which finds your information, no matter which folder it is in. Outlook also has added Color Categories, which let you apply the same color category to e-mail, calendar, and task items so you can visually locate all associated items. Outlook has added flags you can use to create and mark a follow-up item for tracking. The new To-Do Bar is a feature that integrates tasks, e-mail messages flagged for follow up, and calendar information in a toolbar located adjacent to the reading pane.

To illustrate the features of Outlook, this book presents a series of projects that use Outlook to create and send e-mail messages and create and manage a contact list.

Project Planning Guidelines

The process of composing an e-mail message that communicates specific information requires careful analysis and planning. As a starting point, establish why the message is needed. Once the purpose is determined, analyze the intended readers of the message and their unique needs. Then, gather information about the topic and decide what to include in the message. Finally, determine the document design and style that will be most successful at delivering the message. Creating a contact list is simply a matter of who you want to add to the list. The contact list can be used to store people you have frequent contact with via e-mail, telephone, or fax. The contact list can also be used as a mailing list. Each project in this book provides practical applications of these planning considerations.

Project — Communicating Over the Internet

The project in this chapter follows general guidelines and uses Outlook to create the contacts and messages shown in Figure 1–1. To communicate with individuals and groups, you typically send or deliver some kind of message. Telephone calls, faxes, and letters are examples of messages. E-mail is a convenient way to send information to multiple recipients simultaneously, instantly, and inexpensively.

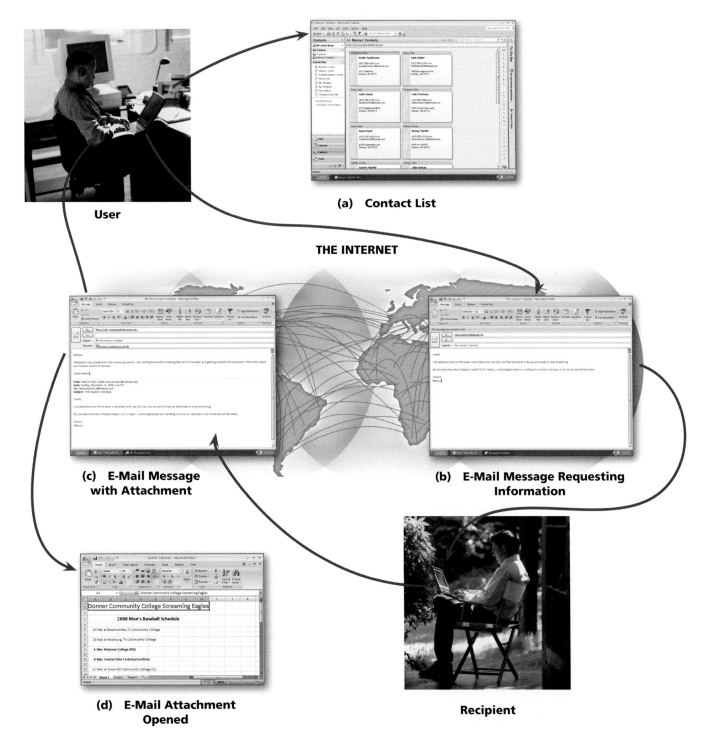

User

(a) Contact List

THE INTERNET

(c) E-Mail Message with Attachment

(b) E-Mail Message Requesting Information

(d) E-Mail Attachment Opened

Recipient

Figure 1–1

As the captain of the Donner Community College baseball team, you use Outlook to keep the players up to date with team information using your school e-mail system. You also use the contact list to store addresses and phone numbers of each member of the team. The project uses the communications features of Outlook to compose, send, and read e-mail messages. In addition to using Outlook's communication tools, this project shows you how to create and organize a contact list. Using the contact list (Figure 1–1a), a user selects a recipient for an e-mail message and then sends an e-mail message requesting information from the recipient (Figure 1–1b). The recipient replies by sending an e-mail message (Figure 1–1c) and includes the requested information as an attachment (Figure 1–1d), or a file included with the e-mail message, that the recipient can open.

Overview

As you read this chapter, you will learn how to communicate over the Internet as shown in Figure 1–1 by performing these general tasks:

- Open and read e-mail messages.
- Print an e-mail message.
- Reply to and forward an e-mail message.
- View a file attachment.
- Create an e-mail signature.
- Compose and format an e-mail message.
- Attach a file to an e-mail message.
- Organize and sort e-mail messages.
- Create and organize a contact list.
- Print a contact list.

Plan Ahead

General Project Guidelines

When creating an e-mail message, the actions you perform and decisions you make will affect the appearance and characteristics of the finished message. As you create an e-mail message such as those shown in Figure 1–1, you should follow these general guidelines:

1. **Choose the words for the Subject line.** The Subject line should indicate the main subject of the message. Use as few words as possible. You should never leave the Subject line blank.

2. **Ensure that the content of the message is appropriate for the recipient.** An e-mail sent to a close friend may be considerably different from one sent to an instructor, coworker, or client. Use e-mail etiquette when composing your message. For work related e-mails, avoid shortening words or using abbreviations (i.e., u for you, r for are, 2 for to, etc.).

3. **Choose the words for the text.** Follow the *less is more* guideline. The less text, the more likely the message will be read to completion. Use as few words as possible to make a point.

4. **Identify how to format various elements of the text.** The overall appearance of a message significantly affects its ability to communicate clearly. Examples of how you can modify the appearance, or format, of text include changing its shape, size, color, and position on the page.

5. **Alert the recipient when sending large file attachments.** Some e-mail servers allow file attachments up to a certain size. If possible, compress large files using WinZip or comparable software. If several attachments are required, you may have to send multiple e-mails.

When necessary, more specific details concerning the above guidelines are presented at appropriate points in the chapter. The chapter also will identify the actions performed and decisions made regarding these guidelines during the creation of the messages shown in Figure 1–1.

Starting and Customizing Outlook

If you are using a computer to step through the project in this chapter and you want your screen to match the figures in this book, you should change your screen's resolution to 1024×768. For information about how to change a computer's resolution, read Appendix E.

To Start and Customize Outlook

The following steps, which assume Windows is running, start Outlook based on a typical installation. You may need to ask your instructor how to start Outlook for your computer.

- Click the Start button on the Windows taskbar to display the Start menu.

- Point to All Programs on the Start menu to display the All Programs submenu.

- Point to Microsoft Office on the All Programs submenu to display the Microsoft Office submenu (Figure 1–2).

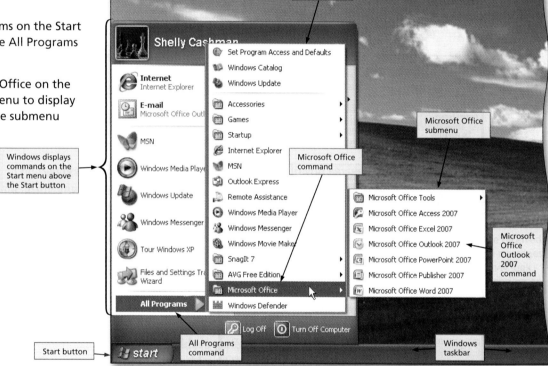

Figure 1–2

[josequinteras123@hotmail.com]), and the recipient's e-mail address (marcuscook1@ comcast.net). Outlook displays the text of the selected message below the message header. Using the View menu, you can display the Reading pane to the right of the message pane (vertically), as shown in Figure 1–5 on page OUT 8, or you can display it at the bottom of the message pane (horizontally) according to your personal preference.

To-Do Bar   The To-Do Bar is a new feature in Outlook 2007. The To-Do Bar keeps e-mail messages flagged for follow up, tasks, appointments, and other calendar information in one place. When displayed, the To-Do Bar contains a Date Navigator, an appointment list, and a task list. The To-Do Bar is displayed by clicking the double arrow button at the top of the To-Do Bar (Figure 1–5).

Working with Incoming Messages

Note: If you are stepping through this project on a computer and you want your screen to appear the same as in the figures in the Mail component section of this project, then you should ask your instructor to help you (or see page OUT 67) to import Marcus' Inbox from the Data Files for Students. Once you have imported Marcus' Inbox, click the plus sign (+) next to the Inbox folder in the Mail Folders list, and then select Marcus' Inbox folder. See the inside back cover of this book for instructions for downloading the Data Files for Students or see your instructor for information about accessing files for this book.

BTW

Reading E-Mail Messages
If Outlook is not the active window on your screen, it still provides a mail notification alert informing you when you receive a new message. Outlook displays a semitransparent Screen Tip momentarily by the Outlook icon in the notification area, showing the sender's name, subject of the message, and the first few words of the message body.

To Open (Read) an E-Mail Message

To view the complete message in its own window, it must be opened. The following step opens the e-mail message from Jose Quinteras.

①

- Double-click the Jose Quinteras message heading in the Inbox Message pane to display the First Practice window (Figure 1–7).

- If necessary, maximize the window.

Q&A

What happens to the message heading in the Message pane after the message is opened?

When you double-click the message heading in the Message pane, Outlook changes the closed envelope icon to an opened envelope icon, and no longer displays the message heading in bold type.

Other Ways

1. Right-click message heading, click Open on shortcut menu
2. Click message heading, on File menu point to Open, click Selected Items on Open submenu
3. Select message heading, press CTRL+O

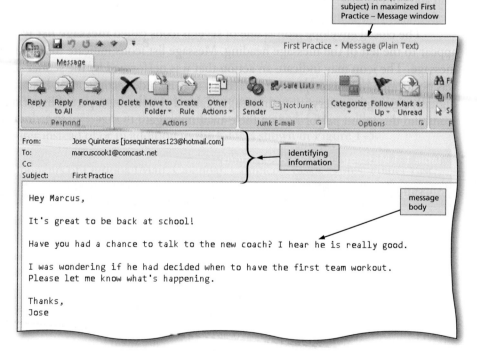

Figure 1–7

Ribbon

The **Ribbon**, located near the top of the Outlook window, is the control center in Outlook (Figure 1–8a). The Ribbon provides easy, central access to the tasks you perform while creating or working with a message, contact, calendar item, or task. The Ribbon consists of tabs, groups, and commands. Each **tab** surrounds a collection of groups, and each group contains related commands. Figure 1–8a illustrates the Ribbon for the Message window.

When you open a message, the Message window Ribbon displays the Message tab. The Message tab contains the more frequently used commands.

To display more of the document in the document window, some users prefer to minimize the Ribbon, which hides the groups on the Ribbon and displays only the Message tab (Figure 1–8b). To use commands on a minimized Ribbon, click the top-level tab.

Each time you open a message, the Ribbon appears the same way it did the last time you used Outlook. The chapters in this book, however, begin with the Ribbon appearing as it did at the initial installation of the software. If you are stepping through this chapter on a computer and you want your Ribbon to match the figures in this book, read Appendix E.

Figure 1–8

Some commands on the Ribbon display an image to help you remember their function. When you point to a command on the Ribbon, all or part of the command glows in shades of yellow and orange, and an **Enhanced ScreenTip** appears on the screen. An Enhanced ScreenTip is an on-screen note that provides the name of the command, available keyboard shortcut(s), a description of the command, and, sometimes, instructions for how to obtain help about the command (Figure 1–9). Enhanced ScreenTips are more detailed than a typical ScreenTip, which usually only displays the name of the command.

BTW

Minimizing the Ribbon

If you want to minimize the Ribbon, right-click the Ribbon and then click Minimize the Ribbon on the shortcut menu, double-click the active tab, or press CTRL+F1. To restore a minimized Ribbon, right-click the Ribbon and then click Minimize the Ribbon on the shortcut menu, double-click any top-level tab, or press CTRL+F1. To use commands on a minimized Ribbon, click the top-level tab.

Figure 1–9

The lower-right corner of some groups on the Ribbon has a small arrow, called a **Dialog Box Launcher**, that when clicked displays a dialog box or a task pane with additional options for the group (Figure 1–10). When presented with a dialog box, you make selections and must close the dialog box before returning to the document. A **task pane**, by contrast, is a window that can remain open and visible while you work in the document.

Figure 1–10

Quick Access Toolbar

The **Quick Access Toolbar**, located by default above the Ribbon, provides easy access to frequently used commands (Figure 1–11a). The commands on the Quick Access Toolbar always are available, regardless of the task you are performing. Initially, the Quick Access Toolbar contains the Save, Undo, and Redo commands. If you click the Customize Quick Access Toolbar button, Outlook provides a list of commands you quickly can add to and remove from the Quick Access Toolbar (Figure 1–11b).

You also can add other commands to or delete commands from the Quick Access Toolbar so that it contains the commands you use most often. As you add commands to the Quick Access Toolbar, its commands may interfere with the document title on the title bar. For this reason, Outlook provides an option of displaying the Quick Access Toolbar below the Ribbon (Figure 1–11c).

Each time you start Outlook, the Quick Access Toolbar appears the same way it did the last time you used Outlook. The chapters in this book, however, begin with the Quick Access Toolbar appearing as it did at the initial installation of the software. If you are stepping through this chapter on a computer and you want your Quick Access Toolbar to match the figures in this book, you should reset your Quick Access Toolbar. For more information about how to reset the Quick Access Toolbar, read Appendix E.

Figure 1–11

Office Button

While the Ribbon is a control center for creating documents, the **Office Button** is a central location for managing Outlook items. When you click the Office Button, located in the upper-left corner of the window, Outlook displays the Office Button menu (Figure 1–12). A **menu** contains a list of commands.

BTW

Quick Access Toolbar Commands
To add a Ribbon command to the Quick Access Toolbar, right-click the command on the Ribbon and then click Add to Quick Access Toolbar on the shortcut menu. To delete a command from the Quick Access Toolbar, right-click the command on the Quick Access Toolbar and then click Remove from Quick Access Toolbar on the shortcut menu. To display the Quick Access Toolbar below the Ribbon, right-click the Quick Access Toolbar and then click Show Quick Access Toolbar below the Ribbon on the shortcut menu.

Figure 1–12

2

- Click the Print button to print the message shown in Figure 1–17.

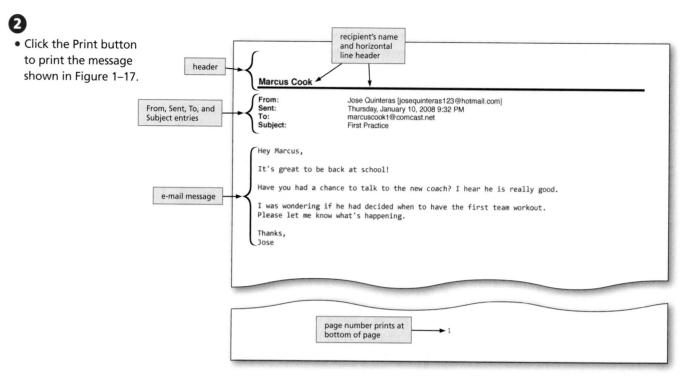

Figure 1–17

Other Ways

1. On File Menu click Print, click OK button
2. Press ALT+F, press P, press ENTER
3. Press CTRL+P, press ENTER

To Reply to an E-Mail Message

The Reply button allows you to reply quickly to an e-mail message using the sender's e-mail address. The following steps reply to the e-mail message from Jose Quinteras.

- If necessary, click the Jose Quinteras message heading in the message pane (Figure 1–18).

Figure 1–18

2

- Click the Reply button on the Standard toolbar to open the RE: First Practice - Message window.

- When Outlook displays the Message window for the reply, if necessary, double-click the title bar to maximize the window.

- Type the e-mail reply (Figure 1–19).

Why is there RE: at the beginning of the Subject line and in the Title bar?

The RE: indicates it is the reply, the subject of the message identifies the title of the window, and Message indicates it is the Message window.

Figure 1–19

3

- Click the Send button to send the message and return to the Inbox window (Figure 1–20).

What happened to the sent message?

Outlook closed the Message window and stores the reply e-mail in the Outbox folder while it sends the message. Outlook then moves the message to the Sent Items folder. The original message in the message pane now shows an open envelope icon with an arrow to indicate a reply has been sent.

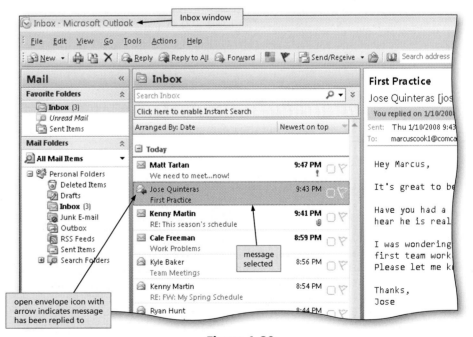

Figure 1–20

New Message Ribbon

The Ribbon for a reply message, new message, or forwarded message is similar to the Ribbon for a Word window (Figure 1–21). The Ribbon provides easy, central access to the tasks you perform while creating a message. The New Message Ribbon, in comparison to the Ribbon discussed earlier, consists of multiple tabs, groups, and commands. As in the previous Ribbon, each tab surrounds a collection of groups, and each group contains related commands. Many of the Ribbon commands will be inactive if the message format is Plain Text. To activate all of the commands, the message must be in HTML or Rich Text format. These formats are discussed later in this chapter.

Figure 1–21

When you open a new mail Message window, the Ribbon displays four top-level tabs: Message, Insert, Options, and Format Text. The **Message tab**, called the primary tab, contains the more frequently used commands. To display a different tab on the Ribbon, click the top-level tab. That is, to display the Insert tab, click Insert on the Ribbon. To return to the Message tab, click Message on the Ribbon. The tab currently displayed is called the **active tab**.

Commands on the Ribbon include buttons, boxes (text boxes, check boxes, etc.), and galleries (Figure 1–22). A **gallery** is a set of choices, often graphical, arranged in a grid or list. You can scroll through choices on an in-Ribbon gallery by clicking the gallery's scroll arrows. Or, you can click a gallery's More button to view more gallery options on the screen at a time. Some buttons and boxes have arrows that, when clicked, also display a gallery; others always cause a gallery to be displayed when clicked. Most galleries support **live preview**, which is a feature that allows you to point to a gallery choice and see its effect in the document — without actually selecting the choice.

Figure 1–22

Message Formats

Outlook offers three message formats: Plain Text, HTML, and Rich Text, summarized in Table 1–2.

Table 1–2 Message Formats	
Message Format	**Description**
HTML	HTML format is the default format used when you create a message in Outlook. HTML supports the inclusion of pictures and basic formatting, such as text formatting, numbering, bullets, and alignment. HTML is the recommended format for Internet mail because the most popular e-mail programs use it.
Plain Text	Plain Text format is understood by all e-mail programs and is the most likely format to make it through a company's virus-filtering program. Plain text does not support basic formatting, such as bold, italic, colored fonts, or other text formatting. It also does not support pictures displayed directly in the message.
Rich Text	Rich Text Format (RTF) is a Microsoft format that only the latest versions of Microsoft Exchange and Outlook understand. RTF supports more formats than HTML or Plain Text, as well as linked objects and pictures.

To Change Message Formats

The following steps change the message format.

1
- With a new Message window active, click the Options tab (Figure 1–23).

2
- Click the appropriate command (Plain Text, HTML, or Rich Text) in the Format group.

Figure 1–23

BTW

Replying to an E-Mail Message
Many e-mail users prefer to reply to a message without including the original e-mail message along with their response. To remove the original message from all e-mail replies, click Tools on the menu bar, click Options, and then click the E-mail Options button in the Preferences sheet of the Options dialog box. In the E-mail Options dialog box, select Do not include original message text in the When replying to a message list.

BTW

Message Formatting
Changing the format of an e-mail message also can help prevent the possibility of virus infection. Many viruses are found in HTML formatted messages. To help protect against viruses, you can configure Outlook to display opened messages automatically in plain text. Click Options on the Tools menu and then click the E-mail Options button in the Preferences sheet of the Options dialog box, select Read all standard mail in plain text in the Message handling area.

To Forward an E-Mail Message

You can forward an e-mail message to additional recipients. The following steps forward the Jose Quinteras e-mail message to the team's coach.

- With the Inbox window active, click the Jose Quinteras message header in the message pane.

- Click the Forward button on the Standard toolbar (Figure 1–24).

Figure 1–24

- When Outlook displays the Message window for the forwarded message, type kennymartin123@hotmail.com in the To text box as the recipient's e-mail address. (If you are stepping through this task, use an actual e-mail address in the To text box.)

- Enter the forwarding message in the message body (Figure 1–25).

- Click the Send button to forward the original message along with the new message to Kenny.

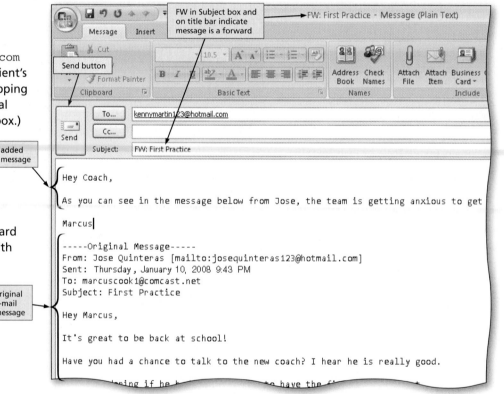

Figure 1–25

Other Ways
1. Right-click message heading, click Forward on shortcut menu
2. Press CTRL+F

To Delete an E-Mail Message

Deleting a message removes the e-mail message from the Inbox folder, saving disk space and making new messages easier to find. The following steps delete the e-mail message from Jose Quinteras.

1

- With the Inbox window active, click the Jose Quinteras message heading in the message pane to select the message (Figure 1–26).

Q&A

Why did the envelope icon for this message change to an open envelope with a forward pointing blue arrow instead of the backward pointing purple arrow?

The backward pointing purple arrow indicated that you replied to the message. The forward pointing blue arrow indicates that you have forwarded the message. The status of the envelope icon represents your last action with the message.

Figure 1–26

2

- Click the Delete button on the Standard toolbar to remove the message from your Inbox (Figure 1–27).

Q&A

Is the message permanently deleted?

Outlook moves the message to the Deleted Items folder. To permanently delete an e-mail message from the Deleted Items folder, click the Deleted Items folder icon in the Mail Folders pane, select the message in the Deleted Items message pane, click the Delete button, and then click the Yes button in the Microsoft Office Outlook dialog box.

Figure 1–27

Other Ways
1. Drag e-mail message to Deleted Items folder in Mail Folders pane
2. On Edit menu, click Delete
3. Press CTRL+D
4. Click e-mail message, press DELETE key

To View a File Attachment

A paper clip icon in a message heading indicates that the message contains a file attachment. The message from Kenny Martin (see Figure 1–28) contains an attachment — in this case, a schedule for the team. The following steps open the message and view the contents of the file attachment.

- With the Inbox window active, double-click the Kenny Martin message heading in the Message pane (Figure 1–28).

Figure 1–28

- If necessary, maximize the RE: This season's schedule – Message window (Figure 1–29).

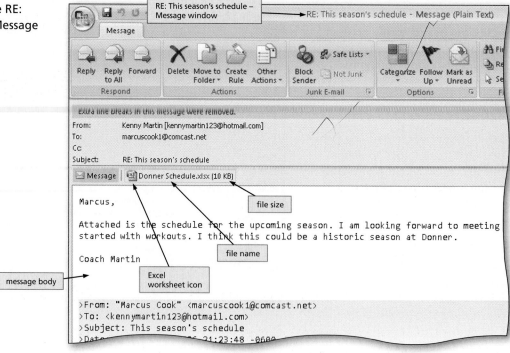

Figure 1–29

3

- Double-click the Donner Schedule icon in the Attachments area to open the Donner Schedule Microsoft Excel file (Figure 1–30).

- If Outlook displays the Opening Mail Attachment dialog box, click the Open button.

 Q&A What type of files can I open?

File attachments can be any type of file; however, files can be viewed only if your computer has the appropriate software. For example, if your computer does not have Excel installed, then you cannot view an Excel file attachment.

4

- After viewing the worksheet, click the Close button on the right side of the title bar in the Excel window to close the attachment and Excel.

- Click the Close button in the Message window.

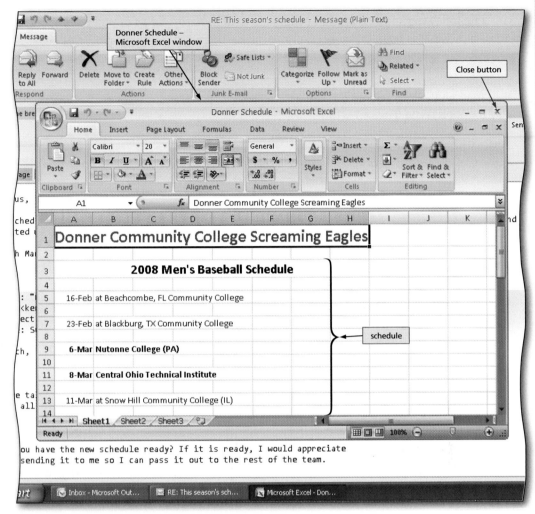

Figure 1–30

Other Ways

1. Double-click file attachment name in Reading Pane

2. Click Save button in Opening Mail Attachments dialog box to save attachment to hard drive or portable storage device

3. On File menu point to Save Attachments to save attachment to hard drive or portable storage device

Working with Outgoing Messages

Before composing a new mail message, you should create an e-mail signature to save time when sending messages.

An **e-mail signature** is a unique message automatically added to the end of an outgoing e-mail message. It can consist of text and/or pictures. The type of signature you add may depend on the recipient of the message. For messages to family and friends, a first name may be sufficient, while messages to business contacts may include your full name, address, telephone number, and other business information. Outlook allows you to create a different signature for each e-mail account created in Outlook.

To Create and Insert an E-Mail Signature

The following steps create and insert an e-mail signature in an e-mail message. The signature will be used by Marcus in his role as team captain.

• With the Inbox window active, click Tools on the menu bar to display the Tools menu (Figure 1–31).

Figure 1–31

• Click Options on the Tools menu to display the Options dialog box.

• Click the Mail Format tab to display the Mail Format sheet (Figure 1–32).

Figure 1–32

- Click the Signatures
  button to display
  the Signatures and
  Stationery dialog
  box (Figure 1–33).

Figure 1–33

4

- Click the New
  button to display
  the New Signature
  dialog box.

- When Outlook
  displays the New
  Signature dialog
  box, type Team in
  the 'Type a name for
  this signature' text
  box (Figure 1–34).

Figure 1–34

5

- Click the OK button.

- Click in the Edit signature area of the Signatures and Stationery dialog box and type `Marcus Cook – Team Captain` as the signature (Figure 1–35).

Edit signature area

Figure 1–35

6

- In the Choose default signature area of the Signatures and Stationery dialog box, select the appropriate e-mail account (if you are stepping through this project, ask your instructor for the appropriate e-mail account).

- If necessary, select Team in the New messages box and the Replies/forwards box to select it as the default signature (Figure 1–36).

7

- Click the OK button to close the Signatures and Stationery dialog box. Click OK in the Options dialog box to close the dialog box.

Figure 1–36

What do I do with my signature now that it is created?

Your signature will be inserted automatically in all new messages as well as reply and forward messages. You also can modify or remove your signatures at any time using the Signatures and Stationery dialog box.

Other Ways

1. Press ALT+T, press O

E-Mail Signatures for Multiple Accounts

You can create unique signatures for different accounts by adding new signatures and selecting a different account in the Choose default signature area of the Signatures and Stationary dialog box (Figure 1–36).

BTW

E-Mail Signatures
Outlook allows you to add signatures to your e-mail messages that you create in Word 2007. Some of the advantages to creating them in Word is the ability to insert pictures and hyperlinks into the signature.

New Mail Messages

In addition to opening and reading, replying to, forwarding, and deleting e-mail messages, you will have many occasions to compose and send original e-mail messages. When you compose an e-mail message, you must know the e-mail address of the recipient of the message, enter a brief one-line subject that identifies the purpose or contents of the message, and then type the message in the message body.

You also can **format** an e-mail message to enhance the appearance of the message. Formatting refers to changing the style, size, and color of the text document.

To Compose an E-Mail Message

The following steps compose a formatted e-mail message to Kenny Martin with an attachment.

1
- With the Inbox window active, point to the New Mail Message button on the Standard toolbar (Figure 1–37).

Figure 1–37

2
- Click the New Mail Message button to open the Untitled – Message window (Figure 1–38).

Figure 1–38

- Type kennymartin123@
  hotmail.com in the To text box,
  click the Subject text box, and then
  type Draft Practice Schedule
  in the Subject text box
  (Figure 1–39).

- Press the TAB key to move the
  insertion point into the message
  body area.

Figure 1–39

- Type the e-mail
  message (Figure 1–40).

Q&A

What if I make a
mistake while typing
a message?

When you enter a
message, you can use
the DELETE key and
BACKSPACE key to
correct errors.
If you are using
Microsoft Word as
your e-mail editor
and you have the
appropriate Spelling
options selected, then
the spell checker will
flag the misspelled words
with a red wavy line. Furthermore, the message will be spell checked before it is sent.

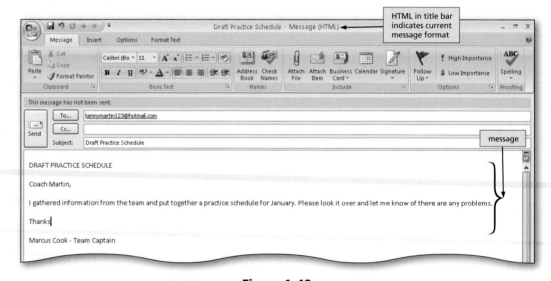

Figure 1–40

To Format an E-Mail Message

Outlook's default message format is HTML, which allows you to customize text with numbering, bullets, alignment, signatures, and linking to Web pages. The following steps center the text, DRAFT PRACTICE SCHEDULE, change the font size to 36-point, and change the color of the text to red. A **font size** is measured in points. A **point** is equal to 1/72 of one inch in height. Thus a font size of 36 points is approximately one-half inch in height.

- Highlight the text, DRAFT PRACTICE SCHEDULE, in the message body and then click the Format Text tab (Figure 1–41).

Figure 1–41

- Click the Center button in the Paragraph group on the Format Text tab to center the selected text (Figure 1–42).

Figure 1–42

- Click the Font Color button in the Font group on the Format Text tab to change the color of the selected text to red (Figure 1–43).

Q&A

How do I pick a color other than red?

To select a font color, click the box arrow on the Font Color button to display a color palette. Simply click a color on the palette to change the color of the text.

Figure 1–43

- Click the Font Size box arrow in the Font group on the Format Text tab to display the Font Size list (Figure 1–44).

Figure 1–44

5

• Scroll down the Font Size list, click 36, and then click the selected text to remove the selection (Figure 1–45).

Q&A Why do I have to select the entire text to change the format?

Because centering is a paragraph format, you can simply click within the text, and then click the Center button. Font size, however, is a character format, so you must select the characters in the entire text before you select a new font size.

Figure 1–45

To Attach a File to an E-Mail Message and Send the Message

Outlook allows you to attach almost any kind of file to your message. You may need to send a Word document, an Excel worksheet, a picture, or other type of file. The following steps attach the Draft Practice Schedule.xlsx file to the e-mail message.

1

• Click the Insert tab on the Ribbon and then click the Attach File button in the Include group to display the Insert File dialog box (Figure 1–46).

Figure 1–46

- With your USB flash drive connected to one of the computer's USB ports, if necessary, click the Look in box arrow and then click UDISK 2.0 (E:) to select the USB flash drive, drive E in this case, in the Look in list as the device that contains the file.

- Click Draft Practice Schedule in the Insert File dialog box (Figure 1–47).

Figure 1–47

- Click the Insert button in the Insert File dialog box to insert the file into the message (Figure 1–48).

Q&A

What if I have more than one file to send?

You can attach multiple documents to the same e-mail message. Simply perform the previous steps for each attachment. Keep in mind, however, that some Internet service providers limit the total size of e-mail messages you can attach. You should keep the sum of the file sizes attached to an e-mail message to less than 1 MB.

④

- Click the Send button to send the message and close the Message window (Figure 1–48).

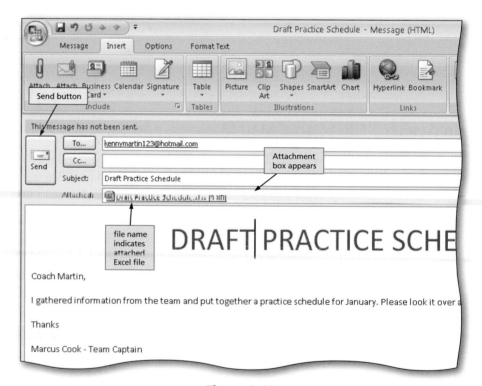

Figure 1–48

BTW

File Attachments
Outlook allows other ways for a file to be inserted into a message. You can drag a file from any folder on your computer to a message, or you can copy and paste a file into a message as an attachment by right-clicking the file, clicking Copy on the shortcut menu, then in the Outlook message, clicking Paste on the Edit menu.

Organizing E-Mail Messages

Keeping track of your incoming messages can be a challenge, especially if you receive a lot of mail. Two features that can help you organize your messages are the Category box and Follow Up flag, located to the right of the message headings. The **Category box** can be assigned one of six different default colors, or you can create your own categories with different colors. Color selection and the meaning of each color are entirely at the discretion of the user. For example, you could assign red to indicate a message from your boss, yellow could mean a message from your best friend, and purple may be a message from your parents.

The **Follow Up flag** can be assigned one of five different flags, or you can customize your own Follow Up flag. These flags are used to remind you to follow up on an issue. When you select a flag, Outlook adds a reminder message in the Reading pane. Outlook also adds a task to the To-Do Bar.

To Categorize E-Mail Messages

Marcus would like to organize his messages. The following steps categorize, flag, and sort e-mail messages.

1

- With the Inbox window active, right-click the Kenny Martin message heading to display the message shortcut menu.

- Point to Categorize to display the Categories submenu (Figure 1–49).

Figure 1–49

Junk E-Mail Filters
A useful feature in Outlook is the Junk E-mail Filter. The filter is on by default. It automatically evaluates whether an unread message should be sent to the Junk E-mail folder. While you can configure the Junk E-mail Filter to your own personal settings, the default settings evaluate several factors, such as content, time the message was sent, and who sent the message. To change junk e-mail settings, click Options on the Tools menu, and then click the Junk E-mail button in the Preferences sheet of the Options dialog box. Make the preferred changes in the Junk E-mail Options dialog box. Note that the Junk E-mail folder is not available if you use an Exchange Server e-mail account.

- Click the Red Category command on the Categories submenu. If the Rename Category dialog box appears, click No.

- Repeat Steps 1 and 2 to categorize the remaining messages in the message pane (Figure 1–50).

Other Ways

1. Right-click Categorize box, click appropriate category color

2. On Actions menu, point to Categorize, click appropriate category color

3. Click the Category button on the Standard toolbar, click appropriate category color

4. Press ALT+A, press I

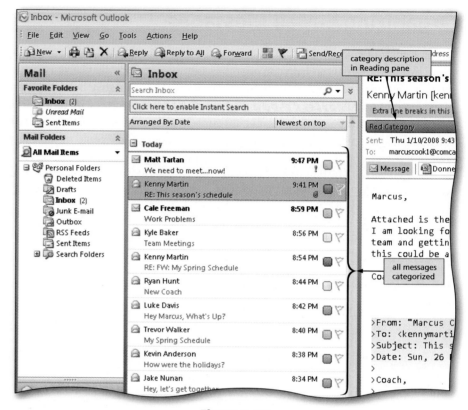

Figure 1–50

To Flag E-Mail Messages

The following steps mark a message with a flag that indicates the message needs to be dealt with today.

- With the Inbox window active, right-click the Kenny Martin message heading to display the message shortcut menu (Figure 1–51).

- Point to Follow Up to display the Follow Up submenu (Figure 1–51).

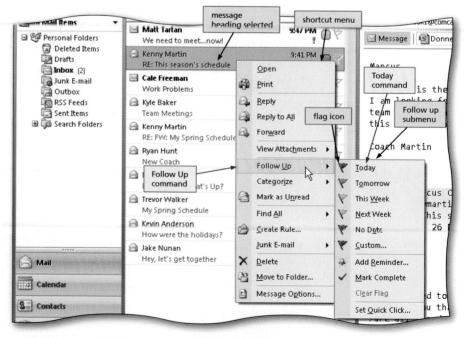

Figure 1–51

2

- Click the Today command on the Follow Up submenu to assign a Follow Up flag with today as the due date.

- Repeat Steps 1 and 2 to add Follow Up flags to the remaining messages in the message pane (Figure 1–52).

- Select different flags as necessary.

Q&A

What does the Follow Up message in the Reading pane mean?

You can select from five default Follow Up flags. The message in the Reading pane corresponds to that selection and assigns a Start date and Due date to the selection (today, tomorrow, this week, and next week).

Figure 1–52

Other Ways
1. Right-click Follow Up flag, click appropriate flag	2. On Actions menu, point to Follow Up, click appropriate flag	3. Click the Follow Up button on the Standard toolbar, click appropriate flag
		4. Press ALT+A, press U

To Sort E-Mail Messages by Category Color

After categorizing and flagging the appropriate messages, you can sort the messages by category color. The following steps sort the messages by category color.

- With the Inbox window active, click View on the menu bar to open the View menu. Point to Arrange By to display the Arrange By submenu (Figure 1–53).

Figure 1–53

- Click Categories on the Arrange By submenu to sort the messages by Category (Figure 1–54).

- Return to the previous view by repeating Step 1 and then clicking Date on the Arrange By submenu.

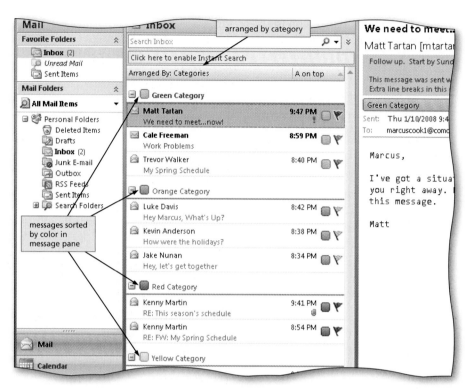

Figure 1–54

To Create and Apply a View Filter

The following steps create and apply a view filter to show only messages from Kenny Martin.

- With the Inbox window active, click View on the menu bar.

- Point to Arrange By on the View menu and then click Custom on the Arrange By sub-menu to display the Customize View: Messages dialog box (Figure 1–55).

Figure 1–55

2

- Click the Filter button to display the Filter dialog box.

- Click the From text box (Figure 1–56).

- Type `Kenny Martin` in the From text box to specify that only e-mail messages from Kenny Martin are to appear.

Figure 1–56

3

- Click the OK button in the Filter dialog box and the Customize View: Message dialog box to close both boxes and apply the view filter (Figure 1–57).

Q&A

How do I know that my other messages have not been deleted?

Outlook displays a message on the status bar and the Inbox pane title bar when a view filter is applied to a selected folder. It also shows the total number of messages remaining in the Inbox folder on the status bar.

4

- Repeat Steps 1 and 2 to display the Filter dialog box.

- Click the Clear All button in the Filter dialog box to remove the view filter.

- Close the Filter and Customize View: Message dialog boxes.

Figure 1–57

E-Mail Message Options

Outlook offers several ways in which you can customize your e-mail. You can either customize Outlook to treat all messages in the same manner, or you can customize a single message. Among the options available through Outlook are setting e-mail message importance and sensitivity. Setting **message importance** will indicate to the recipient the level of importance you have given to the message. For example, if you set the importance at high, a red exclamation point icon will appear with the message heading (Figure 1–58). Setting **message sensitivity** indicates whether the message is personal, private, or confidential. A message banner indicating the sensitivity of the message appears in the Reading pane below the sender's name in the message header, as shown in Figure 1–58.

Along with setting importance and sensitivity, Outlook also offers several delivery options. You can have replies to your message automatically forwarded, save sent messages in a location of your choice (default is Sent Items folder), or delay delivering a message until a specified date and time.

Figure 1–58

To Set Message Importance, Sensitivity, and Delivery Options in a Single Message

The following steps set message importance, sensitivity, and delivery options in a single message.

1
- With the Inbox window active, click the New Mail Message button on the Standard toolbar.
- Enter the message information (Figure 1–59).

Figure 1–59

• Click the Options Dialog Box Launcher on the Ribbon to display the Message Options dialog box (Figure 1–60).

Figure 1–60

❸

• Click the Importance box arrow and then select High in the Importance list.

• Click the Sensitivity box arrow and then select Private in the Sensitivity list.

• Click the 'Do not deliver before' check box in the Delivery options area to select it.

• Select January 14, 2008 in the calendar and 12:00 PM as the time in the respective delivery boxes (Figure 1–61).

Figure 1–61

- Click the Close button to close the dialog box.

How do I know that my settings have been applied to this message?

Notice that the High Importance button on the Ribbon is highlighted (Figure 1–62). While you cannot see it, the recipient of the message will receive the message with a red exclamation

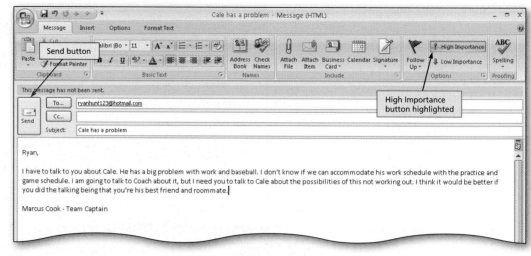

Figure 1–62

point icon and the message heading indicating the e-mail is private, like the one shown in Figure 1–58 on page OUT 38.

- Click the Send button to send the message.

What does Outlook do with the message while it is waiting for the specified date and time to send the message?

Outlook stores the message in the Outbox folder until the specified date and time arrive. At that time, the message will be sent.

To Change the Default Level of Importance and Sensitivity

Outlook allows you to change the default level for either or both of these options. The following steps change the default level of importance and sensitivity for all outgoing messages.

- With the Inbox window active, click Tools on the menu bar and then click Options on the Tools menu to display the Options dialog box (Figure 1–63).

Figure 1–63

2

- In the Preferences sheet, click the E-mail Options button to display the E-mail Options dialog box (Figure 1–64).

- Click the Advanced E-mail Options button to open the Advanced E-mail Options dialog box.

Figure 1–64

3

- Click the Set importance box arrow to display the importance options (Figure 1–65).

- Select High in the Set importance list.

Figure 1–65

- Click the Set sensitivity box arrow to display the sensitivity options.

- Select Private in the Set sensitivity list (Figure 1–66).

- Click the OK button in all three open dialog boxes to close them and return to the Inbox window.

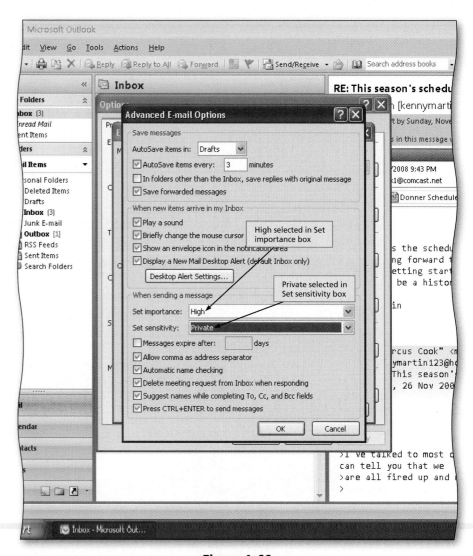

Figure 1–66

Other Ways

1. Press ALT+T, press O

BTW

Rules
Another way to manage e-mail messages is to have Outlook apply rules when receiving and/or sending messages. Using rules, you can have messages automatically forwarded, categorized, flagged for follow up, or apply other options. To create a rule, click Rules and Alerts on the Tools menu, and then click the New Rule button in the E-mail Rules sheet of the Rules and Alerts dialog box.

Search Folders

Outlook offers a feature called the Search Folders folder in the Mail Folders pane (Figure 1–67). The **Search Folders folder** includes a group of folders that allows you to group and view your messages quickly in one of three ways: (1) Categorized Mail, (2) Large Mail, and (3) Unread Mail. **Categorized Mail** messages are messages to which you have assigned a category. These messages are sorted by color. **Large Mail** messages are messages containing very large file attachments. These messages are grouped by size: Large (100 to 500 KB), Very Large (500 KB to 1 MB), and Huge (1 to 5 MB). **Unread Mail** comprises messages that have not been opened or have not been marked as read even though you may have read them in the Reading pane. Figure 1–67 shows messages in the Categorized Mail folder.

BTW

Security Settings
Click the Security Settings button (Figure 1–60 on page OUT 39) opens a dialog box that allows you to apply certain security restrictions on a message, such as encrypting the message or adding a digital signature.

Figure 1–67

Using Contacts

The **Contacts component** of Outlook allows you to store information about individuals and companies. People with whom you communicate for school, business, or personal reasons are your **contacts**. To help organize information about personal contacts, some people keep names, addresses, and telephone numbers in business card files and address books. With the Outlook Contacts component, you can create and maintain important contact information in a **contact list**, which is stored in the Contacts folder. Your contact list is like an electronic address book that allows you to store names, addresses, e-mail addresses, and more. Once you have entered the information, you can retrieve, sort, edit, organize, or print your contact list. Outlook also includes a **Find option** that lets you search for a contact name in your address book while you are using the Calendar, Inbox, or other Outlook components.

When the Contacts folder is open, information about each contact appears on a business card in the default **Business Cards view**. Each card includes fields for name, address, and multiple telephone numbers (home, work, cellular, and so on), e-mail, and Web page addresses. You can choose which fields are displayed on the cards using the View menu.

Previously, an e-mail message was composed, signed, formatted, and sent to Kenny Martin. Kenny's e-mail address was typed into the To text box. The following sections show how to (1) create a personal folder; (2) create a contact list; (3) edit contact information; (4) print contact information; and (5) send an e-mail to a contact.

To Create a Personal Folder

The following steps create a personal folder for Marcus Cook.

- Click the Contacts button in the Navigation Pane to open the Contacts window.

- When Outlook displays the Contacts window, right-click Contacts in the My Contacts pane to display the Contacts shortcut menu (Figure 1–68).

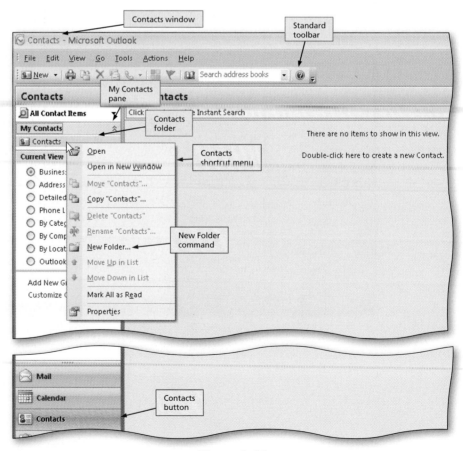

Figure 1–68

2

• Click New Folder on the Contacts shortcut menu to display the Create New Folder dialog box. Type `Marcus' Contacts` in the Name text box (Figure 1–69).

• If necessary, select Contact Items in the Folder contains list.

• Click Contacts in the Select where to place the folder list.

Figure 1–69

3

• Click the OK button to close the Create New Folder dialog box.

• In the Contacts window, click Marcus' Contacts in the My Contacts list (Figure 1–70).

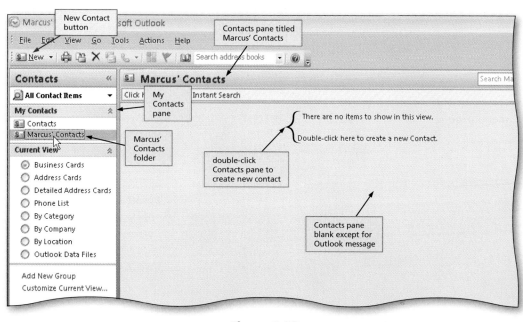

Figure 1–70

Other Ways		
1. On File menu point to New, click Folder on New submenu	2. On File menu, point to Folder, click New Folder on Folder submenu	
	3. Press CTRL+SHIFT+E	

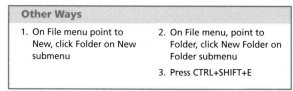

Figure 1–71 illustrates the Standard toolbar located below the menu bar in the Contacts window.

Figure 1–71

Next, you will create a contact list using the information included in Table 1–3.

Table 1–3 Contact Information			
Name	**Telephone**	**Address**	**E-Mail Address**
Kenny Martin	(937) 555-4120	8465 W. 63rd St. Donner, OH 44772	kennymartin123@hotmail.com
Jose Quinteras	(937) 555-7539	8868 Ashwood Lane Donner, OH 44772	josequinteras123@hotmail.com
Kelly Shurpa	(937) 555-9823	214 W. Lincoln Ave. Donner, OH 44772	kshurpa123@hotmail.com
Matt Tartan	(937) 555-0258	5246 Brookfield Ct. Donner, OH 44772	mtartan123@hotmail.com
Jim Osmont	(937) 555-6211	9812 River Rd. Donner, OH 44772	josmont123@hotmail.com
Cale Freeman	(937) 555-3080	7894 Forrest View Lane Donner, OH 44772	calefreeman123@hotmail.com
Kyle Baker	(937) 555-5279	7892 Buckingham Drive Donner, OH 44772	kylebaker101@hotmail.com
Ryan Hunt	(937) 555-1683	8792 Edgewater Lane Donner, OH 44772	ryanhunt123@hotmail.com
Luke Davis	(937) 555-2794	6776 Maplewood Blvd. Donner, OH 44772	lukedavis101@hotmail.com
Trevor Walker	(937) 555-8805	4476 Maplewood Blvd. Donner, OH 44772	trevwalker123@hotmail.com
Kevin Anderson	(937) 555-6309	1021 Ward Rd. Donner, OH 44772	kevanderson123@hotmail.com
Jake Nunan	(937) 555-2148	8924 65th Street Donner, OH 4477	jakenunan123@hotmail.com

To Create a Contact List

The following steps create a contact list.

1

- With the Contacts window active and Marcus' Contacts folder selected, click the New Contact button on the Standard toolbar (Figure 1–70 on page OUT 45) to open the Untitled-Contact window. If necessary, maximize the window.

- Type Kenny Martin in the Full Name text box (Figure 1–72).

- Click the Home text box in the Phone numbers area.

2

- Type 9375554120 as the home telephone number.

- Click the Addresses box arrow and select Home.

- Click the text box in the Addresses area, type 8465 W. 63rd St. and then press the ENTER key.

- Type Donner, OH 44772 to complete the address entry.

- Click the E-mail text box.

- Type kennymartin123 @hotmail.com as the e-mail address and then press the TAB key to complete the contact information for Kenny Martin (Figure 1–73).

Figure 1–72

Figure 1–73

● Click the Save & Close button on the Ribbon to display the Marcus' Contacts window with the Kenny Martin business card in the Marcus' Contacts pane (Figure 1–74).

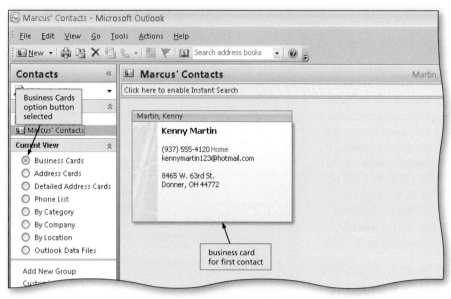

Figure 1–74

● Click the New Contact button on the Standard toolbar.

● Repeat Steps 2 through 4 to enter the 11 remaining contacts in Table 1–3 (Figure 1–75).

Q&A

Is it possible to store information different from what is shown in the Contact window?

By clicking the Details command in the Show group on the Ribbon (Figure 1–73 on page OUT 47), you can enter a contact's department, manager's name, nickname, and birthday information.

Figure 1–75

Other Ways

1. On File menu point to New, click Contact on New submenu

2. On Actions menu click New Contact

3. Press CTRL+SHIFT+C

To Change the View and Sort the Contact List

The following steps change the view from Business Cards to Phone List, sort the contact list in descending sequence, and then change back to Business Cards view.

- With the Marcus' Contacts – Microsoft Outlook window active, click Phone List in the Current View pane of the Navigation Pane.

- With the Phone List in ascending sequence by the File As field, click the File As column heading in the Contacts pane to display the contact list in descending sequence by last name (Figure 1–76).

Figure 1–76

- After reviewing the contact list in Phone List view, click Business Cards in the Current View pane in the Navigation Pane to return to Business Cards view.

Q&A

Are there other ways to sort Outlook information?

If you right-click a column heading in any Outlook component and point to the Arrange By command on the shortcut menu (Figure 1–77), you can see the Arrange By commands.

Figure 1–77

To Find a Contact

A contact record was created for Kelly Shurpa. This record can be found easily by using the Find a Contact box to type a part of the contact name as shown in the following steps.

- Click the Find a Contact box on the Standard toolbar (Figure 1–78).
- Type shu in the text box.
- Press the ENTER key to start the search process.

Figure 1–78

- Outlook opens the Kelly Shurpa – Contact window (Figure 1–79).
- Click the Close button to return to Business Card view.

Q&A

What if there is more than one contact starting with the letters, shu?

If more than one contact with the starting letters, shu, exists, Outlook displays a Choose Contact dialog box with the list of all contacts containing the letters, shu. You can then select the appropriate contact from the Choose Contact dialog box.

Figure 1–79

Other Ways

1. On Tools menu point to Find, click Find on Find submenu
2. Press CTRL+SHIFT+F

To Organize Contacts

To help manage your contacts further, the contact list can be categorized and sorted using Outlook's default color categories, or using your own categories to group contacts by company, department, a particular project, a specific class, and so on. You also can sort by any part of the address; for example, you can sort by postal code for bulk mailings. The following steps assign the baseball players as a contact category with a color designation.

- Click Tools on the menu bar and then click Organize on the Tools menu.

- Click the name bar of the Kevin Anderson contact record.

- Hold down the CTRL key and then click the name bars of Cale Freeman and Ryan Hunt.

- Release the CTRL key.

- Click the 'Add contacts selected below to' box arrow to display a list of categories (Figure 1–80).

- Click Blue Category in the list.

Figure 1–80

- Click the Add button to add the selected records to the Blue Category (Figure 1–81).

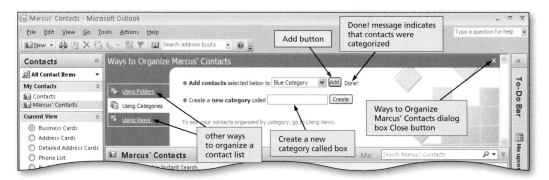

Figure 1–81

Other Ways

1. Press ALT+T, press Z

To Display the Contacts in a Category

The following steps use the Instant Search command to display contacts within a certain category.

- With the Contacts window active, click Tools on the menu bar and then point to Instant Search to display the Instant Search submenu (Figure 1–82).

- Click Instant Search on the Instant Search submenu.

Figure 1–82

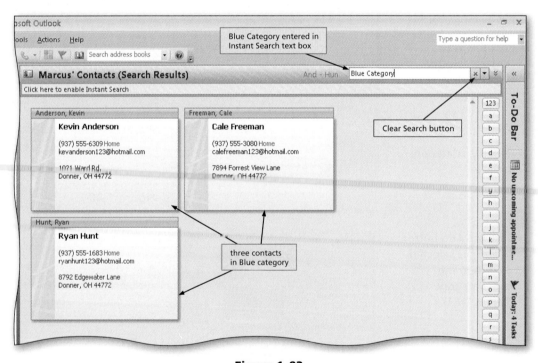

- Type `Blue Category` in the Instant Search text box and then press the ENTER key to display the three contacts that belong to the Blue Category (Figure 1–83).

- After viewing the contacts in the Blue Category, click the Clear Search button to return to the full Contacts window.

Figure 1–83

Other Ways

1. Press CTRL+E
2. Press ALT+T, press I

To Preview and Print the Contact List

The following steps preview and print the entire contact list.

1
- With the Contacts window active, click the Print button on the Standard toolbar to display the Print dialog box (Figure 1–84).

- Click the Preview button to display a preview of the printout (Figure 1–85).

Figure 1–84

Contacts
You can organize contacts from one or more Contacts folders in a personal distribution list. Outlook also detects duplicates and provides the option to merge the new information with the existing contact entry. You also can filter your contact list and then use the filtered list to begin a mail merge from Outlook.

2

- After viewing the preview of the printed contacts list, click the Close button.

- If the preview is acceptable, ready the printer.

- Click the Print button on the Standard toolbar.

- When Outlook displays the Print dialog box, click the OK button.

Q&A

What if I want to print just a single category of contacts?

If you display a category of contacts and then click the Print button, Outlook will print only the contacts in that category.

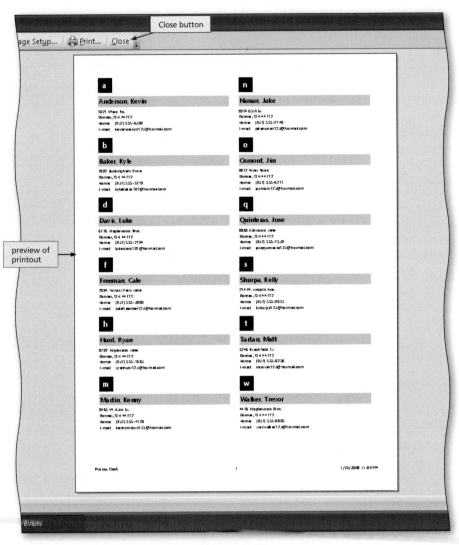

preview of printout

Figure 1–85

Other Ways

1. On File menu click Print
2. On File menu click Print Preview, click Print button in Print Preview window
3. Press CTRL+P

BTW

Business Contact Manager
Outlook 2007 with Business Contact Manager offers complete small business contact management capabilities to Outlook 2007. It allows you to organize customer and prospect information, manage sales and marketing activities, develop and track marketing activities, and centralize project information in one location. Among the capabilities of Business Contact Manager are tools for creating targeted mailing lists, personalizing and distributing print and e-mail marketing materials, and tracking results.

To Use the Contact List to Address an E-Mail Message

The following steps use the contact list to address an e-mail message to Matt Tartan.

- Click the Mail button in the Navigation Pane to display the Inbox window.

- Click the New Mail Message button on the Standard toolbar to display the Untitled – Message window (Figure 1–86).

- When Outlook displays the Untitled – Message window, if necessary, double-click its title bar to maximize it.

Figure 1–86

- Click the To button to display the Select Names dialog box (Figure 1–87).

- Click the Address Book box arrow.

Figure 1–87

- Click Marcus' Contacts in the list.

- Click the Matt Tartan entry in the contact list (Figure 1–88).

Figure 1–88

- Click the To button in the Message Recipients area to add Matt Tartan as the message recipient (Figure 1–89).

Figure 1–89

5

- Click the OK button to close the Select Names dialog box.

- Click the Subject text box and then type `Carwash Fund-raiser` as the entry (Figure 1–90).

- Press the TAB key to move the cursor to the message area.

Figure 1–90

6

- Type the message (Figure 1–91).

- Click the Send button to send the message and close the Message window.

Q&A

Can I add more than one name to the To text box?

You can add as many names as you want to the To text box. You also can add names to the Cc text box. If you do not want those listed in the To text box or Cc text box to know you sent a copy to someone else, send a blind copy by adding the name to the Bcc text box.

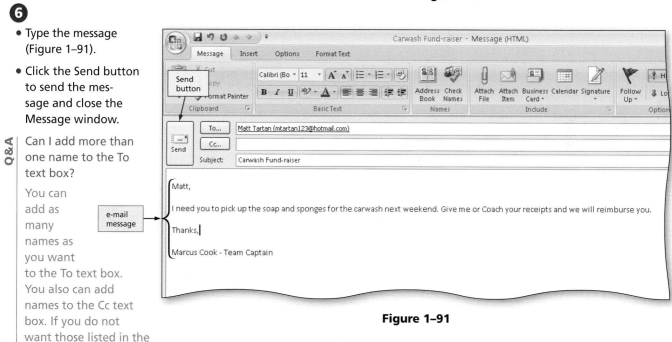

Figure 1–91

Other Ways

1. Click Address Book command on Message window Ribbon

To Create a Distribution List

Outlook can send the same message to a group of recipients using a distribution list. The following steps create a distribution list titled Chemistry Lab Group that includes four members from Marcus' Contacts list.

- With the Contacts window active, click the New Contact button arrow on the Standard toolbar to display the New Contact menu (Figure 1–92).

Figure 1–92

- Click Distribution List to display the Untitled – Distribution List window. Type Chemistry Lab Group in the Name text box, and then click the Select Members button on the Ribbon to display the Select Members dialog box.

- Click the Address Book box arrow and click Marcus' Contacts.

- Select Jake Nunan and then click the Members button to add Jake to the Chemistry Lab Group distribution list.

- Add Kyle Baker and Trevor Walker to the list in the same manner (Figure 1–93).

Figure 1–93

- Click the OK button to close the Select Members dialog box and display the Chemistry Lab Group – Distribution List window showing the members of the Chemistry Lab Group distribution list (Figure 1–94).

- Click the Save & Close command on the Ribbon to close the Chemistry Lab Group – Distribution List window and activate the Contacts window.

Figure 1–94

- Click the Address Book button on the Standard toolbar to display the Address Book dialog box.

- Select Marcus' Contacts in the Address Book list to display the contact list, which now includes the Chemistry Lab Group distribution list (Figure 1–95).

6

- Click the Close button to close the the Address Book window.

Q&A

Can I edit or add to a distribution list after it is saved?

Yes. The Chemistry Lab Group – Distribution List window in Figure 1–94 includes two commands in the Members group on the Ribbon that are useful for modifying a distribution list. The Add New command lets you add a contact that is not already in the distribution list. The Remove command lets you delete names from the distribution list, although they remain in your Outlook contact list.

Figure 1–95

BTW

The Internet
Outlook automatically creates a hyperlink when you type a Web page address or an e-mail address in the text box of a Contact window. If you are connected to an Internet browser, you can click the hyperlink to go to the destination quickly or send an e-mail message.

- Press the ENTER key to display the search results.

- Click the Maximize button on the Outlook Help window title bar to maximize the Help window (Figure 1–101).

Q&A Where is the Contacts window?

Outlook is open in the background, but the Outlook Help window is overlaid on top of the Microsoft Outlook window. When the Outlook Help window is closed, the Contacts window will reappear.

Figure 1–101

- Click the Apply bold, italic, or underline formatting to text link to display information regarding formatting text (Figure 1–102).

Q&A What is the purpose of the buttons at the top of the Outlook Help window?

Use the buttons in the upper-left corner of the Outlook Help window to navigate through the Help system, change the display, show the Outlook Help table of contents, and print the contents of the window.

Figure 1–102

- Click the Close button on the Outlook Help window title bar to close the Outlook Help window and redisplay the Contacts window.

Other Ways
1. Press F1

To Quit Outlook

The following steps quit Outlook.

1 Click the Close button on the right side of the title bar to quit Outlook.

2 If necessary, click the Exit Without Sending button in the Microsoft Office Outlook dialog box so that any messages saved in your Outbox are not sent.

BTW | Certification
The Microsoft Certified Application Specialist (MCAS) program provides an opportunity for you to obtain a valuable industry credential – proof that you have the Outlook 2007 skills required by employers. For more information see Appendix F or visit the Outlook 2007 Certification Web page (scsite.com/out2007/cert).

Chapter Summary

In this chapter you have learned how to use Outlook to open, read, print, reply to, forward, delete, sign, compose, format, and send e-mail messages. You opened and viewed file attachments as well as attached a file to an e-mail message. You learned how to categorize, flag, sort, and set importance and delivery options to e-mail messages. You added and deleted contacts to a contact list. Finally, you used the contact list to create a distribution list and track activities of a contact. The items listed below include all the new Outlook skills you have learned in this chapter.

1. Start and Customize Outlook (OUT 5)
2. Open (Read) an E-Mail Message (OUT 10)
3. Close an E-Mail Message (OUT 15)
4. Print an E-Mail Message (OUT 16)
5. Reply to an E-Mail Message (OUT 16)
6. Change Message Formats (OUT 19)
7. Forward an E-Mail Message (OUT 20)
8. Delete an E-Mail Message (OUT 21)
9. View a File Attachment (OUT 22)
10. Create and Insert an E-Mail Signature (OUT 24)
11. Compose an E-Mail Message (OUT 27)
12. Format an E-Mail Message (OUT 29)
13. Attach a File to an E-Mail Message and Send the Message (OUT 31)
14. Categorize E-Mail Messages (OUT 33)
15. Flag E-Mail Messages (OUT 34)
16. Sort E-Mail Messages by Category Color (OUT 35)
17. Create and Apply a View Filter (OUT 36)
18. Set Message Importance, Sensitivity, and Delivery Options on a Single Message (OUT 38)
19. Change the Default Level of Importance and Sensitivity (OUT 40)
20. Create a Personal Folder (OUT 44)
21. Create a Contact List (OUT 47)
22. Change the View and Sort the Contact List (OUT 49)
23. Find a Contact (OUT 50)
24. Organize Contacts (OUT 51)
25. Display the Contacts in a Category (OUT 52)
26. Preview and Print the Contact List (OUT 53)
27. Use the Contact List to Address an E-Mail Message (OUT 55)
28. Create a Distribution List (OUT 58)
29. Save a Contact List as a Text File and Display it in Notepad (OUT 60)
30. Track Activities for a Contact (OUT 62)
31. Search for Outlook Help (OUT 63)
32. Quit Outlook (OUT 65)

 If you have a SAM user profile, you may have access to hands-on instruction, practice, and assessment. Log in to your SAM account (http://sam2007.course.com) to launch any assigned training activities or exams that relate to the skills covered in this chapter.

BTW | Quick Reference
For a table that lists how to complete the tasks covered in this book using the mouse, Ribbon, shortcut menu, and keyboard, see the Quick Reference Summary at the back of this book, or visit the Outlook 2007 Quick Reference Web page (scsite.com/out2007/qr).

Learn It Online

Test your knowledge of chapter content and key terms.

Instructions: To complete the Learn It Online exercises, start your browser, click the Address bar, and then enter the Web address scsite.com/out2007/learn. When the Outlook 2007 Learn It Online page is displayed, click the link for the exercise you want to complete and then read the instructions.

Chapter Reinforcement TF, MC, and SA
A series of true/false, multiple choice, and short answer questions that test your knowledge of the chapter content.

Flash Cards
An interactive learning environment where you identify chapter key terms associated with displayed definitions.

Practice Test
A series of multiple choice questions that test your knowledge of chapter content and key terms.

Who Wants To Be a Computer Genius?
An interactive game that challenges your knowledge of chapter content in the style of the television quiz show.

Wheel of Terms
An interactive game that challenges your knowledge of chapter key terms in the style of the television show *Wheel of Fortune*.

Crossword Puzzle Challenge
A crossword puzzle that challenges your knowledge of key terms presented in the chapter.

Apply Your Knowledge

Reinforce the skills and apply the concepts you learned in this chapter.

Creating a Contact List
Instructions: Start Outlook. Create a Contacts folder using your name as the name of the new folder. Create a contact list using the people listed in Table 1–4. Sort the list by last name in descending sequence. When the list is complete, print the list in Card Style view and submit to your instructor.

Table 1–4 Contact Information				
Name	**Telephone**	**Address**	**E-mail Address**	**Grade Level**
Greg Sanders	(937) 555-4120	8465 W. 63rd St. Donner, OH 44772	gsanders@isp.com	Junior
Dan Gilbert	(937) 555-7539	8868 Ashwood Lane Donner, OH 44772	dgilbert@isp.com	Freshman
Heather Nichols	(937) 555-9823	214 W. Lincoln Ave. Donner, OH 44772	hnichols@isp.com	Freshman
Valerie Prince	(937) 555-0258	5246 Brookfield Ct. Donner, OH 44772	vprince@isp.com	Junior
Rafael Perez	(937) 555-6211	9812 River Rd Donner, OH 44772	rperez@isp.com	Sophomore
Keith Lee	(937) 555-3080	7894 Forrest View Lane Donner, OH 44772	klee@isp.com	Sophomore

Extend Your Knowledge

Extend the skills you learned in this chapter and experiment with new skills. You may need to use Help to complete the assignment.

Categorizing Contacts and Creating a Distribution List

Instructions: Start Outlook. Using the contact list created in Apply Your Knowledge, create a category for each grade level (freshman, sophomore, junior, and senior) and categorize each student as follows: Greg Sanders – Junior, Dan Gilbert – Freshman, Heather Nichols – Freshman, Valerie Prince – Junior, Rafael Perez – Sophomore, Keith Lee – Sophomore.

Create a distribution list consisting of juniors and seniors. When the list is complete, print the list in Card Style view and submit to your instructor.

Make It Right

Analyze a document and correct all errors and/or improve the design.

Importing Subfolders for the In the Lab Exercises

Follow these steps to import subfolders for the following Make it Right and In the Lab exercises:

1. Connect the USB flash drive containing the Data Files for Students to your computer.

2. Click File on the Outlook menu bar and then click Import and Export.

3. In the Import and Export Wizard dialog box, click Import from another program or file and then click the Next button.

4. In the Import a File dialog box, click Personal Folder File (.pst) and then click the Next button.

5. In the Import Personal Folders dialog box, click the Browse button to access drive E (your USB flash drive letter may be different), select the appropriate subfolder, click Open, and then click the Next button.

6. In the Import Personal Folders dialog box, select the appropriate folder from which to import and then click the Finish button.

Continued >

Make It Right *continued*

Editing a Contact List

Instructions: Start Outlook. Import the MIR 1-1 Contacts folder (Figure 1–103) into Outlook. See the inside back cover of this book for instructions for downloading the Data Files for Students, or see your instructor for information on accessing the files required in this book.

The contact list contains 20 contacts. The five contacts in Table 1–5 need to have their information updated. Locate each contact using the Find a Contact box and change the applicable fields.

Print the revised contact list and submit it to your instructor.

Table 1–5 Revised Contact Information				
Name	**Telephone**	**Address**	**E-mail Address**	**Category**
Jennifer Craig	(916) 555-5686	354 Rutledge St. Condor, CA 95702	jcraig@isp.com	Blue
Andrew Brinckman	(916) 555-4565	8453 Whitcomb St. Condor, CA 95702	abrinckman@isp.com	Blue
Courtney Croel	(916) 555-2348	7456 Brummitt Rd. Condor, CA 95702	ccroel@isp.com	Blue
Ryan Bachman	(916) 555-7410	4654 Ashford Ct. Condor, CA 95702	rbachman@isp.com	Blue
Kris Davids	(916) 555-3647	678 E. 7th Ave. Condor, CA 95702	kdavids@isp.com	Blue

Figure 1–103

In the Lab

Design and/or create Outlook items using the guidelines, concepts, and skills presented in this chapter. Labs are listed in order of increasing difficulty.

Lab 1: Creating a Distribution List and Sending E-Mail

Problem: You are the campaign manager of your mother's campaign for a city council seat. Besides coordinating appearances and advertising, your responsibilities also include soliciting and organizing campaign donations.

Instructions Part 1: Perform the following tasks:

1. Import the Lab 1-1 Contacts folder (Figure 1–104) into Outlook.

2. Create two distribution lists: one consisting of monetary donors, the other consisting of non-monetary donors. Each contact is categorized by type of donation.

3. Print each distribution list and submit to your instructor.

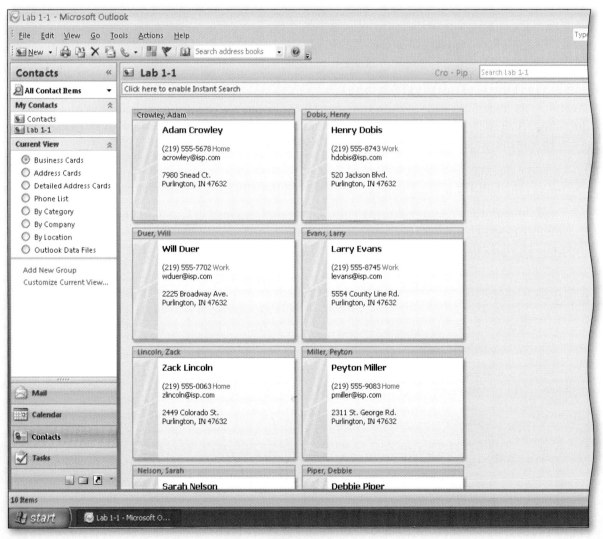

Figure 1–104

Continued >

STUDENT ASSIGNMENTS

In the Lab continued

Instructions Part 2: Perform the following tasks:

1. Compose a message to each group created in Part 1. The message to monetary donors should thank them for their past support and request donations for this year's campaign. The message to non-monetary donors should thank them for their past support and include a request for the same contribution to this year's campaign.

2. Set the sensitivity for each message as confidential.

3. Using Microsoft Word, create a document called Campaign Platform, and include this file as an attachment with your e-mail messages.

4. Set the delivery for each message to March 1, 2008 at 10:00 a.m.

5. Format your messages to monetary donors as Plain Text and your messages to non-monetary donors as HTML.

6. Print each message and submit to your instructor.

Instructions Part 3: Save the Lab 1-1 contact list as a text file. Open the file using Notepad. Print the contact list from Notepad and submit to your instructor.

In the Lab

Lab 2: Flagging and Sorting Messages

Problem: As student director of the Computer Help Center, you are responsible for responding to questions received by e-mail. Some questions require a more timely response than others, so you need a way to sort the questions first by urgency and then by time of receipt.

Instructions: Perform the following tasks:

1. Import the Lab 1-2 Inbox folder (Figure 1–105) into Outlook.

2. Read through each message and apply the appropriate Follow Up flag to each message (Today, Tomorrow, or This Week).

3. After you have flagged each message, sort the messages based on the Follow Up flag.

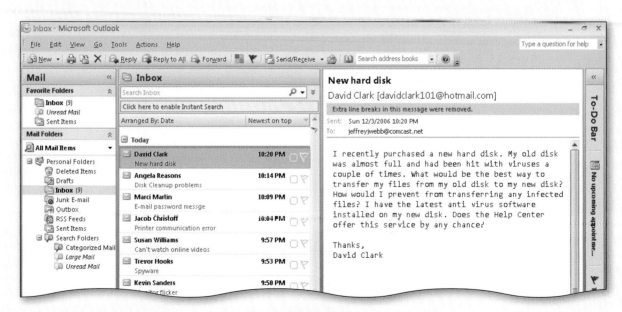

Figure 1–105

In the Lab

Lab 3: Creating an E-Mail Signature, Replying To, and Forwarding Messages

Problem: With all the Computer Help Center messages sorted and flagged, you now have to respond to the messages. You need to perform this task in an efficient manner, as it is the Computer Help Center's policy to respond to questions within three working days. Policy also requires that the name of the person responding, the Computer Help Center's telephone number, and its hours of operation appear on every reply.

Instructions Part 1: Perform the following tasks:

1. Create an e-mail signature consisting of your name, title (Student Director), a telephone number (555-1234), and hours of operation (8:00 a.m. – 8:00 p.m., Closed Sundays).

2. Click the New Message button on the Standard toolbar. Print the blank message containing the signature and submit to your instructor.

Instructions Part 2: Perform the following tasks:

1. Send a reply with the importance set at high to the messages flagged for follow up Today.

2. Forward the messages flagged for follow up Tomorrow. You may use fictitious e-mail addresses for this exercise, because the messages will not actually be sent.

3. Submit printouts of the replies to your instructor.

Instructions Part 3: Perform the following tasks:

1. Clear all the This Week Follow Up flags from the appropriate messages. Use Search Folders to display only the messages flagged for follow up. Make a list of the sender's name, subject, and Follow Up flag type and submit to your instructor.

2. Using information from Microsoft Outlook Help, create a unique signature for a separate e-mail account. See your instructor about setting up a separate e-mail account.

3. Print a blank message containing the signature and submit to your instructor.

Cases and Places

Apply your creative thinking and problem solving skills to design and implement a solution.

• EASIER   •• MORE DIFFICULT

• 1: Create a Personal Contact List

Create a contact list of your family, friends, and colleagues. Include their names, addresses, telephone numbers, e-mail addresses, and IM addresses (if any). Enter the employer for each contact if appropriate. For family members, use the Detail sheet to list birthdays and wedding anniversaries (if any). Print the contact list and submit to your instructor.

• 2: Modify a Contact List

Import the Cases 1-2 Contacts folder into Outlook. You are the manager of the Personnel Department for a large automobile dealership. Your responsibilities include updating the company contact list whenever someone changes positions, receives a promotion, or other changes occur. Byron Taylor has received a promotion to Parts Manager and was rewarded with a private office (Room 3A), private telephone ((812) 555-1278), and his own e-mail address (btaylor@autodealer.com). The information in his current record contains the general telephone number and dealership's e-mail. Make the appropriate changes to Byron Taylor's contact record. Submit a printout to your instructor.

•• 3: Apply a View Filter and Track Contact Activities

Import the Cases 1-3 Inbox folder into Outlook. You work in the IT department of a large company. Every day you receive several e-mail messages about various computer problems within the company. A coworker, Bailey Smithers, has sent several e-mail messages to the IT department complaining that her problem has yet to be solved. You have been told to immediately solve her problem. Apply a filter to the Cases 1-3 Inbox folder to display only the messages from Bailey Smithers. Respond to her latest e-mail message while sending a copy to your supervisor to show that you have found a resolution to the problem. Submit a printout of your reply to your instructor. Add Bailey Smithers to your contact list. Track the activities of Bailey Smithers. List the first five entries from the Activities list and submit to your instructor. After printing your reply message, delete all the messages from Bailey Smithers and remove the filter.

•• 4: Compose and Format an E-Mail Message

Make It Personal

Being involved with your studies, extracurricular activities, and college life in general, can prevent you from keeping in touch with family and friends. Compose an e-mail message to a close relative or friend. Your message should contain information on your class schedule, activities, and new friends that you have made. Compose the message in HTML format. Format the text of your message to enhance its appearance. Use Outlook Help to insert a picture of the campus or your school's logo into the message body. Print the e-mail and submit to your instructor.

•• 5: Compile Contact Information

Working Together

Have each member of your team submit a design of a form for collecting contact information. Have them base the form on available fields in the General and Detail sheets in the Contact window. Have the team select the best form design. After selecting a form, make photocopies for the entire class. Have your classmates fill out the form. Collect the forms and create a contact list from the collected information. Print the final contact list and submit to your instructor.

1 Integrating Office 2007 Applications and the World Wide Web

Objectives

You will have mastered the material in this chapter when you can:

- Integrate the Office 2007 applications to create a Web site
- Add hyperlinks to a Word document
- Embed an Excel chart into a Word document
- Add a hyperlink to a PowerPoint slide

- Create Web pages from a PowerPoint presentation
- Add a hyperlink to an Access report
- Create a Web page from an Access report
- Test a Web site in a browser

1 Integrating Office 2007 Applications and the World Wide Web

Introduction

Integration means joining parts so they work together or form a whole. In information technology, common usages can include the following:

1. Integration during product development combines activities, programs, or hardware components into a functional unit.
2. Integration in manufacturing can bring different companies' products together into an efficiently working system.
3. Integration in marketing combines products or components to meet objectives such as sharing a common purpose or creating demand. It includes such matters as consistent product pricing and packaging, advertising, and sales campaigns.
4. Integration in product design allows a unifying purpose and/or architecture, such as the Microsoft Office System. (The products also are sold individually, but they are designed with the same larger objectives and/or architecture.)

This Integration chapter will show you how you can use the functionality and productivity tools of the Microsoft Office System.

Project — Integrating Office 2007 Applications and the World Wide Web

Many businesses advertise their products and services on the Internet. Companies find it easy to create Web pages using information already saved in word processing, spreadsheet, database, or presentation software formats. The Web pages shown in Figure 1–1 include information about the Makin-It Real Estate Company. This small business specializes in selling homes near the local college campus to first-time homebuyers. The owners of the business want to advertise their services and homes for sale on an attractive Web page.

The project in the chapter follows proper design guidelines and uses Office 2007 applications to create the Web pages and other documents shown in Figure 1–1. The Web page creation capabilities of Microsoft Office 2007 make it simple for you to create an entire Web site using the information available. Word allows you to create and save a document as a Web page. Word also allows you to embed an Excel chart in a document, which can be included in a Web page. PowerPoint provides the same capability and adds a navigation structure for browsing. In addition, an Access report can be saved as a Web page so that users can view database contents online. Several sources of information already exist that can be beneficial to creating a Web page. The following four files of information are supplied to help you get started:

1. A Word document that contains the company letterhead, including logo images, company name, and company address (Figure 1–1a on page INT 4).
2. An Excel workbook with a Bar chart graphically illustrating the company's breakdown of home sales per year (Figure 1–1b on page INT 4).
3. A PowerPoint presentation that contains general information about the company's services (Figure 1–1g on page INT 5).
4. An Access database containing information about homes that currently are for sale through the company (Figure 1–1c on page INT 4).

The Makin-It Real Estate Web site should include the following:

1. A home page with a Bar chart that contains the homes sold by the company per year (Figure 1–1e on page INT 5). Three hypertext links also are included on the home page: Company Services, Homes for Sale, and E-mail for Information.
2. The Homes for Sale Web page (Figure 1–1d on page INT 4) is created from the Access file. Clicking the Homes for Sale link on the home page accesses this Web page. On this Web page, visitors can view the homes for sale from the company, categorized by the type of home.
3. The PowerPoint Web page (Figure 1–1g on page INT 5) displays information about services provided by the company. Clicking the Company Services link on the home page accesses this Web page.
4. Using the E-mail for Information hyperlink, you can create an e-mail message (Figure 1–1f on page INT 5). E-mail is sent to the e-mail address manager@isp.com.

Overview

As you read this chapter, you will learn how to create the Web pages shown in Figure 1–1 by performing these general tasks:

- Insert hyperlinks in the Word document
- Embed the Excel chart in the Word document
- Save the Word document as a Web page
- Add a hyperlink to the PowerPoint presentation
- Save the PowerPoint presentation as a Web page
- Create the Access report
- Add a hyperlink to the Access report
- Save the Access report as a Web page
- Test the Web site

(a) Word Document

(b) Bar Chart in Excel

(c) Access Table

(d) Access Report Saved as Web Page

Figure 1–1

(e) Word Document Saved as Web Page

(g) PowerPoint Presentation Saved as Web Page

(f) New E-Mail Message Created from Hyperlink

Plan Ahead

General Project Decisions

When creating Web pages from many Office 2007 documents, you need to make several decisions that will determine the appearance and characteristics of the finished Web pages. As you create the Web pages shown in Figure 1–1, you should follow these general guidelines:

1. **Choose hyperlink names and locations.** Decide upon the names of the various Web pages and their location on media before creating the Web pages. For example, the first two hyperlinks in Figure 1–1e open Web pages named Company Services and Homes for Sale. The third hyperlink, E-Mail for Information, is easily understood by a Web page visitor.

2. **Ascertain the navigational structure of the Web pages.** The arrows shown between the Web pages in Figure 1–1 are an example of a navigational structure. Determine which pages link to other pages before the Web pages are created. The navigational structure shown in Figure 1–1 is appropriate for a small Web site.

3. **Determine appropriate file names for Web pages.** File names used for each of the Web pages shown in Figure 1–1 need to be determined when planning the pages because the file names are used to create the hyperlinks that are needed to navigate the Web pages. When naming these files, appropriate file names should be used. Save all Web pages to the same location so that they are easier to manage.

4. **Organize the layout of the home page.** Follow good design and visual layout principles to create an inviting home page. The page should not be cluttered, and the user should know what to do without the need for instructions.

5. **Plan the layout of the Access report.** Follow good Access report design guidelines to create the Access report. The fact that the report is to be used as a Web page requires additional thought and planning.

BTW

Web Pages
Making information available on the Internet is a key aspect of business today. To facilitate this trend, the Office 2007 applications easily allow you to generate Web pages from existing files. An entire Web site can be created with files from Word, Excel, PowerPoint, or Access by selecting the Web Page file type in the Save As dialog box.

Adding Hyperlinks to a Word Document

The Web site created for Makin-It Real Estate consists of an initial Web page, called the **home page,** (Figure 1–1e on the previous page) with two hyperlinks to other Web pages, an e-mail link, and a Bar chart. Clicking a **hyperlink**, which can be text or an image, allows you to jump to another location. Text is used (Company Services, Homes for Sale, E-Mail for Information) for the three hyperlinks on the Makin-It Real Estate home page. The first hyperlink (Company Services) jumps to a PowerPoint Web page that contains three Web pages that explain the services offered by the company. A second hyperlink (Homes for Sale) jumps to an Access report that provides a list of homes for sale extracted from Makin-It Real Estate's Homes for Sale Access database. This Web page allows inquiries only; updating the database is prohibited. The third hyperlink (E-Mail for Information) creates an e-mail message. In order to place the three hyperlinks to the left of the Bar chart, a table will be created in the Word document.

To Start Word, Open an Existing Document, and Save the Document with Another Name

The first step in this chapter is to open the Word document, Makin-It Real Estate Letterhead, and save it with the new file name, Makin-It Real Estate Home Page.

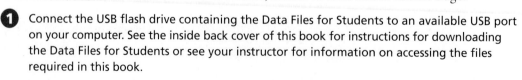

1 Connect the USB flash drive containing the Data Files for Students to an available USB port on your computer. See the inside back cover of this book for instructions for downloading the Data Files for Students or see your instructor for information on accessing the files required in this book.

2 Start Word. Click the Office Button and then click Open on the Office Button menu.

3 Click the Look in box arrow and then click UDISK 2.0 (E:) in the Look in list. (Your USB drive may have a different name and letter.)

4 Double-click Makin-It Real Estate Letterhead to open the Makin-It Real Estate Letterhead document.

5 Click the Office Button and then click Save As on the Office Button menu. Type Makin-It Real Estate Home Page in the File name text box and then click the Save button in the Save As dialog box to save the document as Makin-It Real Estate Home Page.

6 Click the Web Layout button on the status bar to view the document in Web layout view (Figure 1–2).

7 Click the Show/Hide ¶ button on the Ribbon to show hidden formatting symbols.

Figure 1–2

To Insert a Table into a Word Document

The next task is to insert a table with two columns and one row. The left column will contain three hyperlinks. The right column will contain the Bar chart.

The following steps add a table to the Makin-It Real Estate Home Page document.

- Position the insertion point on the second paragraph mark below the company telephone number.

- Click the Insert tab on the Ribbon and then click the Table button on the Ribbon.

- Drag the mouse pointer through the first two cells in the Table gallery and do not release the mouse button (Figure 1–3).

- Release the mouse button to insert the table and close the Table gallery.

Figure 1–3

Other Ways
1. Press ALT+N, T

To Remove the Table Border, View Gridlines, and AutoFit the Table Contents

The table border for the new table is not necessary for the Web page. In order to place the contents in the document properly, however, gridlines should be displayed to serve as a guide for inserting the hyperlinks and chart. The cells in the table also should be formatted to adjust their size automatically to accommodate the data inserted in the table. The AutoFit to Contents option allows you to make the columns in a table automatically adjust to the contents. The following steps remove the border of the table, display gridlines in the tables in the document, and set the AutoFit to Contents option for the table. The heading in the document, including the clip art images, is already included in a table.

- Select both cells in the new table.

- If necessary, click the Design tab on the Ribbon.

- Click the Borders button arrow on the Ribbon to display the Borders gallery (Figure 1–4).

2

- Click No Border in the Borders gallery to remove the borders from the table.

3

- Click the Layout tab on the Ribbon.

- Click the View Gridlines button on the Ribbon to display gridlines in both tables in the document (Figure 1–5).

When should I use gridlines?

Gridlines can be used as a guide when entering text or images. When the document is viewed in your browser or printed, the gridlines do not display or print.

Figure 1–4

Figure 1–5

- Click the AutoFit button arrow on the Ribbon to display the AutoFit gallery (Figure 1–6).

Figure 1–6

- Click AutoFit Contents in the AutoFit gallery to shrink the selected cells to fit their contents (Figure 1–7).

Figure 1–7

To Insert Text for Hyperlinks

After creating the borderless table, you must insert the three text phrases that will be used as hyperlinks on the home page. These phrases (Company Services, Homes for Sale, and E-Mail for Information) allow the Web page visitor to jump to two other Web pages and create an e-mail message. The following steps add the text phrases that are used as hyperlinks.

1
- If necessary, click the leftmost cell in the table to place the insertion point in the cell.

2
- Type Company Services and then press the ENTER key twice.

- Type Homes for Sale and then press the ENTER key twice.

- Type E-Mail for Information but do not press the ENTER key to complete the entry of the three text phrases that will be used as hyperlinks (Figure 1–8).

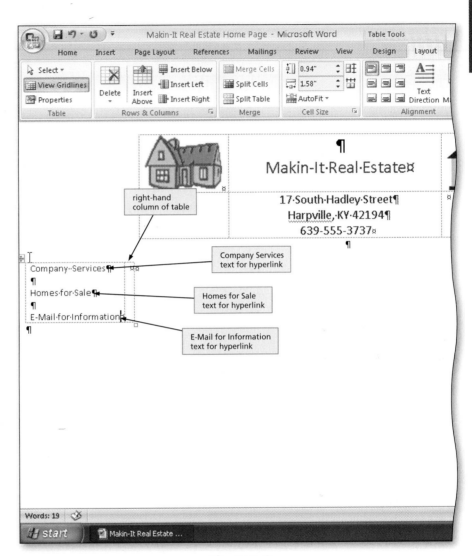

Figure 1–8

To Create a Hyperlink to PowerPoint Web Pages

The **Insert Hyperlink feature** provides the capability of linking to an existing file or Web page, to a place within the current document, to a newly created document, or to an e-mail address. In this chapter, two hyperlinks (Company Services and Homes for Sale) will be created that link to Web pages. The Company Services hyperlink will jump to a PowerPoint presentation that is saved as a Web page using the Web page name, CompanyServices. htm. The Homes for Sale hyperlink jumps to an Access report page using the Web page name, Homes for Sale.htm.

You will create the report later from an existing Access database. The third text phrase (E-Mail for Information) links to an e-mail address, allowing the Web page visitor to send an e-mail message to the company's manager.

The following steps create a hyperlink for the first text phrase.

- Drag through the text, Company Services, in the table to select the text.

- Click the Insert tab on the Ribbon.

- Click the Hyperlink button on the Ribbon to display the Insert Hyperlink dialog box.

- If necessary, click the Existing File or Web Page button on the Link to bar.

- Type CompanyServices. htm in the Address text box (Figure 1–9).

- Click the OK button to assign the hyperlink to the Company Services phrase.

Figure 1–9

Q&A How does the hyperlink function?

After saving the Word document as a Web page, the visitor clicks the text, Company Services, and the CompanyServices.htm file on the USB flash drive is displayed.

Other Ways

1. Right-click selected words, click Hyperlink on shortcut menu
2. Press CTRL+K

To Insert the Remaining Hyperlinks

The following steps add the remaining two hyperlinks.

1. Drag through the text, Homes for Sale, in the table. Click the Hyperlink button on the Ribbon.

2. Type Makin-It Real Estate - Homes for Sale.htm in the Address text box and then click the OK button.

3. Drag through the text, E-Mail for Information. Click the Hyperlink button on the Ribbon and then click the E-mail Address button on the Link to bar.

4. Type manager@isp.com in the E-mail address text box.

5. Type Request for Information in the Subject box and then click the OK button (Figure 1–10).

Figure 1–10

Embedding an Excel Chart into a Word Document

This chapter uses the **Object Linking and Embedding (OLE)** feature of Microsoft Office 2007 to insert the Excel chart into a Word document. OLE allows you to incorporate parts of a document or entire documents from one application into another. The Bar chart in Excel is called a **source object** (Figure 1–1b on page INT 4) and the Makin-It Real Estate Home Page document is the **destination document**. An embedded object becomes part of the destination document. This chapter illustrates using the Paste Special command to embed the Excel object. **Paste Special** inserts an object into Word, but still recognizes the **source program**, the program used to create the object. When you double-click an embedded object, such as the Total Yearly Sales chart, the source program opens within the destination document and allows you to make changes. In this example, Excel is the source program.

To Start Excel and Open an Existing Workbook

The following steps open the Excel workbook in preparation for copying the chart from the workbook.

1 Start Excel. Click the Office Button and then click Open on the Office Button menu.

2 Click the Look in box arrow and then click UDISK 2.0 (E:) in the Look in list. (Your USB drive may have a different name and letter.)

3 Double-click Makin-It Real Estate Yearly Sales to open the Makin-It Real Estate Yearly Sales workbook.

BTW

Hyperlinks
Hyperlinks can link to both external locations and internal locations within the current document. To link to a location inside the current document, select the Place in This Document option in the Link to bar in the Insert Hyperlink dialog box. The Microsoft Office 2007 application then will provide a list of locations within the current document to which you can link.

BTW

Embedded Objects
The advantage of using an integrated set of applications, such as Microsoft Office 2007, is the capability of sharing information among applications. The Object Linking and Embedding (OLE) features of Office 2007 make the integration process more efficient. A chart created in Excel can be included in a Word document using OLE. To edit the embedded object, double-click it. The source program then starts and opens the source object for editing.

To Embed an Excel Chart into a Word Document

The following steps embed the Excel Bar chart into the Word document.

1

• If necessary, click the Total Yearly Sales Chart tab to make the sheet tab active (Figure 1–11).

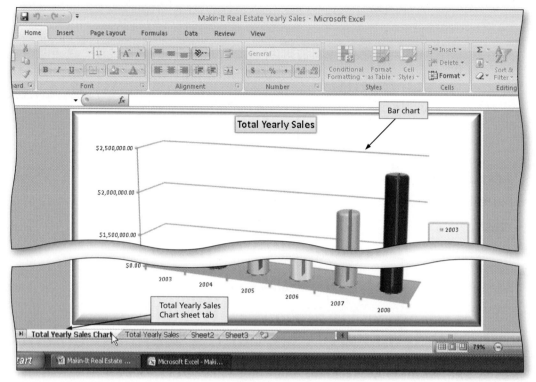

Figure 1–11

2

• Click the white area around the chart area to select the chart and then click the Copy button on the Ribbon to place a copy of the Bar chart on the Office Clipboard (Figure 1–12).

Figure 1–12

- Click the Makin-It Real Estate Home Page button on the taskbar.

- If necessary, click the right cell of the lower table to place the insertion point in the right cell of the table.

- Click the Home tab on the Ribbon.

- Click the Paste button arrow on the Ribbon to display the Paste gallery (Figure 1–13).

Figure 1–13

- Click Paste Special to display the Paste Special dialog box.

- If necessary, click Microsoft Office Excel Chart Object in the As list (Figure 1–14).

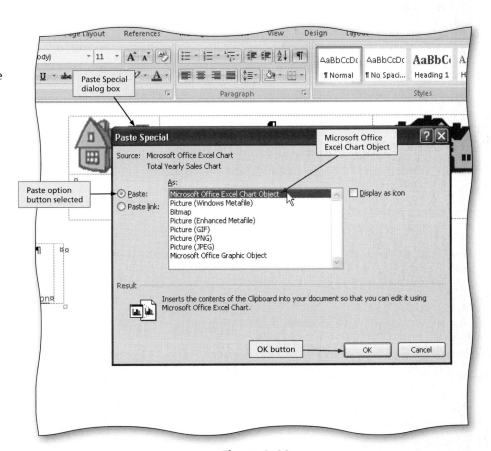

Figure 1–14

5

- Click the OK button to embed the Bar chart into the document (Figure 1–15).

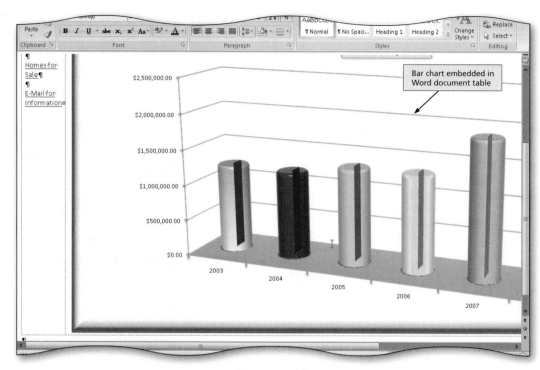

Figure 1–15

Copy Methods

All Office 2007 applications allow you to use three methods to copy objects among applications: (1) copy and paste; (2) copy and embed; and (3) copy and link. The first method uses the Copy and Paste buttons. The latter two use the Copy button and the Paste Special command. Table 1–1 summarizes the differences among the three methods.

BTW

Objects
Objects can be nearly any part of an Office 2007 application or other Windows application. Some examples are Excel worksheets, a paragraph in a Word document, and a slide in a PowerPoint presentation. As long as you use the Paste Special command to paste data in the Clipboard, you can keep data in its native format.

Table 1–1 Copy Methods

Method	Characteristics
Copy and paste	The source object becomes part of the destination document. An object may be edited, but the editing features are limited to those of the destination application. An Excel worksheet becomes a Word table. If changes are made to values in the Word table, any original Excel formulas are not recalculated.
Copy and embed	The source object becomes part of the destination document. An object may be edited in the destination document using source editing features. The Excel worksheet remains a worksheet in Word. If you make changes to values in the worksheet with Word active, Excel formulas will be recalculated. If you change the worksheet in Excel without the document open in Word, however, these changes will not display in the Word document the next time you open it.
Copy and link	The source object does not become part of the destination document, even though it appears to be. Instead, a link is established between the two documents, so that when you open the Word document, the worksheet displays within the document, as though it were a part of it. When you attempt to edit a linked worksheet in Word, the system activates Excel. If you change the worksheet in Excel, the changes also will display in the Word document the next time you open it.

To Change the Size of an Embedded Object

The embedded Bar chart slightly exceeds the margins of the Makin-It Real Estate Home Page document. Reducing the size of the Bar chart will improve the layout of the document. When an Office 2007 document includes an embedded object from another Office 2007 document, you can edit the object in place. When you edit an object in place, the destination document's application displays commands on the Ribbon from the source document's application. For example, when you edit the Total Yearly Sales chart in the Makin-It Real Estate Home Page, the Ribbon changes so that you can use commands from Excel even though you are working in Word.

The following steps reduce the size of the chart by editing the object in place.

1

• Click the View Ruler button above the vertical scroll box.

• If necessary, use the vertical scroll bar on the right side of the Word window to scroll to the top of the document.

• Drag the Move Table Column slider to the right so the border aligns with the left border of the upper table.

2

• Right-click the Bar chart to display the shortcut menu.

• Click Worksheet Object on the short-cut menu to display the Worksheet Object shortcut menu and then point to the Edit command (Figure 1–16).

Figure 1–16

- Click Edit to begin editing the chart in place.

- Click anywhere in the chart to select it.

- Use the scroll bars on the bottom and right sides of the Word window to scroll to the bottom-right of the chart.

- Drag the lower-right sizing handle of the chart up and to the left until the chart is sized as shown in Figure 1–17.

Figure 1–17

Q&A

What happened to the Ribbon?

When you edit an embedded object in place, the destination application, which is Word in this case, displays contextual commands in the Ribbon for the application in which the embedded object was created. You now can edit the Excel chart as though you are working in Excel. This method of editing is much simpler than the entire Excel application opening in order for you to edit the chart.

- If necessary, use the scroll bars on the bottom and right sides of the Word window to scroll to the top of the document.

- Click next to the E-Mail for Information hyperlink in the first column of the table to display the Word Ribbon (Figure 1–18).

Q&A

Why did the Word Ribbon appear?

When you are finished editing an embedded object in place, you can click anywhere outside the embedded object in the destination document to reactivate the destination document's Ribbon commands.

Figure 1–18

To Quit Excel

With the Bar chart embedded in the Word document, you no longer need the Makin-It Real Estate Yearly Sales workbook open. The following steps quit Excel.

1 Right-click the Microsoft Excel - Makin-It Real Estate Yearly Sales button on the taskbar. Click Close on the shortcut menu. If prompted to save changes, click the No button.

2 If the Microsoft Excel dialog box displays regarding saving the large amount of information on the Clipboard, click the No button.

BTW

Resizing
To resize an image proportionally from a corner, you can press and hold down the SHIFT key while dragging a corner sizing handle. To resize vertically, horizontally, or diagonally from the center outward, press and hold down the CTRL key while dragging a sizing handle. To resize proportionally from the center outward, press and hold down the CTRL+SHIFT keys and drag a corner sizing handle.

Viewing the Word Document in Your Browser and Saving It as a Web Page

The next task is to view the Word document in your browser to verify that all information and links in the document are accurate. After verifying its accuracy, you then can save the Word document as an HTML file. Saving the Word document as an HTML file makes it possible for it to be viewed using a browser, such as Internet Explorer.

To Add a Button to the Quick Access Toolbar

Many commands available in Word are not included on any of the tabs on the Ribbon. You can, however, add such commands to the Quick Access Toolbar. One such command allows you to preview a document in a Web browser. This command, Web Page Preview, needs to be added to the Quick Access Toolbar so that the Web page can be previewed. The following steps add the Web Page Preview command to the Quick Access Toolbar.

1

• Click the Customize Quick Access Toolbar button arrow to display the Customize Quick Access Toolbar menu (Figure 1–19).

Figure 1–19

- Click the More Commands command on the Customize Quick Access Toolbar menu.

- When the Word Options dialog box is displayed, click the 'Choose commands from' box arrow to display the Choose commands from list (Figure 1–20).

Figure 1–20

- Click Commands Not in the Ribbon in the 'Choose commands from' list to display a list of commands not in the Ribbon (Figure 1–21).

Figure 1–21

4

- Scroll to the bottom of the list, click Web Page Preview, and then click the Add button to add the button to the Quick Access Toolbar (Figure 1–22).

Figure 1–22

5

- Click the OK button to close the Word Options dialog box (Figure 1–23).

Q&A

Will the Web Page Preview command be on the Quick Access Toolbar the next time that I start Word?

Yes. When you change the Quick Access Toolbar, the changes remain even after you restart Word. If you share a computer with somebody else or if the Quick Access Toolbar becomes cluttered, Word allows you to remove commands from the Quick Access Toolbar. The Web Page Preview button is removed from the Quick Access Toolbar later in this chapter.

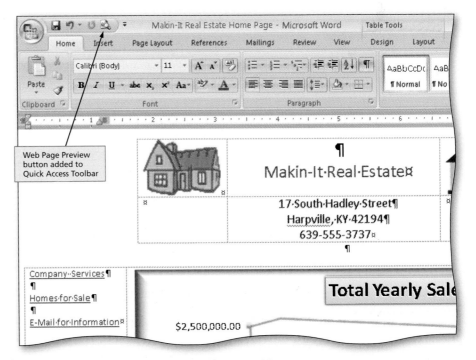

Figure 1–23

To Preview the Web Page

The following steps preview the document in the browser and then save the Word document as an HTML file.

1
- Click the Web Page Preview button on the Quick Access Toolbar to display the Web page in your browser.

2
- If necessary, click the Maximize button on your browser's title bar (Figure 1–24).

3
- Click the browser's Close button.

How should I verify the Web page?

Verify that the Web page contains all information necessary and is displayed as shown in Figure 1–24. The Web page consists of a heading with logo images and the company name, address, and telephone number. A borderless table displays three hyperlinks in the left column and a Bar chart in the right column. The E-Mail for Information hyperlink should display a new message when you click it. The other two links, Company Services and Homes for Sale, do not work because the corresponding Web pages are not available until later in this chapter.

Figure 1–24

Web Page Formatting
Because Word provides formatting options that most Web browsers do not support, some text and graphics may look different when you view them on a Web page. When creating documents for the Web, using Web layout view will ensure that your graphics look the way you want them to when they are viewed as Web pages in a Web browser.

To Save a Document with a New File Name

If the Web page is correct, save it on the USB flash drive as an HTML file. If changes need to be made to the Web page, return to the Word document and correct it. The following steps save the document as a Web page.

1 Click the Office Button and then click the Save As command.

2 Type `Makin-It Real Estate Home Page` in the File name text box if necessary.

3 Select Web Page in the Save as type box.

4 If necessary, click the Save in box arrow and then click UDISK 2.0 (E:) in the Save in list. (Your USB flash drive may have a different name and letter.)

5 Click the Save button in the Save As dialog box. If the Microsoft Office Word dialog box displays, click the Continue button.

Q&A Why should I save the document as a Web page?

Saving an existing Word document as a Web page allows you quickly to get a Word document ready for copying to the Web or to an intranet. One alternative to this is to write the Hypertext Markup Language (HTML) to develop the Web pages. **HTML** is a programming language used for Web page creation. The home page created earlier in this chapter could be created by writing HTML tags (code). For documents that already are in Word format, the easier method is to use the Word Save as Web Page command. This essentially creates the HTML code for you and saves it in a file. While the HTML code is in the file, you do not need to understand HTML code.

To Reset the Quick Access Toolbar and Quit Word

The necessary work with the Word document is complete. The following steps remove the Web Page Preview button from the Quick Access Toolbar and quit Word.

1 Click the Customize the Quick Access Toolbar button arrow on the Ribbon.

2 Click the More Commands command.

3 When the Word Options dialog box is displayed, click the Reset button. If the Reset Customizations dialog box is displayed, click the OK button.

4 Click the OK button on the Word Options dialog box to close it.

5 Click the View Ruler button to close the ruler.

6 Click the Close button on the Microsoft Word title bar.

Q&A Do I need to remove the button from the Quick Access Toolbar?

No. For consistency with this book, reset the Quick Access Toolbar after the added buttons are no longer needed. If you share a computer with others, you should reset the Quick Access Toolbar when you are finished using the computer.

Creating a PowerPoint Presentation Web Page

PowerPoint 2007 allows you to create Web pages from an existing PowerPoint presentation, using the same method used earlier in this chapter to save a Word document as a Web page. The presentation then can be viewed using your browser.

To Start PowerPoint and Open an Existing Presentation

The PowerPoint presentation used in this chapter consists of three slides (Figure 1–1g on page INT 5). The first slide is a title slide, containing the company name and graphics. Slide 2 consists of information about services for home sellers. Slide 3 includes information about services for home buyers. This information can be used in its present format to enhance a presentation about the company's services. As Web pages, you can use this presentation to address a much wider, global audience on the World Wide Web.

The following steps open an existing PowerPoint presentation.

1 Start PowerPoint. Click the Office Button and then click Open on the Office Button menu.

2 Click the Look in box arrow and then click UDISK 2.0 (E:) in the Look in list. (Your USB drive may have a different name and letter.)

3 Double-click Makin-It Real Estate Presentation to open the Makin-It Real Estate Presentation presentation (Figure 1–25).

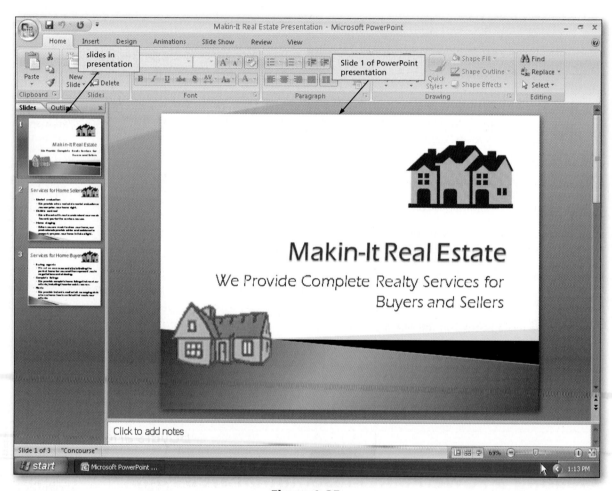

Figure 1–25

To Add Text for a Hyperlink into a PowerPoint Presentation

One of the more important features of Web sites is their capability of linking from one Web page to another using hyperlinks. In earlier steps in this chapter, you added three hyperlinks to the Makin-It Real Estate home page. Once Web page visitors link to the PowerPoint Web pages, however, they cannot return to the home page without using the Back button on the browser's toolbar. This is not a convenient way for Web page visitors to navigate through the Web site. The following steps add a Home link to the first slide of the PowerPoint presentation (Figure 1–1e on page INT 5).

1 Click the Insert tab on the Ribbon.

2 Click Text Box on the Ribbon.

Draw the outline of the text box in the location shown on the slide in Figure 1–26.

 If necessary, click inside the text box.

 Type Home as the hyperlink text (Figure 1–26).

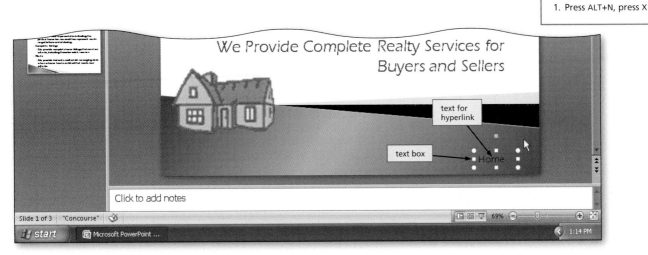

Figure 1–26

To Insert a Hyperlink into a PowerPoint Presentation

After you enter the text for the hyperlink, you can create the hyperlink itself. When clicked, the hyperlink jumps to the Makin-It Real Estate home page created previously in this chapter and saved on the USB flash drive. To create the hyperlink, you will use the Hyperlink button on the Insert tab on the Ribbon.

The following steps create the PowerPoint hyperlink.

1
- Double-click the word, Home, inside the text box you just inserted.

2
- If necessary, click the Insert tab on the Ribbon.

- Click the Hyperlink button on the Ribbon to display the Insert Hyperlink dialog box.

3
- If necessary, click the Existing File or Web Page button on the Link to bar.

- Type e:\Makin-It Real Estate Home Page.htm in the Address text box. (Your USB drive may have a different name and letter.) Click the OK button to add the hyperlink to the text in the text box (Figure 1–27).

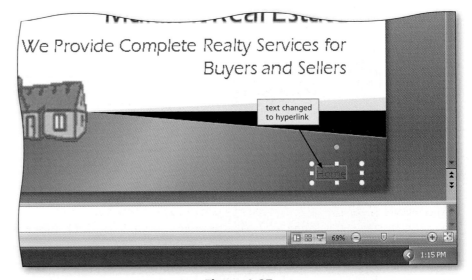

Figure 1–27

To Add a Button to the Quick Access Toolbar and View the Web Page in Your Browser

Just as in the previous section of this chapter, the following steps display the Web page before saving it. It is important to verify all of the Web page navigation features before saving the file. Because the Web Page Preview button is not available on the Ribbon, the button must first be added to the Quick Access Toolbar.

1 Click the Customize Quick Access Toolbar button arrow to display the Customize Quick Access Toolbar menu.

2 Click the More Commands command on the Customize Quick Access Toolbar menu.

3 When the PowerPoint Options dialog box is displayed, click the 'Choose commands from' box arrow to display the Choose commands from list.

4 Click Commands Not in the Ribbon in the Choose commands from list to display a list of commands not in the Ribbon. Scroll to the bottom of the list, click Web Page Preview, and then click the Add button to add the button to the Quick Access Toolbar.

5 Click the OK button to close the PowerPoint Options dialog box.

6 Click the Web Page Preview button on the Quick Access Toolbar to display the Web page in your browser.

7 If necessary, click the Maximize button on your browser's title bar (Figure 1–28).

Figure 1–28

Using Hyperlinks in PowerPoint

Slide 1 of the PowerPoint presentation Web page contains a hyperlink to the home page of the Makin-It Real Estate Web site. Although you created this hyperlink by adding a text box to the first slide, you also can create hyperlinks from existing text or images in a PowerPoint presentation. For example, one of the logo images on slide 1 could be used as a hyperlink to the home page of the Web site. Using one of those images, however, does not give the Web page visitor a clear idea of where the hyperlink will lead. It is more appropriate to create a hyperlink to the home page from text — for example, Home — that makes sense to the visitor.

In addition to any hyperlinks that are added to the presentation, PowerPoint automatically creates hyperlinks in the left column of the Web page, called the **outline**. Using the Expand/Collapse Outline button below the outline pane, you can expand or collapse the outline and navigate through the Web page presentation (Figure 1–28). The text in the heading of each slide is used as the phrases for these hyperlinks. When you click a link, you jump to that particular slide within the presentation. The ease of navigation within a PowerPoint Web page is valuable to the Web page visitor.

BTW

Web Page Publishing
The Web pages created in this project all are stored locally on your computer. Typically, a Web page must be published to a server inside the organization or at your ISP. Microsoft offers a Web Page Publishing Wizard to assist in moving all of the related files and directories that comprise a Web site.

To Save the PowerPoint Presentation as a Web Page

The next step is to save the PowerPoint presentation as a Web page. When you save a PowerPoint presentation as a Web page, the Web page is saved in a default folder. All supporting files, such as backgrounds and images, are organized in this folder automatically. The name of the PowerPoint slide show opened in this section is Makin-It Real Estate Presentation. To simplify the naming of the Web page, the Web page will be saved with the name CompanyServices.htm. PowerPoint uses the name of the saved Web page and adds the string, _files, for the name of the new folder. When saving the current presentation as a Web page, the folder name that PowerPoint Web creates is CompanyServices_files. The default name for the first slide in the presentation is frame.htm. The structure used in the folder organization makes Web page publishing easier because you can keep track of all of the files associated with the Web page. You also can edit the files manually, rather than using PowerPoint.

The steps below save the PowerPoint presentation as a Web page.

BTW

Outline
The outline pane is displayed by default when you view a presentation in a browser. To hide this pane, click the Outline button while in the browser. Click the Outline button again to redisplay the outline pane.

1. Click the Microsoft PowerPoint button on the taskbar.

2. Click the Office Button and then click the Save As command.

3. If necessary, type CompanyServices in the File name text box.

4. Select Web Page in the 'Save as type' box.

5. If necessary, click the Save in box arrow and then click UDISK 2.0 (E:) in the Save in list. (Your USB flash drive may have a different name and letter.)

6. Click the Save button in the Save As dialog box to save the PowerPoint presentation as a Web page.

To Remove a Button from the Quick Access Toolbar, Quit PowerPoint, and Close Your Browser

After saving the PowerPoint presentation as a Web page, you can remove the Web Page Preview button from the Quick Access Toolbar, quit PowerPoint, and close your browser, as shown in the following steps.

1 Click the Customize the Quick Access Toolbar button arrow on the Ribbon.

2 Click the More Commands command.

3 When the PowerPoint Options dialog box is displayed, click the Reset button. If the Reset Customizations dialog box is displayed, click the OK button.

4 Click the OK button on the PowerPoint Options dialog box to close it.

5 Click the Close button on the PowerPoint title bar.

6 Click the Close button on the browser title bar.

BTW

Viewing Web Pages
In addition to Microsoft Windows environments, many environments exist for viewing Web pages. When creating a Web page with special features, such as data access pages, it is important to make sure that the special features are supported within the environment in which the Web page viewers operate. For example, users who view Web pages on Apple Macintosh computers may have a different Web page viewing experience.

Creating a Web Page from an Access Report

The next task in the Makin-It Real Estate Web site creation is to use an Access database to create a report and save it as a Web page. One of the more common purposes of reports is for viewing records in a database via a company's intranet or the World Wide Web. Reports provide a method to make inquiries of large amounts of data in a selective way.

To Start Access and Open an Existing Database

The following steps open an Access database.

1 Start Access. Click the Office Button and then click Open on the Office Button menu.

2 Click the Look in box arrow and then click UDISK 2.0 (E:) in the Look in list. (Your USB drive may have a different name and letter.)

3 Double-click Makin-It Real Estate Homes for Sale to open the Makin-It Real Homes for Sale database (Figure 1–29).

Figure 1–29

To Create a Report Using the Report Wizard

For the Makin-It Real Estate Web site, you do not want the database to be altered by the Web page visitor in any way. The visitors should be allowed to view only the data. Creating an Access report and then publishing the report as a Web page will achieve this goal. The Web page visitors can view all data, but they cannot change the data itself.

The following steps create a new Access report.

- Click the Create tab on the Ribbon.

- Click the Report Wizard button on the Ribbon.

- When the Report Wizard dialog box is displayed, click the Add All Fields button to move all the fields in the table to the Selected Fields list (Figure 1–30).

Figure 1–30

- Click the Next button.

- Click Style in the box on the left and then click the Add button to group the report by Style (Figure 1–31).

Figure 1–31

3

- Click the Next button to display options for sorting records (Figure 1–32).

Figure 1–32

4

- Click the Next button.

- Click the Landscape option button in the Orientation area to select it (Figure 1–33).

Q&A

Why change the orientation to landscape?

When you plan to use a report as a Web page, set the orientation to landscape so that the report takes up as much horizontal space as possible. If portrait is selected, then the Web page visitor might see a large empty margin on the right side of the page.

Figure 1–33

5

- Click the Next button.

- If necessary, click the Access 2007 style in the list on the right (Figure 1–34).

Figure 1–34

6

- Click the Next button and then type Makin-It Real Estate - Homes For Sale in the 'What title do you want for your report?' text box.

- If necessary, click the 'Modify the report's design' option button to select it (Figure 1–35).

Figure 1–35

- Click the Finish button to display the report in Design view (Figure 1–36).

- If necessary, close the Field List task pane.

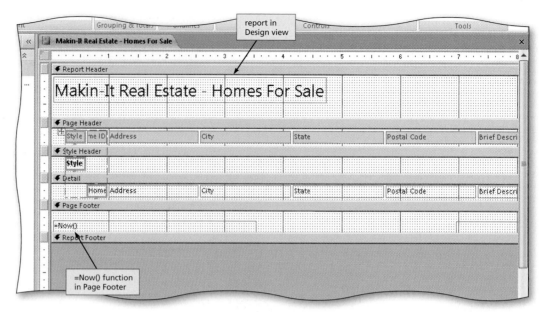

Figure 1–36

To Add a Hyperlink to a Report and Change the Text Background Color

Just as you did on the PowerPoint Web page, you should add a hyperlink on the report that links to the home page. This allows the Web page visitor to return to the Makin-It Real Estate home page without having to click the Back button on the browser's toolbar repeatedly. When you plan to save a report as a Web page, the background color of the elements of the Web page – such as the report title, column titles, and rows – should be changed to a light color, such as white. Browsers do not properly interpret some default colors used by Access for the background colors. The following steps add a hyperlink to the report and change the background colors of the elements in the report to white.

- Click the rightmost text box in the Page Footer area of the report to select it.

- Press the DELETE key to delete the text box.

- Click the leftmost text box in the Page Footer area of the report to select it.

Figure 1–37

- Press the DELETE key to delete the text box that contains the NOW() function (Figure 1–37).

Q&A

Why should I delete these items?

The report will be saved as a Web page. Web pages should not include page footer items such as page numbers because when the report is displayed in a Web browser, it will display as one long continuous page in the browser. There will never be a second page in the Web browser. A report footer, therefore, would be a good design choice, but not a page footer.

- Click the Insert Hyperlink button on the Ribbon to display the Insert Hyperlink dialog box.

- If necessary, click the Existing File or Web Page button in the Link to bar.

- Click the 'Text to display' text box and then type Home as the text to display for the hyperlink.

- Click the Address box and then type e:\Makin-It Real Estate Home Page.htm (Figure 1–38).

Figure 1–38

❸

- Click the OK button to insert the hyperlink (Figure 1–39).

Figure 1–39

- Drag the hyperlink to the lower-left corner of the Page Footer area of the report (Figure 1–40).

Figure 1–40

- Click anywhere in the Style header in the Page header area to select it.

- Click the Plus icon in the upper left corner of the Style header to select all items in the body of the report (Figure 1–41).

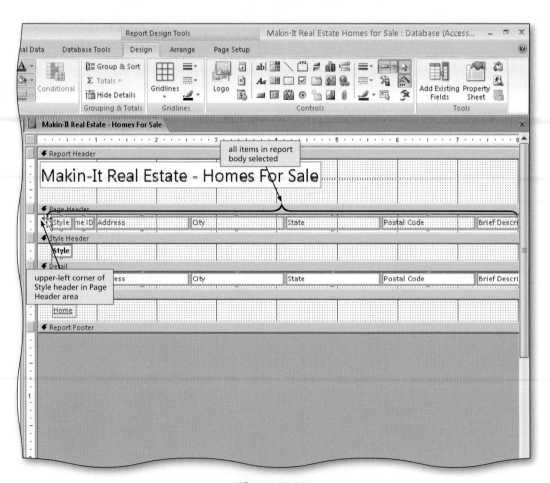

Figure 1–41

6

- Click the Fill/Back Color button arrow on the Ribbon and then click the White color (column 1, row 1) in the Standard Colors area of the Fill/Back Color palette to change the background color of the selected items to white.

- Click the report title in the Report Header area.

- While holding down the SHIFT key, click the Home hyperlink in the Page Footer area to select it.

- Click the Fill/Back Color button on the Ribbon to change the background color of the selected items to white (Figure 1–42).

Q&A

Why should I change the background color of these items?

Some items do not properly display when a Microsoft Access report is saved as a Web page. These items were transparent by default. The Web browser cannot understand transparency. By assigning a background color, you avoid this problem.

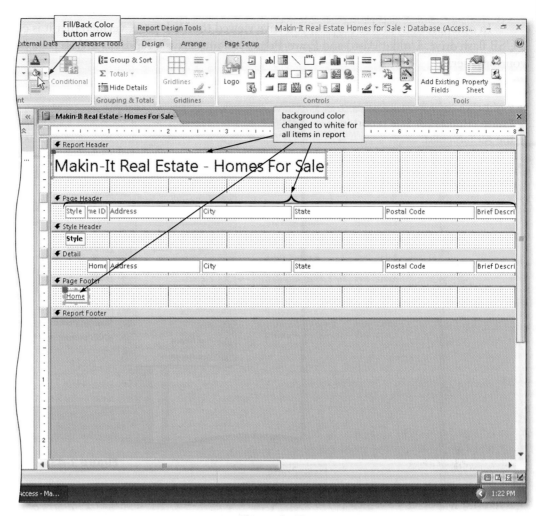

Figure 1–42

Testing the Web Site

The Makin-It Real Estate Web site is complete. To ensure that all the links in the Web site are viable, the following steps open the home page and then thoroughly test the entire Web site.

To Test the Web Site

1 Start your browser.

2 Click the Address bar of your browser.

3 Type `e:\Makin-It Real Estate Home Page.htm` in the Address bar, and then press the ENTER key to display the home page of the Makin-It Real Estate Web site in your browser (Figure 1–46).

Figure 1–46

To Verify the Hyperlinks

All hyperlinks should be tested by clicking them and verifying that they jump to the correct Web page. Three hyperlinks are on the home page: Company Services, Homes for Sale, and E-Mail for Information. The following steps test the links.

1 Click the Company Services hyperlink.

2 Click the navigation buttons to view all slides on the Web page.

3 On the first slide on the PowerPoint Web page, click the Home hyperlink.

4 Click the Homes for Sale hyperlink.

5 On the Access report page, click the Home hyperlink.

6 Click the E-Mail for Information hyperlink to display a new e-mail message with `manager@isp.com` in the To text box.

To Quit E-Mail and Close Your Browser

With the hyperlinks verified, the steps on the next page quit the e-mail program and the browser.

1 Click the Close button on your e-mail program's title bar. Click No if asked to save changes.

2 Click the Close button on your browser's title bar.

Chapter Summary

This chapter introduced you to integrating Microsoft Office 2007 applications. You opened an existing Word document and created a two-column, one-row, borderless table. You then inserted three hyperlinks, embedded a Bar chart from an existing Excel worksheet, and saved that document as an HTML file. You then opened an existing PowerPoint presentation, added a hyperlink to the first slide, and saved this presentation as a Web page. Finally, you opened an existing Access database and created a report, which you saved as a Web page. You saved that report and viewed and tested all Web pages and hyperlinks. The items listed below include all the new Office 2007 skills you have learned in this chapter.

1. Insert a Table into a Word Document (INT 8)
2. Remove the Table Border, View Gridlines, and AutoFit the Table Contents (INT 9)
3. Insert Text for Hyperlinks (INT 11)
4. Create a Hyperlink to PowerPoint Web Pages (INT 11)
5. Embed an Excel Chart into a Word Document (INT 14)
6. Change the Size of an Embedded Object (INT 17)
7. Add a Button to the Quick Access Toolbar (INT 19)
8. Preview the Web Page (INT 22)
9. Insert a Hyperlink into a PowerPoint Presentation (INT 25)
10. Create a Report Using the Report Wizard (INT 29)
11. Add a Hyperlink to a Report and Change the Text Background Color (INT 32)
12. Save the Report and View It in Your Browser (INT 36)

Learn It Online

Learn It Online is a series of online student exercises that test your knowledge of chapter content and key terms.

Instructions: To complete the Learn It Online exercises, start your browser, click the Address bar, and then enter the Web address scsite.com/int2007/learn. When the Integration 2007 Learn It Online page is displayed, click the link for the exercise you want to complete and then read the instructions.

Chapter Reinforcement TF, MC, and SA
A series of true/false, multiple choice, and short answer questions that test your knowledge of the chapter content.

Flash Cards
An interactive learning environment where you identify chapter key terms associated with displayed definitions.

Practice Test
A series of multiple choice questions that test your knowledge of chapter content and key terms.

Who Wants To Be a Computer Genius?
An interactive game that challenges your knowledge of chapter content in the style of a television quiz show.

Wheel of Terms
An interactive game that challenges your knowledge of chapter key terms in the style of the television show *Wheel of Fortune*.

Crossword Puzzle Challenge
A crossword puzzle that challenges your knowledge of key terms presented in the chapter.

In the Lab

Create a workbook using the guidelines, concepts, and skills presented in this chapter. Labs are listed in order of increasing difficulty.

Lab 1: Creating a Web Page in Word with an Embedded Excel Chart

Problem: As vice president of Calamity Jack's Home Disaster Recovery Service, you have created a worksheet and chart in Excel to analyze the sales for the past year. Create a Web page in Word and embed the chart from the Calamity Jack's Sales workbook on the home page. Add a link to a second Web page and an e-mail link to calamityjacks@isp.com below the chart. Create a second Web page in Word by embedding the Calamity Jack's Sales worksheet.

Instructions: Perform the following tasks.

1. Start Excel by opening the Lab 1-1 Calamity Jack's Sales workbook.

2. Start Word and create a new document in Web Layout view. Add a title and subtitle as shown in the Web page preview of the document in Figure 1–47. Select the chart in Excel from the Yearly Sales Chart worksheet, copy it, and use the Paste Special dialog box in Word to embed the Microsoft Office Excel Chart Object. Resize the chart so that it fits in the Word window without the need to scroll to see the right edge of the chart.

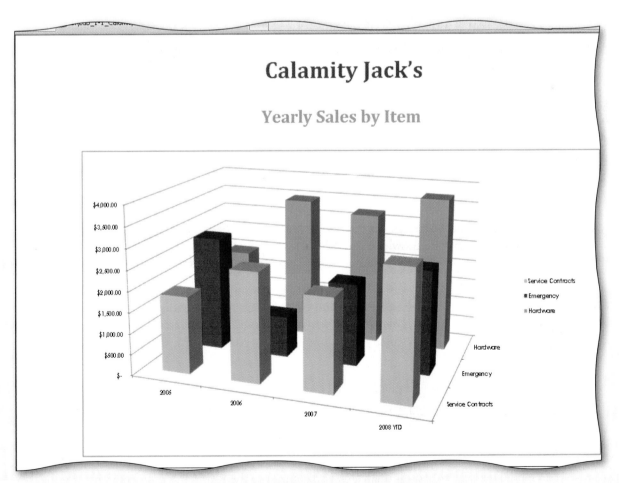

Figure 1–47

Continued >

In the Lab *continued*

3. Add two hyperlinks to the bottom of the page in a centered table as shown in Figure 1–47. The first hyperlink should jump to the Web page Lab_1-1_CalamityJacksSales.htm, which is created next. The second hyperlink creates an e-mail message to calamityjacks@isp.com with the subject About Our Company.

4. Save this file as a Web page named Lab_1-1_CalamityJacks.htm.

5. Create a new document in Word in Web Layout view.

6. Embed the Excel worksheet into the Word page. That is, switch to Excel, select the worksheet named Yearly Sales Analysis, select and copy the worksheet to the Clipboard, switch to Word, and use the Paste Special command in the Paste gallery in Word to embed the Excel Worksheet Object.

7. Save this file as a Web page with the name Lab_1-1_CalamityJacksSales.htm.

8. View the Lab_1-1_CalamityJacks.htm file in your browser (Figure 1–47). Print the Web page. Click the Yearly Sales link to navigate to the Lab_1-1_CalamityJacksSales.htm page (Figure 1–48).

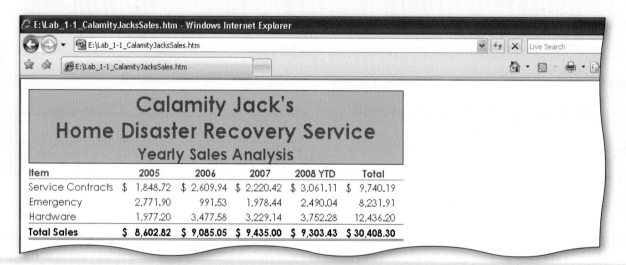

Figure 1–48

In the Lab

Lab 2: Posh Limousine Rental Web Site with an Access Report and an Excel Worksheet

Problem: As the assistant manager of Posh Limousine Services, Matt Ruginis is responsible for keeping track of limousines that are rented on a per-day basis. He would like you to design a site that allows customers to view the availability of limousines for rent. He also wants an e-mail link for customer questions.

Instructions: Perform the following tasks.

1. Start Word. Create a home page for the Post Limousine Availability Web site (Figure 1–49). Add a title and a borderless table below the title. In the left column, insert three hyperlinks. The first hyperlink should go to Lab_1-2_LimousineList.htm (Figure 1–50). The second hyperlink should go to Lab_1-2_LimousineAvailability.htm (Figure 1–51 on page INT 44). The third hyperlink should start an e-mail message to assistantmanager@isp.com. Type the text in the right column. Save the Web page as Lab_1-2_PoshLimousineServices.htm.

Figure 1–49

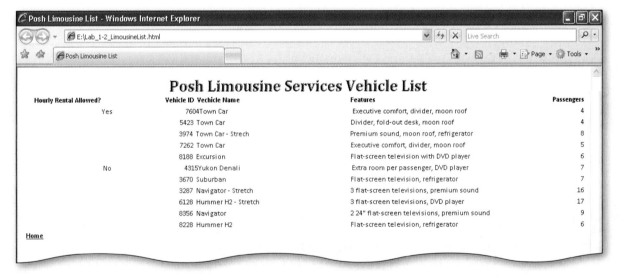

Figure 1–50

2. Start Access by opening the Lab 1-2 LimousineList.mdb database on the Integration Data Disk. Create an Access Report saved as a Web page from the LimousineList table. Create a grouping level using the Hourly Rental Allowed field. Add a title as shown in Figure 1–50. Add a link named Home that links to the Lab_1-2_PoshLimousineServices.htm home page at the bottom of the Access Report Web page. Save the Access Report Web page as Lab_1-2_LimousineList.

3. Start Excel by opening the Lab 1-2 LimousineAvailability workbook on the Integration Data Disk. Create a Web page from the workbook by using the Save As command on the Office Button menu and choosing Web Page as the file type. Use the file name, Lab_1-2_LimousineAvailability.htm.

4. View the Lab_1-2_PoshLimousineServices.htm Web page in your browser. Verify that all links operate properly by clicking each one.

Continued >

In the Lab *continued*

Figure 1–51

In the Lab

Lab 3: Web Site Incorporating PowerPoint Web Pages

Problem: As a part time employee with the Village of Harrust, you have been asked to create a Web page that publicizes the village's summer intern program (Figures 1–52 and 1–53). The specific information for the internships is located in a PowerPoint presentation, which has four pages.

Instructions: Perform the following tasks.

Start Word. Create the Web page as shown in Figure 1–52. Insert two hyperlinks. The first hyperlink should link to Lab 1-3 Village of Harrust Internships.htm, and the second should link to an e-mail address at manager@vilharrust.gov. Use clip art to insert the picture of a municipal building. Save this Web page as Lab_1-3_VillageofHarrustHomePage.htm.

Figure 1–52

Figure 1–53

Open the Lab 1-3 PowerPoint presentation Lab 1-3 Village of Harrust Internships. Add a link named Home at the bottom of the first page of the presentation that jumps to the Lab_1-3_ VillageofHarrustHomePage.htm Web page. Save the PowerPoint presentation as Web pages on the Integration Data Disk. Name the Web pages Lab 1-3 Village of Harrust Internships.htm. View the Web pages in your browser.

Cases and Places

Apply your creative thinking and problem solving skills to design and implement a solution.

• Easier •• More Difficult

• 1: Design and Create a Lawn Care Service Web Site

During your summer break, you and your friends decide to get your exercise by providing lawn care services for local residents and businesses. You plan to offer four services, each at a different rate. To mow a small yard with push mowers, you will charge $15 per week for each quarter acre. To mow a large yard with riding mowers, you will charge $22 per week for each quarter acre. To provide weeding and tree pruning, you will charge $20 per week. Additional lawn care service, including dethatching and fertilizing, will cost $50 for the summer per quarter acre. Create a worksheet in Excel that summarizes each of these plans. Create a Web page using Word that embeds the Excel worksheet; the goal of the Web site is to inform new customers of the services provided. Make sure to include an e-mail address on the Web page.

• 2: Analyze the Cost of Internet Access in a Web Page

You have been asked to research the cost of various types of Internet access for local small businesses. Research the different types of Internet access available to small businesses in your area, and determine the following for each: service provider name, service level, speed, contact name, contact telephone number, contract restrictions, and costs. Create an Excel worksheet and charts summarizing your data and graphing the speed and costs for each service provider. Using Word, create a Web page and embed the worksheet on the home page of the Web site. Create another Web page, and embed the chart(s) from Excel. Create a link to the Excel chart(s) Web page and a link to each service provider's Web page.

•• 3: Design and Create a Customer Complaint Web Page

Your housing association has asked you to help to organize and evaluate complaints from residents. Create an Access database and add eight items to it with the following information for each complaint: complaint number, resident ID number, type of complaint, description, date of complaint, resolution date of the complaint, name of staff member who resolved the complaint, and how the complaint was resolved. From this table, create an Access report saved as a Web page using the type of complaint as the grouping level. Include all of the items in the Access database in the Web page. Use a search engine to find relevant links about each type of complaint – such as drainage, landscaping, and noise – that are relevant to housing associations, and create links to one Web page each for each category at the bottom of the Access report Web page.

•• 4: Design and Create a Summer Internship Web Site

Make It Personal

As an intern for your school's placement program, you have been asked to create a Web page on which students can view information about summer internships available in the local area. Using your own field of interest as a guide, create an Access database and add information to the database about prospective summer internships regarding your area of interest. Include the following fields: organization name, preferred major, type of job, job description, number of positions available, and whether the organization has participated in an internship program in the past. From this table, create an Access report and save it as a Web page using the preferred major as the grouping level. Create a Web page using Word that will act as the Web page for the organization list and create a link to the Access report Web page. Be sure to include a link to your e-mail address on the Web page.

•• 5: Design and Create an Informational Web Site about a Foreign Country

Working Together

Gather basic statistical data about a foreign country, including population, important business and industry, and other demographic data. Have one member of your team create an Excel 3-D Pie chart to summarize the demographic information that you find. Have another member create a PowerPoint presentation that contains at least four major points regarding the country that may make the country interesting to potential visitors, including information about business and industry. A third member should create an Access report saved as a Web page that includes information about popular tourist destinations in the country. Embed the Excel chart into one of the PowerPoint slides. Create a link from one of the PowerPoint pages to the Access report Web page. Save the PowerPoint presentation as Web pages. Include relevant links to Web pages regarding the country.

Appendix A
Project Planning Guidelines

Using Project Planning Guidelines

The process of communicating specific information to others is a learned, rational skill. Computers and software, especially Microsoft Office 2007, can help you develop ideas and present detailed information to a particular audience.

Using Microsoft Office 2007, you can create projects such as Word documents, Excel spreadsheets, Access databases, and PowerPoint presentations. Computer hardware and productivity software such as Microsoft Office 2007 minimizes much of the laborious work of drafting and revising projects. Some communicators handwrite ideas in note-books, others compose directly on the computer, and others have developed unique strategies that work for their own particular thinking and writing styles.

No matter what method you use to plan a project, follow specific guidelines to arrive at a final product that presents information correctly and effectively (Figure A–1). Use some aspects of these guidelines every time you undertake a project, and others as needed in specific instances. For example, in determining content for a project, you may decide that a bar chart communicates trends more effectively than a paragraph of text. If so, you would create this graphical element and insert it in an Excel spreadsheet, a Word document, or a PowerPoint slide.

Determine the Project's Purpose

Begin by clearly defining why you are undertaking this assignment. For example, you may want to track monetary donations collected for your club's fundraising drive. Alternatively, you may be urging students to vote for a particular candidate in the next election. Once you clearly understand the purpose of your task, begin to draft ideas of how best to communicate this information.

Analyze your Audience

Learn about the people who will read, analyze, or view your work. Where are they employed? What are their educational backgrounds? What are their expectations? What questions do they have?

PROJECT PLANNING GUIDELINES

1. DETERMINE THE PROJECT'S PURPOSE
Why are you undertaking the project?

2. ANALYZE YOUR AUDIENCE
Who are the people who will use your work?

3. GATHER POSSIBLE CONTENT
What information exists, and in what forms?

4. DETERMINE WHAT CONTENT TO PRESENT TO YOUR AUDIENCE
What information will best communicate the project's purpose to your audience?

Figure A–1

Design experts suggest drawing a mental picture of these people or finding photographs of people who fit this profile so that you can develop a project with the audience in mind.

By knowing your audience members, you can tailor a project to meet their interests and needs. You will not present them with information they already possess, and you will not omit the information they need to know.

Example: Your assignment is to raise the profile of your college's nursing program in the community. How much do they know about your college and the nursing curriculum? What are the admission requirements? How many of the applicants admitted complete the program? What percent pass the state Boards?

Gather Possible Content

Rarely are you in a position to develop all the material for a project. Typically, you would begin by gathering existing information that may reside in spreadsheets or databases. Web sites, pamphlets, magazine and newspaper articles, and books could provide insights of how others have approached your topic. Personal interviews often provide perspectives not available by any other means. Consider video and audio clips as potential sources for material that might complement or support the factual data you uncover.

Determine What Content to Present to your Audience

Experienced designers recommend writing three or four major ideas you want an audience member to remember after reading or viewing your project. It is also helpful to envision your project's endpoint, the key fact you wish to emphasize. All project elements should lead to this ending point.

As you make content decisions, you also need to think about other factors. Presentation of the project content is an important consideration. For example, will your brochure be printed on thick, colored paper or transparencies? Will your PowerPoint presentation be viewed in a classroom with excellent lighting and a bright projector, or will it be viewed on a notebook computer monitor? Determine relevant time factors, such as the length of time to develop the project, how long readers will spend reviewing your project, or the amount of time allocated for your speaking engagement. Your project will need to accommodate all of these constraints.

Decide whether a graph, photograph, or artistic element can express or emphasize a particular concept. The right hemisphere of the brain processes images by attaching an emotion to them, so audience members are more apt to recall these graphics long term rather than just reading text.

As you select content, be mindful of the order in which you plan to present information. Readers and audience members generally remember the first and last pieces of information they see and hear, so you should put the most important information at the top or bottom of the page.

Summary

When creating a project, it is beneficial to follow some basic guidelines from the outset. By taking some time at the beginning of the process to determine the project's purpose, analyze the audience, gather possible content, and determine what content to present to the audience, you can produce a project that is informative, relevant, and effective.

Appendix B

Introduction to Microsoft Office 2007

What Is Microsoft Office 2007?

Microsoft Office 2007 is a collection of the more popular Microsoft application software products. It is available in Basic, Home and Student, Standard, Small Business, Professional, Ultimate, Professional Plus, and Enterprise editions. Each edition consists of a group of programs, collectively called a suite. **Microsoft Office Professional Edition 2007** includes these six programs, which are Microsoft Office Word 2007, Microsoft Office Excel 2007, Microsoft Office Access 2007, Microsoft Office PowerPoint 2007, Microsoft Office Outlook 2007, and Microsoft Office Publisher 2007. The programs included in the Office suite allow you to work efficiently, communicate effectively, and improve the appearance of the projects you create.

Table B–1

	Microsoft Office Basic 2007	Microsoft Office Home & Student 2007	Microsoft Office Standard 2007	Microsoft Office Small Business 2007	Microsoft Office Professional 2007	Microsoft Office Ultimate 2007	Microsoft Office Professional Plus 2007	Microsoft Office Enterprise 2007
Microsoft Office Word 2007	✓	✓	✓	✓	✓	✓	✓	✓
Microsoft Office Excel 2007	✓	✓	✓	✓	✓	✓	✓	✓
Microsoft Office Access 2007					✓	✓	✓	✓
Microsoft Office PowerPoint 2007		✓	✓	✓	✓	✓	✓	✓
Microsoft Office Publisher 2007				✓	✓	✓	✓	✓
Microsoft Office Outlook 2007	✓		✓				✓	✓
Microsoft Office OneNote 2007		✓				✓		
Microsoft Office Outlook 2007 with Business Contact Manager				✓	✓	✓		
Microsoft Office InfoPath 2007						✓	✓	✓
Integrated Enterprise Content Management						✓	✓	✓
Electronic Forms						✓	✓	✓
Advanced Information Rights Management and Policy Capabilities						✓	✓	✓
Microsoft Office Communicator 2007[1]							✓	✓
Microsoft Office Groove 2007						✓		✓

Microsoft has bundled additional programs in some versions of Office 2007, in addition to the main group of Office programs described previously in this appendix. Table B–1 lists the components of the various Office suites.

In addition to the Office 2007 programs reviewed previously, Office 2007 suites can contain other applications. Microsoft Office OneNote 2007 is a digital notebook program that allows you to gather and share various types of media, such as text, graphics, video, audio, and digital handwriting. Microsoft Office InfoPath 2007 is a program that allows you to create and use electronic forms to gather information. Microsoft Office Groove 2007 provides collaborative workspaces in real time. Additional services that are oriented toward the enterprise solution also are available.

The User Interface

You access commands in Office programs using the Ribbon, Quick Access Toolbar, and Mini toolbars (Word, Access, Excel, and PowerPoint); menus and toolbars (Publisher); or a combination of both methods (Outlook).

The Ribbon

The Ribbon consists of a horizontal bar with a number of tabs, each containing groups of commands (Figure B–1). Command groups reflect tasks. The Home tab on the Ribbon contains the commands for the basic functions of the program. In Excel 2007 for example, the Home tab contains the commands necessary to enter, edit, and format text into an attractive document. Other tabs contain the commands for more specialized tasks, such as Page Layout and Review.

Figure B–1

In addition to the tabs that are on the Ribbon for each program, contextual tabs appear on the Ribbon when using certain features. For instance, in Word, the Picture Tools and Format contextual tabs appear when you insert a picture (Figure B–2). When the picture no longer is active, the contextual tabs disappear.

Figure B–2

Quick Access Toolbar

The Quick Access Toolbar is a small toolbar that appears to the right of the Office Button (Figure B–3). It contains by default just three command buttons but can be customized to contain any command button that you would like to have easily available at all times.

Figure B–3

Mini Toolbar

Like contextual tabs, Mini toolbars are context sensitive, that is, they appear automatically when you perform certain tasks. They provide quick access to appropriate commands when you are working with a particular object in a program. For instance, in Word, a Mini toolbar containing commands used to format text appears when you are working with text (Figure B–4).

Figure B–4

The Gallery and Live Preview

Some Ribbon groups contain a gallery, which provides a group of options that can be applied to a selected object. In Word, for example, text styles appear in a gallery (Figure B–5). When combined with the live preview feature, which allows you to preview a style change in your document before applying it, the gallery is a useful formatting tool.

Figure B–5

Menus and Toolbars

Menus and toolbars, while not prevalent in Word, Excel, Access, and PowerPoint, still appear in Microsoft Publisher 2007 (Figure B–6) and Microsoft Outlook 2007. Menus and toolbars adjust to the way in which you work. You can personalize menus to show only the more commonly used commands. A double arrow at the bottom of the menu allows you to expand the menu in order to view all its commands. As you use commands that are available only by expanding a menu, they automatically become available on that menu the next time you access it. More frequently used buttons appear on the toolbar, while less frequently used buttons do not. Clicking the arrow at the right end of a toolbar displays all buttons. Once you click the arrow at the right end of a toolbar to use a button not displayed by default, that button becomes one of the buttons displayed on the toolbar.

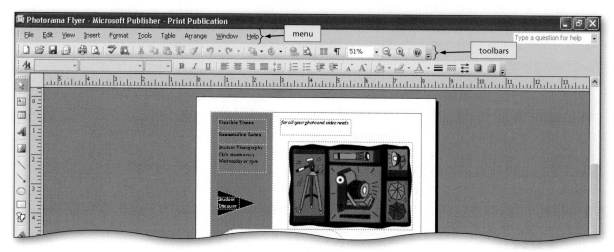

Figure B–6

Office 2007 and the Internet, World Wide Web, and Intranets

Office 2007 allows you to take advantage of the Internet, the World Wide Web, and intranets. The Microsoft Windows operating system includes a **browser**, which is a program that allows you to locate and view a Web page. The Windows browser is called Internet Explorer.

One method of viewing a Web page is to use the browser to enter the Web address for the Web page. Another method of viewing a Web page is clicking a hyperlink. A **hyperlink** is colored or underlined text or a graphic that, when clicked, connects to another Web page. Hyperlinks placed in Office 2007 documents allow for direct access to a Web site of interest.

An **intranet** is a private network, such as a network used within a company or organization for internal communication. Like the Internet, hyperlinks are used within an intranet to access documents, pages, and other destinations on the intranet. Unlike the Internet, the materials on the network are available only for those who are part of the private network.

Online Collaboration Using Office

Organizations that, in the past, were able to make important information available only to a select few, now can make their information accessible to a wider range of individuals who use programs such as Office 2007 and Internet Explorer. Office 2007 allows colleagues to use the Internet or an intranet as a central location to view documents, manage files, and work together.

Each of the Office 2007 programs makes publishing documents on a Web server as simple as saving a file on a hard disk. Once placed on the Web server, users can view and edit the documents and conduct Web discussions and live online meetings.

Using Microsoft Office 2007

The various Microsoft Office 2007 programs each specialize in a particular task. This section describes the general functions of the more widely used Office 2007 programs, along with how they are used to access the Internet or an intranet.

Microsoft Office Word 2007

Microsoft Office Word 2007 is a full-featured word processing program that allows you to create many types of personal and business documents, including flyers, letters, resumes, business documents, and academic reports. Figure B–7 illustrates the top portion of the announcement that students create in Chapter 1 of the Word 2007 section of this book. Chapter 1 of the Word 2007 section of this book contains the steps used to create the flyer.

Figure B–7

Word's AutoCorrect, spelling, and grammar features help you proofread documents for errors in spelling and grammar by identifying the errors and offering suggestions for corrections as you type. The live word count feature provides you with a constantly updating word count as you enter and edit text. To assist with creating specific documents, such as a business letter or resume, Word provides templates, which provide a formatted document before you type the text of the document. Quick Styles provide a live preview of styles from the Style gallery, allowing you to preview styles in the document before actually applying them.

Word automates many often-used tasks and provides you with powerful desktop publishing tools to use as you create professional looking brochures, advertisements, and newsletters. SmartArt allows you to insert interpretive graphics based on document content.

Word makes it easier for you to share documents for collaboration. The Send feature opens an e-mail message with the active document attached. The Compare Documents feature allows you easily to identify changes when comparing different document versions.

Word 2007 and the Internet   Word makes it possible to design and publish Web pages on the Internet or an intranet, insert a hyperlink to a Web page in a word processing document, as well as access and search the content of other Web pages. Figure B–8a illustrates the top portion of a resume that contains a hyperlink (in this case, an e-mail address).

Clicking the hyperlink starts the Outlook 2007 e-mail program, through which you can send an e-mail message to the author of the resume. In Figure B–8b, the Telephone - Message window that allows you to compose a new e-mail message that contains the recipient's e-mail address (lhc@world.net), subject of the e-mail message (Telephone Interview), and a brief message.

(a) Web Page Displaying Resume

(b) E-mail Program

Figure B–8

Microsoft Office Excel 2007

Microsoft Office Excel 2007 is a spreadsheet program that allows you to organize data, complete calculations, graph data, develop professional looking reports, publish organized data to the Web, and access real-time data from Web sites. Figure B–9 illustrates an Excel 2007 window containing a worksheet and 3-D Column chart created in Chapter 1 of the Excel 2007 section of this book.

Figure B–9

In addition to its mathematical functionality, Excel 2007 provides tools for visually comparing data. For instance, when comparing a group of values in cells, you can set cell backgrounds with bars proportional to the value of the data in the cell. You can also set cell backgrounds with full-color backgrounds, or use a color scale to facilitate interpretation of data values.

Excel 2007 provides strong formatting support for tables with the new Style Preview gallery.

Excel 2007 and the Internet   Using Excel 2007, you can create hyperlinks within a worksheet to access other Office documents on the network or on the Internet. Worksheets saved as static, or unchanging Web pages can be viewed using a browser. The person viewing static Web pages cannot change them.

In addition, you can create and run queries that retrieve information from a Web page and insert the information directly into a worksheet. Figure B–10 illustrates a worksheet created by running a Web query to retrieve stock market information for two stocks (Walmart Inc. and Target Inc.). The information in the worksheet was obtained from the MSN Money Web site.

The Refresh All button on the Data tab on the Ribbon allows you to update the last price of the stocks (Last column). Clicking the Refresh All button locates the MSN Money Web site, retrieves current information for the stocks listed in the worksheet, and displays the updated information in the worksheet (Figure B–11). Notice that the stock prices and information in this worksheet differ from that shown in Figure B–10.

Figure B–10

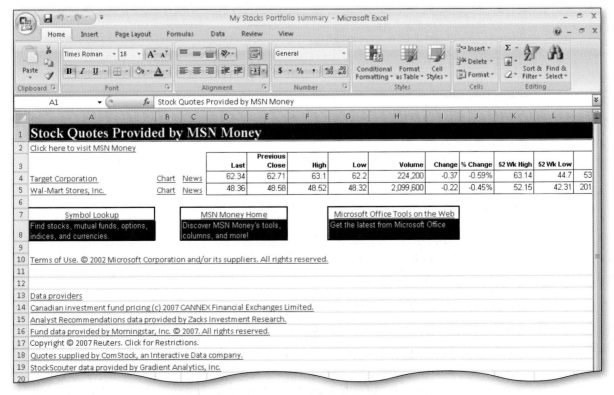

Figure B–11

Microsoft Office Access 2007

Microsoft Office Access 2007 is a comprehensive database management system (DBMS). A **database** is a collection of data organized in a manner that allows access, retrieval, and use of that data. Access 2007 allows you to create a database; add, change, and delete data in the database; sort data in the database; retrieve data from the database; and create forms and reports using the data in the database.

A table from the database created in Chapter 1 of the Access 2007 section of this book is displayed in the JSP Recruiters: Microsoft Access window illustrated in Figure B–12. Chapter 1 of the Access 2007 section of this book contains the steps to create this database.

Client Name	Street	City	State	Postal Code	Amount Paid	Current Due	Recruiter Nu	Add New Field
Alys Clinic	134 Central	Berridge	CO	80330	$0.00	$17,500.00	21	
Berls Hospital	415 Main	Berls	CO	80349	$29,200.00	$0.00	24	
Benton Labs	12 Mountain	Denton	CO	80412	$16,500.00	$38,225.00	24	
ENT Assoc.	867 Ridge	Fort Stewart	CO	80336	$12,750.00	$15,000.00	27	
Ferb Dentistry	34 Crestview	Berridge	CO	80330	$21,000.00	$12,500.00	21	
Family Health	123 Second	Tarleton	CO	80409	$0.00	$0.00	24	
Maun Hospital	76 Dixon	Mason	CO	80356	$0.00	$43,025.00	24	
Peel Radiology	151 Valleyview	Fort Stewart	CO	80336	$31,750.00	$0.00	21	
Tarleton Clinic	451 Hull	Tarleton	CO	80409	$18,750.00	$31,500.00	27	
West Labs	785 Main	Berls	CO	80349	$14,000.00	$0.00	24	

Figure B–12

Access 2007 and the Internet   Access 2007 lets you generate reports, which are summaries that show only certain data from the database, based on user requirements. The database shown in Figure B–13 contains data (Home ID, Address, City, State, Postal Code, Style, Brief Description, Year Built, and Price) about current listings for a real estate company. Figure B–14 illustrates a simple online report created from the data shown in Figure B–13. The report is included on the company Web site and displays up to date information about available listings. The report is displayed in the Makin-It Real Estate - Homes for Sale - Microsoft Internet Explorer window.

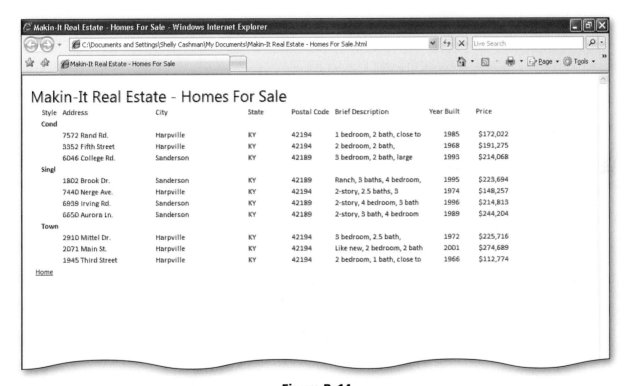

Figure B–13

Figure B–14

Microsoft Office PowerPoint 2007

Microsoft Office PowerPoint 2007 is a complete presentation graphics program that allows you to produce professional looking presentations. With PowerPoint 2007, you can create informal presentations using overhead transparencies, electronic presentations using a projection device attached to a personal computer, formal presentations using 35mm slides or a CD, or you can run virtual presentations on the Internet.

In PowerPoint 2007, you create a presentation in Normal view. **Normal view** allows you to view the tabs pane, slide pane, and notes pane at the same time. The first slide in the presentation created in one of the exercises in Chapter 1 of the PowerPoint 2007 section of this book appears in the Cabo Package - Microsoft PowerPoint window illustrated in Figure B–15. The full window contains the Outline tab with the presentation outline, the slide pane displaying the first slide in the presentation, and the notes pane showing a note about the presentation.

You can include multimedia features such as sounds, movies, and pictures in your PowerPoint 2007 presentations. PowerPoint 2007 includes templates that provide a wide variety of looks for a presentation. PowerPoint 2007 also contains formatting for tables, so that you do not have to create the tables using Word 2007 or Excel 2007. The Table Draw tool available in Word 2007 to draw tables also is available in PowerPoint 2007.

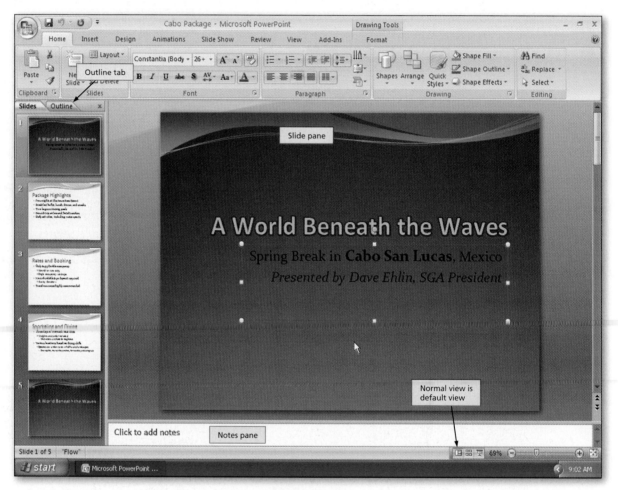

Figure B–15

PowerPoint 2007 and the Internet   PowerPoint 2007 allows you to publish presentations on the Internet or other networks. Figure B–16a illustrates the first slide in a presentation to be published on the Internet. The slide appears in slide view and contains a title (The Benefits of Yoga), a subtitle (A Mind and Body Connection), and a graphical image. The additional slides in this presentation appear in the Slides pane.

Figure B–16b shows the first Web page in a series of Web pages created from the presentation illustrated in Figure B–16a. The Web page appears in the Slide 1 window in the Internet Explorer browser window. Navigation buttons below the Web page allow you to view additional Web pages in the presentation.

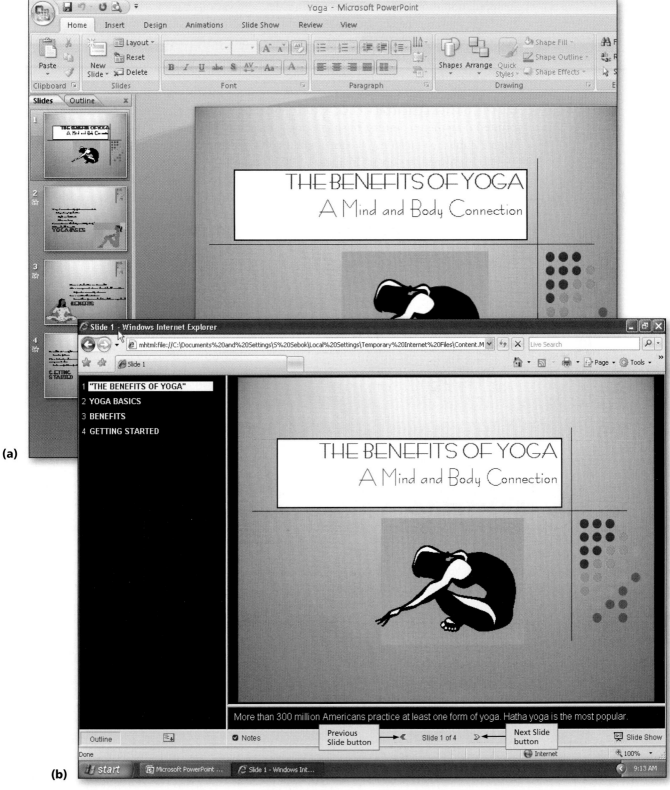

(a)

(b)

Figure B–16

Microsoft Office Publisher 2007

Microsoft Office Publisher 2007 is a desktop publishing program (DTP) that allows you to design and produce professional quality documents (newsletters, flyers, brochures, business cards, Web sites, and so on) that combine text, graphics, and photographs. Desktop publishing software provides a variety of tools, including design templates, graphic manipulation tools, color schemes or libraries, and various page wizards and templates. For large jobs, businesses use desktop publishing software to design publications that are **camera ready**, which means the files are suitable for production by outside commercial printers. Publisher 2007 also allows you to locate commercial printers, service bureaus, and copy shops willing to accept customer files created in Publisher.

Publisher 2007 allows you to design a unique image, or logo, using one of more than 45 master design sets. This, in turn, permits you to use the same design for all your printed documents (letters, business cards, brochures, and advertisements) and Web pages. Publisher includes 70 coordinated color schemes, 30 font schemes, more than 10,000 high-quality clip art images, 1,500 photographs, 1,000 Web-art graphics, 340 animated graphics, and hundreds of unique Design Gallery elements (quotations, sidebars, and so on). If you wish, you also can download additional images from the Microsoft Office Online Web page on the Microsoft Web site.

In the Photorama Flyer - Microsoft Publisher window illustrated in Figure B–17 a flyer created using the Capsules flyer template is displayed.

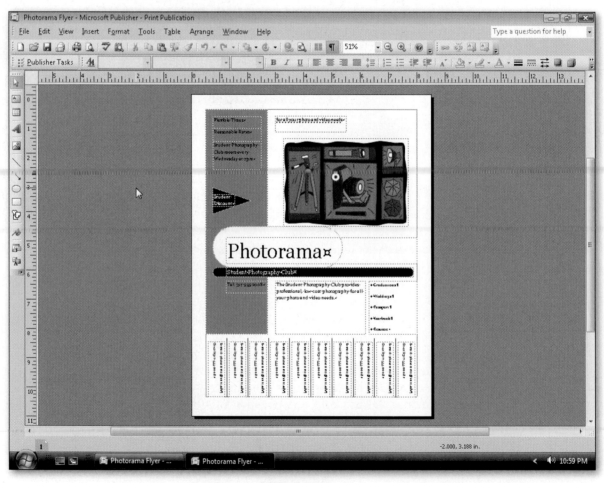

Figure B–17

Publisher 2007 and the Internet   Publisher 2007 allows you easily to create a multipage Web site with custom color schemes, photographic images, animated images, and sounds. Figure B–18 illustrates the Microsoft Internet Explorer window displaying the top portion of the home page in a Web site created using the Convert to Web Publication and the Capsules flyer Template. The home page contains text and graphic images and uses the same template (Capsules flyer) as the flyer illustrated in Figure B–17.

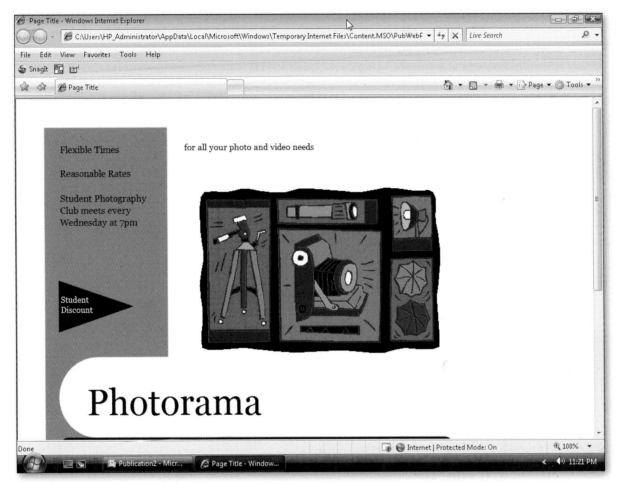

Figure B–18

Microsoft Office Outlook 2007

Microsoft Office Outlook 2007 is a powerful communications and scheduling program that helps you communicate with others, keep track of your contacts, and organize your schedule. Outlook 2007 allows you to view a To-Do bar containing tasks and appointments from your Outlook calendar. Outlook 2007 allows you to send and receive electronic mail (e-mail) and permits you to engage in real-time communication with family, friends, or coworkers using instant messaging. Outlook 2007 also provides you with the means to organize your contacts, and you can track e-mail messages, meetings, and notes with a particular contact. Outlook's Calendar, Contacts, Tasks, and Notes components aid in this organization. Contact information is available from the Outlook Calendar, Mail, Contacts, and Task components by accessing the Find a Contact feature. **Personal information management (PIM)** programs such as Outlook provide a way for individuals and workgroups to organize, find, view, and share information easily.

Figure B–19 shows the Outlook Today - Microsoft Outlook window with the Navigation Pane on the left side of the window and the **Outlook Today page** on the right side of the window. The Outlook Today page contains the current date (Thursday, January 10, 2008); the Calendar area with the currently scheduled events; the Tasks area with a list of tasks to perform; and the Messages area that summarizes the user's e-mail messages by folder. You can customize this page by clicking the Customize Outlook Today button in the upper-right corner of the Outlook Today page.

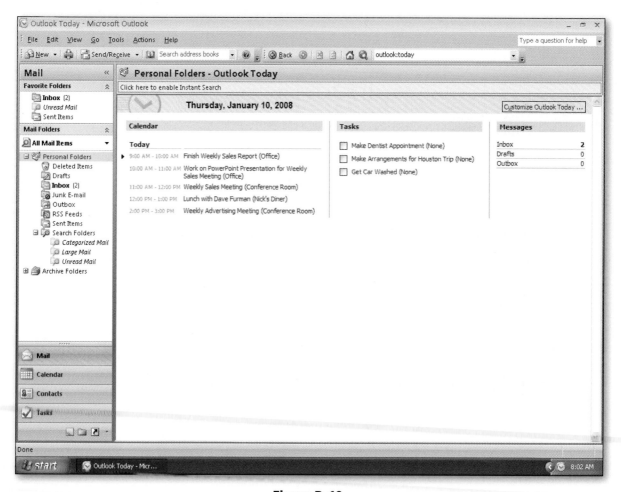

Figure B–19

The **Navigation Pane** is set up to help you navigate Outlook while using any of the components. It comprises one or more panes and two sets of buttons. Although the two sets of buttons remain constant, the area of the Navigation Pane above the buttons changes depending on the active component (Mail, Calendar, Contacts, or Tasks). In Figure B–20, the expanded Mail pane displays the Favorite Folders pane and the All Mail Folders pane. Clicking a button in the Navigation Pane displays the contents of the component's folder with its associated panes in the Outlook window.

In Outlook, click the Mail button in the Navigation Pane to view e-mail messages, click the Calendar button to schedule activities (events, appointments, and meetings), click the Contacts button to maintain a list of contacts and e-mail addresses, and click the Tasks button to view a detailed list of tasks.

When you click the Inbox icon in the Mail pane, the Inbox - Microsoft Outlook window opens and the contents of the Inbox folder (your e-mail messages) and the Reading Pane appear in the window (Figure B–20).

The Inbox message pane contains two e-mail messages. The second e-mail message is highlighted. The contents of the highlighted e-mail message appear in the Reading Pane.

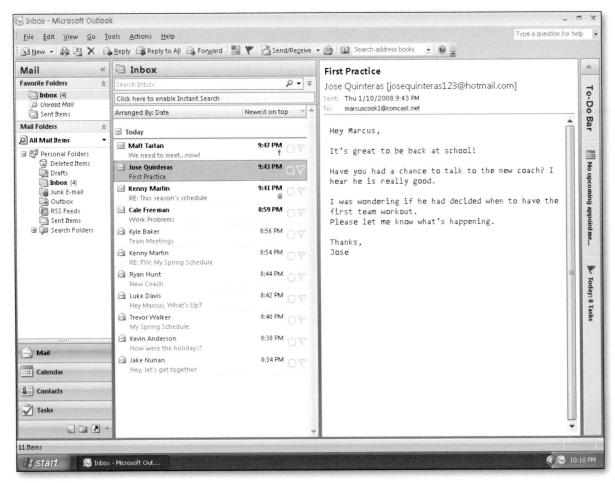

Figure B–20

Microsoft Office 2007 Help

At any time while you are using one of the Office programs, you can interact with **Microsoft Office 2007 Help** for that program and display information about any topic associated with the program. Several categories of help are available. In all programs, you can access Help by pressing the F1 key on the keyboard. In Publisher 2007 and Outlook 2007, the Help window can be opened by clicking the Help menu and then selecting Microsoft Office Publisher or Outlook Help command, or by entering search text in the 'Type a question for help' text box in the upper-right corner of the program window. In the other Office programs, clicking the Microsoft Office Help button near the upper-right corner of the program window opens the program Help window (Figure B–21).

The Help window in all programs provides several methods for accessing help about a particular topic, and has tools for navigating around Help. Appendix C contains detailed instructions for using Help.

Figure B–21

Collaboration and SharePoint

While not part of the Microsoft Office 2007 suites, SharePoint is a Microsoft tool that allows Office 2007 users to share data using collaborative tools that are integrated into the main Office programs. SharePoint consists of Windows SharePoint Services, Office SharePoint Server 2007, and, optionally, Office SharePoint Designer 2007.

Windows SharePoint Services provides the platform for collaboration programs and services. Office SharePoint Server 2007 is built on top of Windows SharePoint Services. The result of these two products is the ability to create SharePoint sites. A SharePoint site is a Web site that provides users with a virtual place for collaborating and communicating with their colleagues while working together on projects, documents, ideas, and information (Figure B–22). Each member of a group with access to the SharePoint site has the ability to contribute to the material stored there. The basic building blocks of SharePoint sites are lists and libraries. Lists contain collections of information, such as calendar items, discussion points, contacts, and links. Lists can be edited to add or delete information. Libraries are similar to lists, but include both files and information about files. Types of libraries include document, picture and forms libraries. Figure B–23 shows an example of a Document library on a SharePoint Workspace Site.

Figure B–22

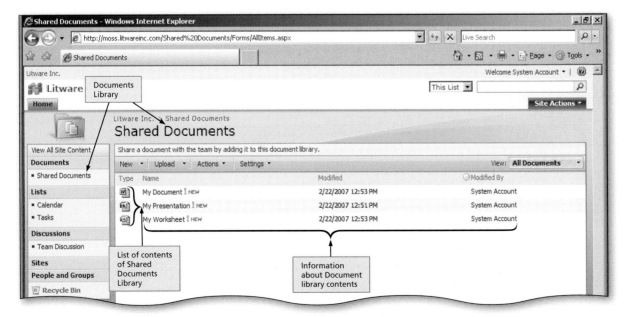

Figure B–23

The most basic type of SharePoint site is called a Workspace (Figure B-22), which is used primarily for collaboration. Different types of Workspaces can be created using SharePoint to suit different needs. SharePoint provides templates, or outlines of these Workspaces, that can be filled in to create the Workspace. Each of the different types of Workspace templates contain a different collection of lists and libraries, reflecting the purpose of the Workspace. You can create a Document Workspace to facilitate collaboration on documents. A Document Workspace contains a document library for documents and supporting files, a Links list that allows you to maintain relevant resource links for the document, a Tasks list for listing and assigning To-Do items to team members, and other links as needed (Figure B-22). Meeting Workspaces allow users to plan and organize a meeting, with components such as Attendees, Agenda, and a Document Library. Social Meeting Workspaces provide a place to plan social events, with lists and libraries such as Attendees, Directions, Image/Logo, Things To Bring, Discussions, and Picture Library. A Decision Meeting Workspace is a Meeting Workspace with a focus on review and decision-making, with lists and libraries such as Objectives, Attendees, Agenda, Document Library, Tasks, and Decisions.

Users also can create a SharePoint site called a WebParts page, which is built from modules called WebParts. WebParts are modular units of information that contain a title bar and content that reflects the type of WebPart. For instance, an image WebPart would contain a title bar and an image. WebParts allow you quickly to create and modify a SharePoint site, and allow for the creation of a unique site that can allow users to access and make changes to information stored on the site.

Large SharePoint sites that include multiple pages can be created using templates as well. Groups needing more refined and targeted sharing options than those available with SharePoint Server 2007 and Windows SharePoint Services can add SharePoint Designer 2007 to create a site that meets their specific needs.

Depending on which components have been selected for inclusion on the site, users can view a team calendar, view links, read announcements, and view and edit group documents and projects. SharePoint sites can be set up so that documents are checked in and out, much like a library, to prevent multiple users from making changes simultaneously. Once a SharePoint site is set up, Office programs are used to perform maintenance of the site. For example, changes in the team calendar are updated using Outlook 2007, and changes that users make in Outlook 2007 are reflected on the SharePoint site. Office 2007 programs include a Publish feature that allows users easily to save file updates to a SharePoint site. Team members can be notified about changes made to material on the site either by e-mail or by a news feed, meaning that users do not have to go to the site to check to see if anything has been updated since they last viewed or worked on it. The search feature in SharePoint allows users quickly to find information on a large site.

Appendix C
Microsoft
Office 2007 Help

Using Microsoft Office Help

This appendix shows how to use Microsoft Office Help. At any time while you are using one of the Microsoft Office 2007 programs, you can use Office Help to display information about all topics associated with the program. To illustrate the use of Office Help, this appendix uses Microsoft Office Word 2007. Help in other Office 2007 programs responds in a similar fashion.

In Office 2007, Help is presented in a window that has Web browser-style navigation buttons. Each Office 2007 program has its own Help home page, which is the starting Help page that is displayed in the Help window. If your computer is connected to the Internet, the contents of the Help page reflect both the local help files installed on the computer and material from Microsoft's Web site. As shown in Figure C–1, two methods for accessing Word's Help are available:

1. Microsoft Office Word Help button near the upper-right corner of the Word window
2. Function key F1 on the keyboard

Figure C–1

To Open the Word Help Window

The following steps open the Word Help window and maximize the window.

- Start Microsoft Word, if necessary. Click the Microsoft Office Word Help button near the upper-right corner of the Word window to open the Word Help window (Figure C–2).

Figure C–2

- Click the Maximize button to maximize the Help window (Figure C–3).

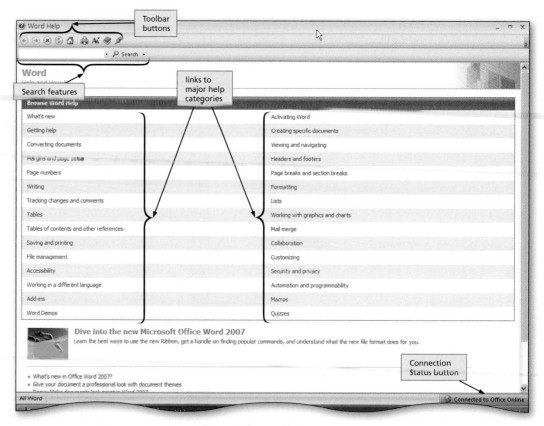

Figure C–3

The Word Help Window

The Word Help window provides several methods for accessing help about a particular topic, and also has tools for navigating around Help. Methods for accessing Help include searching the help content installed with Word, or searching the online Office content maintained by Microsoft.

Figure C–3 shows the main Word Help window. To navigate Help, the Word Help window includes search features that allow you to search on a word or phrase about which you want help, the Connection Status button, which allows you to control where Word Help searches for content, toolbar buttons, and links to major help categories.

Search Features

You can perform Help searches on words or phrases to find information about any Word feature using the 'Type words to search for' text box and the Search button (Figure C–4a). Click the 'Type words to search for' text box and then click the Search button or press the ENTER key to initiate a search of Word Help.

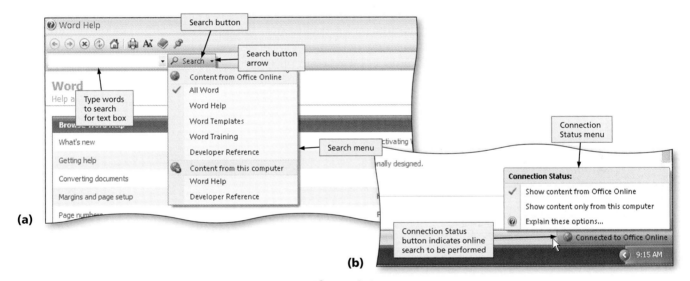

Figure C–4

Word Help offers the user the option of searching the online Help Web pages maintained by Microsoft or the offline Help files placed on your computer when you install Word. You can specify whether Word Help should search online or offline from two places: the Connection Status button on the status bar of the Word Help window, or the Search button arrow on the toolbar. The Connection Status button indicates whether Help currently is set up to work with online or offline information sources. Clicking the Connection Status button provides a menu with commands for selecting online or offline searches (Figure C–4b). The Connection Status menu allows the user to select whether help searches will return content only from the computer (offline), or content from the computer and from Office Online (online).

Clicking the Search button arrow also provides a menu with commands for an online or offline search (Figure C–4a). These commands determine the source of information that help searches for during the current help session only. For example, assume that your preferred search is an offline search because you often do not have Internet access. You would set Connection Status to 'Show content only from this computer'. When you have Internet access, you can select an online search from the Search menu to search Office Online for information for your current search session only. Your search will use the Office Online resources until you quit Help. The next time you start Help, the Connection Status once again will be offline. In addition to setting the source of information that help searches for during the current help session, you can use the Search menu to further target the current search to one of four subcategories of online Help, Word Help, Word Templates, Word Training, and Developer Reference. The local search further can target one subcategory, Developer Reference.

In addition to searching for a word or string of text, you can use the links provided on the Browse Word Help area (Figure C–3) to search for help on a topic. These links direct you to major help categories. From each major category, subcategories are available to further refine your search.

Finally, you can use the Table of Contents for Word Help to search for a topic the same way you would in a hard copy book. The Table of Contents is accessed via a toolbar button.

Toolbar Buttons

You can use toolbar buttons to navigate through the results of your search. The toolbar buttons are located on the toolbar near the top of the Help Window (Figure C–5). The toolbar buttons contain navigation buttons as well as buttons that perform other useful and common tasks in Word Help, such as printing.

Figure C–5

The Word Help navigation buttons are the Back, Forward, Stop, Refresh, and Home buttons. These five buttons behave like the navigation buttons in a Web browser window. You can use the Back button to go back one window, the Forward button to go forward one window, the Stop button to stop loading the current page, and the Home button to redisplay the Help home page in the Help window. Use the Refresh button to reload the information requested into the Help window from its original source. When getting Help information online, this button provides the most current information from the Microsoft Help Web site.

The buttons located to the right of the navigation buttons —Print, Change Font Size, Show Table of Contents, and Not on Top—provide you with access to useful and common commands. The Print button prints the contents of the open Help window. The Change Font Size button customizes the Help window by increasing or decreasing the size of its text. The Show Table of Contents button opens a pane on the left side of the Help window that shows the Table of Contents for Word Help. You can use the Table of Contents for Word Help to navigate through the contents of Word Help much as you would use the Table of Contents in a book to search for a topic. The Not On Top button is an example of a toggle button, which is a button that can be switched back and forth between two states. It determines how the Word Help window behaves relative to other windows. When clicked, the Not On Top button changes to Keep On Top. In this state, it does not allow other windows from Word or other programs to cover the Word Help window when those windows are the active windows. When in the Not On Top state, the button allows other windows to be opened or moved on top of the Word Help window.

You can customize the size and placement of the Help window. Resize the window using the Maximize and Restore buttons, or by dragging the window to a desired size. Relocate the Help window by dragging the title bar to a new location on the screen.

Searching Word Help

Once the Word Help window is open, several methods exist for navigating Word Help. You can search for help by using any of the three following methods from the Help window:

1. Enter search text in the 'Type words to search for' text box
2. Click the links in the Help window
3. Use the Table of Contents

To Obtain Help Using the Type Words to Search for Text Box

Assume for the following example that you want to know more about watermarks. The following steps use the 'Type words to search for' text box to obtain useful information about watermarks by entering the word, watermark, as search text. The steps also navigate in the Word Help window.

- Type watermark in the 'Type words to search for' text box at the top of the Word Help window.

- Click the Search button arrow to display the Search menu.

- If it is not selected already, click All Word on the Search menu to select the command. If All Word is already selected, click the Search button arrow again to close the Search menu.

Q&A — Why select All Word on the Search menu?

Selecting All Word on the Search menu ensures that Word Help will search all possible sources for information on your search term. It will produce the most complete search results.

Figure C–6

● Click the Search button to display the search results (Figure C–7).

Why do my results differ?

If you do not have an Internet connection, your results will reflect only the content of the Help files on your computer. When searching for help online, results also can change as material is added, deleted, and updated on the online Help Web pages maintained by Microsoft.

Why were my search results not very helpful?

When initiating a search, keep in mind to check the spelling of the search text; and to keep your search very specific, with fewer than seven words, to return the most accurate results.

Figure C–7

● Click the 'Brand a document with a watermark or background' link to open the Help document associated with the link in the Help window (Figure C–8).

Figure C–8

• Click the Home button to clear the search results and redisplay the Word Help home page (Figure C–9).

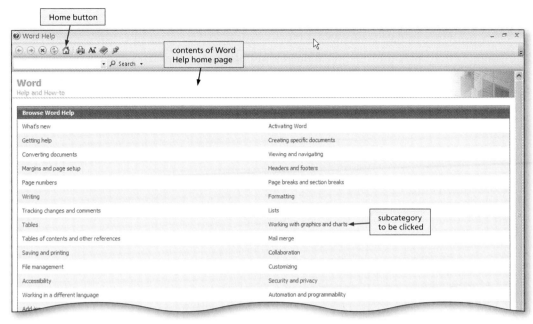

Figure C–9

To Obtain Help Using the Help Links

If your topic of interest is listed in the Browse Word Help area, you can click the link to begin browsing Word Help categories instead of entering search text. You browse Word Help just like you would browse a Web site. If you know in which category to find your Help information, you may wish to use these links. The following steps find the watermark help information using the category links from the Word Help home page.

1

• Click the 'Working with graphics and charts' link to open the Working with Graphics and Charts page.

• Click the 'Brand a document with a watermark or background' link to open the Help document associated with the link (Figure C–10).

 Q&A

What does the Show All link do?

In many Help documents, additional information about terms and features is available by clicking a link in the document to display additional information in the Help document. Clicking the Show All link opens all the links in the Help document that expand to additional text.

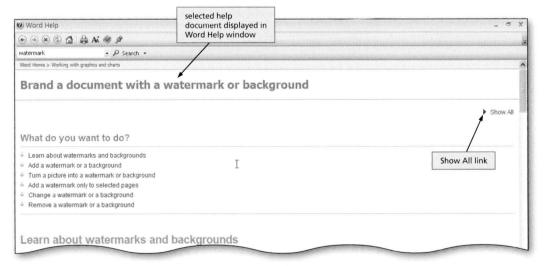

Figure C–10

To Obtain Help Using the Help Table of Contents

A third way to find Help in Word is through the Help Table of Contents. You can browse through the Table of Contents to display information about a particular topic or to familiarize yourself with Word. The following steps access the watermark Help information by browsing through the Table of Contents.

- Click the Home button.

- Click the Show Table of Contents button to open the Table of Contents pane on the left side of the Help window. If necessary, click the Maximize button to maximize the window (Figure C–11).

Figure C–11

- Click the 'Working with graphics and charts' link in the Table of Contents pane to view a list of Help subtopics.

- Click the 'Brand a document with a watermark or background' link in the Table of Contents pane to view the selected help document in the right pane (Figure C–12).

Q&A | How do I remove the Table of Contents when I am finished with it?

The Show Table of Contents button acts as a toggle switch. When the Table of Contents is visible, the button changes to Hide Table of Contents. Clicking it hides the Table of Contents and changes the button to Show Table of Contents.

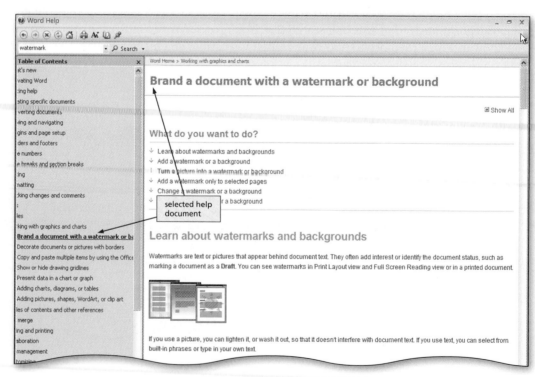

Figure C–12

Obtaining Help while Working in Word

Often you may need help while working on a document without already having the Help window open. For example, you may be unsure about how a particular command works, or you may be presented with a dialog box that you are not sure how to use. Rather than opening the Help window and initiating a search, Word Help provides you with the ability to search directly for help.

Figure C–13 shows one option for obtaining help while working in Word. If you want to learn more about a command, point to the command button and wait for the Enhanced ScreenTip to appear. If the Help icon appears in the Enhanced ScreenTip, press the F1 key while pointing to the command to open the Help window associated with that command.

Figure C–13

Figure C–14 shows a dialog box with a help icon in it. Pressing the F1 key while the dialog box is displayed opens a Help window. The Help window contains help on that dialog box, if available. If no help file is available for that particular dialog box, then the main Help window opens.

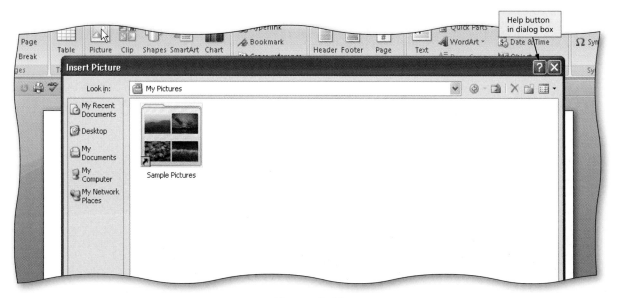

Figure C–14

Use Help

1 Obtaining Help Using Search Text

Instructions: Perform the following tasks using Word Help.

1. Use the 'Type words to search for' text box to obtain help about landscape printing. Use the Connection Status menu to search online help if you have an Internet connection.

2. Click Select page orientation in the list of links in the search results. Double-click the Microsoft Office Word Help window title bar to maximize it. Read and print the information. At the top of the printout, write down the number of links Word Help found.

3. Use the Search menu to search for help offline. Repeat the search from Step 1. At the top of the printout, write down the number of links that Word Help found searching offline. Submit the printouts as specified by your instructor.

4. Use the 'Type words to search for' text box to search for information online about adjusting line spacing. Click the 'Adjust the spacing between a list bullet or number and the text' link in the search results. Maximize the Microsoft Office 2007 Word Help window. Read and print the contents of the window. Close the Microsoft Office Word Help window. Submit the printouts as specified by your instructor.

5. For each of the following words and phrases, click one link in the search results, click the Show All link, and then print the page: page zoom; date; print preview; Ribbon; word count; and citation. Submit the printouts as specified by your instructor.

2 Expanding on Word Help Basics

Instructions: Use Word Help to better understand its features and answer the questions listed below. Answer the questions on your own paper, or submit the printed Help information as specified by your instructor.

1. Use Help to find out how to customize the Help window. Change the font size to the smallest option and then print the contents of the Microsoft Office Word Help window. Change the font size back to its original setting. Close the window.

2. Press the F1 key. Search for information about tables, restricting the search results to Word Templates. Print the first page of the the Search results.

3. Search for information about tables, restricting the search results to Word Help files. Print the first page of the the Search results.

4. Use Word Help to find out what happened to the Office Assistant, a feature in the previous version of Word. Print out the Help document that contains the answer.

Appendix D
Publishing Office 2007 Web Pages to a Web Server

With the Office 2007 programs, you use the Save As command on the Office Button menu to save a Web page to a Web server using one of two techniques: Web folders or File Transfer Protocol. A **Web folder** is an Office shortcut to a Web server. **File Transfer Protocol** (**FTP**) is an Internet standard that allows computers to exchange files with other computers on the Internet.

You should contact your network system administrator or technical support staff at your Internet access provider to determine if their Web server supports Web folders, FTP, or both, and to obtain necessary permissions to access the Web server. If you decide to publish Web pages using a Web folder, you must have the Office Server Extensions (OSE) installed on your computer.

Using Web Folders to Publish Office 2007 Web Pages

When publishing to a Web folder, someone first must create the Web folder before you can save to it. If you are granted permission to create a Web folder, you must obtain the Web address of the Web server, a user name, and possibly a password that allows you to access the Web server. You also must decide on a name for the Web folder. Table D–1 explains how to create a Web folder.

Office 2007 adds the name of the Web folder to the list of current Web folders. You can save to this folder, open files in the folder, rename the folder, or perform any operations you would to a folder on your hard disk. You can use your Office 2007 program or Windows Explorer to access this folder. Table D–2 explains how to save to a Web folder.

Using FTP to Publish Office 2007 Web Pages

When publishing a Web page using FTP, you first must add the FTP location to your computer before you can save to it. An FTP location, also called an **FTP site**, is a collection of files that reside on an FTP server. In this case, the FTP server is the Web server.

To add an FTP location, you must obtain the name of the FTP site, which usually is the address (URL) of the FTP server, and a user name and a password that allows you to access the FTP server. You save and open the Web pages on the FTP server using the name of the FTP site. Table D–3 explains how to add an FTP site.

Office 2007 adds the name of the FTP site to the FTP locations list in the Save As and Open dialog boxes. You can open and save files using this list. Table D–4 explains how to save to an FTP location.

Table D–1 Creating a Web Folder

1.	Click the Office Button and then click Save As or Open.
2.	When the Save As dialog box (or Open dialog box) appears, click My Network Places on the My Places bar, and then click the Create New Folder button on the toolbar.
3.	When the Add Network Place Wizard dialog box appears, click the Next button. If necessary, click Choose another network location. Click the Next button. Click the View some examples link, type the Internet or network address, and then click the Next button. Click Log on anonymously to deselect the check box, type your user name in the User name text box, and then click the Next button. Enter the name you want to call this network place and then click the Next button. Click the Finish button.

Table D–2 Saving to a Web Folder

1.	Click the Office Button, click Save As.
2.	When the Save As dialog box appears, type the Web page file name in the File name text box. Do not press the ENTER key.
3.	Click the Save as type box arrow and then click Web Page to select the Web Page format.
4.	Click My Network Places on the My Places bar.
5.	Double-click the Web folder name in the Save in list.
6.	If the Enter Network Password dialog box appears, type the user name and password in the respective text boxes and then click the OK button.
7.	Click the Save button in the Save As dialog box.

Table D–3 Adding an FTP Location

1.	Click the Office Button and then click Save As (or Open).
2.	In the Save As dialog box, click the Save in box arrow and then click Add/Modify FTP Locations in the Save in list; or in the Open dialog box, click the Look in box arrow and then click Add/Modify FTP Locations in the Look in list.
3.	When the Add /Modify FTP Locations dialog box appears, type the name of the FTP site in the Name of FTP site text box. If the site allows anonymous logon, click Anonymous in the Log on as area; if you have a user name for the site, click User in the Log on as area and then enter the user name. Enter the password in the Password text box. Click the OK button.
4.	Close the Save As or the Open dialog box.

Table D–4 Saving to an FTP Location

1.	Click the Office Button and then click Save As.
2.	When the Save As dialog box appears, type the Web page file name in the File name text box. Do not press the ENTER key.
3.	Click the Save as type box arrow and then click Web Page to select the Web Page format.
4.	Click the Save in box arrow and then click FTP Locations.
5.	Double-click the name of the FTP site to which you wish to save.
6.	When the FTP Log On dialog box appears, enter your user name and password and then click the OK button.
7.	Click the Save button in the Save As dialog box.

Appendix E
Customizing Microsoft Office 2007

This appendix explains how to change the screen resolution in Windows to the resolution used in this book. It also describes how to customize the Word window by changing the Ribbon, Quick Access Toolbar, and the color scheme.

Changing Screen Resolution

Screen resolution indicates the number of pixels (dots) that your computer uses to display the letters, numbers, graphics, and background you see on your screen. When you increase the screen resolution, Windows displays more information on your screen, but the information decreases in size. The reverse also is true: as you decrease the screen resolution, Windows displays less information on your screen, but the information increases in size.

The screen resolution usually is stated as the product of two numbers, such as 1024×768 (pronounced "ten twenty-four by seven sixty-eight"). A 1024×768 screen resolution results in a display of 1,024 distinct pixels on each of 768 lines, or about 786,432 pixels. The figures in this book were created using a screen resolution of 1024×768.

The screen resolutions most commonly used today are 800×600 and 1024×768, although some Office specialists set their computers at a much higher screen resolution, such as 2048×1536.

To Change the Screen Resolution

The following steps change the screen resolution from 800×600 to 1024×768. Your computer already may be set to 1024×768 or some other resolution.

- If necessary, minimize all programs so that the Windows desktop appears.

- Right-click the Windows desktop to display the Windows desktop shortcut menu (Figure E–1).

Figure E–1

2

- Click Properties on the shortcut menu to display the Display Properties dialog box.

- Click the Settings tab to display the Settings sheet in the Display Properties dialog box (Figure E–2).

Figure E–2

3

- Drag the slider in the Screen resolution area so that the screen resolution changes to 1024 × 768 (Figure E–3).

Experiment

- Drag the slider to various screen resolutions in the Display Properties dialog box and watch the changing previews of the desktop. End with the screen resolution set to 1024 × 768.

Figure E–3

4

- Click the OK button to change the screen resolution from 800 × 600 to 1024 × 768 (Figure E–4).

Figure E–4

- Click the Yes button in the Monitor Settings dialog box to accept the new screen resolution (Figure E–5).

Q&A

What if I do not want to change the screen resolution after seeing it applied after I click the OK button?

You either can click the No button in the Monitor Settings dialog box, or wait for the timer to run out, at which point Windows will revert to the original screen resolution.

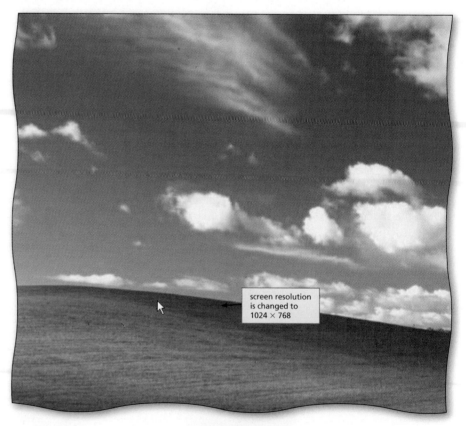

Figure E–5

Screen Resolution and the Appearance of the Ribbon in Office 2007 Programs

Changing the screen resolution affects how the Ribbon appears in Office 2007 programs. Figure E–6 shows the Word Ribbon at the screen resolutions of 800 × 600, 1024 × 768, and 1280 × 1024. All of the same commands are available regardless of screen resolution. Word, however, makes changes to the groups and the buttons within the groups to accommodate the various screen resolutions. The result is that certain commands may need to be accessed differently depending on the resolution chosen. A command that is visible on the Ribbon and available by clicking a button at one resolution may not be visible and may need to be accessed using its group button at a different resolution.

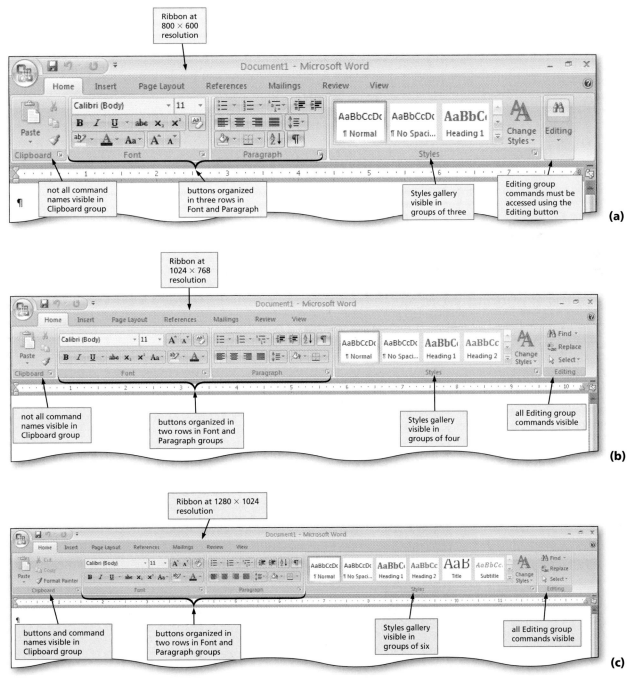

Figure E–6

Comparing the three Ribbons, notice changes in content and layout of the groups and galleries. In some cases, the content of a group is the same in each resolution, but the layout of the group differs. For example, the same buttons appear in the Font and Paragraph groups in the three resolutions, but the layouts differ. The buttons are displayed in three rows at the 800×600 resolution, and in two rows in the 1024×768 and 1280×1024 resolutions. In other cases, the content and layout are the same across the resolution, but the level of detail differs with the resolution. In the Clipboard group, when the resolution increases to 1280×1024, the names of all the buttons in the group appear in addition to the buttons themselves. At the lower resolution, only the buttons appear.

Changing resolutions also can result in fewer commands being visible in a group. Comparing the Editing groups, notice that the group at the 800×600 resolution consists of an Editing button, while at the higher resolutions, the group has three buttons visible. The commands that are available on the Ribbon at the higher resolutions must be accessed using the Editing button at the 800×600 resolution.

Changing resolutions results in different amounts of detail being available at one time in the galleries on the Ribbon. The Styles gallery in the three resolutions presented show different numbers of styles. At 800×600, you can scroll through the gallery three styles at a time, at 1024×768, you can scroll through the gallery four styles at a time, and at 1280×1024, you can scroll through the gallery six styles at a time.

Customizing the Word Window

When working in Word, you may want to make your working area as large as possible. One option is to minimize the Ribbon. You can also modify the characteristics of the Quick Access Toolbar, customizing the toolbar's commands and location to better suit your needs.

To Minimize the Ribbon in Word

The following steps minimize the Ribbon.

- Start Word.

- Maximize the Word window, if necessary.

- Click the Customize Quick Access Toolbar button to display the Customize Quick Access Toolbar menu (Figure E–7).

Figure E–7

- Click Minimize the Ribbon to reduce the Ribbon display to just the tabs (Figure E–8).

Figure E–8

Customizing and Resetting the Quick Access Toolbar

The Quick Access Toolbar, located to the right of the Microsoft Office Button by default, provides easy access to some of the more frequently used commands in Word (Figure E–7). By default, the Quick Access Toolbar contains buttons for the Save, Undo, and Redo commands. Customize the Quick Access Toolbar by changing its location in the window and by adding additional buttons to reflect which commands you would like to be able to access easily.

To Change the Location of the Quick Access Toolbar

The following steps move the Quick Access Toolbar to below the Ribbon.

1

- Double-click the Home tab to redisplay the Ribbon.

- Click the Customize Quick Access Toolbar button to display the Customize Quick Access Toolbar menu (Figure E–9).

Figure E–9

● Click Show Below the Ribbon to move the Quick Access Toolbar below the Ribbon (Figure E–10).

Figure E–10

To Add Commands to the Quick Access Toolbar Using the Customize Quick Access Toolbar menu

Some of the more commonly added commands are available for selection from the Customize Quick Access Toolbar menu. The following steps add the Quick Print button to the Quick Access Toolbar.

● Click the Customize Quick Access Toolbar button to display the Customize Quick Access Toolbar menu (Figure E–11).

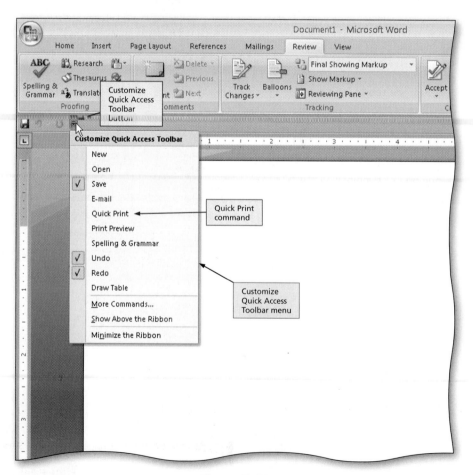

Figure E–11

2

• Click Quick Print to add the Quick Print button to the Quick Access Toolbar (Figure E–12).

Figure E–12

To Add Commands to the Quick Access Toolbar Using the Shortcut Menu

Commands also can be added to the Quick Access Toolbar from the Ribbon. Adding an existing Ribbon command that you use often to the Quick Access Toolbar makes the command immediately available, regardless of which tab is active.

1

• Click the Review tab to make it the active tab.

• Right-click the Spelling & Grammar button to display a shortcut menu (Figure E–13).

Figure E–13

- Click Add to Quick Access Toolbar to add the Spelling & Grammar button to the Quick Access Toolbar (Figure E–14).

Figure E–14

To Add Commands to the Quick Access Toolbar using Word Options

Some commands do not appear on the Ribbon. They can be added to the Quick Access Toolbar using the Word Options dialog box.

- Click the Office Button to display the Office Button menu (Figure E–15).

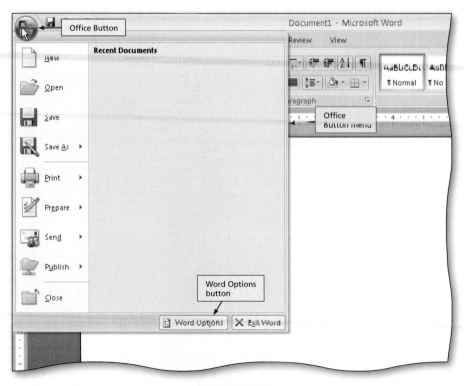

Figure E–15

2

- Click the Word Options button to display the Word Options dialog box (Figure E–16).

Figure E–16

3

- Click Customize in the left pane.

- Click the down arrow to the right of Popular Commands to display the 'Choose commands from' list.

- Click Commands Not in the Ribbon in the Choose commands from list.

- Scroll to display the Web Page Preview command.

- Click Web Page Preview to select it (Figure E–17).

Figure E–17

- Click the Add button to add the Web Page Preview button to the list of buttons on the Quick Access Toolbar (Figure E–18).

Figure E–18

- Click the OK button to add the Web page Preview button to the Quick Access Toolbar (Figure E–19).

Figure E–19

Other Ways

1. Click Customize Quick Access Toolbar button, click More Commands, select commands to add, click Add, click OK

To Remove a Command from the Quick Access Toolbar

1

• Right-click the Web Page Preview button to display the shortcut menu (Figure E–20).

Figure E–20

2

• Click Remove from Quick Access Toolbar to remove the button from the Quick Access Toolbar (Figure E–21).

Figure E–21

Other Ways
1. Click the Customize Quick Access Toolbar button, click More Commands, click the command you wish to remove in the Customize Quick Access Toolbar list, click Remove, click OK 2. If the command appears on the Customize Quick Access Toolbar menu, click the Customize Quick Access Toolbar button, click the command you wish to remove

To Reset the Quick Access Toolbar

1

- Click the Customize Quick Access Toolbar button.

- Click More Commands to display the Word Options Dialog box.

- Click the 'Show Quick access Toolbar below the Ribbon' check box to deselect it (Figure E–22).

Figure E–22

- Click the Reset button, click the Yes button, and then click the OK button, to reset the Quick Access Toolbar to its original position to the right of the Office Button, with the original three buttons (Figure E–23).

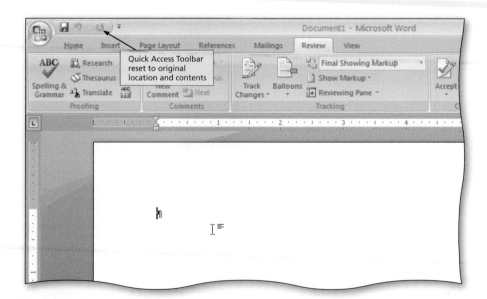

Figure E–23

Changing the Word Color Scheme

The Microsoft Word window can be customized by selecting a color scheme other than the default blue one. Three color schemes are available in Word. The following steps change the color scheme.

To Change the Word Color Scheme

- Click the Office Button to display the Office Button menu.

- Click the Word Options button to display the Word Options dialog box.

- If necessary, click Popular in the left pane. Click the Color scheme box arrow to display a list of color schemes (Figure E–24).

Figure E–24

❷

- Click Silver in the list.

- Click the OK button to change the color scheme (Figure E–25).

Q&A   How do I switch back to the default color scheme?

Follow the steps for changing the Word color scheme, and select Blue from the list of color schemes.

Figure E–25

Appendix F

Microsoft Business Certification Program

What is the Microsoft Business Certification Program?

The Microsoft Business Certification Program enables candidates to show that they have something exceptional to offer – proved expertise in Microsoft Office 2007 programs. The two certification tracks allow candidates to choose how they want to exhibit their skills, either through validating skills within a specific Microsoft product or taking their knowledge to the next level and combining Microsoft programs to show that they can apply multiple skill sets to complete more complex office tasks. Recognized by businesses and schools around the world, more than 3 million certifications have been obtained in more than 100 different countries. The Microsoft Business Certification Program is the only Microsoft-approved certification program of its kind.

What is the Microsoft Certified Application Specialist Certification?

The Microsoft Certified Application Specialist certification exams focus on validating specific skill sets within each of the Microsoft Office system programs. Candidates can choose which exam(s) they want to take according to which skills they want to validate. The available Application Specialist exams include:

- Using Microsoft® Windows Vista™
- Using Microsoft® Office Word 2007
- Using Microsoft® Office Excel® 2007
- Using Microsoft® Office PowerPoint® 2007
- Using Microsoft® Office Access 2007
- Using Microsoft® Office Outlook® 2007

What is the Microsoft Certified Application Professional Certification?

The Microsoft Certified Application Professional certification exams focus on a candidate's ability to use the 2007 Microsoft® Office system to accomplish industry-agnostic functions, for example Budget Analysis and Forecasting, or Content Management and Collaboration. The available Application Professional exams currently include:

- Organizational Support
- Creating and Managing Presentations
- Content Management and Collaboration
- Budget Analysis and Forecasting

Index

3-D
  clustered column worksheet,
    EX 49–54
  pie charts, adding to workbooks,
    EX 204–216
  pie charts, displaying in browser,
    EX 255
64-Bit Edition, Windows XP, WIN 3

A

.accdb files, AC 13
Access
  See also databases
  described, AC 2
  exporting to other applications,
    AC 220–224
  Help, obtaining, AC 61–63
  Navigation pane, AC 126
  program described, APP 12–13
  quitting, AC 35–36, AC 63, AC 127
  referential integrity, specifying,
    AC 185–191
  reports, creating and printing,
    AC 50–56
  sharing data among applications,
    AC 206–229
  starting, AC 12–13, AC 36–38,
    AC 77
  window, using, AC 17–23
Accessories, Start menu, WIN 10,
  WIN 39
Accounting Number Format,
  EX 114–116
accounts, obtaining e-mail, EX 142
activities, tracking for e-mail
  contacts, OUT 61–62
add-ins, installing, AC 209
adding
  See also inserting
  3-D pie chart to workbook,
    EX 204–216
  background colors to Web pages,
    WD 221
  borders to pages, WD 48–50
  buttons to Quick Access Toolbar,
    PPT 148–150
  commands to Quick Access
    Toolbar, APP 39–43
  fields to database tables, AC 157

icons to desktop, WIN 11
records to database tables, AC
  30–33, AC 49, AC 141–148
shapes, PPT 123–130
slide transitions, PPT 130–132
Word table rows, WD 180
additions to documents, WD 57
Address bar, My Computer window,
  WIN 13
address, inside, WD 169
addresses, hyperlink, WD 220
addressing
  absolute vs. relative, EX 186–189
  envelopes, WD 203–204
aggregate functions, AC 117–119
aligning text using tab stops,
  WD 158–160
analysis, what-if. *See* what-if analysis
AND criterion, AC 95–96
animated slide shows, PPT 133
append queries, AC 165
application programs
  See also specific program
  described, WIN 4, WIN 23
  starting, WIN 23
applying
  Quick Style, WD 150
  Word styles, WD 24–25
  Word table styles, WD 176–177
arguments
  in functions, EX 98, EX 105
  Function Arguments dialog box,
    EX 101
arithmetic operations, EX 92
arrangements, OUT 8
art, clip. *See* clip art
Art gallery, WD 49
ascending order, AC 53, AC 192
asterisk (*), Access wildcard, AC 87,
  AC 151
attachments
  adding to e-mail messages,
    OUT 31–32
  viewing e-mail, OUT 22–23
Auto Fill Options, EX 28, EX 171–172
AutoCalculate feature, EX 62–63
AutoCorrect
  in databases, AC 34
  in worksheets, EX 19 EX 96,
    EX 129

vs. building blocks, WD 172–173
  as you type in, WD 91–9
AutoFit
  applying to Word tables, WD 178
  using in presentations, PPT 19
AutoFormat, using while you type,
  WD 162–163, WD 181
AVERAGE function, EX 98–100

B

background colors
  adding to Web pages, WD 221
  changing on Web pages, WD 222
  on worksheets, EX 110–112
background repagination, WD 107
background styles for presentations,
  PPT 97–98
backing up databases, AC 193
best fit, worksheet column width,
  EX 122
BETWEEN operator, AC 95–96
bibliographical lists, creating and
  updating, WD 113, WD 117
bibliography style, changing, WD 95
black slides, PPT 39
blank lines, inserting into
  documents, WD 15
bold
  characters in documents, WD 34
  text in presentations, PPT 25
  worksheet cell entries, EX 38
borders
  applying to worksheet titles,
    EX 110–112
  around pictures in documents,
    WD 45
  bottom bordering paragraphs,
    WD 161
  page, adding to documents,
    WD 48–50, WD 55
  bottom borders on paragraphs,
    WD 161
  box borders, applying to worksheet
    titles, EX 110–112
brackets. *See* square brackets
browser
  default
  Internet Explorer. *See* Internet
    Explorer

Office 2007, APP 6
testing Web pages in, WD 223
viewing, manipulating Web pages using, EX 260–261, PPT 156–157
browsing
Help and Support topics, WIN 58–59
Web by entering URLs, WIN 26
building blocks
creating, WD 170
inserting, WD 172, WD 200
vs. AutoCorrect, WD 172–173
bulleted lists
applying in documents, WD 32
creating as you type, WD 180–181
creating text slides with, PPT 31–32
multi-level, in presentations, PPT 33
presentation with, PPT 3–5, PPT 94–97
in presentations, PPT 29
Business Contact Manager, OUT 54
business letters, WD 166
buttons
See also specific button
adding to Quick Access Toolbar, EX 252–254, PPT 148–150
in My Computer window, WIN 13

C

calculated fields, AC 113
calculating
sums, AC 117, EX 24–26
using AutoCalculate, EX 62
calculations
absolute vs. relative addressing, EX 186–189
formulas, EX 90–91
functions, EX 104
using in queries, AC 113–116
camera ready publications, APP 16
captions, changing query, AC 116–117
cascading deletes in Access, AC 185, AC 188
Category box, Outlook, OUT 33
cells, Word table, WD 173
cells, worksheet
applying styles to, EX 112
copying and pasting, EX 174–177
copying using fill handles, EX 26–28

correcting errors on, EX 63–66
entering column, row titles, EX 19–22
entering text into, EX 18–19
formatting, EX 34–47
inserting and deleting, EX 177–179
moving vs. copying, EX 177
nonadjacent, determining row totals in, EX 194
rotating and shrinking entries in, EX 114
rotating text in, EX 168–171
selecting, EX 15, EX 47
values, and charting, EX 49
centering
data in worksheet cells, EX 113
page contents vertically, WD 50
paragraphs in documents, WD 26
Word tables, WD 179
works cited page title, WD 112
worksheet cells, EX 40–41
certification, Microsoft Certified Application Specialist (MCAS), AC 60
changing
colors in presentations, PPT 21
database primary keys, AC 28, AC 46
database properties, AC 60–61
database structure, AC 26–30, AC 156–161
datasheet appearance, AC 178–180
document properties, WD 130, WD 182
document properties in presentations, PPT 43–45
document properties in documents, WD 50–52, WD 130
e-mail message formats, OUT 19
font colors, WD 193
presentation layouts, PPT 100–103
screen resolution, APP 33–35
text in content control. *See changing*
theme colors in Word documents, WD 39
Word color schemes, APP 46
Word document settings, WD 77–78
workbook themes, EX 109
worksheet cells, EX 49

worksheet column appearance, EX 122–124
worksheet fonts, EX 36–37
worksheet names, EX 140–141
worksheet views, EX 220–223
characters
bold in Word documents, WD 34
formatting in presentations, PPT 21–26
formatting in documents generally, WD 22
leader, WD 158
line break, WD 195
nonprinting, WD 14, WD 25
special, inserting, PPT 114
tab, WD 159–160
tab, in Word tables, WD 178
width in documents, WD 18
charts
adding 3-D clustered column, adding to worksheet, EX 48–54
adding 3-D pie chart to workbook, EX 204–216
inserting titles, data labels, EX 206–209
types, formatting, EX 48
citations
documentation styles for, WD 94–98
editing, WD 98, WD 104–105, WD 110
editing sources, WD 109
inserting, WD 96–97
inserting placeholder, WD 108
parenthetical, WD 76
works cited, in research papers, WD 77
clearing
paragraph formatting, WD 162
worksheet cells, ranges of cells, EX 66–67
Click and Type feature, WD 85
clicking
with mouse, WIN 6
right mouse button, WIN 11
client computers, WIN 2
clip art
inserting into slides, PPT 103–105

inserting into documents,
WD 153–154
resizing, PPT 109–112
Clip Art task pane, PPT 103–104
clip collections, PPT 103–104
Clip Organizer, PPT 103–107,
WD 153
clipboard.
Clipboard
See also Office Clipboard
copying and pasting text using,
WD 119–122
clips
copyright regulations on Microsoft
Clip Organizer clips, PPT 105
importing, PPT 103
moving, PPT 113
closing
database tables, AC 35
e-mail messages, OUT 15
expanded folders, WIN 50
Help and Support Center, WIN 61
tabs on Web pages, WIN 28
windows, WIN 16, WIN 20
Windows Explorer, WIN 50
Word documents, WD 59–60
code, viewing Web page source,
EX 258
collaboration, and SharePoint,
APP 20–21
color schemes in Word documents,
WD 37, APP 46
coloring
graphics, WD 156
text, WD 152–153
worksheet tabs, EX 216–217
colors
background, on worksheets,
EX 110–112
changing font, PPT 118–119,
WD 193
changing in datasheets, AC 179
changing in presentations, PPT 21
changing picture border, WD 45
changing pie chart, EX 213–215
changing theme, WD 150
conserving ink, toner, EX 57
in documents, WD 37
in document page borders,
WD 48–50

Fill and Font Color buttons,
EX 200
font, EX 34, WD 160
in presentations, PPT 20, PPT 21
themes, EX 107
transparent, setting in graphics,
WD 157
in worksheets, workbooks, EX 108
columns, Word table, WD 177–178
columns, worksheet
adjusting, EX 46
changing width, height,
EX 122–126
deleting, EX 180
entering titles, EX 19–21,
EX 87–89
formatting, EX 114
freezing titles, EX 181–182
hiding, unhiding, changing width,
EX 122–124
increasing width of, EX 173–174
inserting, EX 179
planning, EX 16
Comma Style format, Excel, EX 45,
EX 114–115, EX 196
command-line, starting Excel using,
EX 87
command-line interfaces, WIN 4
commands
See also specific command
menu, WIN 8–11
Quick Access Toolbar, APP 39–44,
EX 254, OUT 12–13, PPT 13–14,
WD 10
toggling Ribbon, EX 194
compacting databases, AC 193
comparison operators, using in
criterion queries, AC 94
composing
See also creating
e-mail messages, OUT 27–28
compound criteria in queries,
AC 95–96
computers
clients, servers, WIN 2
logging off, turning off,
WIN 62–64
logging on, WIN 7–8
resolution, decreasing, PPT 5
Concourse theme, using, EX 109

conditional formatting operators,
EX 121–124
conditions in conditional formatting,
EX 118
connections, clients to servers,
WIN 2–3
constants, replacing formulas with,
EX 191
contact lists
creating, OUT 47–48
saving, displaying, OUT 60–61
using to address e-mail messages,
OUT 55–57
contacts
finding, OUT 44, OUT 50
tracking activities, OUT 61–62
using, OUT 44–62
content controls
entering and formatting text in,
WD 197
entering more text in, WD 194
and templates, WD 185–186
contextual tabs, EX 10, PPT 9,
WD 8
converting
hyperlinks to text, WD 163–164
slides from previous PowerPoint
version, PPT 43
copying
backing up. *See* backing up
Excel formulas using fill handles,
EX 95–96, EX 192–193
files by right-clicking, WIN 46
items to Office Clipboard, WD 189
and pasting text, WD 188–192
slides, PPT 40–41
worksheet cell formats, EX 201–202
worksheet cells, EX 26–28,
EX 169–171, EX 174–177
copyright regulations on Microsoft
Clip Organizer clips, PPT 105
correcting
errors on worksheets, EX 63–67
mistakes using AutoCorrect,
AC 34, EX 19–21, WD 91–94
mistakes while typing, PPT 19
spelling in worksheets, EX 127–129
worksheet errors, EX 164
COUNT aggregate function, AC 117

cover letters
  creating, WD 165–182
  described, WD 146
  planning effective, WD 149
creating
  contact lists, OUT 47–48
  cover letters, WD 165–182
  database forms, AC 57–58
  database queries, AC 74–103
  database tables, AC 23–26,
    AC 44–49
  databases, AC 13–17, AC 210
  distribution lists, OUT 58–59
  e-mail messages, OUT 14
  e-mail signatures, OUT 23–27
  e-mail view filters, OUT 36–37
  folders on removable drives,
    WIN 34–35
  folders, OUT 44–46
  letterhead, WD 149–151
  queries, parameter, AC 89–92
  queries, simple, AC 78–80
  Quick Style, WD 90–91
  research papers, WD 74
  resumes using templates,
    WD 183–186
  Web pages using Excel, EX 250–261
  Web pages using Word, WD 216–223
  WordPad document, WIN 38–45
  worksheets, EX 3–4
criterion
  adding fields to design grid,
    AC 85–86
  and update queries, AC 162
  using comparison operators in,
    AC 94
  using compound, AC 95–96
  using in calculating statistics,
    AC 120–121
  using in field not included in
    results, AC 88–89
  using in queries, AC 81–82
  using numbers in, AC 93
crosstab queries, AC 122–125
Crosstab Query Wizard, AC 123–125
currency
  format, setting , AC 25
  symbols and database data types,
    AC 9–10
Currency style, EX 117
current date, inserting, WD 168–169

custom dictionaries for spell-checking,
    PPT 55–58, WD 127
customizing
  Access Navigation pane, AC 126
  My Computer window, WIN 13
  Office 2007, APP 33–46
  Outlook, OUT 5–6
  Quick Access Toolbar, APP 38,
    OUT 12–13
  Word window, APP 37–38
cutting and pasting. See copying,
    pasting

D

data
  centering in worksheet cells, EX 113
  entering into Word tables,
    WD 174–175
data types
  changing in database fields, AC 169
  and database design, AC 5, AC 9–10
Database Design Language
    (DBDL), AC 8
database fields
  deleting, AC 156
  moving in table structure, AC 156
  multivalued, adding, AC 160–161
  using calculated, AC 113–116
database forms, creating, AC 57–58
database management systems, AC–2
database records
  adding to tables, AC 30–33,
    AC 38–40, AC 49
  deleting, AC 148, AC 163–164
  described, AC 4
  duplicates, finding, AC 191
  filtering, AC 148–156
  grouping, AC 52, AC 121–122
  ordering, AC 192–195
  restricting in joins, AC 112
  saving, AC 33
  sorting, AC 97–103
  unmatched, finding, AC 191
  updating, AC 141–147
database tables
  adding records to, AC 30–33,
    AC 38–40, AC 49
  closing, AC 35
  creating, AC 23–26, AC 44–49
  joining, AC 103–107

  and make-table queries, AC 165
  naming, AC 8
  previewing and printing, AC 40–43
  removing from queries, AC 89
  saving, AC 27
  with validation rules, updating,
    AC 169–178
databases
  See also Access
  backup, recovery, repair, compact,
    AC 193
  changing structure of, AC 26–30,
    AC 156–161
  creating, AC 13–17, AC 210
  datasheets. See datasheets
  described, AC 2
  designing, AC 6–12
  exporting to other applications,
    AC 220–224
  importing worksheets into,
    AC 212–215
  maintenance generally, AC 138,
    AC 140
  mass changes, making, AC 162–164
  naming tables, fields, AC 8
  opening, AC 77
  properties, changing, AC 60–61
  querying. See queries, querying
  resizing datasheet columns,
    AC 175–176
  sharing data between, AC 217
  tables. See database tables
  undoing changes, AC 34
  validation rules, using, AC 165–178
Datasheet Formatting dialog box,
    AC 181–184
Datasheet view, AC 30, AC 82, AC 146
datasheets
  changing appearance of, AC 178–180
  changing gridlines, colors, fonts,
    AC 179
  including, removing totals in,
    AC 176–178
  resizing columns in, AC 175–176
  and subdatasheeets, AC 190–191
dates
  formatting of, EX 183–185
  inserting current, WD 168–169
  MLA documentation style, WD 84
DBDL (Database Design
    Language), AC 8

debugging described, EX 135–136
decimal places
  in Access, AC 47–48
  in Excel, EX 23
decisions
  making with IF function,
    EX 189–190
  what-if analysis. *See* what-if analysis
default value, and validation rules,
    AC 165, AC 167
defining database tables, AC 24–26
delete queries, AC 163–164
Deleted Items folder, OUT 7, OUT 21
deleting
  See also removing
  database fields, AC 156
  database records, AC 148
  desktop icons, WIN 21
  e-mail messages, OUT 21,
    OUT 37
  embedded charts, EX 67
  files, WIN 48–49
  placeholders, PPT 112
  text and lines, WD 193
  text from existing documents,
    WD 59
  text from presentations, PPT 58
  text in presentation placeholder,
    PPT 42–43
  text with BACKSPACE key, WD 13
  Word table rows, WD 180,
    WD 186–187
  WordArt from presentations,
    PPT 119
  worksheet cells, EX 177–179
  worksheet columns, rows, EX 180
deletions from documents, WD 58
delimited files, AC 218
demoting text in presentations,
    PPT 34
descending sort order, AC 53, AC 99,
    AC 192
Design view, Access
  clearing design grid, sorting
    records, AC 98–103
  creating queries in, AC 82
  described, AC 31
designing
  See also planning
  database queries, AC 76

databases, AC 5–12
  letterheads, WD 149–150
desktop
  adding icon to, WIN 11
  deleting icons, WIN 21
  organizing windows on, WIN 14
  Start menu, WIN 11
destination area, copying to, EX 27
Dialog Box Launcher
  Access, AC 20
  Excel, EX 11, EX 198
  Outlook, OUT 12
  PowerPoint, PPT 11
  Word, WD 9
dialog boxes
  See also specific dialog box
  described, using, WIN 21
dictionaries
  main, custom, WD 127
  spell-checking. *See* spell checking
dimensions of Word tables, WD 173
disabling database content, AC 38
displaying
  e-mail contacts, OUT 52
  files and folders in Windows
    Explorer, WIN 29–31
  folder contents, WIN 38, WIN 47
  formatting marks in documents,
    WD 14, WD 77
  minimizing and displaying
    windows, WIN 14
  presentations in grayscale,
    PPT 59–61
  rulers in documents, WD 87
  shortcut menus, WIN 11–12
  Start menu, WIN 8–11
  status bar, WIN 30
  system date on worksheets,
    EX 183–185
distribution lists, creating,
    OUT 58–59
Document Information Panel,
    PPT 44, WD 51–53
document properties
  changing in Word, WD 50–52,
    WD 130, WD 182, WD 202
  changing in Excel, EX 54–57
  changing in PowerPoint,
    PPT 43–45
documents
  See also specific products

attaching to e-mail messages,
    OUT 31–32
  creating, saving in WordPad,
    WIN 40–44
  requirements, described, EX 3–5
  Word. *See* Word documents
dollar signs ($)
  entering absolute cell reference,
    EX 187
  in Excel, EX 23, EX 114,
    EX 116–117
domain names in URLs, WIN 25
.dotm files, WD 150
double-clicking mouse, WIN 6
double-spacing, WD 78
downloading
  hierarchy of folders, WIN 35–36
  Internet Explorer, WIN 23
draft quality printing, WD 53,
    WD 130
Drafts folder, OUT 7
drag-and-drop editing, WD 119,
    WD 121
dragging
  right-, described, WIN 21
  windows, WIN 17
  worksheet cells, EX 179
dragging with dropping
  arranging slides, PPT 41–42
  with mouse, WIN 6
  moving worksheet cells, EX 177
Draw Table feature, WD 179
drives, AC 13
  creating folder on removable,
    WIN 34–35
  expanding, WIN 37
  keychain, WIN 32
  network, WIN 32
  organizing, displaying in Windows
    Explorer, WIN 32
  USB flash. *See* USB flash drives
duplicating. *See* copying

E

e-mail
  account, obtaining, EX 142
  described, OUT 2
  E-mail Filter feature, OUT 33
  Inbox, APP 18–19
  spam filter, OUT 14

E-mail Filter feature, OUT 33
e-mail messages
 attachments, adding to, OUT 31–32
 closing, printing, OUT 15–16
 composing, formatting, OUT 27–31
 contact lists, using to address,
  OUT 55–57
 deleting, OUT 21, OUT 37
 flagging, OUT 33–35
 forwarding, OUT 20
 importance, sensitivity, delivery
  options, OUT 38–42
 opening, OUT 10
 outgoing, working with, OUT 23–32
 replying to, OUT 16–17
 rules, applying, OUT 42
 saving in different formats,
  OUT 60–61
 signatures, creating and inserting,
  OUT 23–27
 sorting, OUT 35–36
 view filters, applying, OUT 36–37
 viewing attachments, OUT 22–23
e-mailing workbooks, EX 142–143
editing
 citation sources, WD 104–105
 citations, WD 98, WD 110
 drag-and-drop, WD 119, WD 121
 in-cell, on worksheets, EX 64–65
 Word table cells, WD 175
electronic mail. *See* e-mail
embedded charts
 deleting, EX 67
 in worksheets, EX 49
endnotes, WD 100, WD 106
Enhanced Screen Tips
 Access, AC 20
 Excel, EX 11
 Outlook, OUT 11
 PowerPoint, PPT 10
 Word, WD 9
envelope icon on e-mail message,
  OUT 9, OUT 21
envelopes, addressing, printing,
  WD 203–204
equal sign (=) and formulas, EX 91,
  EX 92, EX 99
error checking worksheets, EX 129
error messages
 database compacting error, AC 193
 #REF!, EX 180

errors, correcting, PPT 58,
  WD 57–60, EX 63–67
Excel
 See also spreadsheets, worksheets
 adding to startup submenu, EX 167
 Auto Fill Options, EX 28,
  EX 171–172
 calculating sums, EX 24–26
 charts, EX 48–53
 creating Web pages using,
  EX 250–261
 described, EX 2–3
 e-mailing workbook within,
  EX 142–143
 Edit mode, EX 63–64
 exporting Access data to,
  AC 221–222
 exporting data from Web sites,
  EX 137–140
 file management tools, EX 259–261
 font type, style, size, color, EX 34–47
 functions, EX 104
 functions in, EX 82, EX 99–105
 Help, EX 7, EX 67–68
 importing into database, AC 212–215
 numeric limitations of, EX 22
 Office Button, EX 14
 program described, APP 9–11
 quitting, EX 59
 selecting cells, EX 15, EX 47
 smart tags, option buttons, EX 96–97
 spell checking worksheets,
  EX 127–129, EX 218
 starting, EX 6–7, EX 87
 what-if analysis, using, EX 162,
  EX 164, EX 223–227
 workbooks. *See* workbooks
 worksheet window, using, EX 9–15
 worksheets. *See* worksheets
exclamation point icon on e-mail
  message, OUT 8
expanding
 area in window, WIN 18
 files, folders, WIN 37
exploding (offsetting) pie charts,
  EX 213–215
Explorer. *See* Windows Explorer
exporting
 data from Access generally, AC 207,
  AC 209, AC 220–224
 XML data, AC 226–227

F
Favorite Folders pane, OUT 7
fields, database
 adding to design grid, AC 85
 changing, AC 46–48
 defining, AC 24–26
 described, AC 4
 naming, AC 8
file attachments, viewing,
  OUT 22–23
file management
 tools, EX 259–261, PPT 155–157
 Windows Explorer, using,
  WIN 45–50
file names, WD 18, WD 53
file specification in URLs, WIN 25
File Transfer Protocol (FTP),
  publishing Web pages via, APP 32
files
 attaching to e-mail messages,
  OUT 31–32
 copying by right-dragging, WIN 46
 deleting, WIN 48–49
 e-mail view, OUT 36–37
 naming Word, WIN 34
 naming database, AC 13, AC 15
 naming presentation, PPT 27
 organizing in Windows Explorer,
  WIN 31–32
 renaming, WIN 47–48
 searching, WIN 51–54
 text. *See* text files
 Word, WD 18
Fill and Font Color buttons, EX 200
fill effects
 adding to presentations, PPT 97–98
 adding to Web page background,
  WD 222
fill handles
 copying formulas using, EX 95–96,
  EX 192–193
 copying range of cells using,
  EX 104–105
 copying worksheet cells using,
  EX 26–28, EX 169–171
Filter By Form, AC 153–154
Filter By Selection, AC 149
filtered Web Page format, WD 218
filtering database records, AC 148–156

filters
    clearing database record, AC 151
    E-mail Filter feature, OUT 33
    e-mail spam, OUT 14
Find and Replace dialog box, WD 124
Find command, locating text using,
    PPT 98
finding
    See also searching
    contacts, OUT 44, OUT 50
    files and folders in Windows
        Explorer, WIN 51–55
Firefox browser (Mozilla), WIN 23
FIRST aggregate function, AC 117
First Lie Indent marker, WD 88
first-line indents, WD 88–89
fixed-width files, AC 218
flags, e-mail, OUT 33–35
floating dollar signs, formatting in
    worksheets, EX 114, EX 116–117
folders
    See also specific folder
    closing expanded, WIN 50
    creating, OUT 44–46
    creating on removable drive,
        WIN 34–35
    creating using WordPad, WIN 38–45
    deleting, WIN 48–49
    described, WIN 11
    displaying contents, WIN 38,
        WIN 47
    downloading hierarchy of,
        WIN 35–36
    expanding, WIN 37
    in My Documents windows, WIN 17
    naming, WIN 34
    organizing in Windows Explorer,
        WIN 31–32
    in Outlook, OUT 7–8
    renaming, WIN 47–48
    saving documents in, WIN 40–44
    saving to, AC 15
    searching for, WIN 51–54
    verifying contents of, WIN 45
    Web. *See* Web folders
Folders pane, Windows Explorer,
    WIN 30
Follow Up submenu, OUT 34–35
Font gallery, PPT 117
font sets, WD 37

fonts
    changing color, PPT 118–119,
        WD 193
    changing color in cell entry, EX 39
    changing in datasheets, AC 179
    changing in worksheets, EX 36–38
    changing size in documents, WD 28
    changing theme, WD 39–40
    coloring, WD 160
    increasing size, WD 151–152
    sans serif, PPT 94
    sizing, WD 23
    using, EX 34
    using in presentations, PPT 20,
        PPT 25–26
footers in documents, WD 79–83
footnotes in documents, WD 99–106
foreign keys, and referential
    integrity, AC 185
Form view, Access, AC 57, AC 143,
    AC 146
Format Painter, PPT 114,
    PPT 119–121, EX 201–203
format symbols, EX 180
formats
    See also specific format
    datasheet, changing, AC 178–180
    e-mail message, OUT 19
    hierarchical, WIN 31
    import support, PPT 106
    saving presentations, PPT 26
    specifying data field, AC 168–169
    undoing on worksheets, EX 66
    verifying using Range Finder,
        EX 106–107
    Web page, PPT 152, EX 256–257
    Word documents, WD 36–40
formatting
    AutoFormat, using while you type,
        WD 162–163
    characters in presentations,
        PPT 21–26
    clearing, WD 162
    conditional, in worksheets,
        EX 118–121
    dates in worksheets, EX 114
    e-mail messages, OUT 27–31
    numbers in worksheets, EX 44–45
    numbers using Excel Ribbon,
        EX 114–118
    pictures in documents, WD 40–42

pie charts, EX 204–216
shapes, PPT 123–130
single vs. multiple paragraphs in
    documents, WD 26–32
system date, EX 183–185
text as hyperlinks, WD 220–221
text in content controls, WD 197
text using Quick Styles, PPT 114–116
text using shortcut keys, WD 86
Web pages, WD 220–223
What-If Assumptions table, EX 203
Word documents generally, WD 22
worksheet cells, EX 34–47
worksheet column titles, EX 42–43
worksheet titles, EX 110,
    EX 199–200
worksheets, EX 33–34, EX 107–114
formatting marks in documents,
    WD 14, WD 77, WD 150
forms
    creating database, AC 2, AC 57–60
    updating databases using, AC 141–148
Formula AutoComplete, EX 99
formula bar, EX 12
formulas
    absolute vs. relative addressing,
        EX 186–189
    copying using fill handles, EX 95–96,
        EX 192–193
    copying worksheet, EX 201–202
    determining values using goal
        seeking, EX 225–228
    entering using Point mode,
        EX 93–94
    entering IF functions in
        worksheets, EX 189–190
    entering into worksheets, EX 90–91
    replacing with constants, EX 191
    version of worksheet, EX 135–136,
        EX 191
forward slashes (/) in HTTP protocol,
    WIN 24
forwarding e-mail messages, OUT 20
freezing worksheet titles, EX 181–182
FTP locations, and Web folders,
    EX 252
Function Wizard, EX 26
functions
    See also specific function
    absolute vs. relative addressing,
        EX 186–189

entering into worksheets, EX 98

generally, EX 82

G

galleries

See also specific gallery

Access, AC 20

Office 2007, APP 5

Outlook, OUT 18

PowerPoint, PPT 9–10

Word, WD 8

Goal Seek command, using for formula values, EX 225–228

grammar checking in documents, WD 16–17, WD 125–126

graphical user interfaces (GUIs), WIN 4, WIN 5

graphics

See also pictures

coloring, WD 156

described, WD 153

resizing, WD 155

setting transparent color in, WD 157

sizing handles on, PPT 109

grayscale

displaying presentation in, PPT 59–61

printing in, EX 57

greater than (>) operator, AC 94

greater than or equal to (>=) operator, AC 94

gridlines

changing in datasheets, AC 179

worksheet, EX 7

grids, adding fields to, AC 85

grouping

database records, AC 52

using with statistics, AC 121–122

groups on Ribbon, EX 9

Grow Font button, WD 151–152

guidelines for planning, APP 1–2

H

handouts, printing presentations as, PPT 133–138

hanging indents in documents, WD 116

hard copies of worksheets, EX 57

hard page breaks, WD 112

headers in documents, WD 79–83

headings

e-mail message, OUT 10

in worksheets, EX 7–8, EX 43

Help

Access, AC 61–63

Excel, EX 7, EX 67–68

Office 2007, APP 19, APP 22–23

Outlook, OUT 62–64

PowerPoint, PPT 63–64

Word, WD 60–61

Help and Support

browsing topics, WIN 58–59

starting, WIN 22, WIN 56–57

using, WIN 56–61

hiding

formatting marks in documents, WD 14

worksheet columns, EX 122

worksheet rows, EX 126, EX 127

hierarchical format, organizing files and folders in, WIN 31

Home Edition, Windows XP, WIN 3

home pages described, WIN 24

Home tab

Excel Ribbon, EX 9–10

PowerPoint Ribbon, PPT 9

horizontal ruler in Word documents, WD 87

HTML (Hypertext Markup Language)

e-mail message format, OUT 19

saving Word documents in HTML format, WD 218–219

viewing Web page source code, EX 258

HTTP (Hypertext Transfer Protocol), Web pages and, WIN 24

hyperlinks

See also links

converting to text, WD 163–164

described, WIN 14

formatting text as, WD 220–221

using in Office 2007, APP 6

Hypertext Transfer Protocol (HTTP), WIN 24

hyphen, nonbreaking, WD 171

I

icons

See also specific icon

Access, AC 37

adding to, deleting from desktop, WIN 11, WIN 21

in My Computer window, WIN 13

IF function

making decisions using, EX 189–190

nesting, EX 195

images. *See* graphics, photographs, pictures

Import Spreadsheet Wizard, AC 211–215

importance, e-mail setting, OUT 38–42

importing

clips, PPT 103

data between databases, AC 217

data into Access generally, AC 206, AC 211

data into Excel using Web query, EX 137–140

files into Clip Organizer, PPT 105–106

vs. linking data in Access, AC 216

worksheets into database, AC 212–215

in-Ribbon gallery, EX 10

Inbox, OUT 7–10, APP 17–18

indenting paragraphs, WD 196

infinity symbol , and referential integrity, AC 188

inner joins, AC 104

Insert function dialog box, EX 98, EX 101, EX 104

Insert mode, EX 64–65, WD 58

inserting

See also adding

blank lines in documents, WD 15

building blocks, WD 172

citation placeholders, WD 101

citations and sources, WD 96–97

clip art into documents, WD 153–154

clip art into slides, PPT 103

clips into content placeholders, PPT 104–105

current date, WD 168–169

e-mail signatures into e-mail
messages, OUT 23–27
footnotes reference marks, WD 100
leader characters, WD 158
nonbreaking space, WD 171
page numbers in documents, WD 82
photographs into slides,
PPT 106–107
pictures in documents, WD 40–42
special characters, PPT 114
synonyms in text, WD 124–125
text into existing documents,
WD 58
Word tables, WD 173–174
worksheet cells, columns,
EX 177–179
insertion point
in Access work area, AC 18
in documents, WD 6
in worksheets, EX 17
inside address and salutation, WD 169
installing add-ins, AC 209
integrity, referential. *See* referential
integrity
Internet
Access and, APP 12–13
e-mail contact links, OUT 59
Excel and, APP 10–11
Office 2007 and, APP 6
PowerPoint and, APP 14–15
Publisher 2007 and, APP 17
Word and, APP 8
Internet Explorer
browsing the Web with, WIN 23–25
described, APP 6
windows described, WIN 24
intranets, and Office 2007, APP 6
italicizing text
in presentations, PPT 21
in documents, WD 36

J

joining
changing join properties,
AC 108–109
database tables, AC 103–107, AC 112
junk e-mail, E-mail Filter feature,
OUT 33
Junk E-mail folder, OUT 7

K

Key Tips
Access, AC 23–26
Excel, EX 15
Outlook, OUT 14
PowerPoint, PPT 15–16
Word, WD 12
keyboard
described, WIN 4, WIN 22
indicators, status bar, EX 9
scrolling in documents, WD 43
selecting range using, in Excel,
EX 97
shortcuts, WIN 22
worksheet formulas, entering using,
EX 91
keychain drives, WIN 32
keys
See also specific key
primary. *See* primary keys
shortcut, WD 86
sorting, AC 98–103
keywords
database properties, AC 60–61
in presentation document
properties, PPT 43
in document properties, WD 50

L

labels
chart data, EX 204
mailing, WD 204
on toolbar buttons, WIN 13
landscape orientation
printing datasheets, AC 40–41
printing worksheets, EX 129–132
for slide shows, PPT 6
LAST aggregate function, AC 117
Layout gallery, PPT 100
layouts
changing presentation, PPT 100–103
presentation, PPT 6
resizing datasheet columns,
AC 175–176
leader characters, inserting, WD 158
left-aligned text in worksheet cells,
EX 18, EX 22, EX 168

Left Indent marker, WD 88
left mouse button, WIN 11–12
less than (<) operator, AC 94
less than or equal to (<=) operator,
AC 94
letterhead
creating, WD 149–151
saving, WD 164
levels, paragraph, PPT 19, PPT 38
line breaks, inserting, WD 194–195
line spacing in documents, WD 78–79
line wraps in presentations, PPT 18
lines
deleting, WD 193
join, AC 105–106
lines, selecting, WD 27
Link Spreadsheet Wizard, AC 211
Linked Table Manager, updating
query links with, AC 216
linking data to databases, AC 211,
AC 216, AC 217
links
See also hyperlinks
bulleted. *See* bulleted lists
creating in workbooks, EX 258
described, WIN 14
Excel worksheet to Access data,
AC 206
opening in tabbed Web pages,
WIN 27–28
updating using Linked Table
Manager, AC 216
lists
bibliographical, creating, WD 113
bulleted. *See* bulleted lists
and data conversion, AC 206
research paper sources, WD 111
live preview, AC 20, APP 5, EX 10,
OUT 18, PPT 9, WD 8
logging off your computer,
WIN 62–64
logging on to Windows XP, WIN 7–8
logical operators in IF functions,
EX 189
Lookup fields
creating, AC 158–160
multivalued, AC 173–174
using in queries, AC 172–175
Lookup Wizard, AC 158–160

M

magnifying. *See* zooming

mail, electronic. *See* e-mail

Mail Folders, OUT 7

mailing labels, creating and printing, WD 204

major sort keys, AC 97, AC 102

make-table queries, AC 165

managing files. *See* file management

margins, changing worksheet's, EX 130–132

mathematical operations
using, AC 113
using AutoCalculate, EX 62–63

MAX function, EX 98, EX 101–102

MAX (largest value) aggregate function, AC 117

Maximize button, WIN 15

maximizing
windows, AC 13, WIN 15
Windows Explorer window, WIN 29–30
Word Help, WD 61

maximums, determining using AutoCalculate, EX 62–63

MCAS (Microsoft Certified Application Specialist), AC 60, AC 122, AC 193

media, removable, in Windows Explorer, WIN 31

Media Center Edition, Windows XP, WIN 3

menu bar, My Computer window, WIN 13

menus
See also specific menu
described, WIN 8–11
Office 2007, APP 6
shortcut. *See* shortcut menus

merging worksheet cells, EX 40–41

message pane, OUT 8–9

messages
e-mail. *See* e-mail messages
error. *See* error messages

metadata
database properties, AC 60–61
Excel document properties, EX 54
PowerPoint document properties, PPT 43

MHTML file format, PPT 154

Microsoft Certified Application

Specialist (MCAS), AC 60, AC 122, AC 193

Microsoft Clip Organizer, PPT 103

Microsoft Office 2007. *See* Office 2007

Microsoft Office Access 2007. *See* Access

Microsoft Office Excel 2007. *See* Excel

Microsoft Office Outlook 2007. *See* Outlook

Microsoft Office PowerPoint 2007. *See* PowerPoint

Microsoft Office Professional Edition 2007, APP 3

Microsoft Office Publisher 2007, APP 16–17

Microsoft Office Word 2007. *See* Word

Microsoft SharePoint, APP 20–21

Microsoft Windows XP. *See* Windows XP

Microsoft Windows XP Home Edition, WIN 3

Microsoft Windows XP Media Center Edition, WIN 3

Microsoft Windows XP Professional, WIN 2

Microsoft Windows XP Tablet PC Edition, WIN 3

MIN function, using, EX 98, EX 102–104

MIN (smallest value) aggregate function, AC 117

Mini toolbar
Access, AC 21
Excel, EX 12
Office 2007, APP 5
PowerPoint, PPT 11–12
Word, WD 9–10, WD 151

minimizing
Access Ribbon, AC 19
Excel Ribbon, EX 10
Outlook Ribbon, OUT 11
PowerPoint Ribbon, PPT 9
windows, WIN 14
Word Ribbon, WD 7

minor sort keys, A 97, AC 102

mistakes
See also AutoCorrect
correcting while typing in

worksheets, EX 19
correcting while typing in documents, WD 91–94

MLA documentation style
applying, WD 95
date format, WD 84
described, WD 76–77
headers, WD 80
works cited page, WD 111

Mode indicators, status bar, EX 9

modifications to documents, WD 58

modifying. *See* changing

money, currency symbols, and database design, AC 9–10

monitors
changing screen resolution, APP 33–35
computer, WIN 4
optimizing resolution, WIN 7

mouse
described, WIN 4
operations described, WIN 6
pointer in Access, AC 18
pointer in PowerPoint, PPT 7
pointer in Word, WD 7
right-clicking, WIN 11
scrolling in documents, WD 43

moving
to another slide in presentation, PPT 46–48
clips, PPT 113
text, WD 119–122
vs. copying worksheet cells, EX 177
windows, WIN 17

Mozilla Firefox browser, WIN 23

MSN MoneyCentral Investor Stock Quotes, EX 139

multi-level bulleted lists, PPT 33

multivalued database fields, AC 160–161, AC 181–184

multivalued Lookup fields, AC 173–174

My Collections, PPT 103

My Computer window, mouse and windows operations, WIN 13–22

N

Name box, using, EX 47

names
changing worksheet, EX 140–141

file, WD 18
finding files and folders using,
  WIN 51–54
user. *See* user names
naming
  database files, AC 13, AC 15
  database tables, fields, AC 8
  folders, WIN 34
  PowerPoint documents, PPT 27
  Word documents, WD 20
  workbooks, EX 29, EX 31
  worksheet, workbook files, EX 29
  worksheets, EX 86, EX 216–217
Natural Wireless Laser Mouse 6000,
  WIN 6
Navigation buttons, AC 38–39
Navigation pane
  Access, AC 126
  Outlook, APP 17, OUT 7–8
Navigation pane, Access, AC 18–19
negative numbers, handling, EX 197
nesting IF functions, EX 195
networks described, WIN 32
New Message Ribbon, OUT 18
nonbreaking spaces, hyphens,
  inserting, WD 171
nonprinting characters, WD 14,
  WD 25
Normal style, setting and resetting,
  WD 23, WD 150
Normal view, APP 14, EX 129,
  PPT 46, PPT 99, PPT 100
NOT (not equal to) operator, AC 94
Notes Page view, PPT 8
Notes pane, PPT 8
Notification area, desktop, WIN 7
NOW function, displaying system
  date on worksheets, EX 183–185
numbers
  calculating. *See* calculating,
    calculations
  entering as text into worksheets,
    EX 24
  entering into range of worksheet
    cells, EX 90
  entering into worksheets,
    EX 22–24, EX 180–181
  formatting in worksheets, EX 44–45
  formatting using Ribbon, EX 114–118
  negative, EX 197

O

Office 2007
  customizing, APP 33–46
  Help, APP 19, APP 22–23
  online collaboration using, APP 6–7
  programs in, APP 3–4, APP 7–19
  user interface, APP 4–6
Office Button
  Access, AC 22–23
  Excel workbook control, EX 14
  Outlook, OUT 13–14
  Word, WD 10
Office Clipboard
  copying and pasting text,
    WD 188–192
  copying graphics using, WD 190
  copying worksheet cells using,
    EX 174–175
Office Collections, PPT 103
Office Theme, PPT 16, PPT 117
offsetting charts, EX 213–214
one-to-many relationships, and
  referential integrity, AC 185
online collaboration using Office
  2007, APP 6–7
opening
  databases, AC 36–38, AC 77
  links in tabbed Web pages,
    WIN 27–28
  presentations, PPT 54–55
  Word documents, WD 56–57
  workbooks, EX 60–61
operating systems, WIN 2
operations, arithmetic, EX 92
operators
  comparison. *See* comparison
    operators
  conditional formatting, EX 121–124
  logical, in IF functions, EX 189
OR criterion, AC 95–96
ordering
  database records, AC 192–195
  descending, ascending, AC 53
organizing
  arranging slides, PPT 41–42
  e-mail contacts, OUT 51, OUT 53
  e-mail messages, OUT 33–37
  files, folders in Windows Explorer,
    WIN 31–32
windows on desktop, WIN 14

orientation, printing, AC 40–41,
  EX 129–132, PPT 6
Outbox folder, OUT 7, OUT 17
outer joins, AC 104
Outline tab, PowerPoint window,
  PPT 8
outlines, printing presentations as,
  PPT 133–138
Outlook
  Contacts, using, OUT 44–62
  described, OUT 2
  e-mail message options, OUT 38–43
  Help, using, OUT 62–65
  Inbox panes, OUT 7–10
  incoming messages, working with,
    OUT 10–23
  organizing e-mail messages,
    OUT 33–37
  outgoing messages, working with,
    OUT 23–32
  program described, APP 17–19
  quitting, OUT 65
  starting and customizing, UT 5–6
overtype mode, EX 64–65, WD 58

P

page breaks
  automatic, WD 107–108
  manual, WD 112
Page Layout View, EX 129–132,
  EX 130–132
page numbers, inserting in
  documents, WD 82
page setup, EX 136
pages
  Web. *See* Web pages
  Word documents. *See* Word
    documents
panes
  See also specific pane
  splitting windows into, EX 222–223
paper clip icon on e-mail message,
  OUT 8
Paragraph Dialog Launcher, WD 158
paragraph formatting, WD 22
paragraph mark (¶), WD 14
paragraphs
  bottom borders, WD 161
  centering in documents, WD 26

changing spacing above, below, WD 50–51, WD 195

first-line indent, WD 88–89

formatting single vs. multiple, WD 26–32

indenting, WD 196

right-aligned, WD 81

spacing in documents, WD 78–79

tab stops, WD 159–160

parameter queries, AC 89–92

parentheses (( ))

  in calculated fields in queries, AC 113

  in Excel functions, EX 100

  overriding formula order of operations, EX 92

parenthetical citations, WD 76

passwords, choosing your, WIN 7

paste area, EX 27

Paste Options button, WD 122, WD 192

pasting

  and copying text, WD 188–192

  from Office Clipboard, WD 191–192

  text, WD 119

  worksheet cells, EX 175–177

paths

  to drives, folders, WIN 32

  in URLs, WIN 25

PDF format

  exporting to, AC 209

  saving documents in, WD 183

  viewing, AC 224

Percent style format, EX 118

Personal information management (PIM) programs, APP 17

photographs

  See also pictures

  inserting into slides, PPT 106–107

  resizing, PPT 111

phrases, searching files using, WIN 54–55

pictures

  applying styles in documents, WD 44

  inserting in documents, WD 40–42

  photographs and Clip Organizer, PPT 105–106

pie charts

  adding 3-D, to workbook, EX 204–216

  exploding (offsetting), EX 213–214

PIM (personal information management) programs, APP 17

pixels described, EX 122

placeholders

  deleting, PPT 112

  deleting text in presentation, PPT 42–43

  inserting citation, WD 101, WD 108

  inserting clips from Clip Organizer, PPT 104–105

  using in presentations, PPT 7, PPT 19, PPT 34

plain text, e-mail message format, OUT 19

planning

  See also designing

  cover letter and resume, WD 149

  cover letters, WD 165

  Excel calculations, EX 24

  charts, EX 48, EX 204

  flyers, WD 12

  graphics in Word documents, WD 41

  pie charts, EX 204

  presentations, PPT 3, PPT 18, PPT 20, PPT 92, PPT 94

  projects, guidelines for, APP 1–2

  research papers, WD 76, WD 83–84

  resume Web page, WD 216

  Web pages, PPT 148

  Word documents, WD 4, WD 23

  worksheet formulas, EX 90

  worksheets, EX 16, EX 85, EX 108, EX 165–166, EX 196

plugging USB flash drive into USB port, WIN 33–34

plus sign (+)

  mouse pointer, EX 8

  file and folder expansion, WIN 37

  in Inbox folder, OUT 10

Point mode, entering formulas using, EX 93–94, EX 101

point size

  in presentations, PPT 21

  in worksheet cells, EX 34, EX 38

pointing with mouse, WIN 6

pop-up menus, Slide Show view, PPT 51–52

portrait orientation

  printing datasheets, AC 40–41

printing worksheets, EX 129

  for slide shows, PPT 6

ports, USB, WIN 32

positioning

  graphics on slides, PPT 113

  paper orientation, printing, AC 40–41

  Quick Access Toolbar, APP 38–39

postal codes, AC 12

PowerPoint

  See also presentations

  creating Web pages using, PPT 146–157

  described, PPT 2–3

  document themes, PPT 16–17

  file management tools, PPT 155–157

  files, naming, PPT 27

  Help, PPT 63–64

  Key Tips, PPT 15–16

  Mini toolbar, shortcut menus, PPT 11–12

  Office Button, PPT 14–15

  program described, APP 13–15

  Quick Access Toolbar, PPT 13–14

  quitting, PPT 52–53, PPT 65

  Ribbon, PPT 8–10

  saving, PPT 26

  starting, PPT 5–6, PPT 53, PPT 92–93

  window, using, PPT 6–8

presentation graphics programs, WIN 23

presentations

  See also PowerPoint; slides

  adding new slide to, PPT 29–31

  animated slide shows, PPT 133

  background styles, choosing, PPT 97–98

  with bulleted lists, PPT 94–97

  changing document properties, PPT 43–45

  changing layouts, PPT 100–103

  changing views to review, PPT 98–99

  correcting errors in, PPT 58

  creating text slide with, PPT 31–32

  creating title slide, PPT 93–94

  creating with illustrations and shapes, PPT 90–108

  deleting text from, PPT 58

  ending, PPT 39–40

  exporting XML data, AC 226–227

formatting characters in, PPT 21–26

opening, PPT 54–55

planning, PPT 3, PPT 92

printing, PPT 61–62

printing as outlines and handouts, PPT 133–138

saving, PPT 26–29, PPT 45–46

saving as Web pages, PPT 153–154

speaker's delivery skills, PPT 90

spell checking, PPT 55–58

transparencies in, PPT 62

viewing in Slide Show view, PPT 48–52

previewing

database tables, AC 40–43

e-mail contacts, OUT 53–54

gallery choices, OUT 18

presentations, PPT 134–136

printouts, EX 60

Web pages, EX 252–255, PPT 151–152

worksheets before printing, EX 132–124

primary keys

changing, AC 28, AC 46

in database fields, AC 4–5, AC 8

and referential integrity, AC 185

Print dialog box, EX 133

Print Layout view, WD 6

print preview

documents, WD 57, WD 201–202

Excel, EX 60

Print Scaling option, EX 137

Print What list, PPT 134

printers, selecting, PPT 136

printing

Access reports, AC 56, AC 111

in black and white, EX 218

conserving ink, toner, EX 57–58, WD 53

database table relationship, AC 188

document properties, WD 130–131

e-mail contacts, OUT 53

e-mail messages, OUT 15–16

envelopes, WD 203–204

handouts, PPT 137–138

mailing labels, WD 204

presentations, PPT 61–62, PPT 136–137

presentations as outline and handouts, PPT 133–138

queries, AC 83

range of pages, AC 43

resumes, WD 185

Word documents, WD 53–55

worksheets, EX 129–135

printouts, EX 57

Professional Edition, Office 2007, APP 3

Professional Edition, Windows XP, WIN 3

programs

See also specific program

described, WIN 23

in Microsoft Office 2007, APP 3–4, APP 7–19

PIM (personal information management), APP 17

on Start menu, WIN 8–10

projects

Access, AC 2–6

cover letter and resume, WD 146–149

creating Web pages using PowerPoint, PPT 146–148

creating Web pages using Word, WD 216–217

financial projection worksheet, EX 162–167

maintaining databases, AC 138–139

Outlook, OUT 3–4

planning guidelines, APP 1–2

presentation with bulleted lists, PPT 3–5

presentations with illustrations and shapes, PPT 90–92

querying databases, AC 74–76

research paper creation, WD 74–76

saving workbook, EX 29–32

sharing data among applications, AC 206–209

Word document with picture, WD 2–4

workbook with chart saved as Web page, EX 251–252

worksheet with embedded chart, EX 2–5

worksheet with formulas, functions, Web queries, EX 82–86

promoting text in presentations, PPT 34

proofreading, WD 76, WD 118

properties

automatically updated, PPT 44, WD 51

database, changing, AC 60–61

database table join, AC 108–109

document. *See* document properties

protecting passwords, WIN 7

protocols. *See specific protocol*

Publisher 2007, PowerPoint and, APP 16–17

publishing

Access reports, AC 225

resumes as Web pages, WD 216–217

Web pages, PPT 148

Web pages to Web servers, APP 32

workbooks, EX 252

punctuation, spacing after, WD 106

Q

queries

append, make-table, AC 165

calculating statistics, AC 117–122

calculations, using, AC 113–116

changing captions, AC 116–117

creating, using, printing, AC 80–85

criteria, using in, AC 81–82, AC 85–86

crosstab, AC 122–125

delete, AC 163–164

designing database, AC 76

lookup fields, using, AC 172–175

omitting duplicates, AC 100–101

parameter, AC 89–92

printing, AC 83

saved, using, AC 92

saving, AC 91

sorting records, AC 97–103

table joins, AC 103–107

top-values, creating, AC 102–103

update, AC 162–163

using compound criteria in, AC 95–96

using criterion in calculating statistics, AC 120–121

using multivalued fields in, AC 181–184

Web. *See* Web queries

wildcards, using, AC 87

querying
 databases generally, AC 74
 multivalued fields on, AC 182–184
question mark (?), Access wildcard,
  AC 87, AC 151
Quick Access Toolbar
 Access, AC 22
 adding button to, EX 252–254,
  PPT 148–150
 adding commands to, APP 39–43
 customizing, resetting, APP 38
 Excel, EX 13, EX 65, EX 258
 Office 2007, APP 5
 Outlook, OUT 12–13
 PowerPoint, PPT 13–14
 removing commands, APP 44
 resetting, APP 45
 Word, WD 10–11
Quick Parks gallery, WD 198
Quick Styles
 applying, WD 150
 creating, WD 90–91
 formatting text using, PPT 114–116
 in Word documents, WD 36
quitting
 Access, AC 35–36, AC 63, AC 127
 Excel, EX 59
 Outlook, OUT 65
 PowerPoint, PPT 52–53, PPT 65
 Windows Explorer, WIN 50
 Word, WD 55, WD 62, WD 132
quotation marks ("") in Access text
  fields, AC 82

R

Range Finder, using, EX 106–107,
  EX 164
range of values, AC 165, AC 166
RE:, in e-mail messages, OUT 17
reading e-mail messages, OUT 10
Reading pane, OUT 9–10
Really Simple Syndication, RSS
  Feeds folder, OUT 7
records, database, AC 4
recovering databases, AC 193
Recycle Bin, WIN 21
redoing and undoing changes, AC 34
redundancy, removing from
  databases, AC 5, AC 10–12

#REF! error message, EX 180
referencing, absolute vs. relative,
  EX 186–189
referential integrity, specifying,
  AC 185–191
refreshing worksheet data, EX 139
relational operators, conditional
  formatting, EX 121
relationships, database
 determining, implementing, AC 9
 and referential integrity,
  AC 185–191
relative vs. absolute addressing,
  EX 186–189
removing
 See also deleting
 commands from Quick Access
  Toolbar, APP 44, EX 254
 panes from windows, EX 223
 redundancy from databases,
  AC 10–12
renaming
 files, folders, WIN 47–48
 worksheets, EX 216–217
repagination, background, WD 107
repairing databases, AC 193
replying to e-mail messages,
  OUT 16–17, OUT 19
Report Wizard, AC 52–55, AC 111
reports
 Access, creating and printing,
  AC 50–56
 creating from database table joins,
  AC 108–111
 publishing Access, AC 225
required fields, AC 165
requirements documents and
  planning worksheets, EX 3–5
research papers
 creating, WD 74
 proofreading, WD 118
Research task pane, WD 128–130
reserved words, symbols
 for database creation, AC 15
 in worksheets, workbooks, EX 31
 folder names, WIN 34
 in Word window, WD 20
resizing
 charts, EX 53
 clip art and photographs,
  PPT 109–112

database fields, AC 84
 datasheet columns, AC 175–176
 graphics using Size dialog box,
  WD 155
 shapes, PPT 125–126
 Word table columns, WD 177–178
resizing graphics in documents,
  WD 46–47
resizing handles, Word tables,
  WD 178
resolution
 changing screen, APP 33–35
 decreasing monitor's, PPT 5
 monitor, optimizing, WIN 7
restoring windows, WIN 15
restructuring databases, AC 138
resumes
 creating using template, WD 183–186
 described, WD 146
 planning, WD 149
 printing, WD 185
Ribbon
 Access, AC 19–21
 Excel, EX 9–11, EX 114–118,
  EX 194
 Office 2007, APP 4
 Outlook, OUT 11–12, OUT 18,
  OUT 48
 PowerPoint, PPT 8–9
 screen resolution and, APP 36–37
 Word, APP 37–38, WD 7–9, WD 86
rich text, e-mail message format,
  OUT 19
right-aligning
 paragraphs, WD 81
 text in worksheet cells, EX 168
right-clicking to copy files, WIN 46
right-dragging described, WIN 21
rotating
 pie charts, EX 209–210
 text in worksheet cells,
  EX 168–171
 worksheet cell entries, EX 114
round tripping MHTML files,
  PPT 154
row selector, AC 28
rows, Word table
 adding, deleting, WD 180
 deleting, WD 186–187
 resizing, WD 178

rows, worksheet
  changing height, EX 126
  deleting, EX 180
  entering titles, EX 21–22
  entering titles into, EX 88
  freezing titles, EX 181–182
  hiding, EX 126, EX 127
  inserting, EX 177–179
  planning, EX 16
RSS Feeds folder, OUT 7
ruler
  displaying, WD 158
  setting custom tab stops using,
    WD 167
  using in documents, WD 87
rules
  database validation, AC 165–178
  e-mail, OUT 42

S

salutation of cover letter, WD 169
sans serif, fonts, using for titles,
    PPT 116
Saved Exports feature, AC 225
Saved Imports feature, AC 219–220
saved queries, using, AC 92
saving
  Access reports, AC 55
  database files, AC 16–17
  database queries, AC 91, AC 107
  database records, AC 33
  database tables, AC 27, AC 44
  Outlook information in different
    formats, OUT 60–61
  presentations, PPT 26–29,
    PPT 45–46
  presentations as Web pages,
    PPT 153–154
  templates, WD 164
  workbooks as Web page,
    EX 256–257
  Word documents, WD 18–21, WD
    87, WD 183
  Word documents as Web pages,
    WD 218–219
  Word documents to Web servers,
    WD 219
  Word documents with same file
    name, WD 53

WordPad documents, WIN 40–44
  workbooks, EX 29–32, EX 106
scaling prints, Excel, EX 137
schemas
  exporting XML, AC 226–227
  Word color, APP 46
screen resolution, APP 33–35,
    PPT 5, WIN 7
Screen Tips
  Access, AC 20
  Outlook, OUT 10–11
scroll bar
  in Access window, AC 19
  in PowerPoint window, PPT 7
  in Word window, WD 7
  in worksheet window, EX 9
scrolling
  using scroll arrows, WIN 18–19
  through documents, WD 43
Search Companion, finding files or
    folders using, WIN 51–55
Search Folders folder, OUT 7,
    OUT 43
searching
  Access Help, AC 61–63
  for database records, AC 145–146
  Excel Help, EX 67–68
  for files, folders, WIN 51–55
  Help and Support topics,
    WIN 56–60
  information using Research task
    pane, WD 128–130
  Outlook Help, OUT 63–64
  PowerPoint, PPT 63–64
  Word Help, APP 24–29,
    WD 60–61
secondary sort keys, A 97
security
  e-mail settings, OUT 43
  password, WIN 7
  untrusted content warning, Access,
    AC 38
Select Browse Object menu,
    WD 118–119
selecting text, techniques for, WD 120
selection rectangle, and resizing
    graphics, PPT 109
sensitivity analysis. *See* what-if
    analysis

sensitivity, e-mail setting,
    OUT 38–42
Sent Items folder, OUT 7
servers
  described, WIN 2, WIN 32
  Office SharePoint Server 2007,
    APP 20
  publishing Web pages on, EX 252,
    WD 219
  Web. *See* Web servers
service packs, WIN 4
shadowing text, PPT 118
Shape Quick Style, PPT 127–128
shapes, formatting, adding,
    PPT 123–130
Shared Collections, PPT 103
SharePoint, and collaboration,
    APP 20–21
sharing, EX 14
  Access data among applications,
    AC 206–229
  workbooks, EX 14
shortcut key, WD 86
shortcut menus
  in Access, AC 21
  displaying, WIN 11–12
  in Excel, EX 12
  PowerPoint, PPT 12
  Word, WD 9–10, WD 102–103
shortcuts, keyboard. *See* keyboard
    shortcuts
shoulder surfing, PPT 96
shrinking
  worksheet cell entries, EX 114
  worksheet, chart appearance,
    EX 220–223
signatures, e-mail, OUT 23–27
Simple Query Wizard, AC 78–80
Single File Web page format, EX 256,
    PPT 152
Size dialog box, WD 155
sizing
  fonts, WD 151–152
  fonts in documents, WD 23, WD 28
  windows, WIN 9–20, WIN 13–15
  worksheet columns using best fit,
    EX 122
  worksheets, EX 9, EX 135–136
sizing handles on graphics, PPT 109

slashes, double, in HTTP protocol, WIN 24

slide indicator, PPT 47–48

Slide pane, PowerPoint window, PPT 8

slide shows
See also presentations
described, PPT 2

Slide Sorter view, reviewing presentations in, PPT 99

slides
adding to presentation, PPT 29–31
adding transitions, PPT 130–132
animated shows, PPT 133
arranging, PPT 41–42
changing layouts, PPT 100–103
creating title, PPT 93–94
described, PPT 6
inserting clip art into, PPT 103
inserting photographs into, PPT 106–107
replacing text in, PPT 59
using bulleted lists, PPT 94–97

Slides tab, PowerPoint window, PPT 8

soft page breaks, WD 107

sorting
contact lists, OUT 49
e-mail messages, OUT 35–36
query records, AC 97–103

source and destination drives, folders, WIN 46

source code, viewing Web page, EX 258

sources, citation, WD 96–97, WD 99, WD 109

SP2 (Windows XP Service Pack 2), WIN 4

spaces, inserting nonbreaking, WD 171

spacing, paragraph, WD 195

spam, e-mail filter, OUT 14

special characters, inserting, PPT 114

spell checking
workbooks, worksheets, EX 127–129, EX 218
presentations, PPT 55–58
Word documents, WD 16–17, WD 125–126

split forms, AC 57–59, AC 63

splitter bar in PowerPoint window, PPT 8

splitting
merged worksheet cells, EX 41
windows into panes, EX 222–223

spreadsheets. *See* worksheets

SQL Server and multivalued database fields, AC 160

square brackets ([ ]), use in parameter queries, AC 89, AC 90

Standard Buttons toolbar, My Computer window, WIN 13

standard deviation aggregate function, AC 117

Standard toolbar, OUT 7–10

Start menu
displaying, WIN 8–11
opening windows using, WIN 16–17
starting application using, WIN 23–24

start pages, WIN 24

starting
Access, AC 12–13, AC 36–38, AC 77
application programs, WIN 23
Excel, EX 6–7
Help and Support, WIN 22, WIN 56–57
Outlook, OUT 5–6
PowerPoint, PPT 5–6, PPT 53, PPT 92–93
Windows Explorer, WIN 31–32
Windows XP, WIN 5
Word, WD 4–5
WordPad, WIN 39

Startup submenu, adding programs to, EX 167

statistical functions, EX 98

statistics
calculating in queries, AC 117–122
using with grouping, AC 121–122
word count in documents, WD 107

status bar
Access, AC 19
displaying XP, WIN 30
Excel, EX 9
PowerPoint, PPT 8
Word window, WD 7

STDEV (standard deviation) aggregate function, AC 117

stock quotes, MSN MoneyCentral Investor Stock Quotes, EX 139

storage folders, WIN 11

storage media for databases, AC 14

style formats in documents, WD 38

style sets in documents, WD 36–38

styles
See also specific style
applying picture in documents, WD 44
applying Word, WD 24–26
background, for presentations, PPT 97–98
bibliography, WD 95
business letter, WD 166
changing worksheet cell, EX 35–38, EX 42–43
footnote text, WD 102–105
MLA documentation style, WD 76–77
modifying using Styles task pane, WD 114–115
using in presentations, PPT 21
Word document, WD 24–26
Word table, WD 176–177
worksheet cell, applying, EX 112

subdatasheets, AC 190–191

submenus
Access, AC 22–23
Outlook, OUT 14
Excel, EX 14
PowerPoint, PPT 15
Word, WD 10

subtitles, selecting for worksheet, EX 16

Sum button, using, EX 97, EX 102

SUM (total) aggregate function, AC 117

sums, calculating, EX 24–26, EX 28–29

support. *See* Help and Support

switching
between documents, WD 189
between tabbed Web pages, WIN 28

symbols
format, AC 168, EX 180
infinity, for many- relationship, AC 188
reserved words. *See* reserved words, symbols

synonyms, finding and inserting, WD 124–125

system date, displaying on
  worksheets, EX 183–185
System Tools programs, WIN 39
Systems menu, My Computer
  window, WIN 13

T

tab characters
  in documents, WD 159–160
  in Word tables, WD 178
tab stops
  aligning text using, WD 158–160
  setting custom, using ruler, WD 167
tabbed Web pages, WIN 27–28
tables
  database. *See* database tables
  Word. *See* Word tables
Tablet PC Edition, Windows XP,
  WIN 3
tablet PCs, WIN 3
tabs
  See also specific tab
  Access Ribbon, AC 19–20
  coloring worksheet, EX 216–217
  New Message Ribbon, OUT 18
  PowerPoint, PPT 8–9
  in Ribbon feature, OUT 11
  worksheet, EX 7, EX 141
  worksheet window, EX 9–10
tag names, citations, WD 101
tags, smart, EX 96–97
task pane
  Access, AC 20
  Clip Art, PPT 103–104
  Clipboard, WD 191–192
  Excel, EX 11
  Outlook, OUT 12
  PowerPoint, PPT 11
  Research, WD 128–130
  Word, WD 9
templates
  creating databases using, AC 13–14
  creating resume using, WD 183–186
  database table, AC 26
  saving, WD 164
  Word, WD 146
testing
  hyperlinks, WD 221
  Web pages in Web browser, WD 223

text
  adding to shapes, PPT 127
  aligning using tab stops, WD 158–160
  bold in documents, WD 34
  coloring, WD 152–153
  converting hypertext to,
    WD 163–164
  copying and pasting, WD 188–192
  data, using in criterion queries,
    AC 86–87
  deleting, WD 193
  deleting from presentations,
    PPT 58
  entering into documents,
    WD 12–15
  entering into worksheets,
    EX 15–19
  entering more in content controls,
    WD 194
  finding and replacing,
    WD 123–125
  formatting using Format Painter,
    PPT 119–121
  formatting using Quick Styles,
    PPT 114–116
  inserting special characters,
    PPT 114
  italicizing in documents, WD 36
  modifying in content control,
    WD 187–188
  moving, WD 119–122
  promoting, demoting, PPT 34
  rotating in worksheet cells,
    EX 168–171
  shadowing, PPT 118
  typing in WordPad, WIN 40
  underlining in documents, WD 35
  wrapping, EX 87–89, WD 14–15
text files
  exporting Access data to, AC 224
  importing into, linking to Access
    database, AC 218–219
text labels on toolbar buttons,
  WIN 13
theme colors, changing, WD 201
themes
  in Excel, EX 34, EX 37, EX 107,
    EX 109
  in PowerPoint, PPT 8, PPT 16–17
  in Word, WD 23, WD 150
thesaurus, WD 124–126

time, updating system, EX 183
tips. *See* Key Tips, ToolTips
title slides, PPT 18–20, PPT 93–94
titles
  centering works cited page, WD 112
  creating title slide, PPT 18–20
  entering worksheet, EX 17–18,
    EX 87–89
  entering worksheet row,
    EX 21–22
  formatting worksheet, EX 199–200
  freezing worksheet, EX 181–182
  inserting chart, EX 206–209
  using sans serif font for, PPT 116
  worksheet rows, columns,
    EX 19–22
To-Do bar, OUT 10
toggling database record filters,
  AC 151
toolbars
  See also specific toolbar
  Office 2007, APP 6
ToolTips
  Enhanced. *See* Enhanced ToolTips
  in Windows XP, WIN 9
top-values queries, AC 102–103
transitions, adding slide,
  PPT 130–132
transparencies, using in
  presentations, PPT 62
transparent colors, setting in
  graphic, WD 157
turning off
  Mini toolbar, PPT 11
  your computer, WIN 62–64
type. *See* fonts

U

UDISK drive, WIN 33
underlining
  text in documents, WD 35
  wavy, for misspelled words, WD 16
undoing
  actions in Word documents,
    WD 32–33
  database changes, AC 26, AC 34
  typing, PPT 19
  worksheet changes, EX 65, EX 180,
    EX 227
unhiding. *See* displaying

Uniform Resource Locators. *See* URLs
unique identifiers in database fields,
    AC 4
update queries, AC 162–163
updating
  bibliographical lists, WD 117
  database records, AC 141–147
  database tables containing
    validation rules, AC 169–178
  PowerPoint slide from previous
    version, PPT 43
  system date, time, EX 183
URLs (Uniform Resource Locators)
  browsing Web using, WIN 26
  described, WIN 24–25
USB flash drives
  creating databases using, AC 14–17
  described, WIN 32
  opening database on, AC 37
  opening Word documents,
    WD 56–57
  removing from port after work,
    EX 69
  saving to, EX 30–32, OUT 32,
    WD 21, WIN 33
USB ports
  described, WIN 32
  plugging USB flash drives into,
    WIN 33–34
user-friendly, WIN 5
user interface, Office 2007, APP 4–6
user names, choosing, WIN 7

V

validation rules, database, AC 165–178
value axis in Excel charts, EX 50
values
  formula, determining using Goal
    Seek command, EX 225–228
  and validation rules, AC 165–167
  version of worksheet, printing,
    EX 135–136
VAR (variance) aggregate function,
    AC 117
verifying
  Excel formulas, EX 106–107, EX 164
  folder's contents, WIN 45

versions
  of Microsoft Office 2007, APP 3–4
  of Windows XP, WIN 2–4
vertical ruler in documents, WD 87
viewing
  database records through forms,
    AC 57–58
  file attachments, OUT 22–23
  PDF, XPS files, AC 224
  presentations in Slide Show view,
    PPT 48–52
views
  changing worksheet, EX 220–223
  Outlook, OUT 49
  PowerPoint, PPT 8, PPT 48–52,
    PPT 98–99

W

warning of untrusted database
    content, AC 38
Web
  browsers. *See* browsers
  Office 2007 and, APP 6
Web browsers, WIN 23
Web Collections, PPT 103
Web folders
  and FTP locations, EX 252
  publishing Web pages using,
    APP 32
Web Page format, PPT 152, EX 256
Web pages
  adding background colors to,
    WD 221
  adding pattern fill effect to
    background, WD 222
  creating using Excel, EX 250–261
  creating using PowerPoint,
    PPT 146–157
  creating using Word, WD 216–223
  described, WIN 24
  formatting, WD 220–223
  previewing, EX 255, PPT 151–152
  publishing to Web servers, APP 32
  saving workbooks as, EX 256–257
  saving presentations as, PPT 153–154
  saving Word documents as,
    WD 218–219
  tabbed, WIN 27–28

testing in Web browser, WD 223
viewing, manipulating using
    browser, EX 260–261
Web queries, importing data into
    Excel using, EX 137–140
Web servers
  publishing Web pages to, APP 32
  publishing Word documents on,
    WD 219
Welcome screen, Windows XP,
    WIN 5, WIN 64
what-if analysis, using in worksheets,
    EX 162, EX 164, EX 223–227
What-If Assumptions table
  Excel, EX 181
  formatting, EX 203
width
  changing worksheet column,
    EX 173–174
  Word table rows and columns, WD
    180
wildcards
  Access, AC 87, AC 151
  database validation rules, AC 165
windows
  See also specific window
  closing, opening, WIN 16–17,
    WIN 20
  minimizing, maximizing, AC 13,
    WIN 14–15
  moving, sizing, resizing, WIN 17–20
  Outlook, customizing, OUT 6
  PowerPoint, using, PPT 6–8
  sizing, WIN 9–20
  splitting into panes, EX 222–223
  Word, using, APP 37–38,
    WD 4–12
  worksheet, EX 9–15
Windows Explorer
  file management in, WIN 45–50
  organizing files and folders,
    WIN 31–32
  quitting, WIN 50
  starting, WIN 31–32
  using, WIN 29–31
Windows Taskbar, WD 188
Windows XP
  described, versions, WIN 2–4
  desktop, using, WIN 8–13

Help and Support, getting, WIN 56–61
keyboard, keyboard shortcuts, WIN 22
logging on, WIN 7–8
starting, WIN 5
user interface described, WIN 4, WIN 6
Windows XP 64-Bit Edition, WIN 3
Windows XP Service Pack 2 (SP2), WIN 4
Wireless Entertainment Desktop 8000 keyboard, WIN 22
wizards. *See specific wizard*
Word
  color schemes, changing, APP 46
  creating Web pages using, WD 216–223
  described, WD 2
  documents. *See* Word documents
  entering text, WD 12–15
  exporting Access data to, AC 223–224
  fonts, font sizes, styles and themes, WD 23
  Help, APP 22–31, WD 60–61
  insert and overtype mode, WD 58
  and the Internet, APP 8
  Key Tips, WD 12
  Mini toolbar, shortcut menus, WD 9–10
  program described, APP 7–9
  Quick Access Toolbar, Office Button, WD 10–11
  quitting, WD 55, WD 62, WD 132
  Ribbon, WD 7–9
  starting, WD 4–5
  tables. *See* Word tables
  window, customizing, APP 37–38
  window, using, WD 4–12
Word documents
  adding page borders, WD 48–50
  applying picture styles, WD 44
  automatic page breaks, WD 107–108
  bibliographical lists, creating, WD 113
  bold characters, WD 34
  building blocks, using, WD 170
  bulleted lists, WD 32

changing spacing around paragraphs, WD 50
changing document settings, WD 77–78
citations, WD 94–98
Click and Type feature, WD 85
closing, WD 59–60
copying and pasting text, WD 188–192
correcting errors in, WD 57–60
counting words in, WD 107
displaying formatting marks, WD 14
documentation styles, WD 76
entering text into, WD 12–14
finding and replacing text, WD 123–125
fonts, font sizes, WD 23
footnotes, WD 99–105
footnotes, endnotes, WD 106
formatting marks in, WD 77, WD 150
formatting paragraphs, characters generally, WD 22
formatting single vs. multiple paragraphs, characters, WD 26–31
grammar checking, WD 125–126
hanging indents, WD 116
inserting clip art into, WD 153–154
inserting current date, WD 168–169
inserting text into existing, WD 58
italicizing text in, WD 36
line and paragraph spacing, WD 78–79
opening, WD 56–57
page borders, WD 48–50, WD 55
page numbers, inserting in header, WD 82
pictures, inserting, WD 40–42
printing, WD 53–55, WD 201–202
proofreading, WD 76
Research task pane, looking up information using, WD 128–130
resizing graphics, WD 46–47
rulers in, WD 87
saving, WD 18–21, WD 165
saving as Web pages, WD 218–219
scrolling around, WD 43
selecting groups of words, WD 33

spell checking, WD 16–17, WD 125–126
spelling and grammar check, WD 16–17
styles, applying, WD 24–25
switching between, WD 189
underlining characters, WD 35
undoing, redoing, WD 32–33
using styles in, WD 36–40
wordwrap, WD 14–15
word processing programs, WIN 23
Word tables
  adding, deleting rows, WD 180
  applying table styles, WD 176–177
  described, WD 173
  entering data into, WD 174–175
  inserting empty, WD 173–174
  resizing columns in, WD 177–178
  selecting, centering, WD 179
  selecting contents, WD 178
WordArt, PPT 119
WordPad
  creating document and folder using, WIN 38–45
  viewing contact lists in, OUT 61–62
words
  counting in documents, WD 107
  finding and inserting synonyms, WD 124
  searching files using, WIN 54–55
wordwrap
  in documents, WD 14–15
  in Word tables, WD 174–175
work area, AC 18–19
work days, EX 195
workbooks
  adding 3-D pie chart to, EX 204–216
  changng themes, EX 109
  creating hyperlinks in, EX 258
  e-mailing, EX 142–143
  naming, EX 29, EX 31
  opening, EX 60–61
  saving, EX 29–30, EX 29–32, EX 106
  saving as Web pages, EX 256–257
works cited, in research papers, WD 77, WD 111

worksheets
  adding 3-D clustered column to,
    EX 49–54
  adjusting column width, EX 46,
    EX 173–174
  aesthetics vs. function, EX 84
  Auto Fill Options, EX 28,
    EX 169–171
  cells, *See* cells, worksheet
  centering cells, EX 40–41,
    EX 113
  changing column width, height,
    EX 122–126
  changing margins, headers,
    orientation, EX 130–132
  changing views, EX 220–223
  changing names of, EX 140–141
  columns. *See* columns, worksheet
  conditional formatting,
    EX 118–121
  copying and pasting cells, EX 175–177
  copying cell formulas, EX 201–202
  copying cells using fill handle,
    EX 26–28
  correcting errors on, EX 63–67
  creating, methodology for, EX 3–5
  debugging, EX 135–136
  determining multiple totals,
    EX 28–29
  entering column, row titles,
    EX 19–22
  entering numbers into, EX 22–24
  entering numbers with format
    symbols, EX 180–181
  entering text into, EX 15–19
  entering titles, EX 87–89

  error checking, EX 129
  fitting entries to cells, EX 174–175
  font type, style, size, color,
    EX 34–47
  formatting, EX 88, EX 33–34,
    EX 107–114
  formatting column titles, total row,
    EX 42–43
  formatting numbers in, EX 44–45
  formatting titles, EX 110,
    EX 199–200
  formulas, entering into, EX 90–91
  freezing titles, EX 181–182
  gridlines, EX 8
  hiding, unhiding columns, EX 122
  in-cell editing, EX 64–65
  inserting cells, EX 177–179
  inserting columns, EX 179
  merging cells, EX 40–41
  naming, renaming, EX 216–217
  planning, EX 16, EX 108
  printing, EX 57–58, EX 129–135
  printing formulas or values version
    of, EX 135–136
  printing sections of, EX 134–125
  rows. *See* rows, worksheet
  selecting cells, EX 48
  selecting cells using Name box,
    EX 47
  spell checking, EX 127–129,
    EX 218
  splitting merged cells, EX 41
  system date, displaying,
    EX 183–185
  working with cells, EX 7–8
World Wide Web. *See* Web

  wrapping, text
    in Excel, EX 87–89
    in PowerPoint, PPT 18
    in Word, WD 14–15

X

XML (Extensible Markup
    Language)
  exporting data, AC 226–227
  importing data into Access,
    AC 228–229
XPS format
  exporting to, AC 209
  publishing Access report in,
    AC 225
  saving documents in, WD 183
  viewing files in, AC 224

Y

y-axis in Excel charts, EX 50

Z

Zip codes, AC 12
zooming
  in Access, AC 42–43
  in print preview, WD 202
  on text, WD 12, WD 193
  in Word documents, WD 45–46,
    WD 50
  worksheet, chart appearance,
    EX 220–223

Quick Reference Summary

In the Microsoft Office 2007 programs, you can accomplish a task in a number of ways. The following five tables (one each for Microsoft Office Word 2007, Microsoft Office Excel 2007, Microsoft Office Access 2007, Microsoft Office PowerPoint 2007, and Microsoft Office Outlook 2007) provide a quick reference to each task presented in this textbook. The first column identifies the task. The second column indicates the page number on which the task is discussed in the book. The subsequent four columns list the different ways the task in column one can be carried out.

Table 1 Microsoft Office Word 2007 Quick Reference Summary

Task	Page Number	Mouse	Ribbon	Shortcut Menu	Keyboard Shortcut
1.5 Line Spacing	WD 86		Line spacing button on Home tab	Paragraph | Indents and Spacing tab	CTRL+5
AutoCorrect Entry, Create	WD 93	Office Button | Word Options button | Proofing | AutoCorrect Options button			
AutoCorrect Options Menu, Display	WD 92	Point to text automatically corrected, point to small blue box, click AutoCorrect Options button			
Background Color, Add	WD 221		Page Color button on Page Layout tab		
Bibliographical List, Create	WD 113		Bibliography button on References tab | Insert Bibliography		
Bibliographical List, Modify Source and Update List	WD 117		Manage Sources button on References tab | select source | Edit button		
Bibliography Style, Change	WD 95		Bibliography Style box arrow on References tab		
Bold	WD 34	Bold button on Mini toolbar	Bold button on Home tab	Font | Font tab | Bold in Font style list	CTRL+B
Border, Paragraph	WD 161		Page Borders on Page Layout tab | Borders tab		

Table 1   Microsoft Office Word 2007 Quick Reference Summary *(continued)*

Task	Page Number	Mouse	Ribbon	Shortcut Menu	Keyboard Shortcut
Building Block, Create	WD 170		Quick Parts button on Insert tab | Save Selection to Quick Part Gallery		ALT+F3
Building Block, Insert	WD 172		Quick Parts button on Insert tab		F3
Bullets, Apply	WD 32	Bullets button on Mini toolbar	Bullets button on Home tab	Bullets	ASTERISK KEY | SPACEBAR
Capital Letters	WD 86		Change Case button on Home tab | UPPERCASE	Font	CTRL+SHIFT+A
Case of Letters, Change	WD 86		Change Case button on Home tab	Font | Font tab	SHIFT+F3
Center	WD 26	Center button on Mini toolbar	Center button on Home tab	Paragraph | Indents and Spacing tab	CTRL+E
Citation Placeholder, Insert	WD 101		Insert Citation button on References tab | Add New Placeholder		
Citation, Insert and Create Source	WD 96		Insert Citation button on References tab | Add New Source		
Citation, Edit	WD 98	Citation Options box arrow | Edit Citation			
Close Document	WD 60	Office Button | Close			
Count Words	WD 107	Word Count indicator on status bar	Word Count button on Review tab		CTRL+SHIFT+G
Color Text	WD 152	Font Color button arrow on Mini toolbar	Font Color button arrow on Home tab		
Content Control, Change Text	WD 187	Triple-click content control, change text			
Copy	WD 189		Clipboard Dialog Box Launcher on Home tab	Copy	CTRL+C
Cut	WD 121		Cut button on Home tab	Cut	CTRL+X
Date, Insert	WD 168		Insert Date and Time button on Insert tab		
Delete Text	WD 59				DELETE
Dictionary, Custom, View or Modify Entries	WD 127	Office Button | Word Options button | Proofing | Custom Dictionaries button			
Dictionary, Set Custom	WD 127	Office Button | Word Options button | Proofing | Custom Dictionaries button | select desired dictionary name | Change Default button			
Document Properties, Set or View	WD 51	Office Button | Prepare | Properties			

Table 1 Microsoft Office Word 2007 Quick Reference Summary *(continued)*

Task	Page Number	Mouse	Ribbon	Shortcut Menu	Keyboard Shortcut
Documents, Switch Between	WD 189	Program button on Windows taskbar	Switch Windows button on View tab		ALT+TAB
Double-Space Text	WD 87		Line spacing button on Home tab	Paragraph	Indents and Spacing	CTRL+2
Double-Underline	WD 35		Font Dialog Box Launcher on Home tab	Font	Font tab	CTRL+SHIFT+D
Envelope, Address and Print	WD 203		Envelopes button on Mailings tab	Envelopes tab	Print button		
File, Create from Existing File	WD 165	Office Button	New	New from existing			
Find Text	WD 124	Browse Object button on vertical scroll bar	Find icon	Find button on Home tab		CTRL+F
Find and Replace Text	WD 123	Browse Object button on vertical scroll bar	Find icon	Replace tab	Replace button on Home tab		CTRL+H
First-Line Indent Paragraphs	WD 88	Drag First Line Indent marker on ruler	Paragraph Dialog Box Launcher on Home tab	Indents and Spacing tab	Paragraph	Indents and Spacing tab	TAB
Font Size, Change	WD 28	Font Size box arrow on Mini toolbar	Font Size box arrow on Home tab	Font	Font tab	CTRL+SHIFT+P
Font Size, Decrease	WD 152	Shrink Font button on Mini toolbar	Shrink Font button on Home tab	Font	Font tab	CTRL+SHIFT+<
Font Size, Decrease 1 Point	WD 86			Font	Font tab	CTRL+ [
Font Size, Increase	WD 151	Grow Font button on Mini toolbar	Grow Font button on Home tab		CTRL+SHIFT+>
Font Size, Increase 1 Point	WD 86			Font	Font tab	CTRL+]
Font, Change	WD 29	Font box arrow on Mini toolbar	Font box arrow on Home tab	Font	Font tab	CTRL+SHIFT+F
Footnote Reference Mark, Insert	WD 100		Insert Footnote button on References tab		CTRL+ALT+F
Footnote, Delete	WD 106	Delete note reference mark in document window	Cut button Home tab		BACKSPACE	BACKSPACE
Footnote, Edit	WD 106	Double-click note reference mark in document window	Show Notes button on References tab		
Footnote, Move	WD 106	Drag note reference mark in document window	Cut button on Home tab	Paste button on Home tab		
Footnote Style, Modify	WD 102		Styles Dialog Box Launcher	Footnote Text	Footnote Text box arrow	Style	Footnote Text	Modify button	
Formatting Marks	WD 14		Show/Hide ¶ button on Home tab		CTRL+SHIFT+*

Table 1 Microsoft Office Word 2007 Quick Reference Summary *(continued)*

Task	Page Number	Mouse	Ribbon	Shortcut Menu	Keyboard Shortcut
Formatting, Clear	WD 162		Clear Formatting button on Home tab		CTRL+ SPACEBAR
Graphic, Insert	WD 153		Clip Art button on Insert tab		
Graphic, Recolor	WD 156		Recolor button on Format tab	Format Picture | Picture | Recolor button	
Graphic, Resize	WD 46	Drag sizing handle	Format tab in Picture Tools tab or Size Dialog Box Launcher on Format tab	Size | Size tab	
Graphic, Set Transparent Color	WD 157		Recolor button on Format tab | Set Transparent Color		
Hanging Indent, Create	WD 116	Drag Hanging Indent marker on ruler	Paragraph Dialog Box Launcher on Home tab | Indents and Spacing tab	Paragraph | Indents and Spacing tab	CTRL+T
Hanging Indent, Remove	WD 86		Paragraph Dialog Box Launcher on Home tab | Indents and Spacing tab	Paragraph | Indents and Spacing tab	CTRL+SHIFT+T
Header & Footer, Close	WD 83	Double-click dimmed document text	Close Header and Footer button on Design tab		
Header, Display	WD 80	Double-click dimmed header	Header button on Insert tab | Edit Header		
Help	WD 60		Office Word Help button		F1
Hyperlink, Format Text As	WD 220		Insert Hyperlink button on Insert tab	Hyperlink	CTRL+K
Hyperlink, Remove	WD 163		Hyperlink button on Insert tab | Remove Link button	Remove Hyperlink	
Indent Paragraph	WD 196	Drag Left Indent marker on ruler	Increase Indent button on Home tab	Paragraph | Indents and Spacing sheet	CTRL+M
Insertion Point, Move to Beginning of Document	WD 24	Scroll to top of document, click			CTRL+HOME
Insertion Point, Move to End of Document	WD 25	Scroll to bottom of document, click			CTRL+END
Italicize	WD 36	Italic button on Mini toolbar	Italic button on Home tab	Font | Font tab	CTRL+I
Justify Paragraph	WD 86		Justify button on Home tab	Paragraph | Indents and Spacing tab	CTRL+J
Left-Align	WD 86		Align Text Left button on Home tab	Paragraph | Indents and Spacing tab	CTRL+L
Line Break, Enter	WD 194				SHIFT+ENTER
Move Selected Text	WD 121	Drag and drop selected text	Cut button on Home tab | Paste button on Home tab	Cut | Paste	CTRL+X; CTRL+V

Table 1 Microsoft Office Word 2007 Quick Reference Summary *(continued)*

Task	Page Number	Mouse	Ribbon	Shortcut Menu	Keyboard Shortcut
Nonbreaking Space, Insert	WD 171		Symbol button on Insert tab | More Symbols | Special Characters tab		CTRL+SHIFT+SPACEBAR
Open Document	WD 56	Office Button | Open			CTRL+O
Page Border, Add	WD 48		Page Borders button on Page Layout tab		
Page Break, Manual	WD 112		Page Break button on Insert tab		CTRL+ENTER
Page Number, Insert	WD 82		Insert Page Number button on Design tab		
Paragraph, Add Space Above	WD 79		Line spacing button on Home tab | Add Space Before (After) Paragraph	Paragraph | Indents and Spacing tab	CTRL+0 (zero)
Paragraph, Decrease Indent	WD 196	Decrease Indent button on Mini toolbar	Decrease Indent button on Home tab	Paragraph | Indents and Spacing tab	CTRL+SHIFT+M
Paragraph, Remove Space After	WD 195		Line spacing button on Home tab | Remove Space After Paragraph	Paragraph | Indents and Spacing tab	
Paragraphs, Change Spacing Above and Below	WD 50		Spacing Before box arrow on Page Layout tab	Paragraph | Indents and Spacing tab	
Paste	WD 191		Clipboard Dialog Box Launcher on Home tab	Paste	CTRL+V
Pattern Fill Effect for Background, Add	WD 222		Page Color button on Page Layout tab | Fill Effects | Pattern tab		
Picture Border, Change	WD 45		Picture Border button in Format tab		
Picture Style, Apply	WD 44		Picture Tools and Format tabs | More button in Picture Styles gallery		
Picture, Insert	WD 41		Picture button on Insert tab		
Print Document	WD 54	Office Button | Print | Print			CTRL+P
Print Document Properties	WD 130	Office Button | Print | Print | Print what box arrow			
Print Preview	WD 201	Office Button | Print | Print Preview			
Quick Style, Create	WD 90		More button in Styles gallery | Save Selection	Styles | Save Selection	
Quit Word	WD 55	Close button on right side of Word title bar			ALT+F4
Remove character formatting (plain text)	WD 87		Font Dialog Box Launcher on Home tab | Font tab	Font | Font tab	CTRL+SPACEBAR
Remove paragraph formatting	WD 87		Font Dialog Box Launcher on Home tab	Font | Font tab	CTRL+Q

Table 1 Microsoft Office Word 2007 Quick Reference Summary *(continued)*

Task	Page Number	Mouse	Ribbon	Shortcut Menu	Keyboard Shortcut
Research Task Pane, Use	WD 128	Hold down ALT key, click word to look up			
Right-Align Paragraph	WD 81		Align Text Right button on Home tab	Paragraph	Indents and Spacing tab	CTRL+R
Rulers, Display	WD 87	View Ruler button on vertical scroll bar	View Ruler on View tab		
Save Document as Web Page	WD 218	Office Button	Save As	Other Formats			F12
Save Document, Same Name	WD 53	Save button on Quick Access Toolbar			CTRL+S
Save New Document	WD 19	Save button on Quick Access Toolbar			CTRL+S
Select Block of Text	WD 33	Click at beginning of text, hold down SHIFT key and click at end of text to select; or drag through text			CTRL+SHIFT+RIGHT ARROW and/or DOWN ARROW
Select Browse Object Menu, Use	WD 118	Select Browse Object button on vertical scroll bar			ALT+CTRL+HOME
Select Character(s)	WD 120	Drag through character(s)			CTRL+SHIFT+RIGHT ARROW
Select Entire Document	WD 120	Point to left of text and triple-click			CTRL+A
Select Graphic	WD 46	Click graphic			
Select Line	WD 27	Point to left of line and click			SHIFT+DOWN ARROW
Select Lines	WD 30	Point to left of first line and drag up or down			CTRL+SHIFT+DOWN ARROW
Select Paragraph	WD 90	Triple-click paragraph			SHIFT+DOWN ARROW
Select Paragraphs	WD 30	Point to left of first paragraph, double-click, and drag up or down			
Select Sentence	WD 120	Press and hold down CTRL key and click sentence			CTRL+SHIFT+RIGHT ARROW
Select Word	WD 59	Double-click word			CTRL+SHIFT+RIGHT ARROW
Select Words	WD 33	Drag through words			CTRL+SHIFT+RIGHT ARROW
Single-Space Lines	WD 86		Line spacing button on the Home tab	Paragraph	Indents and Spacing tab	CTRL+1
Small uppercase letters	WD 86		Font Dialog Box Launcher on Home tab	Font tab	Font	Font tab	CTRL+SHIFT+K
Sort Paragraphs	WD 200		Sort button on Home tab		
Source, Edit	WD 104	Citation Options box arrow	Edit Source			
Spelling and Grammar	WD 125	Spelling and Grammar Check icon on status bar	Spelling	Spelling & Grammar button on Review tab	Spelling	F7

Task	Page Number	Mouse	Ribbon	Shortcut Menu	Keyboard Shortcut
Table 1 Microsoft Office Word 2007 Quick Reference Summary *(continued)*					
Spelling and Grammar Check as You Type	WD 16	Spelling and Grammar Check icon on status bar		Correct word on shortcut menu	
Style Set, Change	WD 37		Change Styles button on Home tab | Style Set on Change Styles menu		
Styles Task Pane, Open	WD 25		Styles Dialog Box Launcher		CTRL+SHIFT+S
Styles, Apply	WD 24		Styles gallery		
Styles, Modify	WD 90		Styles Dialog Box Launcher		
Subscript	WD 86		Font Dialog Box Launcher on Home tab	Font | Font tab	CTRL+EQUAL SIGN
Superscript	WD 86		Font Dialog Box Launcher on Home tab	Font | Font tab	CTRL+SHIFT+PLUS SIGN
Synonym, Find	WD 124		Thesaurus on Review tab	Synonyms | desired word	SHIFT+F7
Tab Stops, Set	WD 158, WD 167	Click tab selector, click ruler on desired location	Paragraph Dialog Box Launcher | Tabs button	Paragraph | Tabs button	
Table Columns, Resize	WD 177	Double-click column boundary	AutoFit button on Layout tab	AutoFit | AutoFit to Contents	
Table Style, Apply	WD 176		More button in Table Styles gallery		
Table, Delete Rows	WD 186		Delete button on Layout tab | Delete Rows		
Table, Insert	WD 173		Table button on Insert tab		
Table, Select	WD 179	Click table move handle	Select button on Layout tab | Select Table on Select menu		
Table, Select Cell	WD 178	Click left edge of cell			
Table, Select Column	WD 178	Click border at top of column			
Table, Select Multiple Adjacent Cells, Rows, or Columns	WD 178	Drag through cells, rows, or columns			
Table, Select Multiple Nonadjacent Cells, Rows, or Columns	WD 178	Select first cell, row, or column, hold down CTRL key while selecting next cell, row, or column			
Table, Select Next Cell	WD 178	Drag through cell			TAB
Table, Select Previous Cell	WD 178	Drag through cell			SHIFT+TAB
Table, Select Row	WD 178	Click to left of row			
Theme Colors, Change	WD 39		Change Styles button on Home tab | Colors on Change Styles menu		
Theme Fonts, Change	WD 40		Change Styles button on Home tab | Fonts on Change Styles menu		

Table 1   Microsoft Office Word 2007 Quick Reference Summary *(continued)*

Task	Page Number	Mouse	Ribbon	Shortcut Menu	Keyboard Shortcut
Underline	WD 35		Underline button on Home tab	Font	Font tab	CTRL+U
Underline words, not spaces	WD 86				CTRL+SHIFT+W
Zoom	WD 46	Zoom Out and Zoom In buttons on status bar	Zoom level button on View tab		

Table 2   Microsoft Office Excel 2007 Quick Reference Summary

Task	Page Number	Mouse	Ribbon	Shortcut Menu	Keyboard Shortcut
AutoCalculate	EX 62	Select Range	right-click AutoCalculate area	click calculation			
Bold	EX 38	Bold button on Mini toolbar	Bold button on Home tab or Font group Dialog Box Launcher on Home tab	Font tab	Format Cells	Font tab	Bold in Font style list	CTRL+B
Borders	EX 111	Borders button on Mini toolbar	Borders button on Home tab or Alignment Dialog Box Launcher on Home tab	Border tab	Format Cells	Border tab	CTRL+1	B
Cell Style, change	EX 35		Cell Styles button on Home tab		
Center	EX 113	Right-click cell	Center button on Mini toolbar	Center button on Home tab or Dialog Box Launcher in Alignment group on Home tab	Format Cells	Alignment tab	CTRL+1	A
Center Across Columns	EX 40	Right-click selection	Merge and Center button on Mini toolbar	Merge and Center button on Home tab or Dialog Box Launcher in Alignment group on Home tab	Format Cells	Alignment tab	CTRL+1	A
Chart, Add	EX 50, 205		Charts Dialog Box Launcher on Insert tab		F11
Clear Cell	EX 66	Drag fill handle back	Clear button on Home tab	Clear Contents	DELETE
Clear Worksheet	EX 66		Select All button on Worksheet	Clear button on Home tab		
Close Workbook	EX 59		Close button on Ribbon or Office Button	Close		CTRL+W
Color Background	EX 110		Fill Color button on Home tab or Font Dialog Box Launcher on Home tab	Fill tab	Format Cells	Fill tab	CTRL+1	F
Color Tab	EX 216			Tab Color	

Table 2 Microsoft Office Excel 2007 Quick Reference Summary *(continued)*

Task	Page Number	Mouse	Ribbon	Shortcut Menu	Keyboard Shortcut
Column Width	EX 46, 122	Drag column heading boundary	Home tab | Format button | Column Width	Column Width	ALT+O | C | W
Comma Style Format	EX 44		Comma Style button on Home tab or Number Dialog Box Launcher on Home tab | Accounting	Format Cells | Number tab | Accounting	CTRL+1 | N
Conditional Formatting	EX 119		Conditional Formatting button on Home tab		ALT+O | D
Copy and Paste	EX 175		Copy button and Paste button on Home tab	Copy to copy; Paste to paste	CTRL+C; CTRL+V
Copy to adjacent cells	EX 27	Select source area | drag fill handle through destination cells	Select source area | click Copy button on Home tab | select destination area | click Paste button on Home tab	Right-click source area | click Copy | right-click destination area | click Paste	
Currency Style Format	EX 116		Currency Style button on Home tab or Format Cells | Number | Currency	Format Cells | Number | Currency	CTRL+1 | N
Cut	EX 64		Cut button on Home tab	Cut	CTRL+X
Date	EX 184	Insert Function button in formula bar | Date & Time | NOW	Date & Time button on Formulas tab | NOW		CTRL+SEMICOLON
Date, Format	EX 113		Font Dialog Box Launcher on Home tab | Number tab | Date	Format Cells | Number tab | Date	
Decimal Place, Decrease	EX 115		Decrease Decimal button on Home tab or Number Dialog Box Launcher on Home tab | Number tab | Currency	Format Cells | Number tab | Currency	CTRL+1 | N
Decimal Place, Increase	EX 118		Increase Decimal button on Home tab or Dialog Box Launcher in Number group on Home tab | Number tab | Currency	Format Cells | Number tab | Currency	CTRL+1 | N
Delete Rows or Columns	EX 180		Home tab | Delete button arrow | Delete Sheet Rows or Home tab | Delete button arrow | Delete Sheet Columns	Delete | Entire row or Delete | Entire column	
Document Properties, Set or View	EX 55	Office Button | Prepare | Properties			ALT+F | E | P
E-Mail from Excel	EX 142	Office Button | Send | E-Mail			ALT+F | D | E
Embedded Chart, Delete	EX 67				Select chart, press DELETE
File Management	EX 259		Office Button | Save As, right-click file name		ALT+F | A, right-click file name

Table 2 Microsoft Office Excel 2007 Quick Reference Summary (continued)

Task	Page Number	Mouse	Ribbon	Shortcut Menu	Keyboard Shortcut
Fit to Print	EX 156		Page Setup Dialog Box Launcher on Page Layout tab		ALT+P | SP
Folder, New	EX 259		Office Button | Save As | Create New Folder button		ALT+F | A
Font Color	EX 39	Font Color box arrow on Mini toolbar	Font Color button arrow on Home tab or Font Dialog Box Launcher on Home tab	Format Cells | Font tab	CTRL+1 | F
Font Size, Change	EX 38	Font Size box arrow on Mini toolbar	Font Size box arrow on Home tab or Font Dialog Box Launcher on Home tab	Format Cells | Font tab	CTRL+1 | F
Font Size, Increase	EX 39	Increase Font Size button on Mini toolbar	Increase Font Size button on Home tab		
Font Type	EX 36	Font box arrow on Mini toolbar	Font box arrow on Home tab or Font Dialog Box Launcher in Font group on Home tab	Format Cells | Font tab	CTRL+1 | F
Formula Assistance	EX 101	Insert Function button in formula bar	Insert Function button on Formulas tab		CTRL+A after you type function name
Formulas Version	EX 136				CTRL+ACCENT MARK
Freeze Worksheet Titles	EX 182		Freeze Panes button on the View tab | Freeze Panes		ALT+W | F
Full Screen	EX 9		Full Screen button on View tab		ALT+V | U
Function	EX 101	Insert Function button in formula bar	Insert Function button on Formulas tab		SHIFT+F3
Go To	EX 48	Click cell	Find & Select button on Home tab		F5
Goal Seek	EX 225		What-If Analysis button on Data tab | Goal Seek		ALT+T | G
Help	EX 67 and Appendix C		Microsoft Office Excel Help button on Ribbon		F1
Hide Column	EX 122	Drag column heading boundary	Format button on Home tab | Hide & Unhide or Hide & Unhide button on View tab	Hide	CTRL+0 (zero) to hide CTRL+SHIFT+) to display
Hide Row	EX 126	Drag row heading boundary		Hide	CTRL+9 to hide CTRL+SHIFT+(to display
In-Cell Editing	EX 63	Double-click cell			F2
Insert Rows or Columns	EX 178		Home tab | Insert button arrow | Insert Sheet Rows or Home tab | Insert button arrow | Insert Sheet Columns	Insert	ALT+I | R or C
Insert Single Cell or Range of Cells	EX 179		Home | Insert button arrow | Insert Cells		

Table 2 Microsoft Office Excel 2007 Quick Reference Summary *(continued)*

Task	Page Number	Mouse	Ribbon	Shortcut Menu	Keyboard Shortcut
Italicize	EX 203		Italic button on Home tab or Format Cells: Font Dialog Box Launcher	Font tab	Format Cells	Font tab	CTRL+I
Margins, Change	EX 130		Margins button on Page Layout tab		
Merge Cells	EX 41		Merge and Center button on Home tab or Alignment Dialog Box Launcher. on Home tab	Format Cells	Alignment tab	ALT+O	E	A
Move Cells	EX 177	Point to border and drag	Cut button on Home tab; Paste button on Home tab	Cut; Paste	CTRL+X; CTRL+V
Move Sheet	EX 217	Drag sheet tab to desired location		Move or Copy	
Name Cells	EX XXX	Click Name box in formula bar, type name	Define Name button on Formulas tab		ALT+I	N	D
New Workbook	EX 67	Office Button	New			CTRL+N
Open Workbook	EX 61	Office Button	Open			CTRL+O
Paste Options	EX 176		Paste button arrow on Home tab		
Percent Style Format	EX 118		Percent Style button on Home tab or Number Dialog Box Launcher on Home tab	Percentage	Format Cells	Number tab	Percentage	CTRL+1	N or CTRL+SHIFT+%.
Preview Worksheet	EX 132	Office Button	Print	Print Preview			ALT+F	W	V
Print Worksheet	EX 132	Office Button	Print			CTRL+P
Quit Excel	EX 59	Close button on title bar Office Button	Exit Excel			ALT+F4
Range Finder	EX 106	Double-click cell			
Redo	EX 65	Redo button on Quick Access Toolbar			ALT+3 or CTRL+Y
Remove Splits	EX 223	Double-click split bar	Split button on View tab		ALT+W	S
Rename Sheet tab	EX 217	Double-click sheet tab	type sheet name		Rename	
Rotate Text	EX 169		Alignment Dialog Box Launcher on Home tab	Format Cells	Alignment tab	ALT+O	E	A
Row Height	EX 125	Drag row heading boundary	Format button on Home tab	Row Height	Row Height	ALT+O	R	E
Save Workbook, New Name	EX 57		Office Button	Save As		ALT+F	A
Save Workbook, Same Name	EX 57	Save button on Quick Access Toolbar	Office Button	Save		CTRL+S
Select All of Worksheet	EX 67	Select All button on worksheet			CTRL+A

Table 2 Microsoft Office Excel 2007 Quick Reference Summary *(continued)*

Task	Page Number	Mouse	Ribbon	Shortcut Menu	Keyboard Shortcut
Select Cell	EX 15	Click cell or Click Name box, type cell reference, press ENTER			Use arrow keys
Select Multiple Sheets	EX 218	CTRL+click tab or SHIFT+click tab		Select All Sheets	
Series	EX 169	Drag fill handle			ALT+E | I | S
Shortcut Menu	EX 12	Right-click object			SHIFT+F10
Spell Check	EX 127		Spelling button on Review tab		F7
Split Cell	EX 41		Merge & Center button on Home tab or Alignment Dialog Box Launcher on Home tab | click Merge cells to deselect	Format Cells | Alignment tab | click Merge cells to deselect	ALT+O | E | A
Split Window into Panes	EX 222	Drag vertical or horizontal split box	Split button on View tab		ALT+W | S
Stock Quotes	EX 138		Existing Connections button on Data tab		ALT+D | D | D
Sum	EX 25	Function Wizard button in formula bar | SUM	Sum button on Home tab	Insert Function button on Formulas tab	ALT+=
Underline	EX 203		Underline button on Home tab or Font Dialog Box Launcher on Home tab	Format Cells | Font tab	CTRL+U
Undo	EX 65	Undo button on Quick Access Toolbar			ALT+2, CTRL+Z
Unfreeze Worksheet Titles	EX 194		Freeze Panes button on View tab | Unfreeze Panes		ALT+W | F
Unhide Column	EX 122	Drag hidden column heading boundary to right	Unhide button on View tab	Unhide	ALT+O | C | U
Unhide Row	EX 127	Drag hidden row heading boundary down	Unhide button on View tab	Unhide	ALT+O | R | U
Web Page, Save Workbook as	EX 256	Office button | Save As | Save as type: arrow | Single File Web Page Or Office button | Save As | Save as type: arrow | Web Page			
Worksheet Name, Change	EX 141	Double-click sheet tab, type new name		Rename	
Workbook Theme, Change	EX 109		Themes button on Page Layout tab		
Zoom	EX 220	Zoom box on status bar or Zoom In and Zoom Out buttons on status bar	Zoom button on View tab		ALT+V | Z

Table 3 Microsoft Office Access 2007 Quick Reference Summary

Task	Page Number	Mouse	Ribbon	Shortcut Menu	Keyboard Shortcut
Add New Field	AC 24	Right-click Add New Field in Datasheet	Insert Rows button on Design Tab	Design View | INSERT	
Add Record	AC 30, 38	New (blank) record button	New button on Home tab	Open | Click in field	CTRL+PLUS SIGN (+)
Calculate Statistics	AC 118		Totals button on Design tab		
Change Colors and Font	AC 180		Alternate Fill/Back Color button arrow or Font Color button arrow or Font box arrow on Home tab		
Change Database Properties	AC 60	Office button | Manage | Database Properties			
Change Gridlines	AC 179		Gridlines button on Home tab		
Change Primary Key	AC 28	Delete field | Primary Key button	Design View button on Design tab | select field | Primary Key button		
Clear Query	AC 98				Select all entries | DELETE
Close Object	AC 35	Close button for object		Right-click item | Close	
Create Calculated Field	AC 113			Zoom	SHIFT+F2
Create Crosstab Query	AC 123		Query Wizard button on Create tab | Crosstab Query Wizard		
Create Database	AC 14	Blank Database button or Office Button | Save			CTRL+S or SHIFT+F12 or ALT+I
Create Form	AC 142		Form button on Create tab		
Create Query	AC 78		Query Design button on Create tab		
Create Report	AC 51		Report Wizard button on Create tab		
Create Table	AC 23	Office Button | Save button	Table button on Create tab		CTRL+S or SHIFT+F12
Customize Navigation Pane	AC 126	Navigation pane arrow | Object Type			
Delete Record	AC 148	Click Record Selector | DELETE	DELETE button		
Define Fields in a Table	AC 24		Right-click Add New Field on Datasheet tab | Rename Column	Right-click Add New Field | Rename Column	
Exclude Field from Query Results	AC 112	Show check box			
Export Query	AC 221		Select query | desired application button in Export group on External Data tab		

Table 3 Microsoft Office Access 2007 Quick Reference Summary *(continued)*

Task	Page Number	Mouse	Ribbon	Shortcut Menu	Keyboard Shortcut
Field Size	AC 46		Design View button on Design tab | select field | Field Size box		
Filter by Selection	AC 149		Selection button on Home tab | select criterion		
Format a Calculated Field	AC 116		Property Sheet button on Design tab		
Format a Field	AC 168	Select field | Format property box			
Group in Query	AC 121	Total row or include multiple fields in query			
Import Data	AC 212		Desired application in Import group on External Data tab		
Include All Fields in Query	AC 85	Double-click asterisk in field list	Query Design button on Create tab | Add All Fields button		
Include Field in Query	AC 85		Query Design button on Create tab | select field | Add Field button		
Join Tables	AC 105		Query Design button on Create tab | bring field lists for tables into upper pane		
Link Tables	AC 217		Access button on External Data tab | select database | OK button		
Lookup Field	AC 172	Data Type column for field | Lookup Wizard			
Move to First Record	AC 39	First Record button			
Move to Last Record	AC 39	Last Record button			
Move to Next Record	AC 39	Next Record button			
Move to Previous Record	AC 39	Previous Record button			
New Item	various	Office button | Open			
Omit Duplicates	AC 100	Open Property Sheet, set Unique Values to Yes	Property Sheet button on Design tab | Unique Values	Properties | Unique Values	
Open Database	AC 37	More button | Open button or Office button | double-click file name			CTRL+O
Open Table	AC 26	Open button		Open	
Preview Table	AC 41	Office button | Print | Print Preview			ALT+F, W, V
Print Object	AC 41, 56	Office button | Print | Quick Print or Print			CTRL+P
Quit Access	AC 36	Close button			

Office Quick Reference

Table 3 Microsoft Office Access 2007 Quick Reference Summary *(continued)*

Task	Page Number	Mouse	Ribbon	Shortcut Menu	Keyboard Shortcut
Referential Integrity	AC 186		Relationships button on Database Tools tab		
Resize a Column	AC 175	In Datasheet view, double-click right boundary of the field selector		Right-click field name | Column Width	
Save Form	AC 58	Office button | Save			CTRL+S
Save Query	AC 91	Save button or Office button | Save			CTRL+S
Save Table	AC 27	Save button	Office button | Save	Save	CTRL+S
Search for Access Help	AC 62	Microsoft Office Access Help button			F1
Search for Record	AC 145		Find button on Home tab		CTRL+F
Select Fields for Report	AC 51		Report Wizard button on Create tab | Add Field button		
Simple Query Wizard	AC 78		Query Wizard button on Create tab		
Sort Data in Query	AC 98		Select field in Design grid | Ascending		
Sort on Multiple Keys	AC 101	Assign two sort keys			
Split Form	AC 57		Split Form button on Create tab		
Start Access	AC 12	Start button | All Programs | Microsoft Office | Microsoft Office Access 2007			
Switch Between Form and Datasheet Views	AC 57	Form View or Datasheet View button			
Update Query	AC 162		Update button on Design tab | select field, Update To row, enter new value	Query Type | Update Query	
Use Advanced Filter/Sort	AC 155		Advanced button on Home tab | Advanced/Filter Sort		
Use AND Criterion	AC 95				Place criteria on same line
Use Criterion	AC 81	Right-click query | Design View | Criteria row			
Use OR Criterion	AC 96				Place criteria on separate lines

Table 4 Microsoft Office PowerPoint 2007 Quick Reference Summary

Task	Page Number	Mouse	Ribbon	Shortcut Menu	Keyboard Shortcut
Add Shapes	PPT 119		Shapes button on Home tab	select shape		
Add Transition	PPT 122		Transition button on Animations tab or More button in Transition to this Slide group on Animations tab	select transition		ALT+D	M
Change Size, Clip Art, Photo, or Shape	PPT 101, 103, 117	Drag sizing handles	Dialog Box Launcher in Size group of Format tab	Size tab	enter height and width values or Size group of Format tab	enter height and width values		
Clip Art, Insert	PPT 96	Clip Art icon in slide	Clip Art button on Insert tab		
Demote a Paragraph	PPT 34	Increase List Level button on Mini toolbar	Increase List Level button on Home tab		TAB or ALT+SHIFT+ RIGHT ARROW
Display a Presentation in Grayscale	PPT 59		Grayscale button on View tab		ALT+V	C	U
Document Properties	PPT 44	Office Button	Prepare	Properties			
Document Theme, Choose	PPT 16		More button on Design tab	theme		
End Slide Show	PPT 54			End Show	ESC
Font	PPT 109	Font button or Font arrow on Mini toolbar	Font button on Home tab or Font arrow on Home tab	select font or Font Dialog Box Launcher on Home tab	Latin text font arrow on Font tab	Font	Latin text font arrow on Font tab	CTRL+SHIFT+F	Font tab	Latin text font arrow
Font Color	PPT 23, 110	Font Color button or Font Color arrow on Mini toolbar	Font Color button on Home tab or Font Color arrow on Home tab	select color or Font Dialog Box Launcher on Home tab	Font color button on Font tab	select color	Font	Font color button on Font tab	select color	CTRL+SHIFT+F	Font tab	Font color button	select color
Font Size, Decrease	PPT 25	Decrease Font Size button or Font Size arrow on Mini toolbar	Decrease Font Size button on Home tab or Font Size arrow on Home tab	size	Font Size arrow	Size	CTRL+SHIFT+LEFT CARET (<)
Font Size, Increase	PPT 24	Increase Font Size button or Font Size arrow on Mini toolbar	Increase Font Size button on Home tab or Font Size arrow on Home tab	size	Font size arrow	Size	CTRL+SHIFT+RIGHT CARET (>)
Help	PPT 63 and Appendix A	Microsoft PowerPoint Help button			F1

Table 4 Microsoft Office PowerPoint 2007 Quick Reference Summary *(continued)*

Task	Page Number	Mouse	Ribbon	Shortcut Menu	Keyboard Shortcut
Insert Photograph	PPT 98, 99	Insert Picture from File icon on slide	Picture button on Insert tab		
Move Clip Art or Photo	PPT 105	Drag			
Next Slide	PPT 47	Next Slide button on vertical scroll bar			PAGE DOWN
Normal View	PPT 91	Normal View button at lower-right PowerPoint window	Normal button on View tab		ALT+V | N
Open Presentation	PPT 54	Office Button | Open | select file			CTRL+O
Preview Presentation as Web Page	PPT 151	[Assumes Web Page Preview button has been added to Quick Access toolbar] Web Page Preview button			
Previous Slide	PPT 50, 51	Previous Slide button on vertical scroll bar			PAGE UP
Print a Presentation	PPT 61	Office Button | Print			CTRL+P
Print an Outline	PPT 122	Office Button | point to Print | Print Preview | Print What arrow | Outline View			
Promote a Paragraph	PPT 34	Decrease List Level button on Mini toolbar	Decrease List Level button on Home tab		SHIFT+TAB or ALT+SHIFT+ LEFT ARROW
Quick Access Toolbar, Add Buttons	PPT 148	Customize Quick Access Toolbar button | select from command options			
Quick Access Toolbar, Reset	PPT 154	Customize Quick Access Toolbar button | More Commands | Reset button			
Quit PowerPoint	PPT 53	Double-click Office Button or Close button on title bar or Office Button | Exit PowerPoint		Right-click Microsoft PowerPoint button on taskbar | Close	ALT+F4 or CTRL+Q
Save a Presentation	PPT 27	Save button on Quick Access toolbar or Office Button | Save			CTRL+S or SHIFT+F12
Save as Web Page	PPT 152	Office Button | Save As | add File name | change Save as type to Single File Web Page | Save button			ALT+F | G
Slide, Add	PPT 29		New Slide button on Home tab or New Slide arrow on Home tab | choose slide type		CTRL+M
Slide, Arrange	PPT 41	Drag slide in Slides tab to new position or in Slide Sorter View drag slide to new position			

Table 4 Microsoft Office PowerPoint 2007 Quick Reference Summary *(continued)*

Task	Page Number	Mouse	Ribbon	Shortcut Menu	Keyboard Shortcut
Slide, Background	PPT 89		Background Styles button on Design tab	select style		
Slide, Duplicate	PPT 40		New Slide arrow on Home tab	Duplicate Selected Slides		
Slide Layout	PPT 92, 94		Layout button on Home tab		
Slide Show View	PPT 49	Slide Show button at lower-right PowerPoint window	Slide Show button on View tab or From Beginning button on Slide Show tab		F5 or ALT+V | W
Slide Sorter View	PPT 91	Slide Sorter View button at lower-right in PowerPoint window	Slide Sorter button on View tab		ALT+V | D
Spelling Check	PPT 55		Spelling button on Review tab		F7
Text, Add Shadow	PPT 110		Text Shadow button on Home tab		
Text, Bold	PPT 25	Bold button on Mini toolbar	Bold button on Home tab		CTRL+B
Text, Change Color	PPT 23	Font Color button or Font Color arrow on Mini toolbar	Font color arrow on Home tab	choose color	Font	Font color button	choose color	
Text, Delete	PPT 42		Cut button on Home tab	Cut	DELETE or CTRL+X or BACKSPACE
Text, Formatting with Quick Styles	PPT 119		Quick Styles button on Home tab	select style		
Text, Italicize	PPT 22	Italic button on Mini toolbar	Italic button on Home tab	Font	Font style arrow	Italics	CTRL+I
Text, Select	PPT 21	Drag to select	double-click to select word	triple-click to select paragraph			
Use Format Painter	PPT 112	Format Painter button on Mini toolbar	Double-click Format Painter button on Home tab	select text with a format you want to copy	select other text to apply previously selected format	press ESC to turn off Format Painter		
Zoom for Printing	PPT 128	Drag Zoom slider on status bar or Office Button	point to Print	Print Preview		Zoom button on View tab	select zoom		
Zoom for Viewing Slides	PPT 127	Drag Zoom slider on status bar	Zoom button on View tab	select zoom		

Table 5 Microsoft Office Outlook 2007 Quick Reference Summary

Task	Page Number	Mouse	Ribbon	Shortcut Menu	Keyboard Shortcut
Address E-Mail Message	OUT 27	Mail button in Inbox window	New Mail Message button on Message tab | To button		
Attach File to E-Mail Message	OUT 31	Attach File button on Standard toolbar in Message window	Attach File button on Insert tab		
Close an E-Mail Message	OUT 15	Click Close button on title bar in Message window			ALT+F, C
Compose E-Mail Message	OUT 27	New button on Standard toolbar	New | Mail Message*		CTRL+N
Create Contact List	OUT 47	New button on Standard toolbar	Actions | New Contact*	New Contact	CTRL+SHIFT+C
Create Distribution List	OUT 58	New Contact button on Standard toolbar	New Contact button | Distribution List*		CTRL+SHIFT+L
Create E-Mail Signature	OUT 24		Tools | Options | Mail Format tab | Signatures button*		ALT+T, O
Create Personal Folder	OUT 44	Contacts button in Navigation pane	File | New | Folder*	New Contacts | New Folder	CTRL+SHIFT+E
Create View Filter	OUT 36		View | Arrange By*	Custom	
Delete E-Mail Message	OUT 21	Delete button on Standard toolbar	Select message | Delete*		CTRL+D or DELETE
Display Contacts	OUT 52	Find a Contact box on Standard toolbar	Tools | Instant Search*		CTRL+E or ALT+T, I
Find a Contact	OUT 50	Find a Contact box on Standard toolbar	Tools | Instant Search | Advanced Find*		CTRL+SHIFT+F
Flag E-Mail Messages	OUT 34	Follow Up button on Standard toolbar	Actions | Follow Up*	Follow Up	ALT+A, U
Forward E-Mail Message	OUT 20	Forward button on Standard toolbar		Forward	CTRL+F
Open E-Mail Message	OUT 10	Double-click message	File | Open*	Open	CTRL+O
Print Contact List	OUT 53	Print button on Standard toolbar	File | Print* or File | Print Preview | Print*		CTRL+P
Print E-Mail Message	OUT 15	Print button on Standard toolbar	File | Print | OK button*		CTRL+P, ENTER
Reply to E-Mail Message	OUT 16	tton on Standard toolbar	Reply button on Message tab		
Save Contact List as Text File	OUT 60	Select name bar of contact | CTRL+A | File | Save As	File | Save As*		
Send E-Mail Message	OUT 31	Send button in Message window	Send button on Insert tab		
Set Message Importance, Sensitivity, and Delivery Options	OUT 38	New Mail Message button on Standard toolbar in Message window	Options dialog box launcher in the Options group on the Message tab		
Sort E-Mail Messages	OUT 35	Arrange By Command on View menu			ALT+V, A, E

indicates a task handled by the Outlook Standard menu instead of the Ribbon